1 MONTH OF
FREE
READING

at
www.ForgottenBooks.com

By purchasing this book you are
eligible for one month membership to
ForgottenBooks.com, giving you
unlimited access to our entire
collection of over 1,000,000 titles via
our web site and mobile apps.

To claim your free month visit:

www.forgottenbooks.com/free470384

ISBN 978-0-265-39012-2
PIBN 10470384

A

Medium of Intercommunication

FOR

LITERARY ·MEN, GENERAL READERS, ETC.

"When found, make a note of."—CAPTAIN CUTTLE.

FIFTH SERIES.—VOLUME NINTH.

JANUARY—JUNE, 1878.

LONDON:
PUBLISHED AT THE
OFFICE, 20, WELLINGTON STREET, STRAND, W.C.
BY JOHN FRANCIS.

LONDON, SATURDAY, JANUARY 5, 1878.

CONTENTS.—Nº 210.

Notes.

THE TRUE STORY OF THE CENCI FAMILY.

The note which appeared in these columns a few weeks ago on this subject was necessarily brief, as its only purport was to call attention to the latest Italian publications on the history of the Cenci. Since then it has occurred to me that some notes on the Cenci family, their trial and execution, may be interesting to those who are not likely to see the books referred to, as the accounts till now accessible to English readers are most grossly incorrect. It appears that a MS. extant in the Minerva Library at Rome is the foundation of a notice in the *Quarterly Review*, in an article "Italian Tours," published in April, 1858. The story, as related there, is a tissue of misstatements, the guilt of Beatrice being the solitary fragment of truth to be found in it. But worse still, in Hare's *Walks in Rome*—a book in the hands of every traveller in Italy—the account of the tragedy is taken from Ademollo, who assumes the innocence of Beatrice. To tell the story correctly, according to lately discovered* documentary evidence, shall be the aim of this paper; and some of the MSS., though not trustworthy in facts, will help in details. These different MS. versions of the story seem to have

* D'Albono's volume on the Cenci is not cut of print, and is published by Nobile, Naples.

been founded on one common original, with variations and glosses by other hands. But they are valuable as traditionary accounts of the family, &c., and certainly some of the touches in them could only have been given by an eye-witness, who might be ignorant of the events that preceded the trial, though he had seen the execution, and was familiar with the features and personal appearance of many of the actors in the sad drama. The subject falls naturally under five heads : the family of Count Cenci ; the murder ; the trial ; the execution ; the survivors.

THE FAMILY OF CENCI.

Francesco Cenci, Magnifico Romano, was born, as he deposes himself, Nov. 11, 1549, and succeeded at thirteen to the wealth amassed by his father, who was clerk and treasurer of the Camera Apostolica. An idea of his fortune may be gained from the fact that for composition for his father's frauds he paid 58,000 scudi, and for fines imposed on himself for various crimes 125,000 sc. His appearance is described thus in a MS. : "Short, well made, large expressive eyes, but the upper eyelid drooping a little, a large prominent nose, thin lips, and a charming smile."

Though stained with nameless crimes, and knowing no bounds to his passions, he cannot have been the bold infidel ordinary accounts have made him. In his will, dated Nov. 22, 1586, after directing that his body shall be laid in the little church of S. Tommaso, which he had rebuilt, he provides an endowment for a chaplain, and leaves several bequests to hospitals and for the dower of poor girls. He was notoriously grasping —his step-daughters speak of his *notoria tenacità* —and of a most restless disposition. Bernardo, his son, describes his father as continually changing house, as he took a fresh fancy into his head.

He married at fourteen Ersilia Santa Croce, of the great Roman family of that name. She died in April, 1584, leaving him seven surviving children ; and though the first years of their married life, owing perhaps to a lawsuit about her dowry, do not seem to have been happy, as his first will, in 1567, attests, yet there is not the slightest evidence that he poisoned her, according to the common story, to marry Lucrezia Petroni. On the contrary, he remained a widower nine years, not remarrying till Nov. 9, 1593.

Between 1567 and 1573 he was, from time to time, under surveillance in his own house, or in prison for assaults ; and Sept. 14, 1572, was banished from Rome for six months. From 1591 to 1594 he was, at times, again in prison, and on trial, for blacker deeds. His evidence is given in full by Cavaliere Bertolotti. From it we learn the reason of his former imprisonments ; his age ; date of marriage ; that during the *sedia vacante* all men used to go about armed ; that he suffered

to the Pope practically admitting his guilt, and requesting to treat with his Holiness through friends and relations. Accordingly, on June 12, 1594, a penalty of 150,000 sc. was inflicted, which was afterwards reduced to 100,000, of which half was paid in August and the rest in instalments the same year. To effect this he had to contract large loans, some of which were not repaid at his death, but which seem to have been satisfied out of the property then confiscated. After 1594 no further proceedings against him have been found.

His possessions comprised some places interesting to the traveller in Italy : Torre Nuova, with its pines and vast farm buildings, so well known to the hunting man at Rome ; the Castle of Nemi, now the property of the Orsini, which still guards its lake, lying like a mirror below, over which still earlier a temple of Diana kept watch, whose priest none could be, according to old legend, unless he had killed his predecessor ; the Castle of Falcognano, and the farms of Testa di Lepre and Castel Campanile, in the Roman Campagna. Besides these he held the Castle of Assergio and other estates in the Abruzzi, and the two Palazzi Cenci in Rome—one at the Ghetto, the other in the Piazza San Eustachio.

Of Lucrezia, his second wife, there is little to be said. She was the widow of a Velli, with three daughters. MSS. describe her as about forty-four, short, with dark eyes, a fresh pink and white complexion, very stout, with auburn hair, but little of it.

Giacomo, the eldest son, and accomplice with Beatrice and Lucretia in the murder, was already out of favour with his father in 1586. Count Cenci, in his will made at that date, precluded him from any share in the estate beyond his *leggitima*, except 100 scudi, "and this for just and reasonable cause."

He had married Lodovica Velli without his father's consent, but documents show still worse was behind. A paper exists, signed by him, in which he promises to repay money unduly appropriated ; among other items, a month's pay for his sisters in the convent of Monte Citorio, which he had kept back, and thirty scudi to replace tapestries which he had *stolen* from the *guardarobba* to which only his father and he had access. In 1594 Count Cenci threw him into prison for a supposed scheme of parricide, which however was trumped up by a servant whom he had chastised. His disposition, however, remained unchanged, and in his last moments he confessed to another fraud on his father—a bill forged for 13,000 sc.

"Elle était petite, avait un joli embonpoint, et des fossettes au milieu des joues, de façon que morte et couronnée de fleurs on eût dit même qu'elle riait. Elle avait la bouche petite, les cheveux blonds et naturellement bouclés."

Another MS. :—

"Erano i capelli del puro color d'oro, piutosto corti che lunghi, ma cosi naturalmente inanellati, che comparivano fatti ad arte."

From a professed acquaintance with her the first writer says (transl.):—

"Elle avait surtout une gaîté, une candeur, et un esprit comique, que je n'ai jamais vu qu'à elle."

The traditions of her beauty are incidentally confirmed by an answer of one of the assassins on his trial. Asked whether he knew Beatrice, he said " Yes " ; asked under what circumstances, he replied, " Havendo grande desiderio di guardare la sua bellezza." Beatrice kept house for her family, and accounts still exist showing the sums paid to her monthly, which were large. Her love story with Monsignor Guerra will be proved to be a fiction ; but though she had a dowry of 20,000 sc. she remained unmarried. Her father kept her in a kind of imprisonment at Petrella. " Come carcerata e sotto chiave," she says in her deposition ; but her young brothers Bernardo and Paolo were treated much in the same way. Bernardo, when asked on trial why they had left Petrella about six weeks before the murder, says, " My father kept us shut up in the Rocca, and would not let us go out." For this severe treatment of Beatrice we shall perhaps later find a reason.

Bernardo, the last of those implicated in the tragedy, though apparently innocent, was the youngest but one of the sons, and was born August 16, 1580. In figure, face, and hair he bore a marked resemblance to his sister. His advocate Farinacci made him out to be only sixteen, and imbecile, but there appears no more foundation for the latter statement than for the former.

The other children were Antonina, the elder daughter, Rocco, Cristoforo, and Paolo, the youngest son, all of whom but Antonina died before the trial.

Antonina is commonly said to have presented a memorial to the Pope detailing her father's cruelties, which the Pope answered by marrying her to Carlo Gabrielli, of Gubbio. Still more, I find in one MS., which has the correct date of the marriage and the real name of the husband, Luzio Savelli, Baron of Riquano, the specific statement that the Pope committed the matter to Cardinal Rusticucci, Vicar of Rome. The cardinal then sent for Count Cenci, obliged him to sign the marriage contract, while in the mean time Antonina was fetched, and married then and there in the cardinal's chapel. Unfortunately for the truth of this story, a steward's account is extant, in which the count is charged for carriages for an excursion to Riquano two months before the marriage, and forty baiocchi are put down for the dolls Antonina gave to the child of Luzio Savelli. Certainly it sometimes happens that "trifles light as air are confirmation strong." Who would have thought that the entry of the hire of carriages on an excursion, and the gift of two dolls to a child, would, after 270 years, clear the dark memory of Count Cenci from a false accusation? Yet these trifling entries prove that the engagement was entered into with the father's consent, and that Antonina was on a visit to her future husband's family two months before her marriage. She appears to have died shortly before the execution of her family in 1599.

Rocco and Cristoforo were two *mauvais sujets.* The latter was killed in a brawl about a woman, in 1598, on the little island of S. Bartolomeo. His murderer was banished; but before the sentence was carried out Giacomo and Bernardo forgave him their brother's death. Accordingly, in the same year, his mother petitioned the Pope to allow her son to return to Rome, next year being the Jubilee. This document, found by Bertolotti, gives a strange insight into the life of the period. She begs for her son's return, as she is old and infirm; besides, "he is ready to marry a tall and handsome girl (*zitella vistosa e grande*), whose father is bankrupt, and mother in bad health, and whose virtue will otherwise be in danger, as she is twenty years old."

Rocco was killed in 1595 by an Orsini; but in 1594 he had been implicated with Monsignor Guerra, a first cousin of his father, in a robbery of silk hangings, linen, tapestry, and a silver basin from Count Cenci's house. The depositions given by the Fiscale are published by Bertolotti. Certainly the Cenci family washed their dirty linen in public. Paolo, Antonina, and Beatrice Cenci gave evidence. The words of Beatrice are interesting, and not very lover-like :—

"I think that M. Guerra helped Rocco to take and carry away the articles in question, because Rocco alone could not carry them away; still more, I say that I think the aforesaid M. Guerra was the contriver of the whole affair, and I say so believing it to be the truth."

The unfortunate Count Cenci has even been charged with the death of Rocco; but from the notes of the inquiry, published by Bertolotti, it is quite evident the murder was the result of an old quarrel.

The last of the family was Paolo, a weakly boy, who died about ten weeks after the murder, and was apparently not implicated in it. All the sons had been in debt, whether owing to their scanty allowance or to their own extravagance it is impossible to determine. Rocco sends a petition from Padua, which town MSS. have changed into Salamanca, alleging that he is utterly destitute — a statement which seems confirmed by other evidence; and we find that in 1595 the Pope, taking the matter into his own hands, really ordered some rents belonging to the father to be applied to the maintenance of the sons. The dissensions and misery of the family life are sketched by Bernardo, who says in his deposition, "My father and my brothers Giacomo and Cristoforo never spoke." Add to this the tyranny exercised by Count Cenci over the younger sons and Beatrice, and the forgery already committed by Giacomo, which perhaps threatened detection, and we see that things were ripening for the parricide.　　　K. H. B.

(*To be continued.*)

NEW YEAR'S GIFTS.

This is a subject which has been well nigh exhausted, but towards the illustration of which there is always some trifle presenting itself to be added to the already huge collection. From the time when branches of vervain, with fruit, honey, and good wishes, were acceptable gifts among the classical people of old, to the period when the custom became an imposition—a tax which the people paid to superiors,—there was no very great interval. Some circumstances connected with the custom are noteworthy. It is difficult, for instance, to discover how the yearly flinging of little pieces of money into Curtius's lake could be a testimony on the part of the citizens of their good wishes for the long life and prosperity of Augustus. Of the new year's gifts contributed to this emperor by the chief citizens, it cannot be said that he made unpraiseworthy use. It is asserted that of money Augustus never put into his own purse, for his private use, more than a penny of the sum presented by each donor. With the rest he substituted gods of gold for those of wood, and set up divine figures in villages which had been lacking such protection and symbols. Perhaps the most welcome tribute Augustus ever received was the heap of gold which was placed at his feet by universal Rome for the rebuilding of his Palatine House, which fire had destroyed. Augustus knew how to accept with dignity.

On the other hand, Caligula had no such knowledge. He was at once a mean and truculent beggar. On the birth of his daughter he declared that he should be ruined by family expenses; and that as to maintaining the grace and glory of the imperial condition, it was out of the question, unless pecuniary aid was afforded. The imperial hint was so very broad, that the weight and value

gestion. Caligula never forgot to make a very significant one towards the close of the old year, namely, that he should be prepared to receive all gifts from his loyal people at the opening of the new year. It must have been a strange sight to see this greedy tyrant stationed under the entrance to his palace, ready to receive the gifts of every imaginable sort which were brought by his lieges with full hands and full laps. Caligula had a sensual delight in walking over gold with his bare feet, or in rolling himself among the glittering heaps. He gave nothing in return for the donations he received; indeed, the custom of making them was one of which he had ordered the restoration. Tiberius had abolished this new year's usage, on the ground that some substantial acknowledgment was due to the givers, and that he really could not afford to pay it.

In the most splendid and abominable of the days of the French monarchy, the Gallic Tiberius, Louis XIV., was lavish with his presents, to make which, indeed, he had but to dip into the people's pockets. In 1672 he delighted that queen of French husseydom, Madame de Montespan, with a new year's gift which disgusted the whole nation. It consisted of two covered goblets and a salver of embossed gold, profusely ornamented with emeralds and diamonds. The value was ten thousand crowns. To the same woman, or rather as flattery to the king, Madame de Maintenon in 1670 gave, as a new year's gift to their illegitimate son, the Duc de Maine, a quarto volume printed in gold letters. The cover was inlaid with emeralds, and the lettering on the back stated that the book contained the various works of an author seven years of age—"Œuvres diverses d'un auteur de sept ans": the author was the little duke himself. The *Courrier de l'Europe* says that the most exquisite and most admired gift ever made at Versailles was that of Madame de Thianges to the above Duc de Maine, in 1685, and which is thus described:—

"C'était une chambre mesurant un mètre de chaque côté, toute dorée. Au-dessus de la porte était écrit en grosses lettres: *Chambre du Sublime.* Au dedans, un lit et un balustre avec un grand fauteuil dans lequel était assis le duc de Maine, fait de cire et d'une grande ressemblance; auprès de lui, M. de La Rochefoucauld, auquel il donnait des vers à examiner; autour du fauteuil M. de Marcillac et Bossuet; à l'autre extrémité Madame de Thianges et Madame Lafayette lisaient des vers. Au dehors du balustre, Boileau, armé d'une fourche, empêchait sept à huit mauvais poètes d'approcher. Racine était auprès de Boileau, et un peu plus loin La Fontaine, auquel il faisait signe d'approcher."

The above gift to a gentleman twenty-two years old seems to have been a pretty wax-work, with portraits of distinguished personages. The *Courrier*

robbed me, you rascal, throughout the preceding year!"   ED.

ABYSSINIAN AND IRISH LEGENDS.

In M. de Cosson's interesting *Cradle of the Blue Nile* he gives the following legend:—

"The native traditions affirm that St. Areed was first struck with the idea of composing the Abyssinian church music by seeing three birds singing on a tree, their number reminding him of the Holy Trinity. He was inspired with the notion of inventing a musical instrument, and forthwith invented a sort of rattle, which is used to this day by the priests to accompany their chants. Delighted with his new musical instrument, St. Areed went to the king and began to perform. History relates that the king was so absorbed in the charms of the music, that he inadvertently rested the point of his spear on St. Areed's great toe, and, gracefully reclining his weight on it, penned the worthy saint to the ground. My own opinion is that the astute monarch resorted to this as a last and desperate resource to induce the saint to bring his performance to an end; but, if this were his intention, he was disappointed, for St. Areed was so carried away with delight at his own harmonies, that he never even noticed the accident, though the ground was covered with his blood. This story is depicted in two paintings in one of the native churches."

Irish traditions relate that, when St. Patrick was baptizing one of the pagan kings of Ireland, the saint's crozier slipped downwards and pierced the foot of the convert, who from motives of reverence, or else believing that the wound inflicted on him was a part of the ceremonial rites, never moved or murmured, but endured the pain until they were over. In the Abyssinian legend the saint of that country is made the sufferer through his zeal for the Church; in the Irish legend the newly converted king is the sufferer; but there is an odd likeness between the two traditions of Christian missionaries in the south-east and south-west. In another part of the same work M. de Cosson gives some curious Abyssinian folk-lore about blacksmiths and all workers in iron. The Abyssinians, he says, regard them with awe, believing that they can transform themselves into hyenas, and can cause people to be possessed with an evil spirit by means of an incantation performed by bending a piece of grass into a circular form. A mythical Irish personage, the Gobhan Saer, who is supposed to have built many old churches in the course of one night by magic, was, I believe, a blacksmith as well as an architect; and the placing an iron coulter of a plough in the fire while milk is being churned is believed to be a sovereign spell against the witch who has charmed away the butter-making powers of the Irish dairy-woman. The wife of a most respectable Protestant farmer in Ireland once told me a long story of the success of this spell in her own farmhouse. Regarding St. Areed's birds, it is worth noting that not only singing, but talking, in fact, preaching birds figure largely in the old Irish legends about St. Brendan and other Irish saints. In the *Journal* of the Royal Historical and Archæological Association of Ireland, a few years ago, there was an account of a very curious ancient instrument, to all appearance a musical one, which was dug up in some county in Ulster. It had small figures of three birds attached to it with rings which could be moved up and down. It was shaped like a modern flute, but by some was conjectured to have been an instrument used by pagan priests in divination.   M. A. H.

NAVAL ARTILLERY IN ANCIENT TIMES : FIRE-ARMS A.C. 1100.—The following statement, suggestive of discussion at the Christmas fireside, is forwarded in the hope that it may be acceptable to the readers of "N. & Q." The statement is taken from a work recently published in Paris (*Les Premiers Habitants de l'Occident*, par M. d'Arbois de Hubainville), and is to this effect :—

The most ancient colony in Spain is Gadeïra, called by the Romans Gades, and at this day Cadiz. If we adopt the chronology of Velleius Paterculus, the date will be about 1100 A.C., and if we are to follow the calculation of the Spaniard, Pomponius Mela, the foundation of the colony will go back so far as to be coincident with the siege of Troy. The Phœnicians encountered resistance in this place, and Macrobius has preserved a legend which refers to Theron, the Iberian King of Northern Spain, coming thither with a fleet to take possession of (and of course to spoliate) the temple of Hercules. The Latin name of Hercules is here the designation of the Phœnician god *Melkarath*, in whose honour the founders of the colony had erected a temple on the eastern side of the little island on which the city is built. The Phœnicians came out to encounter the enemy in their long ships. The battle lasted for some time, without any signal success on either side ; but—all of a sudden—the Iberians were seized with a panic of terror—an unexpected fire consumed their ships to ashes ! The Iberians believed that they saw lions upon the prows of the Phœnician ships, and that these lions poured out against them flashing rays of fire, by which their ships were burned.

Such is the statement of M. Hubainville, ch. iii. pp. 39, 40. The account given by Macrobius of the burning of the Iberian fleet is in these words :

"......Subito in fugam versæ sunt regiæ naves ; simulque improviso igne, correptæ conflagraverunt, paucissimi, qui superfuerant, hostium capti indicaverunt apparuisse sibi leones proris Gaditanæ classis superstantes, ac subito suas naves immissis radiis quales in solis capite pinguntur exustas."—*Saturn.*, lib. i. ch. xx. p. 207 {Leyden, 1695).

Thus it will be seen that the Iberian fleet was destroyed by means of fire that had been discharged from the ships of the Phœnicians. The "lions' heads" were, most probably, the ornamental orifices to the engines from which the fire was ejected, and the destructive material must have been of a similar substance to that of the "Greek fire," the invention, as is generally supposed, of a later time, attributed to Callinicus, and which is described as being "blown out of long tubes of copper." If this be so, the incident mentioned by Macrobius is the earliest record of ships employing artillery, as they do in modern times, for the destruction of an enemy.   WM. B. MACCABE.

LOWLAND ABERDEEN.—Strangers reckon Aberdeen as belonging to the Highlands of Scotland. They have of late, perhaps, had some excuse for this, since its militia regiment has been named the Aberdeen Highland Light Infantry. Nevertheless, the city of Aberdeen and more than three-fourths of the county have been for some centuries entirely devoid of Celtic character. Indeed, there are few districts in which the feeling of antagonism of race has been kept up more strongly, or at least used to be so some years ago, than the Lowlands of Aberdeen. I do not know whether the feeling has been modified of late years ; but at the period to which I allude, some thirty years ago, Highlanders were often characterized as "sweer Hieland breets"—lazy Highland brutes. And still less flattering epithets were often added.

My present object is to inquire whether any readers of "N. & Q." can complete or give a different version of some rhymes which used to be shouted out by boys in reproach of their Highland neighbours :—

> "Hielanman, Hielanman, far ware ye born ?
> Up in the Hielans amang the green corn.
> Hielanman, Hielanman, fat gat ye there ?
> *   *   *   *   *
> Canna get naething but sowins and leeks.
> Lauch at the Hielanman wanting his breeks ! "

In some versions *siddies* or *sids*, the corn seeds out of which *sowins*, a kind of flummery, is made, is substituted for sowins, and in others *ingans* or *sibbies*, an old word for onions, is used. In another version the last three lines are run into two, thus :

> "What got you there ? Sibbies and leeks.
> Lauch at the Hielanman wanting his breeks ! "

My own notion is that there should be six complete lines.

I fear that this year there will be only too much of green or unripe corn in the Highlands. As to the allusion to leeks, it seems to have been introduced mainly as a word to rhyme with "breeks." In former times the Highlanders had scarcely any vegetables, and now they grow very few. I have never heard of leeks being characteristic of Highlanders, as of their Kymric brethren in Wales.
                                        I. M. P.

Curzon Street, W.

would appear to mean dirt ; but it is applied in a variety of ways. The other day, in Rutland, I was talking with an old cottager who had recently been left a widower, and I was inquiring about one of his married daughters, who had promised to come and live with him, and "do for him." The old man represented his household arrangements to be in a deplorable state, and ended the recital of his woes by saying, " If she don't come soon I shall be mucked to death." The words " muck " and " mucky " are usually pronounced " moock " and " moocky." When I said to an old Huntingdonshire farmer, " What a state the roads are in !" he lifted up his hands (as well as his voice) and exclaimed, " Moocky, moocky, woonderful moocky !" This was forcible, if not elegant. A Huntingdonshire woman, whose weekly duty it was to clean the parish church, complained to me of the school-boys, " They owdacious boys make muck all over the church." To the same effect a Rutland cottager the other day, when I asked him to walk into my study, politely excused himself by pleading that he was " all over muck," meaning that his clothes were covered with mud from the ploughed field. It may be noted that a farmer's dream of heaven was that of a place where there were " heaps o' muck."

CUTHBERT BEDE.

CHARLOTTE BRONTE : ELIZABETH BARRETT BROWNING.—*Jane Eyre* was published in 1847 ; *Aurora Leigh* in 1856 or 1857. I note the following points of resemblance between the two stories, conceding that, as a poem, apart from its narrative, *Aurora Leigh* is abundantly original.

Jane Eyre is pressed by her cousin, St. John Rivers, to marry him, but she declines the offer, on the ground that he does not require a wife, but merely some one to help him in his works of benevolence. A similar situation occurs between Aurora and her cousin Romney.

Jane Eyre, an orphan, is left to the care of her aunt by marriage, who dislikes and ill treats her, and dies after a short illness. Aurora Leigh, being an orphan, is taken charge of by her aunt, who misunderstands her and is severe with her, and who dies suddenly.

The proposed marriage between Jane Eyre and Mr. Rochester is interrupted in church, and Jane becomes a fugitive. The intended espousals of Marian Erle to Romney Leigh are prevented by the flight of Marian, whose disappearance is announced in church to the crowd assembled to witness the ceremony.

Rochester has his house burnt over his head. Romney Leigh has his house burnt over his head ;

J. W. W.

NEW WORKS ON WORDS WANTED.—

" It would be both entertaining and instructive were any one to collect the words in English invented by particular authors, and to explain the reasons which may either have occasioned or hindered their being incorporated with the body of the language. In some cases no want of the word has been felt ; in others the formation has been incorrect, or unsupported by any familiar analogy."—*Guesses at Truth* (ed. 1876), p. 219.

" It would form an interesting essay, or rather series of essays, in a periodical work, were all the attempts to ridicule new phrases brought together, the proportion observed of words ridiculed which have been adopted and are now common, such as *strenuous, conscious*, &c., and a trial made how far any grounds can be detected, so that one might determine beforehand whether a word was invented under the condition of assimilability to our language or not."—Coleridge's *Lectures on Shakespeare*, &c. (ed. 1874), p. 266.

WILLIAM GEORGE BLACK.
1, Alfred Terrace, Glasgow.

" CLEANLINESS IS NEXT TO GODLINESS."—I read some time ago in the *Jewish World* that this was in the Talmud. On Sunday, Dec. 3, a Jewish lecturer on the Talmud said :—

" This well-known English phrase had been taught by the Rabbins of the Talmud many centuries ago, both as a religious principle and a sanitary law."

No doubt this was the spirit of the laws in the Pentateuch. But perhaps the Jews may have had the principle from the Egyptians. Plutarch says in his *Isis or Osiris, or the Ancient Religion and Philosophy of Egypt* :—

" You are in the first place to understand this, that these people make the greatest account imaginable of all endeavours that relate to health : and more especially in their sacrifices, purgations, and diets ; *health is then no less respected than devotion*. For they think it would be an unseemly thing to wait upon that Nature that is pure, and every way unblemisht and untoucht, with crazy and diseased minds and bodies."

W. J. BIRCH.

[This saying, quoted by Wesley, has been traced in " N. & Q." to others of similar significance in the Talmud, in Aristotle and St. Augustine. See " N. & Q.," 2ⁿᵈ S. ix. 446 ; 3ʳᵈ S. iv. 419 ; vi. 259, 337 ; vii. 367 ; 4ᵗʰ S. ii. 37, 68, 213.]

OBSOLETE WORDS IN THE ENGLISH BIBLE.— Some works on this subject have been noticed ; but mention has not been made, so far as I recollect, of the earliest : *A Short Explanation of Obsolete Words in our Version of the Bible, and of such as are there used in a Peculiar or Uncommon Sense*, by Rev. H. Cotton, D.C.L., Oxford, Parker, 1832. ED. MARSHALL.

Queries.

[We must request correspondents desiring information on family matters of only private interest, to affix their names and addresses to their queries, in order that the answers may be addressed to them direct.]

"INKLE-WEAVER."—
"They chat together, drink and fill,
 And like two *inkle-weavers* swill."
—*Poems on Several Occasions*, by N(icholas) Amhurst, sometime of St. John's College, Oxford, London, 1720, 8vo., p. 115.
I heard the other day in Berkshire of two persons who had struck up a close intimacy, it was supposed, to outwit their neighbours : "Oh, they are as thick as *inkle-weavers* just at present, but how long it will last," &c. *Inkle* is used in Shakspeare several times, and means a coarse bad kind of tape ; but I should be glad to have any other references pointed out in which the weavers of inkle are in confidential and convivial comparisons.

"SHE'D TAKE UP A STRAW WITH HER EAR" (MS. Commonplace Book of Joshua Peart, of the City of Lincoln, Gentleman, 1726, 4to., pp. 165).—This line occurs in a somewhat homely lyric called "The Gossip's Song," beginning, "Two gossips they luckily met." It is probably to be found in some printed collection of the period. What does the line which I have extracted mean ? The saying was probably proverbial. In Shakspeare, and elsewhere, a wisp of straw is mentioned as appropriate to be shown or mentioned to a scold or "a callet"; and the Horatian *fenum habet in cornu*, meaning he is an ugly customer, literally an ox whose horns require to be blunted with hay, may perhaps each help to explain our quotation.

"LONDONS SCHOLLER-KILLING LETTER."—
"Death lies in ambush like an enemy,
 And brasheth where our sconces weakest be.
 Whether an icecle or drop of water,
 Or gnat, or *Londons Scholler-killing letter*.
 A thousand trickes we see of cunning death ;
 He finds or makes a way to stop our breath."
—"*Lychnocausia sive Moralia Facum (sic) Emblemata*," *Lights Morall Emblems*, authore Roberto Farlæo Scoto-Britanno, London, 1638, sm. 8vo., No. 53.
"Scholler" is "scholar," of course, for we have (supra, No. 46), "The schollar's badge are sallow looks and blanch." But what does the phrase mean, or to what does it allude ?

PARCHMENT LACE.—
"Nor gold nor silver *parchment lace*
 Was worn but by our nobles :
 Nor would the honest, harmless face
 Weare ruffes with so many doubles."
—"The Map of Mockbeggar Hall" (*Roxburghe Ballads*).
What kind of lace was this ?   HORATIO.

MCMAHON FAMILIES.—I am informed that the annals of the Collegiate Church of St. Peter, at Cassel, France (Département du Nord), exhibit in the list of canons of that church three Irish ecclesiastics named McMahon, or "Mac-Mahon." The first and best known of the three is Arthur Augustin de Mac-Mahon, who was Provost of the Collegiate Chapter for the long period of twenty-eight years. He was raised to that dignity by a royal ordinance on March 24, 1682, his immediate predecessor in it having been an Irish priest whose name is recorded as "Mac-Wyer or Magguire." The second canon of the name of Mac-Mahon was Hugh (junior). He was a near relative of the provost, and was one of his heirs. The third canon of the name was Arnould.

It would appear from documentary evidence that the Provost Mac-Mahon was "Archbishop of Armagh, and Primate of Ireland," who had taken refuge in exile from the persecution that threatened him at home. On this and other points I seek for confirmatory details. His testamentary executor was Hugh Mac-Mahon, Bishop of Clogher, who went over to Cassel, and on Feb. 14, 1713, signed the contract of sale of the late provost's house. This house is the present presbytery-house of Cassel, situate in the Grande Place, at the corner of the Rue d'Aire. The arms of the three Canons Mac-Mahon were Or, an ostrich sable, holding in its beak a horse-shoe of the same, pierced argent ; in the sinister corner of the chief a star azure.

The number of Irish dignitaries in the Chapter of Cassel may be regarded as an instructive, and is probably by no means an extraordinary, illustration of the operation of the penal laws in Ireland. Other readers may perhaps be able to cite parallel cases of equal interest, which I should be pleased to see. My primary object, however, is to beg the favour of information from Irish sources as to the Provost Mac-Mahon, Archbishop of Armagh ; Hugh, Bishop of Clogher ; and their family, and the possible relationship between that family and the present President of the French Republic, Marshal de Mac-Mahon. The armorial bearings of the latter are not those of the three canons. For any information on these points, or, failing details, for any references to probable sources of information, I, and I am sure my correspondent, should feel much obliged.
                                JOHN W. BONE, F.S.A.
26, Bedford Place, Russell Square.

SEAMEN AND TATTOO MARKS.—In the *Uncommercial Traveller*, ch. xi., on the wreck of the Royal Charter, there is this remark :—
"It is not impossible that the perpetuation of this marking custom may be referred back to their desire to be identified if drowned and flung ashore."
Is there any foundation for such a supposition ? or is the custom to be traced, as other authorities have it, to a traditional use of the old British habit of staining the skin ? Is it a common

EARLY BRITAIN.—The anonymous geographer of Ravenna has left a list of the British names (under Latin forms) of some old British cities and strongholds, but to the sites of many of them there seem to be no clues but the meanings of their names. Can any of your readers tell me what towns or earthworks answer to the following names ?—

(1.) Punctuobice, Br. *Pwnc-twy-bic*, now Poncdwy-big, Mount two peaks.

(2.) Bannio, Br. *Ban*, a prominence, high ground. Is Banbury on a *ban* ?

(3.) Conderco, *Con-derch*, high point. The Peak of Derbyshire, or what one ?

(4.) Dolcindo, *Dôl-cynad*, the steep ground by the meadow or lealand.

(5.) Melarnoni, *Moel-ar-non-wy*, the bare hill by the Non (or Nen) stream. Could it be by the river Nen ? *Non* means a stream.

(6.) Vindomi, *Gwyn-dom*, the White mound. Said to be St. Mary Bourne. Has it such a mound ? Not, I allow, a very singular mark.

W. BARNES.
Rectory, Winterborne-Came, Dorchester, Dorset.

SUPERSTITION IN YORKSHIRE.—A young woman has singularly disappeared at Swinton, near Sheffield. The canal has been unsuccessfully dragged, and the Swinton folk are now going to test the merits of a local superstition, which affirms that a loaf of bread containing quicksilver, if cast upon the water, will drift to, keep afloat, and remain stationary over, any dead body which may be lying immersed out of sight. Does this singular superstition exist elsewhere ?

EVERARD HOME COLEMAN.

DR. JOHNSON'S METEOROLOGICAL INSTRUMENT. —Sir John Hawkins says that Johnson wrote the dedication to the king for George Adams's treatise on the use of the globes, for which he was gratified with a very curious meteorological instrument. What was this instrument ? Was it amongst the doctor's effects at his death ? Who had it then ? And where is it now ?   C. A. WARD.
Mayfair.

THE MAYOR OF HUNTINGDON AND THE STURGEON.—Mr. Pepys says that on May 22, 1667,
" coming from Westminster with W. Batten, we saw at White Hall stairs a fisher-boat with a sturgeon that he had newly catched in the River ; which I saw, but it was but a little one ; but big enough to prevent my mistake of that for a colt, if ever I become Mayor of Huntingdon."

What is the story ? and who was the Mayor of Huntingdon to whom the diarist refers ?

HIRONDELLE.

do not find any entry of him in the register." Are there any other catalogues of his library except the undated one (? 1694), contents sold by auction at Tom's Coffee House by John Bullord, a copy of which is in the Brit. Mus. Library, and another in the Bodleian, and that of books sold " at Paul's Coffeehouse the 24th of January, 1714/15, by Thomas Ballard," copies of which were to be obtained " at his late Dwelling-Cottage near Clerkenwell " ? or is any catalogue known of his musical instruments or other property ?
GEORGE POTTER.
Grove Road, Holloway, N.

LEIGH, OF CO. WARWICK.—In 1643 Sir Thomas Leigh, Bart., of London, was created Baron Leigh of Stoneleigh, co. Warwick. The second Lord Leigh, grandson of Sir Thomas, had four sons and two daughters. The tale told here is that the eldest son, Thomas, the heir to the estate and peerage, who was born Feb. 3, 1682, murdered his father's footman and fled from his ancestral home, to which he never returned. He would be at the age of eighteen when it is alleged he committed the murder (*circa* 1700). Shortly afterwards it is asserted that Thomas Leigh was living in this town, and the name is to be found on our church registers. I should be glad if any of your Warwickshire readers could confirm, from contemporary records, the legend of Thomas Leigh's crime, and ascertain if for the offence he was outlawed or in any way, directly or indirectly, punished.   JOSIAH ROSE.
Leigh, Lancashire.

SCHOMBERG ARMS.—Seckendorf, in his *History of Lutheranism*, says : " Rhenani (Schombergii) stellam liliatam in scuto gerunt, quam vulgo Clivensem vocant, Misnenses leonem, *alia Helvetici.*" What were the *other* arms the Swiss Schombergs bore ? Where can I find any account of their families ? How were the Schombergs of Ober-Wesel related to, or sprung from, the house of Clèves ?   OTTO.

BRODHURST OR BROADHURST.—Can any reader, learned in family histories, tell me which of these two is the correct spelling of the name I bear ? The name is not a very general one, but is more frequently met with in Staffordshire than elsewhere. I never saw it spelt without the *a* in any other case than my own, but it has always been our custom, so far as I can trace, to spell it so. I should also like to know whether or not the family was originally a Staffordshire one. I believe it has been settled in that county for something like 150 years. It is probable that those who spell

the name in either fashion are derived from a common, though perhaps somewhat remote, ancestor.   J. PENDEREL-BRODHURST.
Colchester.

LEWIS BRUCE, D.D., Vicar of Rainham, Essex, was heir male of the Bruces of Earlshall in 1769. Was he ever married, and, if so, to whom, and did he have any male descendants?   W. B. A.

THE PRONUNCIATION OF "ARE."—I find that inhabitants of North America, whether born in the United States or Canada, pronounce "are" with the *a* long, so as to rhyme with "fare." Is this the old English pronunciation, surviving in our former and present colonies though extinct at home? Clearly it has analogy in its favour, and I do not know of an exception to the long sound of *a* before an *r* followed by *e*. The rule, I take it, is the same, whatever the intermediate consonant. We shorten the *a* in "have," but this may be an innovation. If *äre* is the old English pronunciation, can any of your readers say when the short sound of *äre* was introduced, and when it became current?   DAWSON BURNS.

ST. TYRNOG.—The parish church of Llandyrnog, three miles from Denbigh, N. Wales, is dedicated to St. Tyrnog. I can find nothing about this saint, and should be obliged if any of your readers can enlighten me.   ARTHUR MESHAM.
[Butler does not mention this saint.]

G. AND H. CABOT, OF BOSTON.—In the biography of C. Sumner, by Pierce, in vol. i. pp. 258, 310, and 360, there are references to his friends George and Henry Cabot, of Boston. What connexion has this name with that of the navigators?
HYDE CLARKE.

THE CIRCUS.—Are there any other books, in any language, on the modern circus, in addition to Mr. Frost's *Circus Life and Circus Celebrities* (Tinsley Brothers, 1875)?
J. BRANDER MATTHEWS.
Lotos Club, N.Y.

REGISTER OF PREMONSTRATENSIAN ABBEYS.—In Peck's collections for a supplement to the *Monasticon Anglicanum*, now in the British Museum, are numerous extracts from a MS. register, the marginal reference to which is "Reg. Prem." The extracts are generally of great interest, and often consist of quaint English letters. In Pegge's *Beauchief* this register is mentioned in a note as being (*circa* 1790) in the British Museum. I am told it is not in the Museum now, and possibly the reference in Pegge is an error. I am very anxious to know where it is, and, as the register is of such vast antiquarian importance, I am surprised that I cannot find any clue to its whereabouts. It surely must be well known, and

I should be very thankful to any one who could give me the reference to it. It probably consists of many volumes.   S. O. ADDY.
Sheffield.

AUTHORS OF BOOKS WANTED.—
Tales of the Forest : containing the Lotus-Walker and the Spoiler's Doom, by Snellius Schickhardus (London, Madden, 1853, 8vo.), includes "Songs of the Exile"—subjects Indian—two mythical cuts, and a note : "This volume was printed in 1842. Circumstances prevented its publication at that time."   J. O.

Letters, Conversations, and Recollections of S. T. Coleridge, in 2 vols. (Moxon, 1836).—Joseph Cottle's book is called *Early Recollections of Coleridge*.
J. M. SIMSON.

Replies.

BOOKSELLERS IN ST. PAUL'S CHURCHYARD.
(5th S. viii. 461, 489.)

The subject which DR. SIMPSON has started is one of considerable interest, and one which probably many would be glad to see completely carried out, not only in relation to St. Paul's Churchyard, but also to other parts of the City. A mere list of the booksellers and signs in the cathedral yard, with only brief explanatory notes, would occupy many pages of "N. & Q." In the two lists already given the first date is 1593, but the churchyard had been noted for its booksellers for many years previously. Probably the first bookseller there was Julian Notary, who dwelt "at the sygne of the Thre Kynges, without Tempell barre," in 1510, and who in 1515 had removed to St. Paul's, where he published *The Chronicles of England*, at the sign of the Three Kings, "in powlys chyrche yarde, besyde ye weste dore, by my lordes palyes." Not long after Henry Pepwell was a noted bookseller, at the sign of the Holy Trinity in St. Paul's Churchyard. His will bears date 1539, and in it he desired to be buried in the crypt of St. Faith.

The following list contains a few of the more prominent names and signs of booksellers who had shops in St. Paul's Churchyard between 1515 and 1590. The books which they sold may readily be found in Ames.

Date.	Sign.	Bookseller.
1515.	The Three Kings.	Julian Notary.
1520.	The Holy Trinity.	Henry Pepwell.
1523.	The A. B. C.	Rychard faukes.
1525.	The Meremayde.	John Rastell.
1527.	The George.	John Raynes.
1531.	The Saynte Nycolas.	John Toye.
1536.	Ye Maiden's Head.	Thomas Petyt.
1537.	The Lucreece.	Thomas Purfoote.
1539.	The St. Michael.	Michael Lob'ey.
1544.	The Brazen Serpent.	Reynold Woulfe.
1544.	At the West Door.	Wyllyam Teletson.
1548.	The George.	William Beddell.
1548.	The Hill.	William Hill.
1549.	The Star.	Thomas Raynald.
1550.	The Byble.	Richard Jugge.

1551.	The Lamb.	Abraham Veale.
1551.	The Rose.	John Wight.
1551.	The Red Lion.	Wyllyam Bonham.
1553.	The Holy Gho3t.	John Cawood.
1553.	The Bell.	Robert Toy.
1553.	At the West Door.	John Kingston.
1556.	The Hedgehog.	William Seres.
1558.	The Sun.	Anthony Kitson.
1559.	At the North Gate.	James Burrel.
1559 ?	The Cock.	John Turke.
1561.	In the Church Yard.	Rycharde Watkins.
1563.	The Crane.	Lucas Harrison.
1565 ?	The Black Boye.	Henry Sutton.
1569.	The Lucreece.	Thomas Purfoote.
1570.	The King's Arms.	William Norton.
1570 ?	The Key.	Thomas Hacket.
1571.	The White Horse.	William Williamson.
1572.	The Three Welles.	H. Binneman.
1573.	The Helmet.	Humphrey Toye.
1573.	At the West Door.	Richard Johnes.
1574.	The Green Dragon.	Francis Cradock.
1575.	The White Greyhound.	John Harrison.
1575.	The Grasse-hopper.	Christopher Barker.
1576.	The George.	Tho. Sturruppe.
1576.	The Brazen Serpent.	John Shepherd.
1576 ?	The Red Dragon.	Edward Aggas.
1577.	The Black Beare.	Thomas Woodcock.
1577.	At the S. West Door.	Henry Disle.
1578.	The Three Lillies.	Richard Day.
1579.	The Parat.	And. Maunsell.
1579.	At the North Door.	Edward White.
1580 ?	The Cock.	Robert Redborne.
1580 ?	The Saint Austen.	Heugh Syngleton.
1581.	The Bible.	Myles Jenyngs.
1582.	The Blacke Boy.	Timothie Rider.
1582.	The Mare-maide.	Nich. Ling.
1583.	The Crane.	Tobie Smith.
1584.	The Swan.	Gerrard Dewes.
1587.	The Helmet.	Thomas Charde.

With respect to the note of Dibdin, quoted by Dr. Simpson (viii. p. 489), as to the signs descending by will from father to son, I think there is perhaps a mistake. The passage in Joan Woulfe's will, dated July 1, 1594 (Ames's *Typo-graph. Antiq.*, 1785, p. 597), where she leaves to her son "The chapel house and the brazen serpent," did not mean, as is generally supposed, the house and the sign, but two independent houses—one known as the Chapel House and the other known as the Brazen Serpent. At the dissolution of monasteries Raynold Wolfe purchased from the king the chapel house and ground near St. Paul's, on which he built several houses. On the books that he printed he stamped the foreign device of the brazen serpent, and he adopted the same as the badge of his shop ; but there was no copyright in the sign, and he did not leave it in his will, Jan. 9, 1573-4, to his wife, and she could not have left it to her son twenty years later. It was because any one might take a known sign and adopt it that the term " old " was often added to a sign to distinguish it from a new comer : thus

unfrequently he abandoned it, and adopted the sign of the house to which he moved. About the year 1650 Sam. Gellibrand changed from the sign of the Brazen Serpent to the Golden Ball, but I am unable to say whether this was a change of house or of sign only. There were curious changes at the time of the Restoration. Thus, Hardy's book on *The Epistle of St. John, Part II.*, bears on the title-page, "and are to be sold at Joseph Cranford's shop, the Castle and Lion in St. Paul's Church Yard, 1659"; but at the end of the volume there is an advertisement of " books to be sold at Joseph Cranford's shop, at the sign of the King's Head and Bible in St. Paul's Church Yard."

In working out Dr. Simpson's suggestion it would be necessary to note the earliest and latest publication of each bookseller and of each sign. In doing this it is not always safe to trust to a single date. For example, *A Discourse concerning Auricular Confession* bears on its title-page, " London, Benj. Tooke, at the Sign of the Ship in St. Paul's Church Yard, 1648 "; yet on reading the book it will be found to contain references to J. Boileau's *Historia Confessionis Auricularis* as a work just published. Now, Boileau's book was printed in Paris in 1683 ; hence it is clear that the date of B. Tooke, at the Ship in St. Paul's Church-yard, is a misprint ; it should be 1684, and not 1648. The dates which are given in the preceding list are believed to be those in which books were first sold at the respective signs.

EDWARD SOLLY.

Sutton, Surrey.

In addition to the names and signs given by Dr. Simpson may be named the following, which I find attached to some of my old plays :—

Date.	Sign, &c.	Old Play.	Publisher.
1638.	At his house in Paul's Church Yard, at the signe of the Mary-gold.	*The Martyr'd Souldier* (H. Shirley).	Printed by J. Okes, sold by Francis Eglesfield.
1646.	At the signe of the Prince's Armes, &c.	*The Goblins.*	Humphrey Mosely.
1658.	The Printing Press in St. Paul's Churchyard.	*The Old Couple.*	Samuel Speed.
1637.	The White Lyon in Paul's Church-yard.	*Microcosmus.*	Charles Greene.

W. PHILLIPS.

There is in the Bodleian Library a folio broadside, entitled—

"The Description of a Monstrous Pig, | the which was farrowed at Hamsted besyde London, the xvi day of October, | this present yeare of our Lord God M,D,LXII. [Followed by two rough woodcuts and description.] Imprinted at London by | Alexander Lacy for Garat Dewes, dwellyng in Poules church yard, at the East | end of the Church."

Ames says that Gerard Dewes (no doubt the same person) kept a shop at the sign of the Swan, and used the following rebus:—"Two in a garret casting Dews at dice."

Ames also says that Raynold Wolfe "settled his printing-office in Paul's Churchyard, and set up the sign of the Brasen Serpent."

A further examination of the above-quoted work would yield a long list of early printers, and therefore booksellers, who dwelt under the shadow of the old cathedral, the first named being Henry Pepwell, who sold books at the sign of the Trinity, in Paul's Churchyard, about the year 1502.

GEORGE POTTER.

42, Grove Road, N.

LATIN VERSIONS OF FOOTE'S NONSENSE TALK (5th S. viii. 366.)—There is at least one other version into Latin hexameters besides that quoted by CUTHBERT BEDE. There are two misprints, "equisse" for *equisse*, and "Gargule" for *Garyule*. The following version into Thucydidean Greek lately appeared in the *Cheltonian*:—

Ἐισελθοῦσα δὲ ἐκείνη ἐς τὸν κῆπον, ὡς πέμμα ἀπὸ μήλων ποιήσουσα, λαχάνου φύλλον ἀπεψίλου. Ἐνταῦθα δὲ μεγάλη τις ἄρκτος κατὰ τὴν ἀγυιὰν ὁδοιπορούσα ἐτύγχανεν, καὶ διὰ τῆς θυρίδος τὴν ῥῖνα ἐντεθεικνία, Τὸ τὴν κονίαν, ἔφη, μὴ ἐνεῖναι. Καὶ ὁ μὲν οὕτως ἐτελεύτησεν, ἡ δὲ, ὡς εἶχεν ἀνοίας, τῷ κουρεῖ ἐγήματο. Ἐκαλοῦντο δὲ ἐς τοὺς γάμους οἱ Πραγματο-κρινεῖς, καὶ οἱ Πικκανοὶ, καὶ οἱ Γωβλίται, καὶ δὴ καὶ αὐτὸς ὁ Πανιανδροῦμος ὁ Μέγας ὁ ἐπ' ἄκρου σμικρὸν φέρων κεράτιον. Ἔπαιζον δὲ ἐνταῦθα πάντες Ληπτικὸ-δυναμενο-κίνδα, ὥστε καὶ ἀπὸ τῶν ἐμβάδων φέρεσθαι τὴν κόνιν τὴν πολεμικήν.

The following version by a friend has lately come under my notice:—

βῆ δ' ἰμέναι κήπονδε γυνή· σπεύδουσα πλακοῦντας ποίπνυε μήλοισιν, λαχάνοιο δὲ φύλλον ἀπέσπα· Ἔνθα δ' ἀναίξαν ἄρκτον μέγα χρῆμα θυρέτρην ὦσε χολωσαμένη· Τὸ δὲ μή τοι σμῆμα παρεῖναι· Ῥίμφα δὲ μιν Μοῖρ' ἔσχε, νέον λέχος ἔντυε κείνη κουρεῖ νυμφεύουσα', ἄτη δ' ἄρ' ἔην φρενοδαλής· ἔνθα δ' ἐπορσύναντο γάμον Γαριούλλιον ἔθνος, Γωβλίλιοι, Πικανοὶ, σὺ δ' ἄμ' αὐτοῖς ὄβριμον ἔρνος ἦσθα μέγας μεγάλως Πανίανδρος, κρωβύλον ἄρας κρατὸς ἀπ' ἀκροτάτου πεπυκασμένον· ἔνθα δὲ παῖγμα λαμβανέμεν τὸν ἑταῖρον ἔην, εἶθ' αὐτὸν ἁλῶναι· ἔνθα δ' ἴδοις μέγα θαῦμα· κόνις ὑπένερθε ποδοῖϊν ἔπτατο ἐκχυμένη, πολέμου βέλος ὀκρυόεντος.

While on the subject of curiosities in Latin and Greek versification, may I be allowed to refer CUTHBERT BEDE to Prof. Kennedy's *Between Whiles* (Cambridge, Deighton, Bell & Co.), p. 164? I shall be happy to send the extract either to "N. & Q." or to any reasonable number of correspondents.

Will any correspondent oblige me privately with the meaning of "Cum jure atque cum signo," in *Aul. Gell.*, xvii. 9?   P. J. F. GANTILLON.

5, Fauconberg Terrace, Cheltenham.

Without entering into any invidious criticism of the translations by the Eton Boy of *Punch* and Q. M. R., I think it may please CUTHBERT BEDE and those who have read what he has given to have another and, to my mind, a better translation:—

> "Protenus illa foras sese projecit in hortum
> Pluribus e caulis foliis resecaret ut unum,
> Dulcia conficeret coctis quo crustula pomis;
> Quum subito attonitam vadens impune per urbem,
> Monstrum horrendum ursæ visum est per claustra fernæ.
> Inseruisse caput patulisqu : adstare fenestris—
> 'Usque adeo ne omnis saponis copia defit'?
> Ergo illum leti vis improvisa repente
> Occupat. At miseram quæ te dementia cepit,
> Tonsorem vinclo tecum sociare jugali !
> Jamque aderat studio ludorum accensa juventus
> Jobliliana cohors. Garaniiæque catervæ.
> Impubesque manus Picaninnia. Quos super omnes
> Panjandri regale decus, cui parva coronat
> Bulla apicem, insigni et longe præfulget honore.
> Nec mora, certatum fictæ discrimina pugnæ
> Certa lege cient, capiendi ut cuique facultas
> Sic capiat, capiunt capti, capiuntur et ipsi
> Captores profugiuæ iterum fugientibus instant
> Tunc vero adspicires ocrearum e calcibus imis
> Pulveris ignivomi medicatos sulfure rivos
> Effluere et longos per terram ducere tractus."

This was given to me some time ago by a friend, who attributed it to "Tweed of Oriel." But as a specimen of what can be done with most unlikely words from which to render verse, let me give another. It was given to me some time ago by a Cambridge man, who said it was by one of the "Gepps" of Oxford.

Foote's nonsense English need not be repeated; but this is a translation of a Yankee advertisement which some years back went the round of all the papers:—

> "If you want a real fine unsophisticated family pill, try Dr. Rumbolt's liver-encouraging, kidney-persuading, silent perambulator, twenty-seven in a box. This pill is as mild as a pet lamb, and as searching as a small-tooth comb. It don't go fooling about, but attends strictly to business, and is as certain for the middle of the night as an alarm clock."
>
> "Si forte ægrotis poscas quæ detur alumnis
> Egregiæ pilulam simplicitatis? Adest.
> Hæc jecur instigat, stimulos hæc renibus addit
> Ambulat arcanas hæc taciturna vias.
> Disce repertorem : medicus Rumboltius audit
> 'Ter septem et senas pyxis aperta dabit.'
> Par agno pilul, est ; tenero quid mitius agno,
> Si quis amor dominæ deliciæque fuit.

That the boy or man who can do such translations "need not despair of doing any piece" may, I think, be safely allowed. But the faculty is peculiar, and I doubt whether much advantage would be gained by setting such an exercise, unless it were done quite exceptionally to see whether any boy's mind had a turn for this peculiar work.

GIBBES RIGAUD.
Oxford.

THE FIRST LOCAL NEWSPAPER (5th S. viii. 72, 140, 153, 179, 232, 330.)—Now that the question of the first establishment of the *Stamford Mercury*, and its right to rank as the earliest of our English provincial newspapers, has again been opened in the columns of " N. & Q.," allow me to produce a bit of contemporary evidence bearing on the subject.

Thomas Tanner, afterwards Bp. of St. Asaph, in a letter to Browne Willis, the Bucks antiquary, dated Norwich, Aug. 1, 1706, says :—

" The Norwich Newspapers are the principal support of our poor printer here, by which, with the Advertisements, he clears near 10s. every week, selling vast numbers to the country people. As far as I can learn this Burgess first began the printing news out of London; since I have seen the *Bristol Postman*, and I am told they print also now a weekly paper at Exeter."

Francis Burges, who died at the early age of thirty in 1706, established his press, and probably his newspaper, at Norwich, in 1701 ; and, until we have something more authentically supported than the claim of either Stamford or Worcester, Norwich must be considered as the birthplace of the first provincial newspaper in England.

MR. RAYNER says that he " only gave the *first* paper in each town," and considers that his list was " correct with the exceptions of Manchester and York"; but here we see three more exceptions to his correctness. There may also be added to his list the *St. Ives Post*, of which vol. ii. No. 1, was printed by J. Fisher, Jan. 20, 1718. And here let me note what has escaped the observation of Mr. Worth in his *History of Plymouth*, that the above mentioned Browne Willis, in his *Notitia Parliamentaria*, vol. ii. p. 292, has recorded that " Here [*i.e.* at Plymouth, in 1716] are, by Reason of the great Concourse of People, two Printing Houses to advertise Things, both which subsist chiefly by publishing News-Papers."

This interesting subject might be considerably enlarged upon ; but as I hope ere long to submit my observations to your notice more fully, in publisher's cloth, I will conclude with an endorsement of MR. RAYNER's remark, that " the subject is surrounded with difficulties."

W. H. ALLNUTT.

The claim for 1690, as the year in which it was first printed, is of modern origin, and the manner in which the proprietors fell into the mistake has already been pointed out in " N. & Q." If the age of a newspaper is to be considered established beyond controversy, because the proprietors have affixed " 1695 " on the title-page, what is to prevent a newspaper proprietor from affixing " established 1595 " upon his print? At all events, MR. PATERSON will have to throw over the *Stamford Mercury* in favour of the *Worcester Journal*, the latter print having recently affixed to its title-page " established 1690." There seems to be an animated competition amongst ancient local prints for supremacy as regards antiquity. Those who do not believe in these seventeenth-century dates simply ask for *proof* from those who have faith in them, and it is hardly necessary to add that no proof is ever forthcoming.

In reply to MR. DUNN, I would state that my date of the origin of the *Nottingham Weekly Courant* was the correct one. This paper first appeared on Monday, Nov. 27, 1710. The authority for this statement is excellent (see " N. & Q.," 3rd S. i. 479). WILLIAM RAYNER.
Blenheim Crescent, Notting Hill.

MR. DUNN must certainly be in error in his correction of MR. RAYNER, in stating that the *Nottingham Post* was started in 1719. I have now before me a copy of the *Nottingham Post*, No. 42, July 11 to July 18, 1711. This seems to settle the matter. As neither the name of the author nor the page of the *History of Nottingham* is given by MR. DUNN, I have not referred to any of the histories of that place.

ROBERT WHITE.
Worksop.

A BOTANICAL PUZZLE (5th S. viii. 146, 294, 378.)—The subject of the sudden appearance and capricious distribution of plants is no doubt " a botanical puzzle" not to be easily explained. But when plants present themselves on ground newly turned up, it does not follow that the seeds have lain dormant for a great number of years. Plants are always trying to extend their bounds, and in this they are greatly assisted by winds. As an observant poet has said :—

" How many plants—we call them weeds—
Against our wishes grow,
And scatter wide their various seeds
With all the winds that blow."

A particular soil or unoccupied spot will attract seeds blown about, and they will settle wherever they can find support. Thus old walls are covered by vegetation, and how soon a mass of rubbish abandoned to nature, or disused garden ground, gets covered with the goose-foot tribe and other weeds ! Stonecrops, mouse-ear chickweeds, &c., often cover the roofs of houses, where they were never planted except by natural causes. Snapdragons and the red valerian are very common upon walls, and hawkweeds are sure to mount upon them.

The henbane is a plant that loves manured or freshly turned-up soil, and it consequently appears in such places in what seems a wonderful manner. When walking in the gardens at Wellcombe, near Stratford-on-Avon, I noticed the henbane growing close to the finest flowers ; and in the Worcester Arboretum I once saw henbane actually flourishing within cucumber frames, and in this latter case the seeds must certainly have been recently deposited, though not by the gardener. A clergyman told me that in his churchyard, in Herefordshire, some henbane had sprang up on mould thrown out of a grave, and he thought it must be from disentombed seed that had long lain in the ground ; but it is far more probable that a natural dispersion of seed from some plant not far away in an unnoticed place was the cause. No doubt, as every cultivator knows, seeds are very uncertain in their germination in gardens, and will not come up at the time desired ; but how long seeds may remain under ground in a dormant state is not certainly known. I sowed a dozen or two of the seeds of vegetable marrow in my garden last spring, but only one came up, and I do not expect to see any more of them.

Gardeners dislike old seeds as not likely to be productive ; and, in experiments made at the Oxford Botanic Garden, the produce from seeds, commencing with one year's age and going on to twenty, disclosed the fact of decreasing fertility with every advancing year, so that seeds twenty years old would not germinate at all. But these experiments were made with dry seeds, and possibly in moist earth or under ground vitality may be longer preserved.

Other plants beside the henbane are intruders upon garden or upturned soil, and it does appear rather mysterious how they could come where they were not sown ; but this is not to be arbitrarily determined without due consideration. Last summer a lady applied to me to look at her garden, where she had caused a number of seeds of the vegetable marrow to be sown, but in their place some tall spreading plants had sprung up which she did not know. I found that they were the thorn-apple (*Datura stramonium*). Now the seeds of the Stramonium are so different from those of the vegetable marrow, that the one could not possibly have been substituted for the other ; and the lady assured me that she had never known

the thorn-apple to appear in the garden before the present year. On mentioning this curious fact to a nurseryman, he said that the Datura came up occasionally in his grounds, and had done so last year, though he had never cultivated it.

Every cultivator of even the smallest garden must have had experience how "ill weeds grow apace," and, like the tares mentioned in Scripture as coming up with the wheat, really appear as if "an enemy had done this" spitefully. But natural causes by winds and tempests distribute the seeds of noxious weeds, however vexatious it is, and the industry of man must counteract the operations of nature. It is remarkable that years ago Mrs. Barbauld noticed the henbane as an intrusive garden weed, for, in one of her prose hymns, one of the advantages to be found in that happy celestial "home" she is there depicting for the human family is, that "the poisonous henbane will not grow among sweet flowers."

EDWIN LEES, F.L.S.

Worcester.

With reference to MR. JACKSON's remarks on the spontaneous appearance of henbane, as described by me, in North Lincolnshire, I may say that it has certainly never been cultivated in this district within the memory of man ; nor is there, as far as I am aware, any tradition of its cultivation for medicinal or any other purposes. The most curious circumstance connected with the erratic appearance of this plant is its occurrence in situations which have not been previously disturbed for very long periods of time, such as the sites of old banks and hedgerows, woodlands, and old pasture land, known to have been in pasture for many generations. It is probable, therefore, that the seed has lain dormant not for eight or ten years, but for several centuries. While on the subject of hedgerows, I may remark that many of our fine old fences, particularly such as mark the boundaries of parishes, are of immense antiquity, and undoubtedly take us back to Saxon times. The rough banks, overgrown with blackthorn, wild-brier, and hazel, which formerly fringed so many of our hedges, making excellent cover for game, and sheltering hundreds of fieldfares and redwings in the winter, have now, to the sorrow of the lover of the picturesque, almost entirely disappeared under the modern system of farming. With them is fast disappearing from Lincolnshire the term "mud-fang," by which they were designated.   JOHN CORDEAUX.

Great Cotes.

"QUEM DEUS VULT PERDERE PRIUS DEMENTAT" (5th S. viii. 449.)—The Greek version of this proverb was first pointed out by MR. T. J. BUCKTON in "N. & Q.," 1st S. vii. 618 ; viii. 73. It is met with in a Scholium on the *Antigone* of Sophocles, ll. 615-20, as an old Greek saying, whence

It is cited also by Athenagoras (*In Legat.*, p. 106, ed. Oxon.). Erfurdt quotes, in addition, a fragment of Æschylus preserved by Plutarch (*De Audiend. Poet.*, p. 63, ed. Oxon.; *Euseb. præpar. Evang.*, lib. xiii. c. 3) and by Stobæus (p. 62, ed. Schow) :—

Θεὸς μὲν αἰτίαν φύει βροτοῖς,
ὅταν κακῶσαι δῶμα παμπήδην θέλῃ.

And also four iambic lines by Lycurgus (c. *Leocratem*, p. 198, R.) :—

ὅταν γὰρ ὀργὴ δαιμόνων βλάπτῃ τινά,
τοῦτ' αὐτὸ πρῶτον ἐξαφειρεῖται φρενῶν,
τὸν νοῦν τὸν ἐσθλόν· εἰς δὲ τὴν χείρω τρέπει
γνώμην ἵν' εἰδῇ, μηδὲν ὧν ἁμαρτάνει.

With these lines Heyne compares a trochaic fragment of Archilochus : ἤμπλακον καὶ πόυ τιν' ἄλλον ἠδ' ἄλη (wandering of mind) κιχήσατο (Heyne, *Ad Iliad*, ix. v. 116, *vide* Soph., *Trag.*, Erfurdt, cum Not. Herm., 1830).

MR. BUCKTON also pointed out that the Latin version is found first in the edition of Euripides by Barnes, and the Greek wrongly ascribed to Euripides, who, from the date, could not have been the author.

I would remark that the original passage in the text of the *Antigone* of Sophocles (not the Scholiast's comment) is by far the more poetical embodiment of the idea, and the poet's conclusion very striking in the case of such a victim :—

πράσσει δ' ὀλιγοστὸν χρόνον ἐκτὸς ἄτας,

which MR. BUCKTON, reading πράσσειν, translates, "But that he (the god) *practises* this a short time." In this, however, I venture to differ from him, and should read, with Hermann, πράσσει, and translate it, "But he (the victim) *fares* for the briefest time apart from calamity," *i.e.* his prosperity is but short lived—in Greek phrase, soon κακῶς πράσσει. E. A. D.

[All other kind correspondents on this quotation are referred to " N. & Q.," 1ˢᵗ S. i. 351, 388, 407, 421, 476 ; ii. 317 ; 2ⁿᵈ S. i. 301 ; 3ʳᵈ S. xii. 44, 99, 138, 294, 383, 471 ; 4ᵗʰ S. xi. 243. At the reference in the 2ⁿᵈ S., and at that in the 4ᵗʰ S., BIBLIOTHECAR. CHETHAM. has thrown a light on the age, if not authorship, of this saying which deserves to be kept in mind.]

" THE TOAST," BY DR. WILLIAM KING (5ᵗʰ S. iii. 68, 247, 275, 319, 418, 438.)—I have but just perceived the query of H. S. A. as to the *locus in quo* of a magazine article upon this very curious and most readable satire, entitled *By-ways of History: History of an Unreadable Book.* I hasten to inform him, with the hope that even

of *St. Mary's Hall, Oxford, with Dr. William* King, *Advocate of Doctors' Commons*, &c., whose humorous and satirical works were edited, annotated, and published (1776, 3 vols., 8vo.) by John Nichols of London, who prefaced them with an interesting memoir of the author ; and of whom Pope makes Lintot say, in the letter to Lord Burlington in which he describes his journey to Oxford with the bookseller, " I remember Dr. King could write verses in a tavern three hours after he could not speak." Of the former Dr. William King, author of *The Toast*, we have the very interesting but neglected *Anecdotes of his own Times* (second edit., 1819, 8vo., pp. 252), edited by P. R. Duncan, LL.D., who died Nov. 12, 1863, and of whom an obituary will be found in the *Gentleman's Magazine*, vol. lxi., N.S., p. 122. My own copy of *The Toast* forms one of the numerous pieces in Latin prose and verse which make up the handsome quarto volume entitled *Opera Gul. King, LL.D., Aulæ B. M. V. apud Oxonienses olim Princip.*, and of which, according to a statement of Dr. Bullock, the executor of Dr. King, only fifty copies had been preserved, and were dispersed among the old friends of the author. Mine is a fine copy in half russia, uncut, and fetched ten guineas at the sale of Isaac Reed.

WILLIAM BATES.
Birmingham.

" THE MIDNIGHT OIL " (5ᵗʰ S. viii. 491.)—The history of this proverb is to be seen in Plutarch. In his *Life of Demosthenes*, after speaking of his care in composition, he says :—

" For this many of the orators ridiculed him, and Pytheas in particular told him, ' That all his arguments smelled of the lamp.' Demosthenes retorted sharply upon him : ' Yes, indeed, but your lamp and mine, my friend, are not conscious to the same labours.' "—The Langhornes' *Trans.*, vol. v. p. 273, Lond., 1819.

Plutarch also notices the same anecdote in his treatise, *Reip. Gerendæ Præcepta:* —

" Pytheas said, ' That the speech of Demosthenes smelt of lamp-wicks, and sophistical subtlety, with keen arguments, and periods exactly framed according to rule and compass.' "

Plut., *Opp. Moral.*, Par., 1621, p. 802, E. The proverb, " Lucernam olet," is in the collection of Erasmus, and appears in translation as " It smells of elbow-grease " (*Paremiologia*, by J. Clarke, Lond., 1639, p. 92). The notion of the lamp, or oil, occurs in other phrases, as, " Aristophanis et Cleanthis lucerna " ; " Epicteti lychnulus " ; " Venusina lucerna." ED. MARSHALL.

This phrase first occurs, I think, in Gay's *Trivia*,

bk. ii. 1. 558. Speaking of the bookstalls in the streets of London he says :—

> "Walkers at leisure learning's flowers may spoil,
> Nor watch the wasting of the midnight oil."

The same author makes use of this phrase in the introduction to his *Fables*. The words "midnight oil" are also used by Shenstone, Cowper, Lloyd, and others.   FREDERIC BOASE.
15, Queen Anne's Gate, Westminster, S.W.

The following are earlier than Lamb :—

> "Whence is thy learning? Hath thy toil
> O'er books consumed the midnight oil?"

—Gay's *The Shepherd and the Philosopher* (introduction to the *Fables*), ll. 15, 16.

> "I trimmed my lamp, consumed the midnight oil."
> Shenstone's 11th Elegy, seventh stanza.

LAYCAUMA.

The use of oil (*oleum*) for literary night-work is common and semi-proverbial in the Latin classics. So "oleum et operam perdere" (Plaut., *Pœn.*, i. 2, 119). Cicero (and plenty more) repeat the same phrase. Having got so much from the ancients, the addition of "midnight" is not far to seek, and no great originality would be evinced in the combination. Bacon talks of his "midnight studies."   HORATIO.

"RUBBISH" (5th S. viii. 423.)—MR. PICTON would derive *rubbish* from Italian *robaccia* (the pejorative of *roba*), poor stuff, old goods (Altieri). He says that the history of the word cannot be traced further back than the middle of the sixteenth century, overlooking the article in the *Promptorium Parvulorum* which I have quoted in my *Dictionary*: "*Robows*, or coldyr, petrosa, petro (*i.e.* chippings of stones)." And Way, in his note on the word, cites a payment in the Wardrobe accounts of the year 1480 to "John Carter, for carriage away of a grete loode of *robeux* that was left in the strete after the reparacione of a hous apparteigning to the same Wardrobe." Horman, in his *Vulgaria*, says : "Batts and great *rubbryshe* serveth to fyl up the myddell of the wall." By Palsgrave, Minshew, Cotgrave, Florio, Sherwood, it is treated as synonymous with *rubble*, signifying fragments of old stone or brick, a sense obviously anterior to that of the Italian *robaccia*, worthless goods : "*Robrisshe* of stones, platras" (Palsgrave); "*Rovinazzo* or *ruinazzo*, rubble, rammel, *rubbish* of broken walls" (Florio); "*Rottame*, all manner of broken things, as splinters, shards, fragments, or *rubbish*" (Florio). When we look at the earliest of the forms above cited, *robows* and *robeux*, and also the application of the word to the *rubble* used in building, we may fairly suspect it to have been originally borrowed from the French *repous*, a technical term of masonry signifying concrete or rubble work : "A filling in with rubbish or rubble, *repous*" (Sherwood).   H. WEDGWOOD.

Universal negatives are dangerous things. MR. PICTON in his interesting and learned note asserts that the word *rubbish* "cannot be traced in our language further back than the middle of the sixteenth century." And yet that word, of course in an antiquated form, is of much earlier occurrence. In the *Promptorium Parvulorum*, about 1440, we find : "*Robows*, or coldyr. *Petrosa*, *petro*"; *coldyr*, Prov. Eng. *colder*, being the refuse of corn, and *petro* the clippings of stone, "petrones sunt particule que abscinduntur de petris" (*Catholicon Anglicum*, 1483). The old word, therefore, was evidently synonymous with our *rubble*, detritus, mason's refuse. Mr. Way identifies this *robows* with *robeux* (MS. 1480), *rubbrysshe* (Horman, 1519), *robrisshe* (Palsgrave, 1530), all denoting rough and broken stones. Moreover, is *robaccia* a sixteenth-century word in Italian, with the meaning assigned to it, "coarse, rough stuff"? It certainly does not occur in Florio.
                    A. SMYTHE PALMER.
Lower Norwood, S.E.

"FIFTEENTHS" (5th S. viii. 490.)—Tenths and fifteenths meant such a proportion of property, not so much per cent. It happens that a tenth is ten per cent., but a fifteenth is only six and two-thirds per cent. "Tandem finis Parliamenti erat taxa levanda ad opus Regis, id est, *decima* de clero, et *quinta-decima* de populo laicali" (Walsingham, *Hist. Anglic.*, ed. Riley, ii. 177). In some cases tenths were subscribed by *towns*, and fifteenths by the less wealthy *rural* population (Lambarde's *Peramb. of Kent*, ed. 1656, p. 55). Cf. "And a fifteneth and a dyme eke" (*Richard the Redeles*, Pass. iv. l. 15). I extract these references from my *Notes to Piers Plowman*, where more on the subject will be found. I hope it will appear that these *Notes* contain a good deal of information relative to affairs of the fourteenth century.
                    WALTER W. SKEAT.
2, Salisbury Villas, Cambridge.

This tax was imposed 14 Edw. III. (1340-41), when it was enacted that foreign merchants, and all others which dwell not in cities nor boroughs, and also all who dwelt in forests and wastes and "live not of their gain nor store," should be assessed at the value of a "fifteenth."
                    H. FISHWICK, F.S.A.

ELWILL FAMILY (5th S. viii. 369.)—Your correspondent A. H. will find that there were four baronets of this race, commencing with Sir John Elwill of Exeter, merchant, who was the son of a grocer of that city by his wife, an heiress of Pole. He was educated at the university, and designed by his father for a clergyman ; was knighted at Kensington, April 28, 1696 ; was Sheriff of Devon 6 William & Mary, and on Aug. 25, 1709, was created a baronet. He died in 1717, having been

Surrey, by whom, according to one authority (Halsted), he had no issue, while, according to another (Le Neve), it was his first wife who was childless. Sir John died in 1717, and was succeeded in the baronetcy by his elder son, John, who married Elizabeth, sole daughter and heiress of Humphrey Style, Esq., and through her he acquired Langley Park in Beckenham, co. Kent. Lady Elwill survived till 1731, but Sir John died in 1727, leaving no issue. The monuments of this pair are on the north wall of the aisle of Beckenham Church. The second Sir John was succeeded in title and estate by his only brother, Edmund, who sold Langley Park to Hugh Raymond, Esq. The Elwills appear to have maintained a connexion with Devonshire, where they had scattered landed property, including the manor and barton of Pinhoe, the place of residence of the first baronet. Sir Edmund Elwill died in 1740, and was succeeded by Sir John, fourth and last baronet, who married Selina, relict of Arthur, Lord Ranelagh, and daughter of Peter, the next brother of Allen, first Earl Bathurst. Sir John Elwill died at Totnes, March 1, 1778, and on the 5th of that month his remains were carried through Exeter in funeral procession on the way to his seat at Egham, preparatory to interment in the family vault. It is said that the hearse containing the body of Sir John Elwill was the first carriage that passed into Exeter over the new Exe Bridge. By the marriage of his heiress, Selina Mary, his estates passed into the Bathurst family, as mentioned by your correspondent, who will find fuller particulars in Le Neve's *Pedigrees of Knights*, 454 ; Halsted's *Kent* ; Lysons's *Devon* ; Lysons's *Environs of London* ; Oliver's *Exeter*, 171 ; *Reports on Devonshire Charities*, 1826 ; Nichols's *Collect. Top. et Gen.*, v. 341 ; and other authorities.

ROBERT DYMOND.

Exeter.

This gentleman was not the first but the fourth baronet. The title was conferred upon his grandfather, Sir John Elwill, Knt., of Exeter, by Queen Anne on August 25, 1709, and became extinct on the death of Sir John, the fourth baronet, March 1, 1779 (*London Magazine*, 1779, p. 139), or March 1, 1778, according to Burke's *Extinct Baronetage*. He represented Guildford in the Parliaments elected 1747, 1754, and 1761.

EDWARD SOLLY.

The fourth baronet, grandson of the first, who I think held some appointment under the county of Devon, mar. Selina, dau. of Peter Bathurst, Esq., and relict of the Earl of Ranelagh, but dying

Bicknor Court, Coleford, Glouc.

A. H. will find all the information he asks for in Burke's *Extinct Baronetage*. If he has not access to that work, I shall be glad to extract the article for him.   E. A. WHITE, F.S.A.

Old Elvet, Durham.

DR. WATTS'S PSALMS (5th S. viii. 409.)—In the Psalms as given in the large edition of Dr. Watts's *Works* in six vols., "with selections from his MSS. in 1753," the fourth rendering of Psalm l. is headed, "To a new tune." This carries back this peculiarity, which was at a later date omitted, to the fifteenth edition, 1748, the last during his life.

JOSIAH MILLER, M.A.

My copy is dated 1747, "printed for I. Oswald, at the Rose and Crown, near the Mansion House, and J. Buckland, at the Buck in Paternoster Row, near St. Paul's," and in it appear the words, "To a new tune," to the rendering of Psalm l. beginning, "The Lord the Sov'reign sends his summons forth."   W. PHILLIPS.

The words "to a new tune" and "to the old proper tune," as given by M. D., under Psalm l., from his twentieth edition, 1756, are not interpolations, for I find them exactly as quoted in my first edition of 1719.   J. O.

EDWARD HYDE, EARL OF CLARENDON (5th S. viii. 409.)—The most authentic thing about Clarendon is the *Life* he wrote of himself, as a continuation to his *Hist. of the Rebellion.* The best edition is that of 1875, 2 vols., 8vo, printed from the original MS. in the Bodleian. Then there is T. H. Lister's work on the life and administration of the earl. Also there is S. W. Singer's *Correspondence* of Henry Hyde, Earl of Clarendon, and Lawrence Hyde, Earl of Rochester. The Hon. Agar Ellis wrote an inquiry into his character, 1827, and tried to prove him an unprincipled man of talent. The late Lord Clarendon was his descendant. He belonged to the Hydes of Dinton, Wilts. Notices of him occur in Burnet's *Hist. of his own Times*, and in Evelyn and Pepys.

C. A. WARD.

Mayfair.

CURIOUS CUSTOM (5th S. viii. 446.)—A custom somewhat akin to that spoken of by MR. E. T. MAXWELL WALKER existed recently at Penzance, in Cornwall. In that town it was usual for the mayor and corporation, with the mace-bearers and constables in attendance, to go once a month in state to St. Mary's Church. At the commencement of the first lesson all the constables went out of church to visit the licensed houses, to see that they were complying with the then law in closing during the period of divine service. Some time before the commencement of the sermon the constables returned to the church, so as to be in readiness to accompany his worship on his homeward journey. The new licensing law has now done away with the actual necessity of this observance, and with an increase of the police force all the men are not required in the municipal procession.

GEO. C. BOASE.

15, Queen Anne's Gate, S.W.

REV. WILLIAM GARNETT (5th S. viii. 408.)—It is possible to explain that which puzzles MR. GARNETT. Matriculation is the admission to the *university*, not to the *college*, and the Rev. William Garnett may have had his name down for a time at Trinity, and yet never have matriculated.

C. F. S. WARREN, M.A.

Bexhill.

A William Garnett took his A.M. degree at Queen's College, Cambridge, in 1797. Could this have been the above gentleman ?   SYWL.

PORTRAIT OF BEATRICE CENCI (5th S. viii. 407.) —Cav. Bertolotti, who has written on the Cenci family, is equally desirous with H. C. C. to discover who was the painter of the portrait, and the earliest mention of it. Very curiously, however, he does not seem to be aware it was formerly in the Colonna Gallery, and he has published in *Giornale di Erudizione Artistica*, vol. v. fasc. 9, 10, Firenze, a catalogue of the pictures in the Barberini collection in 1623, where he thinks he has recognized the portrait under the title of a Madonna Egiziaca, by P. Veronese. When he becomes aware of his mistake, he will probably find and publish a list of the Colonna Gallery of the same date. I believe the earliest mention of Guido being employed in Rome is found on July 25, 1609, when he was paid four hundred scudi for some work done at the Vatican.

K. H. B.

In the collection of a relative of mine is a modern picture, painted by a Milanese artist, of considerable merit, though the subject is of the gloomiest kind—Beatrice Cenci after torture. She is about to be immured in a cell, whilst two figures, habited like Familiars of the Inquisition, and whose faces are hidden by cowls, support her slender figure. Her countenance retains traces of great beauty, though racked by suffering. On one side stands an ecclesiastic with his hood thrown back, who has evidently been administering spiritual consolation to Beatrice Cenci, and at the door of the prison stands a man habited as a soldier of that period, with his hand on the key. The picture is of considerable size, and the figures in it

are about one-third the size of life. What its date may be I do not know ; but to my knowledge it has been in the possession of the present family more than thirty-five years.

JOHN PICKFORD, M.A.

Newbourne Rectory, Woodbridge.

A PSEUDO-CHRIST (5th S. viii. 488.)—Beesley's *History of Banbury*, p. 91, contains this sentence :

"In 1219, according to Knyton, in a council of bishops held at Oxford, a blasphemous impostor, who had assumed the name and pretended to the wounds of Jesus, was condemned and was crucified at Adderbury."

This is probably another version of the circumstance stated by ED. D., although there is a difference of four years in the date, and Alderman-bury has been substituted for Adderbury, which is a large village seventeen miles north of Oxford, and nearly four miles south of Banbury.

WILLIAM WING.

Steeple Aston, Oxford.

CHRISTMAS SERVICE FOR THE GIFT OF A MANOR (5th S. viii. 486.)—Peter le Brus gave Henry Percy the manor of Kildale, which became the principal residence of the Percys in Cleveland. It was from hence, doubtless, and not from Pet-worth, that he would pay his Christmas visit to Skelton Castle, a short ride. Skelton Castle passed to the family of Fauconberg on a division of the Brus estates, a few years after this donation of Kildale.

I heard from a venerable Westmoreland statesman, now deceased, a modern instance of a "jocular tenure" almost parallel. "Fifty years ago I was great friends with Mounsey, that they called King of Patterdale. He offered to let me the fishing of Easedale Tarn. 'What rent ?' 'Five shillings.' 'Too much.' 'What will you give ?' 'Three halfpence.' 'Then you must come to Patterdale and pay it on a fixed day.' 'And you must give me my dinner.' So we agreed."   W. G.

DE STUTEVILLE FAMILY (5th S. viii. 447.)—The Lattons of Chilton, co. Berks, derived their descent from this family—at least, according to Ashmole. Many of them were buried in the adjoining church of St. Michael, Blewbury, where a number of their brasses, including shields of arms, if not swept away by recent "restoration," still remain. These bear, among other quarterings, "Ermine, three cross-bows or," by the name of "Sycheville." Whether this may be a perversion of Stuteville I cannot say, but I have never been able to meet with any family of Sycheville or Sychevyle.

ROYSSE.

A list of Stutevilles (originally from Estoute-ville in Normandy), barons by tenure from the time of the Conquest, is given in Nicolas's *Synopsis of the Peerage of England*, and the account includes Nicholas, brother and heir of Robert de Stuteville,

period at Dalham in Suffolk, and there continued for many generations. The pedigree is extant, and their arms are said to have been : Per pale arg. and sab., a saltire engr. ermines and erm. Crest : Paly of six, erm. and ermines, disposed feather-wise. Other grants of arms, differing entirely from the above, were made to the Stutevilles of Devon, Somerset, and Essex. For further particulars it might be well to refer to Add. MS. 17,732, Brit. Mus. Collection, and to Chart. Cat. v. iii.   WM. UNDERHILL.
66, Lausanne Road, Peckham.

The crest of this family is a camel's head couped proper.   HIRONDELLE.

THE EXTINCT IMPERIAL CONSTANTINIAN ORDER OF ST. GEORGE (5th S. viii. 349.)—In M. Maigné's *Abrégé Méthodique de la Science des Armoiries* (Paris, 1860, p. 319) is the following, under the head of orders of the Two Sicilies :—

" 3° Ordre Constantinien, ou de Constantin, appelé aussi Constantinien des Deux Siciles, pour le distinguer d'un ordre du même nom qui appartient au duché de Parme.—Créé, à ce que l'on croit, le 5 août, 1699, par Jean-François Farnèse, duc de Parme ; plusieurs écrivains lui donnent, il est vrai une origine plus ancienne, mais ils se gardent bien d en fournir la preuve. En 1734, Don Carlos, duc de Parme, étant devenu roi de Naples, incorpora cet ordre à ceux du royaume, et en renouvela les statuts en 1759 ; mais, le 23 août, 1816, l'archiduchesse Marie-Louise d'Autriche, ex-impératrice des Français et duchesse de Parme, le rétablit pour ses états, et, pour éviter toute discussion au sujet de la propriété de la grande maîtrise, les deux maisons souveraines de Naples et de Parme convinrent de conférer concurrément les insignes de l'ordre, qui n'admet, sauf quelques exceptions, que des membres de la noblesse.
" Cinq classes : Ecuyers, Frères servants, Chevaliers du mérite, Chevaliers de justice, Chevaliers grand-croix.
" Ruban : rouge.
" Les Chevaliers portent la croix à la boutonnière ; les grands-croix, en écharpe avec plaque."*
                                                  HIRONDELLE.

" STAG " (5th S. viii. 226, 298, 478.)—Cock turkeys in their second year and onwards are very generally called *stags* in Norfolk.   N—N.

SILVERSMITHS' WORK (5th S. viii. 369.)—I have bound up, under the title of *Pugin's Designs of the Fifteenth and Sixteenth Centuries*, published by Ackerman & Co., London, April 4, 1836, two parts on the subject, the first part being generally *Designs for Gold and Silver Smiths*, &c., the second part, *Designs for Church Plate*. It is very likely that Mr. B. Quaritch, the London bookseller, would inform Z. whether these treatises can be

* " L'ordre de Constantin est désigné, dans les anciens auteurs, sous les noms de : Ordre des angéliques, Ordre des chevaliers dorés, Ordre des angéliques dorés sous l'invocation de saint George, Milice Constantine de Saint-George."

THE "DE IMITATIONE CHRISTI" (5th S. viii. 489.)—I have a copy which corresponds exactly with that which MR. KREBS describes, except that the first book wants the engraving of Simeon in adoration. This has no doubt been torn out, as each of the other three books has its engraving. On the other hand, there is opposite the title-page an engraving of an angel standing by a cross, on the top of which is a crown. The title-page itself runs :—
" Thomæ a Kempis | Canonici Regularis | Ordinis S. Augustini | De | Imitatione | Christi | Libri Quatuor. | Editio Nova, Figuris | Illustrata. | Coloniæ | Sumptibus Balthasaris | ab Egmond, 1711."
                                               HENRY A. BRIGHT.

GREGORY CLEMENTS, THE REGICIDE (5th S. viii. 228, 353.)—
" Gregory Clements is hardly worth mentioning. He was at first a merchant, but, failing in that, he sought to thrive by a new trade in bishops' lands, wherein he got a considerable estate. He was turned out of the Rump Parliament for lying with his maid at Greenwich, but was taken in again when they were restored after Oliver's interruption. His guilty conscience and his ignorance would not suffer him to make any plea at the Bar or any speech or prayer at the gallows."—*The Indictment, &c., of Twenty-Nine Regicides,* &c., preface, p. ix, London, for the Booksellers in Town and Country, 1739.
                                                        C. W. J.

LEYLANDS OF LANCASHIRE (5th S. viii. 468.)— There is a pedigree of Leyland of the Grange, Hindley, in Foster's *Lancashire Pedigrees*, published in 1873.   C. J. E.

AUTHORS OF QUOTATIONS WANTED (5th S. viii. 509.)—
" Omne ignotum pro magnifico est."
This occurs in the *Vita Agricolæ* of Tacitus, cap. xxx. He puts it into the mouth of Galgacus, the British general, in the speech to his soldiers before the last fatal battle at the Grampian Hills : " Nos terrarum ac libertatis extremos, recessus ipse ac sinus famæ in hanc diem defendit, nunc terminus Britanniæ patet, atque omne ignotum pro magnifico est."   E. A. D.

This occurs in Tacitus, *Jul. Agric. Vit.*, c. xxx. Tacitus elsewhere uses a similar expression. *Ibid.*, c. xxv., there is, " Ad manus et arma conversi Caledoniam incolentes populi, paratu magno, majore fama, uti mos est de ignotis " ; and in Ann. iv. 23, " Sed missis levibus copiis quæ ex longinquo in majus audiebantur." He had been anticipated by Thucydides, who, in the speech of Nicias, vi. 11, 4, has, τὰ γὰρ διὰ πλείστου πάντες ἴσμεν θαυμαζόμενα, καὶ τὰ πεῖραν ἥκιστα τῆς δόξης δόντα.   ED. MARSHALL.

" Pity is akin to love."
Dryden has this thought expressed in his ode, *Alexander's Feast*, l. 96 :—
" 'Twas but a kindred sound to move,
For pity melts the mind to love."
But was Dryden the author of the thought, or had it grown into a proverb in his day ?   E. A. D.

Shenstone says :—
" I have heard her with sweetness unfold
　How that pity was due to a dove ;
　That it ever attended the bold,
　And she called it the sister of love."
　　　　　　　　　　　　　　Wm. Underhill.
Southern's *Oroonoko*, Act ii. sc. 1.　See " N. & Q.,"
1st S. viii. 89.　　　　　　　　　　　W. T. M.

Miscellaneous.

NOTES ON BOOKS, &c.

Scholæ Academicæ. Some Account of the Studies of the English Universities in the Eighteenth Century. By Christopher Wordsworth, M.A. (Cambridge, Deighton, Bell & Co.)

The one only fault to be found with this interesting volume lies in the circumstance that it is not in the same form as the author's former work, in two vols., *Social Life in the English Universities in the Eighteenth Century.* This premised, nothing but praise remains. The present volume is not only more important than its predecessors, but it is, what one would hardly expect, much more amusing. We have here, in full detail, "the history and method of the old Cambridge test and examination for the first degree in arts, and of mathematics...A place is given to the *trivials* (grammar, logic, and rhetoric), which under the more ancient *régime* led the undergraduate in his four years' march. Classics and moral philosophy (the subsidiary studies of the old *Tripos*) close this portion of the work." This accurately describes the serious history recounted by Mr. Wordsworth. The reader of it will perhaps be surprised to find how much constantly hard and important work was successfully got through in what some have thought an easy and rather idle era. We must add in all fairness that there is many a humorous trait flashing across these scholarly pages about scholars. Richard Porson and the *good* work he did are fully recorded, with all honour, in the *Scholæ Academicæ.*

The Invention of Printing. A Collection of Facts and Opinions descriptive of Early Prints and Playing Cards ; the Block Books of the Fifteenth Century ; the Legend of Lourens Janzoon Coster of Harlem ; and the Work of John Gutenberg and his Associates. Illustrated with Fac-similes of Early Types, by Theo. L. de Vinne. (Trübner & Co.)

The above title-page concisely describes the contents of this beautiful volume. By the words " second edition," on the same page, we see that the work has been appreciated by the public. It is one which undoes a good deal of imaginative history as to the invention and progress of the art ; at the same time it contains new and attractive details, attractively narrated. We hope the second edition may be as successful as the first.

Note-Book of Sir John Northcote, some time M.P. for Ashburton, and afterwards for the County of Devon ; containing Memoranda of Proceedings in the House of Commons during the First Session of the Long Parliament, 1640. From the MS. Original in the Possession of the Right Hon. Sir Stafford Northcote, Bart., M.P. Transcribed and Edited, with a Memoir, by A. H. A. Hamilton. (Murray.)

In the well-told sketch of the life of the above Devonshire gentleman, Mr. Hamilton says that, though Sir John Northcote's name is not to be found in biographical dictionaries among those of the busy politicians of his time, he was nevertheless a man of mark. Brief as the entries in the note-book are, they show that he who made them was a man of ready observation, and not

without foresight. The volume will have an honourable place among the chronicles of the same period.

With the new year Messrs. Cassell, Petter & Galpin have commenced the issue of two new serials, *Science for All*, illustrated, and an illustrated *History of the Russo-Turkish War.*

Commemoration of City Worthies.—A memorial window, in memory of Bishop Pearson, Bishop Walton, and Thomas Fuller, was unveiled on the 1st inst. in the church of St. Martin, Eastcheap. The window is in the Renaissance style, and at its base is the following inscription :—

" In D. O. M. gloriam, et in recordationem
　　　　　THOMÆ FULLER
　　Sacræ Theologiæ Professoris
Qui Anglorum laude dignorum vitas depinxit
　Ecclesiæ Britannicæ annales composuit,
　　　　JOANNIS PEARSON
　　　　Episcopi Cestriensis
Qui Fidem Catholicam interpretatione luculenta explicuit,
　　　　BRIANI WALTON
　　　　Episcopi Cestriensis
Qui compluribus linguis divinas scripturas edidit.
Discrimina donorum, idem spiritus.—1 Cor. xii. 4."

The inscription was written by Archdeacon Hessey.

The City Gates.—While Temple Bar is in course of destruction, the following paragraph may have a certain interest for some of the readers of " N. & Q." :—" As the reign of George II. drew to a close, in the autumn of 1760, a change came over the City of London, which, to many, indicated a new era ; namely, the destruction of their City Gates, in the preservation of which timid Whigs saw safety from the assaults of Jacobites. Read announced the fate of those imaginary defences in the *' Journal '* of August 2nd : ' On Wednesday the materials of the three following City Gates were sold before the Committee of Lands to Mr. Blagden, a carpenter in Coleman Street ; namely, Aldgate for 157*l*. 10*s*., Cripplegate for 91*l*., and Ludgate for 148*l*. The purchaser is to begin to pull down the two first on the first day of September, and Ludgate on the 4th of August, and is to clear away all the rubbish, &c., in two months from these days.'"—*London in the Jacobite Times* (Bentley & Son, 2 vols.).

Wm. Goddard's " Satyricall Dialogue."—I am reprinting, for subscribers only, the three very rare works of this outspoken satirist of the Jacobite times. The only copy of his *Satyricall Dialogue* that I can get at has had its head-lines cut off by one of those binders who have done so much to mangle the book-treasures of antiquity. Another copy of the book was sold at Mr. Corser's sale. Messrs. Sotheby kindly tell me that it was bought by Lilly, but was not in his sale. Can any " N. & Q." man tell me to whom Lilly sold his Corser copy ('twas *not* to Mr. Huth), or where it is now, or where any other copy is ? I want a transcript of the head-lines, and am keeping back my proofs for them. The *Mastif Whelp* and *Neaste of Waspes* are already printed.　　　　　　　　　　　　F. J. Furnivall.
3, St. George's Square, N.W.

Mary Robinson's Grave at Old Windsor.—Will you inform me where I can find a copy of the inscription on Mary Robinson's grave at Old Windsor ? The writing on the tomb is so much effaced that it is impossible to read it. I have found a copy of the verses on the tomb, which are given in Mrs. Robinson's *Memoirs*, by her daughter, but I cannot come across the prose epitaph, which gives dates of her birth, death, &c. The tomb is now being restored, and any of your readers who would supply the information would confer a great favour.　　　J. G.

succeeding editors were Mr. John Sterling, Mr. Duke (editor and proprietor), Mr. T. K. Hervey, and Mr. W. Hepworth Dixon.

Notices to Correspondents.

ON all communications should be written the name and address of the sender, not necessarily for publication, but as a guarantee of good faith.

To CORRESPONDENTS GENERALLY.—We have over and over again cases in which subjects are proposed to be mooted that have been the text of long and almost exhaustive discussion in the earlier volumes of "N. & Q." Our readers will therefore forgive us if we urge upon them the duty of searching the back indexes of "N. & Q." *before* ventilating their questions in its current columns, as then they would write with the latest information on the subject which interests them.

SIKES AND SYKES (5th S. viii. 468.)—MR. EDWARD SIKES (14, Belmont Terrace, Huddersfield) writes:—"I shall be most happy to give your correspondent information to the best of my knowledge on his writing to me at my address. Our family have been in Huddersfield for a long time." MR. G. W. TOMLINSON (24, Queen Street, Huddersfield) writes to the same effect, and adds, "from the nature of the reply it would be better to do it direct."

WEST INDIAN PEDIGREES.—CAPT. FORTE (7, The Paragon, Clifton, Bristol) writes:—"If your correspondent (5th S. viii. 400) will communicate with me I shall be able to refer him to a gentleman who is greatly interested in this subject, and has also in his possession a large number of pedigrees, dating from the seventeenth century."

MR. H. SMITH (Bray, Ireland) writes:—"I pasted a collection of book-plates in the first instance on sheets of paper of a uniform size, arranging them in alphabetical order, and kept the collection in a portfolio. As I purpose having the sheets bound together in book form, may I ask is this arrangement the best, or should I class the collection in order of precedence, from Duke to Esquire, with index at end?"

N. C. (Chelmsford.)—A Latin dictionary would answer the first query. To the second, we reply that Apsley House and old St. George's Hospital were originally of red brick. For the third, see any cookery book. The others could be answered by any intelligent child.

W. G. B. (Glasgow.)—Many thanks for the courtesy in letter marked "private." Absence from town prevented us from profiting by it.

ABIIBA (2, Paragon Buildings, Cheltenham) will feel very much obliged to THUS for a copy of the pedigree which he has kindly proposed to send.

S. L.—We should say that the Irish name *Morrow* is the foolishly English-shaped form of the purely Irish *Morrough*.

R. B. P. and W. H. B.—Letters forwarded.

E. C. B.— Received.

NOTICE.

Editorial Communications should be addressed to "The Editor of 'Notes and Queries'"—Advertisements and Business Letters to "The Publisher"—at the Office, 20, Wellington Street, Strand, London, W.C.

We beg leave to state that we decline to return communications which, for any reason, we do not print ; and to this rule we can make no exception.

LONDON, SATURDAY, JANUARY 12, 1878.

CONTENTS.—N° 211.

Notes on Books, &c.

Notes.

THE TRUE STORY OF THE CENCI FAMILY.

(*Continued from p. 3.*)

THE MURDER.

Rocca Petrella, where the murder took place, lies between Tagliacozzo and Rieti, in the wild valley of the Salto. It did not belong to Count Cenci, but was a fief of the Colonna family, though Francesco Cenci lived there for portions of the last three years of his life. According to one MS. the castle had a tower, and on the first floor a long gallery, open and ruinous, which joined some *fabbriche* beyond. Along this gallery on the night of Sept. 9, 1598, the murderers, Olimpio and Marzio—not the women—dragged their ghastly burden. The charge that Beatrice had hounded them on to kill her sleeping father, by saying she would do the deed herself if they were afraid, was, according to another MS., indignantly denied by Beatrice in the words, "Impossible! not even a tigress could do such a thing; think then if a daughter could!"

The dead body was thrown from the gallery on to an elder tree, where the next morning it was found, and buried after being exposed in the little church. What happened after shall be told in Bernardo's own words, who was with his brother Giacomo at Rome. A contadino had brought a letter to the Palazzo Cenci from Beatrice, announcing her father's death. The two brothers left Rome at once. When they arrived at the Rocca—

"we found a crowd before the entrance......We stayed there about a day, but Signora Lucrezia and Beatrice told us nothing about our father's fall, nor how it happened; they only wept.......My father was already buried when we arrived, and we did nothing about the funeral rites except to give fifteen scudi to Don Marcio, who undertook the matter.......No one came to the Rocca to offer any kindness, respect, service, or sympathy. I did not see where he was buried, for I did not wish to do so."—Bernard. 1 Const.

The next day they left the Rocca.

"When we left, many of the people of the place accompanied us on foot for about a mile. With us Olimpio Calvetti came also on horseback, and his daughter Vittoria riding too, as she was only about eight years old, the muleteers following with our baggage."—*Id.*

These extracts give a graphic picture of the Rocca after the murder,—the sons not giving a look to their father's grave; the paltry payment for the funeral; the fact of no one coming to the Rocca to pay respect to the deceased; the silence of the weeping guilty women; their departure, accompanied by their poorer neighbours, who perhaps loved them; while in their following rode the murderer Olimpio and his little daughter, who, as we shall see, was to be dowered with the price of blood.

They arrived in Rome, and joined the family of Giacomo at the Palazzo Cenci, and within three days the brothers took possession of their father's honours and estates. At the same time they put on mourning for him, which was paid for in 1601 by the Pope, on the petition of the drapers who had supplied it, and Giacomo ordered a magnificent hanging worked with the Cenci arms, as the fulfilment of a vow to Our Lady of Weeping, whose church was opposite his palace. But in their fancied security they could not escape the memories of the black deed that had rid them of a hateful presence. The words of Bernardo show the intimacy that complicity in guilt forced on them with their father's murderer. When asked if before the murder, when Olimpio came to the Palazzo Cenci, he had his meals with the family or alone, Bernardo answers, "Alone; I never was at table with him." After the murder he allows Olimpio "dined with me, my brother, my sister Beatrice, and Signora Lodovica, my sister‑in‑law; we were all at table together."

Suspicion, however, was aroused before Christmas. The authorities at Naples had ordered the arrest of both Marzio and Olimpio, on Dec. 10, as being implicated in the crime. Marzio was taken before long, and his confession—afterwards retracted, according to tradition—was the cause of the arrest of the Cenci. Gaspari Guerra, of Fano, sent a memorial to the Pope in 1601, alleging he had not been paid for the capture of Marzio—in

inquiries were being made at Petrella, they did not attempt flight: as one MS. says, "God refused them this idea that might have saved them."

THE TRIAL.

Some time at the beginning of January the brothers, if not the women, were already in prison. The first examination of Bernardo bears date Jan. 16, and the judges began with him as the youngest, and most likely to confess or contradict himself. Cav. D'Albono publishes the six examinations from his MS. copy of part of the trial. From these we find that to May 2 he firmly maintains his ignorance of any plot against his father's life. There is then an interval extending to August 7, on which day, after repeating his denial, when confronted with Giacomo—it would seem for the first time—he confirms his brother's confession of their mutual guilt. What could have prompted so sudden a confession it is impossible to imagine, as Farinacci distinctly declares torture had not been used at this examination. All we know is that since his last appearance before his judges, on May 2, fresh suspicions had been aroused. Olimpio, the second assassin, formerly *custode* of Rocca Petrella, and dismissed by Count Cenci, who had also *toccato l' onore*—how is not known—was killed on May 17. This fresh murder was committed by three men, one of whom had been steward of Giacomo Cenci. In some way or other, which the evidence does not explain, Monsignor Guerra was later implicated in the crime of the Cenci, and every one has imagined that he and Giacomo procured the murder of Olimpio, in order to dispose of a dangerous witness against them. Bertolotti adopts this idea, that Giacomo availed himself of a proclamation from Naples, setting a price on the head of Olimpio, to have him killed, and thus frustrate justice in its own name. But this theory seems untenable, as in the very proclamation cited by Bertolotti the name of the steward appears as, with the two others, receiving a commission from the Viceroy to take Olimpio alive or dead. Another of the three had also been in service at the Palazzo Cenci, according to the evidence, which is strange, to say the least. Full particulars are given of the murder, which was committed in a most cold-blooded fashion. While Olimpio stopped a moment, to give the tired steward a lift on his horse, he was instantly stunned, and his head, cleft by an axe, was cut off, and carried to the viceregal tribunal.

This occurred on May 17. How or when evidence was obtained against Monsignor Guerra cannot be ascertained. The MSS. declare that, in consequence of his being implicated in Olimpio's evidence, when taken in 1602, he says he ret Rome about the middle of July, in the cardinal's coach and six, ostensibly to pay a visit at Tivoli whence he fled on horseback to Celano, in the kingdom of Naples.

Perhaps this flight made suspicion against the family still stronger; at any rate, on August 7 both Giacomo and Bernardo confessed their guilt. The confession of Bernardo is subjoined, but we must remember his brother later declared him entirely innocent:—

"If I have in past time denied all, I now say that what my brother affirms is true; that is, about the coming of Olimpio some days before my father's death and his consultation with Giacomo. Paolo, and myself when he told us he intended to kill my father because he had 'toccato l' onore,' and sent him away from th Rocca: also that Beatrice our sister was dissatisfied with my father's treatment, as he kept her so shut up tha she would not bear that life any longer, 'non volev stare piu a quella vita,' and therefore had determined t have him killed, and wished Olimpio to do the deed, t which Beatrice was anxious that we should give ou consent."

He then further confesses that Beatrice an Lucrezia gave him details of the murder, whic were confirmed by Olimpio when he came to Rom later, and at the foot of his deposition he writes "Io Bernardo Cenci ho deposto per la verità come sopra."

As for Beatrice, till August 10 she seems t have denied everything, even under torture. Bu strange to write, on that day, when questione *without torture*, she confesses to having parleyed with Olimpio :—

"I told him to do nothing without the consent c my brothers.......He said, 'Your brothers will agre willingly.' So it was settled that he should go to Rom and speak to them.......He came back to Petrella, an told me he had spoken to *Giacomo only*, as he would no have any dealings with boys, and that he had promise Giacomo to kill our father. and that he would keep fait with him, as it would be disgraceful not to do so."

The same day she denies having made any promis of reward to Olimpio, "non havendo mente a mi disposizione." The next day she was called fac to face with the others, and then admitted bavin consented to, if not originated, the promise of dowry of 2,000 scudi to his little daughter, as th price of the murder. The trial was now practicall over, the confessions had been made or extorted and the Pope is said to have ordered the usu punishment of parricides to be inflicted.

A careful study of the documents relating to th trial shows :—

1. That no charge of unnatural conduct o

* The confession of Beatrice is the only part of he examinations found in D'Albono's MSS.

the part of Count Cenci was ever advanced by the family. Farinacci, their advocate, alone depended on the foul accusation to save Beatrice, whose guilt he assumed in the opening words of his defence, considering that if he could save her, he could save the rest, who were guilty in a minor degree. Her imprisonment by Count Cenci may have been caused by some clandestine attachment he had discovered, which had resulted in the birth of the *fanciullo* we shall hear of later. It cannot be supposed that any over-refinement in those days would have prevented some confirmation being given of Count Cenci's criminal passion, by his wife at least, when the lives of four persons were at stake. Tradition asserts that Beatrice always denied the existence of such a passion, and Scolari claims her as a martyr who died rather than stain her good name. Yet how shall we explain that her own advocate put forth this plea? In a letter to Farinacci she says :—" If I had done myself any injury [suicide?] I should have fallen under the malediction of the Holy Father." In another, to Cardinal Aldobrandini, she speaks of herself as

"martyrized and oppressed by my own flesh and blood, from which oppression having besought deliverance oftentimes of the Blessed Virgin, all my prayers and devotions were of no avail, and if I had done myself any injury I should have fallen," &c.

These dark hints may only mean that her life was unbearable, and the mystery must remain a mystery still.

2. The guilt of Beatrice as designer of, or at least abettor in, the plot is certain. She throws the blame on Olimpio, saying that he was always suggesting it to her ; but we cannot suppose that Olimpio, however he might have suffered at Count Cenci's hands, would, to avenge himself, propose a scheme of murder to the daughter. We must remember that Giacomo had his own injuries, his scanty maintenance, his imprisonment, his exclusion from inheritance, and Beatrice her forced captivity, probably made worse by blows, to spur them on, while they found a ready tool in the injured Olimpio.

A woman of twenty-one who could endure the rack without flinching could not have been made of too tender stuff. The days, too, in which she lived were days of blood. Her father had laid an ambush for a near relation at his own palace door ; two brothers had died by the assassin's hand ; and men were then wont to avenge the honour of their wives or daughters by the death of both lovers. Perhaps Beatrice may have thought that her own life was not safe, and that a murder committed by another, who had his own wrongs to avenge, was no longer a parricide. Be it as it may, I leave the question to the judgment of my readers, and pass on.   K. H. B.

(*To be continued.*)

CHAUCERIANA.

JAKK OF DOVER.—
" Any many a Jakk of Dover hastow sold
    That hath be twyes hoot and twyes cold."
                    The Coke's Prologe, 22.

Urry has : "Jack of Dovyr, *Jack-a-dover*, 1239, *i.e.* a fowl or joint of meat done over again, as is explained, *ib.* 1240." Bailey renders "Jack of Dover" a "joint of meat dressed over again." Tyrwhitt says : "The general purport of this phrase is sufficiently explained in the following line ; but the particular meaning I have not been able to investigate." Urry makes a guess from the second line, and Bailey and Tyrwhitt follow suit. At the very first it struck me that as the term "Jack" is frequently applied to large things, the Dover sole, which is both large and far-famed, might be very well termed "Jack of Dover." On referring to one of the old numbers of "N. & Q.," I find that MR. JOHN ADDIS, writing on this word *crux*, says :—"See a note in Hazlitt's *Shakspeare Jest Books*, ii. 366, which seems to settle that the Jakk is a 'sole.' "

JORDANES.—
" And thine urinales, and thi jordanes,
    Thine Ypocras, and thine Galiounes."
                The Prologe of the Pardoner, 19.

Skinner renders *jordains*, double urinals ; Wright gives *jordanes*, chamber pots ; Tyrwhitt says : "This word is in Walsingham, p. 288, ' duæ ollæ, quas *Jordanes* vocamus, ad ejus collum colligantur.' This is part of the punishment of a pretended *phisicus et astrologus*, who had deceived the people by a false prediction. Hollinshed calls them *two jordan pots*, p. 440." The word is from French *jarron*, dim. of *jarre*, a jar, large pitcher ; or *i.q.* Spanish *jarrón*, a large jug, an urn, augmen. of *jarra*, a jug, jar, pitcher ; from Arabic *jarrah*, a jar. Indeed, from the French or Spanish words we have also the slang term *jerry*.

PELL.—
" God save the lady of thys pel,
    Our oune gentil lady Fame."
                The House of Fame, 220.

Speght gives *pel* ; Urry and Tyrwhitt, *pell*, a house, cell ; Skinner renders *pell*, a palace ; Bailey, a house. If it means "house," it is from O. Fr. *pila*, " porte, entrée " ; but I prefer Mr. Morris's rendering, "castle," "fortress." This agrees with Chalmers, who says : " *Pil* in the British and Cornish, as well as in ancient Gaulish, signifies a stronghold or fortress, a secure place. There are a number of old forts called by this name ; as the Peel of Gargunno, the Peel of Gardin, the Peel of Linlithgow, Peel Castle in E. Kilbride, Lanarkshire. The term *pil* or *peel* is unknown to the Irish language or the Scoto-Irish, as well as to the Teutonic." The Cornish has also "*pil*, a hillock, a sea-ditch, a trench filled at high-water,

SWINTON OF THAT ILK.

I met the other day with a document which interested me much—a lease in the Scottish vernacular, by " Jon of Swynton, lord of that Ilk," to the Prioress of the Cistercian nunnery of Cold-stream-on-Tweed. John of Swinton leases to them all his land of " litill Swynton " for ten years, from Whitsunday 1424. The amount of rent is not given, merely " the raward mad and for to be mad to me both temporal and spiritual "—the latter no doubt prayers for his welfare. The deed is undated, but it is executed at Dunbar, in all likelihood about the term when the tenants took possession. Now this was an historical personage ; none other than the John Swinton who figured at the battle of Baugé (April 3, 1421), where he is said by some historians to have overthrown Thomas of Clarence, the brother of Henry V., with his lance, and is usually styled " Sir John," though it is evident from this lease he was not a knight even in 1424. From the mention of Dunbar it is likely he was on the eve of sailing for France, where he was killed at Verneuil (August 27, 1424). The same MS. vol. in which I met with the above lease (the Register of Coldstream, Harl. MSS., Brit. Mus.) reveals another fact in the early history of this old Border family. The first presumed "Swinton" was Ernulf, who obtained from David I. a charter of Swinton, " meo militi Hernulfo " (Coldinghame Charters, No. xii.). In the " Quæquidem," or deduction of title from previous owners, it is said that it had belonged previously to Liulf, son of Edulf, and Udard his son. But not a word is said of any relationship between these three persons and Ernulf, the new grantee, which would have been stated had there been any. Yet they have usually in the Swinton pedigree been set forth as the grandfather, great-grandfather, and father of Ernulf. In another grant of David I. to Ernulf (Cold. Charters, No. xiii.) the lands are said to have been held by " Udard the Sheriff." Still no relationship is given between the two. Indeed, hitherto there has been no evidence that Ernulf ever used the surname of Swinton. He evidently had none before he got the lands. This was pointed out by the learned John Riddell, yet he, though he must have had this MS. chartulary or a tran-script (Adv. Library) in his hands, does not, so far as I have seen, notice the fact that in the eleventh charter, which is granted by " C. Comes " (Cospatric, the third Earl of March, who died before 1166), the fourth witness is " Ern[ulfus]

---

by William Dixon, Prior of Colding-hame, to the Prioress of ·Coldstream, of the same lands, for " al ye tym yat ye land is in warde till us," at a rent of forty shillings annually. This shows that John Swinton was dead, and his heir a minor, wherefore the superior lords, the prior and convent of Coldinghame, had the ·right to take the profits of the lands till the heir's majority. This interesting MS. is soon to be printed by the Grampian Club, under the editorship of " A. S. A.," a gentleman not a stranger in these columns. .

ANGLO-SCOTUS.

THE COURTS OF FLEET STREET.

As one of the principal City thoroughfares, with many historical associations, Fleet Street has been brought prominently under notice by Mr. Noble and others ; and its frays, pageants, churches, celebrated houses, and still more celebrated resi-dents, have each in turn received a full measure of attention. But, as it has been pointed out, Fleet Street, wealthy as it is in these respects, is rich also in another way—in the number of its courts, branching out on both sides, and not by any means to be confounded with the narrow pas-sages remaining in the neighbourhood, and known as alleys.

These courts, originally named, for the most part, from the signs of taverns or other well-known houses to be found in days of yore between Fleet Bridge and Temple Bar, are twenty-three in num-ber, and may be roughly described as cricket-bat shaped, with the handles turned towards the main thoroughfare. Their titles show, as might be expected, a great diversity, and therefore it is somewhat remarkable that, while we find the Crane, Falcon, Popinjay (Poppin), and Hen and Chickens, as well as the Red Lion, Boar's Head, the Hind, and the Hare, there exists at the same time no allusion to fish of any kind—not even to the extent of a solitary mermaid. Royalty is represented by Three King Court and Crown Court ; while episcopacy appears in references to the Mitre, St. Dunstan, Salisbury, and Peter-borough. The Bell also seems to have an eccle-siastical significance, and the Bolt may be assumed to pertain to martial matters or the chase, or both. The classical student is conciliated by allusions to Apollo and Hercules' Pillars ; and family names are discerned in Child's Place and in Pleydell and Johnson's Courts. Finally, to wind up the list, Racquet Court and Wine Office Court speak to us of recreation, and serve to enforce the old warning concerning the deteriorating effect of all work and no play.

Touching the court last named, a story is told

which, as it is not given in Mr. Noble's interesting volume, may be worth recording. It is said that the brilliant and facetious Dr. Maginn had, upon a certain occasion, been dining out, and was proceeding homeward, when he was suddenly brought to a standstill by what may be called, in the language of history, "an intestine commotion ending in a general rising." Whilst steadying himself by leaning for support against Temple Bar, he was accosted by a stranger, who inquired the way to Wine Office Court. "My dear sir," said the doctor, with a rueful pleasantry, "allow me to express my great regret that I am unable to furnish the information you seek. Unfortunately I do not know Wine Office Court, but there," pointing to the roadway, "is wine off his stomach."

Up to the commencement of the present century the majority of the Fleet Street courts was composed of private houses, occupied for the most part by persons of fairly good position, who combined a liking for city life with a taste for peace and quietness, and who could say with Cowper:—

"'Tis pleasant, through the loopholes of retreat,
To peep at such a world; to see the stir
Of the great Babel, and not feel the crowd;
To hear the roar she sends through all her gates
At a safe distance, where the dying sound
Falls a soft murmur on th' uninjur'd ear."

But this has all been changed, and trade, growing too big for the crowded highway, has pushed up side streets and through other openings, and thus it has come to pass that the old residents, with their families, have long since fled to the suburbs or more distant places, and the once retired spots, where trees were planted and gardens cultivated, have been given up to printers, engravers, binders, and other zealous caterers for the ever-increasing demands of a book-coveting and newspaper-loving public.   WM. UNDERHILL.

Lausanne Road, Peckham.

JOHN KEATS.—In *The Life and Letters of John Keats* (Moxon, 1867), Lord Houghton says at p. 3, "He [Keats] was born on October 29, 1795"; and in a foot-note to the statement :—

"This point, which has been disputed (Mr. Leigh Hunt making him a year younger), is decided by the proceedings in Chancery on the administration of his effects, where he is said to have come of age in October, 1816 (Rawlings *v.* Jennings, June 3, 1825)."

In the shorter memoir prefixed to *The Poetical Works of John Keats* (Moxon, 1868), Lord Houghton repeats the same date (p. x). On looking through Leigh Hunt's papers to-day, I found a copy of *The Literary Pocket-Book; or, Companion for the Lover of Nature and Art* (C. & J. Ollier), for the year 1821, which belonged to Mrs. Leigh Hunt, and on the fly-leaf of which is written, by Leigh Hunt : "To Marian Hunt, from her affectionate husband." In the pages for diary

Mrs. Hunt has entered the birthdays of her numerous friends, such as—

January 22. "Lord Byron."
February 10. "Mr. Lamb, born 1775."
March 3. "Mr. Godwin."
April 10. "Mr. Hazlit."
April 27. "Mrs. Wolstonecroft."
May 24. "Mr. Hogg."
July 4. "Mr. Shelley born 1793."
August 17. "Mrs. Novello."
August 30. "Mrs. Shelly."
September 6. "Mr. Novello."
October 18. "Mr. Peacock."
October 19. "Mr. Hunt."

And under date Monday, October 29, is, "Mr. Keats, born 1796 ; told me by himself at the time I entered the date in a former book." It was doubtless on this authority that Hunt, *apud* Lord Houghton, made Keats "a year younger" than his noble biographer. I am aware that a man cannot be regarded as able to give conclusive or even the best evidence of the *date* of his own birth, but it is interesting to know Keats's own belief in the matter, and in the absence of any certificate this is not without a certain value. Was a certificate of Keats's baptism (certificates of *birth* did not then exist) produced in the Chancery case? If so, a copy of it is easily attainable, or a biographer might do what Mr. Charles Kent has recently done, with the assistance of the Rev. Dr. Vaughan, in the case of Charles Lamb. In the absence of any documentary evidence, I should say that this entry by Mrs. Leigh Hunt is of some importance. I may add that under Friday, February 23, Mrs. Hunt has entered, "Mr. Keats died at Rome," "1821" being added by her in pencil. Under November 21 we get "Mr. Proctor"; and December 3, "Miss Lamb, 1764." In their due chronological order Mrs. Hunt has also entered dates of the birth of her children, with, in most cases, the place of birth added.

S. R. TOWNSHEND MAYER.

Richmond, Surrey.

"WHIG" AND "TORY."—In that curiously illustrative book, *London in the Jacobite Times*, it says in vol. ii. p. 352 :—

"Lord Marchmont thought Johnson had distinguished himself by being the first man who had brought *Whig* and *Tory* into a dictionary."

Now does this mean that Johnson was the first to give what his lordship thought the correct definition, or that his dictionary was the first that contained these words? Johnson's *Dictionary*, according to Croker, was published on April 15, 1755. Now I have before me

"Dictionarium Britannicum, or a more Compleat Universal Etymological English Dictionary than any Extant. The Whole Revis'd and Improv'd by N. Bailey. London. printed for T. Cox at the Lamb, under the Royal Exchange, 1730."

In this I find :—

accusing him of favouring the rebellion and massacre of the Protestants in Ireland, gave his partizans the name of *Tories;* but of late the name has been transmitted to those that affect the *style of High Churchmen,* and since the death of King James II. to the partizans of the Chevalier de St. George."

Is this the first edition of Bailey's *Dictionary?* Can any one give a definition published before 1730? CLARRY.

MARRIAGE OF CHARLES I. AND HENRIETTA MARIA.—The following extract, describing the rites observed at the wedding of Charles I. and Henrietta Maria, may fitly find a corner for itself in "N. & Q." It is taken from the treatise by Pope Benedict XIV., *De Synod. Diœces.,* Romæ, MDCCLXVII., lib. vi. cap. v. § 5 (vol. i. p. 154) :—

"In Collationibus Ecclesiasticis Parisiensibus *de Matrimonio, tom. iii. l:b. i. collat* 2, § 5, exhibetur ritus quo celebratæ fuerunt nuptiæ inter *Henrichetam* e Regio Francorum sanguine Principem, et *Carolum I.,* Magnæ Britanniæ Regem, quibus Apostolicam dispensationem *Urbanus* Papa VIII. in eum finem concesserat: quæ nuptiæ descriptæ habentur etiam in Historia, seu Commentario, cui titulus *Mercurius Gallicus,* tom. ii. p. 359. Narrant itaque, matrimonium inter prædictam Catholicam Principem, & hæretici Regis Procuratorem, extra Ecclesiam contractum fuisse ad limina Ecclesiæ Metropolitanæ Parisiensis coram Cardinale magno Franciæ Eleemosynario, a quo tamen benedictio nuptialis data non fuit: deinde Britannici Regis Procuratorem novam nuptam deduxisse usque ad ingressum Chori: ibi vero a prædicto Cardinale celebratam solemni ritu fuisse Missam, adstantibus Rege, & Regina Franciæ, & nova Magnæ Britanniæ Regina, ac universa Regia Familia: sed prædictum Regis Angliæ Procuratorem, quamvis ipse Catholicus esset, cum personam gereret Principis Anglicanæ sectæ addicti, in proximum Archiepiscopi Palatium interim secessisse, donec Missa terminaretur; qua demum expleta, ad reducendam ab Ecclesia Reginam accessit."

The proxy for Charles I. was the Duc de Chevereux. JOHNSON BAILY.

TOWN CROSSES.—In a minute book belonging to the town of Melton-Mowbray, Leicestershire, I find the following as to two of these, formerly standing at the principal entrances to the town :—

"1584. It'm. The stockstone at Thorpe Crosse was sold to John Wythers for towe pense, and to plante or sett one Ashe tree or a thorne, and to renewe the same till yt please god theye growe.

"It'm. The stocke stone at Kettlebye Crosse wᵗ one stone standinge is solde to Willm Trigge for fyve shillings, and he to sett a Tree and husbond yt till yt growe as above-said.'

p. 220, only gives part of the monumental inscription on the Wymberley monument in Pinchbeck Church, and as now the inscription is wholly illegible, it seems but fitting to place on record in "N. & Q." the copy made of it by my ancestor, Maurice Johnson, *the antiquary,* in 1735. The inscription is as follows :—

"Orta
Gulielmo Welde generoso Cestrensi
et
Dorotheæ Georgii Wright, Cant, Equitis
uxor
Gulielmi Wimberli armigh. hujus co. et parochiæ
Sarum Innocentium die
Chori triumphantis Æmula
suam sibi nec minoris Innocentiæ
stolam induta Primo puerperio
ad cœlitis emigravit
et
quicquid habuit terræ hinc totum juxta deposuit
ætatis anno 25 salutis 1656.
Tam gloriose resurgat quam pulchre occubuit."

Arms,—Quarterly, 1 and 4, Azure, two bars, and in chief three bucks' heads caboshed or—Wymberley ; 2 and 3, Ermine, a fess nebulee sable—Sharpe ; impaling Azure, a fess nebulee between three crescents ermine—Weld. On the base of the monument :—

"Etiam præ memoria Bevillis Johannis filiis Thomæ Wymberley armigeri hinc proxime in vicina ecclesiæ Spaldensi in-humati anno MDCXVI. necnon Elizabethæ et
Franciscæ uxorum
filiabus Gulielmo Welbye
prænobili ordine Balnei Equitis Eque villa
Gedeniensi
qui hic juxta jacent sub spe
Christianorum."

On a blue marble, with the arms of Wymberley only, was inscribed on the floor of Pinchbeck Church :—

"Xuvias
Hic deposuit Bevill Wymberley
de Weston
armiger
Obiit 14 die Maii anno {ætat. 46.
{Dom. 1720."

EVERARD GREEN, F.S.A.

SYNONYM FOR A WEDDING FESTIVITY.—In a case recently brought before the magistrates of a town in Worcestershire, one of the witnesses testified that certain events occurred at "a sweetening job." Being asked what he meant by that phrase, he explained to the bench that "a sweetening job" was the festivity that followed upon a wedding. CUTHBERT BEDE.

Queries.

[We must request correspondents desiring information on family matters of only private interest, to affix their names and addresses to their queries, in order that the answers may be addressed to them direct.]

PEGGE'S MONASTIC VISITATION.—In 1789 Dr. Samuel Pegge published transcripts of two MSS., copiously annotated, in one volume. One of these MSS. was the "Annales Eliæ de Trickenham," from Lambeth Library, and the other, "Compendium Compertorum per Doctorem Legh et Doctorem Layton in Visitacione regia provincie Eboracen. et Episcopatu Coventris et Lichf. cum aliis," from the library of the Duke of Devonshire at Chatsworth. This volume, which is described as a 4to. in the *Parentalia* of Dr. Pegge's son, but as an 8vo. in Nichols's *Anecdotes*, is not in the British Museum, nor, strange to say, is there a copy at Chatsworth. I have failed to find a copy in several likely quarters, and as I am wanting to see the book for immediate reference, and for collation with the Chatsworth MS., I should be greatly obliged to any of your readers who could refer me to any public library where it can be found, or who would be kind enough to lend me the book for a few days. J. CHARLES COX.
Chevin House, Belper.

BIRDING-PIECE.—Will some one be so good as to explain the difference between a birding-piece and a fowling-piece? That the terms were not synonymous is evident, for in a statement of arms, armour, and ammunition seized from dangerous and disaffected persons in 1684, we find that both descriptions of arms were taken from the same person, *e.g.* from "William Clutterbuck, of Estinton," co. Glouc., were seized, *inter alia*, one "fowling gunn" and one "birding gunn"; from "Mr. Charles Trinder, of Burton on yᵉ Water," in the same county, were taken, *inter alia*, one "fowling pcice" and one "birding peice"; and so from many others. Moreover, we find the names occurring together in old inventories.
JOHN MACLEAN.
Bicknor Court, Coleford, Glouc.

COMMON ARYAN WORDS FOR AGRICULTURAL INSTITUTIONS.—Professor Max Müller (*Science of Language*, eighth edit., vol. i. p. 246) claims that the Aryans, before their first separation, had advanced to a state of agricultural civilization (see also Bunsen's *Egypt*, vol. iv. p. 562). Now we know from the researches of Sir Henry Maine and others something about this common agricultural civilization; the essential feature being the village community or cultivating household. In the earliest periods the whole community is shifted, at certain seasons, from one tract of land to another; in the later periods, the allotments incident to every householder only, the village itself remaining fixed. In-

stances of the former are found among the Afghans (*Bengal Asiatic Society Journal*, No. iii., 1862, p. 270); of the latter, throughout India (Maine's *Vill. Com., passim*), Russia (Rev. J. Long's *Vill. Com. in India and Russia*), Ireland (Maine's *Early Hist. of Inst.*), England (Nasse's *Agric. Com. of Eng.*), Iceland (Dasent's *Introd. to the Story of Burnt Njal*), and generally through Germany and Scandinavia (see, for instance, J. S. Mill's *Polit. Econ.*, chapter on peasant proprietors, and *House of Commons Commercial Reports*, No. 1590 (1876), p. 457, *et seq.*, and Von Maurer's German works).

I should be glad if any of your correspondents would furnish me with a list of common Aryan words indicating this common Aryan agricultural civilization. Professor Müller, at vol. ii. p. 236, gives "corn" and "tree"; but the list should surely be of some length. It should include words denoting some system of government, and perhaps the method of cultivation.
G. LAURENCE GOMME.

BISHOP YOUNG (BISHOP OF ROCHESTER).—Was he of Italian descent? His arms, as given by Sir B. Burke:—Per saltier, az. and gu., a lion pass. guard. or; crest,— a lion's head guard. or, between two wings ar., each charged with a fleur-de-lis az. Now I have an old "coat of arms," given me lately by a friend, which was borne by an Arthur Young, who was said to have been descended from an Italian family of rank that fled from Italy, on account of religious persecution, and settled in England. His arms:—Gu., a lion statant passive or; crest,—a lion's head guard. or, between two wings ar., each charged with a fleur-de-lis az. At the bottom are the initials A. Y. and the date 1689, all painted on parchment.

I should like to know whether, from the fact of their crests being identically the same, it shows conclusively a relationship. S. W. B.
U.S. America.

ANNIBAL CARACCI painted a dead Christ at the grave, surrounded with four women. Where is the original, and what its history? The engraver was Jean Louis Roullet. I saw recently here a fine specimen of this masterpiece of drawing and engraving. If I am well informed only three copies are known to exist. Where are they, and who are their fortunate owners? On the lower left corner of the engraving are the words: "Annibal Caracci pinxit, Joan. Lud. Roullet del. & sculp^t. Cum privilegio regis." G. A. M.
Washington.

"SCOTTISH SCENERY, OR SKETCHES IN VERSE," by James Cririe, D.D. (Dumfries, Dalton), a large quarto vol. published in 1803.—In his preface the author acknowledges that he has drawn his materials chiefly from the *Statistical History of Scotland*, but the work is curious as containing

1810. Is anything further known of Dr. Crine, and is this his only production?　　　　C. H.
Stirling.

AURORA BOREALIS.—It is said that there is no natural phenomenon unnoticed by Shakespear. Are the Northern Lights the exception to prove the rule, or can any of your readers refer me to any mention of them by our great poet?
　　　　　　　　D. M. STEVENS.
Guildford.

HERALDIC.—The arms borne by Richard Owen, of Morben, co. Montgomery, who, in the early part of the seventeenth century, married the heiress of Lewis Owen, of Peniarth, co. Merioneth, are given in Burke's *Landed Gentry* as Gules, a lion rampant reguardant or; and by others as Argent, a cross flory engrailed sable between four Cornish choughs proper, with a boar's head in chief. What were the actual arms and crest borne by the said Richard Owen, of Morben?
　　　　　　　　LEWIS MORGAN.
Edgbaston.

RAFFAELLE LESS USEFUL THAN A PIN-MAKER. —Who was the prelate that declared Raffaelle to be a less valuable member of society than a pin-maker?　　　　　　　　C. A. WARD.
Mayfair.

THEOLOGICAL BOOKS FROM SPAIN.—In 1872 I bought some books in a Dublin sale room. The catalogues of Mr. Jones, the auctioneer, included some thousand volumes from Coimbra. I understood there were 100,000 volumes consigned to him, and many thousands to other book salesmen. What were the circumstances which led to the dispersion of such a large library, which contained many choice and valuable books?
　　　　　　　　GEORGE LLOYD.
Cramlington.

"THREESTONES."—What meaning is attached (Druidical or otherwise) to the word "threestones," or, as it is in Scotland, "threestanes"?　　M. G.

ROBOTHAM.—Arms were granted in 1560 to Robert Robotham, of "Roskell, in the co. of York," for services done to K. Edward VI. 1. Whereabouts is Roskell? 2. What were the services rendered, and where are they recorded? 3. Where are the pedigrees before that date?
　　　　　　　　J. K. ROWBOTHAM.
Woodbine Cottage, Leeds.

THE WORD "READ."—What a perplexing word is "read"! When I meet with it I frequently

the verb "to lead," or "readed," after that of the verbs "to bead" and "to knead."?　J. W. W.

THE GREENFIELD FAMILY.—Can you furnish information respecting this family? Richard Greenfield married a sister of the Rev. Dr. Odam, Rector of Charleton, Devon. The family resided near Exeter about the year 1775. They held property in Tedburn St. Mary and in Charleton, Devon. Are there any descendants of the family now living, either male or female?
　　　　　　　　R. LL. GWYNNE.
Kilvey, Swansea.

VERE ESSEX CROMWELL.—In the Irish Parliament for 1634 and 1662 he was member for county Down, and was afterwards created Earl of Ardglass. Was he of the same family as the Protector, or related in any way?　　E. Q.
Claughton, Cheshire.

LONDON FOGS.—Is there any mention of London fogs to be found earlier than the following, from Evelyn's *Diary* for the extraordinarily severe winter of 1683/4, which is quoted in Lady Russell's *Life*, vol. i. p. 115?—

"London, by reason of the excessive coldness of the aire hindering the ascent of the smoke, was so fill'd with the fuligenous steame of the sea-coale, that hardly could one see crosse the streetes, and this filling the lungs with its grosse particles exceedingly obstructed the breast, so as one could hardly breath."

Can any of your readers refer me to any satisfactory account of this disagreeable phenomenon? Is it found elsewhere, as in Manchester, in the same intensity? If not, can it be traced in part to the natural features of London, e.g., to the hills on the north or to the river? Has it been observed to depend at all on the state of the wind or of the tide?　　　　　　　　R. E. B.
Chelmsford.

THE WIDOW OF LORD BACON.—Did she remarry? Where did she reside? When did she die?　　　　　　　　PHYLLIS.

HERALDIC.—Whose arms are the following?— Sable, a chevron ermine, between three beavers passant argent, collared argent and sable. Crest: On a coronet, a pelican with wings elevated and vulning her breast, argent, collared argent and sable. Motto: "Assiduitas." They are on a book-plate which has been in my family about a century. Probably a Cheshire or Derbyshire family.　　　　　　　　W. H.

THE CLUBS OF DUBLIN.—Will some kind correspondent of "N. & Q." direct me to information on the above subject? I allude particularly to Dublin club life in the last century, and especially in the last half of it. A speedy reply will be much appreciated by   THE INQUIRER.

DESTRUCTION OF CONSTANTINOPLE. — Mrs. Piozzi, writing in 1816 (Whalley's *Memoirs*, 1863, vol. ii. p. 430), mentions the proposed crusade against Turkey of three great Christian powers, and says :—

"I think there is an account somewhere that Harvey, who first discovered the circulation of the blood, did, in the year 1580, tell, in some long-forgotten treatise of his, how an Eastern prophecy had before then assured mankind that a second attack of united Europeans would be decidedly fatal to Constantinople."

Probably Mrs. Piozzi was confounding together William Harvey, 1569-1658, the great anatomist, and Gabriel Harvey, 1545-1630, the caustic Elizabethan wit ; but what was the prophecy to which she refers, and where is it to be found ?   EDWARD SOLLY.

"CHRONIQUES DE L'ŒIL DE BŒUF."—The reputed author of this work is Touchard-Lafosse. Is this a real or an assumed name ; and where can I obtain any information concerning him ?   J. K.

WAGES AND POPULATION.—Can you refer me to a report of a speech by the present or late Lord Derby, at a gathering of agriculturists, in which the statement is made that a permanent rise in agricultural labourers' wages was improbable, unless they adopted means for the limitation of their numbers, as had been done by the French peasantry?   P. E.

INDIA-RUBBER SHOES.—I always supposed these useful articles a quite modern invention ; but in Miss Roberts's *Women of the Last Days of Old France*, she states (p. 382) that about 1796 a French emigré in Russia obtained resources from "manufacturing india-rubber shoes."   W. M. M.

BOOK-PLATE.—Can any collector give me any information respecting a book-plate which represents a man blowing down an arquebuse, with "R. T. Pritchett" at the bottom of it ? The engraving looks antique, but the paper is apparently modern.   C. G. JARVIS.

PROPHECIES ABOUT TURKEY.—1. Where shall I find some doggerel verses about the Cock and Bull and Bear, quoted at the time of the Crimean war, and predicting the fall of Turkey twenty years afterwards ?

2. What is the prophecy about a certain gate at Constantinople through which the "red Giaours" are to enter ? De Quincey alludes to it.

3. Is it true that the green flag of the prophet is lost ?   H. A. B.

ST. ISHMAEL.—I notice two churches dedicated to this saint in the diocese of St. Davids. Was he a British saint, or by whom was Ishmael canonized ?   W. F. R.

JOHN BURNET, PROCURATOR-FISCAL OF GLASGOW.—Can you procure me information about his pedigree ? He was born March 4, 1799 or 1800, and married a daughter of James Boaz, accountant, Glasgow.   JOHN BURNET, Jun.

TIGER DUNLOP.—In or about 1820 an energetic character was known to old Indians in London by this name, and edited, I think, a literary journal. Can any correspondent name him and the title of his work, as well as the reason for his being so designated ?   J. O.

RHOS, OR "LITTLE ENGLAND BEYOND WALES," PEMBROKESHIRE.—Camden says, "That part of the country which lies beyond the [Milford] Haven is called by the Britains Rhos," or, as he says further on, "Little England beyond Wales." What are the present names of the principal parishes of that district ?   H. G. C.
Basingstoke.

AUTHORS OF QUOTATIONS WANTED.—
"I tremble from the edge of life, to dare
    The dark and fatal leap, having no faith," &c.

I cannot ascertain who is the author of these lines, and the date is not unimportant, because they resemble some well-known lines of the Laureate's *In Memoriam*.   J. R. S. C.

" Thus painters write their names at Co.'
" Where the gaunt mastiff, growling at the gate."
"That strain I heard was of a higher mood."
" But though the treacherous tapster Thomas
    Hangs a new Angel two doors from us."
        " How war may best upheld,
    Move by her two main nerves, iron and gold,
    In all her equipage " (*sic*).
All from Burke's *Regicide Peace*.   S.

Replies.

WORKS ON THE TRADING ROUTES FROM EAST TO WEST, A.D. 476-1492.
(5th S. viii. 369, 435.)

To the works already mentioned I may add :—

Ameilhon. Histoire du commerce et de la navigation des Egyptiens, sous le règne des Ptolémées. Paris, 1766, 12mo.

Arriani Periplus Ponti Euxini, et Maris Erythræi Periplus, Gr. et Lat. cum comment. Guil. Stuckii. Genevæ, Vignon, 1577, fol.

Audiat (L.). Pélerinage en Terre sainte au xve siècle. Paris, 1870, 8vo.

Bayer (Th. S.). Historia regni Græcorum Bactriani in qua simul Græcorum in India coloniarum vetus memoria explicatur. Acc. Chr. Th. Waltheri doctrina temporum Indica. Petropoli, 1738, 4to.

Benjamin Tudelensis. Itinerarium hebraice. Constantinopolis, 1543, 12mo. Cum versione latina et notis

Breydenbach (Bern. de). Sanctarum peregrinationum in montem Syon, ad venerandum Christi sepulchrum in Jerusalem—opusculum. In civitate Moguntina, per Erhardum Renwich, 1486. Fol., black letter. Maps of Venice, Paros, Corfu, Modon, Candia, Rhodes, and plan of Jerusalem. There are several other editions.

Breydenbach (B. de). Le Sainct Voiage et pelerinage de la Cite Saincte de Hierusalem fait et copōse en latin. Trāslate......en françoys par frere Jehā de Hersin. Lyon, 1489. Sm. fol., woodcuts.

Brunet de Presle (W.). Recherches sur les établissements des Grecs en Sicile. Paris, impr. royale, 1845, 8vo., map.

Brugsch (H.). Examen critique du livre de M. Chabas intitulé Voyage d'un Egyptien en Syrie, en Phénicie, en Palestine, &c., au xiv° siècle avant notre ére Paris, 1867, large 8vo.

Capodilista (Gabriele). Itinerario di Terra Santa, e del monte Sinai. 4to., no place nor date. [That journey was made in 1458.]

Clermont-Ganneau (Ch.). Observations sur quelques points des côtes de la Phénicie et de la Palestine, d'après l'itinéraire du pélerin de Bordeaux. Paris, 1875, 8vo.

Depping (Geo. Bernard). Histoire du commerce entre le Levant et l'Europe, depuis les croisades jusqu'à la fondation des colonies d'Amérique. Paris, Treuttel & Würtz, 1830, 2 vols., 8vo.

Derenbourg (J.). Essai sur l'histoire et la géographie de la Palestine d'après les Thalmuds et les autres sources rabbiniques. Paris, 1867, 8vo.

Essai historique sur le commerce et la navigation de la mer Noire. Paris, 1805, 8vo. (by M. Anthoine).

Fabri (F. F.). Evagatorium in Terræ sanctæ, Arabiæ et Ægypti peregrinationem, ed. C. E. Hassler. Stuttgardiæ, 1843-49, 3 vols., 8vo.

Gail (fils). Dissertation sur le périple de Scylax, et sur l'époque présumée de sa rédaction. Paris, 1825, 8vo.

Guillain. Documents sur l'histoire, la géographie, et le commerce de l'Afrique orientale. Paris, 1856-57, 3 vols., 8vo., maps.

Hasselquist (F.). Voyage dans le Levant, contenant des observations sur l'histoire naturelle, la médecine, l'agriculture, le commerce, et particulièrement sur l'histoire naturelle de la Terre-Sainte. Paris, 1769, 2 vols., 12mo.

Henin (Chevalier d'). Histoire du commerce, de la navigation. et des colonies des anciens dans la mer Noire, traduit de l'italien de Formaleoni. Venise, 1769, 2 vols., sm. 8vo.

Hese (Joan de, presbyter). A Hierusalem itinerarius describens dispositiones terrarum, montium et aquarum, &c. Davetrie, par Richardum Pafraet, 1499. 4to., black letter; and other editions.

Huet. Histoire du commerce et de la navigation des anciens. Lyon, 1763, 8vo.

Ibn Batoutah. Voyage à travers l'Afrique septentrionale et l'Egypte au commencement du xiv° siècle, publié par M. Cherbonneau. Paris, 1852, 8vo.

Ibn Khordadbeh. Le livre des routes et des provinces, publié, trad., et annoté par Barbier de Meynard. Paris, 1865, 8vo.

Itinéraires de la Terre Sainte, des xiii°, xiv°, xv°, xvi°, et xvii° siècle, traduits de l'hébreu, par E. Carmoly. Bruxelles, 1847, 8vo., illustrations.

Itinerarium Portugallensium e Lusitania in Indiam et inde in occidentem et demum ad aquilonem ex vernaculo 1843, 8vo.

Labat (Dr. L.). Mémoires sur l'Orient and moderne. Paris, 1840, large 8vo. ports. and map.

La Brocquiere (Bertrandon de). Travels to Pa and his return from Jerusalem overland to Fra 1432 and 1433. Trans. by Th. Johnes from the published by Legrand d'Aussy. At the Hafod Henderson, 1807, large 8vo., plates.

Larcher. L'expédition de Cyrus dans l'Asie sup et la retraite des dix mille. Paris, 1778, 2 vols., maps.

Lettres sur l'Atlantide de Platon et sur l'an histoire de l'Asie. Londres, 1779, 2 vols. 8vo. ma

Ludolphus, rector in Suchen. De terra san itinere hierosolymitano, et de statu ejus et aliis m bus, quæ in mari conspiciuntur videlicet medite Sm. fol., black letter, no place nor date. Severa editions.

Mauroy. Du commerce des peuples de l'Afriq tentrionale dans l'antiquité, le moyen-âge, et les modernes, comparé au commerce des Arabes jours. Paris, 1845, 8vo.

Mauroy. Précis de l'histoire et du comm l'Afrique septentrionale. Paris, 1852, 8vo.

Michel (Francisque). Recherches sur le con la fabrication et l'usage des étoffes de soie, d'argent, et autres tissus précieux en Occident, palement en France, pendant le moyen âge. 2 vols., sm. 4to.

Murad (Mgr.). Notice sur l'origine de la Maronite, et ses rapports avec la France, nation Druze et sur les diverses populations du Liban. Paris, 1844, 8vo.

Œlsner. Des effets de la religion de Moh pendant les trois premiers siècles de sa fondation. 1810, 8vo.

Oppert (J.). Mémoires sur les rapports de l et de l'Assyrie dans l'antiquité, éclaircis par l'ét textes cunéiformes. Paris, 1869, 4to.

Pastoret (de) Dissertation sur l'influence maritimes des Rhodiens sur la marine des Grec Romains, et de l'influence de la marine sur la p de ces deux peuples. Paris, 1784, 8vo.

Pélerinage (un) en Terre Sainte au xv° siècle. 1860, 8vo. (Journey of Guillaume d'Orange.)

Puget de Saint-Pierre. Histoire des Druses, du Liban, formé par une colonie de François. 1762, 12mo., plates.

Rambaud (A.). L'empire grec au x° siècle stantin Porphyrogénète. Paris, 1870.

Ramsay. Les voyages de Cyrus. Paris, 1727, 12mo.

Reinaud (J. T.). Relation des voyages faits Arabes et les Persans dans l'Inde et la Chine ix° siècle de l'ère chrétienne. Texte arabe et Paris, 1845, 2 vols., 18mo.

Reinaud. Relations politiques et commerc l'empire romain avec l'Asie Orientale pendant premiers siècles de l'ère chrétienne. Paris, Im périale, 1863, 8vo., maps.

Relation des voyages de Saewulf à Jérusale Terre Sainte, pendant les années 1102 et 1103, d'après un MS. de Cambridge. Paris, 1839, 4to.

Rey. Etudes pour servir à l'histoire des Paris, 1823, 8vo.

Robiou (F.). Itinéraire des Dix-Mille. Etude topographique avec trois cartes. Paris, 1875, 8vo.

Sauvaire (H.). Histoire de Jérusalem et d'Hébron depuis Abraham jusqu'à la fin du xvᵉ siècle de J. C. Fragments de la Chronique de Moudjir-ed-Dyn. Paris, 1876, 8vo.

Sayous (Ed.). Les origines et l'époque païenne de l'histoire des Hongrois. Paris, 1874, 8vo.

Thurot (Al.). Manuel de l'histoire ancienne considérée sous le rapport des constitutions, du commerce, et des colonies des divers états de l'antiquité, traduit de l'Allemand de A. H. L. Heeren. Paris, 1836, large 8vo.

Tucher (Hans). Wallfart und Reise in das gelobte Land. Hannsen Schönsperger, Augspurg, 1482, fol.; or Nuremberg, same date, fol. There are several other editions.

Vincent (Dean). History of the Commerce and Navigation of the Ancients in the Indian Ocean. 1807, 2 vols., 4to., maps and plates.

Vivien de Saint-Martin. Description historique et géographique de l'Asie Mineure, comprenant les temps anciens, le moyen âge, et les temps modernes, avec un précis détaillé des voyages qui ont été faits dans la Péninsule depuis l'époque des Croisades,......précédée d'un tableau de l'histoire géographique de l'Asie depuis les plus anciens temps jusqu'à nos jours. Paris, 1852, 2 vols., 8vo., maps.

Voyages faits en Terre-Sainte par Thetmar en 1217, et par Burchard de Strasbourg en 1175, 1189 ou 1225; par le baron Jules de Saint-Genois. 4to.

Le saint voyage de Jérusalem, par le baron d'Anglure (1395). Paris, 1858, sm. 8vo.

Voyaige d'oultremer en Jhérusalem par le seigneur de Caumont, l'an 1418, publié par le marquis de la Grange. Paris, 1858, 8vo., plates.

Voyages faits principalement en Asie, dans les xiiᵉ, xiiiᵉ, xivᵉ, et xvᵉ siècles; avec une introduction par P. Bergeron. Leyde, 1729; or La Haye, 1735, 2 vols., 4to.

Ayr Academy.   HENRI GAUSSERON.

JOHN COOKE, THE REGICIDE (5ᵗʰ S. viii. 407.)—
Ludlow says (*Memoirs*, vol. iii. p. 69) that "Mr. John Coke (*sic*), late Chief Justice of Ireland, had in his younger years been the best part of Europe, and at Rome had spoken with such liberty and ability against the corruptions of that court and church, that great endeavours were used there to bring him into that interest. He thought it no longer safe to continue among them, and therefore departed to Geneva, where he resided some months in the house of Signor Gio. Diodati, after which he returned to England and applied himself to the study of the law."

In 1658 Cooke was living in England, and in a letter to the Lord Lieutenant of Ireland, H. Cromwell (Thurlow's *State Papers*, vii. 305), he explains why he had been so long absent from Ireland: "Intending all last year to have returned, had not my wife's consumptive condition and the death of my aged father retarded." There is also preserved in Thurlow (vol. vi. p. 666) a letter dated Dec. 9, 1657, from Northampton, which is of some interest, though it contains no reference to his family. In that curious little volume, *Rebels no Saints*, London, 8vo., 1661, there are several letters of John Cooke's, one of which, dated Oct. 15, 1660, a day before his execution, contains these ex-

pressions addressed to his little daughter, Freelove Cook: "Be obedient to thy dear mother, and good grandmother, and thy loving uncle and aunt Massey. Know that thy dear father is gone to Heaven to thy dear brother." There is a good deal of confusion in respect of his name in books of the time, being spelt Cook, Cooke, and Coke in English histories; Couke and Cowke by Raguenet and Leti.   EDWARD SOLLY.

Noticing this query I have turned up the undermentioned little vol., thinking it might supply an item about this notability in the direction required, but have been disappointed; nevertheless, as it is a curiosity, perhaps you may deem it worth a niche in "N. & Q." :—

"Monarchy no Creature of God's Making, &c. Wherein is proved by Scripture and Reason that Monarchicall Govᵗ is against the Minde of God. And that the Execution of the late King was one of the Fattest Sacrifices that ever Queen Justice had. Being a Hue and Cry after Lady Liberty, which hath been ravished and stolne away by the Grand Potentates of the Earth: Principally Intended for the Undeceiving of some Honest Hearts, who like the poore Iewes cry, Give us a King, though they smart never so much for it. By Iohn Cooke, late of Grayes Inne, Esquire, Chief Iustice of the Province of Munster, in Ireland," &c. 12moʰ, pp. 134. Printed at Waterford, in Ireland, by Peter le Pienne, in the Year of our Lord God 1651.

There is a savagery in the title to this which proclaims the king-killer, Justice Cooke, and a corresponding fanaticism runs through the volume, exhibiting a Puritan of the severest type. It is introduced by an address "To the Supreme Authoritie of the three Nations, the Parliament of the Commonwealth of England," in a style not less rancorous, extending to twenty-seven leaves, and the whole is founded upon the king's speech in which he says, "I must avowe that I owe an accompt of my actions to none but God alone," and which is indeed Justice Cooke's text. In *Rebels no Saints*, 1661, there is a long account of Cooke's behaviour at and before execution, representing him as glorying in the testimony he was bearing to justice, truth, and liberty, only incidentally alluding to my book: "As for that against monarchy," he says, "they will be ashamed to oppose it." My query is, Was the book really printed at Waterford, and by such a printer? The bibliographers say it was reprinted in 1652; Allibone, that another edition came out as lately as 1794; if so, the date might suggest it to have been to forward the original purpose—the downfall of the monarchy.   J. O.

If MR. STILLWELL is not already acquainted with the *Trials of the Regicides*, Lond., 1724, he may see at pp. 298-328 a notice of "Mr. Justice Cooke during his Imprisonment in the Tower and Newgate," with his Speeches and Prayer upon the Ladder." There is also "A Letter to a Friend," p. 310; "A Letter to his Wife," p. 322; and a

Is MR. STILLWELL correct in styling the above a regicide ? His name is not amongst the signatures on the warrant to execute Charles I., and I am under the impression that only those whose signatures appear on the warrant were styled regicides.　　　　　　　　　　　　　　SYWL.

CAROLS (5th S. viii. 491.)—In Parker's *Glossary of Architecture*, third ed., 1840, vol. i. p. 38, the term is thus noted:—"Carol, carrol, carrel, carola (Lat. *studium*), a small closet or enclosure to sit in."

I am well acquainted with the example in the cloisters of Chester Cathedral concerning which Mr. Parker writes, in his book entitled *The Medieval Architecture of Chester*, p. 28 :—" In the west walk (of the cloisters) are the places prepared for the carols of the monks, or their studies, to sit and write in ; . . . . they were so called probably from their being square, *carrels*, or *quarrés.*"
　　　　　　　　　　　　　　J. W. W.

It seems that in some places *carols* was the name given to recesses in ancient cloisters where the monks studied and transcribed manuscripts. It is asked what is the derivation. In Gaelic *cro* has several meanings, among them a hut, a house ; -*ol* is the diminutive from *cxol*, small ; in composition the *c* is aspirated and loses its sound. In some cases a word may be said to be derived from another ; in other instances it may be said to be *derivable* from another : perhaps the latter way is the one here. The early Celtic Christian church was overlaid or superseded by the Roman Catholic, and some terms from a Celtic source may have come into use. Some Celtic words begin in Gaelic with *c*, and in Cornish with *t*: the Gaelic *cro*, a house, is the analogue of the very common Cornish word *tre*.　　　THOMAS STRATTON.

Carrells, carralls, caroles (Fr.), karils, quarrels, quadrils ; so called from their square shape.

Mr. Parker, in his *Glossary of Architecture*, says :—" *Carola* is applied to any place enclosed with skreens or partitions. In Normandy and elsewhere in France the rails themselves are termed *caroles*. Also this term was applied to the aisles of French churches which have skreened chapels on one side."　　　　　　　　　T. F. R.

Carol = *quadrellus*, a pew.　　　J. T. M.

THE WORKHOUSE KNOWN AS THE BASTILLE (5th S. viii. 406.)—I have heard the workhouse

The word does not occur in Messrs. Nodal and Milner's *Glossary of the Lancashire Dialect*, no does Halliwell record it with the above meanin attached to it.　　　　　　　　　ST. SWITHIN.

The term Bastille applied to the workhouse i not local. Forty years ago it was a general terr through England. More, your correspondent ma be informed that such use of the word did no arise from the " lower ten." With the change (the poor laws forty years and more ago appeared large book on the English Bastilles, or a simila title comprising those words, by G. R. Wythe Baxter, if my memory is correct to each initia The book was most voluminous, and most peopl would say now most intemperate. Newspapei adopted the term, and it became at once popula and the one slang word for the new union-houses
　　　　　　　　　　　　　W. G. W.

I remember that every one in the part (Derbyshire where I lived in my young days calle the workhouse " the Bastile." The workhouse wi looked upon as a veritable prison, and it was cor sidered by many quite as great a disgrace to l obliged to go into the one as to be put into th other.　　　　　　　　　　　THOS. RATCLIFFE.
Worksop.

In the days of my youth I always heard th Kidderminster workhouse spoken of as " th Bastile " by the lower classes ; and, since then, have frequently heard the same misapplication (the word in various counties.
　　　　　　　　　　　　CUTHBERT BEDE.

APSLEY FAMILY OF THAKEHAM, CO. SUSSE (5th S. viii. 409.)—I think this the solution (D. C. E.'s question. Alice, eldest daughter an co-heiress of Sir Edward Apsley, and sister to tl Edward Apsley who died a bachelor, *did* mari Sir John Butler, son and heir of Sir Oliver Butle of Teston, Kent, who, however, died before h father and *without issue*. His widow marrie secondly George Fenwick, of Brinkburne, c Northumberland, afterwards a colonel in tl Parliamentarian forces. They had issue tw daughters, named after two of their mothei Apsley aunts—" Elizabeth " and " Dorothy According to the Visitation of Northumberlan 1666, the former married Sir Thos. Haslerig, Noseley Hall, Bart., and had children. The latt married Sir Thos. Williamson, Knt. and Bar of East Markham, Notts, and afterwards of Nor Wearmouth Hall, co. Durham. She died 169 aged fifty-four. "Brunton" Hall is simply a mistake for Brinkburne. "Lady Alice Boteler, wife of George Fenwick," as she is called on her tombstone in America, emigrated there with her second husband in 1639. He was one of the company who held the patent of Connecticut, granted to the Earl of Warwick, in which Lord Say and Sele, Lord Brooke, Sir Arthur Haslerig, &c., were interested. Thos. Lechford, in his *News from New England*, 1641, says "Master Fenwike with the Lady Boteley" were living at Connecticut river's "mouth" in a fair house, and "well fortified: and one Master Higginson, a young man, their chaplain." The lady died shortly after the birth of her daughter Dorothy, Nov. 4, 1645, and was buried at Saybrook. Her remains were removed in 1870, to make room for a railway terminus, and reinterred in the presence of the principal inhabitants of that town; and a long account of the ceremony, and some interesting particulars of her family, appeared in an American newspaper.

George Fenwick soon after returned to England, was governor of Berwick for the Parliament, married secondly Katherine, daughter of his old friend Sir Arthur Haslerig, of Noseley (who was also a Parliamentarian, and much connected with the North), and she survived him, but they had no children. Brinkburne passed into the possession of his brother, Claudius Fenwick, M.D., and his heirs.   J. BOYD.
Moor House.

"THE LOUNGER" (5th S. viii. 409.)—This periodical was projected in 1785 at Edinburgh by Henry Mackenzie, the well-known author of *The Man of Feeling*. Together with a small band of literary friends, he brought out in 1779 a folio periodical called the *Mirror*, which lasted for two years, and has been frequently reprinted in 3 vols., 12mo. In 1785 the idea was revived under the title of the *Lounger*, and 101 numbers were printed. The *Lounger*, like the *Mirror*, appeared first in folio, but was subsequently reprinted in 12mo. The chief contributors were H. Mackenzie and Lord Craig, who wrote more than half the numbers. Besides these, Lord Abercrombie, Frazer Tytler, Mr. Cullen, Dr. Henry, Mr. M'Leod, Bannatyne, D. Hume, Prof. Richardson, and Mr. Greenfield all contributed. The *Mirror* was published at threepence a number, and about four hundred copies were sold of the first issue. When reprinted, Mackenzie and his friends, who were known as the "Tabernacle Club," received one hundred pounds, which they handed to the Orphan Hospital, and enough over to buy a hogshead of claret for themselves. There is an interesting criticism of the *Lounger* in Sir Richard Phillips's *Public Characters* for 1802-3. It is quite safe to say that the *Lounger* contains "some

very readable papers," for some of them will probably last as long as our language. Lovers of Burns have a kindly value for No. xcvii., from the pen of Mr. Mackenzie, which I believe first drew public attention to "the Ayrshire ploughman" (see "N. & Q.," 5th S. ii. 325). Mr. Mackenzie died in 1831. There is a fair biographical notice of him in the *Annual Biography*, vol. xvi. pp. 10-23.   EDWARD SOLLY.

This was a weekly paper of the *Tatler* tribe. It ran through a hundred and one numbers, and appeared on the Saturdays of 1785-7, its first issue being dated February 5 in the former, and its final January 6 in the latter year. It makes three volumes of the *British Essayists*, edited by Alexander Chalmers. The *Lounger* succeeded to the *Mirror*, and was mainly by the same authors—Messrs. H. Mackenzie, R. Cullen, M'Leod, Bannatyne, Alex. Abercromby, W. Craig, and G. Home. *Vide* Chalmers's "Advertisement" to the *Mirror*, wherein he says:—

"In this edition it has been thought proper to furnish the reader with the following table (and a similar one is annexed to the *Lounger*), by which he is informed of the author of every number except the few which were furnished by correspondents neither known at the time nor ever afterwards discovered, and who chuse still to remain unknown to the public."

This valuable table seems to have been forgotten in the case of the *Lounger*, but from that affixed to the *Mirror* I learn that the letters of "John Homespun," which must have amused MR. WING at Stow, were by Mackenzie.   ST. SWITHIN.

The title-page of this work affords all the information that is likely now to be obtained concerning it, namely, that it was a periodical paper published in Edinburgh in the years 1785 and 1786, and in a collected form, in 3 vols., in 1787. Few persons, I imagine, share your correspondent's curiosity respecting the names of the contributors to this bygone but by no means uncommon book, in comparing which in style to the *Spectator* and the *Rambler* he no doubt means that, like these, the *Lounger* was first issued in numbers. With regard to date, it appeared seventy-four years after the commencement of the former, and thirty-five years after the latter of these publications.
                              CHARLES WYLIE.

In the *Lounger* Burns was first brought into notice on his appearance in Edinburgh towards the close of the year 1786. The editor, Henry Mackenzie, in giving a specimen of his poetry, introduces the fact by saying, "My readers will discover a high tone of feeling, a power and energy of expression, particularly and strongly characteristic of the mind and the voice of a poet," &c.
                              JAMES M'KIE.

ABRAHAM FLEMING (5th S. viii. 409.)—He was rector of St. Pancras, London. He was a most

not mentioned by Lowndes at all. His black-letter *Hist. of England* is certainly scarce, but as to its money value I can find no hint. Its mental value as a book is probably *nil.* C. A. WARD.
Mayfair.

PRINTED CALENDARS OF POST MORTEM INQUISITIONS AND ESCHEATS (5ᵗʰ S. viii. 468.)—W. F. C. may see in the account of the "Inquisitiones Post Mortem," in R. Sims's *Manual for the Genealogist, &c.*, Lond., 1856, pp. 123-30, that there are no other printed volumes, but only the four which he has seen in the Bodleian, and which were published by the Record Commission early in the century. But Mr. Sims also gives a list of MS. Inq. p.m. and abstracts, which are in the British Museum, the Bodleian, and elsewhere. The original inquisitions are, of course, in the Public Record Office, where there are MS. calendars.

ED. MARSHALL.

Four volumes only have been printed, exclusive of some referring to Lancashire which form part i. of vol. i. of *Ducatus Lancastriæ*. Copies are in the British Museum and in several public libraries, amongst them the Chetham Library and the Rochdale Free Public Library.

H. FISHWICK, F.S.A.

If W. F. C. will apply to Mr. Sage, Turnstile, Lincoln's Inn, he will be happy to sell him a set of printed calendars of Inq. P. Mortem cheap enough. H. T. E.

AUTOGRAPHS OF SIR JOSHUA REYNOLDS (5ᵗʰ S. vi. 88, 219 ; vii. 18, 176.)—In looking over some waste-paper rubbish at a furniture broker's, a few months ago, I picked up a well-bound quarto volume, containing a collection of the *Discourses* of the great painter, "delivered to the students of the Royal Academy." Inside the cover is the heraldic book-plate of Sir Charles Dance, and on the fly-leaf of each of the discourses, which are the original issues, is the inscription, in slightly varied terms, "George Dance, Esq., from the Author," in the handwriting of the President. This is, of course, George Dance, the Royal Academician, who preceded Sir John Soane, R.A., as Professor of Architecture to the Academy, and who retired from that office in 1806.

In the interesting catalogue of Messrs. Ellis & White, just issued, I see a copy of the *Cento Favole Bellissime* of Verdizotti (Venetia, 1661, 4to.), "Sir Joshua Reynolds's copy, with his autograph and monogram on the title-page." This most interesting and characteristic relic is described as being "in the old binding, preserved in a blue

by G. D. T., is well known, and will often be found impressed upon one of the lower corners of drawings by the old masters which have formed part of his collection. I have seen it, however, upon specimens of such inferior merit and questionable authenticity as to lead me to the suspicion that it may have been forged—a very easy matter —by unscrupulous dealers. It may, however, be that Sir Joshua, on purchasing a lot of drawings, would at once impress his stamp upon them, and huddle them, good, bad, and indifferent, into his cabinet, postponing a more discriminative examination to a moment which never arrived.

WILLIAM BATES.
Birmingham.

INQUISITIONS POST MORTEM (5ᵗʰ S. viii. 426, 516.)—Roger Mortimer, first Earl of March. died " die veneris in vigil' Sc'i Andree," anno 4 E. III. [Nov. 29, 1330] (Inq. p. m. 28 E. III., i. 53).

Edmund, second earl, died at Stanton Lacy, 26 kal. Jan., 5 E. III. (Dugdale's *Baronage*). This was Dec. 7, 1331.

Roger, third earl, died in Burgundy, Feb. 26, anno 24 E. III. [1350] (Inq. p. m. 46 E. III., i. 40). This is the date given by the inquisition, and this was the point to which I called attention. In fact, the probability seems to be that Vincent was right in giving 1360 as the date, since the marriage of William, Lord Greystock, was granted to the earl July 24, 1359 (Rot. Pat. 33 E. III., Part II.), and the office of Clerk of the Marshalsea in the hospice of Prince Thomas is declared vacant by the earl's death, April 20, 1360 (*ib.* 34 E. III., Part I.). I ought to have added a note to my former communication, pointing this out, as the date in the inquisition is probably a scribe's error ; but my point was the difference between the date *given by* the inquisition and the date at which it was taken.

Edmund, fourth earl, died at Cork Dec. 27, 1381 (Inq. p. m. 5 R. II., 43).

Roger, fifth earl, was killed in a skirmish at Kenles (Dugdale), Ireland, July 20, 1398 (Inq. p. m. 22 R. II., 34).

Edmund, sixth and last earl, died at Trim Castle, Ireland (Anderson's *Royal Genealogies*), Jan. 19, 3 H. VI. [1425] (Inq. p. m. 3 H. VI., i. 32). Each of these earls was the son of his predecessor. HERMENTRUDE.

LAKE THIRLMERE (5ᵗʰ S. viii. 469.)—In the *Edinburgh Gazetteer*, 1822, the lake is called Brackmeer ; but Speed, in 1610, names it Thurlemyre, and this designation is also given in Camden and other old writers. In Robert Morden's map in

Cox's *Magna Britannia*, 1720, the name is spelt Thurlemire. In the *Guide to the Lakes*, 1778, the lake is described as "Leather Water, called also Wythburn and Thirlmeer." The latter name is evidently one of considerable antiquity. When was the name Brackmeer, which is suggestive of sea water, first used?   EDWARD SOLLY.

USE OF EVERGREENS AT CHRISTMAS (5th S. viii. 482.)—As an item of Christmas lore, and *à propos* of the reason for using evergreens at Christmas, the following tale, told to Mr. C. G. Leland by an English gipsy, is not out of place :—

"The ivy, and holly, and pine trees never told a word where our Saviour was hiding himself, and so they keep alive all the winter, and look green all the year. But the ash, like the oak, told of him where he was hiding, so they have to remain dead through the winter. And so we gipsies always burn an ash-fire every Great Day." —*The Engl. Gipsies and their Language*, by C. G. Leland, Lond., 1874.

H. T. C.

SERLE'S GATE, LINCOLN'S INN (5th S. viii. 491.) —So called because it was the gate leading to Serle's Court, as New Square was originally called. See Cunningham's *Handbook of London*, 1850, p. 444. The site of New Square was, after the Restoration, the property of Sir John Birkenhead, F.R.S., Master of the Faculty Office and Court of Requests, who died in 1671. It was then acquired by Mr. Henry Serle, or Searle, a bencher of the Inn (Knight's *London*, iv. 372), who died intestate and left his property heavily mortgaged about 1690 (Timbs's *London and Westminster*, i. 176). The Society of Lincoln's Inn purchased this part of Serle's estate about 1697. Hatton, in his *New View of London*, 1708, mentions Serle's Court as the new square designed and partly built by Henry Serle, Esq., who died before it was completed.

EDWARD SOLLY.

MR. WARD is in error in saying that Cunningham does not give the explanation of the name of this gate. If he will consult the 1850 edition, *sub* Serle Street, he will find some particulars of Mr. Henry Serle (who appears to have owned considerable property in this part of London), and the express statement : "The old name for Lincoln's Inn New Square was Serle's Court ; the arms of Serle, with those of the Inn, are over the gateway next Carey Street." MR. WARD may supplement Cunningham's information by a reference to the late W. H. Spilsbury's *Lincoln's Inn*, pp. 81-82.

W. P. COURTNEY.

15, Queen Anne's Gate.

Sir John Birkenhead was the conductor of the Royalist paper, *Mercurius Aulicus*. See Thornbury's *Haunted London*, p. 493. The publisher's name was Illidge, *not* Illidoc.

GEORGE POTTER.

42, Grove Road, N.

Was this gate ever used exclusively as a footway ? and, if so, when was it first opened as a carriage road ?   AJAX.

"CIVET CAT" (5th S. viii. 468.)—Being without information as to the nature of the "certain miscellaneous articles" in which a shop, referred to by CLERICUS RUSTICUS, deals, I can only conjecture that the following extract furnishes a reply to his query :—

"The Civet is common all over Europe as a perfumer's sign, as it was said to produce musk. A Dutch perfumer in the seventeenth century wrote under his sign :

'Dit's in de Civet kat, gelyk gy kunt aanschouwen, Maar komt hier binnen, hier zyn parfumien voor mannen en vrouwen.'

'This is the Civet, as you may see ; but enter. Perfumes sold here for men and women.'"—*The History of Signboards*, p. 162 (London, John Camden Hotten, 1866).

ST. SWITHIN.

Shops in which fancy articles are sold used frequently to bear the above sign, because among those articles was the once favourite scent prepared from a secretion of the so-called civet cat (*Viverra civetta*), an animal nearly allied to the weasels, and a native of North Africa. This scent, as is remarked in the *Guide to the Zoological Society's Gardens*, edited by Mr. P. L. Sclater, is now superseded by purer and more delicate floral perfumes. A graphic account of the way in which these animals were kept, chiefly in Holland, and of the manner of extracting their secretion twice or three times weekly, will be found in Bewick's *History of Quadrupeds*, or indeed in any old work on natural history.   W. R. TATE.

Blandford St. Mary, Dorset.

I will answer this query by proposing another, and that is, Are "shops dealing in miscellaneous articles" called Civet Cats? I think only to this extent, viz. that the civet cat was for long the sign of a perfumer's shop, and in every village the barber and the toyshopman are "two single gentlemen rolled into one."

H. FISHWICK, F.S.A.

[The old gilt figure of the Civet still distinguishes the long-established firm of Gattie & Peirce, perfumers, Bond Street. Shakspeare, in *King Lear*, shows who sold the article in his time : "Give me an ounce of civet, good apothecary, to sweeten my imagination"; and Cowper (*Conversation*, l. 283) lets us know that, in *his* days, gentlemen were perfumed with it like milliners:—

"I cannot talk with civet in the room,
A fine puss-gentleman that 's all perfume."]

COCKER'S "ARITHMETIC" (5th S. viii. 349.)— Having occasion to make search with respect to this name, I made reference to a copy of the work alluded to in the Public Library, Newcastle-on-Tyne, my object being merely to ascertain the author's Christian name. I took no other note, but remember that the date of publication was

man Edward Cocker was, but the name occurs in the neighbourhood of Leeds, near which town Christopher Saxton was also born." According to Thoresby, John Cocker Saxton was buried in Leeds parish church in 1701. The combination of names is somewhat remarkable. The names of Cocker and Crabtree both occur in the registers of Batley parish, near Leeds. Possibly some of your correspondents may be able to throw more light on John Cocker Saxton.

I append a few extracts from registers, together with two partly conjectural tabular sketches, in the hope that by similar contributions the parentage of Edward Cocker may be cleared up, and, if possible, the connexion of his family with the Saxtons made out.

Thomas Crabtree, bd. at=
Batley, Jan. 1675.

1674. | | | 1676. | | 1677.
Robt.=Grace ....= Hannah=Jonas Mary=Thomas
Apple- Crab- Crab- Crab- Beck- Crab- Healey.
yard. tree. tree. tree. with. tree.

1702.
Marmaduke=Dorothy
Faucet. | Crabtree.

Batley Registers.—Thos. Crabtree, buried Jan. 5, 1675
Robt. Appleyard and Grace Crabtree, nupt. Aug. 26, 1674.
Thomas Healey and Mary Crabtree, nupt. Dec. 2, 1677.

? Edward Cocker=

1. Alice, d. of=Richard Hardwick, Clk.,=2. Sarah, d. of
......, Batley, | of Batley; his admin. | ...... Cocker,
bur. May 24, | granted, June, 1639, to | mar. June 21,
1674. | John Thurnam and | 1675.
| Robert Radcliffe. |

Martha, bap. Richard. Edward. Sarah. Susanna,
June 20, 1672, ? if named bap. May
bd. Feb., 1674. after his 13, 1677.
maternal grandfather.

Batley Registers.—Alice, wife of Richard Hardwick, bd. May 24, 1674.
Ric ard Hardwick and Sarah Cocker md. June 21, 1675. h

W. NEWSOME NIGHE.
Newcastle-on-Tyne.

"LADIES' SMOCK" (5th S. viii. 358.) — MR. COLEMAN gives "ladies' smock" as the Dorsetshire

Watts's *Psalms of David* published in 1706, h have been the result of an agreement betw those who brought it out : the law did not terfere with signs until a later date. If Larw and Hotten's *History of Signboards* may trusted, Paris began a reform in the matte 1761 :—

"London soon followed. In the *Daily News*, Novem 1762, we find : 'The signs in Duke's Court, St. Mar Lane, were all taken down and affixed to the front of houses.' Thus Westminster had the honour to begin innovation by procuring an act to improve the paven &c., of the streets, and this act also sealed the doo the signboards, which as in Paris were ordered affixed to the houses. This was enforced by a statu 2 Geo. III. c. 21, enlarged at various times. O parishes were longer in making up their mind; the great disparity in the appearance of the streets ward from Temple Bar, and those eastward, at last the Corporation of London follow the example and a similar improvements. Suitable powers to carry ou scheme were soon obtained. In the 6 Geo. III. the C of Common Council appointed commissions, and in a months all the parishes began to clear away : St. Bot in 1767 ; St. Leonard, Shoreditch, in 1768 ; St. Mar le-Grand in 1769 ; and Marylebone in 1770."—P. 29 For further information I must refer M. D. to book itself. ST. SWITHI

Shortly after the accession of Geo. III., Oct 1760, an Act of Parliament was passed for pa and also for removing the signs and obstruct in the streets of London. The use of signs become universal, and traders sought to ou each other in their size, fittings, and attrac devices, and to project them so far into the st as to encumber the way. See *ante*, Samuel W R.A. (5th S. vii. 72). Jos. J.

The reason of signs being discontinued is far to seek. In 1760 names were first pu doors, and in 1764 houses were numbered. first houses numbered were those in New Bur Street ; the next those in Lincoln's Inn F (*Haunted London*, 458). CHARLES WYLI

"THE THIRD PART OF THE PILGRIM'S GRESS" (5th S. viii. 469.)—I have an old copy of Bunyan's *Pilgrim's Progress*—the part, thirty-second edition, printed for W. J ston, &c., 1767 ; the second part, twenty edition, printed for W. Johnston, &c., 1767. the title-page of this second part : "Note. Third Part, suggested to be J. Bunyan's, i impostor." The third part, twentieth edi printed for L. Hawes & Co., &c., 1765. On

title-page is : "To which is added the Life and Death of John Bunyan, Author of the First and Second Parts (completing the whole Progress)." On the back of the title of the third part, "Licensed and Entered according to Order." This may help in ascertaining the author : "The Preface to the Christian Reader" is signed "J. B." Verses "to his Worthy Friend, the Author of the Third Part of the Pilgrim's Progress, upon Perusal thereto," &c., are signed "B. D."; and other verses, "These Lines are humbly Recommended to the Reader (written upon the Perusal of this Book," &c.), are signed "L. C."	SAMUEL SHAW.
Andover.

THE MISTLETOE (5·h S. viii. 487.)—I have never experienced any difficulty in propagating mistletoe, and can show four trees in my garden at Dulwich all bearing mistletoe, raised from seed inserted under the first or outer skin of the tree by myself.
W. H. CUMMINGS.
Brackley Villa, Dulwich.

THE SHEPHERDS OF BETHLEHEM (5th S. viii. 490.)—In Dr. Edersheim's book on *The Temple* is an interesting suggestion as to their having been Temple officers, whose duty was to take care of and send to Jerusalem the sheep for the daily sacrifices, and that the tidings of the Saviour's birth would thus soon reach the Temple.
J. T. F.
Winterton, Brigg.

FLEMISH (5th S. viii. 475.)—As MR. MORFILL takes exception to Sir Walter Scott's describing burghers of Liége talking Flemish, will he kindly enlighten my ignorance by specifying the limits of the district in which Flemish is, or was, spoken ?
W. M. M.

HUGHENDEN VEL HITCHENDEN (5th S. viii. 491.) —Seventy-five years agone I was a child in "Hitchenden," my father's waggons were so inscribed, and the parish was so called until Mrs. Norris (née Douglas), the wife of the then possessor of Hitchenden House, re-called it by an old and obsolete name—Hughenden. Only a few years since some of the waggons of the farmers of the parish still bore the old name, Hitchenden. I have often bathed in the brook below the house, and have since seen the channel growing a crop of beans, though it is now again running a clear stream. I was not a little puzzled when I last visited the old place to find the church and church-yard, in which I had attended the funeral of an infant brother, brought within the park fences.
R.

ARMS OF ARCHBISHOP HERRING (5th S. viii. 491.)—The present Lord Bishop of Durham, who descends from the marriage of Sir Francis Baring, first baronet, with Harriet, daughter of William

Herring, of Croydon, cousin and co-heir of Thomas Herring, Lord Archbishop of Canterbury (see Burke's *Peerage*, &c., *s.v.* "Northbrook"), quarters the arms of Herring with his paternal coat. Upon his seal as Bishop of Gloucester and Bristol (of which I have an impression in my cabinet) the Herring quarters agree with the blazon given by Moule from the painted windows at Croydon in Lincoln's Inn, viz., "Gu. crusily, three herrings hauriant arg." (see my Supplement to Bedford's *Blazon of Episcopacy* in the *Herald and Genealogist*, vol. vii. p. 443).	JOHN WOODWARD.

SCOTT FAMILY : THE PARENTAGE OF ARCH-BISHOP ROTHERHAM (5th S. vii. 89, 139, 158, 292, 330, 375, 416, 470, 490, 509 ; viii. 29, 79, 370, 389, 410.)—Amongst Alumni Etonenses who passed to King's Coll., Cambridge, in the first list, A.D. 1443, 22 Hen. VI., occur Wm. Hatecliffe, Wm. Towne, John Langport, Robert Dummer, Richard Cove, John Chedworth, *Thomas Scot*, alias *Rotherham*, with the following note :—
"The six Fellows of the first Foundation continued members of the second. On this new Establishment by K. Henry, *Hatecliffe* and *Towne*, A.M., two of the former Fellows or Scholars, came to Eton, and were incorporated and admitted Gremials of the College by Provost Waynflete, *Sept.* 15, 1445, and two days after, viz. *Sept.* 17, they returned to Cambridge, and were readmitted Fellows or Scholars of King's College, together with *Langport* and *Dummer*, on the new Establishment. And this being after the Founder had completed the 21st year of his reign, viz. *August* 31st, consequently it then was the 22d year of Henry VI. *Cove, Chedworth,* and *Rotherham* were admitted Scholars of King's in *July* following."
Also Mr. Foss, whom every one must allow·to be a very good and careful authority, in his *Judges of England* says :—
"*Rotheram, alias* Scot, Thomas (Archbishop of York), adopted the name of his native place. His family was named Scot, and resided at Rotheram, in Yorkshire, where he was born [? baptized] on August 24, 1423."
The above points very much to the fact that Archbishop Rotheram's original surname was Scot : possibly he changed it to Rotheram on his removal from Eton to King's College, a scholar of which he was appointed in July, 1444 ; or, more probably still, did so on coming of age, which must have been just about this time.	SYWL.

QUEEN ELIZABETH (5th S. viii. 266, 313, 394.) —The eulogistic effusions in praise of Queen Elizabeth, as given by MR. KENNEDY, are to be found in Camden's *Remaines concerning Britaine*, ed. 1614, chapter on "Epitaphs," pp. 378-9.
Although deprecating repetition, I would, in this case, venture to ask for their reappearance in the quaint old garb of the period, with the context as given in the book referred to above :—
"Queene Elizabeth, a Prince admirable aboue her sexe for her princely virtues, happy gouernment, and long continuance in the same, by which shee yet suruiueth, and so shall, indeared in the memory not only

.more clung about the barge, usu under water
Wept out their eyes of pearle, and swome blinde after.
I thinke the Barge-men might with easier thighes
Have rowed her thither in her peoples eyes.
For how so ere, thus much my thoughts haue scand,
Sh'ad come by water, had shee come by land.'
Another at that time honoured her with this—H.
Holland :
' Weepe greatest Isle, and for thy mistresse death
Swim in a double sea of brakish water :
Weepe little world for great Elizabeth.
Daughter of warre, for Mars himselfe begat her,
Mother of peace ; for shee brought forth the later.
Shee was and is, what can there more be said ?
On earth the chiefe, in heaven the second Maide.'
Another contriued this Distich of her :
' Spaines rod, Romes ruine, Netherlands reliefe ;
Earths ioy, Englands gemme, Worlds wonder, Natures
chiefe.' "

F. D.

Nottingham.

CARACCIOLO (5th S. vii. 507 ; viii. 74, 132, 412.)
—Has this disputed question been set at rest for
ever ? If Dumas is to be trusted, in a matter of
which proof can be easily obtained, there are now
original documents in the archives at Naples,
taken from the Royal Palace in 1860—where he
copied them—which would throw a different light
on the subject. In his *Storia dei Borboni di Napoli* he gives extracts, from which it appears :—
1. That Ruffo was the *alter ego* of Ferdinand, with
full powers of life or death. 2. That Sir W.
Hamilton wrote in a letter to the king, June 27,
1799, *before* Caracciolo was secured, " It is hoped
he is already taken, and will be hung at the yard-
arm, and exposed from morning to night as an
example." 3. That Nelson wrote to Count Thurn
to say Caracciolo must be tried, and, " if found
guilty, inquire of me what punishment he is to
suffer."

I take these jottings from my note-book, written
down at the time I was reading the book. Among
the documents Dumas mentions the note of Sir
W. Hamilton to Ruffo, which said Nelson would
not break the armistice in any way. According
to Dumas, Ruffo was not satisfied with this, and
persuaded Captains Troubridge and Ball, the
bearers of the letter, to write on the back of it :—

" I Capitani Troubridge e Ball hanno autorità per la
parte di Milord Nelson, di dichiarare a S. Eminenza che
Milord non si opporrà all' imbarco dei Ribelli, e della
gente che compone la guarnigione dei Castelli Nuovi e
dell' Uovo."

They refused, however, to sign it. If this is true,
we know how the promise was kept. A search in

except Foote, who had been sent to a
They say that an infraction of the capi
would be "un attentato abominevole contro
pubblica," and "chiamano risponsabile
a Dio e al mondo chiunque ardisse d' im
l' esecuzione."   K. I

THE TITLE OF "ESQUIRE" (5th S. vii. 3:
viii. 33, 55, 114, 157, 256, 314, 450.)—I
formed that a relative of mine had th
conferred upon him by William IV. Can
your readers tell me if the title was ever co
by that monarch ? if so, if there is any list o
to which I can refer ?   F.

THE " HONOURABLE " MRS. BYRON (5th
345, 416.)—In *Traditional Ballad Airs,*
Christie, M.A., Dean of Moray, the fo
allusion occurs in a note in reference to th
descent of Mrs. Byron, the mother of the p
" Miss Gordon of Gight (lineally descended
second Earl of Huntly and his wife, a dau
James 1. of Scotland) was second wife to Joh
son of Admiral Byron. Their only child v
Byron, sixth baron, the celebrated poet."—Vol
The ballad is also given in the same boo
Gordon of Gight, written on the occasior
marriage to Captain Byron :—
" O whare are ye gaun, Miss Gordon ?
   O whare are ye gaun, sae bonny and bra
Ye 're gaun wi' Johnny Byron
   To squander the lands of Gight awa'."
Gight is in the parish of Fyvie, and in the
of Aberdeen.   JOHN PICKFORD,
Newbourne Rectory, Woodbridge.

AUTHORS OF BOOKS WANTED (5th S. ix
Letters, Conversations. and Recollections of S
ridge, 2 vols., Moxon, 1836. Author, Thomas
                                               G

John Forster calls this, in a letter to Land
of latter, vol. ii. p. 469, a " wonderfully foolish
                                           J. A. I

AUTHORS OF QUOTATIONS WANTED (5
449.)—
             " Toujours perdrix."
An editorial answer to this query will be
" N. & Q." (4th S. iv. 337).   W

A long and careful editorial note (4th S.
supplemented by well-known correspondents a
464.   ED. Ma
             (5th S. viii. 509.)
Napoleon's Midnight Review.—This poem
Austrian poet, Baron von Zedlitz. It has l
translated. The most animated of all the tr

may be found in *Graham's Magazine* (Philadelphia, U.S.) for 1854.   M. N. G.
(5th S. viii. 519.)
" Alackaday ! the well is dry," &c.
also—
" Going, gone ! to Tom Toddle for seven pounds ten," are both to be found in *Rural Scenes.*   E. R. W.

(5th S. viii. 509; ix. 18.)
" Pity is akin to love."
As to the exact relationship in which love and pity stand to each other, there seems to be some doubt:—
" Pity, some say, is the parent
    Of future love."
—Beaumont and Fletcher, *The Spanish Curate,* Act v. sc. 1.
" And some say pity is the child of love."
          Cotton, *Love's Triumph,* v. 5.
                                        St. Swithin.

That the thought is older than Dryden or Butler is clear when we remember Shakspeare's *Twelfth Night:*—
" *Vio.* I pity you.
  Oli. That's a degree to love."
                              D. B. Brightwell.

𝕸𝖎𝖘𝖈𝖊𝖑𝖑𝖆𝖓𝖊𝖔𝖚𝖘.

NOTES ON BOOKS, &c.

The Vision of William concerning Piers the Plowman; together with Vita de Dowel, Dobet et Dobest, Secundum Wit et Resoun. By William Langland (1362-1393 A.D.). Edited by the Rev. Walter W. Skeat, M.A. Part IV. Section I. Notes to Texts A, B, and C. (Early English Text Society.)
The English Works of John Fisher, Bishop of Rochester (born 1459, died June 22, 1535). Now first collected by John E. B. Mayor, M.A: Part I. (Early English Text Society, Extra Series.)
The History of the Holy Grail. English: ab. 1450 A.D. by Henry Lonelich, Skinner. From the French Prose (ab. 1180-1190 A.D.) of Sires Robiers de Boiron. Re-edited from the Unique Paper MS. in Corpus Christi Coll., Cambridge, by Fred. J. Furnivall, M.A. Part III. (Early English Text Society, Extra Series.)
The Bruce; or, the Book of the Most Excellent and Noble Prince Robert de Broyss, King of Scots. Compiled by Master John Barbour, Archdeacon of Aberdeen, A.D. 1375. Edited, with Preface, Notes, and Glossarial Index, by the Rev. Walter W. Skeat, M.A. Part III. (Early English Text Society, Extra Series.)

It is impossible to glance at the four goodly volumes whose titles we have just transcribed, or to turn over their pages, without recognizing in them most valuable contributions to the history of our language and literature ; and, consequently, without feeling how much those who take an interest in such studies owe to the untiring energy of Mr. Furnivall, to whom they are mainly indebted for the establishment of the Early English Text Society, by means of which these volumes have been given to the world. The object for which that society was established was certainly not one to command success, however much it may have deserved it ; but it has achieved it : and Mr. Furnivall will, we are sure, be among the first to recognize how large a portion of that success is owing to the band of learned and hard-working scholars who have enlisted under his banner.

Three of the volumes just described are instalments of large and important works—namely, *The Holy Grail,* edited by Mr. Furnivall, and *Piers the Plowman* and

Barbour's *Bruce*, by Mr. Skeat—and as such will be most welcome to the subscribers. The fourth is likewise an instalment, being the first part of a collection which will have special interest for many readers, namely, *The English Works of John Fisher, Bishop of Rochester ;* and we congratulate the members of the Early English Text Society that a book of this peculiar character has been entrusted to an editor, Mr. Mayor, whose previous labours have shown how especially fitted he is to do justice to the life and writings of the pious Christian prelate who sealed his faith with his blood. We sincerely hope that Mr. Mayor will be able to complete the work here commenced sooner than he anticipates.

Mr. J. Charles Cox has published vol. iii. of his important and interesting work, *Notes on the Churches of Derbyshire* (Chesterfield, Edmunds; London, Bemrose). This third volume contains records of the Hundreds of Appletree and Repton and Gresley. The work is not only well written, but profusely illustrated, admirably printed, and handsomely, that is to say appropriately, bound. All who have a justifiable pride in our churches should possess themselves of this series. It will revive old memories in some, and excite in others a desire to visit these ecclesiastical monuments, and so have joyously reverential memories of their own.—Messrs. Longmans have published a second issue of the small edition of *The Life and Letters of Macaulay.* It is emphatically a handy book. We advise those who read it to note Macaulay's opinions on books, and also how many were, in his estimation, each the very best book of any he ever read.—We have received the first and second parts of *The Norfolk Antiquarian Miscellany,* edited by Walter Rye (Norwich, Miller & Co.). The first part was published in 1873 ; the second in 1877. If subscribers have had to wait, they have now something worth the waiting for, and which they probably could not have obtained so easily by other means.

The Folk-Lore Society.—The published prospectus of the Folk-Lore Society wi1 show that the suggestion first made in " N. & Q." has at length been carried out by the formation of a society having for its object the collecting and printing the fast-fading relics of our popular fictions and traditions, legendary ballads, local proverbial sayings, old customs and superstitions. It is intended to include in the field of the society's labours the folk-lore of aboriginal people. But the extent of the society's operations must of course be in proportion to the amount of support which it receives. In order, however, to carry out one important portion of its work, it is necessary to ask the many country readers of " N. & Q." to forward me the names of any local journals in their neighbourhood which have a folk-lore column. It is essential that as complete a list as possible should be obtained.   G. Laurence Gomme, Hon. Sec.
Castelnau, Barnes.

Temple Bar and Buckingham Street Gate.—Why should not Temple Bar be set up again between the Temple and the Embankment, as an entrance to the gardens, and the beautiful Buckingham Street Gate, now buried and lost, be placed between the garden and the road ? Then, almost in juxtaposition and quite in association with their old names and sites, there would stand two works, one of Inigo Jones, the other of Sir Christopher Wren, each not a little interesting to many who are neither sages nor judges of art.
                                        Wm. Jno. Blew.

The Primroses, Earls of Rosebery.—If, as stated in the *Athenæum* (Jan. 5), the Earl of Rosebery (Baron Rosebery of the U.K.) is about to become proprietor of the *Examiner,* the family name of this peer will once

ON all communications should be written the name and address of the sender, not necessarily for publication, but as a guarantee of good faith.

ATHENRY.—The Annesley case was not the first in Ireland in which a similar question was involved. In the "Remembrances to be thought of touching the Parliament"—the Irish Parliament, 1611 (*Calendar of Carew MSS. preserved in the Archiepiscopal Library at Lambeth*, p. 147)—there is the following passage, referring to a question of summoning certain peers to the above Parliament:—"The like question may be made of the Lord Bourke, of Castleconnell, whose elder brother has a son living, and by his friends called Lord Bourke. His uncle alleges that he is a bastard, but the boy is not yet proved to be so. Upon this allegation only his said uncle assumes the name of Lord. How he may be called to the Parliament (before his right be determined) is to be considered." The "boy" is on the roll of peers with the word "infant" added to his name. By an enactment of 1611 it was unlawful for an illegitimate child to take for his surname any other than his mother's Christian name.

M. E. B.—The descent of the quotation is traced as follows : Seneca (the dramatic writer). who died A.D. 30, has, in his *Thyestes* (Act ii. l. 380), "Mens regnum bona possidet." Byrd, in *Psalms, Sonnets*, &c. (1588), has, "My mind to me a kingdom is." Southwell (*ob.* 1595) has, "My mind to me an empire is," in *Look Home*. Sir Edward Dyer, who died 1607, is quoted in Prof. Morley's *Shorter English Poems*, p. 218, in the lines—
"My mind to me a kingdom is;
  Such present joys therein I find,
    That it excels all other bliss
      That earth affords or grows by kind."

H. R. D. should send his name and address (not for publication).

J. J. P., A. L. G., SWYL, T. K. (Bristol), C. E. B.—Next week.

W. JOHNSON (Philadelphia.)—See "N. & Q.," 5th S. vii. 6, 137, 179, 413.

S. should apply to the publisher of the Hon. Mrs. Norton's works.

W. F. (Glasgow.)—Forwarded to Mr. Lowe.

ANTIQUITAS (" Podmore Family," 5th S. viii. 349.)—We have a letter for you.

SI JE PUIS.—With pleasure next week.

ERRATUM (5th S. ix. 17.)—I see I have written the more familiar word " Easedale " Tarn, instead of *Grisedale* Tarn, which was the subject of King Mounsey's grant. W. G.

NOTICE.

Editorial Communications should be addressed to " The Editor of ' Notes and Queries ' "—Advertisements and Business Letters to " The Publisher "—at the Office, 20, Wellington Street, Strand, London, W.C.

We beg leave to state that we decline to return communications which, for any reason, we do not print ; and to this rule we can make no exception.

LONDON, SATURDAY, JANUARY 19, 1878.

CONTENTS.—N° 212.

Notes.

"GARETH AND LYNETTE."

I have just been reading the story of Gareth in Sir Thos. Malory's *History of Prince Arthur*, and have been greatly struck with the deviations of Tennyson's version from the more ancient story. For my own part I much prefer the prose narrative, which is more consistent and natural. Probably many will be interested in having a brief sketch of each of these versions, told in such a way that they may be readily compared together ; but, before entering on the stories themselves, the reader must be reminded that the word "Gareth" is the only name which the poet has not more or less altered, as the subjoined table will plainly show :

Tennyson.	*History of Pr. Arthur.*
Lynette and Lyonors.	Linet and Lionês.
The Evening-star, or Hesperus.	The Green Knight, Sir Pertolope.
The Noonday-sun, or Meridies.	The Red Knight, Sir Perimones.
The Morning-star, or Phosphorus.	The Blue Knight, Sir Persaunt of India.
Night, or Nox.	The Black Knight of the Black Lands, Sir Peread.
Death, or Mors.	The Red Knight of the Red Lands, Sir Ironside.

The classic names of Hesperus, Meridies, Phosphorus, Nox, and Mors appear to me especially out of character in this British romance.

CHAPTER I.

The Historical Account.—King Arthur was holding his annual Whitsun festival at the city and castle of King Kenedon, on the sands in the borders of Wales, when three men on horseback and a dwarf on foot drew nigh. The horsemen alighted, and, giving their steeds to the dwarf to hold, approached the castle gate. The middle one of the three was young, tall, and broad shouldered, and his "hands were the largest that ever man saw." He entered the presence-chamber leaning on the shoulders of his two companions, over whom he towered a foot and a half in height. "A boon, sir king," he said modestly ; and being told to name it, craved three gifts, one to be granted forthwith and the other two at the next anniversary. All he asked at present was that he might be taken into the king's service for meat and drink till next Whitsuntide. His prayer was at once vouchsafed, and the king ordered his steward, Sir Kay, "to take the young man and treat him as a lord's son." Sir Kay received him sulkily, and from the unusual size of his hands nicknamed him Beaumains (not "Fairhands"*), and put him into the kitchen, but his two companions departed, leaving him behind.

When Sir Launcelot saw how churlishly the young stranger was treated, he rebuked the steward sharply, but Sir Kay heeded him not ; and the young stranger "went to the hall door and sat him down among the boys and lads, and there ate he sadly with them." For twelve months he put up with this insulting treatment, but in all those days "he never displeased either man or child, but was invariably meek and courteous."

The next Pentecost the king held at Carlion in unusual state ; and on Whitsunday a damsel entered, and said, "A lady of great worship is oppressed by a tyrant, who will not allow her to quit her castle, and wants to force himself upon her against her will. She has sent to crave aid of thee, sir king, and hopes you will permit one of your knights to espouse her cause." She refused to give up the name of the lady, but said the oppressor was called the Red Knight of the Red Lands. Then said the king, "If you withhold the lady's name, no Knight of the Round Table can undertake the cause." At this arose the stranger nicknamed Beaumains, and said, "Sir king, I have a boon to ask. I have now been with you for twelve months, and the time is come for me to prefer my other two petitions." "Ask," said the king ; "they shall be granted at my peril."

---

* Tennyson's *Fair-hands* is very improper. We speak of "fine fruit," "fine vegetables," "fine fellows," meaning *large*, but never use *fair* in this sense. "Fine-hands," in the sense of *big-hands*, would do, but "Fair-hands" gives quite a wrong idea. Instead of "Fine-face" and "Fair-hands," the poet ought to have said *Fair-face* and *Fine (i.e.* Big) *hands.*

— — — —, — — — — — — — — — — — —, — — — — —
gracious answer. •

The damsel now broke out indignantly, and cried, " Fie on it, fie, I say ! What, shall no one but a kitchen page be given me ?" And she was exceeding angry, left the presence-chamber, mounted her horse, and departed. At this moment one entered and told Beaumains that a dwarf was at the gate, who had brought a steed and armour. And the young man went and armed himself; then, having taken leave of the king, he rode after the damsel.

Tennyson's Version.—Gareth was the youngest and tallest son of Lot, King of Orkney, and Bellicent (the history says his mother was Morgawse, Arthur's sister), and, thirsting for adventure, he wanted to join his two brothers (the history says his three brothers, Gawain, Agravine, and Gaheris) in the court of King Arthur ; but his mother, in order to quash the wish, said, more in banter than in earnest, she would consent to his so doing on the following conditions : that he concealed his name and served as a kitchen menial for twelve months and a day. She thought his proud heart would revolt from such degradation, but he replied, " The body may be in thrall, yet the mind be free." Next morning ere daybreak he started with two servitors, who had waited on him from his birth, and making his way southwards came to Camelot (the history says King Kenedon, in Wales). On reaching the castle an old warder came out and asked his business, and Gareth said, " We be tillers of the soil, who have left our ploughs to come and see the glories of the king." On hearing this the old greybeard began to banter the strangers ; but, heeding him not, they entered the court and came with other suitors to the great hall, where the king was seated on his throne administering justice, as was his wont. When it came to Gareth's turn, he cried, " A boon, sir king. Grant me for meat and drink to serve among thy kitchen knaves a twelvemonth and a day, but seek not to know my name." The king smiled at the request, and answered, " Then must my seneschal be thy master." And Sir Kay unwillingly took the young stranger in charge, and called him in mockery " Sir Fine-face" and " Sir Fair-hands " (? Big-hands). And Gareth " underwent the sooty yoke of kitchen vassalage " the allotted time.

One day he tilted with Sir Gawain, and, having overthrown him, went and told the king, saying, " Joust can I ; make me thy knight, sir king, in secret." And the king replied, " Make thee my knight ! My knights are sworn to hardihood." And Gareth made answer, " So be it." (Compare this with the original tale, as given above.)

Castle Perilous. Three knights defend the three passages to her castle, and a fourth holds her a captive, wanting to wed her against her will. Send therefore, I pray thee, thy chief man, Sir Lancelot, to deliver her." The king then asked " the fashion of these knights "; and the maid replied, " Three of them call themselves Day, viz. Morning-star, Noon-star, and Evening-star ; but the fourth names himself Night, and oftener Death."

Then rose Gareth and cried, " A boon, sir king. Be this quest mine. Thy promise, king." And Arthur could not gainsay his word, and said, " Go." And all were filled with amazement ; but the damsel was indignant, and cried in her anger, " Fie, O king ! I asked for thy chiefest knight and you give me your kitchen knave." So saying, she left the presence-chamber, mounted her horse, passed " the weird white gate," and rode off. And Sir Gareth found a war-steed ready for him, the gift of the king, and his two companions (in the history they had left) waiting for him, with shield, and casque, and spear. So he armed himself and rode after the damsel.

This is no place for criticism, but I fancy none can read these two accounts and not regret the alterations. The arrogance of the damsel is truly offensive, and her telling the king the name of her sister deprives the poet of a capital point, viz. the impossibility of a Table Knight engaging in an anonymous adventure. I think also the brag of the " meek " Gareth that he could joust, and claiming knighthood of the king in secret, is no improvement, but the reverse.

E. COBHAM BREWER.

Lavant, Chichester.

(*To be continued.*)

"SHAKESPEARE IN FRANCE."

I observe that our editor, in his interesting paper upon " Shakespeare in France " in this month's number of the *Nineteenth Century*, leaves undecided the question as to the earliest mention of Shakespeare in French literature. The subject is of course one of literary curiosity only, for it is certain that our great poet could have had no appreciable influence upon French literature until the days of Destouches and Ducis.

Was not St. Evremond the first Frenchman who discovered our Elizabethan drama ? The

* The history says Lionés or Lyonese, quite another person. Lyonese was sister of Linet or Lynette, daughter of Sir Persaunt of Castle Perilous; but Lyonors was daughter of the earl Sanam, and the unwedded mother of Sir Borre by king Arthur.

Réflexions sur les Tragédies et sur les Comédies Françaises, Espagnoles, Italiennes, et Anglaises of this sadly neglected but very charming writer has indeed no reference to Shakespeare by name, but contains evidence that its author was acquainted with his works, which, as may be naturally supposed, the Gaul was quite unable to estimate. As St. Evremond never took the trouble to acquire our language, his knowledge of Shakespeare must have been obtained from his English friends, and probably from seeing some of the plays performed. Des Maizeaux, in his *Life of St. Evremond* (Lond., 1714), tells us that the *Réflexions* were the result of the writer's acquaintance with D'Aubigny and Buckingham :—

"Being often together, they discours'd about all manner of subjects, but chiefly about the Dramatick Pieces of several nations. Mr. de St. Evremond not understanding the English Tongue, those gentlemen acquainted him with the best Strokes in our most celebrated Plays ; of which he retain'd a clear idea to the very last ; and from these ingenious Conversations resulted his Reflexions on the English Stage."

Dryden also, in an allusion to the work of St. Evremond, makes use of the expression that the writer did not see our theatre with his own eyes. St. Evremond wrote his dissertation about the year 1676.   C. ELLIOT BROWNE.

[With reference to English actors rather than to Shakespeare himself in France, we reprint, from the *Intermédiaire des Chercheurs—Notes and Queries Français*, i. 65, the following account of an English company in France, playing in Paris and at Fontainebleau, when Shakespeare was yet alive. By this it will be seen that the English troop had legal possession of the stage in the great hall of the Hôtel de Bourgogne, and were liable to a fine of one crown every day, during the term agreed upon, if they acted in any other theatre. Further, that they acted before Henri IV. at Fontainebleau, and that the young Dauphin, then five years old, and afterwards Louis XIII., was sufficiently impressed by the English actors to dress himself like them, and to repeat an exclamation which he had caught from them in the words, "Tiph toph, milord !" The name of the piece, as of the actors, is unfortunately lacking.

"COMEDIENS ANGLAIS EN FRANCE SOUS HENRI IV.— Dans l'inventaire des titres et papiers de l'hôtel de Bourgogne se trouvent mentionnés : 1° un bail de la grande salle et théâtre du dit hôtel, passé le 25 mai, 1£98, devant Huart et Claude Nouvel, notaires à Paris, par Jehan Schuis (*sic*), comédien anglais ; 2° une sentence du Châtelet, rendue le 4 juin, 1598, à l'encontre des dits comédiens anglais, tant pour raison du susdit bail que pour le droit d'un écu par jour, jouant par les dits anglais ailleurs qu'au dit hôtel.

"Dans le journal manuscrit du médecin Héroard, qui se trouvait autrefois dans le cabinet de M. de Genas (No. 21,448 de la Bibl. hist. du P. Lelong) il est dit que le samedi 18 septembre, 1604, le roi et la cour étant à Fontainebleau, le dauphin (Louis XIII., qui entrait alors dans sa quatrième année) est mené dans la grande salle neuve, ouïr une tragédie représentée par des Anglais. Il les écoute avec froideur, gravité, et patience, jusques à ce qu'il fallut couper la tête à un des personnages. Le mardi 28, le dauphin se fait habiller en masque et imite les comédiens anglais qui étaient à la cour et qu'il avait vus jouer. Enfin, le dimanche 3 octobre de la même année, l'enfant se fait encore habiller en comédien, et, marchant à grands pas, imite les comédiens anglais, en disant : *Tiph ! toph ! milord !*

"Voilà donc, à l'époque de Shakespeare, des comédiens anglais jouant à Paris, en 1598, et à la cour de Fontainebleau devant Henri IV. en 1604. Serait-il possible de connaître le personnel de ces troupes et les pièces de leur répertoire ?"

By the above account we find that the lease and other documents are only mentioned in the papers connected with the Hôtel de Bourgogne as having existed. If the originals are in existence, they would be well worth examination ; but, without disputing their genuineness, the examiner would have to bear in mind the facility with which "original documents" are occasionally fabricated in France. The so-called autograph letters of Sir Isaac Newton and others may be cited as an example. Then, as to the Dauphin's quotation, "Tiph ! toph ! milord !" where is anything like it to be found in Shakespeare ? Falstaff says to the Chief Justice (2 *Hen. IV.* Act ii. sc. 2), "This is the right fencing grace, my lord ; tap for tap, and so part fair." But there is here no question of a man losing his head, as in the play at Fontainebleau. In *Measure for Measure* (Act i. sc. 2) Claudio's head, according to Lucio, stands "so ticklish on his shoulders that a milkmaid, if she be in love, may sigh it off." Lucio hopes the mediation of Claudio's sister, Isabella, may save her brother's life, "as well for the encouragement of the like [Claudio's offence], which else would stand under grievous imposition, as for the enjoying of thy life, who I would be sorry should be thus foolishly lost at a game of tick-tack." The last words are so near to the French name for backgammon, *tric-trac*, that a French boy could hardly have changed them, as the Dauphin is said to have done, into "Tiph ! toph !" Again, in the passage from *Measure for Measure* there is no "my lord," as in *Henry IV.*, but, on the other hand, there is a man in peril of losing his head. The only question of interest is, was there an English troop of actors in France at the period indicated above ? If this be proved, they may have acted either or both of the plays. If any correspondent possesses a series of the *Mercure Galant*, and will inform the readers of "N. & Q." if, and when, the name of Shakespeare occurs in it, he would render most acceptable service. We would also ask any one who can refer to M. E. Fournier's *Théâtre Français aux 16me et 17me Siècles* to kindly look into it for the same purpose ; and finally, as having some bearing on the question, how long after 1591 did the English military force remain in France as allies of Henri Quatre ?]

BEWICK'S MASTERS.

I have lately turned up the following list of a small collection of old illustrated books which I understood to have been the workshop library of Thomas Bewick. They were distinguishable from his home library by their much used condition, as well as their specialty of old engravings. The books themselves were accidentally destroyed soon after this description was drawn up, but you may think the list worth preserving as indicating Bewick's masters, if masters he had :—

1. Old Vulgate Latin Bible, with Woodcuts. 8vo., old dated stamped binding, 1573.

2. Albert Dürer's Woodcuts of the Passion. 1510. 35 cuts, with 5 duplicates loose in the cover. This copy is printed on blank paper, without any letter-press or inscriptions of any kind. 4to., old vellum.

By Edward Topsell. *Iaggard*, 1607. Full of woodcuts. Folio. Used copy, and not quite perfect. Autograph on title:—"Thomas Bewick's [vign.] Book, 1795."

5. Grimston's Historie of the Netherlands. Full-length copperplates of Kings and Governors. Folio, imperfect.

6. The Herball; or, Generall Historie of Plantes. By John Gerarde. 1597. Frontispiece mounted. Portrait engraved by Rogers, also many hundred excellent wood-cuts. Folio. Autograph in print-hand:—"This curious Book belongs to T. Bewick, Engraver, NEWCASTLE, 1798."

7. Ovidii Metamorphoses. Tomus 2dus. *Lips*, 1621. Many woodcuts.

8. Help to English History. By P. Heylyn. 1675, 12mo.

9. Fabellæ Æsopicæ. Latine. Cum Imaginibus. (*Antv.*) *Raphelengius*, 1604. Many good woodcuts. 12mo, old vellum. Written on the cover:—"Present to T. Bewick from Messrs. Longman & Co., Booksellers, June...79..., London."

10. Fabvlæ Variorvm Avctorvm, Æsopi, &c. *Francof.*, 1660. Many woodcuts. 12mo. Autograph:—"T. Bewick, 1770."

11. Book of Ciphers. 4to., fragment only.

12. School Horace. No cuts.

13. About 100 plates of Hunting, &c. By Jo. Stradanus. Engraved by Galle, &c. Oblong folio, used.

14. Alciati Emblemata. Cuts. Small 8vo., imperfect. Also Bewick's collection of old engraved writing books, in 5 vols., folio, and various others of his shop pattern books.

THOMAS KERSLAKE.

Bristol.

THE PURY FAMILY: A SPEECH IN THE LONG PARLIAMENT.

Some years ago, taking an accustomed stroll among the London bookstalls, I met with a small quarto pamphlet which bore this title :—

"Mr. Thomas Pvry, Alderman of Glocester: his Speech upon that clause of the Bill against Episcopacy the which concernes Deanes, and Deanes and Chapters, at a Committee of the whole House. Printed in the year 1641."

I thereupon very gladly gave the florin or half-crown which was the marked price for it ; and as it is a remarkable speech by a remarkable man, of whom, though he took an important part in the civil war, comparatively but little is known, I propose to occupy some of your space with an account o the speech, and of the speaker and his family.

Thomas Pury was one of the members returned to the Long Parliament for the city of Gloucester in 1641. It was, therefore, during his first session that he made this speech, and the occasion was this. Sir Edward Dering, member for Kent, on May 21, 1641, brought in a Bill "for the utter abolishing and taking away of all Archbishops, Bishops, their Chancellors and Commissaries, Deans, Deans and Chapters, Archdeacons, Pre-

"The Bill for abolition of our present episcopacy was pressed into my hand by S. A. H. (Sir Arthur Haslerig) being then brought unto him by S. H. V. (Sir Harry Vane) and O. C. (Oliver Cromwell). He told me he was resolved that it should go in, but was earnestly urgent that I would present it. The Bill did hardly stay in my hand so long as to make a hasty perusall."

This Bill was distinguished from others of a similar character as "The Root and Branch Bill." The second reading was carried by 139 against 108 (*Parl. Hist.*, vol. ii. p. 815), and went into committee June 11, when Hyde (afterwards Lord Clarendon) was appointed chairman, and it was hotly debated from seven in the morning until night. The debate was resumed the next day and also on June 15, when Sir B. Rudyard, member for Wilton, opposed the Bill, and concluded his speech by saying :—

"I am as much for reformation for purging and maintaining religion as any man whatsoever, but I professe I am not for innovation, demolition, nor abolition."

Thereupon up stood Mr. Alderman Pury, and said, "Mr. Hide, I rise not up to answer the arguments of the learned Gentleman of the long robe that spoke last"; and, having stated why he would not enter upon a technical discussion, he proceeded to say :—

"Here is a copy of the Statutes, Grant, and Foundation of the Dean and Chapter of the City of Gloucester. I have read them over, and doe find first the end wherefore the Lands and Possessions were granted unto them. Secondly, the manner and forme of Government of themselves. And lastly, their several oathes to keep all the Statutes prescribed unto them."

He then read the terms of the grant by Henry VIII., and went on :—

"Mr. Hide, you see wherefore the lands were granted unto Deanes and Chapters, what their Statutes are, and their oathes to keep them. It might be thought these men doe know another or nearer way to Heaven than they teach us, or otherwise that they would not sit in the seate of Perjury as it may seeme they doe without remorse of conscience. For it is notoriously knowne to the City of Gloucester and country thereabouts that not one of the said Statutes before mentioned are, or ever were, during my remembrance, kept, or the matters contained in any one of them performed by any of the Deanes or Prebendes of the said Cathedrall: They come indeede once a yeare to receive the rents and profits of the said Lands, but do not distribute unto the Poore and needy their portion, neglecting altogether the mending of the highwayes and Bridges, and do not keep any common table at all: And instead of Preaching the Word of God themselves, *in season and out of season*, they are and have been the chiefe instruments to hinder the same in others. Infinite are the pressures that many cities near unto Deanes and Chapters have endured by them and their procurement. And whereas it was objected by another learned gentleman of the long robe that the Deanes and Chapters are a body corporate, and that they have as much right unto their lay possessions as any other body politicke, or any City or Towne Corporate; I am of his opinion for such Lands and Possessions (if they have any) which they bought themselves in right of their corporation, or for such Lands as were given them for their owne use, and I am well contented that such lands should be left unto them, but their case is farre different in my opinion; for I have showed you before to what goodly, pious, and charitable uses the said Lands and Possessions were granted unto them. . . . Seeing therefore the said Deanes and Chapters are but Trustees, and the profits of the said Lands so ill imployed by them, contrary to the trust reposed in them; I am cleare of opinion that by a Legislative power in *Parliament* it is fitt to take them away, and to put them into the hands of Feoffees, to be disposed of to such pious, religious, and charitable uses as they were first intended."

He then proceeds to show what are the possessions of the Dean and Chapter of Gloucester ;—

"Above twelve Rectoryes of good value, and about thirty Vicaredges, Pensions, and Portions of Tythes, which being at the first *Deo consecrata*, most fit they should be still imployed for the maintenance of the Gospell, for 'preaching ministers' instead of so many singing men there in orders that cannot Preach. And then there are left to be provided for only the Organist, eight singing boys, two schoole masters, foure poore Almesmen, and some under officers, whose yearly wages come unto about one hundred pound per annum."

He says :—

"The Deane and Chapter have almost the third part of the houses of the City of Gloucester, the old rent of them being yearly about 175 pound, which will well defray that charge with a sufficient surplusage for repairing the highwayes, Bridges, and twenty pound yearely to the poore."

And then proceeds :—

"But over and besides the said yearly revenues before mentioned, the said Deane and Chapter of Gloucester, although but of the last Foundation, and one of the least revenues in this kingdome, yet they have eighteen goodly mannors, and also divers other Lands, Tenements, and Hereditaments, besides the Manors, houses and premises, the old rent of assize of one of the said Mannors being 80 pound *per annum ;* out of which Mannors and Lands, the said Cathedrall being to be made a Parochiall Church, 200 pound *per annum* or more may be allowed for a learned Preaching minister there, and a hundred pound a year a piece, for two such others to assist him, all which stipends within a few years one of the said Mannors will discharge, and also sufficiently repaire the said Cathedrall Church, and then the rest of the said Mannors and Lands may be imployed to other godly, pious, or charitable uses, as the Wisdome of the King and Parliament shall think fit. And sutable to this, but in a more ample proportion of maintenance, will be the allowances of all other Deaneryes in England."

The speech concludes thus :—

"And surely, Sir, if these things take effect I am confident we shall be so far from having a poore beggerly Clergy, as that no kingdom in the Christian world will have a more rich and flourishing Clergy, both for Nur. series, and incouragements of learning : and for their maintenance in more plentiful manner than it is at this present. Please you therefore to put the Question, I am ready to give my ayde thereunto."

This being the substance of the speech, I purpose in a future number to give some account of the speaker and his family.　　　J. J. P.

SECRET OR MYSTIC SOCIETIES.—I have several times called attention to the light which may be thrown on the development of mystic societies in the eighteenth century by collecting accounts of those which existed in Italy. Cornelius de Brujn in his voyages to the East gives an account of his admission into an ascetic society. The works of Van Dael de Oraculis and others on the ancient mysteries had widely spread the notions of initiations, of which we find traces among the Rosicrucians and alchemic sects. The practice of white magic was possibly carried on by small secret conclaves. The ideas of such societies must, as is suggested by early masonic rituals, have been much more ancient, for the scheme of such a system will be found sufficiently displayed five centuries ago in a burlesque tale of Boccaccio. It is the ninth novel of the eighth day of the *Decameron*, where Bruno and Buffalmace fool Master Simon, the doctor, with a sham initiation.

HYDE CLARKE.

MODERN AFFECTATIONS.—

"About five years ago, I remember, it was the fashion to be short sighted. A man would not own an acquaintance until he had first examined him with his glass.......
However, that mode of infirmity is out, and the age has recovered its sight : but the blind seem to be succeeded by the lame, and a janty limp is the present beauty.......
I indeed have heard of a Gascon general who by the lucky grazing of a bullet on the roll of his stocking took occasion to halt all his life after. But as for our peaceable cripples, I know no foundation for their behaviour without it may be supposed that in this warlike age some think a cane the next honour to a wooden leg. This sort of affectation I have known run from one limb or member to another. Before the limpers came in, I remember a race of lispers, fine persons who took an aversion to particular letters in our language......
"This humour takes place in our minds as well as bodies. I know at this time a young gentleman who talks atheistically all day,......and in his degrees of understanding sets up for a Free-thinker, though it can be proved upon him he says his prayers every morning and evening.......
"Of the like turn there are all your marriage-haters, who rail at the noose, at the words ' for ever and aye,' and at the same time are secretly pining for some young thing or other that makes their heart ake by their refusal."

This passage is from the *Tatler*, No. 77, Thursday, October 6, 1709. One of the sentences I have omitted begins, "Some never uttered the letter *h*." This is the first time I ever heard of its being considered "the thing" to drop one's *h*'s.

ST. SWITHIN.

THE ISLE OF MAN A BAD PLACE.—In an account of the Isle of Man, printed by Quiggin, Douglas, 1852, which came into my possession some time since, I found the following epigram written at the back of the title, which is suggestive of Man's not being entitled to be called a "holy island," as some others are. I do not know whether this is a popular idea, or only the result of individual experience, and should like to know

by mortals called the Isle of Man,
That little spot I cannot spare,
For all my chosen friends are there."

No initials are put to this unmanly gibe.

EDWIN LEES, F.L.S.
Worcester.

THE LONGEVITY OF LITERARY LADIES.—The
mayor of Bath (now probably the ex-mayor), Mr.
Jerom Mutch, has published a paper which he
read before a literary society on this subject, and
he gives the following list :—

	Died	Aged
Miss Jane Austen	1816 ...	42
Mrs. Radcliffe	1823 ...	59
Miss Mitford	1855 ...	69
Mrs. Trimmer	1810 ...	69
Miss Jane Porter	1850 ...	74
Mrs. Elizabeth Montagu ...	1800 ...	80
Mrs. Piozzi	1821 ...	81
Mrs. Barbauld	1822 ...	82
Miss Edgeworth	1849 ...	82
Lady Morgan	1859 ...	82
Madame d'Arblay	1840 ...	88
Miss Hannah More ...	1833 ...	88
Mrs. Marcet	1859 ...	89
Mrs. Joanna Baillie ...	1851 ...	89
Miss Berry ...	1852 ...	90
Mrs. Somerville ...	1872 ...	92
Miss Harriet Lee ...	1851 ...	95
Miss Caroline Herschel ...	1848 ...	98
Lady Smith	1877 ...	103

These give an average age of eighty-one. Harriet
Martineau and some others might have been included.

KINGSTON.

COWPER AND THE DRAMA.—By a ludicrous misapprehension of the poet's satire, a writer in the
Mirror for 1839, p. 343, quotes from Cowper's
Task, bk. vi., to prove that Cowper had no dislike
to the theatre. It was in reference to the jubilee
at Stratford in 1769 that Cowper wrote :—

"'Twas a hallowed time, decorum reigned
    And mirth without offence. No few returned
    Doubtless much edified, and all refreshed."

Having quoted these, this writer pleases himself
with the idea that Cowper, "a pious and in some
respects a severe Christian," thought better of the
stage than did his religious friends.

J. R. S. C.

"NEITHER HAWK NOR BUZZARD."—This phrase
is used in North and East Derbyshire, and in
parts of Notts, and is thus applied :—Persons on
being asked how they are will reply, "Oh ! I 'm
neither hawk nor buzzard," which means a state of
being "rather out of sorts." It is mostly used by
women. They also say of a young girl just on the

This Picture with your Eyes,
Remember the end of mortal men,
And where their Glory lies.   "I. E."

The above lines are on a small brass plate on the
wall of Crondall Church, Hants. They are engraved under the representation of a partially
shrouded skeleton. The use of the word *imp*, as
applied to the human race in general, is new to
me.

W. J. BERNHARD SMITH.
Temple.

NEW YEAR'S DAY CUSTOM.—Early in the
morning of each New Year's Day groups of children may be observed in the towns and villages
of South Wales, perambulating the streets, headed
by a boy or girl carrying an apple pierced with
barley or oats on end, bearing a comparison to
thorns, and resting on three legs similar to a
tripod. The children will gather around the door
of some house, the boy or girl carrying the apple
standing in the centre, and the whole will sing
the following medley :—

" I wish you a merry Christmas,
    A happy New Year,
    A pocket full of money,
    A cellar full of beer ;
    My feet are very dirty,
    My shoes are very thin,
    I 've got a little pocket
    To slip a penny in."

The apple-bearer then knocks at the door, exclaiming, "Please give us a penny for singing so
well."

I am informed this procedure is of ancient
origin. I shall be obliged if any of your readers
can inform me whether the custom is prevalent in
any part of the kingdom except South Wales,
and further if any can enlighten me as to its
origin and the object of the pierced apple.

W. WILLIAMS.
Oakfield, Pontypridd, Glam.

[We must request correspondents desiring information
on family matters of only private interest, to affix their
names and addresses to their queries, in order that the
answers may be addressed to them direct.]

A SERVIAN DOCUMENT.—I have come across a
Servian document, of which the following is the
French translation :—

"LETTRES PATENTES.—Au nom du Père, du Fils et du
St. Esprit, Amen. Nous Stephan Doubicha par la grâce
de Dieu Roi de Serbie, de Bosnie, du littoral de la terre
de Khilm, des pays inférieurs et occidentaux de Oussora

et du Podrinia (vallée de la Drina),—Faisons savoir à tous ceux que cela pourrait concerner, qu'ayant succédé, par la grâce de Mon Seigneur Jésus-Christ, à la royauté sur les terres ci-dessus dénommées, Nous avons constaté que Notre père et Notre aïeul avaient donné le village et domaine de Umikolo aux ancêtres de Joupan Wlessimir Semikowitch, en récompense de leurs exploits et services rendus en combattant l'ennemi. ·

"Attendu que le nommé Joupan Wlessimir nous supplie aujourd'hui humblement de vouloir bien confirmer cette donation et faire enregistrer en son nom le dit domaine d'Umikolo, Nous avons arrêté, eu égard aux services signalés qu'il Nous a rendus et au sang qu'il a versé pour notre cause, que la propriété du fief d'Umikolo lui serait confirmée, pour lui et ses descendants. Ont été témoins de cet acte Nos hauts dignitaires dont les noms suivent: Le prince (Kniez) bosniaque, Pawel (Paul) Radimowich, le prince de la terre de Khilm, Vlikachin Milatowitch, le prince de la même terre, Jouvan Radinowœwitch, le voïvode du pays-bas (low-lands), prince Mladen Staninitch, le voïvode d'Oussora, prince Stepan Wilochéwitch, le grand-maître (pristav) de la cour, Joupan Rado Radosanitch, l'adjoint du grand-maitre (ipo-voiti), Branko Siménitch.

"Nous Nous engageons à maintenir la présente donation en jurant sur les Sts. Evangiles et au nom du Père, du Fils et du St. Esprit. Ecrit au Palais de Kruchéwatch, de la main de Thomas Logothète, le 31 du moi de mai de l'an de N.S. 1395.

"Signé: (STEPAN). (L. S.) Signé: (DOUBICHA)."

The original is written on leather in old Servian characters, and has a large seal attached, one side representing a man on horseback, the other a king sitting under an elaborate canopy, with two smaller canopies on each side. The document was brought into Constantinople at the beginning of the Servian war. Can any of your correspondents tell me anything about this document—as to its value or otherwise?

ARTHUR LEVESON GOWER.
British Embassy, Constantinople.

PELHAM FAMILY : REVER VEL TREVE MANOR, CO. SUSSEX.—Can any of your correspondents hailing from Sussex explain to me where the above manor was really situated? I am frequently coming across it in connexion with the Pelham family, but I never can identify it with any particular parish. In De Banco Rolls, Trinity, 18 Ed. IV. m. 321, and Easter, 21 Ed. IV. m. 400, I find it mentioned, first, concerning the abduction of Emma Pelham, dau. and co-heir of John Pelham, Esq., son of Sir John Pelham, Knight, who held the m. of Treve als Ryver ; in the second reference, concerning the partition of the m. between John Pelham's four daughters and co-heirs, viz. Emma, Alice, Isabel, and William Hersy and Elizabeth his wife, another dau. and co-heir. This partition mentions numerous places which appear all to have been in some way connected with the m. of Rever, and, to give it as shortly as possible, was as follows :—Lotgarshall and part of Tolyngton (where is this place?) and free chapel of Rever allotted to Emma Pelham. Issues from Tolyngton allotted to Alice Pelham.

Site of the m. and chief mansion (wherever it was), advowson of free chapel or chantry of Rever, demesne lands of the m., all services issuing from the manors, lands, &c., called Upmerden, Merston, Lynche, Rumboldswyke, and Stopham, and from the m. of Gerecourt in Yapton, all knights' fees belonging to said m. of Rever, and all services issuing from all manors of Cotes and Ludgarsale, and all services issuing from lands called Covertys in Yapton, and from lands in Tolyngton, formerly Parish of Rever als Trevar, in circuit seven miles, &c., in Ludgarsale, allotted to William Hersy and Elizabeth his wife. The three unmarried daughters were under age, and appeared by their guardian, William Covert. The manor was held of Henry, Earl of Northumberland, as of his honour of Petworth ; but where it was situated, or what parish, seven miles in extent, it now represents, I am unable to identify, and shall be much obliged to any one who will help me to do so.

The above is likewise interesting inasmuch as it brings on the stage four Miss Pelhams instead of, as all other accounts give, only one, Isabella, married to John, second son of William Covert, of Sullington.   D. C. ELWES.
5, The Crescent, Bedford.

UNKNOWN PORTRAIT (size, 6 in. in diameter).— I have in my possession a circular portrait, dated 1583, representing a young man in the costume of the period, viz. an enormous, deeply frilled white ruff, and black doublet, quilted in cross pattern. The hair is reddish brown, and the face ruddy ; cheek-bones high, and nose prominent. The portrait is painted on beechwood turned. On the frame is the inscription : "Plus cher Honnevr qve Vie. Aᵒ 1583. ÆTATIS SVÆ 23 &c." Any contributor to " N. & Q." who could furnish particulars relative to the person represented in the above would greatly oblige.   SI JE PUIS.

PERSONAL PROVERBS.—Amongst the proverbial sayings which were common more than two centuries ago, there are a number which appear to apply by name to distinct persons. Who these persons were, and under what circumstances their names thus became household words, is now lost. The following are some of them :—

Banbury—As nice as the Mayor of B.
Bolton—Bate me an ace, quoth B.
Bolton—Wide ! quoth B. when his bolt flew back.
Bumsted—Crack me that nut, quoth B.
Croker—As coy as C.'s mare.
Cumberland—The devil and John of C.
Day—Ware wapps, quoth William D.
Dawkins—Dab ! quoth D. when he hit his wife.
De la Mott—As much deformed as D.'s house.
Doddipol—As learned as Dr. D.
Gilbert—Gip ! quoth G. to his mare.
Jerman—As just as J.'s lips.
Mortimer—Backan ! quoth M. to his sow.

Palmer—What ! again quoth P.
Parnell—Madam P., crack the nut and eat the kernel.
Ploydon—The case is much altered, quoth P.
Roger—As red as R.'s nose, who was christened with pump water.
Russe—He will live as long as old R. of Pottern.
Snelling—Mark S. anon.
Spratt—Jack S. could eat no fat.
Vavasour—What ! nowhere such a V.
Vier—O Master V. we cannot pay you.
Walley—Wide ! quoth W.
Waltham—As wise as W.'s calf.
Weymark—Two heads are better than one, said W.

Probably, if it were known where these sayings first arose, the persons meant by them might be made out. In the case of Jack Spratt, Howell, in his *Proverbs*, 1659, gives a version different from more modern authorities. He prints, "Archdeacon Pratt would eat no fatt." It is curious that in Le Neve's *Fast. Eccl. Ang.* there is, out of many thousand names, only one Archdeacon Pratt, and his name was John. He was Archdeacon of St. Davids from 1557 to 1607, when he died, and appears to have held considerable church preferment, for he was also Prebendary of Southwell, Lincoln, and Bath. An attempt was made to oust him from the former in 1599, but he would not give up, and held it till his death. Was this good man the real original Jack Spratt of the nurseries ? EDWARD SOLLY.

THE MSS. OF DR. BENNETT, BISHOP OF CLOYNE. —This great antiquary of the last century, who, with the Rev. Thos. Leman, walked over the course of nearly all the Roman roads of England, compiled the result of his observations in a series of articles on the Roman roads of each English county. They were intended for publication in the *Magna Britannia* of the Messrs. Lysons. Commencing alphabetically, his notes on Bedfordshire, Berkshire, Bucks, Cambridge, Cheshire, Cornwall, Cumberland, Derbyshire, and Devon were published in the above-named work. Those for Hertfordshire were communicated to Mr. Clutterbuck for his history of that county ; and those for Leicestershire appeared in Mr. Nichols's *History of Leicestershire*. Owing to the death of the Messrs. Lysons, the *Magna Britannia* stopped short at " Devonshire," and the remainder of the bishop's notes was never published. That they existed may be gathered from the fact of his stating in *Magna Britannia*, vol. ii. pt. ii. p. 483, and in vol. v. p. ccxiii, that he places the *Mediolanum* of the Tenth Iter of Antoninus at Chesterton, near Newcastle-under-Lyne, but will treat of the fact at greater length when he comes to examine the Roman towns and roads in Staffordshire. This is confirmed by the MS. notes of Mr. Leman on the margin of his copy of Horsley's *Britannia*

came of his MSS. seems never to have been publicly ascertained. Can any reader of " N. & Q." give this information ? That portion of them relating to Staffordshire is especially needed.
W. THOMPSON WATKIN.
Liverpool.

CANDLESTICKS AT ST. BAVON'S, GHENT.—While paying a visit to the cathedral of St. Bavon, a year or two ago, a person who acted as guide pointed out to me, among other objects of interest, four massive copper candlesticks, standing in prominent positions in the choir. These, he informed me, were stamped with the arms of England, and had once belonged to King Charles I. They are briefly referred to, I find, in Murray's *Handbook*, where it is said that they were probably sold and sent abroad in the interregnum, having previously adorned the chapel of Whitehall, or possibly St. Paul's. My present object is to inquire whether any particulars have come to light showing the original local position of these ecclesiastical ornaments, and under what circumstances they were transferred to Flanders.
WM. UNDERHILL.
Lausanne Road, Peckham.

BREAD AND SALT.—Some years since I called for the first time upon Canon Percy, of Carlisle, at his residence there. When refreshment had been offered and declined, he said, " You must have some bread and salt," with some remarks to imply that it was the way to establish a friendship. These were then brought in and eaten, without anything to lead one to suppose that this was an unusual custom at the house. Was this a practice peculiar to himself or to his family ? or is such a custom prevalent in the North, or in any other part of England ? I have not met with it elsewhere.
ED. MARSHALL, F.S.A.

"THE FAULTY ETHICAL SYSTEM OF SIR PHILIP SIDNEY."—In the prefatory matter in Gifford's edition of the works of Ben Jonson there is a notice of the song which occurs in the play of the *Fox*:—

" Come, my Celia, let us prove
While we may the sports of love,
Time will not be ours for ever," &c.

And the writer says : "This song, unfortunately founded on the faulty *ethical* system of Sir Philip Sidney," &c. Can any reader of " N. & Q." tell me why this censure is applied to Sidney, whom (although not acquainted with his writings) I have always looked upon as a great example of moral purity ? HIGHGATE.

WILLIAM ROGERS, of Weymouth, Dorsetshire, born at Dawlish, Devonshire, married Jan. 22,

1760, Martha Matticks, of Weymouth. He held a commission in the army, and had an estate in Weymouth, known during the latter part of the last century as "Rogers's Folly." It was afterwards used as an hotel. Any further information in regard to his family and history, also his wife's connexions, will be gladly received by
S. P. May.
Newton, Mass., U.S.A.

GLASGOW CATHEDRAL ORGAN OF SIXTEENTH CENTURY.—It is stated by Lawson, in his *History of the Episcopal Church of Scotland*, but on very insufficient authority, that there "still exists in Holland an organ that was removed from Glasgow Cathedral at the time of the Reformation." Is anything known of such an instrument?
R. B. S.

M. W., A DUBLIN SILVERSMITH.—Where am I likely to obtain any information respecting a silversmith with the initials M. W., who worked in Dublin in 1764-65, and used those initials as his mark?
F. M.

THE RED MOUSE.—I have lately seen an allusion to the "red mouse of German literature." Where can I find an explanation of it?
J. WOODWARD.

FELICE BALLARIN, OF CHIOGGIA.—The *Art Journal* for February, 1863, contained an engraving of a picture, by Mr. F. Goodall, A.R.A., of "Felice Ballarin reciting Tasso to the people of Chioggia," a seaport on the Gulf of Venice. In the letter-press description of the picture it is stated that Ballarin was a person who, at the period of the artist's visit to Italy a few years previously, got his living by reading or reciting the works of the Italian poets in the market-place of the above-named town to the street population, which consists principally of fishermen and fruit-sellers, and that he recited with much skill and taste. It would be interesting to know something more of a character who obtained his living in so laudable a manner. Do any of your readers know anything of him? What were his antecedents and education? and is he still living, and charming the good people of Chioggia with Tasso's glowing stanzas? Query, if an English Felice Ballarin were to take to reciting the works of our poets, say of Milton or Spenser, to the fishermen and costermongers in the streets of an English seaport, or, for the matter of that, to the merchants and stockbrokers in the neighbourhood of Lothbury, how many would care to listen to him, and, of those who did, how many would appreciate him?
JONATHAN BOUCHIER.
Bexley Heath, Kent.

ANTI-POPERY HYMNS AND SONGS.—I am very anxious to study some of the English and Latin

hymns and popular anti-Popery songs of the Reformation, and those in vogue in 1553-58. Could any reader of "N. & Q." help me in the matter by telling me where to procure such a collection, if there is one?
ACTON WEST.
[The rest of your query can be answered best at the British Museum.]

OGILVIE FAMILY.—Can any genealogist give information as to the parentage and descent of Conyngham Ogilvie, a commissioned officer in the 51st Line, who sold out A.D. 1811?
C. D. WILLIAMS.
Browne's School, Stamford.

AKARIS OR AKARIUS FAMILY.—Will either of your learned correspondents, ANGLO-SCOTUS or HERMENTRUDE, be kind enough to enlighten me on the following points?—1. Was Geoffrey filius Hervey, who held lands in Westmoreland (in Lowther, Clifton, and Melkanthorpe—Escheat, 8 Ed. II.), the grandson or great-grandson of Hervey Fitz Akaris, of Ravenswath? The arms are exactly the same, except that the tinctures of the former are silver and sable.
2. Was Alice de Staveley the wife of Henry, son of Hervey Fitz Akaris, or of another of his sons named Hervey?
3. Where can I find a reliable account of the grant of any lands or manors in Westmoreland (belonging to Hugo de Morville or Robert Vipont) to any of the family of Hervey Fitz Akaris?
IDONEA.

"FORMES" OF LAND.—I find the following entry in an old account book (seventeenth century): Paid so much "for plowing 8 formes of land." What is a "forme" of land?
PAUL Q. KARKEEK.
Torquay.

TOUCHING FOR THE KING'S EVIL.—When did James I. of England first perform this ceremony? I have, as it were, a remembrance, though not improbably a wrong one, that the custom had been for some time omitted prior to his accession. Was it, or was it not?
B. NICHOLSON.

AUTHORS OF BOOKS WANTED.—
Who is the author of two articles in *Cornhill Mag.*, 1860, vol. i. p. 475, and ii. p. 615, viz., "Ideal Houses" and "Neighbours"? Have any of his writings been published in a separate form?
J. A. RUTTER.

To or *On a Stepmother*.—A poem with this title has been, I believe, incorrectly attributed to Beattie. Who was the author?
SCRIBE.

AUTHORS OF QUOTATIONS WANTED.—
Mr. Bright said, "Some poet, I forget who, has said,.
'Religion, freedom, vengeance, what you will,
A word's enough to raise mankind to kill.'"
—*Times*, Jan. 14, 1878.
W. H. C.

GEORGE WASHINGTON AND THE REV. JONATHAN BOUCHER.

(5ᵗʰ S. i. 102 ; v. 501 ; vi. 21, 81, 141, 161.)

At the above references are certain extracts from the autobiography and correspondence of the Rev. Jonathan Boucher, some of which contain severe animadversions upon the personal character of General Washington. Such animadversions have been so rare during the century of his historical existence, and, when made, so readily refuted, that it does not seem proper that these should continue to stand upon record without some notice. It is true that the grandson of Mr. Boucher, who furnished these extracts, very plainly dissented from the estimate placed upon Washington's character and *status* by his ancestor, and in vol. vi. p. 143, used this language :—

"It is only fair, however, both to Washington and to Mr. Boucher to state that the latter, in after years, appears to have changed, or rather modified, his opinion of Washington's conduct, as, when in 1797 he published a set of sermons on the causes and consequences of the American Revolution, which he had delivered at various times in America, he dedicated the volume to his old friend in terms so friendly, and, at the same time, so independent, that I would gladly insert the dedication here, had not these extracts already extended to what I fear is an unconscionable length."

This is very well and very honourable, so far as it goes ; but I think that, in strict fairness and justice to the memory of Washington, the dedication in question should have been printed side by side or in close juxtaposition with the original damnatory allegations, in order that the bane might not be without the antidote. A copy of the volume mentioned has just come into my possession. It is well enough known, but not likely to be much sought after, and hence thousands who have read Mr. Boucher's letter to Washington (5ᵗʰ S. vi. 161-2), and been affected by its wholesale denunciations of the man to whom it was addressed, but by whom there is no evidence that it ever was received, would probably never see what appears to me a complete renunciation of, and manly apology for, the unfounded charges made more than twenty years before.

This letter is dated "Aug. 6, 1775," and was generally, as Mr. Boucher's grandson candidly explains, the natural outpouring of grief, indignation, and disgust, by a man who considered himself wrongly persecuted on account of his political opinions. It is clear, however, from the internal evidence of the letter itself, that the writer had conceived the notion that for some reason—perhaps the very personal friendship which had long existed between him and Washington—he should be singled out from others who held the same political sentiments and protected in the expression of them, when, by his own admission, they

which he lived. The sting of the letter is in its closing sentences, which must here be repeated in order that the case may be perfectly comprehended. After detailing his grievances, he addresses Washington thus :—

"And yet you have borne to look on, at least as an unconcerned spectator, if not an abettor, whilst, like the poor frogs in the fable, I have in a manner been pelted to death. I do not ask if such conduct in you was friendly : was it either just, manly, or generous ? It was not : no, it was acting with all the *base malignity* of a virulent Whig. As such, sir, I resent it : and, oppressed and overborne as I may seem to be by popular obloquy, I will not be so wanting in justice to myself as not to tell you, as I now do with honest boldness, that *I despise the man who, for any motives, could be induced to act so mean a part.* You are no longer worthy of my friendship : a man of honour can no longer without dishonour be connected with you.* With your cause I renounce you," &c.

The italics are mine, and I use them to bring out more pointedly what I regard as an attack upon the personal rather than the political character of the individual addressed. And yet, two-and-twenty years later—viz. in 1797—on publishing *A View of the Causes and Consequences of the American Revolution*, Mr. Boucher dedicated his volume to the very man whom he had accused of base malignity—the man he so despised, who had acted so mean a part, who was no longer worthy of his friendship, and with whom he could no longer be connected without dishonour—in the following terms :—

"To George Washington, Esquire, of Mount Vernon, in Fairfax County, Virginia. Sir, In prefixing your name to a work avowedly hostile to that Revolution in which you bore a distinguished part, I am not conscious that I deserve to be charged with inconsistency. I do not address myself to the General of a Conventional Army, but to the late dignified President of the United States, the friend of rational and sober freedom.

"As a British subject I have observed with pleasure that the form of Government, under which you and your fellow-citizens now hope to find peace and happiness, however defective in many respects, has, in the unity of its executive, and the division of its legislative powers, been framed after a British model. That, in the discharge of your duty as head of this Government, you have resisted those anarchical doctrines, which are hardly less dangerous to America than to Europe, is not more an eulogium on the wisdom of our forefathers, than *honourable to your individual wisdom and integrity*.

"As a Minister of Religion I am equally bound to tender you my respect for having (in your valedictory address to your countrymen) asserted your opinion that 'the only firm supports of political prosperity are religion and morality'; and that 'morality can be maintained only by religion.' Those best friends of mankind, who, amidst all the din and uproar of Utopian reforms, persist to think that the affairs of this world can never be well administered by men trained to disregard the God who made it, must ever thank you for this decided protest against the fundamental maxim of modern revolutionists, that religion is no concern of the State.

"It is on these grounds, Sir, that I now presume (and I hope not impertinently) to add my name to the list of·

those who have dedicated their works to you. One of them, not inconsiderable in fame, from having been your fulsome flatterer, has become your foul calumniator: to such dedicators I am willing to persuade myself I have no resemblance. I bring no incense to your shrine even in a Dedication. Having never paid court to you whilst you shone in an exalted station, I am not so weak as to steer my little bark across the Atlantic in search of patronage and preferment; or so vain as to imagine that now, in the evening of my life, I may yet be warmed by your setting sun. My utmost ambition will be abundantly gratified by your condescending, as a private Gentleman in America, to receive with candour and kindness this disinterested testimony of regard from a private Clergyman in England. I was once your neighbour and your friend: the unhappy dispute, which terminated in the disunion of our respective countries, also broke off our personal connexion: but *I never was more than your political enemy;* and every sentiment even of political animosity has, on my part, long ago subsided. Permit me then to hope, that *this tender of renewed amity between us* may be received and regarded as giving some promise of that perfect reconciliation between our two countries which it is the sincere aim of this publication to promote. If, on this topic, there be another wish still nearer to my heart, it is that you would not think it beneath you to co-operate with so humble an effort to produce that reconciliation.

" You have shown great prudence (and, in my estimation, still greater patriotism) in resolving to terminate your days in retirement. To become, however, even at Mount Vernon, a mere private man, by divesting yourself of all public influence, is not in your power. I hope it is not your wish. Unincumbered with the distracting cares of public life, you may now, by the force of a still powerful example, gradually train the people around you to a love of order and subordination; and, above all, to a love of peace. ' Hæ tibi erunt artes.' That you possessed talents eminently well adapted for the high post you lately held, friends and foes have concurred in testifying: *be it my pleasing task thus publicly to declare that you carry back to your paternal fields virtues equally calculated to bloom in the shade.* To resemble Cincinnatus is but small praise: be it yours, Sir, to enjoy the calm repose and holy serenity of a Christian hero; and may ' the Lord bless your latter end more than your beginning !'

" I have the honour to be, Sir, your very sincere Friend, and most obedient humble Servant,
" Jonathan Boucher.
" Epsom, Surrey, 4th Nov., 1797."

Here again the italics are mine, for the purpose of contrast. As I said before, I know of no withdrawal of unfounded charges more complete, and no apology more manly, than are embraced in the foregoing dedication. It is alike honourable to the man who wrote it and him to whom it was addressed, and I feel certain that its reproduction will at once do away with any unpleasant and unjust conceptions of the personal character of Washington which may have been produced by the publication of the letter to which it is a perfect antidote. Joseph Lemuel Chester.

" Swallow Holes " (5th S. viii. 509.)— " Swallow holes " are very common in places where the surface consists of, or is underlaid by, limestone, this species of rock being generally full of fissures eroded or enlarged by the action of water. Cases in point are common in North Derbyshire and elsewhere. At the south end of Breconshire, near the Beacon range, is a district extremely interesting both scenically and geologically, lying between the Melltè river and its tributary the Hepstè. The surface seems to be a not very thick capping of millstone grit resting upon carboniferous limestone. East and south-east of Ystrad-felltè, a secluded Welsh village, the moorland contains many fissures and funnel-shaped holes, down some of which the surface streams come to a sudden end, but which never discharge water, that office being left to other holes and crevices in the floors and sides of the numerous deep dingles, and at far lower levels. The whole region seems honeycombed with caves, the gritstone roof having often fallen in : hence the cracks and " swallow holes." The Mellte plays curious tricks at and below the above-named village, sometimes in, sometimes below, its surface channel, until swallowed up by a huge cave (reversing the case of the Castleton cavern), and reappearing half a mile below, forced up by *vis a tergo*, just before dashing over a fine series of waterfalls, below which it receives the Hepstè, and on either side of which its banks present a fine combination of lofty rocks and beautiful hanging woods.

The Hepstè is well worth following up for two or three miles above the junction. First come the series of lower waterfalls, whirlpools, and rapids, then the upper or great Cilhepstè fall, 50 ft. wide by 50 ft. high, where a public footway crosses *under and behind* the water. Here it is best to climb the southern bank and keep for half a mile or so along the moorland, as the side of the ravine is slippery and treacherous; then descending to the stream you find a beautiful series of rock-pools and rapids, and soon come to where, in ordinary times, the river wells up in a lovely rock basin after an underground course of a mile or more. (In flood time the dingle is swept by a furious torrent, amid which the place of ordinary emergence is shown by a curious haycock-shaped jet in mid-stream, proving great hydrostatic pressure below, as the fountain has to fight its way through the strong surface current.) On again along the usually dry bed, note the beauty, as all along, of rock cliff and woodland, and the variation in geological detail, and minor " faults " too small for the Ordnance map (42, S.W., a beautifully engraved sheet), till you come to, Hibernicè, a dry waterfall, about 16 ft. high by 20 ft. wide, near which tongues of dry sand show the blocked mouth of a cave, and prove the sometime exit of the stream there. The frequent absence of the slightest sound of running water proves what must be the vagaries of the hidden river, which, as shown at the falls below, must, even in dry weather, gauge equal to 20 ft. wide by 2 ft. deep.

...ing mysteriously away right, left, or below, more or less, according to weather, the Hepstè's course being decidedly a riddle in more senses than one. Note the more frequent mixture, amid the grit and limestone shingle, of pebbles of "old red" from the roots of the Brecon Beacons. Soon you emerge on the open moors or pastures, and see those mountains a few miles ahead, the chief peak, 2,910 ft. high, bearing N.E. about five miles. This range is well worth a visit, is easily reached from Brecon, and presents in its northern cliffs and slopes a grand geological section of nature's making, as well as proof of a denudation justly called by Ramsay "stupendous." The Hepstè falls are half a mile south of Cilhepstè-coed, and the same distance north of Cilhepstè-fach (see Ord. map); and about two miles more to the south the counties Brecon and Glamorgan are separated by the ravine of the Sychrhyd, or *dry ford*, so called from aqueous freaks similar to those of the Hepstè, which latter name seems akin to the Welsh *Nesp*, "dry" or "barren." The Sychrhyd, besides caves and "swallow holes," presents scenic and geological details of great interest. It lies along a "fault," and amid the coal measures on the south side is a grand gable of limestone, with beautifully arched and, as it were, rib-moulded strata, not yet spoiled by quarrying (*pace* Murray), though that fate has befallen Craig-y-dinas on the Brecon side. The gable is called Bwa maen, "stone bow."

I trust the above will give your correspondent some idea of the cause and working of "swallow holes," caused probably in his case by the erosion of chalk beds beneath the clay, and the falling in of the latter. H. B. BIDEN.
* Sale, Manchester.

"Swallow holes" occur in many chalk districts. Their formation is explained in many geological treatises. An excellent account of them and of their theory is to be found in a paper by Mr. Prestwich, late President of the Geological Society, in the tenth volume of the society's *Journal*.

J. C. M.

I presume these to be similar to the "hell-kettles" already mentioned in "N. & Q." (5th S. iv. 105, 155, q.v.). See also Brewer's *Dictionary of Phrase and Fable*. W. T. M.
Shinfield Grove.

CRACKNEL BISCUITS (5th S. viii. 491.)—"Biscuits" surely surplusage. One asks for "cracknels" simply at any baker's or confectioner's, and the article is at once produced. The translators of our Bible version took a current word, which has

sents of a rustic lover. Dryden also has "tributary cracknels."

In the *Promptorium Parvulorum* (Harl. MS. 221, A.D. 1440, ed. Albert Way, Camden Soc., 1843) occurs:—"Crackenelle, brede. Creputellus, fraginellus (artocopus,* k)." Turning to "Brede": "Brede, twyys bakyn, as krakenelle, or symnel, or other lyke (twyes bake or cracknell, P.†)."

Palsgrave, ed. 1530, and Hollyband, ed. 1593, merely mention *craquelin* as equivalent to cracknel.

In Florio (*A Worlde of Wordes*, 1598) we get, under *spira* (after various other meanings): "Also a cracknell or cake like a trendle, or writhen like a rope."

Cotgrave, ed. 1611, mentions the ingredients, "Craquelin, a cracknell, made of the yolks of egges, water, and flower;‡ and fashioned like a hollow trendle ; hence, also, a little light cap of that fashion."

In 1508 the *craquelin* seems to have been the subject of legal enactment at Rouen. The quotation suggests a labyrinthine archæology of bread-stuffs into which I do not intend to plunge the reader ; for we find in M. Littré's splendid dictionary :—

"*Craquelin*, sorte de biscuit qui craque sous la dent. Craquelin au beurre—nom, dans quelques provinces, de l'échaudé.§ Hist. XVIᵉ S. Il est ordonné que tous les boulangers de Rouen fasse de bon pain blanc, comme mollet, fouache, pain de rouelle, semineaux, cornuyaux, *craquelins*, cretelées. Ordonn. d'oct., 1508, etym. craquer."

In J. Higens's edition of the *Nomenclator* of Adrianus Junius, London, 1585, 8vo., p. 85 (misprinted 65), occurs :—

* Artocopus, "Quivis dulciarius panis et arte laboratus" ; and below, in a secondary meaning in which we approach the sacramental wafer, "panis elaboratus ad opus Domini," Ducange.

† Added in Pynson's printed ed. 1499.

‡ So made at the present day, as a practical "bakester" is good enough to tell me. She adds, moreover, that the cracknels are most troublesome biscuits to bake. They must, in fact, be twice baked and twice boiled. This is the cracknel, A.D. 1878, as some American reader may not know the biscuit, viz. : a very light, crisp biscuit, made of eggs, flour, and water ; circular in shape and concave ; about 2½ inches in diameter ; nearly half an inch in thickness ; perforated in its flatter central portions with 7-10 considerable punctures ; the sides raised and scalloped into 7-10 turret-like rounded projections.

§ "Echaudé, a kind of wigg or symnel," Cotgrave ; "Pastila, a cake, cracknel, or wigge," Skinner. On a cap of the period being nicknamed after the cracknel, cf. the dumpling or the pork-pie hat of modern days.

· "Spira, Cat(o).* Placentæ genus aut panis dulci-
arii a.l spinæ funisve in orhem convoluti modum cir-
cumductum atque implicatum. *Crakelinck*, vel panis,
quem *wielbroot*, quasi *rotarium* nominamus, Flandris est
wiellen, quasi dicas *rotula.* Sive quod rotæ effigiem
habeat, sive quod spinas quasdam circulares in solo
expressas habeat. *A cracknel or cake made like a trendell, or writhen like a rope."*   ·

That is to say, a biscuit shaped as in Cotgrave,
or like what bakers now call "a halfpenny twist."
I have seen what might be called "wheel-bread"
or "little wheels" in Germany, but not to my
remembrance in England. The *pain de rouelle*,
however, of the Rouen enactment (= *rotula, wielbroot*, above) is enumerated as distinct from the
craquelin.

It is interesting to find that the Sussex dialect
has preserved for us an English equivalent for
"crakelinck" in *cracklings*, of which Halliwell says
(*Arch. and Prov. Dict.*): "Cracklings—crisp
cakes. Sussex. More usually called *cracknels.*
See Elyot in voce *Collyra. Cracklings* may be
the older English form of the two."

In Cooper's *Thesaurus*, 1578 (founded on Elyot),
collyra is given : "A loafe of bread, a bunne, a
cracknell, a simnell." Turning to *collyra* in
Andrews's *Latin Dictionary*, 1852, we get "maca-
roni or vermicelli"; while Liddell and Scott, ed.
1840, say of κολλύρα, "probably = κόλλιξ, a
roll of coarse bread." Andrews explains *spira*
much as does the *Nomenclator*: "A kind of
twisted cake, a twist, cracknel." The Vulgate
renders cracknels *crustula*, which last word Cooper
translates "a little crust." In the Latin Old
Testament version of Tremellius (London, 1661,
12mo.) I find cracknels, at 1 Kings xiv. 3,† as
buccellata, "biskets, twice baked, and made in
cakes" (Cooper). In the last folio edition of the
Genevan version of the Bible (Robert Barker,
London, 1616) "or wafers" is offered in the margin
as an alternative explanation of *cracknels* in the
same text.

Tracing cracknel back from the present day,
here are a few more dictionary explanations culled
at random :—

"Cracknel, a hard biscuit."—Nuttall, 1877.
"Cracknel, a hard, brittle cake."—Johnson,
6th ed., 1785.
"Cracknels, a sort of cakes made in shape of a
dish, and bak'd hard, so as to crackle under the
teeth."—Phillips's *New World of Words*, 7th ed.,
1720.

Bailey's *Dictionary* (fifth ed., 1731) defines
in the same words as Phillips (see above), but

* Cato, *de Re Rustica*, 77.
† There appears to be no second mention of cracknels
in the Bible. But compare 1 Sam. ix. 7, where Saul,
about to consult Samuel on the loss of his father's
asses, says : "For the *bread* is spent in our vessels, and
there is not a present to bring to the man of God." A
money gift is then substituted.

omits any reference to the dish-like shape. In
Holtrop's *Dutch-English and English-Dutch Dictionary* (vol. i., 1789 ; vol. ii., 1801, Amsterdam)
we get : "*Kraakeling*, cracknel, a kind of hard,
brittle cake." In the English-Dutch volume :
"Cracknel, *kraakeling*, knapkoek"; the last, however, is in its order rendered "hard gingerbread."

To conclude, most of these authorities are fairly
at one in giving the cracknel as a round, hollow
biscuit. Cotgrave is the most definite ; his ingredients agree with those of the modern cracknel,
and his words, "fashioned like a hollow trendle,"
give its present shape, as does also the analogy of
the cracknel cap. Twenty-six years earlier the
Nomenclator said the same thing, "made like a
trendell," but added, "or writhen like a rope."
There may, therefore, have been another variety of
the cracknel in old days more like the modern
"twist."   HORATIO.

NARES'S "HERALDIC ANOMALIES": "THINKS I
TO MYSELF" (5ᵗʰ S. viii. 469.)—Dr. Edward Nares,
the author of the former book, and Archdeacon
Robert Nares were first cousins. Their grandfather, who was steward to the Earl of Abingdon,
had two sons, George and James. The former,
na. 1715, was called to the Bar in 1741; elected
M.P. for Oxford in 1768; appointed Judge in the
Common Pleas and knighted in 1771; and died
at Ramsgate in 1786. His son, the Rev. Dr.
Edward Nares, na. 1762, was B.A. at Christ Church,
Oxford, 1783; Regius Prof. of Modern History
and D.D. in 1814; and died in 1848. He wrote
several books, amongst which *Heraldic Anomalies*
was published anonymously in 1823. The second
son, James Nares, na. 1716, was instructed in
music by Green and Pepusch ; appointed organist
at York in 1734; became organist to the Chapel
Royal and Mus. Doc., Camb., in 1756 ; and died
at Great James Street, Westminster, in 1783.
He was the father of the Archdeacon, Robert
Nares, na. 1753, elected from Westminster School
to Christ Church, Ox., in 1771 ; F.S.A. and
Librarian, Brit. Mus., in 1795 ; Archdeacon of
Stafford in 1800; and died 1829. He was the
author of many books, of which perhaps his
Orthoepy and his *Glossary* are the best known. I
was not aware that there was any misconception
as to which of these two was the author of the
Heraldic Anomalies. It is rightly given to Dr.
Edward Nares in Lowndes's *Bibl. Man.*, p. 1650,
and in Allibone, *Dict. of Authors*, ii. 1401 (for
biographical details see *Gentleman's Magazine*, liii.
182, and lvi. 622 ; Chalmers's *Bio. Dict.* ; and the
Annual Biography, 1830, p. 430).

It is not so easy to answer the question, Who
was R. L., or Robert Long? without further information. If there is any armorial bearing on
the book-plate it would probably not be difficult to
identify the owner. Failing that, I would suggest

Sutton, Surrey.

•

In "N. & Q.," 2nd S. ix. 230, the late MR. J. H. MARKLAND confirms the assertion in Bohn's *Lowndes* that the Rev. *Edward* Nares, D.D., was the author of both these works; and he states that *his* friend, Archdeacon Robt. Nares, of Stafford, always spoke of the former as having been written by his relative (a first cousin). There is, however, a confusion of names and designations which no doubt can easily be cleared up. In the *Biog. Dict. of Living Authors*, 1816, the authorship of the novel is given, in a long list of more serious works, to the Rev. *Edmund* Nares, D.D., Rector of Biddenden, son of Sir George Nares, a Judge of the Common Pleas, by Mary, daughter of Sir John Strange, Master of the Rolls. His career is fully detailed, and in 1814, on the Professorship of Modern History being conferred upon him, he is stated to have taken his degree of D.D. Here he is called *Edmund*, and so he is called in that very useful little book, the *Brief Biog. Dict.*, but with the title D.C.L. instead of D.D.

In the earliest published volume of the *Clergy List* (1841) the Rector of Biddenden is the Rev. *Edward* Nares, D.D., and, with MR. MARKLAND's testimony, this is no doubt correct. But, so far as the *Heraldic Anomalies* may be concerned, there is plenty of internal evidence in the second edition of that work (1824), in allusions to his ancestor Sir John Strange, to show that, whether *Edmund* or *Edward*, whether D.C.L. or D.D., and with the Archdeacon's disclaimer, there can be no doubt that the Rector of Biddenden was the author of those two amusing and instructive works.

S. H. HARLOWE.

St. John's Wood.

The brothers, Sir George Nares, who was for fifteen years Judge of the Court of Common Pleas, and Dr. James Nares, the composer, were born at Stanwell in 1715 and 1716 respectively. Who were their parents?

James was father to Archdeacon Robert Nares. George had, by his marriage with Mary, third dau. of Sir John Strange, Master of the Rolls, besides daughters, three sons, of whom the eldest, John (Bow Street magistrate), was grandfather of Sir George Strange Nares, who led the expedition of 1875 in quest of the North Pole ; and the third was the Rev. Edward Nares, somewhile Regius Professor of History at Oxford and Rector of Biddenden, co. Kent, and, to my hitherto belief, author of *Thinks I to Myself.* Robert and Edward, born respectively in 1753 and 1762, were therefore first cousins.

The Nares family were deservedly quoted at 5th S. vi. 419, in illustration of the Horatian truth of this assertion quickened by so marked an instance in its favour, I venture to amplify the genealogical information there given, and to add the above query.

H. W.

New Univ. Club.

A reference to the *Handbook of Fictitious Names*, p. 208, will show HIRONDELLE who the Rev. E. Nares was ; see also pp. 63 and 152.

At the same reference GEN. RIGAUD, who asks as to *Thinks I to Myself*, will find his question answered.

OLPHAR HAMST.

THE AGGLESTONE, DORSETSHIRE (5th S. viii. 501.)—I cannot think that MR. PICTON's interesting remarks on this primæval monument (if such it be) will meet with assent from the archæologists of Dorset. All that he states respecting the Danish incursions on the coast of Dorset is historically correct, yet cannot be allowed to justify the inference of this being a Danish sacrificial altar. It is jumping to a conclusion from insufficient premises. The Danes visited this coast, and elsewhere, as roving bands of robbers and pirates, and I question whether such a lawless horde of freebooters would trouble themselves with altars and sacrifices or any kind of religious observance. There is no evidence, in fact, as to this being a Danish monument. It is not an unusual thing for popular opinion, in its ignorance of ancient works, to attribute to the Danes that which does not belong to them. As regards the etymology of the name, Hutchins may have erred in deriving it from *hálig*, holy ; and MR. PICTON's suggestion of the A.-S. *egl*=suffering, sacrifice, is plausible, and may be the more correct derivative ; nevertheless, it would not follow that it has reference to a *Danish* sacrificial altar. The Anglo-Saxons may have applied that term to the monument from a legendary character attributed to it, and handed down for centuries before the Vikings were heard of in these parts. There is indeed some analogy between this rocky mass and the so-called rock idols of Cornwall, described by Borlase, and undoubtedly unconnected with the Danes. If this singular rock had any sacred character at all, it may be reasonably referred to an age anterior to that of Stonehenge, I mean to a pre-historic Keltic age. The walls of Wareham are assigned by Mr. Warne, F.S.A., not without reasonable probability, to the Saxons. See his *Ancient Dorset.*

W. W. W. S.

"SHAKESPEARIAN" OR "SHAKESPEAREAN" (5th S. viii. 41, 136, 160, 273, 357.)—I am glad to find that as regards the general rule MR. WARREN and I are nearer to an agreement than I supposed. That a large proportion (not, as he puts it, all) of my examples are either purely Latin words, or the

English forms of such words, is a natural result of the fact which I set out with noticing, that the suffix -*ian* is only the English form of the Latin -*ianus*. If he repudiates the *e* as a component part of the suffix in the cases of *Shakespearean* and *Gladstonean*, and claims to treat it as part of the name itself, it follows that he must pronounce the words as trisyllables, *Shake-speare-an* and *Gladstone-an*, which seem to me as objectionable to the ear as the spelling he advocates is to the eye. I cannot assent to the doctrine that in forming an adjective from either a proper name or common noun the termination of the latter remains entire, and Mr. Warren could not have furnished a stronger case against his own view than in proposing the name of *Novello*, with a distinct Italian termination. It is a necessary inference from Mr. Warren's rule that he would, in this case, form an adjective by writing the name in full and adding -*an* after the vowel, though he has not ventured to see how it would look in print. He says I should hardly make the adjective *Novellian*. I should indeed avoid coining an adjective from the name at all, holding that as long as it retains its Italian form it is not qualified to receive an English termination. No one has attempted to form an English adjective from the name of Tasso or Ariosto. Mr. Novello might Latinize his name into *Novellus*, or Anglicize it into *Novel*, *Novell*, or *Novelle*, as he might prefer, in any of which forms it would take an adjective, *Novellian*. In fact, we do not form adjectives from all proper names, but only from those which, being suitable in structure, have attained a certain eminence, and in which the inconvenience (which Mr. Warren considers a reason for his canon) of not being able to ascertain the name from the adjective does not arise.

J. F. Marsh.

Hardwick House, Chepstow.

Dr. Pitcairn (5th S. viii. 498.)—The mention by W. T. M. of the eminent and eccentric Scotch physician, Dr. A. Pitcairn, reminds me of an anecdote of him which I do not think is to be found in Dean Ramsay's collection. The doctor hardly ever entered a church. He was, in fact, one of that unsatisfactory class of church-goers dubbed by Mr. Spurgeon "umbrella Christians," who are never seen in a place of worship save when caught near one umbrella-less in a shower of rain. Being in this predicament one Sunday, he went into an Edinburgh kirk, and seated himself in a pew which was occupied by a douce, respectable-looking individual, who was apparently lending an attentive ear to the sermon. The preacher seemed to be much exercised in his mind, and shed tears copiously as he went on with his discourse. Dr. Pitcairn, who could discover nothing in the matter of it to account for this lachrymose display, inclined himself towards his fellow sitter, and whis-

pered in his ear, "What the deil gars the man greet?" to which the other responded behind his hand, "Maybe ye wad greet yoursel', gin ye were up there, and had as little to say."

Hugh A. Kennedy.

Reading.

"Cry matches!" (5th S. viii. 491.)—This expression appears to be nothing more than a conversion of the French "cré matin." I have frequently heard the exclamation used by a friend who had spent some time at the Mauritius, and I presume it was introduced in America by the French Canadians.

A. P.

Thomas Peirce, Mayor of Berkeley (5th S. viii. 491.)—Nothing is known here of his parentage or family, and any investigation is at present impossible, as the ancient parish registers were impounded at the House of Lords after the great peerage case in 1810, and have remained there ever since. The name is an old one in the parish, and still flourishes, under the spelling of Pearce.

There is another epitaph to a Pearce in Berkeley Churchyard, quite as quaint in its way as that of the watchmaker, and I send you a copy of it, in case it may not have already appeared in "N. & Q." It was written by Swift, and is quite characteristic of the caustic dean :—

> "Here lies the Earl of Suffolk's Fool,
>   Men called him Dicky Pearce ;
> His folly served to make folks laugh
>   When wit and mirth were scarce.
> Poor Dick, alas ! is dead and gone,
>   What signifies to cry ?
> Dickys enough are still behind
>   To laugh at by-and-by.
>   Buried June 18th, 1728, aged 63."

J. H. C.

Berkeley.

Old Receipts (5th S. viii. 145.)—Dr. James, in his *Pharmacopœia Universalis* (A.D. 1747), describes garden rue as a plant "greatly esteemed by the ancients, which will appear by its being the principal basis of the famous antidote of Mithridates." The leaves of rue, he says, "mixed with recent butter, and eaten in a morning with bread . . . are an excellent preservative against the noxious influences of a moist and vapid atmosphere and the contagious miasmata of epidemical diseases. The leaves bruised with pepper, common salt, and strong vinegar," &c. The latter compound is to be applied in other cases ; but the doctor further mentions that "strong wine vinegar, richly impregnated with the juice of the rue, applied to the mouth and nostrils, is . . . an excellent preservative against the contagion of epidemical disorders." Galega, *Ruta caprania*, is another species of rue—goat's rue—most probably the herb intended in the "old receipt" ; for, according to Dr. James, "it grows in several

HAMILTON (5th S. viii. 389)—Although I am not able to give N. M. a clue to the present whereabouts of this picture, I may give him a thread, by following which he may ultimately arrive at the desired information.

Some forty years ago, or it may be a little more, I attended the sale of this picture, which I well remember, at Lark Hill, Salford, then a private residence, now a public library and museum. The sale was conducted by Mr. Winstanley, of Liverpool and Manchester. An application to his son or successors may enable N. M. to follow out his inquiry. I have a faint remembrance the picture was sold for about seventy guineas ; but in this I may be mistaken. I had long the catalogue in my possession, giving the names of the purchasers with the prices ; but, on looking for it for the purpose of giving a reply, I have not been able to put my hand on it.　　WILLIAM HARRISON.
Rock Mount, Isle of Man.

SAMUEL ROPER AND THE SEWALL FAMILY (5th S. v. 28.)—Henry Sewall, who was Mayor of Coventry in 1606, married a Margaret Grazbrook, who died in 1632, aged seventy-six. He died in 1628, aged eighty-four. They had the following children :—Anne, married Anthony Power, of Kenilworth, Gent. Henry, bapt. in St. Michael's Church, Coventry, April 8, 1576 ; died at Rowley, New England, 1657, aged eighty-one : he married Anne Hunt, and was the ancestor of one of the most respectable families in America. Richard, vintner of Coventry, will extant ; and Margaret, who married Abraham Randall, of Coventry, Gent. This pedigree is derived from one in Drake's Hist. of Boston, Mass., folio edit., and is said to be of the highest authority. See also the Heraldic Journal for 1865, vol. i. p. 68, and the New Eng. Genealogical Register, 1847, vol. i. p. 111, published in the same place. The arms of this family of Sewall are, " Sable, a chevron between three bees argent." Allibone mentions eighteen authors of the name, most of whom, if not all, were of the New England Sewalls. In the Life and Correspondence of Sir Wm. Dugdale, by Wm. Hamper, 1837, p. 286, is a letter of Samuel Roper to Dugdale, of which the supposed date is 1654, calling him " cozen." A foot-note describes him as " Dugdale's earliest encourager in antiquarian studies," and states he " was a barrister of Lincoln's Inn, and married Elizabeth, one of the daughters of Sir Henry Goodere. He resided at Monks Kirby, and our author has thus mentioned him in his account of it in Warwickshire, p. 50," &c. It is noteworthy that, in a pedigree of the Dugdales in the back of this work, Richard Sewall, who

born at Coventry, where his father was a reputable citizen and clothier. He died Jan. 19, 1693 (vide Calamy, and Sibree and Caston's Independency in Warwickshire). A family of Shewell were early settlers of Pennsylvania, among which occurs the name of Stephen, also of frequent occurrence in the New England family. Elizabeth Shewell of this line was the wife of Benjamin West, R.A., the celebrated painter. B. F. Rodenbaugh, Bvt. Brigadier-General, U.S.A., 23, Murray Street, New York, is collecting information in regard to this family. Prior to 1750 there was a Peter Sewell and Hannah his wife of Wolsingham, England. They had a son Thomas, who married Elinor Cummin, afterwards of Alnwick, and may have had other children. As they are said to have used the same arms as the Coventry Sewalls, I shall be glad to know if there was any relationship.
　　WILLIAM JOHN POTTS.
Camden, New Jersey, U.S.A.

EPITAPH AT YOULGRAVE (5th S. viii. 426.)—The epitaph quoted by DR. GATTY is to be found on a tombstone in Holmesfield Churchyard (near Dronfield, co. Derb.), erected to commemorate a musician named Hattersley. I cannot just now give the date, but I strongly suspect the Youlgrave epitaph is only a copy, and that Holmesfield is its original locality. I have always fancied that Mr. Richard Furness, who died in the neighbouring parish of Dore in 1857, was the author of it.　　CLK.

SIR JULIUS CÆSAR (1st S. viii. 172 ; 2nd S. v. 394 ; xi. 139, 153 ; 4th S. x. 412 ; 5th S. viii. 427.)—The " Mr. S. Laurence Somnel " mentioned by MR. REYNOLDS at the last reference is a misprint of my own name. I have in my possession one copy of Lodge's life of Sir Julius Cæsar and family, and another copy is in the Guildhall Library. The last representative of the Cæsar family was Mrs. Eliza Aberdeen, living at Hammersmith in 1827, the date of the publication of Lodge's work, and who died in 1833, aged 97 years. Most of the materials used for the compilation of the Life of Sir Julius Cæsar were in the possession of this lady. She, however, wishing to place them in safe hands, offered them to Lord Hardwicke, a distant member of the family. My great-grandfather, James Cheatle Gomme, carried out this arrangement for Mrs. Aberdeen, and I have the correspondence which ensued with Earl Hardwicke on the occasion, dating from April 2 to August 4, 1827.

Sir Julius Cæsar's library was sold in 1757 : see Hist. MSS. Com. vol. iii. p. 64. Several of his books were bought by Horace Walpole : see catalogue of sale at Strawberry Hill in 1842.

Mrs. Aberdeen's property was sold in June, 1833, and I have a priced catalogue.

For some notes on several members of the family, see index to *Hist. MSS. Reports, sub voce.* See also Pepys's *Diary*, Feb. 12, 1666 ; Scott's *Peveril of the Peak*, appendix, p. 56, edit. 1848. There are two marble slabs bearing inscriptions relating to the Cæsar family in St. Catherine's Church, near the Tower, of which I have a copy. In conclusion, I may say my little collection of notes is very much at the service of Mr. REYNOLDS.   G. LAURENCE GOMME.

MR. REYNOLDS will find a good account of Sir Julius Cæsar, his ancestors and descendants, in Burke's *History of the Commoners*, 1837, vol. ii. pp. 18-21.

I notice in Mr. James Watts's *Book Catalogue* for December last a copy of the work on the Cæsar family, mentioned at 4th S. x. 412, priced 7s. 6d.   HIRONDELLE.

A Mr. Henry Cæsar was Cursitor for Lincolnshire and Somersetshire for the Court of Chancery in 1691 (*New State of England*, by G. M., 1691, p. 194).   R. PASSINGHAM.

COUSINS (5th S. viii. 427.)—Frederick the Great is a notable instance of a great man whose parents were first cousins.

Ernest Augustus, Elector of Hanover, had, amongst other children, George I. of England and Sophia Charlotte, the wife of Frederick I. of Prussia. George I.'s daughter Sophia Dorothea married her cousin, Frederick William I. of Prussia, the only son of Frederick I. and Sophia Charlotte his wife. Frederick William I. and his wife Sophia Dorothea had, amongst other issue, Frederick the Great.   R. PASSINGHAM.

Celebrated person offspring of cousins—Earl Derby, the Rupert of debate, Prime Minister three times.   HARDRIC MORPHYN.

HOMER'S "NEPENTHES" (5th S. viii. 264, 316.) —As a help towards the meaning of Homer's much-discussed word "Nepenthes," in *Od.* iv. 221, I beg to refer MR. J. LE BOUTILLIER and A. S. W. to two very interesting remarks in the notes to Lane's translation of *The Thousand and One Nights*, viz. note 46 to chap. ii., in which he says :—

"The name of 'benj' or 'berg' is now, and I believe generally, given to henbane ; but El-Kaswenee states that the leaves of the garden hemp are the benj, which when eaten disorder the reason," &c.

And in note 76 to chap. xi. he says :—

"Respecting benj, see note 46 to chap. ii. The following remarks by the celebrated Von Hammer, who regards the benj as hyoscyamus (or henbane), should have been there added : '"Bendj," the plural of which

in Coptic is "nibendj," is without doubt the same plant as the "nepenthe," which has hitherto so much perplexed the commentators of Homer. Helen evidently brought the nepenthe from Egypt, and bendj is still there reputed to possess all the wonderful qualities which Homer attributes to it.'"

                          T. S. NORGATE.

Sparham Rectory, Norwich.

ORIGINAL LETTER (5th S. viii. 425.)—Your correspondent MR. MALDEN says :—"A Turkish history seems to me an unlikely thing for a country gentleman of 1715 to want, even if such a thing had been written." Why such a thing as a Turkish history should not be wanted by a man living in 1715 as much as by one of the present day I am at a loss to understand. That a great many copies of such a book were wanted by "the reading public" is a matter proved beyond doubt. A good proportion of that public then as now, I believe, would be made up of country gentlemen. There can be little doubt that the book referred to is Richard Knolles's *General History of the Turks*. The first edition bears the date 1603 on the title-page. There are other editions of 1610, 1621, 1631, 1638, and 1679. It was republished with a continuation by Sir Paul Rycaut in 1687-1700, in three volumes folio. In the *Rambler*, No. 120, Knolles's *History* is highly spoken of. Raleigh and Clarendon have already been alluded to ; and then the writer goes on to say :—

"None of our writers can, in my opinion, justly contest the superiority of Knolles, who, in his *History of the Turks*, has displayed all the excellencies that narration can admit."

Lord Byron said at Missolonghi, a few weeks before his death :—

"Old Knolles was one of the first books that gave me pleasure when a child ; and I believe it had much influence on my future wishes to visit the Levant, and gave, perhaps, the Oriental colouring which is observed in my poetry."—*Byron's Works Complete*, one vol. edit., 1846, p. 62.

                          EDWARD PEACOCK.

Bottesford Manor, Brigg.

CHESS (5th S. viii. 269, 316, 438, 495.)—I am obliged to MR. KENNEDY for his answer to me ; but I am afraid I must ask leave to rejoin. MR. KENNEDY puts a case—I will accept it—and says my suggestion "creates an unspeakable absurdity." If he had thoroughly followed out my suggestion, I do not think he would have said this. I suppose I ought to have done it myself, but I had thought I should be understood. There is no "unspeakable absurdity" ; for on my suggestion black is *not* "in a position of checkmate" as long as white's knight covers his own king from black's check ; but when white's knight is relieved from this office, his powers of giving check of course return to him, and black's position then *becomes* one of checkmate. Thus, supposing black is so silly as to let his king stay where it is (it not being

mate given by his knight, and wins the game by that move. On the other hand, if black makes any move which has the effect of freeing white's knight, he makes a false move, which he has no right to make, because he exposes his king to an actual check, which, by the laws of the game, he cannot do ; and if he does it inadvertently, he must be dealt with as he would be dealt with if he had played his king into check in any other way.

Mr. Kennedy opposes my definition of check as " such a position of the king that he could be taken if he were not a king," and says, first, that it is " not a position of the king at all." But it appears to me that a king must be in some position, even if he is in check ; he would find it difficult to be in none. Secondly, Mr. Kennedy says that check is " an intimation to him that he is attacked." Very good ; I quite agree. But what is attacking a king, or any other piece, if it is not threatening to take it ? The king cannot be taken, and therefore the intimation is given. Mr. Kennedy and I say the same thing in different words.

Mr. Jarvis, in his short and easy solution of my difficulties, just misses the very point. The point is that the piece which is supposed to give check (and according to the present laws of course *does* give check) *itself* covers the attacking king, that is, its own king.

As to the alteration making obsolete all our chess literature, it would of course do so with some, but by no means all. I have played a good deal of chess in my time, and the case has occurred to me comparatively seldom.

C. F. S. Warren, M.A.

Bexhill.

Prophecies about Turkey (5th S. ix. 29.)—I extract the following notice and version of the prophecy inquired for by H. A. B. from Blavatsky's *Isis Unveiled* (New York, Bouton, and London, Quaritch, 1877), vol. i. p. 261, a work of great research and erudition in matters occult :

"In an old book of prophecies published in the fifteenth century (an edition of 1453) we read the following among other astrological predictions :—

'In twice two hundred years the Bear
The Crescent will assail ;
But if the Cock and Bull unite,
The Bear will not prevail.

In twice ten years again,
Let Islam know and fear,
The Cross shall stand, the Crescent wane,
Dissolve, and disappear."

In a foot-note the modern garb of the prophecy is thus accounted for :—

" The library of a relative of the writer contains a copy fore, an English version, which is said to be taken from a book in the possession of a gentleman in Somersetshire, England."

Temple.

C. C. Massey.

In the fifty-fifth chapter of Gibbon's *Decline and Fall of the Roman Empire*, we have the following :—

" By the vulgar of every rank it was asserted and believed that an equestrian statue in the square of Taurus was secretly inscribed with a prophecy how the Russians, in the last days, should become masters of Constantinople. In our own time a Russian armament, instead of sailing from the Borysthenes, has circumnavigated the continent of Europe ; and the Turkish capital has been threatened by a squadron of strong and lofty ships of war, each of which, with its naval science and thundering artillery, could have sunk or scattered a hundred canoes, such as those of their ancestors. Perhaps the present generation may yet behold the accomplishment of the prediction—of a rare prediction, of which the style is unambiguous and the date unquestionable."

Altrincham.

J. B.

The Dormant Scottish Peerage of Hyndford (5th S. viii. 429, 453.)—William de Carmychel lived in 1350. His great-grandson William, at the battle of Beaugé, broke his spear in an encounter with the Duke of Clarence, for which feat he added to his arms a dexter hand and arm, armed, holding a broken spear, which has since been the crest of the family. His descendant, James Carmichael, was in 1627 created a baronet, and in 1647 Lord Carmichael in Scotland, to him and his heirs male whatever, and died in 1672. He was succeeded by his grandson John, second Lord Carmichael, who was sworn a member of William III.'s Privy Council, and in 1690 was appointed the King's Commissioner of the General Assembly of the Church of Scotland. In Macaulay's opinion (*History*, ch. xvi. 222) he was " a nobleman distinguished by good sense, humanity, and moderation." On June 25, 1701, he was created in Scotland Earl of Hyndford, Viscount of Inglisberry and Nemphlar, Lord Carmichael of Carmichael, by patent to him " et hæredibus masculis et talliæ," &c.

The first Earl Hyndford died in 1710, and was succeeded by his son James (second earl), who died in 1737, and was succeeded by his son John (third earl).

The third earl was a celebrated diplomatist, and a friend of Frederick the Great, from whom he had a grant of an addition of the eagle of Silesia to his arms. He married a daughter of the celebrated Sir Cloudesley Shovel, but, dying in 1767 without issue, was succeeded by his cousin John (fourth earl), the representative of the first earl.

The fourth earl was succeeded by his brother James (fifth earl), who, dying in 1787, was succeeded by his cousin Thomas (sixth earl), the last male descendant of the first earl. He died after 1809, since which time the honours have remained dormant.

Even should the earldom not have been in remainder to the heirs male whatever, as MR. CARMICHAEL seems to think possible, there can now be no doubt that, after the decision of the House of Lords in the Mar and other peerage claims, the heirs general have no claim. (See *Biographical Peerage*, 1809, vol. iii. 146 ; Carlyle's *Frederick the Great*, v. 11, 13, 17, 20, 29, 42, 48, 49, 50, 58, 67, 138 ; iv. 200 ; v. 8, 116, 135 ; vi. 171.)   R. P.

This peerage has been dormant since the death of the sixth earl in 1817. Both the earldom of Hyndford (created 1701) and the barony of Carmichael (1647) were granted with remainder to heirs male and of entail. According to Sir B. Burke (*Extinct Peerage*), Sir Jas. R. Carmichael, Bart., is the heir male of the family. As, however, the common ancestor of Sir James and of the Hyndford line lived some two centuries prior to the creation of the peerage in 1647, it may be somewhat difficult to prove the extinction of all intermediate heirs.   W. D. PINK.
Leigh, Lancashire.

MARY ROBINSON'S GRAVE AT OLD WINDSOR (5th S. ix. 19.)—In *Public Characters*, 1800-1, R. Phillips, St. Paul's Churchyard, I find the following dates :—

"The lady was born on November 27, 1758, at College Green, Bristol.......On December 26, 1800, she expired. She was interred in the churchyard of Old Windsor, agreeable to her particular request, and the following epitaph by Mr. Pratt is engraven on the simple monument erected to her memory :—

"'Epitaph on Mrs. Robinson's Monument in the Church of Old Windsor, by J. S. Pratt, Esq.

Of Beauty's isle, her daughters must declare,
She who sleeps here was fairest of the fair.
But ah ! while Nature on her favourite smil'd
And Genius claim'd his share in Beauty's child,
Ev'n as they wove a garland for her brow,
Sorrow prepar'd a willowy wreath of woe ;
Mix'd lurid nightshade with the buds of May,
And twin'd her darkest cypress with the bay ;
In mildew tears steep'd every opening flow'r,
Prey'd on the sweets, and gave the canker pow'r.
Yet O may Pity's angel from the grave
This early victim of misfortune save !
And as she springs to everlasting morn,
May Glory's fadeless crown her soul adorn !'"
                                      J. F. NICHOLLS.
Bristol.

MAC MAHON FAMILIES (5th S. ix. 7.)—The President of the French Republic, Marshal de Mac Mahon, is, I believe, descended from the Mac Mahons of Clare, and has no connexion whatever with the Mac Mahons of the county of Monaghan, who bore Or, an ostrich sable, in its beak a horseshoe proper. Hugh Mac Mahon, R.C. Bishop of Clogher, was translated to Armagh in 1715, and died August 2, 1737, æt. seventy-seven. He was of the Mac Mahons of Monaghan, but his parentage has not been ascertained. There were also two brothers who succeeded each other as R.C. Bishops of Clogher and also as Primates of Armagh, Bernard and Ross. The first died May 27, 1747, æt. sixty-seven. Ross died Oct. 29, 1740, æt. forty-nine. Their tombstone is in Edergale old churchyard. Of Arthur (or Augustin ?) Mac Mahon, Provost of the Collegiate Church of St. Peter, at Cassel, I have no account, but I think MR. BONE is wrong in supposing that he was R.C. Archbishop of Armagh. In my *History of the County of Monaghan*, p. 206, I have given a pedigree of this illustrious family of Mac Mahon, and found it impossible to identify the three ecclesiastics in question.   EV. PH. SHIRLEY.

AUTHORS OF QUOTATIONS WANTED (5th S. ix. 29.)—

"While the gaunt mastiff, growling at the gate,
Affrights the beggar whom he longs to eat."
                Pope's *Moral Essays*, ep. iii. 1. 195.
                                              H. D. C.

"Thus painters write their name at Co."
                Prior's *Protogenes and Apelles*.

"What though the treacherous tapster Thomas."
                Swift, lines on *Stella*.
                                              J. C. M.

"That strain I heard was of a higher mood."
                Milton's *Lycidas*, l. 87.

"How war may best uphold
Move by her two main nerves, iron and gold,
In all her equipage."
    Milton, *Sonnet to Sir Henry Vane the Younger*.
                                     JONATHAN BOUCHIER.

Miscellaneous.

NOTES ON BOOKS, &c.

A Dictionary of Music and Musicians (A D. 1450-1878). By Eminent Writers, English and Foreign. With Illustrations and Woodcuts. Edited by George Grove, D.C.L. Part I., "A." to "Ballad." (Macmillan & Co.)

HALF a century has gone by since Sainsbury & Co. published their *Dictionary of Musicians*, with Choron's summary of the *History of Music* by way of introduction. It is still a pleasant book, as far as it goes, but long since out of date. Dr. Grove's new *Dictionary of Music and Musicians* promises in this first part to supply much of what was omitted in the old work, and still more of the record of the art and the artists of the fifty years that now remain to be added to the history. The old dictionary began with "Aaron"; the new opens with "A." The former finished its A.s with "Azopard"; the latter goes further, and chronicles "Azor and Zemira." Our elder friend put "Babel," a famous tenor singer of the middle of the last century, at the head of the B.s; our contemporary has a word to say for B itself, and the *aliases* by which it is known (as a

"Scientific Lectures, their Use and Abuse."—The "Story of Dr. Faustus" in the *New Quarterly Magazine* puts the date of the historical Faustus at about the beginning of the sixteenth century.—"Spontaneous Generation," by Prof. Tyndall, in *The Nineteenth Century*, should be read after the *Quarterly* article on the use and abuse of scientific lectures.—*Macmillan* has a paper, "Schliemann's Mycenæ," which may be very profitably read in conjunction with a similarly entitled article in the *Quarterly*. Both allow the value of the discoveries, but dispute the theory built upon them.— The historical paper in *Temple Bar* portrays the eccentric Christina of Sweden, and describes her abdication as a mistake.—In *Cornhill* there is a pleasant paper on "Marivaux," reminding the reader of Vinet's critical chapter on this French dramatist in *The History of French Literature in the Eighteenth Century*. Marivaux's plays may be safely commended to students. The *talk* in them gave the word *marivaudage* to the French language. Some persons who do not care for Marivaux speak of his graceful verbiage as mere dust; but the glittering dialogue is, at all events, gold dust. Voltaire's judgment of him was—"Marivaux weighs a fly's eggs in the web of a spider." "He fatigues me and himself," said a lady, "by making me travel twenty leagues on a piece of wood three feet square."

———

THE ancient barony of Mowbray is no longer in abeyance. The question has been decided by the Queen in favour of Lord Stourton, whose ancestor, William, fifteenth Baron Stourton (1753-1781), married Winifred, eldest daughter and co-heir of Philip Howard, brother of the Duke of Norfolk, who died s.p. in 1777. At the death of this duke, twelve (perhaps thirteen) baronies fell in abeyance between the daughters and co-heirs of the duke's brother Philip. His elder daughter married as above. The younger, Anne, married Lord Petre. The co-heirship of the present Lord Stourton, in right of his ancestress Winifred, the elder daughter, is now settled by the grant to this peer of the older barony. The barony of Mowbray (by tenure) dates from William the Conqueror. The eleventh Baron was created Duke of Norfolk in 1397. The barony of Stourton was created in 1448. The seventh Baron Stourton was hanged for murder in 1557. His attainder for felony does not appear to have prevented the descent of the dignity. The son of the murderer, however, was not summoned to Parliament till nearly eighteen years after his father's execution.

COL. CHESTER, who has done such good service for this country by his work on Westminster Abbey registers, has been for fifteen years engaged in collecting materials for a complete history of the Washington family. The Colonel was led to this from the fact that he had demolished the accepted pedigree of Washington, and left the illustrious President without an ancestor. This result Col. Chester published in the late Mr. J. G. Nichols's *Herald and Genealogist*, vol. iv. pp. 49-63, and the paper was reprinted several times, both here and in the United States. Since that time the Colonel has been collecting evidences and materials for a *Stemmata Washingtoniana*. But it will be some time before he will be in a position to produce the volume.

MESSRS. SOTHEBY, WILKINSON & HODGE announce for Wednesday next the sale of an important collection of illustrations of the Drama and Dramatic Literature.

45. All the separate numbers of the First Series of "N. & Q." are out of print. Our publisher has one complete set from the commencement up to the present time for sale. Many of the subsequent numbers, including the Second Series, up to the present time, may still be had separately. The Fourth Series Index may be had, as also the indexes to all the subsequent volumes.

F. W. F. (5th S. viii. 507.)—Joseph Merlin, born at Huys, between Namur and Liége, Sept. 17, 1735, is said to have been the inventor of roller skates. See "N. & Q," 5th S. v. 509; vi. 36, 336. For *Skating Literature*, see "N. & Q.," 5th S. ii. 107, 156, 318, 379; iv. 177, 437; v. 136.

B. W. S. (Shillingford Rectory.)—On the subject of hats you will find a number of interesting articles in "N. & Q.," at the following references: 2nd S. i. 450; 3rd S. v. 136, 499; vi. 16, 26, 57, 75; viii. 325, 402, 403, 466, 549; 4th S. ii. 286; vi. 360; ix. 444, 517; x. 96, 193, 219, 247, 318.

H. HALL will find the subject of the meeting of Wellington and Blücher, at Belle Alliance, fully discussed in "N. & Q." of the present series, vol. vi. 48, 98, 112, 230, 370.

W. GARNETT (Taunton.)—A correspondent desires to forward you some memoranda bearing on your query, 5th S. viii. 408. To what address should they be forwarded?

SCHOLASTICA.—The plays of Destouches, in prose and verse, fill ten volumes. The writer ranks after Molière and Regnard. His plays are thoroughly readable.

DICA.—Received. Two proofs will be sent. To what length would the other article run?

M. E. will find he has been anticipated. In Farquhar's *Inconstant* (Act iv. sc. 2) the French phrase "Toujours perdrix" takes this form: "Soup for breakfast, soup for dinner, soup for supper, and soup for breakfast again!"

E. D. H.—Any other member of your club could answer these queries in much less time than it takes to write to this effect.

G. O. asks for the best means of taking out mud stains from printed papers without injuring the colour of the paper or print.

J. P. WRIGHT.—We forwarded the words of the song "Good St. Anthony" to MR. TAYLOR, for which he thanks you.

A. C. (Union Club, Brighton.)—Consult *Men of the Time*.

W. D. PINK.—Not received till after the paragraph on the same subject was in type.

WILL the writer of the "Legend of the Comtes d'Albanie" send us his name,—not for publication?

S. R. (Manchester).—The ballad is in *Othello*, Act ii. sc. 3.

E. J. TAYLOR.—Teignmouth will find the lady.

NOTICE.

Editorial Communications should be addressed to "The Editor of 'Notes and Queries'"—Advertisements and Business Letters to "The Publisher"—at the Office, 20, Wellington Street, Strand, London, W.C.

We beg leave to state that we decline to return communications which, for any reason, we do not print; and to this rule we can make no exception.

CONTENTS.— N° 213.

Notes.

ARMS ON THE STALLS IN THE CHOIR OF THE CATHEDRAL AT HAARLEM.

When I was at Haarlem in the autumn of 1873, I made the following notes of the fine series of armorial bearings which are depicted on the stalls in the choir of the Groote Kerk, formerly the Cathedral of St. Bavon. I send them for preservation in "N. & Q.," both on account of their historical interest and because it may easily happen in these times of restoration that future visitors to Haarlem may find the stalls newly scraped and varnished, and those "trumpery old coats of arms" obliterated by those who are ignorant, or careless, of their interest to the genealogist and historian. The brass grille which separates the choir from the nave is supported by a carved base of oak, of which the principal feature is a fine series of shields, each with its single tenant or supporter, but the bearings, which no doubt once adorned the escutcheons, have all disappeared.

SOUTH, OR GOSPEL, SIDE ; EAST TO WEST.

1. Quarterly of four grand quarters :—I. and IV. Quarterly, 1 and 4, Castile, quartering Leon ; 2 and 3, Arragon, impaling Sicily : the whole enté en point Grenada. II. and III. Quarterly, 1, Austria ; 2, Burgundy modern ; 3, Burgundy ancient ; 4, Brabant : over all an escutcheon of Flanders. The whole escutcheon is ornamented

with an open crown, and is surrounded by the collar of the Order of the Golden Fleece. These are the arms either of Philippe le Bel, King of Spain, Archduke of Austria, Count of Holland, Flanders, &c. (d. 1516), or of his son Charles V., afterwards Emperor.

2. Quarterly, 1 and 4, Or, a lion ramp. sa. (Flanders) ; 2 and 3, Or, a lion ramp. gu. (Holland). The arms of the Counts of Holland. The escutcheon is here surrounded in base by the palisade, or hedge, with its gate, which appears on the seals of some of the Counts of Holland (see the seals of William, Duke of Bavaria, Count of Holland, and of his daughter Jacqueline, heiress of Holland, &c., in Vree, Gén. des Comtes de Flandre, plate 60). There is an interesting notice of Jacqueline and her four husbands, among whom were the Duke of Gloucester, brother of Henry V., and François de Borsele (whose arms appear on the Epistle side), in Beltz, Memorials of the Order of the Garter, pp. 341-342.

3. Quarterly, 1 and 4, Or, a lion ramp. gu., armed az. (Brederode) ; 2 and 3, Arg., a lion ramp. gu. (queue fourchée), crowned or (Valkenberg). The arms are surrounded by the collar of the Golden Fleece, on a field semé of flames ; on either side of the shield in base is placed a boar's head couped sa., tusked arg. These are the arms of Regnauld, Lord of Brederode, elected a knight of the Golden Fleece at the chapter held at Tournay in 1531 (Chifflet, Insignia Gentilitia Equitum Ordinis Velleris Aurei, clxxiii.). The Brederodes claimed the highest place among the nobility of Holland, and had attributed to them in common parlance the epithet of "die Edelste," as the Wassenaers had that of "oudste" (=most ancient), and the Egmonts that of "die ryckste." They descended from the old Counts of Holland (Spener, Op. Herald., p. spec., p. 395). The boars' heads were used to accompany the shield in memory of the Order of St. Anthony en Barbefosse, which was in great estimation in Hainault. For the same reason John of Burgundy, Duke of Brabant, another of the husbands of Jacqueline, Countess of Hainault and Holland, assumed two boars as supporters.

4. Gu., ten lozenges conjoined (3, 3, 3, and 1), on the first a lioncel rampant of the field for difference ; the shield surrounded by the collar of the Order of the Golden Fleece. The arms of Philippe de Lalain, Count de Hochstraten (or Hoogstraaten), the head of the younger line of the great house of Lalain, elected at Utrecht in 1546 (Chifflet, No. cciii.).

5. Quarterly, 1 and 4, Gu., three crescents arg. (Wassenaer) ; 2 and 3, Az., a fess or (Leide). Around the shield are four crescents arg., the badges of the family of Wassenaer (see No. 7 on the Epistle, or north, side).

6. Az., three vine shoots fessways, 2 and 1, from

in No. 3, impaling Or, an eagle disp. sa. (probably
for the Counts Nieuwenaar ; the Dutch family of
Honthorst bore the same).

9. Or, a lion ramp. gu., over all a label az.
(Brederode). The shield is placed on a ground
semé of flames, and is ornamented with the collar
of the Golden Fleece. These are the arms of Regnauld de Brederode, probably the elder of the two
knights of the Golden Fleece who had the same
name (vide supra, No. 3). This knight was probably the one elected at Ghent in 1445 (Chifflet,
Insig. Gent. Equit. Aur. Vell., No. xli.). The
label is here given which was used by the Brederodes as a brisure to indicate their descent from
the old Counts of Holland. About the year 1476
the Brederodes discontinued the use of the label,
probably as an indication that they claimed to be
the heirs male of the old counts. But when in
1494 the Archduke Philip claimed the homage of
the nobles of Holland as count of that country, he
insisted that the Brederodes should resume the
use of their former brisure, as accordingly was
done (v. Spener, Op. Her., p. spec., p. 396).

10. A lozenge-shaped shield bearing the
quartered arms of Brederode and Valkenberg (as
in No. 3), impaling, Or, a fess chequy arg. and
gu., in chief a lion issuant of the third ; the arms
of the Counts von der Marck.

11. As No. 3.

12. Arg., three mill-rinds (zuilen) gu. The
arms of one of the several great Dutch families of
Zuylen, whose arms, otherwise called chess-rooks,
are allusive to the name.

13. Zuylen, as No. 12; impaling Lalain (see
No. 4), but without the lioncel brisure.

14. Arg., a cross gu., in each quarter five
barrulets wavy az. ; over all, on an escutcheon arg.,
three horseshoes gu. Behind the shield is placed
a pastoral staff erect, and the whole is surmounted
by a bishop's hat, as in No. 4. As it was only in
1559 that the see of Haarlem was constituted, by
the bull " Supra universas," I naturally expected
that the three ecclesiastical escutcheons would be
those of bishops of Utrecht, given in the same
Supplement to Potthast, Wegweiser durch die
Geschichtswerke des Europäischen Mittelalters, and
to none of the prelates of the fifteenth or sixteenth
century can I attribute the arms.

15. Brederode, as in No. 3 ; on the lion's
shoulder is a small escutcheon of Zuylen, as in
No. 12. The shield is placed on the usual ground

(Arnstein). III. Az., a lion ramp. or ; over
bend goboné gu. and arg. (Heldrun gen.).
shield is ensigned with a count's coronet and
the collar of the Golden Fleece. These are the
of the Counts of Mannsfeld. Two of these
knights of the Golden Fleece—Hoier, e
1516, and Pierre Ernest, elected in 1546 (C
Nos. cxxx. and ccv.).

This completes the series on the south, or C
side of the choir. JOHN WOODWA
Montrose.

THE TRUE STORY OF THE CENCI FAM
(Continued from p. 23.)

THE EXECUTION.

Shortly before the confession of her br
Beatrice had addressed a petition to Ca
Aldobrandini, nephew of the Pope, from wh
extract was given in the last note. It is
July 20, and is found in D'Albono. A
passage is worth quoting :—

" Shut up in prison, and unable to see my brot
relations, I betake myself to your eminence...s
seech you to consider my miserable position, to b
vered from which there is nothing I would n
whether it were bodily or spiritual punishment or
vation to be endured.......In my wretched position
mit to whatever sentence the Holy Father may
on my property and person, pledging myself to
of the said property...for the repairs of any br
bridge, or road, or for the glory of our holy n
for the benefit of the holy souls in purgatory.....
Savella, 20 July, 1599."

The Pope, as we have seen, had, in his ho
the confession of the prisoners on Augu
ordered punishment to be at once inflicted.
advocates and friends wrung from him a d
fifteen or twenty-five days for the defence. S
advocates appeared for the Cenci besides Far
Giorgio Diedi ought to go down to posterity
prisoners' friend, as he was actually impriso
order of the Governor of Rome, after
pleaded their cause too boldly, and a me
exists in which he begs his Holiness not tc
more of his foolish talk. He was instantly re
Farinacci's defence was fatal to the whole :
assuming Beatrice's guilt as originatrix deli
not proving the provocation on which he
her claim to mercy, the charge being articu
sed non probatum.

One more despairing appeal was made
Cardinal by Beatrice on August 20. It is
in D'Albono, and also in a Venetian MS., w
find no less than four memorials in fav
Lucrezia :—

"**Memorial of Signora Beatrice...to his Eminence, &c.**
"In this last extremity I have no other resource than your Eminence's pity, and I beseech you by the bowels of Jesus Christ to hear the dreadful case of myself and my stepmother from our advocate Farinacci, and to procure an audience for him of his Holiness. Then when his Holiness and your Eminence have been good enough to hear the real truth, I am ready to suffer any punishment, and however heavy it will not be hard to bear, considering that it is the holy and just decision of his Blessedness and your Reverence."

The prisoners were evidently expecting death about the 25th of August, as on that day Giacomo made his confession, in which he exonerated Bernardo, and on the 27th he and Beatrice made their wills. The will of Beatrice is still preserved by the notary Gentili at Rome. She directs her body to be laid in S. Pietro in Montorio, and leaves 3,000 sc. to build a wall to protect the approach to the church ; other moneys to twenty-four churches and chapels for masses ; to her former mistress in the convent, and to Lavinia, a pupil there, 300 sc. each ; 200 sc. to Madonna Bastiana, who had waited on her in prison ; with other moneys for the dowry of thirty poor girls. She makes the Company of the Sacred Stigmata of St. Francis her residuary legatees, with the obligation to dower fifteen girls every year, who were to walk in procession on their festival. But there is a special bequest :—

"I leave to Madonna Chaterina,...who lives with Signora Margherita Sarocchi, 300 sc., which money is to be put out at interest, and the interest applied, according to the instructions I have given her, in certain relief...if, however, the person who is to be relieved according to my instructions should be alive," &c.

Of this person we shall find fresh mention in the secret codicil later. The same day Giacomo made his will, appointing as executors the Cardinals Sforza (said to be his godfather), Caetani, and S. Giorgio. On September 8, Beatrice, who had made an unimportant codicil on August 30, executed another, which has only just come to light through the indefatigable researches of Cav. Bertolotti. He relates that, thirty-five years after her death, the then Procurator Fiscal of Rome went to the notary Colonna, declaring that he had been apprised of the existence of a codicil made by Beatrice Cenci, consisting of a sealed letter, which was as yet unopened. Search was made, and the codicil found ; and, after due proof had been given of Beatrice's death, it was opened, and is still to be seen, I imagine. This codicil had been prepared by her confessor, and was deposited with another notary, not the person who had made her will. Bertolotti gives its contents in full. On the back is written :—

"Before witnesses, Donna B. Cenci...affirming she desired to add a codicil...consigned to me this sealed paper...which she declared to contain her codicils, desiring them to be kept secret as long as she lived, but to be opened after her death." (Names of witnesses follow.)

In this codicil she takes off 1,000 sc. from the money left for dowries, and leaves this sum between the two women before mentioned, with the proviso that they are to maintain a poor boy, a ward of theirs, as she had explained to them by word of mouth ; and she also makes provision for this *fanciullo* attaining the age of twenty, when he was to come into possession of the whole sum. The codicil closes with a strict injunction that her wishes shall be carried out without delay, and provides that any future disposition she may make of her property shall not vitiate this bequest. Taking all things into consideration, we cannot be far wrong in believing that she intended, by a late act of reparation, to provide more fittingly for a child. No other trace has been found of the life or death of this child, but in the fact of its existence we may see a motive for Count Cenci's cruelties which hitherto has not been suspected, and which was quite unknown to her contemporaries. Those who know Italian history of that epoch will remember how jealously even the most reckless and vicious men guarded and avenged the honour of their wives and daughters.

The will of Beatrice was, however, never carried into execution. From the archives of the Company of the Stigmata, quoted by Venosta, we learn that repeated applications were made through Cardinal Montalto to the Pope for the payment of their legacy. But after May 18, 1600, no further notice appears.

In the codicil Beatrice provides for a future disposition of her property ; and on Sept. 5 Giacomo had appointed agents to manage his interests in the Abruzzi. Perhaps a gleam of hope had been given them, as the Pope seemed at first inclined to mercy, and is said to have spent a whole night reading the depositions, with many tears. But about the 9th the Santa Croce matricide occurred at Subiaco, making, with the Massimi fratricide, the third tragedy in the great Roman families within one brief year. This decided the Pope for summary justice. The sentence of death was passed on the 10th, though apparently not communicated to the prisoners till the evening. Death by the headsman's axe was awarded to Beatrice and Lucrezia ; to Giacomo branding and quartering, after which his limbs were to be exposed *nei rostri*. Farinacci in the early morning wrung from the Pope the exemption of Bernardo from the capital punishment, on condition of his being present at the death-throes of his relations. Death was commuted for the galleys in these terms : "Afterwards he shall be sent to the galleys for ever, so that life may be a torment and death a release." Entire confiscation of their property was decreed. The Florentine ambassador, however, writing the same day, doubted whether the sentence would be carried out, as all sorts of rumours were afloat of dissatisfaction in the city,

about 11 P.M., the Confraternity of the Florentine Misericordia met at Corte Savella, and in the chapel the condemned women were handed over to them to prepare for death. The night seems to have been spent in the chapel of both prisons in prayers and consolation of the unhappy prisoners. The archives of the Company tell us that next morning, at 9 A.M., the Brothers accompanied the condemned to execution. The sad procession of Giacomo and Bernardo, which had started from the prison of Tor di Nona—now the Apollo Theatre —reached Corte Savella in the Via Giulia at that hour. For the following details I am inclined to trust the MSS., which generally agree, as probably the original account came from an eyewitness.

The brothers were on the fatal cart, on which stood also the executioner with brazier and pincers, and Giacomo, stripped to the waist, was branded in public from time to time. Bernardo, from his girlish look and curling hair, was at first mistaken for Beatrice by the crowds who looked down from windows and housetops in the narrow streets. At Corte Savella the women joined the procession on foot. Both wore loose gowns with wide sleeves, as nuns then wore them, showing the white under-sleeve tight to the wrist, which one still sees in the Campagna. Beatrice was in blue or violet, Lucrezia in black, with long veils of the same colour. Over the shoulders of Beatrice was thrown a scarf of cloth of silver, and her shoes were white velvet with crimson *fiocchi*. Their arms bound to the body with crimson cord, left their hands free to carry a crucifix: Lucrezia weeping; Beatrice firm and self-possessed, her fair hair clustering in curls over eyes too proud to shed a tear. Before them is said to have been carried the banner of the Confraternity, a Pietà painted by Michael Angelo. By the church of San Giovanni, and in front of San Celso ai Banchi, where sympathizing hands rained down flowers and vine-leaves on Beatrice, they passed into the Piazza S. Angelo.

Here a little chapel with compartments had been built, close to the *paleo eminente* on which stood the block. The women and Giacomo were conducted to the separate compartments till all was ready, and Bernardo had taken his place on the scaffold. Lucrezia was the first called out to suffer. We may be spared the horrid details of the execution. Beatrice followed, and without assistance jumped on the plank where the victim must sit astride, with head bent, to receive the fatal blow. Then, we are told, the air resounded

wretched Bernardo, who had fainted at farewell, was carried back to prison m than alive.

The corpses lay exposed at the foot of known statue of St. Paul, with torches round them, Beatrice wreathed with ros smile on her face. Near them hung the q limbs of Giacomo, round them, perhaps,* and dying, crushed or trampled or struck sunstroke. Later they were transferred chapel of the Confraternity, and after Maria were carried to their several grav body of Beatrice, surrounded by tapers, a great following, was borne to S. Pietro torio. As the procession passed (accordin MS.) lights were brought to every win flowers showered down on the bier. The to rest in front of the high altar, but h cannot now be traced. The stone perhaps found on the left of the sacristy door, built wall—its inscription erased—and now bea name of Paolo Toquino. According to one the Republicans, in 1798, rifled many gr the sake of the lead coffins, and the vault church shared the same fate. The body trice is then said to have been found, head lying near it in a silver basin, wl corpses were cast about the church in l confusion. We look in vain, then, for he but her name survives in imperishable tarnished fame. K. l

(*To be concluded in the fourth part.*)

* See Muratori, *Chron.*, 1599.

FOLK-LORE.

FOLK-LORE OF SMYRNA.—Asiatic Greek a person is passing a place where building on, and a stone or plank is built on his he will die within the year. In rever ghost of a person who was so killed at hides in a well in the garden, and comes o night. HYDE CL

TO GET RID OF WHOOPING COUGH.— fisherman, formerly well known at the Keswick, once caught a fish, which he put mouth of a child suffering from whooping He then replaced the fish in the Gret affirmed that the fish, after being placed mouth of the child and returned to the riv the complaint to the rest of its kind, as w dent from the fact that they came to the top to cough. Apart from old Edmondson's fable, it is clear that the superstition did exist in Cumberland.

J. F. C.

Keswick.

CHARMS IN JAPAN.—The prevalence lately of cholera in Japan has caused some of the inhabitants to have recourse to the use of charms. The following extracts are from the *Japan Daily Herald* of Nov. 26, 1877 :—

"The shopkeepers of the Sinsaibashi have suffered considerably by the unhealthy state of Osaka, and the number of houses and shops to let is unusually great throughout the city. Over the door of nearly every house various charms are suspended. Now it is a bunch of onions or a leaf of a *kiri*, but more often it is some printed figure. Sometimes the latter resembles the horoscope of a Western astrologer, but most frequently it is a nondescript figure, which I can compare to nothing on land or sea better than to a featherless chick standing on tiptoe. Occasionally this is varied by multiplying the legs of the creature. Another new charm often to be seen is a rag monkey—the latter as being emblematic of wisdom.

"From the *Osaka Nippo*:—

"'In order to escape cholera, the dogs in the Matsushima and neighbourhood, the cats and birds in Horiye, the monkeys and bears in Nambajinchi, the rabbits in the Temma temple, the deer in the Sakuranomiya temple are wearing charms. One day a man who is fond of tortoises got anxious about those in the Tennoji temple, and was just about to pour a quantity of carbolic acid into the pond, when the priests interfered and reprimanded him.'"

W. H. PATTERSON.

Belfast.

HORSESHOES UNDER ASH TREES.—In grubbing up old stumps of ash trees, from which many successive trees have sprung, in the parish of Scotton, there was found, in many instances, an iron horseshoe. The one shown to me measured 4½ in. by 4½ in. The workmen seemed to be familiar with this fact, and gave the following account :—The shoe is so placed to "charm" the tree, so that a twig of it might be used in curing cattle over which a shrewmouse had run, or which had been "overlooked." If they were stroked by one of these twigs, the disease would be charmed away.

E. LEATON BLENKINSOPP.

[See 5ᵗʰ S. vii. 368.]

EELS A CURE FOR DEAFNESS.—The other day I was at the sluices which drain Lochleven, where there were a woman and a boy. They were beside a big perforated wooden box, in which were many large eels wriggling in an inch of water. The woman was putting one of the eels, two feet or so long, into a bag ; and, in answer to my question, she said it was for a lady in England who was deaf. The doctor had ordered it to cure her deafness. On further inquiry, I learned that it was common to send eels away by her for such a purpose. On asking her if she believed that eels

cured deafness, she answered, " Od, I dinna ken, sir, but thae English doctors shud ken " ; and then she added, " this yin's for a lady near Lunon" ; whereupon I thought of writing to you to inquire whether eels are anywhere in England supposed to cure deafness,—whether any doctors anywhere think so,—and whether there is in any one's eyes a special virtue of healing in the eels that are in Lochleven.

W. HODGSON.

Cupar, Fife.

MEETING EYEBROWS.—In "N. & Q.," 5ᵗʰ S. vi. 286, I noted that while the Danes still profess to know a man who is a werewolf by his eyebrows meeting, the current saying in the south of England is, " It is good to have meeting eyebrows ; you will never have trouble." In China, according to Dr. Dennys, the people say that " people whose eyebrows meet can never expect to attain to the dignity of a minister of state " ; that " ladies with too much down or hair are born to be poor all their lives " ; but that " bearded men will never become beggars."

WILLIAM GEORGE BLACK.

Glasgow.

THE CORPSE CANDLE.—The belief in the appearance of the corpse candle in Wales has not yet died out. Having occasion to visit this part of Wales, which, by the way, is in many particulars one of the most interesting spots in Caermarthenshire, I found a valuable " subject " for folk-lore study—one who cannot speak half-a-dozen words of English. My informant is an aged widow lady. I asked her to-day if she had ever seen the corpse candle, and she positively assured me that she saw it on the night her husband died, and, further, that at the railway station at this place there is to be seen sometimes, late at night, after every one has left, a candle burning in the office, which is a portent of some evil. With all the persuasive powers at my command, I entirely failed in disabusing her mind of this superstitious belief. It is curious to note that the old corpse candle should find an abiding place in a railway station.

J. JEREMIAH.

Trehelig, Llangadock, Caermarthenshire.

VENETIAN FOLK-LORE (5ᵗʰ S. viii. 325.)—In studying the folk-lore of other countries it is curious how we stumble across superstitions which are common to lands other than our own, but which a great majority of people, from a want of wider knowledge, have learned to look upon as peculiarly insular. I fancy if one of the contributors to "N. & Q." were induced to write a book upon comparative folk-lore, he would find many readers, and open up a most interesting field of research. The specimens of Venetian folk-lore furnished by K. H. B., which, from want of any other idea, I will number 3, 6, 9, 21, 27, 32, are

servation in the pages of "N. & Q.," something akin to the specimen which I will call No. 29?—

"Dr. Hardwicke held an inquest this morning at Holloway on the body of William Winckles, a saddler, aged seventy-four, of 4, Mitford Road. On Sunday a strange cat entered his room, which caused the old gentleman to become very much excited, and he declared that something portent would happen before night. The cat was driven out, and the people present laughed at the circumstance, but he appeared very grave. When his son (a watchman) went to his work in the evening, deceased asked if he should take him his supper. The son replied 'Yes.' Shortly before nine, Mr. Billing, of 27, Windsor Road, was passing along that thoroughfare, when he heard a fall, and, upon looking round, saw deceased on the pavement insensible. Before aid could be procured he was dead. His son not getting his supper went home at eleven o'clock for it, and, hearing that his father was dead, exclaimed, 'That strange cat came to warn him of his death!' The medical evidence showed that the actual cause of the death was apoplexy, while suffering from softening of the brain. The jury returned a verdict accordingly."

R. P. HAMPTON ROBERTS.

SERVIAN FOLK-LORE.—The following notice of what is, in all likelihood, an old custom turns up in the war news of the *Scotsman*, Jan. 4, 1878, in a letter from Bucharest, anent the warm reception of Prince Charles there on Dec. 27. After telling of the triumphal arches, the hearty greetings of the onlookers, and so forth, the writer goes on to say :—

"The Mayor of Bucharest presented the Prince with the *customary bread and salt*, and the Prince on receiving it said, 'The army by its bravery and devotion has reached the height of the mission confided to it by the country. God has been with us. Let us, then, go and thank the Almighty for the success that he has granted us.'"

J.

QUEEN EMMA AND THE ORDEAL OF FIRE.—Warton (ii. 97 of the new edition) has a valuable citation to the effect that, upon the occasion of the Bishop of Winchester visiting the priory of St. Swithin in 1338, a minstrel sang ballads in the hall of the priory about Colbrond, and about Queen Emma's deliverance through the ordeal of fire. I know of no earlier authority for the story of Queen Emma than Higden's *Polychronicon*, three hundred years later than the event (bk. vi. Gale, i. 277). It is well known that a similar story is told, full two hundred years earlier, by William of Malmsbury of Gunhild, Emma's daughter, wife of the emperor Henry III., and by other "historians" of St. Cunigund, wife of the emperor Henry II.; also in Percy's ballad of *Aldingen* of Elina, wife

behalf : "Sancte Swythune, tu illar Deus vim patitur," &c. It seems to 1 possible that it is a ballad about Qu which is intended in the prologue to *I man* :—

" ......dykers and delveres, that doth here d
And dryven forth the longe day with *Di*
Dame *Emme*."

It is just this kind of fellow that in (*Accidia*) does not know his Paternoste know "rymes of Robyn Hood and R of Chester." F. J.
Harvard College, Cambridge, Mass.

THE EARLIEST CHURCH DECORATIO *Grantham Journal*, Jan. 5, 1878, is an the service, on the previous Sunday e the Navvies' Chapel, the schoolroom at Tunnel, when

"the chaplain, the Rev. J. P. Davies, M.A., text Genesis x. 2, 'And the dove came in t evening ; and, lo, in her mouth was an olive off : so Noah knew that the waters were aba the earth.' Doubtless, also, Noah took t stuck it up amidst the general rejoicings of It was, so far as he (the preacher) could d earliest instance on record of Church decorat Ark was the Church of that day. So regarded it might teach them a few useful lessons. I in his book called *The Stones of Venice*, had gi account of this olive leaf. Its dark green against the Syrian sky, its under surface of 'as if the ashes of the Gethsemane agony ha upon it for ever,' each sparkling with the w flood, certainly did not present a picture o boughs and bushes in Church. But it was sign or pledge that this leaf brought joy to 1 of the Ark. It told them of hill tops un safety and plenty. And in like manner the texts, the crowns and trefoils, that adorned should do more than lend a simply festive ap their Church ; they should carry their thou magi, the shepherds, the manger, and fix th blessed dogma of the Incarnation."

The preacher's "doubtless" is highly s and its use would sanction every kind o to the Scriptural narrative. His ren: "barbarous boughs and bushes" is also notice. I wonder what the navvies thou sermon and of Noah's church decoration.

NOT A :

INFORMATION FOR THE PEOPLE.—Yo (5th S. viii. 486) that a few years ago, in illustrated almanac, Christmas Day w sented as falling on October 25. I have following remarkable list of dates from a for 1878 appended to an advertisement 1 to my house by a tradesman in this town :—Becket, d. 1863 ; Wesley, d. 1721 ; George VI., d. 1830 (query, when did George V. die ?) ; Louis XI., d. 1843 ; Wellington, d. 1862 ; James II., d. 1801 ; Battle of Worcester, 1642 ; Milton, d. 1694.

Sidney Smith invented a purgatory for his friend Macaulay, which was to consist in the latter's having wrong dates and facts of the period of Queen Anne shouted in his ears, without his possessing the power of correcting them. Had this almanac been sent to the great historian he would not have survived it.

JONATHAN BOUCHIER.

Bexley Heath, Kent.

Queries.

[We must request correspondents desiring information on family matters of only private interest, to affix their names and addresses to their queries, in order that the answers may be addressed to them direct.]

A PASSAGE IN "LYCIDAS."—Mr. Jerram, in his edition of this poem, explains line 46—

" Or taint-worm to the weanling herds that graze "—

by a reference to a kind of spider known as a "taint." May I be permitted to suggest that the " taint worm" is nothing more than the worm which is supposed to be the cause of the " rot " in sheep ? I say supposed, because I believe it is not quite clear whether the worm which infests sheep suffering from that disease is the cause or the effect of the " rot." In support of my theory I may quote from W. Ellis's *Compleat System of Experienced Improvement* (London, 1749). At p. 154 of that work I find : " Or take it in this way—if a sheep, for example, is in good order of body and receives a taint or rot, about midsummer," &c. As Mr. Jerram is a correspondent of "N. & Q." perhaps he will say whether he accepts my suggestion.   B. R.

PETER AND PAUL WENTWORTH.—Are there in existence portraits of Peter Wentworth, M.P., one of the chief men of the Puritans in the reign of Queen Elizabeth, and of his brother Paul ?

P. P. W.

THE RT. REV. HENRY DOWNES, successively Bishop of Killala, Elphin, Meath, and Derry, died Jan. 14, 1734-5, and was buried in St. Mary's Church, Dublin. I am anxious to learn whether any portrait of him exists in private hands. There is none at the palaces of his successors in any of his sees, nor at Trinity College, Dublin. One is much desired for the purpose of engraving, if the original or a photograph can be obtained. Address Colonel Chester, 124, Blue Anchor Road, Bermondsey, S.E.   J. L. C.

AN OLD WORK ON GEOMETRY.—Can any one do me the kindness to give me information about the following book ? It is a small volume (6 in. by 4 in.), of which the title-page is lost, containing four pages of an Address " To the Reader " " Of Geometry in General " ; thirty-eight pages of " The Principles of Geometry " ; 140 pages of " Geometrical Practice upon Paper " ; and six pages of " The Table." Its most notable feature consists of eighty full-page etchings, much in the style of Callot, the upper part of the engraving being a diagram illustrative of the proposition on the opposite page, and the lower part a landscape or figures, some of the latter being very spirited. The type points to the end of the sixteenth or the beginning of the seventeenth century, and I suspect the author to be Thomas Masterson.   B. H. J.

SAMUEL SWAYNE.—Wanted information of— 1. Samuel Swayne, said to have been chaplain to the celebrated Earl of Strafford, and tutor to his children. After the earl's execution he is reported to have taken his son Lord Wentworth abroad, and to have returned and held the living of the two Worthies near Winchester. 2. Samuel Swayne, Univ. of Oxford B.A. 1679, M.A. 1687. The first is said to have been the brother, the second the son, of Rev. Geo. Swayne, who came into Somersetshire with Gilbert Ironside, when he was made Bishop of Bristol, 1666. He held the living of Sutton Crowthorne, co. Somerset (patron Edmond Burton). Whom did he marry ?   OTTO.

FRANCIS COATES, THE PAINTER.—In Nichols's *History of Leicestershire*, vol. iv. p. 399, it is stated that " Francis Coates, Esq., the celebrated painter, is maternally descended from the Lynns " of Southwick, near Oundle, in Northamptonshire. Can any of your readers help me to trace this descent ? A very full pedigree of the family of Lynn will be found in Dr. Marshall's *Genealogist*, vol. i., but no such name as Coates occurs in it. Who Francis Coates was, where he lived, and what he painted, are questions I should also be glad to have answered.   EVERARD GREEN.

Reform Club.

HOLLY TREES IN HEDGES.—Any one who observes the fences by the side of our railway lines may see, as a rule, in the clipped continuous thorn hedges, at intervals varying in length from 100 to 200 feet, young holly trees, planted at the same time with the hedge, and therefore in all cases within the last fifty years. Stephens, in his *Book of the Farm*, gives an elaborate account of the trench-planted hedge introduced by the railway engineer in place of the ditch-and-bank system, but he says nothing of this very noticeable feature. I have met with it in other hedges, whose date, though probably earlier than railway times, can seldom be so well ascertained. Is this custom a survival of the superstition mentioned by Pliny, " Aquifolia arbor, in domo aut villâ sata, veneficia

IRISH CERAMICS.—The following extract from the *Belfast Newsletter*, Jan. 11, 1757, may be of interest :—

"Dublin, Jan. 15.—Monday last died, universally lamented by all true lovers of their country, Captain Henry Delemain, formerly in the Duke of Saxe-Gotha's service, master of the Irish delft ware manufactory, who, by the expense of a large fortune and unwearied application, brought that ware to such perfection as totally to prevent the enemies of our country, the French, from drawing large sums yearly from this country for Burgundy and Roan ware. Mary Delemain his widow carries on said manufactory, and hopes for the continuance of the friendship of the nobility, gentry, and whole kingdom."

Can Delemain's ware now be recognized ?

W. H. PATTERSON.
Belfast.

"MIRACLES FOR FOOLS."—The Rev. Robert Taylor, in his *Diegesis*, p. 15, says that θαυματα μωροις was "a common adage among the Greeks." Can any one furnish evidence of the truth of this statement ?

J. B. S.
Cornbrook.

"HOP$_{\mathrm{G}}$N AGAINST HOPE."—Can any one give the origin or earliest literary use o this nonsensical expression for "hoping against expectation"? It ought to have a pretty long prescription to justify its continued use, and I have met with it, I think, in a book published in the seventeenth century, but cannot now give the reference. Hope sometimes connotes expectation, but I know of no other instance of it as a simple synonym for that word.

C. C. M.

PASCAL.—Under chap. xxv. of the *Pensées de Pascal*—those published since 1843—the following is placed as No. xcviii. :—"Mon ami, vous êtes né de ce côté de la montagne, il est donc juste que votre aîné ait tout." May I ask some one to explain the allusion in the first part, presuming that the latter refers to the law of primogeniture ?

F. DE H. L.
Madras.

JONATHAN BOUCHER wrote a *Glossary of Archaic Words* as supplement to Johnson and Webster, published 1832. Have these words been incorporated in Bell & Daldy's *Webster*, edited by Goodrich and Noah Porter, which has been issued without any date ? or have very many of the old words been omitted ? Is Boucher's book worth anything as an independent work ?

C. A. WARD.
Mayfair.

QUAKERS AND TITLES.—Have Quakers ever used or acknowledged amongst themselves titles of any kind, whether by virtue of office or inheritance by descent or marriage ?

J. BEALE.

OFFICE OF THE STRACHY.—What is the mean ing of the word "strachy"?

Ω.

CHEVALIER ROSLIN.—Can any one tell m anything of him ? See 5th S. viii. 448.

MAG.

THE DEATH OF "A SURVEYOR OF HER MAJESTY CUSTOMS IN ALL HER PLANTATIONS AND COLONIE OF AMERICA."—What gazette or news-letter of 1702 or 1703 would be likely to mention such a event as the above ?

E. R.

MODERN GREEK BIBLE.—Where can one ge a real, that is, a perfect and complete Bible i Modern Greek ? It is to be had neither at the Society for Promoting Christian Knowledge, n at Messrs. Bagster's, nor at the British and Forei Bible Society.

W. J. BLEW.

A "TUCKING" MILL.—What is a "tucking mill ? What was the operation of "tucking," an what was its purport ?

S. W.

"TRA SA."—Can any one suggest the extensic and meaning of the abbreviated words "tra sa in the following extracts from the Court Roll the Manor of Bibury, co. Glouc.?—

"Et quod idem Willelmus fecit insultum et *tra* super Thomam Wykes, ideo in misericordia."

"Et quod Ricardus serviens Thome Benet fecit i sultum et *tra sa* super Thomam Cole, ideo ipse in mise cordia."

"Et quod Felicia Muleward leuauit hutesium ius super Aliciam Foreward, ideo in misericordia, et qu dicta Felicia *tra sa* iniuste de dicta Alicia, ideo in mise cordia."

G. F. W.

WHO WAS THE LAST SURVIVING MEMBER THE IRISH HOUSE OF COMMONS ?—Sir Thom Staples took the chair as the last survivor at lecture on the "Irish Parliament" by Mr. Whit side, in 1862. He is referred to as the last me ber in "N. & Q.," 3rd S. vii. 474. He was bo in 1775. I cannot find his name in the lists members of Parliament in the Dublin director from 1791 to 1801. A John Staples sat duri all that period (Limavady, 1791 to 1796 ; Antr county, 1797 to 1801, in the Imperial Parl ment). Nor is any Thomas Staples mentioned Barrington in his Red and Black lists. In t note in "N. & Q." it is said he sat for Colerai and subsequently for Knocktopher. The representatives of both those boroughs are accounted for in Barrington and the *Cornwallis Correspondence*, as having voted for the Union. A. W. Dublin.

CRYING BABIES.—I happened to be in the hamlet of Clayhanger recently. It is a remote little place on the Devon and Somerset border line. The churchyard is open, and the wind was blowing bleakly. Some small girls were loitering, on their way home from school, amongst the graves, and one of them had an infant in her arms. Presently the baby cried—yea, roared. "Why don't 'ee turn its face to the wind, Sally?" asked an elder girl of the juvenile nurse. Sally, however, evidently did not pay due attention, for presently the shrill command, rather than advice, was repeated: "Do 'ee hear! why *don't* 'ee turn his face to the wind?" This time the exhortation was taken, the child duly turned round, and in less than a minute its piping ceased. Did the breeze half choke it, and thus bring quietness, or did it temporarily give comfort, and soothe the little one? The custom may be general, but to me, a family man and a travelled one, it is novel.
HARRY HEMS.
Exeter.

"GUY'S PORRIDGE POT; with the Dun Cow Roasted Whole: an Epic Poem in Twenty-five Books. Part I. Carefully Corrected and Enlarged by many new Passages and Additional Notes. (Motto.) Second Edition. London: Printed for the Author, and Sold by the Booksellers. 1809." 12mo. pp. xxix-101, and corrigenda (one page). Imprint of Slatter & Munday, Oxford. A squib on Dr. Parr and other Warwick notables.

This has been often ascribed to Walter Savage Landor, but is disclaimed as his work in Mr. Forster's *Walter Savage Landor: a Biography*, 1869 (see vol. i. p. 320). Who wrote *Guy's Porridge Pot?*
ZERO.

AUTHORS OF QUOTATIONS WANTED.—
"I had rather be the victim of a too willing credulity than the slave of an unjust suspicion."—Burke, I think, but I cannot find where.

"I give him joy who stammers at a lie."

"Though women are angels, yet wedlock's the devil."
"Is selfishness for a time a sin,
Stretched to eternity celestial prudence?"
V. S. L.

Replies.

CHRONOGRAMS.
(1st S. ix. 60, 61, Jan. 21, 1854.)

Just three and twenty years ago (how rapidly the years have passed!) I sent to "N. & Q." a dozen chronograms which I had gathered on the banks of the Rhine. I don't know that such ingenious puzzles interest me now as much as they did then;

but yet I cannot resist the temptation, which a casual glance at my former paper (printed at the pages indicated above, when "N. & Q." was still young) has given me, of sending you a few more chronograms to add to your abundant store. If any of your readers should not be familiar with this "strange device," it will suffice to say that in the following sentences the letters used as Roman numerals (M, D, C, L, X, V, I), and these only, when gathered out and arranged in order, will be found to indicate a date desired to be expressed by the composer of the sentence.

1. From the *Disputatio Theologica de Luce Primigenia* of Dr. Johannes Meisnerus (4to., Wittenburgæ, 1680):—

DEO pRIMIGxnIæ LVCIs patrI & satonIs honoR [1660].

2. From a Latin poem addressed by the Carmelite convent at Louvain to Godefridus Hermans (Abbas Tongerloensis), 4to., Louvain:—

sIC enIXe VoVet antIstItI DoMVs pLaCetana [1780].

3. From a congratulatory poem addressed to Antonio Van Gils, of the College of Louvain (4to., Louvain):—

ITa ACCInIt CongregatIo MaIoratana sVo In sACra theoLogIa LoVanII LICentIato AntonIo Van gILs tILbVrgensI [1785].

4. From a congratulatory address to Lucas de Vandenesse (Abbas Averbodiensis) on the fiftieth anniversary of his entering on the religious life (4to., Louvain):—

eX Vero CorDe LVCæ VoVet aMbrosIVs [1786].

5. From a poem addressed to Martin Lamal (4to., Antwerp):—

WY WensChen D'heer MartIno VoLLe IVbIL-Iaeren [1785].

6. From a similar poem addressed to Franciscus Dominicus Hermans (4to., Antwerp):—

geLVxK-WensChInge aen DoMInICVs [1783].

7. From a poem addressed to Godefrid Hermans (Abbas Tongerloensis) on his installation (4to., Antwerp):—

sIC VoVet, ITa affpLaVDIt abbatI goDefrIDo ConVentVs [1780].

8. From the *Carmen Panegyricum* addressed to Gisbertus Halloint (Averbodiensis Abbas) on his jubilee year:—

optIMo patrI et præLato sVo IVbILantI offICIaLes aVerboDIenses [1773].

9-14. From the same volume. The date, 1773, is expressed in each line of the following chronodisticha:—

DIffLVe ConDIgno Læta aVerboDIa pLaVsV:
IVbILa enIM CeLebrat spLenDor honorqVe tVVs.
VoTa et MVLta patrI Defer: sI ConVenIt VLLo,
TaM festo eXoLVas ConVenIt ILLa DIe.
HALLonIDes VIVat CVMæos præsVL In annos,
ADDat ADnVC fLenIs IVbILa pLena, VoVe.

15. But by far the most remarkable instances

Augustæ, 1712). This very curious work contains no less than seven hundred (numbered) chronograms, besides that which I have copied from the title-page, nine others on the engraved frontispiece, and a few more scattered throughout the volume. All these chronograms give the same date, 1712. I will copy a few of these as specimens of the singular, if misplaced, ingenuity of the author ; but, before doing so, it may be as well to transcribe a little more of the title-page, as it will show the occasion on which the work was composed, and will give some information as to the general plan of the book :—

" ConCeptVs...DeIpara: septingentis sacræ Scripturæ, SS. Patrum, ac rationum, necnon historiarum, symbolorum, antiquitatum et anagrammatum suffragiis roboratus, ac totidem præfixis chronographicis annum currentem prodentibus copiose instructus; occasione sæculi hoc eodem anno septima vice absoluti et celebrati a Patribus Benedictinis Liberi ac Imperialis Monasterii ad SS. Udalricum & Afram Augustæ Vindelicorum, combinatus per P. Josephum Zoller," &c.

16. PVRA DeIPARA, OB AQVAS CONGREGATAS MARIA APPELLATA.
17. S. ALBERTVS MAGNVS, DeIPARæ sINE LABE PROTECTOR.
18. VeLLe DeI, EST IPsVM FACERE.
19. CELEBRITAS FESTIVA sINE LABE ConCEPTæ, A SANCTO nICoLAo, ELsINo ABBATI MANIFESTATA.
20. DeIParæ sINE LABE, pRInCIpIVM soLENNE IN GRATIA.
21. LIBER pROPRIA IVLII Cæsaris ManV ConsCRIptVs, EIVs pORRECTO EX AQVIs TRACHIo, AB INTERITV sALVATVs.
22. AVE pVRA A LABE, AMANtI DILeCTA.
23. DeI MATER pVRE ConCEPTA, TERRA VIRGO.
24. ALCVINVs, MARIæ A LABE DEFENSOR.
25. FESTIVITAS ConCEPTIONIs, AB ANsELMo InCHOATA, IN ECCLEsIA RECEPTA.

But enough, and more than enough ; five and twenty chronograms are as much as any one number of " N. & Q." can safely carry. Ample must have been the leisure of the man who could compile, even with the assistance of his brethren, seven hundred of them, to say nothing of the equally ingenious anagrams with which the volume abounds. I will end my paper with a few specimens of these. Zoller takes as his theme the angelic salutation, " Ave Maria, gratia plena, Dominus tecum," upon which he founds no less than a hundred anagrams. I transcribe a few of them :—

1. Ave pura Regina, summo amanti dilecta.
2. Virgo serena, pia, munda, et immaculata.
3. Eva secunda, Agni immolati pura Mater.
4. Magnes cordium, vita animæ, tela pura.
5. Alto Regi amica, tu janua semper munda.
6. Regia nata, evadens luctum amari pomi.

ut in omnibus glorificetur Deus. *Reg. S. Ben.* c. 57.'

W. SPARROW SIMPSON

THE MOTTO OF THE ORDER OF THE GOLD FLEECE (5th S. viii. 328, 375, 477.)—The reply GEN. RIGAUD, at pp. 477, 478, is not unlikely mislead. At the first reference a distinct inqu was made :—" Is there any, and what, mo attached to, this order ? " To this query I ge at p. 375, a distinct, and I believe an entir correct, reply ; and I was at the pains to po out at some length that the words " Pretium i vile laborum" were the true and constant mo of the order, other sentences being merely th attached to the personal devices of the seve sovereigns of the order. GEN. RIGAUD does appear to distinctly dispute the correctness of reply, but at pp. 477, 478, he tells us (what known to everybody) the name of the founder a the date of the foundation, and winds up by scribing the collar, and implying that the wo " Ante ferit quam micet " are the motto of order ; for, if this be not the inference, the lat part of the reply is as irrelevant as the former.

Now these words, " Ante ferit," &c., are c tainly not now, and never have been, the motto the order. They were the words attached to the fl and steel which were the personal device of F lippe le Bon, and were used by him previous the institution of the Order of the Golden Fle (see Palliser's *Historic Devices*, &c., p. 56). It quite true that the flint and steel were afterwa used in the collar, but the motto of the device not become the motto of the order. Clark a Carlisle, who, in an identical paragraph of th works on *Orders of Knighthood*, declare the wo " Ante ferit quam flamma micet" to have b the motto of the ancient sovereigns of Burgun are as mistaken as when, in the same paragra they assert that the flint stones formed the cha of " the ancient arms of the sovereigns of B gundy of the first race." Clark, from whom C lisle copies, was misled by a passage misquo from Paradine's *Devises Héroiques* in Fav Théâtre d'Honneur et de Chevalerie, p. 945 (vol p. 14 of the English edition). But, indeed, e if the statement were correct, the motto of sovereign is not necessarily, or even usually, motto of his orders ; *e.g.*, " Honi soit qui ma pense " is the constant motto of the Order of Garter, while its sovereigns have used " Dieu mon droit," " Semper eadem," " Je maintiendr &c.

J. WOODWARI

· SILVER FORKS (4ᵗʰ S. v. 174, 322, 405, 510, 590; vi. 56, 102, 156, 279; x. 77; 5ᵗʰ S. v. 500; viii. 338.)—In Mr. George Roberts's *Social History of the People of the Southern Counties of England in Past Centuries*, 1856, p. 341, I find the following:—

"A word or two about spoons, knives, and forks used at this date [*i.e.* in 1601]. Common spoons were made of horn. Knives were imported from St. Maloes in 1553, and cost from 2*d.* to 4*d.* each. They were first made in England in 1563. None are referred to as being purchased or in use at this feast [*i.e.* a *Cobb ale*, a great festivity of Lyme, 1601]. Forks are not mentioned. *Silver forks came into fashion for invalids about the year* 1680. Forks are said to be an Italian invention. Old Tom Coryate, whatever kind it may have been, introduced this 'neatnesse' into Somersetshire about the year 1600, and was therefore called *furcifer* by his friends. Alexander Barclay thus describes the previous English mode of eating, which sounds very ventaish, although worse mannered:—

"If the dish be pleasant, eyther flesche or fische,
Ten hands at once swarm in the dishe."
Ford's *Gatherings from Spain.*

Forks were used on the Continent in the thirteenth and fourteenth centuries (Voltaire). Mr. Joseph Haydn, in his *Dict. of Dates*, says:—

"This is reasonably disputed as being too early. In Fynes Moryson's *Itinerary*, reign of Elizabeth, he says: 'At Venice each person was served (beside his knife and spoon) with a fork to hold the meat while he cuts it, for there they deem it ill manners that one should touch it with his hand.' Thomas Coryate describes, with much solemnity, the manner of using forks in Italy, and adds, 'I myself have thought it good to imitate the Italian fashion since I came home to England,' A.D. 1608."

From a passage in that curious work, Coryate's *Crudities*, it has been imagined (says Mr. R. Chambers, in his *Book of Days*) that its author, the strange traveller of that name, was the first to introduce the use of the fork into England, in the beginning of the seventeenth century. He says that he observed its use in Italy only "because the Italian cannot by any means endure to have his dish touched with fingers, seeing all men's fingers are not alike clean." These "little forks" were usually made of iron or steel, but occasionally also of silver. Coryate says he "thought good to imitate the Italian fashion by this forked cutting of meat," and that hence a humorous English friend, "in his merry humour, doubted not to call me *furcifer*, only for using a fork at feeding." This passage is often quoted as fixing the earliest date of the use of forks; but they were, in reality, used by our Anglo-Saxon forefathers and throughout the Middle Ages. In 1834 some labourers found, when cutting a deep drain at Sevington, North Wilts, a deposit of seventy Saxon pennies, of sovereigns ranging from Cænwulf, King of Mercia (A.D. 796), to Ethalstan (A.D. 878–890); they had been packed in a box, of which there were some decayed remains, and which also held some articles of personal ornament, a spoon, and

the fork which is engraved in the *Book of Days*. The fabric and ornamentation of this fork and spoon would, to the practised eye, be quite sufficient evidence of the approximate era of their manufacture, but their juxtaposition with the coins confirms it. In Akerman's *Pagan Saxondom* another example of a fork from a Saxon tumulus is given; it has a bone handle, like those manufactured for common use. It must not, however, be imagined that they were frequently used; indeed, throughout the Middle Ages they seem to have been kept as articles of luxury, to be used only by the great and noble in eating fruits and preserves on state occasions. Chambers also engraves a German fork, believed to be a work of the close of the sixteenth century. It is surmounted by the figure of a fool or jester, who holds a saw. This figure is jointed like a child's doll, and tumbles about as the fork is used, while the saw slips up and down the handle. It proves that the fork was treated merely as a luxurious toy. Indeed, as late as 1652, Heylin, in his *Cosmography*, treats forks as a rarity : "the use of silver forks, which is by some of our spruce gallants taken up of late," are the words he uses. A fork of this period is also engraved in Chambers's *Book of Days; it is entirely of silver, the handle elaborately engraved with subjects from the New Testament. It is one of a series so decorated at present in the collection of Lord Londesborough. In conclusion we may observe, says Chambers, that the use of the fork became general by the close of the seventeenth century.
S. F. LONGSTAFFE.
Norton, Stockton-on-Tees.

PRONUNCIATION OF "ARE" (5ᵗʰ S. ix. 9.)—Consult Mr. Ellis's work on *Early English Pronunciation*, Mr. Sweet's *History of English Sounds*, and Mr. Sweet's *Handbook of Phonetics*. In the case of *are*, the common pronunciation is a survival of the old one ; in the case of *bare, fare, stare*, and all the rest, the pronunciation has suffered change. The final *e* at present merely denotes the *length* of a vowel, it is true, but this involves a long story, and the original force of the final *e* was, in most cases, entirely different. In the case of *are*, the final *e* is due to a survival of the *e* in the old form *aren*, which again was due to the old Northumbrian *aron*, and it *really* means that the word was once dissyllabic.
WALTER W. SKEAT.

I have frequently observed, in conversing with the farmers and peasants of that part of Radnorshire which may be best described, perhaps, by saying that it lies on the right hand of the road leading from Newtown to Llandrindod Wells, that they pronounce the word *are* with *a* long, same as in *care*. The word *calf* is pronounced exactly like *cave*; *have* same as *a* in *cave*; *day, hay, way*, are

that several varieties of Dialects VI. and VII., as classified by Prince Louis Lucien Bonaparte, will be discovered as existing in the south-eastern parts of Montgomery, and the north-eastern and central parts of the county of Radnor. E. R. MORRIS.
Homestay, Newtown, Montg.

RING AND KNIFE MOTTOES (4th S. xii. 517; 5th S. i. 55.)—A correspondent, M. D. T. N., asks for the translation of a ring motto running thus : "vt . coia . cvte . pace . do ."—each word being on a boss. A contemporary asks for the translation of a knife motto (in the B. M.) running thus : " Me petit penvs erit amato me fecit." · The former seems to me to present little difficulty : but the version at the latter reference is simply impossible. Unquestionably, " coia " is an error for cola. Then I read, "Ut colam cutem pacem do," i.e. " In order that I may save my skin I make peace " ; the ring being the pledge of it. The other I can make nothing of. What can it mean ? JABEZ.
Athenæum Club.

THE ULSTER RIBAND (5th S. viii. 428.)—An Ulster riband does not appear to have ever existed but in the imagination of the gentlemen who assembled under the direction of the late Sir Richard Broun. The Ulster badge was granted not to be worn as a jewel, but to be charged on the escutcheon. The recommendations of the " Committee of the Baronetage for Privileges," not having been officially recognized by the Heralds' College, have never been generally adopted. The baronets of the United Kingdom now all bear the badge of Ulster, no baronets of Scotland or Ireland having been created since the Union.
HIRONDELLE.

TIGER DUNLOP (5th S. ix. 29.)—This " remarkable biped," as his biographer calls him, was the subject of No. xxxv. in the " Gallery of Literary Characters " which appeared in Fraser's Magazine, with portraits done by Maclise under the pseudonym of Alfred Crowquill. William Dunlop's portrait and life up to 1833 are in the number for April of that year, and a very fine portrait it is ; the head admirably finished, and expressive of the man who earned his feline by-name by " clearing two or three islands in the Ganges " of tigers.
H. BUXTON FORMAN.

J. VANDERBANK (5th S. v. 408.)—I beg, in tardy vindication of the " omniscience of ' N. & Q.,' " to inform MR. HENRY GIBBS that one of the series of pictures by this artist in illustration

about twelve years ago from Mr. D. Forl picture-dealer, whose present address is Tc Street, in this town. He informed me at the ti that he had had others of the series, but that one which fell to my lot was the last which possessed. WILLIAM BATES
Birmingham.

TRANSLATIONS (5th S. v. 205.)—
" Un bon traducteur est un bienfaiteur. Il sert conducteur électrique aux idées et aux faits, aux couvertes et aux acquisitions, aux variétés infinies génie et de l'art. Il renouvelle le sol intellectuel de nation et de sa race. Rien du passé, rien du présent demeure étranger aux peuples qui emploient vigoure: ment le grand ressort d'éducation mutuelle."—Phila: Chasles, Mémoires.
J. M

" CATALOGUE OF FIVE HUNDRED CELEBRA: AUTHORS " (5th S. viii. 428.)—I purchased book noted by MR. WARD. It is a very inex: incomplete, and somewhat libellous product: It was published anonymously, and the work it affords no clue to its author. It was very sever handled at the time of its publication by Gentleman's Magazine and the Analytical Rev: the critic of the former calling it " a mere c temptible catchpenny." I find no mention of book or its author in Pickering's edition Lowndes, but in Watt's Bibliotheca Britann 1824, is the following : " Marshall, ——. Cha ters of 500 Authors. London, 1788." I shall thankful for any further information respect Mr. Marshall. D. M. STEVEN:
Guildford.

I presume the high price is on the strength the extract from Lowndes, as I gave one shil for my copy at Sir C. Rugge Price's sale (Sothe February 14, 1867, lot 400), and it has Macartney book-plate. I have a note of ano: copy with MS. notes, priced at two shillings sixpence. It was referred to in " N. & Q.," 3: xi. 280. The Gent. Mag. for 1788, pp. 537 819, says the work is a contemptible catchpe: After reading the preface and the promise future editions should be carefully brought de &c., it seems most unlikely that the author she have destroyed any copies. In this work we a conjecture which partly answers a question has several times appeared in " N. & Q." (3: xii. 419), namely, Who was " Anna Matild Under "Robert Merry" (the Catalogue is unpag the author says : " In this publication they I been interspersed with poems by a lady in I land, under the signature of Anna Matilda.

conjecture this lady to be Mrs. Piozzi." If, however, the reviews of the *Catalogue* are good, this conjecture is in all likelihood bad.

OLPHAR HAMST.

I have a copy, and have known it from my childhood. The margins of my copy are well covered with MS. notes by my mother. I have a similar book, published by Colburn, 1816, entitled *A Biographical Dictionary of Living Authors.*

H. T. E.

Clyst St. George, Devon.

MR. WARD will find *Catalogue of Five Hundred Celebrated Authors* in Bohn's *Lowndes,* under the head of "Literature," p. 1369. This *Catalogue,* 1788, was the foundation of a similar work—

"Literary Memoirs of Living Authors of Great Britain, arranged according to an Alphabetical Catalogue of their Names, and including a List of their Works, with Occasional Opinions upon their Literary Character. London, 1798," 8vo., 2 vols.

Lowndes says : "A useful work to the time when it was published. Edited by Dr. Rivers, a Dissenting minister of Highgate."

CRAWFORD J. POCOCK.

Brighton.

RECORDS OF THE WEATHER (5ᵗʰ S. viii. 507.)—If MR. LOWE is not yet acquainted with *A General Chronological History of the Air, Weather, Seasons, Meteors, &c.,* in two vols., 8vo., published in London in 1749, I am sure he will be glad to have his attention called to them. I may add that they were compiled by Thomas Short, M.D. (no author's name given in vols.), author of other valuable works in the last century, and a most careful observer. In White's *Natural History of Selborne* will be found many useful references to remarkable seasons of rainfall, frosts, &c. In the Reports of the Irish Census Commission for 1851, in all four vols., will be found such a mass of information as respects the weather and vital statistics of that country as is hardly to be found elsewhere. I may further (I hope without any charge of personal vanity) refer him to articles Famines, Fevers, Floods, and Frosts, in my *Insurance Cyclopædia.* I am preparing for the Statistical Society of London a paper on the "Famines of the World," wherein is embodied a large mass of facts bearing upon meteorology which I have drawn from a great variety of sources.

CORNELIUS WALFORD, F.S.A.

Belsize Park Gardens, N.W.

DINKEL, ARTIST (5ᵗʰ S. viii. 507.)—I have two small oval water-colour drawings by this artist—one of a lady, and the other of a fury of the time of the French Revolution. The lady has powdered hair and a tall head-dress, with feathers and ribbons and lace ; a yellow ribbon round her neck,

tied in a bow in front ; a pale blue dress trimmed with pale yellow and white : she has very delicate features and complexion. The other is a very bold-faced woman, with dishevelled hair and naked breasts. She wears a white frilled cap, with a broad blue ribbon and strings untied. She has a dark blue dress, and a red kerchief thrown loosely round her neck. They are signed E. I. D.

W. N. STRANGEWAYS.

Stockport.

POPE CALIXTUS II. (5ᵗʰ S. viii. 428) was an author, and among his other writings is a treatise on the discovery of the body of St. Turpinus, Archbishop of Rheims and martyr. In that work, which I do not possess, I should think it most likely that your correspondent would find all the information he desires.

EDMUND TEW, M.A.

LORD ROBERT STUART (5ᵗʰ S. viii. 443.)—Will the writer of this notice furnish the readers of "N. & Q." with any particulars he may have of the family of Penicuik of that Ilk ? This ancient family is about the least known in Scotland, and I, for one, am thankful when any the smallest gleam of light is thrown on its history.

MAG.

"MUCKED TO DEATH" (5ᵗʰ S. ix. 6.)—As a term of reprobation or as an epithet the word *muck* has a very wide range, and is so used in Scotland (at least the Border counties), and to the writer's knowledge throughout the northern counties of England, at least as far south as Cheshire. In Scotland a dirty or slatternly woman or girl is termed a "big heap," a "mucky heap," and, superlatively, a "great mucky heap." If a Scottish southland shepherd comes soaking wet from the hill, or a farmer from the plough in the same condition, each will describe himself as being "wet as muck"; and in Northumbria a pedlar or other dealer will commend his wares to his customers as being as "cheap as muck"; and a drunken man, on both sides of the Border, is termed as "drunk as muck." In Lancashire, where almost every person has a nickname, the unsavoury word is also in current use as an opprobrious epithet. One person will, for example, be best known as "Jock o' Bill's o' Dick's," that is, John, the son of William, the son of Richard, and so on. One young woman, for instance, is called "Jinny o' Mucky Molloy's," from the fact that her mother, Mary or Molly, was a slattern. Near where I reside there is a moorland farm, the name of which is actually "Mucked Earth," and not far off is another farm which has a much "higher" designation. This singular name, I presume, had its origin in the fact that no hay can be grown in this high region of north-east Lancashire, except the fields and meadows receive a liberal top dressing of manure in the autumn and winter months. In the *Vicar of Wakefield*

that she was "all a-muck of sweat." CUTHBERT
BEDE, in describing the farmer's heaven as a place
where there is "heaps of muck," reminds one of
the Highlander's idea of the same place. Donald
is telling a friend that he has dreamt of being in
heaven. "And what a fine place it was!" he
enthusiastically exclaimed; "there were nae less
than fifty pipers a-playing at aince [once]!"
H. KERR.
Stocksteads, Lancashire.

Though I feel sure that CUTHBERT BEDE knows,
some of your other readers may need to be told that
the "heaps o' muck" which entered into the
farmer's dream of heaven consisted not of mounds
of earth or of mud, but of abundance of management, i.e. of farmyard manure, as distinguished
from artificial enrichers of the soil. I think I am
right in saying that muck, management, and
manure are, in Lincolnshire, the positively vulgar,
the comparatively polite, and the superlatively refined name for the same thing. I would refer any
one interested in the subject to Peacock's Manley
and Corringham Glossary (E.D.S.). The Holderness and the Mid-Yorkshire and Whitby glossaries
of the same society give some pleasing examples
of the use of the word muck, which is probably
one that is common to all English folk-speech.
ST. SWITHIN.

A "SNOW" (5th S. viii. 428.)—In the Imperial
Dict. is a woodcut representing a "snow." As the
word is not in the four dictionaries (Richardson,
Latham, Halliwell, and Nares) which I propose
to supplement, I have marked it for insertion in
my glossary, with the following quotation:—

"Far other craft our prouder river shows,
Hoys, pinks, and sloops, brigs, brigantines, and snows."
Crabbe, The Borough, Letter 1.
T. LEWIS O. DAVIES.
Pear Tree Vicarage, Southampton.

A "snow" differed very slightly from a brig, the
difference being that the fore-and-aft sail was not
hoisted on the mainmast, but on a supplementary
mast or spar immediately abaft the mainmast.
The vessel would thus carry a square mainsail and
a fore-and-aft mainsail. There was a picture of a
"snow" in the earlier edition of the Encyclopædia
Britannica, but it is omitted in the later, this
kind of rig having become obsolete. J. C. M.
113, Eaton Square.

Wedgwood says under this word: "Pl. D.
snau, a kind of ship, originally a beaked ship, from
snau, beak, snout." EDMUND TEW, M.A.

A "snow" is described by Webster as
vessel equipped with two masts, resembling
main and fore masts of a ship, and a third i
mast just abaft the mainmast, carrying a trysa
D. M. STEVE
Guildford.

The sail on the third small mast, just abaft
mainmast, and almost similar to a ship's m
was called the trysail, and extended from its
towards the stern of the vessel.
FREDERIC BOA
15, Queen Anne's Gate, Westminster.

In those charming plates of "Shipping
Craft," drawn and etched by E. W. Cooke, wi
found one of a "Prussian snow," looking very
what we know here as a barque.
HARRY SANDA
Oxford.

A "snow" is generally the largest of all
masted vessels employed by Europeans, and
most convenient for navigation. A.

See Smyth's Sailor's Word Book, sub voc.
EDWARD PEACO

"SMOTHERED IN THE LODE AND WORRIE
THE HOSE" (5th S. viii. 408, 433.)—This mu
a mining figure of speech—smothered in
lode (where the mineral is dug) and worried
choked, the original meaning of the word) ii
hose, the shaft or pipe by which the miner
brought to the open surface. It thus sig
doubly smothered before the plot is brought t
light of day. H. V

MARRIAGE OF CHARLES I. AND HENRI
MARIA (5th S. ix. 26.)—I hand you a descrip
of an important historical document, former
my possession, which formed an essential pa
this transaction. It consisted of two folio sl
of about foolscap size fastened together as
leaves, in which state it must have been befor
writing, as this continues from one page to ano
and is not written on separate leaves and a
wards connected. This is the more notice
because the dates of the three parts are in re
order to the succession of them; so that the k
was first written, leaving space before it for
two foreign parts to be written afterward
believe I am sufficiently acquainted with I
Charles's writing to be able to attest it.
notice is all that remains of the document, a
believe all that is known of it, as, unluckily,
no longer in existence.

we may see the bust of Prince William V., Stadtholder in 1766, then nineteen years of age. At his side is the bust of Sophia Wilhelmina, a Prussian princess, whom he married in 1767."

He then describes the figures precisely as they are on W. M. M.'s plate and on my bottle, and says that different plates have different inscriptions. He adds :—

"They were fabricated on the occasion of this marriage, which seems to have been a popular one in Holland, and another plate shows the figures separated by a candle, while lines in Dutch surround them. The letters ' P . W . D . V .,' which we see on many of these services, are the initials of Prins Willem. Deu. V."

From Chaffers's description, then, this ware seems to be Staffordshire and not Leeds pottery, though in many respects very like it. Can any one give me the translation of the two inscriptions on my very quaint bottle, the likenesses on which are certainly approaching caricatures ?   B. J.

The inscription is corrupt Dutch, but not wholly so, as *couleur* is French. In correctly written Dutch it would read :—

" Zal nooit de Oranje
  Klein vergaan,"

—the orange colour will never fade. Is W. M. M. really assured that this plate is of Leeds pottery ? The political allusion points to a much earlier date.
                                        HUGH OWEN.

DICTIONARY OF ENGLISH MALE AND FEMALE NAMES (5th S. vii. 267, 397.)—MR. WARREN will hardly find one which is more satisfactory than the glossary affixed to vol. i. of the *History of Christian Names*, by the author of the *Heir of Redclyffe*, &c. (London, Parker, Son & Bourn, West Strand, 1863).   ST. SWITHIN.

HERALDIC (5th S. viii. 268, 379.)—The arms described are so nearly identical with those borne by the Hutchinsons of this country, that I think they must be the same.

See the *New England Historical and Genealogical Register*, vol. i. pp. 296 and 310, for those borne by Gov. Thomas Hutchinson, the eighteenth Governor of Massachusetts ; and *id.*, xxii. p. 236, for those of the Hutchinsons of Salem, Mass. The "lion rampant" is argent in both cases ; but of the "cross crosslets or" there are eleven in the former, and but eight in the latter ; but the description gives the field as "semée of cross crosslets or," which may account for the discrepancy between both and the one described in "N. & Q."

Col. Joseph L. Chester, of London, has spent time and labour in tracing the Salem branch of the family, and somewhere he concludes that the governor's branch are not entitled to these arms.

The governor's family name is extinct here, but there are descendants from the same parent stock, of whom I am one. He left descendants in England ; for his grandson, the Rev. John Hutchinson,

published in London, in 1828, the third volume of the governor's *History of Massachusetts from* 1749 *to* 1774 ; and one of the governor's sons, Thomas, died at Heavitree, near Exeter, in 1811, aged seventy-one. The governor lived at Brompton till June 3, 1780, and died there.

Perhaps this may meet the eye of some descendants of Governor Hutchinson's, who can give me their version of their pedigree, and say whether or not they are entitled to the above arms—the contrary to which is so confidently asserted by Col. Chester.

I should be much pleased to receive a personal communication in relation thereto.
                                        WM. M. SARGENT.
Portland, Me.

LAKE THIRLMERE (5th S. viii. 469 ; ix. 34.)—On referring to a *perfect* copy in my library of that extremely rare work, Saxton's *Maps*, 1576, I find this lake named " Thurlemyre flu." The singular accuracy of these, the first maps published of England and Wales, is most surprising, as the difficulty of carrying out a survey in this wild and mountainous county three hundred years ago must have been very great.   R. H. WOOD.
Penrhos House, Rugby.

AUTHORS OF QUOTATIONS WANTED (5th S. ix. 49.)—
" Religion, freedom, vengeance, what you will," &c.
Byron's *Lara*, ii. 8, third and fourth lines from the end.
                                        C. W. BINGHAM.

Miscellaneous.

NOTES ON BOOKS, &c.

A Chronicle of England during the Reigns of the Tudors, from A.D. 1485 *to* 1559. By Charles Wriothesley, Windsor Herald. Edited from a MS. in the possession of Lieut.-Gen. Lord Henry Percy, by Wm. Douglas Hamilton. (Printed for the Camden Society.)

THIS interesting volume contains notes made in the reigns of Edward VI., Mary, and in the first year of Elizabeth. Its great value lies in the fact that it tells us as much of the private life of the times as of their public history. In some cases the record of manners will raise a smile ; at others, something graver than a smile. Under 1554 there are these incidents, illustrating a street scene, and how the Spaniards who came over with Philip bore themselves : " Frydaye, the 26 of Octobre, was a Spaniarde hanged at Charinge Crosse which had shamefullie slayen an Englishe man, servant to Sir George Gifforde. There would have been given c. crownes of the strangers to have saved his life." Again, in 1555 : " The xi of Januarie was a Spaniarde hanged at Charing Crosse for slaying an English man at the court gate at Westminster, at Christenmas holydayes, cunningely runninge him thorowe with a rapere whilst 2 Spaniardes held him by his armes, who also were arrayned and cast, but after pardoned by the Queene." The entries of executions in Mary's reign are numerous, and business-like as a ledger account. Here is one sample out of many : " Saturday, 27 Junii (1556), were 13 persons carried from Newgate in three cartes to the end of the towne of Stratford the Bowe and there brent."

Testaments. The compact whole is in two columns; the type small, but clear.

The Theban Trilogy of Sophocles. With Copious Explanatory Notes for the Use of Elementary Students. By the Rev. W. Linwood, M.A. (Longmans & Co.) ADMIRABLY edited in every respect. The student has just enough help afforded him as may serve for encouragement to help himself. Of old the learner was often left with scanty aid, or none at all. Now, there is some danger of going to the other extreme. Mr. Linwood has adopted the happy medium. Moreover, the volume is so neatly got up that a student, on opening it, might find pleasure in the perusal of its attractive pages.

WE have received *Corn and Chaff, or Double Acrostics* (B. M. Pickering),—*The Public Ledger Almanac,* kindly sent to us by Mr. Childs of Philadelphia.—*The Genealogist,* No. 16, edited by Dr. Marshall,—*The New England Historical and Genealogical Register,* No. 125. —*Journal of the National Indian Association,*—and *English Mystics of the Puritan Period,* a reprint from the *New Englander* of an article by R. E. Thompson (Univ. Pennsylv.).

UNIVERSAL CATALOGUE OF PRINTED BOOKS.—The Prince of Wales, President of the Soci·ty of Arts, having referred to the Council the subject of the cost of producing a Universal Catalogue of all Books printed in the United Kingdom up to the year 1600, the Council, to enable them to report to their President, will feel greatly obliged if librarians, publishers, and printers will kindly give replies to the following questions, and return them answered to the Secretary, P. Le Neve Foster, Esq , John Street, Adelphi, London, on or before February 15 :— 1. As it is proposed to issue the catalogue in sections, do you approve of dividing the catalogue into periods, say, of fifty years? If not, please say what other periods you recommend. 2. Do you approve of the size of the proposed page and type? If not, what do you suggest? 3. Would you be willing to attend a meeting of the Council, and give explanations of your views generally on the subject? A specimen of the proposed catalogue may be seen at the Society of Arts', Adelphi, between the hours of 10 and 4, or a copy will be sent for inspection, to be returned.

THE Scotish Literary Club, instituted for the reprinting of rare, curious, and remarkable works pertaining to Scotland, has issued as its volume for 1877 the works of Adam Petrie, "the Scotish Chesterfield," viz. :—1. *Rules of Good Deportment, or of Good Breeding. For the Use of Youth.* 1720.—2. *Rules of Good Deportment for Church Officers; or, Friendly Advices to Them.* 1730. Now first collected.

THE Diploma Galleries of the Royal Academy, containing the works deposited by members on their election as Academicians, and other works the property of the Academy (including the Gibson Sculpture), are now open free to the public, from 11 to 4 daily, Sundays excepted.

in Newgate in the following March. Moliere's origi] comedy satirized hypocritical human nature. Medbou adapted it to calumniate an adverse religious par Cibber used it in his *Nonjuror* (1717) to cast obloquy an antagonistic political faction; and Bickerstaff, v had no religion at all, readjusted the piece in his *Hy crite* (1768) in order to caricature those Dissenters v thought nobody religious but themselves.

F. DE H. L. (Madras.)—The *Parliamentary History England,* 1806-20, as well as the series of the *Parl mentary Debates* (Hansards), give lists of the memb of the House of Commons from a very early period do to the last Parliament of the current reign. The li are prefixed to each new Parliament. Another li from 33 Henry VIII., 1542, to 12 Charles II., 16 arranged in Parliaments, is printed in Willis's *Noti Parliamentaria,* vol. iii. pt. ii Beatson's *Chronologi Register,* 3 vols. 8vo., gives the members of both Hou from 1708 to 1807.

DOUBLE X.—Mrs. Southey, in 1834, publish. *Olympia Morata and her Times.* In 1851, M. Ju Bonnet published his *Vie d'Olympia Morata, Episode la Renaissance et de la Réforme en Italie.* In the latt work the story that Olympia had been a professa Heidelberg was proved to be without foundation.

MR. H. GAUSSERON (2, Bath Place, Ayr) thinks he c give useful information about anti-Popery hymns a songs to ACTON WEST if the latter will send him l address.

HORATIO.—Always glad to hear from you. We w act on your suggestion by printing the comments small type.

VINCENT S. LEAN.—" Cold pudding will settle yo love." See " N. & Q.," 1st S. v. 30, 189.

F. RULE.— We shall be happy to forward to K. N. (; S. viii. 289) the translation.

T. L.—The name of the Russian general responsil for the slaughter of the Turcoman men, women, a children is given in Burnaby's *Ride to Khiva.*

S. W.—The rhymes on the kings of England ca doubtless, be procured of any publisher of childrei books.

WM. FREELOVE.—Has the account been publish before ?

REV. W. ROTHERHAM should write to MR. J. A. VINCENT. We shall be happy to forward a letter to th gentleman.

GEO. GASCOYNE.—See 5th S. vii. 206, under "A Stran Descent."

NOTICE.

Editorial Communications should be addressed to " T Editor of 'Notes and Queries '"—Advertisements ai Business Letters to "The Publisher"—at the Office, 2 Wellington Street, Strand, London, W.C.

We beg leave to state that we decline to return con munications which, for any reason, we do not print; ai to this rule we can make no exception.

LONDON, SATURDAY, FEBRUARY 2, 1878.

CONTENTS.— N° 214.

In Memoriam.

Every reader of "N. & Q." will, I am sure, share the profound regret with which I pen these lines, recording the death of the accomplished gentleman and warm-hearted scholar who has, for the last five years, helped them in their inquiries, ministered to their information and instruction, and tempered their discussions with a geniality and tact which must have won for him, in his character of Editor, the regard that was entertained by all whose good fortune it was to know him as a friend. DR. DORAN died, after a short illness, on Friday, the 25th of January, in his seventy-first year.

Receiving his early education in France and Germany, and gifted with a memory which never failed him, DR. DORAN was eminently fitted to discharge the responsible duties of an editor—duties calling for a combination of firmness in maintaining the character of the journal under his charge with a delicate regard for the susceptibilities of contributors. DR. DORAN was, I believe, under twenty when his 'prentice hand directed the *Literary Chronicle*; and, for the last quarter of a century, hardly a publishing season has returned without producing some valued work from his pen. During the whole of this time he was a constant contributor to various literary journals ; and yet such was his industry, that all this labour did not compel him to withdraw from that society where he was always so heartily welcomed, and where his loss will be so deeply deplored.

My introduction to DR. DORAN was one of the many kindnesses for which I was indebted to his and my good friend, dear John Bruce, who, had he been spared, would have worthily accomplished what I have so feebly attempted—rendered full justice to the high personal character and varied acquirements of the worthy and joyous-hearted man of letters who was laid to his rest in Kensal Green on Tuesday last.   WILLIAM J. THOMS.

Notes.

THE "BORE" ON THE RIVER SEVERN.

The recent work of Prof. Huxley on *Physiography* is distinguished by the lucidity of explanation and the graphic power of description so characteristic of its author. It forms a valuable introduction to the physical study of the earth on which we dwell, and of the innumerable agencies always at work moulding and shaping it as we now inherit it.

In describing the effects of the tidal wave there is one passage which, probably through inadvertence, is calculated to mislead, or, if not misleading, it points out a phenomenon which has certainly not been hitherto recorded. On p. 180, remarking on the rapid rush of water in a narrow strait caused by the tidal wave, he proceeds :—

"If the tidal wave rolls into a narrow estuary, the water becomes heaped up and produces a sudden rush into the channel of the river. Such a wave is called a *bore*, and is well seen in the Bristol Channel at the mouth of the Severn, where at certain seasons the head of water attains to as great a height as *forty feet*."

There is a little ambiguity in this statement. If it is merely meant that the rise and fall of the tide in certain parts of the Severn—about the mouth of the Wye, at Chepstow for instance—is forty feet, it is rather an understatement, fifty feet being not unusual with spring tides under favourable circumstances ; but this is not what is called the *bore*. This term is limited to the effect produced when, in the words of the professor, "the

warranted. Imagine for a moment a perpendicular
wall of water forty feet high ! We read· that in
the Red Sea "the waters were gathered together,
the floods stood upright as a heap," but a rush
such as this would be sufficient to sweep away a
dozen Pharaohs and their armies at once.   No
ship or boat could withstand such a shock for
a moment.
   The great wave which swept along the coast of
Peru a few years ago, and again in 1877, and
which caused such an enormous amount of destruction, was not half this height. The phenomenon
is not peculiar to the Severn, being occasionally
found in the Dee, the Trent, and the Solway, and
on a much larger scale in the Hoogly at Calcutta,
where it only rises about five feet.   On the
Brahmapootra the height is said to exceed twelve
feet, and is so dangerous that no boat will venture
to navigate when it is likely to occur.   In some
of the great rivers of Brazil it is said to reach the
height of fifteen feet, being the greatest known.
   Camden describes the *bore* on the Severn thus :
   " There is in It a daily rage and boisterousness in its
waters, which I know not whether I may call a gulph
or whirlpool, casting up the sands from the bottom, and
rowling them into heaps.   It floweth with a great
torrent, but loses its force at the first bridge.......That
vessel is in great danger that is stricken on the side.
The watermen us'd to it, when they see this Hygre (or
Egre) coming, do turn the vessel, and, cutting through
the midst of it, avoid its violence."—Gibson's *Camden*,
edit. 1695, p. 231.
   Some time ago there was a very graphic account
of this *bore* in the Severn inserted in the *Times*.
The perpendicular height was there fixed at six
feet.
   There must be many readers of " N. & Q." in
the immediate neighbourhood of the banks of the
Severn.   It would be interesting to ascertain what
their experiences of this phenomenon amount to,
and to what extent Prof. Huxley's statement can
be verified. ·   J. A. PICTON.
   Sandyknowe, Wavertree.

BEDINGFIELD OF OXBURGH.

   In a note to p. 151 of Mr. Scott's *Memorials of
the Scott Family of co. Kent* occurs the following :—
   "Blomfield, in his *History of Norfolk*, vol. iii. p. 488,
asserts that Margaret Scott was *widow* of Sir Edmund
Tudenham, K.G., and that her arms (' Three catherine
wheels, &c.') were impaled with those of Tudenham
(' Lozengée argent and gules ') in the chancel window of

field, relict of Sir Edmund, Knight of the
that is, of Sir Edmund *Bedingfield*.   The
Mr. Blomefield mentions three shields *car*
the roof, which exhibited the arms of Bedi
(*i.e.* Bedingfield quartering Tudenham) im
Scot of Scot's Hall, Kent.   Possibly these
passages Mr. Scott cites, and on an apparer
apprehension of which he proceeds as fo
"This confusion of names of Tudenha
Bedingfield in the person of this Sir E
probably arises from the fact[!] that h
equally known by one or the other surnam
(note to p. 151).   Mr. Scott, to make goo
statement, should show from documentary
that *any* of the Bedingfields were ever
"Tudenham."   At least, he has no warra
Blomefield for the double name.   That hi
has carefully set out all the particulars rela
the Bedingfield pedigree in the account (
burgh (vol. vi.), and, since Mr. Scott quot
work as his authority, I cannot understand
can be so misconstrued ; more especially
Blomefield says in his account that he ha
particularly set down the evidence of certai
and other records upon which the pedig
founded, in order that there might be no mi
as mistakes *had* been made with respect
subject.   At p. 150 of his book Mr. Sco
this : "Sir Edmund Bedingfield, or Tude
for he appears to have been known by botl
names, the latter probably in the first insta
heir of his mother (sister and heir of Sir T
Tudenham, beheaded in 1461)," &c.
Margaret Bedingfield, *née* Tudenham, w
mother to Sir Edmund Bedingfield, but
mother, he being son and heir of Thomas E
field, Esq., son and heir of Edmund Bedir
Esq., by his wife the said Margaret Tude
Again, in the note to p. 151 Mr. Scott obs
"There can be little question, therefore, th
heir general [*i.e.* of Lord Wenlock] marrie
kinsman of Archbishop Rotherham was n
than the prelate's sister Margaret, married
Edmund Tudenham or Bedingfield," &c.
truth, however, with respect to this passage
in the first place the heir general of Lord W
was a *male* (one Thomas Lawley, Esq.) ; sec
it is on record that the archbishop had a
certainly, but most assuredly she could nc
been Margaret Scott.   In the same note M
goes on to say :—
   " Looking therefore to the facts[!] of the case
not unmindful of its difficulties [there are no diffi

we come to the conclusion that Margaret Bedingfield (née Scott) conveyed by marriage the manor of Oxburgh to her husband, as heir-at-law of Lord Wenlock, or Archbishop Rotherham her brother."

It seems almost unnecessary to repeat that Margaret Bedingfield, née Scott, was not the heir of Lord Wenlock, or sister or related to Archbishop Rotherham, and that prelate in nowise related or heir to Lord Wenlock. Mr. Scott, before penning the above, might have elicited from the Inquisitions post mortem in the Public Record Office the information that Margaret Bedingfield, née Tudenham, relict of Edmund Bedingfield, Esq., died seised of the manor of Oxburgh, she having inherited it as sister and heir of Sir Thomas Tudenham, who had likewise died seised of the same.* From which it is clear that Margaret Bedingfield, née Scott, second wife of Sir Edmund Bedingfield, cannot by any possibility have been associated with the acquisition of the manor of Oxburgh by the Bedingfields.

JAMES GREENSTREET.

"THE HELIAND," AN OLD SAXON POEM
OF THE NINTH CENTURY.
(Bibliographical Notice.)

I. Manuscripts.—(a) The Cottonian, Caligula A. vii., parchment 8vo., first mentioned in Hickes, *Institutiones grammaticæ Anglo - Saxonicæ et*

* Chancery Inquisitions post mortem, A° 15 Edw. IV., No. 38. This comprises several inquisitions taken in different counties after the death of Margaret Bedyng-felde, widow. In one of them, taken at Norwich, April 25, A° 16 Edw. IV., the jurors say that she was seised, *inter alia*, of the manor of Oxburgh; that said Margaret died Jan. 25, A° 15 Edw. IV.; and that Edmund Bedyngfelde, son and heir of Thomas Bedyng-felde, son of aforesaid Margaret, is cousin (or, as we should say, grandson) and heir of the said Margaret, and aged twenty-one years and more.
Ibid., A° 33 Hen. VI., No. 7, taken at Weybrede, co. Suffolk, Nov. 8, A° 33 Hen. VI., after the death of Thomas Bedyngfelde, Esq. The jurors say that he was seised in fee of a tenement called Skottes, in the vill of Westylton, worth per annum 3s. 4d., and that he held no other lands or tenements in this county; also that he died Oct. 12, A° 32 Hen. VI., and that Edmund Bedyngfelde is son and heir, and aged five years and more.
Ibid., A° 5 Edw. IV., No. 34. Two inquisitions taken after the death of Thomas Tudenham, Knt. In one, taken in co. Norfolk, the jurors say that he was seised, *inter alia*, of the manor of Oxburgh; that said Thomas died Feb. 23, A° 1 Edw. IV.; and that Margaret (else-where in the inquisition she is described as Margaret, late wife of Edmund Bedyngfelde, Esq.), daughter of the aforesaid Robert Tudenham, sister of the aforesaid Thomas, is next heir of the same Thomas, and aged sixty years and more. The other inquisition, taken in co. Suffolk, sets out the Tudenham pedigree in the following manner: first, as below, by an account of the descent of the manor of Ereswell' in said county, which was settled in tail by a fine levied in Michaelmas term, A° 54 Hen. III., the underneath Robert Tudenham

Mæsogothicæ, Oxon., 1689; described by H. Wan-ley in Hickes' *Thesaurus*, iii. 225, and in Schmeller's *Heliand*, vol. ii. p. vii : fac-simile in Schmeller, specimens in Hickes' *Thesaurus.*—The MS. was copied in September, 1768, by C. Frid. Temler for Nyerup, *Symbolæ ad literaturam teutonicam anti-quiorem*, Havn., 1787, No. V., pp. 130-146; also Introd., pp. xix-xxiii.—Copy in the Bodleian, by Francis Junius; another in the Royal Library at Copenhagen, by Friedr. Rostgaard.

(b) Monacensis—in the Royal Library of and Eve his wife being the plaintiffs, and Robert de Westone and Hawisia his wife the deforciants.

Robert Tudenham=Eve.
died seised of it.
|
┌──────────────────────┴──────────────────────┐
Robert Tudenham, s. and   Thomas Tudenham, bro.=
h., seised of it, but ob. s.p.   and h., died seised of it.
|
Robert Tudenham, Kt., s. and h.,=
died seised of it.
|
John Tudenham, Kt., s. and h.,=
died seised of it.
|
Robert Tudenham, s. and h.,=
died seised of it.
|
┌───────────┬──────────────┬──────────────┐
[Robert Tuden-   Thomas Tudenham,   Margaret,   late
ham, ob. s.p.]   Kt. [br. and h.], seis-   wife of Edmund
See below.   ed of it, but ob. s.p.   Bedyngfelde, Esq.

Secondly, by an account, as under, of the descent of the manors of Brandeston and Westerfelde, in said county, which were settled in tail upon Robert Weylond and his wife Cecilia, née Baldok', by a fine levied in Hilary term, A° 19 Edw. II., between Master Robert de Baldok', junior, plaintiff, and the underneath William Weylond, Chivaler, deforciant.

William Weylond,=   Thomas de Baldok'=
Chivaler.
|
Robert Weylond, s. and h.=Cecilia.
|
Margaret, d. and h.=John Tudenham, Kt.
|
Robert Tudenham, s. and h. of Margaret=
|
┌───────────────┬───────────────────────┐
[Robert Tudenham, ob.   Thomas Tudenham, Kt., "son
s.p.] See below.   and heir" (really brother and
heir to Robert), ob. s.p.

Ibid., A° 1 Hen. VI., No. 77. Proof of the age of Thomas Tudenham, brother and heir of Robert Tuden-ham, son of Robert Tudenham, defunct. Taken at Bertoñ, in co. Suffolk, on the Tuesday after the feast of the Epiphany, A° 1 Hen. VI. The jurors say that he was born at Ereswell' and baptized in the church there, and that he was twenty-one years old on the feast of SS. Gordianus and Ephimachus last past (*i.e.* May 10, 1422).

Francis orientalis et episcopatus Wirceburgensis, Wirceb., 1729, ii. 325 : fac-simile in Schmeller. The Cottonian MS. is written in the North Frankish dialect, and probably a translation from the original poem in the Old Saxon dialect of Westphalia, of which the Munich MS. is a copy. Both MSS. belong to the ninth century.

II. Editions.—

1. Heliand, poema saxonicum seculi noni, accurate expressum ad exemplar Monacense insertis e Cottoniano Londinensi supplementis nec non adjecta lectionum varietate nunc primum edidit J. A. Schmeller. Monachii, Stuttgartiæ et Tubingæ, Cotta., 1830, 4to., vol. i., text. —Gloesarium Saxonicum e poemate Heliand inscripto et minoribus quibusdam priscæ linguæ monumentis collectum cum vocab. lat.-saxonico et synopsi grammatica. *Ibid.*, vol. ii., 1840.

2. Heliand, oder das Lied vom Leben Jesu, Urschrift mit Uebersetzung und Anmerkungen von J. R. Köne. Münster, 1855. (The Cottonian text.)

3. Heliand, mit ausführlichem Glossar, herausgegeben von Moritz Heyne. First ed., Paderborn, 1865; second, *ibid.*, 1873. (Collated from both MSS.) Considerable portions in—1. Rieger, Alt- und Angelsächsisches Lesebuch nebst friesischen Stücken. Giessen, 1861.—2. Oscar Schade, Altdeutsches Lesebuch. Halle, 1862.—3. Müllenhoff, Altdeutsche Sprachproben. Second ed., Berlin, 1871.—4. Wackernagel, Gothische und Altsächsische Lesestücke. 1871.

III. Translations.—

1. Kannegiesser. Berlin, 1847.—2. Grein. Rinteln, 1854, and Cassel, 1869.—3. Köne. Münster, 1855.—4. Simrock. Elberfeld, 1856 and 1866.—5. Rapp. Stuttgart, 1856.

IV. Criticism.—

1. Vilmar, deutsche Alterthümer im Heliand als Einkleidung der evangelischen Geschichte. Marburg, 1845 and 1862.

2. Püning, Gymnasialprogramm. Recklingshausen, 1851.

3. H. Middendorf, Ueber die Zeit der Abfassung des Heliand. Münster, 1862.

4. E. Behringer, Zûr Würdigung des Heliand. Würzburg, 1863.—Krist und Heliand. Würzburg, 1870.

5. Windisch, der Heliand und seine Quellen. Leipzig, 1868.

6. Grein, Heliandstudien. Cassel, 1869.

7. Schulte, Ueber Ursprung und Alter des altsächsischen Heliand. Glogau, 1872.

8. Schulte's article in Zacher's Zeitschrift für deutsche Philologie, vol. iv. pp. 49-69. Halle.

9. Heyne's article in *ibid.*, vol. i. pp. 288, *seq.*

10. Grein's article in Pfeiffer's Germania, vol. xi. pp. 209, *seq.*

With regard to the authenticity of a Latin preface to the poem :—Zarncke in Berichte der Kön. Sächsischen Gesellschaft der Wissenschaften Philologisch-historische Classe. 1865.

G. A. SCHRUMPF.
Tettenhall College.

sweetheart is not quite so clear as the reviewer would have us believe. Some time ago, in writing an English grammar, I instanced *sweetheart* as word whose termination had changed its form from *sweet-ard* in order to show a meaning ; in fact, it was a pretty instance of false analogy, *female.* But a colleague of mine absolutely refused to believe the statement, and challenged proof I produced as my authority Prof. Max Müller Rede Lecture of 1868, who compared *sweetard* with the Ger. *liebhart.* When my friend said that authority was not proof enough, I brought forward others—Dr. Richard Morris's *Historical Outline* of *English Grammar,* Messrs. Abbott and Seeley' *English Lessons for English Readers,* Chambers' *Etymological Dictionary,* but all to no purpose So I set to work to make inquiry, and the authorities melted away ; in fact, when the case was fairly put, they kindly helped to show that no proof was forthcoming. The form *sweet-ard* is not in Mätzner's list of words in *-ard.* It cannot be produced from English literature. Bailey's Dictionary gives a *"Saxon swaet-heort"* as sweetheart but I am afraid that is of his own manufacture (it is not in Bosworth), and it would seem to mean *sweet-hearted,* if it meant anything. *Dear heart* and *sweet heart,* which occur a good way back in English, though with a slightly different sense, point to another origin, and hardly leave time for the loss or weathering down of *sweetard.* I do not know how early *sweet-heart,* meaning lover, is found. Shakespeare is quoted ; but the word is in *Roister Doister* (A.D. circa 1550), i. 2, "my *swete hearte* Custance"; and i. 4, iii. 5 ; and in *Euphues to Philautus* (A.D. 1579), p. 114 (Arber's Reprint) : " And although thy *sweete hearte* binde thee by othe alwaye to holde a candle at hir shrine, and to offer thy devotion to thine owne destruction," &c. I removed my rash statement from a second edition after Dr. Abbott wrote to me that it was clear that "*sweetard* was exploded." It is almost a clearer case than *beef-eater,* for which so many authorities and so little proof can be quoted.

O. W. TANCOCK.

"MUGGING TOGETHER."—This expression might be worth comparing with "mucked to death" (5th S. ix. 6). I have heard it in Berks thus used : " They are all, father, mother, and children, *mugging together* in one room" ; that is to say, this family is living in the crowded, dirty, littery state which arises from eating, sleeping, dressing, working, all within the compass of, say, nine feet

square. Halliwell gives *mudge* as a Derbyshire form of mud or dirt. Mr. Wedgwood, under "mucker," to hoard up, observes, "hence *muck* or *mug* appears as a root giving rise to a number of words connected with the idea of privacy or concealment." *Mud, muddle, muck, buck,* &c., seem probably from a separate root, whose fundamental idea is moisture or softness. When we say at the present day, "People are living in hugger-mugger," we mean much what the Berkshire *mugging together* does, the old and proper meaning of living clandestinely being in the main lost sight of. I know not therefore whether to connect *mug, mugging,* in its provincial use, through *mudge* with *muck, mud, muddle,* &c.; or, as seems more likely, with *mucker, hugger-mugger,* &c., and all that class of words.
HORATIO.

THE PUBLIC-HOUSE SIGN OF "THE THREE CHILDREN IN THE WOOD."—Although in Hotten's *History of Signboards* an instance is adduced, from Yorkshire, "among the more uncommon ballad signs," of one called "The Babes in the Wood," no instance is mentioned of the sign of "The Children in the Wood," much less of such a singular sign as that of "The *Three* Children in the Wood." It seems, therefore, worth noting that there was such a sign somewhere in London (as it would seem, in the neighbourhood of Billingsgate) in the year 1770. I find it mentioned in the *Oxford Magazine,* July, 1770 (pp. 26-27), in some "Particulars of the Trial of Peter Conway and Michael Richardson for the Murder of Messrs. Rogers and Venables, on Monday, July 16, at the Old Bailey." The prisoners had been at "The Three Children in the Wood" on the night before the murder, as was deposed to by "— Smith, a publican, who keeps the Three Children in the Wood," and also by their companion, Thomas Blackstone, who "drank with them at the Three Children in the Wood."
CUTHBERT BEDE.

CAPTAIN BOYTON'S PREDECESSOR.—In the *Annual Register* for 1805 (Rivingtons) I find the following curious anticipation of the Boyton life-saving dress, and also of his method of exhibiting its capabilities:—

"A trial was lately made in the river Thames of the life-preserver invented by Mr. Daniel, surgeon, of Wapping. It is composed of waterproof leather, prepared to contain air, and is inflated in half a minute through a small tube, with a cock, which is turned when the jacket is sufficiently expanded; thus prepared it supports the head, arms, and body out of the water, the person wearing it having it at all times in his power, by means of the tube and cock, to increase or diminish the quantity of air. Several persons thus equipped quitted the boats from off the Old Swan, and floated through London Bridge and down the river with the greatest ease and safety, without being obliged to use the slightest exertion to secure their buoyancy, some smoking their pipes, and others playing the German flute, which they did with as much convenience as if on land. In this

manner they proceeded below the London Docks, near the residence of the inventor, Mr. Daniel, where, on their landing, he was greeted with three cheers from the numerous spectators, who were gratified with the sight of such a novel and really useful invention.—*Chronicle,* October 14th."
S. R. TOWNSHEND MAYER.
Richmond, Surrey.

"MANSE."—The term "manse" in Scotland is the universal equivalent for the English parsonage-house, and, as far as I am aware, it is not employed there in any other way than to denote the abode of the minister of a parish. In England the word is now in complete abeyance; but in former times it appears, by the following extracts from the *Sixth Report of the Historical Manuscripts Commission,* p. 291, to have been used as the synonym for an ordinary habitation :—

"1278, Feast of the Invention of the Holy Cross—Agreement between the Prior and Chapter of Ely and John de Walford, physician.—John promises to attend the Prior and Monks. They to supply him and two boys with board, forage for one palfrey, and *a manse* within the court where Stephen the mareschal used to live."
"1278, Morrow of the feast of St. Nicholas, Bishop and Confessor—Agreement between the Prior and Convent of Ely and Nicholaz Dusic of Strahan. They grant to him for his life 2 acres in the vill of Strahan, whereof half an acre, called Croft, lies at Lunewelle, to build him *a manse.*"
"1280, 24th year of Pontificate, Kal. Jan. Durham. Hugh, Bishop of Ely, with the consent of the Prior and Convent of Ely, grants to Symon de la More and Waletham, Kts., that in consideration of the bad ways and long distance from *their manses* of Brame to the mother church of Ely, they may have in the oratory at Brame daily office by a fit chaplain for them and their wives and families. The chaplain is to swear on the Gospels that he will answer to the sacrist of Ely for all oblations and obventions."
HUGH A. KENNEDY.
Waterloo Lodge, Reading.

OWL-PERCH.—Recently, on visiting an old hall in Cheshire, now used as a farmhouse, the tenant said to me, "Now you have been all over the house, except into the owl-perch," pointing to the trap-door leading to the cock-loft. On inquiring afterwards of a tenant farmer if this was a common word in Cheshire, he replied, "I never heard it before, but it is a likely Cheshire word, as in every old Cheshire house there was a hole left in the gable for the owls to go in and out."

Col. Egerton Leigh, in his *Cheshire Glossary,* does not give owl-perch; but he does give "Hattock, a hole in the roof where owls harbour."
W. N. STRANGEWAYS.
Stockport.

OLD STORIES.—A story used to be told in my younger days in the Lowlands of Scotland in ridicule of the Highlanders. It was as follows. Some Highlanders were ignorant of the English language, and as they intended to proceed to the low country in hopes of getting employment, they were primed with three English phrases, which it was hoped would help them on among the Sassenachs. The first phrase was, " We three Hielanmen," intended as a reply to any one inquiring who they were. The next one was, " For the mony and the penny siller"; this was meant as an answer to the question why they had come. In case the questioners should not engage their services, there was a third phrase in reserve, " If you don't, another will."

The Highlanders accordingly set out, and had scarcely crossed the Lowland border when they came on the corpse of a man who had been slain. They stopped to look at it, and while they were engaged in so doing the ministers of justice came up, and, turning to the Highlanders, inquired, " Who did this?" The reply was, " We three Hielanmen." The next question was, " Why did you do it?" The answer was ready, " For the mony and the penny siller." The sheriff, pleased at having so easily made out the evil doers, exclaimed, " You scoundrels, I shall hang you for this." To which the Highlanders complacently replied, " If you don't, another will." On which the poor Highlanders were carried off to jail.

Some years ago I read an exactly similar story, only that it was three monks who set out from their monastery furnished with three sentences, which were in Latin. The first, I recollect, was " Nos tres monachi." I think the second sentence may have been " Pro re est crumenâ." I entirely forget the third. Doubtless some of the readers of " N. & Q." will ·be able to say where the story is to be found. I think it was told in old French. It is possible that a story like this may be current in many parts of Europe. It may also vary in Scotland at different points along the Lowland border. I. M. P.
Curzon Street.

[With variations, this almost universal story comes from the East. In Prussia it takes this form. An Irish recruit, enrolled in the Grenadiers, who were about to be inspected by the "great" Frederick, is told that the king would ask him three questions, which he invariably addressed to foreign recruits on his first recognizing them. The questions would be, " How old are you?" " How long have you been in the service?" and " Are you satisfied with your pay and rations?" The Irish recruit, ignorant of German, was furnished with the

TOY PUZZLE, TIME OF CHARLES I.—Can yo tell me anything about an ancient ornament whic is lying before me? It is a double cross every way in shape like the common puzzle, made up of si bars with different notches, that we have seen i toyshops all our life ; but this will not take t pieces, but each end is heavily mounted in silve and has an engraved device—1. A fleur-de-lis 2. a tower ; 3. a horseshoe ; 4. an anchor ; 5. I. R. 6. R. S. (or S. R.) ; 7. lion rampant ; 8. W. W. 9. a heart pierced with three darts ; 10. a vampire 11. a lion couchant ; 12. a unicorn. All three o the initials have true lovers' knots. J. C. J.

LIFE OF THE DUKE OF SCHOMBERG.—Bayle, ii his Dictionary, speaking of him, says : " He woul deserve a long article here, but not having receivec the memoirs "—what memoirs are these?—" expected, I am forced to defer it to another time.' Did he do so? " He is one of those great mer whose history ought to be written by an able pen I do not doubt but that the Duke of Schomberg his worthy son, has already thought of procurin this honour to his family, and this fine present t(the commonwealth of learning." Has this eve been carried out, or have materials for such a his tory been collected, and where? OTTO.

THE STANDERWICKS OF THE UNITED STATES.— I have been informed that they assume as arms ɛ bloody hand grasping a drawn sword. Are thes Standerwicks descended from Nathaniel Stander wick, who was expatriated in 1685 for participa tion in the Monmouth rebellion? On wha authority and by whom were the arms originally assumed? ANTIQUUS.

" CALLIS," used in Stamford for almshouses What is its derivation, and is it used elsewhere? E. D.

COURTNEY AND AP JENKIN.—When Leonard Calvert, brother of Cecil Calvert, second Lord Baltimore, sailed with two ships from the Isle of Wight on Nov. 22, 1633, and landed at Old Point Comfort, Virginia, America, on Feb. 24, 1634, it is stated that he had with him two or three hundred emigrants with which to establish the English colony of Maryland. Among the emigrants were Lieut. Thomas Courtney, of the Royal Navy, and Ap Jenkin, of Wales, whose son is said to have afterwards married Courtney's daughter. Historical information towards identifying the family from which the emigrant Ap Jenkin emanated, as well as that to which the foresaid

Thomas Courtney belonged, is solicited for an archæological work. LLALLAWG.

"O NIMIS FELIX," &c.—In the *Breviarium Romanum*, pars æstiva, ad Laudes on June 24 (the feast of St. John Baptist), is the hymn commencing "O nimis felix," &c. The second verse is as follows :—

> "Serta ter denis alios coronant
> Aucta crementis, duplicata quosdam ;
> Trina te fructu cumulata centum
> Nexibus ornant."

Will some one of your readers kindly give as literal a translation as possible of these lines, and state something of the allusions contained in them? What is the date, and who was the author of the hymn? H. N.

SOLOMON GRILDRIG.—Who was he? It appears to be a "fictitious name," though it does not appear in OLPHAR HAMST's book. He was "of the College of Eton," and conducted *The Miniature: a Periodical Paper*, 8vo., 1805.
CUTHBERT BEDE.

THE WINDSOR SENTINEL AND ST. PAUL'S.— Years ago I discovered after a weary search, in a newspaper of the period, the name of the famous sentinel at Windsor who heard St. Paul's bell strike thirteen times, and the story I see sometimes repeated without acknowledgment. *Sic vos non vobis.* Piracy and compilation go hand in hand together. What was the "old soldier's" name?
MACKENZIE E. C. WALCOTT.

TOWN MARKS.—In an entry of the business done at a Court Leet and Court Baron held at Melton-Mowbray, Leicestershire, on April 21, 1675, mention is made that they "marked" certain land "with two steps, being the towne marke of Melton." Was this to mark boundaries before the open fields were enclosed? THOMAS NORTH.

JETTON.—Brass, the size of a sixpenny piece, and unusually thick. *Obv.* Laureated head to the left ; legend GVLIELMVS . DEI . GRATIA. *Rev.* The crown of England, with two sceptres in saltire behind it ; in base I . GVINEA . W. Is this a known jetton, or was it ever made to pass for money?
NEPHRITE.

HENRY VAUGHAN.—A Henry Vaughan in 1680 signed an inventory of the goods of an intestate who was formerly at Hythe, Kent. He signs himself "Registrarius." I am particularly anxious, for a literary—not genealogical—purpose, to identify him in his official capacity, and to ascertain when and where he died. WALTER RYE.
St. Anne's Hill, Wandsworth.

JOHN, FIRST EARL OF MIDDLETON.—In Burke's *Extinct Peerage*, 1866, p. 367, we are informed that John Middleton, first Earl of Middleton,

"married secondly, at St. Andrew's, Holborn, in Dec., 1667, Lady Martha Cary, daughter of Henry, Earl of Monmouth, but by her had no issue."
On p. 103 appears the following sentence in the course of a foot-note : "Lady Elizabeth Spelman, daughter of Martha, Countess of Middleton, who was daughter of the second Earl of Monmouth." Which of these conflicting statements is correct? and, if the latter, who are the heirs general of Lady Elizabeth Spelman, and did Martha, Countess of Middleton, leave any other descendants?
J. W. STANDERWICK.

DRAYTON.—What is the derivation of the common English local name *Drayton*? There are eighteen parishes of that name in England, besides four named *Draycot*. A. L. MAYHEW.
Oxford.

JOHN BRINDELL.—The following quaint epitaph deserves a place in "N. & Q." I found it in St. Giles's Cemetery collection. Who was this man of evil life so long? Who was the writer of the epitaph?—

> "The mortal remains of
> John Brindell,
> after an evil life of 64 years,
> Died June 18th, 1822,
> and lies at rest beneath this stone.
> ' Pause, reader ; reflect;
> Eternity, how surely thine.' "
> R. B. CANSICK.

"HOT COCQUAILLE" OR "COCQUALE."—I am told one of the cries in the city of Norwich, on Ash Wednesday, is "hot cocquaille," a species of bun. Your former correspondent, DR. HUSENBETH, gives *cocquaille* as from the Saxon or German, meaning baken in ashes (I quote from memory). Does not the same word mean in Old Norman French egg-shell? And if these cakes or buns are, as I am told, made with eggs, this would seem a better derivation. But, again, eggs were not allowed after Shrove Tuesday. May it not be that some former Bishop of Norwich has granted a dispensation allowing the poor to use the remainder of the eggs on Ash Wednesday, which of course otherwise would be wasted? I should be very glad to learn anything further on this subject. JOHN THOMPSON.
The Grove, Pocklington.

MYSTERIOUS LIGHTS. — The following notice appeared in a recent number of the *Oswestry Advertiser* :—

"From time to time the west coast of Wales seems to have been the scene of mysterious lights. In the fifteenth century, and again on a larger scale in the sixteenth, considerable alarm was created by fires that 'rose out of the sea.' Writing in January, 1694, the rector of Dogelly stated that sixteen ricks of hay and two barns had been burned by ' a kindled exhalation which was often seen to come from the sea.' Passing over other alleged appearances, in March, 1875, a letter by the late Mr. Picton

Can any authorities upon natural phenomena furnish further information on the subject?

EVERARD HOME COLEMAN.
71, Brecknock Road, N.

TIRLING-PIN.—At the recent sale of the effects of James Drummond, Esq., of Edinburgh, two tirling-pins were disposed of : one which came originally from Leith Tower fetched 5l. 10s., and another was secured by a friend of mine for 2l. 2s. My friend has written to inquire from me the mode of the use of the tirling-pin, and not being able satisfactorily to answer his query, it is consequently referred to "N. & Q." Glossaries of Scotch words give the meaning of "tirling" as unroofing, but that of course cannot be the universal application of the word. Amongst Scottish ballads I have found the following allusions to this relic of antiquity, and doubtless there are many others. One from *Lord Beichan*, an Aberdeenshire ballad :—

"And whan she cam' to Lord Beichan's yetts,
She tirl'd gently at the pin,
Sae ready was the proud porter
To let the wedding guests come in."

Another is in *Sweet William's Ghost* :—

"There came a ghost to Marg'ret's door
With many a grievous groan ;
And aye he tirled at the pin,
But answer made she none."

A third instance occurs in *Prince Robert* :—

"O he has run to Darlinton
And tirled at the pin ;
And wha sae ready as Eleanor's sel'
To let the bonnie boy in ?"

JOHN PICKFORD, M.A.
Newbourne Rectory, Woodbridge.

FANS.—There is now open in New York an exhibition of decorative art, including a loan collection of fans. The first loan collection of fans was held at South Kensington in 1870. Of this I have the catalogue. Have there been any other such exhibitions, and did they issue catalogues? Two or three years ago M. Blondel published in Paris a *Histoire des Éventails*. In the September, 1877, number of *Scribner's Monthly* is an admirably illustrated article by Mr. Maurice Mauris on fans. Scattered through the *Art Journal*, the *Gazette des Beaux-Arts*, and *L'Art* are many engravings of fans. Can any reader of "N. & Q." refer me to further sources of information?

J. BRANDER MATTHEWS.
Lotos Club, New York.

Sharpe, while the original of No. 4 (acc⌷ the *Times* of August 27, 1877) was Th⌷ Quincey. Who are the others?

HERALDRY.—What is the crest for th Macginty, or Macgenty—an Irish family A.
Kirkstall.

HERALDIC.—Can any one inform me the following armorial bearings belon appear on two large three-quarter-length ⌷ of about the time of Queen Anne? O⌷ the man, Vaire, four bars gules ; on th⌷ lady, in an oval shield az. an arm in issuing from the dexter, holding three points to the base, all or.

SUTTON MUTTON.—There is a saying, ⌷ of considerable antiquity, in this part o⌷ which has taken the form of a vulgar rh⌷ has been often quoted :—

"Sutton for mutton,
Carshalton for beeves ;
Epsom for *jades*,
And Ewel for thieves."

In the adjoining county of Kent these also known, but in a modified form ; th⌷ are :—

"Sutton for mutton,
Kirby for beef ;
South Darne for gingerbread,
Dartford for a thief."

As Sutton (south town) is a very comm⌷ and there are villages which bear it in twenty-five counties, I should be glad t⌷ these lines are applied in any other counti⌷ Surrey and Kent. EDWARD ⌷
Sutton, Surrey.

AUTHORS OF BOOKS WANTED.—

1. *Politeuphuia, Wits' Commonwealth, or a 1 Divine, Moral, Historical, and Political Ad Similes, and Sentences. For the Use of Sch* N. L., 12mo.) London, 1699.

2. *The Accomplish'd Courtier. Consisting ⌷ tions and Examples. By which Courtiers and State may square their Transactions Prudently a⌷ Order and Method. By* H. W., Gent. (12mo.⌷ 1658.—The dedication is dated, "Ex Musæo ⌷ Bangor-howse primo Januarii, 1658. Stylo ⌷ D̶.

1. *Abra-Mule ; or, Love and Empire: ⌷* London, 1743.

2. *The Yahoo : a Satirical Rhapsody.* ⌷ printed and published by H. Simpson, 1830.

Replies.

GEORGE WASHINGTON AND THE REV.
JONATHAN BOUCHER.

(5th S. i. 102 ; v. 501 ; vi. 21, 81, 141, 161 ;
ix. 50.)

I am very glad that COL. CHESTER has sent
you the dedication to Washington which my
grandfather prefixed to his sermons on the *Causes
and Consequences of the American Revolution*,
published in 1797. As I said at the time, my
reason for not including it in my articles containing the extracts from my grandfather's autobiography was solely because these extracts had
extended to so great a length that I was afraid of
trespassing any further on your space. As it
was, they occupied nearly twenty-four columns
of "N. & Q.," exclusive of the previous extracts
I sent you in February, 1874. COL. CHESTER is
quite right in saying that the "antidote," that is
the dedication written in 1797, should have been
published in close juxtaposition with the "bane,"
that is the damnatory allegations contained in
Mr. Boucher's letter to Washington written in
1775. There is, however, one phrase in COL.
CHESTER's article which I must take exception to.
Mr. Boucher's dedication to Washington is undoubtedly very "manly," and "alike honourable
to the man who wrote it and him to whom it was
addressed," but I cannot regard it in the light of
an "apology." I feel sure that Mr. Boucher did
not mean it for one, as this would have been to
admit that he was wrong in addressing Washington as he did in 1775. From COL. CHESTER's
point of view, as also from my own, he was
wrong, but was he so from his own point
of view? It must be remembered that from
the date of his letter to that of his dedication
twenty-two years had elapsed ; this is a long
period at any time, but especially so when we
remember that these twenty-two years comprised
the two greatest events of the century, the American and French revolutions. In 1775 Washington
was nothing but a revolutionary soldier. I do not
mean that there is any harm in a man's being
what Hampden, Dumouriez, and Garibaldi were ;
but in the eyes of my grandfather—a staunch
church and king man, a Tory of the Tories—a
revolutionist was very much what a Puritan was
in the eyes of Laud, a play-actor in the eyes of
Prynne, or a poacher in the eyes of Squire Broad-
acres. Washington's character had not at that time
fully unfolded itself, and Mr. Boucher, although possessed of considerable shrewdness and penetration,
could no more suppose that his "shy, silent, stern,
slow, and cautious" friend would one day develope
into the wise and noble president who has left
an example to all succeeding ages, than Sir Philip
Warwick could suppose that the Long Parliament
member for Cambridge, whose "plain cloth suit

seemed to have been made by an ill country tailor,
whose hat was without a hat-band, whose voice
was harsh and untuneable," and whose oratory had
nothing but its fervour to recommend it, would some
fifteen years later develope into one of the greatest
rulers that Europe has ever seen. It is perhaps
one of the brightest testimonies to Washington's
pureness of soul, and general nobility of character,
that he should have been addressed in such
eulogistic terms by one who detested his political
principles, and who regarded the revolution of
which he was the guiding spirit as a huge mistake,
not to say a crime.

There is another thing that may have helped to
soften Mr. Boucher towards Washington, namely,
the fact that the dedication was written in
November, 1797, only two years after the final
suppression of the French revolution by the "whiff
of grapeshot," delivered by Citoyen Napoleon
Bonaparte on the 13th Vendémiaire, 1795. May
he not have felt the contrast between the leader of
the American and the leaders of the French revolution? However much we may acknowledge
the necessity for that gigantic bonfire of shams,
the French revolution, it is hardly possible,
with any amount of good will thereto, to extend
much admiration to its leaders ; and Washington
seems grander than ever when we compare him
with Robespierre, Marat, and St. Just, or even
with Danton. It is very possible that my grandfather was struck by this contrast.

COL. CHESTER says there is no evidence that
Washington received Mr. Boucher's letter. As
there is no evidence to the contrary, I should think
it is probable that he did receive it ; but I do not
know what sort of a reply he returned. It will,
however, interest COL. CHESTER to see the reply
(if he has not already seen it) which the great
president returned to the dedication, and for
which I am indebted to *Notes on the Virginia
Colonial Clergy*, by the Rev. E. D. Neill, of
Macalester College, Minneapolis, published last
year in Philadelphia. I do not know from what
source Mr. Neill obtained this letter. From the
somewhat abrupt way in which it begins it appears
to be only an extract from the original letter. It
is dated Mount Vernon, Aug. 15, 1798 :—

"For the honour of its dedication, and for the friendly
and favourable sentiments therein expressed, I pray you
to accept my acknowledgment and thanks. Not having
read the book, it follows of course that I can express no
opinion with respect to its political contents ; but I can
venture to assert beforehand, and with confidence, that
there is no man in either country more zealously devoted
to peace and a good understanding between the nations
than I am; no one who is more disposed to bury in
oblivion all animosities which have subsisted between
them and the individuals of each."

One cannot but regret that after such a "redin-
tegratio amoris" the two old friends had no opportunity of meeting and renewing their former inti-

who dedicated a book to Washington, and who, "from having been his (Washington's) fulsome flatterer, became his foul calumniator." Does any one know to whom my grandfather alludes?

JONATHAN BOUCHIER.
Bexley Heath, Kent.

THE DORMANT SCOTTISH PEERAGE OF HYNDFORD.

(5th S. viii. 429, 453 ; ix. 58.)

I was "pausing for a reply" from your original querist, C. E. G. H., when the further answers of R. P. and MR. W. D. PINK unexpectedly proved the existence of a wider interest than I had anticipated to see roused in what might seem a mere family matter. I think there are good reasons why I should make some further remarks on the subject, partly in correction of both R. P. and MR. PINK, and partly in explanation of what may have seemed an excessive reticence on my own part. I considered the question so entirely one of private genealogical interest that I contented myself with the statement of some bare facts, not clothing them with any names. As, however, both your recent correspondents have mentioned names, I think it right that I should point out some particulars in which they are either inaccurate or not warranted by the facts, and that I should state more fully than in my first reply what are the actual facts of the case.

I may say, at the outset, that I was perfectly cognizant of all the history which R. P. relates, and of a good deal more besides. But I did not think that it bore upon the question asked, and I therefore refrained from inserting it into my reply. As it is, I must say that I do not think any amount of references to Carlyle's *Frederick the Great* likely to help the inquirer into the genealogy of the Carmichaels of Hyndford. In criticism of R. P., I must further observe that it is rather worse than useless to encumber a well-ascertained history with a date of uncertain sound such as he gives for the death of the sixth earl, viz. "after 1809," when it is perfectly well known that Andrew, sixth Earl of Hyndford, died in 1817, as MR. PINK rightly states. Also I must protest against the use of the slipshod expression "Earl Hyndford" for "Earl of Hyndford," the title being derived from a place, and not, like some more modern earldoms, from a family name. It is possible that in another of his mistakes, that of calling the sixth earl *Thomas* instead of *Andrew*, R. P. may have been misled by the erroneous account in the

ancient earldom of Mar, I am not going in the present place to enter. I will only remark that the decision in the case of the claim of the Earl of Kellie affords, so far as I understand it, not the slightest clue to what might be decided in the case of a patent "hæredibus masculis et talliæ." And the recent case of the barony of Balfour of Burleigh is just as much against the theory of R. P. as the earlier case of the earldom of Sutherland. But it would be altogether unsafe to argue from pre-Parliamentary—I had almost said pre-historic—titles to those of a comparatively late period. R. P. may rest assured, however, that in my first reply I purposely minimized the possible rights of the heir male, so as not to be liable to the charge of exaggeration. MR. PINK errs, in a different sense from R. P., in asserting that "both the earldom and barony were granted with remainder to heirs male and of entail." This was only the case with the earldom.

The difficulties attendant upon proof of extinction of intermediate heirs form a class of difficulties which I may assure MR. PINK that I am far from undervaluing. But I have never yet, in the course of a study of the genealogy in question extending now over a period of some fifteen years, met with any proved facts calculated to shake my conviction that the late most distinguished genealogical antiquary and peerage lawyer, John Riddell, was perfectly justified in his opinion that Dr. Carmichael - Smyth of Aitherny, the unquestioned heir male of the Carmichaels of Meadowflat and Balmedie, was heir male general of the Carmichaels of that ilk, both of the older line and of the line of Hyndford. The heir male of Sir David Carmichael of Balmedie is also the heir male of Sir John Carmichael, last of the Captains of Crawford of the line of Meadowflat, whose daughter Margaret was served heir to her father May 24, 1638, Sir John himself having been served heir, in 1595, to his father, grandfather, and great-grandfather. The last of the oldest line of that ilk, Sir John Carmichael, who became involved in difficulties which were among the principal means of the rise of the Hyndford family, was served heir to his grandfather, Sir John, the Warden of the Middle Marches, in 1627, and died *s. p.* at some date, not exactly determined, before July 17, 1649, when his two surviving sisters, Jean and Anna, were served his heirs portioners of line, their elder sister, Margaret, being also then dead.

I do not doubt that Sir Bernard Burke is perfectly capable of defending any judgment on a point of genealogy or peerage law which he may have expressed in any of his works. But I feel bound to state that Sir Bernard's view, doubtfully quoted by Mr. Pink from the *Extinct and Dormant Peerage*, that the chiefship of the name of Carmichael, and the male representation of the Earls of Hyndford and Lords Carmichael, are both vested in the present Sir James Robert Carmichael, Bart., is in exact accordance with the opinion known to have been entertained by the sixth earl himself, as well as by the heritors of Lanarkshire at the time of the earl's death, and by such eminent Scottish genealogists as the late John Riddell and Alexander Sinclair.

C. H. E. Carmichael.

New University Club.

F. Bartolozzi, R.A. (4th S. xii. 110 ; 5th S. ii. 335.)—It is certainly true that this eminent artist was "admitted to the full honours of the Royal Academy"; but it was as a *painter*, not as an *engraver*, that he received this distinction, which, by a law of the body, could not be conferred upon one of the latter class. W. H. Pyne says :—

"Bartolozzi sometimes engraved from his own designs, but he obtained very little acquisition of fame from the attempt; yet he drew the human figure to admiration, and he could paint; for he acquired his diploma in the Royal Academy for a picture which was exhibited at Somerset House."—*Somerset House Gazette* (1824, 4to.), vol. i. p. 353.

Likely enough there was some jobbery in the matter, suggested by the true British admiration of the "foreign." Further on in the same miscellany, in a special article on the engraver, we read :—

"Bartolozzi was a member of the Royal Academy; this is said to have given great offence to Strange, who was unsuccessful in his attempts to be admitted a member of that body, particularly as it was notorious that the picture which the former painted as the preliminary to his academical honours was either wholly executed, or at least touched off, by Canaletti."—*Ibid.*, vol. ii. p. 249.

Elsewhere I have read that it was Cipriani who performed this friendly office for his countryman ; it may have been either or neither, and does not much matter which now. Anthony Pasquin (J. Williams) says :—

"According to the institutes of the Royal Academy, the number of engravers was limited to six, and they are considered in the inferior scale of merit with the painters. Mr. Bartolozzi, conscious of his own strength, presented himself as a painter, and was admitted as such ; and happy were they all to have such an acquisition. All this was just ; for to denominate him a mere engraver would be to circumscribe my language within the limits of ignorance, as he is not only something more, but almost everything that the hope of imitative science can embody. He draws better than any other man in the world, and can give a truth and durability to that design beyond the powers of any other individual in the same department."

When Sir Robert Strange offended Lord Bute,

Mr. Dalton was commissioned to invite to this country the most promising historic engraver he could find in Italy. Bartolozzi, then studying in his native Florence under Wagner, was selected ; and thus there existed a special enmity and rivalry between the two eminent artists. The Englishman no doubt "smoked" the Academic jobbery, the successful issue of which must have been hugely galling to him. In his interesting little work on the rise of the Royal Academy he says :—

"No sooner had the Academicians passed this law, ...which excluded every ingenious engraver native of this kingdom, than they admitted amongst them M. Bartolozzi, an engraver, a foreigner. The Academicians soon felt the disapprobation of the public, for their proceedings were universally condemned. To cover, therefore, their reprehensible conduct, they......said that they had copied that part of their institution which regarded the exclusion of engravers from the Royal Academy of Painting at Paris. This they did when. at the same time, every one of them knew that I had been received a member of that Academy as an engraver."—*Inquiry into the Rise of the Academy of Arts*, 1775, 8vo., p. 112.

An eminent engraver, the late John Pye, writes :

"The alteration subsequently made in the Academy's original law, so far as to allow of six engravers becoming associates, i.e. members of the third class, disqualified them, whatever their merit might happen to be, from rising higher, from holding any office amongst the Academicians, or voting in their assemblies,—and virtually told native engravers, while Bartolozzi was enjoying the Academy's highest honours, that six of them might become appended to the outside of the royal establishment, into which artists of every other class might enter; but that those who did allow themselves to be so appended would thereby recognize a position of degradation as an honour—the just and munificent reward of their merits !"—*Patronage of British Art* (Lond., 1845, 8vo.), p. 191.

It may not be amiss to remind the reader that the "diploma pictures" of the long series of members of the Royal Academy during its century of existence are now on view, and form a most interesting exhibition. William Bates, B.A.

Birmingham.

Archbishop Sharp (5th S. viii. 149, 187, 295.) —The family of Archbishop James Sharp (not "Sharpe"), of St. Andrews, is given incorrectly in Anderson's *Scottish Nation* (iii. 445), and I am unable to admit that his work is "remarkable for accuracy in matters connected with Scotch family history," for I have frequently ascertained it to be just the reverse, in numerous instances, where he repeats the old fables of the asserted origin and descent of so many ancient Scottish houses.

In an article on this archbishop, martyred by the Covenanters, which was furnished by me ten years ago to the pages of "N. & Q." (3rd S. xii. 321, for Oct. 26, 1867), there is a tolerably full account of the members of his family, which, here repeated, with some abbreviations and emendations, may serve as a reply to your correspondents P., T. F., and A. E. F., and establish the question as to which

appears from *The Diary of Mr. John Lamont, of Newton*, 1649-1671 (4to., printed at Edin., 1830):

"1653, April 6.—Mr. James Sharpe, minister of Craill, married one of Randerston's daughters : the marriage feast was att hir father's house in Randerston."—P. 54.

"1655, Jul.—The young Laird of Randerstone, in Fyfe, surnamed Moncriefe, depairted out of this life att Randerstone, and was interred at Craille the 23 of July, 1655."—P. 90.

"1659, Nou.—The Laird of Randerston, elder, surnamed Moncreife, in Fyfe, depairted out of this life at Randerston. He disponed his estate not long before (to defraud his son, a lousse liuer) to his two goodsonns, viz. Kingaske, surnamed Ingels, in Cuper, and Mr. James Sharpe, minister of Craill."—P. 119.

"The day after [Feb. 7, 1662] the Lady Randerston was interred at St. Andrews."—P. 144.

"1663. This summer [Alex. ?] Balfoure, of ......, second son to the deceassed old Laird of Dinmille, in Fiffe, bowght the lands of Randerston att Craill from Mr. Sharpe, Arc. bishope of St. Androws, and Alex. Ingells of Kingaske, the two sonns in law of the deceassed Laird of Randerston. It stood him about sextie thowsande marks or therby. Ther was as mutch gotten as payed the old mans debt, the sellers tochers, and ten thowsande marks more, which was to be giuen to the yowng man formerly mentioned, to helpe his portion. Itt was rentald to him about 25 chald. of victuall, and 100 marks togither."—P. 167.

The date of Mrs. Sharp's death I have not ascertained, but it is believed that she predeceased her husband, fortunate in that she did not survive his melancholy death.

One son and two daughters only were living at the period of the murder ; although, from excerpts from the archbishop's *Household Book*, 1663-1666, it appears that another daughter, *Agnes*, was buried in March, 1666; and in February preceding a son, *John*, was christened, who must also have predeceased his father. The surviving children were—1. *Sir William Sharp*, of Scotscraig and Strathtyrum, in Fifeshire, "who was provided by his father to a competent estate, and married Mrs. *Margaret* Erskine, daughter to Sir Charles Erskine of Camlo, Baronet, Lyon King-at-Arms, by whom he hath a numerous and hopeful issue." There is a difficulty here, as it is stated in Douglas's *Peerage of Scotland* (edit. Wood, ii. 21) that it was the third and youngest daughter of Sir Charles Erskine, *Sophia*, who "married Sir James Sharp of Scotscraig," and no mention is made of his daughter *Margaret*; while Sir James Sharp of Strathtyrum, Baronet, who was the son and successor of Sir William Sharp, and consequently grandson of the archbishop, was still living in the year 1725 ; but whether married, with

Cunningham of Barns, in 1704; but the were "adjudged to Scotstavit in 1743" (East Neuk of Fife, pp. 90, 173, 259, 29 " Mrs. *Margaret*," who was born Dec. 8, 166 christened Feb. 12, 1665 (cf. *Household* ut supra). She married, in 1683-4, the Honourable William Fraser, Master of who was born Nov. 21, 1654, succeeded his father Alexander, *tenth* Lord Salton (at his in his ninetieth year), Aug. 11, 1693, an March 18, 1715, leaving a family of three so four daughters. Lady Salton died at Edir Aug. 29, 1734, in the seventieth year of he her *third* daughter, the Hon. *Mary* Frase married to William Dalmahoy, of Ravelrig was served heir of provision-general to his b John Dalmahoy of Ravelrige, Jan. 21, (*Reg. in Libris Talliarum*, Edinburgen., J 1720). It was his *father*, William of Rav who died at Edinburgh in 1704 ; cf. *The 1* of *Dalmahoy of Dalmahoy, Rotho, Cour Edinburgh* (privately printed 1867), for nu notices of this family. The *elder* William officer in the Scots Horse Guards, or, as st the family pedigree, "Quartermaster t Majesty's Life Guard of Horse," in the year and, in 1687-89, "*late* Quartermaster King's Troop of Guards"; his wife was Martine. "*James* Dalmahoy, Lieutenant Earl of L"[even's regiment ?] in 1676, app have been the fourth son of Sir John Dal of Dalmahoy, Knight, and is mentioned in dated July 24, 1666 (*Reg. of Deeds, Edin* vol. xxv.).

The reference to Fraser's *Family of Baird* William is entitled "*second* Lord Salton," tainly incorrect; he was undoubtedly the el who held that title, which was created by James II. June 28, 1445, in the family of nethy, and carried on by an heir female Frasers of Philorth in December, 1668, firmed by patent of King Charles II. J 1670, and ratified by Parliament on the the same month ; the present possesso seventeenth Lord Salton of Abernethy, Si ander Fraser, being thus the descendant of bishop Sharp : cf. Douglas's and Crawford *ages* (pp. 469, 664, and 435), also Carm *Tracts concerning the Peerage of Scotlan* Edin., 1791, pp. 16, 36-8). The quoted | of the above, relating to the archbishop's th viving children, are from a scarce littl printed at Edinburgh in 1723, entitled *A True and Impartial Account of the Life of the Most Reverend Father in God, Dr. James Sharp,* &c., in 12mo. Though an anonymous production, it is known to have been written by David Simson, the historian of the House of Stewart.

A. S. A.

Richmond.

THE ORIGIN OF THE WORD "NEWS" (5th S. viii. 428.)—The quotation from De Quincey is not the earliest form of the supposed derivation. One of the first correspondents of "N. & Q.," MR. BOLTON CORNEY, stated, in 1st S. v. 178, that it had appeared in an epigram in *Wits' Recreations,* first published in 1640. He copied the following lines from an edition in 1817 :—

"*News.*

" When news doth come, if any would discusse
. The letter of the word, resolve it thus :
News is convey'd by letter, word, or mouth,
And comes to us from North, East, West, and South."

This was the last communication in a discussion which he characterizes as "fierce and tiresome." It commenced with a note by MR. J. U. G. GUTCH, vol. i. p. 270, in which was brought forward the conjecture that the word was derived from a practice of prefixing at the head of newspapers the cardinal points—

N.

E.   W.

S.

It was shown, p. 369, that there was a volume entitled *Newes from Scotland,* which was published in 1591. Its derivation from the German was insisted on at p. 428, and combated p. 487, and defended vol. ii. pp. 23, 81, 82 (where *Olde Newes or Stale Newes* is cited from Baret's *Alvearie* in 1573). The singular form "a news" is referred to from Pepys's *Diary,* at p. 107. The discussion is continued at p. 137, and MR. S. W. SINGER contributes some notes for the elucidation of the subject at p. 180. It is shown at p. 181 that the word was first printed by Caxton in the modern sense in the *Siege of Rhodes,* 1490. The controversy is continued at p. 218, and Dr. Latham's remarks on the use of the word are adduced. It is remarked that "much wit and ingenuity have been wasted on the word," at p. 397. Some remarks are offered in vol. iii. p. 300, upon the early use of it, with a professed disinclination to continue the discussion. No one ventures upon the question in the course of vol. iv., and MR. BOLTON CORNEY, as mentioned above, "just two years after" the first statement, brings the subject to a close in vol. v. p. 178.   ED. MARSHALL.

It is hardly credible that an etymologist should ever think it possible to find the derivation of the word *news,* as quoted by CAVE NORTH, unless it be given as a joke, for if every word was as easily to be traced as this one there would be little difficulty in getting a complete and correct etymological dictionary. *News* is an old genitive, and may be compared with the French article partitive. Likewise, I think, we have to account for *means.* In German such genitives are *nichts, neues.* Not unfrequently the genitive is used adverbially, *e.g. nowadays, needs, sideways,* &c., as in Ger. *morgens, abends,* and thus we have also to explain *of course, of truth, of yore* (cf. Koch's *Eng. Gram.,* iii. 1, § 122). With these forms we may also compare the Low Germ. *van dage* (to-day), *van nacht* (to-night), &c. There are also English datives used in this way, *e.g. whilom, seldom, aye* (cf. *Sources of Standard English,* by Kington Oliphant : this excellent book, so popularly written, ought to be in every Englishman's library ; cf. also Koch, *ib.* § 125). Likewise we must explain *to-morrow, to-day, to-night,* and corresponding with these is the Low Germ. *to jare* (last year). Finally, I may add that Ogilvie is altogether wrong when he says, "*News* has a plural form, but is almost always united with a verb in the singular" (cf. Ogilvie's *Dictionary, s.v.* "News") ; for I think I have plainly enough proved that it is a singular in the genitive case, and this it is always whenever it is "united with a verb in the singular."

F. ROSENTHAL.

Hanover.

No doubt this "theory" is a mere conceit, and has no foundation but in the imagination of some pseudo-etymologist. Wedgwood's explanation is :—

"1. Fr. *nouvelles,* new things, and 2. Dan. *nys,* to get wind of a thing, to get news of it. O.N. *hny'sa,* to search for, spy out; *hnysinn,* curious; Du. *neuselen,* to sniff after, to scent out; *neuswijs,* sagacious, having good scent, curious."

EDMUND TEW, M.A.

I saw the same derivation of *news,* as given by your correspondent, in a small duo. vol. entitled *Antiquitates Curiosæ,* published in 1818. It says :—

"The four cardinal points of the compass, marked with the letters N. E. W. S., standing for North, East, West, and South, form the word *news,* which coming from all parts of the world gave derivation to the word."

Again, under the word in question, Ogilvie's *Ety. Dict.* has the following : "Dr. Trusler gives a fanciful derivation from N. E. W. S., the cardinal points of the compass, because news comes from all directions."

MINNIE DOBSON.

ANTHONY GRIFFINHOOF (5th S. viii. 460.)—It is something for EARLSCOURT to be able to give the date (August, 1814) of the death—though I much fear he will never be able to produce the certificate of burial—of the ever to be lamented Anthony Griffinhoof, author of " *The Maskers of Moorfields, a Vision,* by the late A. G., Gent., edited by W. Griffinhoof, 1815," inasmuch as " Anthony Griffinhoof" is a phrenonym for John Humphreys Parry

book also the Christian name Humphreys is further on spelled Humffreys. Again, Lowndes has, "Griffinhoof, Ant., *i.e.* George Colman the younger," whilst under the head "Colman the Younger" he has, "*Arthur Griffinhoof*, Turnham Green." In Peake's *Memoirs* it is "Arthur Griffinhoofe." The *Biog. Dram.* (1812), omitting the final *e*, says the name "is well known to have been used by Mr. Colman as a *nom de guerre*, through the apprehension that disrepute as a farce writer might have been prejudicial to him as the author of any kind of regular drama." Verily printed "dates and names" appear to be as unreliable as "facts and figures." A word about Colman's *Random Records*, of which Lowndes notes one impression only (and not the first), of the year 1830 (Lond., post 8vo.). In my copy (Lond., Bentley, 1830) there is a MS. note following the words, "End of the Second Volume" :—

"A third time on March 29, 1833. A fourth do. Feb. 20, 1836. How much it is to be regretted that no more volumes have yet appeared. Alas! poor Colman: he was called away on Oct. 26, 1836, aged seventy-four. April 10, 1838; Nov. 7, 1840; May 7, 1842; Feb. 23, 1846 : in all eight times—a sure sign of its interest and ability."

HARRY SANDARS.

"Anthony Griffinhoof" is a pseudonym. See the *Handbook of Fictitious Names*, pp. 55 and 209. If there ever was a real person of this name who was an author, EARLSCOURT will oblige by giving more particulars than he has.

OLPHAR HAMST.

"CHRONIQUES DE L'ŒIL DE BŒUF" (5ᵗʰ S. ix. 29.)—J. K. may not be aware that two *Chroniques de l'Œil de Bœuf* exist, and that the one attributed to Touchard-Lafosse is apocryphal. The true chronicle is anonymous, but is the reputed work of Lebel, a *valet de chambre* of Louis XV.

G. PERRATT.

[Why does not the name of Touchard-Lafosse appear in the *Nouvelle Biographie Générale?*]

THE RED MOUSE (5ᵗʰ S. ix. 49.)—An example of the use of the red mouse in German literature is to be found in the Walpurgis Night scene in Goethe's *Faust.* EDWARD H. MARSHALL. The Temple.

JACK OF HILTON (5ᵗʰ S. viii. 504.)—In Erdeswicke's *Survey of Staffordshire*, edit. Harwood, Lond., 1820, pp. 133-4, occurs the following notice of Jack of Hilton :—

"William Evendon and Thomas Evendon, 25 Hen. VI , by fine gave the manors of Hilton and Essington to Thomas Swinnerton and Elizabeth his wife, and the

its figure hand placed on its breast. This ser performed for upwards of one hundred and forty but has long been discontinued, probably becau two manors have been united in the same lord."

GEORGE M. TRAHER

Jack of Hilton is still carefully preserved though I believe the curious service in wh played so important a part is no longer perf the Vernons being now lords both of the ma Hilton and of that of Essington. Jack has at least one journey to London—to the Archæological Institute. Plott, in his *Hist Staffordshire*, gives an account of this gro service, and also a representation (not, ho entirely accurate) of the figure of Jack of I whom some have considered to be an a Scandinavian idol.

W. J. BERNHARD SM Temple.

MRS. JUDITH WELD (5ᵗʰ S. viii. 507.)—] GREEN consults *Notes on Burgundy*, by C Richard Weld, edited by his widow (L Longmans, Green & Co., 1869), it may he to identify the above.

E. J. TAYLOR, F.S.A. N Bishopwearmouth.

TIGER DUNLOP (5ᵗʰ S. ix. 29, 72.)—M pseudonym in the *Fraser* Gallery was " Croquis" (Fr. *croquis*, a sketch). "Alfred quill" was the pseudonym of a most estimab indefatigable, but mediocre, comic artist, Forrester. G. A. S

"HOPING AGAINST HOPE" (5ᵗʰ S. ix. 68.) at least worthy of remark that *hope* in 1 English merely meant, in many cases, *expect* out implying *desire.* Examples are in Tyr note to Chaucer, *Cant. Tales*, l. 4027 ; Shak and *Cleop.*, ii. 1, 38 ; and "Hope" in 1 *Glossary.* A clear case is that in the speech Tanner of Tamworth, who said, "I hope [*i.* I shall be hanged to-morrow." Another in is in *Piers Plowman*, Text C., Pass. xvii from my note on which I have copied the al WALTER W. SK 2, Salisbury Villas, Cambridge.

Charles Wesley has, in his well-known beginning

"Jesu, lover of my soul,"

and written in 1740, the line,

"Hoping against hope I stand."

It was probably suggested by our not very a translation of the Greek of Rom. iv. 18, against hope believed in hope," referring t

is said in the Old Testament of Abraham's faith in respect to Isaac. The same Greek word for " hope" is used twice in the New Testament verse.
JOSIAH MILLER, M.A.

MODERN GREEK BIBLE (5th S. ix. 68.)—There exists a recent translation of the whole Bible in Neo-Hellenic by the learned archimandrite Neophytos Vambas, who translated the Old Testament from the Hebrew text. He was much blamed for not having conformed to the Septuagint (see Oikonomos, *Treatise on the Septuagint,* 4 vols.). The best Bible commentary in modern Greek is that of Th. Pharmakidis, in seven volumes. If MR. BLEW wishes for any of these works, he may order them through Mr. David Nutt, bookseller, 270, Strand, who has an excellent agent at Athens.
G. A. SCHRUMPF.
Tettenhall College.

Apply to Mr. W. H. Howe, Sudbury, Suffolk, who has, I think, a pocket size, mounted in silver, do. clasps, perfect, in good preservation, and very scarce.   F. HOWE.
27, Hamsell Street, E.C.

"FIFTEENTHS" (5th S. viii. 490 ; ix. 15.)—We meet with the payment of " fifteenths " as far back as the statute of Magna Charta, in the conclusion of which the Parliament grant the king, for the concessions by him therein made, a " fifteenth " of all their movable goods. This taxation was originally set upon the several individuals. Afterwards, in the year 1334, a certain sum was rated upon every town by commissioners appointed in the Chancery for that purpose, who rated every town at the fifteenth part of the value thereof at that time, and the inhabitants rated themselves proportionally for their several parts. This " fifteenth " amounted in the whole to 29,000l., or thereabouts. "Fifteenths" continued in use down to 1624, in which year three " fifteenths " were granted to James I. This was the last grant of the kind, for when in the first Parliament of Charles I. a motion was made for adding two " fifteenths " to the subsidies granted to the king, it was rejected, and the next Parliament was dissolved before this vote of three " fifteenths " passed into law.   FREDERIC BOASE.
15, Queen Anne's Gate, Westminster.

A JACOBITE CONTRIVANCE (5th S. viii. 328, 375, 516.)—It is interesting to learn that another of these Jacobite " perspective" portraits is in existence. The one to which, at p. 328, I referred is at Lower Tabley Old Hall, a " show " place some fifteen miles south-west of Manchester, and accessible enough therefrom by rail or highway. Any reader of " N. & Q." in that city might, on his next spare afternoon, dot down a more exact description of the Jacobite contrivance than I was able to supply above. There is a long and excellent

note in the glossary to Mr. Dyce's edition of Shakspeare on the various " perspectives" of Elizabethan times,* but I find nothing therein directly bearing upon my original query, namely, this very ingenious perversion of optical science to the service of a lost political cause. I should quite expect that allusions would occur in the literature of those times to the distorted portrait and the cylinder. Can none of your readers help me to such a passage ? Imagine a tableful of hot Jacobite squires, with the " contrivance " as a kind of centre-piece to their dessert, pledging the reflected features of the Young Chevalier, and quickly pocketing the cylinder on the intrusion of any dubious visitant. Such an incident has much of the romantic and the picturesque, especially if the party were, as sometimes occurred, marched off to prison straight from their wine and walnuts. How well the author of *Waverley* and *Redgauntlet* would have worked up such materials !   Λ.

SNUFF SPOONS (5th S. vii. 428 ; viii. 275, 396, 497.)—C. G. says, "It is sixty years since snuff spoons were in use." I was at Callander in August, 1874, and, whilst waiting for the train to Stirling, saw a respectable farmer use one. He took it out of his snuff-box and shovelled a quantity of snuff into his nostrils with great gusto, and to my disgust, never having seen anything of the kind before.   L. MACREADY.

I saw one used as naturally as possible by an old man at Norham on Tweed, Dec. 15, 1877. He was a retired exciseman.

I have now before me a large mull, or snuffhorn, made of a buffalo's horn, with silver lid, on which are engraved the letters T. M., surmounted by a falcon (?) on a crest wreath. Near the top is a ring, from which are suspended by chains (1) a snuff spoon, with eight perforations ; (2) a sort of rake ; (3) a simple point ; (4) a fox's foot ; (5) a small ivory hammer. Whether all these instruments were employed in snuff-taking I cannot say. It belonged to the late Mr. Thomas Milson, of Lincoln, wine merchant, and is supposed to have formed part of the paraphernalia of some club to which he belonged. He died about fifty years ago at least.   J. T. F.
Winterton, Brigg.

DEATH OF EDWARD, DUKE OF YORK, 1767 (5th S. vii. 228, 274, 294 ; viii. 192, 215, 238, 397.) —The last three references, while they deem the statement made at p. 192 improbable, ask for the production of the documents on which it is based. With regard to the probabilities (laying aside the variations in the different accounts of the duke's movements, illness, and death, which do not at all harmonize), if an impartial view is taken of

* I have been referred to this note through the kindness of a correspondent.

his interference in politics, while he as angrily replied, resenting also the domineering influence of Bute, who instigated his being ordered out to the Mediterranean so shortly after his return. The duke in his anger, and for other reasons, determined to give up his position and large income, preferring rather to retire into obscurity than be burdened with the many annoyances of his life. In this he but acted in accordance with his family nature, as shown by his brother the king, and the Georges before him, repeatedly threatening to throw up the kingdom and retire to Hanover, rather than be thwarted in their views. Once resolved to carry out this scheme, there can be no doubt the fewer concerned in the secret the better, and so, to avoid having many attendants, the duke went to Monaco.

As regards the production of papers, I cannot see of what use they would now be ; for it must be borne in mind that the duke, to conceal his existence, had to assume a name, and these papers would have to be connected with him before they would be of any value.

Be the probabilities, however, what they may, there is no gain in weighing them, since they will not decide the question of the duke's death at Monaco or elsewhere. But if this is deemed of historical importance, it can easily be determined by a test which is in the hands of the nation, and that is by an examination of the coffin said to contain the body. This is the more necessary as there is no record of a lying in state, and of the body having been seen and identified after the arrival of the coffin in England.   G. D. P.

LEIGH OF CO. WARWICK (5th S. ix. 8.)—The second Lord Leigh had eight children. Of the four sons, Thomas and Lewis both died young (Collins's *Peerage*, 1709), and Edward succeeded afterwards as third Lord Leigh. That the eldest son, Thomas, may have had some share in the death of a servant is quite possible, but that it could be given out that he was dead, and that he should be residing in a neighbouring county under his paternal name, is surely most improbable. Lord Leigh died in 1710, and when his third surviving son, Edward, succeeded to the title and estates, he must have been able to prove that his two elder brothers were dead. It would be difficult to disprove the local legend, but probably the family tombs at Stoneleigh will show when these two young men, or boys, died. The expression used by Collins leads to the presumption that they died infants.   EDWARD SOLLY.

Wokingham in Berkshire), but, in the absence local evidence to the contrary, it seems more t probable that " old " is simply the A.-S. *ald*, wl cognate forms we recognize at a glance on l ing at a map of Northern Europe.

Altenburg, Oldenburg in Germany, and ⌐ bury, Aldborough, Oldborough in England ; Al dorf in Ger. and Althorp in Lincoln ; Ouden: in Holland and Oldland in Glouc., all tell the s tale ; whilst, without leaving England, we l Aldridge in Dev. and Staff. and Oldberrov Worcest., Aldcliff in Lancast. and Oldcleev Somerset, Aldham in Essex and Suff. and Old (cfr. Newham in Northumberland) in Lanc., &

As to " ham," few roots are more frequen English names of places. I have under my ∈ as I write, an unfinished MS. list of them which " ham " occurs nearly one hundred fifty times. It is, of course, the A.-S. *ham*, ⌐ to the Germ. *heim*, Go. *haims*, Lith. *kaimas*, κώμη, a village, a dwelling ; hence the nam that

"Spot of earth supremely blest,
A dearer, sweeter spot than all the rest,"

our own " home."   ALPHONSE ESTOCLE

CHESS (5th S. viii. 269, 316, 438, 495 ; ix. —I beg to assure MR. WARREN that I fully un stood the import of his proposed innovation. answer to a remark of mine he says : " On suggestion black is *not* 'in a position of ch mate' as long as white's knight covers his king from black's check." It is certain, I r that the situation does place black in *a positi* checkmate, although according to MR. WARE proposal the mate is not to take effect unti knight is liberated by the removal of the v king to another square. A position includin(conditions in question is now on a chessb before me, and my assertion may be tested by body who chooses to set up a similar one. I w send it in a diagram, were such a thing admis in " N. & Q." MR. WARREN again says : " posing black is so silly as to let his king where it is," &c. Now if black's best play move his king when the white knight interp as that would be the ordinary and natural n MR. WARREN, it is clear, at once knocks his suggestion to the ground ; but we are supp the black king to be in a state of checkmat that the unfortunate monarch must perforce re immovable. To carry on a *partie* in such cir stances would, I repeat, create an unspeal absurdity, and be a violation of one of the principles of the game of chess, which is to shield the king from harm. If Mr. Warren doubts the correctness of what I state, I would recommend him, when leisure permits, to visit any chess club in his neighbourhood, and propound the case to the leading players of that club, whose opinion, I entertain no doubt, will coincide with mine. Touching the definition of *checkmate*, I by no means coincide with Mr. Warren that he and I "say the same thing in different words."

HUGH A. KENNEDY.

Reading.

BOOKSELLERS (PLAY) IN ST. PAUL'S CHURCH-YARD (5th S. viii. 461, 489; ix. 9.)—I give you a list of a few plays from my collection printed in Paul's Churchyard, which may be of interest to your readers :—

Date.	Sign, &c.	Old Play.	Publisher.
1611.	Sold at his shop near the Great door of Pauls.	Golden Age. Thomas Heywood.	Printed by William Barringer.
1630.	Dwellinge at the Signe of the Crowne in Pauls Churchyard.	A Chaste Mayde in Cheapside. Thomas Middleton, Gent.	For Francis Constable.
1637.	White Lion in Pauls Churchyard.	Hannibal and Scipio. Thos. Nabbs.	Richard Oulton for Charles Greene.
1649.	Princes Arms in St. Pauls.	Tragedy of Thierry, by Beaumont and Fletcher.	Humphrey Moseley.
1649.	Same.	Woman Hater, by same.	Same.

I have no instance prior to 1649 of the addition of St. to Paul's.

| 1652. | At the Three Pigeons and at the Princes Arms in St. Pauls Churchyard. | The Cardinal, by James Shirley. | For Humphrey Robinson & Humphrey Moseley. |

I observe this as the first time I have met with the sign of the Three Pigeons, and the partnership between Robinson and Moseley in this play, although in the same year their joint names are omitted in the next one in this list.

| 1652. | Princes Arms in St. Pauls Churchyard. | The Changeling. T. Middleton and Rowley. | Humphrey Moseley. |

The Crowne, like the Crane, seems to have been an old publishing house. We find :—

| 1630. | At the Crowne in Pauls Churchyard. | The Crvell Brother. Dr. Avenant. | A. M., for John Waterson. |
| 1630. | Do. | The Renegado. P. Massinger. | |

Also published at this house, Drayton's *Muses Elyivm*.

This John Waterson was probably son of Simon Waterson, publisher of Robert Stafforde's description of the globe. JOHN WILLIAM JARVIS.

19, Charles Square, N.

MAC MAHON FAMILIES (5th S. ix. 7, 59.)—I think MR. BONE is not correct in stating that Arthur Augustin de Mac Mahon, who was Provost of the Collegiate Chapter of St. Peter, at Cassel, France, from 1682 to 1710, was "Archbishop of Armagh and Primate of Ireland, who had taken refuge in exile from the persecution at home." I cannot find that Arthur Augustin Mac Mahon was ever Primate of Ireland or Archbishop of Armagh, and at the time mentioned the see of Armagh was filled by other ecclesiastics. Oliver Plunkett was, A.D. 1669, promoted to the see by Pope Clement IX. He was arraigned on a charge of holding treasonable correspondence with the French Court. His accusers were Murphy, chorister of the R. C. Cathedral, Armagh, and certain friars and laymen. He was seized and sent to (the Dublin) Newgate, December 6, 1679, and thence in October, 1680, removed to London. "Here the first attempt to convict him failed, and the grand jury refused to find the bill against him; but additional evidence having been procured, he was in the end pronounced guilty of the crimes laid to his charge, and he was sentenced to be executed on July 1, 1681. He was taken on a sledge to Tyburn, and there executed in the presence of a great concourse. With his latest breath he called on Heaven to witness his innocence, and asserted that it was impossible for him to carry out the plans laid to his charge." Archbishop Plunkett was succeeded by Dominick Maguire, who was appointed in 1681 by Pope Innocent XI. Archbishop Maguire fled to France after the surrender of Limerick, and died in Paris in 1708. He was instrumental in preserving the valuable library of Trinity College, Dublin, during the troubles in the reign of James II. Archbishop Maguire was succeeded in 1708 by Dr. Hugh Mac Mahon. I should think this is the prelate described by MR. BONE as Bishop of Clogher ; he died in 1737. I have thus covered the period from 1669 to 1737, showing that the see of Armagh was filled by other prelates, and that Arthur Augustin Mac Mahon was not Archbishop of Armagh or Primate of Ireland. MR. BONE will find further information in King's *Primer of Irish Church History*, vol. iii. pp. 1242 *et seq.* JOSEPH FISHER.

Waterford.

I have just been reading the Presbyterian Dr. Killen's *Ecclesiastical History of Ireland*, in which I find a disagreement with MR. SHIRLEY as to the Mac Mahon archbishops. At chap. ii. p. 253, and notes, Dr. Killen says that Bryan or Bernard Mac Mahon was archbishop from 1738 to 1747, and was succeeded (according to Brenan) by Ross Mac Mahon. But MR. SHIRLEY says Ross died in 1740. I suppose he is right, as he quotes the tombstone ; but then what is Dr. Killen's mistake, or, rather, Brenan's ? It would seem as if Ross had

is bad enough.
CHARLES F. S. WARREN, M.A.
Bexhill.

[An account of the Mac Mahon family will be found in Mr. Sullivan's *New Ireland;* and a statement of the Marshal being descended from Brian Boru (!) is referred to in *The Secret History of the Fenian Conspiracy.*]

THE FIRST LOCAL NEWSPAPER (3rd S. i. 287, 351, 398, 435, 479 ; ii. 38, 92 ; 5th S. viii. 72, 140, 153, 179, 232, 330 ; ix. 12.)—In reply to MR. RAYNER and MR. WHITE at the last reference, I would refer to the first allusion to this subject (3rd S. i. 287), in which the oldest Nottingham paper is stated to be the *Journal*, 1710, the date of which is corrected in the same series (pp. 351, 435) to 1716. This is altogether wrong. The *Journal* was not started till 1757, and eventually bought up the *Courant*, which was amalgamated with it, and appropriated the *Courant's* date, 1716, as the first date of its own publication. On p. 479 of the same series the *Post* is stated to be the first paper by one correspondent, and the *Courant* by another. The subject seems to have dropped at this time (1862), and was not renewed till last year (5th S. viii. 72) by MR. RAYNER, when he gives the *Courant* as the first paper, and the date 1710. This I corrected (p. 331), and I may say that the date there given (1719) is evidently a printer's error, and I think my copy will be found to be 1716—a mistake I only noticed on my attention being drawn to it by MR. WHITE. And now for my authorities. Deering, in his *History of Nottingham*, says that " Mr. William Ayscough," who died in 1719, " is remarkable for having first established the art of printing in this town about the year 1710." The subject is elaborated in Blackner's *History* of the town, p. 96, wherein he states that, " about six years after the introduction of printing as above named, Mr. John Collyer commenced a newspaper called the *Nottingham Post*, which was continued till 1732 " (this date is no doubt 1723, as given in Bailey's *History*, and most likely a printer's error by transposition), " when Mr. George Ayscough (son of Wm.) began the *Nottingham Courant* in the house where his father commenced the business of printing."
There can be no doubt, I think, that the *Post* was the first paper, and not the *Courant*. By MR. WHITE's copy, July, 1711, he would make the first number of the *Post* appear to date early in 1710, as he states his copy to be 42 ; and I should doubt its having been printed weekly, more likely at uncertain intervals. I should be glad if

Norfolk.
Sparham Rectory, Norwich.
T. S. N.

" CHIC " (5th S. viii. 261, 316, 436, 458.) A Hebrew scholar, a friend of mine, says that t] word *chic* in Hebrew is applied to distinction speaking.
B.

KATHERINE RALEGH (5th S. viii. 309, 515.)- have always understood that one of the last i junctions of Walter Ralegh was : " Bury me wi my father and mother in Exeter Church."
CALCUTTENSIS.

CURIOUS NAMES (5th S. viii. 127, 237, 516.)- have before me " Pindari Carmina, recogno· W. Christ " (Lipsiæ, Teubner, 1873).
P. J. F. GANTILLON.

SAMUEL ROPER AND THE SEWALL FAMILY (; S. v. 28 ; ix. 56.)—I am greatly obliged to M POTTS for his reply to my query. The marria of Alderman Henry Sewall to Margaret " Gr; brook " is (I am informed by COL. CHESTI asserted in a pedigree drawn up by a member the Sewall family, who was born in 1652, and di in 1703.
Since my query appeared I have acquired good deal of information about the Sewalls a the Ropers. The Richard Sewall who marr Mary Dugdale was, I find, the younger son Henry and Margaret. MR. POTTS says his wil] " extant." I do not think this is so; but ι ministration of his effects was granted Jan. 1638-9, to Mary his widow. His eldest s· Richard Sewall, of Nuneaton, Gent., refers in will (proved at Lichfield in 1648) to his " aι Dugdale " ; and his uncle (Sir) Wm. Dugdale ε his " brother Dudley " (husband of his sister Ma were the executors. I find from Hamper's *Lifε Dugdale* that Wood, in stating that Samuel Ro and Richard Sewall were " cousins german," ι quoting the *ipsissima verba* of Dugdale himself Samuel Roper, as I stated in my query, was son of Thomas Roper by Anne, the daughter Alverey " Greisbrooke " (so he wrote his name) Middleton ; and there can be no doubt that M garet " Grazbrook " was her sister ; for Alve had a daughter of that name who is mentioned his will.
The Ropers were an old family at Heanor. : Irish Viscounts Baltinglass were of the sε family. Dr. Fuller (who had married for second wife the Hon. Mary Roper, daughter the first viscount) refers, in his *Church Histι*

to Samuel Roper as his kinsman—"that skilful antiquary and my respected kinsman Samuel Roper, of Lincoln's Inn." Samuel Roper died Sept. 2, 1658. His will, wherein he is called "Samuel Rooper, of Heanour, Esquire," is dated Aug. 31, 1658, and was proved in London on Oct. 14 following. The Roopers of Abbott's Ripton, co. Huntingdon, claim to be descended from him. See their pedigree* in Burke's *Landed Gentry*. H. S. G.

Dr. Pitcairn (5th S. viii. 498 ; ix. 55) may at any time have taken his religious duties too easily, but during the greater part of his professional life in Edinburgh, detesting as he did the revolutionary disestablishment of episcopacy in Scotland, it must have been an unusually heavy shower that drove him, cloakless probably, and certainly "umbrella-less," into a "kirk" at sermon time. His vigorous lines on the death of Viscount Dundee, *Ultime Scotorum*, &c. (indifferently Englished by Dryden), sufficiently express his sentiments :—

"Te moriente, novos accepit Scotia cives,
Accepitque *novos*, te moriente, *Deos*."
" New people fill the land now thou art gone,
New gods the temples, and new kings the throne."
Aberdeen. NORVAL CLYNE.

"THE WHOLE DUTY OF MAN" (5th S. viii. 389, 515.)—I flattered myself I had in my query guarded against the mistake into which MISS BOYD has fallen, namely, that I referred to three different editions of the same book, whereas I spoke of three distinct works, though under almost identical titles. MISS BOYD's note clearly refers to the earliest of the three, though giving it (from the *Literary Churchman*) an author which had never before been suggested. My inquiry (viii. 389) referred to the second book, which even on its title-page states itself to be a different work, and first published 1747, while the first edition of the earlier one was, I believe, in 1657. W. M. M.

The authorship of the *Whole Duty of Man* formed the subject of critical investigation in the *History of Meltham*, near Huddersfield, published by Messrs. Crossley of that town in 1866. This local historical work was reviewed in "N. & Q." of the following year. Two chapters, consisting of thirty-six pages, are devoted to, the inquiry, which is apparently exhausted. Among the different claimants enumerated the name of John Ischam is not included, nor can I find any account of him in biographical books to which I have referred. The only mention of him in Watt's *Bibliotheca Britannica* is the following : " Isham,

* In this pedigree Thomas Roper, of Heanor, is stated to have married Anne, daughter of "Aluzed Gresbroke.'.

John. A Daily Office for the Sick. Lond., 1694, 8vo." As he appears to be put forward as a new claimant to the authorship of the *Whole Duty of Man*, it is of importance to know what are the evidences in support thereof. LLALLAWG.

"PEUESY" (5th S. viii. 288, 356, 518.)—There need be no doubt about the words. T. F. R. has overlooked the horizontal stroke through the stem of the *p*, making "*separale*." The passage reads (the printed book before me) :—
" Item [presentant quod] pratum separale pertinens ad dictam ecclesiam valet per annum xlᵗ. Item [presentant quod] pastura separalis pertinens ad eandem valet per annum xxˢ. Item," &c.—*Nonarum Inq. Com. Wiltes*, p. 173.

JOHN A. C. VINCENT.

EDWARD HYDE, EARL OF CLARENDON (5th S. viii. 409 ; ix. 16.)—I am much obliged to MR. C. A. WARD for his reply ; but the question I asked related to the earl's family, not to himself. Could he further oblige me by pointing out where I could find the pedigree of the Hydes of Dinton, Wilts ? EDMUND RANDOLPH.
Ryde.

COPIES OF SHAKSPEARE, FOL. 1623 (5th S. vii. 247, 277, 455 ; viii. 78.)—A copy is in the small but valuable library of Sir William FitzHerbert, Bart., the Hall, West Farleigh, Kent.
W. M. M.

AUTHORS OF QUOTATIONS WANTED (5th S. ix. 69.)—
" I give him joy that 's awkward at a lie."
Young's *Night Thoughts*, night viii.
G. F. S. E.

Miscellaneous.

NOTES ON BOOKS, &c.

Lectures on Mediæval Church History ; being the Substance of Lectures delivered at Queen's College, London. By Richard Chenevix Trench, D.D., Archbishop of Dublin, Chancellor of the Order of St. Patrick. (Macmillan & Co.)

THOUGHTFUL and thought-inspiring in a very high degree, refined in expression and language, and sober in judgment, this volume cannot fail to be welcome to all students of history. The lectures of which it is composed do not, indeed, themselves constitute a history of the mediæval church, neither could they be used merely to "cram up" for an examination. Dates are only rarely introduced, and foot-notes, with references to authorities, are entirely absent. This is a peculiarity not to be recommended for general adoption, though no doubt, in the case of the volume before us, any information which the hearers of Abp. Trench may have sought was supplied orally in the lecture-room. The world at large, however, has not this advantage, and we should have been glad to have seen something more, which could not but have been instructive, of the process by which the writer arrived at his conclusions. In the case of a volume covering so large a field both of time and subjects, it is impossible to do more than hint at the many beauties which it contains. But at a moment

region of its birth, a region where it was not without its fitness, and has obtained a dominion not limited but universal.......The despotisms of the East are not accidents, but the legitimate outgrowths of the Koran; and *so long as this exists as the authoritative book, they too must exist with it*." Written years ago, this sentence is full of applicability to the present circumstances of Eastern Europe. With every desire to be just towards those who have attempted, though at the eleventh hour, to establish a constitutional form of government in the Ottoman Empire, we fear that the teaching of history is with Abp. Trench, and against the possibility of free parliaments under the rule of the "shadow of God upon earth." Those who value a loving appreciation of high qualities, combined with scrupulous fairness of historical judgment, will welcome the Archbishop of Dublin as a guide and companion through the intricate paths of mediæval church history.

Ancient History from the Monuments.—The History of Babylonia. By the late George Smith. Edited by Rev. A. H. Sayce. Assistant Professor of Comparative Philology, Oxford.— *The Greek Cities and Islands of Asia Minor.* By W. S. W. Vaux, M.A., F.R.S. (S. P. C. K. Depositories, London.)

THE two further instalments, now before us, of the series of volumes dedicated to telling the tale of ancient history by means of its monuments, give a very favourable view of the intelligent activity with which the Society for Promoting Christian Knowledge is fulfilling the useful task which it has set before itself. Nobody could be more competent than Mr. Sayce to take up the thread of the work left unfinished, though nearly ready for press, by the late Assyrian explorer, George Smith. Those who are not acquainted with Mr. Smith's larger works will find here a brief but clear *précis* of the historical results of his labours, to which Mr. Sayce has appended occasional notes, together with tables explaining the meaning of the names met with in Babylonian history, which will add greatly to the convenience of the student. In the *Cities and Islands of Asia Minor*, Mr. Vaux unfolds a story of more directly Western interest. bound up with indelible memories of Homeric song and Greek and Roman oratory, as well as with the early days of Christianity. The blue waves of the Ægean wash the shores of which he tells us, just as they did in the days of the blind old man of Chios. It is a kaleidoscope of history, in which Priam and Xerxes, Cicero and St. Paul, by turns attract our attention, and in which the latest results of the excavations of Mr. Wood and Dr. Schliemann.

IF Mr. Gladstone's article, "The Peace to Come," forms, from the present circumstances of the country, the most important feature of *The Nineteenth Century* for this month, it may be truly said that Mr. Knowles has supplied the public with other equally attractive and generally interesting matter. The articles on Ritualism, Spinoza, and Mrs. Siddons cannot fail to find many a reader.

The Cornhill Magazine opens with a new story, entitled "Within the Precincts." In "Over the Balkans with General Gourko" is a spirited account of the perils

writes:—"I am sure there is not a contribu 'N. & Q.' who will not mourn for our late Editor a father—a father both kindly and wise; as kindly he wisely suppressed as when he courteously acc the communications sent him. A week has not e since I wrote to thank him for the kindly receptioi which I, a stranger both to him and to fame, ha from him." It is a melancholy satisfaction to knou these words do but give expression to the sense caused to numerous contributors to "N. & Q." t death of their common friend.

Notices to Correspondents.

ON all communications should be written the nam address of the sender, not necessarily for publicatio as a guarantee of good faith.

P. T.—A note on Sir John Vanbrugh, by Cunningham, will be found in our Second Series, p. 7, and another at p. 116 of the same volume was buried in St. Stephen's, Walbrook.

W. A.—
"Where sprawl the saints of Verrio or Laguerr
Pope, *Moral Essays*, Ep. iv.

E. T. M. WALKER asks in what numbers of J he will find Thackeray's story of *The Ho(Diamond;* also, how many volumes of the poets, by Rev. G. Gilfillan, have been published.

W. F. C.—With regard to the Middle Hill Libr the late Sir Thomas Phillipps, apply to Mr. Fer Cheltenham.

M. P.—The fullest account is to be found in *A of the Last Century* (Bentley & Son, 1876).

M. E. C. WALCOTT (" The Old Soldier at St. Pa —Anticipated, 5th S. viii. 512.

L. C. R.—A short time since the *Builder* gave scription of the removal of the obelisk to Paris.

J. G.—W. GARNETT TAUNTON, 22, Charles S Brighton, will be glad to hear from you.

J. W. W. asks for the best English work on bai currency, and commerce in Austria and Hungary.

A LADY (" Cockades ") should refer to " N. & Q S. i. 126, 255; v. 81; vi. 94.

L. N.—We cannot undertake to answer q privately.

J. BORRAJO.—See Wheeler's *Noted Names of Fi(*

G. R.—Letter to Montrose forwarded.

F. RULE.—Forwarded to K. N.

N. M.—Letter forwarded to E. S.

NOTICE.

Editorial Communications should be addressed to Editor of 'Notes and Queries '"—Advertisement Business Letters to "The Publisher"—at the Offic Wellington Street, Strand, London, W.C.
We beg leave to state that we decline to returr munications which, for any reason, we do not print to this rule we can make no exception.

CONTENTS.— N° 215.

Notes on Books, &c.

Notes.

ARMS ON THE STALLS IN THE CHOIR OF THE CATHEDRAL AT HAARLEM.

(*Concluded from p. 62.**)

NORTH, OR EPISTLE, SIDE ; EAST TO WEST.

1. Quarterly, 1, Sa., a lion ramp. or (Brabant), impaling Burgundy ancient ; 2 and 3, Burgundy modern ; 4, Or, a lion ramp. gu. (Holland), impaling Burgundy ancient. Over all, Or, a lion ramp. sa. (Flanders). This is an inversion of the usual coat of the Dukes of Burgundy, which is Quarterly, 1 and 4, Burgundy modern ; 2, Burgundy ancient, impaling Brabant ; 3, Burgundy ancient, impaling Holland. See Vree, *De Seghelen der Graven van Vlaendren* (plate 33, *et seq.*), and his *Généalogie des Comtes de Flandre.*

2. Quarterly, 1 and 4, Gu., three mill-rinds arg. (Zuylen, *v.* No. 1, Gospel side) ; 2 and 3, Sa., a fess arg. (Borselen). Here the usual arrangement of the quarters is inverted.

3. Sa., a fess arg. (Borselen) : the escutcheon crowned with a count's coronet, and surrounded by the collar of the Golden Fleece.

4. The same in all respects as No. 3.

5. The same as Nos. 3 and 4, with the collar, but without the coronet. These four stalls bear

* The reader is requested to supply the omission of the tincture of the lozenges in the arms of Lalain (No. 4, p. 61 *ante*) ; it is argent. The third quarter of the arms of the Counts of Mannsfeld (No. 16, p. 62) is for Heldrungen, not "Heldrun gen," as printed.

---

the arms of members of the great family of Borselen, Marquesses of Veere, or Campvere, and Flushing. The head of the family was considered the " premier noble de Seeland " (Spener, *Op. Her.*, p. 661). Three of this family were Chevaliers of the Toison d'Or :—(1) Francis de Borselen, Stadtholder of Holland, fourth husband of Jacqueline, Countess of Holland, Hainault, Zealand, and Friesland, daughter of William of Bavaria, K.G., Count of Ostrevant (afterwards reigning Count of Holland, &c.), by Mary of Burgundy. Allusion has already been made to this marriage, of which the Duke of Burgundy so strongly disapproved that he arrested Borselen and compelled the princess to cede her states to him. Jacqueline died at Teilingen in 1436, after which event Philip of Burgundy released Borselen, gave him the county of Ostrevant, and invested him with the Order of the Golden Fleece. He died in 1470 (Chifflet, *Insig. Gent. Equit. Ord. Vell. Aur.*, No. xlii. ; Beltz, *Memorials of the Order of the Garter*, pp. 341-2). According to Chifflet his arms were those blazoned in No. 2 above, but with the quarters reversed, Borselen being in 1 and 4, Zuylen in 2 and 3. This is confirmed by the series of arms of the Knights of the Golden Fleece in Notre Dame at Bruges, and in the church of St. Bavon at Ghent. In both places I noted that the Zuylen quartering is put in 2 and 3, Borselen in 1 and 4.—(2) Henry de Borselen, Seigneur de Veere, Comte de Grandpré, was nominated Knight of the Golden Fleece at the same chapter, held at Ghent in 1445. He bore Borselen plain, without the Zuylen quartering (Chifflet, No. xliv.). In the series at Notre Dame at Bruges the arms are Borselen quartering Zuylen. At Ghent the Borselen arms alone appear.—(3) The last of the knights was Wolfart de Borselen, Comte de Grandpré, Seigneur de Veere. He was elected at Bruges in 1478, and bore the arms of Borselen alone (Chifflet, No. lxxix.). He died without male issue by his wife, Charlotte de Bourbon-Montpensier. Their daughter and heiress, Anna de Borselen, brought the marquessate of Veere and Flushing to her husband, Philip of Burgundy, Lord of Beveren, who was a son of " le grand bâtard de Bourgogne," Antoine, Comte de la Roche, Chevalier de la Toison d'Or, son of Duke Philippe le Bon. Philip of Beveren styles himself " Knight of the Golden Fleece, Councillor of the Order, Chamberlain of the King of the Romans (Maximilian of Austria, husband of Mary of Burgundy), and Governor of the Archduke (their son) ; Lieutenant-General of Artois, and Admiral by Sea." See his titles given at length from a charter, dated 1493, in which he pledges himself for the observance of the treaty of peace between Maximilian and Philip of France, drawn up at Senlis (Vree, *Généalogie des Comtes de Flandre*, tome ii. p. 392). On the extinction of the line of Philip, two gene-

of Frederick the Great (see Triers, *Einleitung zu der Wapen-künst*, p. 308).

6. Quarterly, 1, Or, a bend sinister gu. (Baer); 2 and 3, Or, chevronny gu. (Egmont); 4, Arg., two bars counter embattled gu. (Arkel). The escutcheon is surmounted by a count's coronet, and surrounded by the collar of the Golden Fleece. In base are two badges, each consisting of a pair of *broyes* closed or, the lines az. These are the inverted arms of the Counts of Egmond, of whom four were Knights of the Golden Fleece, the last being the famous but ill-fated Lamoral von Egmond, who was executed at Brussels during the regency of the Duke of Alva for Philip II. of Spain. The one here commemorated was probably John, Count of Egmond (Chifflet, No. cxlix.), one of the twenty new knights created by Charles V. at his extension of the order. The order had previously been conferred on his progenitor, Jean, Count of Egmond and Lord of Baer, in 1491, in the blazon of whose arms Chifflet (No. ci.) correctly places Egmond in the first and fourth quarters, Baer (a bend *dexter*) in the second, and Arkel in the fourth. The reason of the inversion in the present instance will be given below.

7. Quarterly, 1 and 4, Az., a fess or (Leide); 2 and 3, Gu., three crescents arg. (Wassenaer). The arms are surrounded by the collar of the Golden Fleece; around it are four crescents arg., the two in chief placed upon a golden letter J. These are the arms and badges of Jean, Seigneur de Wassenaer, Viscount of Leyden, created Knight of the Golden Fleece at the same time as No. 6 above. As given by Chifflet (*Insig. Gent. Equit. Vell. Aur.*, No. cxlvi.) the arms correspond in arrangement with those already described in No. 5 on the Gospel side (*ante*, p. 61), Wassenaer being in the first and fourth quarters. Here, consequently, the arrangement is inverted.

8. A lozenge-shaped shield of Brederode and Valkenberg (see No. 3 on the Gospel side), impaling Or, a lion ramp. (contourné) gu. Around and above the shield are the flames, while the boar's head badges are arranged in base, as in No. 3 of the Gospel side, and the well-known Burgundian badge of the saltire-raguly also appears among the flames.

9. Quarterly, 1 and 4, Az., three fleurs-de-lis or, over all a bend sin. gu. (Bourbon); 2 and 3, as No. 3 on the Gospel side, but with the quarterings in reversed order. Over all, Borselen. This coat, of which, as in the instances above, the placed in the first and fourth quarters, Bourbon-Montpensier in the second and third, and Borselen over the whole (see Vree, *Généalogie des Comtes de Flandre*, plates 126, 127), I am inclined to suspect that in the second and third quarters the reference should be rather to No. 2 than to No. 3. I may have erred in the reference, though my pencil note is quite distinct.

10. Brederode only; on the shoulder of the lion a small escutcheon of the same (for Holland?), viz. Or, a lion ramp. gu.

11. Arg., two chevrons az. The shield is ensigned with a count's coronet, but I am unable to say what family it indicates.

12. Quarterly, 1 and 4, Or, a lion ramp. gu., a label azure for *brisure*: see No. 9 on the Gospel side (Brederode); 2 and 3, Arg., three zuilen gu. (Zuylen).

13. Quarterly, 1 and 4, Or, a lion ramp. sa. (Flanders?); 2 and 3, Arg., fretty sa.; on a chief or three *canettes*, or martlets, of the second (...?). The second and third quarters (which in reality are probably intended for the first and second of the shield, as will be presently explained) seem to be those of the family of D'Estrees.

14. Egmond, &c. (as No. 6 above).

15. Brederode (Or, a lion ramp. gu.); on the shoulder of the lion a small escutcheon of Mark: Or, a fess chequy gu. and arg.

16. Quarterly, 1 and 4, Arg., a mill-rind gu., in base a rose of the second (....?); 2 and 3, Or, a cross vert (....? perhaps for the Burgundian family of St. Croix, which bore the same). A pastoral staff is placed in pale behind, and an episcopal hat above the shield (see my note on No. 14, Gospel side).

This concludes a series which I think is of considerable interest and importance. I have only to remark that that curious inversion of the quarters and of the position of the charges in several of the coats on the Epistle side (see Nos. 1, 2, 6, 7, 8, 9), which cannot fail to strike any one who has a decent knowledge of continental heraldry, arose simply from the ancient custom—of which we find analogous examples at Dijon and elsewhere—of making the position of the quarterings, charges, and crests depend upon that of the high altar of the church. Thus, in several of the above instances, the quarterings which were ordinarily borne in the first and fourth places of the shield are transferred to the second and third, because on the north, or Epistle, side the second place was nearer to the high altar than the first, and was therefore, for the time being, the more honourable. This is how we come to find here the "repeated" coat of a family borne in the second and third, rather than in the usual first and fourth places. This again is how the bend of Baer becomes converted into a bend sinister in the shield of Egmond. The bend of Bourbon-Montpensier undergoes a similar change, and in No. 8 the lion is *contourné*. I have already noticed in "N. & Q." (4ᵗʰ S. xii. 444; 5ᵗʰ S. i. 155) that at Dijon, on the Epistle side of the choir, all the helmets and crests of the Knights of the Golden Fleece were turned to the sinister, in order that they might look towards the high altar, and that the old stall plates of the Knights of the Garter in St. George's Chapel at Windsor show that the same custom obtained in England also.

JOHN WOODWARD, F.S.A. Scot.

Montrose.

SHAKSPEARIANA.

THE OBELI OF THE GLOBE EDITION IN "HAMLET."—Act i. sc. 1, ll. 117, 118 :—

"†As stars with trains of fire and dews of blood,
Disasters in the sun."

Any one who observes the similarity in the commencement of the two lines—

"As stars—
Disasters—"

must see how very easily a printer's error may have arisen from transposition. I read :—

"Disasters from the sun—as dews of blood,
And stars with trains of fire."

Act i. sc. 3, ll. 72-74 :—

"For the apparel oft proclaims the man,
And they in France of the best rank and station
†Are of a most select and generous chief in that."

Punctuate l. 74 thus :—

"Are, of a most, select and generous, chief in that."

By "of a most" I understand "for the most part." Polonius says that in France men of rank in general show fine taste, and are unsparing of expense, chiefly in the matter of dress.

Act i. sc. 4, ll. 36-38 :—

"The dram of †eale
Doth all the noble substance †of a doubt
To his own scandal."

The conjecture is surely reasonable that "eale" is a misprint for "evil." That granted, the second line may be restored without adding to or taking from it a single letter :—

"The dram of evil ·
Doth o' the noble substance fall a doubt
To his own scandal."

"Fall" in the sense of "let fall" we find in the *Comedy of Errors*, Act ii. sc. 2 :—

"As easy mayst thou fall
A drop of water in the breaking gulf";

and in *Antony and Cleopatra*, Act iii. sc. 2 :—

"Fall not a tear."

As illustrative of the meaning of the passage, compare Ecclesiastes x. 1 :—

"Dead flies cause the ointment of the apothecary to send forth a stinking savour : so doth a little folly him that is in reputation for wisdom and honour."

Act iii. sc. 4, ll. 161-165 :—

"That monster, custom, who all sense doth eat,
†Of habits devil, is angel yet in this,
That to the use of actions fair and good
He likewise gives a frock or livery,
That aptly is put on."

The meaning seems to be—That monster custom, who destroys the sense of shame, though by habit a devil, is yet an angel in this, &c. The word *habit* is used in its two senses of "wont" and "dress." Custom, which usually appears in garb a devil, is yet an angel in this respect, that his wardrobe also affords for the use of actions fair and good a suitable frock or livery.

Act iii. sc. 4, ll. 168, 169 :—

"For use almost can change the stamp of nature,
†And either......the devil, or throw him out."

Read :—

"And tether the devil, or throw him out."

As an unruly beast he must either be confined or expelled.

Act iv. sc. 1, ll. 38-44 :—

"Come, Gertrude, we'll call up our wisest friends;
And let them know, both what we mean to do,
†And what's untimely done......."

There may be no lacuna here, but merely a broken line, of which there are so many in *Hamlet*. If we read "both" in l. 39 as a pronoun, the whole passage may be made intelligible, with no change but in punctuation :—

"Come, Gertrude, we'll call up our wisest friends;
And let them know, both (of us), what we mean to do :
And what's untimely done
(Whose whisper o'er the world's diameter,
As level as the cannon to his blank,
Transports his poisoned shot) may miss our name,
And hit the woundless air."

In order to prevent suspicion that any mischief was intended to Hamlet, the King was anxious it should be known that Hamlet's mother as well as he saw the propriety of his temporary exile : hence the force of "both." Being followed by "and," it has not unnaturally been mistaken for a conjunction ; but in Act ii. sc. 2, l. 29, we find "both" followed by "and," where "both" is evidently a pronoun. Speaking for Rosencrantz and himself, Guildenstern says :—

"We both obey, and here give up ourselves."

Act v. sc. 1, l. 68 :—

"Go, get thee to †Yaughan : fetch me a stoup of liquor."

Yaughan is probably the name of a vintner, not of a place.

Act v. sc. 2, l. 118 :—

"I know to divide him inventorially would dizzy the arithmetic of memory, †and yet but yaw neither, in respect of his quick sail."

in his plainest mood, Laertes was beyond his comprehension.

Act v. sc. 2, ll. 196-202 :—

"Thus has he—and many more of the same bevy that I know the drossy age dotes on—only got the tune of the time and outward habit of encounter ; a kind of yesty collection, which carries them through and through the most †fond and winnowed opinions ; and do but blow them to their trial, the bubbles are out."

I believe Warburton is right in substituting "fanned" for "fond." The men of whom Osric was a specimen had "got the tune of the time and outward habit of encounter"—could go the round of courtly observances ; they were possessed of "a kind of yesty (frothy) collection" of words, "which carried them through and through the most fanned and winnowed opinions"—which served for the interchange of conventional commonplaces ; "but blow them to their trial, the bubbles are out"—test their knowledge of aught beyond those, and their utter ignorance was manifested. R. M. SPENCE, M.A.
Manse of Arbuthnott, N.B.

"MACBETH," II. 3.—

"Porter.......Who's there, i' the name of Beelzebub? Here's a farmer [&c.]......Knock, knock ! Who's there in the other devil's name?"

I do not remember having seen any explanation as to who the "other devil" may have been ; but I think it may be found in the following extract from James I.'s Dæmonologie :—

"The knauerie of that same deuil ; who as hee illudes [=deludes] the Necromancers with innumerable feyned names for him and his angels, as in special, making Sathan, Beelzebub, and Lucifer to be three sundry spirites, where we finde by diuers names giuen to the Prince of all the rebelling angels by the Scripture.......And the last, to wit, Lucifer, is but by allegorie taken from the day Starre (so named in diuers places of the Scriptures) because of his excellencie (I meane the Prince of them) in his creation before his fall. Euen so I say he deceaues the Witches, by attributing to himselfe diuers names : as if euery diuers shape that he transformes himselfe in, were a diuers kinde of spirit."
—Book iii. ch. v. (p. 76, first ed.).

I neither say nor mean that the Porter was a witch, but that which was a witch-belief was doubtless a popular belief. B. NICHOLSON.

"PEERETH."—What is the meaning of the word peereth in

"As the sun breaks through the darkest clouds
So honour peereth in the meanest habit" ?
Taming of the Shrew, iv. 3.

Does it mean simply (as its etymology from paroir might show) "appeareth," or is it from par, a

gracefully inspired son of a grocery and whiske dealer in Dublin ; Reboul was a working baker i Nismes. The Irish bard was born in 1779 ; Jea Reboul in 1796. The former died in 1852 ; the Frenc child of song in 1864. In the year 1816, whe Moore was thirty-seven years of age, and Rebou only twenty, the Irishman published the first c his Sacred Songs. The dedication to the poet friend Dalton is dated May, 1816, and the song were mostly written in the preceding year. In th first number is the following song, for which Si John Stevenson furnished the music :—

"This world is all a fleeting show,
For man's illusion given ;
The smiles of joy, the tears of woe,
Deceitful shine, deceitful flow ;
There's nothing true but Heaven.

And false the light on glory's plume
As fading hues of even ;
And love, and hope, and beauty's bloom
Are blossoms gathered from the tomb ;
There's nothing bright but Heaven.

Poor wanderers of a stormy day,
From wave to wave we're driven ;
And fancy's flash and reason's ray
Serve but to light the troubled way ;
There's nothing calm but Heaven."

The Sacred Songs were soon after published in Paris. They are also included in an edition o Moore's Works, in 4 vols., "printed by Fain," and sold by Galignani in 1821. A year before M Thierry wrote an essay on the Melodies, and their author, Moore, became well known and highly appreciated in France. In 1829 Madame Belloc published a translation of the Melodies; and the Sacred Songs must at least have been known to her. About this time Reboul is said by a writer in the Irish Monthly to have written a sacred song called "Soupir vers le Ciel," and which runs thus :—

"Tout n'est qu'images fugitives,
Coupe d'amertume ou de miel,
Chansons joyeuses ou plaintives
Abusent des lèvres fictives :
Il n'est rien de vrai que le ciel.

Tout soleil naît, s'élève, et tombe,
Tout trône est artificiel.
La plus haute gloire succombe ;
Tout s'épanouit pour la tombe,
Et rien n'est brillant que le ciel.

Navigateur d'un jour d'orage,
Jouet des vagues, le mortel,
Repoussé de chaque rivage,
Ne voit qu'écueil sur son passage,
Et rien n'est calme que le ciel."

The above poor version of Moore's song is in the Œuvres de Jean Reboul, with no indication that it is a translation. The writer adds that "it is very unlikely that a Nismes baker should know English, especially forty or fifty years ago." It is more than sixty years since Moore published the *Songs*, and Reboul may have seen some prose translation of them, such as there used to be of the *Melodies*, in French literary papers. The imperfect lines claimed by Reboul read very like a version by an educated Englishman, who, with all his ability, could catch neither the grace of the original nor the charm of the French ballad lyre.   D. N.

A QUAKER SPELLING REFORM.—Several of the early Quakers tried their hands at the barbarous amusement which some people pleasantly call spelling reform. That curious book, "*The Arrainment of Christendom*, Printed in Europ, 1664," is printed entirely in a new spelling. The following is a portion of the prefatory notice :—

"The Corrector to the Reader, concerning the Orthografy or Spel-ing herrin us'd.

"Reader,—Wonder not to see me Spel, as thy self dayly speakest, & hearest others sound words. I hav heer indevored to spel as we. speak, for the advantag' sâk which I know wil therby ensù if practised, I., To Children in learning to read, whos tender capacitys âr over charged, memorys burthened and dul'd with harsh spel-ing, by which they âr kept longer in learning.

"II., To Men and Women in wryting, who thô they hav learnd to read wel enuf, when they com-to wryt, âr at a los how to spel aryt as its cal-ed.

"III., To strangers in learning English, who âr discoraged & almost put out of hôps of ever learning to speak, read & wryt good English. And al this only throuh the present harsh manner of spel-ing, scars to be comprysd in Rûls, which is the only means strangers abroad hav for learning to speak, & for al, thô in England, to read & wryt trû English. Besyds the multitùds of superfluos Letters in the present Speling, al which is amended & avoyded by spel-ing & wryting simply as we speak: As no les than 5. in the word Righteousness (as thus commonly spelt) âr avoyded by speling it thus, *Ryteosnes*, & no les than 6. letters in the word. *Though*, spelt thus, *Thô*. Which do as perfectly sound the words as the other, tho ny twys so many letters. Wherfor I hav thus don, 1., Chiefly for the benefit of strangers, in al words in which the letter (i) is sounded as (y), which no other Nation but ours doth, I hav ûs'd (y). The old English way, throuh chang' of which, into (i) such confusion is happend in sounding that letter somtyms ôn way, as in King, Thing, &c., and somtyms another way, as in Kind, Mind, Child, &c., that a stranger cannot by Rûls be tauht when to sound it as in the former words softly, or as in the lat-er words fully as (y). Which being spelt with (y)., Kynd, Chyld, &c., is remedied.

"2. The letter (e) wher it is mût and maketh not a syllabl, but only the former syllabl long, I hav left out: strangers commonly in that câs pronouncing môr syllabls than ther âr, as ti-me for time, lo-ve for love, ti-mes for times, &c. Which being writ-en tym, lov, tyms, &c., ther ìs but ôn syllabl for them to sound. And how is it pos. sibl otherwys to giv certain Rûls when to sound the (e) and when not; seing in the word plases; it must, and in times, it must not be sounded? And for compensing the us of the (e) viz. of distinguish a short from a long syllabl, I hav oft ûs'd the Accents, (ˊ) or (ˋ). Which, doth again distinguish (as e did) betwixt words of dyvers signifi.

cations, thô of the sâm letters. As mad from made thus, mâd. hat from hate thus, hât. on from one thus, ôn. us from use thus, ûs. Which yet âr sufficiently distinguish'd by the sens."

George Fox appears to have spelled like a Leicestershire peasant.   C. ELLIOT BROWNE.

THE "MARSEILLAISE."—The following, from the *Times* of Feb. 1, 2, and 4, should find a corner in "N. & Q.":—

"Sir,—The late Baron de Bunsen used to assert that the 'Marseillaise' was an old South German, perhaps Aleatian, air adapted by Rouget d'Isle on the reception of the Marseilles regiment at Strasburg, whence it spread like wild-fire throughout France. I should be glad if this supposition could be fairly examined. Having the volume of Rouget de l'Isle's compositions before me, I am struck by the immense superiority of this melody over all the rest, the only one that shows anything of a similar vigour being the song of the fabulous destruction of the 'Vengeur,' the chorus of which, 'Mourons pour la patrie,' was attached to the 'Parisienne' of 1830.

"Were this origin authenticated, the French might find some consolation in the knowledge that 'God Save the King' was composed by Lully, and first produced on the visit of Louis XIV. and Madame de Maintenon to the convent of the Desmoiselles de St. Cyr. Some years after it was happily and unscrupulously appropriated by Dr. John Bull, organist of St. Paul's.—I am, Sir, yours obediently,   HOUGHTON."

"Sir,—The discovery that Rouget de Lisle, when composing the music of the 'Marseillaise,' at Strasburg, where he was stationed as a French officer in 1792, was —consciously or unconsciously—under the charm. of some reminiscences of a German *Volkslied*, belongs to Dr. F. K. Meyer, for many years the friend and secretary of Baron Bunsen, and for a time German librarian to the Prince Consort. Lord Houghton will find. the arguments in support of this theory and the music of the German song in a little pamphlet, s.l.e.a., *Zwanzig Vaterländische Gedichte, nebst einem Aufsatz über den Ursprung der Marseillaise, von F. K. M.*—Your obedient servant, "M. M."

"Lord Houghton says that 'God Save the King' was composed by Lully, first produced on the visit of Louis XIV. and Madame de Maintenon to the convent of St. Cyr, and some years after 'happily and unscrupulously appropriated' by Dr. John Bull, organist of St. Paul's. I am sorry to destroy so fair and coherent an edifice ; but St. Cyr was founded in 1686, while Bull was buried at Antwerp, March 15, 1628. Bull was organist of the Chapel Royal and Gresham Professor, but there is no trace of his having been organist of St. Paul's. The history of 'God Save the King' is curiously meagre and obscure ; but I believe I am right in saying that there is nothing to give Lully, and very little to give Dr. John Bull, any share in its composition.   G. GROVE."

H. Y.

[See MR. CHAPPELL's note, 5ᵗʰ S. viii. 209.]

"UXORICIDE."—The *Chicago Tribune* of Sept. 6, 1877, records a "probable murder" arising from jealousy. The details need not be given of what the reporter considers "may prove an *uxoricide*." This is surely one of the latest additions to the "American" language. It is perhaps with a view to the prevention of wife-murder that this terrific word has been invented.   WILLIAM E. A. AXON.

Stockport.

LATIN AS AN OFFICIAL LANGUAGE IN THE NINETEENTH CENTURY.—In an official document now before me I read :—

" Deeds of gift, as written and passed in the offices of the Great Seal and Quarter Seal of Scotland, are in Latin, being literal translations of the terms of the royal warrants upon which they proceed, and it has therefore been thought better to give the terms of the warrants."

This is an instance of Latin being in actual use as a language at the present day. It would be interesting to know of other cases in this country in which Latin is the compulsory orthodox language employed. H. Y. N.

Queries.

[We must request correspondents desiring information on family matters of only private interest, to affix their names and addresses to their queries, in order that the answers may be addressed to them direct.]

THE PRICES OF CORN, LABOUR, AND PRODUCE, HOME AND FOREIGN, BETWEEN 1401 AND 1582.— I shall be under great obligations to any reader of " N. & Q." who may be able and willing to give me any information, from original documents in his possession, as to prices of corn, labour, and produce, home and foreign, between 1401 and 1582. I have already a large mass of information for this period of English history, but the statistics in my possession are broken and unequal. I am led to believe that documents containing such information may be in the hands of private gentlemen ; for I obtained some time ago some very valuable figures from the late Mr. Walbran, who possessed documents of Fountains Abbey for the fifteenth century, and I have consulted some purchases made from the private collection of a Kentish antiquary, and now in the British Museum, for the parish of Sutton at Hone during the same period. I am not inquiring for documents in public collections.
JAMES E. THOROLD ROGERS.
8, Beaumont Street, Oxford.

" IT IS EASIER FOR A CAMEL," &c.—It may have occurred to many of your readers, as it has to me, that the phrase, repeated by three of the evangelists in the New Testament, " It is easier for a camel to go through the eye of a needle, than for a rich man to enter into the kingdom of God," is not only hyperbolical, but also wanting in that propriety which usually characterizes the metaphors employed by Jesus Christ in his parables. Now I can distinctly remember read-

door or gate of which was only opened for the sage of camels, carriages, &c.), was called ' needle's eye," and it struck me at once that if metaphorical name for a wicket was known Palestine at the time of our Saviour's preacl the propriety of the metaphor would be un stood by all his hearers, while the difficulty of camel's passage, that is, the moral of the parr remained the same. Unfortunately I omitte follow the good advice contained in your me and I did not " make a note of it," and I l now forgotten the name of the book in whit found it. My present object is to inquire whe any of your travelled or learned contributors confirm the existence of such an appellation f small door or wicket in any Eastern country must admit that, although I have since res some time in Persia, and occupied myself ' Oriental literature, I have not been able to con from my own experience the accuracy of the st ment above referred to. My thoughts have, l ever, been lately directed to a subject which I almost forgotten than a metaphorical ph precisely similar in another country and langu On reference to the Purgatorio of Dante, cant verse 16, there occurs the following line : " noi fossimo fuor di quella cruna," the poet and conductor Virgil having just been creeping thro a " narrow passage," termed here a " cruna," " the eye of a needle," and is so properly explai by the Italian commentator, " la fenditura quella via, angusta come la cruna d'un ago." scholars know how numerous are the instance: an apt metaphorical expression being found many different peoples and languages, and I h some one of your readers will be able to conl the sense herein suggested for the " needle's e in the parable. CH. A. MURRAY
Cannes.

DANA.—What is the origin of this name, wl is so well known as a literary one in the Stat In England we have it thus :—towards the of the late century the Hon. Helen Kinna daughter of the sixth Lord Kinnaird, married Rev. Edmond Dana, Vicar of Uttoxeter.
HYDE CLARKE

" CLOISTER PEALING."—Can any old Wy hamist explain the origin at Winchester of curious custom of " cloister pealing"? At particular time of the year, called cloister ti because anciently the boys learned their less in the college cloisters during the summer mon! the juniors assailed the prefects with a series satirical lampoons, attacking them on every possi point—their personal appearance, extraction, old school scandals, &c., and with complete impunity. The twentieth part of the impertinences uttered would, at other times, have brought the direst consequences on the offenders, but at this time (it usually lasted for perhaps twenty minutes for three or four days) it was allowed to pass unnoticed.

J. R. B.

NAME OF ARTIST WANTED.—On a fan in my possession is a very beautiful classical composition, drawn delicately in sepia, and in the margin is the inscription, "Eques D. Nicolaus Capulus calamo delineavit." Can any of your readers help me to discover the artist? The work is probably of the beginning of the last century. TEUCER.

BADGES.—I have before me some badges in modern painted glass which simulate the Tudor style. They are all surmounted by the crown imperial, and are as follows : 1. Gu., planta-genista ppr. ; 2. Gu., a portcullis or ; 3. Az., a fleur-de-lis or ; 4. Az., a rose az. and gu. ; 5. Gu., on a tower or an owl az. ; 6. Gu., a tree eradicated, leaves ppr., trunk and branches az., roots or.

No. 1 is, of course, the name-giving badge of our Plantagenet kings ; 2, 3, and 4 were adopted by Henry VII. ; but what do 5 and 6 profess to represent?—for I fancy they may have been copied from fifteenth century examples. It has occurred to me that 6 may be intended for the hawthorn bush of Bosworth Field—it will not do for the tree root of Edward III.—and that 5 may have been a badge assumed by Henry VII. as Earl of Richmond. The arms of the town of Richmond are given by Guillim thus : " Gu., an inner border arg., over all a bend ermin"; but on the elaborate cover of Baines's *Yorkshire Past and Present* the bearings of the place are represented as being "Gu., an owl ar., over all a bend ermine." What has the owl to do with Richmond? If anything, my view of badge 5 may be confirmed.

ST. SWITHIN.

RUDSTONE OBELISK.—In the churchyard of Rudstone, near Bridlington, in Yorkshire, there is, or was, a very remarkable monolith, somewhat similar in character to the stones at Burrowbridge, and probably, like them, brought from a quarry some miles distant. In Cox's *Magna Britannia*, 1731, vi. 529, it is described as " an obelisk of Ragg or Milstone grit, standing in the churchyard, and of a very great height." In the *Universal Magazine* for March, 1782, there is an account of this stone and an engraving of it, from which it would appear that the stone is about three feet by seven feet, and fifty feet high ; half being buried in the ground and half above it. This length of the stone is said to be given on the authority of " experiments" made by Sir William Strickland, but the nature of these experiments is not indi-

cated. Is the real size of this stone accurately known? and is there any quarry from which it might have been brought nearer to Rudstone than that at Ilkley, from whence it has been supposed that the Burrowbridge monoliths were brought? According to Camden's *Britannia* (Gibson's edit., 1722, ii. 874), the distance from Ilkley to Burrowbridge is about sixteen miles ; but the distance from Ilkley to Rudstone is probably not much under fifty miles. EDWARD SOLLY.

THE DIAMOND NECKLACE OF MARIE ANTOINETTE.—I have read in some memoirs that (contrary to the received idea that the necklace was broken up) it was seen, years afterwards, on the neck of a Russian lady—I think, at any rate, in Russia. The lady who wore it was connected by marriage with some of the most intimate friends of Marie Antoinette. Is there any foundation for such a story, or what can have given rise to it ? K. H. B.

Naples.

MILTON QUERIES : (3) "IL PENSEROSO."—What is the meaning of the line?—

" And the mute Silence hist along."

The context is almost too well known to require quoting. The poet invokes Melancholy :—

" First and chiefest with thee bring
Him that soars on golden wing,
Guiding the fiery-wheelèd throne,
The cherub Contemplation,
And the mute Silence hist along.
'Less Philomel will deign a song."

" 'Less " is, of course, "unless"; but "hist along," what is that? One annotator kindly informs us that "hist" is hushed, the same as whist." But " hushed along " is to me just as incomprehensible as "hist along." What part of speech is "hist" in this passage ? J. DIXON.

ST. PAUL'S SCHOOL.—Is there any history of St. Paul's School containing biographic notices of the scholars educated there ?—any work of a similar kind to Rev. H. B. Wilson's *History of Merchant Taylors' School*, or the *Admission Register of the Manchester School*, edited by Rev. J. F. Smith ? R. INGLIS.

" THE PALACE OF TRUTH."—What is the name of the French piece from which Mr. Gilbert's *Palace of Truth* is derived or adapted ? H. J. S.

JAMES BRUCE.—In Gough's *Camden's Britannia*, ii. 112, under head of " Cley, Norfolk," I find the following extraordinary statement. Can any of your readers throw light upon it ?—

" The fishermen of this place accidentally falling in with James, son and heir of *Robert Bruce*, King of Scotland, who was going to France for education, with a bishop and the Earl of Orkney, made them prisoners, and sent them to Henry IV., who lodged them in the

sea-sickness."
It is clear this James was not the son of King
Robert Bruce. Who was he? W. B...A.

REVELATION, CH. XIII.—I have seen it lately
suggested in print (though I regret to say I did
not make a note of it) that, in the Chaldee or
Aramaic language, the letters which express the
number of the beast (Rev. xiii.) form the name
Nero. I should feel greatly obliged to any of
your correspondents acquainted with those languages who would tell me if there is any truth in
this. J. C. M.

HERALDRY.—Is either of the following coats
of arms borne by any English family of the name
of Bolton?—Argent, on a chevron gules, three
lions passant gardant of the first; or, Argent, on
a bend gules, between two fleurs-de-lis azure,
three lions' heads or. Crest in both cases, "A
stag's head pierced through the nose with an
arrow or." SENEX.

BACON'S ESSAY "OF A KING."—Bacon's *Essays*
(Glasgow, Urie, 1752) has the fourteenth essay
entitled "Of a King." This essay does not appear
in Bohn's Standard Library edition. Why has it
been suppressed? M. N. G.

"NOTES OF A RECRUITING OFFICER."—I remember to have read in some magazine, I believe
about the year 1861, an article entitled "Notes of
a Recruiting Officer." It contained statistics of
the respective average height, breadth of chest,
&c., of the English, Irish, and Scotch members of
the British army. Having some present necessity
for referring to this, can any one oblige me with
the name and date of the magazine in question?
H. N.

AUTHORS OF BOOKS WANTED.—
The Tutor of Truth.—My copy has no date, but it
must have been published before 1790. M. N. G.

AUTHORS OF QUOTATIONS WANTED.—
The following verses, written on a slip of paper, I
found between the leaves of a novel recently purchased
from a second-hand bookseller. Could any obliging cor-
respondent furnish me with the name of the author of
these lines?—
"*In Praise of Tobacco.*
Mighty aroma, thine the power
To ripen to the full-blown flower, &c.
The Smoker.
His manner easy, person neat,
Whilst modest pride doth hold her seat, &c."
Translated from the French by T. B."
G. PERRATT.
"In the glow of thy splendour
Descend from above,
O beautiful mother
Of beautiful love!" H. P. ROCHE.

(U W. VIII. 420., IXI 10.)
I feel honoured by the critiques of two gentle
men so well known in the philological world a
MR. H. WEDGWOOD and MR. SMYTHE PALMER
Like Cassius, I am "always glad to learn of nobl
men." I ask, however, space for a few words in
reply.
In writing my paper I had not, as my critic
suppose, overlooked the article in the *Promptorium*
Parvulorum. I had before me both that and
MR. WEDGWOOD'S notice in his *Dictionary*; but
I thought then, and still think, that the reference
is irrelevant.
The two words *rubble* and *rubbish*, which are
continually confounded, have really nothing to d
with each other. Their origin is different, and
their meaning entirely separate.
I claim to know something about *rubble*, having
in years gone by, had largely to do with rubble
constructions. I never met with a mason's
labourer who did not perfectly understand the
essential difference between the one and the other
Rubble is thus described by Gwilt in his *En
cyclopædia of Architecture:* "A wall which consists of unhewn stone is called a rubble wall
whether mortar is used or not. The uncoursed
rubble wall is formed by laying the stones in the
wall as they come to hand, without gauging o
sorting." It is the *opus incertum* of Vitruvius
described in the eighth chapter of the second
book of his work on architecture. The term
rubble is also applied to the stone chippings mixed
with mortar used in Roman and mediæval buildings to fill in the core of a thick wall. This is
undoubtedly the sense of the word *robows* in the
Promptorium. It is translated *petrosa, petro,* and
made equivalent to *coldyr* and to *schuldere,* both
of which are similarly translated by *petrosa*
Petro is correctly rendered by Mr. Way as the
chippings of stone. So in the *Catholicon,* "Pe
trones sunt particule que abscinduntur de petris."
In the note appended, reference is made to a
document of 20 Edw. IV. (1480) for payment fo
"cariage away of a grete loode of *robeux* that wa
left in the strete after the reparacyone made upon
a hous," &c. The *robeux* here may be fairly in
ferred to correspond with the *robows* in the tex
above. Words of French derivation ending in
eau or *eu* commonly interchange their final syl
lable into *el,* as Beau-voir = Bel-voir; Chapeau
Chapel-lerie, &c. It would not be therefore sur
prising to find *robow* altered to *robel* or *rubbel.*
By the courtesy of a fair correspondent o
"N. & Q." I have been favoured with some ex
tracts from the parochial accounts of the church o
St. Michael extra Portam at Bath. The date i
not given, but from the style they are evidentl

of the sixteenth century. One item is for a sum paid "pro equo ad cariendum *rubyll*"; another "pro ablacione de *rubyll* coram campanile." There are other entries of the same kind, all evidently connected with repairs or building, as items are inserted of payments " hominibus laborantibus ad lapifodium."

So far as my researches go, I can find no instance of *rubble* having any other meaning than that of undressed stone fragments or chippings. The derivation suggested by Mr. WEDGWOOD from French *repous* is a very probable one. The term is now limited, according to Littré, to a mixture of mortar and chippings in the core of a wall, the word *moellon* being used as the equivalent to our *rubble*. The employment of *moellon*, however, cannot be traced further back than the end of the sixteenth century, some time before which the word *robows* had been introduced into English.

I maintain, therefore, that *rubble* cannot, under any circumstances, be identified with *rubbish*. Now a few words as to *rubbish*. Mr. Way's note in the *Promptorium*, under " Robows," says that " in later times the word was written *rubbrysshe*," on which he quotes from Horman's *Vulgaria*, "Battz and great *rubbrysshe* serveth to fyl up in the myddel of the wall "; and he quotes also a similar passage from Palsgrave. According to my view of the case, *robows* and *rubbrysshe* are entirely different words, which cannot by any process be made to coalesce. My statement remains uncontradicted, that our word *rubbish* cannot be traced further back than the sixteenth century. When once introduced, from its general aptitude it might be applied to waste stone or any other material. The authorities given for the identity of the two words are very weak. Minshew's note gives no information whatever. Both Cotgrave and Sherwood evidently considered that *rubbish* meant rubble, since they make it equivalent to Fr. *moellon* and *repous*, but of *rubbish* in the modern sense of waste material of all sorts they give not the slightest intimation. This is not difficult to account for. The word was at that time comparatively new, and had not settled down to a general acceptation of its meaning. It is to be noted that neither Cotgrave, Sherwood, nor Minshew give any example or illustration of its use.

The conclusions at which I arrive are the following. Both *rubble* and *rubbish* are words of foreign origin, the former most probably from the French, introduced about the fourteenth century, and always restricted to its original meaning. The latter is of much later introduction; and, although liable at first to be confounded with the former, it cannot be shown that it has ever been generally employed in any other sense than that of waste material, exactly corresponding to the Italian

robaccia, from which I think there is strong probability that it has been derived. The omission of the word from early Italian dictionaries is not surprising. The "aumentativi" and "peggiorativi," one, *accio*, *ino*, &c., may be applied to any word, and even now very few of them are inserted in the dictionaries.

I have to apologize for the length to which these remarks have extended.   J. A. PICTON.
Sandyknowe, Wavertree.

PAUPERS' BADGES : VAGRANTS' PASSES (5th S. viii. 347, 513.)—MR. PATTERSON has given a copy of a "Licence to begge," temp. Elizabeth, which appears to have been issued by the magistrates in session, and addressed to the particular justices residing within the hundred in which the poor person was to ask alms. Can any one give a copy of a vagrants' pass ? It is evident that the beggar had an exciting time of it in the sixteenth and seventeenth centuries. When he appeared in a town he certainly received relief, but it was frequently accompanied by a whipping which must have left so strong an impression upon his mind as well as upon his body that he probably did not pay the same locality a visit for some time afterwards.

In the accounts of the constables of Melton-Mowbray, Leicestershire, I find :—

1602. Geven to Robert Moodee for wippin to pore folks ...   ij^d

And gave them when the were wipped ...   ij^d

The infliction of this punishment was sometimes deputed to a boy with what must have been a most brutalizing effect :—

1602. Geven to Tomlyn's boy for whippin a man *and* a woman ...   ij^d

And gave them when the went ...   ij^d

1601. P^d and geven to a poore man and his wiff that was wipped 0 0 4

Again :—

1625-6. Payd for whipping 6 vagabonds ... 00 00 06

After the twopennyworth of whipping and the twopennyworth of alms a pass was given :—

1625-6. Payd for pass and wax to make passes for wagrants wch was punished ... 00 00 03

This pass appears to have saved the back of the recipient at the next place he visited :—

1602. Geven to one that was whipped at buxminster ij^d

and from which village he, I presume, brought a pass ; but if he did not pass on he took the consequences :—

1601. P^d and geven to bluett that was taken vagrant *after* his wipping 0 0 2

P^d more for wipping 0 0 2

THOMAS NORTH, F.S.A.

The Act of Parliament, 8 and 9 Will. III. cap. 30 provides that on and after Sept. 1, 1697, every person receiving parish relief shall wear upon the

one days with hard labour and whipping. The portion of the Act having reference to the wearing of badges was repealed in 1810 by 50 Geo. III. cap. 52. The custom of wearing badges is alluded to in that quaint bit of county history (which all Salopians should make themselves acquainted with), Gough's *Antiquities and Memoirs of the Parish of Myddle*, p. 171 (Shrewsbury, Adnitt & Naunton, 1875). B. R.

The children in a charity school at Amsterdam wear distinctive clothing to prevent them from frequenting taverns or gin-shops. I have seen the boys wearing coats half red and half black, the division being vertical. The proprietors of any taverns, &c., are liable to a penalty for serving intoxicating liquors to these charity children.

FREDERICK E. SAWYER.
Brighton.

[Mr. Walford, in *Old and New London*, mentions, with reference to a hospital of Our Lady and St. Catherine at Newington, that in 1551 " their proctor, William Cleybrooke, being dispossessed of his home, was fortunate enough to obtain a licence to beg."]

THE DE STUTEVILLE FAMILY (5th S. viii. 447; ix. 17.)—One representative of this family is Sir Peyton Estoteville Skipwith, of Prestwould, co. Leicester, Bart. Robert Estouteville, son of Robert Estouteville and Adeliza, dau. of Ivo, Count de Beaumont, was in 1170 Justice Itinerant in counties Cumberland and Northumberland. He married Erneburga, dau. and heiress of Hugh Fitz Baldric, said to have been a great Saxon thane, and through her became possessed of large estates, among which was Schypwic, now called Skipwith, a small town in the East Riding of Yorkshire. He left three sons—Robert, Osmond, and Patrick. The youngest of these, Patrick, had by gift from his father Skipwith, and assumed that name in lieu of his patronymic, and from him in a direct line is descended the above Sir Peyton Estoteville Skipwith. Their arms were, Argent, three bars gules, to which was added by one of the members of the Skipwith family, on account of marrying the heiress of the De Langtune family, a greyhound in chief sable, collared or. Their crest is, On a wreath a turnpike gate ppr. Motto, " Sans Dieu je ne puis." SYWL.

ST. MARY MATFELON (5th S. vii. 225, 314.)— Two etymologies have been suggested in your columns—*matta fullonum* and *mate* (daunt) *felon*. It might be to the point to compare Richard Cœur de Lion's tower, or engine of war, named

The King continues :—
"I have a castel I understond
Is made of timbre of Inglond,
With six stages ful of towrelles,
Well flourished with cornelles;
Therin I and many a knight
Against the Frensh shall take the fight.
That castel shall have a sory nom,
It shall be hight the Mate-Gryffon."
Henry Weber's *Metrical Romances*, Edinburgh, 8vo. 3 vols.; see vol. ii. p. 73, " Richard Cœr de Lion
ZER(

THE BIRTHPLACE OF SUNDAY SCHOOLS (5th viii. 367.)—Some correspondence having ta place upon this subject in the *Gloucesters Chronicle*, a further communication to this e: has recently appeared :—

" It is a fact which does not admit of dispute that first Sunday School was opened by the late Rev. T Stock, A.M., and was held in the house of the late Ja King, in St. Catherine Street. That house—the h in which James King lived, and in which the first : day School was held by the late excellent Rev. T Stock—is still standing, undefaced and unaltered. have written to the Rev. Jonathan Mayne to endea to induce him to make some inquiries respecting Bible during his numerous pastoral visits. We may get possession of that interesting Bible, but we ma; possession of the house. I look upon that old hou St. Catherine Street as a sacred relic which shoul carefully preserved. It should be valued by the citi and corporation of the city of Gloucester as sacredly carefully as Stratford appreciates and preserves birthplace of Shakespeare. Will our mayor, will corporation, will the Church of England clergy, their congregations, will the citizens of Gloucester, mit the ' birthplace of Sunday Schools ' to be remo desecrated, or destroyed ? "

It appears that in the *Gentleman's Maga*: 1831, the Rev. J. Evans wrote : " I took order Gloucester in 1783, about three years after commencement of this institution " (Sur Schools). The first school he said " was hel in the house of Mr. King, of St. Catherine Stre who " possesses a Bible given at the comme ment of this institution." James King w: bricklayer. The writer who speaks so autho tively above signs simply by initials, so that value of the evidence cannot be judged.
KINGSTO

EDWARD FARR (5th S. viii. 429.)—I am ena to answer MR. INGLIS'S inquiry respecting Edward Farr. He died at Iver, Bucks, on D(1867. He had a fluent and versatile pen, to w his honourable and indomitable industry, in midst of other avocations, allowed but little I have before me a list of his works in his

biography, poetry, &c., amounting to thirty-eight volumes, and the list by no means exhausts the number of his productions. Among these was *A New Version of the Psalms of David*, adapted to *Psalmody*, which received the commendations of James Montgomery. Perhaps the most important of his labours was a *Continuation of Hume and Smollett's History of England, to the Tenth Year of the Reign of Queen Victoria*. This he did in conjunction with Dr. W. H. Russell. The history was afterwards ably continued by Mr. J. Goodall.   J. W. Dalby.
Richmond, Surrey.

Lowland Aberdeen (5ᵗʰ S. ix. 5.)—As a native of Aberdeen, I may be supposed to know something of the feelings of its inhabitants (I speak only of them, not of the Lowlands in general) towards the Highlanders; and I can truly say that, so long as I lived in Aberdeen (twenty-four years, up to the year 1819), I never remember hearing a word of displeasure or dissatisfaction expressed regarding them; but they were looked upon as a brave and loyal race, whose antipathies to the Saxon and deep-rooted prejudices had been long overcome by measures and acts of goodwill and beneficence on the part of Government and individuals. There was, and I suppose still is, a Gaelic kirk in Aberdeen for enabling the Gaelic-speaking few—for by far the majority of the inhabitants were of Anglo-Saxon or Danish descent—to attend divine service in their native tongue; for there certainly was a minister attached to the church in my time, and I always heard him mentioned with great respect in that capacity. I cannot complete or give a different version of the rhymes quoted by I. M. P., but I remember hearing an expression which seemed to convey a sly smile at the predatory habits of the "Heelenmen" in old times, and it was this: "Ye fand faar the Heelenman fand the tengs," *i.e.* you found it where the Highlandman found the tongs, that is, by the fireside, alluding to the raids of the Highlanders on their Saxon neighbours for purposes of plunder in the wild old times. I sign my name to this in the old Anglo-Saxon spelling, as I came well known in Aberdeen, although since I came to England I have omitted the *h*, which I see is still retained by my Scotch cousin and fellow-townsman the Bishop of Rupertsland.   John Machray.
Oxford.

Yorkshire Superstition (5ᵗʰ S. ix. 8.)—On January 24, 1872, a boy named Harris fell into the stream at Sherborne, Dorsetshire, near Darkhole Mill, and was drowned. The body not having been found for some days, the following expedient was adopted to discover its whereabouts. On January 30 a four-pound loaf of best flour was procured, and a small piece cut out of the side of it, forming a cavity, into which a little quicksilver

was poured. The piece was then replaced, and tied firmly in its original position. The loaf thus prepared was then thrown into the river at the spot where the boy fell in, and was expected to float down the stream until it came to the place where the body had lodged, when it would begin to eddy round and round, thus indicating the sought-for spot. An eye-witness of this experiment, from whom I received this account a few days after it happened, told me that no satisfactory result occurred on this occasion.   C. H. Mayo.
Long Burton.

St. Tyrnog (5ᵗʰ S. ix. 9.)—There is no saint of this name. The parish church of Llandyrnog is dedicated to Twrnog or Teyrnog, a brother of St. Tyfrydog, and son of Arwyste Geoff ab Peithenyn by Tywynwedd, the daughter of Amlawdd Wledig. Twrnog was one of the British saints, his festival being observed on June 26.   W. Williams.
Oakfield, Pontypridd, Glam.

The parish church of Llandyrnog, in the diocese of St. Asaph, was founded originally by Tyrnog, a saint of the sixth century, and brother of Deifar or Diheufar and Marchell, the respective founders of Bodfari and Whitchurch (*Hist. of Diocese of St. Asaph*, by the Rev. D. R. Thomas, London, 1874, p. 413).   George M. Traherne.

This saint is probably the same as St. Tigernach, who was a bishop in Ireland, and died in 550. See Butler's *Lives of the Saints*, April 5.
                                                    C. J. E.

Bishop Yonge of Rochester (5ᵗʰ S. ix. 27.)— There were two Bishops of Rochester surnamed Yong or Yonge. The first was Richard Yonge, who was consecrated Bishop of Bangor in 1400, and translated to Rochester in 1407. To him are assigned the arms, Per saltire az. and gu., a lion pass. gard. or. The other was John Yong, consecrated Bishop of Rochester in 1578. To him Dethick, Garter, "confirmed" the same coat, with the addition of two fleurs-de-lis gold in pale. There is not, so far as I am aware, any ground for believing that the prelates were related or of Italian descent.   J. Woodward.

The Clubs of Dublin (5ᵗʰ S. ix. 28.)—Your correspondent may find abundant information regarding club life in the Irish metropolis in Gilbert's *History of the City of Dublin*, Dublin, 1854-59, 3 vols., 8vo. An index to the work has been printed, but is not to be found in every copy.
                                                    Abhba.

Sweet-heart (5ᵗʰ S. ix. 84.)—The origin of this phrase is much earlier than O. W. T. supposes. It is due to Chaucer, and to his great influence. In *Troilus and Creseide*, bk. iii. l. 988, we have, "Lo! herte mine!" In the next stanza

etymologies are too clever to be true. Ingenuity is the sworn foe of true philology.

WALTER W. SKEAT.
Cambridge.

THE MAYOR OF HUNTINGDON AND THE STURGEON (5th S. ix. 8.)—The story referred to by Pepys dates to the year 1624, when there was a great flood on the river Ouse. Several inhabitants of Huntingdon, Godmanchester, and Brampton·were watching the flood, and saw a dark object floating towards them on the water. The Huntingdon folks guessed it to be a sturgeon ; the Godmanchester people surmised that it was a black hog ; and the Brampton men pronounced it to be a dead donkey ; and they were right. In Rider's *British Merlin* it states that, in the year 1624, " the two Bailiffes and York, the constable of Huntingdon, siezed Sir Robert Osborn's ragged colt for a sturgeon"; and this account, with the colt instead of the donkey, agrees with Pepys's mention of the anecdote. The story gave rise to the contemptuous expressions, "Huntingdonshire sturgeons" and "Godmanchester black hogs." See *The History of Huntingdon*, 1824, without an author's name, but the preface signed "R. C." These were the initials of Mr. Robert Carruthers, who at that time was a junior master in the Huntingdon Grammar School.

CUTHBERT BEDE.

What Pepys referred to in the passage quoted is thus explained in a note by Lord Braybrooke (Pepys's *Diary*, May 22, 1667) :—

"During a very high flood in the meadows between Huntingdon and Godmanchester, something was seen floating, which the Godmanchester people thought was a black *pig*, and the Huntingdon folk declared was a *sturgeon ;* when rescued from the waters it proved to be a young donkey. This mistake led to the one party being styled ' Godmanchester black pigs' and the other 'Huntingdon sturgeons,' terms not altogether forgotten at this day. Pepys's colt must be taken to be the *colt of an ass.*"

Lord Braybrooke probably was unable to ascertain the name of the Mayor of Huntingdon when this was said to have taken place.

EDWARD SOLLY.

SCHOMBERG : SCHÖNBERG ARMS (5th S. ix. 8.)—There are two Swiss families named Schönenberg (which we may take to be the same name as Schönberg) whose arms are known to me. The one bore, Per fess gu. and arg. (*Wappenbuch von Zürich*, Taf. 4, No. 76 : a fourteenth century MS. published in 1860, in fac-simile, by the Antiquarischen Gesellschaft in Zürich) ; the other bore, Gu., a lion ramp. arg., crowned or (Sieb-

G. AND H. CABOT, OF BOSTON (5th S. ix. The *North American Review* for Nov.-Dec., contains a short notice of the *Life and Lette* George Cabot, by H. C. Lodge (Boston, I Brown & Co.). This biography may perhaps Mr. Cabot's ancestors. M. N.

CHRONOGRAMS (1st S. ix. 60, 61 ; 5th S. ix. —On medals of the seventeenth and early i eighteenth centuries, struck on the Conti chronograms frequently occur.

Upon a set of twelve remarkable medals markable for the fineness of work and from being struck in *hard wood*—now before me, memorating various battles between the] garians and Turks, coronation of the Em] Joseph, various treaties, &c., this ingenious me of arranging the date occurs on several.

The coronation medal has, upon a scroll t the bust, VIVat IosephVs teVton Le re DeLICIVM, which, added together, give the of the medal, 1735, or perhaps 1739.

Another, upon which a Turk is flying fron rays of light issuing from a Greek cross carrie an angel, has the inscription—IMbeLLes tV CrVX atqVe eCCLesIA VInCVnt, or 168 Several others are adorned in the same cu manner. J. HENI
Devonshire Street, W.C.

["One curious feature in the tomb" (that of Lu Stuart, Duke of Richmond and Lennox, 1623-4, (of James I., in the chantry on the south side of I VII.'s Chapel at Westminster) "deserves notice.] inscription the date of the year of the duke's de apparently omitted, though the month and day are tioned. The year, however, is given in what is ca chronogram. The Latin translation of the verse Bible, ' Know ye not that a prince and a great me this day fallen?' (the words uttered by David i lament over Abner) contains fourteen Roman nu letters, and these being elongated into capita MDCVVVIIIIIIII, which give the date 1623. remarkable that words so appropriate to this nob should contain the date for this identical year ; shows much ingenuity on the part of the writer inscription that he should have discovered it." *Builder,* June 19, 1875.]

WAS ST. PETER A MARRIED MAN ? (5th S 346, 453, 492.)—My critics do me good servi rejecting the hypothesis that the passage 1 Cor relates to matrimony. For, if the text has n reference—if St. Paul claims for himself an or three other apostles a special privilege (privilege, in the case of the married 'Pete likely to have caused some little jeal γυναῖκα περιάγειν who should not be his '

there remains one only passage of Scripture on which to rest the theory of St. Peter's being married. My acquaintance with the Greek,tongue is, I own, not extensive ; and I am not able to determine the question whether the person who provided a meal might or might not have herself waited on the guests, or whether the waiting and the catering were necessarily performed by different people. I think I have read in tales of Eastern hospitality of the host personally seeing to the comfort of his guests.

As to the conjecture that St. Peter would not have had patience to endure a household composed of such mixed elements as a wife, a mother-in-law, and a brother, it is not easy to argue ; common experience, I am told, supports my view. If, as ETONENSIS urges, the house was joint property of Andrew and Peter, one can only admire the benevolence of the younger brother in suffering the elder to take such a *pars leonina* of the common possession. MR. TEW seems to infer from St. Matt. xix. 27 that St. Peter had forsaken his wife at this early period of his apostleship, which of course puts a different face upon the question. Why, in that case, he had not also forsaken his house, his brother, and his mother-in-law, is a point worthy of inquiry.　　EDWARD H. MARSHALL.
The Temple.

Whether MR. E. H. MARSHALL is right in his conjecture is a separate question. But it appears to me that what he chiefly tries to establish, namely, that St. Peter's wife was dead, and not with him, is not very unlike what has elsewhere been advanced. Cornelius a Lapide, on St. Matt. viii. 14, has : " Socrus hæc erat S. Petri ; ipse enim a conjugio vocatus est a Christo, tumque reliquit uxorem et filiam ex ea genitam." The absence of St. Peter's wife, as supposed, is explained in the one case by the supposition of her death, in the other by the supposition of her having been put away. It is entirely a question for conjecture.
　　　　　　　　　　　　　　CLERICUS.

ON THE USE OF THE WORD "SYDYR" (CIDER) BY WICKLIFFE (5ᵗʰ S. viii. 464.)—The word occurs in Chaucer (*The Monke's Tale*, 65) as *siser :*—
" This Sampson neyther *siser* dronk ne wyn."
　　　　　　　　　　　　　R. S. CHARNOCK.
Boulogne-sur-Mer.

THE EAST (5ᵗʰ S. viii. 465.)—That the morning sun dances on Easter Day is still believed in many parts of Devonshire. See *Trans. Devon. Assoc.*, vol. viii., 1876, p. 57; see on "An Easter Day Sun," "N. & Q.," 1ˢᵗ S. vii. 333.
　　　　　　　　　　　　W. PENGELLY.
Torquay.

BRODHURST OR BROADHURST FAMILY (5ᵗʰ S. ix. 8.)—The name Broadhurst is a well-known one at Congleton, in the county of Chester, and has

been so for many years. Congleton is close on the borders of Staffordshire, but whether the Broadhurst family came from that shire to Congleton I cannot say. I should rather incline to the belief that it was an old Cheshire family. The name would be found constantly occurring in the municipal records of that ancient borough ; and it may be worth noting additionally that few towns in England possess such an excellent and entire collection of them as Congleton does. In 1875 Mr. Earwaker collected and had bound up in nine large volumes, for the Corporation, the ancient charters and records of that borough, and it is needless to say that his care was only equalled by his zeal.　　　　　JOHN PICKFORD, M.A.
Newbourne Rectory, Woodbridge.

" KEX " (5ᵗʰ S. viii. 169, 454.)—Allow me to correct a little misprint in MISS PEACOCK'S quotation of *Piers Plowman*. It must be B., Passus xvii. l. 219, and not 119. The reading of text C., Pass. xx. l. 185, is the following :—
" As doþ a kyx oþer a candele þat cauht has fuyr, and blaseþ."
There cannot be the slightest doubt that its meaning is hemlock, as given at the latter reference ; yet in the above-cited line it must mean a candle, for the preceding lines contain the following :—
" As glowing coals do not give light to workmen,
Who are working and awaking in winter nights,
As does a *kex or candle* that has caught fire and blazes."
　　Cf. *Piers Pl.*, B. xvii. l. 217.
May not small strips of kex have been used in the fourteenth century as wicks, as nowadays we find rushes used ? Then also the line quoted from Peroy's *Rel.* is quite clear, meaning that the wives of Tottenham came with kex-candles and rush-candles, and the same it would mean in *Piers Plowman*.
I cannot well believe that kexes without any preparation would be able to burn as a candle. Another way to explain the sense would be to assume that the whole stalk was used as a wick in torches ; then, of course, kex would stand for a torch. Maetzner, in his *Sprachproben*, ii. p. 414, says nearly the same as Halliwell.
　　　　　　　　　　　　F. ROSENTHAL.
Hanover.

I believe with MISS MABEL PEACOCK that *kex* means the hemlock. " As dry as a *kence* " is a very common expression in the district within which she resides, but I never heard the word pronounced as kex or kexes.　　W. E. HOWLETT.
North Lincolnshire.

ADVERBS : " OVERLY " (5ᵗʰ S. viii. 406, 475.)—In the original example given by M. D. H. this word was rightly called an adverb. In the two quotations from Hall, and the one from Sanderson, put forward by E. A. D., it is an adjective. As

Shinfield Grove.

OLD WORDS WITH NEW MEANINGS (5th S. vii. 424 ; viii. 354.)—Please add to my note on this subject :—

The Bible Word-Book: a Glossary of Old English Bible Words. By J. Eastwood, M.A., and W. Aldis Wright, M.A. London, Macmillan, 1866.

The following further works are mentioned by Mr. Wright in his preface to the above :—

1. A Short Explanation of Obsolete Words in our Version of the Bible, &c. By the Rev. H. Cotton, D.C.L. Oxf., 1832.

2. A Glossary to the Obsolete and Unusual Words and Phrases of the Holy Scriptures, in the Authorized English Version. By J. Jameson. London, 1850.

3. Motes upon Crystal ; or, Obsolete Words of the Authorized Version of the Holy Bible, &c. Part I. By the Rev. Kirby Trimmer, A.B. London, 1864.

ROBERT GUY.
Shawlands, Glasgow.

"THE BOTHIE OF TOBER-NA-VUOLICH" (5th S. viii. 88, 198, 395, 435, 474.)—I have not Arthur Clough's poem to refer to, and I have not been in that part of Braemar. It is asked what is the meaning of the above and of *Toper-na-Fuosich,* and which of them is the right name. *Bothie* is a hut or cottage, from the Gaelic *both,* a hut. *Tobar* is a well ; it is wrong to spell it with a *p* or an *e.* *Fiosaiche* is a diviner, one who tells what is to happen in the early future. *Bealach* is a pass between hills, or between a hill and a river. In some circumstances *b* becomes *bh,* sounded like *v.* It is from *beul,* the mouth. Perhaps the name means the Well of the Soothsayer, or possibly the Well of the Pass. I do not know if it be a real name. If it be, perhaps the latter explanation may suit the characteristics of the spot.

THOMAS STRATTON, M.D.
Stoke, Devonport.

"THE SHEPHERD OF HERMAS" (5th S. viii. 410, 455, 511.)—MR. E. H. MARSHALL speaks of "an English *edition* of this book," and I do not know whether he has overlooked or not the fact that Hone's is a mere reprint of Archbishop Wake's. If he has not, I beg his pardon.

C. F. S. WARREN, M.A.
Bexhill.

JOAN PLANTAGENET, LADY TALBOT (5th S. viii. 328, 375, 396.)—Beatrice was married to Sir Gilbert Talbot not later than 1413, for she is called his wife in a charter dated at Blakemere on Monday after the feast of St. Luke, 1 Hen. V. (Oct. 23, 1413). She was, therefore, the mother of Ankaret Talbot, who was heir also to her

Talbot, died on Christmas Day, 1447, Willia: Fetteplace being her son and heir, aged twent; four years. No mention is here made (Inq. i Hen. VI. No. 7) of Thomas Fetiplace, but I fin that Sir Gilbert Talbot, by charter dated Sept. 1 1 Hen. V. (1413), appointed Thomas Fetiplas i be steward of the manor and hundred of Bampto: co. Oxford, with yearly wages of fifty shilling and also steward of the manors of Shryvenham, c Berks, and of Swyndon, &c., co. Wilts, with year: wages of thirty and twenty shillings respectivel Mr. J. M. Davenport, in *Lords Lieutenant an High Sheriffs of Oxfordshire,* gives as sheriff ' the county with Berks, in 14 Hen. VI., S Thomas Fetiplace, of Childrey, Knight ; and, : the course of a long note appended to the nam he says that "in the reign of King Henry tl Sixth the family received a great addition ' blood and honour, by marrying Beatrix, daught of the King of Portugal ; which match is me: tioned, and allowed of, in the pedigree of tl Kings of Portugal. The Fetiplace that marrie the Daughter of Portugal, was Thomas Fetipla: Esquire, of Childrey, in Bucks, the Sheriff, wl was the Father of James [or *William,* as by tl inquisition above quoted], the Father of Richar who &c. (*Delafield's MSS.*)."

Beatrice, formerly wife of Thomas, Earl : Arundel, died *sine herede* Oct. 23, 1439 (Inq.] Hen. VI. No. 28). JOHN A. C. VINCENT.

THE WINDSOR SENTINEL AND ST. PAUL'S (5 S. ix. 87.)—In a volume of newspaper cuttings i my possession is a tale called " The Thirteen Chime : a Legend of Old London." It is unfo tunately not dated, but was apparently issue about thirty years ago. The sentinel's name is Mark Huntly. T. W. C.

JETTON (5th S. ix. 87.)—The piece of bra described as a *jetton* is a weight for a guinea. Tl old scale boxes were often fitted with a number similar weights, with the name of the coin of whi they were the weight. D. T. M.

SOUSA OR SOUZA FAMILY (5th S. viii. 48, 17 518.)—As SIGMA has appealed to me, I am gl: to be able to send the following information.

The Sousas derived their origin from Mart Affonso Chichorro and Affonso Diniz, who were tl natural sons of King Affonso III. by two siste Sousa. The two families issuing from these roy bastards bore different arms. The descendants Affonso Chichorro quartered Portugal and Leo: those of Diniz quartered Portugal with the arms Sousa. This and other information as to their an

and crests is found in the following extract :—
" Sousas procedem de Martim Affonso Chichorro
e de Affonso Diniz, filhos del Rey D. Affonso III.
que cazaraõ com duas netas de meni Garcia de
Sousa, neto do Conde D. Mendo o Sousaõ, em
quem veyo a ficar esta Familia. Os que procedem
de Martim Affonso Chichorro,esquartelaõ as Quinas
de Portugal com as armas de Leaõ : tymbre hum
Leaõ das armas com huma grinal da sobre a cabeça
de prata, florida de verde. Os que vem de Affonso
Diniz trazem as mesmas Quinas esquarteladas com
quadernas de meas Luas ; tymbre hum Castello de
ouro lavrado de preto. As Luas dizem ser as armas
antigas dos Souzas, ajuntaraõ he os Leoens pela
descendencia, que traziaõ dos Reys de Leaõ, assim
como as Quinas por virem dos de Portugal "
(Nobiliarchia Portugueza, p. 333).

The original Sousa arms were—Gu., four
crescents arg. (the meas Luas of the quotation
above), arranged in cross, so that the points are all
turned towards the centre of the shield ; at least
they are so represented in a drawing of them which
I copied some years ago.

As the illegitimate Sousas were born before the
House of Braganza came to the throne of Portugal, the arms of that kingdom quartered by them
are the Quinas only, without the bordure which
now encloses them.

Rietstap, Armorial Général, only gives the arms
of one of the branches mentioned above, and
blazons them—Quarterly, 1 and 4, Arg., a lion
passant (? rampant) gu., Leon ; 2 and 3, Portugal.

There are no Soziers, or Sosiers, in Rietstap, or
in Siebmacher's Wappenbuch. There are several
French families of Sohier ; none have the slightest
connexion with the Sousa family or with the
Azores.   J. WOODWARD.
Montrose.

" STONE BUTTER " (5th S. viii. 508.)—Steinbutter,
in French beurre de montagne, beurre de roche, is
composed of clay, alum, iron, and rock oil. We
call it rock butter. The following is Buchanan's
definition :—" Native alum mixed with clay and
oxide of iron, usually in soft masses of a yellowish-
white colour, occurring in cavities and fissures in
argillaceous state."   G. A. SCHRUMPF.
Tettenhall College.

The stone butter about which your correspondent
inquires is the Bergmehl of German quarrymen.
It is found in beds, sometimes thirty feet thick,
and is entirely composed of the siliceous cases of
microscopic animals. It contains nothing nutritious,
being pure silica, but may be swallowed in small
quantities without injury.   J. C. M.

" DAME " AND " LADY " (5th S. viii. 451 ; ix.
75.)—The title Dame was of wider application
than P. P. supposes. In a Bible I have, printed
by Rouland Hall, Geneva, 1560, Genesis xvi. 8, 9,
is thus rendered :—

" 8. And he sayde, Hagar Sarais maide, whence
commest thou? and whither wilt thou go? And she
said, I flee frō my dame Sarai.
" 9. And the Angel of the Lord said vnto her, return
to thy dame, and humble thyselfe vnder her hands."
                                     J. R. DORE.
Huddersfield.

" ESTRIDGES " (5th S. vii. 326, 385, 458.)—It
seems to be pretty well agreed that the falcon is
meant by Shakspere in the passage,
          " All plumed like estridges."
There can, however, be little doubt that the word
was also used with reference to the ostrich :—
" The peacock not at thy command assumes
Her (sic) glorious train, nor estrich her rare plumes."
                                     Sandys.
Neither here nor in the passage from Drayton's
Polyolbion, quoted by MR. PICKFORD, does the
word seem from the context to refer to the falcon.
A falcon's plumes could hardly be described as
" rare," and as ostrich feathers were undoubtedly
used as plumes for knights' helmets, it seems to me
more probable that these are referred to in Dray-
ton's line :—
" The Mountfords all in plumes, like estriges, were seen."
                                     ROBERT GUY.
Shawlands, Glasgow.

MRS. JUDITH WELD (5th S. viii. 507 ; ix. 94.)—
Mrs. Judith Weld, buried at Gateshead-on-Tyne
in 1656, was the second wife of the Rev. Thomas
Weld, a well-known Puritan minister in New
England for many years. In 1624 he was Vicar of
Terling, in Essex, but thought it prudent, to avoid
persecution, to retire to America. From 1632 to
1641 he was minister of Roxbury. In the latter
year he returned to England, and never visited
America again. For many years, until after the
Restoration, he was minister of Gateshead, and is
said to have died there on March 23, 1661/2.
Several of his works, some of them very curious,
are in the British Museum. Further particulars
of his life will be found in William Allen's
American Biog. Dict. (third edit., 1857), F. S.
Drake's American Dict., and James Savage's
Genealogical Dict. of First Settlers of New England.   W. P. COURTNEY.
15, Queen Anne's Gate.

SAMUEL ROPER AND THE SEWALL FAMILY (5th
S. ix. 28 ; ix. 56, 98.)—The claimants, in England
as well as in America, to bear the arms of the
old Saxon family of Sewall appear, almost without
exception, to be in error in respect of the coat.
There is some reason for supposing that John
de Sewell (the manorial orthography is Sewelle
in Domesday Book), who accompanied Edward
the Black Prince into Aquitaine, bore, Sable, a
chevron between three butterflies argent, and that
this was the heraldic cognizance of his family
subsequently.   PAPILIO.

·directly for want of an address, but who, if one of the Cogan family, will feel interest in matter which would overload the pages of "N. & Q." The little book I printed for the amusement of a friendly circle was published by William Lewis, of Bath, at the price (I believe) of 1s. 6d.

HENRY JULIAN HUNTER.
10, Regent Terrace, Penzance.

JOHN HOOK (5ᵗʰ S. vi. 447 ; viii. 509 ; ix. 75.) —He was the son of William Hook; "·born of genteel parents in Hampshire"; sent to Trin. Coll., ·Oxford, 1616 ; Vicar of Axmouth, in Devon ; went to New England as a Nonconformist, and was colleague with Mr. Davenport in the church of New Haven, in New England. In the time of the Commonwealth he returned to England, and was made Master of the Savoy and chaplain to Oliver ·Cromwell. He died March 21, 1677, and was buried in the "New Artillery Garden." For an account of him and his writings see Wood's *Athenæ Oxonienses* and the *Nonconformists' Memorial* (ed. 1802, i. 184, and ii. 271). In Thurloe's *State Papers*, i. 564, there is a letter from him to Oliver Cromwell, dated from New Haven, Nov. 3, 1653, in which he thanks the Lord General for his bounty and the favour which his son has found in his eyes. After the death of Mr. John Hook, in 1710, his papers passed into the hands of his ·successor in the ministry at Basingstoke, Mr. Jefferson. It would be worth while to try and trace what became of them subsequently.

EDWARD SOLLY.

SIR JULIUS CÆSAR (1ˢᵗ S. viii. 172 ; 2ⁿᵈ S. v. ·394 ; xi. 139, 153 ; 4ᵗʰ S. x. 412 ; 5ᵗʰ S. viii. 427 ; ix. 56.)—The other day, in crossing Northumberland Avenue, I encountered a country cart, on the side of which appeared the owner's name, "Jeremiah Cæsar, Peckham, Surrey." In "The London Directory for 1878 I find eight persons of the name of Cæsar, of whom three are also named Julius. A. J. M.

PROCLAIMING AN EARL'S TITLES AT THE ALTAR (5ᵗʰ S. vi. 447 ; vii. 15, 390.)—There seems to be no doubt that, at the burial of the last member of an historical family, some ceremony denoting the fact of extinction was wont to be performed at the side of the grave. In 1464 Otto, Duke of Stettin-Pommern, died without heirs, it having been arranged that the Hohenzollerns were to succeed. Carlyle, in his *History of Frederick the Great*, bk. iii. c. iii., thus describes the scene at the grave :

kin ; these tokens we must send to his Grace at Wol with offer of our homage.'"

They were sent accordingly, and several centu passed before Prussia could get Stettin-Pomm
R. PASSINGHAM

MANDRIL (5ᵗʰ S. viii. 186, 295, 477.)— word is used here of a plug inserted into a ho piece of wood which has to be turned in a la in order to connect it with the revolving par the machine. It is pronounced *maundril*.
J. T. 1
Winterton, Brigg.

"MAULEVERER" (5ᵗʰ S. vii. 344, 478 ; viii. 379, 517.)—Whilst admitting your correspond to be correct in assigning Arncliffe in Clevel as the ancient abode of this family, yet the fol ing quotation from the *White Doe of Rylston* Wordsworth would induce the supposition th had in days of yore some connexion with Cra

" Pass, pass who will yon chantry door,
And through the chink in the fractured floor
Look down, and see a griesly sight:
A vault where the bodies are buried upright !
There face by face, and hand by hand,
The Claphams and *Mauleverers* stand ;
And in his place, among son and sire,
Is John de Clapham, that fierce Esquire—
A valiant man, and a name of dread
In the ruthless wars of the White and Red—
Who dragged Earl Pembroke from Banbury Churc
And smote off his head on the stones of the rcb
Canto

There is the following explanatory note upon passage by the author :—

" At the east end of the north aisle of Bolton Pi Church is a chantry belonging to Bethmesly (qy. Be ley) Hall, and a vault where, according to tradition from the Mauleverers) were interred upright. Joh Clapham, of whom this ferocious act is recorded, v man of great note in his time: he was a vebei partisan of the House of Lancaster, in whom the s of his chieftains, the Cliffords, seemed to survive."

Well do I remember on my first visit to Bc Priory, in 1852, looking in vain for the "gri sight" through the crevices in the "fractu floor" of the chantry, and coming to the clusion that the legend was traditional. On last visit, in 1869, the nave of the priory had un gone an entire restoration, which had given a · cold appearance to it. The slabs in the chant the end of the north aisle, traditionally saic cover the sepulchre of the Claphams and Ma verers, had been levelled with the floor, as fa I can remember. It may perhaps be worth w adding a query—whether on the restoration any human remains were found buried in an upright position under these large slabs of stone. Wordsworth mentions his having visited Bolton Priory for the first time in 1807, when he no doubt heard the tradition. The *White Doe of Rylstone* was composed in the same year.

JOHN PICKFORD, M.A.

Newbourne Rectory, Woodbridge.

"SKAL" (5ᵗʰ S. viii. 509.)—This word is in Old Norse *skál*, pl. *skálir, skálar*, and means a drinking bowl. It is akin to the English word "scale," denoting the dish of a balance, also to "scale, shell, shale," German *schale*. The meaning "drinking bowl" occurs for the Old High German *scála*, the Middle High German *schále, schal*, the Old Saxon *scala*, the Danish *skaal*, and the Swedish *skál*. In the Swedish language "dricka en skål" means "to drink a bowl, a health," as "dricka ens skål," "to drink one's health." The following quotation from Paul Warnefrid's *History of the Langobards* gives an additional instance of *scala* = drinking bowl:—"In eo prœlio Albwini Cunimundum occidit caputque illius sublatum ad bibendum ex eo poculum fecit, quod genus poculi apud eos (*i.e.* the Langobards) *scala* dicitur, lingua vero latina patera vocitatur."

G. A. SCHRUMPF.

Tettenhall College.

The Swedish salutation, "Er skål!" "Your health!" (in Danish *skaal*) has its origin in pledging one another's health in the flowing bowl (Sw. *skål*, Icel. *skál*, Dan. *skaal*).

A. L. MAYHEW.

Oxford.

WYVILL BARONETCY (5ᵗʰ S. viii. 88, 496.)—My query as to the American branch of this family has elicited several replies from across the Atlantic. A descendant of the family informs me that the male line of Marmaduke Wyvill (who should have inherited as eighth baronet) is still in existence. The said Marmaduke died in 1809, leaving issue three sons—Marmaduke, Darcy, and Walter. The eldest deceased leaving an only child, a daughter, who is still living, married, and has issue. The second and third sons both left male issue. I am further informed that the marriages, births, and deaths of this branch of the Wyvill family are very carefully kept.

W. D. PINK.

Leigh, Lancashire.

"TATTERING A KIP" (5ᵗʰ S. viii. 508.)—Halliwell gives, "To tatter, to make a fool of any one (Middlesex)"; while "kip" is said by the same authority to be "the skin of a small or young beast."

W. F. R.

Worle Vicarage.

A "kip" is a word used in Ireland for "bordelle" or "brothel," and "to tatter a kip" meant to make a raid on an establishment of the kind and to break the windows, &c.   W. H. R.

[REV. P. J. F. GANTILLON refers our querist to 3ʳᵈ S. viii. 483, 526; ix. 48.]

SILPHIUM (5ᵗʰ S. viii. 449.)—H. C. C. will find an admirable and exhaustive article on silphium in the *Journal de Pharmacie et de Chimie* for Jan., 1877. It is written by M. Thérincq, Attaché au Muséum d'Histoire Naturelle de Paris, and published in full in pamphlet form, *La Vérité sur le prétendu Silphion de la Cyrenaïque*, chez Lauwereyns, 2, rue Casimir Delavigne. In it he upsets the claim put forward by Dr. Laval to the rediscovery of the long-lost plant of the Cyrenaica, and proves to his own satisfaction that the so-called *Thapsia silphion* is no other than the well-known *T. garganica*.

T. B. GROVES.

RAFFAELLE LESS USEFUL THAN A PIN-MAKER (5ᵗʰ S. ix. 28.)—So said Josiah Tucker, Dean of Gloucester, at a meeting of the Society for the Encouragement of Arts. See Northcote's *Life of Reynolds*, vol. ii. p. 78.   R. R.

Boston, Lincolnshire.

BIRDING-PIECE (5ᵗʰ S. ix. 27.)—I take it that the birding-piece was what we should now call a pea rifle, carrying a very small ball, and used, as was the stone bow or prod—a cross-bow for the discharge of bullets or stones—to kill small birds. The fowling-piece, on the other hand, was a large gun with smooth bore, often fired from a rest, and charged with slugs or "hail shot," employed for the destruction of wild ducks, wild geese, or to slaughter a covey of partridges sitting, as we see the fowler about to do in Rubens's great picture in the National Gallery.

W. J. BERNHARD SMITH.

Temple.

In an old inventory and valuation, dated Sept. 20, 1672, in my possession, I find the following:—"Five old Musketts and foure old Burden Peeces, at 5s. pr. peece, 2l. 5s." Further on in the same is:—"One Fowling Peece, 1l. 15s."

J. H. COOKE.

AUTHORS OF BOOKS WANTED (5ᵗʰ S. viii. 470.)—
Almegro, a Poem, is by Emma Roberts.
W. H. ALLNUTT.

(5ᵗʰ S. viii. 469; ix. 53.)
Thinks I to Myself was a very popular book in Northumberland in my young days. I have often heard my mother affirm that it was written by a Captain Beresford, whom she knew personally. He was, I believe, one of the Waterford family.   E. LEATON BLENKINSOPP.

(5ᵗʰ S. ix. 88.)
Abra-Mule: a Tragedy [by Dr. Joseph Trapp], acted at the new theatre in Lincoln's Inn Fields.—A copy of the first edition in 4to., 1704, is in the Dyce collection at

This tragedy was first acted in 1704, and revived in 1710, 1721, 1735, and 1744 (see Genest, *Some Account of the English Stage*, vol. ii. pp. 304-5, and also the Index).
A. BELJAME.

AUTHORS OF QUOTATIONS WANTED (5th S. viii. 90, 119, 159, 179.)—
"And thou, Dalhoussy, the great god of war," &c. If A. C. B. can point out where these lines are found in Blackmore, the question of authorship will be settled. Otherwise, and in absence of authority for his statement, they may be set down as Pope's own. They are marked "anonymous," and Dr. Warton informs us (see his edition of Pope's *Works*, 1822, vi. 207, 222) that most of the passages so marked are quoted from the poet's own youthful poems, and several such passages are specified by him. Where, on the other hand, the quotations are from Blackmore—and of these there are at least forty or fifty —instead of being marked "anon.," they have appended to them precise references in the notes. G. F. S. E.

(5th S. viii. 229.)
"Talis cum sis utinam noster esses."
Said by Agesilaus, the Spartan king, to Pharnabazus, the Persian general. See Plutarch's *Lives: Agesilaus.*
(5th S. viii. 307.)
"I do not love you, Dr. Fell," &c.
The student who made this extempore translation of Martial's epigram was Tom Brown, not John Locke. See *T. Brown's Works*, vol. iv. p. 100.

Miscellaneous.

NOTES ON BOOKS, &c.

The Talmud. By Joseph Barclay, LL.D., Rector of Stapleford, Herts. With Illustrations and Plan of the Temple. (John Murray.)

IT may truthfully, we think, be said of our country that everything relating to the Holy Land is sure of exciting interest among the reading public. The celebrated *Quarterly* article on the Talmud by the late lamented Emmanuel Deutsch is an instance in point. Yet our contemporary literature, at least the periodical portion of it, does not seem to devote much space to this subject, apart, of course, from the publications of the Palestine Exploration Fund and the *Transactions* of the Society of Biblical Archæology. Dr. Barclay, indeed, in his list of authorities chiefly followed by him in the preparation of his present work, only cites, besides the *Quarterly* article, one from the *Edinburgh Review* for July, 1873, and one from the *Law Magazine and Review* for August, 1872, on the "Growth of Jewish Law." Dr. Barclay does not appear to have known either Weill's book on *La Femme Juive: sa Condition Légale d'après la Bible et le Talmud*, or Prof. Thonissen's *Etudes sur le Droit Criminel des Peuples Anciens de l'Orient*, a portion of which is dedicated to Jewish law. But what Dr. Barclay has studied he has carefully presented to his reader in clear language, and he possibly desired rather to set forth the Talmud as the "wise men" had handed it down, and the "master builders" had built it up, than as foreign scholars had conceived it. The result is an undoubtedly interesting volume, from which a very good idea may be obtained by the Gentile reader of that "extraordinary

parent of much Oriental heresy, and must t in the creation of Mohammedanism. But, 1 there are deep and true sayings to be f(Talmud, and Dr. Barclay's book is well w attention of the student of history, as an ill the influence of tradition in moulding relig among a people who with truth said: "The the labour vast; but the labourers are slot the reward is great, and the Master of the h(for despatch."

The Bibliotheca Cornubiensis. By G. C. W. P. Courtney. Vol. II., P—Z. (Longn

THE publication of this volume marks an literature of its class. It purports to give details, with copious references to books authors who have had the luck to be born i or who have been in any way connected v written about that county. The biographic followed by complete bibliographical (we u in its most scientific sense) lists of printe manuscripts. The work, however, contains of facts concisely and accurately stated, wit such a number of English authors, that s better discard the notion of its being confin wall, and treat it as if the title-page read, " A of Some English Authors." If an author ha land of mines his county by adoption, M and Courtney have adopted him also, thou born in Timbuctoo. Nobody, it is imagine plain of this; on the contrary, most studer inclined to regret that the work is not univer we have the exact model of what a true D English Authors should be. There is no slips no hurrying over names—none of that 'oosen so much complaint has been made with regai works of reference. From the accurate nature of the information given in its page conclude that it had come from the persons even if we were not especially told so. It h that obtaining information from authors t a disadvantage, and true as this may be criticism, it cannot be doubted that it is a p the present instance. Messrs. Boase and (not indulge in either criticism or comment latter takes the form of facts. Facts, fact they—not by insisting on this in words, but Thus it is we are enabled to appreciate the cance of the instances they give in their which we need not make further reference say that not only in these cases but in every meet hard facts concisely stated. They h criticism, the facility and pleasure of which h than one bibliographer into a labyrinth in v lost himself.

The sources from which information has b comprise the whole range of English literatu very date of publication. Works of history travels, science, and fiction, all have been rai the slightest reference to the authors' si recorded. We observe that our columns hav used. In one of our early numbers there was a communication from our esteemed corresp JAMES CROSSLEY as to the authorship of Pt Accordingly, under Robert Paltock's name, bibliography of that delightful work of fi

article well illustrates our observations upon the accuracy of the bibliography of this work. The authors have solved the Gordian knot of "full" or "abbreviated" title-pages by giving titles in full, and that of the *Life and Adventures of Peter Wilkins, a Cornish Man*, occupies twenty-six lines. The remarkable part of the article on Paltock, and that which unfortunately distinguishes it from the others in this work, is the absence of biography. Interesting as it would be to have some knowledge of Robert Paltock, his name seems likely to remain in the same category as that of the lamented Edward Cocker, of arithmetical celebrity. Directly after Paltock's name occurs that of the author of another popular and anonymous work, *Philosophy in Sport made Science in Earnest*, in which Dr. Paris had the invaluable aid of that great artistic genius whose death we are all now mourning. Those who make anonymous works their study will find an ample field, and tolerably easy work, for they are invariably distinguished by the word "[anon.]." Finally, the printing and general get-up of the volume are all that could be desired; and considering that we have upwards of five hundred closely printed pages of double columns, it will compare in cheapness with any continental publication.

L'Intermédiaire des Chercheurs et Curieux (Notes and Queries Français). (Paris, Sandoz et Fischbacher.) WE are glad to see that our French contemporary and namesake continues to flourish. It contains much interesting and curious matter, as well as some valuable contributions to historical and philological science. Under this last head we would particularly note a carefully written paper in the number for January 25, 1878, on the "Orthography of Geographical Names," the author of which analyzes the documentary history of some local names in Alsace. This is, of course, rather a delicate subject since 1871; but it is temperately handled by the writer, and there can be no question that the list analyzed by him is that of a group of names of Roman not Teutonic origin. Oddly enough the French printers have turned "*Rubeus Mons*" into "*Rubens Mons*," as though their heads had been full of the recent Antwerp centenary, which would have been more excusable in a Belgian than in a French *Notes and Queries*. The future biographer of Pius IX., who is doubtless on the look-out for materials, may be glad to make a note of the story (for the truth of which we of course cannot vouch) that the first pontiff who outlived the years of Peter took snuff, in full pontificals, at his coronation in 1847.

WE can only hope that Professor Bryce will be induced to give us three such papers on Jerusalem, Athens, and Rome, as the one on Constantinople in this month's *Macmillan*.

IN *Old and New London*, Part LXII. (Cassell), so closely does Mr. Walford run with the present times that in his description of Blackheath and its former terrors he refers to the ludicrous attempt last year at the revival of the practice of highwaymen. This number has a peculiar interest for the inhabitants of S.E. London.

WE have received the first number of a new monthly issue of the *Irish Church Society's Journal* (Dublin, E. Ponsonby), which, by its combination of matters of general and special interest, and its appreciative notices of the Literature of the day, gives promise of a useful career, both as a Theological and Literary organ, refined in its tone, while firm in its expression of opinion.

MESSRS. DEAN & SON announce for immediate publication the one hundred and sixty-fifth annual edition of *Debrett's Peerage, Baronetage, and Knightage*, amplified, improved, and remodelled by Robert H. Mair, LL.D.

GEORGE CRUIKSHANK.—"N. & Q." will scarcely allow so great a genius and so good a man as George Cruikshank to pass from among us without a word of tribute to his memory. Although to the rising generation he appears as a figure of the past, his work has, in truth, but just ended, and the time for estimating the exact value and extent of his genius has not yet arrived. Whether his pedestal shall be as high as that of Rowlandson, Gillray, or of Hogarth, or whether it shall rise far above theirs, must be left to another generation to decide. I do not propose to attempt the most condensed sketch of that active, varied, laborious life, but shall confine myself almost exclusively to a few personal traits.

The clever portrait of Cruikshank by Maclise, in *Fraser's Magazine*, will at once present itself to the mind of each one of your readers. The great artist is there portrayed, with pencil and paper in hand, seated on a beer barrel, with a tobacco pipe, &c., at his side, with his eagle eye (that did not lose its brightness to the day of his death) fixed eagerly on some object which he is sketching. In that portrait of Cruikshank at forty years of age the Cruikshank of 1878 was immediately recognizable. But the surroundings were, since many years, entirely changed. The frequenter of public-houses, where only could be met those types of character which he has immortalized, had quitted his old haunts—had once and for ever, in *The Bottle, The Drunkard's Children*, and numerous other similar productions, stamped with eternal ignominy the great vice of the age—had become a teetotaler, and nobly set the example of practising—rigidly practising—what he himself believed to be right, and what he never failed to inculcate. Cruikshank was happy in the possession, to the very last, of both mental and physical activity. He was a man of progress; he went with the times, and had sympathy with the young generation springing up around him. He eagerly joined the Volunteers, and became a leading figure in the movement. In early life he had been destined for the sea, and only escaped being sent on board a man-of-war (those were the times of the press-gang) by hiding away. When mentioning to me once that episode in his life, which must have changed his whole career, and deprived the world (as I then suggested to him) of such a fund of amusement and instruction—"Well," answered Cruikshank, with a simplicity that was one of the great charms of his conversation, "well, I should have done my duty and become an admiral."

It was not my good fortune to know Cruikshank in early life; but for several years I was proud to count him among my most honoured friends. What pleasant evenings were those when, with the works of bygone days before us—those of his father (Isaac Cruikshank), of his brother (Robert), and his own—I sat by his side as, with the little magnifying glass which he always used, he examined the etchings, the very existence of many of which he had forgotten, and passed his remarks upon them as the circumstances connected with them were brought to his memory. "Ah ! that was my work when a very little fellow; let me sign it." "In that etching I helped my father; he did this part, and I did that." "This is the joint production of my poor brother and myself." "Capt. Marryat designed this, and I only etched it," &c. Never was a man more ready to impart information, or more desirous to accord to every one his due.

It has been said by a leading contemporary that Cruikshank was too jealous of his reputation. I never found him so. Jealous he undoubtedly was—and, perhaps, rightly so—of his share of the conception of one or two of the great works of fiction which he had illus-

was inspired by, and adapted ·his·verses to, the designs of·Rowlandson. But Cruikshank.always appeared to me .free from jealousy ·as far ·as·his particular ·branch of art was concerned, and was ever·ready ·to award his meed of praise to those who were striving after their laurels in ·his profession. I may mention two incidents in proof of this assertion.

Not very long ago I had received some etchings by a German artist—simple subjects, representing children in their various occupations. I laid them before Cruikshank, who, after examining them very attentively, exclaimed, " They are beautiful ; I should like to have been the.artist who did them ! " One evening a rising young English artist met Cruikshank at.my house, and submitted to him some specimens of dry point which he had just done. The old·man, ·in the fulness of his enthusiasm and the generosity of his nature, said to him, " They are very clever ; I was never able to do such work."

The complete list of George Cruikshank's almost numberless productions has yet to be made, for Mr. Reid's admirable catalogue—unfortunately too expensive for the million, whose artist George Cruikshank undoubtedly was—is not perfect. The .moment is surely propitious for a reprint of that work at a price which would ensure its more general circulation. Perhaps some of the contributors to " N. & Q." ·will undertake the interesting task of supplying the omissions referred to through your columns. For some time before his death George Cruikshank was engaged in writing his memoirs, and it is to be hoped that he has left in a forward state the MS. of a ·work which cannot fail to have an interest not only for the world of art, but for the public in general. H. S. ASHDEE, F.S.A.
46, Upper Bedford Place, W.C.

CHURCH AND DISSENT IN 1676.—A very scarce and interesting record is preserved in the William Salt Library at Stafford. It is a religious census of the province of Canterbury for the year 1676, and its origin is thus set forth in a certificate which two of the bishops have attached to the returns for their respective dioceses :— " In pursuance of a letter to me directed from the Right Reverend Father in God, Henery, Lord Bishop of London, to give an account of the number of Inhabitants, Papists, and other Dissenters within my Diocess, these are to certify that, according to the retorns to me made by the Ministers and Churchwardens of ye several parishes in the places abovesaid according to the most exact computation, this is a true retorne." The Volume is manuscript, beautifully written, and was formerly in the library of the Duke of Sussex. Certain errors of spelling lead·to the supposition that the copy was made from another manuscript, and not from a printed report; thus we have Ultoxeter for Uttoxeter, Itam, for Ilam, and Alurton for Alveton or Alton. The object of the census has not yet been discovered, or the authority by which the Bishop of London issued the " letters " referred to. Perhaps some of our readers can throw light on the subject. The information contained in the volume is tabulated in four columns—the names of parishes, the number of Conformists, the number of Papists, and the number of Nonconformists.

ROYAL ARCHÆOLOGICAL INSTITUTE.—Feb. 1.— G. T. Clark, Esq., in the chair—Mr. W. M. Flinders Petrie read a paper on " Ancient Roads."—Mr. Soden Smith exhibited and described a pectoral cross of the sixteenth century, covered with emblems and inscriptions, and

Notices to Correspondents.

ON all communications should·be written the nam address of the sender,·not necessarily for publicatio as a guarantee of good faith.

".A CURIOUS CUSTOMER."—The subject of thi; posed haunted house has been mooted ,·alrea ".N. & Q.", without eliciting any further inforr than you possess. The late Lord Lyttelton wr these columns : " It·is quite true that there is a ho Berkeley.Square (No. 50) said to be haunted, an unoccupied on that account. There are ·strange about it, into which ·this deponent cannot enter.' " N. & Q.," 4th S. x. 372, 399, 490, 506 ; xi. 84, 187

A RESIDENT IN WEST KENT (" Kentish Men " Men of Kent.")—See " N. & Q.," 3rd S. vii. 324 viii. 92, 131. The West Kent men are styled " K men," and those of East Kent " men of Kent."

E. N. HENNING.—You will find that much inf tion has already been given, ante, p. 53. Is it poss supplement it ?

L. N. T.—Marchand de brie-à-brac is a dealer iron, copper, brass, pictures, &c.

H. R. D.—No man can have a right to style h such unless he has taken a degree at some recoç university.

H. J. WAITE (Darlington.)—For " Cock and Story," see our 1st S. iv. 312 ; v. 414, 447 ; vi. 14 209 ; 2nd S. iv. 79 ; viii. 215 ; and 3rd S. iii. 169.

SHELDON HALL.—A proof will be sent. We always be glad to receive your communications.

H. G. A. should address his query to Science (Hardwicke, 192, Piccadilly).

D. T. M.—Please accept the initial letters assig this number. The single one is already appropriat

R. F. PITT wants to know which is the best w the Protestant religion. [Has he tried Chillingwo

W. P. H.—We shall be glad to have the inscript not already printed.

C. PETTET.—It is not an English word, and the not subject to the rules of English grammar.

TIBIA AMNE (sic) and GUY PAGANUS have sent no and address.

C. ST. S.—Apply to any large general bookseller

F. L. S. H.—It is impossible to answer such a qu

E. R —See Monk (M. G.) Lewis's Tales of Wonc

G. C. B.—Many thanks.

L. BARBE.—Proofs shall be sent.

K. N. and W. H.—Letters forwarded.

W. H.—Portland, Maine, U.S.A.

F. G. H. P.—No.

NOTICE.

Editorial Communications should be addressed to Editor of ' Notes and Queries ' "—Advertisement Business Letters to " The Publisher "—at the Offic Wellington Street, Strand, London, W.C.

We beg leave to state that we decline to return munications which, for any reason, we do not print to this rule we can make no exception.

LONDON, SATURDAY, FEBRUARY 16. 1878.

CONTENTS.—N° 216.

Notes.

QUEEN KATHARINE DE VALOIS.

The following, we have reason to know, is a fuller and more accurate summary than has hitherto appeared of the paper read by the Dean of Westminster, on the 31st ultimo, at a meeting of the Society of Antiquaries, held at Burlington House, at which the Earl of Carnarvon presided.

The paper read was upon the depositions of Katharine de Valois, the Queen of Henry V., the remains of the Queen having on that very day been placed in the chantry of Henry V., after many remarkable removals and vicissitudes. The Dean exhibited upon a screen the drawings made of the contents of a box in which, in 1778, the remains of Queen Katharine de Valois were laid, when placed in St. Nicholas's Chapel, in the vault of the Villiers, beyond that of the Percies. This latter vault having been opened in December last, upon the occasion of the burial in the Abbey of the late Lord Henry Percy, the opportunity was taken, by the sanction of Her Majesty the Queen, to remove the royal remains to the chantry of Henry V., which stands on the site of the original "Reliquary" of the Abbey. Katharine de Valois, the Dean remarked—"the Kate of the never-to-be-forgotten scene in Shakspeare's *Henry V.*"—was on the day of her funeral conveyed by water to St. Katharine's Church, of which, as Queen Consort, she was the patron; thence to St. Paul's, where

another service was held; and thence to the Abbey, and interred meanly in the Lady Chapel. In the time of her son Henry VI. it was proposed to move the body further down, and to erect a tomb more "honourably apparelled"; but it remained undisturbed until Henry VII.'s Chapel was erected, when the old Lady Chapel was destroyed, and with it her tomb, and the bones were removed to the vacant place on the south side of her husband's sepulchre. Various writers, the Dean showed—Pepys and Fuller among them—testified to the fact that the bones were, from time to time, exhibited. Till the eighteenth century they were thus exposed, and the Westminster scholars of those days were stated to have misused the remains. Finally, to avoid this scandal, they were enclosed in a wooden chest and were placed underneath the tomb of Sir George Villiers, beyond the Percies' vault. There they rested until, as stated, the funeral of Lord Henry Percy, in December last, rendered it possible to obtain the restoration of the remains to a fitting depository. Upon the box was a leaden plate with this inscription :—

> Katharine de Valois,
> Queen to Henry V.,
> 1437,
> deposited in this Chapel of
> St. Nicholas
> by Benjamin Fidoe,
> Clerk of the Works
> at Westminster Abbey,
> 1778.

The box was only nailed together in a rough way, and, having fallen away, the bones were visible in a rude sheet of lead. The upper part of the body had been, previous to its last burial in 1778, much disturbed, and several portions of it were missing. In conclusion, the Dean described the spot in Henry V.'s chantry where the remains of the French princess and English queen, fittingly placed in a proper covering, are now re-entombed between the Plantagenets and the Tudors, and near to the memorials of her husband's victories, by which he won her to be his bride, in the chapel which had been built under her own auspices. The new coffin bore, besides the old plate, a new plate, with the following inscription :—

> The former Chest,
> which for 99 years had decayed
> in the Villiers' Vault in the Chapel of St. Nicholas,
> was Removed thence,
> and this new Chest including
> the Royal Remains
> was, with the sanction of Queen Victoria,
> Placed here
> in this Chauntry of King Henry V.
> by Thomas Wright,
> Clerk of the Works at Westmr Abbey,
> in the Presence of
> Arthur Penrhyn Stanley, D.D.,
> Dean of Westminster,
> A.D. 1878.

The coffin is placed, with the fragments of the

--- ...., .g... ....,
'Requiescunt tandem,
Varias post vices,
Hic demum jussu Victoriæ Reginæ deposita,
Ossa Catharinæ de Valois,
Filiæ Caroli Sexti, Franciæ Regis,
Uxoris Henrici Quinti,
Matris Henrici Sexti,
Aviæ Henrici Septimi.

Nata MCCCC,
Coronata MCCCCXXI,
Mortua MCCCCXXXVIII.

In the course of the discussion the Dean repeatedly expressed his obligations to Mr. George Scharf, Mr. Doyne C. Bell, and also to Mr. Poole, the Master Mason, and Mr. Wright, the Clerk of the Works at Westminster Abbey ; and Mr. Doyne Bell added his testimony to that of the Dean in speaking of the reverential care which, on the occasions of such investigations, characterized all those concerned, down to the humblest workman. [See p. 140.]

"GARETH AND LYNETTE."

(*Continued from p. 42.*)

CHAPTER II.—THE COMBATS.

The History of Prince Arthur makes the order of the four combats to be, first, that with the Black Knight of the Black Lands (night), then that with the Green Knight (dawn), then with the Red Knight (noon), and then with the Blue Knight (evening) ; but Tennyson, evidently misled by the modern custom of beginning day with the morning and ending it at night, has not only deranged this natural order, but has been led into the anomalies of a *blue* morning and a *green* evening. There cannot be a doubt that green is more naturally associated with youth, strength, and hardihood than with old age and decay. It is very true we speak sometimes of a "green old age"; but the phrase is meant for a paradox, otherwise it would have no force at all. So again in the same misapprehension has driven the poet to make the *blue* star (or Blue Knight) the representative of morn's young beam, whereas "the blue star of evening" is a household phrase. Instead, therefore, of following the natural order of the old story, the black night, the green dayspring, the red noon, and the blue twilight, the poet begins with the Blue Knight, which he calls morning ; then takes the Red Knight, or noon ; thirdly, the Green Knight, which he makes "the green" evening star ; and, lastly, the Black Knight. Still stranger will this perversion appear when it is remembered that the story calls the Blue Knight an Indian or Eastern king, and not a Western knight, like the Green and Red. It is the Eastern

of changing the historic order, he might, if he chose, have made the Green Knight morning, and the Blue Knight evening. It was quite optional with him, and he made the change because he chose to do so. Plausible as this seems at first sight, it manifestly is not the case. Having made the first blunder, the poet was driven of necessity into the second. Green may glow into red or languish into blue, and blue may lead up to black ; but Tennyson felt it would be an outrage against common propriety to separate the blue from the red. It was absolutely indispensable to make black lighten into blue, and to bring the red and the green together. The history makes the blue evening darken into night, and the green morning glow into red noon. The poet makes blue the luminous abatement of black, and green the languishing of red, and thus far preserves a just propriety ; but, by the fatal error of beginning his day at the wrong end, he makes the blue morning dawn from the dark night of the past day, and was then compelled to make green the languishing and fading shade of red, instead of the living vigorous dawn which grew brighter and redder to the perfect day.

Of course, as Tennyson has changed the Green Knight into the Blue and the Blue Knight into the Green, we must not compare the combat of Tennyson's Blue Knight with the Blue Knight of the old story, but with the Green, and the Green Knight of the prose romance with the Blue Knight of the idyll. These combats I shall therefore omit, as the change of colour would involve considerable confusion, and the error which lies at the base of the two combats is fatal to their working out.

COMBAT WITH THE BLACK KNIGHT (*Historical Account*).—When Sir Gareth overtook the damsel, she turned on him in scorn. "What dost thou here, dish-washer? Thou savourest of kitchen grease and tallow. Return to thy clouts and dishes ; thou art an offence to me." "Damsel," said Gareth, "say what ye list ; I'll not leave thee till I have achieved this task, and I will achieve it or die in the attempt." "Thou ! thou, a washer of dishes, achieve my adventure ! You will find the broth too hot, I warrant, for such as thou." So saying, she rode on, and Gareth followed.

At nightfall they came to the Black Lands of the Black Knight, whose name was Peread, and saw in a hawthorn bush a black banner and a black shield, and beside them stood a black spear and horse, and on a black stone sat a knight in black harness. When the damsel saw him, she cried aloud, "Flee, Scullion, flee for thy life !" "Nay, fair damsel, it is for cowards to flee." Then came forth the Black Knight, and said, "Damsel, whom have we here ? Is this thy champion from King Arthur's court ?" " No champion of mine, sir knight, but a kitchen drab who forces himself on me." " So, so !" said the Black Knight ; " I 'll soon put him on his feet, and strip him of his conceit, though to fight with such a one will surely shame me." On hearing these words of scorn, Sir Gareth answered, " Sir Knight, thy words are big and swelling, but words I heed not. This land I mean to pass, maugre thy threats and lets." " Say you so ? Come on, then !" and he drove his horse till the two combatants came together like thunder, and the spear of the Black Knight brake, and Sir Gareth thrust him through both his sides, and he swooned, and forthwith died.

Then Gareth armed him with the Black Knight's armour, and took his horse, and rode after the damsel ; but she still cried, " Off, off, I say ! Out of the wind, thou kitchen knave ! Thou art an offence to me. Alas that such a caitiff should slay so good a knight !" And Gareth answered, " Damsel, ride on ; I follow."

This allegory is full of beauty, and will bear the closest examination. It describes the destruction of night by the rising day, but, inasmuch as the dawn is still partial darkness, the dayspring rides on the Black Knight's horse and in the Black Knight's armour. It will be observed that Gareth (the god of nature) kills the Black Knight, but not the others. The Green Knight is spared, and entertains Gareth ; for the rising sun is not slain, but cherished, by the hot noon. So the life of the Red Knight is spared, for eve is a part of the same day. And the Blue Knight is not only suffered to live, but in his castle Gareth and the damsel take their evening meal and pass the night. The day is over, and our hero sleeps till he rises the next morning to another day of toil.

Tennyson, with less consistency, makes the horse of the Red Knight slip in a river stream as the knight was about to give Gareth a fifth stroke, and the noonday sun " was washed away " by the running water. This will bear no criticism. There are not five strokes, or hours, between noon and eve, and to make the " sun washed away " before twilight is strange, if not more than strange. So again the poet makes Gareth hurl the Green Knight over the bridge, and say to him, " There sink or swim." If the Green Knight is morning, as in the history, the allegory is destroyed by this " dramatic stroke "; if evening, as the poet supposes, how much more beautiful is the original story. But we must return to the Black Knight, which, as I have said already, is the first of the four combats in the history and the last in the idyll.

Tennyson's Version.—Then came they in sight of Castle Perilous, and beside it was a huge black tent with black banner, and a long black horn hung beside the banner, which Gareth blew till the walls echoed. Thrice blew he the horn, when from the tent came forth a knight in night-black armour, riding a night-black steed, but spake no word. " Fool !" said Gareth, " men say thou hast the strength of ten ; can ye not trust then to your thews, but must think to scare us by your devices ?" Still the Black Knight answered not a word, but, putting spurs to his horse, rushed on his opponent. Gareth was ready for the knight, and with one stroke split his skull in twain, one half of which fell to the right and the other half to the left.

In this version the poet must be credited with two good points—one, the silence of the Black Knight, which is a decided improvement on the older story ; and, secondly, the splitting of the head in twain, in my opinion the best and most original thought of the whole poem, although it would not have suited the prose narrative. Night, as the close of day, belongs to two days—one half of the head falls to the day which is ended and one half to the day which begins on the morrow ; so, as the poet puts it, " one half falls to the right and one half to the left." Beautiful and apt as this idea undoubtedly is, it would not suit the prose romance, which begins day from the preceding eve, so that the head is not split in twain, but when night dies " its ebon spear is snapped, and the knight, being thrust through both his sides, swoons and dies." The thrust " through both his sides," and the " swooning of night " before daybreak, are equally graphic and pertinent. But as the poet, either by mistake or otherwise, has reversed the original order of the combats, he has, in a measure, compensated for the fault by a fine thought, both original and true.

E. COBHAM BREWER.

Lavant, Chichester.

(*To be continued.*)

SPIRITUALISM, ANCIENT AND MODERN.

" The prophet is a fool, the spiritual man is mad."— *Hosea* ix. 7.

Against Praxeas, Tertullian says he got his notions of the Trinity from the revelations of the Paraclete. In the *De Anima*, ii., he says : " The true system of prophecy has arisen in the present age." Chap. ix. he says : " The soul's corporeity was a mystery revealed by the Paraclete to a Montanist sister." He gives particulars of the alleged communication which exactly agree with those of the spiritualists of the present day. Montanus was the Paraclete ; Prisca and Maximilla were his associates, mediums, sisters, or prophetesses. However, as Tertullian does not give a name to her, the sister in question may have been another than those mentioned—one possessed with whom he was acquainted :—

" We have now amongst us a sister whose lot it has been to be favoured with sundry gifts of revelation,

in the reading of the Scriptures, or in the chanting of
psalms, or in the preaching of sermons, or in the offering
up of prayers—in all these religious services matter and
opportunity are afforded to her of seeing visions. It may
possibly have happened to us, whilst this sister of ours
was rapt in the spirit, that we had discoursed in some
ineffable way about the soul. After the people are dismissed at the conclusion of the sacred services, she is in
the regular habit of reporting to us whatever things she
may have seen in visions (for all her communications are
examined with the most scrupulous care, in order that
their truth may be probed). Amongst other things she
says, 'There has been shown to me a soul in bodily shape,
and a spirit has been in the habit of appearing to me;
not, however, a void and empty illusion, but such as
would offer itself to be even grasped by the hand, soft
and transparent, and of an ethereal colour, and in form
resembling that of a human being in every respect.' This
was her vision, and for her witness there was God, and
the apostle most assuredly foretold that there were to be
spiritual gifts in the Church (1 Cor. xii. 1-11; also
Romans i. 11). Now, can you refuse to believe this,
even if indubitable evidence on every point is forthcoming for your conviction? Since, then, the soul is a
corporeal substance, no doubt it possesses qualities such
as those which we have just mentioned; amongst them
the property of colour, which is inherent in every bodily
substance."

The evidence which is not to be resisted is proclaimed every day by our modern spiritualists.
I have heard it and seen it in print, where it is a
sister that is the medium, and communicates to
the writer* when a vision or inspiration does not
occur to himself. Here we have the soft substance
which is so often mentioned by the spiritualists,
either in a hand or being handled, the whole body
sometimes appearing. Tertullian, too, allows that
he sometimes caught the infection and went on
rhapsodizing in the manner we have in his
works, which is treated as sane theology. His
theory of colours might recommend it to Mr.
Gladstone.

Here, however, it may be said, is admission of
collusion between Tertullian and the sister. She
may have only interpreted his thoughts, or become
acquainted with them and delivered them in correspondence with those he imagined.

Colours entered into all systems of sacred and
profane theology. The Bible, Philo, and Josephus
treat of them. In all mythologies they are, down
to the Chinese and Japanese. Colours were symbols. Those who are interested in colours, as
many are in Chinese or Japanese, or have theories
of colours, as Mr. Gladstone, might find a fertile
field of research in these theological speculations
upon the properties of colours. W. J. BIRCH.
Oxford and Cambridge Club.

---

* Mr. Maitland in *The Soul, and How it found Me.*

ᴇxᴇᴛᴇʀ ᴘᴏꜱꜱᴇꜱꜱᴇꜱ ᴀ ᴄᴏʟᴏᴜʀᴇᴅ ᴇɴɢʀᴀᴠᴇᴅ ᴍᴀᴘ,
by 13¾ in., in which the city and its subu
delineated in that curious combination o
and elevation which distinguishes the maps
Tudor period. It is nearly certain that th
formed part of the Oxenden and Warley (
Warley collection, sold at Church House,
Street, Canterbury, on January 4, 1870, an
obviously the parent of the reduced and n
less complete copies engraved by Franci
Abraham Hogenberg for Braun (or Bruin
Hoefnagle's *Civitates Orbis Terrarum*, 1572-
for Speed's *Theatre of Great Britain*, edit.
for Izacke's *Memorials of Exeter*, edit. 1677
with more perfection of detail, for Lysons's
Brit., Devon, 1822. Mr. Brodie's map h
following title on the upper edge:—

"Isca Damnoniorum, britanice Kaier penhue!
Saxonice Monketon: Latine Exonia: Anglice Exea
vel Excestre et nunc Vulgo Exeter: vrbs pers[n]t
Emporium celeberrimum."

In an oblong compartment near the right
lower corner is the inscription: "Opera e
pensis Joannis Hokeri generosi ac huius Ci'
quæstoris, hanc tabellā sculpsit Remigius H
bergius. Anno Dñi 1587." In the top left
corner are the royal arms, with the letters "]
over the crown. In the top right-hand corn
the arms of Exeter, with the augmentatio
helm, crest, and supporters granted in 156'
without the motto "Semper Fidelis," bestow
Queen Elizabeth. In the lower left-hand c
are the arms, with six quarterings, of John H
the learned Chamberlain of Exeter (for who
engraving was made), with the motto "
Mortem Vita," and near the lower right corn
a pair of compasses extended on a scale, and
forming a triangle (Hoker was a Freemason).
impressions, evidently from the same plate
uncoloured, are known to exist in Exeter, o
them being in my own possession. These tw
pressions have been divided or folded dow
middle, as if for insertion in a book, the 1
hand portion differing from Mr. Brodie's in
omission of one of the trees close to Exe Br
and in the incomplete obliteration of the comp
and scale, which are replaced by some lin
shading less carefully executed than those o
original. These discrepancies have given r
the suggestion that the right-hand half of
original plate had been damaged and re-engra
but this is disproved by a careful comparison
a magnifying glass, which shows that the min
strokes and even the accidental defects of
Brodie's copy are reproduced in the two ot
The former is believed to be a unique impre

made for John Hoker himself from a plate which was soon afterwards slightly altered for publication, as above described. The evidence afforded by the plate itself of its having been engraved from a drawing by John Hoker is amply confirmed by documents in the Record Room of Exeter Guildhall. Bound up with his MS. account of the city, of which he was the first chamberlain and the first and best historian, are three or four rude coloured sketch plans, on which his own handwriting is to be easily recognized, and which were obviously essays for the drawing (if not the identical drawings) on which the engraving is founded. No one of these forms by itself a representation of the entire city, as shown in the engraving, and yet a comparison of their details conclusively proves that Hoker, the artist, and Hogenbergius, the engraver, were working in concert. If any of your numerous readers are acquainted with other impressions of this interesting map, they may possibly be in a position to decide whether the belief in the uniqueness of Mr. Brodie's copy is well founded or otherwise.   R. Dymond.
Exeter.

Sir Thomas Adams, Bart., Lord Mayor of London, and President of St. Thomas's Hospital.—On the south side of the chancel of the church of St. Mary and St. Margaret, Sprowston, co. Norfolk, is a large and costly marble monument to the memory of Sir Thomas Adams, Bart., who was formerly Lord Mayor of London, on which are life-size recumbent figures of himself, with his chain and robes of office, and his wife weeping above him, while on either side are two smaller figures, also weeping. There is a long Latin inscription. Sir Thomas was born at Wem, in Shropshire, in the year 1586. He was educated at the University of Cambridge, and afterwards commenced business as a draper in London. He rose to be sheriff in 1639, and was made Lord Mayor in 1645. At various times he represented the City in Parliament, and was chosen President of St. Thomas's Hospital, which institution he saved from ruin by discovering the frauds of a dishonest officer of the institution. He was subsequently dignified with the title of the "Father of the City," and became an intimate friend of King Charles II., to whom he remitted in various sums about 10,000l. when that monarch was in exile. When the restoration of that king was agreed upon, Mr. Adams (he being at that time seventy-four years of age) was deputed by the city of London to accompany General Monk to Breda, in Holland, to congratulate his Majesty, and escort him to this country; for which service the king, after the restoration, knighted him in the month of December, 1663, and some time afterwards advanced him to the dignity of a baronet. As a public benefactor Sir Thomas's character stands

highly conspicuous. He gave the house of his birth at Wem as a free school to the town, and liberally endowed it. He also founded the readership of Arabic at Cambridge, both of which events took place before his death. He was also at the expense of printing the Gospels in Persian and sending them to the East, that he might (as he quaintly expressed it) "throw a stone at the forehead of Mahomet." He died at the age of eighty-one on February 24, 1667, his death having been hastened by his falling to the ground while stepping out of a coach. His body lay in state for several days at his residence in Ironmongers' Hall, London, and on March 10 his remains were solemnly conveyed to St. Catherine Cree Church, London, attended by the Lord Mayor and Aldermen, the members of the Drapers' Company, the governors of St. Thomas's Hospital, and Heralds-at-Arms, where a funeral sermon was preached by Dr. Hardy (at that time Dean of Rochester). The body was placed in the vestry of that church, and on the 12th of that month removed in a hearse and buried in the chancel of Sprowston Church. In the welfare of St. Thomas's Hospital Sir Thomas exhibited great interest. He purchased Sprowston Hall of Sir Thomas Corbet (who was the last baronet of his family) in 1645. The arms of the family were Ermine, three cats passant azure.
Walter P. High.
Norwich.

Dante and Milton.—In your "Notices to Correspondents" (5th S. viii. 480) you quote a passage from Paradise Regained, canto iv., in which the poet says that a tempest is to the whole frame of heaven and earth as inconsiderable and harmless "as a sneeze to man's less universe." This you justly characterize as bathos. It is remarkable that Dante, in his Paradiso, has been guilty of a comparison which is equally bathos. In the thirty-second canto St. Bernard says to the poet:—

"Ma perchè il tempo fugge che t' assonna,
Qui farem punto ; come buon sartore
Che, com' egli ha del panno, fa la gonna."

It must be remembered that at this moment St. Bernard and Dante are supposed to be in "the heaven which is pure light," the poet being rapt in admiration of the White Rose of the Blessed ; it is accordingly rather startling to hear the saint talking of cutting his coat according to his cloth. Considering the time and place it is, I suppose, the most extraordinary simile in all literature. Let any one read the marvellously ethereal description of the White Rose, with the angels flying about amongst the ranks of the Blessed, and plunging into the river of light, and then, in the midst of all this light and angelic music and motion, think of a tailor cutting cloth : the shock is like that of a cold douche ! Milton and Dante are, after Shakespeare, the two

call up the same ideas as a tailor in our days, as mediæval dresses were so much more magnificent and costly than our own. This may be so; but I am nevertheless of opinion that for the poet to introduce the idea of a tailor—or, as Cary translates it, "workman"—cutting cloth, however rich, in Paradise (and such a Paradise!) was "the most unkindest *cut* of all."

In the fifteenth canto of the *Inferno* there is also a simile of a tailor, which, although quaint, is picturesque, and much more appropriate than the other. A band of spirits in the seventh circle meeting Dante and Virgil:—

"Si ver noi aguzzavan le ciglia,
Come vecchio sartor fa nella cruna."

As I am on the subject of tailors, will some one tell me why the old lady in the *Midsummer Night's Dream*, when the victim of Puck's mischievous trick, cries "tailor"? Why tailor any more than cobbler, hosier, or barber?

JONATHAN BOUCHIER.
Bexley Heath, Kent.

ANOTHER FOREIGN CRITIC ON SHAKSPEARE.— The estimate of Shakspeare by the Abate Andrès, quoted 5th S. iii. 223, led me to refer to the opinion of another clerical foreign critic, the Abate Antonio Riccardi, whose *Manual of Universal Literature* was published at Milan in 1831. I find him scarcely more complimentary to our great dramatist than his predecessor. After having given him credit for the sublimity of his thoughts and the energy of his characters, he continues :—

"Con tutto ciò non abbiamo di lui un dramma solo, nel quale le poche bellezze originali non sieno oscurate da molti e più grandi difetti. Le sue terribili pitture provano piuttosto la forza del genio, che la cognizione del cuore umano; e il filosofo amico dell' uomo si consola, non trovando che produzioni esagerate e colossali, che non hanno il loro modello nella natura. I suoi drammi sono mostruosi : senza unità nel disegno, senza morale nell' azione, senza decoro nell' espressione, accozzano insieme di tutto, stravaganza, orridezze, oscenità, incoerenze, bassezze le più biasimevoli. Si trova spesso nella medesima opera il comico più basso col tragico più sublime," &c.

And the worst part of all is that

"intanto il generale entusiasmo per questo autore ha perpetuato i suoi difetti sul teatro Inglese, e ne ha sbandito il buon gusto sino a questi tempi."—Pp. 393, 394.

C. W. BINGHAM.

BLACK BARLEY : THE FEAST OF THE BIRDS.— About thirty years ago, being at the Gogerddan Arms, Aberystwith, Mr. Powell Davis the landlord, who also farmed some land in the vicinity, informed me that he had grown some extraordinary black barley, said to be famous for its malting property, that had a history attached to it which I

cut. I felt interested at his account, and gave me the address of the person who ha him, by whom it was publicly advertised to the advertiser to send a small quar friend of mine, an agriculturist in the division of Northumberland, who got su sow a rood of land. The barley gre' promised an abundant crop; but so s ripened it attracted all the birds of th who appeared to have some mode of con ing the news, as they came in flocks and grain in the ear as it ripened. A boy was with a gun to fire powder charges, but i of the gun the birds prevailed, so that ir the product was less than the quantity sown. The circumstance of this grain col many birds excited considerable curio several farmers and others came from a d see the crop and the birds which it collect recollect rightly, my friend would not the experiment the following year, as the terfered with his other grain crops, a: with those of his neighbours (who did no when they could not obtain the coveted l

About the same period some new whea troduced, said to have been obtained fron of an Egyptian mummy, and went by 1 of "mummy wheat," which produced seve from one stalk. I have seen it figured popular periodical. From some cause ne black barley nor the "mummy wheat" w vated. The reason why the former could fitably be grown has been explained. J. Barbourne, Worcester.

Queries.

[We must request correspondents desiring in on family matters of only private interest, to : names and addresses to their queries, in ordei answers may be addressed to them direct.]

HOGARTH CARICATURED.—Can any r form me who is the "A C" whose in: on the etching I am about to describ 8½ × 6½ in., drawn with considerable free spirit, and a good deal of coarse humour. resembling Hogarth, but with dog's legs, at work before an easel, palette and mah hand; a curly tail peeps from his lon; coat; an enormously fat nude female fi; of ordinary proportions, and another of . hag-like form, are posed in quaint at and a stumpy black-clad man* (the "dur

* Probably Dr. John Hoadly, who assisted B writing the *Analysis of Beauty*.

noisseur") is evidently vastly pleased with the painter's work. A satyr grins from above, holding a mirror in which are reflected a fool's cap, bells and bauble. A middle-aged cherub, with the well-known *Line of Beauty* in his mouth, floats overhead, and several minor figures complete the designs, which contains half a score of satirical allusions to the *Analysis of Beauty*.

Under the print occur the words: "Puggs GRACES Etched from his ORIGINAL Daubing A C Invt et Sculp Publish'd According to Act of Parliame't 1753-4"; and the lines:—

> "Behold a Wretch who Nature form'd in spight,
> Scorn'd by the Wise; he gave the Fools Delight.
> Yet not contented in his Sphere to move
> Beyond mere Instinct, and his Senses drove
> From false Examples hop'd to pilfer Fame
> And scribl'd Nonsense in his daubing Name
> Deformity her Self his Figures place }
> She spreads an Uglines on every Face }
> He then admires their Ellegance and Grace }
> Dunce Connoisseurs extol the Author Pugg,
> The sensles, tasteless, impudent Hum Bugg."

Was the artist's needle inspired by personal hatred, or was it only a weapon hired by Wilkes or Churchill?   J. ELIOT HODGKIN.

[This is Satirical Print, Brit. Mus., No. 3242, and as such described in the published catalogue of those works. It is by Paul Sandby—one of a numerous category produced by that worthy and others, foes to Hogarth. "A. C." doubtless, as Mr. Scott of the Print Room suggests, stands for Annibale Carracci, *i.e.* according to Sandby's whim, "Scratchy"; he not unfrequently indulged himself in this fashion. If we are to believe Wilkes and Churchill, they were on intimate terms with Hogarth at the period indicated by the date, 1753-4, and therefore neither of them is likely to have had to do with this satire. It was prompted by the "personal hatred" of P. Sandby, one of the supposed causes of which was Hogarth's resolute opposition to the institution of an "Academy" for artists under *dilettante*, royal, noble, or rich patronage, which Sandby and his party desired. This prompted Hogarth's and B. Thornton's attacks, *e.g.* the Sign Board Exhibition, on the fussy "patronage" of the Society of Arts of that day and some other big-wiggeries, much abhorred by the Englishman, who wished painters to help themselves. The print refers to this opposition in the inscriptions, "No Salary Reasons against a Publick Academy, 1753," and "Reasons to prove erecting a Publick Academy without a wicked Design to introduce Popery & Slavery in to this Kingdom." These passages are ironical, of course. The fat nude woman is probably Mrs. Hogarth. "Pugg" refers to the nose of Hogarth, his small stature, and dogmatic air. There are at least two states of this etching; on the back of one of them is an address "To the Publick" in mockery of the *Analysis of Beauty*, and proposing the publication of "An Analysis of the Sun."]

MONBOUCHER FAMILY.—Can MR. VINCENT, to whom I am very much indebted for his interesting addition to the Halsham family (5th S. ix. 76), give me any information concerning the above family? I came across it in tracing the Skipwith pedigree, for I find that Sir William Skipwith, eldest son of Sir William Skipwith, Chief Justice of England, married Katherine de Aswarby, and

had an only daughter Elizabeth, who married "Georgio domino Moni Bourchier," and died without issue (*Vis. of Yorkshire*, 1584-5 and 1612, edited by Joseph Foster, 1875, p. 634). On tracing this gentleman it appears, from an Inq. p. m., 10 Hen. IV., No. 33, that he died without issue, leaving his wife Elizabeth living, and that his brother Ralph, aged twenty-six and upwards, was his heir, not only to his paternal properties, but to some of those that he obtained through his marriage. As this latter property, not very long after, appears in the possession of the Tirwhite family, I wish to know how it passed from Ralph Monboucher's hands. Did Elizabeth Skipwith marry for a second time a Tirwhite? The property I am anxious more particularly to trace is the manor of Bigby, in ancient times spelt Bekeby, and with it Kettleby, both in co. Lincoln. Can MR. VINCENT or some other of your correspondents inform me anything as to Ralph Monboucher's end, by inquisition or otherwise?   SYWL.

"IN RANCONTEN."—I shall be glad if any of the readers of "N. & Q." can offer me any suggestions as to the significance of this term. It is a business expression, and has, I believe, some connexion with the goldsmith's or banker's trade. I have met with it in several accounts in the ledgers of Alderman Edward Backwell (who was a great banker) of 1663, but in every instance the account in which the term was met with was that of a goldsmith and banker, as, for instance, cf. Vyner, Colvill, Snow, or others. In the account of Hinton & Co., who were goldsmiths at the Flower-de-Luce, in Lombard Street, in 1663, I find they were credited "by money in Ranconten," and debited "to them in Ranconten"; again, Sr Wm. Ryder pays Alderman Meynell "in Ranconten" so much. In a ledger of 1668 the term was not used.   F. G. HILTON PRICE.
Temple Bar.

"FIRST AN ENGLISHMAN AND THEN A WHIG."— What is the old Venetian proverb which Macaulay parodied in this sentence (speech delivered Jan. 29, 1840)?   P. C.

THE "COW AND SNUFFERS."—Near Llandaff, in Glamorganshire, there is an old roadside inn rejoicing in the name of the "Cow and Snuffers." I have frequently wearied myself in endeavouring to trace the possible origin of the name. However, a short time since I read, in the *Cardiff Times* :—

"The 'Cow and Snuffers' was so named by the late Sir Robert Blosse, of Gabalva, father of the present Dean of Llandaff, and its odd nomenclature has often exercised the ingenuity of antiquarians, but no satisfactory solution of the problem of its origin has as yet been forthcoming."

Can any reader of "N. & Q." throw any light on the subject? I may add that the old sign-

emphasis he laid on the words "crocodile and mummy," when playing the part of Bayes in the *Rehearsal.* I have searched my copy, dated 1796, in vain for any such expression.   H. CROMIE.

KEATSIANA.—How much older than John Keats was his friend and patron Charles Armitage Brown, the retired Russia merchant? What was Miss Fanny Brawne's subsequent married name? What was the exact height of John Keats? Byron somewhere calls him a manikin; and the poet himself, in one of his letters to his relatives in America, is angry because a lady has said of him, "Oh, he is quite the little poet."   ZERO.

THE WHITEHALL CHALICE.—I have a chalice bought some years ago from Lambert & Rawlings, which they called the Whitehall Chalice, from some legend that it was used in the Roman service at the Chapel Royal there. It is silver gilt, and screws off into three pieces, so as to be comparatively easy to pack into a small space. I remember being told it had been exhibited some twenty years ago at some great exhibition in the City, perhaps at the Guildhall. The catalogue gave the history of this chalice, according to my informant, but I foolishly delayed to follow up the clue. Does any one know when such an exhibition of artistic treasures took place, or where a catalogue is to be obtained?   K. H. B.

"ST. AUGUSTINE'S CONFESSIONS."—I have before me the following book :—

" S. Augustine's CONFESSIONS : With the Continuation of his *Life* to the End thereof, Extracted out of *Possi.dius,* and the *Father's* own unquestioned WORKS. Translated into *English.* S. Aug. *De Bono Persever.* c. 20 [quoted]. Printed in the year 1679."

There is no publisher's name, and the preface of two pages is neither headed nor signed. Who was the translator?   A. J. M.

AN INEDITED(?) CRITICISM OF CHARLES LAMB'S. —In the last edition of *Chambers's Cyclopædia of English Literature,* 1876, ii. 97, it is stated :—

"Charles Lamb, in a communication to the *London Magazine,* says of Lord Thurlow : ' A profusion of verbal dainties, with a disproportionate lack of matter and circumstance, is, I think, one reason of the coldness with which the public has received the poetry of a nobleman now living; which, upon the score of exquisite diction alone, is entitled to something better than neglect. I will venture to copy one of his sonnets in this place, which, for quiet sweetness and unaffected morality, has scarcely its parallel in our language.' "

Then follows the well-known sonnet, " O melan-

Talfourd, 4 vols., 1849–1850, Mr. Shepher 1875, and Mr. Kent, 1 vol. (1877); no Babson's *Eliana,* 1864.   WM. BUCE 87, Union Street, Glasgow.

COLERIDGE OR WALPOLE.—The late I Collins commenced an article with the " ' Summer has set in with its usual sev Coleridge said." An eminent publisher i hands the paper was placed inserted Wa Coleridge. Can any of your readers tell n this remark of Walpole's is to be fot whether Coleridge ever wrote anything kind likely to mislead Mortimer Collins, usually so accurate in his quotations ?
                                                              FRANCES Co
5, New Burlington Street, W.

MORTON, IN DUMFRIES.—In 22 Edw Feb. 16 (1348), there is a grant from Edw of the manor of Morton, in the co. of Dun Scotland, which had belonged to Willi Heriz, to Stephen de Swynnerton, for l services in war, &c., to hold to the said and his heirs for ever (*Rot. Scot.,* vol. i. p the Stafford Library). Can any of your refer me to any subsequent account of the and of the family of the grantee ? If Ste mained in possession it is probable he cha name to "de Morton."   M

BADGES.—I shall be glad to be all supersede my former query (*ante,* p. 107) following :—1. Gu., planta-genista ppr.; 2 portcullis or; 3. Az., a fleur-de-lis or; 4 rose *arg.* and gu. ; 5. Gu., on a tower or *arg.* ; 6. Gu., a tree eradicated, leaves ppi and branches *arg.,* roots or. In my form munication I used ar. as the abbrevia *argen.* This your printer mistook for az., a consequence, the beauty of the badges been fairly set forth.   ST. SWI
[*Az.* was plainly written in each case.]

MISTRESS (OR LADY) FERRARS.—Whe find some account of Mistress Ferrars (c Ferrars, as she is sometimes called), who b to a gang of highway robbers that infeste fordshire in the last century, and who is said been put to death in front of her own l Market Cell, near Market Street, in that c
                                                              C. I

REGINALD HEBER.—About the middle last century there lived in Chancery Lane having prenomen and family name similar of the estimable Bishop of Calcutta, but whose pursuits seem to have been ,somewhat different from those of the pious prelate. The works of the one are too well known to require recapitulation ; those of the other seem to have been limited to *An Historical List of Horse-Matches run* 1753, and in subsequent years.

"Reginald" not being a very common first name, and being conjoined in both instances with "Heber," also not a very frequent designation, I am led to ask if there might have been any family connexion between the two. The bishop could not have been the son of the other person referred to ; *his* father was a divine of some repute, who succeeded to a brother's estate in· Shropshire in 1766, and subsequently, at the demise of his brother's widow, in 1803, to the family estate in Yorkshire. It would be then only in that county that we might trace the connexion, if any, between the two men similar in name but so different in their pursuits ; though, if I may be pardoned the remark, I would say that each was an ardent lover of his race.   PHILIP ABRAHAM.

147, Gower Street.

GERMAN MEASLES.—Why is this malady so named ? If the term were popular—but it is hardly that yet—one might suppose *German* to imply that the malady was spurious ; that it simulated the genuine malady, as "German" silver does the pure metal. Is not German here *germanus,* akin to, as in cousin-german ? Or is this type of measles so common in Germany that it has become thus designated ? Perhaps some medical reader of "N. & Q." will throw light upon the origin of the term.   HENRY ATTWELL.

Barnes.

"LIBERTY AND PROPERTY !"—Voltaire frequently alludes to this as the recognized national watchword of Englishmen. Fielding makes the electioneerers in *Pasquin* agree that

"We 'll fill the air with our repeated cries
Of 'Liberty and Property !' and 'No Excise !'"

To how late a date did the words continue in use as a familiar phrase ?   CYRIL.

AUTHORS OF BOOKS WANTED.—

Autobiography of a Country Curate ; or, Passages of a Life without a Living. 2 vols. in 1. London, Smith, Elder & Co., Cornhill, Booksellers to their Majesties, n.d., post 8vo., pp. 276 and 257.
   JOHN PICKFORD, M.A.

Law Quibbles : | or, A | Treatise | of the Evasions, Tricks, Turns, and Quibbles, | commonly used in the Profession of the Law, | to the Prejudice of Clients, and | others ; Necessary to be perus'd by all | Attornies, those who are or may be | concern'd in Law Suits, Trials, &c. to avoid | the many Abuses, | Delays, and Expences, | introduc'd into Practice. | With | An Essay on the | Amendment and Reduction | of the Laws of England. | The Third Edition, Corrected. | To which is added, | A New propos'd Act of Parliament, for a | thorough Regu-

lation of the Practice of the Law. | And also | The Contents of Divers late Statutes, relating to | Vexatious Arrests, Attornies and Solicitors. | Bribery. Forgery and Perjury, &c. | In the Savoy | printed by E. & R. Nutt, and R. Gosling | (Assigns of Edw. Sayer, Esq), for L. Corbett, at | Addison's Head without Temple Bar. 1729.
   HIRONDELLE.

Wanted reference to a "piece" called *New Potatoes.*
     S.

AUTHORS OF QUOTATIONS WANTED.—

"Instead of useful works, like Nature's grand,
Enormous cruel wonders crush the land."
   R. C. A. P.

"Plus negabit in una hora unus asinus quam centum doctores in centum annis probaverint."
   E. MARSHALL.

"How can we admire, when we are all starving ?
So less of your gilding, and more of your carving."

Can any of your readers complete this epigram, of which I remember only the last two lines, and say the occasion of its composition ? Martial has a similar one, on some ostentatious but stingy Roman (book iv. 78, *In Varum*).
   JOHN CLARKE.

Replies.

THE NANFAN FAMILY.

(2ⁿᵈ S. viii. 228, 294, 357 ; 5ᵗʰ S. viii. 472.)

The following stray notes, collected for another purpose, though by no means exhaustive, will tend to throw some light upon the history of the family of Nanfan, and the question of there being still existing any légitimate descendants of that family. There can be no doubt, I think, that the family was Cornish, though they possessed property in Worcestershire. Of their connexion with the latter county I am unable to say anything. It is situate beyond the range of my researches.

The first of the name of whom I have any knowledge is Henry Nanfan, who was Keeper of the Fees of the Duchy of Cornwall in 1374 (Ministers' Accounts, Duchy of Cornwall, 48 Edw. III.). In 1386 Henry Nanfan held, as one of the trustees, certain manors belonging to the family of Bodrigan (Ped. Fin., 10 Rich. III., Michs.). In 14 Rich. II. Thomas Nanfan was one of the jurors upon an inquisition concerning the franchises of the priory of Plympton, in the manor of Lanow, in Cornwall. The same Thomas and Johanna his wife, in 1397, were parties to a fine for the settlement upon them and their heirs of the manor of Penfons and other lands in the same county (Ped. Fin., 20 Rich. II., Easter). John Nanfan was Sheriff of Cornwall in the 7th and 18th of Henry VI., and, according to tradition, was a servant to one of the Erysy family, *temp.* Henry V. In 1431 Richard Beauchamp, Earl of Warwick, John Nanfan, Esq., and others, levied a fine of David Halep and Margaret his wife of the manor of Trethewell, in the parish of St. Eval, Cornwall, and divers other manors and lands, and the advowson of the

for ever. (All these manors and lands had been parcel of the possessions of John Billon, of Trethewell, who was living in 1396, and would seem to have been carried in marriage to David Halep by Margaret his wife, for she was clearly the inheretrix. Was she the daughter and heir of John Billon, or of Walter his brother? For information upon this point I should be grateful.) John Nanfan presented to the church of St. Tudy, 1444. He is believed to be the son of the last mentioned, was Sheriff of Cornwall in the 29th and 35th Henry VI., and is the first of the county sheriffs on the Pipe Rolls styled "Esquire," that title not being usually given to the sheriffs until about the middle of the reign of Henry VIII. In 1453 he was made Governor of the Islands of Guernsey and Jersey (Pat. Roll, 31 Hen. VI., m. 25), and three years later collector of all the customs, &c., there (Pat. Roll, 31 Hen. VI.; m. 5). To him succeeded Richard Nanfan, whom we find in the Commission of the Peace for Cornwall in 1st Henry VII. (Pat. Roll, 1 Hen. VII., part i. m. 33). In the same year he is styled "Esquire of the King's Body," and two years afterwards he received a grant from the king of the manors of Bliston, Camanton, and Helston Tony, in Cornwall, in tail male, to hold by the service of one knight's fee (Pat. Roll, 3 Hen. VII., part ii. m. 15). In this grant he is also styled "Esquire of the King's Body." He was dubbed a knight by the king before Christmas, 1488 (anno 4), on the way towards Kingston, when the king sent him ambassador into Spain (Cott. MSS., Claud. III.). He was Sheriff of Cornwall in 1489. Sir Richard Nanfant died Jan. 1, 1506-7, and it appears from the inquisition taken thereupon that he was seised, inter alia, of the manor of Trethewel, &c., and the advowson of the church of St. Tudy, and that he enfeoffed Richard, Bishop of Exeter, and others, to hold to them and their heirs in fee to the use of the said Richard Nanfant and his heirs, and to the performance of his last will; and that afterwards the said bishop and the others suffered a recovery in the said manors, &c., to Thomas Bradbury, James Erysy, and Robert Tredonek, to hold to them and their heirs, by virtue of which the said parties were seised in fee to the same uses; and that afterwards the said Richard, by his last will, dated Nov. 10, 1506, and proved in the court of the Archbp. of Cant., April 16, 1507, devised all the said manors, &c., to the said James Erysy to hold to him and his heirs for ever, and directed the above-mentioned Thomas Bradbury and Robert Tredonek to make a sufficient estate in law to the said James. The jury find that John Bollys is room of Sir John Salusbury-Trelawny at Tr Cornwall, Baronet.

The will of Sir Richard Nanfan, dated a stated, is, I think, of sufficient interest to be with some fulness, especially as it would s dispose of the claims of the Nanfans of Wo shire to be legitimate descendants of the He gives his body to be buried in the pl the north side of the "south yle of the Chu Seint Bart'hus spitell in West Smythfeld, L where I use to sett in my pewe there. It. myn Executor shall purvey and ordeyne venyent tombe according to my degre, to be and set o'er my body wth a scripture to be in latten of all suche offices as I have ha occupied in this world, to be fixed vnto the tombe." Bequeaths for the good of his soul v legacies. Gives to Dame Margaret, his w much plate of silver and silver gilt as shall a to the value of 100 marks, 20l. in money, gives to John Nanfan his great red horse tha from Calais; gives a ship of silver,* price vjs. to be offered to St. George in Southwarl another like ship of silver, of a like price, to George in Cornwall. Devises all his manor in Cornwall, as stated above, to James Erys his heirs and assigns for ever; gives to Eli Welles an annuity of 10l. as long as she sh of good lyvyng, guyding, and governance; gi John Nanfan, his bastard son, all the resi his lands and manors in the county of Worcest to his heirs for the term of thirty years, rem to him and the heirs male of his body; in d remainder to the right heirs of testator. Ap Thomas Wulcy, clerk, and the said James Esq., executors (Prob. April 16, 1507; Adea P.C.C.). Soon afterwards a pardon and under the Great Seal was granted to T Wulcy, clerk, and James Erysy, executors will of Richard Nanfan, Knt., late the king's of Calais, and sheriff of the counties of Woi and Cornwall, for all offences committed h said Richard (Pat. Roll, 22 Henry VII., p m. 3).

It remains to say a few words of Dame Ma the relict of Sir Richard Nanfant. She d 1510. In the inquisition taken thereupon th say that John Nanfan, clerk, and John I were seised of four messuages in South Beau Devon, and, being so seised, gave the sa Richard Nanfant, Esq., and the said M Nanfant, then his wife, and the heirs of bodies; in default of such issue, remain

---

* A standing vessel in which to burn incense.

Robert Holbeine and Johanna his wife, and the heirs of the body of the said Johanna ; in default, remainder to the right heirs of the said Margaret. The jury say that the said Margaret died without heirs of her body, and that the messuages descended to a certain Philip Holbeine, as son and heir of the aforesaid Robert and Johanna. And they say the said Margaret died April 6, 1510. By her will, without date, she directs her body to be buried in the church of the Exaltation of the Cross, within the Hospital of Seynt Bartholomew in Westsmythfeld, London, with her husband ; gives to James Erysy her great bed, &c.; the residue to Thomas Crewker, master of the said hospital, and the brethren and sistren of the same, which Thomas she appoints her executor, to the intent, inter alia, that the said master, brethren, and sistren shall specially pray for the souls of Richard Nanfan, Knt., and Margaret his wife, brother and sister of the chapter of the said hospital, and for the soul of Thomas Clemens and all Christian souls (Probate April 8, 1510 ;' Benett, 27).

I must apologize for the length of these notes, and will refrain from offering any comments upon them. The facts will speak for themselves.

JOHN MACLEAN.
Bicknor Court, Coleford, Glouc.

Claiming descent from this family, I feel an interest in all connected with it, and should be glad to know if any of its descendants in the male line are living. I have searched for persons of this name in various directories, both London and county, but hitherto in vain. The following note is copied from Old Worcestershire Houses (p. 36), which contains engravings of Birtsmorton Court :—

"Mr. William Nanfan died in Newport Street (Worcester) in 1869. He claimed to be the lineal descendant of Sir Richard Nanfan, Knt., who, in the reign of Henry VII., was Captain and Treasurer of Calais, Keeper of Elmley Castle, and Hereditary Sheriff of Worcestershire ; and to be entitled to Birts Morton Court, and the broad lands attached to it."—From Berrow's *Worcester Journal*, Jan., 1870.

An officer of this name served, on the British side, in the American War of Independence. Authors of this name, whose works are in the British Museum Library, are :—

Nanfan, Bridges—Essays Divine and Moral, 1681. Sermons and Essays on Eccles. xii. 1.
Nanfan, John—Answer to a Passage in Mr. Baxter's Book, intituled, A Key to Catholics (1660?).

I have not met with the title of any work by Gervaise Nanfan.   H. BOWER.

DEATH OF EDWARD, DUKE OF YORK, 1767.
(5th S. vii. 228, 274, 294; viii. 192, 215, 238, 397 ; ix. 95.)

It is much to be regretted that G. D. P. does not give us the authentic information of what really occurred at Monaco, which he says is in his possession (viii. 192). If the papers to which he refers really contain authentic information, or even only information which may possibly be proved by other facts, and so rendered authentic, their production would be of great use. In place, however, of giving us any one fact, G. D. P. contents himself with a few problematical suggestions of what might have been the case, and then treats these suggestions as established facts. Thus he tells us that "the duke had sufficient cause for acting in the way he did." What evidence is there that the duke acted at all ? Again, he asserts that "the duke in his anger, and for other reasons, determined to give up his position and large income, preferring rather to retire into obscurity than be burdened with the many annoyances of his life." Now what evidence is there that he made any such determination, or that his life was full of annoyances ? He was then a handsome, popular young prince of the blood royal, of the age of twenty-eight, with an income of 20,000l. a year, and free to enjoy life in any way he chose with one exception—he was not free to interfere in the government of his brother's kingdom, or to speak and vote in Parliament against his brother's ministry ; and this both the king and his ministers pointed out to him. Travelling through Europe under the convenient title of the Earl of Ulster, fêted and caressed in each court that he chose to visit, accompanied by faithful and attached attendants, we are asked to believe that he formed the ghastly and absurd scheme of acting his own death, giving up everything, and retiring from the world to live and die in poverty, obscure and nameless.

It is suggested that the duke was likely to do such a thing because more than once the King of England, being also Sovereign Prince of Hanover, has, when much troubled with the vexations of his English government, been reported to have said, "I would rather resign the English crown, and retire to my Hanoverian dominions." It is easy to believe that a king governing two distinct countries, and who had endless anxiety and trouble from the one, and nothing but pleasure and gratification from the other, might talk of resigning the troublesome charge. This, however, supplies no argument to render it at all probable that a prince, enjoying all the pleasures and none of the heavy responsibilities of government, would —not talk of resigning part of his occupation, but voluntarily give up everything but his bare life.

It would be hardly too strong an expression to say that the duke could not have carried out the farce of his supposed death alone, and without very clever assistants. Three or four of his personal attendants, Colonel St. John, Colonel Morrison, Capt. Wrottesley, and Mr. Edward Murray, were in constant attendance, and must either have been parties to the alleged fraud or would have

diately after the duke's death the body was opened and embalmed, and there is a reasonable certainty that some at least of his attendants must have seen and identified the body as that of their much loved master. We are at present a very long way off from any necessity for opening the coffin which was so solemnly deposited in Westminster Abbey on Nov. 3, 1767. All known evidence leads to the conclusion that it really did contain the body of the duke. An assertion has been made that it did not, and it is the evidence on which this assertion is made that is now asked for. If it was to be stated that Queen Anne did not, as commonly believed, die on Aug. 1, 1714, but that to escape the constant worry of her ministers (and it was commonly said that she was worried to death when the Privy Council quarrelled before her till two in the morning on July 27, 1714) she had it given out that the queen was dead, but that in fact she quietly escaped to France or elsewhere, every one would say, "Have you one fact of evidence to support this fiction?" In the same way I would now ask with regard to the Duke of York, who is commonly believed to have died at Monaco on Sept. 17, 1767, Is there any one fact known to make it appear probable that he was alive later than that day? Are there any facts connected with his pecuniary accounts, or the administration of his property, or letters to or from his friends or attendants, which warrant the assertion now made?

EDWARD SOLLY.

SHELDON HALL, WARWICKSHIRE (5ᵗʰ S. viii. 285.)—As the descendant of a former owner of Sheldon Hall, I shall be happy to give you any help. In the Inq. p.m. of Humphrey Stafford, Duke of Bucks, 38 Hen. VI., the manor of Sheldon—*i.e.* East Hall—and West Hall formed part of the possessions of that nobleman. In the Inq. p.m. of Sir Edward Devereux, Knight and Bart., 1622, Sheldon was left to his son Sir George, Knight (Dugd., *Baron.*). It descended to Pryce Devereux, tenth Viscount Hereford, at whose death, in 1748, I believe it to have been sold. Lord Digby in 1622 was Lord of the Manor. Sir Edward Devereux built Castle Bromwich, which, according to Dugdale, was sold in 1657 to Sir J. Bridgeman, whose descendant still holds it.

HEREFORD.

Tregoyd, Hay, R.S.O.

P.S.—Since writing the above I find Sir George Devereux's mother, Lady Devereux of Castle Bromwich, was an Arden of Park Hall, and Mrs. Arden's (her mother) sister (they were Throck-

A PASSAGE IN "LYCIDAS" (5ᵗʰ S. ix. 67.)—In my note on *Lycidas*, l. 46, I did not mean positively to adopt the explanation of "worm" as "spider," but merely to suggest the possibility of Milton's having availed himself of a poetical licence of this kind. In that case my citation from Sir T. Browne's *Vulgar Errors* would be to the point. But from what I have learned since the publication of my book, I am inclined to think that Milton meant nothing of the kind, and that he alludes to certain maggots (commonly known as "flukes") which infest the livers of sheep, and are the effect of cold and damp. This was first pointed out to me in a notice that appeared in the *Westminster Review*, Oct., 1874. If a new edition is wanted, I shall omit the reference to the "spider," and substitute what I now believe to be the true explanation.   C. S. JERRAM.

Windlesham, Surrey.

I presume the word ought to be written "*tainct-worm.*" Take the following passage:—

"There is found in the summer a kinde of spider called a *tainct*, of a red colour, and so little of body that ten of the largest will hardly out-weigh a grain. This by country people is accounted a deadly poison unto cows and horses, who, if they suddenly die and swell thereon, ascribe their death thereto, and will commonly say they have licked a *tainct.*"—Sir T. Brown's *Pseudodoxia Epidemica*, ed. 1650, p. 179.

The worthy author goes on to state that he has administered the *tainct* to calves, horses, dogs, and chickens without their suffering any inconvenience. Perhaps, he suggests, another insect is to be blamed, the *buprestis*, or "burst cow," the *cruca* (canker-worm), or the like; which *buprestis* (in Greek the sweller up of oxen) seems to be of very similar habits to the *tainct*, to wit, "a poisonous beetle which, being eaten by cattle in the grass, causes them to swell up and die."

Such dictionaries as I have at hand seem to have based their definitions of the *tainct* on Sir T. Brown's account, viz. :—

"*Tainct*, a small red spider, infesting cattle in summer."—Cole's *Dict.*, edit. 1701.

"*Tainct*, a little red coloured insect, being a kind of spider that annoys cattle in the summer time."—Phillips, *New World of Words*, edit. 1720.

"*Tainct*, a small red spider, troublesome to cattle in summer time."—Bailey's *Dict.*, fifth edit., 1731.

"*Tainct*, a kind of red coloured spider, very common in the summer time."—Halliwell, *Arch. and Prov. Dict.*, 1840.

Tainct seems curiously enough connected with a set of words in several European languages giving a parallel double meaning of scabbiness or scurf, and of a moth or rodent worm. For instance, take Fr. *teigne*, scurf or a hot scabbiness on the head ; also a moth (Cotgrave). It. *tigno*, a mite, a wezell, a meal-worm, a corn-worm, a nut-worm, a grub, a cheese-grub, a moth that devoureth clothes ; *tignoso*, that hath a scald head ; *tarma*, a moth or worm breeding in woollen clothes ; *tegna*, the head-scurf, the dead scald (Torriano). Span. *tina*, a moth ; *tina de la cabeca* (of the head), the scurffe or white scaule (Minshew, *Span. Dict.*, 1623). I have heard it said in Cheshire of a very bald man, " He has the moth." Apparently in Latin the double meaning holds, but the worm or vermin meaning is more large and general. Lat. *tinea*, a gnawing worm, a moth, wood, beehive, or figtree worm, one in the human body, used also of lice (Andrews's *Dict.*). *Tinea*, a gnawing ulcer in the head (Phillips).   HORATIO.

EAR-RINGS : GEN. XXIV. 22 (5th S. viii. 361, 453.)—The word "ear-ring" here is probably due to the *inaures* of the Vulgate, which in like manner may be derived from the ἐνώτια of the Septuagint. The use of the word is treated of in the article in Smith's *Dict.* But to the occurrence of it, as there noticed, it may be added that St. Jerome explains, in his *Commentary on Ezekiel*, xvi. 12, how the special word *inaures* came to have a general use, which may also apply to our " ear-ring ":—" *Et dedi inaurem super os, sive, nares tuas.* Verbum Hebraicum Nezem (נֶזֶם), qui interpretatus est ἐπιρρίνιον, omnes *inaurem* transtulerunt : non quo inaures ponantur in naribus, quæ ex eo quod de auribus pendeant inaures vocantur : sed quo circulus in similitudinem factus inaurium, eodem vocabulo nuncupatur : et usque hodie inter cætera ornamenta mulierum, solent aurei circuli in os ex fronte pendere, et imminere naribus."—*Opp.*, tom. v. col. 134, ed. Migne, Par., 1845.

The passages in which the word occurs sometimes have no specification of the use, as Gen. xxiv. 22, Judg. viii. 24 ; sometimes state for the nose or forehead, as Gen. xxiv. 47, Ezek. xvi. 12 ; sometimes for the ears, as Gen. xxxv. 4. A comparison of the renderings in our version, and of the marginal readings, with the Hebrew, leads to the supposition that our translators felt uncertain about the meaning of it in different passages. The article *u.s.* observes "that it originally referred to the nose-ring, as its root indicates, and was transferred to the ear-ring " ; and that " in the majority of cases the kind is not specified, and the only clue to its meaning is the context."

ED. MARSHALL.
Sandford St. Martin.

Rebecca's jewel was a Nezem (nose-ring) נֶזֶם, as proved by Proverbs : " A Nezem of gold in the *nose* of a swine : woman fair, of averted taste " ; סָרַת טַעַם perhaps contradicting, illogical, but not indiscreet or imprudent (בְּלָא תְּוִשִׁיָּה). Ear-

ring is more connected with אֹזֶן, the listening organ, and is possibly the נְטִיף (ear-drops) of Isaiah iii. 19, as Mr. Sharpe translates. .I hold that whereas Palestine was the archaic crossing country of mercantile caravans (like modern Belgium), the indigenous language incorporated foreign words of products of nature and art. Thus why do the Germans say, " Das Thermometer (*Wärmemesser*) zeigte 17 Grad (*Stufen*, *Tritte*) Kälte," and let the Greek and Latin displace the *indigenous* words ?   S. M. DRACH.

MAC MAHON FAMILIES (5th S. ix. 7, 59, 97.)— I see that in my note on this subject the date of the death of Ross Mac Mahon has been inadvertently wrongly printed ; it was 1748, not 1740, Ross having succeeded his brother as Roman Catholic Primate for one year. As several of your readers appear to take an interest in these brothers, I will here give an *exact copy* of their tombstone, copied by myself on August 18, 1852, from the original in the old graveyard of Ematris or Edergole, in the barony of Dartrey, and county of Monaghan. On a flat stone in Edergole Churchyard :—

HIC IACET BERNARDUS ET ROCHUS
MAC MAHON FRATRES GERMANI U-
TERQUE SUCCESSIVE EPISCOPUS CLOG-
HIRENSIS UTERQUE ETIAM SUC'ESIV-
E ARCH-ARMACANUS TOT'S HIBN. PRIM-
ATI. QUORUM NOBILISSIMI GENERIS
MEMOR PIETAS ATQUE ÆMULA DOC-
TRINA VITAQUE TI'ULIS NON IM-
PAR MERENTEM PATRIAM DECO-
RAVERE. BERNARDUS OBIIT DIE 27
MAII, 1747, ÆTAT 67, ROCHUS DIE
29 OCT., 1748, ÆTAT 49.
AMBO PARES VIRTUTE
PARES ET HONORIBUS AMBO.
THIS MONUMENT WAS ERECTED
BY MR ROGER MAHON BRO : TO THE
DECEASED PRIMATS. ANNO DOM: 1750.

EV. PH. SHIRLEY.
Ettington Park, Stratford-on-Avon.

VERE ESSEX CROMWELL (5th S. ix. 28.)—There was no relationship between the Welsh family from which the Protector was descended and that of Thomas Cromwell, who was created Earl of Essex in 1539. About that time Morgan, the son of William ap Yevan, had taken the more permanent family name of Williams, and married the sister of Thomas Cromwell. The family then assumed the designation of Cromwell als Williams. The first who bore this double name was Sir Richard Cromwell als Williams of Hinchinbrooke, the great-grandfather of the Protector. His son, Sir Henry, also adopted it, but his grandson, the father of the Protector, was styled only Robert Cromwell, and after this time the old Welsh name of Williams was wholly lost in this branch of the family in that of Cromwell.

Hence the Protector could not trace any blood

created Earl of Ardglass, but succeeded to the title in 1682, on the death of his nephew the third earl, and died in 1687, when the title became extinct.

EDWARD SOLLY.

E. Q. will find, upon referring to the pages of Burke, that this nobleman was not created Earl of Ardglass, but succeeded to that dignity as fourth earl upon the decease of his nephew in 1682. The Earls of Ardglass were the descendants of Gregory Cromwell, the son and heir of Cromwell, Earl of Essex. The Protector derived his Cromwell descent and name through the marriage of his great-grandfather, Sir Richard Williams, with the sister of the vicar-general. W. D. PINK.
Leigh, Lancashire.

LONDON FOGS (5th S. ix. 28.)—Is it not the case that fogs in the London valley are caused by the great rarefaction of the air, owing to the quantity of gas that is burned during the night? Fogs begin about the time that the gas is extinguished, about 8 A.M., and become most intense at 10 or 11 A.M. W. S. L.

HERALDIC (5th S. ix. 28.)—The arms and crest are those of a branch of the family of Hartopp; but the beasts are otters, not beavers.

J. WOODWARD.

See Harleian Society's Publications, vol. ii. p.196.
G. J. A.
Clifton Woodhead, Brighouse.

THE WORD "READ" (5th S. ix. 28.)—"Red" would certainly be a better way of writing the past tense of the verb "read." It is not improbable that a corrupt pronunciation may result from the present mode of spelling the word. The verbs *eat* and *beat* have to some extent undergone this change for the worse, which they might have escaped had their past forms been written, according to their better pronunciation, *et* and *bet*.
W. SPURRELL.
Carmarthen.

"THREESTONES" (5th S. ix. 28.)—The Auld Wives' Lifts, Stirlingshire, are of this class. It is customary to creep on hands and knees between the upper and two lower stones. They are said to be Druidical. JOHN BULLOCH.

A SERVIAN DOCUMENT (5th S. ix. 46.)—The document cited by MR. LEVESON GOWER is clearly the confirmation of a gift of land to a certain Zhupan (a title, not a proper name) Vlesimir by Stephan Dabisha, the Ban of Bosnia, who also

not be utterly destroyed in this gr is well known to scholars what a n able MSS. (far more important 1 been lost while these unfortunate been under Turkish rule.

The Logothet was the title of the of the Bosnian and Servian princes can form an opinion without seei document, there would appear to b racies in the translation; but you not be wearied with these minutiae.
W.]

INDIA-RUBBER SHOES (5th S. ix. ber these well some forty or forty They are not to be met with no made of the genuine article, not of the goloshes of the present day, ar every way more substantial.
Pendleton.

THE ISLE OF MAN A BAD PLACE —I have often heard the epigram N to, but could never gain any partic One conjecture which seemed to m that the last line (which, by-the-by "choicest," not "chosen") refers about the end of the last century, of Man, affording an immunity fr the favourite haunt of broken-dc worn-out *roués*, and generally of 1 lived "not wisely, but too well."

"NEITHER HAWK NOR BUZZARD' —"Too high for the hawk, and buzzard," were the words in which friend of mine delivered judgmen monial prospects of a well-educate the daughter of a tradesman in a cc

Θαύματα μώροις (5th S. ix. 68 *Reviews*, "On the Study of the Evic tianity," by Baden Powell, p. 115 gone further, and have considered of miracles as little more than is e: ancient proverb, θαύματα μώροις, posed to be nearly equivalent to tl evil generation seeketh a sign,' &c. —From a foot-note, *Letter and Spt Wilson, 1852.*" The Greek words on them may have only been ta Powell from Mr. Wilson, and by N the *Diegesis* of Taylor. None of authorities, and it is well known

Taylor scarcely ever did, and therefore he is not depended upon.   W. J. BIRCH.
Oxford and Cambridge Club.

PELHAM FAMILY : REVER VEL TREVE MANOR, CO. SUSSEX (5th S. ix. 47.)—In the late Mr. Mark Antony Lower's *Historical and Genealogical Notices of the Pelham Family*, printed for private circulation some five years ago, he records at p. 29 how, in the 28th of Henry VI., Sir John Pelham and Alice his wife had a grant from his father of the manor of Treve with the knight's fee, advowson of the free chapel there, and all reversions belonging to it. Mr. Lower further states that this manor of Treve is a place *unknown*, but that on the death of Sir John it devolved on an *only* daughter, Isabella, married to John Covert, second son of William Covert, of Sullington, co. Sussex. We can now, I venture to think, identify this manor of Treve, and that from the circumstance of its appearing in the De Banco Rolls, as recorded by your correspondent, under the title of Treve *als Ryver*. The manor of Rever is mentioned in a Subsidy Roll, Henry IV., 1411-12, relating to the county of Sussex, as follows. John Pelham holds the manors of Pelham, *Ryvere*, and Nutbourne, which are worth yearly, beyond reprises, 66*l.*, viz. :

Manor of Pelham	...	...	...	... £10
Manor of Ryvere	...	...	...	40
Manor of Nutbourne	...	...	....	16

Rever or River was at Tollyngton, in Domesday Tolintune—a parish in the hundred of Rotherbridge, situate a mile from Petworth. There is known to have been a chapel there, and in local nomenclature we still find enclosures called Chapel Field, Lady Field, Chantry Field, &c. Lotgarshall, anciently Lodekersale, Lotegershale, and now Lurgashall, is likewise in the hundred of Rotherbridge, five miles from Petworth, and in the rape of Arundel. This clearly is the locality allotted to Emma Pelham. The other places referred to are close at hand : Upmerden, in the rape of Chichester ; also Merston, or Mersitone ; likewise Lynche, or (as in Domesday) Lince ; Rumboldswyke, one mile from Chichester ; and Stopham, or Stopeham, in the same hundred as Lotgarshall and Tollyngton.

There is yet another place which may have some connexion with these possessions. I mention it merely from a certain significance in the name. Treyford is also in the rape of Chichester. In Domesday it occurs as Treverde. Before the Conquest it was held by Alard of Earl Godwin, but there is a break in its history from this period to the sixteenth century, when Sussex antiquaries associate it with the Aylwins, an ancient county family.   JOHN EDWARD PRICE, M.R.S.L.
60, Albion Road, Stoke Newington.

There is a manor called River in the parish of Lurgashall. This parish is situate in the rape of Arundel, and is distant about five miles south-west from Petworth.   D. M. STEVENS.
Guildford.

Lotgarshall and Ludgarsale are doubtless the present parish of Lurgashall, near Petworth, and Tolyngton would probably be Tillington parish, close to Petworth. The river Rother runs through part of the latter parish, and that portion of the village is known as River and River Common. There are three farms also in the parish named, respectively, River Farm, Little River Farm, and River Park Farm. Tillington and Lurgashall parishes join. I hope this may prove of use to MR. ELWES ; but if he wishes for further information, and will communicate with me, I will try to obtain it for him.   E. E. STREET.
Grayling Well, Chichester.

The following note under "Tillington," in Hussey's *Churches of Kent, Sussex, and Surrey*, p. 296, affords a clue to the identification of Tolyngton and the manor of Rever :—

"At River, in the northern part of Tillington [near Petworth], was once most probably a chapel, the names Chapel Field, Lady Field, Soul Field, and Chantry Field being still known there ; and a stone coffin was dug up on the premises of River Farm."

To this Hussey adds his authority—Horsfield's *Sussex*, vol. ii. p. 181.   E. H. W. DUNKIN.

EARLY BRITAIN (5th S. ix. 8.)—" Conderco, Con derch, high point. Peak (of Derbyshire, or any other)." The Derbyshire "Peak" is, *pace* Ordnance map and other authorities, *not* a hill, but a large tract of the country, so that places many miles apart, *e.g.* Hathersage, Castleton, Bakewell, Buxton, &c., are said to be *in* it as a district, not *on* it as a mountain. Kinder-scout, often miscalled the *Peak*, is not even a high point, but a lofty plateau two miles or more long, E. to W., about half as wide, N. to S., and 2,088 ft. high, at the new Ordnance datum, on the S.W. corner. In wet weather its surface drainage falls down the western cliffs in a grand shoot, which after heavy rain has been seen from Manchester glittering in the setting sun, but at other times steals away down crannies in the millstone grit of the upland, to leak out among the *débris*, hundreds of feet below, as the Kinder brook *en route* Hayfield, &c. Kinder-scout is at any rate good early British, Kin(cin)-dwr-scwd meaning in Cymraeg "high water cataract," a name sufficiently appropriate, as the source must be 1,800 ft. above sea level. Not far off are the Cluther rocks—Cymraeg again. Cluder (pronounced *Clidder*) meaning a confused heap or litter. Near Snowdon are Y Glyderfawr and Y Glyderfach, Great and Little Cluder, and those who have ascended them, as all Snowdon tourists ought to do, will see how true the title is.   H. B. BIDEN.
Sale, Manchester.

have only the *Poésies en Patois de Liége* of Si-
monon (1845).　　　　　　W. R. MORFILL.

BRISBANE OF BRISBANE (5th S. viii. 208, 293,
397, 516.)—In the year 1840 there were issued the
family pedigrees of Brisbane of Bishoptoun, Brisbane Macdougall of Mackerstoun, and Hay of
Alderstoun, framed from authentic documents by
William Fraser, printed upon two large sheets of
drawing paper.　　　　　　T. G. S.
Edinburgh.

"Go to" (5th S. viii. 28, 94, 138.)—No one has
pointed out, I think, that in French familiar conversation one is always hearing "Allez!" used
interjectionally in the sense of defiant raillery;
indeed, a vulgar Frenchman's argument, like Dog-
berry's, is interlarded with it at every point.
　　　　　　VINCENT S. LEAN.
Windham Club.

RAFFAELLE LESS USEFUL THAN A PIN-MAKER
(5th S. ix. 28, 117.)—R. R. points out that this
expression was used by Tucker, Dean of Gloucester,
at a meeting of the Society for the Encouragement
of Arts. A very similar comparison is put by
Voltaire into the mouth of the *blasé* Venetian
nobleman Pococurante, in the novel *Candide:*—

"'Ah, voilà quatre-vingts volumes de recueils d'une
académie des sciences,' s'écria Martin; 'il se peut qu'il
y ait là du bon.' 'Il y en aurait,' dit Pococurante, 'si
un seul des auteurs de ces fatras avait inventé seulement
l'art de faire des épingles; mais il n'y a dans tous ces
livres que de vains systèmes, et pas une seule chose
utile.'"

I fancy the above quotation was written before
Tucker made the depreciatory remark concerning
Raffaelle. The story of those philosophical but
not exemplary young people, Candide and Cuné-
gonde, is known to have been much read in
England at the close of the last century.
　　　　　　ALBAN DORAN.
20, Lower Seymour Street, Portman Square.
[Voltaire died in 1778 and Tucker in 1799.]

"SILE" (5th S. viii. 26, 138, 318.)—This appears
to be an interesting word. In the sense of to
strain it can have nothing to do with A.-S. *syl=*
filth, soil, a word with cognate forms in most
European languages. Its root must rather be
sought in the first two letters *si*, and the *l* be
regarded as a secondary element, probably indicating a diminutive form. Such a root is widely
extended with the signification of sifting or strain-

preserved in the common speech of th
of England. French *seau*, of which the
form is *seille*, only means a bucket ; Lat.
　　　　　　C.

This word is common all over the north
land, where it signifies the passing of milk
a fine wire sieve. The vessel in which th
inserted is termed a *milsie* or *milsey*.
word be merely a corruption or abbreviatic
might naturally arise from hasty pronunc
milksieve? And may not *sile* be a simila
tion or diminutive of *settle?* for settling an
which are the removing of foreign or
ingredients or substances, have the sam
view. This seems to have as much probe
going back to Saxon roots to find the g
of the word. G. S., who thinks the Scot
of the word is *sine*, appears to be confu
entirely different words. *Sine*, or, more
syne, means since or ago, *e.g.* "Auld lar
Anglicè (paraphrase), "Long, long ago
G. S. seems to have been thinking of ou
word *synd*, which I have sometimes he
nounced *syne*, which signifies to rinse or
wash.
Kelso.

The Scottish form of this word, as
Jamieson's *Dictionary*, is certainly *sile*,
sine, as supposed by G. S. It is a transit
signifying to strain, and derived from t
Gothic word *sil-a*, colare, whence also *sil*, a
It is also to be found in Dr. Webster (ec
by Goodrich and Porter), where the ety
sila, Swedish and Armorican ; *sielen*, Low
siolaidh, Gaelic ; and *siol*, Irish ; all ha
same meaning—to strain or filter. The
rather uncommon, but still used in some
of Scotland and perhaps in the northern
England, and almost invariably with ref
the straining a liquid through a sieve or
　　　　　　A.
Richmond.

The same word is preserved in *silt*,
familiar enough in Lincolnshire as descri
fine deposit left by the tide on "war
Silt is a valuable word, as we have no oth
describes the dregs left by water-straining
　　　　　　E.

THE FIELDFARE (5th S. viii. 286, 354,
—The belief that the fieldfare is a migrant

have been accepted in Chaucer's time from the proverbial phrase, "Farewell, feldefare!" in *Rom. of Rose*, 5513, and *Troil. and Cres.*, iii. 861, which Tyrwhitt could not understand.

VINCENT S. LEAN.

Windham Club.

DRAYTON (5th S. ix. 87.)—The name Drayton is one of those curious evidences of the succession of races which abound in our land. The first syllable is British, signifying "town." *Tre* (pronounced *dra*), or, as it often for the sake of euphony becomes, *dre*, enters into the formation of the names of many places in the Principality. Every Drayton, therefore, may be looked upon as an ancient British town which was in existence when the Saxons came, who, not perhaps exactly understanding the meaning of the term *dre*, called the place *Dra*-ton. There is a similar curious instance in the name of a parish in Cumberland—Torpenhow—where there is a hill called Torpenhow Hill, concerning which Hutchinson, in his *History of Cumberland*, ii. 353, says : "Every syllable of which word, in the several languages of the people which successively did inhabit the place, doth signify after a sort the same thing." "The Britons call a hill *pen*. The Saxons succeeding them called the place Tor-pen, *i.e.* pinnacle pen. They who came next Torpen-how, that is the 'how or hill Torpen.'" Hutchinson also gives two other probable derivations, which I will only refer your readers to.   W. F. MARSH JACKSON.

AKARIS OR AKARIUS FAMILY (5th S. ix. 49.)—I am sorry that I am quite unable to answer IDONEA's queries except as regards one item. The supreme authority for grants of manors at any period is the Patent Roll, and that is to be seen at the Public Record Office.   HERMENTRUDE.

OFFICE OF THE STRACHY (5th S. ix. 68.)—I presume Ω. refers to the well-known passage in *Twelfth Night*, Act ii. sc. 5. I believe the word is now generally received as meaning the *general*, or military governor of the place, from στράτηγος, strategy, stratgy, stratchy, *strachy*.

If your correspondent will turn to Charles Knight's *Pictorial Edition of Shakspeare*, he will find in a note on the place nearly as much information as it is possible to collect on the point. Halliwell notices the word, but imperfectly.

• W. T. M.

Nearly all to be said on this noted and almost desperate Shaksperian crux may be found *in voce* "Strachy" in the Glossary (vol. ix. p. 419) of Dyce's *Shakespeare*, second edition, 1867.   HORATIO.

" TRA. SA. " (5th S. ix. 68.) is an abbreviation for " traxit sanguinem." In the Court Rolls of the Manor of Titsey such entries as the following occur frequently, although not in an abbreviated form.

In 4 Hen. IV. : " Juratores presentant quod Johes Helyar injuste 'traxit sanguinem' de Valentino Mory "; and again, in 7 Hen. IV. : "Presentant quod Rob'u' Stonhurst injuste et contra pacem 'traxit sanguinem' cum una Rakestel de Simone Coffyn." "Item quod Joh^na uxor Johis Lambe contra pacem 'traxit sanguinem' de Alicia uxore Thome Cheseman cum pugillo suo ad insultum ipsius Johannis."   G. L. G.

Titsey Place.

The third passage surely should read, "Et quod Felicia Muleward levavit hutesium *in*juste super Aliciam Foreward, ideo in misericordia." A proper raising of a hue and cry could hardly be finable. Probably the transcriber has read "hutesium" for "hutesiu [with an abbreviation mark over the final *u*] in."   WALTER RYE.

In the court rolls which I have examined " extraxit sanguinem " is commonly used, and the contraction takes the form of "extra. sa." or "ex. sa."   K. P. D. E.

AN OLD WORK ON GEOMETRY (5th S. ix. 67.)—The work inquired for by B. H. J. is—

. "Practical Geometry ; Or a New and Easy Method of Treating that Art, whereby the Practice of it is render'd plain and familiar, and the Student is directed in the most easy manner thro' the several Parts and Progressions of it. Translated from the French of Monsieur S. Le Clerc. The Fourth Edition. Illustrated with Eighty Copper-Plates. Wherein, besides the several Geometrical Figures, are contain'd many Examples of Landskips, Pieces of Architecture, Perspective, Draughts of Figures, Ruins, &c. London, Printed for T. Bowles, Print and Map-seller in St. Paul's Church-Yard ; and J. Bowles, Print and Map-seller, at the Black Horse, Cornhill. MDCCXLII."

This title-page is taken from the copy in the Educational Library at the South Kensington Museum.   R. O. Y.

FANS (5th S. ix. 88.)—The Liverpool Art Club held a special exhibition of 176 fans in the clubhouse in the late autumn of last year (1877). An interesting and instructive introduction to the catalogue was contributed by Mr. G. A. Audsley, of Liverpool. The Wyatt collection of 148 fans, given to the nation by the late Sir M. Digby Wyatt and Lady Wyatt, a short time prior to the death of the former, is exhibited at the South Kensington Museum. Each fan is separately described by a label mounted with it. The collection consists of English, French, Italian, Flemish, Dutch, German, Chinese, and Japanese fans.

GEORGE WALLIS.

South Kensington Museum.

[It is announced that an exhibition of fans and a competition in the art of fan-making are about to be held in the City, under the auspices of the Fan-Makers' Company—a guild founded in 1709, under a charter granted by Queen Anne, and which it is understood a vigorous attempt is now being made to resuscitate.]

~~~~ ~~~~~~ ~~~~~~~~, ~~~. ~~~ pp. ~~~ ~~~ ~~~,
edit. of 1809), was son of Henry Hyde, of Pyrton and Dinton, co. Wilts, who married Mary, dau. and heiress of Edw. Langford, of Trowbridge (*vide* Hutchins's *Dorset*, vol. ii. p. 494, 2nd ed., 1803). He was third son of Lawrence Hyde, of West Hatche (*vide* Sir R. C. Hoare's *Wilts*, and also E. Kite's *Brasses of Wilts*, Tisbury Church), who was third son of Robert Hyde, of Norbury and Hyde, Cheshire (Inq. p. m., 22 Hen. VIII.), for whose pedigree to time of King Henry III. *vide* Ormerod's *Cheshire*, vol. iii. p. 394.

Besides the family located at Dinton, as mentioned above, there were also Hydes of Denton, Lancashire (*vide* Baines's *Hist. of Lancashire*, vol. iii. p. 167).   H. BARRY HYDE.
Univ. Coll., Durham.

THE WINDSOR SENTINEL AND ST. PAUL'S (5th S. ix. 87, 114.)—The story mentioned by T. W. C., called "The Thirteenth Chime : a Legend of Old London," originally appeared in the *Illuminated Magazine*, about the year 1843 or 1844—I think in either the third or fourth volume of that periodical, which was issued in quarto form, and was edited by Douglas Jerrold. It was illustrated by John Leech and Kenny Meadows, and, though well got up and conducted, its career was a very short one—to the best of my recollection, only running over two years.   JOHN PICKFORD, M.A.
Newbourne Rectory, Woodbridge.

FELICE BALLARIN, OF CHIOGGIA (5th S. ix. 49.) —I spent a long summer day at Chioggia (pronounced *Chioza*) in 1875, exploring the place, and observing the folk and their ways ; and I saw and heard nothing of Felice Ballarin or any other rhapsodist. True, I did not ask about Felice, for I had forgotten Mr. Goodall's graceful picture ; but a brilliant Sunday afternoon was just the time when he might have been expected to appear. As to Tasso, Byron says somewhere that in his time there were only three gondoliers who could recite him. I heard of *one* gondolier who could do so in 1875, and only one. MR. BOUCHIER asks whether English fishermen and costermongers would care to hear Milton or Spenser recited. Certainly they would not ; for, if they are "worldlings," they prefer beer ; and, if they are devout, they probably go to some philistine preacher who knows no more of Milton and Spenser than they do. But I can testify that in Yorkshire, at least, the fisher folk will listen to verse with interest, and even enthusiasm, if it be written in their own dialect. Let me add that Chioggia is a pleasant and primitive place ; rude, indeed, but not unworthy of its renown as the scene of the famous war of Chioggia. The old white *zendale* of Venice is still

~~~~~ ~~~~~ ~~~~ ~~ ~~~~~ ~~~~ ~~~~~, ~~~ ~~~ ~~~~~
of the maidens, which is innocently performed in public. In all the side streets are long rows of girls, lying prone on their backs at every doorstep, their bare brown feet extending over the stones, their heads on their mothers' laps ; the mother, meanwhile, combing out her daughter's thick black tresses, and—well, giving them that minute inspection which there is not time for during the week.
A. J. M.

SOLOMON GRILDRIG : "THE MINIATURE" (5th S. ix. 87.)—A short account of the *Miniature* is printed in Mr. Maxwell Lyte's *History of Eton College*, pp. 350-51, 384, where it is stated that "Stratford Canning (now Lord Stratford de Redcliffe) was the working editor." The magazine was pecuniarily a failure, but its owners were relieved from all anxiety on this point through the purchase of the unsold copies by Mr. John Murray. This circumstance is said by Mr. Maxwell Lyte to have introduced that publisher to George Canning, the cousin of the principal editor of the magazine. With Canning's assistance Murray took a fresh start in business, and by the aid of Canning's friends, many of whom were writers in the *Miniature*, he was enabled to set on foot the *Quarterly Review*.   W. P. COURTNEY.
15, Queen Anne's Gate.

The word Grildrig is taken from Gulliver's *Voyage to Brobdingnag.* Gulliver says : —
"She gave me the name Grildrig, which the family took up, and afterwards the whole kingdom. The word imports what the Latins call *nanunculus*, the Italian *homunceletion*, and the English *mannikin*."
It was a happy name for the editor of a paper written for boys by boys.   A. H. CHRISTIE.

BREAD AND SALT (5th S. ix. 48.)—In the North Riding, twenty or thirty years ago, a roll of new bread, a pinch of table salt, and a new silver groat or fourpenny piece were offered to every baby on its first visit to a friend's house. This gift was certainly made more than once to me, and I recollect seeing it made to other babies. The groat was reserved for its proper owner, but the nurse who carried that owner appropriated the bread and salt, and was also gratified with a half-crown or so, the tribute of those to whom she unveiled for the first time that miracle of nature, the British infant. The same custom, I believe, prevailed among the poor, except that the groat was omitted. Does it prevail still, in any rank of life ?   A. J. M.

FRENCH PROVERB (5th S. viii. 406, 516.)—Cotgrave, edit. 1611, renders this proverb somewhat differently, "'Nulle maison sans passion' : Pro. 'No house without some humour,'" meaning,

apparently, without some ailment, mental or bodily, inside it.   HORATIO.

·ANTI-POPERY HYMNS AND SONGS (5ᵗʰ S. ix. 49.) —Flacius Illyricus, *ob.* 1575, published *Varia Doctorum Piorumque Virorum de Corrupto Ecclesie Statu Poemata.* Bapt. Mantuanus, *ob.* c. 1577, wrote a poem, *De Calamitatibus Temporis.* In the former of these ACTON WEST will find various pieces on the subject of his query. The latter is a poem in several books relating to the same subject.   E. M.

AUTHORS OF BOOKS WANTED (5ᵗʰ S. ix. 108.)— *The Tutor of Truth,* 3 vols., 12mo., 1779.—The author was Samuel Jackson Pratt. An obituary notice in the *Gentleman's Magazine* for Oct., 1814, gives a full account of his life and literary career, which closed at Birmingham on Oct. 4 of that year. As a poet, novelist, and dramatic author he was one of the most prolific writers of his day. In his early works he assumed the name of Courtney Melmoth. It is said that " no man who ever attained public distinction was more exempt from envy." However this may be, it is certain that Mr. Pratt met with a most unfriendly critic in the compiler of *Literary Memoirs of Living Authors,* 1798, who, after three pages of sarcasm, finishes by saying that "if he ever wrote for fame, he seems mightily to have mistaken the means of obtaining his object."   W. H. ALLNUTT.

AUTHORS OF QUOTATIONS WANTED (5ᵗʰ S. ix. 108.)—

" In the glow of thy splendour."

The above is a very poor translation of some extremely beautiful lines in one of Metastasio's minor poems, *An Epithalamium on the Marriage of "Il Principe della Rocca."* The original begins thus:—

" Scendi propizia
   Col tuo splendore,
O bella Venere,
   Madre d' amore."   S. L.

𝕸𝖎𝖘𝖈𝖊𝖑𝖑𝖆𝖓𝖊𝖔𝖚𝖘.

NOTES ON BOOKS, &c.

Non-Christian Religious Systems.—Islam. By J. W. H. Stobart, B.A., Principal, La Martinière College, Lucknow.—*Buddhism.* By T. W. Rhys Davids, Barrister-at-Law, late of the Ceylon Civil Service. (S.P.C.K. Depositories.)
WE have here two more instalments of the useful series in course of publication by the venerable society. Mr. Stobart's volume on Islam does not profess to be anything more than a compilation from the best known authorities. The subject chosen by Mr. Stobart is a most interesting one at the present crisis, whether we turn our eyes to Turkey, Persia, or British India, and we should have been glad to have had some touches of personal experience of Mahometanism in our Indian Empire from one who must have a certain familiarity with it. From a philosophical point of view the Shia sect is the most interesting division of Islam, and it is also the only one in which there has been a development in the direction of asceticism—a point not noticed by Mr. Stobart, though it was very ably treated in the *Home and Foreign Review* during its short but brilliant career. The Wahabee reform, to which the Principal of La Martinière does draw the attention of his readers, is one of no little importance as a source of occasional outbursts of fanaticism

in British India. Mr. Stobart's judgment of the founder of Islam seems to strike the balance fairly between exaggerations on either side.
Mr. Rhys Davids is one of a small band of Buddhist scholars in this country, which has lost a mighty athlete by the lamented death of Prof. Childers. The manual produced by so competent a specialist is therefore a compilation of a far higher than the average calibre. The subject is a most perplexing one, from its superficial likenesses to Christianity. Buddhist monasteries, Buddhist rosaries, even a Buddhist Pope, so to speak, all combine to puzzle the Christian student of a religious system which "ignores the existence of God." The English Roman Catholic Bishop of Clifton, who is stated to have been leading the recitation of the rosary at the Vatican when Pius IX. was *in articulo mortis*, was doubtless far from thinking how a similar function might be at that moment in progress among the snows of Ladakh or on the shores of the Yellow Sea. Yet it is not necessary to suppose that either was derived from the other, for Prof. Monier Williams points out in a recently published letter that in each case similar causes probably produced like effects. It is calculated that there are at least 200,000 Buddhists in European Russia, so that, independently of its importance as a factor in the politics of the Far East, the subject is well worthy of study by Europeans. Those who have not leisure for the larger works of Spence Hardy, Alabaster, &c., may with confidence take Mr. Rhys Davids for their guide to the general features of this remarkable religious system. But we should like to understand how Mr. Rhys Davids reconciles in his mind the apparent antinomy, which we feel unable to reconcile, in his account of Nirvana, as being a moral condition and yet implying, he admits, the cessation of individual existence. Both works are provided with suitable maps, which cannot fail to add to their utility, but why is the map illustrating Buddhism bound into its volume upside down? Can this be a feature of hitherto unknown Buddhist ritual?

The Reform of Convocation (Rivingtons) is the title of a speech delivered at the Lichfield Diocesan Conference of 1877 by one who, whether as Dean of the diocese or as having been elected Prolocutor of Canterbury in four successive Convocations, is entitled to a respectful hearing. Dean Bickersteth's views embody perhaps the minimum of reform which is likely to be acceptable to those who think that Convocation exists for other than merely ornamental purposes.—*Prototypography* (Toronto, Copp, Clark & Co.) is the somewhat startling heading of an historical sketch of early Continental and English printing, contributed to the Canadian Institute Caxton Celebration by Dr. Scadding, Canon of the Cathedral Church of St. James, Toronto. The works of the Aldine, Elzevir, Plantin, and other great presses are briefly passed in review, but the author takes no notice either of the Veronese press, which certainly had native printers as early as 1472, or of the Italian claim for the invention of the art by Panfilo Castaldi of Feltre.—Mr. Alfred Dawson, F.R.A.S., in a *Theory of Gravity and of the Solar Process* (Reading), is not satisfied apparently with the fact that gravitation has been "invented," and that the "verbal statement of the law is left, a grand mysterious postulate," but wishes to probe the mystery, and solve the difficulties which surround it. We are willing to grant the "materiality of matter," and to admit a doubt as to the materiality of the "magnetic fluid," but having made these allowances we still find ourselves enveloped in a certain nebula of doubt as to what we have learned from Mr. Dawson's laboriously constructed hypotheses.—Dr. Spencer T. Hall, M.A., sends us a handy guide to *Pendle Hill and its Surroundings* (Simpkin, Marshall & Co.), in which he

& Co.), asks the pertinent questions. "Why go to Russia? Why write anything about it?" He himself furnishes us with the answer that, in his case at least, "both of these desires were irresistible." As he confesses to thinking Mr. Gladstone "restless and emotional," and Lord Beaconsfield a "special-pleading novelist, devoid of statesmanship," we are hardly surprised that he should sum up the situation in the words, "Everywhere is darkness, distrust, falsehood—leading to chaos."

QUEEN KATHARINE DE VALOIS.—MR. SCHARF explained the drawings on the screen referred to *ante*, p. 121, which were made by him from the remains when the box was first opened. He described the bones as much destroyed on the upper surfaces by the action of quicklime. The front of the skull was entirely wanting. No vestige of the body remained. All the ribs and vertebræ had been removed, and the collar-bones and those of the neck rested immediately on the hips. The arms were complete, although the bones of the fore arms were turned round the reverse way. The feet were perfect, and the muscles of the legs remained undisturbed and were remarkably well preserved. A large quantity of cere cloth had been gathered together round the lower extremities. The bed of the lead on which the remains lay was composed of *débris* of the coffin, fragments of bone, and the cere cloth more or less acted upon by the lime. One rib alone—the uppermost—was found, and all the teeth had disappeared. Although dried and mummified at the period when seen by Fuller, Pepys, and Dart, the appearance of the remains was now entirely altered by exposure to damp during ninety-nine years in the depository adjoining the Percy Vault in St. Nicholas's Chapel. Judging from the measurement of the bones, Queen Katharine of Valois must have been remarkably tall.

[The above would have been appended to our first Note had it not reached us at too late an hour.]

RELICS OF FIRE WORSHIP IN SCOTLAND.—A few days ago I cut the following from the *Daily News*:—"On the last day of the year, old style, which falls on January 12, the 'intival of 'The Clavie' takes place at Burghead, a fishing village near Forres. On a headland in that village still stands an old Roman altar, locally called the 'Douro.' On the evening of January 12 a large tar-barrel is set on fire and carried by one of the fishermen round the town, while the assembled folks shout and halloa. If the man who carries the barrel falls it is an evil omen. The man with the lighted barrel having gone with it round the town carries it up to the top of the hill, and places it on the 'Douro.' More fuel is immediately added. The sparks as they fly upwards are supposed to be witches and evil spirits leaving the town. The people therefore shout at and curse them as they disappear in vacancy. When the burning tar-barrel falls in pieces the fisherwives rush in and endeavour to get a lighted bit of wood from its remains. With this light the fire on the cottage hearth is at once kindled, and it is considered lucky to keep in this flame all the rest of the year. The charcoal of the Clavie is collected and put in bits up the chimney, to prevent the witches and evil spirits coming into the house. The 'Douro' (*i.e.* the Roman altar) is covered with a thick layer of tar from the fires that are annually lighted upon it. Close to the 'Douro' is a very ancient Roman well, and, close to the well, several rude but curious Roman sculptures can be seen let into a garden wall." H. A. W.

Wordsworth's, with name inside and date 1820. Sm size, 18*s.* 6*d.*" HORATIO.

ACCORDING to the Report just issued the English Diale Society have made arrangements for work with referen to Cheshire, Cumberland, and Somersetshire.

Notices to Correspondents.

ON all communications should be written the name a address of the sender, not necessarily for publication, b as a guarantee of good faith.

CORRESPONDENTS generally are requested to send the communications as letters—*not* by book post

SETH WAIT ("Douglas Queries.")—Have you not be anticipated by our correspondents (5th S. viii. 471 Possibly you might be able to supplement by a short nc the information there given.

F. ROSENTHAL (Hanover.)—Many thanks. Please se another copy, and run your pen through the not making other necessary corrections in the margin.

UNEDA will, on consideration, see that his query co cerning a "great mathematician" may possibly refer a gentleman still living. The portrait was that of *Eliz beth*, Duchess of Devonshire.

L. H.—The chronogram on Queen Elizabeth, indic ting the year of her death, MDCIII., is--
"My Day Is Closed In Immortality."

W. F. R.—*Dunnage*=loose substances laid on t bottom of a ship as a bed for heavy goods (Stormontl *Eng. Dict.*).

J. M.—
"Arma amens capio, nec sat rationis in armis."
Æneid, ii. 314.

D. F. (Hammersmith.)—The usage referred to directed by the Rubric in the Marriage Service.

J. M. (Perth.)—Please let your notes be as brief possible.

H. R. M.—*Ye Gentlemen of England* is altered fro an old ballad by Martin Parker in the Pepys collectio for you.

SENEX ("Heraldry," *ante*, p. 108.)—We have a lett for you.

HORATIO.—"Lycidas" too late.

W. F.—Constrained to decline—with thanks.

S. A. PHILLIPS.—Baron Stourton and Mowbray.

A. F. G. LEVESON GOWER.—A proof shall be sent.

W. B. NEGLEY (Pittsburg, U.S.A.)—Letter forwarde

A. J. (Brechin.)—Please repeat.

R. S. KILGOUR.— Answer not enclosed.

ERRATA.—P. 111, col. 2, l. 16 from top, read *Arrey Gloff ab Seithenyn*. P. 114, col. 2, l. 29 from top, 1 "Bucks," read *Berks*. P. 115, col. 1, l. 14 from botto for "argillaceous state," read *argillaceous slate*.

NOTICE.

Editorial Communications should be addressed to "T Editor of 'Notes and Queries'"—Advertisements a Business Letters to "The Publisher"—at the Office, Wellington Street, Strand, London, W.C.

We beg leave to state that we decline to return co munications which, for any reason, we do not print; a to this rule we can make no exception.

LONDON, SATURDAY, FEBRUARY 23, 1878.

Notes.

THE TRUE STORY OF THE CENCI FAMILY.

(*Concluded from p. 64.*)

THE SURVIVORS.

Bernardo Cenci, though spared from death, was destined to drag out long years of suffering and poverty. The most contradictory accounts have been given of his fate. According to some he was released within a few days on payment of a fine ; according to the MSS. cited by Hillard, *Tour in Italy*, Oriental precautions were taken lest any heirs of his should disturb those who had taken possession of the family property. For the true story we are indebted again to Cav. Bertolotti, though Venosta, in his notes to *Beatrice Cenci* (Milano, Barbini, 1873), which are often correct, has a glimmering of the truth. He has found entries in the archives of the Company of the Stigmata which show that in the following March some of the members visited Bernardo at Tordinona, and presented him with a candle weighing one pound as a token of sympathy and gratitude for the interest he had shown in their society. He was sent later to the galleys at Civita Vecchia. In a petition to the Pope that he may be transferred to the fortress (St. Angelo ?) he says he has been dangerously ill, as the air and water are so unhealthy that even the fish die.

Another memorial was favoured by the French ambassador, praying that the galleys might be com-

muted for banishment. The prayer was granted ; and on March 21, 1606, he reports himself to the Governor of Rome as having been released, but prays that he may be allowed to return to his home, where he is greatly wanted. But his troubles did not end with his release. From his banishment at Naples he sends continual petitions for restoration to his honours and rights, and complains of the enmity of his sister-in-law, who is averse to his being put in possession of his houses, &c., and who is trying to raise a fresh trial against him at Naples. His poverty was extreme. He does not say whether the allowance made him by the Pope in prison had been stopped, but he tells Cardinal Borghese that he owes fifty ducats, and will have to go into a hospital, and that while his sister-in-law is enjoying farms and palaces, which bring her in at least 8,000 scudi yearly, he is dying of hunger. Moreover, she uses her money to obtain his imprisonment in the Vicaria, from which poor people like himself can never get out. About the same date Lodovica Cenci addresses a letter to the Pope :—

"Most holy Father,—Lodovica Velli......humbly sets before your Holiness the fact, that as long as there was an idea of releasing Bernardo from the galleys......she was silent, not wishing to appear to thirst for the blood of her relations. But now that great interest is being used, not only to bring him back to the very house where your petitioner lives with her children, but also to put him in possession of the property of which he was justly deprived,......she prays that orders may be given to the Governor of Rome that Bernardo shall not be allowed to live in the house with your petitioner and her children, else with the continual sight of him the remembrance of the old wounds of this unhappy family would be brought up again. Who can be secure of a youth who did not even spare his own father?"

In fact, though suffering at first from great poverty, Lodovica and her children had in 1600 been put in possession of the whole Cenci property, on payment of 80,000 sc., with the exception of Torre Nuova, which had been sold to the Borghese family by the Fisco to satisfy Count Cenci's creditors, who were said to press for payment—of the loans, as I suppose, that he had contracted in 1594. To keep the property in her children's hands was now the object of Lodovica's life, and she did not hesitate to repeat the charge of parricide, of which her own husband had declared Bernardo innocent. Unhappy family, indeed, always fated to be divided against itself !

These wretched dissensions continued, with what result is not evident. In the course of them a memorial occurs from Lodovica, asking that her advocate may consult the *processo*, which is not accessible to the public. This is confirmed by a document reprinted by D'Albono, the existence of which, I believe, has often been denied, namely, the entire prohibition under penalties of any publication relating to the Cenci tragedy. It runs thus :—

volunt, et despicere. Et sicut nobis nuper exponi fecerunt dilecti filii Præsidens et Officiales ex libello prædicto, et impio labore quærunt lucrum, et secreto curant imprimi......et libellum impressum vendere in dicta nostra alma urbe...inhibemus et prohibemus universis Christi fidelibus præsertim librorum Impressoribus et Bibliopolis:......maturaque deliberatione declaramus (ut non dare materia funestam historiam repetendi), libellum prædictum......tam in magno quam in parvo folio in odium auctoris......et per præsentes injungimus ut pœnas prædictas in contravenientes irremisibiliter exequantur. "Datum Romæ sub annulo Piscatoris Sep. 11, 1600, Pontificatus nostri anno decimo."

It would be curious to find this printed book, and it must be remembered that no authentic copy of the process is accessible, except the portion possessed by D'Albono, the so-called MS. copies being merely relations of the affair with a few quotations from the evidence.

Bernardo returned to Rome on a free pardon, granted him by Paul V., and on August 3, 1614, married his relation Clizia Cenci, and died in 1626, leaving several children. His widow, by an arrangement with the family, obtained 20,000 sc. for her children. The family of Giacomo sold many of the Cenci estates—Testa di Lepre to Card. Borghese in 1612, and Falcognano to Card. Barberini, with Bernardo's consent, in 1622 for 53,000 sc. It is strange, if the family lived at the Palazzo Cenci, that no trace of the names of the children of Giacomo or Bernardo appears in the little chapel. A Ludovico Cenci and Laura Lante, 1861, lie in Our Lady's Chapel, which is painted with cherubs sporting among flowers and graceful arabesques, the gift of Valerio Cenci. The arms of the Cenci are on the walls, but not a name recalls the children or grandchildren of Count Francesco.

The absurd story is often repeated in Rome that the Villa Borghese was the property of the Cenci, and was alienated by Paul V. There is no foundation for this statement. We have seen that the Borghese twice bought estates from the Cenci, but the first time when an Aldobrandini was Pope, which family was not yet allied to the Borghese. It does not appear that any relation of Clement VIII. reaped any benefit by the condemnation of the Cenci, and according to the system of fines then prevalent, 80,000 sc. does not seem much for the family to pay to enter on a confiscated estate.

As for the legal questions that divided the family I must leave them to lawyers, as they are wrapped in hopeless mystery for ordinary readers. There were several claimants — the children of Giacomo, Bernardo, and the three other branches of the Cenci family. As far as I can gather, the claims of Bernardo were opposed on the ground

was only entitled to his *leggitima*, and that, any other heirs in the immediate family of Cenci, the property was to go to the other bra How it was decided I cannot discover. Th remains that, of the two Cenci palaces at one bears the name of Bolognetti, the ot Maccarani, both branches of the Cenci family whether they have come into possession by i decision, or by the failure of direct heirs to Cenci, has not yet been made public.

Mario Guerra was tracked by an anon letter, and brought to Rome in 1602, an banished to Malta, whence he returned late was even employed about the Papal Court was alive in 1633. Bertolotti has found st his depositions, but they do not throw any on his implication in the guilt of the Cenci.

Our task ends here with the survivors of concerned in the tragedy. Till the Vatican are accessible we shall probably know little though we are nearer to the truth than thos wrote but a year ago. The secret, however, provocation which made Beatrice stain her with her father's blood is buried with her. can only hazard surmises, and make every ance for weak fellow-creatures, whose surrou and influences were so different from our ow

It was in the little church of S. Tomm Cenci, built by Count Cenci, and at whos Beatrice was baptized, that the writer first th of reopening this dark page of history. The of a November morning shrouded the cha S. Francesco, where Giacomo and Bernardo a nameless grave, and dimly burning tapers fitful light over the members of a confrat who were chanting the psalms for the dead. setting of the scene was in harmony wit thoughts it called forth of the family sufferings and crimes we have retraced. Ho we better turn and close the last sad page of story than with the words then echoing th the vaulted roof—

"Requiem æternam dona eis, Domine."

K. H.

ST. MARY'S CATHEDRAL, TRURO : THE N OF THE STALLS IN THE CHOIR.

The Right Rev. Edward White Benson, for Chancellor of Lincoln Cathedral, but since Ja 1877, first bishop of the newly formed dioc Truro, has since his appointment been grad regulating the affairs of the Cornish churcl getting the cathedral establishment into a Under the sixth section of the Bishopric of Act, 39 and 40 Vict., c. 54 (Aug. 11, 1876

Ecclesiastical Commissioners were authorized to submit to Her Majesty in Council a scheme for founding honorary canonries in the cathedral church of Truro and for allowing the non-residentiary canons of Exeter holding benefices in the new diocese of Truro, and consenting to the transfer, to become honorary canons in the cathedral church of Truro. The necessary scheme of the Ecclesiastical Commissioners was duly laid before the Council on April 30, 1877, and published in the *London Gazette* of the 4th of the following month. Twenty-four honorary canons in all can be created under the scheme, of which number the bishop was allowed to appoint eight during the first year of his episcopacy, exclusive of any who might be transferred from the cathedral church of Exeter. To the present time only one of the old non-residentiary canons of Exeter, viz. the Rev. Arthur Christopher Thynne, Rector of Kilkhampton, has consented to become an honorary canon of Truro.

The bishop has exercised the power conferred on him, and on Jan. 17, 1878, installed the first eight canons in St. Mary's Cathedral. On the back of each stall is painted the name of the saint after whom it is named, and below this appear in the Latin tongue the commencing words of some appropriate psalm. The stalls have been named by the bishop, with the assistance of the Rev. C. W. Boase, of Exeter College, Oxford, and it may be of interest at this time to give some short account of the holy men after whom these seats are called. Further particulars of some of them, which space will not permit of being inserted here, will be found in the two volumes of the *Bibliotheca Cornubiensis*.

Stall 1. St. Neot was born of noble parentage in the former part of the ninth century, and is generally stated to have been related to King Alfred the Great. In his youth he took the monastic habit at Glastonbury, and pursued his studies with such application that he became one of the best scholars of the age. After being ordained, he retired to a manor in Cornwall, where he led an ascetic life, and died at Ham Stoke, July 31, 877, being buried in a church which he had founded, and which was called after him Neot-stoke or St. Neot.

Stall 2. St. Aldhelm was the first Bishop of Sherborne, and was ordained there in 705 by Brithwald, Archbishop of Canterbury. He died May 25 in the year 709.

Stall 3. St. Corentin was born in Brittany, where he became a preacher, and after visiting Ireland came into Cornwall. He was consecrated Bishop of Cornwall by St. Martin, Bishop of Tours. The cathedral of Quimper, in Brittany, and the church of Cury, in Cornwall, are dedicated to his memory. From the Exeter Martyrology it appears that his day was kept on May 1.

Stall 4. St. Conan was the first Bishop of Cornwall, 925-40, in the reign of King Æthelstan. A charter still extant, and dated 930, bears a signature which is thought to be that of the bishop.

Stall 5. St. Piran was born at Ossory or Cape Clear Island, and came from Ireland to Cornwall to preach Christianity to the natives of that county, where he died about the year 540, and was buried at Perranzabuloe. The Cornish tinners took him for their patron saint, and kept his feast on March 5. The three churches of Perran-ar-worthal, Perranuthnoe, and Perranzabuloe are dedicated to this saint. The history of the lost church of Perranzabuloe has been written by the Rev. C. Trelawny Collins Trelawny and the Rev. William Haslam, and much discussion has been caused by these books, the former of which ran to seven editions.

Stall 6. St. Buriena was another Irish saint, who came into Cornwall and settled in a wild district near the Land's End, where King Æthelstan was founding a church. Her day is June 4. The church is that of St. Buryan, now a rectory, but formerly famous as a rich sinecure deanery.

Stall 7. St. Carantoc, or St. Cairnech, was a disciple of St. Columb, and flourished in Cornwall about 433. He was one of the original compilers of the early Brehon law of Ireland, and was buried at Dulane, in Meath. His feast is kept on May 14. Crantock is now a vicarage; it was formerly a collegiate church.

Stall 8. St. Cubi, Cebi, or Kebi, was a cousin and contemporary of St. David of Wales. After being in Ireland for some time he returned to Anglesey whilst Maelgwn was reigning in North Wales about 550. He was present at the Synod of Brevi in 569, and died about 570. The parish church of St. Cuby is dedicated to this saint, and his feast is kept on November 8.

Stall 9. St. German, a native of Gaul, was born about 380 of Christian parents. He was famous for his piety and virtue, and having entered the priesthood was advanced to the dignity of Bishop of Auxerre anno Domini 425. He travelled through England, Wales, and Scotland, preaching against Pelagianism, and attended the General Council of the Clergy at St. Albans, where he argued on the same heresy. The church of St. Germans is dedicated to this holy man. This place was at one time the seat of the early Cornish bishopric, the town of Bodmin, the original bishopric, having been burned by the Danes. Here it continued until the reign of Canute, when it was united with that of Crediton, and Cornwall and Devonshire were placed under the jurisdiction of one bishop, whose see was fixed at Exeter. From that period Cornwall had no bishop of its own until the appointment of Dr. Benson on Jan. 16, 1877, as before stated.

THE AUTHORS OF THE "BIBLIOTHECA CORNUBIENSIS."

name given by pastrycooks, implying that a piece of meat and pastry is old and hard (Roquefort *in v.* 'Jaquet'). The remaining part of the expression is probably a punning repetition of the same idea. I am informed that a heated-up dish is still among waiters called a *dover* or *doover*, doubtless *do over*."

This is very ingenious, and conveys the views of a great authority on this vexed passage. In 1843 the Percy Society, in their "Early English Poetry, Ballads, &c.," vol. vii., reprinted

"Jack of Dover, his Quest of Inquirie, or his Privy Search for the Veriest Foole in England. London, Printed for William Ferbrand, and are to be sold in Pope's Head Alley, over against the Taverne Doore, near the Exchange, 1604. 4to."*

This tract was also reprinted in *Shakespeare Jest-Books*, edited by W. C. Hazlitt (London, Willis & Sotheran, 1864). The note at p. 366, alluded to by DR. CHARNOCK, is as follows :—

"A 'Jack of Dover' in the vocabulary of the fishermen is, I believe, a term for a *sole*, the soles of Dover being celebrated. Whether Chaucer, in the *Prologue to the Coke's Tale*, intends a *sole* when he speaks of a 'Jack of Dover' is, however, a question which I am content to leave to the new editor of Chaucer.† But I may mention that it has been pointed out to me by Mr. F. S. Ellis, of King Street, Covent Garden, the well-known bookseller, that a *dover* is still the cant word among innkeepers for a *dish of any kind* which has been warmed up a second time (Fr. *réchauffé*), and it appears to me likely enough that the original phrase was 'Jack of Dover,' the two former words, with the liability to abbreviation common to all proverbial phrases, falling gradually into disuse."

"Jack of Dover" appears merely to have been used as a catchpenny title to this skit, and neither the import nor the application of the name seems any the clearer from its perusal. Mr. Wedgwood's reference to Roquefort is so all-important in the discussion of the present *crux* that I shall give the passage just as it stands in *Glossaire de la Langue Romane*‡ :—

"*Jaquet, jaket :* impudent, menteur. C'est sans doute de ce mot que les pâtissiers ont pris leur mot d'argot *jaques*, pour signifier qu'une pièce de volaille, de viande, ou de pâtisserie cuite au four, est vielle ou dure."

* A later edition, *The Merry Tales of Jacke of Dover, or his Quest*, &c. (as in former edition), Lond., 1615, 4to. Both in the Bodleian Library. I copy these descriptions from *Shakespeare Jest-Books*.
† In a prefatory note, however, Mr. W. C. Hazlitt says : " It is evident that the term 'Jack of Dover' is used here (as the book title and in the book) in quite a different sense from the one in which it is found in Chaucer (*Prologue to the Cook's Tale*)."
‡ *Glossaire de la Langue Romane*, par J. B. B. Roquefort, Paris, 1808.

English waiter would pronounce the last element *doover* exactly. But somehow I do not think the *dover* of innkeepers is the *dover* of Chaucer.§

On a passage so obscure as the present it may perhaps be permitted to venture a third suggestion. Might not the "Jack of Dover" be a corruption or a parallel form of the *hake* or *haak*|| of *Dover ?* For, on turning to Bosworth's *Dictionary*, we find Anglo-Sax. *hacod*, Plat. Du. *heket*, Germ. *hecht*,¶ Monsee Gloss. *hæcid*, Mid. Lat. *hacedus;* a pike, mullet, bakot; *hakeds*, a large sort of pike ; "*lucius piscis, mugil*," Elfric's *Gloss.* We find in Bailey "*hakeds*, a sort of large pike fish taken in Ramsay Moor." In Halliwell (*Arch. and Prov. Dict.*) "*haked*, a large pike, Cambridge." Now it seems highly probable that our wide-spread word *jack*=pike is rather connected with *hacod*, *haked*, *hake*, than with any of the numerous *jacks* which spring from the root *jacobus*. Moreover, in Cotgrave, first edit. 1611, occurs "*brochet de mer*, the sea-pike, the cod-fish " ; and again, "*lus*, a pike ; *lus marin*, a cod-fish." Indeed, *merlucius*, the vague post-classical term for the cod-fish and its congeners, is only the *lucius*** or pike of the sea. *Poor-john*,†† which is *hake* salted and dried, twice mentioned in Shakspeare, and occurring in other dramatists of his time, bears in all likelihood a merely accidental connexion with *jack*,‡‡ in the

§ A stubble goose is mentioned four lines after "Jack of Dover."
|| *Merluccius vulgaris*, the hake, a scaled fish quite distinct from *Morrhua vulgaris*, the cod-fish, but much jumbled therewith both in old days and now in popular parlance, especially when each fish is salted as in stock fish, ling, haberdine. So *haaf-fishing* is the fishery for cod, ling, tusk, &c. Off Orkney and the Shetlands *ling* means cured hake, but the *ling* is also a distinct fish, allied to the cod, *Lota molva.*
¶ So far Bosworth goes with Rider (*New Univ. Engl. Dict.*, 1759), who says : " *Hakod* (A.-S. *hacod*, Bel. *heket*, Teut. *hecht*). a fish of the non-spinous kind, &c., called by some a pike."
** Cf. *lachs*, the Rhine salmon ; *lax*, a salmon (Halliwell).
†† "A haak or poor John. a fish, merlucius."—Littleton's *Lat. Dict.*, ed. 1724. The *Nomenclator*, 1585, explains the then acceptation of two rather indefinite terms, viz , *Asellus salitus*, labordean, moluc, a babberdine ; *Asellus arefactus*, a stockfish. Another instance of a nickname given to fare of this kind is *buckhorn*, i.e. dried whiting. " for its hardness," Cotgrave.
‡‡ Richardson gives a quotation from King, in which *poor jack* seems at first sight used as = *poor-john*. This is very tempting, but I do not feel at all sure that *poor jack* means here more than thin or inferior pike. *Poor-john* is derived by Mr. Wedgwood from the last two syllables of Fr. *habordean*, haberdine ; Du. *labberdaan* or

sense in which I propose to take it of an equivalent to *hake*.* At any rate, there seems to be a curious parallelism of nomenclature between the cod-fish in its wider sense and the pike or jack.
                                                                ' HORATIO.

May I be allowed to submit to your readers a solution of the *Jakk* of Chaucer in the *haak* or *hake* of the present day ?   C. PETTET.

THE MORAYS OF BOTHWELL, "PANETARII SCOTIÆ," AND THE DOUGLASES.

Lately reading Father Theiner's *Monumenta Vetera,* I noticed a document which interested me. It is usually said by the authorities that Archibald Douglas, Lord of Galloway, afterwards third Earl of Douglas, married Johanna, *daughter* and *heiress* of Thomas Moray, the last "Panetarius" and Lord of Bothwell, who died in England of the plague while a hostage for the ransom of David II. in 1361. Indeed the learned John Riddell, in his *Stewartiana,* p. 97, while discussing the various branches of the "De Moravii," says, on the authority of Gray's MS. *Obituary and Chronicle* (Adv. Library), written early in the sixteenth century, that Thomas Moray died at Newcastle in 1366, and Archibald Douglas married Johanna, his heiress, and brought her from England, after offering to do battle for her with five Englishmen—a highly romantic story. But the compiler of this obituary, writing about 150 years after these events, could have no special means of acquiring the above information. And if the following quotation from Theiner is correctly taken from the Vatican archives it is clear he was wrong on more points than one. On p. 318 a dispensation by Pope Clement VI. occurs, dated x Kal. Aug. (July 23), 1361, whereby his Holiness permits the marriage of Archibald of Douglas, Knight, of the diocese of Lothian, and Johanna de Moravia, *relict* of Sir Thomas de Moravia, *widow,* of the diocese of Glasgow. This beyond doubt identifies the Lord of Galloway and the Lady of Bothwell. That the latter, however, was the *widow,* not the *daughter,* of Thomas Moray is quite new. For these papal dispensations, though they often make sad work of Scottish surnames and names of places, never misstate the character in which the parties seek authority to marry, and hence we may take it that Johanna was the widow, not the daughter, of Thomas Moray. This view is fortified by the fact that he must have been a young man. His mother,

Christian Bruce, sister of King Robert, and the widow successively of Gratney, Earl of Mar, and Sir Christopher Seton, married Sir Andrew Moray in 1326. Thomas, her second son, could not have been born before 1328 ; hence at his death he was not more than thirty-three, and was more likely to have left a buxom young widow than a marriageable daughter. If this view is correct, it explains an armorial shield still visible in the Kirk of Both well, founded by Archibald Douglas *c.* 1400, which puzzled me when writing a paper on the church some years ago for the Scottish Antiquaries. At the north spring of the interior arch of the east window is a shield, impaling, on the dexter side, three stars (2 and 1) within the royal tressure ; in chief three stars ; on the sinister side, three stars (2 and 1), but no tressure. Exactly opposite, on the outside wall, is the shield of Archibald Douglas, the bloody heart on an ermine field, and three stars in chief. The former coat is doubtless that of Thomas Moray and Johanna. · He, as the son of Christian Bruce, bore the royal tressure ; she, as of another branch of the Morays, did not ; and as wives and widows then usually kept their maiden surnames in deeds, she must have been a Moray. The point is decidedly interesting. For if, as it has been remarked, the appropriation of the Bothwell estates by the Douglases through the marriage of the heiress, while there were, it is highly probable, near *male* relatives to whom these should have gone, was a proof of their overwhelming power, much more was this the case if they acquired them by marriage of the widow merely of the last Moravia of the chief line.

There are in Theiner's great work some other curious documents illustrative of eminent Scottish families, to which attention may be called again.
                                                            ANGLO-SCOTUS.

MOSES WITH HORNS.—In a work on art,† by an American artist, recently published, the following passage occurs :—

"What a time (*sic*) has been made over Michael Angelo's 'Moses' with horns! Michael Angelo felt that *Moses must have horns!* To represent him he must have something more than a man with a full beard ; and you must accept these horns just as you would a word some poet had felt the need of and had coined."—P. 48.

I question very much if Michael Angelo felt anything of the kind. In the seventeenth century this was a subject of frequent discussion, the question being put in this form, "What 's the reason that Moses is generally painted with horns ?" We find it thus propounded in an early volume of the old *Athenian Mercury,* 1691 ; and what appears to be a plausible explanation is given in these terms :—

"The Reason is plain ; from a mistake of the Vulgar

---

abberdean. I suspect *haberdine* and *hake* are radically connected.

* Connected perhaps in another direction with Du. *haak. hoek,* a hook, and our obsolete *hake,* with the same signification. *Hake* means also provincially to gape, perhaps as a pike does. But compare also to *hawk, heck, keck,* &c., all connected with the idea of spitting, coughing, &c.

† *Talks about Art.* By W. M. Hunt. With a Letter from J. E. Millais, R.A. (Macmillan, 1878.)

self, whence the phrase of *lifting up their Horns,*" &c.

As to the rendering of the Hebrew I do not pretend to speak ; but, right or wrong, the passage, as above, is to be found in the Vulgate, and it is more likely, I think, that Michael Angelo and others should follow it in their representations of Moses than that the great painter should conceive an idea so far-fetched as that attributed to him in the work referred to, and that he should be followed in it by other masters.

ALEX. FERGUSSON, Lieut.-Col.

THE SIGN OF "THE SQUIRREL," ALVELEY.— Although the sign of "The Squirrel" is not mentioned (in the singular number) in Hotten's *History of Signboards,* first ed., p. 163, yet it is by no means an uncommon sign for a public-house. There is at least one sign of "The Squirrel" that deserves mention. It is in Shropshire, in the parish of Alveley, about eight miles from Kidderminster, on the road to Bridgenorth. In the coaching days the coaches from Worcester to Shrewsbury, including the famous "L'Hirondelle" and "Hibernia," used to stop there. It was also, and I believe still is, an inn much frequented by anglers who take a holiday to fish in the neighbouring river, the Severn. But the squirrel of this inn sign is chiefly worthy of mention as being a heraldic squirrel. It was the armorial bearing of the lady on whose property the house was situated, Miss Lee, of Coton Hall, who married (the late) John Wingfield, Esq., of Tickencote Hall, Rutland.

CUTHBERT BEDE.

"ENGLISH TAPESTRY AT WINDSOR."—This is the heading of a short account of this work in the *Times* of January 15. It is there stated that "it was about the time of Charles I. that tapestry weaving was introduced into England, when a factory was opened at Mortlake, in Surrey." Now, according to Fuller, "this manufactory was set up by Sir Francis Crane about the year 1619, under the patronage of King James, who gave him two thousand pounds to build a house therewith for that purpose." In 1623 the celebrated Francis Cleyne, a native of Bostock, in Lower Saxony, was employed as limner, and he "gave designs, both in history and grotesque, which carried these works to great perfection." For his services the king made him a free denizen, and granted him a pension of 100*l.* for life. Within two months after the accession of Charles I. he granted an annual pension of 2,000*l.* to Sir Francis Crane for ten years, one moiety of which was in satisfaction of a debt of 6,000*l.* for two suits of gold tapestry de-

supposed to have been of some s Dugdale says "the art itself v England by William Shelden, Es of the reign of Henry VIII."

Teignmouth.

PLATFORM.—The way in whic] formerly used, as contrasted with : ing, was discussed by various c the second, third, and fourth seri(It was shown by MR. SALA (3ʳᵈ "platform" was used in the sens(until quite the latter part of the tury. But it is curious that, whil so employed during the preceding also sometimes used at that time sense of esplanade or raised walk. in *Hamlet* is, "Elsinore ; a plat castle"; and yet in another pla Part I. Act ii. sc. 1) Shakspeare m: the equivalent of *plan:*—

"To gather our soldiers, scatter'd a
And lay new platforms, to endam(

The word can hardly be used her(sense of ramparts.

THE OLD HOSTELRY, "THE BRI TOWN.—The author of *Old and* his notice of this hostelry, enter, genious speculations as to the origi I would suggest, as a more pro] than any that have been advanced Jacobite Boniface of the period house from the name of the ship, brought William, Prince of Orang when he came to supplant his ruler of these realms. W. S.

THE EAR-LOBE.—If the ear-lo] the conventional limit of the line and is in the line of the chin, the] hanged — such is the orthodox f ear in England would be regarded even among the lower classes, and H·

CHERUB.—The seal of William (Aberdeen, appended to a charter to the Carmelite monastery in tha bears his arms, with helmet, crest, (see Laing, *Catalogue of Scottish* p. 41). The arms are a chevro fleurs-de-lis in chief, and a crab in named charge is, of course, allusiv as is also the crest, which is a cl (head and wings). I take this a that at the date of the seal the modern pronunciation of the Greek χερούβ, with the soft *ch*, which I suppose we derive from the French *chérubin*, had not been introduced.

I have lately heard of one or two instances in which clergymen have resumed the old mode of pronunciation, but it sounds a little affected to modern ears.   J. WOODWARD.

Montrose.

Queries.

[We must request correspondents desiring information on family matters of only private interest, to affix their names and addresses to their queries, in order that the answers may be addressed to them direct.]

"HEADS OF THE PEOPLE."—This book, first published eight and thirty years ago by the Vizetellys, has just been reissued, in two handsome volumes, by the Messrs. Routledge. The "Heads" were drawn by Kenny Meadows, and engraved on wood by Orrin Smith, the descriptive letterpress being written by Douglas Jerrold, William [Makepeace] Thackeray, Sydney Laman Blanchard, Samuel Lover, Leigh Hunt, R. H. Horne, Mrs. Gore, Wm. Howitt, and other popular and rising authors. The editor was, I believe, Laman Blanchard. The new edition is an exact reprint of the old, Kenny Meadows's sketches being reproduced with all their original force and individuality. The editor, in his preface, lays stress on the claim to the merit of *fidelity* for these so-called "Portraits of the English"; but to us of a later generation they seem to have been broad caricatures. I have had the good—or ill—fortune to see two or three "Fashionable Authoresses," "Young and Old Lords," "Retired Tradesmen," and "English Paupers" of the present day, and making due allowance for change in style of dress and some little mental progress, I can scarcely bring myself to believe that Kenny Meadows's "Heads" *were* faithful portraits of the respective types delineated. I shall be glad to have some information respecting Miss Winter, who wrote the article on "The Family Governess"; E. Howard, who described "The Midshipman," "The British Sailor," and "The Greenwich Pensioner"; J. Ogden, who contributed the papers on "The Chimney Sweep" and "The Retired Tradesman"; E. Chatfield ("Echion"), who wrote "The Old Lord"; and Richard Brinsley Peake, who represented "The Theatrical Manager." I shall be greatly obliged also to any readers of "N. & Q." who can identify for me the following anonymous contributors, viz., "Alice" ("The Old Housekeeper," "The Farmer"); "A Knight of the Road" ("The Commercial Traveller"); "Hal. Willis" ("The Street Conjuror"); "Godfrey Grafton, Gent." ("The Exciseman"); "An M.P." ("The Whig," "The Tory"); "James Smythe, Junr." ("The Poor Curate");

"A Bachelor of Arts." ("The Dowager," "The Collegian"); "Nimrod" ("The Coachman and Guard," "The Sporting Gentleman," "The Jockey"); "Arthur Armitage" [qy. is this a *nom de plume?*] ("The Spitalfields Weaver"); and "Akolonthos" ("A Radical M.P."). "Paul Prendergast" is, according to the "Contents" pages, P. [qy. Percival?] Leigh.

S. R. TOWNSHEND MAYER.

"GROUSE."—I should be greatly obliged to any one who would furnish me with an instance of the use of this word (in whatever fashion it may be spelled) older than 1603, when it occurs in an Act of Parliament (1 Jac. I. cap. 27, sect. 2). I should also be glad to learn whence the late Mr. Yarrell could have obtained the information that our word *grouse* "is considered to be derived from the Persian word, *groos.*" He would certainly have never made this assertion, which he published in 1840, without some authority for it. I am told by Persian scholars that there is no such word in that language, and it would seem as if *grouse* were cognate with the old French *greoche* or *griais*—the modern *grièche.*   ALFRED NEWTON.

Magdalene College, Cambridge.

P.S.—I take the opportunity, which correcting the proof of the above affords me, of adding that, since I wrote it, I have found *gryse* used in an Act of the Scottish Parliament (1551), but what it actually means there seems open to doubt.

THE MARQUIS ESTERNULIE.—In a work entitled *Les Faux Don Sebastien, Etude sur l'Histoire de Portugal*, par Miguel d'Antas, Paris, 1866, p. 27, the following allusion to the creation of an Irish marquis by the Pope appears:—

"Un Anglais, Thomas Esternulie, nouvellement créé Marquis de Lenster par le Pape, avait embarqué cette petite troupe à Civita Vecchia, sur un navire genois, pour la conduire en Irlande et combattre avec les soldats de hérétique reine Elizabeth."

In a note upon this passage the author says:—

"Nous ne garantissons pas l'orthographe du nom de l'Anglais commandant les Italiens. Conestaggio le nomme le Marquis Thomas Esternulie; Fr. Bernardo da Cruz, Estucli, Marquis de Lenster; et Mendoça, le Marquis Sternoile. Aucune de ces orthographes ne nous paraît toutefois être la vraie. Peut-être serait-ce Sterling ou Stucley."

Can any one inform me who this so-called Marquis Esternulie was, and what was the real name or title? It is almost certain that he was killed in Morocco when Don Sebastian was killed and his army annihilated.   A. LEARED, M.D.

12, Old Burlington Street.

JUNIUS: DR. FRANCIS AND "THE CON-TEST."—Indirectly connected with the Junius mystery is the question of the authorship of *The Con-Test.* I am aware that it is usually attributed to Dr. Francis. What is the evidence? In the last

·· he has not been a little pleased ·to hear men eminently distinguished for their learning, judgment, and probity, named as the author of this paper. But his pride has been most signally flattered by a French translation of *The Con-Test*, published abroad, wherein this performance is attributed to a gentleman no less admired for his genius than esteemed for his morals. And the writer hopes to be excused for not having hitherto corrected a mistake which did him so much honour, and gave his writings such authority."

Who was the translator of *The Con-Test?*

C. ELLIOT BROWNE.

GENTLEMEN.—You have pretty well exhausted esquires. Will you allow me to ask wherein consisted the difference between esquires and gentlemen in the last century? In a list of Poor-Law Guardians, dated 1792, I find gentlemen, clerks, and esquires; and in a list of benefactors to Shrewsbury School there is an entry dated 1609, in which one "Thomas Baldwine of Duddlesbury" is described as "in the County of Salop, Gentleman," but the last word is erased, and "Esq." substituted. A. R.

Croeswylan, Oswestry.

BINDING OF E.D.S. PUBLICATIONS.—Will any one who knows "what's what," and something also of what is coming, give advice as to the arrangement in binding of the E.D.S. publications? A paper cover is not calculated for long service, and I am thinking of getting a more lasting uniform in its place. Now a dictionary or a glossary has as much right as an alderman to be portly; and to my mind no work of the E.D.S., with perhaps one exception, is sufficiently bulky to claim a binding for its own exclusive accommodation. I should like to keep together, as much as possible, the dialects of the same county or of adjacent districts, but shall be glad to know how others think the glossaries, &c., may be most conveniently grouped for reference.

ST. SWITHIN.

"GIVE PEACE IN OUR TIME."—It is deplorable that any of the petitions of the Church in her magnificent Litany should be unintelligible. To me, as to many of my friends, the petition for peace has an unfortunate resemblance to that peace "which passeth all understanding." What is the precise meaning of "in our time"? What are we to understand by the assigned reason for the urgency of the petition? Surely "in reason's ear," and to our ordinary common sense, there need be no anxious desire for peace if the Almighty fight for us. "If God be for us, who can be against us?" (Rom. viii. 31.) The whole thing reads to me as if some clause had been wrongly omitted on revision : e.g., "Give peace in our time, O Lord ; but if thou wilt send us war, 'the weapons of our warfare are not carnal,' for there is

Athenæum Club.

MISS L. S. COSTELLO was author of *Wortley Montagu*, a burletta, acted at Theatre in the Easter season, 1839. I: in print?

In Genest's *History of the Stage* it is that on March 15, 1817, Miss Costello, tenham, appeared at Covent Garden as *Cymbeline.* Was this lady from Chelte L. S. Costello? and did she perform in characters at Covent Garden? R.

GOLDSMITHS KEEPING RUNNING CAS carried on the business of John Colvil bard Street, who was Pepys's own gol who died *circa* 1672-77, after losing a John Lyndsay, or Lindsay, a goldsmith siderable way of business.

Is it known who succeeded to the b the following great goldsmiths?—Hint the Flower-de-Luce, Lombard Stree Rowe, of the George, Lombard Stree Hornboy, of the Star, Lombard Str Snell, of the Fox, Lombard Street ; Tl wood, or Carwood, over against the They were all in existence in Charles and the last five are named in the li smiths in the *Little London Directory* o F. G. HILTO

Temple Bar.

JOHN PHILLIPS : " THE SPLENDID SI I have picked up within the last few da old bookstall, a nice little copy of " *Several Occasions.* By Mr. John Ph Student of Christ Church, Oxon. The Th London, printed for J. Tonson, E. Cu Jauncy. MDCCXX." It contains the po Splendid Shilling," " Cyder," " Blenhe to Henry St. John, Esq.," &c., with " Tl Character of Mr. John Phillips. By The Third Edition. London, printed I next the Temple Coffee-house in Fl MDCCXX." Can any one inform me wh of that edition are scarce? FATHER Birmingham.

COAT OF ARMS.—Can any corresp me, from my unskilled description, to lies the following arms belong? Dex shield, a bend between two muzzled be sinister, on a bend three fieurs-de-ly two horses' heads erased. The arms ar in a Norfolk church. Both the effigy tion are gone.

A PRINT.—Can any of your readers find the painter and engraver of an eng

also its value? It is a proof before letters, I think. It was bought for a Bartolozzi. On the left side is an old man, resting on a tombstone, talking to three females; two females standing in the centre, the one on the right apparently dressed in white; on the right is a female sitting on a grave with her hands crossed, and a dog sitting down by her side. Between second and third female is a small church, with tower fully shown, surrounded by trees; in the right rear houses, and in the left background a mansion. What church is it?

R. B. CANSICK.

2, Cavendish Road, N.W.

HUGH LE PAUPER, EARL OF BEDFORD.—Hugh de Bellomont, surnamed the Pauper, who was the youngest son of Robert de Bellomont, Earl of Leicester, obtained the earldom of Bedford from King Stephen, with the daughter of Milo de Beauchamp, upon the expulsion of the last-named personage. Dugdale adds that, "being a person remiss and negligent himself," this Hugh de Bellomont "fell from the dignity of an earl to the state of a knight; and in the end to miserable poverty." Where can further particulars be found? Thoroton, in his *Antiquities of Nottinghamshire*, mentions Sabina, widow of Hugh de Bellomont. Was this the daughter of Milo de Beauchamp? A. E. L. L.

Highfield, Nottinghamshire.

GIPSIES IN ENGLAND.—What is the earliest notice we have of the existence of gipsies in England? K. P. D. E.

SHANDYGAFF, a drink compounded of beer and ginger-beer. What is the derivation of the word?

F. G. W.,

Oxford and Cambridge Club, Pall Mall.

SEPULCHRAL MOUND.—On the beach at the head of a bay variously called Towyn, Two, or War Horses Bay, a short distance from the South Stack lighthouse, Holyhead, is a large mound or hillock composed of human bones and dry sand. The apex of the mound is covered to a depth of two feet with a mixture of peat and pebbles, and over that a layer of flat stones. The side towards the land is covered with grass, but that towards the sea has been partly swept away by the action of the weather. About a quarter of a mile inland is a large stone set on end. I inquired of various inhabitants in the neighbourhood, and the only information I could get was that a great battle had been fought here, and a prince killed and buried where the stone stands. Can any one give me further information? B. B.

"DIE BIBEL, DER TALMUD, UND DAS EVANGELIUM."—Is this treatise, announced in the November number of the foreign book circular of an English publishing house, the same as one advertised a year or two ago in a London periodical, by the same author (E. Soloweyczyk), under the title *La Bible, le Talmud, et l'Evangile?* Does it give any information regarding the views entertained by the Jews (modern or ancient) concerning the Bible, the Talmud, and the Gospel, or does it represent merely the author's individual position towards these three books? JAY AITCH.

WRESTLING IN FRANCE.—I want to get some information about the past and present history of wrestling in France—in which province most practised; whether more popular among the peasantry or the inhabitants of towns; at what seasons of the year the meetings are generally held; what prizes are given; and any other particulars pertaining thereto. Does any book of travels or other work contain a description of the pastime as witnessed in France? I do not want an account of French wrestlers in England. SIDNEY GILPIN.

THOMAS DE CHEDDAR.—In the chancel of Cheddar Church, Somerset, is a brass memorial of Isabel, wife of Thomas de Cheddar, with her arms, Vert, three fleurs-de-lis and a label of three points or (and these were repeated in the windows before the recent restoration). Of what family was she? I have searched the county histories, but they do not give the required information. S.

MONDAY "NEXT" AND MONDAY "FIRST."—The former is invariably used by the English, and the latter by the Scotch. Taking the English usage to be the correct form of expression, I should be much obliged if any critical contributor to "N. & Q." would be good enough to inform me why it is so. THOMAS WATKIN.

THE USE OF FIRE-SHIPS.—The *Pall Mall Gazette*, in an article on the passage of the Dardanelles by the Russian admirals Orloff and Elphinstone, asserts that fire-ships were then, in 1770, "as great novelties as torpedoes are now." This is hardly true; for, to go back no further than the Spanish Armada, we find that it was "eight fire-ships" which, at the very crisis of the engagement off Gravelines, turned the scale in favour of the English. Is not the use of these instruments of naval warfare, however, of much older date than the sixteenth century? D. C. BOULGER.

"LE DÉLUGE."—Can any one give me information as to the whereabouts of a picture called "Le Déluge," painted by Charles Gleyre, a Swiss artist? The picture came to England in 1855, and has since been lost sight of. V. W.

CHANDOS.—In what edition of Pope, or in what other literary production, can a full copy of Chandos's letter to him be perused? Johnson comments on an extract, which alone he gives.

JOHN PIKE, F.S.A.

(5th S. vii. 241, 264, 296, 338, 471; viii. 304.)

My friend Mr. Van Voorst has not only kindly placed at my disposal some particulars of editions of White's *Natural History of Selborne* not seen by me, but has also given me a copy of two which I had not before possessed. I am thus enabled to supplement my former notes. The most important information I am now in a position to furnish is with respect to the *quarto* edition of 1813, mentioned by several writers, but erroneously supposed by me to be but a large-paper copy of the *octavo* (in 2 vols.) of the same year. This edition proves to be self-standing, and to the generosity of my friend I owe a very good copy. Its description is as follows :—

*1813. The | Natural History | and | Antiquities | of | Selborne, | in the | County of Southampton. | To which are added, | The Naturalist's Calendar ; | Observations on Various Parts of Nature ; | and Poems. | *By the late Rev. Gilbert White,* | formerly Fellow of Oriel College, Oxford. | A New Edition, with Engravings. | London : | Printed for White, Cochrane, and Co.; | Longman, Hurst, Rees, Orme, and Browne ; J. Mawman ; S. Bagster ; | J. and A. Arch; J. Hatchard; R. Baldwin; and T. Hamilton. | 1813. 4to., pp. x-588.

There are twelve copper-plates ; eight of the nine from the original edition unaltered, except that the line containing the date of publication, &c., is wanting. The missing plate, that of "*Charadrius himantopus,*" has been re-engraved, and is the same as that in the 8vo. edition of 1813. A "View of the Residence of the late Rev. Gilbert White" is inserted as a tailpiece to the biographical sketch, as well as a "Copy of a Picture in Selborne Church, supposed to be painted by John de Maubeuge ; the Gift of the late Benjamin White, Esq.," which faces p. 314, but does not seem to be mentioned in the letter-press ; while, finally, the well-known plate of the "Hybrid Pheasant" is added.

Mr. Van Voorst tells me that some copies of this edition were issued on large paper, one of which, a splendid example, is in Prof. Bell's possession.

The next addition and correction I have to make refers to Jesse's edition before mentioned by me (5th S. vii. 264). This formed a volume of Bohn's "Illustrated [not Scientific] Library," and the title runs thus :—

*1851. The | Natural History | of | Selborne; | with | Observations on Various Parts of Nature ; | and | the Naturalist's Calendar. | By the late | Rev. Gilbert White, A.M. | Fellow of Oriel College, Oxford. | With Additions and Supplementary Notes by | Sir William Jardine, Bart., F.R.S.E., F.L.S., M.W.S. | Edited, with further Illustrations, a Biographical Sketch of the Author, | and a Complete Index, by | Edward Jesse, Esq. | Author of "Gleanings in Natural History," &c. &c. | With Forty Engravings.

1849, and no doubt such have not seen such a copy has the engravings (which are woodcuts) on separate a very ordinary character. Bewick's ; the best are si The other notes furr Van Voorst indicate an lowing, edit. Jardine (C in 1826, and edit. New Y others bearing date 1860 lished by Bell & Daldy), can say nothing. These have not exhausted the su

Finally, I have to recor of an edition of this class fairly said to throw all it shade. Its description is

*1877. The | Natural Hist Selborne, | in the County of | Rev. Gilbert White, | forme Oxford. | Edited by | Thomas &c., | Professor of Zoology in London : | John Van Voorst MDCCCLXXVII. 2 vols., 8vo. Antiquities, | Naturalist's Ca Various Parts of Nature, Vol. ii. | Correspondence, S Garden Kalendar, Animals | Roman-British Antiquities, &

Magdalene College, Cambri

THE "BORE" ON THE S &c. (5th S. ix. 81.)—Altho say about the "bore" on recalls to my mind some pe violence of the "bore" on such of your readers as me Calcutta, this tidal wave w an exciting scene often wit dire effects upon the ship boats and other small cra the Strand Road, runnin Palaces and the river. W on, the observer, at low we but a long slimy bank, when suddenly the air is cries, all along the line ir multitudes of boatmen flyi and other craft ; for the di it rounds the point at Fo upon them, crashing, smas everything, and at once stream into an impetuous about the shipping outsid ing adrift the vessels from

at once filling the river and covering its banks with the stranded boats taken unawares, and too late to reach the comparative safety of the offing. It is now many years since I obtained my own personal acquaintance with the effects of the Hooghly bore. The Hindoo festival of the Doorga Pooja affords the Calcutta folk a fortnight's holiday, and on the occasion of one of these breaks in Indian life I and a couple of friends elected to recreate ourselves in a river trip. Chartering a suitable budgerow, and charging it with a sufficiency of creature comforts, books, guns, &c., we set out, in the month of October, in an up-country direction, visiting Barrackpore, the foreign settlements of Serampore, Chandernagore, and Chinsurch, all now exchanged by the Danes, French, and Dutch for small extensions of territory at their own sea-board stations. When the time for our return approached, we 'bout ship, and commenced dropping back to Calcutta; but, having a friend at Dukinsore, we anchored there, and spent our last evening on shore. The night was one of the calmest, and the moonlight the finest I ever saw. On returning on board at ten o'clock, after directing our manjee to drop down to Calcutta during the night, we proceeded to prepare for rest, and were half undressed when the well-known cry of " The bore ! the bore !" saluted our ears; and before we could take any precautions the crest of the wave came dashing down upon us, starting the budgerow from her mooring, flooding her deck and cabins, and but for our friend on shore, who had heard the alarm, we should have been swept into the seething waters, the dingy he had pushed off to our aid just reaching us as our boat sank. Luckily we had a refuge with our friend. At low water, in the morning, we had access to the wreck, but found everything mashed up, and had to find our way to Calcutta by dawk (palanquin conveyance), reaching our homes certainly more in the character of distressed mariners than that of holiday excursionists.   J. O.

With reference to the tidal bore, I may say I have had some little experience of the phenomenon. At the beginning of 1857 I went to live at Bridgwater. That town is situate about six miles from the bay of that name. The river Parret, after running from the bay in serpentine form a distance of twelve miles, passes through the town of Bridgwater, where, a few days after I went to live there, the bore made its appearance. It was estimated by those who witnessed it (including myself) that the tidal wave was from six to ten feet high. Probably it would be nearer six feet than ten, but it certainly exceeded six. Fortunately there were not many vessels in port at the time, but some of them were drifted from their moorings by the force of the wave, and considerable damage was done. The bore had only been seen

in the Parret, I believe, once before 1857 by any one living, and I believe I am correct in saying that it has not been seen there since. The bore on the Severn only appears at long intervals, and I have spoken with those who have seen it many years ago. I should say that the account given by Mr. Buckland in the *Times* about three years ago as to the bore which then appeared on the Severn was not at all exaggerated when it was stated to have been six feet high. I have always understood that these remarkable occurrences were confined to the Severn, the Parret, and the Humber, and I should doubt whether the Trent has ever been much affected by them.   J. Ingamells.

Newcastle, Staffordshire.

"Hot Cocquaille" or "Cocquale" (5th S. ix. 87.)—*Coquille* certainly, as Mr. Thompson suggests, means in Cotgrave *inter alia* "the shell of an egg," but might not the derivation of the Norwich Ash Wednesday bun be connected more likely with "*Pain coquillé*, a fashion of a hard-crusted loafe, somewhat like our Stillyard Bunne,"* which occurs in Cotgrave also ? The *cocket-bread* of many of our old dictionaries may be also suggested, of which Coles (1701) says, "Wheaten next to wastel or white bread"; Kersey (1715), "The finest sort of bread or cakes"; Minshew (1627), "A distinction of bread in the statutes of bread and ale made anno 51 Hen. III., where you have mention of *cocket-bread*,† *wastell-bread*, bread of trete (bran ?), and bread of common wheat." As to Stillyard bun, we find in Minshew :—

"*Stilliard*, Guilda Teutonicorum, is a place in London where the fraternitie of the Easterling merchants, otherwise the merchants of the Haunse and Almaine, are wont to have their abode. It is so called Stilliard, of a broad place or court, wherein steele was much sold, q. *steele-yard*, upon which that house is now founded."

In Blount's *Glossographia*, 1656, this is almost word for word repeated, and the following added : "The place is now only famous for Rhenish wine, neat's tongues, &c. The Lord Herbert (of Cherbury) in his *Henry VIII.* calls it the *stilly art*, but gives no reason for that denomination." The locality is moreover given as "near the Thames," and Bailey, who boils down the foregoing considerably, says, "Still-yard, a place in Thames Street," &c. Among, therefore, the *et ceteras* of foreign delicacies which follow the Rhenish and the neat's tongues, I presume the Stillyard bun is to be added, and this or a similar foreign cake might, through the agency of Easterling merchants, have also been naturalized at Norwich. The very

---

* "*Cook-eel*, a cross-bun, Eastern Counties." So Halliwell; but Mr. Thompson's spelling seems preferable.

† Possibly related to *cochet*, a present in meat, wine, or money, which a newly married man made to his companions (Gloss. in Ducange, and Carp. Supplem. *in v.* "Cochetus").

what schoolboys now play as " knucks " or " dibs," *cockall* being given in Torriano, the *Nomenclator*, and Minshew's *Spanish Dict.* as a knuckle-bone.* The ancient and still surviving romp of *hot cockles* is probably not connected in any way with the Norwich bun.   HORATIO.

When at school at Norwich more than fifty years since, Valpy's boys at some time of the year —I do not remember the precise time—had a sort of Bath bun for breakfast. They were about two inches square and had a slight flavour of allspice. I do not think they were made with eggs, but merely dough. We were glad of a little butter to eat with them. They were ticketed in the shops as *cookeals.*   D. T. M.

"SCOTTISH SCENERY," &c., BY JAMES CRIRIE (5th S. ix. 27.)—Dr. Cririe put out a feeler in his *Address to Loch Lomond*, anon., n.d. but 1788, before he published his bulky three guinea volume. The first was transmitted to Robert Burns by Peter Hill, his bookseller, and acknowledged by the poet in a glowing commendation upon the unknown author. I have a copy of the *Address*, a thin quarto which was incorporated in the larger *Scottish Scenery* of 1803. Burns upon the specimen offered adjudged the doctor an equality with Thomson, a rank not confirmed apparently by the coldness with which the larger work was received. The *Edinburgh Review* and other critics seemed to ignore the poet in their high approval of the publisher's spirit in venturing upon so expensive a work, with its fine illustrations and notes. Dr. Cririe was one of the masters of the Edinburgh High School when he published his specimen, and at a later period minister at Dalton, Dumfriesshire, and died in 1835. Notwithstanding the Ayrshire poet's high appreciation of the doctor's *Address*, I do not find that the poets fraternized when they had the opportunity of becoming better acquainted.   J. O.

Of this reverend gentleman biographical particulars will be found in Dr. Thomas Murray's *Literary History of Galloway*, Dr. W. Steven's *High School of Edinburgh*, Dr. Scott's *Fasti*, and other works. Born at Newabbey in April, 1752, he was, by the early death of his father, necessitated to engage as a cow-herd. Nearly self-taught, he became schoolmaster at Lochrutton, and in May, 1777, was elected master of Wigton Grammar School. In 1781 he was promoted to the mastership of the Grammar School of Kirkcudbright, from which office he, in November, 1787,

* So Cotgrave also :—" *Osselet*, a little bone ; *osselets*, the game termed *cockall*, or knucklebones."

Licensed to preach by the Pre burgh on March 30, 1791, he 1801, ordained minister of Dalton of Lochmaben. The University 1802, conferred on him the deg died Jan. 5, 1835, in his eighty Cririe was an accomplished lingu *Scenery*, which appeared in 1 publication.   CH₄

Grampian Lodge, Forest Hill, S.E.

I do not know *Loch Kettrin*, b upon the various ways in which t until it settled down to the fai Sir Walter Scott, who may be s covered " this lake and its surrou tourists were concerned—was at call it Loch Cateran, from the (laws, who lived in the caves of Rob Roy's country (see his no *Maid of Perth*). MacCulloch a Cateran. The author of the me work (referred to in Scott's intr *Roy*), *The Trials of James, Dur M'Gregor, three Sons of the cel* (Edinburgh, 1818), calls it Loc *The Travellers' Guide through Sc* in the same year, 1818, it is callec and it so appears in a large map " A Guide to Loch Catherine an inscribed, by permission, to Wa 1818." In Sir Robert Gordon's name appears as Kennerin ; an given in Alexander Gordon's " I 1727. In a proclamation issue Council, in 1610, against the exces and Caterans, it is spoken of as I Walter Scott's poem of *The Lad* published in May, 1810, and i Katrine " to many a reader who of such a lake. In fact, Mac Scott that he had " a Scottish was not even inserted."   Ct

FRANCIS COTES (NOT COATE: born in London in 1726, died the first members of the Royal eminent portrait painter in cray was a pupil of Knapton. Hi: Queen Charlotte, with the Princ her knees, was exhibited by the umberland in the Portrait Ex The Duke of Argyll possesses a the beautiful Miss Gunnings by Sir Brook Bridges, the Earl o the Rev. W. Weller Poley pos

amples of Cotes's skill as a portrait painter in oil. Many of his portraits have been engraved.

John L. Rutley.

5, Gt. Newport Street, W.C.

Francis Cotes, R.A., was the son of an apothecary of great respectability, who lived in Cork Street, Burlington Gardens. His full-length portrait of the queen of George III., with the infant Princess Royal in her lap, was engraved by Wm. W. Ryland. Walpole names several portraits by him. In 1766 he was a member of the Society of Incorporated Artists of Great Britain ; but, serious contentions arising in that body, he withdrew, and with three other of the seceding artists successfully petitioned the king to favour the establishment of an academy, and thus became one of the founders of the present Royal Academy of Arts, the first exhibition of which was opened in 1769. Cotes did not, however, live to enjoy his triumph, as, having been afflicted early in life with stone, he fell a victim to that disease before he had attained the age of forty-five, on July 20, 1770. He died at his residence in Cavendish Square, and was buried at Richmond, Surrey.

There was also a younger brother, Samuel Cotes, who painted miniatures, and who was a constant exhibitor in the early years of the Royal Academy. See Walpole, *Painters in the Reign of George II.*; Edwards, *Anecdotes of Painting*; Pye, *Patronage of British Art.*   Jos. J. J.

"Inkle-weaver" (5ᵗʰ S. ix. 7.)—The proverb referred to is well known here, and often used in a ludicrous sense, or by persons who perhaps know no more of the subject than the traditional sound, yet who have somehow a notion that it is a forcible expression. The author of the couplet quoted by Horatio must have belonged to the latter class. Where inkle is still remembered, the mode of its manufacture, and the smallness of profit it could ever have brought, the idea of inkle-weavers as convivial drinkers or riotous livers is absurd and unknown. The only distinction that I am aware of between those who wove inkle and weavers of larger webs was the small space and simple frame required for the former, while the latter must have ample space, fixed looms, and ponderous appliances. Moreover, I have only heard of inkle (one of the smallest of domestic industries) as made by women ; a row or a circle of whom might sit on the same bench, or by the same fire, each with her frame on her knees (I have seen fringe made on such a frame), except that for the inkle there was no roller for the warp. That was usually *run*, or passed round some post, in an apartment behind ; the same might have served several workers, to circle round to them as it was wanted, and they chose to draw it, and thus they were close, or thick, in proximity and interest while their work lasted, seldom more than a day at

once. The adjective *thick*, kind, intimate, in its figurative sense, would give increased significance to the phrase. No doubt there was a good deal of gossip and kindly unity among those whom I imagine to have been the inkle-weavers referred to, in days when, in the great houses, many women were employed in spinning, and by whom, after the more important spinning for household use, the inkle was made. It was made in country houses, I suppose, generally ; and in Shakespeare's time, we know, for sale—carried about by pedlers, and by poor persons later, till superseded by smoother fabrics, when it was sometimes irreverently called " beggar-inkle."

I am in possession of a frame of dark polished oak, on which I have seen an aged relative make inkle. She died, many years ago, at the age of eighty-seven ; and, when spinning was quite left off, used to buy knitting cotton to make the inkle, which she always thought so much better for many household purposes than bought tape, or anything from shops. I could give a specimen, if Horatio would like it, taken from the hanging of a bedstead, of inkle of unbleached linen thread, at least, I believe, a hundred years old, in proof of its not being " bad "—it is apparently as tough as ever— and one also of that made of knitting cotton, soft and pliable, and very durable, though not smooth.

M. P.

Cumberland.

Cowper, writing to Lady Hesketh from Weston Underwood, under date May 6, 1788, says :—

" When people are intimate, we say they are as great as two inkle-weavers, on which expression I have to remark, in the first place, that the word *great* is here used in a sense which the corresponding term has not, so far as I know, in any other language ; and, secondly, that inkle-weavers contract intimacies with each other sooner than other people, on account of their juxtaposition in weaving of inkle."—Southey's *Cowper*, vol. vi. p. 153.

W. F. R.

" Lord ! why she and you were as great as two inkle-weavers. I am sure I have seen her hug you as the Devil hugg'd the witch."—Swift, *Polite Conversation* (conv. i.).

T. Lewis O. Davies.

Pear Tree Vicarage, Southampton.

Keatsiana (5ᵗʰ S. ix. 128.)—Fanny Brawne married Mr. Lewis Lindo, who afterwards changed his name to Louis Lindon.

A. C.

The exact date of the birth of Mr. Charles Armitage Brown could be ascertained by a letter to his son, his Honour, Major Charles Brown, Taranaki, New Zealand. Miss Brawne became the wife of a Mr. Lindon, and left several children who are still alive. Keats was not much more than five feet in height.

D.

In the *Gentleman's Magazine* for Feb., 1874,

... the honour or dishonour to spell its name with an *i*. Like Mr. Weller, we are very particular about the spelling ; and, whenever the taste and fancy of the speller would insert a *y*, we at once exclaim, " Put it down an *i*, put it down an *i !* " Why I know not, as Bill Sikes is not one to be proud of. The name is, I believe, derived from the Anglo-Saxon *sich*, interpreted by Somner as *sulcus aquarius*, a water-course or water-furrow. Northern topography abounds with the word *syke*, which is usually applied to a small running stream or rivulet. The arms in use, from a remote period, are derived from the same source, being Argent, a chevron sable, between three heraldic fountains, or sykes. Has the above derivation anything to do with the Staffordshire expression, "Don't syke," when a person catches his breath in bathing ?

JOHN CHURCHILL SIKES.
Godolphin Road, Shepherd's Bush, W.

Sikes is the surname of an old Yorkshire family appearing in deeds from 1300. The usual spelling now is Sykes ; but it was formerly written Sicks, Siches, Sikes, and Sykes indifferently. The *Yorkshire Archæological Journal* gives a photo. of a thirteenth century deed referring to the Flockton Sykeses, and I have seen numerous references at Wakefield dating from that time. There is no reason to doubt the etymology is from *sike*, a ditch. The name appears as *del* (of the) *Siche*. Blount's *Dict.* gives " *Sich*, a little current of water, *inter duos sikettos*." It occurs frequently as a local name—Slead Syke, Shaw Syke, &c.

J. HORSFALL TURNER.
College House, Idle, Leeds.

I can introduce SIKES to at least one family who held to the Sikes orthography. They are traceable to Lutterworth, in Leicestershire (where Nichols says that the name was not uncommon, and where it was also, to my own knowledge, to be found in the parishes of Markfield and Ashby de la Zouch), but were long connected with Hackney—according to the inscription on the family tomb, " upwards of one hundred years," and, in fact, 170 years, since John Sikes is found to have purchased the manor of Kingshold, in Hackney (which he resold in 1698 to Francis Tyssen), in 1694, and his great-grandson, Henry Sikes, the last male representative of the family, died and was buried there, at the age of ninety-one, in 1864. The arms they bore—Gu., three clusters of sedges or—seem still to point, if less directly than the Sykes bearing of three fountains, to the traditional

been distinguished by a different In some early wills I have found *Siks* and *Sicks.*
New Univ. Club.

I have carefully looked over Directory, and cannot find a si Sikes amid its numberless Sykese on the contrary side, predominate all but to the same extent. Abou1 is no difficulty. It is local from *s* lish (especially Yorkshire) for a look upon it as a fact that his " Tyke." The desinent *s* occurs in a this class ; as, for instance, Burns Bridges, Hayes, Styles—Styles Stiles is almost unknown. C. V Manchester.

N.B.—Speaking of a Tyke r Yorkshiremen spell this word *tike*

OLD STORIES (5th S. ix. 86.)—A of the story related by I. M. P *Contes ou les Nouvelles Récréat Devis de Bonaventure des Peri* Jacob, Bibliophile, et Charles No(Nouvelle xxii.). It is told of thr by their father to study for the (where they wasted their time i idleness, and found themselves w Latin when he suddenly summor The three phrases which they t learn are, "Nos tres clerici," "Pro b " Dignum et justum est." In a (given in Cuthbert Bede's *White* 1865, pp. 100-103), it is three H who are near being hanged thro ledge of English. The phrases Highland men," " The money in t right and good reason." I. M. P.' is very interesting, and any simil memory would, I venture to thin to other readers of " N. & Q." be have been trying without succes unbound back numbers a note of th and possibly from the same source Argyllshire stories. One was the No. xvi. of *A C. Mery Talys* (ed. 1864), *Of the Mylner that Stale* Tayler that Stale a Shepe ; Wolf' *Das Beste Essen von der Welt märchen*, von J. W. Wolf, Göttin 1851, pp. 404-407) ; and Croke1

Aghadoe (Killarney Legends, a new edition, London, Tegg, s.a., cap. vii.). I have versions from Galway and Belfast, in the former of which the tale is made to explain a common Irish proverb, "'Nuair is cruaidh don chailígh, caitfid sí rith" ("When it goes hard on the old woman she must run"). Among out-of-the-way printed variations may be named one from *Inis-Eóghain (Inishowen,* by Maghtochair, Derry, 1867), and one in *A New Riddle Book or a Whetstone for Dull Wits* (Derby, s.a.), a chap-book.   DAVID FITZGERALD.
Hammersmith.

M. W., A DUBLIN SILVERSMITH (5ᵗʰ S. ix. 49.)
—If I mistake not, the reference here is to Matthew West, of No. 15, Skinner Row, Dublin, and, if so, your correspondent cannot, I think, have any difficulty in ascertaining particulars of his honourable and successful career in business. Matthew West (? the same) was one of the sheriffs of Dublin, 1810-11 ; Alderman Jacob West was Lord Mayor, 1829-30, having previously served as sheriff ; and James West was sheriff, 1856. The name, I may add, is well known in Dublin.
                                   ABHBA.

F. M. would be able to get the information he requires at the Dublin Assay Office. I find that they marked plate, &c., previous to 1646. I should think they could tell him about M. W.   AGA.

THE FIRST LOCAL NEWSPAPER (3ʳᵈ S. i. 287,351, 398, 435, 479 ; ii. 38, 92 ; 5ᵗʰ S. viii. 72, 140, 153, 179, 232, 330 ; ix. 12, 98.)—I have consulted all the references to the *Stamford Mercury* which have appeared in " N. & Q." within the past ten years, and while I admit that no one has been able to furnish direct proofs of its existence prior to 1712, there still remain one or two points which I should like to have cleared up. When was that numbering adopted which would seem to give colour to the claim to date from 1695 ? The late MR. ALEXANDER ANDREWS, in an explanatory note (4ᵗʰ S. x. 357, Nov. 2, 1872), gives the proprietors as his authority for the statement which appeared in his *History of British Journalism,* published in 1859. The earliest issue of Mitchell's *Newspaper Press Directory* in my possession is that for 1857, and here I read, under the head *Lincoln, Rutland, and Stamford Meicury,* the following : "Established 1695, and has been uninterruptedly printed weekly for 159 years." There is evidently either a clerical or a typographical error here, as 159 years dating back from 1857 would give 1698, not 1695. This is corrected in 1858, when 159 is found to have grown during the twelve months to 163, and in 1877 it stood at 182. The last issue at the date of writing is that for February 1, 1878, the number being 9537, and assuming the weekly publication to have been uninterrupted, this would throw the date of its commencement back to the latter part of 1695. Now as the numbers on the earliest known copies would make the date of the commencement the early part of 1712, and as the volumes were then half yearly ones, when did the present system of annual volumes and numbering from 1695 commence ? And what were the circumstances which led to this change being introduced ? - Satisfactory answers to these questions—and of course to be satisfactory they should be supported by evidence—would set the vexed question finally at rest. The first query might easily be answered by a reference to the office files, which are stated by one correspondent to be complete from 1770 ; and as the paper is too well established to be dependent for its reputation and standing upon a spurious antiquity, I have no doubt but the proprietors would willingly afford any correspondent of " N. & Q." residing in Stamford or its neighbourhood access to the files. If it was in existence from 1695 to 1712, the latter was probably the date of its re-establishment under a new proprietary.; but there ought, to justify the modern claim, to be some evidence forthcoming respecting the first seventeen years of its history. If there is no better authority given for adopting the date 1695 than a mere *ipse dixit,* I shall certainly throw that date to the winds. I quite agree with MR. RAYNER that the subject of fixing the dates at which early provincial newspapers were commenced is one surrounded with difficulties. It is no unusual thing for the projector of a new journalistic venture to adopt the title of a defunct newspaper, and foist his bantling upon the world as a full-fledged print of thirty, forty, fifty, sixty, or seventy years' standing. Mr. Grant was misled by several of these pretenders by writing his third volume of the *Newspaper Press,* and I could give names, if necessary, of other papers which are now in a similar way sailing under false colours. Again, the majority of our present provincial dailies were originally published weekly, and in many cases there is nothing to show in the press directories that they were not always dailies. A compiler who would set himself to the task of hunting up and supplying dates in cases of the above nature where such are wanting would confer a boon both upon the newspaper world and upon the community at large.
                          ALEXANDER PATERSON.
Barnsley.

[MR. W. HODGSON is referred to vol. iii. of Grant's *Newspaper Press* for the history of the *Mercurius Caledonius.*]

A "TUCKING" MILL (5ᵗʰ S. ix. 68) is a fulling mill, *i.e.* for scouring, cleansing, and thus pressing and smoothing woollen cloths, such as kerseys, serges, and the like, and "tucker" is an old and common word for a fuller. Skinner (*Etymolog. Anglic.,* s.v.) says : " *Tucker,* fullo à Teut. *tuch,*

or tucking mills are said to have been introduced into England in the thirteenth century ; and at Tiverton, in Devon, there were fifty-six fulling or tucking mills about the year 1730, according to Dunsford (*Hist. of Tiverton*, part iv. p. 216). The name has in some places survived the art, for a mill near Southmolton, Devon, on the river Mole, though now only used for grinding grain, is still called the Tucking Mill. E. A. D.

Now that my *Notes to Piers Plowman* are printed, a simple reference to the index helps me to answer several questions. I quote the following from p. 26 : " A *tucker*, now chiefly used as a proper name, is the same as a fuller of cloth ; and a *tucking-mill* means a fulling-mill for the thickening of cloth. A description of the process of fulling or felting may be seen in *The English Cyclopædia*, 1861, Arts and Sciences Division, vol. viii. col. 1000." And see *Piers Plowman*, text A., prologue, l. 100.
WALTER W. SKEAT.
2, Salisbury Villas, Cambridge.

To the noise made by the hammers used in the process of "tucking" we are indebted for " the unparalleled adventure achieved by the renowned Don Quixote with less hazard than any was ever achieved by the most famous knight in the world."
ST. SWITHIN.

A complaint was made to Edw. IV. (*Stat. of Realm*, vol. ii. p. 474) that hats, caps, &c., hitherto made in the wonted manner with hands and feet (" mayns et pees "), are now made in an inferior manner by the use of mills, *i.e.* tucking mills. In the days of its prosperous woollen trade Bristol had its Guild of Tuckers, with its Hall in Temple Street. The trade also gave a name to a street, a short bit of which remains to this day.
J. F. NICHOLLS.
Bristol.

" POMPS " (5th S. ix. 78.)—When the villagers on the Mendips could not " pomps" to use certain remedies for their complaints, they meant to say that they could not " promise " to use them. Not unfrequently to the question in the Catechism, " What did your godfathers and godmothers then for you?" they reply, "They pomps and vows three things in my name." THOMAS CONEY.

Your correspondent A. T. has not, I think, given quite accurately either the word or its meaning. It should be " pompster," which is rightly explained by Mr. Williams, in his *Somersetshire Glossary*, as " to tamper with a wound, or disease, without

MR. PATTERSON for some interesting particu of Henry Delemain and his widow to 4th S 573 ; v. 50. I recommend him also to consul he has not done so already) Mr. Chaffers's *M* and *Monograms on Pottery and Porcelain*, an may find an answer to his inquiry. I do happen to have a copy of the work at hand.
ABHBA

EAR-RINGS : GEN. XXIV. 22 (5th S. viii. 361, 4 ix. 133.)—The Breeches Bible (1599) gives word " abillement," with a marginal note " e ring." Nose-rings were and are at least as c mon as ear-rings. The juvenile comment referred to in 5th S. viii. 453 should know th single ear-ring is not uncommon, however.
HIC ET UBIQUI

THE BIRTHPLACE OF SUNDAY SCHOOLS (5th viii. 367 ; ix. 110.)—The following quotation f a marble tablet in the parish church of Bre bears upon this subject, so far as relates to S land :—" Mr. Blair, about the year 1760, ir tuted a Sabbath Evening School in Brechin, first, it is believed, that was opened in Scotla Mr. Blair, who was a St. Andrews student, licensed by the Presbytery of Dundee in 1 (Scott's *Fasti*), was appointed first to the ch of Lochlee, next, in 1733, to the second, and s sequently to the first, charge of Brechin. He c in 1769, and left a family by his wife, Chris Doig, who was heiress of the property of Cc stone, near Brechin. A. J

THE WINDSOR SENTINEL AND ST. PAUL'S S. ix. 87, 114, 138.)—I first read the story vol. i. of Chambers's *Book of Days*, pp. 2 an and although the subject has also been mentio in " N. & Q.," 2nd S., it might be well to say t the name given in " The Thirteenth Chime " be Huntly, but his real name was John Hatfi He died at his house in Glasshouse Yard, Ald gate, June 18, 1772, aged 102, and a notice of appeared in the *Public Advertiser* a few d afterwards. GIBBES RIGAUI
Long Wall, Oxford.

HERALDRY (5th S. ix. 108.)—The Bolton fan (Lanc. and Yorks) bear the following arms : on a chev. gu. three lions pass. guard. or (anot ar.). Crest : A buck's head erased ar., attired gorged with a chaplet vert, pierced through neck with an arrow of the second. See the *Bri Herald*, vol. i., by Thomas Robson, 1830.
E. J. TAYLOR, F.S.A. New
Bishopwearmouth.

"UXORICIDE" (5th S. ix. 105.)—I am no great friend to new words, but this is a perfectly legitimate formation. And why is it worse than *infanticide?*   C. F. S. WARREN, M.A.

BACON'S ESSAY "OF A KING" (5th S. ix. 108.) —This is said not to be by Bacon, and is placed in the appendix of S. W. Singer's edition of the *Essays*, Lond., 1857, p. 223. For this reason see p. xxxiv.   ED. MARSHALL.

SWEET-HEART (5th S. ix. 84, 111.)—I did not really neglect Chaucer, but quoted the phrase from him in my inquiries among the "authorities," of whom one objected that in Chaucer the meaning was not a lover, but merely sweet heart. I am very glad MR. SKEAT says otherwise.
O. W. TANCOCK.

A plain prose instance of *sweetheart :*—
"Myne owyn *swete hert*, in my most humylwyse, I recomaund me on to you, desyryng hertly to here of your welfare."—*Paston Letters*, No. 866 (Gairdner's edition), dated A.D. 1482 (from a wife to her husband).
HALIFAX.

MODERN GREEK BIBLE (5th S. ix. 68, 95.)—I am much obliged by MR. SCHRUMPF's reply. Will he kindly add a few words about "Oikonomos" and its bearing on the Seventy? There would seem, then, to be of the Old Testament a version by the Archimandrite Hilarion (Horne, Introd., vol. ii. part ii. p. 91) from the LXX.; another by the Archimandrite Neophytos Vambas from the Hebrew ; and, besides these, one of the Bible Society from the English version of the Hebrew. Of the New Testament we have a version by Maximus Calliergi (so Horne, ii. ii. 91), Geneva, 1638, 4to. (two columns, old and new Greek), altered and printed at Chelsea and London, 1810, 12mo. (two columns, old and new), and again at London, 1814, 12mo. (new only), beside other reprints of the Genevan quarto of 1638 at the beginning of the last century. The Bible Society's New Testament, appended to their Old in the *Holy Scriptures* (Oxford, 1872, 8vo.), differs greatly from that in those former editions as being more anciently worded—more like to the old Greek text. The versions of Scripture in the two modern Greek editions of the Book of Common Prayer (Bagster's edition, 1820, and that of the Society for Promoting Christian Knowledge, 1839) differ somewhat from each other, as they both do from the Bible Society's translation, and in a much greater degree from that of London (1814), Chelsea and London (1810), and Geneva (1638), all above mentioned. The earliest version is the most vernacular.
W. J. BLEW.

SHEEP LED BY THE SHEPHERD (5th S. vii. 345, 477 ; viii. 79, 218, 377, 478.)—CUTHBERT BEDE says that the custom on the Cheviots of the sheep following the shepherd was "a realization of Scrip-

ture reading, and a Northern picture of Eastern life," and that he has "never witnessed the sight elsewhere." CUTHBERT BEDE has only to cross over to this pretty seaport and take a walk into the country to see the shepherd and dog in front and the sheep following, the custom being common all over France and Italy, and from this custom came the expression sheep-followers. The chief use of the dog is to keep the sheep within bounds where there are no hedges, by parading up and down or round and round, as indicated by the simple motion of the hand of the shepherd. In Italy the shepherd usually carries one of those long, light Italian reeds, and if a sheep should stop to crop the grass he gently taps it on the back with the reed, and the sheep immediately moves on.
HENRY G. ATKINSON.
Quai de la Douane, Boulogne-sur-Mer.

"RALPH WALLIS, THE COBLER OF GLOUCESTER" (5th S. viii. 388, 494.)—I shall be glad of a note of any tracts by, or pertaining to, Ralph Wallis, in addition to—
Magna Charta ; More News from Rome, 1666.
Room for the Cobler of Gloucester, 1668.
The Life and Death of Ralph Wallis, 1670.
The Young Cobler of Gloucester, 1713(?).
With any other scraps upon shoe-making or shoe-makers for a bibliographical list of broadsides, ballads, histories, &c.   JOHN TAYLOR.
Northampton.

ANTLERS OF THE RED DEER (5th S. viii. 428, 458.)—On this point the late Mr. Collyns of Dulverton, in his interesting *Notes on the Chase of the Wild Red Deer*, writes :—
"The ancients imagined that the horn of the stag possessed great medicinal virtues, especially the right or off horn, which it was said was rarely found, and consequently was the more highly prized. To account for the scarcity of shed or cast horns, a notion obtained currency that the hind is in the habit of eating the horn, and I think Mr. Scrope says that the late Duke of Athol once found a dead hind which had been choked by part of a horn that remained sticking in her throat, and quotes this as a circumstance corroborative of the popular belief. I may say that I have not found any mention of this habit in the old works to which I have had access, and which I have consulted, although the ancient writers on hunting were certainly men of great observation, and by no means unwilling to give credence to and report any peculiar habit or property attributed to deer."

During a short visit that I recently paid to Scotland, I made many inquiries on this subject, and I was informed by keepers and hillmen of great experience and undoubted veracity that it is a common occurrence for the hinds to eat the cast horns ; and they go so far as to say that unless the horns are picked up within a short time after they are dropped, the chances are that they will be found mutilated and partially destroyed by the hinds. In our country I have never, from my own experience or from reliable information, discovered

is dedicated and given to nature, and that the foure elements do every of them take a portion. Isodore is of another opinion, saying that the hart doth hyde his first heade in the earthe in suche sort that a man shall hardly finde it."—*Art of Venerie*, p. 42.

WADHAM J. WILLIAMS.

Taunton.

CAROLS (5th S. viii. 491 ; ix. 32.)—With regard to *carols*, a name sometimes given to recesses in cloisters, in my note (*ante*, p. 32) I ought to have mentioned that Cornish has *crow* or *crou*, meaning a house of some kind. The three Gaelic dialects (Scotch Gaelic, Irish, and Manx) often begin words with *c* or *g*, where the Kymric dialects (Welsh, Cornish, and Armoric) begin them with *d* or *t*. At the same time each of the two groups has a few instances where both ways are followed. It would take up too much space here to give a list of these. THOMAS STRATTON.

A BOTANICAL PUZZLE (5th S. viii. 146, 294, 378; ix. 12.)—It may be added to the notes on this subject that the Rev. W. Jackson, M.A., F.R.S., in his recently published *Handbook to Weston-super-Mare and its Vicinity*, in speaking of Worlebury, draws attention to the occurrence of the *Cochlearia officinalis*, which, he says, was " unknown in the neighbourhood before the Worlebury pit circles were examined, when its seeds were thrown out from the pits and germinated after a sleep of many centuries" (p. 65). And again : " Below Spring Cove, and near the first turnpike, the botanist may be pleased to observe Scurvy-wort (*Cochlearia officinalis*), self-sown from the ancient Celtic pits, and now abundant" (p. 165). Very abundant the plant certainly is now, with its glossy succulent leaves, amid the old hut circles, and down the rocky sides of the fortress-city. I do not gather from Mr. Jackson's work when the excavations of which he speaks were made, but from a paper by the Rev. F. Warre in the *Trans-actions* of the Somerset Arch. Society I imagine they took place in 1851. It would, I think, be very interesting to learn the precise grounds for the statement, and whether care has been taken to eliminate possible sources of error. One must in inferences of this kind beware of the *post hoc ergo propter hoc* theory. In a little work, *The Flora of Weston*, published in 1856, the plant is mentioned, with no note of its being in any way a recent in-troduction. Brean Down is there given as another "habitat." W. F. R.

Worle Vicarage.

At Framlingham, in Suffolk, is a slight elevation immemorially called Broom Hill. The origin of at least, had ever known or heard of br ing there *or anywhere else in the parish.*

About twenty years ago, however, i struction of the Framlingham bran G. E. R., a cutting was made through I and the banks of the cutting proceeded the name of the place by producing th year a profuse crop of broom, which s there luxuriantly. Whence came the it was produced by plants that flourish gave name to the spot not less than before, we have an instance of very vitality. If, however, it was recent seed, it must have come from a consid tance, and was fortunate in finding a su in an unoccupied spot, possessing the si vantage of being ready named for its re (

Inner Temple.

AUTHORS OF BOOKS WANTED (5th S.
My New Pittayatees is by Samuel Lover found in a cheap edition of his works p Charles H. Clarke, Paternoster Row, in a " The Parlour Library." EVERARD HOME

My New Pittaytees, by Samuel Lover, is giv of Carpenter's *Penny Readings in Prose a* Dec., 1865.

AUTHORS OF QUOTATIONS WANTED 129.)—
" Pray less of your gilding," &c.

The epigram MR. CLARKE inquires for, the not quoted it correctly, is no doubt one to p. 159 of *Hunting Songs and Miscellaneo* R. E. Egerton Warburton (second edit., 12m Longmans, 1860) :—

``` 
    ‘You see,’ said our host, as we entered his
      ‘ I have furnished my house à la Louis Qu
    ‘ Then I wish,’ said a guest, ‘ when you as
      You would furnish your board à la Louis
    The eye, can it feast when the stomach is
      Pray less of your gilding, and more of you
```

There is something like the last line but on epigram ; but the play on the word " carvin the point of the epigram turns, is necessaril the English, and this is merely a versificati have seen related as a joke by Lord Alvanle; at Mr. Greville's ; but I cannot give a refer J. .

" Plus negabit," &c.

I have met with a note made by me in v attributed to Dr. Johnson, on the authority *Review*, vol. 1. p. 520. ED.]

(5th S. ix. 108, 139.)

" In the glow of thy splendour."

Vide a fair translation of Metastasio's *Hy* (" Scendi propizia," &c.) by E. Kenealy ir

Magazine, p. 138, Aug., 1842, in original metre. Other Italian *poemetti* are also to be found in that year's magazine by the same hand, which in p. 139 has baptized the elder D'Israeli by Israel instead of Isaac.

SAMEDI.

Miscellaneous.

NOTES ON BOOKS, &c.

The Life of John Milton. By David Masson. Vols. IV. and V. (Macmillan & Co.)

THE new volumes of Mr. Masson's *Life of Milton* cover the whole period of Milton's career from the execution of Charles I. to the restoration of his wandering son. The sudden changes of English government during this epoch might have induced any biographer to stray somewhat from the strict range of his subject, but Mr. Masson falls a willing victim to the temptation. The cause of every alteration in government from Commonwealth to Protectorate — the never-ending changes fell at last into disunion and anarchy, and ended in the return of Charles II.—is minutely described. Under all these varied forms of rule the services of Milton were employed in state administration, and many of the changes were supported by his pen. While we allow that his biographer could not omit to mention the actions in Church and State in which he was engaged, we cannot but add that in Mr. Masson's volumes the life of the poet and letter-writer is often sacrificed to the discussion of internal politics. In the first sixty-four pages of the fourth volume the name of Milton is mentioned but once. More than one hundred and fifty pages of its successor are occupied with the history of the Protectorate of Richard Cromwell and the events which led to the restoration of Charles; in only two of them will the name of Milton be found. The industry and accuracy of Mr. Masson must ever extort admiration, but for a living picture of Milton's life we must wait until a biographer has arisen who can make a fit use of the materials which Mr. Masson's labours have collected.

Exactly a fortnight after the king's death, and four days after the publication of *Eikon Basilike*, Milton issued a bold and singularly opportune vindication of the conduct of the Parliament in deposing and killing their sovereign. This pamphlet secured for him the prominent position of "Secretary for Foreign Tongues" to the Council of State, and led them to impose upon him the task of counteracting the sympathy roused in every heart by the circulation of thousands of copies of the royal book. From that time he was immersed in controversy with Salmasius and his satellites. They poured upon him all the expressions of abuse which their knowledge of the refined vocabulary of the Latin language could supply, and received in return a good deal more than they gave. For these controversies Milton's dream of a History of England was neglected, for them the compilation of a Latin dictionary was abandoned as soon as it was contemplated. The lines of *Paradise Lost* which were written in these years can be counted on the fingers of the hands. Poetry was discarded for politics, and when Milton was not engaged in his chamber in repelling the attacks of foreign disputants, he was summoned to the council chamber to turn into Latin Cromwell's stirring despatches on behalf of the suffering Protestants of the Continent. Only a few sonnets remain to prove that his affection for the Muses was undiminished, but these must be ranked among the highest products of his poetic genius. The stateliness of thought embodied in the noble sonnets to Cromwell and Vane, and the deep feeling breathing through the simple words of his sonnet to his "late espoused saint," he never surpassed.

Though the chapters which depict the struggles of English politics must draw from the reader the frequent expression of a wish that Mr. Masson had adhered more closely to the legitimate lines of his biography, they often throw fresh light on the events of English history. There are many lessons to be learned from the list of members (v. 453) of the restored Rump Parliament of 1659, carefully annotated to show the parts they had played in the successive changes of the Commonwealth. The substance of a crowd of pamphlets is condensed in the histories of the new sects (v. 15-27) which swarmed in the first Protectorate of Cromwell. In a few pages Mr. Masson has sketched the careers of the English men of letters during the rule of Cromwell, and has drawn up instructive tables of those who cordially adhered to his cause, and those who tacitly obeyed or actively opposed his government. His researches have illustrated the lives of Marvell, Needham, and the friends who solaced by their conversation the vacant hours of the blind poet.

In the last days of 1651 Milton was forced by ill health to remove from his chambers in Whitehall Palace to a "pretty garden-house" in York Street, Westminster. Sadly had the neighbourhood deteriorated in two centuries and a quarter, but the house still remained (to use the words of Jeremy Bentham's tablet) "Sacred to Milton, Prince of Poets," and but little altered in its structure from the time when the blind bard groped from one room to another. Never more will the eager pilgrim forget the squalor of the neighbourhood in gazing on the house of Milton ; last year it vanished, and his desire to realize its appearance must be satisfied by the descriptions of Hazlitt and Mr. Masson. Milton entered it in December, 1651, and he occupied it until the threatening pamphlet of L'Estrange, full of eager anticipations of the vengeance of Charles against the controversialist who had justified the death of his royal father, warned him to seek safety in obscurity. Mr. Masson's next and last volume will deal with Milton's life in seclusion, and there will be less justification in his forgetting the subject of his biography in describing the history of his times.

Poetry for Children. By Charles and Mary Lamb. To which are added Prince Dorus and some Uncollected Poems by Charles Lamb. Edited, Prefaced, and Annotated by Richard Herne Shepherd. (Chatto & Windus.)

AT length Charles Lamb's many lovers have the luck to recover the lost " *Poetry for Children, Entirely Original*, by the Author of *Mrs. Leicester's School*." Every collection of Lamb's works hitherto made has had to do without it, because no copy was forthcoming to print it from till last year. Now Messrs. Chatto & Windus gain much credit by the issue of a careful, handy, pretty reprint of this collection, of the newly recovered humorous poem "Prince Dorus," known to be Lamb's by an entry in Crabb Robinson's *Diary*, and of a few other uncollected trifles of Lamb's that were worth collecting. Mr. R. H. Shepherd, as editor, gives useful bibliographical details, and attempts to apportion the *Poetry for Children* between Lamb and his sister—not very successfully, but also by no means dictatorially. Lamb told Manning that *his* verses were "but one-third in quantity of the whole " ; three poems are known to be his ; and Mr. Shepherd suggests twenty-six others on supposed internal evidence. They are by no means the twenty-six best ; and one point in the evidence is in some cases fallacious : thus, three poems are left to Mary Lamb's account because we "cannot imagine" Charles "making *sex* rhyme with *protects*,...*withdrawn* with *forlorn*,...or *Anna* with *manner*" ; yet, in the course of the poems ascribed

Fine description, you've only your young sister Mary
Been taking a copy of here for a fairy"—
while in his acknowledged poem "The Three Friends"
(p. 74) is no less lax a rhyme than *feature* and *greater*.
The book is a priceless one, and all lovers of Lamb must
get it; but the apportionment of the poems will probably
have to wait till some authentic and decisive document
turns up, as in the case of Hood and Reynolds's *Odes and
Addresses to Great People*.

Debrett's Peerage, Baronetage and Knightage, and *House
of Commons and the Judicial Bench*, 1878. (Dean &
Son.)
FOURTEEN years ago we welcomed the reappearance of
Debrett amongst the Peerages as that of an old friend
with a new face, adding that Debrett was for years *the*
(if not the only) Peerage which the fashionable world
consulted. We may now add that so many improvements
have taken place in it, and such additions made to its
usefulness, that it bids fair to resume the important
place which it once held as a high authority on all
matters connected with the titled classes of this country.
One only has to compare Debrett of the past year with
that for the present one to appreciate the improvements
that have been effected by Dr. Mair. A special feature
of the present issue is that the succession to Peerages,
which will be separated on the demise of the present
incumbents, is set forth in a manner at once brief and
intelligible.

MESSRS. PARKER & Co., Oxford, and Mr. Murray,
London, have just published two volumes of very remarkable interest—*The Catacombs of Rome* and *Tombs in and
near Rome, Sculpture among the Greeks and Romans,
Mythology in Funeral Sculpture, and Early Christian
Sculpture*. These are two more splendid volumes, giving
additional illustrations of both life and death in ancient
and in Christian Rome, which volumes we owe to Mr.
John Henry Parker, C.B., to whom we are already indebted for an attractive volume on the Colosseum as
compared with other amphitheatres. Although the
reader may not invariably agree with his learned and
modest guide, Mr. Parker's Volumes deserve the highest
praise. The text is sufficient for the reader, who may
pleasantly and profitably spend hours over the numerous
illustrations, all giving a history and offering suggestions
to be thought over independent of what may be found in the
author's text. Between text and plates the reader passes
through very unwholesome places without any fear of
catching the Roman fever, though these books may well
tempt him to risk the malaria.

"GOD SAVE THE KING" AND HENRY CAREY.— In
the controversy at present going on in the *Times*,
respecting *God Save the King*, errors are so abundant
that it would require many pages to expose them all.
The latest assertion is that Carey spelt his name without
an *e*. Fact is better than fiction, and I possess over two
hundred works published by himself, in all of which he
spells his name Carey. The same form was adopted by
his son, John Saville Carey.
I may add that it is my intention to write the history
of *God Save the King*, and to publish, for the first time,
evidence I have recently acquired respecting Bull's MS.
and also two forgeries in connexion therewith.
W. H. CUMMINGS.
Brackley Villa, Thurlow Park Road, Dulwich, S. E.

anecdotes, or facts about him to favour me with then
valuable. Information about his early days will be particular
valuable. BLANCHARD JERROLD.
Reform Club, Pall Mall.

A COMPLETE set of the Second Series of "N. & Q,"
half calf, may be had of our publisher.

Notices to Correspondents.

ON all communications should be written the name an
address of the sender, not necessarily for publication, bi
as a guarantee of good faith.

H. A. B.—"Lumen de cælo" is, we believe, th
correct version of the prophecy concerning the la
Pope's successor. For the prophecies of St. Malac
respecting the Popes, see "N. & Q.," 3rd S. i. 49, 77, 17
359; 4th S. viii. 112, 296. Please forward your other quer
OLIM ("Shakspeariana"); H. ("Christchurch, Hants".
B. ("Letter of Bp. Hacket"); BEDALE ("Exell
Family"); and —— ("Rev. R. Clarke"), have sent r
name and address. In the last instance the query is in
complete.

W. D. B.—Four different forms of expression may I
used: "tanto, quanto"; "quanto" alone; "cos
come"; "altrettanto che." The natural correlative (
tanto is of course *quanto*, though the form to which yo
allude may be used colloquially.

K. H. B.—In the wedding ceremony at these marriage
the left hand is given. The children resulting from suc
unions, though considered legitimate, are not entitled t
succeed to their fathers' estates.

SETH WAIT.—We have forwarded your communicatio
to our correspondent MR. C. H. E. CARMICHAEL, Ne
University Club, S.W., who will be glad to hear fro
you.

ECLECTIC.—Are not the people mentioned still living
The question should be referred to some lawyer pra
tising in the Divorce Court.

A. IRELAND.—A proof shall be sent with pleasure.

F. ROSENTHAL.—You mentioned certain misprint
which we should wish to see corrected in the margin (
the copy to be sent.

A. G. W. should apply to some flag-maker to th
Admiralty.

REV. W. ROTHERHAM.—Letter forwarded. In du
course.

H. KREBS.—Your query is suited to *Science Gossi
(Hardwicke, Piccadilly).

ST. SWITHIN.—*Az.* and *arg.* are the proper abbrevii
tions. Proof shall be sent.

S. should refer to the Hon. Mrs. Norton's works in th
Free Library at Manchester.

TIBIA AMNE having referred to *ante*, p. 135, will pr
bably deem it necessary to rewrite his reply.

S. F.—Forwarded to MR. THOMS.

NOTICE.

Editorial Communications should be addressed to "Th
Editor of 'Notes and Queries'"—Advertisements an
Business Letters to "The Publisher"—at the Office, 2(
Wellington Street, Strand, London, W.C.
We beg leave to state that we decline to return com
munications which, for any reason, we do not print; an
to this rule we can make no exception.

LONDON, SATURDAY, MARCH 2, 1878.

CONTENTS.— N° 218.

Notes.

A LADY CONTEMPORARY OF QUEEN KATHARINE OF VALOIS.

The re-interment of the remains of Queen Katharine of Valois recalls to my mind an in- teresting hour which I spent with a second cousin of her husband's, a lady exactly contemporary with the queen herself, on March 5, 1875, an account of which may not be uninteresting to your readers.

While the restoration of the choir of Tewkes- bury was being carried on, it was considered by the committee that the opportunity ought to be used for the purpose of gaining further information, if there was any to be gained, respecting the great families of De Clare and De Spencer, who repre- sented the founder, and whose bodies had been buried there for many generations. Several dis- coveries were made, and not the least important among them was that of the body of Isabel, great- granddaughter of Edward III., and second wife of the great Earl of Warwick and Albemarle, who succeeded the Duke of Bedford as Regent of France, and who is commemorated by the well- known brazen effigy in the Beauchamp Chapel at Warwick.

This lady was the daughter and only child of Thomas Despencer, thirteenth Earl of Gloucester, who was put to death at Bristol six months before her birth, which took place on July 26, 1400, and of Constance, the daughter of Edmund of Langley, fourth son of Edward III. At eleven

years of age she was married to Richard Beau- champ, Earl of Abergavenny and Worcester, and four years afterwards bore him a daughter at Hanley Castle, the Lady Elizabeth Beauchamp, from whom the families of Abergavenny and Despencer are descended. The Earl of Aber- gavenny was killed at the siege of Meaux, on March 18, 1421, and was buried between the pier of the tower and the first pillar of the arcade on the north side of Tewkesbury choir, a beautiful chantry, which is the original model of the still more beautiful Beauchamp chantry at Warwick, being erected by his widow over his grave.

Two years and a half afterwards, on Nov. 26, 1423, the Lady Isabel was married to her late husband's cousin, who was also named Richard Beauchamp, and was the fifth Earl of Warwick. The British Museum possesses a very beautiful pictorial life of this earl, drawn in sepia by Rous, one of his chaplains, the forty-six quarto-sized drawings illustrating his career from his birth to his burial. His attendance at the marriage of Henry V. gives occasion to a fine drawing of that ceremony, in which it is not too much to suppose we find a contemporary portrait of Katharine of Valois at the most interesting day of her life. Lord Warwick died at Rouen Castle on April 30, 1439, and his body was brought home to England by his widow and their son Henry, afterwards Duke of Warwick and King of the Isles of Wight, Guernsey, and Jersey. The sorrowing lady could travel no further than London, and went to be nursed by the loving hands of the sisters minoresses of St. Clare, whose house stood in the Minories, near the Tower. Here Henry VI. went to visit her, and after acceding to some parting request which she made respecting her son and Tewkesbury Abbey, the good king took his leave of her with the words, " May God, whom you worship with an upright heart, grant thee thy heart's desire and fulfil all thy mind."

The Countess of Warwick died on St. John the Evangelist's day, December 27, 1439, and there is a pen-and-ink drawing of her as she lay upon her deathbed, and in the act of delivering her will to the Abbot of Tewkesbury, in a MS. volume in the possession of Sir Charles Isham. On January 13, 1440, she was buried with much state in the choir of Tewkesbury Abbey, an inscription around the top of the Abergavenny chantry stating that her grave was " I. choro I. dextra patris sui," her father's grave being elsewhere recorded as being " under the lamp which burned before the Blessed Sacrament." The will handed to the abbot gave minute directions respecting her monument, which is said to have been "a very handsome marble tomb, exquisitely carved." Her orders were " that her statue should be made all nakyd with her hair cast backward, according to the design and modell that one Thomas Parchalion had for

but on the side thereof the statues of poor men and women in their poor array, with their beads in their hands" (Dugdale's *Warwick.*, p. 330, ed. 1656, from a copy "ex dono Authoris"). The monument has entirely disappeared ; but, guided by the inscription on the chantry, I searched for the grave on the south side of the choir, a little to the right of the spot under the key-stone of the groining of the easternmost bay. We soon came upon a large stone, the top surface of which had remains of ancient mortar upon it, and which, being on the old level of the floor, was no doubt the base of the monument. On the under side of this stone was inscribed a long cross in shallow lines, together with, here and there, intersecting circles, that looked like sketches of designs for tracery, such as I once found, in a more finished stage, on the under side of stall desks at Over, in Cambridgeshire. Across the upper limb of the cross there was deeply cut, in black-letter of fifteenth century date, the inscription, "Mercy Lord Jhu." Beneath this slab there was a grave of very fine masonry, 7 ft. 0½ in. long, 2 ft. 5 in. wide, and 3 ft. deep. At the bottom lay the body of Lady Warwick, wrapped in a close shroud of linen, which had become of a rich brown colour, tinged either by age or by the spices used in embalmment. The left arm and hand protruded through the shroud, and indicated that nothing but bones remained within, at least in that part of the body. The rest of the body was perfectly enclosed in its envelope, but a small opening occurred above the forehead, and through this was seen a mass of auburn hair in its natural condition, but somewhat coloured, like the shroud, by the embalming spices. Around the body lay the fragments of a wooden coffin, which had been covered, on the outside as well as the inside, with a damasked purple silk, of Oriental fabric, such as that which was often used for lining the leather flaps covering episcopal seals. The body measured 5 ft. 8 in., but as the feet lay straight this was more than the natural height of the living person. When these facts had been observed, a tile was placed in the grave with the inscription, "This grave was opened during the restoration of 1875, and, after having been inspected, was reverently closed and restored to its original condition," the inscription being signed by the chairman of the restoration committee and myself. The covering slab was then replaced, and now lies (as do the

* Dugdale gives an engraving of the countess kneeling at a prayer-desk, and clad in a mantle with her own and her husband's arms upon it, from the east window of the Lady Chapel, Warwick.

latter heaped tiles and] upon the young Duke of died, at the early age of : Castle, and was buried at ' too much to conjecture th also a friend of Queen K curious coincidence that, t same year and dying in respective relics should ha' at the same time.

Beverston Rectory.

EARLY ALLUSIONS 1

In one of the elegies ac Charles Deodate there are s to describe certain dramas poet during a visit to town tragedies are thus particula
" Puer infelix ind
Gaudia, et abrupto flendu:
Seu ferus e tenebris iterat
Conscia funereo pectora to
The only guess at these all that of Warton in his edit (Lond., 1785). He says : first couplet he perhaps Romeo. In the second Richard III." This opinio: Hamlet are concerned, is a Prof. Masson in his *Life of* terizations of Shakespeare's see any special appositenes: is at least doubtful how far used with propriety in conr the turn of the second cou] *Spanish Tragedy* rather tha lines necessarily refer to pl in London ? In the previ comedy, the allusions are t to Ruggle's *Ignoramus*, ai *Fraus Honesti*, none of wl to have seen upon Banks therefore, that illustrations or, at any rate, from mode would accord better with which pervades this gracefu
Peter Anthony Motteux, of the *Gentleman's Journal* Frenchman who was able 1 poet. His journal has s illustrate the state of popul: speare. In December, 169 the Rymer controversy :—
"Mr. Rhymer's Book, whic] with so much Impatience, i

A *Short View of Tragedy*, &c., being dedicated to the Right Honourable the Earl of *Dorset*. Mr. Rhymer, like some of the *French* that follow *Aristotle's* Precepts, declares for Chorus's, and takes an occasion to examin some Plays of *Shakespear's*, principally *Othello*, with the same sevirety and judgment with which he criticised some of *Beaumont* and *Fletcher's* in his Book called, *The Tragedies of the last Age*. The ingenious are somewhat divided about some Remarks in it, though they concur with Mr. Rhymer in many things, and generally acknowledge that he discovers a great deal of Learning through the whole. For these Reasons I must forbear saying any more of it, and refer you to the Book it self."

Dennis's reply is also noticed :—

"We are promised a second Part [of the *Impartial Critick*], wherein Mr. Dennis designs to prove, that, tho Shakespear had his faults, yet he was a very great Genius, which Mr. Rymer seems unwilling to grant. I am only sorry that the time, which the perusal of the many excellencies which are diffus'd thro Shakspear's Plays, requires, will keep Mr. Dennis very long from giving us that Book."

In February, 1693, the editor printed Sir Charles Sedley's lines on Shakespeare :—

"We have had a Comedy, call'd *The Wary Widow, or Sir Noisy Parrot*, by Henry Higden, Esq.; I send you here the Prologue to it by Sir Charles Sedley; and you are too great an Admirer of Shakespeare, not to assent to the Praises given to the Fruits of his rare Genius, of which I may say as Ovid to Græcinus,

Quos prior est mirata, sequens mirabitur Ætas,
In quorum plausus tota Theatra sonant."

It is satisfactory to find that Shakespeare was properly estimated by the first English literary journal. About this time, however, the small fry of contemporary dramatists appear to have looked upon his writings in the light of a vast quarry of old material, free to be carted away when wanted, dealing with him very much after the manner of the grantees of the old abbeys with their noble ruins. One of the most honest of these men was Charles Burnaby, who in the preface to his *Love Betrayed*, 1703, says bravely :—

"Part of the Tale of this Play I took from *Shakespear*, and about Fifty of the Lines; Those that are his, I have mark'd with Inverted Comma's, to distinguish 'em from what are mine. I endeavour'd where I had occasion to introduce any of 'em, to make 'em look as little like Strangers as possible, but am affraid (tho' a Military Critick did me the honour to say I had plunder'd all from Shakespear) that they wou'd easily be known without my Note of distinction."

Here is a specimen of Burnaby's treatment of the "strangers," from a speech of Moreno, Duke of Venice :—

"Poor Cæsario ! thou art too young for Cares,
Or thou hadst known, they follow us in Sleep.
Physicians poyson in their Sleep,
Lawyers undoe in their Sleep,
Courtiers get new Grants in their Sleep......
Nothing in Nature's quite at rest,
But the slick Prelate."

Amongst earlier allusions not given in the *Century of Prayse* are the following : an allusion to *Venus and Adonis* in *Cornelianum Dolium*,

1638 ; a mention of Falstaff by Lord Chancellor Jeffreys in Lady Ivy's case, 1684, reported in the *State Trials*; two interesting allusions to Shakespeare in Sir John Suckling's *Letters*. A quotation from the *Merry Wives*, written by the fifth Earl of Montgomery in a copy of Inigo Jones's *Stonehenge*, was printed in the second volume of your Fifth Series.   C. Elliot Browne.

Chaucer, "Prologue," l. 52: "The Borde Begonne."—I think I have found out yet more solution of difficult passages in Chaucer. A well-known puzzle is that in l. 52 of the *Prologue* :—

"Ful ofte tyme he had the *bord bygonne*
Aboven alle naciouns in Pruce."

The difficulty is, does it mean that the knight had been placed in the seat of honour at table, or that he had "begun the tournament," whatever that may mean ? Now the usual meaning of *bord* certainly "table." The puzzle is to know if there was such a phrase as "to begin a board" in the sense of sitting highest at table. The answer is yes ; and all the while it occurs in Gower, *Conf. Amantis*, ed. Pauli, vol. iii. p. 299, where every one has overlooked it hitherto. The whole passage in Gower is most explicit, and should be consulted :—

"At souper tyme netheles
The king, amiddes al the pres,
Let clepe him up among hem alle,
And bad his mareschal of his *halle*
To setten him in such degre,
That he upon him mighte se.
The king was sone set and served ;
And he, *which hadde his pris deserved*,
After the kinges owne worde,
Was made *begin a middel borde*,
That bothe king and quene him sigh."

That is, he occupied the place of honour at a table in the middle of the hall.
Walter W. Skeat.

Cambridge.

The Son of Theodore, King of Corsica.—On the night of Wednesday, February 1, 1797, an old man walked from a coffee-house at Storey's Gate to Westminster Abbey. Under one of the porches there he put a pistol to his head and shot himself dead. He proved to be Col. Frederick, son of Theodore, King of Corsica, who, about forty years before, had been buried in a pauper's grave in the churchyard of St. Anne's, Soho. The Colonel was a benevolent, eccentric, moneyless gentleman, well known in London. The son of the King of Corsica once dined at Dolly's with Count Poniatowski, future King of Poland, when they had not enough money between them to pay the modest bill. Distress, it is said, drove the poor Colonel to suicide. Such is the accepted fact ; but contemporary history had another and a very curious version of the Colonel's death. The account below

man, Son of the late Theodore, King of Corsica, was found murdered under the West Porch of Westminster Abbey, facing Tothil-street. No fire-arms were found near the place, nor any thing that could lead to a discovery of the means by which the deed was perpetrated. After a minute inquiry yesterday, the following is a circumstantial account of the transaction, as related by a lad who was near the place at the time of the murder, William Colvin by name.—About half after nine o'clock on Wednesday night, he states his being at a pump near the church-yard of the Abbey, when he saw two men talking together near the Porch door, one of whom he heard say to the other, 'If you don't give me some money, I 'll blow your brains out.' The other (whom he describes to be the Colonel) replied, 'If you don't get about your business, I shall call out for assistance, and have you taken into custody.'—That immediately after he heard the report of a pistol, and saw the Gentleman fall; the other then turned round to look if any body was near, and on seeing this lad, ran after him, and took him by the collar; that his mouth was then stopped with a handkerchief, to prevent his calling out; in this state the fellow brought him back to the place where the deceased was lying, and swore if he made the least noise he would blow his brains out. He then held him between his knees whilst he searched the deceased's pockets, and saw him take out of his breeches pocket a green purse (as he believes), containing some money, and out of his coat pocket a red and white handkerchief, which he put into his breast; that he then took a paper out of his own waistcoat pocket, and put it into that of the deceased; it contained something, but cannot say what it was. The lad further states, that he was then released by the man, who, on going away, gave him a violent blow on the breast, which stunned him. After recovering himself, he ran after him, and saw him ram something into his pistol. He overtook the ruffian, and caught hold of the skirt of his coat; the man disengaged himself, and ran towards the House of Commons. On the lad calling out 'Stop Thief,' a person near the place threw a pail after him, which hit the man's heels; after which he saw no more of him. To corroborate the above account, the Colonel's dress was exactly as the boy had described it. When the body was taken to St. Margaret's bone-house, the paper was found in the waistcoat pocket, which had been stated to have been put in by the man who shot the Colonel, and which paper contained some gunpowder. The most diligent search is making after the villain who perpetrated the deed."

Of course he was never discovered.   D. N.

A WELSH PARSON OF THE SEVENTEENTH CENTURY.—The following story is perhaps known to Lord Macaulay's schoolboy, in which case I must apologize for offering it to "N. & Q." But Lord Macaulay himself has not referred to it in the notes to his famous third chapter. It may be one of the "sources too numerous to mention" from which he drew the materials for that chapter. I found it the other day, when looking for something else, in an anonymous law book, The Gamester's Law, a 12mo. of about 130 pages, published in 1708. It is the one gleam of humanity in a chaos of dog-Latin and Norman French. After

" But tempora mutantur; our Gracious and our Reverend Bishops will not Patro Custom or Allowance. And, that the igr were misled, and thought such Pastimes of Mirth appears by this story of a Welsh (a poor Boy) was bred up at School, and bei Lad at his Books, used to assist some Ger that went to the same school. Afterward trip to the University and got a Degree and in process of time, upon some occasion com in a tattered Gown: One day a Gentleman to School with him, meets him, and kne (saith the Gentleman) I am glad to see t do? I thank you (Noble Squire) replied Gentleman invited him to the Tavern, ar Discourse of their School and former Con Gentleman ask'd him where he lived? J in Wales. The Gentleman askt him if he v The Parson replied he was, and that he ha seven Children. Then the Gentleman en value of his Benefice, the Parson answered 9l. per Annum. Pugh! quoth the Gen canst thou maintain thy Wife and Childr O! Sir, quoth Jack, shrugging his Shoulde the Church-yard, my Wife sells Ale, and I and after Evening Service (my Parishior kind to bring their Dogs to Church) I bring and bate him, and for about two Hours we and Shove, Staff and Tail till we are all thirsty, and then we step in to our Joa stoutly of her Nutbrown Ale, and I pro saith he, we make a very pretty Business of

The tutoiement of the "Noble S deference of poor Jack, the slight an tuous way in which his education, his University," and his taking Orders ar as if he had gained nothing, socially tually, by these things—all this is though by no means novel. Perhap ordained by one of those Whig bisho trived to bring the Church in Wale utter disrepute.

ETYMOLOGY OF "LOZENGE."—We the following meanings of this word: with four equal sides, having two acu obtuse angles; a rhomb; 2. a small ca &c., often medicated, originally in the lozenge or rhomb, but now usually gives Fr. losange, Gr. λοξος, oblique corner. Dufresne gives losengina, lozeng scutaria." I find no losange, lozange, c Littré for the sweetmeat. He renders

"1. Terme de blason. 2. Parallélogran quatre côtés sont égaux sans que les angles 3. Terme de plain chant. Note figurée e qui vaut la moitié de la carrée ou brève; le donc une semi-brève.......Etym. Berry, osar incertaine. Scheler, d'après Gachet, pense n'est pas selon toute l'ancien français losar flatterie, qui est une autre forme de lou comme il déduit: jadis les armes des fan encadrées dans les rhombes ; on aura dit que ces armoiries, destinées à exalter les seigneurs par des allégories, étaient des *losanges* ou *louanges ;* puis le nom de *losange* aura passé à l'encadrement même. Cela est ingénieux, probable même, car le sens du blason est le premier et le plus ancien ; mais il faudrait quelque intermédiaire pour le rendre sûr."

Bescherelle, who gives the parallelogram as the primitive meaning of the word, says, "*losange, lozange,* du Lat. Barb. *laurengia ;* fait de *laurus,* laurier, par ce que cette figure ressemble à quelques égards à la feuille de laurier ; selon d'autres, du Gr. λοξος, oblique, parce que les angles du losange ne sont point droits." Fleming and Tibbings's *Dict.* has "*losange, lozange* (figure à quatre côtés égaux, ayant deux angles aigus et deux obtus), lozenge." Cotgrave gives "*losenge,* a losenge, the form, or a thing of the forme, of an ordinarie quarrell of glasse, &c., as in lozenge" ; and "*lozenge,* a lozenge ; a little square cake of preserved herbs, flowers, &c. ; also a quarrell of a glasse-window ; any thing of that forme ; also guile, deceit, fraud, cousenage." The sweetmeat is rendered in modern French by *pastille,* and, when not of a round form, by *tablette.* That the word for the sweetmeat may be altogether a different word is quite possible. I am, however, disposed to think it is the primitive word from which the others have been derived. It would appear to be from the Arabic *lawzīnaj,* a confection of almonds (*lawzīyāt,* sweatmeats in which almonds are used, almond confections ; *lawzat,* preserved fruit ; Persian *lawzīna,* any food in which almonds form a part ; from *lawz,* an almond (Mod. Arab. *lûza,* Heb. חל, *lūz,* the almond tree) ; found also in Syriac. Freytag (*Lex. Arab.-Lat.*) gives "*lawz,* nom. gener., *lawzat,* nom. unit., *amygdalum* ; *lawzinaj* (Pers. *lawzīna*), dulciarium opus ex amygdalis" (quoting *Kam.*). Meninski has "Arab. *lews,* amygdalum ; *lewzīnej,* dulciarium ex amygdalis ; Pers. *lawzīne,* id." Kieffer and Bianchi (*Dict. Turc.-Franç.*) have "*levzínedj* et *levzînè,* s. Arab., pâtisserie d'amandes ; *levz,* amande, s. Arab., *levz ul-hind,* coing (fruit)." Shakespear (*Hindustani Dict.*) gives "*lauz,* an almond, a kind of sweetmeat, s. Arab" ; "*lauz-iyát,* sweetmeats in which almonds are mixed, s. Arab." ; "*lauz-ina,* a confection of almonds, Arab. Pers." The Sanscrit has three words for the sweetmeat, and six for the quadrangular figure. R. S. CHARNOCK.

Junior Garrick Club.

CURIOSITIES OF CRICKET.—Amongst the novel matches of last season was one played at Shalford (Surrey), between eleven Heaths and eleven Mitchells, the former all belonging to Shalford, while the latter team was composed of men from Holmwood, Felday, Ockley, and Littleton. The Mitchells won on the first innings by seventeen runs. It was stated in the newspaper (*Surrey Advertiser*) from which this is derived that the victors had already vanquished eleven Mileses and eleven Muggeridges, and that they were about to challenge eleven named Lucas. These eleven (Lucases), all connected by family ties, had then recently played a match near Horsham. During the same season eleven women of Elstead "handled the willow" and defeated eleven ladies of Thursley, the Thursley team having previously beaten the Elstead. One of the fair ones was described as being "a batswoman of considerable local repute." Another showed "an excellent defence" until "she was well caught by the bowler." When Thursley went in (first innings) "they were quickly disposed of," the bowling of Mrs. —— and Mrs. —— "proving of so destructive a character that no less than seven 'ducks' eggs' appeared in the score." A Miss —— is described as "a promising young player," "her defensive powers as a cricketer being well brought out." Two other ladies "each batted in good form." Elstead scored forty-four and twenty-eight ; Thursley, seventeen and forty-nine. I did not learn whether the tie was played off, each team, as I have said, having won a game. I find it recorded that in 1846 eleven brothers Colman were in one set, and in a previous year a Mr. Pagden, with four of his sons and six of his nephews, won a match. More recently the Brotherhoods mustered an eleven in Gloucestershire, and it is said that eleven Lytteltons, with the late baron at their head, once took part in a match. KINGSTON.

[A few years ago there was a match at the Surrey Oval between eleven Greenwich pensioners with one arm and eleven other Greenwich pensioners with one leg. There was excellent play on both sides. The one-armed lost. They were less handy than their fellows in picking up the ball.]

DANTE'S "PURGATORIO."—In Mrs. Oliphant's *Dante,* the first of the series of "Foreign Classics for English Readers," there is a mistranslation (p. 117) which should be corrected in the next edition. In the third canto of the *Purgatorio,* ll. 118-120, Manfredi says to the poet,

"Poscia ch' i' ebbi rotta la persona
Di due punte mortali, io mi rendei
Piangendo a Quei che volentier perdona."

Mrs. Oliphant has rendered the last line, "Weeping to Those who willingly pardon," instead of "to Him who willingly pardons." *Quei,* although usually plural (for *Quelli*), is here singular. Volpi, in his *Indice,* says, in reference to this passage, "*Quei* per quello in terzo caso"; and Cary, Wright, and Longfellow all translate it as *Him.* The singular verb *perdona* shows that the pronoun is also singular. I have thought it possible that Mrs. Oliphant may understand the poet to mean the Trinity, as she writes "Those" with a capital ; but I think there can be no reasonable doubt that he simply means God, and this is the view which

culars of an old bell, which may be of interest to some of your readers :—

"Efforts are being made to collect sufficient funds for the restoration of the parish church of Brailes, Warwickshire. The tower of this ancient church contains one of the heaviest peals of six bells to be met with in this country. Unfortunately these are so badly hung and out of repair that twenty men and boys find it a toilsome and difficult task to bring out their melody, and the tenor and third bells are badly cracked. The former is a mediæval bell, weighing about 34 cwt., and much admired by archæologists. It bears the arms of the Underhill family, with the following legend, probably a stanza of some ancient Ascension hymn :—

' Gaude quod post ipsum scandis,
Et est honor tibi grandis
In celi palacio.' "

It is proposed to recast this bell, exactly reproducing its interesting features, and also the other cracked bell.   F. S.
Churchdown.

ANECDOTE OF GEORGE III. AT WEYMOUTH.—
I had been writing to a lady, upwards of seventy years of age, and in my letter had said something about Weymouth. In her reply the lady thus wrote :—
"I never think of Weymouth without an anecdote of our old king, George III. My mother was one day walking there when she saw a little girl run up to the king, saying, 'Mr. Ting! Mr. Ting! I have dot on a new flannel pettitoat !' at the same time affording him ocular demonstration thereof. Whereupon the king, with his well-known good-nature, patted the child on her head, bestowing seemly commendation on the utility of the newly acquired article. Such was the simplicity of childhood and the benevolence of riper years."

If, as I imagine, this anecdote has not yet been in print, I think that it deserves preservation in these pages.   CUTHBERT BEDE.

THE " CIRRUS."—Looking for a word in Rich's Illustrated Companion to the Latin Dictionary my eye fell, as one's eye always does, on something else, and that was :—

" Cirrus in vertice. A tuft of hair drawn up all around the head, and tied into a bunch on the occiput, as was the practice of athletes, wrestlers, boxers, &c."

Any one who has noticed lately the mural decorations of the metropolis must have observed an animated portrait of a celebrated clown, "Little Sandy," that exhibits a cirrus in vertice most strikingly. Now I would ask, is this a whim of "the drollest of the droll," as he is termed in the bills, or is it a tradition of the circus that has come down to us from the time of the Romans? I have observed that the Spanish bull-fighters have their hair cut very short with the exception of a cirrus,

PRAYER AND CREED.—Subjoined is an e transcript of a small Anglo-Saxon text, which some years since, but it is no longer in existe and I hesitate to send even this printed because I doubt if I could find another if should not print it. It was a small vellum in the finest preservation, having perhaps kept between the leaves of some old boo devotion. It may have come from Byland Al since a large collection of the charters of abbey was also in the same house. Except to accommodate the printer, it was necessa render the characters proper to Anglo-Saxon ordinary letters, I can answer for its literal e ness, having collated the proof with the origin

Her is gebed & geleafa
Hit gedafnath th
Ic lufige & wurthige
God ana & symle
Fæder Sunu & Halgan gast
Wæt ic sothe wile
Thurh godes gife
Sy god fultume
A. on minum gebede
Swa his wylla sy ;
                                         A M H

As I remember, the final N was uncomm protracted in length.   THOMAS KERSLAK
Bristol.

THE ORDER OF THE GARTER AN EPIC ORDER.—The following not generally known is extracted from an article entitled "Petti Knights," in All the Year Round for Februar the present year—an article to which I we direct the attention of your readers :—

" The Order of the Garter, itself the most glorio extant orders of knighthood, was originally founde the benefit of both sexes, and was worn by them fo first hundred and fifty years of its existence.......In reign of Richard the Second, the two daughters of Duke of Lancaster—Philippa, wife of John, Kin Portugal, and Catherine, wife of Henry, Prince of turias—were also Knights of the Garter. I am c aware that, up to this point, the Garter Roll prove more than that the ladies of the family of the sover were admitted to the order ; but in the succeeding re the limits of knighthood were largely extended. An the names occur those of the Countesses of Buckingt Pembroke, Salisbury, Huntingdon, Kent, Derby, W moreland, Arundel, Warwick, and Richmond ; the La Mohun, Le Despencer, Poynings, Swynford, Fitzwa De Ros, Waterton, and Burnell. The last lady Kn of the Garter was Margaret Beaufort, Countess of R mond, mother of Henry the Seventh."

                                         H. Y. N

Queries.

[We must request correspondents desiring information on family matters of only private interest, to affix their names and addresses to their queries, in order that the answers may be addressed to them direct.]

JOHN CARVER.—The first governor of the Pilgrim Fathers was John Carver. He appears in the compact as bringing his wife to New England, and his family numbered eight (Baylie's *Memoirs of Plymouth Colony*). His son Jasper died on Dec. 6, 1620, before the landing. John Carver, the governor, died from a sunstroke on April 5, 1621, and his wife died six weeks later. He is "supposed to be one of Robinson's church who emigrated from England to Holland, and first appears as the agent of the church. It is also said that he had once possessed a large property which had been impaired during his exile" (Baylie's *Memoirs*). Dr. Belknap, in his *American History*, says, "We have no particulars of the life of Mr. Carver previous to his appointment as one of the agents of the Congregational church in Leyden."

I have an idea that Governor Carver was possibly descended from Deryk Carver, a Brighton brewer of good property, who was burned at the stake at Lewes, Sussex, in 1554 (see Foxe's *Book of Martyrs*). Perhaps some of your American readers could throw light on the subject.

FREDERICK E. SAWYER.
Brighton.

A WASHINGTON LETTER.—At a sale, June 2 and 3, 1830, by Messrs. Southgate, Grimstone & Wells, of No. 22, Fleet Street, there was sold an autograph letter, written by John Washington to Messrs. Cary & Sons of London, containing instructions concerning a tombstone. If the present possessor of that letter will communicate with COL. CHESTER, 124, Blue Anchor Road, S.E., he will confer a great favour.

"MARQUIS" v. "MARQUESS."—I recently observed on the visiting card of a nobleman holding a prominent public position that he adopts *marquis* for the orthography of his title. Having always been under the impression that *marquess* is the preferable form of spelling, it would be interesting to others as well as to myself if some of your correspondents could throw light on the subject, and at least collect instances of the various ways in which the word has been spelt by noblemen of historical celebrity.
MARCHIO.

DOVE FAMILY.—About the year 1700 the Governor of "Plymouth Dock," as it was then called, was a man of the name of Dove. I should be much obliged to any of your correspondents who could give me any information about him or his family (ancestors or descendants). I have reason to believe that he belonged to the family of

Camberwell, co. Surrey, and I should much like to verify this belief. This family is referred to in Manning and Bray's *History and Antiquities of the County of Surrey*, vol. iii. p. 427, where it is mentioned that there is a pedigree of the said family in one of the Surrey Visitations.

I should be grateful also for any information about this family. Manning and Bray say nothing more than that they trace their descent to Henry Dove, who fell on Bosworth Field fighting for Richard III., and that the wife of this Henry Dove was a daughter of Thomas Brereton, of Cheshire.
P. E. D.

THE REPORTERS' GALLERY IN THE HOUSE OF COMMONS.—Who first called the Reporters' Gallery in the House of Commons a fourth estate of the realm? Macaulay adopts the expression in his essay on Hallam and in the third chapter of the *History*.
P. C.

[The expression is often applied to the Press, and therefore may possibly have been extended, by analogy, to the gallery occupied by its representatives.]

THE ROYAL CROWN OVER A CIVILIAN CREST.—A county militia regiment, having the designation of "Royal," and as such entitled to bear the insignia of royalty, has lately adopted for its badge the crest of its colonel. Would it be right or wrong, in ordering a die for the plate or paper of the regiment, to put a royal crown over the civilian crest, with the name of the regiment underneath? or should the royal crown be divided in some way from the crest or badge, so as to show that the person bearing the crest is not himself entitled to bear also a regal crown?
C. T. J. M.

UNIVERSITY OF LONDON.—I have never seen the name of my University in Latin, and, as there is more than one Latin form which the name might legitimately take, I should feel obliged if some one would say whether there is any official document issued by, or relating to, the University in that language, or what the Latin terms are (if any) in any way used or recognized by the Senate or by Convocation to designate the University itself, and the handsome Government edifice in Burlington Gardens at present officially styled in English "University Building."
A GRADUATE OF LONDON.

WARTON AND JOHNSON.—Where is the anecdote to be found of Dr. Johnson saying to Dr. Warton, "I am not accustomed to be contradicted," and Dr. Warton's answer, "It were better for yourself and your friends, sir, if you were"?
J. R. B.

QUEEN ANNE AND GEORGE II.—I have an old brown pottery tankard (gallon size), with the incised date 1730, and the name of the owner, "Mary Bayly." Round the rim of the tankard is

have formed the subject of the toast.   S. J.

Manchester.

NORFOLK A BIG GOOSE-GREEN.—Some celebrated character (such as Charles Fox) has said of Norfolk that it is (or was) one big goose-green interspersed with hamlets, or a succession of hamlets connected by a goose-green. I shall be greatly obliged if any of your readers can give me a reference to the original, or the name of the author of the saying.   T. S.
Norwich.

FRIESIC LEGENDS.—The titles of any collection of Friesic legends or popular songs will be welcome to the querist.   He has Scheltema's *Friesche Spreckworden.*   F. L.

A PAINTING BY GUERCINO DA CENTO.—Will some of your learned friends complete the following fragment, which appears on the open book held by a Cumæan Sibyl painted by Guercino?—

SALVI CASTA SION
PER MVLTAQV PASSA PVLL
SIBILLA CVM⁴

I should be glad to be able to put it in an intelligible shape.   E. A.

"CHARLOTTE."—Derivation wanted of this term, peculiar to French and English cookery-books, as applied to a "charlotte russe," "charlotte de pommes." The result being a "little house" for the apples, &c., can it be corrupted *chalet*, *chalotte*, *charlotte?* Is there any *etymological* dictionary of culinary terms?   GREYSTEIL.

URCHENFIELD.—It is a curious fact, hitherto unexplained, that in a large district of Herefordshire at least five of the peculiar legal customs of Kent were anciently in force, though unknown in other parts of England. In Urchenfield—the Arcenefelde of Domesday—a territory lying all around King's Capley, the inhabitants, like the men of Kent, possessed the customs of (1) partible descents, (2) freedom from escheat for felony, (3) dower of half the husband's lands, (4) devisability of "purchased" lands, and, according to Domesday, the still more remarkable Kentish right of (5) being placed in the van of the army ("Cum exercitus in hostem pergit, ipsi per consuetudinem faciunt avauntwarde, et reversione redrewarde"). Can any of your readers suggest how this identity of customs arose, or inform me if any trace of it still survives?   CYRIL.

BRAMPTON PARK, HUNTS.—I from a well-engraved plate, o(place. On it is : "Published D(ham, 39, Strand." The view : Finley, and engraved by T. Hig has probably appeared in some end of it is a sitting female figur ing Dress." I should be glad to work in which the view may ha\ any other description of the parl WY/
33, Bloomsbury Street.

WILLIAM, THIRD BARON OF V Who were the "other issue" (mentioned under the family of £ head of Marlborough, and what
Lowbourne, Melksham.

AN ENGRAVING.—I have a engraving of three foxhounds' h coloured hounds on each side coloured hound in the centre. readers tell me from whose paint and the probable engraver? It i letters."

A BANBURY STORY.—In *The* by Nicholas Cox, 1696, I read :— "Now, by the way, let me give caution : be sure whilst you are dres him not again naked, his Body be penetration of the air, whilst you ar story to some comrades that acciden stable." What is a "Banbury story"? W. N.
Stockport.

THE LORD OF BURLEIGH.—Yo familiar with *The Lord of Burlei* which Tennyson gives a poetic romantic incident in the history Exeter. Can any of them sup prose version upon which it is lil founded his poem? Northampton.

INVITATION CARDS OF THE E TURY.—A friend of mine has, invitation to an evening party : Mann and one from a Duchess o written on the backs of playing cards. I should like to know whether the custom was general; when and whence introduced, and its meaning; and whether such invitations were issued for card parties only or otherwise.   A. B. H.

"ROYD."—What is the meaning of the word *royd?* It is used in many places in this district, such as Longroyd Bridge, Highroyd (district), Coteroyd (house), Royd House, Royd Hall, &c.
W. H. C.
Huddersfield.

GODMOROCKE.—In the year 1636 Sir Ferdinando Gorges, of Ashton Phillips, co. Somerset, granted to Arthur Champernowne, of Dartington, two large tracts of land lying on the extreme south-western frontier of Maine, in New England, one to be called Dartington, and the other Godmorocke. The latter was not then a local name in New England. Its origin, like Dartington, must be found in England. I have not been able to find Godmorocke in any English gazetteer or county history. I shall be obliged to any one who can tell me anything about it.
C. W. TUTTLE.
Boston, U.S.A.

SIR JOHN WOODVILLE.—Did Sir John Woodville, who was slain with his father, Earl Rivers, at Edgecot Field, leave an only daughter and heiress, Anne, who was married to Sir John Helwell of Whissendine? A descent from this match is claimed in Nichols's *Leicestershire* for the Sherards of Stapleford, on the faith of " two very old pedigrees on vellum." Can the statement be proved, or disproved, on more satisfactory evidence?
CLK.

THE WOOD FAMILY OF OR ABOUT LEIGH, LANCASHIRE. — Will some correspondent of " N. & Q." give what information he can respecting the Wood family of or about Leigh, Lancashire? One of them, Elizabeth Wood, I believe, married about 1734 Edward, the son of Thomas, eldest son of Baron Leigh, of Stoneley, Warwickshire. All information will be thankfully received by   J. HENRY WHITEHEAD.
24, Clarendon Street, Cambridge.

"THE LASS OF RICHMOND HILL."—I have been for some weeks endeavouring to discover the author of the above song, and whether the Richmond is in Surrey or Yorkshire. One very circumstantial account gives " McNolly," author of *Robin Hood,* as the composer, and the county as Yorkshire; while a great authority on the subject of the present day states it to have been composed by Mr. James Hook, grandfather of Theodore Hook, and Surrey as the county. Can any of your readers place the matter beyond a doubt?   QUAVER.

CHARLES LAMB.—When he left Islington he hired that "gamboogey" furnished cottage at Chaseside, Enfield, which he quitted after a year to board and lodge at Westwood's, next door. Was the "gamboogey" cottage Leishman's, with whom he had formerly boarded and lodged? Whereabouts in Edmonton was his *first* removal before finally going to Mr. Walden's, Church Street, where he died?   QUIVIS.
[Charles Lamb died Dec. 27, 1834.]

TOM TOMPIER.—A picture of this person is represented with a clock. Is he known to fame? and if so, who and what was he?   W. P.

DR. CHILLINGWORTH.—Does any portrait of Chillingworth exist? If so, where is it? and has it been engraved?   J. J. P.

ST. SUNDAY.—Where shall I find any notice of this saint? There was at Drogheda, in 1649, " a strong round tower next the gate called St. Sunday's." See Carlyle's *Lett. and Speeches of Oliver Cromwell,* ii. 53.   ANON.

SIR FRANCIS BURDETT.—One of our customers is in possession of a large silver vase, which was purchased at the sale of Sir Francis Burdett's effects after his death. He has been given to understand that it was a presentation vase, either commemorating Sir Francis's return from imprisonment in the Tower, or his retirement from Parliament. We have been requested to ascertain its history, and have been advised to make application to " N. & Q." The Hall mark on the vase would seem to be of the year 1810, but of this we are not certain.   T. & W. BANTING.
27, St. James's Street.

AUTHORS OF BOOKS WANTED.—
Commutation of Tythes in Ireland injurious not only to the Church Establishment, but to the Poor. London, 1808. 8vo.
History of the Campaign on the Sutlej and the War in the Punjaub, &c. London, 1846. 8vo.   ABHBA.

AUTHORS OF QUOTATIONS WANTED.—
" And often in my heart I cry,
How beautiful is youth ! "
JOHN A. BLAGDEN.

Replies.

PERSONAL PROVERBS.
(5ᵗʰ S. ix. 47.)

MR. SOLLY'S interesting note on this subject opens out a wide field of inquiry. These apparently personal proverbs are very numerous in our national parœmiology. A list of two or three hundred might be without much difficulty compiled. Yet, on more minute investigation, in a very large percentage of these no special person

some passing skit in a town must be connected with the mayor of that town as its concrete and visible spokesman or representative. When, however, a Christian or other name is localized, as in Mr. Solly's list, "John of Cumberland" and "Old Russe of Pottern," the presumption is greatly strengthened that an actual person is meant. Next, the proverbs which contain common surnames merely are in many instances impersonal. 1. Where the surname is different in independent versions of the same proverb, or where the same surname figures in different proverbs. 2. Where there exists an alliterative connexion between the surname, which is a common one, and a hingeing word in the saying, e.g. 3. Bolt and Bolton.† 3. Where the surname comes in as a mere tag in the formula, "Quoth Dawkins," "Quoth Mortimer,"‡ and the like. 4. The surname may be merely an obsolete or corrupted word which is no surname at all. But, with all these deductions, there will be left a noteworthy residuum where an actual man is meant, as Plowden,§ of whom we have definite information, and some three or four in our present list, of whom particulars may be somewhere or some day forthcoming. I venture to append a few remarks on Mr. Solly's list. The interpretation of proverbs is the slipperiest of all etymological tasks, so that I speak in all cases without the smallest wish to dogmatize. H. refers to *English Proverbs and Proverbial Phrases*, by W. Carew Hazlitt, 1869 ; R. to Ray's *Collection of Proverbs*, the page references being to the first edition, printed at Oxford in 1670.

Banbury: As nice as the Mayor of B.—Halliwell gives, As *wise* as the Mayor of Banbury, who would prove that Henry III. was before Henry II. These civic magistrates were favourite proverbial butts. The respective mayors of Huntingdon, Northampton, Altrincham, Over, Hartlepool, Halgaver (an imaginary place), London (in four proverbs), Banbury, York, &c., all

* When the proverb treats of an animal it becomes Tom, Dick, or Harry's animal for the same reason.

† To avoid repetition, I may say that the following numbers in Mr. Solly's list seem to be suspiciously impersonal from connecting Christian names or common surnames with an alliterative match-word in the proverb—2, 3, 5, 8, 11, 14, 15, 21.

‡ This tag is, I need hardly say, in our language as old as Hendyng and his proverbs, and doubtless much older. It often winds up a black-letter broadside ballad.

§ A hasty glance through Ray for the purpose of this note has suggested from his pages the following certainly alluded to personages:—Duke Humphry, Hobson, the Cambridge carrier, William of Wickham, Lord Keeper Egerton, Lady Donne, Robin Hood and his *entourage* of course, plenty of saints.

her (R., p. 163). Without the tag it mont and Fletcher (*Prophetess*, Act i. ye an ace of a sound senator." In N are quoted which give the whole pro best must crave their aces of allowance (H., p. 358). The alliterative connexion and Bolton is evident.

Bolton : Wide ! quoth B. when his l Halliwell says "flew backward," which rect. H. gives a variation, "Wide ! p. 475. The latter version shows how t moulded ; when docked of the second stood, "Wide ! quoth Bolton." But this alliteration being *de rigueur*, so any con a *w* was substituted.

Bumsted : Crack me that nut, quoth has *knak me that nut;* but the rest of tl more modern growth seemingly " (I p. 214, gives as above. Here, as in *We*₃ tag being an uncommon surname and n suspect a real allusion.

Croker : As coy as C.'s mare.—I find H., p. 60 (but R., p. 202, gives as Mr. S coy as a oroker's mare." It may, perhap as quiet as a crocker or crock-dealer's ho a restive jade would smash all the eartl round in such carts. Croker meant saffron, which is less appropriate.

Cumberland : The devil and John of This should be John a Cumber, a great S He appears in Anthony Munday's play. *John a Cumber*, 1595. Here is a quotatic by Nares *in v.* " Cumber ":—

" Ile poste to Scotland for brave *John*
The only man renownde for magick
Oft have I heard *he once beguylde th*
And in his arte could never find his

Day : Ware wapps, quoth William D likely wasp; but it may mean a large which *wapps* and *whips* signify, and the those walking below some hay-loft. C quoth Grubber," &c. (H., p. 447).

Dawkins : Dab ! quoth D. when he Dawkin, a foolish person; dawkingly wis North (Halliwell). R. adds more, whic homely to quote. I have heard in Ber Daniel when he —— in a well." Both I kins and I suspect, mythical individu reappears as the hero of another sayin; kin, the devil is in the hemp " (H., p. 34

De la Mott : As much deformed as I gets a glimmer here : *houss*, large, co (Halliwell). *Mot*, a jade, still in use, *dollimop*, a servant wench, as altered t house can hardly be called deformed.

Doddipol : As learned as Dr. D.—Th to be a surname. See Richardson *in v.* " pole," " perhaps from dote and pole." stances given of its use here is one : " B our curate is naught, an ass-head, a c latine, and can do nothing " (Latimer, *before K. Edward*). Sterne uses the w *Shandy*.

Gilbert : Gip ! quoth G. to his mare ill rubbing, quoth Badger, when his

Note (by Ray), "This is a ridiculous expression, used to people that are pettish and froward" (see H., p. 141). *Badger* is a pedlar. *Gip*=gee up, as in other proverbs commencing, "Marry, come up," &c.

Jerman: As just as J.'s lips.—"'Just as Jerman's (German) lips.' In apparent allusion to the firm compression habitual among the Germans" (H., p. 251). But Cicero (Off. 3, 17, 68) speaks of *germana justitia*, genuine, sincere justice, and the proverb may merely be *germane lips*, a literalism from some Latin adage.

Mortimer: Backan ! quoth M. to his sow.—Should be *baccare*, go back ; etym. doubtful. See *Taming of Shrew*, Act ii. sc. 1. Nares explains this as made in ridicule of some man who introduced Latinized English words upon trivial occasions. Compare Goodyer's pig, John Gray's bird, Pedley's mare, Kettle's mare, Jackson's hens, Jackson's pigs, Bunny's bear, Teague's cocks, Wood's dog, and many more birds and beasts, which appear proverbially with their respective owners, who are probably merely so many John Does and Richard Roes. But just as our law realized its fictions in supposed individuals, so the clown found it much more telling and definite to say, "As lazy as Ludlam's dog, who leant against a wall to bark," than to say, "As lazy as a dog, who leans," &c.

Mosse : He found him napping as M. found his mare. —"Till day come catch him, as Mosse his grey mare, napping," quoted by Wilbraham, *Ches. Gloss.*, p. 58, H., p. 287, from the *Christmas Prince*, 1607, was still current in Cheshire in Wilbraham's time. See also R., p. 187. Mosse occurs still in Cheshire as a common surname. I fancy that "finding a mare's nest" is connected somehow.

Mumford : Mock not, quoth M.—Mock not (quoth Montford) when his wife called him cuckold (R., p. 186). Compare one Benson exactly in the same domestic embarrassment. "I hope better, quoth Benson, when his wife bid him come in, cuckold" (H., p. 212).

Nicholas : Good night, N., the moon's in bed.—Here St. Nicholas is probably meant, the patron saint of boys. In boys' games to cry "Nicholas" meant that the speaker will break off (see Halliwell *in v.*). This may be the converse of

"Boys and girls come out to play,
The moon doth shine as bright as day."

Or the proverb may allude to thieving, "St. Nicholas's clerks," 1 *Henry IV.*, ii. 1. *Moon-men*, thieves, robbers (Hall).

Noble: Gramercy, forty pence, Jack N.'s dead.— Given by R., p. 215. The coin is here intended. The noble was worth 6s. 8d., the modern solicitor's fee ; forty pence would be the half noble. The meaning is, thank you for half, failing the whole, or may allude to the cessation of nobles to be coined in the ninth year of Henry V. They first appeared under Edward III., 1334. The noble reappears in a Cheshire proverb (R., p. 217); "Right, master, right. Four nobles a year is a crown a quarter" ; and of a prodigal it is said, he will "bring his noble down to nine-pence."

Palmer: What ! again quoth P.—What, again ? quoth Paul, when his wife made him cuckold the second time (H., p. 451). Mumford, Montford, Benson, Palmer, and Paul all are in analogous domestic situations.

Parnell: Madam P., crack the nut and eat the kernel. —He that will eat the kernel must crack the nut. R., p. 84, gives both. *A pretty parnel*, amatorcula, petronilla. *Pratling parnel*, an herb, sanicula maculosa (Littleton's *Lat. Dict.*, 1724). *Parnel* or *Pernel* was used as a Christian name ; it is Petronilla contracted. It is probably brought in here as the only available rhyme to "kernel."

Ploydon : The case is much altered, quoth P.—This is "Plowden's proverb: the case is altered," or "The case

is alter'd, quoth Plowden." In this case alone it seems certain that a particular individual is intended, viz. Edmund Plowden, an eminent lawyer in Queen Elizabeth's time, born 1518, died 1585. Two accounts (too long to quote) of how the saying arose may be read in R., p. 162, or in H., p. 361. The general readiness of lawyers to argue on either side is satirized.

Roger : As red as R.'s nose, who was christened with pump-water.—He was christened with pump-water. It is spoken of one that hath a red face (Ray). I don't see the humour of *pump-water ;* but in Berks I have heard a thin damsel called "as straight as a yard of pump-water." *Roger* only appears as a jingle to *red*, as it is one to *right* in this : "'Right, Roger, your sow is good mutton'" (R., p. 191).

Russe : He will live as long as old R. of Pottern.— Here is, I take it, a genuine personal allusion. Potterne is near Devizes, in Wilts. Some local correspondent would perhaps kindly say if this old Parr of the neighbourhood be still remembered. This worthy is named *Rosse* with more likelihood in H., p. 198, and it is added, "who lived till all the world was weary of him."

Snelling : Mark S. anon.—Anon was the old waiter's "Coming, sir. immediately." Is this Mark Snelling connected with Du. *maaken*, to make ; *snell*, quick ; *snellen*, to run at speed ? But Mark Snelling may have been in his time as classical as the "plump head-waiter at the 'Cock.'"

Spratt : Jack S. could eat no fat.—I do not think Archdeacon Pratt can be intended. In Clarke's *Parœmiologia*, 1639 (quoted H., p. 249), a parallel version is already in existence :—

"Jack will eat no fat, and Jill will eat no lean,
Yet betwixt them both they lick the dishes clean."

Compare "Jack Sprat would teach his grandame" (R., p. 108), and "Little Jack Dandy-prat was my first suitor" (Halliwell's *Nursery Rhymes*, 1844, p. 149); and again, ib., p. 40, "Jack Sprat had a calf." These varying versions seem to indicate that no particular person is meant.

Vavasour : What ! nowhere such a V.—This comes from, or at least through, Chaucer, who sums up his description of the "frankeleyn" :—

"A schirreve had he ben, and a counter ;
Was nowhere such a worthi vavaser."

That is, such a worthy member of the lesser gentry; but this expression may be older than Chaucer, as poets often imbed in their text pre-existing proverbs.

Vier : O Master V. we cannot pay you.— *Vie*, to wager or put down a certain sum upon a hand of cards (Halliwell). Nares supplies many quotations of its use. Torriano mentions a *signore* or director of the game of *mora*, when played in the English fashion.

Walley : Wide ! quoth Wally.—Perhaps diminutive of Walter, a softer form than "Watty." If a surname, should be written Whalley ; common in Lancashire. Cf. "Wide ! quoth Wilson," *supra*.

Waltham : As wise as W.'s calf.—R. adds (p. 203), that ran nine miles to suck a bull. I have myself heard in Berks of one who had gone a fruitless errand, "He went all that way to suck a bull adrye." "Waltham must be a place, not a man, viz. Waltham in Essex :—

"For Waltham's calves to Tiburne needes must go."

Quoted in H., p. 446, from the *Collection of Seventy-nine Black-letter Ballads and Broadsides*, London, Joseph Lilly, 1870, p. 226. Cf. also "an Essex lion" (*i.e.* a calf). But another version (H., *ib.*), quoted from Skelton's *Colyn Cloute*, runs, "As wise as Walton's calf." Ray has, p. 227, "Essex calves," with a note on their celebrity and the handsome monuments of butchers in that county, whose epitaphs style them *carnifices*.

hardly be connected.

HORATIO.

P.S.—Since writing the above I have stumbled on a rather obscure commentary of the *Jerman* proverb in a varied form. Torriano, 1659, *in v.* "Bocchata," says :—" Also a word much used, when one is about to tell a thing, and knows not very certainly what it is, also that one knows nothing of it in the least, or that a schollar would fain learn and read his lesson and cannot ; and that we by some signe, or voice would let him know, that he is out, we use then to crye *Bocchata*, as in English, Tush, Pish, *jump as Germins lips*, yea, in my other hose." H., p. 370, quotes from Herbert, 1640, " The German's wit is in his fingers."

JOHN COOKE, THE REGICIDE (5ᵗʰ S. viii. 407 ; ix. 31.)—I have, bound up in a volume of sermons, a tract of sixteen pages, without date, entitled— "The Court of Justice : | or | The Tryals | of King Charles's Judges. | Being an Account of the Arraignment and Condemnation | of Twenty-Nine of those barbarous Traytors, that Cut | off the Head of King Charles the First. | Ten of which (viz. | Thomas Harrison, John Carew. *John Cooke*, Hugh | Peters, Thomas Scot, Gregory Clement. Adrian Scroop, John Jones, | Francis Hacker, and Daniel Axtell) were Executed, and their | Quarters set upon the several Gates of the City. Also, an | Account of what they said in their own Defence, and the Speeches | they made tending to justifie that horrid and abominable Fact. | London : Printed by J. Bradford, at the Bible in Fetter-Lane."

In the centre of the page are portraits of the ten regicides, with King Charles in the centre. The tract gives a full report of the trial, with the arraignment, list of jurors, &c.

Cooke was tried on Monday, Oct. 14. The Solicitor-General opened the case as follows :—

" My Lords, his (Cooke's) Part and Portion will be different from those Tryed before him : They sat as Judges to the Sentence of the late King, and he, my Lord. stood as a Wicked Instrument of that Matter at the Bar, and here doth subscribe and exhibit a Charge of High Treason (a Scandalous Libel against our Soveraign) to be read against him, and made large Discourses and Aggravations thereon, and would not suffer His Majesty to speak in His Defence : He press'd that Judgment might be given against the King ; and also did say, *That He must Die, and Monarchy with him*."

The evidence and defence are given at some length, Cooke "making a very long and learned defence," pleading his privileges as a member of the bar, &c. There is a horrible description of the barbarous executions. They, the prisoners, on different days, generally the day following their condemnation, "betwixt 9 and 10 of the Clock in the Morning were upon a Hurdle drawn from Newgate to Charing Cross, where, within certain Railes lately there made, a Gibbet was erected, and they were hanged with their faces

divided into Quarters, which v Newgate upon the same Hurdles

Cooke and Peters were exec former's head was set on a po end of Westminster Hall, look and his quarters exposed in lil tops of some of the city gates.

There is also an account (executioner, William Hulet. guilty, but apparently not exe in evidence that a man name the king's head off, and Hul the defence he called " son declared they heard the comn don own he did it.

I shall be glad to know i and whether any further ex readers of " N. & Q." There of the evidence given agains scribed as " a very comical Booted Apostle."

Solberge, Northallerton.

It has always appeared to r tice has been done to the mem The remarkable part of his *Creature of God's Making*, i work itself is worthless, thou printed without the preface. interesting in recording the in Bill Courts of Ireland. Of co Restoration, but were afterwa when, reinstituted. More th heard it had been said by a tion for misgovernment in Ire " that those courts had been is quaint, but the statements torical, and deserve a notice th in Irish or English writings of

TF

ST. ISMAEL (5ᵗʰ S. ix. 29 Ecton's *Thesaurus* and Bacon': are the two best authorities f churches in England and We name of the saint of the t diocese of St. Davids, about made, is not " Ishmael," but I *Mart. Rom.*, at June 17, has ‖ " Chalcedone sanctorum martyr et Ismaelis, qui pacis causa apud pro Rege Persorum legatione fung jussu idola venerari compellere animo recusarent, gladio feriuntur

As the names of these sa Butler's *Lives of the Saints*, t Ribadeneira's *Lives* may be ad

. "Ce mesme jour souffrirent le martyre les saincts Manuel, Sabel et Imael [*sic*], Martyrs, a Calcedoine. C'estoient trois freres, qui auoient esté instruits en la foy & religion Chrestienne dés leur jeunesse ; et de tres noble famille. Comme l'Empereur Julian se preparoit à faire la guerre au Roy de Perse, qui s'apelloit Sapor... Sapor luy enuoya ces trois freres icy en ambassade, pour traiter & conclure la paix auec luy à Calcedoine, où il estoit auec son armée. Il arriua qu'vn iour de grande Feste des idoles, ces saincts ambassadeurs n'ayans pas voulu sacrifier comme les autres, furent acusés vers l'Empereur d'estre Chrestiens, lequel les fit aussi-tost emprisonner, iusques au lendemain seulement, de peur de troubler la Feste. Il tâcha par belles paroles de leur persuader de sacrifier : mais voyant que c'estoit en vain, il se mit en colère, et se seruit de menaces : toutesfois il n'auança non plus d'vne façon que d'vne autre, bien qu'il en vint aux effects. Il les fit cruellement fouetter, puis leur fit attacher les mains & les pieds auec des clous : & déchirer leurs corps aueo des ongles, & des crochets de fer ; pendant lequel tourment ils furent consolés par vn Ange. En apres, voyant qu'ils persistoient en la foy de Jesus-Christ, il leur fit brûler les costés, auec des lames de fer ardentes, ficher des alénes & poinctes de fer entre la chair & les ongles des mains & des pieds, & des clouds sur leurs testes : puis les fit decoler, le dix-septiéme iour de Iuin, l'an de nostre Seigneur trois cens soixante-trois."
— *French Translation,* tome i. p. 659, Par., 1660.

ED. MARSHALL, F.S.A.

There are two churches of this name in the diocese of St. Davids, and dedicated to this saint, viz. St. Ismael, in Carmarthenshire, at the mouth of the river Towy, and St. Ismael in the hundred of Rhos, Pembrokeshire.

St. Ismael (not Ishmael) flourished in the sixth century. He is supposed to have been a suffragan bishop of the episcopacy of St. Davids. He was a son of Budig, the son of Cybydan, a native of the western division of Brittany, called in French Cornouailles, and in Breton Kerneo ; and, being compelled to flee his native country, sought refuge in Demetia, or rather that portion of it now called Pembrokeshire. Aircol Lawhir (Aircol the Long Hand) was monarch of Demetia at the time. Whilst in the latter country Budig married Arianwedd, the daughter of Enlleu, son of Hydwn Devu, and the sister of St. Teilo, by whom he had issue two sons, Ismael and Tyfei, both of whom were consecrated by their mother to religion. Ismael founded the churches of St. Ismael, near to Kidwelly, in Carmarthenshire, and Camrose, Uzmaston, Rosemarket, St. Ismael, and West Haroldston, all in Pembrokeshire. His brother Tyfei was accidentally killed when a child by one Tyrtue, but he is described as a "martyr," although it is difficult to conceive how his death can be attributed in any manner to his connexion or belief in any particular creed. He was buried at Penaly, in Pembrokeshire, and he is the patron saint of Lamphey, or, according to Giraldus Cambrensis, "Llantefei," but, according to Browne Willis, "Llantiffi," in that county.

St. Ismael is recorded in *Liber Landavensis* to have been consecrated Bishop of St. Davids on the

death of St. David ; but his name does not appear in the lists given of the bishops of that diocese, and it is probable that he was only a suffragan bishop under his uncle St. Teilo.

W. WILLIAMS.

Oakfield, Pontypridd, Glam.

COMMON ARYAN WORDS FOR AGRICULTURAL INSTITUTIONS (5th S. ix. 27.)—Our present knowledge of the comparative vocabulary of the Aryo-European languages does *not* justify the supposition that the Proto-Aryo-Europeans lived in a state of agricultural civilization. It is only after the separation of the Proto-Aryan and Proto-European languages that we meet with agricultural terms. The only possible objection to this is a word which means "fieldfruit, rye," and is common to both languages, viz. Zend *yava,* Persian *jav,* Greek ξέα, Lithuanian *java ;* but the knowledge of , a plant does not prove its cultivation. The only direct proof would be in the names of the chief processes of agriculture, and those are the very names which differ. The connexion between the European root *sā,* Latin *sero,* Gotic *saian,* Lithuanian *sé-ti,* Bulgarian *sé-jati,* and the Sanskrit *sasya,* "edible fruit," Zend *hahya,* "cereal," is very uncertain, and probably accidental. On the other hand, we have a large number of agricultural terms peculiar to each language. Thus Proto-Aryan *kars,* "to plough," literally "to draw," *i.e.* furrows" (Sanskrit *krish,* Zend *karesh,* Persian *kishtan, kushtan,* and numerous derivatives or compounds), but Proto-European *arāya* (Greek ἀρόω, Latin *arāre,* Lithuanian *ar-ti,* Bulgarian *ora-ti,* Gotic *arjan).* How the word "tree" can have anything to do with this question I fail to see entirely, for it does not denote a fruit-tree, but merely "wood," as Sanskrit *dāru,* "timber" ; Greek δόρυ, "lance-shaft." The Proto-Aryo-European word is *dru,* Sanskrit *dru,* Greek δρῦ-ς, Bulgarian *drŭ-kolŭ,* "a stake" ; Gotic *triu ;* Old Saxon *trio, treo ;* Anglo-Saxon *treó ;* English *tree.*

The first attempt to give an account of the civilization of the Proto-Aryo-Europeans was Kuhn's *Zur ältesten Geschichte der indogermanischen Völker,* Berlin, 1845, reprinted in Weber's *Indische Studien,* i. 321-363. The other two works of interest are A. Pictet's *Les Origines Indo-Européennes, ou les Aryas Primitifs,* and A. Fick's *Die ehemalige Spracheinheit der Indo-Germanen Europas.*

G. A. SCHRUMPF.

Tettenhall College.

The most instructive and original work on this subject is *Les Origines Indo-Européennes, ou les Aryas Primitifs,* par Adolphe Pictet, 2 vols., Par., 1859-63. The chapter on agriculture (2e partie, pp. 73-121) investigates the following terms, retracing them through the different Indo-European languages to their Sanskrit root :—1. Soil and field ; 2. furrow ; 3. spade and axe ; 4. plough and

H. KREBS.
Taylorian Library, Oxford.

"CALLIS" (5th S. ix. 86.)—Compare *calisses* (Grose), almshouses. This is probably a more correct and more definite form than *callis*. I feel disposed to connect the word with *cullison*, a corruption of *cognizance*, that is, the badge worn by the paupers in such houses. I take this quotation from Halliwell and Wright's edition of Nares, 1876 :—"Then will I have fifty beadsmen, and on their gowns their *cullisance* shall be six Milan needles" (Brewer's *Love-sick King*). See in Nares, under *badge* and *cullison*, for a good account of their badges of poverty and servitude.   HORATIO.

WHO WAS THE LAST SURVIVING MEMBER OF THE IRISH HOUSE OF COMMONS? SIR THOMAS STAPLES (5th S. ix. 68.)—About thirty years ago the question was discussed in company who were the Irish members of Parliament then living. We examined the list of the division on the Union, but could not find the name of Sir Thomas Staples. As the last act was carried by a majority of one, we may suppose every vote was of the greatest importance. Sir Thomas was connected with my family, and I took occasion to ask him if he had ever been in Parliament. His answer was, "I had everything to constitute a member of Parliament. I was returned for a borough, I took my seat, and I voted on a question. But, as my father and I took different views on the question of the Union, I was advised to resign my seat." His father, whom I have seen, was the Rt. Hon. John Staples, of Lissan, in the county Tyrone, for many years a member of the Irish Parliament. He died between the years 1818 and 1820. The baronetcy came to Sir Thomas from Sir Robert Staples, of the Queen's county, a distant relation. I was with Sir Thomas at Lissan on March 29, 1858 ; and, though past eighty years of age, he put me out of breath in walking up a hill. We spoke of the death of his contemporary Quentin Dick, who was also an Irish M.P., and he said he was then the only surviving member of the House of Commons. He told me that he had gone the north-east circuit with Quentin Dick, who was the owner of a gig. "You may suppose," he added, "our journey was not very comfortable, as his wheels were polygons." Sir Thomas was a fine benevolent old gentleman. I have seen an excellent portrait of him by Catterson Smith in one of our exhibitions. The late Lord Charlemont survived Sir Thomas. I do not know if he had ever been in the House of Commons. I suppose not from what Sir Thomas said.   H.

He did not represent Coleraine in the Parliament. Possibly he may have sat time at the end of the preceding Parl the room of George Jackson, who January, 1796.   ALFRED B.] Preston.

If A. W. will be good enough to refe viii. 16, he will find that I took an ea tunity of correcting the inaccuracy resp late Sir Thomas Staples, Bart., which ha in p. 474 of the preceding volume.

THE "COW AND SNUFFERS" (5th S. May not the origin of this singular pu sign be an English corruption of th We know that the "Goat and Compass rupted from "God encompasses Us," that Whistle" was originally the Saxon '' Wassail," equivalent to "a lass and a "Venus and Bacchus," and that "Bull ar signified Boulogne Mouth or Harbour. T branch of the Keltic language supplies that commence with the consonants *sn* Gaelic branch affords "coin," dogs, an hair" (pronounced *snavair*), a swin "snamhach" (*snavach*), swimming. If derivation of "Cow and Snuffers," the signify "The Swimming Dogs," a nam some parts of the country to otter snamhair" pronounced by a Keltic spec sound very like "cow and snuffers" to Saxon or English ear.   CHARLES M Reform Club.

"In a play of George Colman, entitled the *the Wags of Windsor*, the following lines occ
'Judy's a darling ; my kisses she suffers ;
She's an heiress, that's clear,
For her father sells beer—
He keeps the sign of the *Cow and the Sn*
The same song also occurs in the *Irishman in the Happy African*. At Llandaff the sign is by a cow standing near a ditch full of reeds with a pair of snuffers placed as if they had the cow's mouth. The oddity of the combin probability pleased a publican who had hear and adopted it forthwith as his sign, leaving ment of the objects to the taste of the sign Larwood and Hotten's *Hist. of Signboards*, p
ST. S

I should imagine that the sign was in the sake of the rhyme.

PASCAL (5th S. ix. 68.)—In Havet's the *Pensées*, 1852, the number of the *pen* F. DE H. L. is No. iii. If he will turn to or chapter iii. as he calls it, No. vi see that Pascal there argues that the a country constitute justice; and he adds that hardly is anything so just but that a change of climate changes it. "The meridian decides the truth," and he closes the paragraph saying, "Plaisante justice qu'une rivière ou une montagne borne! Vérité au deçà des Pyrénées, erreur au delà !" This splendid sarcasm he has borrowed from Montaigne and improved. All that he means to say with regard to the law of primogeniture is that it may be just, *i.e.* legally established, in France and unjust in Italy, the Alps in such case forming the only differentiation of eternal and immutable truth; or as between France and England, it is the Channel justice. A grand thing verily is truth when a casuist's definition of it hangs upon a mere geographical accident such as this.

C. A. WARD.

Mayfair.

THE ANGLO-SAXON O (5ᵗʰ S. viii. 368.)—I think you will find in the Saxon surname "Cleborne" (now spelled "Cliburn" in the map of Westmoreland), and in the curious Saxon motto of that family, "Clibbor ne sceame," two interesting examples of the short *o*.   C. J. HUBBARD.

SUTTON MUTTON (5ᵗʰ S. ix. 88.)—In Warwickshire this ancient and vulgar rhyme is thus rendered :—

> "Sutton for mutton,
> Tamworth for beeves;
> Brummagem for blackguards,   •
> Coleshill for thieves."

Nowadays the first two places mentioned have lost their characteristics. It is to be feared that the last two, however, still preserve theirs faithfully. There is an old saying about the Oxfordshire Sutton ; it refers to its church spire, and runs thus :—

> "Bloxham for length,
> Adderbury for strength,
> But King's Sutton for beauty."

This rhyme suggests another, related to me one time by an aged dame. It has nothing to do with MR. SOLLY'S query, but perhaps I may be allowed to give it a resting place in "N. & Q." Here it is then :—

> "Hayley, Crawley, Curbridge, and Coggs,
> Witney spinners and Duckington dogs,
> Finstock-upon-the-hill, Fawder down derry,
> Beggarly Ramsden, and lousy Charlbury;
> Woodstock for bacon, Bladon for beef,
> Handborough for a scurvy knave,
> And Coombe for a thief."

J. DEVENISH HOPPUS.

Camden Street, N.W.

I remember the following as current in the district in Yorkshire in which I was born :—

> "Sutton boiled mutton,
> Brotherton beef;
> Ferrybridge bonny lass,
> And Knottingley thief."(?)

Sutton is a small hamlet twenty miles south of York.   W. W. P.

Slightly varied, the rhyme of which MR. SOLLY gives two versions is, I think, to be found in many parts of the country. In South Staffordshire it takes this form :—

> "Sutton for mutton,
> Tamworth for beef;
> Walsall for a pretty girl,
> And Birmingham for a thief."

The Sutton here referred to is Sutton Coldfield, near Birmingham. I used to hear the rhyme in Staffordshire in my schooldays, but I do not know that I have heard it since.

J. PENDEREL-BRODHURST.

Colchester.

The version of this saying which I have always heard has evidently a more Midland origin than those quoted by MR. SOLLY :—

> "Sutton for mutton,
> Tamworth for beef;
> Walsall for bandy legs,
> And Brummagem for a thief."

HERMENTRUDE.

QUAKERS AND TITLES (5ᵗʰ S. ix. 68.)—The term Quaker was originally given in ridicule. This Christian body called itself "The Society of Friends." The titles they use are "Friend" (sometimes "Neighbour"), "Dear Friend," "Respected Friend." There are no hereditary offices or officers. The only paid officers are the registrars of London and Dublin. Their ministers are not "appointed" but "acknowledged." Any one has the right to speak in their meeting, either for worship or discipline. If his or her communications are approved of, he or she is "acknowledged" to be a divinely appointed minister ; if the communications are disapproved of, the speaker is requested to keep silent. Those selected to judge of such matters are called "Elders," whose appointment is national, but there are in each locality officers who are called "Overseers." The elders and overseers are of both sexes. The government of the society is purely republican or theocratic. There is no president or chairman at any of their meetings, the theory being that wherever two or three are gathered together Christ is spiritually present, and presides thereat. In each meeting for business, or "discipline" as the term is, a clerk is appointed : in the provincial and national meetings the appointment is special or for the occasion ; in the local or monthly meetings the clerk is permanent. These officers are never addressed by their titles. In case of a difference of opinion at any of the meetings, the clerk is expected to take "the sense of the meeting," and record it ; but questions are decided more by the weight of opinion than majority of votes. Quakers object to the word "Reverend" on the ground that it is one of the names of the

addressed by those who do not belong to their body, and considerable offence has been taken at their being addressed " Mr." instead of " Esq.," though the latter is wholly inapplicable to a Friend.　　　　　　　　JOSEPH FISHER.
Waterford.

MILTON QUERIES (5th S. ix. 107.)—
    "And the mute Silence hist along."
Hist I consider to be an imperative, with the meaning of *hush! silence!* The sense. will be this : Mute Silence may go about (along) saying to every one *hist!* so as to bring all to silence, excepting Philomel, who may deign a song in her sweetest and saddest way (plight).
　　　　　　　　　　　　F. ROSENTHAL.
Hanover.

The meaning of the line—
    " And the mute Silence *hist* along "—
is fully explained in Richardson's *Dictionary* by the quotations given there under the word *hist*. It is an interjection and exclamation commanding silence, apparently formed from the Latin *nota silentii, 'St*, which is a common interjection alike in French, German, and Russian.　　H. KREBS.
Taylorian Library, Oxford.

Hist is imperative. This verb is generally compared with the Latin *nota silentii, St!* cp. " st, st tacete " (Plautus, *Epidicus*, 2, 2, 1). The line is thus paraphrased by Masson (*Milton*, iii. 382) : " Move through the mute Silence saying *hush!* telling the silence to continue unless the nightingale should deign to break it with one of her songs."
　　　　　　　　　　　　A. L. MAYHEW.
Oxford.

I find in Chambers's *Glossary of Obsolete and Rare Words and Meanings in Milton's Poetical Works* that *hist* (verb intransitive) means " to come stealing along crying *hist!* " That makes the meaning of the passage quite clear : " And the mute Silence comes stealing along," &c.
　　　　　　　　　　　　GORILLA.

Does not *hist* mean " listen to "? an imperative addressed to Melancholy. " Listen to the silence " is not an unknown idea.
　　　　　　　　C. F. S. WARREN, M.A.

POPE AND " THE REHEARSAL " (5th S. ix. 128.) —The following extract from Dr. Johnson's "Life of Pope " (*Lives of the Poets*, vol. iv. p. 119, ed. 1794) will explain the difficulty :—
    "After the *Three Hours after Marriage* had been driven off the stage by the offence which the mummy and the crocodile gave the audience, while the exploded

claps, which indicated contempt of the play.

An article entitled " Colley Cibber & Temple Bar for November, 1872 (vol. xɪ will explain why MR. CROMIE failed to words " crocodile and mummy " in his coɪ *Rehearsal*. Cibber availed himself of t limited licence for '*gag*'" afforded by t to introduce an allusion to a farce, the jɔ position of Pope and Gay, entitled *Thr after Marriage*, and it is in this piece o that the offending words occur. The stoɪ told in the article referred to above ; but ɪ of " N. & Q." is too valuable to warrant ɑ at length from so easily accessible a sourc
　　　　　　　　　　　　JOHNSON ɪ
Pallion Vicarage.

" THE PALACE OF TRUTH " (5th S. ix. 1 *Palais de la Vérité* is one of the " Contes ɪ of Madame de Genlis.
　　　　　　　　C. F. S. WARREN,
Bexhill.

" THE WHOLE DUTY OF MAN " (5th S. 515 ; ix. 99.)—It may safely be said that Isham, who published the *Daily Office for* &c., in 1694, could not have written tɦ *Duty of Man*. He was born in 1651, anɖ Ch. Ch., Oxford, at the age of fifteen, ɪ consequently he was about six years old · book in question was printed in 1657.

W. M. M. inquires who wrote the *Nɐ Duty of Man* and the *New Week's Pre* In the *London Magazine* for August, ɪ fiftieth·edition of the *Week's Prepaɪ* announced ; but I have not found any to the first appearance of the newer woɪ latter, however, must have gone throuɡ editions, for Darling, *Cyclo. Biblio.*, p. 21 tions the thirty-fourth edit. as London, ɪ date. In reference to the *New Whole Dɪ* is a curious article in the *Universal Maɡ* March, 1761, in which John Hinton, the ɪ who resided at the King's Arms, in Street, gives the reasons which inducec publish it, alleging that the old work, hundred years old, was quite obsolete, ɑ little affected the generality of readers." that the work was printed only for him ; article is incomplete, having probably ɭ tinued on the wrapper of the journal, ʋ removed in binding. If Hinton was publisher of the *New Whole Duty*, that perhaps afford a clue to the writer or ɑ name.　　　　　　　　　　　EDWARD

. THE ISLE OF MAN (5ᵗʰ S. viii. 127, 251, 298, 470.)—MR. HARRISON is pained or astounded that I wrote, "The sovereignty of this island was never purchased by Government." No sovereignty lay there, but only a lordship, therefore no more could be purchased. Sovereignty lies where the jurisdiction is absolute and uncontrolled. I quoted Lord Coke that, in relation to the Isle of Man, in public oaths allegiance was reserved to the Crown of England ; that appeals from decrees or judgments in the Isle of Man lay to his Majesty in Council ; that appeals could be had in causes of so low a value as five pounds. MR. HARRISON ignores these conclusive proofs, and then to support the sovereignty of the lords of Man gives an imperfect quotation from Blackstone— quotes up to a semicolon, and leaves out the last clause ! The words, "and then an Act of Parliament is binding there," MR. HARRISON left out. He must have seen the statement that an English Act of Parliament made for the Isle of Man was as binding there as any one made for England was binding in Middlesex. MR. HARRISON knows that in 1666 Bishop Barrow and Archdeacon Fletcher purchased for a thousand pounds of Charles, Earl of Derby, the impropriations, rectories, and tithes of the island, and that the deeds of this transaction were confirmed under the great seal of England. MR. HARRISON knows that the bishop of the island is, and was, a suffragan of the Archbishop of York. Would that be so if the sovereignty lay in the island ? More still, MR. HARRISON knows that the earls of Derby could only nominate and not appoint a bishop : the right of approbation lay with the King of England. MR. HARRISON knows that if the earls of Derby delayed a nomination, then the kings of England could nominate and appoint a bishop. King William III. sent for the Earl of Derby and insisted that he should nominate a bishop at once, or he would nominate one and present him with the appointment.

Camden, or his continuator, distinguishes the lordship of the island from the old kingship. When there were kings they were crowned and consecrated. But the Stanleys as lords were only publicly proclaimed and installed. A king can create nobles and give titles ; the lords of Man never could do anything of the sort—they could not even create an esquire. W. G. WARD.

Ross, Herefordshire.

F. BARTOLOZZI, R.A. (4ᵗʰ S. xii. 110 ; 5ᵗʰ S. ii. 335 ; ix. 91.)—In his interesting reply MR. BATES says : "Mr. Dalton was commissioned to invite to this country the most promising historic engraver he could find in Italy. Bartolozzi, then studying in his native Florence under Wagner, was selected." This is not quite correct. Bartolozzi's engagement to engrave under Wagner had expired. He went to Rome upon the invitation of Cardinal Bottari, where he established his reputation by his fine plates of the life of St. Nilus, and by a series of portraits for the new edition of Vasari. He then returned to Venice, and it was there that Mr. Dalton engaged him to engrave a set of drawings by Guercino, and afterwards invited him to England to continue engraving for him for the annual payment of 300l.

So highly was Bartolozzi's figure drawing appreciated, that in some engravings he did the figures, and another engraver the landscape. There is hanging before me now a very fine print, published by E. Woollett, 1787, from a painting of Dido and Æneas, then in possession of the Russian Empress Catherine. The figures are painted by L. T. Jones, the landscape by F. Mortimer ; the figures are engraved by F. Bartolozzi, R.A., and the landscape by Wm. Woollett. There is so much elegance, grace, and spirit in these figures, they seem so to blend with the landscape, and give such force and effect to the whole picture, that one can at once realize the charm and power of the engraver's special gifts in figure drawing.

G. M. PASSENGER.

Southampton.

"CAT-GALLAS" : "CRATCH" : "CRADGE" : "CRADLE," &c. (5ᵗʰ S. vii. 148, 237, 435.)—In this part of the country cat-gallas is the usual term for two sticks stuck upright into the ground, with a third laid a-top, in the form of a gallows, for jumping over. It is about big enough to hang a cat upon ; hence, probably, its name. Scratch-cradle is not a corruption of it, but is a trick game, played by two children with a bit of string crossed in a peculiar manner, and wound round their two hands. It is also called see-saw and cradge-cradle. Cratch is the name of an implement used by butchers when they kill pigs. It is a strong oblong frame of wood, with cross-bars about three inches apart, and strong projecting handles at each end. It also stands on four strong feet. The doomed pig is wembled upon it and tied down preparatory to the fatal thrust, and he is rembled upon it when dead. The word is not used to describe anything else. Cradge-cradle is probably so called because to "set a cradge" is to perform a feat not easily imitated, and the great art of the game is for each player to take the crossing and interlacing thread from the fingers of the other's hands without letting any part slip, and by skilful alterations in the position of the fingers to put it into fresh combinations. To cradle is to support or strengthen by pieces of wood let into and crossing each other at right angles. All these words are in common use in the county of Lincoln. R. R.

Boston, Lincolnshire.

"NINE MEN'S MORRICE" (5ᵗʰ S. vii. 466, 514 ; viii. 51, 218, 238.)—In Douce's Illustrations of

merrils,' from *merelles* or *mereaux*, an ancient French word for the jettons or counters with which it was played. The other term, *morris*, is probably a corruption, suggested by the sort of *dance* which in the progress of the game the counters performed. In the French *merelles* each party had three counters only, which were to be placed in a line in order to win the game. It appears to have been the *Tremerel* mentioned in an old fabliau. See Le Grand, *Fabliaux et Contes*, tom. ii. p. 208.

"Dr. Hyde thinks the *morris* or *merrils* was known during the time that the Normans continued in possession of England, and that the name was afterwards corrupted into 'three mens morals' or 'nine mens morals.' If this be true, the conversion of *morals* into *morris*, a term so very familiar to the country people, was extremely natural. The doctor adds that it was likewise called nine-penny or nine-pin miracle, three-penny morris, five-penny morris, nine-penny morris, or three-pin, five-pin, and nine-pin morris, all corruptions of *three-pin*, &c., *merels* (Hyde, *Hist. Nerdiludii*, p. 202)."

Charles Knight, in a note to the same passage, says:—

"'Nine men's morris' was a game played upon their spacious commons by the shepherds and ploughmen of England. The game, it is said, was brought into England by the Normans........A rude series of squares and other right lines were cut upon the turf, upon which were arranged eighteen stones, divided between two players, ‖who moved them alternately, as at chess or draughts, the winner being he who had taken or impounded all his adversary's pieces."

ROBERT GUY.

PELHAM FAMILY : MANOR OF PELHAM, SUSSEX (5ᵗʰ S. ix. 47, 135.)—Several correspondents have pointed out the locality of the manor of "Rever vel Treve." Can any one inform me where the manor of Pelham, in Sussex, is?

That there is such a manor in *Sussex* is evident from the quoted Subsidy Roll, Henry IV., 1411-12.
C.

"DATALER" (5ᵗʰ S. viii. 346, 456.)—I never heard this word, which I spell *datleler*, till I came to live in this neighbourhood. It is pronounced *dât'ler*, and signifies a man employed by the owners of coal mines underground (but not in getting coal) at so much a day. A labourer who thus goes to work underground goes "a-dat'ling."
THOS. RATCLIFFE.
Worksop.

THE WINDSOR SENTINEL AND ST. PAUL'S (5ᵗʰ S. ix. 87, 114, 138, 156.)—I find that I must claim my own discovery. The story of the sentinel is in the *Public Advertiser*, Friday, June 22, 1770, and was reprinted by me in my *Memorials of Westminster*, published in January, 1849, p. 198.
MACKENZIE E. C. WALCOTT.
Oxford and Cambridge Club, S.W.

(1804-14) by a French lady at a Northern Co I do not know, however, if the articles are of value as authority. L. H. 1

ST. PAUL'S SCHOOL (5ᵗʰ S. ix. 107.)—In Knig *Life of Colet* (Clarendon Press edition, 1823) forty pages of biographical notices of a few scho educated here, but there are none of later than the beginning of the eighteenth cent: Some additional names (but no biographies) given in the *Prolusiones Literariæ* of the sch 1848. W. D. SWEETIN(
Peterborough.

LONDON FOGS (5ᵗʰ S. ix. 28, 134.)—These ; are not caused by the rarefaction of the air, or the consumption of gas, nor yet by the hills on north, nor by the river. The peculiar atmosph condition termed an anti-cyclone is the real cᴄ of these annoying visitations ; the wind is t blowing round a well defined circle, in the ce: of which the air is tranquil, and consequently smoke, condensed vapours, &c., cannot escapᴇ they do when there is a direct onward moven of the wind. The pressure of the atmospherᴇ such times is almost invariably greatly in exceₛ the average in the midst of the anti-cyclone, wʰ by preventing the rise of the smoke, &c., incre the intensity of the fog. Whenever, therefore anti-cyclone occurs with London at or near centre, there must necessarily be a "London f the density of which will be in proportion to smoke evolved at the time. The same phenomeᴇ may be observed in other places within the ₛ cyclonic circle, but of course in a less degre density. S. 1

"IN RANCONTEN" (5ᵗʰ S. ix. 127.)—I wᴇ venture to suggest that the term is derived { the French "rançon," and that the cases allᴜ to by your correspondent are compositions money to release anything deposited in kind fact, a ransom. JOHN PARKı:

AUTHORS OF BOOKS WANTED (5ᵗʰ S. viii. 4 ix. 53, 117.)—
Thinks 1 to Myself.—MR. BLENKINSOPP should corroborative evidence in support of Captain Bereᴇ if he really thinks there is anything in the claim ɴ For myself I think there is nothing, and, moreover, your correspondent must be mistaken. If the claim been made on behalf of the Rev. James Beresford t would have been some semblance of probability. was the author of the *Miseries of Human Life*, and just possible some mistake has occurred between t two works, published within a few years of one anoᴏ As against MR. BLENKINSOPP's claimant we have

printed authority of the *Biographical Dictionary of Living Authors*, 1816, which has been uncontradicted for over sixty years. What else did Captain Beresford write, and is his name mentioned in any biographical dictionary?

O. H.

ꟿiscellaneous.

NOTES ON BOOKS, &c.

Walks in London. By Augustus J. C. Hare. 2 vols. (Daldy, Isbister & Co.)

THE innumerable works already published on London have, for the most part, been compiled by antiquaries whose lives were passed in ransacking the national records for the groundwork of their labours or in poring over the contents of vast libraries for anecdotes to enliven their pages. The years which they employed in collecting the materials which their successors are now able to use without stint Mr. Hare has spent in foreign lands. Thus he can compare the neglected buildings of old London with the treasures of which other cities boast, and can contrast the unequalled glories of a London sunset with the clear skies of Italy. Artistic skill is not always found combined with literary talents, but the happy union of these qualities enables Mr. Hare to set before the eyes of his readers faithful representations of the picturesque objects which may be seen, but usually are left unnoticed, in our streets. Some of these illustrations will preserve the memory of antique houses and curious spots doomed soon to pass away. Many of the porches which used to adorn the houses of Queen Anne's Gate have already been destroyed by the ravager, but their memory cannot wholly perish when one of them is pictured in these pages. If all the mansions of Berkeley Square should lose the fine specimens of ironwork which bear witness of the days when footmen extinguished the flambeaux which they carried at the back of their masters' carriages, a glance at Mr. Hare's illustrations will revive the recollection of their appearance. There is abundant evidence in these volumes that their author is well acquainted with the choicest products of our modern literature ; it is not less obvious that he cannot be praised for his knowledge of English literature or English history in the past. Mr. Hare must either have perused the compilations of his predecessors to little purpose or have corrected his proof-sheets very hastily. He could not otherwise have passed such misprints as that the famous Evelyn lived in 1583 ; that the murder of Miss Ray occurred in 1799 ; that 1763 was the date of the great storm which devastated London ; or that 1640 was the time of the plot of the infamous Titus Oates. Dogget, who left the money for the race of the Thames watermen on the 1st of August in every year, did not die in 1821, and the death of that poor poet, Ambrose Philips, did not happen in 1762. Bishop Andrewes should not be stated in the same page to have died in 1626 and 1628, nor Thomas Goodwin to have died in 1643 and yet to have lost his preferment at the Restoration. It was certainly not Secker that refused to crown William and Mary, and Sacheverell's appointment to St. Andrew's, Holborn, rested on stronger foundations than a page of Swift. Savage, the friend of Dr. Johnson, is said by Mr. Hare to have died in Newgate, and the date of 1602 is assigned for the death'of Milton's second wife. Harrington, the author of *Oceana*, is styled a poet of the Commonwealth, and the physician of James I. is called Sir Thomas Mayerne. Again, Mr. Hare falls into error in saying that the books of Dr. Williams's library are now preserved in Somerset House, and he imports a fresh mistake into the vexed question of the old statue in Leicester Fields by the assertion that it came from the Duke of Buckingham's seat at Canons.

Before issuing a fresh edition of *Walks in London* he would do well to submit its statements to the strictest revision. If he will at the same time excise from his pages the long list of pictures in the National Gallery, and reduce to juster dimensions his account of the monuments in Westminster Abbey, the permanent value of his book will not be impaired. The grace of his style and the merits of his pencil will give it a wide popularity in the present day, but only by a careful correction of its errors can he insure its use by the students of future years. Mr. Hare's next venture in the world of letters will, we hope, possess all the merits and lack all the defects of *Walks in London.*

Letters of John Keats to Fanny Brawne, written in the Years MDCCCXIX. and MDCCCXX., and now given from the Original Manuscripts. With Introduction and Notes by Harry Buxton Forman. (Reeves & Turner.)

THIS dainty little book, creditable to the microscopic industry of its editor, contains an Introduction of lxvii pages and 128 pages of love letters addressed by John Keats to his sweetheart, Mistress Fanny Brawne, of Wentworth Place, Hampstead. We cannot judge of these letters by comparison with other love letters, for whither should we go to find those others ? Not, certainly, to the printed records of the law courts, nor to the many reams of faded writing that lie in old desks, to be burned when their owners die ; no, nor yet to Mrs. Browning's *Sonnets from the Portuguese*, nor to Dante's *Vita Nuova.* Howsoever, we and all men have here before us for judgment the sacred and confidential utterances of a dying poet's only love—utterances which add nothing to our knowledge of the poet's character and life, and of which the publication can only be excused, if excusable at all, by the pride of possession and by the eagerness of admiring curiosity. In one place (Letter 28) Keats says he would like to have Shakspeare's opinion about the correspondence. So should we ; for we rather think that, if Shakspeare had been consulted, he would have remembered Ann Hathaway and replied accordingly. All strong emotion is evanescent, just because it is strong ; and even if its purpose holds, the tried and placid love of middle age will look back with somewhat of disdainful pity on the records of its youth, unless, indeed, they be in verse, and good verse. Keats himself, if he had lived, would never have allowed these letters to be published ; nor is it, we think, any answer to this to say that he did *not* live, or to say that we have already stolen from Mr. Samuel Pepys, a very different man, his secret outpourings on the subject of Mrs. Knip. As to the letters themselves, they are of course deeply interesting to all who care for Keats ; but we knew before that he was full of ardour, and combativeness, and sensitiveness, and adoration for beauty, and they do little more than confirm this knowledge. Yes, they do one thing more : they show us the sad and bitter working of illness and physical decay upon his spirit and his heart. And surely it is not well for those who love his poetry to see him thus ; the painful impression as to his later personality which this book gives will be with them when they turn again to *Endymion*, or *Lamia*, or the sonnets. But there is nothing feeble, nothing unmanly or sentimental, in these letters. They are full of force, fire, hurried vigour, and passionate tenderness ; all expressed in that odd and flighty English in which Keats's prose is so often bound. The charm of feeling is present everywhere, but the phrases seldom rise to great literary excellence. Once he says (Letter 2), "Even when I am not thinking of you, I receive your influence and a tenderer nature stealing upon me. All my thoughts, my unhappiest days and nights, have I find not at all cured.

Only once does he slip unconsciously into metre, in this gracious line—

"I want a brighter word than bright, a fairer word than fair."

And what, in those days of trial and coming death, was Keats's creed? "My Creed," he says, "is Love, and you are its only tenet." "I wish to believe in immortality—I wish to live with you for ever." "I appeal to you by the blood of that Christ you believe in." These passages Mr. Forman (by an " elegant μείωσις," we suppose) calls " shifting from the moorings of orthodoxy."

Well, we will draw the veil here, and say one last word as to the book in its commoner aspects. It is, we believe, all new to the public, except that about twenty lines from the letters are quoted by Lord Houghton in the memoir prefixed to the Aldine edition of Keats, 1876, and except a short passage from Letter 17 (p. 57) which appears in the memoir of Mr. Dilke prefixed to The Papers of a Critic. The readers of "N. & Q." may be reminded that several other letters and fragments of or about Keats have appeared of late years in the Athenæum and elsewhere.

[From a Correspondent.]

The Plays and Poems of William Shakespeare, with the Purest Text and the Briefest Notes. Edited by J. Payne Collier. 8 volumes. (Privately printed for the Subscribers.)

CRITICISM on a work printed only for private circulation would be out of place ; but there are two or three points of great curiosity and interest about this book which call for notice in " N. & Q." An edition of Shakspeare in eight 4to. volumes, limited to fifty-eight copies, is, and will probably long remain, unique ; and an edition of Shakspeare brought out by one who commenced his study of the poet before he was nineteen, and continued that study until, in his ninetieth year, he gives to his friends the result of that long continued deliberation, is a work that will long remain without a parallel in Shakspearian literature. One whose good fortune it has been to have enjoyed the friendship of John Payne Collier for the last forty years hopes he may be permitted to call attention to this last labour of love on his part, and to congratulate him on having been permitted thus to crown the arch of his long, zealous, and devoted study of Shakspeare.

MR. JOSEPH BROWN, Q C., has been moved to deliver his testimony on Eastern Christianity and the War (Edward Stanford) in language which amounts to a strong indictment of a form of Christianity evidently very foreign to the ecclesiastical sympathies of the learned author. It appears to us that the shade of Knox is hardly the most suitable ghost to evoke to decide upon the " gross superstitions of the Greek Church." But we certainly hope, with the learned writer, that " the friends of humanity and civilization would feel greatly relieved if their country could rid itself of any partnership with a despotism which is a curse to so many millions of men."—Lieut. Charles Worthy, late of H.M. 82nd Regiment, publishes some useful contributions to the history of Devonshire and its worthies in two separate pamphlets, A Memoir of Bishop Stapledon and a History of the Manor and Church of Winkleigh (Plymouth, W. Brendon). But we should have been glad of evidence, which Lieut. Worthy does not furnish, to convince us of the fact in genealogy which he assumes in his account of Winkleigh, that the modern Gidleys are the descendants and representatives of the mediæval De Gidleys,

Association, vol. xxxiii., an interesting paper on [?] of the Ancient Kingdom of Damnonia outside Cor[?] in Remains of the Celtic Hagiology, read at the B[?] Congress. The subject is one which has been but worked, and of some of those who have given most [?] tion to it we must regretfully speak as the late Bish Brechin and the late Dr. John Stuart.—To a recen lication of the Grampian Club, Genealogical Memo the Family of Robert Burns and of the Scottish . of Burnes, edited by the Rev. Charles Rogers,] (Edinburgh, William Paterson), we must object in l that there is no " Scottish House of Burnes." utmost that Dr. Rogers has to tell us is of tenant far doubtless respectable, but certainly not armigerou[?] as certainly not baronial. This is the more to be reg[?] since we should be the last to dispute either the fa the great poet of the Lowland Scots tongue or the service in India of his distinguished kinsma[?] Alexander Burnes, "linguist, diplomatist, and trave

"GOD SAVE THE KING."—Kindly correct an er my note, ante, p. 160. Carey's son's name was G Saville Carey, not John Saville Carey.

WILLIAM H. CUMMI[?]

A COMPLETE set of the Second Series of " N. & half calf, may be had of our publisher.

CONTENTS.— N° 219.

Notes on Books, &c.

Notes.

MR. GLADSTONE ON THE TOPOGRAPHY OF THE HOMERIC POEMS.

The opening article in the October number of *Macmillan* (the last number that, at the time of my writing, has reached this remote dependency) raises a question which seems well fitted for discussion in the columns of "N. & Q."

In this most enjoyable article on the geography of Homer, Mr. Gladstone deals in a very interesting and ingenious manner with a question which has been a puzzle to all commentators on Homer since the days of Strabo—the question of the identification of Dulichium. On two occasions at least Homer expressly speaks of Dulichium as an island.[*] In *Od.* ix. 21-24 Odysseus describes his island home to Alcinous as forming a portion of a group of four islands lying close to one another. This group, in addition to conspicuous Ithaca, consisted of Dulichium, Samos, and wooded Zacinthos—

Δουλίχιόν τε Σάμη τε καὶ ὑλήεσσα Ζάκυνθος.

As a matter of fact there are in this group but three islands, Ithaca, Zante, and Cefalonia. The first two are easily identified. But if Samos be identified with Cefalonia, there is not a fourth, as

[* The references to Dulichium in the *Iliad* and *Odyssey* given in Smith's *Dictionary of Greek and Roman Geography* are, *Il.* ii. 625 (catalogue of the ships) ; *Od.* i. 245 ; ix. 24 ; xiv. 397 ; xvi. 123, 247.—ED.]

Mr. Gladstone puts it, *in rerum naturâ*. Mr. Gladstone then adds: "Plainly therefore the poet is not in accordance at this point with the actual geography ; that is, he is in error. But his error may not have been more than partial. . . . He believed Cefalonia to be not one island, but two, Doulichium and Samos." Mr. Gladstone then goes on to maintain the supposition that the poet may have described the group from personal recollection, but a recollection based on a limited personal observation. The poet, looking towards Cefalonia from Ithaca, and mistaking the bay at Same that indents the former island for a strait, might have easily carried away the impression of the existence of two islands. This supposition, which is so ingeniously conceived and so admirably set forth by Mr. Gladstone, may, I think, be shown to be unnecessary. My own belief is that Samos and Dulichium were, in the time of Homer, the two divisions of Cefalonia. Any other supposition leads to a dilemma, perhaps even to an absurdity.

Reasoning by analogy, I would suggest that there is no absolute ground for assuming that this island, in the days of Homer, had one name that covered the whole area. Because an island is a physical whole, we naturally—nay, universally— come to think of it as having a name embracing the whole. But this notion is not always in accordance with fact. If I am not mistaken, the outer division of the Hebrides furnishes a case in point. Are not people constantly in the habit of speaking and writing of the *islands* of Lewis and Harris as if these were two distinct islands, whereas they are the two divisions of one island? I spent three months in the Hebrides at one time, and I have heard Highlanders and Islesmen mention Lewis and Harris a hundred times, while conversing in their native language, but always in such terms as might convey the impression that these were separate islands. So far as I know, there is no historical evidence that these two portions of the island were ever embraced under one comprehensive name.† What is still more remarkable, they are in different counties, Lewis being in the civil jurisdiction of Ross-shire and Harris being in Inverness-shire. Let us now suppose that, separated by an interval of 2,500 years from the present time, in the future, as Homer is in the past, a Gaelic bard should become the object of intense admiration to the learned on the coast of Asia Minor ; let his hero be a Mcleod of Skye, whose territories embraced Harris (as was actually at one time the case) ; let us suppose that the names of Harris and Lewis have been dropped utterly out of all recognition, and that the whole island is embraced under one name ; the bard, following

[† Except in so far as the entire group, from Barra Head to the Butt of the Lewis, is known as "The Long Island."—ED.]

separate from Harris. The learned commentators of Asia Minor would, in that case, experience a difficulty of exactly the same kind as now meets us in the case of Homer and Dulichium. There are other interesting points in the analogy. Samos is the rugged (παιπαλοέσσα) ; Harris is mountainous, Lewis is flat. Dulichium was much larger and more populous than Samos ; so is Lewis than Harris. In both cases indentations of the sea serve to mark off the larger and northern portions from the smaller and southern portions. The Ionian as well as the Hebridean island, viewed from a distance, would present the appearance of two islands, and this circumstance may have had a considerable share in perpetuating the notion of a physical division, while in both cases the origin of the division was what may be termed dynastic, a Celtic chief and the βασιλεύς of the Homeric poems being pretty much the same.

Upon this question, then, I think we may reasonably come to the following conclusions : 1. That the larger, more populous, and more fertile portion of Cefalonia, including the whole of the northern and western part, was the Dulichium of Homer ; 2. That the highland region in the south-east, adjacent to Ithaca, was Samos, the portion of Cefalonia over which Odysseus held sway ; 3. That Homer, employing the conventional language of his time, speaks of these two divisions as if they were separate islands, just as a modern poet, using the every-day language of the Western Isles, might speak of Lewis and Harris as if they were two islands. I have no doubt that some of the learned contributors to " N. & Q." will be able to furnish additional illustrations by way of clearing up this *quæstio vexata* of Homeric scholars.   JOHN CARMICHAEL, M.A.
Melbourne.

SAMUEL BAILEY OF SHEFFIELD,

PHILOSOPHICAL ESSAYIST, METAPHYSICIAN, WRITER ON POLITICAL ECONOMY AND FINANCE, POET, AND SHAKESPERIAN CRITIC.

On May 10, 1873, a letter from me appeared in " N. & Q." (4th S. xi. 384) on Samuel Bailey and his works. I then stated that his writings include twenty-one separate publications, two of them having reached a second, and one a third, edition ; that Sir James Mackintosh, Brougham, Bentham, James Mill, J. Stuart Mill, Grote, Austin, Molesworth, W. J. Fox, and other distinguished writers, had expressed most favourable opinions regarding his first work, *Essays on the Formation and Publication of Opinions*, 1821 ; and that General Perronet Thompson, the well-known political economist, wrote an article in the *Westminster Review* of a highly eulogistic character on Mr.

article I have given a striking passage (? graphical list of Bailey's writings belo None of Mr. Bailey's works are even ? Lowndes, nor does his name appear ir graphical division of Knight's *English C* It never found its way into *Men of the ?* the date of his death (1870); nor doeç place in the *Nouvelle Biographie Ge* Didot Frères (1855-66), edited by Dr.] almost exhaustive work of its kind Vapereau's *Dictionnaire Universel des* porains (Hachette & Co.) ; nor in the *S* to all *Historical and Biographical Dictic* Jal, 1872, where one might almost have to find the name without fail. Allibo *Critical Dictionary of English Literat* an imperfect list of his works up to] has been called " the Bentham of Hal A friend who knew him, and who was t capable of appreciating the philosopł racter of his intellect, and the rare and vigour of his style, remarked t were many points of resemblance in int character between him and Turgot, the ɪ French economist and financier. In my cation to you of nearly five years ago I furnish you with a bibliographical anʲ logical list of Bailey's writings, if you (it would be of interest to the readers of ' As you intimated your readiness to accept now the pleasure of sending you the con All the works named are in my possessiʲ two of the pamphlets, Nos. 6 and 11. T still in search of, and should be glad Should any of your readers wish for mʲ than I have supplied, regarding any of named, I will willingly furnish them.

Mr. Bailey was at one time a candida representation of Sheffield, but was unç He was one of the directors of the Sheffı ing Company, and assiduous in his atten interests. It is said he formed two attι but he never married. He was very n in the management of his time, rising re six o'clock summer and winter, and waɪ ably punctual in his habits, engagements, pations. His repugnance to business strong, and he sought refuge in retiremen and composition were a real enjoyment and change of employment always affo a quiet relief. He never persevered in st he felt weary. His self-command was vɪ Turgot, in writing to Condorcet, says, " the satisfaction resulting from study supe other satisfactions." This was precisely h ence. These particulars have been given viving relative, who adds that marriaȷ have improved him amazingly. It was of regret with those who knew him that he had not been sent in early life to one of our universities ; he would have been in his element there, and would have found kindred spirits. He was born in Sheffield in 1791, and died January 18, 1870.

Mr. J. D. Leader, of Sheffield, in a paper on Bailey read before a local Literary Society some years ago, said :—

"He affords a remarkable instance of a man of great attainments and much industry failing to make that mark in the world to which he might fairly have aspired. Had he been successful in his efforts to enter Parliament in the prime of his days, he would have been drawn out of himself, and might probably have taken a high place among statesmen. As it was, he fell back upon his own thoughts, and passed his days in philosophical speculation."

An article on Bailey and his writings (the only attempt I have met with to give some account of his works) appeared in the *British Controversialist and Literary Magazine* for July, 1868 (London, Houlston & Wright), but the writer does not seem to be aware of the existence of his unacknowledged productions (Nos. 10 and 14). Mr. Bailey himself pointed out several inaccuracies in this paper. He was never discouraged by the non-appreciation of his works by the general public. He often said that he did not expect people in general to read his books. His critics and reviewers he sometimes pronounced incompetent to judge of their worth. His own estimate of them remained unshaken ; and he was certainly appreciated by some whose opinion he highly valued.

The most fitting monument to the memory of Samuel Bailey—who, in addition to the services he has rendered in the departments of philosophic thought and economical science, has bestowed substantial benefits in the shape of a munificent money bequest to his native town, Sheffield (90,000*l.*)—would be a carefully edited and uniform edition of his works, which, although not likely to sell largely, would still find their way into public libraries and a few private ones, and would be prized by all students and thoughtful readers. No author of this century has written with greater force and clearness, or with more powerful reasoning, on the right and duty of free inquiry in every department of human thought, on the imperative necessity of candid, temperate, and fair discussion, and on that much neglected part of morality, the conscientious formation and free publication of all opinions affecting human welfare. We have never had a more earnest or strenuous advocate of intellectual liberty and free discussion than Samuel Bailey. His style is truly admirable, its characteristics being perspicuity, accuracy, and precision—not a word wrongly placed, not a word that could be spared. All his works were most carefully prepared and long thought over, and subjected to frequent revision before publication. He was one of the most

conscientious and clearest of thinkers, and no one can study his works, especially the two numbered 1 and 5 in the following list, without having his ideas enlarged, and his mental horizon extended. To thoughtful and earnest young men and women, who care for and can appreciate something higher than the ephemeral and vapid literature of the hour, these two bracing volumes would be invaluable companions. All his writings, including a selection from his unpublished MSS., which I believe are numerous, might be comprised in seven or eight volumes. I have reason to know that the prospectus of such an edition will soon be issued.

BIBLIOGRAPHICAL LIST OF THE WRITINGS OF THE LATE SAMUEL BAILEY OF SHEFFIELD.

1. Essays on the Formation and Publication of Opinions, and on other Subjects. London : Printed for R. Hunter, successor to Mr. Johnson, St. Paul's Churchyard, 1821. Pp. vi-284.

The Same. Second Edition, Revised and Enlarged. London, R. Hunter, 1826. [There are only a few verbal alterations in the text. The additional matter is thrown into the form of an appendix of notes and illustrations, in which the author has extended, supported, and elucidated some of the doctrines contained in the *Essays*. The appendix extends to thirty-two pages of smaller type than that of the text.]

The Same. Third Edition. London, J. Green, 1837. [Issued at a reduced price, with a view to secure for the work a more extensive circulation and a wider influence.]

2. Questions in Political Economy, Politics, Morals, Metaphysics, Polite Literature, and other Branches of Knowledge, for Discussion in Literary Societies or for Private Study ; with Remarks under each Question, Original and Selected. London, R. Hunter, 1823. Pp. viii-400. [Eighty-three questions for discussion are presented in the above departments of literature.]

3. A Critical Dissertation on the Nature, Measures, and Causes of Value ; chiefly in Reference to the Writings of Mr. Ricardo and his Followers. London, R. Hunter, 1825. Pp. xxiii-232. Notes and Illustrations, pp. 23.

4. A Letter to a Political Economist ; occasioned by an Article in the *Westminster Review* on the Subject of Value. London, R. Hunter, 1826. Pp. 101.

5. Essays on the Pursuit of Truth, on the Progress of Knowledge, and on the Fundamental Principle of all Evidence and Expectation. London, R. Hunter, 1829. Pp. vi-301. [An article on this work appeared in the *Westminster Review*, No. 22, which was republished in Nov., 1829, and extensively circulated. The critic (General Perronet Thompson) thus characterizes the author's first production : "If a man could be offered the paternity of any comparatively modern books that he chose, he would not hazard much by deciding that, next after the *Wealth of Nations*, he would request to be honoured with a relationship to the *Essays on the Formation and Publication of Opinions*.......It would have been a pleasant and an honourable memory to have written a book so *totus teres atque rotundus*, so finished in its parts, and so perfect in their union as the *Essays on the Formation of Opinions*. Like one of the great statues of antiquity it might have been broken into fragments, and each separate limb would have pointed to the existence of some interesting whole, of which the value might be surmised from the beauty of the specimen."]

The Same. Second Edition, Revised and Enlarged. London, Longman & Co., 1844. Pp. vi-278. [In this edition the first essay (On the Pursuit of Truth) has been

to it a few notes. The third essay in the original edition was *On the Fundamental Principle of all Evidence and Expectation.* In this edition the essay is not reprinted, for reasons given by the author.]

6. A Discussion of Parliamentary Reform. By a Yorkshire Freeholder. [I have not seen this pamphlet. Date probably 1831.]

7. The Rationale of Political Representation. London, R. Hunter, 1835. Pp. ii-419. Notes and Illustrations, pp. 14.

8. The Right of Primogeniture Examined, in a Letter to a Friend, occasioned by the Debate in the House of Commons. April 12, 1836. By a Younger Brother. London, Ridgway & Sons, 1837. Pp. 63.

9. Money and its Vicissitudes in Value; as they affect National Industry and Pecuniary Contracts; with a Postscript on Joint-Stock Banks. London, Effingham Wilson, 1837. Pp. 224.

10. Letters of an Egyptian Kafir on a Visit to England in Search of a Religion, enforcing some Neglected Views regarding the Duty of Theological Inquiry, and the Morality of Human Interference with It. London: Printed for the Author by G. H. Davidson, Tudor Street, Blackfriars, 1839. Pp. ii-159. [The author never included this in the list of his published works. The late Blanco White declared that the author of this work had drawn a picture which he (Blanco White) might, with perfect accuracy, make a part of his own biography. The author, under the veil of questioning the authenticity of the Koran and the religion of Mahomet, shrewdly argues against a passive acquiescence in a blind and traditionary belief in theological doctrines taught by nurses, parents, preceptors, and priests of all sects and denominations. In the second and enlarged edition of *Essays,* &c. (No. 5), the author twice makes quotations from *Letters of a Kafir.* The book is extremely scarce, in consequence of the whole impression having been destroyed by fire, except about fifty copies. In a letter in my possession, in Bailey's own handwriting, he says:— "The work was never in the hands of a bookseller, although a few copies were dispersed amongst reviews, &c. I believe there are not more than twenty-five copies in existence, except what I have in my hands."— Jan. 20, 1847.]

11. A Defence of Joint-Stock Banks and Country Issues. 1840. [I have not seen this pamphlet.]

12. A Review of Berkeley's Theory of Vision, designed to Show the Unsoundness of that Celebrated Speculation. London, Ridgway, 1842. Pp. 239.

13. A Letter to a Philosopher, in Reply to some Recent Attempts to vindicate Berkeley's Theory of Vision, and in Further Illustration of its Unsoundness. London, Ridgway, 1843. Pp. 68.

14. Maro; or, Poetic Irritability. In Four Cantos. London, Longmans, 1845. Pp. 85. [Mr. J. D. Leader, of Sheffield, a few years ago read a paper to a Literary Society on "Samuel Bailey as a Poet," criticizing this work. He said:—"It is a poem describing the feelings and the disappointments of a young poet, who would print, in spite of friendly advice not to do so, and who, out of an edition of 1,000 copies, only sold ten. There are in it lines of pungent satire and vigorous, able description, but no imagination. The authorship was kept a profound secret. As a poet he has not made his mark in the world, but his efforts in rhyme only cause us to form a higher estimate of those powers of mind which,

16. Discourses on Various Subjects; read Literary and Philosophical Societies. London man & Co., 1852. Pp. 276. [The subjects are : Mutual Relations of the Sciences—On the Mam Fossil Elephant, discovered at the Mouth of the On the Changes which have taken place in the Language, especially during the Three Last Cen On the Science of Political Economy—On the l formation of the Calendar in England—On the Principles of Physical Investigation—On the Mer Causes of Thunder—On the Paradoxes of Vision-Theory of Wit.]

17. Letters on the Philosophy of the Human First Series. London, Longmans, 1855. P Notes and Illustrations, pp. 18.

18. Letters on the Philosophy of the Human Second Series. London, Longmans, 1858. Pp. 2

19. Letters on the Philosophy of the Human Third Series. London, Longmans, 1863. P Notes and Illustrations, pp. 9. [In the abov series of Letters, altogether extending to 800 pa author discusses the various systems of menta sophy, and analyzes the psychological probler sented in them.]

20. A Glance at some Points in Education, who has Undergone the Process. [Privately P A Pamphlet. 1865.

21. On the Received Text of Shakespeare's D Writings and its Improvement. Vol. I. London mans, 1862. Pp. 241. Appendix, pp. 22. [Pr —Proposed Emendations—Indeterminate Rea Verbal Repetitions—Conclusion—Objections Obv

22. On the Received Text of Shakespeare's D Writings and its Improvement. Vol. II. I Longmans, 1866. Pp. 413. [Proposed Emenda Dissertations on Hamlet's Soliloquy—On Shake Metaphors—On an Assertion of Malone's—O jectural Emendations—On some still existing regarding Shakespearean Criticism—On the S Shakespeare's Text as Left by his Contemporarie

ALEX. IREL.

Inglewood, Bowdon, Cheshire.

P.S.—Since the above was written, I fin in the admirable new edition of the *Encycl Britannica* (now in course of publication editor has devoted a column and a half to and his writings. The writer of the notic not seem to know of the existence of the una ledged volume, *Letters of an Egyptian Kafir* says:—"There are few authors of modern who have written more elegantly or clea with more originality of treatment, on the v problems of psychology and political science the *Theory of Reasoning* he speaks as "a th ful discussion of the nature of inference, a able criticism of the functions and value syllogism." The *Letters on the Philosophy Human Mind* (three series, 1855, 1858, and he considers "at once the most considerab the most valuable of his contributions to s science. . . . The *Letters* contain in clear and language a very fresh discussion of many of the powerful problems in philosophy, or rather in psychology. . . . His handling of the moral sentiments is one of the best specimens of his general style of psychological analysis." In the supplement to the latest edition of *Chambers's Encyclopædia* (1877) a brief notice of Bailey, with a list of his works, is given. The list, however, omits *Maro* and *Letters of an Egyptian Kafir*. The writer says:—" Mr. Bailey's works on the *Pursuit of Truth* and the *Publication of Opinions* gave a great impetus to liberal and advanced views. His writings generally are distinguished by independent thinking, logical precision, a careful English style, and warm aspirations for the improvement of mankind. His treatises on the mind, while abounding in original suggestions, extend and enforce the views of the school of Locke in metaphysics, and what is termed the doctrine of utility in morals."

A RARE PAMPHLET.

The following are the title-page and contents of a very curious pamphlet, date 1768 :—
"An Original Camera Obscura; or, the Court, City, and Country Magic-Lantern. In which every one may take a peep, laugh, and shake their noddles at each other, go away well pleased, and your humble servants the Lords! Ladies! and Gentlemen! Being an Account of the most Curious and Uncommon Collection of Manuscripts (warranted original) ever yet offered to the Public. With as Curious and Uncommon a Dedication to the Right Honourable the Earl of Cheatum. To be Sold by Auction on Midsummer Day O.S. by Mr. Smirk, at a Great Room in Soho Square. Being the select Part of a Library of a Gentleman of Virtu (*sic*) not far from St. James's, going to retire, and sold by his express order, with many Curious Particulars, &c. 'Hominem pagina nostra sapit' (Martial).
  'Since all have got a gentle touch,
    Your money here you will not grutch;
  Why so? Because the account is such
    As will in fun give twice as much.'
London : Printed for J. Wilke in St. Paul's Church Yard, 1768."

The lots offered for sale are numerous (sixty in number), and the author in describing them lashes most unsparingly the follies and vices of the age. Take the following as a sample. Lot 32 :—
"Cornuti Contenti, or 'Anything for Peace at Home.' A Farce of Great Humour, frequently acted both in the City and at the Court End of the Town for the Benefit of all Refractory and Jealous Husbands, by whom it is absolutely necessary to be read and seen, and to whom it is Dedicated. At the end of the First Act is an Original Dance : The City Wives, or 'The good-natured Husbands taking their Leave before they go to their Clubs or Parish Meetings.' At the end of the Farce, before the Epilogue, is another original Dance called 'The Court Ladies'; or, Go you, my dear, to Sir John's and visit Lady H**. Finely bound in Vellum and adorn'd with curious Copper-plates of the Dances, which are introduced by a City and Court Gallant with a Pole in their Hands, on the Top of which is a Noble Pair of Branchers doubly Tipped with Gold. With some Well-known Faces in the City and at Court, holding a Bag in

each Hand, and Grinning to think how they had got so much Smart Money. By an Eminent Merchant in the City, and a noble Lord not far from Court.
      ' Comis in uxorem ! '
  'Oh ! blessedness of such a life !
  When man is civil to his wife.'"

As a pendant to the above take the following (lot 48) choice piece of satire, evidently directed against the clergy. It is a picture in miniature of the fox-hunting, place-seeking parson of the period, and shows the dead spiritual level to which the age had sunk :—
  "Opus Operatum; or, Much Business in a Little Time. A very ingenious Poem in Quarto, neatly bound in sheep, and covered with *Crape*, containing an admirable Set of Rules, designed for the use and benefit of those Gentlemen of the *Clergy* both in *Town* and *Country* who are unhappily fallen into a *dreaming* way and infected with a *drawling* tone, at the same time have three or four churches to serve the same morning or afternoon. By an honest country Curate upon *forty* Pounds per annum, who *prays*, *preaches*, and rides *four* times on a Sunday, and *makes nothing on't*, tho' the churches are between three and four miles distant from each other. To which is added an Encomiastic Ode on the noble *spirit* and *generosity* of those fat *Pluralists* and *Dignitaries* of the Church who from their so many *hundreds* per annum can afford to *squeeze out* thirty or forty (if *treble* or *quadruple* duty) to their Curates. Dedicated to a very *worthy* Bench.
  "N.B.—The poem is adorned with a most Curious *Frontispiece* of a *Mezzotinto*, finely engraved by an Eminent Hand, and done from an *original* design of *Hogarth's*, of half-a-dozen Dignitaries sitting in the *Chapter-room*, five with *book* before them, supposed to be explaining some Divinity Points in the Greek or *Latin* Fathers, while the sixth is gathering together his *dividend* and says, with a leering grin to his reverend and learned Brethren, ' O'' my conscience, Brothers, I do think that the *Church of England* is the very *best constituted* (at the same time sweeping the money off the table into his broad Beaver) Church this day upon the face of the Earth.'
      ' Nam quis me scribere plures
  Aut citius possit versus ? quis membra movere
  Mollius ? Invideat quod et Hermogenes ego canto.
  Qui studet optatam cursu contingere metam
  Multa tulit fecitque puer, sudavit et alsit.'   *Hor.*
  ' With *Pen* or *Mouth*, who can discourse
    Faster than I ? or *ride* their *Horse*
  With *greater* speed from church to church,
  And many good souls leave in the lurch!   .
  For *Gaming*, *Drinking*, *Sporting* clean,
  I'm said to raise the *Squire's* spleen :
  He, then, that fain would reach the *prize*—
  A Mitre—must with half-shut eyes
  Hear, see, and *say* nought, but look wise ;
  Must love *Quadrille*, *Whist*, and *Fatigue*,
  Talk *Politics* and *Court*-Intrigues :
  Ride hard, and *swear* through thick and thin,
  To gain *more* votes than canvassing !
  By *these* he soon will reach the station,
  And disregard all defamation.'
  " N.B.—The above paraphrastical imitation of Horace is supposed to be no bad receipt to make a B—p, with a *quant. sufficit* of each *ingredient*."

But the times were different, and national vices required powerful remedies for their extirpation.
                                           A. CUTLER.

118) I wish to observe that there is, I believe, at least one means of information which I think has not yet been exhausted. Your columns have shown us that Paltock was of Clement's Inn. Though that Inn has been threatened, and had a narrow escape of being swallowed up by the new Law Courts, it has not yet shared the fate of Lyons Inn, and a search through its registers might produce some information. Possibly the fact of the book being dedicated to Elizabeth, Countess of Northumberland, may some day lead to information.

As every reader has not access to the early volumes of " N. & Q.," it may be useful to show shortly what previous communications have been about. In 1ˢᵗ S. ii. 480 (1850) the late DR. RIMBAULT asked if the author's name was known. In vol. iii. 13 (1851) the late MR. G. J. DE WILDE, in reply, quoted the advertisement to Smith's Standard Library edition of *Peter Wilkins*, showing how the author's name was discovered, as referred to presently. In vol. ix. 543 (1854) the name of the author was again asked for, but, being three years after the first question, the answer then given appears to have been entirely forgotten, for though there is an editorial note the name of the author is not stated. MR. BATES wrote a reply (x. 17), and quotes *The Town*, vol. i. p. 157, which discourses of "Clifford's Inn" as the residence of Robert Pultock (*sic*), a mistake for "Clement's Inn," to which the remarks are, however, in the present day, equally applicable. On p. 112 the author's name is again given, with the source first referred to in vol. iii. On p. 212 MR. JAMES CROSSLEY quotes the original assignment to Robinson & Dodsley by "Robert Paltock of Clement's Inn, Gentleman," dated January 11, 1749, then in his possession. He also says he thinks he has traced Paltock's hand in another work. In 3ʳᵈ S. xii. 445 I pointed out that the *Memoirs of the Life of Parnese* was by "R. P.," and I suggested that it might be the book MR. CROSSLEY referred to, the title of which he had not then, and has not since, communicated to "N. & Q." OLPHAR HAMST.

MR. THOROLD ROGERS'S " HISTORICAL GLEANINGS."—Mr. Thorold Rogers, in his *Historical Gleanings*, first series, falls into a singular error with respect to the "Butcher" Duke of Cumberland. At p. 92 (the closing sentences of the paper on Walpole) he speaks of this duke as having been, by his marriage, the cause of the Royal Marriage Act. He is evidently unaware, first, that William, Duke of Cumberland, the

* 1ˢᵗ S. ii. 480; iii. 13; ix. 543; x. 17, 112, 212; 3ʳᵈ S. xii. 445.

words) the presumed progenitor of Olive," was a duke of another cr strange to find any one confus Duke of Cumberland, son of George nephew Henry Frederick, Duke of brother of George III. It is yet perhaps, that the mistake seems n been publicly noticed.

CHARLES POVEY.—In "N. & Q.,' under the above heading, there is a curious character, to which the editor a P.S. intimating, in the vague phras author, that "the large quarto and oc with other small pieces I have writ (number," with the natural exclama how few of this voluminous autho known to the present generation of bi! Looking over the half-dozen or so of we can fix upon the magniloquent evident that, instead of volumes an he simply means that his writing many pieces, or subjects he has han *Visions of Sir Heister Ryley*, his *Me Thoughts*, and indeed all his books ! he has copious indexes of "princi treated of, and it will not be difficult 600 pieces, or subjects dilated upon, a Povey's astounding figures to the indicated.

THE FRENCH "NOTES AND QUER: LATE DR. DORAN.—We are sure th: of "N. & Q." will be pleased to see graceful acknowledgment of DR. DO so promptly made by our French cc *L'Intermédiaire des Chercheurs et Cu* issue for the 25th of February:—

"Nous n'attendrons pas l'époque du bila: annuel pour enrégistrer ici la perte qu'a (confrère d'Outre-Manche, le *Notes and Q* lui faire nos condoléances. Le savant Dr. son directeur depuis 1872 (vii. 5), vient c était renommé comme un causeur on n informé (*full of information*). Nos lecteur: sans doute qu'il fut, à maintes reprise aimables et obligeants correspondants. M: breuses occupations, il se plaisait à nous p: de bon collaborateur (*contributor*), et le pl langue française.......M. Doran faisait, il) mois (*Int.* x. 475, 10 Août, 1877), à *l'Inte* communication, la dernière que nous ayc sur la question, alors débattue, des vérit: du Maréchal de MacMahon.......Une n(Anglaise (*The Nineteenth Century*) publia Janvier, son dernier travail, un article int speare en France,' sur les imitations e plus ou moins singulières des œuvres du turge en langue française."

Queries.

[We must request correspondents desiring information on family matters of only private interest, to affix their names and addresses to their queries, in order that the answers may be addressed to them direct.]

COPPER : SCHOCHELADE.—

"In time to come my wrath t' appease, when I shal haply meane,
The fairest of thy Cities all, by grounde to raze it cleane,
Thinke not my minde then to withstand, for *copper* thou mightst get.
Sith herein to content thee now thy wil I nothing let."
Arthur Hall's transl. of Homer, 1581, *Jupiter to Juno*, beginning of book iv.

" Quand i'auray entrepris
A l'aduenir pour mon ire appaiser,
De tes Citez la plus belle raser,
Ne pense pas alors contreuenir
A mon decret, mal t'en pourroit venir.
Veu mesmement qu'à ton intention,
Je me consens à la destruction
De la Cité," &c.
Hugues Salel's Fr. transl. (from which Hall's was made), 1555.

" At Mydon mazde Antilochus a waightie stone did throw,
He crusht his arme, constrayning him the bridle to let go :
Beside this blow, he on his face gaue him a *schochelade*,
Wherby he fel downe to the ground islaine by his blade."
Hall's transl., book v.

" Mydon s'estonna,
Voyant venir le coup d'vne grand pierre,
Qu' Antilochus sur le bras luy desserre :
Le contraignant la bride habandonner.
Oultre ce coup luy vint encor' donner
De son espée à trauers de la face :
Dont il tumba roide mort en la place."
Salel's Fr. transl.

Are there any other examples of the use of these two words, and what is their derivation ?
W. H. ALLNUTT.
Oxford.

LOWER FAMILY, CORNWALL.—Can any one inform me what became of Elizabeth Lower, only child of Sir William Lower, Knt., the dramatist? Sir William was devisee under the will of his cousin, Thomas Lower, of St. Winnow, proved April 13, 1661, *inter alia*, of the manor of St. Winnow, and barton of Clifton in the parish of Landulph, Cornwall, to hold to him and the heirs male of his body, desiring him to continue the same in the name and family of Lower. Sir William died about a year afterwards, his daughter being then under age, as appears from his will dated August 16, 1661, and proved May 17 following. Did Elizabeth Lower marry? and if so, whom? If she died unmarried, where was she buried, and when? Where was Sir William buried? Through the courtesy of the Vicar of St. Winnow and the Rector of Landulph I have ascertained that he was not buried at either of those

parishes. Was he buried at St. Clement Danes, London ?
Thomas Lower, above mentioned, devised certain of his estates to his " sister Dame Dorothy Drummond." Who was this lady's husband, and had they issue? and if so what? JOHN MACLEAN.
Bicknor Court, Coleford, Glouc.

" A PROVERB IS THE WISDOM OF MANY AND THE WIT OF ONE."—A local newspaper ascribes this saying to Lord (John) Russell. In *Chambers's Journal* it was, I think, credited to Sydney Smith. The general impression is that it is of much older date. Can you decide the matter ? J. D. N.

"DANDY PRATTES": "ROMANS GROTTES": "GALY HALFPENY."—These terms are used in State papers of the time of Henry VIII for certain small foreign or adulterated coin which had currency in England at that period. Can any numismatist tell me what they are? "Galy halfpeny" seems to be meant for " Calais halfpenny."
E. M. T.

HARDWICKE HALL.—On one of the pillars of the porch to Hardwicke Hall, erected by the celebrated Countess of Shrewsbury, whose existence had till recently been altogether overlooked, is engraved in bold antique letters, about an inch in height :—

" Hic locus est, quem si verbis audatia detur
Haud timeam magni dixisse palatia cœli."

Can any of your correspondents give information as to the authorship of this couplet ?
A. W. W.

ARMS OF MOORE AND FARWELL FAMILY.—I have lately come across a family of Moore who for the last century or longer have borne the following arms, Erm., fretty sa., on a chief sa. three lions ramp. or. As I can find no grant of such bearings to any family of that name, can any of your readers inform me to whom and when these arms were granted? and can any of your readers either lend me a copy or inform me where I can see or purchase the *Genealogical Dictionary of New England* (Savage), as I particularly wish to see it for the families of Farwell and Moore, scions of both of which established themselves early in America? C. T. J. MOORE, F.S.A.
Frampton Hall, near Boston.

PETRUS DIDONENSIS.—There was a certain Petrus Didonensis who fought with Geoffrey Martel, Count of Anjou, for the county of Saintonge in 1060. What is the meaning and what the derivation of the epithet Didonensis ?
K. N.

THE BETHUNE FAMILY OF CAITHNESS.—I ask for information concerning the family of Bethune, believed to be descended directly from the De

friend of the late Sir John Sinclair, the statistician. I should be very glad to get some information.

B. A. A.

THE LONGLEAT MSS.—Among the papers of the Marquis of Bath preserved at Longleat, which are calendared in the appendix to vol. iii. of the Report of the Historical Manuscripts Commission, are copies of three letters by Oliver Cromwell. Two of these are printed in Mr. Carlyle's *Letters and Speeches of Oliver Cromwell*, but I cannot find the third there, which is thus described :—

" 1655. Nov. 19, Whitehall.—Oliver P. to Col. Norton —asks him to assist Col. Goffe, who will be at Winchester to-morrow."—P. 195.

I am anxious to see a copy of this letter. If it has already been printed, I shall be much obliged to any of your readers who will direct my attention to the place where it occurs. In the same collection, vol. xx. (p. 192 of Report), mention is made of six other letters by Oliver Cromwell. Have these been printed? EDWARD PEACOCK.
Bottesford Manor, Brigg.

AMEN CORNER.—There is a spot near St. Paul's so called. There is also a spot in the extreme point of the college meads at Winchester so called. Can any good antiquary explain the term? Did it denote the end of a processional service or litany? J. R. B.

THE ORDER OF THE LION AND SUN OF PERSIA. —There seems to be much uncertainty about this Persian decoration. Carlisle and Burke give little information on the subject, and other authors even less. Is the order divided into two or more classes? and, if so, what constitutes the difference between these grades? Is it simply in the size and design of the star and badge, or in the privileges (if any) which the order carries with it? There are also gold and silver medals: obverse, lion and sun; reverse, a Persian inscription. For what services and to whom were these given?
GEO. CLEGHORN.

DR. NEBENIUS'S WORK ON THE GERMAN CUSTOMS UNION.—Has this work ever been translated into English? C. A. WARD.
Mayfair.

" As."—What is the meaning of this word in such an expression as " The concert was to have taken place *as* Tuesday " ? Is it short for " as it were "? I know one family every member of which uses the word in this way, and I have supposed it to be a provincialism. I have come across two passages in print lately where the same use

Society it is stated that the next division of will take place *as* at the end of 1879.
W. D. SWEET
Peterborough.

" THE BRISTOL MEMORIALIST," printed f published by W. Tyson, Clare Street,] 1823, 8vo.—Who edited this volume ? W the author of one or two papers in the mis having the signature " My Uncle "?
In a list of Bristol authors in the abov there occurs the name of Thomas Churnick, of *Jehoshaphat, and other Poems* (no date). any Bristol reader of " N. & Q." give me th of this volume, and any information regardi author ? R. INC

ARMS OF SIR JOHN EDWARDS, FIRST AN BART.—Would some reader of " N. & Q." tell me the arms of Sir John Edwards, of field, M.P. for Montgomery in the first Parl of Queen Victoria ? I shall be greatly oblig the information. W. M.

THE SURNAME " WOOLY H."—In the c yard of St. Mary's, Cheltenham, Glouceste there are two inscribed head-stones recordii deaths of several members of this family, 18 the name being given as " Wooley H." on the stones. There does not appear to be an son so named at present in Cheltenham. name to be met with elsewhere? and what meaning of the letter " H." ? I know the n Fetherston H. and its meaning. AB[ ]

SERVANTS' HALL FORFEITS.—I was readi other day a rhymed list of the old forfeits i bers' shops, and this recalled another catalo penalties, also versified, which I had not th of for some twenty years. These forfeits lettered in oil paint on panel, and hung f about the fireplace in a servants' hall, in s country house in the north of England. A] hold of some twenty servants were in the h[ ] dining here daily, and, doubtless, order was times difficult to keep. I remember that or feit was incurred by profane swearing, an[ ] fragment of the rest comes back to me :—

" Whoever——
Or cuts more bread than he can eat,
Shall to the box one penny pay
Or be burnt in hand without delay."

I should date this forfeit list about the mid the last century. Certainly the alternative p savours strongly of the bull-baiting and b drawing period. Can any of your correspon who have seen a similar list, supply the rest of the rhyme ?   ZERO.

ROYAL AND IMPERIAL FAMILIES OF FRANCE.— Where shall I find a full pedigree or account of the above, giving all the issue of Louis Philippe's sons, dead as well as living, and the same of the Bonaparte dynasty ?

FAMILY OF EYTON OF LEESWOOD.—Can any of your readers tell me if John Eyton, of Leeswood, who married Susan Puleston (*temp.* Charles I.), had by her a son John, who was ancestor of the present Eyton of Leeswood ?   C. H.

COTGREAVE PEDIGREE, OF NETHERLEGH HOUSE, NEAR CHESTER.—I have in my possession a letter stating that, in 1844, a pedigree of the above family—the work of Randle Holme, anno 1672, from documents compiled by the learned antiquary William Camden, anno 1598—was in existence. From inquiries I have made I find that the pedigree has been lost. It contained the descents of three generations of the Burse-Blades in the county of Durham, and Stockport, Cheshire, with armorial bearings, &c. I should feel obliged if any of your numerous readers, having come across this pedigree, would kindly communicate with me.
F. A. BLAYDES.
Hockliffe Lodge, Leighton Buzzard.

A NOVEL ABOUT BIRMINGHAM.—Wanted, the name of a novel, and that of its author, which treats learnedly of a place called Stirningham (?) (*i.e.* Birmingham), and of which the hero is John Maurice Baskette.   H. C.

ARMS ON ANCIENT TOMB.—In the parish church of Wellingore, Lincolnshire, there is a fine alabaster "altar tomb," with the effigies of a knight in armour and lady, about which I am desirous of ascertaining more than is at present known, viz. that in Gervase Hollis's *Church Notes*, taken *c.* 1634, the three shields on the south side of the tomb bore the following arms :—1. Sable, two lions passant arg., crowned or—*Dymoke;* 2. Sable, three bars arg. ; 3. Arg., on a fess gules three fleurs-de-lis or—*Disney.* The knight wears the (SS.) Lancaster collar ; and the costume of both figures is that of 1400 to 1450. Can any one tell me to what family the arms on shield No. 2 belonged, or give any further information ?
JOHN FERNIE.
Wellingore Vicarage, Grantham.

BOWING TO THE ALTAR.—Can any of your readers kindly give me any information concerning the old custom of "bowing to the altar" on entering and leaving church ? I should be glad to know whether the custom has been preserved in any of our old parish churches, as well as in any cathedrals and college chapels ; also, the name of

any book or article that has been written on the subject, and any references to it that occur in theological authors of the sixteenth and seventeenth centuries.   F. W. L.
Oxford.

AN OIL PAINTING.—I have an oil painting, painted apparently about ninety years since, a landscape, with tree, water, and figures, the signature on which is "Œram," in old English. Who used this signature ?   T. McM.

AUTHORS OF BOOKS WANTED.—
A Vindication of the Literary Character of the late Professor Potson. By Crito Cantabrigiensis. Camb., 1827. 8vo.
An Address to the Curious in Ancient Poetry.—This work is mentioned by Ritson in a note to the preface to his *Quip Modest,* 1788.   C. D.
The Post-Captain ; or, the Wooden Walls well Manned, comprehending a View of Naval Society and Manners.—This is the title of a chap-book still printed and extensively sold in Ireland. It is chiefly remarkable for the amount of naval slang introduced. Is the author known ?   W. H. PATTERSON.

AUTHORS OF QUOTATIONS WANTED.—
" O world, as God has made it, all is beauty ;
And knowing this is love, and love is duty,
What further can be sought for or declared ? "
T. W. C.

Replies.

ST. GEORGE.
(5th S. viii. 447.)

GEN. PONSONBY will find the whole question about St. George discussed in Peter Heylin's *Historie of St. George,* who wrote to answer the assertion made by Calvin, followed by Dr. Reynolds in his *De idol. Eccles. Rom.,* that St. George of England is identical with George the Arian ; also in a paper read by Dr. Samuel Pegge before the Society of Antiquaries in 1777 against a work of Dr. John Pettingal. He may also consult Baring-Gould's *Lives of the Saints* (vol. for April). A remarkable paper was read by Mr. Hogg, published in the *Transactions of the Royal Society of Literature,* vol. vii. part i., which distinctly proves that St. George the Martyr was honoured as a saint before the time of George the Arian. In the *Christian Remembrancer* of 1863 I wrote an article which gives a compendium of the history of St. George and of the whole question. With regard to GEN. PONSONBY'S query as to when St. George became the patron saint of England, we find from Heylin that the three soldier saints who were invoked at the dubbing of a knight were SS. Maurice, Sebastian, and George, as seen from Baronius, *Annot. in Rom. Mart.,* 23 Ap. Selden says that in the old French ceremonial St. George alone was invoked. " Alors

as well as Christians in the East. Dean Stanley (*Sinai and Palestine*, p. 274) mentions a chapel (*marabout*), near the ancient Sarepta, dedicated to St. George under the title of El Khonda, in which "there is no tomb inside, only hangings before a recess. This variation from the usual type of Mussulman sepulchres was, we were told by peasants on the spot, because El Khouda is not yet dead. He flies round and round the world, and those chapels are built wherever he has appeared."

The first idea of St. George becoming the patron saint of soldiers undoubtedly originated with the Crusaders. The following is from Robert, the Benedictine monk of Rheims, who wrote somewhere about the year 1120 :—

"Dum sic certatur, et tam longi certaminis prolixitas nostros fatigabit, nec numerus hostium videretur decrescere, Albatorum militum innumerabilia exercitus visus est de montibus descendere, quorum signifer et Duces esse dicuntur, Georgius, Mauritius, Demetrius : quos ut primum vidit Podiensis Episcopus, exclamavit magna voce, dicens, O milites ecce vobis venit auxilium quod promisit Deus."

Of course the Moslem fled, and the Christians slew innumerable hosts ; the enthusiastic Bishop of Puy reckons the slain at one hundred thousand. No wonder, then, that St. George received all honours from the army. It was from the Crusaders, therefore, that the fame of St. George spread over the West, and he became the patron of soldiers. At the same time it must be remembered that he was known in England long before the Crusades as a saint, for we have one hundred and sixty-two old parish churches dedicated to him, some of them before the Conquest. The church of the parish from which I make this communication is of Saxon or Danish foundation, being mentioned in Domesday. It is dedicated to SS. George and Laurence. The monastery at Thetford, as old as the time of Knut, also dedicated to St. George, and St. George's, Southwark, are well-known examples of many others which might be named. We cannot, however, maintain that he was constituted the patron saint till the time of Edward III., though some have affirmed that he became so on the return of Richard I. from the Crusades. It appears probable that down to Edward III. St. Edward was considered as the patron. The following is from Thomas of Walsingham :—

"At the siege of Calais, in 1349, Edward III., moved by some sudden impulse, drew his sword, calling out, 'Ha! St. Edward! Ha! St. George!'"

His soldiers, animated by these words and the action of the king, fell on the French and routed them.

In 1348 the king founded the chapel of St.

so continued till 1415, the third yea[r] when at a Council held at Oxford bishop Chicheley the festival was ra[ised to] *duplex*, and put on a level with Ch[ristmas,] cessation of all servile work being e[njoined].
E. LEATON-B[

Springthorpe Rectory.

I have never seen an exact date gi[ven] George was made the patron of the Garter by Edward III., and the bann[er] was white, with the red cross, unt[il] James I. (1603), when the cross o[f] was added, and in 1801, at the "un[ion" of Ire]land, the cross of St. Patrick comple[ted the].
Jack. Sir Harris Nicolas says :—

"The cross of St. George was worn [by] the armour by every English soldier in and subsequent centuries, even if the cus[tom] vail at a much earlier period, to indicat[e] the service of the Crown.

"On the invasion of Scotland by Ric[hard II.] it was ordained that 'everi man of what e[state] or nation they be of, so that they be of o[ne] a signe of the armes of Saint George, lar[ge] and behynde, upon parell that yf he be sla[ine] to deth, he that hath so doon shall not [die] for defaulte of the crosse that he lacketh. enemy do bere the same token or cross notwithstandyng if he be prisoner, upon

A similar ordinance was adopted by the government of his army in Fran[ce.]

St. George was honoured in Fra[nce] the sixth century, but it was not til[l] the Crusaders to Europe, who ascribe at Antioch to his intercession, that honour paid to him reached its full and he was elected patron saint of t[he] Genoa as also of England.

With regard to the election or ch[oice of] saints I should be glad to know ho[w it] took place, for I met lately with passage, which I should like explain[ed.] *Textus Roffensis* Thos. Hearne publ[ished] a translation of Leonard Hutten's *Antiquitatibus Oxoniensibus*, in wh[ich is a] short account of the different pa[rishes,] whom churches and religious hou[ses are] dedicated, and speaking of St. Ge[orge] which of old stood within the precir[cts of] Castle, he says :—

"In the Westerne suburbs therefore o[f Oxford] find little more worthie observation th[an the] whereof wee have alreadie spoken ; I m[ention] of S[t] George, the Abby of South Osne[y and] North Osney, the Parish Church of S[t] Glocester Hall. The only thing to be e[xcepted] saints S[t] George and S[t] Nicholas were.

St George, hee was a Military and a Martiall S^t; and *in sortitione Gentium,* when all Countries cast lotts what peculiar Saint every one should have to it selfe, it fell out that as St Dennis happened to the French, St James to the Spaniard, St Patrick to the Irish people, St David to the Welch, St Andrew to the Scotts, St Anthony to the Italian, St Marke to the Venetian, soe St George happened to the English: but *quo jure,* and how we maie deduce our title and claime to him, I leave that to men more skilfull and studious of those things. All that I can saie is, that hee delivered a King's Daughter from a Dragon neare to the Citty of Lysia when shee was ready to be devoured (as Petrus de Natalibus reporteth in his Legend), and that hee suffered Martirdome att Militena under Decianus the President in the persecution of Dioclesian."

The date of martyrdom was April 23, 290; April 23, 1192, Richard I. defeated Saladin. When did this election of or casting lots for saints take place? GIBBES RIGAUD.

Oxford.

Butler, in his *Lives of the Fathers, Martyrs, and other Principal Saints,* under April 23, says of this saint :—

"He is at this day the tutelar saint of the republic of Genoa, and was chosen by our ancestors in the same quality under our Norman kings. The great national Council held at Oxford in 1222 commanded his feast to be kept as a holiday of the lesser rank throughout England."

Chambers says, "At the Council of Oxford in 1222 his feast was ordered to be kept as a national festival."

Edward III. made St. George patron of the Order of the Garter, instituted, according to Clark, Jan. 19, 1344, but Sir Harris Nicolas is of opinion that the order was not definitely established till the latter part of 1347.

HERBERT H. FLOWER.

How St. George became the patron saint of England is unknown, but the most probable guess is that it was by a simple confusion of names that he was allowed to usurp the place of St. Gregory, who had so large a share in converting our island to Christianity. The names Ge-org-ius and Gre-gor-ius differ "by little more than a single letter" (Mr. S. Sharpe's *Hist. of Egypt,* vol. ii. p. 315).

If the dragon is really the embodiment of Athanasian error, as the author states just before, the adoption of the emblem of George and the dragon is strange in a country where the Athanasian Creed is upheld by law. S. FOXALL.

Birmingham.

The extraordinary popularity of St. George in Western Europe seems to have dated from the period of the Crusades, and to have been owing to the belief in his active interference in favour of the Christian hosts at the battle of Antioch, which led to the recovery of Jerusalem. The red cross was, I suppose, first displayed on the English flag when the first "Union Jack" was formed, and a national ensign invented, under James I., in 1606. It is, perhaps, a noteworthy fact that the saint whose emblem is there conjoined with that of St. George, to wit St. Andrew, contributed in hardly less degree, by a miraculous revelation, to this same victory.

May I be allowed to append to this reply a query? Does not St. Bridget or Bride claim equal devotion with St. Patrick, the apostle of Ireland, as patroness of that country? and is there any other instance of such divided national honours?

H. W.

New Univ. Club.

USTONSON OF TEMPLE BAR.
(5th S. ii. 288.)

The name of Ustonson must be dear to all "brothers of the angle," as honest Izaak phrases it. It was probably about the middle of last century that it first appeared, as indicating the new proprietor of an already well-known emporium of all sorts of fishing tackle, &c. I have one of his bills before me, which runs as follows :—

"To all Lovers of Angling.
ONESIMUS USTONSON,
Successor to the late
MR. JOHN HERRO,
at the
[Here come woodcuts of a Crown and a Fish]
No. 48, the bottom of *Bell Yard,* near *Temple Bar,*
LONDON,
Makes all sorts of Fishing Rods, and all Manner of the best Fishing Tackle, Wholesale and Retail, at the lowest Rates; sells the right KIRBY'S HOOKS, being the best tempered of any made, which cannot be had at any other Shop; the best sort of Artificial Flies, Menow Tackle, Jack and Perch, and Artificial Menows; and all sorts of Artificial Hooks, made upon the said Hooks, in the neatest Manner, for Pike, Salmon, and Trout; Spring Snap-Hooks; Live and Dead Snap, and Live Bait Hooks, Trowling Hooks of various Sorts; the best Sort of Treble and Double Box, and Single Swivels; Gimp, with Silver and Gold; the best and freshest *India* Weed or Grass, just come over; likewise a fresh parcel of superfine Silk Worm Gut, no better ever seen in *England,* as fine as a Hair, and as strong as Six, the only Thing for Trout, Carp, and Salmon; the best Sort of Multiplying Brass Winches, both stop and plain; Woved Hair and Silk Lines, and all other Sorts of Lines for Angling; various Sorts of Reels and Cases; and all Sorts of Pocket Books for Tackle, Menow Kettles, and Nets to preserve Live Bait; Fishing Paniers and Bags; Variety of Gentle Boxes and Worm Bags; Landing Nets and Hooks; Fishing Stools; Wicker and Leather Bottles; and many other Curiosities, in the Way of Angling. All Sorts of Trunks to shoot Darts and Pellets.

N.B. Turnery Ware of all Sorts, Brushes, &c."

This is dated "May 6th, 1768." Below we have another announcement under the same date :—

"St. Anne's Lane, Aldersgate.
To all LOVERS OF ANGLING,
CHARLES KIRBY,
Nephew of THOMAS KIRBY, lately deceased, and Son of CHARLES KIRBY, Grandson to TIMOTHY,

Sellers of Hooks, called KIRBY HOOKS, do hereby declare my Engagement with

> MR. USTONSON, at No. 48, the Bottom of
> Bell Yard, near Temple-Bar, London,
>
> The old Original Shop, for whom I make, and for no other Person.
>
> At the above Shop are made and sold all Sorts of Fishing Rods, and
>
> Tackle, both Wholesale and Retail."

Mem.—The secret of tempering fish-hooks, " so as not to snap, and yet not to bend with the force of the fingers," is said to have been communicated to the original Kirby by Prince Rupert, in the reign of Charles I. (*Rural Sports*, by Rev. W. B. Daniel, 1801, 4to., vol. i. p. 156).

The house and name of Ustonson must have continued to flourish through the following three quarters of a century. I next find it mentioned in a charming book, which, the delight of the readers to whom it is specially addressed for its *matter*, is hardly less appreciated by older " boys " for its genial scholarly *manner* and the artistic excellence of its woodcut illustrations—points in which, I venture to say, it has scarcely found a superior, if, indeed, a rival. Query, Who was its author? The passage appears to me to possess sufficient merit and interest to justify its entire transcription :—

" ANGLING has long held a high rank among the sports of the people of England; poets have written in its praise, and philosophers have delighted in its practice ; it is not confined to particular places, ages, or grades of society; wherever the brook wanders ' through hazy shaw or broomy glen,'—wherever the willow-branch laves in the streamlet,—wherever the Trout leaps at the May-fly, or the Pike lurks in the bulrushes, or the Salmon springs up the waterfall,—there also are Anglers. To enjoy this fine pastime the mountaineer descends to the valley-stream, the Magister Artium quits his learned halls and collegiate ease for the banks of the deeps, the weirs, and the tumbling bays of Cam, the citizen his shop and beloved ledger for a hickory rod and a creek in the Roding, and the courtier his rich Turkey carpet, ottoman and lustre, for ' nature's grassy foot-cloth,' the rough bark of a felled river-side tree, and the sparkling surface of a rippled stream. The boy who was but ' breeched a Wednesday ' often spends his holiday hour on the bank of a brook, with a crooked pin for his hook, a needleful of thread for his line, and an alder switch for his rod ; and the grey-headed statesman—nay, even Royalty itself—has occasionally relaxed from the grave duties attendant on such a superior station, from weighing the balance of power, and determining the fate of nations, to wield the rod and cast the mimic fly. George the Fourth, in the later part of his life, was very partial to Angling. Virginia Water, which covers nearly one thousand acres, afforded ample scope for this re-creation, and a magnificent fishing apparatus was made by command of His Majesty by USTONSON of Temple Bar. When presented, the King was pleased to express his admiration at the great ingenuity and taste displayed in the manufacture of it, and appeared surprised that

inches broad, and three inches in with the richest crimson morocco l sloped with double borders of gold ing alternately the salmon and bas forms a rich gold wreath of the r(rock, intertwined with oak-leav(centre of the lid presents a splen(the Royal arms of Great Britain a] is fastened with one of Bramah's handle, eyes, &c., are all double lined throughout with Genoa sky-t part of the lid tufted. On either partitions for the books or cases for which are the most chaste and beau be imagined. The angling book richest Genoese crimson velvet, th(a diadem of solid gold, the top ; Royal arms richly worked and (the shield appear the rose, thi Within the book is a beautiful em reel, studded with silver, which co] &c., for bottom-fishing, and likewi infinite variety of artificial bait (The fly-book, on the outside, very other, with this difference, that t with a double G. R., enclosed in a embroidered wreath, representing and thistle. This book is full of c the different seasons, &c., and all (manufacture. The books are l watered tabby silk, correspondin{ In the centre of the box, on a rais(sky-blue velvet, are the landing rin{ is beautifully worked, and the l coloured silk. On each side are ring, &c. (in separate partitions' maker's name, and the crown of have extra joints, tops, &c., and m be adapted to any sort of fishing. landing stick, are richly carved an emblematical devices, and the entir(ledged to be the most beautiful spe(has ever been manufactured."—] seventh edit., Lond., Vizetelly, squ

We are not informed of the sportsman made of his daint measure of success which rewa whole matter is more suggestiv than a true Nimrod of the stre the ingenuity of Mr. Ustons(mind the marvellous qualities intellectual, insisted upon by condition of piscatory success, a modern sporting writer that: tities of Fish with the hook ε test, many a *Miller's Boy* m! matched against the very *Si:* of Anglers."

Further on, in the same ex informed :—

" Mr. Ustonson, of Temple Bar most excellent line for Natural F its peculiar construction, is admirably adapted for carrying the light natural fly across a stream."—P. 119.

What I have extracted may not be without interest to readers generally, from its proper merit, and may perchance help the special querent to determine the date of his broadside.

WILLIAM BATES, B.A.

Birmingham.

LIVING ENGLISH POETS, OR THE BRITISH PARNASSUS (5ᵗʰ S. viii. 444.)—The following persons ought to be included in any list of living English poets, as they are all well known to readers of poetry, and many of them, by name at least, to the general public:—William Harrison Ainsworth; William Allingham; Thomas Ashe; William Cox Bennett; John Stuart Blackie; Richard Doddridge Blackmore; Frances Browne; Edward Capern; Joseph Edwards Carpenter; Eliza Cook; Thomas Cooper; William James Richmond Cotton; William John Courthope; Isa Craig; Austin Dobson; Sir Francis Hastings Doyle; William Ewart Gladstone; Dora Greenwell; John A. Heraud; Mrs. Eleanora Louisa Hervey; Rev. William Edward Heygate; Alsager Hay Hill; Edward Vaughan Kenealy; William Charles Mark Kent; Rev. Herbert Kynaston; Rev. Frederick George Lee; Marquis of Lorne; Denis Florence McCarthy; Charles Mackay; Lord John Manners; Theodore Martin; Nicholas Michell; Mrs. Sibella Elizabeth Miles; Lewis Morris; Arthur Munby; Edward Byron Nicholson; Thomas Herbert Noyes; Francis Turner Palgrave; Bessie Rayner Parkes (Mrs. Belloe); Harry Cholmondely Pennell; John Plummer; Compton Reade; William Sawyer; Lord Selborne; Lord Southesk; Ashby Sterry; William Stigand; Henry Sewell Stokes; Rev. Samuel John Stone; Most Rev. Richard Chenevix Trench; Martin Farquhar Tupper; Charles Turner.   FREDERIC BOASE.

15, Queen Anne's Gate, Westminster.

ZERO's list being a very general one, I think that several more names deserve to be mentioned. At the present moment I can remember, amongst others, the following:—Roden Noel, Professor Plumptre, Henry J. Byron, Miss Muloch, Whyte Melville. If William and Mary Howitt are still living—which I hope they are—I would give them a high place in the list. •

J. W. W.

` ZERO and his authorities have all omitted several who have quite as good a right to be on this list as some that are so—for instance, Mr. Bickersteth, author of Yesterday, To-day, and for Ever, Canon Bright, Gerard Moultrie, W. C. Dix. If Frederick Locker is on the list, so should Austin Dobson be; and if either of them, a study of the Athenæum's occasional articles on " Recent Verse " would pro-

bably disclose a few more with claims quite equal.   CHARLES F. S. WARREN, M.A.

Bexhill.

ZERO should add to his list : John Addington Symonds, Alaric A. Watts, F. E. Weatherley, and Charles G. Dodgson, better known as " Lewis Carroll."   EDWARD H. MARSHALL.

The Temple.

REGINALD HEBER (5ᵗʰ S. ix. 128.)—The name of Reginald has been a common one in the Heber family since the time of Henry VII. Reginald Heber, the bishop's father—born 1728, Rector of Chelsea, 1766, which he exchanged in 1770 for the living of Malpas, in Cheshire, which he could hold in conjunction with his own family living of Hodnet, Salop—had three sons : Richard, the well-known collector of books; Reginald, the Bishop of Calcutta; and Thomas Cuthbert, who died unmarried, Rector of Marton, in 1816. He died on Jan. 10, 1804, leaving his estates of Marton Hall, Yorkshire, and Hodnet Hall, Salop, to his eldest son, Richard, the book collector, M.P. for Oxford University, 1821-2. When he died the question was raised in the Gentleman's Magazine, vol. lxxiv. p. 519, whether he was in any way related to an old bachelor who had borne the same name of Reginald Heber, who died at Hadleigh, in Essex, about the year 1796, and left his property there to strangers. This brought a reply from Mr. Churton (Gentleman's Magazine, vol. lxxiv. p. 807), stating that both Reginalds were probably of the same old Yorkshire family, and that the sister of Reginald Heber, of Hadleigh, married the Rev. W. Smith, Dean of Chester, 1758-87, but neither she nor her brother seems to have left any children. There is nothing to show that this Reginald Heber was the author of the Historical Book of Horse-Races and Cockings for 1755, published in Feb., 1756, &c., but it seems very probable that he was. Possibly an examination of his will, which must have been proved about the year 1796, might throw some light upon the matter.

EDWARD SOLLY.

The innate love of horses which distinguishes the true Yorkshireman makes it very probable that Reginald Heber, of Chancery Lane, belonged to the same stock as his illustrious namesake the missionary Bishop of Calcutta. The representative of one branch of the family, Thomas Heber, of Holling Hall, would seem to have been at any rate suspected of tastes much more questionable than those of the ordinary " sporting man," as we find him, on March 30, 1676, brought before Walter Hawkesworth, Esq., on a charge of burglary. See vol. xl. of the publications of the Surtees Society, pp. 222-3, where, it is only fair to say, the editor states his opinion that the accused was " probably acquitted."   This Thomas was grandson of

in the pedigree of the main line at this time. See Dugdale's *Visitation of Yorkshire*, pp. 54 and 34 of the Surtees Society's thirty-sixth volume.

CLK.

Your correspondent notices the fact that the author of *An Historical List of Horse-Matches* run 1753, and in subsequent years, was living in Chancery Lane about the middle of the last century, and that he bore the same Christian and surname as the famous Bishop of Calcutta, Reginald Heber, which he thinks remarkable, as neither of those names is common. I can quote, however, a much earlier instance. In a MS. list of Yorkshire contributors to the Patriotic Fund raised by Queen Elizabeth to meet the expenses incurred in opposing the Spanish invasion, in 1588, is included the name of "Reginald Heybar." Doubtless this is only an old form of spelling this ancient Yorkshire family name.

JAMES H. FENNELL.
14, Red Lion Passage, W.C.

"ST. AUGUSTINE'S CONFESSIONS" (5th S. ix. 128.)—The translation mentioned is from the prolific pen of Abraham Woodhead, printed in 1679, the year subsequent to his death; see *Athenæ Oxonienses*, Bliss's edition, 1817. Anthony à Wood says :—"He hath written very many things, some of which were published in his lifetime and some after his death, all without his own name or initial letters of it set to them." E. W. T.

THE BARONY OF FITZWARINE (5th S. viii. 447.) —An examination of the pedigree of the Chidiock family would have shown the compiler of the lineage of "Delafield of Fieldston" in Burke's *History of the Commoners* that there is no mistake in the *Extinct and Dormant Peerage* regarding William, Lord FitzWaryn, nor confusing of his descendants with those of Robert, Lord FitzPayne. The fact is that the last Sir John Chidiock, who died in 1450, leaving two daughters co-heirs, was the representative and heir of both Robert, Baron FitzPayne, and William, Baron FitzWaryn, for his great-grandfather, Sir John Chidiock, Knt., married Isabel, only child and heir of Robert, last Baron FitzPayne. The son and heir of this marriage, the second Sir John, was father of the third Sir John Chidiock, Knt., who married, about the year 1396, Eleanore, daughter and sole heir of Sir Ivo FitzWaryn, Knt., who was son and heir of Sir William FitzWaryn, K.G., Baron FitzWaryn. They were the parents of the fourth and last Sir John Chidiock, Knt., who thus united in his own person the heritage and rights of both baronies, which are now in abeyance between the descendants and representatives of his two daughters

The Delafield descent, as given in *Commoners*, is not reliable on some poin instance, in the absence of proofs and reference to authorities, there are rea doubting, if not altogether rejecting, the match with Hankford, and the descei William, Lord FitzWaryn. In the first case, Sir John Delafield birth, as represented, could not have tak before 16 Hen. VI., 1437, is stated to have in 35 Hen. VI., 1456-7, Elizabeth, siste Richard Hankford, father of Anne, Cou Ormond. Neither this Christian name marriage of a sister of Sir Richard Han met with elsewhere. Sir Richard's father, Hankford, Esq., died in 1419, at which t son and heir (the future Sir Richard) was ; be twenty-one years old and more, ai husband of Elizabeth, sole child and heir (last Lord FitzWaryn; consequently Richard's sisters must have been born befo We have notices of three of his sist Christina, who was married, in or before Robert Warre, Esq., of Hestercombe; J who was first wife of Sir Theobald Gorge and Blanche Hankford. Query, is it 1 that a Sir John Delafield, who was born in 1437, would marry in 1457 a lady who must have taken place before 1419, ai probably, was born nearly at the beginnin century, as her brother was born in the p one ?

In the second case, viz. the Delafield c descent to the ancient barony of Willia FitzWaryn, K.G., as asserted in the *Com* Eleanore FitzWaryn is reputed to have sole daughter and heir of Sir Ivo, son anc William, Lord FitzWaryn, and at the tim father's death in September, 1414, she wz to be more than thirty years of age, and t of Sir John Chidiock, Knt., and through h and her issue the heirs general of Willia FitzWaryn, are now recognized and fou Lord Stourton and Lord Arundell of Wai stated above. But this barony of Willis Waryn, K.G., became extinct at his death as neither was his son and heir Sir Ivo, 1 any of his descendants, ever summoned t(ment as Baron FitzWaryn.

Possibly the Delafields may descer another family of the name of FitzWaryn. were two other FitzWaryns, living in the b(of the fifteenth century, who bore the : William. One was William FitzWaryn, Appulton, in Berkshire, a manor which he i from his mother, Margaret, daughter of G sister and heir of Thomas de la Mote

William was son and heir of John FitzWaryn, of Aston-in-Monslow, Salop, and he died in 14 Hen. VI., 1436, leaving a daughter and heir, Alice, then aged twenty-four years, and wife of John Gerald. The other William FitzWaryn was father of Catherine, wife of William Westbury, one of the Justices of the Court of King's Bench from 1426 to 1449. They had a son and heir, John Westbury, father of Agnes. She became sole heir on the death of her brother, William Westbury, under age, and without issue. On the death of her mother Alice in 1482, then wife of John Newburgh, Agnes was wife of Robert Leversege.

B. W. GREENFIELD.

Southampton.

"GROUSE" (5th S. ix. 147.)—It is evident from the price at which it is taxed that *gryse*, in the Scottish Act of 1551, is not grouse. In the earlier part of the clause we find little moorfowl (common grouse) taxed at 4*d*.; blackcock and grayhen (black-game), 6*d*.; the dozen poutis (young grouse), 12*d*. At the conclusion we come to *gryse* (doubtless young pig), 18*d*.

There can, I think, be no doubt that PROF. NEWTON is right in referring the name, as I have done in my *Dictionary*, to the O. Fr. *griais*, *griesche*, *greoche*, speckled, grizzled, parti-coloured; although Littré questions the authority on which such a meaning is attributed to the word. He admits, however, that in Fr. *pie grièche*, a shrike, the word *grièche* exactly corresponds to the German *bunt*, parti-coloured, in *buntspecht*, the German name of the same bird. He also cites the expression of "une nonnain *griesche*," which can hardly signify other than a grey or black-and-white nun. In a writer of the thirteenth century the name of *greoche* is given to the quail, also a bird of speckled plumage: "Contornix est uns oisiaus que li François claiment *greoches*." It is perhaps from this latter form that we must explain the English *grouse*, while the name *grice*, by which Cotgrave designates the bird, would be a mere adoption of Fr. *griesche*. In his dictionary we have *griais*, grey, or of the colour of a starling; *griesche*, grey, or peckled as a stare; *perdrix griesche*, the ordinary or grey partridge; *poule griesche*, a moorhen, the hen of the *grice*, or moorgame. H. WEDGWOOD.

31, Queen Anne Street.

Whatever be the origin of this word, it is not, I believe, to be met with in any of the old Scottish Acts, though mention of the bird as "mure-foule" is frequent. With regard to *gryse* there is no difficulty. It is not, unfortunately, the desiderated plural of *grouse*, as I think PROF. NEWTON is inclined to hope it may prove to be. I can quite understand a reader being somewhat misled by the passage of the Scottish Act of Parliament of 1551 where the word occurs. It is an Act

"maid vpone the prices of all wylde foulis and tame foulis ," by the " Quenis grace......havand respect to the greit and exhorbitant derth rysin in this realme vpone the wylde and tame foulis, for putting of ordour heirto and remeidie heirof......It is......statute and ordainit be the Quenis grace, &c......that the wylde meit and tame meit vnder writtin be sauld, in all tymes cumming, of the prices following......Item the *gryse* xviij.d.," &c.

This, however, it must be observed, is not "wylde foule," it is "tame meit," and means simply *young pig*.

The word is still in common use, and occurs in an old Scotch proverb, more quaint than elegant, namely, "Lay the head of the sow to the tail of the *gryce*," equivalent to "first count the cost," or "calculate all available resources."

ALEX. FERGUSSON, Lieut.-Col.

Edinburgh.

"ROYD" (5th S. ix. 169.)—Dr. Morris, in an interesting pamphlet on the *Etymology of Local Names* (London, Judd & Glass, n.d.), gives Royd thus: "Rode, Rod, Royd, land cleared or grubbed up." Among his illustrations of the various forms occur Hol-royd, Orme-rod, Ack-royd. But it appears to me that not unfrequently Dr. Morris's illustrations of local names want some further confirmation, *e.g.*, under this very heading are given Mount Ruti (of whose position in the map of Europe we are not informed) and Ruthyn (said by McCulloch to mean the Red Fortress in Welsh), the situation of which in Denbighshire constitutes an *à priori* improbability of its representing a Teutonic etymon. PHILOLOGUS.

BLACK BARLEY: THE FEAST OF THE BIRDS (5th S. ix. 126.)—I can fully endorse the statements of J. B. P. About twenty years ago I was induced to purchase a sack of black barley, of fine plump appearance, which I was told would ripen very early—and so it did, drawing such a cloud of small birds from far and near that for *four* bushels sown I harvested just *three*. So ended my experiment with a loss and a recollection that Benjamin Franklin once wrote, "Experience keeps a dear school, but fools will learn in no other."

WILLIAM WING.

Steeple Aston, Oxford.

"FIRST AN ENGLISHMAN AND THEN A WHIG" (5th S. ix. 127.)—The old Venetian proverb is, "Prima Veneziani, e poi Cristiani." It was used at the time of the Interdict. GORILLA.

"PLATFORM" (5th S. ix. 146.)—Allow me to remind your correspondent that "platform" in the stage direction of the first scene of *Hamlet* is not Shakespeare's, but was introduced by Theobald. It does not occur in the quartos or folios.

C. ELLIOT BROWNE.

THE WHITEHALL CHALICE (5th S. ix. 128.)— The exhibition must surely be the magnificent

gentry, colleges, corporations, &c., contributed their finest old plate. P. P.

BINDING OF E.D.S. PUBLICATIONS (5th S. ix. 148.)—At the Conference of Librarians held last October at the London Institution, there was exhibited a specimen of binding, cheap and durable, which might be useful in such cases as mentioned by ST. SWITHIN. As well as I can remember the following is a description of it : Take a piece of American cloth (to be bought at any draper's or upholsterer's) ; cut it to the height of the publication to be bound, the length to be somewhat more than equal to the breadth of the sides and back. At one end glue over a piece of thin lath or millboard, equal to the height of the work, through which, at about one inch from each extremity, should be inserted, and likewise glued in, the ends of a piece of elastic, to be afterwards turned over, as in a pocket-book or purse. When this is done, sew in, at the distance of its own width from the glued end, No. 1 of the publication, then No. 2 next to it, and so on ; fold over the loose end, then bring the elastic round, and the thing is complete. I must confess that the above description is rather long, and perhaps not altogether understandable. If, therefore, ST. SWITHIN cannot make head or tail of it, or does not think the binding good enough, I would suggest one of the French inventions procurable in the City, or one of Stone's boxes.

J. BORRAJO.

WARTON AND JOHNSON (5th S. ix. 167.)—The particulars of the disagreement between Johnson and Joseph Warton will be found in Dr. Wooll's memoir of Joseph Warton. As I have not a copy of this work, I regret that I cannot supply the precise reference, but it will probably prove most convenient for the inquirer to know that Wooll's account of this unfortunate quarrel is reproduced in Boswell's *Johnson* (edit. 1835), vol. vii. p. 323, as a note to Johnson's letter to Thomas Warton, numbered 373, and dated May 9, 1780.

W. P. COURTNEY.

15, Queen Anne's Gate.

FAMILY OF SERGISON (3rd S. xi. 379.)—Though I am aware that MR. M. A. LOWER is deceased, there may be others interested in having his query answered. This may give a clue to the locality. The *Public Gazetteer*, a newspaper published at Dublin, contains this marriage. The name is evidently the same as Sergison, which is a very uncommon name, and has probably undergone some extraordinary changes in spelling :—

" Married April 2 [1761], in Cork, Mr. Francis Sergerson (son to John Segerson, of Ballinskellie, in the county of Kerry, Esq.) to Miss Aghern, with 800*l*. fortune."

in the Parliamentary Writs in 1320 shire. The following work might giw of the arms, &c. :—

" The Heraldic Calendar : a List of th Gentry whose Arms are Registered and corded in the Heralds' Office, Ireland. 8vo. By William Skey, St. Patrick P. Register of the Heralds' Office."

WILLIAM JO

Camden, New Jersey.

ARMS OF MOORE OR MORE (4th £ Being disappointed in obtaining an query I inserted some few years a; arms of the Moore family, I will the question in the hope that some of correspondents may be able to give a of the coat in question. The arms Chancellor's family from the time of the present day are, Ar., a chev. between three moorcocks ppr., but of the Roman Catholic families of E the arms of the Mores of Bamboro " Or, a torteau charged with a moc two lions passant gardant in pale g; many flaunches ar., each charged wi lis sa." Were it not for the mc introduced I should have imagined t those of some other family given l More, but as the work was compiled antiquary I cannot accede to such o own theory is that the latter coat w one of the Mores who attended the ; and spent his fortune in their behalf bearings, instead of being simply aug; loyalty, are the royal and family arms It is a unique instance of such a th the correct version ; but if any of yo give me a more intelligible one I sl obliged. C. T. J. Moc

Frampton Hall, near Boston.

PUREFOY (5th S. ix. 106.)—Th Michael's Church, Coventry, a mural a very quaint Latin inscription, to ' foy, surmounted with shield of thirt; also another to the memory of Anne the family arms in a lozenge. The getting very defaced, as the arms a stone. JOE

There is a family of this name in Col. Bagwell Purefoy took the l addition to his paternal cognomen a his maternal uncle. JOSE;

Waterford.

THE DIAMOND NECKLACE OF M NETTE (5th S. ix. 107, 178.)—This h subject of a query in the last number of *Inter-médiaire* (Paris, Sandoz et Fischbacher), where it is stated that a portion, but it is believed only a portion, of the necklace was sold in England by the Count de Lamotte, the husband of Jeanne de Valois, for the sum of 300,000*l*. The French querist asks whether the other fragments can be traced. I may add that a long and interesting chapter is devoted to the countess, whose name is there written De la Motte, in the first volume of the *Reminiscences of Prince Talleyrand*, edited from the papers of the late M. Colmache, private secretary to the Prince, by Madame Colmache (London, Henry Colburn, 1848). Mention is there made of a lady, designated as the wife of the Count de M——y, a quasi-*émigré*, who did not return to France during the reign of Napoleon, being the cause of great excitement at one of the Northern Courts by appearing with

"a necklace of the exact pattern of that concerning which all Europe had been roused before the Revolution —the only difference being that the three scroll ornaments which are so remarkable, and to which I (the extract is given as from a letter to Talleyrand when Foreign Minister, from the ambassador at the Court referred to) could swear as being the same, are held by a chain of small rose diamonds instead of the *rivière*, by which it was joined before."

The work from which I quote goes on to state that the Emperor took the story more gravely than the Court, and caused Prince Talleyrand to ask for a drawing of the necklace, which the ambassador found means to obtain, and which was found to correspond with that preserved among the "pièces du Procès" in the archives. The younger Boehmer is said to have declared his

"full and entire conviction that the jewel was the same, from the remarkable circumstance of a mistake having occurred in the execution of the middle ornament, one side of the scroll containing two small diamonds more than the other, and which he remembered had much distressed his father, but which could never have been discovered save by a member of the trade."

We are further told by Madame Colmache that it was "then remembered, and by the Emperor himself first of all," that the mother of this Countess de M——y had been

"attached to the person of Marie Antoinette, and that she had retired from Court, and gone to reside abroad soon after the trial of Madame de la Motte; and what is still further worthy of remark is the fact that the family of the lady in question did not return to France even after the Restoration, and have continued to dwell abroad ever since."

Perhaps somebody not bound to secrecy can supply the missing links in the name "M——y" before the publication of Prince Talleyrand's autobiography. Russia seems to be the country hinted at in Madame Colmache's *Reminiscences*.

C. H. E. CARMICHAEL.

EDWARD FARR (5th S. viii. 429 ; ix. 110.)—MR. DALBY will, I am sure, gladly accept an emenda-

tion which I venture to offer in regard to one of the items in his enumeration of the literary productions of the late Mr. Edward Farr. The historical work written by Mr. Farr, in conjunction with Dr. W. H. Russell and others, was not, as MR. DALBY states, the *Continuation of Hume and Smollett*, but an entirely distinct and complete work, called the *National History of England, Civil, Military, and Domestic* (Collins & Co.). The latter work is similar in plan to Knight's *Pictorial History of England*, but more condensed, extending, however, to four bulky vols., royal 8vo., and carrying down the record to the close of 1873. Mr. Farr wrote the whole of vol. i. and two-thirds of vol. iii. Death stayed his hand at that stage of his labours, when the unwritten portion of his task, represented by one-third of vol. iii. and one-half of vol. iv., fell to me for completion. Dr. W. H. Russell wrote rather more than a quarter of the final volume. An elaborate introductory chapter to the opening volume was contributed by Lord Brougham, and constitutes in all likelihood the very latest of the multifarious writings of that eminent veteran *littérateur*. J. GOODALL.
Dulwich.

Mr. Farr published two volumes entitled *Select Poetry, chiefly Sacred, of the Reign of Queen Elizabeth and of the Reign of James I.*, London, J. W. Parker, 1847. W. M. M.

OFFICE OF THE STRACHY (5th S. ix. 68, 137.)— According to Ducange, *s.v.*, *Straticus* meant the prefect or chief magistrate of any state, city, or province ; and it is worth noting that Ducange quotes a Dalmatic charter of the year A.D. 1036 as containing the word :—"Romani Imperii dignitatem gubernante . . . Michaele . . . *Stratico* universæ Dalmatiæ" (ch. Dalm., *ap.* Joh. Lucium, A.D. 1036); and another of Italy, where one is named as "Miles regius *Straticus* Salerni suique districtus" (Ughell. *De Archiepisc. Salernit.* A.D. 1337). We may remark that Shakespeare has laid the scene of *Twelfth Night* in "a city of Illyria and the coast near it," no very great distance from Dalmatia. But as to this, "valeat quantum." The conjectures of some commentators are curious and amusing. Johnson says, "Here is an allusion to some old story which I have not yet discovered"; Steevens proposes to read "*Starchy* for *Strachy*," and would explain it as "the place for *starching*," and hence "the Lady of the *Starchy*," as the lady who had the care of the linen, some of which, of course, was *starched!* But this, as Malone observes, is not "the heavy declension," which Shakespeare meant, of a woman from the "starchy" to the "wardrobe." Malone also remarks that "in the old copy the word 'Strachy' is printed in italics as the name of a place would be." One more curious verbal but accidental coincidence may be mentioned. In the Provençal dialect the

and certainly the supposed marriage of Malvolio and Olivia would have been a *mésalliance* beyond all doubt, and Olivia would have been another lady of a "mariagi estraçat." E. A. D.

THE WINDSOR SENTINEL AND ST. PAUL'S (5th S. ix. 87, 114, 138, 156, 178.)—The story mentioned by T. W. C. and MR. PICKFORD was called "The Thirteenth Chime : a Legend of Old London," by Angus B. Reach. It appeared in the *Illuminated Magazine*, edited by Douglas Jerrold, vol. ii. pp. 196–200 (1843). It is illustrated with a large wood drawing by Sir John Gilbert, representing the false friar falling dead at the feet of the king (Henry VIII.), with Mabel Lorne, who had struck the thirteenth chime, clinging to her lover, Mark Huntley, who had been arrested on the false charge of sleeping on his post when on duty as a sentinel at Windsor Castle. I fancy that the *Illuminated Magazine* was completed in two volumes. It contained articles by Douglas Jerrold, Angus Reach, Miss Pardoe, Miss Costello, Samuel Lover, Mark Lemon, H. F. Chorley, Lewis Filmore, Miss Toulmin, Mrs. Postans, Charles Hooton, G. A. A'Beckett, Albert Smith, R. B. Peake, R. H. Horne, Laman Blanchard, Wilkie Collins, F. B. Palmer, &c., together with some of those authors mentioned, under their pseudonyms, by MR. MAYER (p. 147) as contributors to the letterpress of *Heads of the People*, viz., " Paul Prendergast," "Piers Shafton, Gent.," "Sylvanus Swanquill," "Libra," "Mourant the Monk," &c., whose names are not given in Olphar Hamst's *Handbook of Fictitious Names*. In the "Literary Pseudonyms" given (by Mr. G. F. Pardon) in the *Bookseller*, May 4, 1875, "Paul Prendergast" in *Heads of the People* is given as "Jerrold D.," and not P. Leigh. The *Illuminated Magazine* was profusely illustrated by Kenny Meadows, John Leech, John Gilbert, Crowquill, Hine, Henning, Prior, C. Martin, Fussell, Lee, Hamerton, &c. In the second volume are two large coloured etchings by John Leech. It seems strange that such an excellent magazine should have had so brief an existence. It is worth noting that some of the articles in the magazine were illustrated by the editor's eldest son, William Blanchard Jerrold, then in his twenty-seventh year, who, six years after, was married to the only daughter of his godfather, Laman Blanchard, another of the contributors to the magazine. Neither Olphar Hamst nor Mr. Pardon gives Mr. Blanchard Jerrold's pseudonym, "Fin-Bec." CUTHBERT BEDE.

BOOK-PLATES (5th S. viii. 200, 298, 397, 517.)— There are two Scottish book-plates which, although exceedingly rare, occasionally turn up here, viz. :—

Mar. This family had two book-plates, them being a fine representation of the ol Tower, an object of uncommon interest travellers from its having been occupied by Mary and Darnley.

Many years ago the original copperplate Birnie arms was presented to me, but not made any use of it. T. Edinburgh.

I have recently acquired an old book-pla of Sir Rt. Clayton, Lord Mayor of Londo plate is beautifully designed, and must work of a known engraver. It is date and as there does not appear to be any re "N. & Q." of so early a plate, I think it a to send the account of it.

A note of any book-plates prior to 1700 I am sure, be appreciated by many of your J. WI

CLOCK STRIKING (5th S. viii. 187, 276, The bewildering effect of the foreign clock on Wordsworth is alluded to in the *Prelu* sixth :—

" The second night,
From sleep awakened, and *misled by sound*
Of the church clock telling the hours with stro
Whose import then we had not learned, we n
By moonlight, doubting not that day was ni

. . . From hour to hour
We sate and sate, wondering, as if the nigh
Had been ensnared by witchcraft."
Centenary ed., vol. v.

A few lines further on he speaks of the produced by

" The clock
That told, *with unintelligible voice,*
The widely parted hours."
WILLIAM GEORGE B

HAWARDEN (5th S. viii. 229, 335, 477) in Domesday *Haordine*. The second Pennant's *Tours in Wales*, 1810, i. 124 :—

" Genealogists tell us that *Roger Fitz-Valerii* one of the noble adventurers who followed the fo *William* the Conqueror, possessed this castle, an frequent contests with the *Welsh*, often saved by retreating to it ; and from that circumstanc called *Howard's Den.* But, with high respect t blood of all the *Howards*, it does not appear tl name was then known : with more probability d historian say that *William*, the son of *Fitz-Val* ceived the addition of *de Haward*, or *Howard*, accident of being born in this place."

Another note :—

" *Harw*, B. from *garw*, rough. Ex. : Harw-ar Harwarden (Flints), the camp on the rough Flavell Edmunds's *Traces of History in the* Places, 1869, p. 189.
HIROND

"TOBER-NA-FUOSICH" (5th S. viii. 88, 198, 395, 435, 474; ix. 114.)—A Highland friend, to whom I wrote asking the probable original of this phrase, tells me that in his earlier days, when convivial society was not over delicate, he has heard given as a rather dubious after-dinner toast, "Tober-na-feusag," for the meaning of which your readers can refer to a Gaelic dictionary.   T. F. R.

A "TUCKING" MILL (5th S. ix. 68, 155.)—There is a large village near Camborne, in Cornwall, called Tuckingmill.   O. W. TANCOCK.
Sherborne.

"CIVET CAT" (5th S. viii. 468; ix. 35.)—Other signs or names for shops dealing in miscellaneous fancy articles are "The Noah's Ark" and "The Little Dustpan." The meaning of the latter name is not very apparent.   CUTHBERT BEDE.

"SKAL" (5th S. viii. 509; ix. 117.)—It has struck me that our word "skull" may be only another form of the Norse *skål*. Is this so? History states that Norsemen used skulls as drinking cups; in fact, the revengeful delight of drinking ale out of their enemies' skulls was one of the chief pleasures in Valhalla.   M. C. BAYNES.
Horsham.

PORTRAIT OF BEATRICE CENCI (5th S. viii. 407; ix. 17.)—I have nothing to say on the portrait, attributed to Guido, of Beatrice Cenci, though perhaps I am capable of saying something, beyond the protest against Mr. Story's remark that the head-dress is incongruous, as H. C. C. interprets him. If it is true, or was believed to be so at the time this celebrated work of art was painted, there could be nothing incongruous in representing the young woman carried off to execution after various tortures by the perhaps not final one of hanging her up by the hair of her head, with a cloth or turban round it. Happily it is not now, I hope, possible to repeat the experiment, and see if a young woman so treated would like to go bare-headed to execution if she could avoid it. To me the cloth about the head embodies what has passed current and is perfectly consistent with the narra-tive. I do not here attempt to say one other word on the horrible subject.   J. C. H.

Miscellaneous.

NOTES ON BOOKS, &c.

Literature Primers—Greek Literature. By R. C. Jebb, M.A. (Macmillan & Co.)
THE Professor of Greek at Glasgow has had to con-dense the story of a literature of world-wide fame within the short compass of a primer. The task might seem a thankless one, but it demanded an able scholar to set before us the results of the latest thought on the subject in such terse language, at once epigrammatic and vivid in its portraiture of the past. Here the student may find the key-note of the Hesiodic poetry, whose mission was "to utter true things," as distinguished from the Homeric poetry, which moves among "visions of the heroic past, to which the poet's art gives an ideal glory"; and hence he may carry away a pleasant picture of Sophocles, "gentle among the shades, even as he was gentle among men." The power of ancient Greece made itself felt in later days in the eloquence of the "Golden Mouth" and the subtlety of John of Damascus. Let us hope, with Mr. Jebb, "that the literature of Greece—in its recovered vigour still so young—will continue to enrich the language that it inherits."

Books I. and II. of the Aeneid of Vergil. By F. Storr, B.A. (Rivingtons.)
MR. F. STORR, in his new edition of the author whom he calls "Vergil," is happiest as an annotator, illustrating the poet's language. We presume that the boys for whose benefit he gives such grammatical explanations as "*que* epexegetical," "concessive, consecutive, and virtual oblique, subjunctive," will understand what he means to impress upon them. But we fail ourselves to understand Mr. Storr's grammar when he writes of "accusatives plurals." What we find most commendable is Mr. Storr's system of illustrating the text in his notes by quotations from Milton, Spenser, Shakspeare, and other English classics, as well as from Greek and Roman literature. What we like least about his work is the theory of "following the MSS., even at the sacrifice of uniformity."

Epochs of English History—England during the Ameri-can and European Wars, 1765-1820. By O. W. Tan-cock, M.A. (Longmans & Co.)
MR. O. W. TANCOCK'S "Epoch" is an important and interesting one, comprising, as it does, the creation of the United States out of our lost New England colonies, and the erection of our Indian empire on the ruins of the Moghul power. Mr. Tancock, on the whole, does justice to the character of Warren Hastings; but he seems to us to misunderstand the true position of the Zemindars, just as Lord Cornwallis misunderstood it. They were middlemen, who contrived to get themselves taken for the owners of the soil by Government officials whose ideas of land tenure were limited to a strictly English groove, unrelieved by the study of archaic systems. We are glad to recognize in the three works above noticed fresh testimony to the great improvement which has taken place of late in the preparation of text-books for the younger generation of students.

The Sonnets of Michael Angelo Buonarroti and Tommaso Campanella. Now for the first time translated into Rhymed English. By John Addington Symonds. (Smith, Elder & Co.)
THIS is a real addition to our poetic literature. Michel-angelo's sonnets we already knew something about; but we can scarcely be said to have had a really poetic version of the series; and there was no likelihood of a satisfactory version being brought out until the original text, as garbled by the great-nephew of the poet, had been superseded by a text from Buonarroti's own manu-scripts. Of such a text Mr. Symonds is, we believe, the first in England to avail himself; and we congratulate him and English readers heartily on the result; for, having read the sonnets carefully, we cannot find one which is not a beautiful poem, or which betrays by any constraint of style its foreign origin : they might all have been written in English. Michelangelo, then, is here re-interpreted to us in a truly satisfactory manner ; but, beside this, we have placed before us a new poet of no mediocre sort. Very few of us knew anything about Tommaso Cam-panella beyond what Mr. Symonds had told us before ; but a more original and thoughtful poet it would be difficult to find, or, we may add, one more marked in indi-

promisingly grotesque at times in his imagery: a very daring Italian poet, in fact, teeming with spiritual life, and here rendered into excellent English poetry.

THE *Amateur's Kitchen Garden* (Groombridge & Sons) is another of Mr. Shirley Hibberd's instructive and valuable guides, of which it may be said by those who have studied his former works, "Good Master Pease-blossom, I shall desire you of more acquaintance." The present volume opens with the laying down of some principles for the formation of a kitchen garden, which are of so unattainable an altitude of excellence in our variable climate that the author at once proceeds to qualify them. His subsequent remarks will restore the reader's courage by showing him, from Mr. Hibberd's own experience, what may be got out of the most unpromising soil and unfavourable situation by careful attention to sound general principles, and the adaptation of them to particular cases. The work is well and liberally illustrated with drawings, plans, and diagrams, which add greatly to its utility as a book of reference on the numerous questions likely to perplex the amateur gardener.

IT will be no matter of surprise if, at the present time, Sir Garnet Wolseley's article on " England as a Military Power in 1854 and in 1878 " forms the most attractive feature of *The Nineteenth Century*. Sir Garnet writes : "The conditions to be fulfilled by our army are so totally different from those of the German army, that it is as unprofitable to draw any comparison between the systems upon which each is based, as it would be utterly and entirely impossible to apply that of Germany to England."—In the *Cornhill* Mr. W. G. Palgrave has a thoughtful article, " The Three Cities," admirably descriptive of Hong Kong —" Il Rè Galantuomo," by Mr. J. Montgomery Stuart, in *Macmillan*, has a mournful interest that will not be confined to these isles.

FROM Mr. C. Herbert we have received Parts I., II., and III. of the late Mr. Pinks's *History of Clerkenwell*. This reprint will be deservedly appealed to by all residents who take an interest in the history of their parish.

MESSRS. LONGMANS & Co. announce as ready for issue the new edition of *The Ritual of the Altar ;* it has been carefully revised by competent liturgists.

THE " DIES IRÆ " IN ENGLISH.—The Rev. C. F. S. WARREN (Ellerslie, Bexhill, Hastings) writes :—" I wish, with some idea of an essay or pamphlet on the subject, to collect as many English versions of the *Dies Iræ* as possible. I have copies, I believe, of all the well-known modern versions, and of two or three older or less common ones, that is, of the one in the Office of the B. V. M., 1687, and an anonymous one in the *Christian Remembrancer* (old series, vii. 315) ; also of those by Crashaw, Lord Roscommon, Scott, Chandler, Williams, Alford, Irons, Caswall, Lee, Singleton, Blew, Trench, Stanley, Hoskyns-Abrahall (*Christian Remembrancer*, Jan., 1868), and the one in the St. Andrew's Hymn-book, of which I should be glad to know whether it is an independent version or only Williams's greatly altered. Of these I have no copies: Sylvester (*Works*, 1621, p. 1214), Drummond, Worsley, *Irish Ecclesiastical Journal* (May and June, 1849), " *Dies Iræ, in Thirteen Original Versions*, by Abraham Coles, M.D., New York, 1860." And I shall be thankful for references to any other versions. I cannot of course *ask* any corre-

any book containing a version which I could be sent me by post, I would make th the book as soon as possible, and pay the registration if necessary."

Notices to Correspondents

ON all communications should be written address of the sender, not necessarily for pu as a guarantee of good faith.

SCOTUS may like to know that the word refers are not the operative words of ei contract or the ecclesiastical ordinance In canon law the prevailing doctrine is th are themselves the ministers of the sacrar valid, as was laid down by Pope Nich Rescript to the Bulgarians, " solo eorum quorum conjunctionibus agitur." Whe the word *worship* to signify "honour," *endow* to signify the second right whicl acquires by marriage, viz. maintenance. lated *worship* by " corpore meo te dignor," Bucer had previously rendered it in like meo corpore te honoro." Both sentences the oldest substratum of one of the old the Book of Common Prayer, and they ap have been said in the vernacular tongue.

T. CEALLAIGH.—Miss Nagle, the mothe Burke, was great-niece of Miss Ellen Nagl Sylvanus Spenser, the eldest son of the son, Richard, died on August 2, 1794, at th six, within a few days of his election as M. in succession to his father.

B. H. J. (*ante*, p. 67.)—MR. W. HOUGH Road, E.C.) writes :—" I have a copy of quired for by B. H. J., which he can see o

HIC ET UBIQUE.—" Yᵉ long towell all al is termed a " houselling cloth." Its u several churches at the present day. But 2ⁿᵈ S. i. 144 and 5ᵗʰ S. ii. 522.

W. M. SARGENT.—We have forwarded obligingly sent by you to our corresponden

GEO. A. M. (Pascal, Caracci, and othe sent no name and address.

ANGLAISE.—They are, in all probabilit the Clare family.

VAUGHAN.—Has our correspondent cons Lee's *Glimpses of the World Unseen* ?

KINGSTON.—The answer has been giv p. 39.

J. S. T.—*Chamois* is the usual spelling.

J. SMITH.—The latter, of course.

J. D. (Belsize Square.)—See p. 500 of ou

ERRATUM.—P. 136, col. 2, l. 13, for ' *South*.

NOTICE.

Editorial Communications should be addr Editor of ' Notes and Queries ' "—Adver Business Letters to " The Publisher "—at Wellington Street, Strand, London, W.C.

We beg leave to state that we decline t munications which, for any reason, we do r to this rule we can make no exception.

LONDON, SATURDAY, MARCH 16. 1878.

CONTENTS.—N° 220.

Notes.

"GARETH AND LYNETTE."

(Concluded from p. 123.)

CHAPTER III.

I have before observed that the story of Gareth and Lynette is an allegory—a Bunyan's *Pilgrim's Progress* in fact—in which life is a day; then comes the death struggle, then the victory and wedding with the Lamb. The four knights who keep the passages are night, morn, noon, and eve; the "day of life" consisting of the embryo state, youth, manhood, and old age, which keep man from the lady of Castle Perilous, or the bride which is in heaven. The story says that man's struggle with death endures a whole day; his whole life is a combat with moral and physical death. Tennyson makes it a single stroke, a momentary contest; then death is vanquished, and man rises into new life. There is a sense, no doubt, in which this is true; but if Gareth represents the Christian warrior fighting his way to heaven, his struggle with death is no single blow. The physical wrench of life is momentary, that is, the interval between life and death is a mathematical line without breadth or thickness, but that is not the death struggle suited to the allegory before us.

The Prose Story.—After Sir Gareth had conquered the four knights who kept the passages of Castle Perilous, the last and greatest combat remained to be achieved. It was that with Sir Ironside, the Red Knight of the Red Lands, who held the lady in captivity. Lionés is informed by the dwarf of all that had befallen the four knights, as "the bride" is informed by man's ministering angel of every action of his life; and the story goes on to say that while the dwarf was still speaking Gareth and Linet came in sight. At length they reached the sycamore tree (used for mummy coffins, as it was supposed), on which hung an ivory horn, the largest ever seen, and Gareth blew a blast so loud and long that the castle trembled, the knights started in their tents, and all the inmates of the castle rushed to the windows. Sir Ironside armed himself; blood-red was his armour, blood-red his shield and spear, blood-red the charger on which he rode. "Look!" said Linet, "yonder is my sister, and yonder the foe." Then curtseyed the Lady Lionés down to the ground, holding up her hands in supplication. With that Sir Ironside called out bravely, "Leave thy looking, sir knight; lo, here am I, and I warn you that lady is mine." After a few more words the damsel withdrew, and the two knights addressed themselves to battle. When they came together either smote other "so that the peytrels, sursengles, and croupers burst," and both combatants fell to the ground. Then drew they their swords and ran together like fierce lions; they reeled from side to side, they hewed each other's harness into splinters, and still they fought from morn till noon. At noon the Red Knight's strength was greatest. It went on increasing till that hour and then it waned. Awhile they rested to gain breath, and then fell to again, "trasing, raising, loyning, staggering, panting, bleeding"; now butting like two rams, now goring each other as two wild boars, now grovelling on the ground, now hurtling together, and thus fought they from noon to vesper-song. Their armour was so hacked that their naked bodies were seen through the huge gaps [sickness and decay]. At length the sword of Gareth fell from his hand and the knight lay prostrate, but Sir Ironside fell also. "Oh," said the damsel, "my sister is looking on, sobbing and weeping. I fear me her heart will break." On hearing this Sir Gareth took new courage, leapt to his feet, caught up his sword, and began the fight anew. So thick his strokes hailed down that Sir Ironside was vanquished, and Sir Gareth ran to unlace his helmet and slay him, when he yielded, and craved mercy. Death was overcome of victory, and the achievement was accomplished. [In the prose story the hero does not immediately marry the bride, because the notion of purgatory of necessity caused an interval; but after this lapse of time] Sir Gareth married the Lady Lionés, and King Arthur gave them great riches and many lands [an inheritance incorruptible, undefiled, and that fadeth not away].

Tennyson's Conclusion.—Instead of this grand

As Minerva sprang from the cleft head of Jove, so from the cleft head of Tennyson's knight, called Mors or Death, "issued the bright face of a blooming boy," who prayed Gareth to spare him, pleading that his three brothers (the history says four) bade him "stay all the world from Lady Lyonors, and never dreamed the passes would be past." Then, adds the poet, "sprang happier days from underground," and Sir Gareth wedded the damsel Lynette.

I confess I can never read this ending without a pang. Lynette of course represents what Bunyan calls the City of Destruction, or the carnal man within and without. As the flesh chides the Christian, and disparages all he says and does, so Lynette flouts Gareth, scandalizes him, disclaims him, and depreciates all his victories. To make the Christian soldier fight the fight and finish his course, and then marry Lynette instead of the true bride, is revolting (2 Pet. ii. 22), and spoils the allegory. The prose story says Sir Gaheris married Linet. Sir Gaheris was wedded to the world, but Sir Gareth had fought the good fight and his bride awaited him in Castle Perilous.

" Pictoribus atque poetis
Quidlibet audendi semper fuit æqua potestas.
Scimus. . . . .
Sed non ut placidis coeant immitia non ut
Serpentes avibus geminentur, tigribus agni,"

and to marry Gareth with Lynette is to wed a dove to a rattlesnake, a tiger to a lamb.

But bating the poetical and moral objection to this ending of the idyll, a far more serious objection lies against the poet for false coining. It seems to me that a poet has no more right to issue established fable with a wrong image and superscription than he has to falsify an historic fact. Who would tolerate a modern poet who should choose the tale of Troy divine and make Helen elope with Glaucus, and then add, "though Homer says she ran away with Paris"? Who would tolerate the marriage of Pyladês with Hermionê, though "he who told the tale in older times" says that she married Orestês? We are accustomed to think of Hecuba as Priam's wife and Penelopê as the wife of Ulyssês, and it offends our memory to reverse the order. If Tennyson wished to make a new story, he had the infinity of names which imagination can invent at his disposal; but the story of Gareth and Linet had been already appropriated, and if he wished to tell it anew, the main facts ought to be preserved. Once allow the gist of established facts to be tampered with, and it loses for ever its great charm, and all its value for purposes of illustration.

E. COBHAM BREWER.

And either......the devil, or throw him out
With wondrous potency."

In the Clarendon series Hamlet the editors i their note, pp. 189-90, after giving the variou conjectures as to the missing word, say : " It seem more probable that something is omitted which i contrasted with 'throw out,' and this may hav been 'lay' or 'lodge.'" Long before the public tion of this edition I had adopted the view tha the word had contrasted with "throw out," and s thought Bailey, and proposed "house." Bu neither "lay" nor "lodge" contrasts with "thro out," for the evil spirit was not laid in some hol or corner of, say, the liver or lights of the possesse person, and there confined harmless, but wa thrown out from that person, to be "laid" els where. One has heard of a spirit being "laid i the Red Sea"; but he was not laid there becaus he had committed his pranks there, but was "laid there after having been expelled or thrown ou from his chosen place or person.

It is quite true that Hamlet only intends t press abstinence from ill doing. But this is onl one half of the results of custom, and he firs speaks philosophically of the effects of custor generally ; in fact, he begins with the other hal the persistence in ill custom, for he calls it "th monster custom," and "of habits devil," whil afterwards both aspects are comprised and seen i "For custom can almost change the stamp (nature." Nor is this introduction of both effec —that of persistence and that of abstinence- superfluous or unnecessary, for it affords him double argument, or an argument of double forc Custom, says he, is a devil or an angel ; it ca almost change our nature. Continue your guilt- make a custom of it—and it will eventually gai such empiry over you that it will be most difficu —nay, impossible—to throw it off. Disuse it, (use abstinence, and each attempt will be mor easy, till at last you can throw off the temptatio with wondrous power. (And I take it that th "wondrous potency" belongs equally to both th opposite or contrasting verbs.) Founding on these considerations, I woul therefore read :—

"And either [throne] the devil, or throw him out."

"Throne in" is used in Coriolanus, and "throned seven times by Shakspere. I prefer it also to an synonymous word for three reasons : first, it i more forcible than any other ; secondly, the re petition of the letters gives us a very commo cause of elision by a compositor or copier : thr i found in the second syllable of the preceding wor "either," and the th in the succeeding "the" thirdly, the alliteration of the two emphatic an opposing words, " throne " and " throw off," is in the manner of Shakspere, and according to the fashion of the day.   BRINSLEY NICHOLSON.

P.S.—Since writing this I have read in a late number of " N. & Q." (5ᵗʰ S. ix. 103) MR. R. M. SPENCE'S suggestion " tether." But besides other objections, there is, first, the great and worse than unnecessary cutting out of " either," and, secondly, even when that is done, the impossibility of scanning the line as one of five feet.

A FEW NOTES ON " HAMLET."—
" Now to my word ;
It is ' Adieu, adieu ! I remember me.'
I have sworn 't."   Act i. sc. 5, l. 110.

The interpretation of " watch-word " is unsatisfactory. I can perceive no sense, literal or metaphorical, in which the Ghost's injunction is a watch-word to Hamlet.

Is it possible that " my word " may here mean my cue, in allusion to the practice of the stage ? The Ghost's last words are the signal to Hamlet to perform his part, as he had sworn. The interpretation is open to the objections that I can produce no parallel passage, and that if Shakespeare had meant "my cue," he would probably have used the technical term, as he has done in many other places ; but the idea is perhaps worth consideration. If inadmissible, there remains another conjecture, namely, that the allusion is to the word, mot, or motto, accompanying an heraldic achievement, in which sense it is used in Pericles, Act ii. sc. 2, ll. 20, 30, 33.

" Yes, by Saint Patrick, but there is, Horatio."
Act i. sc. 5, l. 136.

This has been objected to as being not only an anachronism, but out of keeping, in making the Danish prince asseverate by St. Patrick instead of St. Ansgarius. Tschischwitz (may good luck guide safely into type a name unpronounceable by English organs, except, perhaps, in the act of sneezing) points out, in relation to the passage, the connexion of St. Patrick with purgatory, but only to remark on the association of the idea of purgatory with that of "inexpiable crime," ignoring the fact that St. Patrick's Purgatory was not the general receptacle of departed souls, as recognized in Roman Catholic doctrine, but an earthly cavern, said to have been placed under his charge with peculiar privileges. Whoever, in true repentance, &c., remained therein for a day and a night was to behold the torments of the wicked ; and, after four-and-twenty hours of as much horror as the managers of the establishment could contrive for him, was promised exemption from purgatory after death. The reference to St. Patrick by Hamlet, fresh from the revelation just made by the Ghost of his state of torment, was therefore quite in keeping, if we can get over the anachronism which pervades the whole play. It assigns to Christian times, and even with a reference to the English Danegeld (iii. 1, 178), a story which, so far as it rests on the quasi-historical authority of Saxo Grammaticus and the Scalds from whom he derived his traditional facts, belongs to a period long anterior to the Christian era.

" To sleep ! perchance to dream ! Ay, there 's the rub."
Act iii. sc. 1, l. 65.

The commentators have not noticed, or not sufficiently noticed, the parallelism of Hamlet's soliloquy with § 32 of the Apology of Socrates. It was pointed out in a privately printed paper, entitled Shakespeare—Rara avis in terris, Juv., by K[enrick] P[rescott], 1774. The resemblance in the comparison of death to a sleep with or without dreams is very striking. The neglect of this illustration is the more remarkable as Addison must have had Hamlet's soliloquy in his mind in writing that of Cato, in which, on the authority of Plutarch, he has based the thoughts on an examination of the reasoning in Plato's works, in which this Apology of Socrates is to be found.

" When he himself might his quietus make
With a bare bodkin."   Act iii. sc. 1, l. 75.

As it has been thought worth while to discuss whether the primary meaning of this word is a dagger, or whether it is the name of a diminutive instrument contemptuously applied to a dagger, I venture (at the risk of a snub from some of your philological correspondents, who do not receive very graciously the attempts of qutsiders to trespass on their ground) to give my notion of the etymology of the word, which I take to be this. From Baldach, where was manufactured a textile fabric of gold thread and silk, the Italians, who imported it into Europe, called it Baldachino, which became in English Bawdekin, and Baudkin, and eventually cloth of Bodkin. The stiff material would require a special needle for its manipulation, which would naturally be called a Bodkin needle, and at length a Bodkin.

" As this fell sergeant, death
Is strict in his arrest."
Act v. sc. 2, l. 347.

This passage would not have needed a note had it not been the subject of a curious slip on the part of Lord Campbell. In his Shakespeare's Legal Acquirements Considered, following and amplifying a note of Ritson, who, like his lordship, should have known better, he says : " Hamlet represents that death comes to him in the shape of a sheriff's officer, as to take him into custody under a capias ad satisfaciendum." A sheriff's officer is not a sergeant. The functionaries present to Shakespeare's mind were the sergeants at arms, the executive officers of the two Houses of Parliament and of the High Court of Chancery. At best the passage is open to the criticism that there is a want of force and dignity in comparing an

To call this figure a " fell sergeant " is less objectionable ; and, at all events, an arrest under the direct authority of the highest courts of judicature in the kingdom conveys a less degrading idea than an arrest by a sheriff's officer on a *ca. sa.*, with its contemptible associations of the sponging-house and the gaol.　　　JOHN FITCHETT MARSH.

Hardwick House, Chepstow.

INDEX TO MATTERS ABOUT BELLS.—The following indexes to matters relating to church bells will }'o do^bt b^o interesting to many of your readers. They are reproduced from two volumes on the bells of Somerset by your old and valued correspondent, the Rev. H. T. Ellacombe :—

Index to Matters about Bells treated of in " Hittorpius de Divinis Officiis," fol., Paris, 1610.

P. 1202. Campana cum sonat, quasi populus ad placitum per præconem convocatur.

P. 1215 d. Campanæ loco tubarum introductæ in ecclesia.

P. 1201 d. Campanæ cur sonantur in processionibus.

P. 1181 c. Campanæ sunt prophetæ.

P. 1181 c. Campanarum significatio.

P. 1218 d. Campanarum sonus quid denotat.

P. 1218 c. Campanas per signa dantur, quæ olim per tubas.

P. 1218 d. Campanæ ubi primum repertæ.

P. 1218 d. Campanæ unde hoc nomen sortitæ.

P. 665 c. d. Campanæ Signa vocantur.

P. 665 c. Campanæ a Campania, et nolæ a Campaniæ civitate sic vocatæ.

P. 276 b., 369 b. c. Campanæ nunc, quod in veteri testimonio, tubæ.

P. 396 b. Campanas movere presbyterorum munus.

P. 1181 c. Campanæ quid mystice significant.

P. 147 c., 471 a. b. Campanæ triduo ante pascha silent: Lignorum sono populus vocatur.

P. 910. Campanæ nunc populum convocant, sicut olim tubæ.

P. 859 c. Campanæ predicatores significant.

P. 859 c. Campanarum classicum trinum in diebus festis.

P. 954 b. Campanæ cur non sonant tempore passionis domini.

P. 1210 a. Campanarium quod in alto locatur quid designat.

Index to Matters about Bells treated of in the " Commentaries on the Decretals of Gregory IX.," by Em. Gonzalez Tellez, Venice, 1756.

Tom. i. p. 132, note 3. Campanarum pulsatio semper fuit prohibita tempore interdicti.

Tom. i. p. 221, n. 4. Campanarum pulsatio in receptione episcoporum et abbatum.

Tom. i. p. 443, n. 3. Campanarum origo, et a quo tempore earum usus in ecclesia cæperit.

Tom. i. p. 444, n. 7. Campanæ certis horis ad ecclesiæ officia peragenda pulsantur.

Tom. ii. p. 180, n. 6. Campanarum pulsatio in receptione episcoporum, et principum secularium.

Tom. v. p. 320, n. 6. Campanæ apud antiquos monacho perforatæ, vel fractæ fuerunt, et quare.

Tom. v. p. 328, n. 7, 8. Campanæ quare in Oratorii monachorum poni non debeant.

Tom. iii. p. 100, n. 2. Campanulæ usum in elevation sacratissimæ hostiæ quis primus instituerit.

Tom. iii. p. 574, n. 3. Campanulæ pulsatio ad eleva tionem et delationem SS. Eucharistiæ, ad infirmos, al ecclesia præcepta.

H. Y. N.

HAYLEY THE POET.—The following letter from William Hayley, the friend of Cowper, addressed to Joseph Hill, Esq., and accompanying a copy o Cowper's translation of *Milton's Latin and Italian Poems*, which was dedicated to Mr. Hill, is,] think, worth preserving :—

"April 3, 1808.

" My Dear Sir,—You gratified me extremely by the celerity and kindness of your letter concerning our anxious Editor of Homer. I have written to warn him against making a too hasty bargain with a bookseller In his hymeneal bargain he cannot be too rapid, for he will gain a treasure indeed. I have had a perfect ac count of the lovely Damsel from one of her old intimate friends. May Heaven render this amiable pair as per manently happy as their friends can wish !

" And now, my dear Sir, I have to entreat your pardor for a liberty that you will see I have taken with your name, without asking your leave.

" If I have sinn'd against your known Modesty, pray recollect with indulgence that trespasses against modesty even of the finest female texture are often allowed to be justified by warmth and sincerity of affection.

" Having loved Cowper as I did *intensely*, it were im possible for me not to regard, and not to wish, that the public might witness my regard, for his most approved friend.

" To gratify a few select individuals with an early sight of the Milton, before any copies of it can be pre pared for circulation at St. Paul's, I dispatch a few books from Chichester. Have the kindness to forward the copy directed to Theodora, and do me the favour to accept the other as a little token of kind remembrance from your frequently obliged

"and ever affectionate

" HERMIT."

The book was printed at Chichester, but published by Johnson in St. Paul's Churchyard, London.

EDWARD SOLLY.

HANNIBAL'S SOFTENING THE ROCKS.—The following passage from Pole's new *Life of Sir William Fairbairn* (Longmans, 1877), p. 59, seems so strikingly illustrative of the well-known account in Livy, xxi. 37, as to deserve a place in " N. & Q." Fairbairn himself is the narrator, and is describing the way in which his father many years before had cleared the surface of a new farm, on the banks of the Conan, near Dingwall. What ever may be said of Livy, no one will be disposed to accuse the great engineer of romancing :—

"The whole surface of the farm was nearly covered with whins and rocks, and to remove these my father adopted an ingenious method. Having cut down the brushwood and piled it upon the large blocks of whinstone, the fuel was ignited, and, the stones becoming heated to almost a red heat, the ashes were ·cleared away, and a small stream of water being applied from a bottle, the rapid condensation, or rather contraction, caused a fracture of the rock in any required direction."

J. H. L.

HEADINGS OF LETTERS.—In the sixteenth and seventeenth centuries it was still by no means unusual to place at the top of letters and documents a sacred name, monogram, or short sentence. Shakespeare refers to the custom in his *Henry VI.* (part ii. Act iv. sc. 2) :—

"*Jack Cade.* What is thy name ?
Clerk. Emmanuel.
Dick. They used to write it on the top of letters."

A list of such would be curious. I append a few from the original MSS. :—

"Emmanuel" appears at the head of the accounts of the chamberlains of the borough of Leicester for the year 1578-9, and several subsequent years : also at the head of a letter addressed by Alderman Robert Heyricke, of Leicester, to his brother Sir Wm. Heyricke, of London, dated April 8, 1618.

"Jesus" is placed at the head of the accounts of the churchwardens of Melton - Mowbray, Leicestershire, made Dec. 8, 3 Ed. VI.

"I.H.C." heads the accounts of the churchwardens of St. Martin's parish, Leicester, for the year 1546.

"I.H.C." and "I.N.R.I.," the first monogram within a shield, the second on a label passing through the upper part of the letter H, head a rent roll of the Guild of Corpus Christi, in Leicester, for the year 1535.

"Laus Deo" is placed at the top of a letter addressed by Mr. John Bonnyt, of Leicester (a young man), to his friend William Heyricke, then in London, on Dec. 5, 1579.

"Salutem in Chr'o" is affixed to a letter written to the same gentleman by his nephew the Rev. Tobias Heyricke, of Houghton, Leicestershire, and dated Jan. 14, 1616-7.

Some years ago, in my *Chronicle of St. Martin's Church, Leicester,* I suggested the inquiry whether these sacred words, &c., were used to attest the truth and correctness of what followed ; whether they were used as a kind of benediction by the writer ; or whether their use was only an instance of the blending of the religious and secular which was so prominent a feature in all the relations of life in past times. Perhaps some readers of "N. & Q." may have something to say on that point.   THOMAS NORTH, F.S.A.

THE PASTON LETTERS.—There is a curious mistake or misreading in Mr. Gairdner's excellent edition of the *Paston Letters*, vol. iii. p. 212 : " Ther is com up ter [there ?] at Caster v or vj barell." The editor's query is an odd slip, especially as the phrase is repeated in the very next letter on the opposite page : "v barell ter, iiij copil oris and gret plante [plenty] of wreke of the schyppe." The word is barrels of *tar*. If an illustration were needed, compare "*tery* and *abyd*," *i.e.* "*tarry* and abide," p. 313.   O. W. TANCOCK.

AN ANCIENT LEGEND.—The publication of a history of Rothwell, a place possessing considerable interest, though strangely neglected by antiquaries in the past, has brought out additional information. My attention has been directed to the fact that the Rev. John Ray, naturalist, when visiting this quarter, records in his *Itinerary*, dated Aug. 3, 1661, the following curious legend. I quote the exact words :—

" Then we rode through a bushet or common, called 'Rodwell Hake' (Rothwell Haigh), two miles from Leeds, where (according to the vulgar tradition) was once found a stag with a ring of brass about its neck, having this inscription :—

' When Julius Cæsar here was king,
About my neck he put this ring ;
Whosoever doth me take,
Let me go for Cæsar's sake.' "

It is a well ascertained fact that the great Roman general did not penetrate so far north. Possibly the animal in question may have been chased from the southern parts of Britain until it reached this uncultivated open region, as yet probably untrodden by the Roman soldier.

This tale, floating in the minds of the inhabitants of old Rodwell (Rothwell) some 217 years ago, was then inexplicable, and, if there was any truth or foundation in the incident, must have existed, and been handed down from generation to generation, for more than a thousand years previously. It has now died out. If, however, any of your readers can throw light upon the subject, show its possibility or absurdity (though I believe there is some kind of truth even in legends), I shall be gratified.

THE AUTHOR OF THE "HISTORY OF ROTHWELL."

Elm Cottage, Rothwell, near Leeds.

THE RED HAND OF ULSTER : CALVERLEY OF CALVERLEY.—Every reader of "N. & Q." will doubtless know the tradition connected with the red hand on the shield of the Holt family of Lancashire (see Timbs's *Ancestral Stories*), but I have nowhere seen it recorded that a similar tradition attaches to the paternal coat of the Calverleys of Calverley, Yorks.

Walter Calverley, Esq., in 1605, murdered two of his children, and attempted the murder of his wife and other child, "at nurse." This became the subject of the play, *The Yorkshire Tragedy,* falsely (?) attributed to Shakespeare. Walter's great-grandson, Walter of Calverley and Esholt, was created a baronet by Queen Anne, Dec. 11, 1711. The tradition obtains that in consequence of the murder the family are required to wear the "bloody hand" on their shield. Many are the inquiries for it by persons coming from a distance

"Historic Certainties ; or, the Chronicles of Ecnarf."—I have only lately noticed, and some other readers of "N. & Q." may not have done so, that the authorship and object of this work have been stated in print. In the article "Miracles" in Smith's *Dict. of the Bible*, the present Bishop of Killaloe, Dr. W. Fitzgerald, as "W. F.," after the mention of Abp. Whately's *Historic Doubts*, remarks, "the argument of which the writer of this article has attempted to apply to the objections of Strauss in *Historic Certainties ; or, the Chronicles of Ecnarf*, Parker [Son & Bourn], Lond., 1862." There had been earlier editions, for there was a "new edition" in 1861.

Ed. Marshall.

HYDROPHOBIA.—Perhaps the following quotation from Dr. Kitchener's *Traveller's Oracle* may serve to show that the present raid against dogs is not a novel one :—

"*Imprimis, Beware of dogs.*—There have been many arguments pro and con the dreadful Disease their bite produces—it is enough to know that multitudes of Men, Women, and Children, have died in consequence of being bitten by Dogs. What does it matter whether they were the victims of Bodily Disease or Mental Irritation? The life of the most humble Human Being is of more value than all the Dogs in the World—dare the most brutal Cynic say otherwise? There is no real remedy but cutting the part out immediately. If the bite be near a large Blood-vessel, that cannot always be done, nor when done, however well done, will it always prevent the miserable Victim from dying the most dreadful of Deaths !

"Well might St. Paul tell us 'Beware of Dogs,' First Epistle to Philippians, chap. iij. v. 2.

"*Therefore*, never travel without a good tough Black Thorn in your Fist, not less than three feet in length, in which may be marked the Inches, & so it may serve for a Measure."

Surely Dr. Kitchener's advice is wise, but his yard stick serves to show us, with his remarks thereon, how great our distance of just fifty years is from his time of coaches, and valets, and pistols, and self-imposed frights.   A. Harrison.
St. Leonards.

THE MAN OF THE SEA.—In a recent work on the *Land of the Incas*, full of interesting and suggestive matter, there is an illustration, taken from some old Peruvian palace or temple, of a combat between "The Man of the Earth and the Man of the Sea," in which the latter appears as a monstrous crab from the waist upwards. It is curious, as bearing upon the author's theory of the origin of the Peruvian race, that when in China I purchased (at Pekin) a very beautiful and curious little phial of porcelain, on which a similar combat was depicted, the crab-man being identical.

Sp.

on family matters of only private interest, to affix their names and addresses to their queries, in order that the answers may be addressed to them direct.]

"PHILOSOPHY IN SPORT."—The recent death of George Cruikshank revives (if it were possible) the interest felt in his multitudinous designs, especially those that were produced in the early and mid years of his long and honoured life. These would include his illustrations to the three volumes, *Philosophy in Sport made Science in Earnest*. This work was published anonymously. On the title-page of vol. i. of my copy is written in pencil, by some previous possessor of the volumes (which came to me uncut !), "By Dr. Paris." Am I right in assuming that this was the Dr. John Ayrton Paris who afterwards became President of the College of Physicians? He is only mentioned in Olphar Hamst's *Handbook of Fictitious Names* under the "titlonym" of "A Physician," and as author of *A Guide to the Mount's Bay and the Land's End*, second edit., 1824. He had practised at Penzance. How many editions has *Philosophy in Sport* gone through? My copy is a "new edition," 1831. On referring to a list of works illustrated by George Cruikshank—made by me through very many years—I see that a sixth edition was published in 1846 ; another edition (query what ?) is mentioned in 1853 ; another edition, probably the first, is dated 1821, and was offered in a second-hand book catalogue for 15s. A copy of Cruikshank's "Bank Note" was recently offered in a similar catalogue for 2l. 2s.   CUTHBERT BEDE.

HERALDIC.—I have seen the following coats of arms in fifteenth century glass, and desire information respecting the bearers, who, I have reason to believe, were connected with Worcester or Worcestershire :—

1. Arg., within a bordure wavy or and sa., on a fesse of the third betw. three cocks' heads erased, of the same, wattled of the second, a mitre ppr.

2. Az., a bend or betw. six martlets of the same.

3. Gu., a fesse or betw. six pears pendent of the same.

4. Parted per pale baron and femme, 1, Gu., a chevron argent ; 2 (nearly destroyed), Arg., a fess sa. ?

5. Quarterly, 1, England ; 2 and 3, France modern ; 4 (much defaced, but apparently), quarterly, 1 and 2, England ; 3 and 4, France modern.

I think that No. 1 may be the arms of Alcock, Bishop of Worcester, who was translated from that see to Ely in 1486. His tomb is to be seen in Ely Cathedral, on the north side of the chapel which he built. "Upon the tomb itself," says Murray, "and in the glass of the east window is the bishop's rebus or device—a cock on a globe. His shield of arms (three cocks' heads) is over the south door." I should like to see this coat rather more vividly "in my mind's eye" than the above notice enables me to do. I have a note—I think from Robson's *British Herald*—that Alcock, Bishop of Ely, bore Ar., a fesse betw. three cocks' heads erased sable, within a bordure gules charged with eight crowns or.

No. 2 probably belongs to some family of Tempest.

No. 5 is a most curious achievement. It is the only example I can remember of England taking the *pas* of France modern—heraldically, of course, I mean.   ST. SWITHIN.

THOMAS FAMILY.—Can any reader of "N. & Q." give me particulars of the biography of the following persons?—

1. John Philip Thomas, queen's lessee of mills at Kenchurch, and occupant of the demesne lands of Grosmont manor, Monmouthshire, in 1591.

2. Evan Thomas, of Swansea, South Wales; b. *circa* 1580, d. 1650 (?). Was he the E. Thomas who, in 1657, published a bitter attack on the Quakers, called "*An Exact History of the Life of James Naylor* : to be sold at his (Thomas's) house in Green Arbor"? Or was he the Evan Thomas who was a member of the Owennydion or Bardic College of Glamorgan in 1620?

3. Philip Thomas, who was in the East India Company's service in 1621, possibly was a messenger of the Commissioners for Charitable Uses in 1638, and was in partnership with one Devonshire, at Bristol, Eng., before 1651 ; previous to that year, probably before 1645, he married Sarah Harrison, and in 1651 he came to Lord Baltimore's province of Maryland, in America, with his wife and three children, Philip, Sarah, and Elizabeth. His first land grant is dated Feb. 19, 1651-2. Having printed a history of the family to which these Thomases belong, I am anxious to get additional information for a proposed supplement of corrections and additions.

LAWRENCE BUCKLEY THOMAS.
54, M'Culloh Street, Baltimore, U.S.A.

COLETI ÆDITIO.—Is any edition of the *English Accidence* drawn up by Dean Colet, and found prefixed to early copies of Lily's *Grammar*, known to exist of an earlier date than 1534? There is one of that date in the Library of Magdalene College, Cambridge ; and Knight, in his *Life of Colet*, refers to one printed in the same year by Wynkyn de Worde. Can any one say where a copy of this latter is now to be met with? Knight's description of it as "inter MSS. regios" in the Public Library at Cambridge has proved to be of no avail.   J. H. L.

PAPAL MEDALS.—1. Bronze, size 18. Obv., CLEMEN . XII . PONT . MAX . AN . III ; half figure of the Pope in benediction. Rev., a fortified palace in the sea being attacked by two or three vessels, a town in the distance on cliffs ; leg., PUBLICÆ . INCOLVMITATIS . PRESIDIO ; in the exergue, DORICÆ . VRBIS . LŒMOCOMIVM . 1734. 2. Bronze, size 13. Obv., MDIII . PIVS . III . PONT . MAX ; bust to the left. Rev., the Pope seated, with priest on each side, giving blessing to a man kneeling on one knee with hand on his heart, beside him on the paved floor a flag ; leg., SVB . VMBRA . ALARVM . TVARVM ; date in exergue. I am desirous of discovering the reasons for striking these two medals, both of which are excellent works of art, especially the second, and as Francisco Piccolomini was Pope only for about a month, it is probable that it was struck by his successor.   NEPHRITE.

A CANDLE PRESENTED AS A TOKEN OF SYMPATHY.—In the "True Story of the Cenci Family" (*ante*, p. 141) the following occurs :—

"He [*i.e.* Bertolotti] has found entries in the archives of the Company of the Stigmata which show that in the following March some of the members visited Bernardo at Tordinona, and presented him with a candle weighing one pound as a token of sympathy and gratitude for the interest he had shown in their society."

Is the presentation of a candle as a token of sympathy and gratitude made elsewhere than in Italy? Any information about this curious custom I should feel much obliged for.
R. P. HAMPTON ROBERTS.

"AN UNLAWFUL COTTAGE."—Among the House of Lords MSS. calendared in vol. iv. of the Historical Manuscripts Commissioners' *Report*, p. 33, is a petition from Richard Allibone, from which it appears that Allibone was charged with letting "an unlawful cottage." What is an unlawful cottage? It would seem that the premises were really his own, for Dr. Clark, the person before whom he was called, ordered them to be leased to another person.   CORNUB.

THE JENNENS CASE.—I do not propose to question either the soundness or the justice of the law as laid down by my Lord Coleridge in the renewed attempt, reported in the papers of the 5th inst., to prove heirship in this historical case. I presume, however, that some distinction would be drawn between the rights to *real* property after an undisturbed (if it can be said to have been "undisturbed") possession of seventy-three years, and the distribution of *personalty*. Whatever claim the present holders may have to the real estate, they surely do not include all those who could have claimed to participate in the enormous personal property. Who are the heirs? The late Mr. Collen, Portcullis Pursuivant of Arms, devoted

the case. What has become of Mr. Collen's papers? ALFRED SCOTT GATTY.

EMBLEMS.—I have recently purchased a most remarkable work of art, of which the following is a brief description, as it may give some correspondent who can answer my query an idea of the *special* meaning of the emblems I wish to have explained, and which have, I believe, various significations or interpretations. The work is executed on a single piece of thick paper four feet long by three feet wide, and contains (exquisitely drawn and illuminated in gold and colours) between sixty and seventy separate pictures illustrating passages in the Old Testament. It also contains a number of masonic emblems, 50,000 letters (forming Biblical texts), and innumerable scrolls, borders, &c., beautifully drawn and coloured. Every bit of the work is done by hand, and at the bottom are the signatures of L. Gilder and E. Detas; no date. It contains the following emblems, which I wish interpreted:—A peacock opposite a lamb with banner, an owl opposite an eagle, a lion opposite a stag. I hope to be able to get a photograph taken successfully of this extraordinary and unique specimen of skill and patience, and shall be glad to supply any readers of "N. & Q." who wish to form an idea of the whole work with copies at about cost price. GEO. MACKEY.
4, Cherry Street, Birmingham.

GAINSBOROUGH v. ZOFFANY.—I have a picture which for two generations has been attributed to Gainsborough. It bears on the back an inscription: "The Lady Maria Clapham, daughter to Sir Thomas Clapham, of Yorkshire, wife of Lord Visc^t Shrievesboro', of Shropshire." Authorities tell me that the picture is by Zoffany. It represents a lady who, beyond question, has negro blood in her veins. The tradition in my family runs to the effect that there was once a male figure, supposed to be her husband, to whom the lady is offering a casket. This male figure was cut out and destroyed by the gentleman for whom the picture was painted, and the lady's portrait was sold.
I should be glad to know any particulars relating to Sir Thomas Clapham, his daughter, or Lord Viscount Shrievesboro' of Shropshire.
FREDK. BOYLE.

MELLON.—Can some of your readers solve the following queries?—1. As to the origin or history of naming St. Mellings House, Cornwall, N.W. of Saltash. 2. St. Mellans, Monm., N.E. of Car-

Donegal. 7. Clonmellan, co. West·
land. 8. M. de la Melloniere, briga
French troops, who with five battalions
the town of Drogheda to surrender at
of the Boyne. Is it known where he w
and if he left any descendants? GEO.
335, E. 16 Street, City, New York.

RHODES FAMILY.—In what paris·
counties of Notts, York, and Derby w
of this name seated in the sixteenth
teenth centuries? The race is an ancie
its name has been spelled, at various
Rodes, Rhodes, Roods, Rhoads, Roads,
B.

GRIMALDI.—He was an Italian acto
related to Joseph Grimaldi the clo
known where he lived in London? It
at the time of the Gordon riots, when
to protect their windows and ex
Protestantism, were wont to write "N
in large letters on their doors, tl
sarcastically put up "No Religion."
C. A
Mayfair.

"THE CRYPT" was published in 182
The editor was the Rev. Peter Hal
papers in this magazine were writt
Meredith. Who were the other contril

THE "ATHALIAH" AND "ESTHER" ·
—Have these, as acted at the Théâtr
been performed on the public stage in
any time? R.

MILTON'S "ANIMADVERSIONS UPO·
MONSTRANT'S DEFENCE AGAINST SME·
—1. "You wanted but hey pass to
your transition *like a mystical man of ·*
(Bohn's edit. *Prose Works*, vol. iii. p.
this a proverb? 2. "A device ridicul
to make good that old wife's tale of a ce
of England that sunk at Charing-cross ·
at Queenhith" (*ibid.*, p. 73). Wha·
Milton refer to? 3. "Scarce be ·
varnish a *vizard of Modona*" (*ibid.*, p.
is the reference? WILLIAM GEORG·
1, Alfred Terrace, Hillhead, Glasgow.

AN OLD BOOK.—I have a small volu·
ing three separate treatises. I give
title-pages below. The book is in ·
dition. What is its value?
1. "The Booke of Husbandry very P·
Necessary for all Maner of Persons. Made

Author Fitzherberd, and now lately Corrected and Amended, with divers Additions put thereunto. Anno Domini 1568. Imprinted at London by John Awdely, dwellyng in little Britayn Streete without Aldersgate." Fol. lxix (with a table of contents).
2. "Xenophons Treatise of Housholde. Anno M.D.LVII." Fol. lxiiii. "Imprinted at London in Paules Churche Yarde at the Signe of the Lambe by Abraham Wele" (no table of contents).
3. "Surveyinge. Anno Domini 1567" (in the scroll below, 1534). Fol. 67 (with a table of contents, but no printer's name).

C. M. BARROW, B.A.

THE JEWS.—Were Janin, Halévy, Prévost Paradol, Giuglini, and Grisi, and are Rubinstein, Wagner, and Patti, of the Jewish race? D.

AUTHORS OF BOOKS WANTED.—
The Chimney Corner, or Auld Langsyne: being Sketches of Scottish Manners, Customs, and Characters. By A. T. B., Scot, Cor. Memb. S.A.S. Edin., 1866.
J. G.

Replies.

ST. GEORGE.
(5th S. viii. 447 ; ix. 189.)

"Whatever may be thought of the real origin of the story of St. George the Martyr of Cappadocia, there can be no doubt that it has been incorporated with an Arian legend of the Arian George, Bishop of Alexandria, murdered by the Alexandrian mob, and that from this union has sprung the story in its present popular form. In this legend (told at length in the Acta Sanctorum, April 23, pp. 120-123) the contest of St. George is for the Empress Alexandra (in whom we can hardly fail to see the type of the Alexandrian Church), and his enemy is 'the magician Athanasius,' who, besides the identification resulting from his name and his repute for magic, is further indicated to be the celebrated theologian by being called the friend of Magnentius. As time rolls on, and the legend grows in dimensions, George becomes the champion on his steed, rescuing the Egyptian princess, and Athanasius the wizard sinks into the prostrate dragon."—Lectures on the Eastern Church, p. 244.
A. P. S.

HERALDIC: HUTCHINSON FAMILY.
(5th S. viii. 268, 379 ; ix. 79.)

I can easily answer the doubts and uncertainties of MR. SARGENT. In endeavouring to ascertain the correctness of a coat of arms, it is of course necessary to go to the fountain head. As he is inquiring for particulars of the Hutchinson family, I may perhaps briefly say that the reputed founder of the family in England was one Uitonensis (this is evidently a Latin form), who accompanied Harfager, King of Norway, in his invasion of England in the vicinity of the river Humber in 1066 (see Burke's Landed Gentry, in v. H.) ; that at the battle of Stanford Bridge, near York, which took place on or about September 25 that year, Harold, King of England, encountered the Norwegians and beat them, with great slaughter ; but as William of Normandy landed on the coast of Sussex on the 29th of the same month, Harold was constrained to leave before he had fully settled his affairs with the Norwegians, as described by William of Malmsbury and all the chief historians of that period, and hurry south to oppose the Normans at Hastings, where he met his death. Of the Norwegians in the north, thus quietly left to themselves, some returned to Norway, but many resolved to settle in England, and amongst these Uitonensis is believed to have gone to Middleham, or Bishop Middleham, in Yorkshire. This much of the early account rests mostly on tradition, as appears in Burke, except that the circumstances of the invasion and movements of the mixed host of the Scandinavians are detailed in the pages of credible history. We do not stand upon firm ground until we come down to the year 1282, when Barnard Hutchinson, of Cowlam, in the county of York, heads the authentic pedigree of the family given in the quarto edition of The Memoirs of Colonel Hutchinson the Regicide. I suppose I may call this pedigree authentic, inasmuch as on the second page of the preface it is stated to have been originally traced by Henry St. George, King of Arms. From Barnard Hutchinson descended John, James, William, Anthony, William, William, and William, this last being described as of Wykome Abbey, co. Ebor. There were several offshoots and younger branches which I need not dwell upon here. My only business is to trace the branch which went to Boston, in Massachusetts, in the reign of Charles I. I have stopped at the third William, of Wykome Abbey, who lived in Queen Elizabeth's time, and here this pedigree stops with him, and carries on only the younger branch of Anthony, which produced the regicide. And now I come to the first grant of armorial bearings. Although amongst the most ancient and the most savage nations it has been the custom for warriors to paint devices on their shields, it was not until the Middle Ages, in Europe, that heraldry became erected into a science and an honour. It was a science from the scrupulousness of the laws by which it was governed, the reasons for its adoption, the advantages of its use in a barbarous age, or the intricacy of its regulations ; and it was an honour as coming direct from the sovereign, and conferred upon such as distinguished themselves in battle, or otherwise did good service to king and country. And during the period when no man dare bear coat armour unless it had been regularly granted to him, or unless he had properly inherited it from one who had, heraldry

"tinker, tailor, 'pothecary, or thief," who makes money enough behind the counter to set up "a one-horse shay," may look about amongst the richest of his neighbours of the same name, copy his coat of arms, paint it on the panel of his "shanderidan," and then sport it as his own. If a coat of arms has been used by a family from the period of the early years of George III. it may be presumed to be genuine and that they have a right to it; dating since that period, it may be looked upon with suspicion. A coat of arms, however, is merely a sort of hieroglyphic a man's family name, borne by himself and all his male descendants only (unless male heirs fail, when females succeed), and lawfully begotten, of course. That is the simplest way of putting it.

When I was a child, I can recollect seeing an old coat of arms, framed and glazed, hanging against the wall in my late father's private room. The same now hangs in the room where I am writing; and as it is my authority for the family armorial bearings, of undoubted age, and, as I believe, the strongest argument that any of my name can produce, I will describe it. The vellum on which the painting is executed measures 11¼ × 8¼ inches; the red and blue colours employed have stood well, especially the red, the blue being slightly slate colour, and where the gilding has worn off a green ground appears underneath, which may have been purposely placed there, or may be a stain given to the vellum by the vehicle used as gold size by the artist. There is a squire's helmet of large size above the shield and supporting the crest, and the ducal coronet of the latter is set off with five full strawberry leaves, instead of three strawberry leaves and two points, as it is the custom to depict the ducal coronet in modern heraldry; and, lastly, there is a label underneath the shield, but, remember, there is no motto. I may further add that the mantling, in red and white, is very profuse, filling up all the picture to the frame. Beneath this achievement there is a description of it in the quaint language of the old heralds, which is quite as valuable as a guide and as an authority as the painting itself. It runs thus :—

"He Beareth, parted per Pale, gules & Azure, a Lyon Rampant Argent, Armed & Langued or: yᵉ feild Charged wᵗʰ Cross Crossletts of yᵉ 4ᵗʰ: for yᵉ Crest a Cockatrice azure, Crestᵉᵈ, Weloped, & Armed Gules. Issuing out of A Ducall Crown or: & is Borne by the name of Hutchinson of Linconᵗⁿshire."

Guided by this description, no person who is conversant with even the merest rudiments of English heraldry could emblazon the arms wrong; and

"charged with cross crossletts," not semée. The number of cross crosslets does not appear to be material. In this old coat the number is seven on the dexter, gules, red, right, or in front of the lion, and six on the sinister, azure, blue, or behind him, making thirteen in all. I look upon it merely as a matter of convenience to the artist how many may be packed in without overcrowding. I have found eight a convenient number where the lion is a good size. This painting on vellum appears to have been folded and kept in a book before it was framed, as there is a crease across the middle. It is still in the frame that held it in my childhood days, and presenting the same appearance. A few years ago, fearing that worms and worm-holes would work entire destruction to it, I dosed it well with benzine, which is said to be a good thing to arrest the progress of these destroyers. Wishing to know something of the early history of this painting, and believing that it is likely to have been done for Edward Hutchinson, who lived at Alford, in Lincolnshire, for forty-five years, and was buried there Feb. 14, 1631, and that it was taken to America by his eldest son William in 1634, and brought back by the Governor in 1774, I took it some years ago to the Heralds' College for examination. From the fact of its being described as " Borne by the name of Hutchinson of Lincolnshire," it may be inferred that the bearer was the only person of that name then in the county, or else that he was the principal one. I learned at the Heralds' College that a coat of arms similar to my painting was granted to Edward Hutchinson, of Wickham, in Yorkshire, July 4, 1581. The following is a verbatim copy of the statement given me by Mr. Planché :— " Arms as in Painting, granted to Edward Hutchinson of Wickham, Yorkshire, by T. Flower, Norroy, July 4, 1581. J. P. Planché, Rouge Croix, April 30th, 1855." Now Edward of Yorkshire received his grant in 1581, and Edward of Lincolnshire baptized his eldest son on the 14th of August, 1586 (as I have seen in the Alford register), being a space of only five years, which is coming pretty close. I am not contending that the two Edwards are one and the same person, but it is hard to escape the inference that the one at Alford was the son or grandson of the one at Wickham. If so, we ascertain the period when this branch left Yorkshire, and became "Hutchinson of Lincolnshire." The heralds did not deny that my painting might be as old as the period under consideration, though they were not certain. They declared it to have been evidently done by a professional artist; that it was not the original painting (which perhaps they have), but that it was an early copy of it. It has long been my wish to look up the evidence of the supposed link between the two Edwards, but a check in not yet having discovered the will of Edward of Alford, and too many other irons in the fire, have prevented. This Edward of Alford had four sons: William, who went to America in 1634 ; Samuel, who died a bachelor of seventy-seven ; Richard, the ancestor of the Earls of Donoughmore ; and John, who may have been the parent of such of the name as still favour that county.

Well, so much for the old painting. The next modicum of evidence I have to produce is a large silver tankard, with handle and cover, which was the private drinking mug of Thomas Hutchinson (born in 1674), the governor's father, with the family arms on an oval shield, surrounded by Jacobean foliage and scroll-work, engraved on the front of it. The rampant lion has the end of his tail incurvate, according to a practice not uncommon with the old heralds, but the one on the vellum has his tail excurvate, as most usually represented. And here we have nine cross crosslets, the lowest one being in the middle, on the pale. In the early days of the colony at Boston, Massachusetts, church plate was probably not easily procurable, so he gave this tankard to the Old North Church for the sacramental wine, and there it remained until about 1870, when, owing to alterations that were being carried out in the city, the church plate was offered for sale, and the tankard was purchased by a descendant of the governor, when it was removed to England, where it now is, and, I am happy to say, once more restored to the family.

Next comes a seal which belonged to Governor Hutchinson. It has twelve cross crosslets. Here is the very mistake in it with respect to dexter and sinister, made by the engraver, to which I have alluded above ; and that this really is an error and absolutely wrong is plain from this fact, namely, that it does not correspond with more ancient authorities actually in the governor's possession.

On turning to the American engraving of the governor in the *New Eng. Hist. and Gen. Reg.*, I see that the shield under the portrait bears eleven cross crosslets, and the coronet has five full strawberry leaves, like the vellum painting.

A word about mottoes, and I have done. Although mottoes may not be subjected to the same strict rules that regulate the rigid accuracy of the charges and tinctures, it would be well that those who assume mottoes should always keep to the same ; and it would be still better if people did not sometimes filch the mottoes of their neighbours. I do not see that any of the name ever used a motto until the time of the American revolution, a century ago, when the governor, for

his unflinching and disinterested loyalty, having twice declined a baronetcy offered to him by the king (Aug. 15 and Nov. 5, 1774), and suffered the loss of all his property in America by riot and confiscation, assumed the following, "Libertatem colo, licentiam detestor," and this is engraved on his seal. On the American engraving the motto given is "Non sibi, sed toti"; but I do not know any authority for this, or whence it came. "Fortiter gerit crucem" belongs to the Donoughmore branch. The Salem branch has adopted the words "Gerit crucem fortiter," which is a mere transposition of the preceding ; but no link to connect the two branches has yet been discovered beyond probability.

To distinguish different offshoots as connected more or less nearly with the main stock, heralds make slight alterations in the tinctures or charges of armorials ; thus, in the coat borne by the Earls of Donoughmore, the cross crosslets are silver instead of gold, and with Hutchinson of Cornforth, and afterwards of Whitton House, in the county of Durham, the lion is gold instead of silver, and so on.

So far from the correctness of the assertion that the governor's branch had no coat armour being unimpeachable, it may rather appear that all other branches had to go to it for their various heraldic bearings. The weak point in my argument is this : I have not proved that Edward of Alford was next heir to Edward of Wickham, however reasonable the assumption may be ; but from Edward of Alford—say the date 1586, when his eldest son was baptized—down to the present time, I cannot doubt that the family has regularly borne coat armour, which is a space of 292 years.

At the present time I am the chief or eldest representative in England of Edward Hutchinson of Alford, and next to me comes my cousin, the Rev. W. P. H. Hutchinson, who luxuriates in one of the Duke of Sutherland's comfortable livings in Staffordshire. Peter Orlando Hutchinson.
Old Chancel, Sidmouth, Devon.

"Whig" and "Tory" (5th S. ix. 25.)—Dr. Johnson was certainly not the first writer of a dictionary who gave these two words, nor can much be said respecting the correctness of his definition of their meaning. In the case of *Whig* he only gives, "the name of a faction," and then quotes the well-known passage from Burnet's *History of his Own Time*, vol. i. p. 43, deriving the term from the Scotch carters' expression, "Wiggam." In the case of *Tory* Dr. Johnson says more, for he explains it as

"A cant term derived, I suppose. from an Irish word signifying a savage. One who adheres to the antient constitution of the State, and the apostolical hierarchy of the Church of England, opposed to a *Whig*,"

and gives illustrations of its use by Addison and

Their principles are the same, though their modes of thinking are different. A high Tory makes government unintelligible: it is lost in the clouds. A violent Whig makes it impracticable: he is for allowing so much liberty to every man that there is not power enough to govern any man. The prejudice of the Tory is for establishment: the prejudice of the Whig is for innovation. A Tory does not wish to give more real power to Government, but that Government should have more reverence. Then they differ as to the Church. The Tory is not for giving more legal power to the Clergy, but wishes they should have a considerable influence, founded on the opinion of mankind: the Whig is for limiting and watching them with a narrow jealousy."

The definition given in Bailey's first folio dictionary, 1730, is also to be found in his first octavo dictionary of 1721, and is also to be met with in earlier dictionaries.

In dictionaries prior to the Revolution, though both *Whig* and *Tory* are given, it is not in their political meaning. Thus Skinner, in his *Etymologicon*, 1671, gives "*Tory Rory*, *Irish Tory*, or *Thory*—Insanus, nisi, quod suspicor Hibernicæ sit originis. *Whig*, serum." The derivation of the two words, *Tory* from the Irish, and *Whig* from the Scotch, whether from *Wiggam* or *Wey*, has been very fully discussed already (see 1ˢᵗ S. iv. 164, 281, 492; vi. 520; x. 482; xi. 36; 2ⁿᵈ S. iii. 480; 3ʳᵈ S. viii. 460). EDWARD SOLLY.

I have just been presented with two copies of Bailey which are numbered on the back i. and ii. respectively. The book which claims to be vol. i. is by many years the younger of the two : it is of "the one and twentieth edition," and is not mentioned in the E.D. Society's *Bibliographical List*. MR. BAILEY notes it, "N. & Q.," 5ᵗʰ S. ii. 515. Vol. ii. bears the date 1727. It was issued as a kind of supplement to the first volume of the *Dictionary*, which had been for some years before the public. It consists of two parts bound together. The title-page at the beginning of the book announces the "Universal Etymological English Dictionary, in Two Parts. . . . Vol. II."; another title-page, which occurs about one-third from the end of the work, introduces "An Orthographical Dictionary, showing both the Orthography and Orthoepia of the English Tongue," and is "Vol. II." likewise. Consulting the former part of this edition of 1727 on CLARRY's question, I do not find the word *Whig*, as a noun, with its definition, but the paragraph concerning *Whiggish* is there, as in the edition of 1730, and *Tory* is there too ; but the clause beginning "also the enemies," and ending with "Tories," does not appear. In that part of the dictionary called "Orthographical," and above referred to, Bailey has :—

"*Whig*, un ennemy du despotism, F. Qui adversatur dominum despoticum, L.

This was all "for the sake of foreigners an acquaintance with the English Tong

In the fifth edition of Bailey's *Un: mological English Dictionary* (1731), have a copy, the definition attached t in 1730 is to be found *sub** "A Wh have an addition : "*Whiggism*, the Practices of Whigs." A somewhat planation is given of *Tory* than that CLARRY :—

"*Tory*, a Word first used by the Protestant signify those Irish common Robbers and M stood outlaw'd for Robbery or Murder : nov given to such as call themselves High-Chur the Partisans of the Chevalier de St. Georg
ST.

CLARRY wishes for earlier definition Here are some in 1685 by the worthy Frenchman and teacher of French. I to see ourselves as others see us. The Gaul is quite plaintive on "ces odieux" :—

"*Whig* (terme écossois naturalisé), un fana un visionaire, un enemi du gouvernement. (dont on noircit aujourd'hui les mecontents en echange de celui de *Tory* que ceux-ci partisans de la Cour.

"*Whig* signifie aussi une sorte de petit tres petite biere.

"*Tory*, voleur d'Irlande, coureur de marais que les Tory's (*sic*) d'Irlande sont à peu prè Bandits d'Italie, ou les Cossaques de l'Ukra ne vivent que de vols et de rapines. En A les esprits se sont aigris malheureusement de années, il s'est fait deux puissans Partis, l'u et l'autre des mecontents, qui se disting aujourd'hui ces deux noms odieux de *Tory* —*A Short Dictionary, English and French*, *French and English*, by Guy Miege, Londoi

These next definitions are of a later dat but likely enough some of the earlier Phillips contain substantially the s ments.† I have unluckily only a lat refer to. They will read but tamel last :—

"*Whig*, whay, or very small Beer; also contradistinguished from *Tory*, and given were against the Court-Interest in the Charles II. and James II ; a Fanatick Fellow.

"*Whiggism*, the tenets and practice o a Fanatical or Rebellious Humour.

"*Tory*, an Irish Robber or Bog trotter name given to the stanch Royalists, or H the time of King Charles II. and James I World of Words, or Universal English I

* *Whig* without the article is "Whey, B very small Beer."
† *A New World of Words*, 1658, 166: 1678, 1696, 1700.

Edward Phillips, sixth edit., edited by John Kersey, London, 1706, folio.

HORATIO.

Your correspondent CLARRY asks whether the 1730 edition of Bailey's *Dictionary* was the *first* edition. Watt, in his *Bibliotheca Britannica*, refers to a *fourth* edition of Bailey, printed in 1728, and Lowndes, in his *Bibliographer's Manual*, alludes to an edition printed in 1726.

E. C. HARINGTON.

The Close, Exeter.

See the *Percy Anecdotes, s.v.* "Whig and Tory." Defoe, in his *Review of the British Nations,* defines the word *Tory* in reference to the Irish freebooters. These references show that the terms were current long before 1730.   FREDK. RULE.

[MR. C. L. M. STEVENS (Guildford) refers CLARRY to an exhaustive note by his father on this subject in 1ˢᵗ S. iv. 281.]

OBELISK IN RUDSTON CHURCHYARD (5th S. ix. 107.)—This obelisk still stands in Rudston Churchyard, and was seen a few months since by me. In an interesting little book on this subject, by the Rev. P. Royston, he states that on measuring the stone himself he found the dimensions to be as follows : 25 ft. 4 in. high ; 6 ft. 1 in. E., 5 ft. 9 in. W., in width ; 2 ft. 9 in. N., 2 ft. 3 in. S., in thickness. Mr. Royston also gives an extract from the parish register stating the stone to be as large underground as above, but does not say what was the nature of the experiments made by Sir Wm. Strickland by which this conclusion was arrived at.

As to the origin of the monolith many theories have been started. Some believe it to be of Druidical origin, and to have formed part of a trilithite, similar to some of those at Stonehenge. Mr. Thos. Thompson, an eminent Yorkshire antiquary, believed the stone to be the Beauta stone - of a Viking named Rudd (hence the name of the village), who was buried here, and that the stone itself was brought from Denmark to be erected over his grave. He says also that a Danish gentleman who visited England, having seen a saga at Copenhagen which relates this story, was at considerable trouble to visit the place and verify the account. This view has, however, been gravely disputed, since there appears to be a doubt as to the existence of the saga in question. Can any of your readers give information respecting this ?

EAST YORK.

There is a paper on this stone, by Dr. Samuel Pegge, in the *Archæologia*, vol. v. p. 95. He gives two reports of its dimensions, preferring that which he quotes from Mr. Willan, namely, that the length of the stone, including the half which is underground, is 16 yards, its breadth 5 ft. 10 in., and its thickness 2 ft. 3 in. Prof. Phillips says it is "29 feet above the surface, and is reported to

be rooted even deeper underground." It is not, he asserts, of the same kind as the Boroughbridge stones, "but consists of a finer-grained grit, such as might easily be obtained on the northern moorlands, about Cloughton, beyond Scarborough, to which ancient British settlement a road led from Rudston by Burton Fleming and Staxton " (*The Rivers, Mountains, and Sea Coast of Yorkshire*, p. 106).

The author of Murray's *Yorkshire* considers " it is worth remarking that a part of the Roman road which crosses the Wharfe at St. Helen's ford, at Tadcaster is known as Rudgate. Little Rudstone is a village on the Wolds about 4 miles S. ; and near Drewton (adjoining S. Cave and a little N. of the Humber) is the name of Rudstone Walk, apparently marking the line of an ancient road."

ST. SWITHIN.

THE "MARSEILLAISE" (5th S. ix. 105.)—If the *Marseillaise* is a German and not a French air, does this account for the use Schumann has made of it in his very fine and characteristic song, *Die beiden Grenadiere*, introducing the air with grand effect at the conclusion of the song, at the words "So will ich liegen"? One would hardly think that Schumann would take the air unless it were German in its origin. I should add he does not give the song note for note from beginning to end. Is it possible that Schumann's version is the German *Volkslied*, improved upon, as the case may be, by the French officer ?   H. A. W.

"THE ILLUMINATED MAGAZINE" (5th S. ix. 198.)—CUTHBERT BEDE has a sharp memory, but in his notes of last Saturday he has committed the, to me, very grave error of adding ten years to my age. I was in my teens when I illustrated some of my father's articles in the *Illuminated*, having been born in December, 1826.

Let me add that one of the *noms de plume* in the magazine, viz. "Luke Roden," was that of Dr. Alfred Wigan, uncle of the distinguished actor. "Piers Shafton, Gent.," was Mr. George Becke, my father's solicitor. The late Herbert Ingram was the proprietor of the magazine.

BLANCHARD JERROLD.

Reform Club.

THE FOURTH ESTATE OF THE REALM (5th S. ix. 167.)—I am not aware that the reporters' gallery has ever been called the "fourth estate" ; but the newspaper press was so designated by Mr. Brougham, if my memory does not deceive me, in one of his numerous speeches in the House of Commons.   C. ROSS.

I have always understood that Edmund Burke was the author of the dictum that the press is the fourth estate of the realm. I am not aware that any one ever applied that expression to the

Colchester.

A PAINTING BY GUERCINO DA CENTO (5th S. ix. 168.)—The answer to E. A.'s query will be found on p. 389, l. 15, of the *Oracula Sibyllina a D. Johanne Opsopœo Bretanno cum interpretatione latina Sebastiani Castalionis* (Paris, 1599). The line is "Salve casta Sion, permultaque passa puella," a translation of χαῖρε ἀγνὴ θύγατερ Σιὼν καὶ πολλὰ παθοῦσα. The Latin continues :—

"Ipse tibi inscenso rex en tuus intrat asello,
Erga omnes mitis, juga quo tibi, quo juga demat
Intoleranda tibi, quæ fers cervice subacta,
Solvat, et exleges leges violentaque viucla."

The allusion, of course, is to the triumphal entry into Jerusalem.   E. C. PERRY.
King's College, Camb.

INVITATION CARDS OF THE EIGHTEENTH CENTURY (5th S. ix. 168.)—I have often heard the late Mortimer Collins say that it was a usual thing in the last century to write notes on the backs of playing cards as well as invitations. He attempted to imitate the custom himself, and often sent a note (generally in verse) on a playing card by post ; but, as cards in these days are always ornamented on the back, he was compelled to use the front only, and would manage to put address, stamp, and note on an ace, deuce, or trey of any suit.   FRANCES COLLINS.
5, New Burlington Street.

CATSKIN EARLS (5th S. viii. 308.)—The trimming of an earl's robes was originally of catskin, but at some period subsequent to 1529 it was changed to ermine. The earls created before that date were, however, allowed the privilege of wearing the catskin trimming, though I believe they seldom, if ever, avail themselves of it. The only earldoms still remaining, which were in existence previous to the change, are those of Shrewsbury, Derby, and Huntingdon.   RIVUS.

"PLATFORM" (5th S. ix. 146, 195.)—If the word "platform" in the stage direction for the opening scene of *Hamlet* be due to Theobald, and not to Shakspeare, I presume that Shakspeare is responsible for the word in the second scene of Act i. :—
"Upon the platform, where we walked."
And also—
"Upon the platform 'twixt eleven and twelve."
                                         JAYDEE.

THE ISLE OF MAN (5th S. viii. 127, 251, 298, 470; ix. 177.)—The following Parliamentary papers do not seem to be known to your correspondents on this matter, so I beg leave to note them as items of information : (1) Acts respecting the Duke of Athol's Claim of further Compensation

Duke of Athol respecting the Sale and C of the Isle of Man, 1829 (252), xxi. 127
                                         G. LAURENCE

"ROYD" (5th S. ix. 169, 195.)—R Rod, simply and in composition, are many place names in England. The wo a clearing, land first brought under c See Halliwell, *sub voc.* "Rode-land" *Words and Places*, p. 502, under Jamieson, vol. ii., under "Roid." T exist in one form or another in all th tongues. Old Ger. *riuti, riutjan ; l reuten, rotten;* A.-S. *wrotan.* The En source. Icelandic or Old Norse *hrjóð* explained by Holmboe (*Det Norske Spr* 1852), "et opryddet eller aabent Sted i en Mark" ("a cleared or open place in a Mark"). Hence the Danish *rode* op the same meaning. *Rod, Royd, Rode,* ar place names in South-east Lancashire, W shire, and Cheshire, in such combi Ormerod, Blackrod, Martinroyd, Boothro royd, Holroyd, North Rode, Odd Rode, (of the Trent it occurs in the forms of Roa (of which latter there are more than a doze alone), Rodborne, Rodborough, Rodmar nell, &c. Germany is fruitful in simila Winzinge-rode, Nessel-rode, Wernige-r gen-roth, &c. In the Middle Ages Rod(equivalent to Lat. *novale,* "terra roa newly brought into cultivation. *Roa* plained by Ihre (*Glossarium Suio,* "terram incultam excisis arboribus saxis ad cultum redigere." *Rotten,* ac Wachter (*Glossarium Germanicum*), is terram sive id fiat aratro, aut fodiendi in quod faciunt coloni, sive rostro, quod faci In this sense it is equivalent to our ' The original radical is *rut,* from an earl (see Graff, *Althochdeutscher Sprachsch* p. 489).   J. A.
Sandyknowe, Wavertree.

[See 5th S. iii. 151, 212, 292, where will be : by MR. WEDGWOOD and MR. SKEAT.]

THE FIRST LOCAL NEWSPAPER (3rd 351, 398, 435, 479; ii. 38, 92; 5th S. vii 153, 179, 232, 330; ix. 12, 98, 155.)— can satisfy most of MR. PATERSON's inqu *Stamford Mercury* was originally publish yearly volumes, and was so published up of 1730—in all thirty-six half-yearly voli published. No earlier volume is known th commencing Thursday, January 5, 171! would make January 3, 1712/3, the c ment of the paper. No. 18 of vol. x.

1717, was shown in the Caxton Exhibition last year, being No. 1838 in the catalogue. Parts of vols. vii., x., xiv., xv., xxi., xxiii., xxiv., and xxv. are in Stamford. In January, 1731, the paper was first published in one yearly volume, and a fresh numbering was begun, and the volume for 1731 is No. 1. The paper of June 30, 1826, is No. 4971, vol. 95. The paper of the following week, July 7, 1826, is marked No. 6833, vol. 131, and in that paper is the following editorial note :—

"It may be useful to some of our readers to state that vol. 131 and No. 6833 which stand at the head of our paper denote the number of years and weeks for which the *Stamford Mercury* has been printed. One of our predecessors in the property, on succeeding to it after the paper had been published weekly for nearly 40 years, thought proper to recommence the numerical distinction, beginning again with No. 1, and from his time the progression has been regularly observed, until the number of the present week would have been 4972; but we have availed ourselves of the occasion of enlarging our paper to add together the two series of numbers, and thus to show the whole period during which the *Mercury* has been printed, viz. 131 years, or 6,833 weeks. We possess a file of the paper 110 years old."

Thus to 95 *yearly* volumes 36 *half*-yearly volumes were improperly added, and in 1826 the paper had been printed 113, and not 131, years. There was a newspaper printed in Stamford earlier than the *Stamford Mercury* of 1712.   Jos. Phillips.
Stamford.

I have the *Stamford Mercury* from Feb. 28, 1722, to Oct. 15, 1724. The first is vol. xxi. No. 9. The vols. are half-yearly, and the numbers weekly.   W. H. Duignan.

According to Burton's *Chronology of Stamford,* "the first *Stamford Mercury* was printed by Thompson & Bailey, in the house now occupied by Miss Booth, in St. Martin's, about 1712."
   J. Ward.
Leicester.

"The earliest instance of the printing of a newspaper in any prominent town in Great Britain occurred in Newcastle, during the sojourn of Charles I. in the North, in 1639. He was attended by Robert Barker, the Royal Printer, who issued a news-sheet from time to time."
The above quotation is from Reid's *Handbook to Newcastle-upon-Tyne,* which states that the first number of the *Newcastle Courant* was published Aug. 1, 1711.   W. M. E.

Personal Proverbs (5th S. ix. 47, 169.)—I lately heard a man, in reply to a request to move on, use these words, which are perhaps worthy of being preserved : "I'm on the road now, says Conway."   Boileau.
Shrewsbury.

John Taylor, the water poet, in a poem written in 1622, when visiting Hull, termed *A Very Merry Wherry Ferry Voyage, or Yorke for my Money,* thus alludes to "Bate me an ace" :—

"But late an ace he'll hardly win the game,
An if I list I could rake out his name."

Ray in a note has the following :—
"Who this *Bolton* was I know not. One of this name might happen to say, *Bate me an ace,* and from the coincidence of the first letters of these two words, *Bate* and *Bolton,* it grew to be a proverb."
   John Symons.
Hull.

"One Wiemark was called to an account for saying the head of Sir Walter Raleigh (beheaded that day) would do very well on the shoulders of Sir Robert Naunton; and, having alleged in his own justification that 'two heads were better than one,' he was for the present dismissed. Afterwards, Wiemark being, with other wealthy persons, called on for a contribution to St. Paul's, first subscribed a hundred pounds at the Council Table, but was glad to double it after Mr. Secretary had told him 'two hundred were better than one.'"—*Anglorum Speculum,* edit. 1684, p. 783.
   Wm. Underhill.

F. Bartolozzi, R.A. (4th S. xii. 110; 5th S. ii. 335; ix. 91, 177.)—Mr. Bates's reply (*ante,* p. 91) reminds me that I have in my possession an old engraving with which I should like to form a closer acquaintance. It represents a youth dressed in loose flowing garments, a shepherd's crook resting against his right shoulder, sitting with both arms extended right and left in an earnest, expressive posture of appeal to a fair maiden. As I interpret the picture, he is addressing her in the words which are printed on a decorative ribbon round the lower portion of the picture. Between and above these two figures a Cupid with wings extended hovers in the air, entreatingly looking towards the maiden. The picture is about five inches high, and is garnished by an oval decorative wreath of flowers, foliage, fruit, and grain. Under the inscription before referred to and round the floral decoration appear the two names "G. B. Cipriani" and "F. Bartolozzi, Sculp*,* 1777."

Martin Archer Shee, R.A., in his *Elements of Art,* published in 1809, says of Bartolozzi, "He was one of the most distinguished characters that ever adorned the annals of art in any country."
   J. Bennett Aitken.
Lorne Terrace, Fallowfield, Manchester.

Chronograms (1st S. ix. 60, 61; 5th S. ix. 69, 112, 140.)—I have a copy of an inscription on an old tomb in which a chronogram is introduced. The clergyman who first kindly sent it to me said he was puzzled by it. On taking the tall letters out and adding them up, I found they gave the date of the deceased's death, 1648 :—"In piam Thomæ Chafe, generosi memoriam. . . . Animam exspiravit xxvto Die Novem. Anno Salutis 1648. eXVVIas sVas eXUIt MeDICVs." He was a counsellor at law.   W. K. W. C. Chafy.

Inventor of Roller Skates (5th S. viii. 507 ; ix. 60.)—In an article "Rinks and Skates," written

in the skating scene in the ballet of "Les Plaisirs de l'Hiver," produced at Her Majesty's Theatre in 1849. This led to a note and illustration, published in the "Varieties" of the *Leisure Hour*, Feb. 17, 1877, in which a fac-simile is given "of an old Dutch picture representing a skater who performed publicly between the Hague and Schevening, in August, 1790." Your correspondent should have a look at this engraving.

CUTHBERT BEDE.

"RUBBISH" AND "RUBBLE" (5th S. viii. 423; ix. 15, 108.)—To the authorities already cited may be added the following extract from Baret's *Alvearie*, which seems explicit enough as to the equivalence in 1580 of *rubbish* and *rubble:*—

"Old rubble occupied, or put in use againe. Rudus redivivum, Vitru. ἐρείπιον ἐπισκίναστον.

"To throw or carrie out rubble, as morter and broken stones of old buildings. Erudero, &c., Var. ἐξηρειπιόω.

"Curet et nettoyer une place de toutes ordures, comme de pierres, platras,* et autres.

"Shardes or peeces of stones broken and shattered, rubble, or rubbish of old houses. Rudus, ruderis, Liu. ἐρείπιον.

"A lateng of rubbish, a paving with rubble and like matter tempered with lime. Ruderatio, &c., Vitru. ἐρειπίωσις."

This gives us the word *rubbish* in its modern form at a date earlier than Minshew, Cotgrave, Florio, or Sherwood. Baret is fifty years later than Palsgrave, but in the latter we only get the older form *robrisshe*.

There are also two other forms, *rubbage* and *rubbidge*, at least as old as the seventeenth century, and both still used provincially.

But at least in provincial England *rubble* has not always been restricted to its original meaning of masons' refuse—we ought, perhaps, to add plasterers' refuse—for we get :—

"*Rubbles*, a miller's name in some counties for the whole of the bran or outside skin of the wheat, before being sorted into pollard, bran, sharps, &c."—Simmonds's *Dict. of Trade Products*, London, 1858.

Compare this with the Suffolk definition of *colder* at vol. i. p. 86, of Way's *Promptorium*, "light ears and chaff left in the caving sieve after dressing corn," and we shall get in these *rubbles* a valuable light on "Robows or coldyr."

The Fr. *rebut*, "the refuse, offals, outcasts, or leavings of better things" (Cotgrave), may be compared.

HORATIO.

GENTLEMEN (5th S. ix. 148.)—The explanation seems simple, as in our own time all who are of habit and repute gentlemen are styled socially Esquire.

---

* "*Plastras*, rubbish ; clods, or peeces of old and drie plaister."—Cotgrave.

---

being styled Gentleman, might have Esquire. I could name records in wl alterations have been found to have be handwriting *different* from that of any nected with the records. In the Matrie Oxford there are entries which suggest in these respects. Thus, for example, of the sons of two brothers (sons of an great and ancient estate by his wife, tl of Sir Roger Townshend, of Reynham) styled "armiger" and the other "plebe fathers were of the same lineage ai armigers, duly distinguished by mark But the Oxford registrar of the perioc thought that mere competency was th of the plebeian !

MISTRESS (OR LADY) FERRARS (5th *Mirth and Metre*, by Frank E. Sn Edmund Yates (London, Routledge & wherein the history, tale, or legend is versification under the heading "Mac hame," with a note that the legend is a story current in the part of Herts scene is laid. WILLIAI Steeple Aston, Oxford.

JOHN PHILLIPS : "THE SPLENDID (5th S. ix. 148.)—I do not think the bc to by FATHER FRANK is very scarce. dates from the same year (1720), prin son, and contains two engravings by l gucht—(1) a portrait of the author ; (scene illustrative of the poem on cider. Nottingham.

The *Splendid Shilling*, by Phillip: literary value whatever, and not worth current coin of the realm than its title

A.

SAMUEL BAILEY, OF SHEFFIELD (5th —I have read with great interest MR. paper in your last number. Mr. Ba saw, but I had some correspondence and can testify to his having been a c man of business, as well as a rema cise and perspicacious writer on ab jects—subjects which now appear to be to men who delight in a cloud of wore their ignorance under a succession of hi formulæ, which prove nothing and me and leave the most important question they found them.

When I published what was then a tion of the essays on *The Formation* ai *tion of Opinions*, I thought I was doin towards the promotion of free philosophical thought. I paid Mr. Bailey 50*l.* for the copyright of the third edition, which I issued at 5*s.* 6*d.*, and which resulted in a heavy loss to me.

The late Mr. Joseph Hume called upon me several times, and was anxious that a still cheaper edition should be issued ; but, as neither he nor his friends were willing to take any share in the risk, I was compelled, as a matter of business, to decline the undertaking.

It seems to me that the entire absence of verbiage or rhetorical ornament will always prevent Mr. Samuel Bailey's works becoming popular.
J. GREEN.

AMEN CORNER (5ᵗʰ S. ix. 188.)—Is it possible that because the "Pater Noster" ends with "Amen," so Amen Corner was considered a suitable name for the end of Paternoster Row? Stow (*Survey*, edit. 1754, I., bk. iii. ch. viii. p. 665) says that Paternoster Row was so called "because of Stationers or Text Writers, that dwelled there ; who wrote and sold all sorts of Books then in use, namely, A·B·C or *Absies*, with the *Paternoster, Ave, Creed, Graces,* &c. There dwelled also Turners of Beads, and they were called *Pater-noster makers.*" It will be remembered that Ave Maria Lane and Creed Lane are hard by Paternoster Row. Stow adds that Creed Lane was "lately so called," and says only that "Amen Lane is added thereunto."   W. SPARROW SIMPSON.

THE SON OF THEODORE, KING OF CORSICA (5ᵗʰ S. ix. 163.)—There is a remarkable attraction in a horrible story ; many like to read it, and not a few are willing to revive it when it is forgotten. The account of the "murder" of poor old Colonel Frederick, on Feb. 1, 1797, is an illustration of this. Any one who will take the trouble carefully to read over the statement of the boy Colvin, who asserted that he was a witness of the murder, will, I think, come to the conclusion that the story is most highly improbable. No boy would be at all likely to grapple with an armed cut-throat in a dark churchyard on a winter night ; no burglar who had just committed a murder would be at all likely to hold a boy between his knees whilst rifling the pockets of the man he had just killed ; and no boy thus held, under such circumstances, could possibly speak to the colour of the purse and handkerchief abstracted from the corpse. But whilst we are considering whether the story is at all probable, common sense seems to suggest the question whether there was not an inquest held. The answer is short and to the purpose. There was a full investigation, and at the inquest, held on Feb. 3, William Colvin confessed "that all he had before said was false, and that he knew nothing further concerning the transaction than that he met a boy on Wednesday night, in St. Margaret's Churchyard, who informed him the body of a man was lying under the porch of the Abbey gate, opposite Tothill Street."

On the inquest it came out that Col. Frederick was in great trouble ; had recently said he should destroy himself ; a few days before had borrowed a pistol ; and the jury were satisfied that he had died by his own hand in a fit of temporary insanity. I think, therefore, we must not say "contemporary history had another version," but rather "rumour, as is too often the case, promulgated a lie."
EDWARD SOLLY.

THE USE OF FIRE-SHIPS (5ᵗʰ S. ix. 149.)—Mr. BOULGER is right in supposing that the use of fire-ships is of much older date than the sixteenth century. They were employed by the Rhodians in the great naval victory which they, in alliance with the Romans, gained over Antiochus off Myonnesus, B.C. 190. See Livy, xxxvii. 30.
R. M. SPENCE.
Manse of Arbuthnott, N.B.

THOMAS DE CHEDDAR (5ᵗʰ S. ix. 149.)—The wife of Thomas de Cheddar was Isabel Scobhill, or Scobhull (Harl. MS. 807) — a Devonshire family whose shield bore Argent, three fleurs-de-lis gules, in chief a label of three points azure. This corresponds with the tinctures of the shield in the east window in Cheddar Church, as described by Collinson, iii. 575. The inquisition on her death, as Isabel Cheddar, widow, was taken in 1476 (Escheats, 16 Edw. IV., No. 67).
B. W. GREENFIELD.
Southampton.

SHANDYGAFF (5ᵗʰ S. ix. 149.)—A short time since I asked an Essex man if he had ever heard of the drovers' expression a "shant of gatter" for a "pot of beer." He answered I must mean *shandygaff.*   R. S. CHARNOCK.
Junior Garrick.

"Ale and ginger-beer ; perhaps *sang de Goff,* the favourite mixture of one Goff, a blacksmith." —*Hotten's Slang Dictionary.*   FREDK. RULE.

SNUFF SPOONS AND MULLS (5ᵗʰ S. vii. 428 ; viii. 275, 396, 497 ; ix. 95.)—Rams'-horn mulls fitted up in silver and cairngorm, with the snuff spoon, hare's foot, &c., chained to them, are very generally displayed in the jewellers' shops in Edinburgh. I was told they were an ornament with Scotch regiments at the table ; and I believe they find favour also with young men who sport the kilt and stalk deer.   P. P.

"ESTRIDGES" (5ᵗʰ S. vii. 326, 385, 458 ; ix. 115.)—I often have heard people in Derbyshire pronounce the word ostrich, *ostridge.*
THOS. RATCLIFFE.

OLD RECEIPTS (5ᵗʰ S. viii. 145 ; ix. 55.)—The various virtues of rue have been expressed in Latin

as it is often proved in time of pestilence, for a nosegay of rue is a good preservative."—Thos. Cogan, *Haven of Health*, 1590, p. 41.

Nor has this belief, or at least the results of it, altogether disappeared. I remember noticing many years ago, at the Old Bailey sessions, that tufts of rue were placed on the front of the dock, whilst others, stuck in the penholes of the ink-stands about the court, brought the doubtful charm under your very nose. The custom is perhaps still observed, and that it originated in the intention of staying infection is manifest, for a less agreeable bouquet, except in relation to health, could hardly have been chosen.

VINCENT S. LEAN.

Windham Club.

"THE THIRD PART OF THE PILGRIM'S PROGRESS" (5th S. viii. 469 ; ix. 36.)—I have the twelfth edition of this part, without any date, "to which is added the life and death of John Bunyan, author of *the first and second part*; completing the whole Progress." The italics are not mine. I think we may infer that Bunyan was *not* the author of the part in question. This third part is bound up with the twenty-second edition of the first and second parts, published in 1727.

C. L. PRINCE.

"STAG" AMONGST POULTRY (5th S. viii. 226, 298, 478 ; ix. 18.)—I have always understood the term "stag" to mean a game-cock which has completed his first year. M. M. H.

"DATALER" (5th S. viii. 346, 456 ; ix. 178) is in common use in the West Riding of Yorkshire, and is applied to any person who works as a "day labourer," no matter what kind of employment that may be. H. E. WILKINSON.

May this word not be from the same root as the Scottish *daidler*, a person who idles his time? Applied to a labourer in a coal mine not working at a specific task, the word may mean, reasonably enough, a kind of "dd man" or "hanger on," ready to do any job he can put his hand to.

J. D. D.

VARANGIANS (5th S. i. 113, 358.)—Dr. Vilhelm Thomsen, Professor of Comparative Philology in the University of Copenhagen, gives the following explanation of this word in his lectures on the *Origin of the Ancient Russ*, delivered in Oxford in 1876, and recently published. He says that *Varangian* was originally a designation of the Scandinavians, and more particularly of the Swedes, citing in proof passages from Byzantine,

Wáring, and in Leo Ostiensis, *Guaran,* *Gualani.* *Vœringjar* is connected with a found in different Teutonic languages, the ancient form of which is *vârâ.* The meani *vârâ* is (1) truth, faithfulness ; (2) plighted truce, peace ; (3) pledged security, prote(Akin to *vârâ* are O.N. *vœrr,* safe, snug, (*vœri,* abode, shelter ; *vœringr,* one who shelter and safety somewhere ; cp. A.-S. *wœr(* =advena. So *Varangian* means primar "denizen," or μέτοικος, and took its rise a: the Scandinavians to denote the Swedish se in Russia. The name was afterwards given t imperial body-guard at Constantinople, whicl at first mainly a Scandinavian corps.

A. L. MAYH

Oxford.

DROWNED BODIES RECOVERED (5th S. i 111.)—Similar trials for discovering the bod the drowned have been described in 1st S. iv. 251, 297 ; and a variation in the methoo narrated by me in 4th S. viii. 395.

W. D. SWEETI

Peterborough.

THE PRONUNCIATION OF "ARE" (5th S. 71.)—MR. BURNS finds "that the inhabita1 North America, whether born in the United S or Canada, pronounce *are* with *a* long, so rhyme with *fare.*" I cannot speak for Ca but I have been in seventeen of the States i Union, and in a pretty long life I have only heard the word *are* pronounced to rhyme *fare,* and that was by a gentleman in this cit; was a native of England. It is pronounce and ought to be spelt so. W.

Philadelphia.

"BEEF-EATER" (5th S. vii. 64, 108, 151 335 ; viii. 57, 238, 318, 398, 478.)—The folli passage gives an instance of the word earlier those usually quoted, and, as I think, str supporting MR. SKEAT :—

"*Steward.* These impudent, audatious serving-me Scarcely beleeve your honours late discharge.
1st Servant. Beleeve it? by this sword and buckle Stript of our liveries, and discharged thus?
Mavortius. Walke sirs, nay walke ; awake yee d drones
That long have suckt the honney from my hives; Begone yee greedy beefe-eaters ; y' are best; The Callis Cormorants from Dover roade Are not so chargeable as you to feed."
—*Histrio-mastix,* iii. 1, 93-101 [*circa* A.D. 1585-] Simpson's *School of Shakspere,* vol. ii. p. 47.

O. W. TANCC

Sherborne.

"DAME" AND "LADY" (5ᵗʰ S. viii. 451 ; ix. 75, 115.)—J. R. D. forgets I was answering the direct inquiry, who were the persons equally described as Dame or Lady in a legal document. Dame in the wider sense of "mistress" had, I presume, become so common, that it was hardly thought complimentary enough in parlance for a baronet's lady. But it is most useful in documents and on monuments, for it admits the Christian name, which Lady would not always do. Dame Mary Bacon is a baronet's lady ; Lady Mary Bacon must at least have been an earl's daughter.   P. P.

AUTHORS OF BOOKS WANTED (5ᵗʰ S. ix. 189.)— "Crito Cantabrigiensis," the author of A Vindication of the Literary Character of the late Prof. Porson, was Thomas Turton, D.D., Regius Professor of Divinity in the University of Cambridge [afterwards Dean of Westminster and subsequently Bishop of Ely, ED.].
                                   FR. NORGATE.

AUTHORS OF QUOTATIONS WANTED (5ᵗʰ S. viii. 509 ; ix. 38.)—
Napoleon's Midnight Review.—I remember reading a translation by my early Scottish acquaintance and friend, the late Leitch Ritchie, to whom, indeed, I first showed the original, in the Foreign Quarterly Review, and thought it very spirited and characteristic of the weird-like original.   J. MACRAY.

(5ᵗʰ S. viii. 90, 119, 159, 179 ; ix. 118.)
"And thou, Dalhousy, the great god of war,
      Lieutenant-colonel to the Earl of Mar !"
This association of the names of Mar and Lord Dalhousie appears to refer to the battle of Bothwell Bridge (June 22, 1679), where Mar was colonel of a regiment of foot and Dalhousie served in a subordinate capacity. (The latter was not engaged in the Jacobite rising of 1715.) See Swift's Memoirs of Captain Creichton, vol. x., Scott's edit. of Works. I have an impression of once seeing a poem, or part of one, by a Scotch rhymer, containing the couplet in question. Swift, when compiling Creichton's memoirs, may have come across it, or Arbuthnot, being a Scotchman, may have been familiar with it, and one or other of them probably repeated the lines to Pope.   NORVAL CLYNE.

(5ᵗʰ S. ix. 129, 158.)
"Plus negabit," &c.
It was Lord Chancellor Eldon (vid. Swift's Life, i. 88) who remembered Dr. Johnson setting down Dr. Mortimer, the Rector of Lincoln College, after he had several times interrupted him by saying "I deny that," with the question, "Don't you know what an ancient writer says ?" But whether Dr. Johnson really quoted, or only pretended to quote, does not appear so certain.
                                        E. H. A.

Miscellaneous.

NOTES ON BOOKS, &c.

A Dictionary of English Philosophical Terms. By Francis Garden, M.A. (Rivingtons.)
THERE can be no doubt that it is very important for a student to "know the origin of words which he encounters," whether in old writers, in ordinary reading, or in common conversation. The work before us supplies to a considerable extent the want thus indicated,

and within the limits of its convenient size will doubtless prove a handy book of reference, while the passages cited from Dante, Spenser, Shakspeare, Hooker, &c., add to its interest. There are some lacunæ which, in view of modern controversies, we would suggest to Mr. Garden to fill up in a future edition. He gives an account of Optimism, why not also of Pessimism ? So much has lately been written concerning Schopenhauer and Leopardi, and the question "whether life is worth living," that such an omission seems remarkable. Mr. Garden's definition of Law as "a general command or a general prohibition, the prescription of a general rule or a general procedure," errs, to our thinking, in the introduction of a word bearing so strict a technical sense as "procedure," and the entire account of Law would bear curtailment. The force of the juridical identification connoted in Roman law by the term persona is not adequately brought out, although it is well worthy of consideration on account of its influence both upon theology and philosophy in Western Europe. Mr. Garden deserves the thanks of the student for the help which he has already afforded, and we hope he will be encouraged to make his book still more useful in the future.

The Poetical Works of John Milton. With Introductions by David Masson, M.A. LL.D. The Globe Edition. (Macmillan & Co.)
IT was a happy thought to add to the Globe series the poems of Milton ; and it was as desirable as natural that the text should be that of the Cambridge edition of Prof. Masson, which is not likely to be bettered. Milton's own second edition (that of 1674) is of course followed in regard to the arrangement of Paradise Lost, that being the only course to pursue in a standard edition as distinguished from a fac-simile reprint. In regard, however, to minutiæ of text, the editor of course follows neither of Milton's eminently inconsistent though by no means carelessly printed editions. Prof. Masson holds that, though Milton took all the pains a blind man could to get his epic correctly printed, he is not to be held responsible for every detail of ortho-graphy and punctuation ; and in these respects, holding this view, he has unquestionably a right to modernize and systematize, especially in a popular edition. We have had an exact reprint of Milton's first edition and a fac-simile of the same ; and it ought to be worth some publisher's while to issue a fac-simile of the second edition, as the first in which the poem was divided into twelve books, and as containing things not in the first edition, while varying as from it in details. Prof. Masson's introductions form an admirable literary history of Milton's poetry.

Gleanings from the Records relating to Exeter. By W. Cotton and Archdeacon Woollcombe. (Exeter, Jas. Townsend.)
THE records of the "ever faithful" city of the West are pregnant with interest. During the Wars of the Roses the influence of the Courtenay family threw the power of the city into the support of Henry and his hapless queen : for their sake its citizens willingly spent their stores of wine and money. Exeter was besieged by Perkin Warbeck on his attempt to wrest the crown of England from Henry VII., but the attacks of Warbeck's deluded supporters on the city gates ended in disastrous failure. The king entered Exeter in triumph, and, with his usual generosity, rewarded its services by the present of a sword and cap of maintenance. The chapter on the siege of Exeter in 1549 by the Cornish rebels illustrates an event which, if successful, would have completely altered the course of our national history. At the beginning of the great rebellion Exeter was held by

gutter; and his successor, though duly elected, refused to act, and was fined 400*l.* for disobedience. Several royal letters are extracted.from the city archives, the most important relating to the siege of 1549, and a summary is printed of a curious collection of Acts of Parliament (1649-52) preserved in the chapter library. Devonshire sadly wants a new historian; when one does arise his labours will be lightened by the publication of these valuable documents.

MR. JOHN BATTY'S *History of Rothwell* (Rothwell, published by the Author) must, we should think. entirely exhaust all that there is to be said on points interesting to Yorkshiremen and others concerning the antiquities, the history, and the manufacturing and mining industry of that portion of Deira. Mr. Batty gives instances from the parish registers of Rothwell of two women who were recorded as centenarians,—"Jane Garon, widow, Oulton," buried Sept. 11, 1805, aged 100, and " Ann England, widow, Royds Green," buried June 29, 1803, aged 103. The story of Jane Garon, or Garrand, is related with some circumstance in a foot-note derived from Taylor's *Supplement to Leeds Worthies;* both cases may be commended to the notice of Mr. Thoms. The Rothwell registers appear to commence at a very early date, 1538, and still earlier information may exist, Mr. Batty thinks, among the Dodsworth MSS. in the Bodleian, if the Nostell Coucher Book has found its way into that collection—a point on which some of our Oxford correspondents may be able to enlighten us.

IN the compass of a handy book of reference for the office, *The Law relating to Trustee and Post Office Savings Banks* (Hardwicke & Bogue and Butterworths), Mr. U. A. Forbes, of Lincoln's Inn, has brought together a mass of information, both as to the Statute Law and the decided cases governing the two classes of savings banks, such as cannot fail to be of great practical utility to all who have to deal with these most valuable institutions. —Mr. Edward Preston has published, under the title *Unclaimed Money, a Handy Book for Heirs-at-Law and Next of Kin* (Allen and Reeves & Turner), a condensed and revised reprint of letters originally written for the *Newcastle Weekly Chronicle,* and which, in this new and more widely accessible shape, will whet the appetite of many a possible heir to untold gold.—From the able propounder of that brilliant vision, " Hygeia, the City of Health," which held a Social Science Congress in rapt attention, we receive with pleasure an earnest pleading for the *Future of Sanitary Science,* an address delivered before the Sanitary Institute of Great Britain, by B. W. Richardson, M.D., LL.D., F.R.S. (Macmillan).—In his *Genealogical Memoirs of the Scottish House of Christie* (London, printed for the Royal Historical Society), Dr. Charles Rogers stands on somewhat firmer ground than in his previous publication respecting the family of Burns. We cannot but regret, however, that anxiety to make out a good case should lead him so far astray from the paths of the undeniable Christies of the sixteenth century as to claim for their family tree a " Dominus Cris'inus," perpetual vicar of the church of Lochalveth, in Moray, in 1333. We could ourselves present Dr. Rogers from memory with the legend " Hec est crux Cristini," which we remember amid fragments of "a broken chancel with a broken cross," by the shore of St. Brandon's Sound. But we do not consider that we

(1st S. iii.) for information about the descendants of Alexander Cumming, of Coulter, is still living, I shall happy to forward to him a pedigree which sets the pretty exhaustively."

MR. J. R. LYELL is preparing an historical accou the Scotch family of Bonar.

LONDON, SATURDAY, MARCH 23, 1878.

CONTENTS.—Nᵒ 221.

𝔑𝔬𝔱𝔢𝔰.

A SALISBURY MISSAL.

A fine copy of the above has recently come under my notice, a description of which will, I think, be not without interest to the readers of "N. & Q.," specially as it will be seen in the course of description that it is marked by not a few peculiarities. The handwriting, which is very clear and beautiful, marks the date of the MS. as c. 1400, and this date is confirmed, amongst other indications, by the absence from the Calendar of the feast of St. Winifred, which was ordered to be celebrated as a double festival by Henry Chichley, Archbishop of Canterbury, in 1415. The Calendar, with which the MS. commences, agrees with those found in the earlier copies of the Missal, but differs in the following important particulars from the later MSS. and from the printed books.

It makes no distinction between Principal and Minor Doubles, but marks thirty-two days simply as Festa Duplicia. The following festivals are omitted :—Mar. 17, St. Patrick ; Apr. 30, St. Erkenwald (the feast of his translation, Nov. 14, is also omitted) ; May 6, St. John Port. Lat. ; May 7, St. John of Beverley ; May 9, Translation of St. Nicholas ; May 24, Festum Sancti Salvatoris ; July 22, Visitation of B.V.M. ; July 16, Translation of St. Osmund (the "Depositio S. Osmundi," Dec. 4, is also absent) ; Aug. 6, Transfiguration ; Aug. 7, Festum Nominis Jesu ; Oct. 2,

St. Thomas of Hereford ; Oct. 17, St. Etheldreda ; Oct. 19, St. Frideswide ; Nov. 3, St. Winifred. St. Tecla is substituted for St. Cecilia on Nov. 22, but this is manifestly merely a clerical error, as St. Tecla appears on her own day, Sept. 23.

The following days, which appear as red-letter festivals in the later Missals, only appear in black letter :—Apr. 28, St. Vitalis ; July 15, St. Swithun ; Sept. 16, ·St. Edith ; Sept. 22, St. Maurice ; Oct. 1, St. Remigius ; Oct. 25, SS. Crispin and Crispinian ; Nov. 13, St. Brice. On the other hand, the octaves of two festivals of the B.V.M., the Assumption and Nativity, are in red letter.

A notable addition is the insertion in red letter on June 7 of the translation of St. Wulstan. This would seem to point to the probability that the MS. belonged to some church in the diocese of Worcester.

Each month is preceded by the line indicating the Egyptian or Evil Days, e.g. January is headed by the verse, "Prima dies mensis et ·vii trūcat ut ensis," and, to make assurance doubly sure, the unlucky days in each month are also indicated by a capital letter D. The days so marked do not, however, in every case accurately agree with those indicated by the head-line. At the foot of each month is noted the length of the day and night.

· Passing from the Calendar to the body of the MS. we find that it begins with the "Benedictio salis et aquæ. Omnibs d'nicis p' anū fiat b'ndictio salis & aque hoc modo." Then follow the Propria for the following Sundays and festivals, agreeing throughout with the Salisbury use :—The First Sunday in Advent ; ·Christmas Day [Propria for one mass only, ·the Tertia Missa] ; St. Stephen ; St. John [to the Introit for this day is added the note, "ī tpē pasc. alla. alla." : this would indicate that though the festival of St. John Port. Lat. finds no place in the Calendar, yet it was observed, and that the Propria for the one festival served also for the other, with the addition, should the feast of St. John Port. Lat. fall within the Easter season, of the Alleluia] ; Holy Innocents ; St. Thomas of Canterbury ; Circumcision ; Epiphany ; Easter Day ; Easter Monday ; Easter Tuesday ; Easter Wednesday ; Ascension Day ; Whitsun Day ; Whit Monday ; Whit Tuesday ; Trinity Sunday ; Corpus Christi. The usual Kyries and special prefaces follow, and are succeeded by :—

"Hᵒ mᵒ incipiāt' onĭs pfac' ad missā p' toᵘ anū tā in feriis q'm ĭ fĭs vid' hoc modo. Per omnia scla sclorum. Amē. D'ns nohiscū. Et cū spū tuo [hic eleuet sac'man']. Sursū corda. Habem' ad dn'm. ·Grās agamus dnō deo n'ro. Dignum et justū est.
"Hec est pfacō cotid ·& dr' cot. p' annū n' ĭ fĭs & p' oct in quibs pprie hēant'. Ita tn' qd onis pf totius an'i sub hoc tono diir sive ppe hēant' sive n' tam ĭ feriis q'm in fĭs secundū usū earū.
"Vere dignum, &c. Sanctus, &c. Et ideo cum angelis, &c."

broken into three parts ; but no mention is made of three distinct acts of fraction, each accompanied by its appropriate words. There is no response of the deacon ("Et cum spiritu tuo") to the salutation of the priest, " Pax tibi & sce coelie dei."

The order of the closing prayers is also somewhat peculiar, as will be seen from the comparative view given below ; the upper arrangement shows the usual order, the lower one that of the MS. under consideration :—

Gratias tibi ago, &c. Cleansing of vessels. Quod ore sumpsimus, &c.
Hæc nos communio dne purget, &c. Washing of hands, &c.
Communio.
Post Communio.
Ite missa est.
Placeat tibi sancta Trinitas, &c.
In nomine, &c.
In principio. St. John i. 1-14.

Quod ore sumpsimus, &c. Cleansing of vessels.
Hæc nos communio, &c. Chalice placed by priest on paten, &c. Gratias tibi ago, &c., or Adoremus crucis signaculum per quod salutis sumpsimus sacramentum.
His dictis sacerdos corpore inclinato junctisque manibus tacita voce in medio altaris dicat hanc orationem.
Placeat tibi, &c.
In nomine, &c.
In principio. St. John i. 1-14.

Propria follow for twenty-nine saints' days, including three " Missæ de sancta Maria," one mass " In natali unius apostoli," and one " In natali unius evangelistæ." Sixty-four Propria follow for various votive masses, commencing with Missa de Trinitate and ending with five Missæ generales.

There are many indications that this MS. belonged to a chantry. The omission of the Propria for almost all Sundays throughout the year proves that it could never have been intended for use as an ordinary service book. Frequent mention is made in the rubrics of the chapel as distinguished from the choir, e.g. in the first of the three Missæ de sancta Maria :—

"Missa de sancta Maria quotidie per adventum in capella et in choro," &c.
" Sciendum est quod quotidie per totum annum dicetur sequentia in capella ad missam beatæ Mariæ, similiter ut in choro," &c.
" Notandum est quod in omnibus festis beatæ Mariæ ......dicetur eadem missa in capella quæ dicenda est in choro."

On a blank page facing the Canon of the Mass is written, " Orate pro bono statu magistri Johannis Michelgror' armigeri uxoris suæ et filiorum et filiarum eorundem," whilst on the upper margin of another page of the Canon is written :—

ppicietur deus. Amen."

The festivals of St. Thomas of Canterbur unerased in the calendar, nor has the ser his day been defaced. The title "papa" escaped erasure. The MS. concludes wit] unimportant Communia, each marked margin with a capital letter for con\ of reference. Three prayers, copies of the Secretum, and Communio of the second Missæ generales, are written on a bla at the end of the MS. in handwriting of th half of the sixteenth century. In thes significant alterations have been made " dominum papam regem et episcopum m in the original, the later copy reads " reg copos et abbates nostros." The clause, ' famulorum tuorum in salutis tuæ pros dispone," is omitted.

The copy of the Secretum, " Deus qui s corporis tui hostia totius mundi solvisti &c.," has been almost completely erased. unimportant verbal changes are made in t of the Communio, the only alteration of portance being the introduction before tl of the Blessed Virgin of the words, " ser virginis."

I would close this somewhat lengthy des with one or two queries. Is there any kno of the Sarum Missal which corresponds one I have described ? Can any corres} skilled in the local history of the diocese (cester or of its cathedral church (to a c which this Missal may have possibly be recognize the names of any of those for th of whose souls prayers are asked, and so ; MS. a local habitation ?

It may perhaps be well to note that here described is in the possession of the Scott Moncrieff, Vicar of Christ Church, land, that it is in beautiful condition, a the exception of the missing illumination in every respect.

I shall be glad to send a list of the titl sixty-four votive masses. JOHNSON F Pallion Vicarage.

SIR RICHARD GRENVILLE.
The noble struggle of Sir Richard (against the overwhelming strength of the fleet has been briefly described in the English of Kingsley in Westward Ho, greater length by Froude in vol. ii. pp. of his Short Studies on Great Subjects,

stirring lines of the Poet Laureate (entitled *The Revenge, a Ballad of the Fleet*), printed in the March number of *The Nineteenth Century*, have again drawn public attention to his glorious death. The scanty particulars of his career which are preserved in the biographical dictionaries justify the insertion in " N. & Q." of a more extended notice of the valour and virtue of one of England's noblest heroes.

. Sir Richard's father was Sir Roger Grenville, a captain in the navy, who perished with the crew of the Mary Rose when she sank at Spithead, in the sight of Henry VIII., on July 18, 1545. He married Thomasine, daughter of Thomas Cole, of Slade, Devon. The eldest son by this marriage was Sir Richard, who was born in the west of England about the year 1540, and entered at a very early age into the service of his country. He first distinguished himself when only sixteen in the wars in Hungary, under the Emperor Maximilian, against the Turks, for which his name is recorded by several foreign writers (Carew's *Survey of Cornwall*, edit. 1811, p. 176). In 1570 and 1584 he was chosen member of Parliament for county of Cornwall, and after serving the office of sheriff in 1577, he was knighted by Queen Elizabeth. During his shrievalty he was called upon to arrest Francis Tregian, Esq., of Golden in Probus, for harbouring Cuthbert Mayne, the first Roman Catholic priest who was put to death under the Act of 1571. Mayne was executed at Launceston Nov. 29, 1577, and his patron, after enduring a long imprisonment, was exiled.

On May 19, 1585, Sir Walter Raleigh's first colonists for Virginia, under the leadership of Ralph Lane, sailed from Plymouth in seven ships, commanded by Sir R. Grenville. An account of the voyage was published under the following title :—

" A Briefe and True Report of the Newfoundland of Virginia......Discovered by the English Colony, there Seated by Sir R. Greinvile, Knight, in the Yeere 1585, which remained under the Government of Rafe Lane, Esquire......at the especiall Charge and Direction of the Honourable Sir Walter Raleigh, Knight, Lord Warden of the Stannaries.......By Thomas Hariot.......Imprinted at London, 1588." 4to.

On Sir Richard's arrival in America he took possession of Virginia in the queen's name, and stored the country with cattle, fruits, and plants, for the use of the settlers. During his passage back to England he encountered a Spanish ship returning from St. Domingo with a cargo of sugar and ginger. His own boats being lost or disabled, he hastily put together some boards of chests, and succeeded in reaching the Spaniard. As soon as Sir Richard and his men had boarded the Spanish vessel his temporary boat fell to pieces. In 1586 he paid a second visit to Virginia, and on his return voyage landed on the Azores, where he pillaged the towns and took many Spaniards prisoners.

On the first news of the proposed descent of the Armada in 1587, he was employed in surveying the maritime defences and in reviewing the trained bands of Cornwall and Devon. In the following year, on the appearance of the foreign fleet, we find him entrusted with the care of Cornwall, and coming forward himself with 303 men, armed with " 129 shott, 69 corsletts, and 179 bowes."

The great event of his life in 1591 has been so often narrated that it will only be necessary briefly to allude to it here, the more particularly as Tennyson has within the last few days retold the story in noble verse. Whilst commander of the Revenge, with only 140 men fit for fighting, he was attacked on August 31 by a Spanish fleet, consisting of fifty-three ships, most of them larger than the Revenge, with 10,000 soldiers and mariners. Disdaining to fly, he kept the enemy at bay for upwards of a whole day, and was only captured when all his ammunition was spent, he himself mortally wounded. Being taken on board the Spanish admiral's ship he was treated with the courtesy which his valour so well deserved, but died on Sept. 3 or 4. Previously to his death, the Spanish captains being around him, he said, in their language :—

" Here die I, Richard Grenville, with a joyfull and quiet mind, for that I have ended my life as a true soldier ought to do that hath fought for his country, queen, religion, and honor, whereby my soul most joyfully departeth out of this body, and shall always leave behind it an everlasting fame of a valiant and true soldier that hath done his duty, as he was bound to do."

The account of this action was almost immediately published, the writer of the narrative being Sir Richard's old friend, Sir Walter Raleigh. The title of the work is :—

" A Report of the Trvth of the Fight about the Iles of Açores this last Sommer, betwixt the Reuenge, one of her Maiesties Shippes, and an Armada of the King of Spaine. London, Printed for William Ponsonbie, 1591." 4to., 14 leaves.

In 1595 Gervase Markham wrote :—

" The Most Honorable Tragedie of Sir Richard Grinuile, Knight. Bramo assai, poco spero, nulla chieggio. At London, Printed by I. Roberts for Richard Smith, 1595." 8vo., no pagination, A to G in eights.

This is one of the scarcest of English books : only two copies are known : one is in the Grenville Library, British Museum, having been purchased by Thomas Grenville at Bindley's sale in 1818 for 40l. 19s., and the other is among the books bequeathed to the Bodleian Library by Malone. For reprints of this and the previously mentioned work the readers are referred to " No. 27, Edward Arber's Fac-simile Reprints," to which is prefixed an interesting preface containing most of the details of Sir R. Grenville's adventurous life that are found in this notice. Further particulars of the Grenville family will be found in *A Complete Parochial History of Cornwall* (1868),

Devon, Knight, by Catherine his wife, a daughter of George Neville, Lord Abergavenny. She was buried in the Grenville aisle in Bideford Church, Nov. 5, 1623. By this lady Sir Richard had four sons and three daughters. Bernard, the eldest son, married Elizabeth, daughter and co-heiress of Philip Bevill, of Killigarth, in Talland, and by her was father of the famous Sir Bevill Grenville, who was mortally wounded at the battle of Lansdowne, July 5, 1643, whilst fighting valiantly for King Charles I.

When Martin Llewelyn, an Oxford poet, wrote an elegy on the death of Sir Bevill, he summed up the praises of his hero with an allusion to the noble "sea action" of Sir Richard Grenville in these words :—

"Where shall ye next fam'd Grenvill's ashes stand?
Thy grandsire fills the sea and thou the land."

THE AUTHORS OF THE "BIBLIOTHECA CORNUBIENSIS."

BIBLIOGRAPHY IN FRANCE.

It is to be regretted that bibliography has so few staunch votaries in this country, and that we have allowed the French to outstrip us in almost every branch of this most interesting science.

While we are waiting, possibly in vain, for the long promised publication of the late Mr. Samuel Halkett's researches in our anonymous and pseudonymous literature—while new editions, brought down to the present time, of Watt's *Bibliotheca Britannica* and Lowndes's *Bibliographer's Manual* have become absolutely necessary—our neighbours d'Outre Manche have done for their literature all and more than this. The great work of Quérard, *La France Littéraire* (10 vols.), in addition to the two supplementary volumes prepared by the author, has been ably continued in *La Littérature Française* (6 vols.), and again by M. Otto Lorenz in his *Cat. de la Librairie Française* (4 vols.), which, with the two additional volumes completed last year, brings the register of French publications down to 1875. *Les Supercheries Littéraires Dévoilées* of Quérard has been republished (3 vols.) with vast additions, and the *Dict. des Ouvrages Anonymes* of Barbier, similarly augmented, is on the eve of completion, and it is intended that the two works of this new edition shall be brought together by one general index embracing both.

Passing now to less important publications, if we compare the ordinary trade catalogues of French and English booksellers, the superiority of the former cannot fail to be noticed; they frequently tion of the books which their issuers hav Among these I would specially poin *Bulletin du Bouquiniste* of F. A. Aubry Jan. 13, a. c.) and Techener's *Bulletin phile*. Both these journals of literature tion to interesting notes appended to offered for sale, contain separate in articles by the most distinguished bibl of France. The *Bulletin du Bibliophi* the forty-fourth year of its existence, h a vast repository of bibliographical lea comprises articles of the greatest interes which are not to be found elsewhere, k Peignot, Paul Lacroix, Gustave Bru indeed, by the *élite* of French bibliograp have, unfortunately, no similar publicati

On April 1, 1876, was issued No. 1 of *seiller du Bibliophile*, a literary journal er by all the improvements of modern ty and destined, as its title implies, to t tion of the beautiful, the curious, and th books. This charming publication ca abrupt termination by the premature and death (Sept. 27, 1877) of its proprietor, chief contributor, M. M. C. Grellet. *Le Conseiller du Bibliophile* has ceased t has been followed by a journal on almost plan, and "got up" with even more typ splendour, *Le Moniteur du Bibliophile*, the first number, March 1, is before i first number contains, among other matte notices upon "La Bibliothèque de la Paris," "L'Imprimerie particulière des C upon Armand Barthet, author of the *M Lesbie*, and the first instalment of a later work by Alfred de Musset, *L'Anglais d'Opium*, a translation from De Quincey.

I would likewise mention another literar as yet also in its earliest infancy (two only published), *Miscellanées Bibliograp* less important work than that immediat mentioned, and more chatty and anecc which it is proposed to insert quest answers somewhat after the manner of " In conclusion, let me notice the *Cata Ouvrages, Écrits, et Dessins poursuivis, s ou condamnés depuis 21 Octobre*, 1814, ju *Juillet*, 1877, par M. Fernand Drujon, of part, 96 pages, has appeared. This catal tains matter and notes not to be foun similar publication.

Let us wish success to these worth takings of our neighbours and ende emulate them. H. S. A

THE TWO ROBBERS, ST. LUKE XXIII.—The well-known sentence expressing the lesson of the history of the two robbers has often been the subject of an inquiry in "N. & Q." On looking at various commentaries in the endeavour to trace it, I have not found it in any very early writer. There are two forms in which it is expressed, and one of them turns on the use of the words "despair" and "presumption," and the other on that of "hope" and "fear."

The former has appeared in "N. & Q." as: "Unus erat ne desperes, unus tantum, ne præsumas." And it has been also traced in an English form to the Πατρικὸν Δῶρον of H. Delaune, published in 1651.

I have traced the latter form as far as Avancinus, *Vita et Doctrina Jesu Christi*, Hebd. v. Quadr. fer. vi., p. 138, ed. Westhoff, Mon. Westph., 1854, the first edition of which was published at Vienna in 1657. It occurs there as a part of the text, without any notice of its being a citation from another writer, as :—"Duo sunt ad latus Christi, unus convertitur, quis non speret? Unus damnatur, quis non timeat, etiamsi sit apud Jesum?" It afterwards appears in a similar form in Quesnel, *Reflexions sur le N. T.*, published in 1693-4, as :—"Un se convertit a la mort, esperez, un seul craignez."

It does not seem probable that the sentence in either form is from a very early writer, as it is not cited in patristic commentaries, in which it is common to find any very remarkable sentence from the Fathers repeated continually.

ED. MARSHALL.
Sandford St. Martin.

TWO OLD SCOTCH PHRASES.—Two instances of the survival of old Scotch phrases have recently been met with:—1. In a newspaper from the north of Scotland I lately read the advertisement of the intended sale, on a certain day, of a well-known garden. The notice closed with the statement that the plants, &c., might be inspected "betwixt and the day." This form is historical. When Archbishop Laud made, in 1637, the ill-advised attempt to force his service book upon the Scottish people, under threats of a "charge of horning" for non-compliance, the proclamation to the sheriffs enforcing the use of the book ran, " . . . take especial care that every parish betwixt and Pasch next procure unto themselves two at least of the said books," &c. Dr. Hill Burton, in his *History* (vi. 438), notes how the learned editor of *Reliquiæ Liturgicæ* has been misled into attempting to fill up the supposed ellipsis in the clause in question; but, in fact, there is no omission, the phrase being an old Scotch law term, still, I believe, occasionally in use as it was in the time of Charles I.

2. The expression "well-?" or "ill- favoured" in England, and the Scotch form, "ill-faured," are common enough; but the use of the verb "to favour" is, I imagine, rarer now in both countries than it once was. Not long ago, in East Lothian, I heard it said of a little village girl that she "favoured her mother." Some one too quickly answered, "It would be bad of her if she did not." In reality the expression used is the old Shaksperean phrase meaning to "resemble in feature," as in the examples given in the large edition of Johnson's *Dict.* :—

"The complexion of the elements is *favoured*
Like the work we have in hand."   *Julius Cæsar.*

Or, more recently, from the *Spectator* :—"The porter owned that the gentleman *favoured* his master."

I am acquainted with a family in Scotland where a solemn-faced urchin of five is said to "favour Oliver Cromwell"; but I am not aware if this use of the word is still common in any part of England.

ALEX. FERGUSSON, Lieut.-Col.
United Service Club, Edinburgh.

WALTER SCOTT : TENNYSON.—In reading the Waverley Novels, which I am now doing again with greater delight than ever, I often come across passages which remind me of scenes or expressions in the *Idylls of the King*. The quotation given below, from the last chapter but one of *The Fortunes of Nigel*, will, when compared with a well-known magnificent portion of "Guinevere," serve to illustrate what I mean :—

" As the eye of the injured man (John Christie) slowly passed from the body of the seducer to the partner and victim of his crime, who had sunk down to his feet, which she clasped without venturing to look up, his features, naturally coarse and saturnine, assumed a dignity of expression which overawed the young Templars, &c. 'Kneel not to me, woman,' he said, 'but kneel to the God thou hast offended, more than thou couldst offend such another worm as thyself. How often have I told thee, when thou wert at the gayest and the lightest, that pride goeth before destruction, and a haughty spirit before a fall? Vanity brought folly, and folly brought sin, and sin hath brought death, his original companion. Thou must needs cast duty, and decency, and domestic love, to revel it gaily with the wild and with the wicked; and there thou liest, like a crushed worm, writhing beside the lifeless body of thy paramour. Thou hast done me much wrong—dishonoured me among friends—driven credit from my house, and peace from my fireside; but thou wert my first and only love, and I will not see thee an utter castaway, if it lies with me to prevent it.—Gentlemen, I render ye such thanks as a broken-hearted man can give....Rise up, woman, and follow me.'

" He raised her up by the arm, while, with streaming eyes and bitter sobs, she endeavoured to express her penitence. She kept her hands spread over her face, yet suffered him to lead her away."

J. W. W.

"To HAVE THE DANES."—Looking into John Parkinson's *Theatrum Botanicum*, fol., 1640, a "herbal of large extent," occupying 1688 pages, and full of woodcuts, I found that he gives this

indices, I note it as the best and most curious example of the terror caused by these sea soldiers along the coasts, and, it may also be said, in the inlands of England. The Danewort or dwarf elder—I again quote Parkinson—is supposed to be so called " from the strong purging quality it hath, many times bringing them that use it unto a fluxe."   B. NICHOLSON.

LICENCE TO EAT FLESH IN LENT.—The following entry in the parish register, which I have been permitted to see, is of some interest, and worthy of record :—

" March yᵉ 22ⁿᵈ 1632. A license was granted to Mary yᵉ wife of Thomas Bishop of Witney for her eating of flesh in time of her sicknes bearing date March yᵉ 15ᵗʰ 1632 in hæc verba.

" Whereas Mary yᵉ wife of Thomas Bishop alias Martin of Witney is fallen notoriously sick and for her health desiring leave to eate such flesh in the prohibited time of lent to bee eaten of persons notoriously sick by yᵉ statute of 1 Jac: I William White curate of yᵉ pariᵇh of Witney aforesaid by vertue of yᵉ statutes 5 Eliz: et 1 Jac: in that case respectively provided doe give leave unto yᵉ said Mary Bishop for the space of eight daies after yᵉ date hereof if her sicknes last soe long to eate such flesh as is not repugnant to yᵉ statute of 1 Jac:

" In witnes whereof I have hereunto sett my hand this 15ᵗʰ day of March 1632.

" Her sicknes continuing this license was continued unto her during yᵉ time of her sicknes Ita. testor.
                                       " GUIL: WHITE."

This is copied exactly as it appears in the book.
                          JOHN H. CHAPMAN, M.A., F.S.A.
Woodgreen, Witney, Oxon.

WITCHCRAFT IN PENNSYLVANIA.—The following is an extract from the minutes of the Provincial Council of the colony (William Penn was the Proprietary and Governor at the time) :—

" At a Council held at Philadelphia yᵉ 21st of 3 Mo. 1701,
                       Present
           The Proprietary and Governor,
" Edward Shippen, Samuel Carpenter, Griffith Owen, Thos. Story, Humphrey Murray, Caleb Pusey, Esq'rs.

" A petition of Robt. Guard and his Wife being read, setting forth that a certain Strange Woman lately arrived in this Town, being seized with a very Sudden illness after she had been in their Company on the 17th Instant, and Several Pins being taken out of her Breasts, one John Richards, Butcher, and his Wife Ann charged the Petitioners with Witchcraft, & as being the Authors of the said Mischief; and therefore Desire their Accusers might be sent for, in order either to prove their Charge, or that they might be acquitted, they suffering much in their Reputation, & by that means in their Trade.

" Ordered that the said John & Ann Richards be sent for; who appearing, the matter was inquired into, & being found trifling, was Dismissed."
                                             UNEDA.

WORDS ONCE OBSCURE.—Abp. Trench, in a lecture on Plutarch's *Morals*, goes at some length into the English of the Coventry physician, Dr.

archbishop cites a few of the words Hol. thought necessary to include in " an explana along the coasts, and of certain obscure words," and append to volume. A little later Joshua Sylvester, in translation of *Du Bartas, his Divine Weekes Workes*, in like manner gives a similar glos " of the *hardest* words." The following is a lis some of the most noticeable ones : Asylum, anɪ cataract, chaos, colony, dialect, domain, duel, taph, epitome, heroic, idea, legislator, paraɪ problem, sympathy, type, theory.
                                  CH. ELKIN MATHEWɪ

A PRECIOUS CRYPTOGRAPH.—Students of se writing may find a profitable as well as pleaɪ which is given in the second volume of Brewsɪ *Life of Newton*. It embodies Sir Christoɪ Wren's latest invention as to the longitude, beɪ he had an opportunity of revealing which he d
                                             CYRIɪ

MODERN FORMS OF SUPERSTITIONS.—Seeing new moon through glass cannot have been unlu in England when we had no window glass, noɪ parts of the East where they have none.   ' origin is most likely a substitution for seeing new moon in a lake or pool, the shadow being, pre-historic mythology and philology, a form eɪ valent to ghost or soul. Horseshoes cannot be remote antiquity, and the use of this form (5ᵗ ix. 65) is possibly derived from the crescent of moon.   HYDE CLARKɪ

THE WILL OF PETER THE GREAT.—From formation which has reached me since the publɪ tion of my letter on this subject in the *Morn Post* of Monday last, I have good reason to beli that the existence of some such " testament p tique " is regarded as a fact by one of the high authorities on Russian history and Russ politics. I shall therefore feel greatly obliged references to any allusion to such a documen more especially to works dated earlier than 180
                                        WILLIAM J. THOMS
40, St. George's Square, S.W.

MR. COLLIER'S REPRINTS.—Your correspond who forwarded the notice of Mr. Collier's privat printed edition of Shakespeare, *ante*, p. 180, woɪ be doing a great kindness to myself, and, I doɪ not, to many other lovers of our early Englɪ literature, if he would furnish a complete list the various series of reprints which Mr. Colɪ has issued during the last few years. I am aw of the list given in the supplement to the last e tion of Lowndes, but that, having been publish in 1864, is necessarily very incomplete.
                                             M. C. R.

Queries.

[We must request correspondents desiring information on family matters of only private interest, to affix their names and addresses to their queries, in order that the answers may be addressed to them direct.]

PETROLEUM.—May not the occasional allusions to oil wells in old books of English travel encourage the notion that petroleum will be found in this country ? Several of these wells are noticed in the appendix to Dr. Russel's *Dissertation on Sea Water*, ed. 1760, from which I enclose an extract respecting one of them that you may perhaps think worth insertion. This Dr. Russel was a little bit crazy on the marvellous virtues of sea water, but to him belongs the merit of having been the first physician to introduce Brighton as a health resort.

" *Of the Burning Well at Brosely in Shropshire.*

" Brosely is a village in Shropshire, four miles northeast of Wenlock, seven north by west of Bridgnorth, and fourteen south-east of Shrewsbury. It was discovered about the year 1711, and is seated about an hundred yards from the river Severn, in the neighbourhood of mines of coal and iron, there being coal works on every side, though none very near it.

" A candle being put down into the well, it will take fire at the distance of a quarter of a yard, darting and flashing in a violent manner to the height of 1820 inches. It is hotter than common fire, and boils any thing much sooner ; for it will boil a common tea-kettle in nine minutes, and broil mutton chops or slices of bacon very soon, with an excellent flavour. It will reduce green boughs to ashes very soon, or anything else that will burn ; but the flame may be put out by holding a wet mop over it ; however, the water itself is extremely cold, and as soon as the fire is out it seems as cold as if there had been none there. Hence it appears that this water is impregnated with a sort of liquid bitumen, called *petrolæum*, that is, rock oil. This water has ceased burning since the year 1752, on the account of an earthquake, if it has not recovered this faculty since 1755."

J. O. HALLIWELL-PHILLIPPS.
Brighton.

SIR JULIUS CÆSAR'S MSS.—Every student of history deeply regrets that the most interesting collection of manuscripts formed by Sir Julius Cæsar, the Master of the Rolls, who died in 1636, was dispersed in a public auction in St. Paul's Churchyard, by Mr. Paterson, in 1757. There were several thousand documents, but the sale, which lasted three evenings, consisted of 188 lots. For the most part they were bought by six buyers, who secured 139 lots. These were—Mr. Webb, 56 ; Mr. Dancer, 20 ; Mr. Snelling, 19 ; Messrs. Chambers and White, 15 each ; and Walpole, 14 lots. At that time the trustees of the British Museum were not so well represented at book sales as they are now, but they bought two lots at a cost of 2l. 4s. Subsequently they acquired from the executors of Lord Lansdowne the 56 lots which he had purchased at the sale of Mr. Webb's collections. It

would be interesting to know what has become of the other MSS. Horace Walpole bought 14 lots at a cost of 43l. 5s., and at the Strawberry Hill sale in 1842 eight lots are mentioned as being from the Cæsar collection ; but besides these there are at least five other lots which must have come from the same source, namely, Nos. 85, 93, 154, 155, and 156 (sixth day's sale). Lodge, in his *Life of Sir Julius Cæsar*, 1827, though he mentions with regret the dispersal of the MSS. in 1757, does not seem to have been aware that Horace Walpole had bought any of them. Two lots which Col. Cæsar bought in 1757 were perhaps amongst the Aberdeen MSS. mentioned by MR. GOMME (5ᵗʰ S. ix. 56). I should be glad to know where the MSS. sold at Strawberry Hill now are.
EDWARD SOLLY.

" CATALOG. MUSÆUM SEPTALIUM " AT MILAN (PRINTED) : DID JOHN RAY SEE A KALEIDOSCOPE THERE IN 1664 ?—In his (own) *Curious Travels*, date March 6, 1664 :—

"We saw there, at the Museum or Gallery of Seignior Manfredus Septalius (Settala), son of Ludovicus Septalius, the famous physician, a box with a multitude of looking-glasses so disposed as by mutual reflexion to multiply the object many times, so that we could see no end of them ; a plain plate of glass with so many spherical protuberances wrought upon it that if you looked through it upon any object you saw it so many times multiplied as there were protuberances of segments of spheres upon the plain of the glass ; likewise a speculum of the same fashion, by looking upon which through the former you see your face as many times multiplied—product of sum of protuberances of one glass by sum of protuberances of the other ; several concave burning specula of metal—saw experiment of burning by reflexion : several engines counterfeiting perpetual motion—understood their intricacy ; automata and clocks, two cylindrical ones moving by rolling down inclined plane without weight or spring ; large crystal with drop of water in it, making air bubble move upwards ; *Indian* feather pictures [ef. Oxford Ashmolean brooch.—S. M. D.] ; fictitious china or porcellane of his own making, hardly distinguishable from true ; natural history curiosities ; crystal is ground and polished by a brass wheel with powder of *Smiris* in water, smoothened with powder of *Sassemort*, a stone found in river hard by ; telescopes, microscopes, musical instruments and pipes of his own making ; chemical oils extracted by him without fire ; crystal glass of his making nearly equalling Venetian for transparency," &c.

Query, is this *printed* Catalogue extant in English libraries? Consult I. M. Visconti, *Exequiæ in S. Nazzaro*, 1680, 4to., with portrait. He died 8 ides Feb., 1680, æt. 80. " Musæum Septalium D. Pauli Mariæ Terzago," p. 20, for this *Exequiæ*.
S. M. DRACH.

WHY IS " AXE " SPELT " AX " IN THE OXFORD PRAYER BOOKS ?—Just two years ago I asked in these pages why *penny* was spelt *peny* in the Oxford Prayer Books. This query was duly answered and satisfactorily disposed of. After a two years' interval a " Teacher " writes to the *Times*, and propounds the same question. The

reasonable inquirers on this subject. I now ask another question concerning the orthography of the Prayer Book, as printed at the Oxford University Press. Why is *axe* spelt *ax* (see the Commination Service)? I have looked at various editions, of various sizes, from a large type folio copy to a duodecimo, and in all of them I find *ax*; therefore it is clear that the elision of the final *e* is done "of a purpose." But from what purpose?
CUTHBERT BEDE.

NUMISMATIC.—To what province (*curia*) does this coin belong?—Copper, formerly plated, size of a half farthing, very thin; probably a heller. Obv., a leaping goat on a grated doorway, and between two towers; leg., MON . NOVA . CURLÆ . RETHIGÆ. Rev., a religious motto, a floreated cross, and the date 1739. I am inclined to think it is Swiss, and in that case it would be one of the divisions of the Batz. NEPHRITE.

ARMS OF LORD CONYERS.—It is stated in Debrett's *Peerage* that no arms of Lord Conyers are registered at the Heralds' Office. Would not the arms of the last Earl of Holdernesse descend to his present representative? Surely an old family like that of Lane-Fox would have had arms granted them. What is the explanation?
Bητα.

WINGREAYES.—In the seventeenth century there appears to have been a place of this name situate in the county of Derby. Was it a hamlet or farm of the parish of Pentrich? The name has disappeared. Can its locality be identified?
BARBATUS.

"BIBLIOTHECA PARVULORUM."— Under the above title two little works were printed some years ago, one of which, with the separate title of *Sacra Academica*, was a collection of Latin prayers, "now or lately used in certain colleges and schools in England." The date of this was 1865. Can any one inform me who the editor was? Messrs. Rivington, the publishers, appear to have preserved no memorandum on the subject. Can any one also inform me whether any copy is known to exist of the St. Paul's School Prayers earlier than the one there reprinted of 1655?
J. H. L.

OLD PROTESTANT BIBLES IN IRELAND.—Are there still many of the Bibles printed in the sixteenth and seventeenth centuries in Ireland? I should have thought that nearly all perished in 1641 or in 1690, except perhaps a very few in some of the Dublin churches. Between 1642

lish Bible, which was in ? was besieged and taken by which was also in the sam when great part of it was bu of James II. It seems to through the care of the ch Denny, the owner of Tralee with whose descendant, tl remains. There are several in it in the chaplain's wri send Mr. J. J. Howard for *logica et Heraldica* in a littl of another old black-letter tant Bible printed at Am served in a family in Kerr also to give an account of sidering the state of the between 1641 and 1650, it i these books escaped dest Bible seems to have been o chained to reading-desks in halls of mansion-houses, attached to such houses. know if any seventeenth ce the Cork churches or at St. Denny of 1641, the owner c Bible which has been so st the great-grandson of Sir Henry VIII.) and his wife Modbury, the aunt of Sir V Humphrey Gilbert, but w to our remembrance as th Askew.

"THE EIGHTEEN TRU Robert Heyricke, of Lei brother, Sir William Heyri don, on Jan. 2, 1614-15, sa you received my letter on S that, I thank you, you este the eighteen trumpeters, wl and will esteem yours, God than trumpets and all the n Christmas." Who were "th

PAINTING BY COSWAY have a print from a paintin in 1793 by Colnaghi, wit "Michal y Izabella z Lasoc presents a lady and gentle arm in front of a balustrade at Venice I find the same p ences—engraved by Sloane published by Schiavonetti my surprise, "Prince and l

there any clue to this riddle? The librarian at the palace was anxious to know who *Umwlorg* could be, whom he has down in his catalogue as an artist otherwise unknown.

Another query. I have a large mezzotint of a charming portrait of Mrs. Cosway, apparently painted by herself. Is it of any value?

K. H. B.

SHELDON FAMILY.—Margaret, daughter of the Rev. George Roberts, D.D., Rector of Hambledon, in Buckinghamshire, and wife of the Rev. Thomas Machon, Prebendary of Lichfield and Master of Sherburn Hospital, in this county, is described in her monumental inscription at the latter place, where she died 1669, as "orta nobili familiâ Robertorum et Sheldonorum." I should be exceedingly obliged for any information about her family and her descent from Sheldon.

E. A. WHITE, F.S.A.

Old Elvet, Durham.

A LEGEND OF RUSHTON HALL, NEAR KETTERING.—In *Once a Week* for April 9, 1864, appears a legend in verse, signed ·A. H. B., chronicling a romantic story about Bryan, second Lord Cullen, of Rushton Hall, who jilted an Italian lady for a Miss Trentham, of Trentham Hall, Staffordshire (now the seat of the Duke of Sutherland), and, cursed by the woman whom he had forsaken, his life was blighted and his prospects ruined. Can any of your readers refer me to an earlier and fuller version of the story?   JOHN TAYLOR.

Northampton.

THE "CHAMIARE."—In Calderwood's *History of the Kirk of Scotland* (republished by the Wodrow Society in 1842), in an account of the "vehement frost" of Feb., 1607, it is said that the sea in the Firth of Forth "froze so far as it ebbed, and sundry went ships upon ice, and played at the *chamiare* a mile within the sea-mark." What was the *chamiare*, and where can one get any account of it?   R. R. MACGREGOR.

IRISH NAMES.—Has the syllable "agh," which terminates so many Irish names (Curragh, Armanagh, Kavanagh), any particular meaning? Does it signify the genitive case—of?   NAP.

WORDSWORTH'S LINES "TO LUCY."—Who was the author of the parody on Wordsworth's lines *To Lucy*, beginning—

"She lived amid th' untrodden ways"?

JOHN DRUMMOND.

Croydon.

AUTHORS OF BOOKS WANTED.—

Heaven open to All Men; or, a Theological Treatise, in which, without Unsettling the Practice of Religion, is solidly proved, by Scripture and Reason, that all Men shall be Saved or Finally made Happy. Third edition, pp. 115. Anon. Robinson, n. d.   J. O.

A Description of Barrington Park, in Gloucestershire. 4to.

Letter to the Queen on the State of the Monarchy. London, 1838, 8vo.

Remarks on the Maintenance of Macadamised Roads. [By J. F. B.] Dublin, 1843, 8vo.

Brill, near Dorton Spa: a Poetical Sketch. London 1843, 8vo.   ABHBA.

Replies.

A TIRLING-PIN.

(5th S. ix. 88.)

The following extract from *The Traditions of Edinburgh*, by Robt. Chambers (1825), will give the information sought by MR. PICKFORD. Speaking of a house in Mylne Square, the second and third flats of which were formerly occupied by Lord Justice Clerk Alva (1742–68), he says :—

"This house had a *pin* or *risp* at the door, instead of the more modern convenience, a knocker. The pin, canonized in Scottish song, was formed of a small square rod of iron, twisted or otherwise notched, which was placed perpendicularly, starting out a little from the door, bearing a small ring of the same metal, which an applicant for admittance drew rapidly up and down the *nicks* so as to produce a grating sound. Sometimes the rod was simply stretched across the *vizzying hole*, a convenient aperture through which the porter could take cognizance of the person applying; in which case it acted also as a stanchion. These were almost all disused about sixty years since (say 1765) when knockers were generally substituted as more genteel. But knockers at that time did not long remain in repute, though they have never been altogether superseded, even by bells, in the Old Town. The comparative merits of knockers and pins were for a long time a subject of doubt, and many knockers got their heads twisted off in the course of the dispute. Pins were, upon the whole, considered very inoffensive, decent, old-fashioned things, being made of a modest metal, and making little show upon a door; but knockers were thought upstart, prominent, brazen-faced articles."

In addition to the instances quoted by MR. PICKFORD, I may refer to the ballad of *Willie and Annie* :—

"He is on to Annie's bower,
    And *tirled* at the pin,
And wha was sae ready as Annie hersel
    To open and let him in?"

In the fine ballads of *Burd Ellen* and *The Bent sae brown*, and many others, mention is also made of the "tirling at the pin." Burns alludes to it in *Verses written on a Window of the Inn at Carron* :—

"But when we *tirl'd* at your door
    Your porter dought na hear us."

Mr. Chambers adds, in a note :—

"Corvex, a clapper or ringle, is one of the *voces* in a list of ' Parts of a House,' which we find in a small Latin vocabulary published in 1702 by Andrew Symson ; from which we may conjecture that ' risps,' under the name of *ringles*, were in common use about the beginning of the last century."

The instrument appears to have been exclusively Scotch. I can find no trace of it in any of our old

ment, published in 1825, the same year as Mr. Chambers's *Traditions*, after quoting from Skinner's *Miscellanies*

> "I hope it's nae a sin
> Sometimes to *tirl* a merry pin,"

he proceeds :—

"*To Tirl at the Pin.* It has occurred to me that this is probably the same with E. *twirl,* 'to turn round, to move by a quick rotation.' This idea has been suggested by the notice in *Gl. Antiq.,* '*Tirling at the door-pin,* twirling the handle of the latch.'"

The learned doctor is probably right in his etymology, but his ignorance of the instrument and of the way in which it was used is very remarkable.

J. A. PICTON.

Sandyknowe, Wavertree.

Tirl in Lowland Scotch is used for a rap, a stroke, a tap ; *tirling* for the tremulous, thrilling motion produced by repeated knocks. Hence the cognate term *to dirl*=to tingle, to vibrate ; as also probably the word *to thirl*=to perforate, to drill, to bore. Thus the word came to be used for the expedient whereby notice was given to open a closed or locked door, the earlier expedient for which was the tirling-pin. The best description I can recollect of it is given by Sir Walter Scott in *Peveril of the Peak,* where Julian seeks an entrance into the residence of his lady love at the Black Fort :—

"An iron ring contrived so as when drawn up and down to rattle against the bar of notched iron, through which it was suspended, served the purpose of a knocker ; and to this he applied himself," &c.—Vol. i. ch. xi. p. 199 (vol. xxviii., 12mo. edit., 1833).

In process of time this contrivance was replaced by the primitive door-latch, which may even yet be seen in old out-of-the-way cottages, in which the wooden bar inside was lifted by a wooden lever projecting outside. It was the practice of intruders to rattle this up and down to attract attention—gently when the lads came to see their sweethearts, violently when an impatient visitor sought admission. This in turn was superseded by a latch lifted by a string, which did not allow of such rough handling ; and now the pretentious brass knocker is gradually finding its way to the doors of farmhouses and dwellings hitherto contented with simpler appliances.   W. E.

Doubtless many of your correspondents will be able to supply information about the tirling-pin, but I venture also to give a reply to MR. PICK-FORD's query from the circumstance that in the house in this city in which I was born, and spent some fifteen years of my life, there was upon the back door a tirling-pin, with the use of which I

capable of considerable mod
understood that the door w:
drum or resonator, capable o
within a very faint sound.
was the common practice to
agitate) the ring only, giving
which was enough to obtain
children would sometimes be
and seizing the ring, and pull
drive it rapidly up and down
a volume of sound enough
Sleepers. Between those ext
or risp, could give endless
alarms.   THOS. A. C

16, London Street, Edinburgh.

Tirl, v.a., according to Jam
is a word of various meaning,
to turn, twirl, thrill ; to un
that "tirling at the pin," in t
was equal to turning, lifting
the door, and was not alwa
within, as in the case of "Sw
But there is no allusion i
tirling-pins as would be so
scribed in the query. Sur
been large weapons of offen
wall, in Northumberland, wa:
given to a place and family w
was first pierced, or broken.
of the wild and lonely little l
between the fells, whose
accounted as unequal to it
lose all its old significance if
to become a gigantic reservoi

Cumberland.

A very common mode of
twirling-pin is a piece of w
on one side, which, being ro
"Unroofing," the meaning
quotes, is because the roof is
the wind. See Dr. Jamies
not far off which has a ver
thirl, to bore, perforate, whe
from the narrow passage bet
the lake. Of this Dr. Jam
amples ; but he refers with
of the word *thrall,* from th
xxi. 6 of *thirling* a slave's ea

It is still usual in Scotlan
at a door, to say that he o
door.

Edinburgh.

Mr. Pickford may see an illustration of two forms of the risp or tirling-pin in the *Gentleman's Magazine* for February, 1870, p. 378.

R. R. MacGregor.

Edinburgh.

"Skal" (5th S. viii. 509; ix. 117, 199.)—Mr. Baynes may see the relation between our *skull* (of the head) and the Norse *skål*, Old English *skull* or *scoal*, a bowl, discussed at great length in Jamieson's *Scottish Dictionary*. Unfortunately the writer adopts the preposterous conclusion that the word acquired the sense of a drinking vessel from the unpleasant habit of our ancestors of using the skulls of their enemies for that purpose. Now in the first place it is extremely improbable that an implement in universal use, like a cup or a bowl, should have taken its name from so exceptional an origin as being made out of a human skull must always have been. And in fact the general sense of a hollow receptacle is anterior to the particular application to the hollow case of the head or skull. The Icelandic *skål* and the equivalent Danish *skaal* are never used alone in the confined signification of a skull, but with some qualification showing the particular purpose or nature of the hollow. The Icel. *skål* is a bowl, the scale of a balance; *hjarnskål*, the brainpan or skull. So we have Danish *suppe-skaal*, a soup-plate; *sukkerskaal*, a sugar-basin; *drikke-skaal*, a drinking-cup; *hofte-skaal*, the hollow of the hip-bone; *hjerne-skal*, the skull. The general sense of the word is still more apparent in the case of the German equivalent *schale*, a cup, dish, shell, &c.; *hirn-schale*, the brainpan; *nuss-schale*, *eierschale*, *muschelschale*, *äpfelschalen*, &c.

When Warnefrid, in his *Acts of the Lombards*, says that Alboin, having slain Cunimund in battle, made a goblet of his skull, and adds, "quod genus poculi apud eos *schala* dicitur," it is plain that he does not mean to confine that appellation to a goblet made of a skull, because he immediately proceeds, "linguâ vero Latinâ *patera* vocitatur."

H. Wedgwood.

In the literary dialect of Scandinavia the words for skull and bowl are respectively *skalle* and *skaal* (or, as it is also written, *skål*). With both these Norse words I believe our *skull* is connected. The Danish term for *shell* is *skal*, and I think that this word is the original one, from which are derived *skalle*, *skull*, and *skaal*. What more natural than to use the word for *shell* in a slightly altered form to denote that important cavity in which is enclosed the mechanism of the brain, and in another slightly varied form to denote a drinking vessel? Indeed the earliest goblets of a seafaring race would probably be large shells. I believe that the idea of the ancient Norsemen drinking from out of the skulls of their enemies originated in a mis-

taken translation of a passage in an old saga—at least I have so read in some work on the Norse race. Might not the translation of the passage be "drinking from the shells (or drinking vessels) of their enemies," the words for *shell* and *skull* being alike in derivation, and nearly alike in form?

Nicolai C. Schou, Jun.

Chorlton-cum-Hardy, near Manchester.

Parchment Lace (5th S. ix. 7, 75.)—This turns out, after all, to be merely a corruption of the Fr. *passement*, a lace, Ital. and Span. *passamano*. It is not bone or bobbin lace at all, but the silk galloon trimming of modern ladies' dresses, or the gold and silver braid or twist lace of the courtier or the officer's uniform. The story is rather a long one. After reading the Roxburghe ballad I turned to Halliwell, and merely finding, "Parchment, a kind of lace," I felt there was more to be known, and wrote my original query. There should have been a cross reference at *parchment* to *passamen*, and *vice versâ*. There was none. I only turned up the latter word in Halliwell a day or two since, viz. :—

"*Passamen*. A kind of lace (Fr.). In a parliamentary scheme, dated 1549, printed in the Egerton Papers, p. 11, it was proposed that no man under the degree of an earl be allowed to wear *passamen* lace."

Now hear once more the ballad :—

"Nor gold nor silver *parchment* lace
Was worn but by our nobles."

In this case the *passamen* or *parchment* would be of gold or silver. Let us see if we can support this by evidence external to the context also. Cotgrave gives :—

"*Passement*, a passing, pacing, going, &c., a carrying or conveying over; also a strayning through; also, a lace, or lacing; *passementé*, laced; *passementier*, a lace-maker, a silke weaver."

In Miege, 1685, we get, "lace, dentelle; *passement*; lacet." Under *passement*, "a lace (such as is used upon livery clothes)." In the Dutch, "*passement*, Galoen, lace; een kleed met goud passement belegd, a coat trimmed with gold lace" (Holtrop, 1801). Span. *passamano de oro, de seda*, a broad gold lace, any kind of silk lace (Minshew, 1623). In Torriano's edition of Florio occur :—

"*Lace, passamano, trina, opera*; Galloone lace, *passamano*; to lace with galloone, *passamentare*; *passamano* d'argento, di seta, d'oro, silver, silk, or gold lace."

As to bobbin or bone lace, see in Cotgrave under *dentelle*, "small edging (and indented) bone-lace, or needleworke." Again, in Miege, "fuseaux a dentelles, bones for bone-lace." Or take the Italian equivalent in Torriano, "*lavoro di canatiglia*, a small edging bone-lace." I am told that the silk "galloon trimmings" for ladies' dresses are, or were recently, once more in fashion.

Horatio.

... ... Museum there is a very interesting account of the mode of working needle or point lace, too long for "N. & Q.," and not likely to be cared for by the gentlemen readers. I need only add the pattern was first traced on a sort of green parchment : hence the above name.

EMILY COLE.

Teignmouth.

JOHN BANKS, AUTHOR OF THE "HISTORY OF PRINCE EUGENE": FLEETWOOD'S "LIFE OF CHRIST" (5th S. viii. 335.)—Now that the name of John Banks of Sunning has found its way into "N. & Q.," it may be worth while to see if we cannot discover some more of the productions of an author who wrote "with spirit and perspicuity," and yet through modesty condemned himself to obscurity. A few years ago, when, I believe, it was the intention of somebody to reprint Fleetwood's *Life of Christ*, so popular with our forefathers, and to look up the author if possible, it was discovered that he was either confounded with William Fletcher of Queen Anne's time or totally unknown ; no one could put his finger upon "the Rev. John Fleetwood, D.D." Even the editor of Darling's *Cyclopædia*, a work devoted to sacred literature, is forced to admit himself at fault, his note to the life in question being : " This is probably an assumed name. The life of our Saviour has long been a popular work." This appearing to me to be an interesting question to solve, I have been trying to look up the first edition of the book at the British Museum, but cannot get further back than an unnamed one, published by Cooke, apparently in numbers, as such books were then often put forth, and dated no earlier than 1767, affording no clue to its author or time of origin. In the order in which Cibber places Banks's productions, his *Life of Christ* precedes that of Cromwell in 1739. It may therefore be worth while looking up a folio *Life of Christ* of about that period to see if it will fit the following character of such a work ascribed to him. "He" (Banks), says Cibber, "engaged in a large work in folio entitled the *Life of Christ*, which was very acceptable to the public, and was executed with much piety and precision." Is it, then, an extravagant idea that the work under this title which held its popularity well into the present century should be the work of John Banks? We have seen that all his works were anonymous ; but it may be that he was under the impression that a clerical name was indispensable in this case, and so have committed the pious fraud of fitting it with one of his own concoction ; or rather, perhaps, the publisher, finding it an un-

notice in the list of his authorities. Benson is the author of another life, in like manner makes no allusion to h

COCKER'S "ARITHMETIC" (5th S. 35.)—I was recently reading a pape reason to believe) Prof. De Morgan, p *Athenæum* for October 18, 1862, pp. is a notice of the two volumes, by 1 of *Correspondence of Scientific Men teenth Century*, and certain letters 1 the same year as Prof. Rigaud's (were edited by Mr. Halliwell for tl Society of Science : these last run 1 1682, the former from 1606 to pas1 paper has some interesting anecdot(mation with regard to many, and am(following passages about Cocker may 1 to MR. POTTER :—

" There is one mention of 'Mr. Cock English graver and writer, now a schoolm(ampton.' This is the true Cocker : his , are specimens of writing, such as engra\ including some on arithmetic, with copper] and space for the working ; also a book of stationers, with specimens of legal hand\ recorded somewhere that Cocker and a1 name we forget, competed with the It beauty of their flourishes. This was his r in these matters l'e was great. The eig his book of law-forms (1675), published Cocker's death, has a preface signed ' J. 1 John Hawkins, who became possessed of C —at least he said so—and subsequentl famous Arithmetic, a second work on L metic, and an English Dictionary, all Cocker. The proofs of this are set o1 Morgan's *Arithmetical Books*. Among m1 roborative circumstances, the clumsy fo1 claring that Cocker to his dying day r solicitation to publish his Arithmetic, ma in the preface an *Ille ego qui quondam* o have been instrumental to the benefit of n of those useful arts, writing and engraving with the same *wonted alacrity*, cast this m mite into the public treasury.' The boc comparable in merit to at least half-a How then comes Cocker to be the im Arithmetic? Unless some one can show we have never found, that he was so b matter is to be accounted for thus.

" Arthur Murphy, the dramatist, was t of letters and ended by being the transla1 though many do not know that the two friends had tried to make him a man of no doubt he had been well plied with co1 metic. His first dramatic performance *The Apprentice*, produced in 1756, is young man who must needs turn actor best known books of the day in arithmeti Cocker and Wingate. Murphy chooses the name of an old merchant who delights in vulgar fractions, and *Cocker* to be his arithmetical catchword. 'You read Shakspeare! get Cocker's Arithmetic! you may buy it for a shilling on any stall; best book that ever was wrote!' and so on. The farce became very popular, and, as we believe, was the means of elevating Cocker to his present pedestal, where Wingate would have been, if his name had had the droller sound of the two to English ears."

GIBBES RIGAUD.

Long Wall, Oxford.

AN OLD PORTRAIT OF MAHOMET II. (5th S. viii. 89, 216.)—It may be interesting to contributors to know that the portrait of Mehemet II. by Gentile Bellini, formerly in the Zeno Palace at Venice, is now in the possession of Mr. Layard. A full account of this picture, with an engraving, will be found in Crowe and Cavalcaselle's *History of Painting in North Italy*.

It would be interesting if MR. FENTON could trace the history of the picture of Mehemet II. in his possession, and could compare it with the engraving mentioned above.

If there were any doubt as to its identity, I should venture to suggest that his picture represents, not Mehemet II., but one of the Janissaries, from the fact that a rose was borne by one battalion of these as their emblem.

If MR. FENTON should have any photographs of his picture, I should be very much obliged if he could let me have one. The fact of the existence of these portraits is curious, as Mussulmans are, I believe, strictly forbidden by their religion to have a portrait taken in any form.

I am endeavouring to obtain further information as to the representation of the rose in the picture, which I hope to be able to send for insertion on a future occasion.

A. F. G. LEVESON GOWER.

British Embassy, Constantinople.

MOORE AND REBOUL (5th S. ix. 104.)—The "Rogueries of Tom Moore" are as familiar to us in phrase, from the learned trifling of Father Prout, as *Les Fourberies de Scapin*, from the brilliant comedy of Molière. I feel sure, however, that the suspicion raised as to the originality of the sacred song, "This world is but a fleeting show," is without ground, and that the Irish melodist is in no way indebted to the pistorial poetaster of Nismes. Your correspondent D. N. states :—

"In 1829 Madame Belloc published a translation of the *Melodies ;* and the *Sacred Songs* must at least have been known to her. About this time (*i.e.* 1829) Reboul is said by a writer in the *Irish Monthly* to have written a sacred song called 'Soupir vers le Ciel,'" &c.;

and adds that "Reboul may have seen some prose translation of them," &c. Now the fact is, Madame Belloc's translation was published in 1823, instead of 1829, and it actually includes "a prose translation" of the song in question,

being No. lix. of the *Mélodies Irlandaises*. The reader may like to have it before him :—

"Ce monde entier n'est qu'une ombre fugitive, où les illusions se succèdent rapidement; les sourires de la joie, les larmes de la douleur sont de faux semblans, qui brillent aux yeux de l'homme pour le tromper, pour l'attendrir. Il n'est rien de vrai que le Ciel!

"L'éclat des ailes de la Gloire est faux et passager, comme les teintes pâlissantes du soir; les fleurs de l'Amour, de l'Espérance, de la Beauté, s'épanouissent pour la tombe. Il n'est de brillant que le Ciel!

"Pauvres voyageurs d'un jour orageux, chassés de vague en vague, l'éclair de l'Imagination, le rayon plus calme de la Raison, ne font que nous montrer les dangers de la route. Il n'est rien de calme que le Ciel !"—*Les Amours des Anges et les Mélodies Irlandaises de Thomas Moore*. Traduction de l'Anglais. Par Mme. Louise Sw-Belloc, Traducteur des Patriarches. Paris, chez Chasserian, 1823, 8vo., p. 196.

The *Irish Melodies* were originally published in seven separate numbers, the first of which appeared in 1807, and the sixth in 1815, the seventh being without a date. This I get from my copy (Lond., 1823, small 8vo.), which contains the "original advertisements." The dedication of the *Sacred Songs* in my copy of the *Works* (Paris, Galignani, 1827) is dated May 22, 1824 ; but they had clearly appeared (at least No. i., containing the poem in question) some time previously.

WILLIAM BATES.

Birmingham.

MORTON, DUMFRIESSHIRE (5th S. ix. 128.)—Probably your correspondent will find in regard to the barony of Morton all that he wants in my volume, *Drumlanrig and the Douglases*. It was granted by Robert Bruce to his nephew, Sir Thomas Randolph, and when, at the fatal battle of Durham, Oct. 17, 1346, Thomas, Earl of Moray, was killed, his heroic sister Agnes, Countess of Dunbar, became sole possessor of his vast estates, and among them of the baronies of Morton and Tybaris. Edward III. would no doubt claim the lands of those whom he had defeated, and confer them on his friends, Scotch or English. Nowhere had I seen that the barony at that early period had belonged to the Herries family, as seems to have been the case from the charter referred to by your correspondent. They were powerful in those days in the south of Scotland, and by intermarriages with the Maxwells became Earls of Nithsdale. Morton barony belonged almost without a break to the Douglases of Dalkeith, and is now in the possession of the Duke of Buccleuch and Queensberry, whose ancestor, the first Earl of Queensberry, bought it in 1618 from Douglas of Coshogle.

The early history of the Herries family is obscure. There is in Drumlanrig muniment room an original charter of Sir William de Heriz, undated, but about 1290, granting charter to Sir William de Karleol (Carlyle) and the Lady Margaret his spouse (sister of King Robert Bruce) of an acre of land in the tenement of Raynpatric. William

"Dominus de Nithsdale," 1323. This Robert may have been the father of the William Fitz-Heriz mentioned in the charter, but we have no proof of it. Stephen de Swynnerton is never mentioned, so far as I have seen, in connexion with Morton. Can he be an ancestor of the Swinton family in Berwickshire, who may have thrown in their lot with the English and been thus rewarded? Would your correspondent give the words in the charter which designate the barony?

C. T. RAMAGE.

"CARPET-KNIGHT" (5th S. iv. 428 ; v. 15, 54.) —The phrase was not much illustrated in the few notices which were quoted. The following passages point to one who stays at home on the carpet instead of going to the open battle-field. Stucley, anxious to go to the wars, answers his father, who wishes to keep him from doing so :—

"Father, unless you mean I shall be thought
A traitor to her Majesty, a coward,
A sleepy dormouse, and a *carpet squire,*
Mix not my forward summer with sharp breath
Nor intercept my purpose being good."
Play of Stucley, ll. 751-55.

"Stukley, thou know'st I am a soldier
And hate the name of *carpet-coward* to death."
Play of Stucley, ll. 1053-4.

The play is quoted from The School of Shakspere (A.D. 1605). O. W. TANCOCK.

FELICE BALLARIN, OF CHIOGGIA (5th S. ix. 49, 138.)—A. J. M.'s note is both interesting and tantalizing. He has told us just enough about Chioggia to make us wish for more. I am sure others of your readers would join with me in requesting him to add a few more details respecting the manners and customs of this Adriatic town to those which he has mentioned at the latter of the above references. Will he also describe more particularly the glass cases in which the infants are taken to be baptized? He says that the name of the town is pronounced Chioza. Is this by the uneducated only, or is it the general pronunciation throughout the peninsula? I believe Italian proper names are always pronounced as written, at least by the educated classes, and that such anomalies as "Burlington" for Bridlington, "Wilscombe" for Wiveliscombe, "Bruff-by-Sands" for Burgh-by-Sands, "Gloster" for Gloucester, "Wooster" for Worcester, &c., are unknown in Italy. JONATHAN BOUCHIER.
Bexley Heath, Kent.

MR. BOUCHIER may be interested to hear that my gondolier, of whom I have made inquiry, writes word : "Felice Ballarin is still alive, and still recites at Chioggia, but is old and very poor.

be at Venice in May, and will endeavo Felice himself. K.
Nice.

"PHILOSOPHY IN SPORT" (5th S. ix. CUTHBERT BEDE is quite right in assur Philosophy in Sport is by Dr. John Ayrt It was originally anonymous, and the name did not appear on the title-page ninth edition in 1861. The work was l lished in 1827, and not in 1821, as state bookseller's catalogue referred to by C BEDE, the figures "21" being no doubt a error. For an account of Dr. Paris and pi of the editions, illustrations, and the caricatured in Philosophy in Sport, C BEDE is referred to the Bibliotheca Corn vol. ii. pp. 421-23. WESTMIᴺ

I have this book, "fifth edition, with (able additions, 1843," in which year it ᴡ me by Dr. J. A. Paris, President of the C Physicians, who wrote in it, "From the a his young friend T. L. O. Davies." It haᵢ cation to Miss Edgeworth, dated Februarᵧ
T. LEWIS O. Dᵢ
Pear Tree Vicarage, Southampton.

JAMES BRUCE (read STUART), PRI SCOTLAND : GOUGH'S CAMDEN'S "BRIᴛ (5th S. ix. 107.)—This is a mistake. Stewart, then only son of Robert Stewaᵣ Scotland, and who afterwards ascended the throne as James I., was meant. All ᵗ ticulars given in the extract from the B regarding the capture and release of Jam apply to the case of James Stewart, ex locality and the date. The date 1473 iᵢ wrong, the reign of Henry IV., in which t is said to have occurred, having ended i and all the authors cited below concur iᵣ that the capture of James Stewart took Flamborough Head. This was in 1405 1424 he was liberated by the English, and at Scone as James I. of Scotland. All the kings of that name were Stewarts, so that hend it is merely a mistake in the name Bruce, instead of James Stewart. See Scotichronicon, lib. xv. c. 18, and lib. x Buchanani Rerum Scoticarum, lib. x. c. 1 ton's History of Scotland, vol. ii. p. 384.
R.

This sentence is quite correct save in tw In place of Robert Bruce, read Robert I in place of saying that the young princ leased in 1473, read 1423. As the passaᵨ in Gough's Camden it is simply nonsense,⸴

been often quoted and reproduced. In Gibson's Camden, 1722, i. 468, it is merely stated that a son and heir to the King of Scotland was intercepted at Clay, in Norfolk, in 1406 ; but in Cox's *Magna Britannia*, 1724, iii. 264, the story is told as given by Gough—that the young prince was the son of Robert Bruce, and that he remained a prisoner in the Tower of London till the time of Edward VI.! In truth Prince James Stewart, afterwards King James I. of Scotland, was detained in England from 1406 till 1423, about eighteen years ; but Gough makes the term of his imprisonment sixty-seven years, and Cox makes it 141 years. There seems also a doubt raised as to where the prince was taken, whether Flamborough Head or Clay. The version given by Holinshed will, I think, render this clear. He says, A.D. 1406 :—

"But it fortuned, that as they sailed neare to the English coast, about Flamborough Head in Holdernesse, their ship was taken and staied by certeine mariners of Claie (a town in Norfolke) that were abroad the same time ; and so he and all his companie being apprehended the thirtieth of March, was conveied to Windsore."

The young Prince James and the Earl of Orkney were sent to the Tower, but the attendant bishop, as Walsingham says, "per fugam lapso." The strange blunder of introducing the name of Bruce into this story probably arose from a hasty and careless reading of the circumstance as described by Buchanan.   EDWARD SOLLY.

James, second son of John Stuart, reigning over Scotland as Robert III., became the prisoner of Henry IV. in 1405. Capgrave says :—

"In this yere the Scottes ledde the Kyngis son of Scotland into Frauns to lerne that tonge and eke curtesie. And men of Cley in Northfolk took the schip in whech was the child with a bischop and the erl of Orkeney & led him to London to the Kyng."

Stow's account of the transaction will bear repeating :—

"The Scots sent James, sonne of Robert King of Scots, being but nine yeeres old, towards France, there to be brought vp and to be instructed in the pleasant eloquence of the French tongue, whom certaine Mariners of Clee in Norffolke tooke on the Seas and with him a Bishop and the Earle of Orkney, to whom his father had committed him, and they brought him into England and deliuered him to the K. who forthwith burst out into a laughter and said, surely the Scots might have sent him to mee, for I can speake French. The Bishop escaped and fled, but the Earle of Orkeney and the said James the young lad was sent to the Tower of London, where he remained Prisoner till the second yeere of Henry the sixt, which was above eighteen yeeres."

Soon after the prince's return to Scotland he ascended the throne as James I. His fame as a poet still survives in *The King's Quair* and, as many think, in *Peblis to the Play*. From his use of the seven-lined stanza employed by Chaucer it is sometimes called " rhyme royal." James married Lady Jane Beaufort.   ST. SWITHIN.

REVELATION, CH. XIII. (5ᵗʰ S. ix. 108.) — In the Chaldee or Aramaic, commonly known as the Syriac language, the letters which express the number of the beast, as given in Rev. xiii. 18, do not form the name of Nero. In the Syriac or Aramaic version of the New Testament published by the British and Foreign Bible Society, the numbers 666 are given, not in figures, but in words, as they stand in the English version, " Six hundred threescore and six." But the Hebrew New Testament, translated from the Greek, and published by the Society for Promoting Christianity among the Jews, gives the numbers 666 as a single word, according to the Jewish style of expressing dates. This word is *Turso* (תרסו), a term without any significance in Hebrew, but which in the Chaldee of the Targums may be translated *his shield*. It is made up of the following numbers : Tau, 400 ; Rēsh, 200 ; Samech, 60 ; Vau, 6=666. The Syriac letters for these numerals, it may be stated, exactly correspond with the Hebrew.   M. G. KENNEDY.

Waterloo Lodge, Reading.

It is in Renan's *L'Antechrist* that it is shown that the number of the beast in (I think, as far as my recollection serves) Hebrew spells " Cæsar Nero." I have not the work now at hand, nor—being ignorant of Hebrew—am I able to say, of my own knowledge, that the Frenchman's assertion is correct.   MIDDLE TEMPLAR.

J. C. M. will find this in Moses Stuart on the Apocalypse, p. 788, as the solution which Prof. Benary, of Berlin, gives of the number of the beast. Curiously enough, it seems that while one form of the Hebrew name of Nero amounts to 666, another amounts to 616, the reading of the Codex Ephræmi.   C. F. S. WARREN, M.A.

See Reuss, *Histoire de la Théologie Chrétienne*, i. 327.   A. L. MAYHEW.

Oxford.

WILLIAM, THIRD BARON OF WORMLEIGHTON (5ᵗʰ S. ix. 168.)—William, second Baron Spencer of Wormleighton, who died in 1636, left by Penelope, eldest daughter of Henry Wriothesley, Earl of Southampton, thirteen children. These were— 1. Henry (third baron) ; 2. Robert, created Viscount Teviot, ob. s.p. ; 3. William, of Ashton Hall, Lanc., ob. s.p. ; 4. Richard, d. unmar. ; 5. Thomas, and 6. John, both ob. inf. ; 7. Elizabeth, mar. to John, Baron Craven, secondly to Henry Howard, and thirdly to William, lord Crofts ; 8. Mary, ob. inf. ; 9. Anne, mar. to Sir R. Townshend ; 10. Katherine, ob. unmar. ; 11. Alice, mar. to the Earl of Drogheda ; 12. Margaret, mar. to the first Earl of Shaftesbury ; 13. Rachel, a posthumous child, ob. inf. Henry, the third Baron Spencer of Wormleighton, born 1620, created Earl of Sunderland in 1643, and slain

-ob. inf. EDWARD SOLLY.
Sutton, Surrey.

"CHARLOTTE" (5th S. ix. 168.)—I have always understood that the dishes in question were so called from the partiality of Queen Charlotte, wife of George III., to them, or else the name was given by the originator of them in honour of his royal mistress. They have no such recondite derivation as suggested by your correspondent. G. L. G.
Titsey Place.

In Harl. MS. 4016, which contains bills of fare for banquets, receipts, &c., from about 1380 to 1425, or thereabouts, the spelling of this word is *charlette*. HERMENTRUDE.

RACINE'S "ATHALIAH" AND "ESTHER" (5th S. ix. 208.)—Two translations of *Athalie*, bearing the name *Athaliah*, are mentioned in Lowndes : one, 1822, is by J. C. Knight ; the second, 1829, by Charles Randolph. Genest mentions another by Duncombe. *Esther; or, Faith Triumphant*, 1715, is by Brereton. None of these pieces and no version of either play has, I believe, ever been played in England. It is of course difficult to speak with absolute certainty on such a subject.
JOSEPH KNIGHT.

ROYAL AND IMPERIAL FAMILIES OF FRANCE (5th S. ix. 189.)—The best and fullest modern account known to me of the whole of the branches of the house of Bourbon, from the Capetian era down to the time of Louis Philippe, as well as of the Bonaparte dynasty, is to be found in Bouillet's *Atlas Universel d'Histoire et de Géographie*, published by Hachette (Paris and London). The genealogical tables compiled by Mr. Hereford B. George are dynastic rather than genealogical, in the strict sense, and would therefore probably not be so suitable to your correspondent.
C. H. E. CARMICHAEL.

"THE BRISTOL MEMORIALIST" (5th S. ix. 188.) —William Tyson, F.S.A., edited this book, and was the writer of many of the papers in it. He died in 1851.

For nearly twenty-five years he was connected with the *Bristol Mirror* (which, in 1865, was incorporated with the *Bristol Times and Felix Farley's Journal*), and contributed to it hundreds of articles relating to local history and antiquities, his knowledge of which was second to none. He also wrote occasionally for the *Gentleman's Magazine*, and corresponded with Southey, Payne Collier, John Britton, Sir R. C. Hoare, &c. For a fuller

They are by John Evans, the author logical *History of Bristol* and other was one of the unfortunate people k fall of the Brunswick Theatre, Lond 1828. He was a clever but not a vei man. A list of his works is in the p. 143, and a notice of his life in *Gent.* i. 375. W.
Bristol.

TOUCHING FOR THE KING'S EVIL (5 —In reply to DR. NICHOLSON's Quest think there is any authority for su' this custom had at all fallen into d period prior to the accession of James contrary, Queen Elizabeth used a sii or form of ceremonies to that first es Henry VII., a slight variation occu prayer used during the Elizabethan rei in the days of Henry VII. I have book a copy of the prayer used by El where it was taken from I forget. It —"Omnipotens Deus, æterna salus ои sperantium, exaudi nos te precamur ni lorum tuorum hic presentium, pro qu cors auxilium tuum imploramus, ut sa tibi gratias agant in sancta Ecclesi Jesum Christum Dominum nostrui James I. discontinued using the sign in giving the coin or medal; but reigns of Edward VI. and Queen E are told, when the "strumosi" came to the manner was "to apply the sign to the tumour, which raising of је if some mysterious operation were im that wise and learned king (James practically discontinued it, but orde expunged out of the service." The use was, however, reverted to by James I given, the angel noble, by Queens Elizabeth bore the following inscri Domino factum est istud, et est mirí of King James I. had "A Domino istud" only.

William Beckett, in his *Free an* *Enquiry into the Antiquity and Effica ing for the Cure of the King's Evil* (Lo implies that Queen Elizabeth at one p reign did for some little time disc touching; yet Tasker tells us that duri "many thousands were healed," the he held monthly, and even daily.
J. A. SPARVEL-BAYL

Your correspondent will find some

information in Mr. Stephens's *Editions of the Common Prayer Book*, vol. ii. pp. 990-1005, note, from which I extract the following :—

"From the reign of Edward the Confessor until the reign of George I. a power of healing diseases by 'touch' was claimed by the sovereigns of England......That the kings of England for several centuries exercised their touch for the cure of scrofulous complaints is proved by abundant historical authority, and scarcely any of our old historians who wrote during a period of at least 500 years have omitted taking notice of this strange and unaccountable fact. [Then follows a series of authorities.] The Form of Healing occurs often in the Common Prayer Books of the reigns of Charles I., Charles II., James II., and Queen Anne. The Latin form was used in the time of Henry VII., and was reprinted in 1686 by the king's printer. From registers duly kept it is ascertained that from 1660 to 1682 the number of persons touched for the king's evil amounted to 92,107. But in 1683 a proclamation was ordered to be published in every parish in the kingdom, enjoining that the time for presenting persons for the ' public healings' should be from the Feast of All Saints till a week before Christmas, and after Christmas until the first day of March, and then to cease till Passion Week. George I. made no pretensions to this miraculous gift, and it has never been claimed by his successors."

The religious ceremony used "at the healing," as given by Bishop Sparrow, may be seen in his *Collection of Articles, Canons, &c.*, p. 165, edit. 1671. The form, however, varied slightly in the different reigns.   E. C. HARINGTON.
  The Close, Exeter.

James I. was not supposed to possess this royal virtue when king of Scotland, but the power is said to have come to him immediately after his accession to the English throne. A proclamation of March 25, 1616, forbade patients to approach the king during the summer. DR. NICHOLSON is mistaken in thinking that the exercise of this superstition was in abeyance for any time prior to James I., as Elizabeth repeatedly went through the ceremony. In common no doubt with other searchers in old parish registers, I have frequently come across instances of certificates granted by their parish priest to those seeking to be royally healed. The latest instance that I have noted in this county is in the Measham registers, under March, 1687. A folio Prayer Book of 1706, now before me, has the office "At the Healing" on a leaf between the Form of Prayer for the Accession and the Articles. With respect to this may I ask another question ? What is the earliest and latest edition of the Prayer Book containing this office, and is the form used by Queen Anne the same as that of other post-reformation monarchs ?
                        J. CHARLES COX.
  Belper.

THE MARQUIS ESTERNULIE (5th S. ix. 147.)— Thomas Stukeley was a native of Devonshire, but, on the side of his mother, he claimed descent from the family of Macmurrough-Kavanagh, of Ireland.

According to another account he was a natural son of Henry VIII. All versions agree in describing him as a man noted for his daring and almost reckless character. He first appeared in public life about the time that Elizabeth became queen, and in 1563 was one of a band of adventurers who projected the exploration and occupation of Florida. This enterprise, despite the support accorded to it by the queen, fell through, and Stukeley had to look to other scenes than the New World for the advancement of his worldly affairs. He appears, even in this early stage of his career, to have been considered by his associates as one of a fickle if not treacherous disposition, and his reputation for probity never seems to have been very great. His plausibility was undoubted, and we find him, shortly after the Florida scheme failure, in the train of Sir Henry Sidney, the Lord Deputy of Ireland. So useful did he make himself in this new capacity, that Sidney entrusted him with the charge of the negotiations that were being carried on with Shane O'Neill in 1567. This confidence in Stukeley was not approved of by the queen, who expressed her dissatisfaction to Sidney upon the subject. The natural consequence of that hint of royal displeasure was that Stukeley passed under a cloud ; and, when he petitioned the Lord Deputy for various appointments as the reward for his services, he was met with a refusal. In a fit of spleen he thereupon entered into relations with the Irish party, and notably with Sir James Fitzmaurice, the great "patriot" or "archplotter," whichever view we may feel inclined to take of Irish politics of that age. By the instructions of Fitzmaurice, Stukeley went on a mission to the Pope, Gregory XIII., who granted the Irish a Bull authorizing them to fight for the recovery of their independence. The Pope also fitted up a small expedition at his own expense, which was afterwards to be maintained by Philip of Spain, and over which Hercules Pisano was made general, and Stukeley admiral. In numbers this force "for the conquest of Ireland" did not exceed eight hundred men, of whom a large number were highwaymen pardoned for their past offences by participation in this expedition against the heretic. Before the departure of the small flotilla Stukeley was created Lord of Idrone, and, subsequently, some higher rank still. I am unable to find any verification of the statement of the various authorities quoted by DR. LEARED, that Stukeley was created Marquis of Leinster, and this is, perhaps, made still more doubtful by the assertion of O'Daly that the Pope was dubious of Stukeley's fidelity to the cause. These suspicions were to some extent verified, for on his journey to Ireland he put into the port of Lisbon, where the King of Portugal, Don Sebastian, was busily preparing for his expedition against Morocco, and Stukeley, indifferent to his promises to Fitzmaurice, who

personal advantage. In the fatal battle of Alcaçar he and most of his followers perished by the side of the unfortunate Sebastian; and thus terminated a career which, even in the troubled age which witnessed it, was far from being monotonous or uneventful. D. C. BOULGER.

This is evidently Sir Thomas Stucley, that bold and adventurous traitor to Elizabeth, concerning whom I quote as follows from the *Saturday Review* of Jan. 26, 1878 :—

"Stucley had actually set out from Rome [for Ireland, in 1578, just three hundred years ago] with a body of Italian volunteers—banditti amnestied on this condition—but at Lisbon he was persuaded by the crusading King Sebastian to take part with him in the invasion of Africa which was to unseat Muley Moluck from the throne of Morocco. In this unfortunate expedition Stucley embarked, and its result, as is well known, was the disaster of Alcazar, where, 'on the fourth of August, three kings *in re* and one *in spe* were slain.'"
A. J. M.

The name Estucli, applied *alias* to the Marquis Esternulie, betrays our old friend Stukeley, of whom Froude gives a good account, and of whom mention is made in Kingsley's *Westward Ho!* The old *Life of Stukeley* rarely appears in catalogues. I have never seen it, and should be glad to know what titles he received from the Pope. I have a copy of a papal passport granted by him to Gregory Sylvester and others, in which he is described as "Thomas Stewkley, Knt., Baron of Rosse and Idrone, Viscount of Murrewes, &c., &c., General of our most Holy Father Gregory the XIII. P.M."
H. J. H.
Penzance.

ARMS ON AN ANCIENT TOMB (5th S. ix. 189.)—In Papworth and Morant's *Ordinary of British Armorials* the arms inquired for by MR. FERNIE (Sable, three bars argent) are said to be borne by several families : Eaton of Worcester ; Haughton and Houghton of Lancester, Chester, Hants, Sussex, and London ; Lea of Lancaster ; Porter of Warwick ; Sir William Scharlow. MR. FERNIE may possibly be able to identify the coat of arms at Wellingore by consulting pedigrees of the Dymokes and Disneys.
W. SPARROW SIMPSON.

The arms about which MR. FERNIE inquires, viz. Sa., three bars arg., are those borne by the old Lancashire family of Houghton or Hoghton. Sir H. Hoghton, of Hoghton Tower, adds a canton or, charged with a rose and a thistle. In the ancient

gomery, bore the following arms :—(1 and 4, quarterly gu. and or, a fess bet lions passant gardant all countercha Edwards ; 2 and 3, Sa., on a fess arg. b chief a lion ramp. of the last, and in ba de-lys or, three snakes interlaced ppr., of Garth. Greenfields in Machynlleth, gomery, was the baronet's paternal est he derived Garth from his mother, Corn and heiress of Richard Owen, of (Llandidloes, co. Montgomery. Sir John only child and heiress, Cornelia Mary, the fifth and present Marquess of Lon Lady Edwards, the baronet's widow a1 wife, and mother of Lady Londonderry,
A

PORTRAIT OF DR. CHILLINGWORTH (169.)—Bromley, *Catalogue of Engrave Portraits*, mentions one of him, "witl bury, Locke, and Woolaston," " mezzo gives neither painter nor engraver. L.

There are these entries in Evans's Ca *Engraved British Portraits:*—Vol. ii. N "Chillingworth, Wm., 8vo., 1s. Barret No. 10447, "Tompion, Thomas, celebrat maker, ob. 1713, fol. *Scarce*, 5s. Smith." ED. MAR

SEPULCHRAL MOUND, TOWYN-Y-CAP ix. 149.)—There is a description of th by the Hon. William Owen Stanley in th of the *Royal Archæological Institute,* p. 223. From his description, and my (vation, there may there be seen the r human bodies in three or four tiers. The ment of the sea has laid bare one port mound, exposing the bones. The bodies with the feet inwards, converging to t The foundations of the chapel still rem: summit of the mound. DE(

The tradition of the neighbourhood a the battle took place during the Roma of Britain, and as we know that th landed in Anglesey, the story does not se probable one. I have, however, never to collect authentic particulars of the eve I know Towyn Bay well.
R. P. HAMPTON R

" DON'T SIKE " (5th S. ix. 154.)—In the origin of this expression I ough remembered that the word *sike* in Cha

to sigh. Hence when the Staffordshire folk say "Don't *sike*" to a person catching his breath in bathing, they evidently mean, "Don't gasp or sigh."   JOHN CHURCHILL SIKES.
Godolphin Road, Shepherd's Bush, W.

"THE LASS OF RICHMOND HILL" (5th S. ix. 169.)—
"Mr. Upton, who wrote the above song, wrote many others for the convivial entertainments at Vauxhall Gardens towards the close of the last century. The music of this song, composed by Mr. Hook, father of the late Theodore Hook, was long popularly ascribed to the Prince of Wales. It was a great favourite with George III."—*The Illustrated Book of English Songs*, Ingram & Co., Strand (n.d.), 8vo.
                                        ZERO.

" *The Lass of Richmond Hill* was written by Leonard MacNally, Esq., barrister, and the Richmond is in Surrey. This information is given by his grand-daughter."
Thus to me his granddaughter, who is my aunt. Mr. MacNally died in 1820. He had a good deal of connexion with the "United Irishmen," for which see Mr. Frost's *Secret Societies*.
                            C. F. S. WARREN, M.A.
Bexhill.

A LADY CONTEMPORARY OF QUEEN KATHARINE DE VALOIS (5th S. ix. 161.)—May I be permitted to ask the REV. J. H. BLUNT if he has not made a mistake in saying that Queen Katharine and Isabel, Countess of Warwick, were "both born in the same year and died in the same year"? Was not the queen born Oct. 27, 1401, fifteen months after the countess, and did she not die Jan. 3, 1437, about three years before her? Would he also oblige me by giving any particulars of the remains of the countess's father, Thomas, Lord Le Despenser, who, as I was told recently at Tewkesbury, was found close beside his daughter?
                                    HERMENTRUDE.

USTONSON OF TEMPLE BAR (5th S. ii. 288; ix. 191.)—Is MR. BATES aware that there is still a firm in existence bearing the name of "Kirby, Beard & Co."?   J. BORRAJO.

"MUCKED TO DEATH" (5th S. ix. 6, 73.)—By the Sussex peasantry this elegant expression is in common use, and, as in the examples given by MR. KERR, the word is employed as a verb, and mostly in the sense of forcible or summary expulsion. Thus you will frequently hear one person saying to another, "I'll muck you out," or "If you don't mind what you're at, and mend your ways, the master will pretty quick muck you out." It is rarely, as in other counties, used in the sense of manure, for which these people have *mending* or *dressing*.   EDMUND TEW, M.A.

Muck is used with various meanings in many parts of Scotland. It is generally used as synony-

mous with manure, but it is also applied to anything that is mean or vile. I have heard it used in particular of the dirt of pig-sties, and the island of Muck (which is notorious both for its pigs and its dirt) and the mountain Ben Mac Dhui seem to point to the same meaning.
                                    FRANCIS ANDERSON.

INVITATION CARDS OF THE EIGHTEENTH CENTURY (5th S. ix. 168, 214.)—The following well-known epigram shows that invitations written on playing cards were not unusual ; it is by the Rev. Mr. Lewis, minister of Margate from 1705 to 1746, in reply to an invitation to dinner by the Duchess of Dorset written on a ten of hearts:—
"Your compliments, lady, I pray you forbear,
    Our old English service is much more sincere :
You sent me ten hearts—the tithe 's only mine ;
    So give me one heart, and burn t' other nine."
                                            H. P. D.

I possess a playing card (the ten of clubs) split, so that the interior affords space for writing, with the address written on the back, being a note from Sir John Danvers, dated Swithland, Jan. 29, 1757, to my great-grandfather, "the Rev. Mr. Statham, at Mountsorrell."   H. W. S.

HARDWICKE HALL (5th S. ix. 187.)—The lines referred to by A. W. W. as being engraved on one of the pillars of the porch of Hardwicke Hall may be found in Ovid's *Metamorphoses*, lib. i. ll. 175-6.
                                        J. HENRY.

AUTHORS OF BOOKS WANTED (5th S. ix. 189.)— *The Post-Captain* is, I believe, by Dr. Moore, the author of *Zeluco*.   P. J. F. GANTILLON.

Miscellaneous.

NOTES ON BOOKS, &c.

The Relations between Ancient Russia and Scandinavia, and the Origin of the Russian State. By Dr. Vilhelm Thomsen. (Oxford and London, Parker & Co.)
THIS interesting little volume is one of the good fruits borne in a short space of time by the bequest of the Earl of Ilchester for the encouragement of Slavonic studies in the University of Oxford. The trustees of this fund having, in 1876, invited a Scandinavian *savant* to lecture on a Slavonic subject, that gentleman naturally gave his course a Scandinavian turn, as he straightforwardly confesses in his preface. Dr. Thomsen's English is, on the whole, remarkably good, but there are occasional quaint or obscure passages, which it seems to us his English friends might have made more conformable to our usage in revising his sheets. With regard to the main thesis of Dr. Thomsen's lectures, the Scandinavian origin of the founders of the Russian State, we must say that his book somewhat reminds us of the tilt which the worthy knight of La Mancha ran against the windmills. We were quite conscious of what Gibbon and his annotators had said on this subject, and what in more recent times had been said by Lappenberg, Thomsen and other leading historians; and as those authorities all concurred in laying down the Scandinavian origin of Rurik and his companions, we did not feel

...... ground in his discussion of the philological evidence adducible from the names of the Dnieper rapids. We do not observe that he quotes Lappenberg at all, though in his work on *England under the Anglo-Norman Kings* there might have been found interesting proofs of the existence of the name Varangian ·in Neustria as well as in Norway. Lappenberg cites Varengeville and the Varangerfjord as examples, in widely different localities, of the recurrence of " an appellation that may be understood to signify all Northern Vikings in general," and of which he further says, " it is well known that the Northern people that visited Russia were so called." Gibbon gives " corsair" as the meaning of Varangian, and it is perhaps quite as likely to signify "wanderer" as " denizen" or " metoecus," though we may remember that after all a " metic" was a foreigner. The list of Scandinavian proper names and other words given in the last lecture and appendix are of considerable philological and historical interest.

The Agamemnon of Æschylus. Transcribed by Robert Browning. (Smith, Elder & Co.)

MR. BROWNING has for once expounded his motives. Since the issue of the fine but ill-starred essay on Shelley, recalled because the letters it preceded turned out to be forgeries, we have had from the poet no prose exceeding a few lines in length ; but here, in front of the *Agamemnon*, we have seven pages of preface. From this we learn that he who is admittedly the profoundest thinker among living English poets, and has the credit of being the hardest to read, considers the *Agamemnon* " very hard reading indeed," and holds that a faithful translation of it should also be hard reading, and that the "magniloquence and sonority of the Greek" are not to be coveted in comparison with the virtue of being "literal at every cost save that of absolute violence to our language." Hence it is not strange that we get a highly valuable book, but one which must be read over and over again to yield the full measure of beauty and instruction it contains. To be conducted through a tragedy of Æschylus by so vigorous and subtle an intellect as Mr. Browning's is no small benefit for any one who cares for more than the "bells and jingle" of poetry: *Balaustion's Adventure* and *Aristophanes' Apology* had taught us to expect that much, from his mode of taking us through two tragedies of Euripides. But we hold one of the foremost aims of translation should be to make a beautiful work as beautiful as possible in its new guise ; and we doubt whether Mr. Browning has made the *Agamemnon* as beautiful as he could. Indeed, in some parts of his version vigour and subtlety are so exquisitely blended with perfect turn of phrase that we are led to regret the frequent absence of beauty elsewhere. The iambic line with dissyllabic ending, selected for the bulk of the work, we cannot, after several readings, find to be·well adapted to the requirements of the poem and our language—not so well adapted as the ordinary blank verse used by Mr. Fitzgerald, and, before him, by Thomas Medwin. Mr. Fitzgerald's *Agamemnon* is a superbly beautiful poem, nowise hard to read, and hence not fully faithful, according to Mr. Browning's criterion. Medwin's version is elegant and easy, with certain echoes of Shelley in it. Mr. Browning's is infinitely more literal than either, but certainly not so well

sent us for incorporation, while we shou indebted to the authors of unpublished ɡ would forward us in advance any plaɪ letters A—F, this being the probable ex part. Jᴀ British Museum.

" IDEL ": " WHAT'S IN A NAME ?"— " It is proposed to adopt the above (whic sensible spelling) for Idle, near Leeds, dents are requested to address their le inhabitants are more indolent than othe are not, as may be premised from the locally pronounced *rust*. We hope orthography will be universally and pron

LONDON, SATURDAY, MARCH 30, 1878.

CONTENTS.—N° 222.

Notes.

THE PURY FAMILY, &c.

(Continued from p. 45.)

Alderman Pury was descended from a family which appears to have been already settled in Gloucester in the reign of Henry VII. In 1506 one Walter Pury gave 20l. a year to the poor of the parish of St. Mary de Crypt, in which parish the family lived, and where most of them are buried. Thomas Pury, mercer, was sheriff of the city in 1541 and mayor in 1550, and again in 1560. He died April, 1580, and is buried in the chancel of the church of St. Mary de Crypt, where there is a monument to his memory, with arms and a long Latin inscription signifying that he was son and heir to William Pury, younger brother to John Pury, of Cokeham, in the county of Berks, Esq., by his wife, the sister and co-heiress of John Cooke, Esq., four times mayor of the city. It also states that he was connected by marriage with Sir William Danvers, Kt., one of the Justices of the Common Pleas under Henry VII., and with Richard Pates, who was Recorder of Gloucester and member for the city *tempore* Mary and Elizabeth. Another monument in the same church to the memory of Alderman Pury describes him as "nuper Major hujus civitatis Glocestriæ, filius Gualteri, filii Thomæ Pury Armigeri, juxta inhumati," so that the alderman was grandson of Thomas Pury above mentioned. It is probable

that in early life he was engaged in trade or manufacture, as was by no means uncommon in those days with members of good families, but he was afterwards "of the profession of the law." The old Royalist pamphlet, entitled *The Mystery of the Good Old Cause*, says that he was "first a weaver in Gloucester, then an ignorant country solicitor"; but no more credence is to be given to the scandal of the Royalists under Charles II. than to that of the Puritans under Oliver Cromwell. Whatever he was, he had become a man of mark in his native city, for he was sheriff in 1626 and a successful candidate at the election March 24, 1639-40, when he was elected (to the Long Parliament) in preference to William Singleton, who had been a popular mayor and also a former member, and William Lenthall, the Recorder, afterwards better known as "Speaker Lenthall," who appears to have resented his defeat, since in an undated and unpublished letter, written many years after, and when he was again a candidate, he says:—"I have noe assurance of Electiō there, it being wth mighty hand and much power labored against me. Only this I can say, if they chewse me not I shall disdayne to beare the name of Recorder amongst them."

There is a long and interesting letter calendared in the last publication of State Papers, 1639-40 (Domestic), written from the bishop's palace at Gloucester on March 24, 1639-40, the day of the election, by John Allibonel to Peter Heylin, from which it would seem as if Pury had some Quaker tendencies, for, describing the candidates, he mentions Pury, and says, "Whom nothing has so much endeared as his irreverence in God's house, sitting covered when all the rest sit bare, whose cause is earnestly presented by the aforesaid Nelmes and Edwards," previously described by him as "strong and rank Puritans." Mr. Webb, in his admirable introduction to the *Bibliotheca Gloucestrensis*, says: "He had raised himself into notice by his talents and industry, and was possessed of considerable influence amongst the citizens. In the House he zealously pressed every innovation of Church and State, and, being a speaker of some ability and a man of business, was frequently engaged in their numerous committees." When the Act for publishing scandalous clergymen and others passed, March 10, 1641, he was appointed one of the commissioners for carrying it into execution in the city and county of Gloucester (Husband's *Ordinances*). Like Sir Simonds D'Ewes, May, and Burton, he took notes of the proceedings in the Long Parliament, and these existed until a recent period, but cannot now be found, and are believed to have been destroyed. On Nov. 30, 1641, he moved that the famous Dr. Chillingworth should be brought to the bar of the House for having said that some members of the House were guilty of treason, and that they should be accused within a day or two; whereupon it was ordered that the serjeant's deputy should bring him forthwith to the House, and if he should refuse to come, that he should apprehend him as a delinquent and bring him (D'Ewes's *Journals*, Nov. 30, 1641). Mr. Webb says:—" He was in determined hostility to the king, and on the approach of danger hastened down to Gloucester, where himself and his son held military commands, and proved themselves amongst the most resolute defenders of the city." He was a deputy lieutenant for the city, and in 1642 was appointed to communicate with the Earl of Essex, who was then engaged at Worcester in settling the militia. He was also in communication with Waller during the latter's visit to Gloucester in June, 1643 (see a very gentlemanly letter from Waller to Lady Scudamore, *Hist. Intro. Bib. Glo.*).

Certainly some stout hearts were needed at that time, for the condition of the city and the garrison was very low, and neither the citizens nor the soldiers appear to have much relished the prospect of a siege. Amongst the Tanner MSS. in the Bodleian are some unpublished letters written before and after the siege, some of which have been copied for me by my good friend Kyffin Lenthall, the Recorder of Woodstock, and which give a very graphic picture of the state of things under which, nevertheless, in defence of their liberties, Pury and his compatriots determined to resist their sovereign. In a letter to Mr. Speaker Lenthall, dated from Gloucester, July 29, 1643, Col. Massie (so he spells his name) complains bitterly of the privations of the garrison, and says :—

" Alderman Pury and his citizens I dare say are still cordiall to us, but I fear 10 for one to enclyne the other way of the rest, w'ch I see by the fayling of the citizens help to amend and better our decaying works, yet neither they nor y° country since Bristoll's losse yeald any obedience unto my warrants, and for lack of force of our owne well paid and cared for, I am enforced to doe as I can, not as I would."

On the same day the officers of the garrison addressed a most urgent letter to the same effect to the Speaker, "for the most noble houses of Parliament these—Haste, Haste : post Haste." This is signed by Massie and thirteen officers, including Alderman Pury and his son ; and in the margin, by way of postscript, Massie writes :—

" The Treasure of this City is so exhausted that no more money can be raysed either to pay my Lo. Stamford's Regim¹ or Collon¹ Stephen's, but we both joyntly are in great necessity, & both looke for Reliefe w¹ᵗ⁰ut wch neither can possibly subsist. Edw. Massie."

Nevertheless Pury and his party held out, and resisted alike privations, threats, and promises. Dorney, the Town Clerk of Gloucester, in his *Exact Relation*, says :—

" After the unexpected surrender of Bristol, the City of Gloucester was assaulted with severall letters, messages, & such verball solicitations by divers of the king's army of no meane quality, thereby pretending our good,

and expressing of their love to care of us, but really intending their own sinister ends and our destruction. Among the rest there came a letter on Friday, August 4, dated August 3, from a Captain of a troope of horse in the king's army to Mr. Alderman Pury, one of the burgesses of the Parliament for this city, full of persuasive oratory for the yeelding up of this city, with great promises as heretofore of preferment, and braggs of the greatness of the army that was then on their march coming against us...but Mr. Alderman Pury (whose fidelity is sufficiently known to be so firm to the Parliament that it is not to be shaken by promises or threats) thinking it not worthy of, so accordingly sent no answer." —See this letter in full, Fosbrooke, pp. 81-82.

When the king was advancing some were wavering, and Mr. Webb says :—

" There is good ground for believing that Pury and his party counteracted anything like a return towards loyalty in the other authorities ; for both the mayor and governor seem to have hesitated, the former upon his oath, and the latter upon his ancient service and allegiance."

Alderman Pury and his son signed the reply to the king, refusing to surrender the city except " as his Majesty's command should be signified by both houses of Parliament" ; and Mr. Webb thinks that "many historical conjectures have been more groundless than that Pury was greatly instrumental to all the consequences that awaited Charles and the kingdom."   J. J. P.

[For particulars of Thomas Pury, Rector of Beverston, 1563-1617, see pp. 149-159 of *Dursley and its Neighbourhood*, by Rev. J. H. Blunt.—Ed.]

(*To be continued.*)

MAGDALEN COLLEGE, OXFORD, AND GIBBON THE HISTORIAN.

I came lately across an interesting specimen of private printing in Magdalen College library, and a note of it may be acceptable to some of your readers. A small quarto tract of forty-four pages was printed by the Rev. James Hurdis, D.D., at a small press of his own at Cowley, near Oxford. The title of it is :—

" A | Word or Two | in Vindication | of | the University of Oxford, | and of | Magdalen College | in Particular, | from the | Posthumous Aspersions | of | Mr. Gibbon.
'Nulla mihi, inquam,
Religio est.
At mî ; sum paulo infirmior; unus
Multorum; ignosces.'   *Hor.*"

The name of Hurdis is now unknown to the general reader, but he was known as the Sussex poet in his day. He was a friend and correspondent of the poet Cowper. The author of *The Task* looked over some of his writings and gave his *imprimatur*. The first edition of Hurdis's poetry was printed at his private press at Cowley by himself and his sisters, but after his death all his poetry was published (1808) in three volumes, with a large subscription, for the benefit of his two sisters, who were in reduced circumstances.

James Hurdis was the son of James Hurdis, of Bishopstone, in Sussex. He was born in 1763, entered at St. Mary Hall, Oxford, Feb. 28, 1780, was elected Demy of Magdalen, 1782, probationer fellow, 1786, proceeded M.A., 1787, and published his first poem, the *Village Curate*, in 1788. In 1785 he went to the curacy of Burwash, in Sussex (his rector being the Rev. John Courtail, Archdeacon of Lewes), and here he remained for six years. In 1791 Hurdis was appointed to the living of Bishopstone ; but the loss of a favourite sister in the following year caused him a deep sorrow, and he moved in April, 1793, with two sisters, to a small house at Temple Cowley, near Oxford, and in the same year was elected Professor of Poetry in that university. In 1797 he took the degree of D.D. ; in 1799 he married Harriet, daughter of Hughes Minet, Esq., of Fulham ; and on December 23, 1801, he died, after three days' illness, in his thirty-eighth year.

It must have been during the last five years of his life (probably about the years 1796-97) that this *Vindication* of Oxford and Magdalen College was printed by Hurdis and his sisters at their press at Cowley.

The historian Gibbon was entered at Magdalen College in 1752 as a Gentleman-Commoner. He was only at Oxford about fourteen months (half of which period was vacation), and he died in 1794. The first edition of Gibbon's *Memoirs* was brought out by Lord Sheffield in Aug., 1795 ; and the feelings of Hurdis were strongly roused by the false and unfair attacks of Gibbon on his *alma mater*, and he wrote his *Vindication* with warmth, in strong nervous English, and entirely turned the tables on the historian. There is one part which I think well worth putting on record as showing how solid an education was given one hundred years ago, at any rate in *one* college—a thing much doubted by those of the present day. Gibbon declared that he learnt nothing at college because nothing was taught there, and "the obvious methods of public exercises and examinations *are* totally unknown in Magdalen College." Hurdis says that even if the system was not quite the same when Gibbon was an undergraduate, which was thirty years before Hurdis's time, still he *ought* to have known that terminal examinations were in existence there when he (Gibbon) wrote, and he gives the curriculum. Hurdis says :—

"At the end of every term from his admission till he takes his first degree every individual undergraduate of this college must appear at a *public examination* before the President, Vice-President, Deans, and whatever Fellows may please to attend, and cannot obtain leave to return to his friends in any vacation till he has properly acquitted himself according to the following scheme :—

" In his *first* year he must make himself a proficient,
" In the first term, in Sallust and the *Characters* of Theophrastus.
" In the second term, in the first six books of Virgil's *Æneis* and the first three books of Xenophon's *Anabasis*.
" In the third term, in the last six books of the *Æneis* and the last four books of the *Anabasis*.

" In the fourth term, in the Gospels of St. Matthew and St. Mark, on which sacred books the persons examined are always called upon to produce a collection of observations from the best commentators.

" During his *second* year the undergraduate must make himself a proficient,
" In the first term, in Cæsar's *Commentaries* and the first six books of Homer's *Iliad*.
" In the second term, in Cicero *de Oratore* and the second six books of the *Iliad*.
" In the third term, in Cicero *de Officiis* and Dion. Hal. *de Structurâ Orationis*.
" In the fourth term, in the Gospels of St. Luke and St. John, producing a collection of observations from commentators, as at the end of the first year.
" During his *third* year he must make himself a proficient,
" In the first term, in the first six books of Livy and Xenophon's *Cyropædia*.
" In the second term, in Xenophon's *Memorabilia* and in Horace's *Epistles* and *Art of Poetry*.
" In the third term, in Cicero *de Naturâ Deorum*, and in the first, third, eighth, tenth, thirteenth, and fourteenth of Juvenal's *Satires*.
" In the fourth term, in the first four Epistles of St. Paul, producing collections as before.
" During his *fourth* and last year he must make himself a proficient,
" In the first term, in the first six books of the *Annals* of Tacitus and in the *Electra* of Sophocles.
" In the second term, in Cicero's *Orations* against Catiline and in those for Ligarius and Archias, and also in those of Demosthenes which are contained in Mounteney's edition.
" In the third term, in the *Dialogues* of Plato, published by Dr. Forster, and in the *Georgics* of Virgil.
" In the fourth term, in the remaining ten Epistles of St. Paul, and the Epistles General, producing collections as before."

He adds :—

" The above exercises are imposed upon every student, of whatever denomination. He has to attend, besides, his tutor's lecture once a day, and must produce a theme or declamation once a week to the dean.
" The undergraduates were also required to attend three distinct lectures in every term, that is, twelve in a year, from three regular lecturers appointed by the college from the body of the fellows."

The whole of this *Vindication* is interesting, and the printing from the private press at Temple Cowley most respectable.   GIBBES RIGAUD.
18, Long Wall, Oxford.

MR. ARBER'S REPRINTS.—The contents of Mr. Arber's *English Garner : Ingatherings from our History and Literature*, are of the most varied character ; and, although I would not say with the alderman in the *Spectator*, "too many plumbs, and too much suet," it is not easy to appreciate the conflicting flavours of this very miscellaneous dish. An enemy might point out that the book has no arrangement, and does not pretend to have any, even in its table of contents ; that it has no index ; and that its first twenty-four pages, for instance, contain no less than eight incongruous pieces. But I am no enemy to Mr. Edward Arber. On the contrary, I feel, and proclaim emphatically, the great and, as yet, imperfectly recognized services he has done for all English-speaking folk, by providing them with a marvellously cheap and most carefully edited series of reprints of many of our best English writers of the sixteenth and seventeenth centuries. And therefore I am provoked, as by the shortcomings of an old friend, when I find him dealing with those very centuries and those very writers in a way so different. For here, in *An English Garner*, we have *Astrophel and Stella* side by side with a list of carriers' carts, and a bridal ballad next door to a wine merchant's bill. We have explanations not only given, but actually bracketed in the text, of the commonest old words, which any one who reads his Bible must know ; as *targets* (p. 16) and *to let* (p. 107). We have the spelling modernized throughout, even in the lovely poems of Sidney and Spenser which give its chief value to the *Garner*. This last proceeding may be a boon to those young persons who need to be taught that to *wot* means to *know*, and to *let* means to *hinder ;* but even to them it is a fatal boon, for it will prevent them from ever enjoying the archaic charm, the *genius loci*, of an old edition. It injures the rhyme (or rather *rime*) too, as Mr. Arber himself confesses ; and, what is worse, it may spoil the rhythm, as it does on p. 253, where, by leaving out the first *e* in the word "chapelets," Mr. Arber has debited Spenser with a halting line. There is another fault which is graver still. All the verse in this volume is accentuated. I must not now occupy your space by protesting against the monstrous and criminal innovation of *accents* in English ; but, if any one should observe that it has crept securely into the later editions even of Tennyson, I would reply that a man like Mr. Arber, a skilled archæologist editing Elizabethan poets, is doubly bound to set his face against that vain and fondly invented thing.

I have spoken out as to these blemishes, because some of them are the result of tendencies that have increased, are increasing, and ought to be diminished, and because all of them are important in a work which is meant, one may presume, for intelligent and educated students. But let no one undervalue the merits of this *English Garner*. They are real, great, and novel. It is not only that the book exhibits industry and wide research, nor that it gives us, for a few shillings, reprints of rare or unique tracts of value and interest ; nor even (though this is much) that it has brought *Astrophel and Stella* within the reach of every one. Had these poems, with Mr. Arber's able and lucid introduction to them, and with Spenser's *Elegies* to boot, been issued separately as an "English reprint," they would have been a joy even to those who possess the original folios, just as the travels and adventures of the *Garner* would have delighted us the more if they too had been published as a separate collection. But in spite of all its incongruities the book has one special and exceeding merit. The best of its verse and the best of its prose, taken together, exhibit, as no other recent collection exhibits, a conspectus of the literary England of Elizabeth— a near and intimate view of that devout and ardent spirit, that new-found delight in the name and glories of their country, which the Englishmen of those great days felt, and had a right to feel.

Mr. Arber promises three or four volumes of his *Garner* annually. For the sake, then, of these and of their readers, I trust that he will sift and winnow his harvest, will restore, at least to the poets, their spelling, and will forbear to insult them and us by the use of accents. Let him but do this, and to his future *Ingatherings* a hearty and unfaltering welcome is assured.

A. J. M.

Temple.

Port Royal and Vivisection.—A curious illustration of the way in which errors arise and are perpetuated occurs in Principal Tulloch's recent work, *Pascal* (Blackwood & Sons, 1878). On p. 176, in a note, he says :—

"The following passage from Fontaine's *Memoirs,* quoted by Cousin (B. Pascal, p. 132), gives an interesting and lively glimpse of the philosophical discourses at Port Royal ; it may not be without some application to the modern no less than the original Cartesian doctrine :— 'How many little agitations raised themselves in this desert touching the new opinions of M. Descartes. There was hardly a solitary who did not talk of *automata*. To beat a dog was no longer a matter of any moment. The stick was laid on with the utmost indifference ; a great fool was made of those who pitied the animals as if they had any feeling. They said they were only clockwork, and that the cries they uttered were no more than the noise of some little spring that had been moved, and that all this involved no sensation. They *raised* the poor animals upon boards by the *fore* paws, in order to dissect them while still alive, and to see the circulation of the blood, which was a great subject of discussion.'"

On reading this passage I felt assured that the original must mean "*nailed* by the *four* paws." On referring to Cousin's *Pascal*, second edit., 1844, p. 41, I found, "on *élevoit* par les *quatre* pattes." This showed that *four* is the right translation ; but how to account for *raised?* It occurred to me that *élevoit* might easily be a misprint for *clouoit ;* and on referring to Fontaine's *Mémoires de Port-Royal*, Utrecht, 1736, vol. ii. p. 53, I found accordingly, "On *clouoit* de pauvres animaux sur des ais, par les *quatre* pattes." Thus by two misprints, one in French, *élevoit* for *clouoit*, and one in English, *fore* for *four*, the meaning has been impaired, if not destroyed. W. B. Hodgson.

Bonaly Tower, near Edinburgh.

An Analysis of Poets' Corner.—The recent "poetic wedding," as one of the morning papers termed it, of the son of Mr. Tennyson and the daughter of Mr. Frederick Locker, in Westminster Abbey, has set me thinking of that most celebrated south transept of the great minster known to all men as Poets' Corner, and I have come to the conclusion that this renowned corner, although undoubtedly one of the most interesting spots in the world on account of the great writers whose ashes lie there, is not quite so much of a *Poets'* Corner as it is popularly supposed to be. Let me explain myself more clearly. The seven greatest poets of our country are, I presume (I name them in chronological order), Chaucer, Spenser, Shakspeare, Milton, Shelley, Byron, Wordsworth. To these I ought, perhaps, to add an eighth, Elizabeth Barrett Browning. Of these eight how many lie in the Abbey?—only two, Chaucer and Spenser. Let us now come down a few steps in the poetic ladder, and mention some who, though great, are not quite so great as the above-mentioned monarchs of Parnassus—for instance, Ben Jonson, Fletcher, Dryden, Pope, Gray, Cowper, Keats, Coleridge. Of these eight again only two are in the Abbey— Ben Jonson and Dryden. Let me once more take another eight : Marvell, Cowley, Thomson, Collins, Goldsmith, Crabbe, Campbell, Mrs. Hemans. Only two of these again are in the Abbey—Cowley and Campbell. Neither do Marlowe, Beaumont, Herbert, William Browne, Vaughan, Waller, Herrick, Shenstone, Chatterton, Hood, Moore, Southey, Leigh Hunt, or Keble repose in the Abbey. Perhaps I ought not to go to Scotland ; and yet I hardly know why, as the writings of Burns and Scott, especially of the latter, are surely as much a part of English literature as those of Spenser or Wordsworth. If, then, we wish to visit the last resting-places of Scotland's two greatest poets, we must seek them not in Westminster, but the one in Dumfries, the other in Dryburgh Abbey.

I have now gone through the greater part of our poets of eminence, and I think that any one who has been kind enough to follow me up to this point must agree with me that, when we think of the multitude of England's singing birds, it is rather the exception than otherwise to find a poet buried in the Abbey. It is true that in Poets' Corner are buried Addison, Johnson, Macaulay, and, in another part of the Abbey, Lord Lytton, and that all these more or less wrote poetry. But they were not, strictly speaking, poets. It is their prose writings that have gained them their great and lasting reputation with mankind.*

I trust that no one will suppose for a moment that I wish to speak depreciatingly or disrespectfully of Poets' Corner, a spot which must ever be dear to all true lovers of poetry were it for the sake of Edmund Spenser alone. All I wish to point out is that it is curious, when we come to closely examine into the matter, to find that out of the

* I am not acquainted with the Rev. H. F. Cary's own poetry, but I presume that Cary, however accomplished as a translator, is hardly entitled to be ranked amongst our really original poets.

great number of England's poets only a small proportion lie in the Abbey. To sum it up, four very eminent poets are there—Spenser, Chaucer, Ben Jonson, Dryden ; half-a-dozen of secondary merit— Cowley, Campbell, Congreve, Prior, Gay, Drayton ; and, finally, a few others who were perhaps not so much children as step-children of the Muse, and who lived, to use a phrase of Charles Lamb's, in the suburbs of her graces. " Non ragioniam di lor, ma guarda e passa."   JONATHAN BOUCHIER.

Bexley Heath, Kent.

BARONIES OF MOWBRAY AND SEGRAVE.—Anent the revival of these two old English peerages it may be interesting to note the numerous baronies in fee to which Lord Segrave, Mowbray, and Stourton is co-heir :—

With Lord Petre.

1295. Furnival	...	...	Abeyance 1777.
1308. Strange	...	...	,, ,,
1320. Lucy ...	...	...	,, 1368.
1331. Talbot...	...	...	,, 1777.
,, Talbot of Goderich	...	,, ,,
1349. Dagworth	...	...	,, 1359.
1470. Howard	...	...	,, 1777.
1509. Darcy ...	...	...	Forfeited 1538.

With Lord Petre and the Earl of Carlisle.

| 1295. Greystock | ... | ... | Abeyance 1569. |
| 1459. Dacre of Gillesland | ... | ,, ,, |

With Lords Arundell of Wardour and Clifford of Chudleigh.

| 1299. Fitz-Payne | ... | ... | Abeyance 1354. |

Also to moieties of the following :—

With Lord Petre.

| 1295. Giffard | ... | ... | Abeyance 1322.* |
| ,, Verdon | ... | ... | ,, 1316.† |

With Lord Petre and the Earl of Berkeley.

| 1294. Braose of Gower | ... | Abeyance 1326.‡ |

With Lord Petre and the Earl of Carlisle.

| 1308. Boteler of Wemme | ... | Abeyance 1369.§ |
| 1375. Ferrers of Wemme | ... | ,, 1410.§ |

With Lords Petre, Arundell, and Clifford.

| 1264. Gant ... | ... | ... | Abeyance 1297.‖ |
| 1322. Kerdeston | ... | ... | ,, 1361.¶ |

To represent, even in part, such an array of distinguished baronial houses is in itself a noble heritage.   W. D. PINK.

Leigh, Lancashire.

* The other moiety in abeyance between the daughters of the late Lord Audley, Sir R. Knightley, Bart., and Sir B. Wrey, Bart.
† Co-heirs to other moiety :—Baroness Le Despencer, Earl of Loudoun, Lady Bertha Clifton, Lady Vict. Kirwan, Countess of Romney, W. Lowndes, Esq., W. S. Lowndes, Esq., Duke of Buckingham, M. E. Ferrers, Esq., and H. T. Boultbee, Esq.
‡ Representatives of other moiety unknown, but vested in the heirs of Bohun of Midhurst.
§ Co-heirs to other moieties :—Lord de Clifford, Hon. R. Marsham, and the Earl of Albemarle.
‖ Other moiety between Lord de Mauley and the heirs of Radcliffe of Mulgrave.
¶ Other moiety between Lords Arundell and Clifford and the heirs (if any) of Alice Chaucer, Duchess of Suffolk, the presumed grand-daughter of the poet.

Breviary, the great storehouse from which four-fifths of our service book were taken, nothing similar occurs, and indeed Wheatley (Common Prayer, ch. v. sec. xi.) distinctly says that this collect was "made new at the compiling of the Liturgy." The expression has always struck me as an odd one, and to tell the very truth, I fancied that it was a kind of side hit at Calvinism. But in reading the *Soliloquies of St. Augustine*—I think a little read book—I have just lighted on the following passage :—

"Cum enim cunctis præsideas, singula implens, totus semper ubique præsens, cunctorumque curam agens quæ creasti, *quia nihil odisti eorum quæ fecisti.*"—*S. Augustini Soliloquia, c. xiv. § 2.*

This seems clearly to show the origin of our prayer for the first day of Lent. I do not know that it has been pointed out before.   H. CROMIE.

WEEPING CROSS.—There is a tradition at Caen that in one of the many troubles of her married life Queen Matilda went outside the gates on a pitiful errand to a weeping cross. In a visitation by the bishop early in the fifteenth century at Chichester there is a record of another weeping cross. I use the quaint rendering made by a capitular antiquary about a hundred years ago :—
"That besides the paupers of the foundation [of St. Mary's Hospital] was used for 13 other paupers to have a mess of broth when the Custos was there; and if not, then a mess of seeded water at the North Gate, called Weeping Crosse."
                    MACKENZIE E. C. WALCOTT.

Queries.

[We must request correspondents desiring information on family matters of only private interest, to affix their names and addresses to their queries, in order that the answers may be addressed to them direct.]

THE OXFORD AND CAMBRIDGE BOAT-RACE, 1829.—Who was the builder of the boat used by Oxford in the first Oxford and Cambridge race, which took place June 10, 1829 ? Is there any drawing of the boat extant ?   SCULLER.

HAMMOND AND CICERO.—Hammond, on Heb. ii. 16, quotes the following explanation of the word ἐπιλαμβάνεσθαι as from Cicero *In Pisonem :*—
"Retinere ad salutem, id est, manu aut lacinia prehendere, ac retinere eum qui se it perditum."
I cannot find this passage in the Oratio *In Pisonem,* nor in any work of Cicero. Could any of your readers inform me where it occurs ?   T. F.
Oxford.

COOPER OR COWPER FAMILY.—In working out the senior branch of this family I am much

---

John Cooper, of Strode, = Mary Challenor.
in Slinfold parish.

| Rob. C., el-dest son, of Strode. | = Agnes Farn-fold. | John C., 2nd son, ob. s p. | Wm. C., 3rd son, *quibus* ob. s p. Cowper the well-known poet. | de=... the Earls and the |
| Ralph C., eldest son, of Strood. | = Alice, d. and co-h. of Thos. Burgh. | John C. 2nd son, ob. s p. | | |

| Ralph C. of dest son. | = Dorothy Michel-borne. | George C., mar. and had issue Geo. and Mary, who both ob. s. p. | Robert C. (Was this the Robert bur. at Slinfold, Feb. 13, 1663 ?) | |

| Thos. C., s. and h, bur. at Slinfold, April 26, 1648. | = Barbara Goring. | Edward C., bapt. July 31, bur. at Slinfold, fold, Aug. 10, 1622. | Mary,bu. Oct. 12, 1624. | Dorothy, bap. Nov 26, 1626, of Greatham, and had issue. |

| Ralph C., el-dest s. bur. Au.15, 1639. | Henry C, 2nd s., bur. Sept. 22, 1652. | Edward C., =Martha 31, 1639, 20, 1678. | John-son. | Thos. July 14, 1642. | Ralph July Nov. 2, 1643. | Mary, Aug. 12, 1634. |

Henry C. of Strood, only=Sarah Smith. son. ob. March 22, bur. at Slinfold, Ap. 1, 1707, æt 58.

Edw. C., bap. Ap. 10,=Jane Weeks. Other issue. 1694, bur. July 30, 1725.

Now, this latter part must be wrong ; for how could a man only ten years of age have a son, which Edward Cooper, who was buried in 1678, must have done if the above dates are correct ? My belief is that Berry concocted this latter Henry, and that the pedigree here should be as follows :—

Ralph C. = Dorothy Michelborne.

| Thos. C., bur. Apr. 26, 1648. | = Barbara Goring. | Henry C., bur. Sept. 22, 1652 | Edwd. C., bur Aug. 10, 1622. | Mary. | Dorothy, m. Thos. Mill. |

| Ralph C. | Henry C., bur.=... Apr. 1, 1707. | | Edward C., bur. 1678. | Thos Ralph. | Mary. |

Edward C., bur. =Jane Weeks. July 30, 1725.

I shall be glad of any help towards a correct solution of this point.   D. C. ELWES.
5, The Crescent, Bedford.

"SORRY" STATESMEN.—In Peter Heylyn's *Cosmography,* 1703, p. 944, after mentioning the report that Prince Madoc of North Wales had discovered a western continent, on which he settled, and the rumour that some smattering of Welsh had since been found there, it is added, " in which regard some sorry statesmen went about to entitle Queen *Elizabeth* unto the sovereignty of these countries." On this statement a reply to the following queries is solicited :—

1. Who were the persons here described as "sorry statesmen"?

2. In what way did they "go about" or attempt to entitle Queen Elizabeth to the sovereignty of the western continent?

3. By what contemporary writers is the fact recorded?   LLALLAWG.

"FORTAKE."—I was asking my way of a little girl in Dorsetshire the other day, and she said, "If you keep straight on, you can't *fortake* your way." Is this a known word? It seems formed strictly after the analogy of *forbear, forget, forego,* &c.   R. E. B.
Bournemouth.

THE CASTLE OF BISHOP'S STORTFORD.—I believe that in 1850 the top of the mound on which the castle of Stortford formerly stood was uncovered, the foundations of the castle chambers disclosed, and a plan of them taken. By whom was this done? Has any account of the transaction ever been published?   J. L. G.
Bishop's Stortford.

DEMOGRAPHY.—It is said that it is proposed to found a chair of Demography at Moscow. What is the professor to teach?   A. L. MAYHEW.
Oxford.

ROBINS OF LANGFORD-BUDVILLE, SOMERSET-SHIRE.—In the churchyard of this parish, on the west side of the south porch of the church, is a stone altar-tomb, the inscription on which is all but illegible, and as it records the deaths of two persons whose burials do not appear in the Langford-Budville parish registers, it seems but fitting to lay it up in your storehouse of the past.

The inscription is on the south side of the tomb, and is as follows :—

"Corpora bina facit thalamus genialis in unum
  Sic duo nunc uno marmore tecta jacent.+
Roger Robins, who died yᵉ xiii. of Feb., 1667,
  and Wilmot his wife, yᵉ xxiii. of May, 1668."

The parentage and arms of Roger Robins I should be glad to ascertain. His wife Wilmot was a daughter of William and Mary Blewet, of Thorn St. Margaret, a parish adjoining that of Langford-Budville.   EVERARD GREEN, F.S.A.
Reform Club.

DELAFIELD OR DE LA FELD FAMILY.—I should feel obliged to any of your correspondents who would supply some of the missing dates, localities,

and authorities in the earlier part of the pedigree of "Delafield of Fieldston" in Burke's *Commoners,* which is referred to by MR. GREENFIELD in "N. & Q.," *ante,* p. 194. I am especially desirous of learning in what part of Lancashire Hubertus de la Feld held lands 3 William I., and John de la Feld 12 Hen. I. A family of De la Felds was seated at Sowerby, near Halifax, *temp.* Ed. I., and as this place then formed part of the possessions of the Duchy of Lancaster, I infer that they were descended from the Hubertus referred to, who is said to have been one of the companions of the Conqueror.

The De la Felds of the West Riding of Yorkshire bore the same arms as those of Madley, co. Hereford, Sable, three garbs arg.

In Symonds's *Diary,* published by the Camden Society, is a description of the monument of Walter and John Felde in Madley Church, on which was the kneeling figure of a knight in armour of the thirteenth century, his surtout embroidered with this coat.

I shall be pleased to receive any information relating to the Delafields or De la Felds of an earlier date than the fourteenth century.
                                              OSGOOD FIELD.
4, Grosvenor Mansions, S.W.

"THE POYSONING" OF SIR EUSEBY ANDREW.—In *Reliquiæ Hearnianæ,* vol. ii. p. 787, Oxford, 1857, is recorded, 1733 :—

"Nov. 10. Sir Justinian Isham hath a little 4to. MS. on paper, which I read over yesterday, being delivered to me by his brother, Dr. Euseby Isham, Rector of Lincoln College, being Dr. John Cotta's opinion about the death of Sir Euseby Andrew. The doctor [Cotta] thus entitles it—My opinion at the Assizes in Northampton demanded in Court, touching the poysoning of Sir Euseby Andrew, more fully satisfied.—Signed, John Cotta; and then he adds—My evidence in open court delivered at the Assizes at Northampton, three several times upon commande."

Can any of your readers inform me in whose possession this interesting MS. now is?
                                              JOHN TAYLOR.
Northampton.

CHARLES SLOPER, D.D., Chancellor of the diocese of Bristol, by will dated Aug. 3, 1827, left certain moneys for distribution of Bibles amongst the poor of the "ancient city of Bristol." Wanted his coat of arms.
                                          J. F. NICHOLLS, F.S.A.
Bristol.

EQUAL USE IN WINE AND FIRE.—Sir W. Gull stated, in his examination before the Select Committee of the House of Lords on Intemperance, that "One of the minor Greek poets writes thus : 'There is an equal use in wine and fire to dwellers upon earth'" (Lords' Reports, Aug. 14, 1877). Which of the minor poets says this?
                                              ED. MARSHALL.

"MANORBEER."—Can you furnish me with the probable derivation of Manorbeer, the reputed birthplace of Giraldus Cambrensis?   •
                                        INQUIRER.

THE WHITEHEAD FAMILY OF SADDLEWORTH. —Will some antiquary, well up in the history of families in the West Riding of Yorkshire, give what information he can respecting this family in that county?   AD FINEM FIDELIS.
St. John's College, Cambridge.

MANOR OF MERE, STAFFORDSHIRE.—The indexes to the Inquisitiones post mortem and other public records occasionally mention the above, coupling it with Clent and Handsworth, in the extreme south of the county, and others elsewhere held by the same owner. In one instance it occurs with Clent and Old Swinford, another Staffordshire lordship, and Hagley, in the shire of Worcester, the latter lying in a direct line between those two and abutting on each. An extent in 8 Hen. IV. mentions the advowson as well as the seigniory of Mere, still joined with the above and other manors in the shires of Worcester and Stafford close upon them, and two in Warwickshire, near Birmingham. Can any of your topographical correspondents point out its situation and the parish in which it lay, possibly under some different name? for Stourbridge, in Old Swinford, was then called Bedcot. There is a parish called Maer near Whitmore, quite in the north of Staffordshire.   J. S. E. H.

LINCOLNSHIRE TOPOGRAPHY. — In Nichols's edition of Fuller's Worthies, vol. ii. p. 33, a collection of the monumental inscriptions in this county, by the Rev. Robert Smyth, is mentioned, and also collections in the library of the Rt. Hon. Sir Joseph Banks, K.B. I wish to know where these two collections may be found at the present time.   G. M. W.

TOKENS OF THE SACRAMENT.—Can any of your correspondents give me any information as to the use of tokens of the Sacrament in the English Church? Some old token books of St. Saviour's, Southwark, still exist. What were the tokens? Were they metallic? Are any preserved?
                                        R. W. C. P.
Beith, N.B.

ANGUS PARLANCE.—In Forfarshire the fatted ox killed for the Yule festivities is called a märt. Whence is the derivation of the word?
                                        JOHN CARRIE.
Bolton.

PETRUS DE NOBILIBUS FORMIS.—I have an early engraving inscribed, in the place where one would expect the name or mark of the engraver, "Petri de Nobilibus Formis." What engraver's

name has been thus Latinized, or can any other explanation be given of the inscription? I have searched in vain in Bryan and Brulliot for any name beginning with Adel, Edel, Ethel, &c. The subject is six nude figures of boys, of somewhat too large a growth to be called amoretti. One carries a small flag, another has his finger on his lip, and the remaining four have both hands raised, as if playing at some game.   J. F. M.

AN ANCIENT CAST LEADEN COFFIN has been found under the road at Crayford, Kent, near to Hall Place, the reputed residence of the Black Prince. I send the following notice, which appears in a local paper, and inquire whether from such data the period when the person lived may be gathered, and whether the inference from the scallop shells is a fair one :—
"On Tuesday morning last, as the excavators for the West Kent main drainage were continuing the work about thirty yards east of the gate of the Iron Church, and on the north side of the road, they came upon a cast leaden coffin containing the remains of a female probably about twenty years of age, as the 'wisdom teeth' were not yet grown. The coffin was of cast lead, wider at the head than the feet, but not shaped at the shoulder as in modern ones. On the lid was a crossed line, a St. Andrew's Cross, from the centre of which proceeded a straight line to about two-thirds of the coffin's length; then a short line at right angles to this, forming a foot, and two slanting lines from the extremities of this line to the lower corners of the lid. On the coffin in various positions were seven scallop shells. The scallop shell was, it is said, the badge of a pilgrim to the Holy Land. Hence the suggestion that this young female had made such a journey."
                                        GEO. SAVAGE.

KING ALARIC.—Can any one inform me in what poem, naming the author, the burial of King Alaric in the river's bed is related?
Where can I find the anecdotes of the chain of Canynge?   W. H.

CHEADLE, STAFFORDSHIRE.—A manuscript without date, but written during the latter part of the eighteenth century, in the William Salt Library at Stafford, says with reference to Cheadle
"This ancient town seems to have been of much higher degree of consideration in days of yore than it is at present, since within memory some of the heads of the first families in the county have not only graced the election of mayor of Cheadle with their presence, but have actually been elected mayor in regular annual succession."
Was Cheadle ever a corporate town? What is the origin of the name of Cheadle, which is given to four places in Cheshire and two in Staffordshire?
                                        J. INGAMELLS.
Newcastle-under-Lyme.

POPULATION OF ROME AND THE ROMAN EMPIRE UNDER AUGUSTUS.—According to Döllinger's statement (Heidenthum und Judenthum, pp. 1, 3) the inhabitants of "Rome under Augustus" may have

amounted to about two millions of people, and those of the Roman empire perhaps to one hundred millions. How can this statement be verified?
H. KREBS.
Taylorian Library, Oxford.

WEST INDIES : BARBADOES. — From which ports in England did vessels sail for the West Indies (Barbadoes especially) between 1590 and 1650? Are there any lists of the ships and names of their passengers at either Barbadoes or at the English ports? and, if so, where are they to be seen now? I am aware of Hotten's book.
C. MASON.
3, Gloucester Crescent, Hyde Park, W.

AUTHORS OF BOOKS WANTED.—
Real | Life in Ireland ; | or, the | Day and Night Scenes, | Rovings, Rambles, and Sprees, | Bulls, Blunders, Bodderation, and Blarney, | of | Brian Boru, Esq., | and his elegant friend | Sir Shawn O'Dogherty, &c. | Printed by B. Bensley, | Bolt Court, Fleet Street. | Published by Jones & Co., 3, Warwick Square ; and | J. L. Marks, Piccadilly ; and sold by all Booksellers | and Newsmen in Town and Country. | 1821.   HIRONDELLE.
There is a very amusing novel which gives an account of the invasion of Ireland by the French under Hoche in 1795 or 1796. What is the name of it, also that of the author and publisher?   R. W.

A Sentimental Journey, intended as a Sequel to Mr. Sterne's, through Italy, Switzerland, and France. In 2 vols. fcap. 8vo. By Mr. Shandy. Printed for T. Baker, Southampton; and S. Crowder, Paternoster Row, London. MDCCXCIII.   FREDK. RULE.

The Tripe Supper.—About thirty or forty years ago there appeared in some serial a piece of poetry thus entitled. Wanted the name of the serial.   A. W.

AUTHORS OF QUOTATIONS WANTED.—
"Crying we come, and groaning we must die ;
Let us do something 'twixt the groan and cry."
Query correctly quoted.   S. H. ATKINS.

Replies.

HERALDIC : HUTCHINSON FAMILY.
(5th S. viii. 268, 379 ; ix. 79, 209.)

I did not feel called upon to make any response to the remarks of MR. SARGENT (ante, p. 79), because it was evident that one who was not convinced by the facts stated by me in a respectable and well-known journal, mysteriously designated by him as "somewhere," would not be open to conviction, let any additional evidence be what it might. If any one is curious on the subject, he will find my paper in the New England Historical and Genealogical Register, vol. xx. (1866), pp. 355-367, copies of which will be found at the British Museum, and elsewhere in London. By every statement in that paper I still stand.

Now that a veritable descendant of Governor Hutchinson, and "the eldest representative in England of Edward Hutchinson of Alford," has

entered the lists, I feel bound to defend my own position, and at the same time expose the utter baselessness of his. I shall not require very much space, because my arguments will take the shape of incontestable facts, and facts may well be allowed to speak for themselves.

MR. P. O. HUTCHINSON very wisely admits that he has not proved Edward Hutchinson of Alford, who was buried there Feb. 14, 1631-2, to have been the next heir of Edward Hutchinson of Wykeham Abbey, in Yorkshire, who had the grant of arms in 1581, but it is evident that he thinks he was. He does not contend that "the two Edwards are one and the same person," but declares that "it is hard to escape the inference that the one at Alford was the son or grandson of the one at Wickham." He may escape that inference very easily. He could have escaped it if he had ever taken the pains to consult authorities so well known as the Heraldic Visitations of Yorkshire, when he would have discovered that the eldest son of Edward Hutchinson of Wykeham Abbey was only eleven years old in 1584, just two years before the baptism of the first child of Edward Hutchinson of Alford. This of course disposes at once of the theory that the latter was either son or grandson of the former. When Edward Hutchinson of Wykeham made his will on Feb. 20, 1590-1, a fact of which MR. HUTCHINSON appears wholly unconscious, all his children, by his own declaration, were still minors ; and yet by that time Edward Hutchinson of Alford was the father of at least three children.

It will be seen therefore that, instead of one of these Edwards being the descendant of the other, they were contemporaries in early life, although one outlived the other more than forty years. Hence, as the arms granted to Edward Hutchinson of Wykeham, in 1581, were confirmed to him and his descendants, any claim to them by the descendants of Edward Hutchinson of Alford is simply absurd and not worth considering.

The immediate ancestors of Edward Hutchinson of Alford are perfectly well known, not a link in the chain of evidence being wanting, as will be seen by referring to my paper already quoted, in which all the details are set forth. The Christian name of his grandfather has not been ascertained, but it is certain, from the wills of the family, that he left four sons and one daughter. One of the sons, Christopher, was a clergyman, becoming incumbent of South Leasingham, in Lincolnshire, in 1522, and of Scremby in the same county in 1526, and dying in 1556. Another son, William, was a respectable tanner in the city of Lincoln, and rose to be sheriff of that city in 1541, alderman in 1545, and finally mayor in 1552. He died in 1556-7. The daughter, Alice, married James Remington, who described himself in his will as a "husbandman."

The youngest son, John Hutchinson, was apprenticed in Lincoln, Sept. 23, 1529, to Edward Atkinson, a glover of that city. He was also one of the "good apprentices," for, like his elder brother, he subsequently occupied the minor civic posts, and was eventually twice mayor of Lincoln—in 1556 and 1564. He died during his second mayoralty, on May 24, 1565, and was buried in the church of St. Mary-le-Wigford. He had eight children, none of whom need concern us except his fifth and youngest son, Edward, who was apprenticed, May 27, 1577, to Edmund Knight, alderman and mercer of Lincoln. He was constantly named in the wills of the family, and was executor of that of his cousin Christopher (son of his uncle William) in 1592, when he was described as of Alford, and a mercer. He is thus perfectly identified as the Edward Hutchinson of Alford who was father of William Hutchinson, the early emigrant to New England, and ancestor of Governor Hutchinson.

Taking the antecedents of his family into consideration, what are the probabilities of their descent from any heraldic family of the name? I leave this question to be answered by any one who chooses to take the trouble.

MR. HUTCHINSON admits that his ancestor Governor Hutchinson and his descendants, himself included, used and still use the precise arms which were granted to Edward Hutchinson of Wykeham and his descendants in 1581. But, as it has been shown that they were not, and could by no possibility have been, his descendants, what becomes of their right so to use them? To avoid this difficulty he appears to intimate that the governor's right to arms is unimpeachable, and that probably the Wykeham branch derived their right through some connexion with his line! That suggestion may go for what it is worth. But, as it may be deemed extremely valuable by some persons, I will now present them with another fact, of which they also seem unconscious, viz. that, when the heralds were making their visitation of Lincolnshire in 1634, Thomas Hutchinson of Thedlethorpe in that county, who was a grandson of William Hutchinson, mayor of Lincoln, already named, and therefore second cousin of Edward Hutchinson of Alford, presented his pedigree and claimed the right to the well-known arms of Hutchinson. On this original pedigree the heralds wrote the ominous words "Respited for Proof."

It is proper that I should say just here that the grant of arms to Edward Hutchinson of Wykeham in 1581 was not an original grant, but a confirmation. In other words, he had established his descent from the family bearing those arms, and they were confirmed to him as of right; but the heralds assigned him an entirely new crest, and that crest belonged only to him and his descendants. Now if, according to the new theory, Governor Hutchinson and his descendants may possibly have

had a right to the Hutchinson arms, they certainly had no right to the Wykeham crest, not descending from the man to whom that crest was granted. And yet it is precisely the crest which they did and do use, and which was painted on the old vellum by which its present possessor sets such store. It was doubtless this coat and crest which the Wykeham family was still in existence, at no great distance, he failed to establish his claim, in 1634, to any connexion with them or their ancestors.

It appears to be a most difficult lesson to learn that there were Hutchinsons and Hutchinsons, i.e. those who belonged to the heraldic families and those who did not. But, until this lesson is learned, we shall no doubt find every one of the name claiming the arms, not because he has a right to them, but solely because his name is Hutchinson.

One word as to the vellum painting which has been referred to. MR. HUTCHINSON is very confident that it is at least as old as the emigration of his first American ancestor, though he admits that the heralds to whom he showed it "were not certain." Any one who knows our dear old friend Mr. Planché will quite understand his indisposition to throw cold water on the enthusiasm of his client, and how he looked and acted when he said, "It may be so old, but I am not certain," being actuated by his anxiety not to hurt his questioner's feelings and his determination not to compromise his official honesty. I venture to think that the date of this painting, and of the arms on the drinking cup of the governor's father, may be safely fixed at quite a century later.

I think I can readily recognize, from the florid description of the picture, the handiwork of one of several old acquaintances of mine who have given me no end of trouble during the twenty years in which I have been investigating the English history of the New England settlers. Early in the eighteenth century there sprang up in Boston a number of professional herald-painters and engravers, whose occupation appears to have been to furnish elaborate coats of arms to anybody and everybody who wanted them. They do not appear to have required from their clients both "name and county," being content with the name alone. If a man's name was Smith, and any family of that name ever bore arms, they had no hesitation in assigning those arms to that particular Smith, his descendants have borne them and are proud of them to this day. I have little doubt that the precious Hutchinson vellum painting was the work of one of these unscrupulous gentry. The description of it quite accords with their well-known style, and Mr. Planché was fully justified in the doubt he evidently entertained of its antiquity. I think it highly probable that Thomas Hutchinson, the governor's father, who was a contemporary with the earliest of them, employed them to paint the picture and engrave his drinking cup, and that such is their only authority.

The point to be remembered is this, that on the authority of this painting and its cognates, by whomsoever and whensoever executed, the descendants of Edward Hutchinson of Alford, from the time of Governor Hutchinson's father down to the present day, have claimed and used, not only the arms confirmed to Edward Hutchinson of Wykeham in 1581, but the particular *crest* then specifically granted to him and his *descendants.* As I have clearly shown that they did not descend from Edward Hutchinson of Wykeham, I may safely leave the question of their right to those arms and that specific crest, I will not say to the decision of scientific genealogists, but to the common sense of any of my readers.

JOSEPH LEMUEL CHESTER.

TOUCHING FOR THE KING'S EVIL : FORMS OF PRAYER (5th S. ix. 49, 236.)—Your correspondent MR. J. CHARLES COX asks for information about the forms of prayer used at the ceremony of touching for the king's evil. In 1871 I printed in the *Journal* of the British Archæological Association (vol. xxvii. pp. 282-307) a collection of "Forms of Prayer recited at the Healing." The series of forms there published comprises the ritual of Queen Mary, transcribed from the original MS. used by herself, now in the possession of Cardinal Manning, by whose great courtesy I was allowed to copy and to print it ; the Office used by Queen Elizabeth, from Dean Tooker's *Charisma sive Donum Sanationis;* the Office used in the reigns of Charles I. and II., from Beckett's *Free and Impartial Enquiry;* that used by Charles II., from L'Estrange's *Alliance of Divine Offices;* that used by James II., from a copy printed by Henry Hills in 1686 ; two Latin versions, 1713 and 1727, from Latin Prayer Books of those respective dates ; and the English form used by Queen Anne, which I have printed from a Prayer Book dated 1715. I hope at some future time to print, perhaps with a few additional observations, another form, *temp.* James II., differing from that above mentioned in that in the above named ritual the Office is entirely in English, whilst in this (which I have not yet printed), although the rubrics are in English, the prayers and Gospels are in Latin. Mr. Maskell has, however, already edited this Office in his *Monumenta Ritualia,* iii. 330-334.

You could not possibly spare the space which

would be needed to give a very brief account of each of these Offices, or even to indicate the variations between them.

I should be glad to be informed how long the "Forma Strumosos Attrectandi" continued to be printed in the Latin translations of the Book of Common Prayer. I have it in Parsel's Latin Prayer Book, sixth edition, 1744, and seventh edition, 1759. Both these editions contain also the forms for the Fire of London and for the Opening of Convocation. I have not seen any later editions in which the Office at the Touching is found.

And when did the English prayers "At the Healing" cease to be annexed to the Book of Common Prayer? I find the Office in the folio Prayer Book "printed by John Baskett, printer to the University" of Oxford, in 1721. An edition published in 1724 is mentioned in the *Archæological Journal* for 1853, p. 194, but this I have not seen.

A correspondent, writing to me in 1876, informs me that the Office is to be found in a duodecimo edition of the Prayer Book printed in 1749 by "Thomas Baskett, Printer to the Kings most Excellent Majesty : and by the assigns of Robert Baskett." He says that the copy concerning which he writes "has prefixed a portrait of the king, said to be 'sold by Rd Ware at ye bible & Sun, Warwick Lane, at Amen Corner.'" But he adds, " I suspect, however, that the title does not indicate the *true* date, and that the volume is really the edition of 1724, the metrical Psalms at the end bearing that date following the Oxford imprint." An inspection of the volume would probably clear up the point. In 1724 Geo. I. was king, and the edition of that date would pray for him and, possibly, his queen, Sophia Dorothea, who did not die till Nov. 2, 1726 ; whereas in 1749 Geo. II. was on the throne, and his queen, Wilhelmina Caroline Dorothea, died Nov. 20, 1737, so that no queen's name would be found in a Prayer Book of this date. Of course I am aware that this test is not complete—the leaves or sheets containing the name of the regnant king or queen may have been inserted in an earlier edition ; but probably the book would bear traces of such alteration in the quality or bookmarks of the paper. I shall be indebted to any correspondent who has a copy of this volume if he will allow me to see it, or will communicate to me the results of his own observations upon it.

W. SPARROW SIMPSON.

THE TOMB OF EDMUND OF LANGLEY, DUKE OF YORK (5th S. viii. 443.)—I have seen four accounts of the finding of the remains in this tomb, excluding such as were manifestly copied from each other. The first, which alone had the appearance of coming from an eye-witness, stated that the bones found were those of one male and two females. The second affirmed them to be those of Edmund of Langley, his wife Isabel (though I think it called her Blanche), and their daughter Constance. This tallied with the first, as the ages of these three persons at death were 61, 38, and 42 ; they had, therefore, all arrived at maturity. At the same time, as matter of fact, Constance was not one of the three, for she was buried at Reading—unless evidence can be offered, entirely unknown to me, showing that her corpse was removed from Reading to Langley. The third account, however, said that the bones were those of Edmund, "Blanche" his wife, and their twin daughters—that is, of one male and *three* females—whether all mature, or one woman and two infants, was not stated. Unless, again, some undiscovered evidence can be shown to the contrary, these twin daughters, whether babies or women, are wholly mythical, for the only known daughter of Edmund was Constance Le Despenser. But the fourth account dropped one infant, and presented us with "Edmund, his wife Blanche, and their infant daughter Constance," which Constance, when she died, was forty-two years of age or thereabouts.

Now, can and will no person come forward who was present at the opening of the tomb, and tell us once for all what bones were really found ? Was it a man and one woman, or ·two, or three women ? Were they women or infants ? If they were children or a child, was it, or were they, certainly female ?

This last question is more significant than appears on the surface. The eldest son of the Black Prince was buried at Chilterne Langley, or, more correctly, Children's Langley, since it takes its name from the nursery palace which stood there. I do not know whether the church of Chilterne Langley is now in existence, but I do know that on consulting two excellent county maps and a good topographical dictionary I fail to find a trace of the spot. As Chilterne Langley was in the immediate vicinity of King's Langley, it strikes me as possible—but I beg that I may be understood as offering the conjecture as a conjecture only—that if the church of Chilterne Langley were destroyed, the coffin of Edward of Angoulême *might* have been removed to the nearest royal sepulchre—that of his uncle at King's Langley. I would therefore ask, Was there any indication of the remains of a male child of seven years old ?

Surely some person was present competent to give these particulars. I trust that he may have been a reader of " N. & Q." HERMENTRUDE.

THE ORDER OF THE GARTER AN EPICENE ORDER (5th S. ix. 166.)—Was the Garter ever worn on the leg by a lady member of the order so that it might be visible ? The hoops of the last century were larger and shorter than the later fashion of crinolines ; the petticoats also were shorter, so that the sight of the fair wearer's garters was a circumstance that was duly expected and provided for. The writings of the essayists of the time make us aware of this. The poetry of the age is also concurrent in its testimony. Here is a recipe for a dress of that period :—

> " Let her hoop extending wide
> Show what beauty ne'er should hide,
> Garters of the softest silk,
> Stockings whiter far than milk."

There is the Scotch song of the same period, " There 's gold in your garters, Marion " (see Mr. Robert Chambers's learned note thereon), from which it would seem that, in dancing, the young lady's garters were plainly visible, from the swaying motion of the wide hoop. Lady Mary Wortley Montagu, in describing a young lady lounging back in her chair, says :—

> " While the stiff whalebone with the motion rose,
> And thousand beauties to the sight disclose."

In the exhibition of the museum of the Archæological Institute, held at Peterborough, July, 1861, Mrs. Gordon Canning, of Hartpury Court, Gloucestershire, exhibited the garters of Henrietta Maria, Queen of England. They were of fine gold wire, embroidered with silk, and were given by her servant, Sir Thomas Bond, to his daughter, who was maid of honour to Mary d'Este. At the recent double wedding, at Berlin, of the Princess Charlotte, eldest daughter of the Crown Prince of Germany, and granddaughter of Queen Victoria, and the Princess Elizabeth of Prussia, second daughter of Prince Frederick Charles, the usual quaint ceremonies peculiar to the German Court were observed. After the performance of the *Fackeltanz,* or torchlight procession, with the accompanying polonaise, the newly-married couples were conducted to their apartments ; upon which " the lady-stewardess of the brides gave to each of the guests a small velvet or silk ribbon, in the Prussian colours, with the portraits of the princesses, each ribbon representing a piece of the bride's garter." CUTHBERT BEDE.

FRIESIC SONGS AND LEGENDS (5th S. ix. 168.)— The Friesic literature is not rich in poetry of any kind. Bendsen mentions in his work, *Die Nordfriesische Sprache*, that popular songs are used on various occasions by the country people, but it does not appear that many of them have been printed. The following list is not very extensive, but it includes all the songs or minor poems that I have been able to find in the course of a careful research. I have never met with a collection of Friesic legends, but the old chronicles will probably meet the requirements of F. L. as nearly as anything that the language contains. The titles of some of them are given below :—

Friesche Rymelarye, in trye deelen forschaet. By Gysbert Japicks. Ed. E. Epkema, Lieauwert, 1821.—To this edition are prefixed three poems in the Friesic language by the editor, Isaac de Schepper, and A. Tymens.

Friesche Rymlary. By Althuysen. 1755.—This work I only know from an advertisement by a bookseller at Leeuwarden.

Eenige Friesche Gedichten. By Wassenbergh. At the end of his *Taalkundige Bydragen tot den Frieschen Tongval*, 1802.

Metrische Sprachproben.—Five poems as an appendix to Bendsen's work, *Die Nordfriesische Sprache.* The last is a part of an old country song, but the first is only a translation of Mrs. Hemans's poem *The Better Land.*

To these may be added a Friesic song on St. Stephen by Hamckema, referred to in Hoeufft's *Oud-Friesche Spreekwoorden* (p. 219); a poem by J. Hilarides, mentioned by Adelung (*Mith.*, ii. 235) as contained in Gabbema's *Verhael van Leuwarden*, 1701; and a Morning Song in Heimrich's *North Friesic Chronicle*, s. a., 1616, of which a part is given in Wiarda's *Alt-Fries. Wört.* (p. 32, Appendix).

Chronicles :—

Croniike ende warachtige beschryvinghe van Frieslant. By Ocke Scharl. Leeuw., 1597.

Chronique ofte historische Geschiedenisse van Vrieslant. By Winsemius. 1622.

De Geschiedenissen kerckelyck ende wereldtlyck van Frieslant tot 1583. By Schotanus. 1658.

Gesta Fresonum, uit de Apographa Juniana. Ed. De Crane, 1837.

Die olde Friesche Cronike, met aantt. van E. Epkema. 1853.

Some assistance may also probably be gained from *De Vrije Fries*, a collection of papers issued by the Friesic Historical and Antiquarian Society, Leeuwarden, 1839-1873.   J. D.

Belsize Square.

The best modern collection of Friesic tales, &c., is *Rimen en teltsjes fen the broarren Halbertsma.* In *Iduna* F. L. will find specimens of various authors. It is a periodical published by the "Selskip for Fryske tael en skriftekennisse."

Amongst more ancient authors Gysbert Japix takes the first place.

In the *Catalogue* of the Frisian Society's Library (Br. Mus. Ac. 965-2) many more titles can be found.   D. G. Brandsma.

Curiosities of Cricket (5th S. ix. 165.)—I should be obliged to Kingston for a reference to the precise number, or to the date, of the newspaper from which he quotes an account of a match in 1877 between eleven women of Elstead, in Surrey, and eleven women of Thursley. These two are not the only villages which have produced a female eleven. The women of Angmering, in Sussex, for instance, had, and perhaps have still, a good reputation as cricketers.   A. J. M.

I find in my note-book a newspaper account of a match played in 1855 (where I know not) between Earl Winterton's club and the 2nd Royal Surrey Militia, in which the military eleven were all re-

moved in their first innings without scoring even one run. The match was the more extraordinary because one of the noble earl's bowlers was a fast bowler, while there were several good bats opposed to him.   John Churchill Sikes.

Godolphin Road, Shepherd's Bush, W.

The Lyttelton cricket match was "Lytteltons *v.* Hagley"—the late Lord Lyttelton, his two brothers, and his eight sons against an eleven of Hagley. I rather think, but am not sure, that the match was won by the Hagley men.

C. F. S. Warren, M.A.

Bexhill.

Tom Tompier, or Tompion (5th S. ix. 169.)—Tompion, who was originally a blacksmith, died in 1713, aged seventy-five, confessedly the best watchmaker in Europe, and was buried in Westminster Abbey (see Col. Chester's *Westminster Abbey Registers*, p. 278, and Noble's *Continuation of Granger*, vol. i. p. 315). His portrait was painted by Kneller, and finely engraved in mezzotint by Smith. In the time of Queen Anne a "Tompion" was as well understood to mean a watch as a "Manton" in the time of George IV. to signify a gun. I should be glad to know where the portrait of worthy old Thomas Tompion, mentioned by W. P., is preserved.

Edward Solly.

[See *ante* (Chillingworth), p. 238.]

At p. 111 of Mr. Wood's *Curiosities of Clocks* one Tompion is reported to have died of the plague which was in 1665. At p. 293 it is said that Tompion died in 1713.

"His portrait, engraved in mezzotinto by Smith after a painting by Kneller, which represents him in a plain coat, showing the inside of a watch, was published in 1697."

At p. 297 Tompion is said to have followed the funeral of Quare, who died in 1724. The portrait in question may probably represent the younger Tompion. The terminal E of the inscription may mean no more than "effigies," but if one may guess it to be an F, representing "filius," much interest attaches to it.   Gwavas.

Parsons who were also Publicans (5th S. ix. 164.)—There is a note on "A Welsh Parson of the Seventeenth Century," whose wife kept the village ale-house. In *Good Words* for March is an article by Henry Nairn, "A Clergyman of the last Century," giving an account of "wonderful" Robert Walker. In the preliminary remarks the writer says :—

"In addition to the above-named methods of making money, the curate was usually the village publican, and it was not an uncommon sight to see the reverend host playing cards and drinking beer on a Sunday morning with his customers, until the church bell summoned them to perform the different characters of minister and

I quote this as a parallel passage to the example from Wales brought forward by your correspondent.

CUTHBERT BEDE.

The parsons of the seventeenth century will contrast favourably, notwithstanding their wives and bears and ale, with their predecessors of the two preceding centuries ; for the late Dr. Doran, in one of his most interesting volumes, tells us that, "in the reign of Henry VII., the Carnarvonshire gentlemen and farmers urgently prayed the government for protection against their own clergy. A papal decree authorized the prelates to deal with their clergy for crimes unutterable." " The prelates," adds Dr. Doran, " might keep a layman for ever in prison on a charge of heresy, but for the grossest outrage against God and nature they could not touch a hair on the head of a priest." He then draws a delightful picture of Bernard Gilpin, the Westmoreland rector of the sixteenth century, whom the death of Mary Tudor " alone saved from the martyrdom for which he was daily dressed and prepared." Perhaps Gilpin has gone out of fashion in these enlightened days when learned divines of their Church find fault with Ridley and Latimer :—

> " The moles and bats in full assembly find
> On special search the keen-eyed eagle blind ! "

M. A. H.

DANTE'S " PURGATORIO " (5ᵗʰ S. ix. 165.)—

> "Io mi rendei
> Piangendo a quei che volentier perdona."

MR. BOUCHIER has undoubtedly detected an error in Mrs. Oliphant's translation of this passage. The pronoun here must be singular, for Dante could not have been guilty of making a plural pronoun agree with a singular verb. I am, however, unable to agree with your respected correspondent that the " Quei " is derived from the pronoun *Quel* or *Quello*, either in the dative or otherwise. If the dative had been intended there would have been no occasion for the preposition *a* before it. I cannot but think that the " Quei " here is merely a Dantesque abbreviation of the peculiar pronoun *quegli*, which is undeclinable. The Italians have three expressive demonstrative pronouns, all unchangeable, the meaning of which may be explained thus :—

" Questi," *this* (being or object near to me, the speaker).

" Cotesti," *that* (being or object near to you, the person spoken to).

" Quegli," *that* (being or object at a distance from both of us).

I have a strong opinion that Dante intended to use the last of the three in a shortened form. *V.* Biagioli's *Italian Grammar*, 3rd edit., p. 103.

M. H. R.

Milton referred, in No. 2, to a popular ballad which confused the two queens of Henry III. and Edward I., both named Alianora, of whom the one was very unpopular for the exaction of her dues payable at Queenhithe, and the other was known to the masses by her memorial at Charing Cross. If MR. BLACK will refer to Miss Strickland's *Lives of the Queens*, vol. i. p. 448, he will find a note on the subject.

HERMENTRUDE.

THE LINCOLN MISSAL (5ᵗʰ S. ix. 168.)—There is a fragment of one in the Bodleian Library (Tanner MS. iv. 133, sæc. xv.). It is printed in the appendix to the York Missal (Surtees Soc., vol. lx. p. 341), and commented on in the preface to the same volume.

J. T. F.

Bp. Hatfield's Hall, Durham.

ST. SUNDAY (5ᵗʰ S. ix. 169.)—I am inclined to think that there is some confusion about this name, and that it arose from mistaking " S. Dominicus" for " dies dominica." I am led to this conjecture from the fact that I found St. Dominick's Abbey, Cork, called St. Sunday's Abbey in an inquisition taken about the end of the reign of Queen Elizabeth. There is a celebrated well in the north suburb of Cork called Sunday's Well, from which a large district takes its name. There is no mention of St. Sunday in the *Martyrology of Donegal*, nor does the name occur in that most valuable work of Dr. Aug. Potthast, *Wegweiser durch die Geschichtswerke des Europäischen Mittelalters von* 375-1500, supplement, Berlin, 1868. This is a perfect Clavis AA.SS. In this work we have nine mentions of Dominicus and two of Dominica, one of the latter a saint and martyr. D'Alton, in his *History of Drogheda*, vol. i. p. 120, says :—

" The Dominican Friary, or Abbey of Preachers Friars, under the invocation of St. Mary Magdalene, was situated in the north part of the town, near Sunday's Gate, and immediately adjoining the town wall."

Here again we have some connexion between St. Sunday and the Dominican abbey. I shall feel much obliged to be set right in this matter.

R. C.

Cork.

With the beatification of Sunday we may compare the Russian deification of Friday, a day worshipped by the superstitious peasants as late as the eighteenth century under the name of *Pyátnitza*, *i.e.* Fifth (day). See *Regulations of the Russian Church*, Consett, 1727.

A. L. MAYHEW.

Oxford.

Perhaps St. Dominic, from Dies Dominicus. Gobat, however, in his *Travels in Abyssinia*, records the sage remark of a native :—" What a very holy man Sunday must have been, for the other saints' days come but once a year, but St. Sunday has a day once a week!" P. P.

Mr. Hare's "Walks in London" (5th S. ix. 179.)—May I, as a member of the Inner Temple, put on record my protest against Mr. Hare's description of the hall of this honourable society? a description which applies to our former hall, but not to the new one, opened on May 14, 1870.
Edward H. Marshall.
Temple.

The Great Bell at Brailes, co. Warwick (5th S. ix. 166.)—F. S. calls attention to the great bell at Brailes, which having been cracked years ago has been reproduced by Messrs. Blews, of Birmingham. This bell has been particularly noticed before in the fifth vol., fourth series, of "N. & Q.," at pp. 315, 352, 407, 436, 499, 568, 609. The cross and stamps were noticed with engravings in Willis's Current Notes, vol. v. p. 29, 1854. After consulting living authorities on ancient hymns I have failed to discover whence this inscription is taken. It is considered to be the latter stanza of an Ascension Day hymn, the word "ipsum" referring to "Christum" in the former stanza. The peculiar initial cross with the two shields are figured in Mr. Tyssen's Church Bells of Sussex and in my Bells of Devon. By the kindness of the Vicar of Brailes, a ring with the inscription entire has been cut out, and kindly presented to me. The metal is of unusual thickness for that part of a bell, being 1½ in. The diameter of the ring is 31 in. For further particulars I would refer the reader to my former communications in this periodical. H. T. Ellacombe.
Clyst St. George, Devon.

Mr. Thorold Rogers's "Historical Gleanings" (5th S. ix. 186.)—C. T. B. has missed at least two public notices of Mr. Rogers's curious mistake. In a letter signed with my name addressed to the Standard and Morning Herald, under date July 7, 1869, and published in the course of the following week, this, with many other of Mr. Rogers's errors, was exposed. Attention was also drawn to them in a very pungent letter to the Manchester Courier, signed "Diogenes," dated April 20, 1870, and written by an Arnold prizeman of Oxford. A second letter from me appeared in the Standard of April 16, 1870, in which Mr. Rogers's inaccuracies in his second series (the error pointed out by C. T. B. is in the first) are set forth. Some of these curious errors seem worth commemorating in "N. & Q." Thus at p. 177, first series, Lord Lytton is confounded with his brother, the author of Historical Characters. The London Gazette of February, 1688, is said at p. 13 to be "full of congratulatory addresses on the birth of the Prince of Wales," who was not born until June 10, 1688. At p. 8

Morley and Sheldon are spoken of as the "managers of the Hampton Court Conference" instead of the Savoy Conference. At p. 105 the great Edinburgh reviewer is called "Jeffreys." At p. 175 Cobbett is said to have been returned for Oldham in 1830, that borough not having been enfranchised until 1832. At p. 19 (second series) the date of the Plague is given as 1662. At p. 164 Potter, the well-known companion of Wilkes, is said to have died Irish Secretary, an office which he never held. At p. 190 Compton, Bishop of London, is described as "one of the seven who stood their trial in the last year of James II." At p. 239 Mr. Bamber Gascoyne, a not altogether unknown member of Parliament, is resolved into two persons, "Gascoigne and Bramber." Alfred B. Beaven, M.A.
Preston.

The Surname "Wooly H." (5th S. ix. 188.)—"H." may stand for the surname "Head," or it may represent "Aitch," whence the patronymic "Aitchison." R. S. Charnock.
Junior Garrick.

The Order of the Lion and Sun of Persia (5th S. ix. 188.)—The Order of the Lion and Sun is divided into three classes, each similar in design, differing only in size. Vide Chronique de tous les Ordres de Chevalerie, puisée dans des Sources authentiques, par H. Schulze, Berlin, 1855. The Persian inscription on the medals states the service for which they were given. J. Hamilton.

Maffled: Mabled: Mobled (Fr. Mouffles): Moffled: Muffled: Muff (5th S. viii. 446.)—Your correspondent K. P. D. E. has, by your kind permission, "registered" in your pages the word maffled. Will you allow, with the same kindness, the cognate words written above by its side to claim kindred there and have their claims allowed? Maffled is no doubt rightly interpreted from that great master of honest English, R. Southey. Still there is reason to believe the word of foreign origin, Dutch, German, or French, for each nation has here a word, idem sonans, to express the same idea. But what I wish to call attention to is the twofold signification of these words. The muffling of the face or hands or body has by a very usual figure of speech suggested a muffling of the intellect. The French word muffles denotes that which does certainly embarrass the play of the hands, for the word means gloves without fingers, and applied intellectually the corresponding English term alluded to by Southey signifies beyond a doubt "confused in intellect," or according to the not unfamiliar vulgarism of late years, instead of saying she was maffled, one might say she was a muff. I think that your correspondent's and Southey's word may be really the word employed by the player in Shakspere, doubted by

Hamlet, but authoritatively accredited by that experienced critic Polonius :—

" That's good: *mobled* queen is good,"   •

where of course not the mind but the person was *mobled*, wrapt up ; or was it the mind ? You see the son seemed to hesitate, having his mother in his mind's eye. Whichever Shakspere meant, here is an authority for the sage Polonius :—

" The pale-fac'd Night beheld thy heavy chear,
And would not let one little star appear,
But over all her smokey mantle hurl'd,
And in thick vapour *muffled* up the world."

Drayton, *Hist. Epistles.*

Stafford.   T. J. M.

I remember hearing an old lady, born and residing in South Yorkshire, speak of a person as " moffling " whose mind and thoughts had become impaired by reason of old age.   J. S.

" As " (5th S. ix. 188) in the expression given by MR. SWEETING is no doubt intended by those who use it to imply " as might be," but it is no more to be tolerated than " the " headache, or " which his " for *whose*, or such like vulgarisms of middle-class English. A friend of mine (well bred and born it is true) said to me a few days ago, " We expected him *as* yesterday " ; but then all her life has been spent in the retirement of a Gloucestershire parsonage.   G. L. G.
Titsey Place.

This term, thus used, may be now a provincialism, but it is of venerable age in the English language. " *As* yesterday there came to this town an Englishman," writes Lord Lisle to Secretary Cromwell (Lisle Papers, i., art. 30) about 1536 ; and " This is to advertise you that as yesterday open war was proclaimed at Bullen betwixt the French King and themperor " (*ib.*, i. 1), June 17, 1536. I take it to mean " on that day which is now yesterday."   HERMENTRUDE.

AN OIL PAINTING (5th S. ix. 189.)—If T. McM. can give no more exact description I would recommend him to inquire whether his picture is not by Gerard Edema. This painter's works are usually tall, and of reddish colour. His signature resembles the letters given, " Œram."

GWAVAS.

SIR JOHN WOODVILLE (5th S. ix. 169.)—Unless it can be proved that Sir John was married twice —of which I know no evidence—I should think his daughter a very problematical person, since his bride, at the time of their marriage, was certainly aged fifty-six, probably sixty-seven, and, according to tradition (though the fact is not so), eighty.

HERMENTRUDE.

" BIBLIOTHECA PARVULORUM " (5th S. ix. 228.) —This commencement of a series which promised

to be of much merit and interest was issued by Rev. John William Hewett, M.A., under whose name it will be found mentioned in Crockford's *Clerical Directory.* The *Sacra Academica* is a particularly interesting little volume.

W. D. MACRAY.

MILTON QUERIES (5th S. ix. 107, 176.)— " And the mute Silence," &c.

None of the replies which have been kindly offered to my query make this line intelligible. If *hist* be " an exclamation enjoining silence," who uses it here ? What we want is a verb, without which, either expressed or understood, no sentence can be complete. The suggestion in Chambers's *Glossary*, that *hist* means " to come stealing along crying hist," is quite amusing. A whole sentence implied in an interjection ! Mr. Masson's " paraphrase " suggests words which Milton might have written, but did not write. What MR. KREBS calls Richardson's full explanation explains nothing. " And the mute Silence," &c., as it stands is nonsense. Now we know that Milton could not write nonsense. How then are we to account for a line which is a blot on one of the most beautiful poems in our language ? Perhaps a slip of the pen or a printer's error may explain the case. *L'Allegro* and *Il Penseroso* were composed while Milton was in full enjoyment of sight, and no doubt were carefully copied out by him for the press. They were first printed in 1645, but were not reissued till 1673, when Milton was already blind. I have not access to the edition of 1645. Will any of your readers who have the opportunity of examining it kindly tell me how Milton there spells the word " haste," in " Haste thee, Nymph," in *L'Allegro* ? The first editions of *Paradise Regained* and *Samson Agonistes* are now before me, and in both poems *haste* is always printed " hast." In the passage just quoted from *L'Allegro* " haste " is used as a verb active ; Shakspeare also so uses it in " let it be so hasted." Will not the substitution of *haste* for " hist " make sense of the line we are considering ? The poet says to Melancholy, " First bring with thee Contemplation " ; if he added, " And haste along (*quasi* hasten on) Silence," that would be plain English.   J. DIXON.

P.S.—I have just found out that the line was long since mentioned in " N. & Q." as requiring explanation (see 4th S. i. 179).

I notice the following coincidence in another branch of languages. Num. xiii. 30 :—" And Caleb stilled (סׄם) the people." Here the radical is םׄם, and the imperative is *has* (in English letters), meaning hist, hush, be silent.

H. F. WOOLRYCH.

HENRY INGLES (5th S. vi. 490 ; vii. 14, 99.)— As an old Rugbeian, and one of your readers who

would welcome an answer to this query, may I draw the attention of J. P. E. to the recent recurrence of the name in the Rugby School register? The entries, which may serve to direct him to a quarter whence the desired information might be obtainable, are those of (1) William, son of Henry Ingles, Esq., 29, St. Andrew's Square, Edinburgh, entered Feb., 1859, and (2) Walter Chamberlayne, son of Henry Ingles, Esq., Chapel House, Guildford, entered Sept., 1866.   H. W.
New Univ. Club.

THE TRUE ORIGIN OF THE WORD "PUMPER-NICKEL" (4ᵗʰ S. xi. 136, 226.)—Accompanying an illustration of the old "Pernickelthurm" at Osnabrück, in Westphalia, a short history of the name of the black bread for which this province is famed is given in a recent number (Nov. 24, 1877) of the *Illustrirte Zeitung* of Leipzig.
According to the story generally current in Germany, a French cavalry soldier, at the period of the Napoleonic invasion, early in this century, being unable, in the course of his foraging, to procure any other than the heavy black bread peculiar to Westphalia, exclaimed in disgust that it was only good for his charger Nickel—"bon pour Nickel"; which expression became eventually gradually corrupted into "Pumpernickel."
This legend is, however, according to the writer of the note in the *Illustrirte Zeitung*, quite devoid of any foundation, the true version being as follows. In the year 1450, there being a great dearth and want in the neighbourhood of Osnabrück, a worthy magistrate of the town undertook to bake bread on his own account, and to distribute it among the starving poor. This bread he called "bonum paniculum"; and it was indeed of so good a quality that even after the famine was past the inhabitants continued to bake bread after the same fashion, calling it, moreover, by the same name, which got to be modified into "Bun-panickel," from which the transition is easy to "Pumpernickel." The site of the oven where this bread was baked is now marked by a round tower, with a conical roof and a chimney. This stands in the eastern part of the town of Osnabrück, and is known as the "Pernickelthurm."
J. C. GALTON.
New University Club.

ROWE FAMILY (5ᵗʰ S. vi. 289, 375, 494; vii. 74, 372.)—A family of this name was resident and possessed property at Plawsworth, in the palatinate of Durham, from the middle of the seventeenth century to about the middle of the present one.
A small heraldic painting of the holy lambs of these folk recently came into my possession. It is scarcely worth ARROW's acceptance, but nevertheless, if he will let me know·his address, he is most welcome to it.   E. A. WHITE, F.S.A.
Old Elvet, Durham.

SIR DRUE DRURY (5ᵗʰ S. viii. 349, 393.)—MR. PINK will find complete pedigrees of the three branches of the Drury family in the *History and Antiquities of Hawsted and Hardwick*, by the Rev. Sir John Cullum, Knt., London, 1813.
FREDERICK E. SAWYER.
Brighton.

ROBIN HOOD SOCIETY (5ᵗʰ S. viii. 351, 378.)—For some notices of this society see the *Connoisseur*, Nos. i., ix., xxxv., xxxvii.   O.

RICHARD BRINSLEY SHERIDAN (5ᵗʰ S. viii. 149, 236, 395.)—Has MR. J. BRANDER MATHEWS seen *Sheridiana; or, Anecdotes of the Life of R. B. S.*: his *Table-Talk and Bonmots*, London, Henry Colburn, New Burlington Street, 1826? It is an interesting work of 334 pages, and is embellished with an engraved portrait of the wit and orator.
T. B. GROVES.
Weymouth.

ARMS OF MOORE OR MORE (5ᵗʰ S. ix. 187, 196.)—In the parish church of Cranborne, county Dorset, on a monument of the Hoopers is the following coat of arms,—Hooper impaling Moore, viz. Erm., on a chev. betw. three Moors' heads couped ppr., two swords conjoined in point ar., hilts or, for Ann, ob. 1637, "one of the daughters and co-heiresses of John Moore, of Hantshire, serjeant-at-law, wife to Edward Hooper, of Boveridge, Esq.," ob. 1664. Symonds, in his *Diary* (Camden S., 1859), notices this coat, and adds this derogatory remark as regards Hooper:—"He was the serjeant's clerke; no gentleman; now living (1644); a rebel; on command, 7,000*l*. p. annum." Hutchins, in *History of Dorset*, first edit., vol. ii., Index to Arms, gives the following:—
"1. More of Manston, A., a fess G. betw. 3 Eaglets S., guttee A.
2. More of Hawkchurch, A., 2 Bars engrailed Az., betw. 9 martlets G.
3. More of Melplash, A., on a fess betw. 3 morecocks Sa., 3 Mullets O."   T. W. W. S.

PUBLIC-HOUSE SIGNS (5ᵗʰ S. ix. 127, 174.)—Is it proved historically—for conjecture is often misleading—that the tavern sign, "Goat and Compasses," is a corruption of the words, "God encompasses us," and that this latter sentence was ever used as the sign of an inn? It seems to me unlikely, and I doubt the derivation. But, if proved, will it help to the origin of the "Salmon and Compasses," the sign of an inn near the Agricultural Hall, Islington? There used to be a curious sign on the Quay at Exeter, viz. the "Anchor and Bodices," the connexion between the two not being obvious, unless, indeed, they are both regarded as stays.   CROWDOWN.

DR. MACKAY explains the "Pig and Whistle" as standing for "*Piga* and *Wassail*," which he

says are the Saxon equivalents of "a lass and a glass.". May I point out that this explanation is unsupported by one atom of evidence, and is absolutely untenable? A.-S. *piga* = "a lass" is of doubtful authority. Bosworth queries the word; there is no instance of it in this sense in old English writers. It is common enough in the Scandinavian languages, but according to Mr. Vigfusson it is a late word, occurring for the first time in Norway about 1400 A.D.　　　　　A. L. MAYHEW.
Oxford.

The sign, "Who'd a thought it?" appears over the door of a public-house in Radnor Street in this city. Is it a corruption, or merely a modern invention?　　　　　W. SLATER.
Manchester.

JOHN PHILLIPS : "THE SPLENDID SHILLING" (5th S. ix. 148, 216.)—Thomas Park, the bibliographer, on receiving a copy of Phillips's *Cider*, wrote on the flyleaf :—

"A Present from the Rev. Mr. Dunster, Feb., 1803.
　　　Impromptu on receiving it.
Some People give Perry and call it Champagne,
Not so gives of Petworth the Rector !
'Tis CIDER he tells us his vessels contain,
But in tasting it proves to be NECTAR.*
　　　　　　　　　　　　　　　"T. P."
　　　　　　　　　CH. ELKIN MATHEWS.

QUAKERS AND TITLES (5th S. ix. 68, 175.)—The Friends have certainly Scriptural authority for calling no man "Master," or, in other words, for not addressing any man by the title of "Mr.," if they adhere to the strict letter of the passage in Matt. xxiii. 8. But I would ask, in all sincerity and respect, by what title do they address their male parent, as in the following verse to the one I have alluded to it is said : "Call no man your father upon the earth, for one is your Father, which is in heaven"?　　　H. E. WILKINSON.
Anerley, S.E.

I do not think the Friends were so thin-skinned a hundred and fifty years since. I have two of their marriage certificates. In that of 1710 they call themselves "the people of God called Quakers," and "the people called Quakers" in 1737. As I descend from one of these marriages, I have of course no wish to be disrespectful, but a few days since we were discussing the date and origin of the song whose chorus is

"Merrily danced the Quaker's wife," &c.

and as we none of us knew perhaps some correspondent of "N. & Q." can help us.　　　P. P.

"HOPING AGAINST HOPE" (5th S. ix. 68, 94.)—The Vulgate renders παρ' ἐλπίδα (Rom. iv. 18) by *contra spem*, from which the English "against" comes. It was translated in Wiclif's version

　　　* "Us Nectar ingenium."

"agens hope," but Tyndall, in 1526, introduced "contrary to hope," which remained in most of the versions until "against" was resumed in the A.V. 1611. Coverdale in the meanwhile has "where nothing was to hope"; and a version—I think one of the Geneva translations—published by Barker in 1583 has, "which Abraham above hope, believed under hope." The idea contained in παρ' ἐλπίδα is well represented in these lines of the *Antigone* :—

ἀλλ', ἡ γὰρ ἐκτὸς καὶ παρ' ἐλπίδας χαρὰ
ἔοικεν ἄλλῃ μῆκος οὐδὲν ἡδονῇ,
ἥκω.—　　　　　　Vv. 392–4, ed. Gaisf.

The exact idea is of something beside and beyond hope, and Dr. Vaughan, in his edition of the *Epistle to the Romans*, translated the two words, ch. i. 25 and iv. 18, "beyond hope."

There is a note by Canon Lightfoot on παρ' ὅ ἐνηγγελισάμεθα ὑμῖν which illustrates this use of παρά. He remarks :—

"On the interpretation of these words a controversy on 'tradition' has been made to hinge, Protestant writers advocating the sense of 'besides' for παρά, Roman Catholics that of 'contrary to.' The context is the best guide to the meaning of the preposition......The idea of 'contrariety' therefore is alien to the general bearing of the passage, though independently of the context the preposition might well have this meaning."—*Ep. to the Galatians*, i. 8.

This explanation seems a better one than that which supposes that "hope" means one thing in the former part of the sentence, and another, viz. "expectation," in the latter part.
　　　　　　　　　　　ED. MARSHALL.

This expression can indeed plead "a pretty long prescription to justify its continued use." It is only St. Paul's saying in Rom. iv. 18, παρ' ἐλπίδα ἐπ' ἐλπίδι ἐπίστευσε, translated in the Genevan version, "above hope believed under hope"; in the Bishops' version, "contrary to hope believed in hope"; and in the authorized and Rheims versions alike, "against hope believed in hope." I fail to see why the expression should in any way be regarded as "nonsensical." That St. Paul's words should have become proverbial shows how their epigrammatic and vivid force has been universally approved. And as to the apostle's use of them, there is a good note in the margin of the Bishops' version :—"That is, which believed and hoped for those things which God did promise when as to men's reason they were without hope."
　　　　　　　　　　　W. D. MACRAY.

ST. JOSEPH (5th S. iv. 450 ; v. 74 ; viii. 472.)—It so happens that I have lately referred to the *Whole Works* of the Rev. John Lightfoot, D.D., Master of Catharine Hall, Cambridge, edited by the Rev. John Rogers Pitman, A.M., London, 1823, 13 vols., which contain *inter alia* Hebrew and Talmudical exercitations upon parts of the

New Testament. Those on St. Matthew's Gospel are contained in vol. xi., at p. 355 of which I find the following, in which for the Hebrew words I have substituted dots :—

"'They stoned the son of Satda in Lydda, and they hanged him up on the evening of the Passover. Now this son of Satda was son of Pandira. Indeed Rabb Chasda said, The husband [*of his mother*] was Satda ; her husband was Pandira ; her husband was Papus, the son of Juda : but yet I say his mother was Satda,...... namely, Mary, the plaiter of women's hair ; as they say in Pombeditha,......she departed from her husband.' These words are also repeated in Schabbath : ' Rabb Bibai, at a time when the angel of death was with him, said to his officer, Go,......bring me Mary, the plaiter of women's [*hairs*]. He went and brought to him ......Mary, the plaiter of young men's [*hair*], &c. The Gloss : The angel of death reckoned up to him what he had done before ; for this story of Mary, the plaiter of women's hair, was under the second Temple, for she was the mother of N., as it is said in Schabbath.'

"'There are some who find a fly in their cup, and take it out, and will not drink ; such was Papus Ben Juda, who locked the door upon his wife, and went out. Where the Glossers say thus : ' Papus Ben Juda was the husband......of Mary, the plaiter of women's hair ; and when he went out of his house into the street, he locked his door upon his wife, that she might not speak with any body ; which indeed she ought not to have done ; and hence sprang a difference between them, and she broke out into adulteries.'"

The names above represent the following persons : Ben Satda, or the son of Satda, Jesus ; Satda, Mary Magdalene, who is called his mother ; Papus Ben Judas, her husband ; Pandira, the reputed father of her son. There would appear to be some confusion between Pandira and *pandar*, as well as between Pandira and *panther*. The name Magdalene is supposed to mean plaiter of women's hair.

Those of your readers who would like to learn something of the state of society in Jerusalem about the Christian era will derive much assistance from Lightfoot's exercitations. Though very orthodox in his opinions, and very bitter against the Jews, and especially against the Pharisees, he appears to be very candid.   PARKFIELD.

According to ancient Jewish tradition, the family name of Joseph, the father of Jesus of Nazareth, was Pandira ; see Babylonian Talmud, Tract. Sabbath, fol. 104^b, and Tract. Sanhedrin, fol. 67^a. These references are not to be found in any modern copy of the Talmud, having been deleted by the censor, but may be seen in any old edition, such as that published in Venice in the year 1520.   M. D.

ARCHBISHOP SHARP (5th S. viii. 149, 187, 295 ; ix. 91.)—I must take exception to an expression in the communication of A. S. A. (ix. 91), in which he speaks of Archbishop Sharp as "martyred by the Covenanters." Assassinated the archbishop was, "martyred" he was not. A

martyr is one who, having presented to him the alternative of apostasy or death, deliberately prefers the latter. James Sharp would fain have purchased his life at any price ; but he found the stern fanatics into whose hands he had fallen as scornfully distrustful of his promises as they were deaf to his piteous appeals for mercy. The man who had never shown mercy met with none. He who had never hesitated to deceive was not believed when terror had made him for the time probably sincere.

As to the character of this "martyr," I refer your readers to Bishop Burnet's *History of His Own Times*, under date 1665. The bishop says :

"There were no more Scottish councils called at Whitehall after Lord Middleton's fall. But, upon particular occasions, the King [Charles II.] ordered the privy councillors of that kingdom, that were about the town, to be brought to him, before whom he now laid out the necessity of raising some more force for securing the quiet of Scotland : he only asked their advice how they should be paid. Sharp very readily said the money raised by the fining was not yet disposed of ; so he proposed the applying it to that use. None opposed this, so it was resolved on. And by that means the Cavaliers, who were come up with their pretensions, were disappointed of their last hopes of being recompensed for their sufferings. The blame of all this was cast upon Sharp, at which they were out of measure enraged, and charged him with it. He denied it boldly, but the King published it so openly that he durst not contradict him. Many to whom he had denied that he knew anything of the matter, and called that advice diabolical invention, affirmed it to the king. And the Lord Lauderdale, to complete his disgrace with the king, got many of his letters which he had writ to the Presbyterians after the time in which the king knew that he was negotiating for Episcopacy, in which he had continued to protest with what zeal he was soliciting their concerns, not without dreadful imprecations on himself if he was prevaricating with them, and laid these before the king, so *that the king looked upon him as one of the worst of men.*"

R. M. SPENCE, F.R.H.S.
Manse of Arbuthnott, N.B.

AUTHORS OF BOOKS WANTED (5th S. ix. 229.)—
Brill, near Dorton Spa: a Poetical Sketch, was written by Rev. Rich. Walker, B.D., formerly Fellow and school-master of Magdalen College, Oxford. He died about ten years ago.   W. D. MACRAY.

(5th S. ix. 189, 239)

The Post-Captain.—I find at the latter reference that this work is thought to have been written by Dr. Moore, author of *Zeluco*. As a grandson of Dr. Moore I can speak confidently that that is incorrect. I am aware that it has been attributed to him, but I have been assured by my father that there was not the least truth in the assertion.   J. C. MOORE.

AUTHORS OF QUOTATIONS WANTED (5th S. ix. 189.)—

"O world, as God has made it, all is beauty," &c.
These lines are from Robert Browning's poem, *The Guardian Angel : a Picture at Fano.*   FREDK. RULE.

Joseph Gostwick. (Longmans & Co.)

MR. GOSTWICK brings a wide induction of examples from the most varied forms and periods of English literature to bear upon the illustration of his text, which in itself forms a considerable body of rules, exceptions, and examples likely to be of great value to the teacher and the advanced student. For elementary purposes we should think it too elaborate, unless in the hands of a well-trained teacher, able to boil down his materials in the course of instruction. And we should hope that such a teacher would be able to correct the somewhat hazy views of early British history which Mr. Gostwick suggests in his introduction, where he appears to think that the Roman province of Britain was "governed by a Roman army." That Roman law penetrated into Britain, that Roman municipia and colonies were established there, that Roman arts and science flourished there—in a word, that Roman civilization was introduced wherever the Roman eagles advanced, Mr. Gostwick appears quietly but firmly to ignore. On the other hand, he is very strenuous in his assertion that "from the time of Alfred" (or, as it is put in another place, "from the time of Ælfric") "to the present one language has been always spoken by the people." If Mr. Gostwick were to test this statement by giving out a passage from Alfred's *Orosius* or Ælfric's *Homilies*, to be done without reference to books, we think he might see cause to estimate the extent of the changes produced by Romance infusions more highly than he does at present. We cannot say that we like "E. I." and "E. II." to represent what used to be called Old English, or Anglo-Saxon, and Middle English, nor yet such *formulæ* as "Present and Past Progressive"; but we appreciate the value to students of Mr. Gostwick's careful analysis of the varying influence of the Northern, Midland, and Southern dialects over the idioms of the existing English language, and we are sure that his book will amply repay the study required to master it.

Lessing's Fables. Edited, with Notes, by F. Storr, B.A. (Rivingtons.)

RESTLESSLY moving from place to place, from Berlin to Breslau, from Hamburg to Wolfenbüttel, sharply criticizing his neighbours wherever he went, Gotthold Ephraim Lessing made his mark upon the literature of his native land alike by the keenness of his satire and the weight of his polemical mallet, which he brought heavily to bear upon conventionality and imitation. Mr. Storr has found Lessing's fables very useful as a German primer, and he now introduces them, in a convenient form, arranged with a view to the graduation of difficulties, and accompanied by short notes and a glossary, as well as an introduction embodying the pith of Lessing's teaching on the subject of fables. In his glossary Mr. Storr adds the useful feature of cognate English words, prefaced by the abbreviation "et.," to signify etymological connexion. We should, however, have thought it preferable to have used "cf.," as they are often subjects for comparison rather than assignment of direct etymological kinship. And we question whether a boy is not likely to be puzzled rather than helped by such a combination as "et. lay, laity, lewd," to illustrate *Leute*, and "et. to loaf," as illustrating "*laufen*, to run," if he is not in the hands of a very careful master.

SIR GEORGE GILBERT SCOTT.—It is with deep regret that we record the great loss which Art in this country has sustained by the death of Sir George

ing his numerous and absorbing engagements, Sir Gilbert found time to send us occasional communications, which were always welcome to the readers of "N. & Q."

WE understand that immediately after Easter a choice private collection, rich in caricatures, etchings, and illustrated books by the late George Cruikshank, will be offered for sale at Sotheby's. The collection contains many etchings and woodcuts signed by George Cruikshank, but not hitherto known to be his, also several pieces of vocal music, the title-pages of which were designed and engraved by him; among these will be found the *Great Gobble Gobble*, believed to be unique.

MESSRS. REEVES & TURNER are about to publish *The Life and Times of James Catnach (late of the Seven Dials), Ballad-Monger*, edited by Charles Hindley. The number of copies issued will be limited.

Notices to Correspondents.

ON all communications should be written the name and address of the sender, not necessarily for publication, but as a guarantee of good faith.

ABHBA.—St. Aidan, who is commemorated on Aug. 31, was a native of Ireland, and a founder of Hij, the great monastery which his countryman. St. Columba, had founded. He became a bishop, and fixed his see in the isle of Lindisfarne. His death took place on Aug. 31, 651. Butler also mentions another St. Aidan, Bishop of Mayo, commemorated in the Irish Calendary on Oct. 20, who died in 768.

L. H.—John Gother, the son of Presbyterian parents, was a convert to the Church of Rome when quite a youth, and became a priest. He was born at Southampton, and died at sea on his way to Lisbon on Oct. 2, 1704. *A Papist Misrepresented and Represented* is his chief work.

T. C. ROWLATT asks for the name of a good set of notes or comments upon the *Idylls of the King* or upon Tennyson's poems generally. [You should supply yourself with the indexes to the respective volumes of "N. & Q."; by their means you could solve many of your difficulties.]

A CORRESPONDENT asks what is the earliest period at which one can find the name of Grant mentioned in England and Scotland.

F. F. G.—A note on the "Prose Chronicles of England called the Brute," by Sir Frederick Madden, will be found in "N. & Q.," 2ⁿᵈ S. i. 1.

FRED. W. FOSTER.—We shall be glad to have your lists. Your former query was answered *ante*, p. 240.

A YOUNG NATURALIST should address his query to *Science Gossip* (Hardwicke, Piccadilly).

TRUTH.—No charge; but your reply has been anticipated. See *ante*, p. 234.

R. M. SPENCE.—Next week.

NOTICE.

Editorial Communications should be addressed to "The Editor of 'Notes and Queries'"—Advertisements and Business Letters to "The Publisher"—at the Office, 20, Wellington Street, Strand, London, W.C.

We beg leave to state that we decline to return communications which, for any reason, we do not print; and to this rule we can make no exception.

Notes.

EMBLEMS OF THE PASSION.

Among the many valuable pictures at Grimsthorpe Castle, Lincolnshire (the Baroness Willoughby de Eresby), is an oil painting on panel, hung in one of the bedrooms, and representing the emblems of the Passion in a highly ingenious way. The picture is on a thick panel, about 24 by 16 inches in size, and of the Dutch school. I was unable, on a close inspection, to discover any signature or monogram of the artist. Affixed to the frame is a recent manuscript, which I take the liberty to copy, as it gives such an excellent description of this curious painting :—

" Description by one who is not an art critic.
 "26/4/76.

"A panel picture of unusual subject and unusual merit. The dark object on the dexter side does not explain itself, but the inscription in Greek and Latin hanging from the crown of thorns reveals the design of the artist, which is to gather into one group all the objects of the Crucifixion, leaving it to the imagination to suggest that they have been thrown together after the body of the Lord had been removed. There hangs loosely the rough scarlet mantle that had been thrown over the Lord ; there is the lanthorn, and there are the weapons that had been carried by the band who went to take Jesus. There is—in the best style of Gerard Douw —the brazier which contained the fire by which Peter warmed himself ; there are the mallet, the hammer, the strong nails, used in the act of the crucifixion ; there are the rods for the scourging, the cords for the binding, the lance for the piercing of the Lord ; there is the reed

with the sponge, the heavy pincers for withdrawing the nails from the wood, the keg for the supply of the vinegar, the pieces of silver for the traitor, the dice with which the soldiers cast lots for the seamless garment. There is great harmony in the sombre hues of the picture, the only light being the slight glare from the written inscription, and a sober glitter from the brazen pan for the coals. Who was the painter ? H. M."

To me the picture seems roughly executed, but I agree with the (ex)bishop suffragan of Nottingham in his general description, and in the forcible representation of the brazen pan, which is very finely represented. Was it, however, "the brazen pan for coals"? I am of course aware, both from classical and Biblical literature (cf. Jer. xxxvi. 22), that such pans of metal were used for fire, though I think that such pans would be furnished with handles, and probably also with legs. The brass pan in this picture is destitute of either, and I would suggest that the Dutch artist intended it to represent the basin in which Pilate washed his hands. I would also suggest that " the dark object on the dexter side" was intended to represent, from the Dutch artist's ideas, the side of the fireplace at which Peter and the rest warmed themselves. It is carried up square and dark to about two-thirds of the picture, ending at the top in a right angle. At a short distance from it, and of less than half its height, is a slender upright, shaped at the top like a crutch. I imagine that this is intended for one of the two "dogs" that would be on either side the fireplace, according to the painter's notions. He has also treated the weapons in the picture according to his own ideas. The scarlet robe hangs over, and down the side of, what looks like a roll of matting or wicker-work, and the white scroll bearing the inscription also hanging from it, and helping the colouring as well as the composition. But probably this matting or wicker-work is designed to convey a definite idea of something connected with the Crucifixion. If so, what could it be?

I have before me a drawing that I carefully made, in the year 1854, from a flat tombstone in the churchyard of Leigh, between Worcester and Malvern. A cross is sculptured on the centre of the stone, with an ornamental wreath of vine and corn hanging over the arms of the cross and down the two outer sides of the stone. Twined in the upper portion of the wreath is a label with the text, " For as often as ye eat this bread and drink this cup, ye do show the Lord's death till he come." On the top of the cross is the pelican in her piety ; underneath is the scroll for the inscription, beneath which, at the arms of the cross, hangs the crown of thorns. On the left arm of the cross stands the cock ; behind the arm are a ladder and a spear. On the right arm of the cross stands a chalice, something like a modern coffee-pot (for the vinegar ?) ; behind the arm are a second ladder and the reed with the sponge. Down the front a volume (?), a hammer, a pair of pincers, two twisted nails, two more twisted nails, a short sword bound together with an ear, and beneath this there may have been another emblem, but the stone is here defaced. The earliest inscription on the two slabs on this stone is 1797.

In Bishop Stanbury's Chapel in Hereford Cathedral (circa 1470) there are eighteen shields, on which are sculptured various emblems of the apostles, arms of the see and deanery, &c. The third shield is described in the Rev. F. T. Havergal's *Visitors' Hand-Guide to Hereford Cathedral* as being carved with "instruments of the Saviour's Passion." I have now before me a photograph of this exquisite chapel, but the shields are on a small scale, and I cannot make out with certainty the various "instruments." What are they? They are not mentioned in Jones's *Guide to Hereford Cathedral and City.*

Four miles south-west of Oundle, Northampton-shire, is the very remarkable unfinished building, Liveden, a cross-shaped stone structure, built in the reign of Queen Elizabeth by Sir Thomas Tresham, of Rushton, the father of Francis Tresham, who was one of the conspirators in the Gunpowder Plot. The building was probably designed for monastic purposes, and is well described and illustrated in *The Ruins of Liveden, &c.*, by T. Bell (of Barnwell, 1847). One of the illustrations represents seven "Emblems on Liveden Ruin." I copy the letter-press description given of them by Mr. Bell :—

"Upon the second story, in stone compartments, also running throughout the building, are singular sculptures, executed with much care, emblematical of the sufferings and crucifixion of our Saviour. These are in circles of about eighteen inches in diameter, and are supposed to represent:—

"1. The purse containing the money for which Judas betrayed Christ, and round the border the thirty pieces of silver.

"2. The lanthorn, torches, a spear, and a sword.

"3. The cross, ladder, hammer, and nails.

"4. The seamless garment and dice, to represent the casting lots for it.

"5. The crowing cock to awaken Peter, and the scourges with which Pilate scourged Jesus.

"6. The X within the circle is 'Christus,' the P in the middle of the cross ' Pontifex '; the wreath round the circle, in which there is neither beginning nor end, is emblematical of eternity, or ' in Æternum '—' Christ a priest for ever.' The circle is sometimes formed of a serpent with the tail in the mouth.

"7. The I.H.S. and Cross. 'Jesus Hominum Salvator,' and round the border ' Esto Mihi ' and I.H.S.

"These sculptures are repeated throughout the whole of the building, with the abbreviations I.H.S. and X.P.S."—Pp. 33, 34.

By the awakening of Peter, Mr. Bell probably meant the awakening of his conscience. He omits mentioning the pincers, crown of thorns, two spears, and two swords, and there are one or two points in which I think that he is wrong. But

original interpretation of emblem 6, and what supposes to be the letter P as the initial "Pontifex." This is certainly a novel explanat of the cross of Constantine ! CUTHBERT BEDE

LONDON BELL-FOUNDERS IN THE LAST CENTURY.

The following letter, written on a double sh of folio paper, and addressed to "Suckling Sp love, Esq., at Beverley, Yorkshire," is copied fi the original in my possession. On the two ins pages is *printed* the long "List of the Peals Bells hung by Samuel & Robert Turner, B Hangers to Messrs. Lester & Pack, Bell-Found in White-Chapel, London," which is copied bel At the side of this list is a most curious represen tion of "St. Nicholas's Steeple, Newcastle," sho ing the ringers ringing the bells, &c. As it not likely that many copies of this list can ha been preserved, it will probably be of service those of your readers who take an interest in ca panology. The spelling, &c., is followed *literat et verbatim.*

"London, July 31ᵗ, 1770

"Sir,—I trouble you with these lines concerning y Bells in the Minster, I have been informed that ᵧ ordered the Carpenter to Rite to me but I never recei any from him, if I had I should have return'd an ansᵥ again, I should be Glad to wait on you, and you n depend on it's being done in the bist manner, ther nobody in your part of the Country that knows ᵪ thing about such work, your Carpenter might Build · frame, and I would give him Directions and a Plan, you think Proper I would come down and sett the C penter to work on the frame and I could give you Estimate of the Expence of the rest of the work, bu should be glad of an answer by the return of the Pᵢ for it would suit me to come down next week, for ᵗ Week after I am going to Put up a new Peal of Eiₗ Bells at Carisbrook in the Isle of white.

"I am, Sir, your Obᵗ Hble Serᵗ,
"SAML. TURNER.'

A LIST
of the Peals of Bells hung by Samuel & Robert Turn Bell-Hangers to Messrs. Lester & Pack, Bell-Founders White-Chapel, London.

The Number of Bells in each Peal and Weight of the Ten

Sᵗ PETER's in the CITY of EXETER	10	67
Sᵗ Peter's, Colchester, Essex ..	8	21
Coper Seale, Essex	5	14
Ridge in Herts	3	12
Harrow on the Hill, Middˣ ...	6	24
Middleton in Yorkshire... ...	4	9
Chiswick, Middˣ	6	14
Little Bentley, Essex	5	15
Rickmansworth, Herts... ...	8	23
Sᵗ Peters, York Minster... ...	10	53
Steple Bumstead, Essex... ...	5	14
Sᵗ Leonard, Colchester, Essex ...	6	18
Gainsbrough in Lincolnshire ...	8	20
Sᵗ Margarets, Lynn, Norfolk ...	8	30
Terrington Sᵗ Clemᵗ, Norfolk ...	6	16
Twyford in Hampshire	6	12
Arith in Kent	6	17
Hertford in Hertfordshire ...	8	21

noorn in Cornwall	0	10
ıg Crondon, Bucks ...	8	20
ıat Maisington, Bucks	6	28
bymalzard, Yorkshire	4	15
sworth, Oxfordshire...	6	5
ɔleby, Leceistershire...	5	15
ʒal Exchange, London	8	20
vsham in Kent ...	8	16
cley in Yorkshire ...	3	8
ıning in Berkshire ...	6	25
ıckington, Oxfordshire	6	12
·tsea in Hants ...	6	12
lhurst, Susex ...	6	12
ɔrton in Suffolk ...	5	13
Saints, Colchester, Essex	5	9
·kell in Yorkshire ...	3	10
ingdon in Berkshire ...	8	19
ɔon, Middx ...	6	14
Nicholas Chaple, Lynn	8	16
ɔreditch, London ...	10	29
·erington in Cambridgeshire	6	17
ell in Surry... ...	6	14
cingham in Barks ...	6	21
lston in Cornwell ...	6	17
ıworth, Middx ...	8	19
w Shoreham, Sussex...	6	15
Sidwells, Exeter ...	8	18
·hmond, Surry ...	8	19
lton, Yorkshire ...	8	15
ıat Heasley, Oxfordshire	6	15
ılford in Surry ...	8	25
ɔhns, Norwich ...	6	12
nesley, Yorkshire ...	6	14

J. P. EARWAKER, F.S.A.
ngton, Manchester.

SLANG PHRASES.

Reader (an extinct literary periodical) pub-n 1864 some notes on slang words, forwarded ous contributors. Dictionary makers will ly not think of looking there for them. If, ɹr, you reprint them in " N. & Q.," they can-to be at hand when wanted. I therefore ıu my cuttings reduced to alphabetical order.

smith's Daughter.—A key. I have never met s word in print, but have heard it frequently in ıtion.

—" Of thys cometh golde in their brydles, in ɪdles, and in theyr spurres, so that theyr spurres ghter then theyr aulters. Of this cometh theyr ɪs wyne presses and their full sellers, *blotking* ys vnto that. Of this cometh their tunes of swete —1532, Sir T. More, *Confutacion of Dr. Barnes,* i., Works, 1557, fol. 808, col. 1.

lbrim.—A Quaker. This word clearly owes its ɪ the peculiar hat worn by the Society of Friends.

ıe *living Jingo!*—Southey is said by a recent ɔ have used this expression in his works. Where? *ffre's " Tightner."*—" I asked him [a young black ɪ at the Cape] to sing; and he flung himself at my an attitude that would make Watts crazy with aɳd crooned queer little mournful ditties. I n sixpence, and told him not to get drunk. He h, no ! I will buy *bread enough to make my belly*

Clay.—A pig's *clays* are the horny coverings of its toes (Northamptonshire).

Culsh.—Useless, valueless lumber.

Dolly.—Silly, foolish (?). " You are a chit and a little idiot," returned Bella, " or you wouldn't make such a *dolly* speech."—Charles Dickens, *Our Mutual Friend,* book i. chap. iv.

Dymminges Dale.—" But......there is no remedy with vs, but that Tindal wil nedes dampne vs all into *Dymminges dale.*"—1532, Sir T. More, *Confutacion of Tyndale,* Works, 1557, fol. 719, col. 2.

Farmer, &c.—A hare (Kent).

Fizz.—To fly (?). " Speaking generally, old maids may be grouped into two great classes : those who take to poodles, and those who take to tracts—those whose yearning for something to love and pet has severed all hope of husband and children, and those who, from their forced celibacy, become a kind of Protestant nun, differing from the Roman Catholic species much as bluebottles differ from drones. Drones live an idle, gregarious, and monotonous life, in a comparatively speaking inoffensive way ; but the bluebottle is always rushing about by itself, *fizzes* fussily into some poor man's cottage, buzzes incessantly and distractingly, knocks its blunt head two or three times against what it doesn't understand, and at last is off, to the unutterable relief of the nerves."—A *tête-à-tête* Social Science Discussion in the *Cornhill Magazine,* No. 59 (Nov., 1864), p. 575.

Gallows Grass, &c. : Hemp.—" Hempe is called in...... English, Neckeweede and *Gallowgrasse.*"—1578, Lyte's translation of Dodoen's *Historie of Plantes,* fol. 72.

Golken.—" But yet to make me sorye, that euer I was so far ouersene, as to take away hys gay *golken* worde of spirituall rulers from him, he beginneth as it were with a great thret and sayth."—Sir T. More, *Debellacion of Salem and Byzance,* Works, 1557, fol. 1020, col. 2.

Hand-em-down.—A second-hand garment (Northamptonshire).

Hemp : Stretch Hemp, sb.—A candidate for the gallows. " [He] feareth [not] to mocke the sacrament, the blessed body of God, and ful like a *stretch hempe,* call it but cske, bred, or starch."—1532, Sir T. More, *Confutacion of Tyndale,* Works, 1557, fol. 715, col. 1.

To Maund : Maunder : Pad.—
" And every man to keep
In his own path and circuit.
Hig. Do you hear ?
You must hereafter *maund* on your own *pads,* he says.
. . . . . .
. . . Thou art our chosen,
Our king and sovereign, monarch of the *maunders.*"
1622, B. and F., *The Beggar's Bush,* ii. 1.

Mazarine.—" I had procured a ticket through the interest of Mr. ——, who was one of the committee for managing the entertainment and a mazarine" [a common councilman, from their wearing mazarine blue cloaks]. —1761, *Annual Reg.,* p. 238.

Mourning Shirts.—" We say *mourning shirts,* it being customary for men in sadness *to spare the pains of their laundresses.*"—Thos. Fuller, *Pisgah Sight,* p. 98.

Muckforks.—The hands or fingers. " Keep your *muck-forks* off me."—Low.

Mum-glass.—" A cant word for the Monument, erected in *Fish Street,* near *London Bridge,* in commemoration of the dreadful fire in 1666, which consumed the greatest

Shakspeare :—

> "*Kate.* I'faith, sir, you shall neuer neede to feare,
> I-wis it is not halfe way to her heart ; •
> But, if it were, doubt not, her care should be
> To combe your *noddle* with a three-legg'd stoole,
> And paint your face, and vse you like a foole."
> *The Taming of the Shrew*, Act i. sc. 1.

Oxford Clink.—" A play upon words is called an *Oxford clink* by Leicester, in Strafford's *Let.* i. 224."—Southey, *Com. Book*, Coll. " Cromwell."

Paper.—This word is applied by commercial men to bills and promissory notes, which are briefly spoken of as " paper." In *theatrical slang* the word is applied to "orders," or free tickets of admission. Thus, in speaking to a friend respecting the crowding of a theatre, he replied to me by saying, " Yes ; they have very full houses, I know ; but three-fourths are *paper*,"—meaning thereby that three-fourths of the audience had been admitted without payment, but with a printed order.

Pinch.—To steal.

Resurrectionist : Resurrection-man.—Both these terms are applied to men who gain a livelihood by exhuming corpses from graveyards and selling them to doctors for dissection. Both words are inserted in Worcester's *Dictionary*. The *Quarterly Review* is there quoted as an authority for the first, and Campbell for the second.

Rody.—Streaked alternately with lean and fat. This very common word seems to be exclusively applied to bacon which presents this appearance. Halliwell gives the word *roded*, and explains it " lean mingled with fat." It is marked by him as being used in the Western counties ; but I have heard it frequently used in the North, in the Midland counties, and in London too.

Sea : at Sea.—Unable to grasp at the meaning of another's speech. " ' But, Byng, have you an idea what a medical student is?' ' What what is?' said I, thinking he was speaking of some little known disease. ' A medical student—a student of medicine !' ' What he is?' I asked, still more *at sea*."—From a *tête-à-tête* Social Science Discussion in the *Cornhill Magazine*, No. 59 (Nov., 1864), p. 577.

Sneak (verb and noun).—This school term I was surprised not to find inserted. One who carried information to the preceptor, or told tales generally, was always called a " sneak." And, again, when something was about to be done which the boys wished to keep from the master's ears, if a known tell-tale was near, one would say, " Don't do anything before ——; he'll *sneak*."—*i.e.*, give information to the schoolmaster.

Sottes hoffe : Goffe.—" These thinges being thus, when he liketh hymselfe well, and weneth he eateth as properly as a camel daunseth, in calling it my faith, and the Popes faith, and the diuels faith, eueri man I wene that wel marketh the matter, wyll be likely to cal his proper scoffe but a very cold conseeit of my *goffe*, that he found and tooke vp at *sottes hoffe*."—1532, Sir T. More, *Confutacion of Tyndale*, Works, 1557, fol. 711, col. 1.

Soup-shop.—The meaning of this term is fully explained in the passage quoted :—" ' Enough !' repeated the guard, ' may be it's too much ! I don't like to think bad of an old acquaintance, but there 's loads of plate at the Abbey, and I ain't such a greenhorn as not to know that there are plenty of *soup-shops* in London—tho' I never heard of one in Lombard Street afore !' ' To the uninitiated of our readers, it may be as well to explain that, by the term *soup-shops*, the speaker meant

recognition of the plunder is no longer possible."—From " Woman and her Master," by J. F. Smith, chap. cxxxv., in the *London Journal*, No. 491, vol. xix. p. 322.

Strap.—Credit. This is a vulgar term, synónymous with " tick," which is inserted in the *Slang Dictionary*.

Swig : Swinging (soft *g*).—" It is not like Lucina, who gets a hearty *swig* at the caudlecup . . . a *swinging* bellyful of good cakes at the blithemeat."—1770, Phil. Skelton, *Works*, v. 216.

Tiddlywink.—A " leaving shop " where money is lent on goods without a pawnbroker's licence (Northamptonshire).

To tip the Wink.—

> " If some alluring girl, in gliding by,
> Shall *tip the wink*, with a lascivious eye,
> And thou, with a consenting glance, reply."
> Dryden's trans. of Persius, Sat. iv.

Two-eyed Steak.—A dried herring or bloater. This amusing term is, I believe, new. A few weeks ago said my groom to my housemaid : " Wouldn't you like what I am going to have for breakfast?" " What is it?" " A *two-eyed steak*," which turned out to be a Yarmouth bloater.

To wet.—" Must I stay till, by the strength of Terse claret, you have *wet* yourself into courage?"—Shadwell, *Humourists*.

ANON.

CURIOSITIES OF HISTORY.—On Feb. 4, at the Castle Assembly Rooms, Hastings, a lecture on the Lord Mayors of London was delivered to "a numerous and appreciative audience." The *Hastings Times* of Feb. 9 gives a full report, from which I cut a noticeable passage :—

" Henry VIII. was a strange fellow. He had a notion that one part of the royal privilege was to take any number of wives, whose heads he could chop off at a minute's notice. He came at last to rather a teaser—Queen Catherine of Aragon—and with her he had some difficulty. She came from Spain, then a powerful nation, and not to be played with. He had his eye on Anne Boleyn, and how should he get rid of Catherine? He had a friend—one of the most astute and sagacious priests England has ever produced—Cardinal Wolsey. Henry in a hurry sued for his divorce, and Pope Clement refused it, wanting still to exert the papal influence in the land. While the king was still puzzled by the Pope's refusal, Wolsey stepped in and said, ' We will take off Catherine's head, and establish your right to be your own pope and the head of the Church.' This was a bold stroke, and Henry was thus made head of the Church and Defender of the Faith. Anne Boleyn became his queen by an entire ecclesiastical revolution. Poor Anne Boleyn did not last long, but she had done her work ! From that time the people of England have had religious liberty ; but if Henry had been a good man the Reformation would not have come so soon. The time was ripening for it. The press was beginning to do its work, and people were becoming more alive to their true interests, but this hastened the matter."

The manner of the above is striking, and some of the matter will be new to the readers of " N. & Q."

FITZHOPKINS.

Garrick Club.

BARONS OF THE ISLE OF MAN : THE PRIOR OF ST. BEES AND OTHERS.—The following extract from the St. Bees College *Calendar* for 1878 (St. Bees, J. Reay ; London, Whittaker) may not be without interest, as having a direct bearing on the question of the powers and privileges of the mediæval kings and lords of Man. It is unfortunate that no dates should be given ; but I think, from the mention of a Scottish and an Irish abbot as sharing the rank of the Prior of St. Bees, we may assume the period indicated to be between 1266, the date of the cession of Man to Scotland by Magnus IV. of Norway, and 1343, the date of its final acquisition by the English :—

"Whilst on the subject of the priors of St. Bees, their rank as barons of the Isle of Man cannot be justly overlooked. As the abbot of the superior house, St. Mary's at York, was entitled to a seat among the Parliamentary barons of England, so the Prior of St. Bees was Baron of the Isle of Man. As such he was obliged to give his attendance upon the kings and lords of Man whensoever they required it, or at least upon every new succession in the government. The neglect of this important privilege would probably involve the loss of the tithes and lands in that island, which the devotion of the kings had conferred on the priory of St. Bees. An abbot from Ireland, and another from Scotland, were also constrained by the same religious liberality to appear in Man as barons when called upon."

I shall be glad if any correspondent can furnish the names of the Scotch and Irish religious houses which gave barons to the Isle of Man. I incline to believe that the Scotch house may have been Saddell in Kintyre, an offshoot of the Cluniac foundation at Paisley, favoured by the Lords of the Isles of the race of Somerled, who had himself married a daughter of Olaus, King of Man.

C. H. E. CARMICHAEL.

TABLING.—It was the custom in English cathedrals to have a punctator (a pricker in), who noted appearances and absences at divine service. An interesting relic of a tablet for entering and marking the names of officiants, celebrants, and hebdomadaries remains at Chichester, still in use. Thus in St. de Offensa is mentioned "intitulatus ad debitum officii cujuscunque secundum cotidianas tabulæ inscriptiones." It is a MS. Ordo Prædicandi, with the names of the preachers in their course written in double columns. Attached to each name is a round hole, and a pin suspended by an iron chain on the outer side is inserted into these holes successively to note the preacher for the following Sunday or holy day.

MACKENZIE E. C. WALCOTT.

THE BISHOP OF DURHAM IN 1722.—Dr. Doran was mistaken (*London in the Jacobite Times*, vol. i. p. 364) in stating that the bishop who appeared at a review on horseback in the king's train dressed in a lay habit of purple, with jack-boots and his hat cocked, and a black wig tied behind him like a military officer, was Nathaniel, Lord Crewe. It

was William Talbot, his successor, lately translated from Salisbury. The mistake is the more pardonable as Lord Crewe is often (though wrongly) said to have died Sept. 18, 1722, instead of Sept. 18, 1721, the latter date being the correct one.

E. H. A.

SCHOOL BOOKS.—In a minute book belonging to the town of Melton-Mowbray, Leicestershire, I find the following entry :—

"The names of the schoolebookes given by Mr. Chamb'lin and left in the schoole at M' Stokes his death, Julye first, 1673 :—Martineus ; Lexicon Geographic ; Erasmus Adiges ; Calopin ; A Greek Lexicon ; Votius Etomologicon ; Skynlau Pentaglot ; Mintius ; Budens Comitaries ; Poetica's Dixnarie ; A Quadrupal Dixnarie ; Goldmans Dixnarie."

Notes on any of the above will be acceptable.

THOMAS NORTH.

A FRIGHTFUL STORY.—"We," that is to say, two young English ladies travelling with their father at Nice in 1865,

"noticed a lady with two attendants, and were exceedingly startled on hearing her speak, her voice having a curious spasmodic effect, *like the bark of a dog*. We have since been told that she is a Russian countess, whose story is very sad and strange. A serf on the estate of a great noble, she lost her voice in the terror of some sudden attack of her master's dogs. Her life was saved ; but all *human* power of speech was gone. The count, in a sudden access of remorse or pity, married her, giving her the shelter of his name, and sending her here with a handsome provision for her life."

This extraordinary story may perhaps be garnered in "N. & Q.," though its interest is mainly physiological. I extract it from *Beaten Tracks ; or, Pen and Pencil Sketches in Italy*, a pleasant and ingenuous book, whose two fair authors are known to at least one friend of mine. But though we may fully rely on what they say, it does not follow that what they heard from others is equally credible.

A. J. M.

CURIOUS NAMES.—In the *Guardian* for Oct. 17 it is stated that "Mr. Zaphnath-Paaneah Isaiah Obed-Edom Nicodemus Francis Edward Clarke, a bloater merchant at Lowestoft, has been poisoned by taking a lotion in mistake for a draught." Among the marriage entries in my parish register for the last quarter occurs the name of "Alice Juddery, widow, daughter of William Peterkin." The name of the Rev. Field Flowers Goe is to be seen in the list of speakers at the Croydon Congress.

T. F. R.

A GOLDEN KEY.—It may be interesting to some of your readers to know that an ornamental steel key fetched the enormous price of seventy guineas at a sale at Messrs. Foster's in Pall Mall, about three weeks ago. It certainly was a beautiful key, the handle and shaft being of bright steel, elaborately ornamented and pierced, and was supposed to be of French manufacture of the fifteenth century. I may add that some of the ornamental keys that my firm are sending to the forthcoming Paris Exhibition are, I think, equal in design and workmanship to this one referred to ; and I hope, if they are ever sold for the benefit of my descendants, they will fetch the same price.

J. C. CHUBB.

Queries.

[We must request correspondents desiring information on family matters of only private interest, to affix their names and addresses to their queries, in order that the answers may be addressed to them direct.]

ST. MARK'S DAY, IN THE SARUM BREVIARY, A FAST.—Can MR. BAILY, or any other of your correspondents learned in matters liturgical, explain why St. Mark's Day is marked in the Sarum Breviary as a fast ? It appears in the Calendar as follows (I quote from a Breviary printed at Paris in 1555, and I put italics for red letters) :—"*xvii. c. vii. cal. Marci euange. infe. du. iii. lec. Jeiu. Letania maior. Ultimum pasc. 25.*" And the rubric in the "proprium de sanctis" directs that if the festival falls in Easter week it is to be deferred "*de ieiunio vero tunc nec de proces. q. solet fieri eo die, nichil fiat nec post nec ante i. illo anno.*" If it fell on a Sunday after the octave of Easter, the whole service for St. Mark's Day was to be used with a "memory" of the Sunday, "*tamen de ieiu. nec de pces. q. solet fieri post mis. de sancto marco : nihil fiat eo anno.*" But if it fell on a week day after the octave of Easter, "*fiat ieiun' & proces. more solito.*" It is obvious to suggest that the fast was to be observed on the day preceding the festival. But if so, the word "Jeiu." in the Calendar should be placed on April 24 : the vigil before a festival is always so marked in the Calendar. Moreover, St. Mark does not appear among the saints who bid us fast (*i.e.* who have vigils), according to the lines which appear in the Calendar under the month of June :

"Petrus cum paulo : iacobus cum bartholomeo :
Thomas, andreas, pariter cum simone iudas.
Ut ieiunemus nos admonet, atq. mattheus."

A. COMPTON.

Chadstone, Northampton.

NEVILLE QUERIES. — Margaret Neville, of Hornby, wife of Thomas Beaufort, Duke of Exeter, speaks in her will of "my nephew the Earl of Warwick." How did this relationship come about? In Rot. Pat., 4 Hen. VI. part 1, I find mention of "Willielmus Lucy, miles, et Margareta uxor ejus, . . . pro nomen Willielmi filii Walteri Lucy, et Margareta Nevill, consanguinea nuper Comitis Marchie (Mar. 5, 1426)." I find myself confirmed by Harl. MS. 807 in the conclusion that this was a daughter of John Neville, of Raby, and Eliza beth Holand, of Kent. Was her husband a Luc beth Holand, of Kent. Was her husband a Luc of Charlcote ?
Was Margaret Neville, wife of Sir Willia Gascoyne, the daughter of (1) Ralph Neville second son of first earl, and Mary Ferrers, or (2) o John Neville of Wymersley, son of the said Ralph or (3) of Ralph, second earl, and Margaret Cob ham ?
What is the true date of death of Ralph, thir Earl of Westmoreland ?
What was the Christian name of the second wif of Ralph his son, daughter of William Paston ?
Was Anne, wife of Sir William Conyers, the daughter of Ralph, third earl, or of Ralph his son

HERMENTRUDE.

"A FORLORN HOPE."—In the Dutch expressio "de verloren hoop van een leger," the forlorn hop of an army, are we to understand *hoop* in the sens of "hope," or in the sense of "a band of men" This expression is given in the Eng.-Dutch par of the Tauchnitz Dutch Dictionary ; but unde *hope* the phrase given is "de forlorene kinden," translation of the F. phrase *enfans perdus*, whicl see in Cotgrave. The sense of "troop" or "band seems the better ; but how is it understood i Holland, and how was it formerly understood there

WALTER W. SKEAT.

JOHNNY GILPIN.—An old newspaper of Nov. 1790, has the following notice :—

"The gentleman who was so severely ridiculed for ba horsemanship, under the title of Johnny Gilpin, died few days ago at Bath, and has left an unmarried daughter with a fortune of 20,000l.—Nov. 1790."

Is this gentleman's name remembered ?

J. E. J.

THE "STEAM HORSE."—Where is a poem thus called, of which this, I believe, is the first verse ?—

"But now unheard I saw afar
His cloud of windy mane,
Now level, like a blazing star,
He thunders through the plain."

FLEUR-DE-LYS.

HON. CHARLES HOWARD'S WIVES.—He was fourth son, and sixth child, of Henry Bowes, fourth Earl of Berkshire and eleventh Earl of Suffolk ; was born October 13, and baptized at Elford, co. Stafford, October 27, 1717, and died issueless October —, 1773, being buried at St. Edmund's, Salisbury ; twice married, first to Susannah —— (?), who died August 1, 1764, aged 71 years. She is said to have been an heiress, and was previously married to Thomas Lane, Lieut. R.N., about 1711, by whom she had a son Thomas, who died 1796, and was buried in the same tomb as his mother at Abbots Langley, in Herts. They were both living together—mother and son—in 1753 at "Iskcal" Wood, a distant part of the parish of Ishcal (?),

close to Wolverhampton, in Staffordshire. Mr. Howard married secondly, 176— (?), Mary ——— (?), widow of Henry Collings, or Collins, who survived her husband, giving up her claim when his will was proved by his creditors in 1773. The peerages give no assistance ; and any additional particulars as to parentage, &c., of these wives are requested, with dates.   A. S. A.
Richmond.

THE PROVOSTS OF THE COLLEGIATE CHURCH OF ST. EDMUND, IN SALISBURY.—In the list of the above I find that Hatcher's *History of Sarum*, p. 701, gives the name of Peter Courtney in 1464, and of Thomas Thurlby (*sic*) in 1534. Can any of your correspondents kindly throw any light on the question whether this Peter Courtney is identical with Peter Courtney who in the same year became Archdeacon of Wilts (being already Archdeacon of Exeter), and was afterwards successively Bishop of Exeter and of Winton, dying in the year 1492? And, further, is there anything to show that this Thomas Thurlby is identical with the bishop who was consecrated to Westminster in 1540, and died ex-Bishop of Ely in 1570? Hatcher, having to mention this bishop in another place, adopts the same unusual spelling of the name. From what source did Hatcher derive his list of the provosts of St. Edmund's? No reference is given.   G. H. B.

TENNYSON : "ARRIVE AT LAST THE BLESSED GOAL" (*In Memoriam*, Poem lxxxiii. stanza 11). —I am very loath to question Tennyson's use of the English language, but I would ask whether "arrive" is correct, in the sense of "attain," in the line—

" Arrive at last the blessed goal."

I should also be glad to learn the date of Dr. Tennyson's death, the Poet Laureate's father. Would it be in 1835? Hallam died in 1833. In Poems xxix. and lxxvii. two Christmas anniversaries are recorded ; if there was no interval these would be in 1833 and 1834. In Poem ciii. another Christmas is mentioned, away from Somersby, and after Dr. Tennyson had died. I find that Somersby is mentioned in the *Clergy List*, and G. A. Robinson succeeded in 1831.   A. G.
[The Rev. George Clayton Tennyson, D.D., died at Somersby, Lincoln, March 16, 1831, aged 53.]

"WILD TURKEYS."—What birds were specified as "game" in several old Irish Acts of Parliament under the name of "wild turkeys"?   ABHBA.

LAUD'S EXECUTION.—Is it known by whom Laud was executed? Was it by the headsman of the Tower? and was it by the "bright execution axe," which was used for his royal master four years afterwards, and which the High Court of Justice, by warrant to the officers of ordnance,

ordered to be delivered up for that purpose? Is that warrant in existence? If so, where is it to be found?   L. E. I.

BETWEEN DOVER AND CALAIS.—What were the usual means of transit from the one place to the other between 1700 and 1780? Was it by *regular* Government or private packet boats, *both* English and French, or by ordinary sailing boats, &c.? Are there any lists of the passengers conveyed across both ways? and, if so, where are they to be seen now?   C. MASON.
3, Gloucester Crescent, Hyde Park, W.

A TURNPIKES ACT MARRIAGE.—I extract the following from the *Times :*—

" It is said that when a certain head of a college in Oxford wanted to marry, the authority of Parliament was sought and obtained in a clause attached to an Act relating to turnpikes."

To what does the above refer?
                                    CLERICUS RUSTICUS.

LINCOLN'S INN.—Is there any published account, historical and architectural, of Lincoln's Inn up to the year 1856? If not, will any one tell me whether any courts have been pulled down in Lincoln's Inn since 1800?   R. M.
[The late Mr. W. H. Spilsbury, Librarian of Lincoln's Inn Library, published in 1850 *Lincoln's Inn, its Ancient and Modern Buildings, with an Account of its Library.* A second edition appeared in 1873.]

BLOMEFIELD'S "HISTORY OF NORFOLK."— Where is to be seen the late Mr. Dawson Turner's copy of Blomefield's *History of Norfolk*, a catalogue of the prints, drawings, &c., in which appears in Woodward's *Norfolk Topographer's Manual?* Add. MS. 23020 professes to be Mr. Turner's copy, but does not seem to be the one in question.   C. H. A.

SALTIMBANQUES, ACROBATS, AND SHOW PEOPLE IN GENERAL.—Where can I obtain some information as to the mode of life of saltimbanques, acrobats, and show people in general? I wish particularly to ascertain the manner in which children are trained and prepared for these performances. But generally I should be glad to be enlightened as to the available literature, either French or English, of the subject.   C. R. F.

NAVAL MEDICAL OFFICERS.—Is there any book giving a biographical account of physicians and surgeons who have served in the royal navy, on the same principle as W. R. O'Byne's *Naval Dictionary* of officers ranking from admiral to third lieutenant? If so, where can one be obtained?
                                    DUNELM.

GOD'S CHURCH AND DEVIL'S CHAPEL.—Alderman Robert Heyricke, in a letter giving an account of a dispute arising from the preaching of a sermon

THE ANCIENT BARONY OF COURTENAY OF OAK
HAMPTON.—Some eleven or twelve years since I
asked your readers who were the heirs of the
ancient barony of Courtenay of Oakhampton,
created by writ of summons 1299, but no answer
would appear to have been given. I am inclined
to repeat the question, as I cannot suppose so important a fact to be unknown to, at all events, the
more studious correspondents of " N. & Q."
J. W. STANDERWICK.

MR. MICHAEL BRUCE was sent to London, a
prisoner, in the autumn of 1668 by order of the
Scottish Privy Council at the desire of Charles II.
On arrival he was confined at the Gate House,
Westminster. He was sentenced while there to
be transported to Tangier, but procured a connivance, and was allowed to choose his place of
banishment, when he named the " wild woods of
Killinchy," his former parish. Can any of your
readers tell me in what public records I am likely
to find an account of his trial in England, and
other orders referring to his banishment to Ireland? I have got all the account of the proceedings against him in Scotland from the Privy
Council records there. W. B. A.

FRANCIS FOSTER BARHAM, THE ALIST.—Can
any reader supply a complete list of the writings of
the " Alist" Francis Barham?
WILLIAM E. A. AXON.
Bank Cottage, Barton-on-Irwell.

WILLIAM JACKSON, OF EXETER.—The late Sir
John Herschel, in a letter to the writer of this
query, says : " Jackson, I believe, wrote other
literary works beside the *Four Ages* and his
Thirty Letters, but I cannot recollect them." His
musical compositions are well known ; perhaps
some of your readers may be able to give the
information I seek. W. H. C.

JOHN EVELYN.—I have an old verse translation
of Lucretius, in which are numerous verses addressed to the translator by John Evelyn, Nahum
Tate, A. Behn, and others. Did Evelyn ever
write any other verses? and, if so, where are they
to be met with? LEONARD BOLINGBROKE.

" AQUIBAJULUS."—What is the meaning of this
word? It occurs in the foundation charter of
Cobham College, Kent, *temp.* Edw. III.
Gravesend. W. H. HART.

UNENCLOSED COMMONS.—Does there exist any
printed or other list of commons in England still

description of the dungeon at
makes it to be
" *Below* the surface of the l
Is this correct ? I remember Albe
that, when you were inside the pr
touch the bars of the window, but
not reach them when you were in
lake. CUTH

" LORD ELLIS."—Who was " Lor
of Monte Cassino and Bishop of S
See Hare's *Days near Rome*, vol. i.

AUTHORS OF BOOKS WANTED.—
$Poems$ for Youth. By a Family C
1820, pp. iv-106.
The World : a Poem. In six books.
The Art of Verse: a Poem, with l
For Young Bards. By a Practitioner.

AUTHORS OF QUOTATIONS WAN
1. " Excessive Lucan."
2. " Ultima ratio regum."
3. Some beautiful lines, called *Drift*
describing the musings of a voyager
Italian water. After speaking of an out
" Our happier one
Her course hath run
From lands of snow to lands of
4. " Sic eat, o superi, quando fidesque
Deficiunt, moresque malos sperar
5. " On one sole art bestow thine wh
And with the craft of others se
Be it thine aim but to attain per
It is no little matter to excel."
(From memory, and possibly inaccurate
DAVI

In what part of Sir Philip Sidney'
Verse occur beginning,—
" My true love hath my he
I cannot find it in the edition, in three
These words have been set to music but
Blumenthal. A

Replies.

" IT IS EASIER FOR A CAM
(5th S. ix. 106.)

I am not unaware that this, amc
theories, has been advanced as an s
dation of the much disputed passage
our notice by SIR CHARLES A. M
unfortunately, like all the rest, fa
most important *desideratum*, the
authority which recommends itsel
ance of those most competent to i

impartial estimate of its worth. Polè, in his *Synopsis Criticorum*, seems to me to have gathered up, from all sources open to him, all that has been, and in my opinion can be, said upon it, or, at least, all that is worthy of consideration, and so, with the editor's permission, as the work is a bulky one, and, I presume, not within the reach of all to whom these presents may come, I will give, *in extenso*, the passage from the original (written in Latin, and, as such, of course for scholars), and for the general reader append a translation. He says :—

"Κάμηλος et *camelum* animal, et *funem nauticum*, sive *rudentem*, significat apud Judæos 'Ελληνίζοντας. Huc facit quòd et vox Arabica בל, et Syrica גמיל, utrumque significant. [Hinc variant.] 1. De rudente loquitur : Id suadent, 1. Analogia major inter rudentem et filum quod solet per foramen acûs induci. 2. Quòd ita Syri et Arabes hìc intelligunt. 3. Quod vox κάμηλος ita sumitur in Suida, et in Scholiaste Aristophanis ; (at hi scribunt κάμιλος) et in Phavorino; qui tamen hanc significationem hoc unico testimonio probat. Sed nec κάμιλον ita sumi ulli Scriptoris idonei auctoritate confirmatum reperio. Nec eum Julius Pollux inter instrumenta nautica memorat. Habent et Talmudici simile proverbium. De camelo animali loquitur. Proverbium est de re quæ aut nullo modo, aut difficulter admodum fieri potest ; usitatum apud Talmudistas, de elephanto, &c. Sub initio Gemaræ, 'Dicunt homines, Non est elephas qui iret per foramen acûs.' Ibidem, cum aliquis incredibilia narrat, respondent, 'Forte ex Pombodita tu es, ubi traducunt elephantem per foramen acûs.' Christus autem *elephanti* loco substituit *camelum*, tanquam animantis genus in Syriâ vulgò notius ; ut alibi oculum posuit pro *dentibus*, Matt. vii. 5, 'Ejice ex oculo tuo,' &c., pro quo in Ebræorum paræmia est, *ex dentibus tuis*. Absurdum videtur hoc de *camelo* sumptum proverbium. Sed quò absurdius hoc est et impossibilius eò verior est Christi sententia. In talibus adagiis nihil necesse est exactam inter partes collatas comparationem institui, cùm soleant ornari ὑπερβολαῖς. Tale erit illud Jer. xiii. 23, simile et illud Latini veteris, 'Citiùs locusta pepererit Lucam bovem.' *Foramen acûs* intellige quod acus vel habet, vel facit. Quod hic est τρύπημα, a τρυπάω, *terebro*, id Marc. x. 25, et Luc. xviii. 25, est τρυμαλιά, a τρύω, *perforo ;* unde ἡ τρύμη, *foramen.** Non ineleganter autem dives turgens ac tumens opibus, quæ ipsi sæpe magis oneri sunt quàm usui, ut quas bajulat aliis potius quàm sibi, camelo comparatur, et angusta porta quâ intratur ad vitam, de quâ suprà vii. 14, foramini acûs."

* This idea is evidently borrowed from St. Jerome, who, in his curious comment on the passage, says : " Si legamus Esaiam (lx. 3) quomodo cameli Madian et Epha veniant Hierusalem cum donis atque maneribus : et qui prius curvi erant et vitiorum pravitate distorti, ingrediantur portas Hierusalem ; videbimus quomodo et isti cameli quibus divites comparantur, cum deposuerant gravem sarcinam peccatorum, et totius corporis pravitatem, intrare possit per augustam portum et arctam viam quæ ducit ad vitam."

By κάμηλος the Hellenistic Jews understand both the *camel* and the rope called by mariners a *cable;* and the reason which makes for this is, that the Arabians and Syrians alike use the word with this twofold meaning. On this view, however, opinions vary. They who take it for a *cable* do so because, as they say, there is greater analogy between this and a thread which passes through a needle's eye ; 2. Because it is used in this sense by the Arabians and Syrians ; and 3. Because it is so taken by Suidas, the Scholiast upon Aristophanes (although these write it κάμιλος), and by Phavorinus, who bases his opinion upon this single authority only. For my own part, I find it supported by the authority of not one writer of any note, and Julius Pollux makes no mention of it in his treatise on nautical implements. The Talmudists have a proverb very similar. There can be no doubt that *camel* is the proper word, and the allusion is to something which cannot possibly be done, or, at least, without the greatest difficulty. The Talmudists give the *elephant*, &c. ; and in the commencement of the Gemara we find the saying, " There is no elephant that can go through the eye of a needle"; and so when they hear people relating things very incredible, they remark, " Perhaps, my friend, you are a native of Pombodita, where they drive an *elephant* through the eye of a needle." Our Lord, however, substitutes *camel* for *elephant*, most likely because the animal was better known in Syria ; just as in Matt. vii. 5, he puts *eye* for *teeth*, "ejice ex *oculo* tuo," *from your eye*, whereas in the Hebrew proverb it is "ex *dentibus* tuis," *from your teeth*. There is a seeming absurdity in the proverb, as taken from a camel ; but in proportion to this, and the utter impossibility which it involves, so much greater is the truth of Christ's saying ;† and in adages of this kind it is by no means necessary that between the several members of them the comparison should be strictly accurate, as they usually have in them much of hyperbolical embellishment. Of such are Jer. xiii. 23, and that old Latin saying, " Sooner shall a locust give birth to a Lucanian ox " (elephant).

Now bear in mind that the *eye* of a needle is either the *hole* in the needle itself or the hole which the needle makes. The word in Matthew is τρύπημα, from τρυπάω, *to bore, pierce through;* in Mark x. 25 and Luke xviii. 25 it is τρύμαλια, from τρύω, *to perforate*, whence ἡ τρύμη, *a hole, an eye*.

Now a man loaded and swollen out, as it were, with riches, often more of a burden than of use to

† Our Lord, of course, did not mean to say that *no* rich man should " enter into the kingdom of God," but such only should not, as he himself explains it in the Gospel of St. Mark, " that*t rust* in riches." Zacchæus was " *very* rich," yet Christ said to him, " This day is salvation come to this house."

him, and which he carries for others rather than for himself, may not inaptly be compared to a (loaded) *camel*, and, in like manner, the narrow gate which leads to (eternal) life be likened to the eye of a needle, see Matt. vii. 3.

Now this, to my mind, is exhaustive of the subject, and conclusive in showing that *camel* and nothing but *camel* is the proper rendering of the word. It is true that Origen and Theophylact lean to *cable*, and in this view are followed by some commentators of a later date. Whitby is very positive, and dismisses it as a question beyond dispute. Hammond, on the contrary—a much safer guide and far more learned—adheres to *camel*, and supports his opinion by arguments and authorities almost identical with those of Pole. By none, ancient or modern, as far as I can find, is there a word said about any " small door or wicket " appropriated to the use of foot passengers only. And I cannot help thinking that this, like *cable*, has only been resorted to as a convenient escape from an apparent difficulty. It is another instance of cutting the Gordian knot.

No doubt, as Pole suggests, the " phrase " is hyperbolical, but I think it is too much to say that it is " wanting in that propriety which usually characterizes the metaphors employed by Jesus Christ in his parables." Apart from this, we must bear in mind that our Lord in his discourses was scrupulously careful, not only to avoid saying anything that would offend the prejudices of the people, but took especial pains to adapt them, as far as he could, to their prevailing customs, modes of thought, and manner of speaking. Hence, when he found a proverb current among them which exactly expressed the important truth which he wished to inculcate, he adopted it at once, not troubling himself to consider whether in its character it was altogether congruous and consistent, but only whether it was calculated to convey the amount of conviction which he desired to produce. Had it been original, instead of being adopted, very likely it would have been different—less hyperbolical, and more in accordance with probability.

EDMUND TEW, M.A.

Patching Rectory, Arundel.

Among the notes to Matt. xix. 24, in Kitto's *Pictorial Bible*, mention is made of the Indian proverb, " An elephant going through a little door," or " through the eye of a needle," where the little door is the equivalent of the needle's eye. I may mention another familiar work, D'Oyly and Mant's Bible, published in 1817, where one of the notes on the above passage is a quotation from Thomas Harmer's *Observations on Various Passages of Scripture* (he died in 1788):—

" In the East the doors are frequently made extremely low, sometimes not more than three or four feet high, to prevent the plundering Arabs from riding into the inner court: still, they train their camels to make their wa; though with difficulty, through these doorways. It wa probably, in allusion to this practice that this proverbi; expression was formed."

These references are sufficient to prove that " th metaphorical name for a wicket " had received th notice of Scripture commentators " more tha; thirty years ago." For a very modern exampl I would refer your correspondent to the *Sunda: Magazine*, Dec., 1877 (in which is the continuatio; of Hesba Stretton's serial story, " Through ; Needle's Eye "), where, in the article " Sunda; Evenings with the Children," Mr. John Macgrego (" Rob Roy ") gives a rude sketch of " The Town gate of Siout," with the following explanation :—

" You see there is one wide opening, but this gate i closed at sunset, and, after that, you can get in only b the *small* gate, which is very narrow, and lower tha the other. Many camels go into the town every da with their loads in large broad packages hanging wid on each side of the camel's hump. When the high broad gate is closed, the camel cannot get in throug] the narrow gate unless he stoops down on his knees an; has his load taken from his sides. You will see a curiou verse about this in the 19th of Matthew. I think w may learn from this verse that if a boy or girl is to ente the kingdom of Heaven, that is, to become a disciple o Jesus on earth, and an heir of glory with him in Heaven it is necessary to go in very humbly, and to leave ou load of sin and cares, and worldly thoughts, and earthl, things outside the ' needle gate,' because ' He hath born our griefs and carried our sorrows.' Look for this i; Isaiah liii."

Mr. Macgregor, apparently, leaves the childre; under the impression that the camel has not t resume his burden when he has got through th " needle gate." CUTHBERT BEDE.

The supposed fact that the foot passengers' gat; into an Eastern city is known as the " needle' eye " has been very generally noticed by com mentators, but modern investigation seems rathe inclined to discredit it. Canon Farrar says tha the explanation " seems to need confirmation (*Life of Christ*, c. xlvi.), and refers his readers t an article of his own on the subject in the *Ex positor*, vol. ii. The comparison of any difficult; with that of a camel or an elephant passing throug] the eye of a needle appears to have been a familia simile to Oriental hearers. Burder (*Oriental Lite rature*, vol. ii. p. 392) quotes, from Lightfoot, th Jewish saying, " It may be that thou art of Pum beditha, where they can bring an elephant throug; the eye of a needle "; and in *Oriental Custom* (vol. ii. p. 214) gives the proverbs, " A came in Media dances in a rabe—a measure which hel about three pints. No man sees a palm-tree c gold nor an elephant passing through the eye of needle." In the Koran, also quoted by the sam industrious gatherer, we read in chap. vii. (Sale' translation), " Verily they who shall charge ou signs with falsehood, and shall proudly rejec them, the gates of heaven shall not be opene;

unto them, neither shall they enter into paradise until a camel pass through the eye of a needle."

Even if we take the saying in its most literal sense, as a Western mind would naturally conceive of it, there is scarcely more hyperbole in it than in that other proverbial utterance of our Lord, recorded in St. Matt. xxiii. 24, " Ye blind guides, which strain at (or out) a gnat and swallow a camel."

In the Rev. J. G. Wood's *Bible Animals* (p. 243) there is a spirited little woodcut of a "Camel going through a ' needle's eye.'" The author says :

" We will now turn to the metaphor of the camel and the needle's eye. Of course it can be taken merely as a very bold metaphor, but it may also be understood in a simpler sense, the sense in which it was probably understood by those who heard it. In Oriental cities there are in the large gates small and very low apertures called metaphorically ' needles' eyes,' just as we talk of certain windows as ' bulls' eyes.' These entrances are too narrow for a camel to pass through them in the ordinary manner or even if loaded. When a laden camel has to pass through one of these entrances it kneels down, its load is removed, and then it shuffles through on its knees. ' Yesterday,' writes Lady Duff Gordon from Cairo, ' I saw a camel go through the eye of a needle, *i.e.* the low arched door of an enclosure. He must kneel and bow his head to creep through ; and thus the rich man must humble himself.'"

ST. SWITHIN.

There is this notice of a gate at Jerusalem which answers to the description :—

" It is explained otherwise : that at Jerusalem there was a certain gate, called the needle's eye, through which a camel could not pass but upon its bended knees, and after its burden had been taken off; and so the rich should not be able to pass along the narrow way that leads to life till he had put off the burden of sin and of riches, that is, by ceasing to love them."—*Glossa* ap. S. Anselm., in *Catena Aurea*, on St. Matt. xix. 24, vol. i. p. 670, Oxf. tr., 1841.

But Maldonatus observes as to this :—

" Alii pejus in urbe Jerosolymitana portam quandam fuisse fingunt, quæ foramen acus appellaretur, adeo humilem, ut cameli per eam, nisi exonerati, ingredi non possent."—*Comm. in* iv. *Evang., ad loc.*

Lightfoot has shown, *ad loc.*, that such a proverb occurs in the Talmud, with the substitution of the elephant for the camel. But there is a remark of Rud. Stier upon this which should be kept in mind, that interpretation may not degenerate into literalism :—

" Proverbially figurative discourse has always this character, that the outward letter is not to be pressed in t e particulars, as it is in a proverbial proposition, but that a background of spiritual meaning all the more deep opens itself up for application."—*The Words of the Lord Jesus*, Edinb. tr., vol. iii. p. 34, 1851.

Maldonatus also, *u.s.*, has some remarks to the same effect, as to its being taken as a proverb.

ED. MARSHALL.

I think, from the following extract from the *Letters and Memoir of Bishop Shirley*, p. 415,

8vo. London, 1849, that the passage referred to is from Lord Nugent's *Travels:*—

" By the way, I met the other day with an interesting illustration of what follows (Matt. xix. 24) about the camel and the needle's eye. Lord Nugent, when at Hebron, was directed ' to go out by the needle's eye,' that is, by the small side gate of the city. And, in many parts of England, the old game of ' thread the needle ' is played to the following words :—

' How many miles to Hebron ?
Threescore and ten.
Shall I be there by midnight ?
Yes, and back again.
Then thread the needle,' &c.

Now this explains, and modifies, one of the strongest and most startling passages of Scripture on the subject of riches, for the camel can go through the needle's eye but with difficulty, and hardly with a full load, nor without stooping."

EV. PH. SHIRLEY.

See Plumptre (Rev. E. H.), *Bible Educator*, i. 365.   K. P. D. E.

THE OXFORD AND CAMBRIDGE BOAT-RACE, 1829 (5th S. ix. 246.)—I am sorry not to be able to answer SCULLER's query with anything like certainty. My impression is that the boat was built at Oxford, as in those days almost all our boats were ; but if not, then I should have no doubt that Searle, of London, was the builder. Our stroke (Rev. T.) Staniforth, of Storrs Hall, Windermere, is (I believe) still alive and flourishing. I should think he could give SCULLER a decisive answer.

C. WORDSWORTH, Bp. of St. Andrews.
Bishopshall, St. Andrews.

[See p. 280.]

THE BIRTHPLACE OF SUNDAY SCHOOLS (5th S. viii. 367 ; ix. 110, 156.)—Fourteen years ago, after considerable research and local inquiry, I was enabled to state definitively the date and locality of the first, or parent, Sunday School. In the *Gloucestershire Chronicle* of Dec. 17, 1864, I wrote :—

" The first Sunday School in this city [Gloucester] was opened in the year 1780 by Stock and Raikes jointly, at the house of a Mr. King in St. Catherine's parish. Mr. King was steward to Mr. Pitt, sometime M.P. for this city, and the house I allude to still stands, and is, I believe, next or near to the ' Queen's Head ' public-house. The *second* school was established by Mr. Raikes (who had deserted the first) in the parish of St. Mary de Crypt, at the house now occupied by Mrs. Lappington [in the Southgate Street]; and the *third* was opened at the back premises of No. 103, Northgate Street by Mr. Stock singly."

In the same paper I advocated the erection of a memorial window to Stock and Raikes as "joint founders of Sunday Schools "; and I am glad to learn from the *Gloucester Mercury* that my suggestion has not been forgotten, and that funds are being raised for the insertion of a " Stock and Raikes Memorial Window " in the church of St.

John the Baptist—the Rev. Thomas Stock having been for many years rector of that parish. See *Churchman's Shilling Magazine*, August, 1868, art. " Who was the Founder of Sunday Schools ?" *Robert Raikes, Philanthropist and Journalist: a History of the Origin of Sunday Schools*, by Alfred Gregory (Hodder & Stoughton, 1877) ; and an article on the " Origin and Growth of Sunday Schools in England," *London Quarterly Review*, No. xcix., April, 1878.

S. R. TOWNSHEND MAYER.

About thirty or forty years ago the following account of some Sunday schools established many years before Mr. Raikes, of Gloucester, established his, appeared in the papers. I shall be glad to know whether the facts there recorded have received due attention at the hands of the recent biographer of Mr. Raikes, whose work I have so far not had the pleasure of reading :—

" Whatever be the issue of the question, so far as Mr. Stock and Mr. Raikes are concerned, there is a town which can show that a Sunday school was established in it full fourteen years prior to the formation of the school or schools at Gloucester. In the year 1769 a Sunday school was commenced by Miss Ball, at High Wycombe. She was a lady of great piety, and of rather uncommon earnestness in doing good. Her custom was to assemble as many as thirty or forty children on Sunday morning, to hear them read the Scriptures and repeat the catechism and the collect, preparatory to going to church. A place is still pointed out in the remarkably fine church of High Wycombe as having been occupied by the Sunday scholars of Miss Ball. An old servant, who when young was my nurse, was one of those scholars, and still lives, in conjunction with sundry individuals, to bear testimony to the facts which I have stated. In a *Memoir of Miss Hannah Ball*, recently ' revised by John Parker, Gent., and published by Mason, 14, City Road,' it is further stated that ' Miss Ball continued this school for many years, and also met the children every Monday to instruct them in the principles of Christianity.'—Rev. W. H. Havergal, Rector of Astley, in *Midland Counties Herald*."

E.

CHIOGGIA (5th S. ix. 49, 138, 234.)—I am afraid that a single day's experience hardly entitles me to give that fuller description of Chioggia which MR. BOUCHIER is good enough to ask for. I went there chiefly to look on the scene of that great year of warfare, when " Doria's menace " was *not* fulfilled, and the horses of St. Mark remained unbridled. I found a quiet, old-world fishing town, built, like Venice, on islands—a half dozen of islands or peninsulas, that lie or seem to lie side by side, like the fingers of a hand, stretching outward from the Paduan shore, towards the southern end of the *murazzi*, between which and Chioggia flows the channel into the open sea. But Chioggia does not face the Adriatic : outside its group of islets lies a land-locked basin, and beyond that another *murazzo*,—or rather a great natural dune, that overlooks the main. On the top of this dune stands a row of houses ; unromantic lodging-houses,

I mournfully observe : for the place, remote as it seems, has visitors in summer ; and it looks for all the world as Blankenberghe in Flanders used to look when first I knew it, more than twenty years ago. But Chioggia itself is altogether old fashioned and piscatory. Fishing boats lie along its little quays and in the channels of the basin ; fishermen stand chatting at the corners ; fishergirls (as I have already said) unfold their populous tresses at the doors. And there is plenty of room for every one. The High Street of the town runs from end to end of the chief island, and looks almost as wide as Regent Street. At its seaward end stands (of course) the Lion of St. Mark, on his pillar : the landward end is joined to the shore by an ancient bridge, beyond which rises the town gateway, spanning the level road to Padua. And from the pillar to the bridge this broad, quiet street winds to and fro, between houses never, so far as I remember, very old or very picturesque, but, on the other hand, never modern, and therefore never mean. Some of them are arcaded, like those of Bologna. And under one of these arcades I found—oh joy !—a *café* which actually owned a teapot, and could and did produce therefrom a decent cup of tea. The side streets, where the fisherfolk live, run down to the little quays—tall cool wynds, where the houses are adorned, sometimes with creeping vines, sometimes with out-of-window clothing. The two churches of the town stand in the High Street. They are (I speak as a man) not remarkable for antiquity or beauty ; but they have the broad naves, the wide and lofty arches, to which one is accustomed in Venice ; and they have mural monuments, with coats of arms and long Latin inscriptions, to worthies of the seventeenth and eighteenth centuries. The larger church is the cathedral : for Chioggia is a bishopric ; the smaller, dedicated to S. Andrea, is older than the cathedral, but was restored, I see, in 1734. And thus we come to the christenings, and the babies in their glass cases. The case is simply a box of glass with a gabled roof, also of glass ; the whole edged with metal at the angles, and looking like a transparent Noah's Ark. Inside lies the baby, on its back, on a pallet of white silk or satin ; and Monna Catarina, who has brought the thing to church under her arm, sets it down somewhere near the font, lowers the glass front, which is hinged at bottom, and takes out the infant ; who, fortunately, never screams, because he is tightly swaddled, head and all, and his hapless visage is powdered with that soft white dust which in England is not unknown to children. These awe-inspiring circumstances apparently compel him to silence ; and, whatever may be thought of them, I can strongly recommend the glass-case method to any afflicted parent who suffers from the cries of a teething child.

It is not easy to reconcile the topography of Chioggia, as I saw it, with the accounts of the war, nor with such maps as I have access to. The houses on the outer dune which I have spoken of are part of the rival village or town of Sotto Marina ; and I believe, but am not sure, that the dune itself is a part of the Isle of Brondolo, which did such good service to Venice by hemming the Genoese in, while Contarini watched the channel at one end and Pisani at the other. As to the name of the town : in the *Carta Amministrativa del Regno d'Italia*, of 1813, it is given as Chioggia ; in Col. Procter's *History of Italy* (a book not so well known, I think, as it deserves to be) and in the *Sketches from Venetian History*, which is based on Daru, it appears as Chiozza ; in the eighth edition, 1854, of the *Encyc. Britannica* it is Chioggia only ; in the ninth edition, 1876, it is Chioggia or Chiozza. I, however, was told to call it Chioza ; I did so, and was understanded of the people, who themselves called it Chioza in my hearing—both the natives and the educated Italians—on board our steamer. This is all I feel competent to say on the subject, except that, howsoever spelt, the word represents the Latin *Claudia*, Fossa Claudia being the ancient name of the town. But is MR. BOUCHIER right in saying that all Italian names are pronounced as they are written ? To go no further from Chioggia than Venice, you have, *e.g.*, the Giudecca, written so, but pronounced *Zuecca*.

One word more, I pray you, as to the voyage home. Heart of man could scarce conceive a more enchanting sight than that September sunset. It burnished the smooth lagoon, and filled the soft sea air with mellow golden light ; it shone in lucid clouds of ruby and amber high above the purple mountains of Verona and the grey Euganean Hills, where the soul of Shelley seems to linger yet. And we on board, being all, except myself, Italians, enjoyed it tranquilly, in silence—spellbound, it seemed, even the humblest of us, by this ineffable beauty of the " spectacles gratis que Dieu donne." So we glided on to Venice in the moonlight. And a few nights afterwards, being out on the lagoon in a gondola, under all the glory of a cloudless full moon, my gondolier suddenly exclaimed, as if to himself, " O bellissima sera !" and broke into some snatch of song about the loveliness of the time. In such a night the British boatman would have been thinking surlily of his supper and his fare ; in such a night the Yankee boatman would have (being paid to do so) have called my attention to the advertisement of old Dr. Jacob Townsend's sarsaparilla, inscribed, in letters three feet long, upon the most beautiful rock or tree whereon the moon was shining. And thus, since empire means insolence and dulness, thus it is that

" Westward the course of empire takes its way."

A. J. M.

P.S.—I see that MR. BOUCHIER asks about the

manners and customs of Chioggia. Of these I am not competent to speak, further than I have spoken, except to say that the Sunday aspect of the place was eminently quiet and respectable, and slightly dull, in spite of sea and sunshine. In the forenoon people went to High Mass ; in the afternoon the better dressed folk strolled calmly in the High Street, or sat in due decorum outside the few inns and *cafés*. Certain boys, daring swimmers, leaped from the mooring posts into the harbour, and swam about our ships in hopes of coin ; and this was the only excitement I saw.

It will be remembered that the salt works between Chioggia and the Po were of great importance in the middle ages. I have said nothing of their present state, for Dr. Johnson's reason : " Ignorance, madam, pure ignorance."

TOUCHING FOR THE KING'S EVIL : FORMS OF PRAYER (5th S. ix. 49, 236, 251.)—I possess a copy of the Prayer Book printed, by permission of John Baskett, by Start in 1717. It is duodecimo and, I believe, very rare. Every leaf is printed from a copper-plate and illustrated in a most beautiful manner. It is a book I value greatly. I have examined it carefully. It does not contain the Office for touching for the king's evil, nor is there any mention of the queen in the prayers for the royal family. Can any one give me the reason for the omission of her name throughout the book ? I shall have pleasure in showing this volume to DR. SPARROW SIMPSON at any time.

BENJ. FERREY.

THERF CAKE (5th S. viii. 508.)—(Cf. *derbes Pumpernickel* in Börne.) The origin of the word *therf* is Teutonic. In Old High German it is *dërb*, *dërp*, *dërap*, and in Middle High German *dërp;* Anglo-Saxon has *theorf*, *thärf*, *therf*, and Frisian *therve*, *derve*. Connecting these adjectives with the Gotic verb *ga-tharban*, Anglo-Saxon *thearfan*, " to be in want of," we may perhaps interpret *therf* to mean " (bread) which is in want of leaven." In Old Slavonic the word *trjeba* not only denoted unleavened bread or cake, but also the sacrificial offering of such cake, and even the temple itself where the offering was made.

The modern German adjective *derb* means " pressed firmly together," as opposed to " loose," hence thickset, strong, coarse, both in the proper and in the figurative sense. The Bavarian dialect has the verb *derben* (cf. German " verderben "), which is applied to plants, and means " to wither." It is therefore possible to interpret *therf* to mean originally " thick, massive, in consequence of being dried," so to speak " crystallized." This interpretation seems to be borne out by the Greek τράφειν, " to cause (milk) to coagulate, curdle " ; τρόφις, τροφόεις, " massive " ; τραφερή, " mainland " ; ταρφέες, " thick " ; τάρφος, " thicket." The modern German *bieder*, " rough and ready, straightforward, honest," used to be spelt *biderbe*, and is evidently to be traced to the same origin as *derb*.

G. A. SCHRUMPF.

Tettenhall College.

This word, which we find in *Piers Plowman*, A. vii. 269, is totally English or Anglo-Saxon, and not Danish. It is, however, strange that Langland has avoided it in his later versions, B. vi. 284 and C. ix. 306, nor have I found it in another work of that time in my possession. I should think that in some dialect or other it is still living, and it would be an interesting work for the Dialect Society to search for it. The A.-S. ·forms are *þeorf, þerf, þorof, þärf, þearf*. The translation given by A. D. is quite correct. In the Latin version it is given by "sine fermento, azymus." In the Old Testament we read :—"And healdaᵹ *þeorfe* mellas" (Exod. xii. 17) ; "*þeorfne* hláf þu scealt ëtan seofan dagas" (Exod. xxxiv. 18). In the following places it is used substantively :—"And ëtaᵹ *þeorf* seofon dagas" (Exod. xii. 15) ; "Ge sceolan ëtan on aefon *þeorf* oᵹ þone däg" (Exod. xii. 18). O.H.G. forms are *dërap, dërb, dërp* ; O. Fris. *therve, derve*. The Gothic form is lost, but it would not be difficult to construct it analogous to the cognate languages.

F. ROSENTHAL.

17, Burgstrasse, Hannover.

Halliwell gives it as Anglo-Saxon. The word is common enough in our early writers, occurring frequently in Wycliffe—*e.g.* St. Mark xiv. 12, where, however, neither the A.-S. version nor the Gothic assists one, the one reading "azimorum," the other " azwme."

W. F. R.

Dr. Stratmann (*Dict. of Early Eng.*) gives as the derivation of *therf* A.-S. *þeorf*, O. Icel. *þiarf*, O· High Ger. *derber*. See Mr. Skeat's note to his edition of *Piers Plowman* (E. E. Text Soc.), Passus ix. 306.

SIDNEY J. HERRTAGE.

Lavender Hill, S.W.

COLETI ÆDITIO (5ᵗʰ S. ix. 207.)—A good and perfect copy of this work remains in the Cathedral Library, Peterborough, of the date 1527. This is seven years earlier than the date given by J. H. L. The contents are in English, but the title is Latin :

" J₀annis Coleti Theologi, Olim decani diui Pauli, ædítio una cum quibusdam G. Lilij Grammaticæs Rudimentis."

W. D. SWEETING.

Peterborough.

LICENCE TO EAT FLESH IN LENT (5ᵗʰ S. ix. 226.) —I have just come upon the following extract from Grantham parish register in Street's *Notes on Grantham:*—

" Memorandum. That Ann, wife of Ralph Nidd, had a licence granted and given her the 9th day of March, 1618, to eat flesh according to the statute made in the fifth year of the reign of Elizabeth, late queen, of famous

memory, by Thomas Wicliffe of Grantham, Gen· Alderman of the said town, and Thomas Deane, (which Ann Nidd, continuing and abiding in th sickness and weak estate, desireth her licence to newed and registered according to law, which i₈ done, this present Tuesday, March 16th, 1618. Testor. Thomas Deane, Vic. Austr., Richard (William Wright, Churchwardens."

It will be observed that Ann Nidd's former li was valid for eight days, like that first grant Mary Bishop, *alias* Martin, at Witney.

ST. SWITH

WORDSWORTH'S LINES " To LUCY " (5ᵗʰ 229.)—It has been already noted in your col that the author of the parody for whom DRUMMOND inquires was Hartley Coleridge.

W. T.

THE WILL OF PETER THE GREAT (5ᵗʰ ⁺ 226.)—In answer to MR. THOMS, I have a ₈ idea that a copy of the will is given in H₍ *Mémoires Secrets de la Russie*, published i₁ century, from some supposed memoirs of Vill₍

K. H.

THE JEWS (5ᵗʰ S. ix. 209.)—Halévy was a and the names of Meyerbeer and Mendelssohr be added—the former, I believe, of Jewish the latter certainly of Jewish origin, if not b₍ the faith. Of present musicians, composers. performers may be remembered Joachim Rubinstein, the former born in the faith, the professing the Jewish faith now. Wagner, I understood, is a Roman Catholic, and Patti wise. Are Wieniauski and Jaell and Au Jewish birth or faith ?

H. A.

HAMMOND AND CICERO (5ᵗʰ S. ix. 246.)— most likely that Hammond quoted from me₁ which in this instance failed him. The n₍ passage to it which I can refer to in which the is contained is Suetonius, *Claud.*, xv. :—" quoque a majoribus natu audiebam, adeo (dicos patientia ejus solitos abuti, ut descende e tribunali non solum voce revocarent, s₍ lacinia togæ retenta, interdum pede appreb detinerent."

ED. MARSHA

THE JENNENS CASE (5ᵗʰ S. ix. 207.)— reference to MR. ALFRED SCOTT GATTY's qu₍ to who are the heirs to the *real* and *personal* perty of William Jennens, of Acton, who di 1798, I was, had my case, reported in the p of the 5th ultimo, been *argued*, in a positi prove my lineal descent from that gentleman.

In justice to both the past and present me₁ of my family, it ought to be distinctly under by the press and the public that the *real* pro my counsel was instructed to claim had only *sixteen* years in the possession of the defend wherefore it will be easily seen that, if Mr. brick had mentioned this fact, instead of asse

Jerusalem, but doubtful if they ever arrived there, for there is no historical account of their having been seen or heard of afterwards, and now it seems to be hopeless that they ever will be.

D. WHYTE.

Gibbon is my authority for the statement that those sacred relics were preserved at Rome till the time of the invasion of Genseric. I refer W. M. M. to chap. xxxvi. Will he kindly state whether the story about the golden candlestick having been taken by Maxentius to the battle of the Milvian Bridge, and there lost, is merely a popular tradition in Rome, or whether there is any historical mention of the fact ? R. M. SPENCE, F.R.H.S.
Manse of Arbuthnott, N.B.

"TOOT HILLS" (5ᵗʰ S. vii. 461 ; viii. 56, 138, 298, 358, 478.)—These hills were evidently look-out stations in the neighbourhood of some camp or military station. The name still lingers in the modern term "tout," as applied to a fellow who makes his living by "touting," or picking up information in connexion with race-horses. The "toot" or "tout hills" were stations from which the military "tout" kept watch and ward. There are two "Toot" or "Tot Hills" in this neighbourhood, both within the lines of old encampments.
JOHN CORDEAUX.
Great Cotes, Ulceby.

PEN FROM AN ANGEL'S WING (5ᵗʰ S. viii. 66, 154, 337, 357.)—I have met with this idea in an old magazine of the last century. The correspondent who sent the following lines stated that he transcribed them from an old copy of Milton's *Paradise Lost :*—

"To Mr. John Milton,
"On his Poem entitled *Paradise Lost.*
"O thou, the wonder of the present age !
An age immerst in luxury and vice ;
A race of triflers ! who can relish nought
But the gay issue of an idle brain !
How couldst thou hope to please this tinsel race ?
Tho' blind, yet with the penetrating eye
Of intellectual light thou dost survey
The labyrinth perplex'd of Heaven's decrees,
And with a quill, pluck'd from an angel's wing,
Dipt in the fount that laves th' eternal throne,
Trace the dark paths of Providence divine,
'And justify the ways of God to man' !
"F. C. 1680."
S. F. LONGSTAFFE.
Norton, Stockton-on-Tees.

HERALDIC (5ᵗʰ S. viii. 147, 254.)—There is at least one exception to the rule SIR JOHN MACLEAN and P. P. lay down so authoritatively. One says, "An heiress in no case conveys a crest"; the other, "Women cannot give their children what they never possessed themselves. They have no crests, and therefore cannot transmit them." On April 20, 1559, 1 Eliz., William Heroye, Cla-rencieux, "ratifyed and confyrmed" to an ancestress

of mine, described as "Margerye Cater, doughter and heire of John Cater, of Letcombe Regis, yn the Countie of Berkshire, gentilman, wyfe to William Hyde, of South Denchworth, yn the Countie of Berkshire, Esquyre," the ancient arms and *crest* of her family, "to have and to houlde the said armes and *creaste* vnto the saide Margerye Cater, gentlewoman, doughter to the aforesaide John Cater, and unto all the posteritie of the saide John Cater for evermore."

Here is a special grant of a crest to a woman. She surely had a right to use it, and her "posteritie" derive from her, male and female, "for evermore." HENRY BARRY HYDE.
1, Belsize Park Gardens, N.W.

"A MONKEY ON THE HOUSE" (5ᵗʰ S. viii. 289, 433.)—May not ·this expression have something to do with the slang word *monkey,* which in my parish (St. Giles's) means a padlock ? In many senses a mortgaged estate may be said to be locked up for a time. JOHN CHURCHILL SIKES.
Godolphin Road, Shepherd's Bush, W.

THE FOURTH ESTATE OF THE REALM (5ᵗʰ S. ix. 167, 213.)—The exact reference to Macaulay's mention of the Reporters' Gallery as a fourth estate of the realm is *Essays,* vol. i. p. 210 (8vo. edit.), in a paragraph near the end of the essay, beginning with the words, "The privileges of the House of Commons." The other passage is in chap. iii. of the *History,* vol. i. p. 366 (8vo. edit.). The writer says that the coffee-house orators "soon became what the journalists of our own time have been called, a fourth estate of the realm." P. C.

QUEEN KATHARINE DE VALOIS (5ᵗʰ S. ix. 121.)—I do not know whether the following notice of the state of the tomb of Catherine of Valois in 1631 was mentioned by the Dean of Westminster to the Society of Antiquaries, but it is not in the summary in "N. & Q." Weever, in his *Funeral Monuments,* Lond., 1631, p. 475, has :—

"Here lieth Katherine, Queene of England, wife to the foresaid King Henry the Fifth, in a chest or coffin with a loose couer to be seene and handled of any that will much desire it, and that by her owne appointment (as he that sheweth the Tombes will tell you by tradition) in regard of her disobedience to her husband for being deliuered of her sonne Henry the Sixth at Windsore, the place which he forbad. But the truth is that she being first buried in our Ladies Chappell here in this Church, her corps was taken up ; when as Henry the Seuenth laid the foundation of that admirable structure his Chappell royall, which haue euer since so remained, and neuer reburied. She was the daughter to Charles the Sixth, King of France : she died at Bermondsey in Southwarke, the second of Ianuary, Ann. Dom. 1437."

Her epitaph, "Hic Katherina jacet," &c., is given as it is in T. J. Pettigrew's *Chronicles of the Tombs,* Lond., Bohn, 1857, p. 300, where it is stated that it is "supposed by Dart to have been written by Skelton whilst he lay hid from Wolsey's fury." But there are two various readings: l. 13, "Tuddero," Pet.; "Tiddero," Weev.; l. 16, "Britannia," Pet.; "Britanna," Weev. The former will not scan. ED. MARSHALL.

"ESTRIDGES" (5th S. vii. 326, 385, 458; ix. 115, 217.)—I cannot accept MR. GUY's general agreement "that the falcon is meant by Shakspere in the passage in 1 *Hen. IV*. iv. 1"; nor do I see the relevancy of the quotation from the *Faerie Queen* describing the flight of the eagle, which MR. PERRATT would array in the borrowed plumes of the ostrich.

In the first place the *estridge* was the recognized name for the ostrich a hundred years before Shakspere wrote this play, and for at least fifty years after, as the following extracts will show :—

> " The Estryge that wyll eate
> An horshowe so great
> In the stede of meate,
> Such fervent heate
> His stomake doth freat;
> He can not well fly,
> Nor synge tunably," &c.
>
> John Skelton (1460-1529), *Phyllyp Sparrow*, l. 478.

And in his *Speke, Parrot*, l. 80, we find :—

> " Io dien serveth for the erstrych fether,
> Io dien is the language of the land of Beme."

This vulgar error (if it be one, and not a mere exaggeration of the fact that the ostrich is a coarse feeder) is put into Jack Cade's mouth in 2 *Hen. VI.*, iv. 10; and Sir Thos. Browne, in seriously discussing it, is prepared, like the bird, to swallow the horseshoe, but has doubts on the digestive process. While it serves to settle what is meant by the estridge, it carries down the word to the middle of the seventeenth century :—

> "They have keen Estridge stomachs, and well digest
> Both Iron and Lead, as a Dog will a Breast
> Of Mutton."
>
> " On the Creeple Soldiers marching in Oxford," *Clarastella : Occasional Poems*, by Robert Heath, 1650, p. 24.

> " No ; the State-Errant fight, and fight to eat ;
> Their Ostrich-stomachs make their swords their meat."
>
> John Cleveland, " The Rebel Scot," *Poems*, 1661, p. 35.

Now for the passage itself. By dispensing with the comma which in the 4to. of 1599 and in the folio of 1623 stands after "eagles," or by moving it two words back, the sense, I contend, becomes perfectly clear, one figure growing naturally out of the preceding one :—

> " All furnisht, all in Armes,
> All plum'd like Estridges, that with the wind
> Bayted, like Eagles having lately bathed,
> Glittering in Golden Coats like Images,
> As full of spirit as is the month of May,
> And gorgeous as the Sun at Midsummer,"

i.e. the plumes on their helmets fluttered with the breeze, as do those of the ostrich when in running he flaps his wings, like the eagle (notably the osprey) shaking the water from his plumage after

a dip in the sea (see Cotgrave, art. "Debatis, the bating or unquiet fluttering of a hawke "). It is just possible that the " eagles " may claim the glittering golden coats of the next line, and that to the images (or pictures) belong the spirit and colour of May and Midsummer ; but this would involve taking further liberties with the punctuation.

The entry of "Estrych-falcon" in Halliwell's *Dictionary* seems responsible for the confusion which has arisen on this subject. He calls it "a species of large falcon, mentioned in the old metrical romance of *Guy of Warwick*. Shakspere seems to allude to this bird in *Ant. and Cleop.*, iii. 11."

I have only been able to find "Gerfawcon" in the printed copies of the two MS. versions of *Guy of Warwick ;* and I observe that Halliwell describes this bird also as "a kind of large falcon," with a reference to p. 26 of the Abbotsford Club text. Surely this passage in Shakspere does not require the discovery of any such hybrid :—

> "To be furious
> Is to be frighted out of fear, and in that mood
> The dove will peck the Estridge,"

i.e. the mildest creature will, in a paroxysm of rage, make puny attacks on the most overwhelming of foes, the dove being taken as the type of submissive weakness, as the ostrich is of aggressive strength. Our English proverb says, in a like sense, " Tread on a worm and it will turn."

VINCENT S. LEAN.

Windham Club.

INVENTOR OF ROLLER SKATES (5th S. viii. 507 ; ix. 60, 215.)—In addition to the information already given by CUTHBERT BEDE on this subject, I beg to suggest that there is another notice of " artificial " skating in England besides those recorded in these columns, to be found in the *Annals of Sporting*, Oct., 1823, under the head of " Skating " :—

> " A skate has been invented which renders this amusement independent of frost. It is like the common skate, but instead of one iron it has two, with a set of small brass wheels let in between, which revolve and enable the bearer to run with great rapidity on any hard, level surface, and to perform, though with less force and nicety, all the evolutions of skating. A patent has been obtained for this invention, and it is now exhibited at the Tennis-court, in Windmill-street."

At this same place pugilistic displays, &c., had for some time been usual. JULIAN MARSHALL.

OLD RECEIPTS (5th S. viii. 145 ; ix. 55, 217.)—Rue, unsavoury as it is, has long been considered a most virtuous herb in preventing infection, hence its use at the Old Bailey. At the trial of the Mannings, after the conviction the female prisoner in her fury seized the sprigs of it which lay on the dock, and dashed them on the floor of the court. " The smell of a Yahoo continuing very offensive, I always keep my nose well stopped with rue, lavender, or tobacco leaves " (*Gulliver's Travels*, part iv. chap. xii.). I have seen in public-houses in London, especially in those on the Surrey side of the bridges, bottles of gin containing rue, which was much used as a dram by the cattle drovers entering London in the early morning. It was also employed as a vermifuge.

W. J. BERNHARD SMITH.

Temple.

THE ISLE OF MAN A BAD PLACE (5ᵗʰ S. ix. 45, 134.)—Is not this a mere play upon words not referring to the isle, but to man himself?—" Give me mankind, and then take all the rest." P. P.

𝔐iscellaneous.

NOTES ON BOOKS, &c.

British Mezzotinto Portraits. Described by J. C. Smith. Part I. Adams to Faber. (H. Sotheran and J. Noseda.)

THOSE who saw the fine collection of mezzotint engravings after Reynolds and Gainsborough at the Burlington House Exhibition of Old Masters this year, will at once appreciate the utility and value of this extremely well devised catalogue. At Burlington House there was no possibility of any classification beyond maintaining an agreeable balance of form and tone, regulated of course by the various conditions of size and shape. The catalogue gave as much valuable and ready information as was needed for the purposes of a cursory visit, and the preparation had been much aided by Dr. Edward Hamilton's comprehensive catalogue of the engraved works of Sir Joshua Reynolds. No less than 103 individual engravers, and mostly mezzotinters, have devoted themselves to the reproduction of the works of this great artist. Dr. Hamilton has classified his subjects according to the names of the persons represented. Mr. Chaloner Smith, on the other hand, adopts the name of the artist as his guide, noticing those portraits only on which the mezzotinto process has been employed. Mezzotinto is his principal theme. The art itself, as is well known, does not date further back than the reign of Charles II., and it suddenly reached complete mastery at the hands of John Smith in reproducing the works of Sir Godfrey Kneller. In early times engravings in this style were inelegantly termed "scrapings," and in Germany the phrase " black art " is still employed to denote it. The velvety appearance of the black produced by this process has also led to the adoption in Germany of the appropriate term " Sammet-stich," or velvet-engraving.

It would appear almost impossible to comprise within four octavo volumes, according to the announcement in the prospectus, this vast number of names and their subdivisions, were it not that Mr. Chaloner Smith has adopted a clever system of abbreviations and employed types of different sizes, although producing a violent contrast. The plan of his undertaking is thus stated in his own words : " This work is intended to describe all mezzotinto portraits published in England, Ireland, and Scotland, down to the early part of the present century ; not including those by engravers such as S. W. Reynolds and Charles Turner, whose principal works were produced at a more modern date." His technical definitions of " platemark," " subwidth," and " inside border " will be found useful to collectors.

His system of what he calls "handing" is far superior to that adopted in the South Kensington portrait catalogues and in the Burlington House portrait descriptions. He justly applies the terms right and left to

those of the spectator facing the picture. This obviously natural course is universally adopted in continental guides and numismatic descriptions. A short warning to the unwary against applying a broad meaning to the word *excudit* might have been useful. Although strictly meaning publisher or issuer of the plate, it is liable to be mistaken for engraver, and this in some cases has led into difficulties. The frontispiece to this volume, showing, side by side, what extensive changes can be made in one and the same plate, is admirably executed, on a reduced scale, by the " Photogravure " process of Messrs. Goupil & Co. It was used in the engraved illustrations for the catalogue of Mr. James Anderson Rose's fine collection, recently dispersed by Messrs. Sotheby. In those plates the minute silvery line engravings of Wierix and Beatrizet, among others, were produced with marvellous fidelity, and now we find the process equally well adapted to render the fulness and richness of mezzotinto. These prints lie flat, on the same paper as the rest of the book, and the pages are not distorted, to the prejudice of the binding, as too frequently happens in modern books devoted to galleries of art, where starched photography takes the place of reproduction by means of genuine metallic engraving.

As the remaining volumes appear, we may briefly comment on distinctive features as they occur, and for the present will only record our admiration at the earnest and thorough manner in which Mr. Smith has carried out his undertaking, not only as regards the main subjects, but down to the minutest points of detail. The labour and research to produce this result must have been immense, and the author has manifestly enjoyed the advantage of access to the choicest collections of engravings illustrating the subject.

Catalogue of Prints and Drawings in the British Museum. Division I. Political and Personal Satires. Prepared by Frederic George Stephens, and containing many Descriptions by Edward Hawkins, late Keeper of the Antiquities. Vol. III., Parts I. and II. (Printed by Order of the Trustees.)

THOUGH in art, as in poetry, satire does not occupy the foremost place, its importance and interest are universally recognized; and nowhere more warmly than in England, the birthplace of those great masters of pictorial satire, Hogarth, Gillray, and Cruikshank. Those who would study the comic history of England at greater length than in the two volumes published by Gilbert A'Becket under that title will find it written at full in the wonderful collection of caricatures and satirical engravings preserved in the Print Room of the British Museum. But fortunately they may do it more comfortably at their own firesides, by means of the elaborate catalogue of them, of which a further portion (the third volume, in two parts) has just been published. To the great credit of all who have had part and parcel in the good work—first to the originator of it, we presume Mr. Reid, the learned and courteous head of the department ; secondly to the Trustees for having fallen into the suggestion ; and thirdly and especially to Mr. Frederic George Stephens, to whom, at Mr. Reid's suggestion, the preparation of the catalogue was entrusted, and who has justified to the fullest the recommendation of his chief, by the production of a catalogue valuable not only for the minute and accurate descriptions it gives of the various engravings enumerated in it, but for the vast amount of curious illustration of social, personal, and political history which he has brought to bear upon them from contemporary writers, ballads, broadsides, pamphlets, and periodicals—a body of information which could scarcely have been gathered together except by one working in the Museum itself. The parts or the catalogue now issued contain descriptions of nearly eighteen hundred prints, published between March, 1734, and 1760; and how full these descriptions are may be judged from the fact that they occupy upwards of twelve hundred pages, and include the most complete account of the matchless works of Hogarth which has yet been given to the world. Mr. Stephens's introduction, on the political importance of artistic satire and the progress of political art in England, will be read with great interest; but that our notice may not be as long as the bulky volumes to which it refers, we will bring it to a close with an expression of our satisfaction at seeing the name of Edward Hawkins on the title-page of a book which would have delighted that good man and lover of satirical art.

Spelling Reform, from an Educational Point of View. By J. H. Gladstone, F.R.S. (Macmillan & Co.)

THE distinguished President of the Chemical Society has been up the Tamar to a place which he calls Cothele—an orthography different from that employed by the Earl of Mount Edgcumbe in giving an account to the British Archæological Association (*Journal*, vol. xxxiii. p. 1) of an estate which came into his family by the marriage of William de Edgcumbe with Hilaria de Cotehele, in 1353—and has come back dismayed to find that whereas he was himself acquainted with " twenty-seven ways of pronouncing it in accordance with the analogy of English words and names," the mode in which the name fell " from the lips of one who could be depended upon " was different from all his own modes. The only adequate remedy which our author sees for such a state of things is a Royal Commission, which Mr. Matthew Arnold would fain have established as a permanent institution. The extracts given by Mr. J. H. Gladstone from reports of foreign systems constitute a valuable feature of his book, whatever be our judgment on the views enunciated in the text.

THE OXFORD AND CAMBRIDGE BOAT-RACE, 1829 (*ante,* p. 271.)—I can inform your correspondent SCULLER, upon the authority of *Bell's Life,* that the cutter in which the Oxford men rowed against the Cantabs in 1829 belonged to Balliol, and was built by King. The Cambridge crew succeeded King at Oxford, or Messrs. Searle can furnish SCULLER with dimensions, or perhaps even afford him an opportunity of inspecting the drawings made for the ships in question. My rowing recollection does not go so far back as 1829, but I remember racing boats built not long after that time, and wondrous craft they were compared to the frail and swift outriggers of the present day. There used to be a gangway fastened along the thwarts from stroke to bow, and each man walked along this gangway, oar in hand, till he reached his proper place. Racing boats were then much pinched in both fore and aft, but more so at bow's thwart than at stroke's. This made it rather hard lines for poor No. 1, for he not only had to contend against the disadvantage of keeping time and stroke with an oar shorter inboard than any of the others, and consequently very badly balanced, but he had to endure more than his fair share of scolding from the coxswain, whose great idea of " principles of rowing and steering " in those pre-scientific days seemed to be that it was at least judicious to select for his severest censure the man who was furthest off from him. BARTHOLOMEW LANE.

HERALDIC BOOK-PLATES.—MR. HENRY PECKITT (Carlton Husthwaite, Thirsk) writes:—"I am just commencing my fifth folio volume of book-plates, and shall be glad of an opportunity of exchanging duplicates or

of purchasing old plates .... If any one "...... plate for insertion I will at once acknowledge it. I a separate collection, ' Foreign Ex Libris,' which I be glad to make additions to by purchase."

THE Rev. W. W. Skeat is a candidate for the Profe ship of Anglo-Saxon at Cambridge. His thor acquaintance with our language in all its s peculiarly fits Mr. Skeat for the Chair just found the University by a legacy from the late Dr. Boswo

WE are sure our readers will be glad to have attention drawn to the very admirable article on late Dr. Doran, by Mr. J. C. Jeaffreson, in this mo *Temple Bar.*

NEXT week we shall have " A Reminiscence of G Cruikshank and his *Magazine,*" from the pen of C BERT BEDE.

Notices to Correspondents.

ON all communications should be written the name address of the sender, not necessarily for publication as a guarantee of good faith.

FREDK. RULE.—The fact was sufficiently establi *ante,* p. 53. On this subject E. NARES HENNING (l borne) writes:—"There was a Mr. Beresford, of M College, Oxford, who was a contemporary and frie Dr. Nares in his early days, and who was the auth *The Miseries of Human Life,* which came out abou same time as *Thinks I to Myself,* and may have l the error. Referring to your *Notices* to Correspond *ante,* p. 120, I do not see how the account of the I family can be supplemented materially, but I sha glad to answer, as far as I am able, any further ques that may be put." See *ante,* p. 275.

F. L. P.—In Murray's *Handbooks,* those reliable most useful *compagnons de voyage,* the traveller in country, whether Italy or elsewhere, will be sure to the information desired.

J. E. CUSSANS.—We shall feel much obliged if you send us a note stating, if such be the case, that son ference to the story will be found in your forthco *History of Hertfordshire.*

P.—The following will probably suit your req ments : Rietstap, *Armorial Général des Familles N et Patriciennes de l'Europe,* Amsterdam, 1875. at twenty shillings in Quaritch's *General Catalog Books,* 1875-7.

H. A. S.—Many thanks for your letter. } hesitate to write. Forward query about "I Officers." Your note, if possible, next week. *ante,* p. 268.

H. A. W.—Your reply will appear, and a proof be sent. We should appreciate an original note o missal referred to by yourself.

GEO. PRESSLY (Knockmaroon.)—The story mu nearly as old as cards themselves.

F. ROSENTHAL.—Second copy received.

H. B. C.—See *ante,* p. 239.

Y. N. E. (Frome) should send name and address

ERRATUM.—P. 244, col. 1, l. 21, for " wot " read i

NOTICE.

Editorial Communications should be addressed to ' Editor of ' Notes and Queries ' "—Advertisements Business Letters to " The Publisher "—at the Offic Wellington Street, Strand, London, W.C.

We beg leave to state that we decline to return munications which, for any reason, we do not print to this rule we can make no exception.

LONDON, SATURDAY, APRIL 13, 1878.

CONTENTS.—N° 224.

Notes.

A REMINISCENCE OF GEORGE CRUIKSHANK AND HIS "MAGAZINE."

In the summer of 1853 Mr. George Cruikshank was projecting a monthly serial, to be published by Mr. D. Bogue, and he wished me to write for it, and also to contribute to its pages from month to month a humorous story of modern life, to be illustrated by himself with page etchings. This made it necessary for me to go up to London on several occasions to have personal interviews with Mr. Cruikshank, and to consult with him on various details relative to the proposed periodical, which eventually took the shape of "*George Cruikshank's Magazine*," edited by Frank E. Smedley (Frank Fairlegh)." No. 1 appeared in January, 1854, and No. 2 in February; after that "the deluge." The *Magazine* was a short-lived failure, and is probably only now remembered from Cruikshank's marvellous etching in No. 1 of "Passing Events: or the Tail of the Comet of 1853," a large folding plate, and one of his choicest and most ingenious productions. This etching alone is enough to preserve *George Cruikshank's Magazine* from oblivion, though there were other folding plates that deserve to be remembered, and one of them, "Trying to cure a Bear of a sore Head," might readily be adapted to the present political crisis.

Though the *Magazine* proved to be "one more unfortunate," I have many pleasant memories of my connexion with it, not the least pleasant being that it introduced me to the personal friendship of George Cruikshank, with whom I had hitherto only exchanged letters. The story that I wrote for him was of course strangled in its birth, but it was subsequently published in a complete form, under the title, *Love's Provocations*. One day, when I went up from the country to see him, early in October, 1853, I found him smarting from the effects of Dickens's article, in *Household Words*, Oct. 1, "Frauds on the Fairies," directed against the letterpress of "George Cruikshank's Fairy Library," another publication which, although containing some exquisitely fanciful etchings, only lived to three numbers; for I believe that the fourth, *Puss in Boots*, though advertised ten years after (in 1863) as "in preparation," was never published.

It was very evident from that article, "Frauds on the Fairies," and also from a previous one from the same pen, called "Whole Hogs" (*Household Words*, Aug. 23, 1851), that Dickens considered Cruikshank to be occasionally given over to the culture of crotchets, and to the furious riding of favourite hobbies. But in all these things it is indisputable that the great moral artist was firmly persuaded that he was acting in the cause of suffering humanity, and engaged upon some work for the amelioration of his fellow creatures. And whatever was the act, and however small and trivial it might appear in the sight of the majority, Cruikshank threw himself into it heart and soul, and, like everything else that he put his hand to, he did it with all his might.

I had a very striking evidence of this, which I imagine will be entirely new to the reader. At one of our interviews at his own house, relative to his projected magazine, he showed me some woodblocks, on which were his own designs, and which he had already gone to the expense of having carefully engraved by (if I remember rightly) Mr. T. Williams. He then explained to me the nature of the designs and the special object for which he had prepared them. I must continually have noticed (he said) an evil that was patent to every one, both indoors and out of doors, in the streets, and railway carriages, and omnibuses, and all public vehicles. It was an evil not confined to the young or the old, it was most injurious in its effects, and it only required the public attention to be pointedly directed to it to have it stopped and put down. This was what he desired to do with his pencil, and it was for this that he sought the co-operation of my pen.

Now, what does the reader imagine was this evil that had obtained such a hold upon the nation? It was nothing more or less than the habit of ladies and gentlemen, and boys and girls, placing the handles of their sticks, canes, parasols, or umbrellas to their mouths, and either sucking them or tapping their teeth with them! Suiting the action to the word, and acting the characters, Cruikshank showed me how the gent of the period tried to make himself look excessively knowing by sucking the ivory or bone handle of his cane; how the young lady, and even the very little girl, made their morning calls and sucked their parasol handles—a sure sign of great *gaucherie;* how other ladies, even elderly ones, who ought to know better, did the same in carriages and omnibuses, thereby running the risk of having their teeth broken if the vehicle gave a sudden lurch; and how even grave physicians carried their gold or ivory headed canes up to their lips. (I here reminded Mr. Cruikshank that if they did so it was in traditionary keeping with an old custom dating from the days of the Great Plague of London, when every doctor who carried "fate and physic in his eye" had a cunningly devised box for aromatic scents fixed on the top of his cane, so that he might hold it under his nose whenever he visited an infectious case.)

Cruikshank spoke most gravely on this "hideous, abominable, and most dangerous custom," an evil that he was determined to try to put down, and for this end he had prepared the designs that he showed to me, and which had been already engraved. These illustrations he wished me to work into letterpress, which should first appear in the projected magazine, and should then be reprinted in the form of a small pamphlet. He did not desire to make money by the publication of this pamphlet; on the contrary, he intended to have many thousand copies printed at his own expense, and to employ men to distribute them gratuitously to the public. There were to be men posted outside every railway station in London, and as each cab or carriage rolled from under the gateway, one of the pamphlets was to be tossed into the vehicle. The omnibus travellers were to be liberally dealt with in the same way, and by these means Cruikshank was quite sanguine that the reform which he so much desired would be effected in a few months, and that he should once more feel the satisfaction of having conferred a public benefit upon his generation.

I could not see in this a very promising subject for my pen; but, as the article was to make its first appearance in the new magazine, I agreed to write something in furtherance of the object that he had in view, and to incorporate the illustrations that he had prepared. After awhile I took Mr. Cruikshank the article that I had written. He was more than disappointed with it—he was horrified. I had treated that grave and earnest question in a light and jocular spirit! It would only amuse instead of warn the reader!—it would never do! and so on, with a great deal of action of hands and head. I argued that it was more likely to make the desired impression upon their minds, if they read what I had written, than they were presented with a grave, sermon-lik treatise on the theme. But my arguments faile to move him, and he asked me to write anothei and far more serious, paper on the subject. Thi I declined to do, and requested him to get som other author to carry out his ideas.

Whether he ever did so or not I do not know The collapse of the new magazine in its earl infancy prevented the appearance in that quarte of George Cruikshank's tilt against stick an parasol sucking, and I am not aware if th engraved blocks of which I have spoken were ev made public. If any one is sufficiently curious t know the nature of the manuscript that I sut mitted to Cruikshank, he may do so by referrin to *Motley*, by Cuthbert Bede, published by Jame Blackwood in 1855. There he will find eigl pages taken up by an article, illustrated by mysel called "Dental Dangers," which is, *verbatin* printed from the manuscript that I had written fc Mr. Cruikshank—which, however, I called "Tak Care of your Teeth!"

In that paper I spoke of a lady in an omnibu whose set of false teeth were projected into he opposite neighbour's lap through a sudden jolt (the vehicle while she was sucking her paras(handle. This led me to tell Cruikshank an anec dote that I had then recently heard, and whicl as it has not been in print, I may here narrate; fc Cruikshank laughed very heartily at it, and sai that he should like to make an illustration to it and asked me if I could not write a paper o country rectors and their adventures, in which might be introduced, and which he would furthe illustrate. Very likely this suggestion might hav been carried into effect if Mr. D. Bogue ha carried on the *Magazine*. As it was, it was lost t the world. But here is the anecdote, which I tol to Cruikshank as it had been told to me.

An old rector of a small country parish had bee compelled to send to a dentist his set of false teet in order that some repairs might be made. Th dentist had faithfully promised to send them bac "by Saturday"; but the Saturday's post did nc bring the box containing the rector's teeth. Ther was no Sunday post, and the village was nir miles from the post town. The dentist, it aftei wards appeared, had posted the teeth on tl Saturday afternoon, with the full conviction tht their owner would duly receive them on the Sur day morning in time for his service. The ol rector bravely tried to do that duty which Englan expects every man to do, more especially if he is a parson and if it is a Sunday morning; but, afte he had mumbled through the prayers, with equ difficulty and incoherency, he decided that would be advisable to abandon any further attempi to address his congregation on that day. Whil the hymn was being sung, he summoned the cler to the vestry, and there said to him, "It is quite useless for me to attempt to go on. The fact is that my dentist has not sent me back my artificial teeth; and as it is impossible for me to make myself understood, you must tell the congregation that the service is ended for this morning, and that there will be no service this afternoon." The old clerk went back to his desk; the singing of the hymn—in "the singing gallery"—was brought to an end; and the rector, from his retreat in the vestry, heard his clerk address the congregation as follows :—" This is to give notice! as there won't be no sarmon, nor no more sarvice this mornin', so you'd all better go whum [home]; and there won't be no sarvice this arternoon, as the rector hain't got his artful teeth back from the dentist !"

I should have liked to have seen George Cruikshank's rendering of this anecdote; and I am sorry that his version of the "artful teeth"—an idea that amazingly tickled him—was lost to the world through circumstances over which we had no control. It would have made a choice supplementary sketch to his series in the "History of a Toothache." For teeth are amongst, if not *the* "Greatest Plague in Life" (another theme for Cruikshank's designs), from the time that we cut them until the time that they "cut" us, in an age "when the *grinders* shall be few in number." I beg to observe that I am not responsible for this interpretation of the text from Ecclesiastes, for it was so applied by Bishop Rudd when he preached before Queen Elizabeth, and desired to remind her majesty that she was sixty-three years of age, and that age had its infirmities in the loss of teeth, and that nine times seven was the grand climacteric of life. Although good Queen Bess kept her temper sufficiently not to interrupt Bishop Rudd in his sermon—as she had interrupted Dean Nowell on a previous occasion, when she called to him from the royal pew that he should "retire from that ungodly digression and return to his text"—she was by no means pleased with his admonition, but said that he might have kept his arithmetic to himself, though she plainly saw that the greatest clerks were not always the wisest men.

This subject, with similar anecdotes, might have afforded a favourable opportunity for the exercise of George Cruikshank's pencil in his new *Magazine*; but, like my paper, "Take Care of your Teeth !" it was not destined to see the light in the pages of that short-lived periodical. It was edited, as I have said, by Frank Smedley, whom it was needful that I should see personally with reference to my contributions—another of my pleasant memories in connexion with the *Magazine*, for I then met Smedley for the first time.

He told me that, as in my own case, he had not known Cruikshank personally until his projected *Magazine* brought them together, although Cruikshank had illustrated *Frank Fairlegh*. The great

artist's first call upon Smedley was made only a few days previous to my own, and Smedley gave me the following account of it. "He was shown into this room, while I was sitting at that writing-desk by the window. I wheeled my chair round" (poor Smedley had to use a self-acting wheeled chair) "and advanced to meet him. Thus I had my back to the light, and he was facing the window. He appeared so amazed at seeing me such a cripple as I am, that he could not overcome his wonder, but kept exclaiming, 'Good God! I thought you could gallop about on horses!' and the like expressions. I explained how it was; and we then proceeded to discuss business details. It was a very hot, sultry day, and Cruikshank had walked fast; he was very heated, and his face and forehead were very red. His hair was blown about; and, instead of sitting quietly on a chair, he was standing up and gesticulating wildly. I have a sense of the ludicrous, and I had the greatest difficulty to keep from laughing, or to look him in the face. For all this time, in the very centre of his capacious and very red forehead, there was a round something of ivory, not plain, but carved in circles, and as big as a large button. I wondered what it could be. Was it some Temperance badge ? Was it some emblem of office in some secret society, in which he held rank as a Great Panjandrum with the little button atop ? For the life of me I could not divine what it was. And all the time he was holding me with his glittering eye, and going through a whole pantomime of gesticulations. Suddenly, and to my intense relief—for I was beginning to feel that I could not bear the mystery much longer—the ivory badge fell from his forehead and dropped on to the hearthrug at his feet. Cruikshank looked at it with bewilderment, and said, ' Wherever did that come from ?' 'From off your forehead,' I replied. 'From off my forehead !' he echoed, as he rubbed it fiercely. 'Yes,' I said ; ' it has been there ever since you entered the room.' Cruikshank seized his hat and looked into its crown, when it appeared that the ivory circlet had dropped from the ventilating hole in the crown of the hat as Cruikshank had walked to my house, and that it had found its way down to his forehead, where, what with the heat of his head and the fragments of glue on the ivory, it had become firmly fixed, and would perhaps have remained there for some hours longer if he had not accompanied his conversation with so much action. When he found out the truth, and fully realized the absurdity of the situation, he burst into such a hearty roar of laughter as I have not heard for many a day. This was my first personal introduction to George Cruikshank."

CUTHBERT BEDE.

M. DAVID CLEMENT AND ROBERT BARNES, D.D.: AN EXTRAORDINARY BIBLIOGRAPHICAL BLUNDER.

A former bibliographical correspondent of "N. & Q.," writing from the other side of the Atlantic, declares himself reluctant to advance "a charge of carelessness against Clement" on the ground that he "is not often justly liable to such reproach" (1st S. iv. 440). Now that author's *Bibliothèque Curieuse* is unquestionably valuable for the carefulness and minuteness of his collations, and is generally, so far as I have proved it, trustworthy, whatever may be thought of M. Clement's excessive liberality in the attribution of the quality of rarity to the works he describes—an error, if it be one, which will readily be excused by the bibliophile who consults him for the identification of some of his own cherished treasures. I for one have often wished that he had lived to complete his labours. But "Bernardus enim non videt omne,"*—one of such consultatory *excursûs*, which I had occasion recently to make, has resulted in the discovery of an extraordinary blunder on Clement's part—a blunder sufficiently remarkable in itself, but rendered still more so by the sweeping censures of his bibliographical predecessors into which it has betrayed him, a blunder, too, which appears to have hitherto escaped detection.

The case stands thus. At tom. ii. p. 440, under the name Robertus Barns, Clement notices a work, the general title of which he quotes as follows :—

"Scriptores duo Anglici Coaetanei ac Conterranei; De Vitis Pontificum videlicet: Robertus Barns & Johannes Baleus quos a tenebris vindicavit, veterum testimoniis ne quis de fide illorum dubitaret confirmavit, & usque ad Paulum Quintum hodie regnantem continuavit Johannes Martini Lydius Francofurtensis Minister Verbi Dei Veteraquini. Lugduni Batavorum, Excudebat Georgius Abrahami A Marsse, 1615. Sumptibus Henrici Laurentii Bibliopolæ Amstelodamensis. Cum Gratia & Privilegio illustrium D.D. Ordinum Generalium. In 8vo. *Rare.*"

To this he subjoins a note, which contains assertions so astonishing that I must beg to be allowed to quote his own words at some length. Bayle it seems, in his great *Dictionary*, objects to Seckendorf's assertion that Barns's *Vitæ Romanorum Pontificum* may be reckoned a lost work, and cites in opposition to it the edition of Lydius, Leyden, 1615 (as above), which, he adds, is by no means extremely rare. Upon this statement of Bayle's M. Clement comments as follows :—

"Si elle n'étoit pas extrêmement rare, il auroit du faire ses éforts pour la voir, & il auroit trouvé, qu'il étoit dans l'erreur : puis qu'il n'y a pas un mot de Barns dans tout le Volume : qui doit sa naissance à l'imposture & à l'artifice criminel de celui qui l'a fait imprimer : ce qui a seduit tous les Savans qui ont parlé de cette Edition.

* Whence this proverbial saying? I have failed to trace its paternity even through the voluminous indexes of "N. & Q."

Il est étonnant que l'Auteur du *Thesaurus Bibliothecal* qui avoit ce Livre devant lui, lorsqu'il composa l'artic 226 que l'on trouve *ibid.* Vol. II. p. 297, n'ait pe remarqué cette tricherie. J'ai confronté l'Editic trompeuse de Lydius avec celle de Rob. Barns, qui e ici dans la Bibliothèque Roiale, & je n'y ai rien trouv qui vienne de ce Docteur."

Thus far Clement. And now, after such positive statement, and such severe censures upo men like Bayle, Schwindel, and the host of ur named *savans*, implying at the least gross careles ness on their part, not to mention the imputatio of deliberate fraud and trickery to the poor biblic pole of Amsterdam, will it be readily believed tha there is not a word of truth in that statement, an that the censures based upon it apply to the cen surer, not to the censured !

A fine copy of the work in question now lie before me. Let me briefly but faithfully describ the contents of this very bulky little tome. Th general title differs from Clement's transcript a before cited in the following particulars : a comma follows "Anglici," "Romanorum" with a full stop after it follows "Pontificum," and "quos" begin with a capital Q. I note these *minutiæ* chiefly because the correctness of Clement's transcript even in the matter of punctuation will be have been so implicitly relied on by your American correspondent (*loc. sup. cit.*). On the reverse o the title is a sort of *imprimatur* entitled "Ivdiciv ac Censvra Facvltatis Theologicæ, Academiæ Lei densis," and subscribed "Johannes Polyander.' Then comes Lydius's dedication to the States General, filling six pp. After which, withou separate titles but with distinct pagination, follow 1. "Johannis Lydii . . . Continvatio Historiæ I. Balei," &c., pp. 1–358 ; 2. "Præfatio Joannis Balei ad Lectorem," pp. 1–9 ; "Onvs sev Prophetia Romæ, Lavrentio Hunfrido authore" ; "In Mino tavrum Romanvm Carmen, authore Christ. Soth."; "Joannes Parkhvrstus Anglus, de verbis Apostoli. 1. Tim. 3" (all in Latin verse), pp. 10–13 ; "Avthorvm Nomina," &c., pp. 14, 15 ; "Papæ Sacrificorum filij," p. 16 ; "Acta Romanorvm Pontificum . . . ex Joannis Balei . . . maiore Catalogo Anglicorum scriptorum desumpta," &c., pp. 17– 587 ; "Breve Paralipomenon ad Balæum," subscribed "Pontanus Isacius," pp. 3, unnumbered ; 3. "Pontificvm Romanorvm Vitæ, per Robertum Barns Anglum descriptæ," pp. 1–264.

Our unfortunate author and critic must have relied upon a single copy, which in this case happened to be an imperfect one. The moral from this is obvious.

The *Vitæ* of Robert Barns are not, I need hardly add, contained in the edition of his *Whole Workes*, London, by John Daye, 1573. They have never, I believe, been translated into English, nor has the original Latin been published in England. I have no opportunity of referring to the original and only(?) separate edition, that published at Basle in 8vo.,

without date, but in 1568. Perhaps some of your readers who may be able to compare it with the Leyden edition of 1615 will kindly inform us how far the latter is a faithful reproduction of the former. Clement speaks doubtfully of another edition without date in 4to., entered in *Catal. Librorum Bibliothecæ medii Templi Londinensis*, 1734. Is such an edition to be found there or elsewhere, or is it an erroneous reference to the Basle 8vo.?   H. A. S.
Breadsall, Derby.

PALM SUNDAY.—The subjoined paragraph from the *Monmouthshire Beacon* newspaper seems entitled to a place in " N. & Q.":—

"FLOWERING SUNDAY IN MONMOUTH AND DISTRICT.— Notwithstanding that the tendency of the present day is to neglect and let die out the old customs and habits of our forefathers in favour of other and new-fangled ideas, yet the old custom known as Flowering Sunday, on which the graves of departed friends and relatives are adorned with flowers and garlands, and a general and spontaneous visit seems to be paid to our churchyards and cemeteries, still finds great favour, and unflaggingly bears the test of time. The pretty custom of flowering the graves on Palm Sunday is essentially a Welsh one, and although it may be observed in the Forest and in some other districts immediately around Monmouth and the Principality, yet this yearly habit will not be found to obtain in other parts of the country, although it is by no means a novelty to see flowers placed by loving hands on the graves of departed friends all the year round. The custom of keeping up Flowering Sunday—which is un-doubtedly a very ancient one — is one of the most beautiful and affectionate that can be imagined. Flower-ing Sunday in Monmouth and its neighbourhood was observed with no lack of interest. All Saturday—and indeed with many days previous to Saturday—the great desire seemed to be to obtain flowers for the Sunday's offerings, and all descriptions of Flora's treasures, from the wax-like exotic to the homely grown flowers, and the primrose, cowslip, and daffodil, were culled for the decoration of the churchyard. The flowering of graves is not confined to one section of the community; it can be and is indulged in by rich and poor alike. The flowers were formed into crosses and placed on the tombs, or woven into wreaths and hung upon the head-stones; in other instances they were arranged into immense and graceful bouquets, or, in the case of the humbler class of graves, the flowers were tied in bunches and laid upon them. One grave was adorned with a fine cross of varied coloured greenhouse flowers, with an emblematic representation of the Good Shepherd; many others were adorned with crosses composed of the choicest blooms; and in one case two tombs side by side, and belonging to the same family, were adorned with large crosses composed of moss and primroses. In several instances wreaths of cypress and other foliage and flowers were entwined around the crosses at the head of the graves; in others the tombs were bordered with ivy leaves, and bouquets of flowers laid upon them; moss baskets containing flowers were the choice of others; whilst chaplets of flowers and foliage and im-mortelles were the decorations placed upon many a friend's resting-place. One particularly simple and pretty decoration, at the tomb of some young children, was chaplets of field daisies grouped together, whilst many of the graves were edged around with flowers or evergreens and the surface laid out like a garden. Some of the humbler graves were literally covered with grow-ing primroses and other modest flowers, whilst there was scarcely a grave in the cemetery but showed some mark of the remembrance of the living for the departed. The general appearance of the cemetery was as if it were carpeted with flowers of various hues. The tombs and stones had been in many cases repainted or washed, and the graves had been trimmed up, and in some instances returfed. The tombs and graves in the old churchyard were extensively decorated with flowers, but not nearly so much as was the case at the cemetery. Amongst the decorations we noticed that the tomb of an old and very liberal supporter of the church and cemetery had been repainted and decorated with flowers in a very attractive manner. A large concourse of visitors attended the cemetery on Sunday, and many also were those who visited the various churchyards in the neighbourhood. But amidst the general ' flowering' many a fine old but dilapidated tomb in some of the churchyards—showing that the occupants had filled no inconsiderable position in their day and generation—was now left without adornment; the last friend and relative seemed to have died away, and none was left to call them to remem-brance."
                                CHARLES ROGERS.

PRIMITIVE COFFINS.—Among the Bghai tribes, who are found in Burmah, coffins are made, as with the Chinese, of a single log of wood with a place for the corpse hewn out.[*] Lieut.-Colonel M'Mahon in his work[†] makes mention of those seen by him during his visits to Karen tribes when in charge of the Toungoo district, British Burmah. He notes having seen such coffins among the Bghais, the Gaykhos,[‡] and the Red Karens.
When on a visit to Copenhagen last summer, in the Museum of Northern Antiquities in that city I saw in one of the rooms three or four large oak coffins which are whole trunks of trees hollowed out so as to form a receptacle for the body. In one of these are the remains of a skeleton—the skull, hands, and feet—and the remnants of the clothes in which the body was habilitated when first laid in the coffin. There is a reference to these coffins in Murray's *Handbook to Denmark*.
The analogy here shown in the funeral usage of two very different races is interesting. The coffins which I saw at Copenhagen belong, as classified by Mr. C. Thomsen, the late director of the museum and an eminent archæologist, to the bronze age. So that what were in use by the primitive inhabitants of Denmark many ages ago may now be found uni-versally used by the Bghai tribes of Burmah; per-haps from a remoter antiquity.
                                R. P. HAMPTON ROBERTS.

PARISH PAYMENTS.—Let me make a note that among the payments to the poor of Stoke, in the parish of Bradford, Wiltshire, for the thirteen

* Mason's *Burmah*.
† *Karens of the Golden Chersonese*.
‡ See also Bishop Bigandet's *Legend of the Burmese Buddha* for information concerning the coffins of these people.

weeks ending March 21, 1795, is that of four shillings to Oliver Cromwell, and among the incidental payments of the same parish is one of three shillings to John Cromwell. See Eden's *State of the Poor* (1797), vol. iii. pp. 789, 791.

ALICE B. GOMME.

TWIN TOES.—Where the division between the toes is not complete, and they are partially joined, they are called twin toes. Cases must occur, as they are reputed to be lucky. In one case an eight months' girl has twin toes. The maternal grandmother (supposed to be an eight months' child) has also twin toes. HYDE CLARKE.

CICERO ON LONDON DRIVERS.—In Temple's *Introduction to the History of England* there is an account of the soldiers who rode in chariots armed with scythes fastened to the ends of the axletrees, which did great execution in time of battle. Swift probably had this in his mind when, in his *Tale of a Tub*, section ix., he quotes Cicero's opinion of English drivers. He says :—

"Cicero understood this very well, when writing to a friend in England, with a caution among other matters to beware of being cheated by our *hackney coachmen*, who, it seems, in those days were as arrant rascals as they are now."

Temple only thought of the British warriors and their dangerous scythes ; and Cicero, in his letter to Trebatius, probably only meant to caution his friend against the dangerous charioteers. But Swift, with his exuberant fancy and keen sense of humour, gave a double meaning to the passage, and suggested that Cicero meant to say that the English drivers were always rogues.

EDWARD SOLLY.

TONY LUMPKIN.—Some novelists and dramatists have taken great pains to make names which shall suit their ideas of the characters they describe. How Dickens toiled to this end is recorded. The name of the rustic hero of *She Stoops to Conquer* seems like a happy hit of the same kind by Goldsmith. To note its appearance in real life may therefore be worth while. Henry Lumpkin was a witness at the Corsham petty sessions last week, as reported in the *Bath Herald*.

HAROLD LEWIS.

THE THIRTEENTH CHIME.—One clock in England, to my knowledge, is in the habit of striking thirteen every day, and I heard it do so in June last. This thirteenth chime may be heard at Worsley, near Manchester, the seat of the Earl of Ellesmere, and the reason thereof is as follows. The Worsley estates were formerly the property of the eccentric Duke of Bridgwater, originator of the Bridgwater Canal. His grace was walking over his place one day, when building operations were going on, at a few minutes after 1 P.M. Workingmen were sitting idle. "Not heard the clock

strike ?" "No." "How's that ?" "On strikes once, and, not hearing it, hadn't a secon chance." "I'll put that right ; shan't have th excuse again." Nor did they, for next day th clock struck thirteen times at one o'clock, an continues to do so to this day.

EDWARD H. MARSHALL.
The Temple.

CERTIFICATES OF BIRTH.—Here are two odd spelt and rendered ones. The originals may I seen any day in the office of the city surveyor Exeter :—

"Exeter. Thise is to Silifey that I comfine Sarah — of a daed bon Child living in the piarah of Mry Mage Feb. —, 187-. Witness my hand, —— Madwife."

"Thise is to certifie that I comfine M™ —— of a de Borne child. Liveing in the of St Edmons, March - Wittiness, witnss my hand, ——."

It is satisfactory to notice that the "daed b Child" is certified as "living" in each instanc The "madwife" appears as uncertain about th spelling of her name as she does about that of th Exeter parishes. "Mry Magers" means St. Ma Major's, and "St Edmons," as will be surmise St. Edmund's. HARRY HEMS.
Exeter.

SINGULAR SURNAMES.—In Grand Street, Ne York, is the sign of the firm of Bearup & Carr her. In another part of that city is the firm Late & Early. A few years ago the firm of D & Evening was in existence in Philadelphia.
M. E.
Philadelphia.

Queries.

[We must request correspondents desiring informatic on family matters of only private interest, to affix the names and addresses to their queries, in order that th answers may be addressed to them direct.]

THE AUTHOR OF "THREE COURSES AND DESSERT."—I should be much obliged if any your readers could and would afford me some pa ticulars of the life and work of Charles Clarke, th author of the above work and of the *Cigar*. W he a journalist as well as a solicitor ?

BLANCHARD JERROLD.
Reform Club, Pall Mall.

EDMUND WALLER.—The first authorized editio of Waller's poems appeared in 1645. It wa however, as the preface explains, put forth in con sequence of the previous publication of an un authorized edition, very likely compiled durin his imprisonment in the Tower, which lasted t November, 1644. Is any copy of this prior issu known ? If so, when was it printed, and does i contain the *Battell of the Somer Islands ?*
J. H. L. Y.

"AD QUEM DIU SUSPIRAVI."—There is a very fervent thanksgiving hymn after Communion which begins with this line. I have seen it attributed to the famous priest, Prince Hohenlohe, but I think it must be earlier than this century. As a translation of this poem is included in a little book, *Eucharistic Verses*, which I am now printing, I am anxious to find out at once its authorship.

> MATTHEW RUSSELL, S.J.
> 87, St. Stephen's Green, Dublin.

PRINCESS SCHWARZENBERG.—Can any of your readers refer me to an authentic history of the case of the Princess of Schwarzenberg, which is frequently referred to in medical works, but which seems so extraordinary that the story is probably apocryphal ? This lady is said to have perished one evening in a fire at Paris (the date I do not find given), and a living child is said to have been removed next day by the Cæsarian section.

> F. R. C. P.

["Charles Philip, Prince Schwarzenberg, Feld-Maréchal in the Austrian service, born at Vienna 1771 (distinguished himself at Hohenlinden, &c.), married 1819; was sent as ambassador to St. Petersburg, and then to Paris, where he negotiated the marriage of Napoleon with Marie Louise. During a ball which he gave in Paris, on the occasion of this marriage, in 1810, a terrible fire broke out, causing the death of a number of distinguished persons, and amongst the victims was his own sister-in-law." There is no hint of the further particulars related by F. R. C. P. The above is from Bouillet, *Dict. d'Hist. et de Géogr.*]

PUNISHMENT IN IRELAND IN THE EIGHTEENTH CENTURY.—In the *Dublin University Magazine*, vol. lxxxv. p. 91, Mr. Oliver J. Burke, barrister-at-law, writes the history of Connaught, in which he says :—

"A man was indicted at the Leitrim Assizes for highway robbery, for which he was condemned, and the presiding judge passed the following sentence :—' That he shall be confined in some low dark room, where he shall be laid on his back, and shall have as much weight as he can bear laid upon him, and no more ; that he shall have nothing to live on but the worst bread and water, and the day that he eats he shall not drink, and the day that he drinks he shall not eat, and so shall continue till he dies.'"

Is there any such recorded punishment in England at the same period ? Who was the judge ?

> SETH WAIT.

CIPHER IN REIGN OF QUEEN ELIZABETH.—I have just bought a curious book of devotions written in England in the year 1576. The beginning and end have religious and moral poetry. The whole of the middle of the book is written in cipher, the same prayers and ejaculations being repeated many times. On the bottom of one page, partly concealed by the stitching, there is the name W. Fisher. The ciphers are of two kinds. In one the vowels are expressed by numerals, and in the other the vowels are expressed by

courthand *m*'s, *n*'s, and other fictitious letters, with peculiar tails, the tail alone signifying the vowel, the rest being put in to make it look like regular courthand. Is anything known of a Catholic William Fisher of the date ? Are there any letters among the correspondence of the time written in a similar manner ?

> J. C. J.

THE "VIOLA SANCTORUM."—I have a copy of the *Viola Sanctorum* with the following at the end :—" Viola sanctor' finit feliciter. Anno d'ni 1487, x. kall' Septēbrio Argentinē' impressum per Johannem prüf." Can any one inform me if this is the first edition ? also who was the printer ? If you can give me any information respecting this book I shall feel much obliged. JOHN HALL.

HAMPDEN PEDIGREES.—Will some reader kindly give me full references to the books and manuscripts which contain the most complete pedigrees of the family of John Hampden, the patriot, during the seventeenth and eighteenth centuries ? O. C.

ANNIS-WATER ROBBIN.—A pamphlet of 1650, speaking of a lady of apparently a domineering and overbearing temper, suggests that now her husband is dead "the fittest mate for her upon earth must needs be Annis-water Robbin." What is the meaning of this ? J. E. J.

MAYNELLS OR MANELL.—May I ask for illustrations of this rare word ? Canon Eston in 1455 left money "iiijᵒʳ pulsatoribus pulsantibus in le Maynell et le belfrey " at Chichester, and a computus of 1534 mentions " bells in le Manells." In 1544 " the Great Bell in the choir " occurs ; this hung in " Le Steple," the central tower, in distinction to the detached " Berefridum vulgo Raymond's tower," called " novum campanile " in a will 1436. Manell is the central tower. Possibly Raymond, locally called Ryman, was the " W. Ryman serviens Comitis de Arundel," who is mentioned in the earl's will, 1415, at Lambeth. Is it main-hele ? William Rowe, residentiary, in 1456 desired to be buried " ante magnam crucem in navi ecclesiæ," and bequeathed 20s. " ad reparacionem ecclesiæ super le hell ibidem " (Wills, Stockton, 5). The rood loft stood between the western pillars of the tower.

> MACKENZIE E. C. WALCOTT.

LEEDS POTTERY.—I shall be obliged for a translation of the following words on the rim of a plate, and an explanation of the subject in the centre :—

> " De Vryheyd Spwnd Een groote boog
> Om Vryheyd te ver Kryge
> Maar die on Vryhevd Leeft om hoog
> Doet d' Aarsche Vryheyd Zwyge."

A female holding in right hand what looks like a cap of liberty on a spear, pointing with the left to an open book with the letters ENG DIENS, her feet

" Voor V. Field." I will not at all say that I have copied the words or letters entirely correctly; I have given what they seem to be. A lion standing with a scimitar in the right paw held out, and seven arrows in the left ; an eye in a cloud over-looking both. H. A. W.

A " COTTACEL."—What is a " cottacel" of land ? The term occurs in a deed of grant from the Dean and Chapter of Winchester. T. F. R.

LADY CHARLOTTE JOHNSTON.—I want to know the date of the death of this lady, youngest daughter of George, Earl of Halifax, first wife of General James Johnston, of Overstone, Northants. Her portrait was painted by Sir Joshua Reynolds, and an engraving of it was in the recent collection exhibited at Burlington House. H. M.
Athenæum.

CHAPELS OR ALTARS OF ST. CATHERINE.—Was there any rule or custom in regard to situation in ecclesiastical buildings of the chapel or altar of St. Catherine ? For instance, the chapel of St. Catherine at Westminster was the chapel of the Infirmary and apart from the Abbey.
W. L. R.

ROMAN CITIES IN BRITAIN.—What authors should I consult, besides Nennius, Zosimus, Ptolemy, and the Antonine Itinerary, to obtain a complete list of these so far as they are known ? And where are they identified with modern towns?
G. O. M.

A RUSSIAN FUNERAL CUSTOM.—As I learn from Dr. King's reliable work, *The Rites and Ceremonies of the Greek in Russia* (Lond., 1772), there is an ancient custom among the Russians (though not prescribed by their liturgy, yet sanctioned by tradition) to give the deceased two written documents placed in his coffin, containing (1) the confession of his sins, (2) the absolution declared by the priest. Is there any nation contemporary or in history (besides the ancient Egyptians) where a similar custom has been or is still observed ? Did or do the Greek Christians in Greece and in the Levant follow such a custom ?
H. KREBS.
Taylorian Library, Oxford.

ST. GOVAN.—Will some hagiologist kindly refer me to an account of this sainted personage, or favour me with replies to the following questions, viz. :—In what age did St. Govan live ? Was the saint male or female ? What particular legend connects the name of this saint with a well near Milford Haven, formerly celebrated for the miraculous cures by its water ? Is there not a place of the same name near Glasgow? Are not Govan and Gowen synonymous ? T. W. W. S.

College, Oxford, Judge in the Co in 1828, and who was supposed 1853.—I shall be glad of any acc given of him.

SENSITIVE PLANT TOY.—Ha there was a well-known toy made material, said to be the leaf of th This material was cut into fig fish, men, &c., and these, when le of a warm hand, curled up a variety of shapes. Some you sought my aid in procuring sor but they appear to be already 1 ties, for I have asked for then shops in London, and found then unknown, and apparently not to however, some good-natured read me on the traces of them.
JOHN W.
26, Bedford Place.

DANTE.—*Inferno*, canto xxx version, " Nimrod's howl of fury
" Raphel mai amech izabi
Are these words mere nonsense explained as an attempt at some

Bishop Hatfield's Hall, Durham.

SIR GEORGE DOUGLAS, of P; at Pinkie, married Marion, daug] James Douglas, of Parkhead. J James married Elizabeth, gran of Michael, Lord Carlyle, and Carlyle 1609. Can any of you the pedigree of Sir George D driech ? Whose son was he ? J mate ?

LUCREZIA BORGIA AND OUR I I lately heard an Italian gentle her Majesty Queen Victoria wa Lucrezia Borgia. Was there ar much truth in his statement ?
Reform Club.

A " FEMALE HERCULES."—Ir Montagu, dated Jan. 9, 1752, says : " We are assured that or surprising strong woman was Countess of Holderness's, before of persons of the first quality. find an account of this surpris feats ?

" THE BLUE BELLS OF SCOTL the *Blue Bells of Scotland*, and t was it written ?
[" Ritson," says Mr. W. Chappell, *Olden Time*, " prints this song in

Chorister, 1802, under the title of 'The New Highland Lad.' He says, in a note, 'This song has been lately introduced upon the stage by Mrs. Jordan, who knew neither the words nor the tune (although not at all like a Scotch air) is included in Johnson's *Scots' Musical Museum* (vi. 566). It has been entirely superseded in popular favour by that of Mrs. Jordan. 'The Blue Bell of Scotland, a favourite ballad, as composed and sung by Mrs. Jordan at the Theatre Royal, Drury Lane,' was entered at Stationers' Hall on the 13th of May, 1800, and the music published by Longman & Co."]

An Old Print, dated 1790, represents a low thatched cottage and outbuildings. It is lettered "Revolution House, Whittington, near Chesterfield, where convened England's preservers and the plan devised which raised her present glory, and regain'd her freedom lost." What does this refer to ?

B. B.

Blechynden and Bache.—I shall feel much indebted to any one residing at Oxford who will forward me information as to the place of birth of the following graduates :—

Richard Blechynden, of St. John Baptist's College, who graduated as Master of Arts on March 22, 1672, and as Bachelor of Divinity on June 5, 1679.

Richard Blechynden, of the same college, who graduated as Bachelor of Civil Law on April 27, 1691, and Doctor of Civil Law on February 13, 1695.

William Bache, of Christ Church, who graduated as Master of Arts on November 12, 1692.

WILLIAM DUANE.

Philadelphia.

Milton : "Paradise Lost" illustrated by George Cruikshank.—To Mr. Hunt's *Popular Romances of the West of England* (1865) is prefixed a drawing of Giant Bolster's stride of six miles, which puts the figure in perspective. In a P.S. to his letter of explanation Cruikshank says :—

"The first time that I put a *very large* figure in perspective was about forty years back, in illustrating that part of *Paradise Lost* where Milton describes Satan as

'Prone on the flood, extended long and large,
Lay floating many a rood.'

This I never published, but possibly I may do so one of these days."

Was this illustration to Milton ever published, and if so, when ?   William George Black.
1, Alfred Terrace, Hillhead, Glasgow.

The Name Skelhorn.—From what source was the name Skelhorn derived ? What is its probable meaning, and to what race or country does it belong ?   Inquirer.

St. Valentine.—I have read the following in the *Contemporary Review*. Is it the fact ?—

"Valentine has nothing to do etymologically with St. Valentine, but comes from *Galantins*, a Norman word for a lover."   Clericus Rusticus.

Authors of Books Wanted.—

A Generall Treatise of Serpents, Divine, Morall, and Naturall.—The epistle dedicatory, of which a fragment remains, is addressed "To the Reverend and Right Worshipfvll Richard Neile, D. of Divinity, Deane of Westminster, Maister of the Savoy, and Clearke of the King his most excellent Maiesties Closet."

Frederic Wagstaff.

[Dr. *Neale* was Dean of Westminster 1605-10.]

The affianced one. By the author of *Gertrude.* Lond., Bull. 1831. 12mo. 3 vols.   ʃ

Albany: a novel. By the author of *Beau Monde.* Lond., A. K. Newman, 1819. 12mo.

Alice Maine: a true tale. By A. W. D. Lond., 1842. 12mo.

An Alpine tale, suggested by circumstances which occurred towards the commencement of the present century. By the author of *Tales from Switzerland.* Lond., Westley, 1823. 12mo. 2 vols.

Ambition: a practical essay. By Beppo Cambrienze. Published by Cadell & Davies, Strand, London. Swansea, printed by T. Jenkins. 1819. 8vo. pp. viii-54.

R. T.

Authors of Quotations Wanted.—

" *The Art of Book-keeping.*

How hard when those who do not wish
To lend (that's give) their books
Are snared by Anglers (folks who fish)
With literary hooks,—
Who call and take some favourite tome,
But never read it through ;
Thus they commence a set at home
By making one at you.
I, of my ' Spencer ' quite bereft,
Last winter sore was shaken ;
Of ' Lamb ' I've but a quarter left,
Nor could I save my ' Bacon,' " &c.   A. R.

" Hayle blessed Virgin, mother to thy Syre,
Virgin which shalt bring foorth thy Maker deere :
Him that gave life to thee thy selfe shalt beare,
And with thy breast shalt feede thy nourisher."

These lines are in a book of quaint prints of New Testament history, printed at Amsterdam by Cornelis Danckertz about 250 years ago.   J. R. Dore.

" The greatest happiness which a man can possess, to have the power of doing good."   Beta.

Replies.

"GIVE PEACE IN OUR TIME."
(5th S. ix. 148.)

I cannot see my way to your correspondent's difficulty. To my mind the meaning is clear upon the surface, independent of which it is supported by the strongest Scriptural authority. Thus Hezekiah said to Isaiah, " Is it not good if peace and truth be in my days ?" (2 Kings xx. 19) ; and Jehoshaphat prays, "We have no might against this great enemy that cometh against us ; neither know we what to do ; but our eyes are upon thee" (2 Chron. xx. 12). " The precise meaning " is, no doubt, that which the words in their literal sense convey—"in our time," that is, during the time in which we live; and the petition is almóst a parallel to that in the Lord's Prayer, "Give us this day our daily bread." And it no more follows, because we pray for peace only "in our time," that we do not desire it also for them who come after us, than because we ask merely for bread *for the day* that we do not wish that we may have it the day after. The *present* alone is ours—the future rests with God.

As for the "unfortunate resemblance" (is it not rather an unfortunate expression?), it only holds so far as all qualities coming under the same category must, more or less, resemble one another. But the likeness is with a difference. The peace here prayed for is an *outward general* peace, whether of the Church alone or the world at large. But that of the benediction, "the peace which passeth understanding," is an *inward personal* peace—that which "keeps the heart and mind in the knowledge and love of God." Still, though not identical, it has not only a "resemblance" to the former, but is as intimately and necessarily connected with it as cause is with effect. For as "wars and fightings" come from the "lusts that war in our members" (James iv. 1), so, *per contra*, does peace *outward* come, to any extent, from a corresponding principle *within*. And it is when this shall have become universal and pervading that men "will beat their swords into ploughshares, and their spears into pruning hooks, and learn war no more" (Isaiah ii. 4).

I know of no "assigned reason for the urgency of the petition" beyond what may be gathered from the Scriptures, either directly or by implication; such as "Pray for the peace of Jerusalem," &c. (Ps. cxxii. 6); "I exhort, therefore, that . . . . prayers . . . . be made for kings . . . . that we may lead a quiet and peaceable life," &c. (1 Tim. ii. 1, 2); with many passages of a like nature.

"There need be no anxious desire for peace" (in this I entirely agree with JABEZ), nor yet for anything else, and *ought* not to be, because we are strictly warned against it; but this surely "in reason's ear," and to our ordinary common sense, is no reason why we should not pray for peace, because the Almighty fighteth for us. If so, there would be no need of prayer at all; since, as the "Giver of *all* good," and as "knowing our necessities before we ask," we might set ourselves at ease, and leave him to do with and for us as he would. But as we are *commanded* to ask that we may receive, and *told* that "we have not because we ask not," we may be certain that prayer *for all things* is a duty the most positive and incumbent upon us.

It is incorrect to place these petitions in the "magnificent Litany" of our Church. They are not there, but in the versicles which immediately precede the second collect in the Order of Morning and Evening Prayer. They are, moreover, of very high antiquity, having had use in the Church upwards of one thousand years. Palmer (*Origi: Eccl.*) thus speaks of them:—

"The versicles which follow the Lord's Prayer : described by Amalarius in A.D. 820 (Amal., *De C* lib. iv. c. 4), and they are found in the Anglo-Sa: offices (*Appendix to Hickes's Letters, ad primam*). Th varied, however, in different Churches of the West, e: where the same prayers in general were used; but our verses and responses are found in the ancient rit of the English churches, both before and after t Norman Conquest; and they occurred in the same pl: which they occupy at present."

EDMUND TEW, M.A.

It is a delicate and difficult matter to touch up points of theology without provoking a cont: versy or stirring other questions. I deprecate bo and write merely from a literary point of illust: tion of two passages. What an antiphon is to t psalm this versicle with its response is to t collects for peace, for grace to live well, and : aid against perils. It breathes the same spirit the "Da propitius pacem in diebus nostris" in t Missal, on which Albinus wisely comments. T Church prays for temporal, that there may be hindrances to her spiritual, peace:—

"Ecclesia deprecatur '*pacem in diebus nostris*,' qu et post nos alii, et post ipsos alii usque ad finem sec similiter orabunt. Cur autem ipsam pacem postul subjungit, scilicet, 'ut ope' [id est, auxilio et protectio 'misericordiæ Dei adjuti,' quantùm ad interiorem ligionis devotionem pertinet '*simus* semper à pecc: liberi': quantùm ad exteriorem pacem, simus 'et omni perturbatione securi.'"—*De Divinis Officiis*, 79,

It was also said on certain days "ad Vespe: et Laudes," and reminds one of the "dones pac: protinus" in the "Veni Creator."

The same thought recurs elsewhere in our s: vices, for instance, in the Collect for the Seco Sunday after Epiphany and in that for the Fi: Sunday after Trinity: "Qui cœlestia simul terrena moderaris . . . pacem Tuam nostris conce temporibus"; "Da nobis ut mundi cursus pacif *nobis* Tuo ordine dirigatur, et ecclesia Tua tra quillâ devotione lætetur." *Nobis* is not represent in the Prayer Book version.

I must observe that this versicle occurs as o of "the suffrages next after the Creed," and not the "magnificent Litany." It also led Burn thinking of "wars and tumults," into one of l numerous blunders, which was corrected by t learned Bishop Lloyd, of Oxford. The meaning the response seems to be suggested by Ps. lix. l Vulg., "Da nobis auxilium quia vana sal hominum"; and more directly by 2 Chr: xxxii. 8, "Cum eo brachia carnea: nobiscu autem Dominus Deus noster ad præliandu prælium nostrum."

On the Pax Dei, which is peculiar to the Engli service and taken literally from the Epis. to t Philippians, iv. 7, the best commentary is th given by a Spanish writer, summarizing St. Thomas Aquinas:—"La tranquilidad de conciencia, que nace de una viva esperanza en Dios, servira como de una salvaguardia á vuestros espiritus, para que, mediante la gracia de Jesu Christo, no abandoneis jamás el camino de la verdad." Νοῦς is equivalent to "humana cogitatio," as the Collect for the Sixth Sunday after Trinity renders "Qui diligentibus Te bona invisibilia præparasti . . . quæ omne desiderium superant," "Such good things as pass man's understanding . . . which exceed all that we can desire"; recurring to 1 Cor. ii. 9 (Is. lxiv. 4), "Eye hath not seen," "Nec in cor hominis ascendit quæ preparavit Deus iis, qui diligunt Illum," so my Spanish commentator says, "Las fuerzas naturales del hombre no puedan comprehendar esta sabiduría, que se contiene en la doctrina del Evangelio, y que Dios de toda eternidad ha preparado para la gloria de sus fieles." There is no conflict with human "reason" or reasoning; the Latin version is "quæ exuperat omnem sensum."

MACKENZIE E. C. WALCOTT.

It is true that the exact relation between this versicle and response is not perhaps quite clear at first sight. But it may be explained in two ways: 1. By giving to the response a more general sense than JABEZ appears to give; that is, by applying it, not to the particular help to be sought in the wars against which the versicle prays, but to the general help to be sought at all times and in all misfortunes. God only fights for us, he only defends us against evil and gives us good; therefore he only can give us peace in our time. 2. But the deeper and preferable explanation is this. The divine help promised to us is surely no reason whatever why we should take the less care to avoid any danger in which we may need that help, or why we should pray the less earnestly against the danger. Nay, rather, the great goodness of God in promising us that help of which we are so utterly unworthy should give us a stronger motive still; for the promise is not unconditional, but is to be claimed, the help promised asked for, and the danger in which we need it struggled and prayed against. In the same way we say in the Psalm, "There is mercy with thee, *therefore* shalt thou be feared." God's mercy is·great, but we fear him none the less for that, because we know that we do not deserve that mercy; nay, we fear him the more, because we know it might be withdrawn from us. There can hardly be a better commentary on this versicle and response than the old proverb, "God helps those *who help themselves*." The religious proverbs of this class are good and true; and if we could be so unconventional, they would supply us priests with admirable texts for sermons.

In respect of JABEZ'S suggestion about "some

clause wrongly omitted in revision": if he will look at the original Latin in Blunt's *Annotated Prayer Book*, or at the original English in Keeling's *Liturgiæ Britannicæ*, he will see that it is groundless; and if he will consider the nature and character of a versicle and response, he will see that it is impossible.

CHARLES F. S. WARREN, M.A.

Bexhill.

There is no clause wrongly omitted on revision here, the words being a translation of the "antiphon" which formed part of the "memoria de pace" in the Sarum services, from which our "second collect for peace" is taken. "Da pacem Domine in diebus nostris. Quia non est alius qui pugnet pro nobis nisi tu, Deus noster." As for the meaning of the phrase, we do not assign God's fighting for us as the reason why we dread war, but as the reason why we seek peace only at his hands. "Si vis pacem para bellum," says an adage often quoted in these days. It is because God fights for us and defeats all our enemies that we enjoy peace. As for the words "in our time," I suppose we may paraphrase them, "Whatever thy providence hath provided for future, grant to us now peace." Hezekiah, when he heard of the judgments upon his house and people, was yet thankful that there would be peace and truth in his days (Is. xxxix. 8). I suspect the words are from some part of the Latin Bible, though I cannot succeed in finding their equivalents in our version.

A. C.

Dickinson on the Prayer Book has the following remarks on this versicle :—

"The clauses, 'Give peace in our time, O Lord;' 'Because there is none other that fighteth for us, but only thou, O God,' have suggested to some a difficulty. As has been said, 'The connexion between this petition and its response is not very obvious at first sight; the former evidently supposes a state of war (and war seldom ceased in the rude times in which these versicles were framed), while the latter implies that God alone can give the victory, which will secure peace as its result' (Procter). 'Give peace in our time,' &c. The emphatic word here is 'peace.' That is what we, as Christians, should desire; and we ask God to aid our cause, that we may have it. It is he who 'reaketh the bow and knappeth the spear in sunder,'who also 'maketh wars to cease in all the earth.' It is he who maketh even our enemies to be at peace with us; 'and therefore we commit our cause to him who 'hath 'the government upon his shoulder,' for he is also the 'Prince of Peace.'"

JOHN CHURCHILL SIKES.

Godolphin Road, Shepherd's Bush, W.

There is some want of an easily seen connexion between the petitions. I have always, however, read the ellipse in a way different from that which JABEZ suggests. "Give peace in our time, O Lord"; we appeal to thee, for thou only canst give peace, thou only art the Lord of Hosts. Then the words "in our time" would be not at all

"For there shall be peace and truth in my days," and "none other that fighteth for us," an echo of the words of Joshua xxiii. 10, "The Lord your God it is he that fighteth for you." There is a passage which has struck me as curiously parallel in Virgil, Æn., x. 18-19 :—

"O Pater, O hominum divumque æterna potestas—
Namque aliud quid sit, quod jam implorare queamus ?"

—"O father, O everlasting ruler of men and gods, for who else is there to whom we can appeal ?"

O. W. TANCOCK.

Sherborne.

This versicle with its response, not from the Litany, but from the Order of Morning and Evening Prayer, occurs in the Roman Breviary as the antiphon before the collect, "Deus a quo sancta desideria," &c. It runs as follows : "Da pacem, Domine, in diebus nostris, quia non est alius qui pugnet pro nobis, nisi tu, Deus noster." This citation will perhaps furnish an answer to the questions that JABEZ has raised. The expression "in our time" then represents "in diebus nostris." The assigned reason for the urgency of the petition is seen to be this, that there is none other *to fight for us*, and therefore none other that can give us peace by subduing our enemies, but he to whom the prayer is addressed. Our translation, by rendering the words "qui pugnet pro nobis" as "that fighteth for us," has passed over the force of the subjunctive mood, and thus obscured the connexion between the two clauses of the petition. It will also be evident from the above that no clause has been wrongly omitted on revision, as JABEZ has suggested. C. H. MAYO.

Long Burton.

I fail to see the difficulty which JABEZ and others, as I know, find in this petition and its response. Surely it means, "Give peace in our time"=in our lives, "O Lord"; because there is none other that fighteth for us"—and therefore no other can give us peace by vanquishing our enemies. How far it is wise or desirable to pray for temporal peace is a separate question, and scarcely suited to your columns. It always strikes me as painfully resembling a petition for a delay of the Lord's coming. HERMENTRUDE.

I presume that JABEZ alludes to the Litany of the Established Church. I am not acquainted with it ; but if he will refer to the "Officium Parvum Beatæ Mariæ Virginis, ad usum Romanum," in any edition of the Roman Breviary, he will find these words in the commemoration "Pro Sanctis" at the end of Lauds and Vespers. The prayer runs thus :—

"Omnes Sancti tui, quæsumus Domine, nos ubique adjuvent: ut dum eorum merita recolimus, patrocinia sentiamus: et pacem tuam nostris concede temporibus: et ab Ecclesia tua cunctam repelle nequitiam," &c.

Horæ B. M. V. of the fifteenth century and
EQ
Athenæum Club.

"Give peace in our time, *because* there other that fighteth for us, but only thou." Church prayer has a strange sound to mode Surely the significance of the words mus changed. I find the passage also in Henry Prayer Book. Where can I find the ans this difficulty ? It must have struck many me. L. A

Athenæum.

I wonder to how many priests and deacor are bound to recite the passage twice a matins and evensong, any objection has oc Surely the "reason assigned" is to be ta a general expression of trust in God to " the right." So "Deliver us from evil, *fo* is the kingdom," &c. J. 1

Bp. Hatfield's Hall, Durham.

THE OXFORD AND CAMBRIDGE BOAT-RAC (5th S. ix. 246, 271, 280.)—The Christ racing boat, in which the Oxford crew pu Henley, June 10, 1829, was built by D King, of Oxford, as was every racing boat, best of my memory, during the four ; 1827, '8, '9, and '30—that I pulled in the Church boat, except the Exeter boat, which derstood was built at Saltash.

I am not aware that any drawing of th was taken, at any rate I never heard of it.

THOS. STANIFC

Storrs, Windermere.

BINDING OF THE ENGLISH DIALECT SO PUBLICATIONS (5th S. ix. 148, 196.)—Ther doubt but that the best way of binding cations of a society like the Early English the English Dialect Society is, in theory, every separate work in a separate volume. if a work extend only to a few pages, it nevertheless, if complete in itself and not to addition, be bound by itself and be I lettered with a title sufficiently distinctive. is the scientific and theoretical method.

But it often happens in practice that method is inconvenient, as multiplying the of volumes and the cost of binding. As extent to which the right rule should be through, it is simply impossible to give me a few general hints. It becomes a purely ; matter, and depends on the peculiar requi of the owner of the volumes. This being : only speak for myself, and say what I ha with my own books, with such slight amer as experience has dictated. I must prem I am merely "a working man," and pa regard to the outside of the book, but only aim at the convenience of getting at the inside as soon as possible. I also wish to avoid expense, and have to resort, in consequence, to the practice (wholly incorrect) of binding together as many of the publications as will comfortably go into one volume.

For brevity, I use the numbering of the publications as shown on the wrapper of No. 19, *i.e.* An Outline of the Grammar of the Dialect of West Somerset.

Nos. 1, 5, 6 make a volume of "Reprinted Glossaries."

Nos. 2, 8, 18 make up the "Bibliographical List." Together with these I have bound up all the reports, advertisements, &c. hitherto received, and a copy of Mr. Ellis's *Varieties of English Pronunciation*, containing the account of Glossic. The disadvantage is, that future reports will have to go somewhere else; but there is some advantage in having the old reports disposed of.

Nos. 3, 12, 9, and 13 (observe the order) make a volume of Original Glossaries, marked C. 1 to C. 7.

No. 4 may go by itself, or, conveniently enough, with Nos. 11 and 17.

No. 6* by itself. No. 15 by itself. But Nos. 14 and 16 (both Yorkshire) go together well enough.

No. 10 should wait for the present. So should No. 7, to go with No. 19, and the Glossary of West Somersetshire which is yet to come.

This reduces the whole set to seven volumes (complete), and leaves a few incomplete parts over. It is better not to *number* the volumes, but to *letter* them so as to show the contents.

WALTER W. SKEAT.

A FRIGHTFUL STORY (5th S. ix. 265.)—The story of the Russian countess who barks like a dog is partly true. She is a well-known lady.
D.

PUBLIC-HOUSE SIGNS (5th S. ix. 127, 174, 257.) —The tenacity with which mankind cling to a plausible idea or a favourite crotchet is most remarkable. More than thirty years ago I heard that the sign of the "Goat and Compasses" was a corruption of "God encompasseth us." I hear so now, and I suppose I shall hear it again thirty years hence, if I live so long, unless "N. & Q." will aid in stamping such nonsense out. I said then what I now repeat—that signs were used because nine-tenths of the people could not read; and to suppose, under these circumstances, that a sign would take the place of a legend, is the most preposterous suggestion that was ever propounded. These signs were primarily heraldic in honour of the lord of the soil or the patron; hence the un-lettered world was favoured with directions and sign-posts portrayed by chromatic illustrations of lions, dragons, bulls, stags, horses, goats, &c. Then, in addition, there were the cognizances of guilds, trades, and handicrafts. There is, or was, in Bermondsey, a public-house known by the sign of the "Three Compasses, the House of Call for Carpenters." Are we therefore to infer by a parity of reasoning that this sign was a corruption of the "Trinity encompasseth us"? There is one house in London bearing the sign of the "Goat and Star," and two that of the "Goat in Boots." Would any one dare to affirm that the star of the former alludes to Bethlehem? And I am very much afraid we should be obliged to make an irreverent interpretation of the "Goat in Boots."

What, then, is the common-sense view of the case? The Carpenters' Company was incorporated in 1476, and its arms were a chevron engrailed between three compasses sable. The company never appears to have had a crest. A publican who had already the sign of the "Goat," in honour perhaps of the house of Russell, may have been desirous of attracting the custom of the carpenters, and he added the arms of that guild; the sign would soon then fall into the "Goat and Compasses." Or, what is more probable, he of the "Goat," being a Free-mason, would append the emblems of the craft, the square and compasses—they may be seen on most public-houses now. And what could be more easy than for the goat and compasses to be combined in the sign, without the aid of a black-letter legend to lead the way and be corrupted?

At the back of Guy's Hospital, in Southwark, is the sign of the "Ship and Shovel," an hostelry that for generations and generations has been much affected and patronized by the medical students. Now would the sapient conjecturer who published the dogma about "God encompasseth us" (I call it dogma because it has become an article of faith with an unreasoning majority) have asserted that this sign, seeing its association with medical students, was a corruption of "Shape your scalpel," which is quite as near and as logical a conclusion as the conversion of the goat? No; the simple solution is that the public-house being near the wharves and granaries in Tooley Street, where the corn-meters and corn-porters most did congregate, the founder of the institution to obtain their custom doubtless hoisted the emblems of their employment. Good beer and skittles subsequently attracted the alumni of St. Thomas's and Guy's, and not an aphorism of any famed operator.

In conclusion, permit me to say that to endeavour to find a profound, a mythical, or a religious interpretation for any sign that the humour or ingenuity of a Boniface may have set up by which to advertise his calling or to attract his thirsty customers, appears idle, absurd, and an evidence of a perverted ingenuity.
CLARRY.

"THE NEW WHOLE DUTY OF MAN" (5th S. viii. 389, 515 ; ix. 99, 176.)—Who was the author of the *New Whole Duty of Man* and the *New Week's Preparation?* I am unable to say, but that they were both originally published by Edward Wicksteed, at the "Black Swan" in Newgate Street, near Warwick Lane, there is no doubt. The *New Whole Duty* was first issued in 1741, and the copy I have seen contains an advertisement to the effect that the *New Week's Preparation* was published in two parts, of which the first had then reached a second edition, and the two parts might be purchased separately or bound in one volume. In 1742 Wicksteed was the publisher of a St. Asaph visitation sermon preached by Dean Powel, at the end of which are advertised both the books under discussion, of which the *New Week's Preparation* is stated to be "The Fourth Edition, very much enlarged and improved." The publisher further adds :—

" *Pray observe* this *carefully.*

" The *Spurious* Editions of this Book being *very imperfect* as well as *incorrect,* and consequently a great *Abuse* and *Imposition* upon the Publick ; the *Proprietor* EDWARD WICKSTEED thinks it necessary to *distinguish* such Copies as are *Correct* and *Genuine,* by subscribing his Name to this Notice upon the Back of the *Title-Page.*
" EDWARD WICKSTEED."

Wicksteed was also the original publisher of Hoppus's *Practical Measuring,* 1736. In 1718 he was a bookseller at Wrexham. At what precise date he left that town for the busier life of the metropolis I am not prepared to state. He was, however, from 1730 to 1736, in partnership with Thomas Ward in Inner Temple Lane, and from the latter date till 1742 was a publisher on his own account at the "Black Swan," as above mentioned. This is all I have as yet been able to discover about him, and shall feel obliged to any reader of " N. & Q." who can furnish us with the date of his death or further particulars of his antecedents.

W. H. ALLNUTT.
Oxford.

I have a copy printed by Roger Norton for John Baskett, 1719, and a second part, *Private Devotions for Several Occasions,* London, printed by W. Burton for John Baskett, 1720. Was John Baskett the author of this work, or did John Baskett have it printed for the author ? AGA.

LONDON FOG (5th S. ix. 28, 134, 178.)—The pre-eminence enjoyed by London in respect of fogs is due to a variety of causes that are apparent to the most casual observer ; but there is one primary agency to which all others are of secondary importance, and that has but rarely obtained attention. The London fog consists of water, soot, sulphur, and ammonia, curiously blended; the mountain mist and the sea fog consist almost wholly of pure water in a state of minute mechanical division. That the burning of coal and coal gas, and the emanations from myriads of living creatures crowded into a small space, should aggravate the offensive and poisonous properties of the Lo[n] fog is natural and inevitable. But these are [i] contributories—they do not originate the fog ; add to it its distinguishing characteristics, make it a thing to be dreaded by all excep[t] most robust. The London fog is primarily a duct of the London climate, a feature of physical geography of the London basin, and valley of the Thames is the breeding ground of which, in the first instance, it arises. The trough of the river operates at times in condu[c] into and through the metropolis a body of air charged with more moisture than it can in solution. This moisture is in part precipit[a] and so rendered visible, and a further stage of precipitation gives it the character of a mou[n] mist, that may not only be seen, but felt as a deposit that wets the beard and forms a fil[t] humidity on all rough woollen garments. this extreme precipitation is of rare occurr[e] for the atmosphere is not often still enough to mote it, the movement being much greater appears, even when the fog is densest and t appears to prevail a dead and a deadly c Proximity to the sea and the immensity of trough (which includes marshes and flats as as the river itself) account both for the abun[d] humidity and its continual movement onw usually from east to west or from west to ea[s] the general direction of the river and the low l[i] on either side of it. Observation of the phenom[e] will soon show that in intensity it does not respond with the periodical lighting of the but with the periodical movement of the tid the river. If we ignore the tide-table, it appear that the fog observes no rule in going coming, for at one time it will clear off in forenoon and thicken again in the evening, an another the order of events will be reversed. the tide-table will throw direct light upo[n] variations, and as a matter of course it is al[w] subject to instant dissipation when a frie breeze springs up and saves us from asphyxia. there is not much information available on subject, it may be proper to say that in *Pictorial World* of Nov. 24, 1877, I have deavoured both to explain the origin of a Lo[n] fog and indicate how its worst features mig[h] considerably mitigated and perhaps prevented
SHIRLEY HIBBER[T]

BETWEEN DOVER AND CALAIS (5th S. ix. 26 The usual means of transit between 1770 and are rather graphically described by M. La C[o] in his *Observations sur Londres et ses Envi avec un Précis de la Constitution de l'Anglete sa Décadence,* a book which went through editions before 1778. I translate the pa which will answer part of MR. MASON'S q although it does not clear up the doubt whether any list of passengers was taken in the last, as I believe it has been during the greater part of the present, century :—

"The packet boats cross *daily;* they are safe and their captains well known. Those from Calais to Dover are English. They only charge ten shillings, but they put you to further charges by obliging you to get into a boat a mile from shore whenever you do not arrange with the captain to land you at his own expense and risk. If you are rich you can have a little vessel to take you over for five louis, and land you at the harbour without further charge.

"You must give the sailors (of the packet boats) half-a-crown for drink, without which portmanteaux, night-caps, canes, pistols, eatables, and, above all, bottles of Burgundy, become invisible. Arrived at length in harbour, one is surrounded by the inquisitive, visitors, Custom House spies, and English and French innkeepers. The safest plan is to call for Mr. Marié, a big, good-looking, and very honest man, who will accompany you to the Custom House, and help in having your trunks searched. By giving the searcher (if he be alone) five shillings he will get things over for you very quickly, if you are not suspected of having hidden goods either on your person or in your carpet bag.

"Mr. Marié undertakes to pay porters and other small expenses of the packet boats, for every one wishes to have money to drink without having done anything for you. Arrived at Mr. Marié's house you take tea, and before supper time you can walk about the town and harbour. Then you start at one in the morning, either by Mr. Marié's diligence or by the mail. When there are as many as three travellers the mail is the quicker and cheaper; the coach (diligence) costs twenty shillings, luggage fourpence a pound. The chambermaid, the waiter, coachman and guard, breakfast and dinner, come to twelve or fifteen shillings. Thus the expense from Dover to London comes to about 2*l*. 17*s*. when all is reckoned up."

La Combe's book furnishes many interesting particulars about London and Englishmen a century ago. But these are not *à propos* of the query, to which this is partly an answer.

FREDK. HENDRIKS.

DEMOGRAPHY (5th S. ix. 247.)—The propriety of this title as indicating a branch of the science of man was discussed at some of the meetings of the Paris Anthropological Society in 1876. On April 20 of that year a paper was read by Dr. Topinard on "Anthropology, Ethnology, and Ethnography," and in the discussion which followed M. Dally proposed the substitution of Demography for Ethnography ; but it was shown by M. Broca that this term had been invented by Achille Guillard to express the statistics of the human race ("la statistique humaine"), and that it had therefore already a special connotation. In the discussion on June 1, following upon a paper by M. A. Hovelacque on "Ethnology and Ethnography," the question was again raised. Littré was cited as giving the following account of Demography : "La description des peuples quant à la population considérée suivant les âges, les professions, les demeures," &c. (*Dict. de la Langue Française*). But M. Lagneau, who quoted Littré,

also pointed out that the terms Ethnology, Ethnography, and Demography were almost synonymous in their etymological signification. It would seem to result from these discussions that it is open to the new Moscow professor either to be a teacher of anthropology, or simply an exponent of the results arising from study of the statistics of the Russian people, the "Demos" among whom he dwells. But it appears to me most probable, from the fact of Moscow being the centre of the Pan-Slavist idea in a scientific as well as a political sense, that the occupant of the new chair of Demography will principally devote himself to Anthropology.

C. H. E. CARMICHAEL.

New Univ. Club.

GIPSIES IN ENGLAND (5th S. ix. 149.)—The Gipsies landed in this country early in the reign of Henry VIII. They appear to have had some difficulty in settling here, for by 22 Hen. VIII. cap. 10, after reciting, "forasmuch as before this time divers and many outlandish people calling themselves Egyptians, using no craft nor feat of merchandise, have come to this realm," &c., it is enacted that thenceforth "no such person be suffered to come within this the king's realm under certain penalties, and that the Egyptians then in this realm have monition to depart within sixteen days after proclamation of the Act."

JOHN CHURCHILL SIKES.

Godolphin Road, Shepherd's Bush, W.

"The first we hear of them (the Gipsies) in England was in the year 1530" (Rees). See further Simson (Walter), *Hist. Gipsies*, Lond., edit. 1865, 8vo. ; Hoyland (J.), *Hist. Survey*, 1816, 8vo. ; Grellmann, *Versuch*, Gött., 1787.

R. S. CHARNOCK.

Junior Garrick.

MR. ARBER'S REPRINTS (5th S. ix. 243.)—A. J. M. decides, himself being a sort of Cer-berean triplet of proposer, seconder, and voter, that all reprints should be reprinted in fac-simile. But he either does not know, or is unable to understand, that as Mr. Arber did do so in his "English Reprints," and does do so in other works still, he must have had some reason for not doing it in the *English Garner*. This reason A. J. M. will find in Mr. Arber's prospectus. The "Garner" series is for the younger or for the general reader ; the other series, viz. "The English Scholar's Library," "The English Reprints," &c., all in their antique spelling, are for more advanced students, such, for instance, it may be, as A. J. M. Though no schoolmaster, I know that those for whom the *Garner* is principally intended are deterred from such reading by the unaccustomed spelling, forms of letters, and interchanges of *u* and *v*. Besides, I see harm, and not good, in un-settling a young person's memory as to whether he should spell *city* as *cite, citye, citty, cittie,* or -*cittye,* causing him to be refused a good situation "because he is an ill-bred lout."

A. J. M. is also strongly opposed to its being a "miscellany." One might content oneself with avowing a belief that its intents are thereby greatly promoted, as well as its charms, and that all palates, or the same palate at different times, will find a relish. But Mr. Arber's published intent suffices as an answer. For myself (one against one) I like it both as a miscellany and as a very excellent one, spite even of A. J. M.'s aversion (I presume as an out-and-out teetotaller) to seeing a "merchant's wine bill"—which it is not—side by side with a bridal ballad.

A. J. M.'s third objection is to the accents. One who has not seen the book will probably, from the description, conceive pages peppered with accents of all kinds, acute, grave, and circumflex—nay, even add the marks of the long and short quantities. What is the case? In English the past -*ed* is rarely pronounced as a separate syllable, but for emphasis, rhythm, or necessity poets have the licence of making it one. And now-a-days we mark this for distinction's sake -*èd*. Is this "a monstrous and criminal innovation"? It may be unnecessary to A. J. M.'s poetic ear, but I know that its absence would baulk many in reading the line. I open, say, at *Astrophel and Stella,* and find one example *(lovèd)* on the second page, and have gone on to the ninth without finding another. But its rarity is its *raison d'être,* and many think this "vain invention" a real advance and benefit. A. J. M. might as well object to the possessive apostrophe, or to the present use of inverted commas to mark a quotation. BRINSLEY NICHOLSON.
306, Goldhawk Road.

GRIMALDI (5th S. ix. 208.)—Grimaldi, not an actor, but a pantomimist, came to England as dentist to Queen Charlotte in 1760. It was he who during the Gordon riots assured the mob that in his house there was "no religion at all." At that time he resided in a front room on a second floor in Holborn, not far from, and on the same side as, Red Lion Square. The anecdote is related by Henry Angelo in his *Reminiscences* (vol. ii. p. 152), who states that it was told to him by Grimaldi himself. The hero of this adventure was the father of the celebrated clown, who was born in Stanhope Street, Clare Market, in 1778. The memoirs of Joseph Grimaldi (edited by "Boz") furnish all the information your correspondent is likely to get, if not all he desires, on the subject of his inquiry. CHARLES WYLIE.

That quaint and sterling Shakesperean actor, the late John Pritt Harley, once at a Drury Lane Theatrical Fund dinner described our "Old Joe" as "the mortal Jupiter of practical joke—the

Michael Angelo of buffoonery, who if he was *Grim all-day* would surely make *you* chuckle at night."
HARRY SANDARS.

NAME OF ARTIST WANTED (5th S. ix. 107.)—What is the subject represented on the fan What school did the painter belong to? A answer to these questions might help in findin out his name. Nicolaus Capulus may be a fanc name. Without much effort of imagination though I confess it requires some, we may suppos a genial and skilful artist, after a campaign i which he may have been wounded, spending hi time in more peaceable quarters, and relaxing wit drawing. The knight or horseman ("eques"), afte handling the sword ("capulus") successfull ("nicolaus"), now handles the pencil, and does no care to have his true name inscribed on such trifling thing as a fan(?). GEO. A. M.
Washington, D.C.

THE ANCIENT BARONY OF COURTENAY OF OKE HAMPTON (5th S. ix. 268.)—I think I can giv MR. STANDERWICK some satisfactory evidence tha the rightful heirs to this ancient barony are th Vyvyans of Trelowarren, Cornwall. My uncle however, Sir R. R. Vyvyan, Bart., of Trelowarrel has never attempted to get the title revived in h favour, although I believe he possesses the nece sary pedigrees, &c., to substantiate his claim. I Burke's *Peerage and Baronetage,* p. 1220, col. art. "Vyvyan," it will be seen that "John Vyvya mar. Elizabeth, eldest dau. of Sir Hugh Courtena and one of the co-heiresses of Edward Courtena Earl of Devonshire, and hence lineally descended &c. This marriage took place *circa* 1520. M uncle, when M.P. for Okehampton (1831), pu chased the ruins of the old castle at that place, being thought at the time that he would endeavo to revive the title, but although pressed by mar relatives and friends, he made no attempt to do s It is through Eliz. Courtenay that the Vyvya claim would proceed.

I append my address, should MR. STANDERWIC wish to write to me on the subject.
EDWARD R. VYVYAN.
142, Queen's Road, W.

AN ANCIENT LEADEN COFFIN (5th S. ix. 248.)- The probability is that the coffin found at Cra ford, Kent, is Roman. The escallop is a commo ornament on coffins of this kind. For informatic on this subject refer to Mr. Roach Smith's *Co lectanea Antiqua,* vol. iii., where there is a exhaustive article on it, and an excellent engra ing of several specimens of these antique relic It is therein stated that in all such coffins found this country the lid is made to overlap the und part by an inch. This may help to test tl accuracy of the suggestion now offered.
T. W. W. S.

"COPPER" (5th S. ix. 187.)—Is not this word connected with the Aryan root *kop*, which appears in the same form as a Scandinavian word for "head," and from which the modern Ger. *kopf* is derived? From this root also are traced the Greek κεφαλη and the Latin *caput*. If I am right in this conjecture, the word *kopper* (or "copper," as the author of the passage quoted by MR. ALLNUTT spells it) can easily be applied, as it seems to be in Hall's translation of Homer, to a blow on the head. The words "header" and "head" would then be synonymous with *kopper* and *kop*.
NICOLAI C. SCHOU, Jun.
Chorlton-cum-Hardy, near Manchester.

"MEMOIRS OF WELFORD" (5th S. viii. 89.)—The title-page of the book inquired for reads as follows :—*Memoirs of Welford ; to which are added several Poems and Songs*, Paisley, printed by J. Neilson, 1816.   ANSELM KEANE.

COTGREAVE PEDIGREE (5th S. ix. 189.)—From the description given by MR. BLAYDES of the letter in his possession, I dare venture to say that it bears the signature of that maker of pedigrees, William Sidney Spence.

The pedigree from which he offered to extract the few descents for his clients was generally described as "the work of the great Camden," or "of Randle Holme," from documents compiled by the great Camden," and it invariably contained an ancestor who was "slain while fighting" in some great battle. See "N. & Q.," 1st S. ix. 221, 275, and 3rd S. i. 8, 54, 92.   H. S. G.

UNENCLOSED COMMONS (5th S. ix. 268.)—A. J. K. should consult the Return presented to the House of Commons (1874, No. 85) relating to Commons and Common Field Lands in each Parish of England and Wales. The following are the headings of the return :—

Parish, township, district, &c.
Total area.
Area of commons : Apparently capable of cultivation —Apparently mountain, or otherwise unsuitable for cultivation.
Area of common field lands.
G. LAURENCE GOMME.
[E. W. F. next week.]

THE WHITEHEAD FAMILY OF SADDLEWORTH (5th S. ix. 248.)—There is a note about this family in the *Manchester School Register*, vol. i. p. 56 (Chetham Soc., vol. lxix.). I have a strong suspicion that the Whiteheads of Saddleworth were a branch of the Whiteheads of Nateby, in Garstang, co. Lanc., and shall be glad to communicate with AD FINEM FIDELIS direct if he will favour me with his address.   H. FISHWICK, F.S.A.
Carr Hill, Rochdale.

WEST INDIES : BARBADOES (5th S. ix. 249.)—According to some notes I have, taken probably from one of the histories of Barbadoes or from the State Papers in the Record Office, the first English vessel touched at Barbadoes in 1605, the second in 1625, the third, sent by Charles I., in 1627, the fourth in 1628.

There is a list of original landowners in Barbadoes in 1638 in a little book in the British Museum.

This reply is a very insufficient one to MR. MASON's queries, and many persons would, I believe, be thankful to have them carefully and fully answered.   G. F. B.
Westminster.

CHIOGGIA (5th S. ix. 49, 138, 234, 272.)—I am much obliged to A. J. M. for his courtesy in complying with my request that he would give us some account of Chioggia. May I trespass just once more on his good nature? He says that, as a proof that Italian names are not invariably pronounced as written, the Giudecca in Venice is pronounced *Zuecca*. This bears upon a passage in Dante, and is therefore doubly interesting. The last belt of the ninth circle of the *Inferno*, in which the great poet has condemned Brutus and Cassius to unmerited punishment, is called Giudecca. Would an Italian in reading this aloud pronounce it *Zuecca*, or is this only the Venetian pronunciation?   JONATHAN BOUCHIER.

SERVANTS' HALL FORFEITS (5th S. ix. 188.)—Our original copy was lettered in oil on a panel, and I think the line ran :—

"He that breaks the least command
Shall forfeit burning in the hand,
Or to the butler pay a penny."

This had given offence, for the word "burning" was nearly scratched out ; and in getting a few copies printed (about forty years since to give to a friend), that line only was altered as below :—

"*Rules to be observed at this House.*
The orders of this room are such
That no one eat or drink too much ;
Yet spare not either bread or meat,
But cut no more than you can eat.
Let no idle word be spoke,
Yet merry be and pass a joke ;
But yet what joke may happen here
Shall not be spoken of elsewhere.
Swear not, nor tell a thing untrue,
For each reproof severe is due.
Whatever bones be left at meat
Let them be saved for dogs to eat ;
Not to be cast upon the floor,
But to be placed without the door.
He that lies the long'st in bed
Shall serve the rest with beer and bread ;
Not if he 's ill, but only they
Who idly sleep their time away.
The butler must enforce this rule,
And all obey (nor, like the mule,
Too stubborn be), for he acts right
His master's wishes ne'er to slight.
This room must neat and clean be kept,

Each morning *early* will be swept.
That each in turn the cloth remove,
This is a plan I much approve.
The hours for meals you must attend;
Upon the bell's call then depend.
Men in the kitchen must not go;
They plague the cook they surely know;
She serves your meals, then be content;
Vex her but once, you 'll soon repent.
He that breaks the least command
Shall not be punished by the hand,
But to the butler pay a penny :
Mind, I 'll not be disobeyed by any.
The sum by him is to be spent
And all the rest to be content,
Or given unto them that need it.
So this is all—and mind you heed it."

P. P.

ROYAL AND IMPERIAL FAMILIES OF FRANCE
(5ᵗʰ S. ix. 189, 236.)—*A Genealogical Chart showing all the Branches of the Royal Family of Bourbon*, by Fredk. J. Jeffery, F.G.H.S., published by
J. Camden Hotten, London, 1869, will probably
be of service to your correspondent.   H. M.

ANNIBAL CARACCI (5ᵗʰ S. ix. 27, 75.)—Of the
"Three Marys" there is no duplicate by the artist.
It is 3 ft. 7 in. long by 3 ft. high, is in splendid
preservation, and shows very little trace of injury
or repair. The "Three Marys" was lent in 1857
by the late Earl of Carlisle to the Manchester Art
Treasures Exhibition, where it was a very popular
attraction, the attendance of a policeman being
generally required on busy days to make people
pass on. Besides the old engraving by Rouillet
mentioned by G. A. M. there is another, also in
line, about the same size and date ; and a third in
line was published during the Art Treasures
Exhibition. There is also a mezzotint, one of the
series called "Gems of Art," and it has been
engraved in one of the annuals. In connexion
with this subject it may be worthy of note that
the price paid for the entire Orleans collection of
Italian and French paintings was 43,000*l.* They
were each carefully valued by Mr. Bryan ; and,
after the original purchasers had made choice of
the pictures each wished to keep, the whole was
publicly exhibited for six months. The sales to
the public during the exhibition amounted to
31,000 gs., the receipts from the exhibition and
sale by auction of the residue reached 10,000*l.*
more, so that the paintings selected by the three
noblemen, the Duke of Bridgwater, Earl Gower,
and the Earl of Carlisle, now forming the gems of
the Ellesmere, Stafford, and Castle Howard galleries, and whose united value, according to Mr.
Bryan's estimate, was 39,000 gs., really cost the
fortunate buyers comparatively nothing.

G. D. T.
Huddersfield.

A PSEUDO-CHRIST (5ᵗʰ S. viii. 488 ; ix. 17.)—
The personation of Christ is apparently not a

---

unique occurrence. Witness the following fanatical conspiracy. An article entitled "Fanaticism
in Cheapside, A.D. 1591," by Mr. Fredk. Ross,
appeared in the *City Press* of Oct. 7, 1876, the
main features of which are as follows :—

In the early part of the year 1591 a maltster,
named Hackett, "gave out that he was commanded in a vision to assume the sovereignty of
Europe, and eventually that he was Jesus Christ
himself." He had duped into the belief of these
assertions two men, Coppinger and Arthington,
the former of whom he nominated his Prophet of
Mercy, the latter his Prophet of Judgment. Coppinger, who appears to have been more confederate
than dupe, hoped to reap some worldly advantage
by the connexion—to marry a rich widow, and
for the success of this object he and Hackett often
prayed together. He also pretended to have had
a vision in which it was revealed to him that
Hackett was the predestined king of Europe, and
that he and Arthington, his prophets, were to prepare the way for him. They accordingly went
together to anoint their king, who informed them
that

"he had already been anointed by the Holy Ghost, and
bade them go into the City and declare aloud that Jesus
Christ had come, with his fan in his hand, to purge and
judge the world ; and to tell the citizens that if they do
not believe the report, to come to Walker's house, by
Broker-wharf, and see him, and to kill him if they can."

The two prophets then proceeded to Cheapside
crying aloud, "Christ is come ! Christ is come !
Repent ye of your sins ; repent, and implore the
mercy of God." They then mounted upon a cart
near the cross, and proceeded to proclaim their
mission to the assembled citizens and 'prentices.
Their language soon became more inflammatory.
They inveighed bitterly against the queen and the
government,

"asserting that she and they were the enemies of God,
and the emissaries of the devil; that 'God had spewed
them out of his mouth'; and that by his command
they hereby formally deposed her and proclaimed
Hackett lord of the realm; further, that he should
eventually become king of the world."

The citizens, unable to stand tamely by and hear
such treasonous language levelled against their
beloved queen, hooted and yelled at the orators.
The proceedings coming to the knowledge of the
authorities, orders given for the apprehension
of the offenders, who, after being examined before
the Lord Mayor, were committed to Bridewell.

"Hackett, the pretended Messiah, was try'd and convicted at the Old Bailey of treason, put upon the rack,
and confessed all things, whence he was carried to the
place of execution in Cheapside, where, instead of showing the least sorrow for his crimes, he committed the
most horrid and execrable blasphemies against God, and
detestable imprecations against the queen and her
ministers ; and his associate, Coppinger, refusing all
manner of sustenance, dy'd the next day in Bridewell."

Arthington, on hearing of the execution of

Hackett, acknowledged himself deluded, and wrote imploring the Chancellor and Treasurer to intercede with the queen on his behalf. Her Majesty agreeing to a suspension of judgment, he was removed to the Ward Street Compter, where he published his *Recantation and Confession*. He was eventually pardoned and retired to his native place in Yorkshire. He was a member of an old Yorkshire family, seated for many centuries at Arthington of the Wharfe, of which they were lords of the manor.   G. Perratt.

The Bishops Yonge of Rochester (5th S. ix. 27, 111.)—I am induced by Mr. Woodward's note to ask whether further information can be given respecting the two bishops. From what family or families were they descended? Burke gives the coat, "Per saltire, az. and gu., a lion pass. guard. or," as having been granted by Dethick to "Young, Bishop of Rochester," and not as having been confirmed by him with an augmentation. If this statement be correct, those arms must have been granted to the second Bishop Yonge, Dethick's contemporary; but, if Mr. Woodward's account of the arms be the right one, is not a relationship between the two prelates proved by the sameness of their armorial bearings? It is worthy of notice that about the time of the first Bishop Yonge there was a family of that name resident at Bryn Yorkyn, co. Flint, and descended from Tudor Trevor, Lord of Hereford, of which was Morgan le Yonge, who bore "Gu., a toison or."   S. G.

"Inkle" (5th S. ix. 7, 153.)—Peter Pindar says in some lines put in the mouth of Canning's mother, *apropos* of her son's fortunate marriage:—

"The pride of the Scotts may be hurt
If they hear we sold bobbin and inkle."

I quote from memory, and with the impression that "inkle" here serves the exigencies of rhyme rather than the desire to express the extremity of contempt.   Gwavas.
Penzance.

Bread and Salt (5th S. ix. 48, 138.)—The custom of giving to a baby, on its first visit to a friend's house, bread, salt, an egg, and a silver coin, with occasionally a packet of sugar, is still observed in the West Riding of Yorkshire (Doncaster and Barnsley) and in the county of Durham. My children usually returned from their first excursion with quite a load of these provisions.
                    W. N. Strangeways.
Stockport.

Sikes and Sykes (5th S. viii. 468 ; ix. 154.)—Six is, I suppose, another form of this name. James Six, Esq., F.R.S., was a very distant connexion of mine. He published, as I see from Allibone, two or three small scientific papers. His only son, James Six, Fellow of Trin. Coll., Cam.,

Chancellor's Med. 1778, died at Rome 1786, æt. twenty-nine; and his daughter Mary married the late George May, Esq., of Herne, and had a large family.   C. F. S. Warren, M.A.
Bexhill.

Authors of Quotations Wanted (5th S. ix. 268.)—
"My true love hath my heart, and I have his."
The little poem of which the above is the first line is in Sir Philip Sidney's *Arcadia*, bk. iii. (edit. 1674), p. 357. Two of the three stanzas of which the poem consists are included in Mr. Palgrave's *Golden Treasury*. Mr. Palgrave in his preface says that the few instances in which he has omitted anything from a lyric are specified in the notes; but he has not always kept to this rule. There is no mention of the omission of the last verse in the above-mentioned poem of Sidney's, nor of the omission of a stanza in Wordsworth's lines suggested by a picture of Peel Castle in a storm.   Jonathan Bouchier.

See Dr. Grosart's edition of Sir P. Sidney, vol. ii. p. 254.   R. R.

Miscellaneous.

NOTES ON BOOKS, &c.

The Thirty-nine Articles of the Church of England. A Historical and Speculative Exposition. By Rev. Joseph Miller, B.D. (Hodder & Stoughton.)

It says a good deal for the zest with which the Lancashire intellect pursues any subject in which it becomes interested that Mr. Miller should have sprung out of what appears to have been a course of parochial lectures. We much fear that few parishes south of Trent would have cared for disquisitions concerning the "Principium quod" and the "Principium quo," and the dangers of Docetic and Monarchian leanings, however orthodox the lecturer might be. We hope that Mr. Miller will be encouraged to continue his work, of which the present volume is properly but the first instalment, dealing only with the first five Articles. His method of printing the Latin and English texts in parallel columns, with a foot-note embodying the source and the theological bearing of each Article, is very commendable. We observe that at p. 87 Mr. Miller appears to call the title "Theotokos" a "Eutychian or Monophysite heresy," and he is somewhat hard, it seems to us, on Monarchianism. For he does not point out that there is a sense in which the Eastern Church is strongly Monarchian, as any one who remembers or has studied the discussions at the last Bonn Conference would recognize. But of course the sense in which Oriental Churchmen press the one 'Αρχή is a sense not contradictory to the procession of the Spirit *through* the Son, as the language of their own doctors testifies. We cannot say that we altogether like some of Mr. Miller's terminology, which is often peculiar—we should prefer "factor" and "Levitical," for instance, to "moment" and "Levitual"; and there are some errata not comprised in Mr. Miller's list, which should be rectified in a future edition.

The Romans of Britain. By Henry Charles Coote, F.S.A. (F. Norgate.)

We wish heartily to recommend this book to the notice of our readers because, as a repertory of facts, it is invaluable, and because it takes up a phase of early English history which should not by any means be lost sight of. The author explains in his preface that the present work is a recension of his *Neglected Fact in English History;* and we feel sure that those who know this

before us. We are not, however, prepared to accept all Mr. Coote's conclusions, for to a great extent they are the conclusions of an advocate, and a powerful one, rather than of an impartial historian. With an ingenuity which is certainly remarkable he labours to prove, not only that English institutions are the lineal descendants of Roman institutions, but that Englishmen are descendants of a Roman population which once occupied Britain—a population made up of Latins and Latinized Belgic-Teutons. The fact of calling ourselves by a Teutonic name, English, goes for nothing with Mr. Coote —nay, is a positive error of about 1,300 years' standing. Mr. Coote complains of the excessive Teutonism of those historians who differ from him, and we, on the other hand, are inclined to complain of his excessive Romanism. He claims almost all our early history as in reality being, not English, but Roman. We think he claims too much, and does not pay sufficient attention to those scholars who can see our Teutonic element in our speech, in our land communities, and in our popular local institutions. But having said this much, we must bear favourable testimony to the real value of his researches. Let us particularly note the section devoted to municipalities. The details he supplies in support of his theory are numerous and, as a rule, accurate. This makes us the more surprised to find that on p. 267 he rests his assertion, that the hide already existed in Cornwall when that part of the country was first conquered by the Anglo-Saxons, upon a charter in the Codex Diplomaticus granting three *mansæ*, not *hidæ*, situate at Lesmanaoc and Pennarth, neither of which places can, so far as we know, be identified with modern localities. Does Mr. Coote identify them? Again, on p. 465, he founds the force of an argument, which to us seems quite capable of standing on its own merit, upon the fact of a charter of King Æthelbyrht not being dated, whereas upon turning to his reference we find that it bears date April 28, 604. In a book so full of valuable details such items as these must be considered in the light of blemishes. A few printer's errors should be corrected in a future edition, which is certain to be called for, and it should be noted that the title of Mr. Kemble's *Saxons in England* is wrongly given on p. 231.

The Place of Iceland in the History of European Institutions. Being the Lothian Prize Essay for 1877. By C. A. V. Conybeare, B.A. (Oxford and London, Parker.)

THE age which saw the colonization of Iceland by Norsemen seeking a refuge from the "overbearing of King Harold" was one of great activity throughout the whole Scandinavian race. Athens and Byzantium saw their keels and battle-axes no less than did fair Neustria and remote Thule. Light was the hair and bright were the cheeks of Jarl, the typical ancestor of the free man of noble birth among the Northern folk, who stood so high among men, and bore himself so doughtily, that between the earl and the king there was in those days a difference in little more than name. Therefore, in speaking of the "Republic" of Iceland, we must be careful to bear in mind that under that designation is comprised a state of society not antagonistic to that of other portions of the Scandinavian race, but itself the older form of that society in its purity, as it existed before the "overbearing of King Harold," with such local differences as the special circumstances of Iceland called forth. It is a picture well worth studying, were it only for the sake of the great jurist Njál and his noble life, so nobly spent for his country. Mr. Conybeare has treated an interesting subject carefully and with general moderation of tone. The real lesson which

excessive reverence for the letter of the law as contrasted with its spirit, or, as we might put it; the danger of a system of law untempered by equity. Some of the well-known general features of the history which Mr. Conybeare relates might with advantage have been abridged to make room for the expansion of this thesis, which he perceives but does not develope.

MR. C. BROWN has nearly ready for the press the *Annals of Newark-upon-Trent.* If any of our readers possess information relative to the past history of the town, and will communicate with Mr. Brown (30, Stodman Street, Newark), he will feel much obliged.

THERE is in the press (Pollard, Exeter), and will be published shortly, *The Plant-Lore and Garden-Craft of Shakspeare,* by Rev. Henry N. Ellacombe, M.A., Vicar of Bitton, Gloucestershire. In this work every passage will be quoted in which Shakspeare names any tree, plant, flower, or vegetable production.

IT has been proposed to complete, by public subscription, the restoration of the exterior of the North Transept of Westminster Abbey as a memorial to the late Sir George Gilbert Scott.

Notices to Correspondents.

We must call special attention to the following notice:—
ON all communications should be written the name and address of the sender, not necessarily for publication, but as a guarantee of good faith.

H. A. S.—The paragraph from *London in the Jacobite Times* shall be copied and forwarded so as to enable you to frame the query. The other matter was clearly a *lapsus calami.* Our publisher has secured the edition referred to, and of which you say you have a copy. It is now out of print. Bibliography is most certainly a favourite subject with the readers of "N. & Q."

WILLIAM BETHELL.—What does our correspondent think of this reading?—
" Virtue did strike my heart with wonder,
Beauty did wound my eyes with love,
And speech did charm my ears with delight."

J. K.—For information respecting the toast "Church and Queen," see 1st S. x. 146; 3rd S. vi. 91; xi. 517.

E. E. P. should consult a second-hand bookseller and a collector of old prints.

F. W. F.—Received with thanks. It shall be done as you wish.

S.—We shall be very glad to have the list of Mr. Collier's Reprints.

E. W. B. is thanked for his communication, which he will see has been anticipated, *ante,* p. 295.

H. G. GRIFFINHOOFE.—"Philpot Family" next week.

COL. J. H. JOLLIFFE and KINGSTON.—Letters sent.

ALPHONSE ESTOCLET.—Received. Next week.

JOHNSON BAILY.—Proof as soon as possible.

A. C.—See *ante,* p. 256.

NOTICE.

Editorial Communications should be addressed to "The Editor of 'Notes and Queries'"—Advertisements and Business Letters to "The Publisher"—at the Office, 20, Wellington Street, Strand, London, W.C.

We beg leave to state that we decline to return communications which, for any reason, we do not print; and to this rule we can make no exception.

LONDON, SATURDAY, APRIL 20, 1878.

CONTENTS.—N° 225.

ﬡotes.

DICE.

The siege of Troy is the date usually assigned for the invention of dice playing. Isidorus of Seville attributes it to a warrior of the name of Alea, from whom, he says, the game took its name :—

"Alea est ludus tabulæ inventa à Græcis, in otio Tro- jani belli, à quodam milite, nomine Alea, à quo et ars nomen accepit."—*Orig.,* l. xviii. c. 57.

He is followed in this by Hugo von Trumberg, a Ger- man poet of the beginning of the fourteenth century. In a poem which he entitles *Der Renner* he men- tions "Aber," probably a slip of the pen for "Aleo," which the rhyme requires, as the inventor of what he calls *Schachzabel,* "a game which gives rise to much sin and mischief":—

"Nun ist ein ander Spiel
Des Herren pflegen, von dem doch viel
Sünden und Schaden kommt gerne,
Schachzabel ich euch das Spiel nenne.
Das fand ein Ritter, hiess Aber,
Vor Troja, dess doch venig fro," &c.

Schachzabel, it is true, is often used to mean chess, but it is evident from the following passage, in which he enumerates the various *throws* and the "Sünden und Schaden" which follow them, that he refers to a game of chance played with dice :—

"Von Zincken quater Essen
Sigt mancher in Kummers-Fressen,
Von Zincken quater Dreyen
Mag mancher Waffen schreyen.

Von Zincken quater Duss
Hat mancher ein ungerathen Huss.
Von quater dreyen Zincken
Muss mancher Wasser trincken.
Von Zincken Dreyen und quater
Weint manches Mutter und Vater.
Von Zincken quater Duss und Sess
Muss Mege, Luckart und Agnes
Unberathen bleiben ; wann es lang thut
Ihr Vater, das erbarme Gott."

Suidas, though agreeing with Isidorus and Hugo as to the date of the invention, differs from them as to the inventor. Instead of the unknown Alea he mentions Palamedes, famous for his knowledge of mathematics and of astronomy. According to his interpretation of the game which he calls τάβλα, and which seems to have resembled the modern backgammon, the board represented the world, the dice-box heaven, whence all good and evil proceed. The passage is as follows in Wolf's translation :—

"Tabula nomen ludi ; hanc Palamedes ad Græci exer- citus delectationem magnâ eruditione atque ingenio invenit. Tabula enim est mundus terrestris, duodenarius numerus est Zodiacus, ipsa vero area, et septem in ea grana sunt septem stellæ Planetarum. Turris est altitudo cœli, ex qua omnibus bona et mala rependuntur."

To these authorities we may add Sophocles, who also attributes the invention of dice to Palamedes, in a play bearing the hero's name, and quoted by Eustathius as follows :—

οὐ λιμὸν οὗτος τόνδ' ἄπῶσε σὺν θεῷ
εἰπεῖν, χρόνου τε διατριβὰς σοφωτάτας
ἐφεῦρε φλοίσβου μετὰ κοπὴν καθημένοις
πεσσοὺς κύβους τε τερπνὸν ἀργίας ἄκος.

If, however, as is usually received, the Greek ἀστράγαλος and the Latin *talus* are the κύβος and the *alea* in their primitive form, we have the authority of Homer for fixing their origin at a time anterior to the Trojan War. It was after having slain the son of Amphidamas in a quarrel at dice that Patroclus was sent from home to be brought up with Achilles, in the house of Peleus :—

ἀλλ', ὁμοῦ ὡς ἐτράφημεν ἐν ὑμετέροισι δόμοισιν,
εὖτέ με τυτθὸν ἐόντα Μενοίτιος ἐξ Ὀπόεντος
ἤγαγεν ὑμέτερόνδ', ἀνδροκτασίης ὑπὸ λυγρῆς,
ἤματι τῷ, ὅτε παῖδα κατέκτανον Ἀμφιδάμαντος,
νήπιος, οὐκ ἐθέλων, ἀμφ' ἀστραγάλοισι
χολωθείς. *Il.* xxiii. 84-88.

Herodotus, however, differs essentially from the authors already quoted. He utterly ignores Pala- medes and the siege of Troy, and asserts that all the games that were played by means of the κύβος, of the ἀστράγαλος, and of the σφαίρα were invented by the Lydians. Stranger than this divergence from the generally received opinion is the origin which he assigns to these pastimes. It was not for recreation and amusement that the Lydians had recourse to them, but for the purpose of assuaging, or at least of forgetting, the pangs of hunger. Being reduced to half rations during a time of ramine, they hit upon the expedient of fasting one day and eating the next, and, in order to render this enforced abstinence less noticeable to their stomachs, of spending the whole of the fast day in the excitement of gambling :—

Φασὶ δὲ αὐτοὶ Λυδοὶ καὶ τὰς παιγνίας τὰς νῦν σφίσι τε καὶ Ἕλλησι κατεστεώσας, ἑωυτῶν ἐξεύρημα γενέσθαι. ἅμα δὲ ταύτας τε ἐξευρεθῆναι παρα σφίσι λέγουσι, καὶ Τυρσηνίην ἀποικίσαι, ὧδε περὶ αὐτῶν λέγοντες· ἐπὶ Ἄτυος τοῦ Μάνεω βασιλῆος σιτοδείην ἰσχυρὴν ἀνὰ τὴν Λυδίην πᾶσαν γενέσθαι· καὶ τοὺς Λυδοὺς τέως μὲν διάγειν λιπαρέοντας· μετὰ δὲ, ὡς οὐ παύεσθαι, ἄκεα δίζησθαι· ἄλλον δὲ ἄλλο επιμηχανᾶσθαι αυτῶν. ἐξευρεθῆναι δὴ ὧν τότε καὶ τῶν κύβων καὶ τῶν ἀστραγάλων καὶ τῆς σφαίρης, καὶ τῶν ἄλλεων πασέων παιγνιέων τὰ εἴδεα, πλὴν πεσσῶν. τούτων γὰρ ὧν τὴν ἐξεύρεσιν οὐκ οἰκηϊοῦνται Λυδοί. ποιέειν δὲ ὧδε πρὸς τὸν λιμὸν ἐξευρόντας· τὴν μὲν ἑτέρην τῶν ἡμερέων παίζειν πᾶσαν, ἵνα δὴ μὴ ζητέοιεν σιτία· τὴν δὲ ἑτέρην σιτέεσθαι, παυομένους τῶν παιγνιέων.—Lib. i. c. 49.

The original die of the ancients was, as has already been remarked, the *talus*, a small bone found in the foot joint of certain animals. According to Pliny's definition, "rectum in articulo pedis os est, ventre eminens concavo, in vertebra ligatum" (Pliny, b. ii. c. 46). Later on the *talus* used in playing was made in imitation of this bone, and consisted of six uneven and unequal sides. Of these six sides two were broad and flat, and bore the numbers one and six respectively. Ace was termed *canis* or *vulturius* by the Romans, and κνὼν or χῖος by the Greeks. Six, the highest and best throw, was called *Venus* and χῶος. Two narrower sides, of which the one was slightly concave, the other slightly convex, bore the four and the three respectively. The extremities were not marked by any figures, two and five not occurring in the game. Such is the explanation given by one of the commentators on Martial, ii. l. 14 :—

"Formam seu figuram talorum tute conjectare potes, cum ad similitudinem talorum, qui in pedibus animalium sunt, effecti dicantur, et maximè Leonis, nec rotundi planè nec quadrati. Sex habent latera, sed quatuor tantum in usu ludentium, duo quippe sunt incurva, ut illis talus vix posset insistere, consistit tamen aliquando rectus: duo illa incurva Græci κεραίασν, id est, antennas appellitant."—Raderus *ad Mart.*, ii. l. 14.

To this we may add Sabellicus's commentary on a passage in Suetonius :—

"Tali latera suum singula numerum faciebant, latus quod unitatem habuit Canis sive Canicula appellabatur, et quia minimus is erat numerus, damnosus erat. Latus huic oppositum Venus dicebatur sive Cous, senarium continens, qui omnium maximus, sex lucrificiebat nummos : reliqua duo Chius et Senio dicta, ternarium ille, hic quaternarium continens. Chius tres nummos, senio quatuor lucrantes. Binarius et senarius in talo non erat numerus."

The throw called Venus also received the Basilicus from being that which determined election of thè *rex convivii*, or master of the r Hence the allusion in Horace :—
"Quis udo
Deproperare apio coronas
Curatve myrto? Quem Venus arbitrum
Dicet bibendi?"   Horat., l. ii. od

To obtain the favour of a lucky cast it was cus ary for players to invoke the gods or somet their mistresses :—
"Talos arripio, *invoco almam meam nutricem* Herc
Jacto Basilicum."   Plaut., *Curcul.*, ii.

The lowest or unlucky cast was known as *dam canes*, an expression which we find in Propertiu
"Me quoque per talos Venerem quærente secund
Semper *damnosi* subsiluere *canes.*"
Prop., l. iv. eleg. v

To prevent cheating, or at least to render it easy, the dice were thrown *through* an instru which was variously termed *turricula, bu: fritillus.*

"Quærit compositos manus improba mittere talos
Si per me (turriculam) misit, nil nisi vota faci

This instrument was funnel-shaped, open at ends, and notched or grooved inside to preven dice from sliding evenly through. This exp the following passage in Ausonius :—

"Vidimus et quondam tabulæ certamine longo,
Omnes qui fuerant, enumerasse bolos,
Alternis vicibus quos præcipitante rotatu
Fundunt excisi per cava buxa gradus."

Amongst the Greeks these primitive dice : to have been considered childish. We are that Phraates, King of the Parthians, sent go dice to Demetrius, King of Syria, as a repr for his levity : "Regi Demetrio in opprob puerilis levitatis, taxillos aureos à rege Parthc fuisse datos (fertur)" (Joh. Sarisb., *de N Curial.*). The *tesseræ* or κύβοι were prec similar to the modern dice, and require no fu description. As regards the games in which were used, they seem to have been chiefly thr number, πλειστοβολίνδα, προαιρέσιμον, διαγραμμισμὸς. In the first of these, which usually played with three dice, the highest won the stakes. Three aces were the worst three sixes the best throw, and it was from game that the expression, ἢ τρεῖς ἑξ, ἢ τρεῖς κ ("neck or nothing"), was derived. Such at : is the explanation given by the commentators
"Qui plura puncta attulisset, abibat victor; qui tria tantum puncta ceciderant, infelicissimum jac faciebat, ideoque certissime perdebat. Non erat e qui posset inferius punctum adducere. Indeque ad ludi speciem referendum est istud proverbium ἢ τ ἑξ, ἢ τρεῖς κύβοι."—Salmasius, *ap. Souter ad* ι κύων.

The second of these games, προαιρέσιμον, se to have been very similar to that still in ve amongst German students. The winning nur was determined before each main by each of the players in turn. Thus the highest odd or the highest even number might be selected, or again the product of the numbers of two of the dice divided by the third—indeed, any arbitrary combination, without regard to the rules in use for the other games. Ovid seems to allude to some such combination in the following distich :—

" Et modò tres jactet numeros, modo cogitet aptè
Quam subeat partem callida, quamque vocet."
De Arte Amandi, l. ii.

The third of the games which I have mentioned was played with dice, counters, and a board. Though critics and commentators have thought it worth their while to write long dissertations on the subject, all that we know about it is merely conjectural. The *tabula*, or board, seems to have borne some resemblance to our modern back-gammon board. It is at least described as consisting of twelve lines on each side : " Constat ex bis senis lineis seu viis, scilicet ab utraque parte ludentium." The men, or counters, were thirty in number, fifteen being of one colour and belonging to one player, fifteen of another and belonging to his adversary. They were called *calculi*.

" Discolor ancipiti sub jactu calculus astat,
Decertantque simul candidus atque niger :
Ut quamvis parili scriptorum tramite currant,
Is capiet palmam quem sua facta vocant."

We may gather from this that this game was not one of mere chance, but that it also required some skill, and that a good player could turn even unlucky casts to his advantage. This is alluded to by Terence in the *Adelphi* :—

" Ita vita est hominum quasi cum ludas tesseris,
Si illud quod maximè opus est jactu, non eadit ;
Illud quod accidit, id arte ut corrigas."
Adel., iv. 7.

It was consequently easy for a courteous player to manage his game so as to lose even against an inferior adversary. This is what Ovid advises lovers to do when playing with their mistresses :—

" Seu ludet, numerosque manu jactabit eburnos ;
Tu male jactato, tu male jacta dato."
De Art. Am.

This game was so well known that many of the terms used in it became household words. It is thus that Cicero employs " reducere calculum " : " Itaque tibi concedo, quod in duodecim scriptis solemus, ut calculum reducas, si te alicujus dati pœnitet " (Cicero, in frag. *Hortens*.). The proverb, κινήσω ἀφ' ἱερᾶς, was an allusion to the line, " linea sacra," which divided the *tabula* into two parts. When all the counters had reached the last division they were said to be " ad incitas," an expression which we find used figuratively in Plautus :—

" Sy. Profecto ad incitas lenonem rediget, si eas
abduxerit.
Mi. Quin prius disperibit, faxo, quam unam calcem
civerit."
Pœnul., iv. 2.

The well-known exclamation, " Jacta est alea," was in use long before Cæsar uttered it, or at least its Greek equivalent, ἀνερρίφϑω ὁ κύβος, on the bank of the Rubicon.

Though forbidden by the laws, " vetita legibus alea," dice playing seems to have been the favourite amusement of the Romans under the emperors. Augustus was addicted to it, as we learn from Suetonius :—" Notatus est et ut pretiosæ supellectilis Corinthiorumque præcupidus, et aleæ indulgens " (*Octav. Aug.*, c. 71). Claudius is said to have made it the subject of a treatise, and to have invented a board on which he could play in his carriage or litter : " Aleam studiosissime lusit, de cujus arte librum quoque emisit. Solitus etiam in gestatione ludere, ita essedo alveoque adaptatis, ne lusus confunderetur " (Sueton., *Claud. Cæs.*, c. 33). And Domitian devoted all his leisure, early and late, to the dice-box : " Quoties otium esset, alea se oblectabat, etiam profestis diebus, matutinisque horis " (Sueton., *Flav. Domit.*, c. 21).

But gambling was not a vice of civilization alone. Tacitus records that it was carried to such an extent among the Germanic tribes that players often staked their liberty on a cast of the dice. Amongst the wild Huns, if we admit the authority of the following extract, gambling seems to have been the chief object in life :—

" Ferunt Hunnorum populos omnibus bellum inferre nationibus, fæneratoribus tamen esse subjectos ; et cum sine legibus vivant, aleæ solius legibus obædire, in procinctu ludere, tesseras simul et arma portare, et plures suis quam hostilibus ictibus interire. In victoriâ suâ captivos fieri, et spolia suorum perpeti, quæ pati ab hoste noverint. Ideoque nunquam belli studia deponere, quod victi aleæ ludo, cum totius prædæ munus amiserint, ludendi subsidia requirunt bellandi periculo."—*Ambrosius l. de Tobia*, c. 10.

To transcribe all the hard things that have been said of gambling by both pagan and Christian writers would far exceed our limits. One remark, however—it is from Aristotle—is so apt and so brief that it deserves a place. Gamblers, he says, are worse than thieves—the latter expose themselves to peril for the sake of gain, but the former rob their friends, οἱ δὲ ἀπὸ τῶν φίλων κερδαίνωσιν, οἷς δεῖ διδόναι. To this may, in conclusion, be added an epigram, from an unknown author, bearing the quaint epigraph :—

" In tesserâ quot latera, tot patibula.
" Quæris, cur facies bis monstret tessera ternas ?
Scilicet in sese tot gerit illa cruces.
Ludentis prima est : Socium manet altera : rursum
Tertia spectantem ; quarta docentis erit ;
Quinta inventoris, sed judicis ultima muti
Qui cruce non subolem sustulit atque patrem."
L. BARBÉ.

Bückeburg, Schaumburg-Lippe. .

It was through Daines Barrington that Gilbert White's papers on the *Hirundinidæ* were presented to the *savants* of the Royal Society, and through Barrington's encouragement, as the fifth published letter of Gilbert White to him shows, the simple, unobtrusive parish priest of Hampshire was induced to commence that *Natural History of Selborne* which ranks among the most delightful publications of our country. The debt of gratitude which the whole world owes to this pompous antiquary for the gift of a book eagerly devoured both by the scientific student and the ignorant tyro can never be repaid. After this tribute of praise I shall not be deemed guilty of ingratitude to the memory of Daines Barrington if I extract from Charles Lamb's essay, *The Old Benchers of the Inner Temple*, the following extraordinary anecdote, showing how little the receipt of White's delightful letters had benefited his best-loved correspondent : "When the accounts of Barrington's treasurership came to be audited, the following singular charge was unanimously disallowed by the bench : ' Item, disbursed Mr. Allen, the gardener, twenty shillings for stuff to poison the sparrows, by my orders.' " To me it is indeed marvellous that the favourite friend of the ardent naturalist of Selborne should ever have been seduced into ordering the destruction of these cheerful visitants to the dull courts of the Temple.

Permit me now, Mr. Editor, to ask in your columns a few questions which arise from Professor Bell's edition of this English classic. In p. xlix of the introductory memoir there is printed an extract from an unpublished letter to Pennant. I own to a feeling of pain that the letter has not been printed in full : if there is no impediment to its publication would it not be well for it to be given to the world in the columns of " N. & Q." at this late hour? Gilbert White says in the twenty-second letter to Pennant (dated Jan. 2, 1769), " I am well acquainted with the south hams of Devonshire"; and in the account-book under date of June 30, 1752, is a payment of four pounds (the carriage first to London and then to Oxford costing with the "porterage into the cellar" a further sum of 19s.) for a "hogshead of cyder from the Southams of Devon." The cider must have proved a great success, for in May of the following year Gilbert White paid 1l. 17s. 6d. for a half hogshead, as a present for his father, and a like sum for the same quantity as a present to his "uncle White." In letter 31 to Pennant ring-ousels are said, on the authority of "an observing *Devonshire* gentleman," to frequent some parts of Dartmoor and to be bred there ; the same statement occurs in letter 39, and in letter 22 to Daines Barrington swallows are said, no doubt on the authority of the same Devonshire gentleman, to have arrived at South Zele in that

county on April 25 in 1774. Is the name of this gentleman known, and at what period of his life did Gilbert White obtain his knowledge of the South-hams district of Devonshire? The seventh letter to Churton, containing the sentence, " I will take care of your *Rex platonicus* and hope I shall bring it you at Exeter," suggests that Churton may have drawn him into the West, ⸗but the last word I venture to think should be read Easter. The thirty-eighth letter to Barrington concludes with what Gilbert White terms a "lovely quotation" from Lucretius. Mr. Bell reprints from a review of White's *Selborne*, which appeared in the *Topographer* for 1789, a translation of this passage originally published in *Sonnets and other Poems*, [Anon.] Lond., Wilkie, 1785, and adds that he had not succeeded in discovering its author. It may save a future editor some trouble if I state that the translation was by Sir Egerton Brydges ; I feel but little doubt that the review in the *Topographer* was also from his pen. The first edition of *Sonnets and other Poems* appeared without the author's name in March, 1785, but a new edition in the same year, and a subsequent edition in 1795, bore his name on the title-page. Is Hatt's *History of Oxfordshire* (p. xxi of memoir) an error for Plot's? The date 1770, assigned to letter 35 to Barrington, should be 1777. Gray's *Beggar's Opera* (ii. 262, note) is of course a provoking misprint for Gay's. I cannot but think that if letter 13 to Samuel Barker were shown to the head of the Rashleigh family, he could suggest a solution for the illegible name of the place where Mrs. Rashleigh saw rushes in use in 1775.

P. W. TREPOLPEN.

THE PURY FAMILY, &c.

(Continued from p. 242.)

When the siege commenced Pury was equally active in arms and in council, and attempts to seduce him were renewed, but without effect. In Dorney's *Diurnall* we read :—

"Thursday, 17th August. This day a printed paper, conteyning the king's message and our answer thereto, was sent out of the king's army unto Mr. Alderman Pury, with a persuasive letter for the surrendering up of the citie, the close of which printed paper runs thus :—'Let the world now judge, if his Majestie could have sent a more gratious message to his most loyall subjects, and whether these desperate rebels deserve any mercy, who after so many offers do still refuse a pardon ; but since their returning this rebellious answer they have set their own suburbs on fire, which surely is not to keep the city either for King or Parliament.' [A copy of this 'printed paper' is amongst the Tanner MSS.] At the same time there was also sent unto him certain specious considerations and reasons subtilly composed to satisfie conscience in the delivering up of the citie, notwithstanding the late oath and protestation, wherewithall the said Capt. Pury being not convinced, did not divulge the same till after the seige was raised."

It appears also that Pury with others became

security for moneys raised to support the garrison, for in a letter dated May 19, 1646, signed by "Lau. Singleton, Maior," and others, and addressed "To the worshipple oʳ Honoured frynd, John Lenthall, Esq., a member of the Honᵇˡᵉ House of Com's," they say :—

"We have often represented oʳ necessitous condic'on to the Honᵇˡᵉ House of Com'ons, but have not yet obtayned any effectual meanes for supply of moneys to discharge ·oʳ city lands and Mr. Alderman Pury and others, who undertooke for moneys borrowed and arrears taken up for the Parlᵗ forces here in oʳ great extremity to keep them fro' mutiny, nor yet to satisfy the remaynder of oʳ Billett money or oʳ great losses for the necessary defence of the place."

The sufferings of the citizens were in truth very great, for it appears by a presentment of the Grand Jury in July, 1646, that 241 houses had been destroyed, with the goods in them, and that the value, which they say will be rather found undervalued than overvalued, amounted (inclusive of 2,000l. for the damage done to the meadows surrounding the city) to 28,720l. It was probably in consideration of the liability he had undertaken for these losses and for engagements for the supply of the city and garrison that the Parliament afterwards awarded him compensation. It appears that the Parliament awarded him 4l. a week. Mr. Webb says he was one of the earliest that obtained reparation for losses, and it was assigned to him out of the estate of the Marquis of Worcester. The Royalist pamphlet before mentioned says he "had 3,000l. given him, and Mr. Gerrard's place in the Petty Bag worth 400l. per ann." His subsequent devotion to the cause of the Parliament appears to have brought upon him the enmity of the soldiers when the army and Parliament quarrelled, for in 1647 his house in London was attacked and he himself was assaulted, for which the House sent some of his assailants to Newgate.

He was elected mayor of the city in 1653, and ·continued to represent it in Parliament until 1656, when he was succeeded by his son, to be hereafter mentioned. But though so far retired from public life he was by no means indifferent to the welfare ·of what he deemed to be "the good old cause," and when, upon the death of Oliver Cromwell and the abdication of Richard, the designs of the king's friends became apparent, and Massie, soldier of fortune as he was, had changed sides and was hovering about the country with the view of securing the city, we learn from the Commons' Journals, July 30, 1659, that Alderman Pury and his son raised and armed 300 foot in Gloucester, for which they received the thanks of Parliament by letter from the Speaker. He died August 13, 1666, and is buried in the church of St. Mary de Crypt, where there is a monument to his memory. Of such a person and in such times the reputation accorded to him by partisans and ·opponents must have been very conflicting, but his speech recorded in a former number of "N. & Q." appears to have given great offence to the Church party during his life and long after his death. Of this the learned Fosbrooke, in his History of Gloucester, published in 1819, affords an amusing illustration, for, speaking of the Civil War, he writes (p. 213) :—

"At this period a person who under the wise administration of Elizabeth would probably have been a sycophant took advantage of the times to recommend seizure of the Chapter property, that tenants who held their estates under leases nearly equal to freehold might be turned into rack-renters, and highways might be kept in repair by persons who never used a road for the benefit of those who did. It is not a shadow of difference to the publick whether a clergyman or a layman is landlord of an estate; but in all ages there are men who substitute regular habits and austere deportment for honour and sentiment, who were they in the army would for knavery be broke in a week. We know Joseph Surface and Blifil; and this person, of the name of Pury, made a fortune by the rebellion, being Signior Manuel Ordonnez in Le Sage, who never walked out without downcast eyes and counting his beads, and gained a good estate by managing the concerns of the poor.......It is needless to observe that these remarks allude to the speech of Master Thomas Pury, which as merely seditious is not here printed."

The italics are those of the learned historian, who probably felt relieved after this ebullition.

J. J. P.

Temple.

(To be continued.)

BISHOPSTONE CHURCH: THE EARLIER STYLES OF ECCLESIASTICAL ARCHITECTURE.—James Hurdis, D.D. (ante, p. 242), is buried at Bishopstone; at least, a mural tablet erected there by his sisters records that he died in 1801, aged thirty-eight. I confess, however, that when I visited this church in the year 1875, in company with a friend, we passed lightly by the grave of Hurdis, and spent our time in studying the features of the early styles of architecture, of which we have here so interesting an example. The tower consists of four stages, with a corbel table and capping, and resembles that at Newhaven, both being early Norman. The circular heads of the small windows are formed of one stone ; and in this feature, which occurs also in the sills of the windows of the north aisle, we recognize the transition from the style which generally prevailed before the Conquest. The porch is lofty and curious, and is, perhaps, the oldest part of the whole building. From the nave you pass into the chancel through an Early English archway, exhibiting shadowed mouldings, capitals with projecting foliage, and the square abacus, which last is a special feature of the earlier development of the first pointed style. So much is this the case that I scarcely think there is an example of a square abacus in the whole of Salisbury Cathedral, at all events above the ground floor, and that although we have at Salis-

building. On the other hand, at Chichester the square abacus is a common feature in the earlier example of the same style which is there presented ; and from Salisbury you have only to pass on to the curious remains of the church at Amesbury to find this feature occurring again. I need hardly mention what every ecclesiologist is well aware of—that the churches on the seaboard of Sussex afford a favourable field for the study of the Norman, pre-Norman, and Early English styles. Early English woodwork is not common, but there is a good specimen in the curious building known as St. Mary's Hospital, at Chichester, and again at Findon, near Worthing. But I must pause, and bring these somewhat disjointed observations to a close.

No one that loves to ponder reverently and humbly over the thoughts and records which our forefathers have left impressed on the walls and sculptured pillars of our ancient churches, but must mourn over and often resent the intrusion of the modern restorer, who has so often confounded old and new, with his imitations and his confusing process of alteration and adaptation. Would that the Society for the Preservation of Ancient Buildings, or some similar body, might exert an influence to arrest the progress of "restoration," as it has often been carried on in our obscurer villages as well as in the more public edifices. It is not now too late for the archdeacons or other local authority to take in hand the business of exercising some superintendence over restorations ; and at least they might provide us with some reliable record whereby we may distinguish the old from the new, before the memory of recent changes has entirely passed away.

S. A.

Turnham Green Vicarage.

ILLUSTRATED VISITING CARDS AND TRADESMEN'S ADDRESS CARDS.—Some years ago (I regret that I cannot furnish the date) I think that I sent you a short contribution on the subject of the pictorial visiting cards of the last century, in the hope that some of your correspondents would respond, and that, after a few good examples set, the present tasteless uniformity of "pasteboards" might be varied by a recurrence to the beautiful productions of a less utilitarian age. A reference to Chambers's *Book of Days* (June 5) will give an idea of what might be done nowadays, and if the demand arose the greatly neglected art of vignette engraving would doubtless speedily experience a revival. The cognate branch of industry, that of the engraving of tradesmen's vignette address cards, only needs an intelligent resuscitation to become general. The cheapness of lithography has done much to debase the style of these appeals to a race of customers whom we must, I fear, consider less appre-

A study of such remnants of a bygone fashi trivial though they may appear, will be well paid, and I shall be glad to correspond with any your subscribers who may happen to have spe mens of cards or plates of either of the varietie have mentioned, and to receive offers of them fr any who may have them for disposal. I inch heraldic book-plates in these last remarks.

J. ELIOT HODGKIN.

9, Dynevor Gardens, Richmond, Surrey.

SALE BY CANDLE.—"N. & Q." contains ma notices of this old method of sale ; the followi passage from the *Fourth Report of the Histori MSS. Commission* may therefore be interestii It is from the Calendar of the House of Loi MSS. for October, 1641 :—

" Affidavit of Solomon Smith respecting the sale the St. John Baptist, by the candle, at the Red L tavern at Ratcliffe in the afternoon of the 25th of Se last. After the reading of their lordships' order a w candle, above an inch in length, was set on the edge o knife, and he that should bid most for the said sb apparel, and furniture, before the said candle was o should be the buyer, at which time the ship was boug by George Warner for 1,600*l.*"

EDWARD PEACOCK.

MOSES'S ROD.—It may interest some of yo readers to know that in the library of the Briti Museum exists a representation of the rod wi which Moses smote the rock. See Vendrami A., *Museum Vendramenum*, 4to. 1627 (MS.), p. *Verga dell' arbore, con il quale Mosè percosse pietra.*" It is a very crooked stick, being intend to express the force of the blow. LOUIS FAGAN.

OLD SPELLING OF "VELVET."—Mr. H. C. Coo in his *Romans of Britain*, p. 35, just publishe instances the old spelling "welvet" for his arg ment as to the use of the letter *w* in the Engli language. I have come across another spelli of this word, which perhaps may be worthy of note, namely "welwet." Among the parish recor of Hammersmith is a list of the property of t church in 1670, in which the following item occu: as printed in the local newspaper : " 1 Pulpit wi a cloth and cushion of welwet."

G. LAURENCE GOMME.

Queries.

[We must request correspondents desiring informati on family matters of only private interest, to affix th names and addresses to their queries, in order that t answers may be addressed to them direct.]

A DEVONSHIRE CUSTOM.—Mrs. Bray, in h *Traditions of Devonshire*, describes a curio custom formerly prevalent, and perhaps still knov in that county, at harvest time. She says :—

" When the reaping is finished, towards evening t labourers select some of the best ears of corn from t sheaves. These they tie together, and it is called the *nack*. The reapers then proceed to a high place. The man who bears the offering stands in the midst, elevates it, while all the other labourers form themselves into a circle about him. Each holds aloft his hook, and in a moment they all shout these words: ' Arnack (or *ah nack*), arnack, arnack, wehaven (pronounced *wee-hav-en*), wehaven, wehaven !' This is repeated three several times."

What is the meaning of these strange words? No one has ever yet explained—or, as far as I know, attempted to explain—them, but it seems to me that they are a remnant of the ancient speech of the British people (the Gaelic), spoken in these islands before the Roman, Saxon, and Danish invasions, two thousand years ago, and not yet wholly extinct in Scotland and Ireland. *Arnach,* which is like no Saxon or Anglo-Saxon word, is, I think, derived from the Celtic or Gaelic *air* or *ar*, to plough, whence *airean*, a ploughman, a husbandman, and *aireanach*, pertaining to husbandry, corrupted, when the meaning had been lost, into the Devonshire word *arnack. Wehaven*, in like manner, is a corruption of *eubhach* (pronounced *eu vach*), a cry, a shout, and *eubhaichean*, or *euvaichean*, shouts and huzzas, whence the apparent gibberish cited by Mrs. Bray would signify " Husbandry! husbandry! (or the fruits of husbandry) huzza! huzza! huzza !" Perhaps some of the philological correspondents of "N. & Q." may be able to throw further—or different—light upon the question.   CHARLES MACKAY.
Fern Dell, Mickleham, Surrey.

CHEVALIER D'EON.—Are the papers entrusted by the D'Eon family to M. Gaillardet, and on which the life of this extraordinary personage by M. Gaillardet is mainly founded, still in existence? If so, can they be consulted and where?

THOMAS CHALLONER, THE REGICIDE.—Can any Clerkenwell antiquary tell me whether this gentleman, a son of Sir Thomas Challoner, was a resident in Clerkenwell, "in the spacious fair house built by his father," at the time of the trial of Charles I.?   WILLIAM J. THOMS.

"THE GOLDEN AGE ; OR, ENGLAND IN 1822-3," &c.—A friend, knowing I am much interested in Cheshire books and authors, has kindly presented me with a copy of an octavo pamphlet published anonymously in 1823, and bearing the following title :—

"The Golden Age; or, England in 1822-3: in a Poetical Epistle to a Friend Abroad. Second Edition, enlarged [two quotations, one Latin, the other English]. London, printed for James Ridgway, Piccadilly, 1823." Pp. 63.

In the preface the author writes :—

"The public having thought the following trifle worthy a second edition, and having indulged in various surmises respecting its author, I have seized this oppor. tunity of setting all further doubt at rest by putting my name to a work which will at least show that I value the

good of my country far above the present sunshine of court favour, or the more remote contingencies of honours and preferment."

This is signed " J. Jobson, LL.D., Slutchby in the Fens, May 29, 1823," which is obviously fictitious. The special interest of this copy, however, consists in the fact that some previous possessor has written on the title-page, evidently about the time the pamphlet appeared, " This poem is by E. Davenport, Jun., Esq., son of Mr. D., one of the present members for Cheshire," and adds on the fly-leaf, " In the first edition the author prefers these two lines as a beginning :—

' Friend of my secret thoughts, who best can tell
How in my country I have loved to dwell.' "

Davies Davenport, of Woodford and Capesthorne, Esq., was M.P. for Cheshire from 1806 to 1830. His eldest son, Edward Davies Davenport, was born April 27, 1778, and at this time would be about forty-five years of age. Can any of your correspondents send any further particulars concerning this poetical pamphlet, or in any way throw light upon its authorship?
    J. P. EARWAKER, F.S.A.
Withington, near Manchester.

WILLIAM DE ROOS, OF YOLTON.—This person had a grant from Edward I., in the thirty-fifth year of his reign, to hold weekly markets and annual fairs in his manor of Haltwhistle, in the county of Northumberland, which manor by settlement, on the marriage of his daughter, passed to the Musgraves. Nicholson and Burn suppose this William de Roos, of Yolton, to be identical with William de Roos, Lord of Kendal, second son and heir of his mother, Margaret de Brus, wife of Robert de Roos, Lord of Wark. This could not be, as his father's name was Alexander (*vide* Hodgson, ii. 3, 115, and the Yorkshire Visitation, 1575). Was Alexander a younger son of Robert de Roos, Lord of Hamlake and Wark, who married Isabella, daughter of William the Lion, and obtained with her the manor of Haltwhistle ?   E. H. A.

"MR. BONNEILE'S BOOK."—The Bermuda Company, writing in 1616 to Captain Daniel Tucker, say :—

" Because we conceave that Mr. Bonneile's Book lately sett forth, recommended unto vs by his Matie, will be of special use for the instructing of the people in the raising of those rich and staple comodities wch wee most earnestly desyre and in some pte hope may be raised wee thought it good at present to send some of them."

The receivers were to pay half a pound of tobacco apiece for the copies. The Bonneile in question was probably David Bonneile, or Bonnel, " born in Norwich, the son of an Alien, a merchaunt," living in East Cheape in 1618. Can any reader oblige me with the name of the book? There are several works in the British Museum by authors of the

LLYN CORN SLWC.—Can any reader of "N. & Q." tell me the meaning of this name of one of the smallest of Welsh llyns, situated amid the rugged summits of Craig Ddrwg, in Merionethshire?

J. L. WALKER.

THE BLESSING OF CRAMP RINGS.—Mr. Pegge, in his *Curialia*, has annexed to the service in use for the royal healing a service, taken from a folio Prayer Book of 1710, for the blessing of cramp rings. Is there any known history of this public superstition?

GWAVAS.

MRS. CRANMER'S MARRIAGE.—The celebrated Cranmer was married, I believe, whilst the old canonical law of marriage was in force. Was he afterwards remarried to the lady?

F.S.A.

MILTON'S FIRST WIFE, MARY POWELL.—On Oct. 26, 1643, the House of Lords ordered that Mrs. Mary Powell should have a pass to go into Berkshire and return again to London (*Journals*, vol. vi. p. 273). Was this the first wife of Milton? The uncertainty of the date of the poet's marriage with Mary Powell of Forest Hill, near Oxford, provokes the inquiry. According to Phillips he was married to this lady about Whitsuntide (May 21) that year, and shortly afterwards she left her husband's home, to return about Michaelmas. The register of the marriage had not been found when Mr. Masson was writing the second volume of his *Life of Milton* (p. 505).

JOHN E. BAILEY.

EMBER DAYS.—The usual derivation given of the term "ember days" is, as in Ogilvie's *Dictionary*, the Saxon root *ymb*, about, and the Gothic word *ryne*, a course or race, hence ember days are explained to be " days which recur at certain seasons in the *course* of the year." May I inquire whether any etymological objection can be made to the much simpler derivation from the usual sense of the word *embers*, viz. as meaning cinders or hot ashes, from the Danish word *eine*, to steam or smoke? No one doubts that the term Ash Wednesday is to be derived from the ancient connexion of *ashes* or *cinders* with days of abstinence. Why should not the expression " ember days" be similarly explained, these days being also days of fasting or abstinence?

G. F. W. MUNBY.

Turvey Rectory.

"ALICE IN WONDERLAND."—One of your correspondents, speaking of living English verse-writers, stated that the real name of "Lewis Carroll" is Mr. Dodgson. In the list of "Pen Names" prefixed to Whitaker's *Reference Catalogue of Current Literature* Mr. D. C. Lutwidge is said to

FORD : HEINS.—Can you give n tion as to the family of Ford? Tw Nonconformist ministers in Suffolk as to a painter named Heins, of Nor portraits by him?

PHILPOT AND PHILLPOTT FAM manor of Hoggeston or Hoxton, *Environs of London*, says :—
" In 1485 John Philpot died seized (*in* manor of Hoggeston with the appurtena son John his heir......No records are to the site known, probably it was Balmet to have belonged to Sir John Philpot in the seventeenth century."

And writing of the manor of Ascl End, he says :—
" In the reign of Richard III. it was Sir John Philpot, who settled it upon hi he married Alice Stourton......I think the manor of Mile End continued ma family of Philpot, as it appears by the that Sir George Philpot resided in that l middle of the last (*i.e.* seventeenth) cent

Lysons mentions (vol. ii. p. 452) Stepney of " Elizabeth, wife of Sir pott, of Mile End, Knt., Aug. 11, 1t

Can any one give me, or tell m trace, Sir George's descent from the pot who died in 1485? also what ants Sir George left?

Lysons, treating of Hackney, me Phillpott as having been buried 1 Robinson, in his *History of Sto*l describing the tomb, gives the dat 1730," adding "aged 35. Also Phillpott, mother of the above said.'

The Hackney burial register ha 1750 respecting a Mrs. Mary Philpo Hackney Philpots (the name is v connected with the Philpots of Mile how? The Hackney Philpot arms cross or, between four daggers propei or—an augmentation granted Philpot when Lord Mayor of Lond older arms.

RELAYED OR RELAID?—What participle of *relay*? Should we say, *relayed* this year," or *relaid*? In *la lay*, *inlay*, and *overlay* we make th *aid*, but in *delay*, *allay*, and all ot end with *ay*, except *slay*, we make i

CORSICAN SEAL.—When the gall tunate Baron Neuhoff was accepte sicans as their king in 1736, one measures was to establish a mint, a

time he caused a great seal to be prepared. This seal is one inch and seven-eighths in diameter, and bears a shield surmounted with a royal crown, two savages with clubs as supporters, and the motto "In te Domine speravi." The bearing on the shield appears to be, Party per pale sable and argent, three links of a chain and a Moor's head couped proper. Horace Walpole, who took a kindly interest in the ex-king (*World*, No. viii., Feb. 22, 1753), had a great seal of Corsica, which was sold at Strawberry Hill in 1842, but I have reason to doubt whether it really was *the* great seal, and should be glad to know what has become of it. I should also like to know when the broken chain became part of the national arms. It might have been adopted when the Moorish yoke was first cast aside, or when the rule of Genoa, which was quite as hard to bear, was revolted from.
EDWARD SOLLY.

MINIATURE OIL PAINTING ON COPPER OF KING CHARLES I., in a substantial gold case, enamelled blue, oval shape, adapted to be worn by a ribbon round the neck; size 2 in. by 1¾ in. Three of these were said to be taken by Sir Peter Lely after sentence of death on the king. Can any one give information as to any of these miniatures?
C. R. L.

WHOEVER "HEARS THE WHISTLERS" WILL DIE.—A novel published not very long since alluded to this superstition. The scene was laid in Cornwall. It illustrates Spenser's *Faery Queene*, ii. xii. 36. What was the name of the novel?
O. W. T.

A WELSH MANOR.—The text of an old MS. in the College of Arms leads me to ask your Welsh contributors if there is a manor called "Radnor" in Flint or Denbigh, and if it belonged before 1500 to a Jenkyn Mathew.
M.

AUTHORS OF BOOKS WANTED.—
Essays, Moral, Philosophical, and Stomachical, on the Important Science of Good Living. By Launcelot Sturgeon, Esq., Fellow of the Beef-Steak Club, and an Honorary Member of several Foreign Pic-Nics, &c. 1822.—Who was the real author of this satirical work?
FREDERIC WAGSTAFF.

Our Staple Manufactures: a Series of Papers on the History and Progress of the Linen and Cotton Trades in the North of Ireland. Belfast, 1855. 8vo.
A Few Words on the Eastern Question. London, 1860. 8vo.
The Gothic Renaissance: its Origin, Progress, and Principles. London, 1860. 8vo.
A Familiar Epistle to Robert J. Walker, &c. From an Old Acquaintance. London, 1863. 8vo.
ABHBA.

Who is the compiler of *The Book of Familiar Quotations*, &c., third edition, dedicated to Dr. T. Herbert Barker, Whittaker & Co., 1862?
J. D.

Hermit in London.—It consists of a series of sarcastic sketches on various subjects.
`LEFTWICHE.

AUTHORS OF QUOTATIONS WANTED.—
" I tremble from the edge of life to dare
    The dark and fatal leap, *having no faith*,
    No glorious yearning for the Apocalypse,
    But like a child that in the night-time cries
    For light I cry, forgetting the eclipse
    Of knowledge and of human destinies."
                                        J. R. S. C.

" Filled the stage with all the crowd
    Of fools pursuing and of fools pursued,
    Whose ins and outs no ray of sense discloses,
    Whose deepest plot is how to break folks' noses."
                                    J. BRANDER MATTHEWS.

What " old poet " wrote the lines,
" Vast plains and lowly cottages forlorn,
    Rounded about by the low wavering sky"?
They do not sound old.   J. D.

Replies.

" O NIMIS FELIX," &c.
(5th S. ix. 87.)

Paul the Deacon, who entered the monastery of Monte Cassino on the conquest of Lombardy by the Franks, and died between 790 and 796, wrote in praise of St. John Baptist the well-known hymn commencing " Ut queant laxis." The first syllable of each half line of the first stanza suggested, as is well known, to Guido Aretino what is technically called " sol-faing." In the Sarum Breviary, as well as in the Roman, this hymn of fourteen stanzas is divided into three portions, of which the first, " Ut queant laxis," is appointed for vespers ; the second, " Antra deserti," for matins ; and the third, " O nimis felix," for lauds of St. John Baptist's Day. Mr. Copeland's translation of the stanza, " Serta ter denis" (in *Hymns of the Week and Hymns of the Season*), expresses the sense accurately, and will guide H. N. to a literal translation :—

" While some with wreaths of increase thirty-fold
    Are crownèd, other some twice thirty wear,
    Thee with thrice glorious weight
    The hundredth fold adorns."

The allusion is to the closing words of the parable of the sower, " and bringeth forth some an hundredfold, some sixty, some thirty." St. Jerome and St. Athanasius assign the yield of the hundredfold to virgins, of the sixty to widows, and of the thirtyfold to the faithful and holy wedded. St. Cyprian gives the hundredfold to martyrs, the sixty to virgins, the thirty to the married. St. Augustine (*De Virginitate*, xlv.) alludes to four interpretations :—

" What the meaning is of that difference of fruitfulness, let them see to it who understand these things better than we ; whether the virginal life be in fruit an hundredfold, in sixtyfold the widowed, in thirtyfold the married ; or whether the hundredfold fruitfulness be ascribed unto martyrdom, the sixtyfold unto continence, the thirtyfold unto marriage ; or whether virginity, by the addition of martyrdom, fill up the hundredfold, but

thirtyfold arrive at sixtyfold, in case they shall be martyrs; or whether—what seems to me more probable, forasmuch as the gifts of Divine grace are many, and one is greater and better than another, whence the apostle says, *But emulate ye the better gifts*—we are to understand that they are more in number than to allow of being distributed under those different kinds."

St. John Baptist, celebrated in the hymn as virgin, "nesciens labem nivei pudoris," and martyr, "præpotens martyr," is reckoned to have filled up the hundredfold, and therefore to be adorned with the richest crown. Daniel, *Thesaurus Hymnologicus*, vol. i. p. 211, has a long and interesting note on the stanza; and Valentianus, *Hymnodia Sanctorum Patrum*, p. 410, gives a summary of all that has been written upon it.

WILLIAM COOKE, F.S.A.
The Hill House, Wimbledon.

This is the third portion of a hymn appropriated to the festival of the nativity of John the Baptist, of which the first portion is sung at matins, the second at lauds, and the third at vespers. It is of very early date, and bears a curious history. Paulus, a monk of Aquileia, whose date is not known, but probably in the sixth or seventh century, having lost his voice, addressed this hymn to John Baptist as most likely to help him, because at his birth his father Zacharias recovered his power of speech, and he himself was "the voice crying in the wilderness." Hence the hymn was adopted for use on St. John's Day, and John came to be considered the patron saint of singers and songs of the Church. It is said also to have been used as a charm against hoarseness or loss of voice (Gavanti, Th. iii. p. 475). It was probably for this reason that Guido of Arezzo (A.D. 1030) adopted the first syllables of the half lines of the first verse as the basis of his musical notation, Ut, Re, Mi, Fa, Sol, La:—

" *Ut* queant laxis *Re*sonare fibris,
*Mi*ra gestorum *Fa*muli tuorum,
*Sol*ve pollute *La*bii reatum,
Sancte Johannes."

The entire hymn will be found in Daniel's *Thesaurus*, vol. i. p. 205. The reading of the verse referred to by H. N. is somewhat different from that given by him:—

" Trina centeno cumulata fructu
Te sacer ornant."

The meaning of it is thus explained by a quotation from a note of Hilarius:—

" Tres ordines hic notantur......*conjugati, continentes*, et *virgines*. Serta ter denis, &c., i.e. triginta coronant conjugatos......Illa serta duplicata in sexagesimum fructum coronant continentes......Aucta centeno fructu coronant te, S. Johannes, qui es virgo."

G. B. BLOMFIELD.

Romsée, in his *Praxis Divini Officii*, tom. iii. 347, says of this hymn that it was written by Paul the Deacon, that he was a monk of Monte Cassino,

and died as the beginning of the third
The same authority gives the following of the second verse:—

" Ante horum versuum elucidationem,
et facit aliud quidem centesimum, aliud ai
mum, aliud verò trigesimum. Et *Marci*, c
verso *unum trigesimum, unum sexagesimi*
centesimum. Porrò significatur merita
crescere tantum usque ad trigesimum, in
gesimum, et in aliquibus usque ad cente
posito sensus est: *serta* seu coronæ (gallic
aucta ter denis augmentis, id est, triginta
feris, seu floribus alios *coronant*, seu dec
cata illa serta id est, sexies denis, seu se
mentis quosdam vestiunt, sed trina se
multiplicata te *Joannem centum nexibus* fl
Hoc est summatim. *Joannem Baptistam*
perfectionis et sanctitatis pervenisse, et coi
cœlis ad præmium superioris ordinis.

" Vel rectiùs et litteræ conformiùs in
describuntur aureolæ, quæ virginibus, d
martyribus in cœlo reservantur: ii qui virg
in terris solum coluerunt, unam tantum in c
nempe virginum consequuntur; idque sig
verbis: *Serta ter denis alios coronant au*
Qui verò virgines simul et doctores fue
palmam recipiunt juxta illud hymni *duplic*
Qui autem virginitati et doctoris officio sime
martyrium, tribus palmis decorantur; c
sanctus *Joannes Baptista* fuerit virgo, p
doctor et martyr, de eo cantatur *trina te fru*
centum nexibus ornant. Sed quare cent
dantur et non nonaginta, cum cuilibet vii
tantum tribuantur? Huic responderi pc
sanctum *Joannem* sanctitate extraordinariâ
tum: undè Christus de eo dixit: *inter na*
non surrexit major Joanne Baptistâ; ideòq
illius supra mensuram ordinariam extollitur

I find this translation of the verse in
The Day Office of the Church, the hymn
at lauds on the Nativity of St. John B

" He who bare thirty-fold bright garlands ·
He who bare sixty double glory shareth,
But his rich chaplet who three hundred l
Holy one, decks thee."

Let me add this query: How is it
seems to leave out this important h
Hymni Latini Medii Ævi?   I

The People's Hymnal has tried to tr
hymn in the original sapphics, but h
ceeded. *Ex uno disce omnes:—*

" Saints with their crowns shall glitter, s
crease
Thirty-fold, some with double wreaths sh
Yet shall no other diadem of glory
Glitter like thine."

CHARLES F. S. WARR

These lines occur, as cited by H. N.
Brev. Rom., as published under the :
Pope Urban VIII., Antv., 1630. Bu
and fourth lines are printed in th
Eccles. Sarisb., Littlemore, 1850 :—

" Trina centeno cumulata fructu
Te, sacer, ornant."

Paulus Diaconus, *al.* Paul Winfried, the writer of the hymn, was a Benedictine of Mount Casino at the close of the eighth century.

ED. MARSHALL.

JONATHAN BOUCHER'S " GLOSSARY OF ARCHAIC WORDS " (5ᵗʰ S. ix. 68.)—I do not know the edition of Boucher published in 1832, but I possess part i. (said to be all that was published) of what is entitled—

" A Supplement to Dr. Johnson's Dictionary of the English Language, or a Glossary of Obsolete and Provincial Words. By the late Rev. Jonathan Boucher, A.M., Vicar of Epsom, in the County of Surrey. London, Longman & Co., 1807."

With this part, which ends with the letter A, the following advertisement was issued, which will show the intention and scope of the *Glossary*, and to what extent the author had proceeded with the work at the time of his death :—

" As the late Mr. Boucher announced his intention, by a prospectus in the year 1801, and again in 1802, of publishing a supplement to Dr. Johnson's *Dictionary*, it may require explanation why no greater part than what is contained in the following pages is now presented to the public. It may, therefore, be necessary to premise that an alteration in the arrangement of the learned author's materials was one of the principal causes which retarded the completion of his labours in lexicography. He was induced to undertake the formation of a provincial glossary about twelve or fourteen years ago, both from the knowledge which, as a native of Cumberland, he possessed of our northern dialects, and from the conviction, which his literary studies had produced, that many difficult passages in the best writers, both in prose and verse, would receive explanation and illustration from the ' honest kersey' language of our unlettered peasantry ; and the various communications which he received from friends in remote parts of the kingdom enabled him, in a very few years, to advance as far as the letter T. He had likewise directed his attention to the collecting of references for obsolete words, which at first had appeared to be, though a necessary, yet a subordinate, part of his work.

" At this period, however, a maturer consideration of his subject led him to abandon the plan of a double glossary, and to recast the whole anew, by blending provincial and obsolete words together under one alphabet; and, although the public may now perhaps have cause to lament that his original course was not persevered in, yet it must be confessed that the division of a dictionary of English words into two parts would have been objectionable in many respects, more particularly as various instances must have occurred of the extreme difficulty of deciding whether a word which was formerly provincial was not now obsolete, or whether a word supposed to be obsolete was not still provincial. It will be seen that many, usually considered as no longer in use, are still prevalent in the distant counties.

" In combining the two classes of words, Mr. Boucher had proceeded as far as the letter G, and having de. termined to complete the whole in four parts, making two thick quarto volumes, he would probably have published the first part, consisting of six letters, in the year 1804 had not death, which regards not the labours of the learned, deprived philologists of the gratification that was preparing for them.

" Under all the circumstances of difficulty which must

attend a posthumous publication, it is not to be expected that in times like the present his family should hazard the very great expense of printing a work which in bulk would probably be equal to Dr. Johnson's *Dictionary*. It being, however, conceived that, with such revision as it was thought proper to make, even a small part of the intended glossary might prove acceptable to those to whom the structure of language is an interesting inquiry, the letter A (though less attractive perhaps than many subsequent letters) has been prepared for the press, and is now submitted to the judgment of the public. It must depend not only on the result of that judgment, but on various considerations of a private nature, whether the first part will be followed by the remainder, or any part of the remainder, of the supplement. It will be proper, however, to apprise those respectable persons who subscribed their names in expectation of a complete work, that although Mr. Boucher was in the most flattering manner encouraged to prosecute his arduous undertaking by a list of nearly eight hundred subscribers, not the slightest claim is now presumed to be obtruded on that list to patronize a part only of what they subscribed for. If, however, from any intrinsic merit, that part shall appear to them, and to the public in general, to deserve a place on the same shelf with Johnson, the family and the friends of the lamented author will experience the satisfaction that they have not, from a mistaken zeal for his posthumous fame, sullied the literary character which he acquired while living.—Jan. 1, 1807. "

On the fly-leaf of my copy is the subjoined extract of a letter from Mr. Southey, dated Keswick, Jan. 11, 1827, showing the poet's keen appreciation of the merits of the work, and also that an endeavour was made at that time (*i. e.* 1827) to publish the remaining portion of Mr. Boucher's MS. :—

" I thank you for the specimen of Mr. Boucher's *Glossary*—nothing can be better than this *Glossary*. I doubt whether there is anything else of the kind so good —anything which exhibits at once so wide a range of knowledge and such acuteness. The Royal Society of Literature should purchase the manuscript and take measures for completing it. If the task were fairly undertaken they might reckon upon much gratuitous co-operative labour, and would be certain of repaying themselves.

" If I lived and moved among the operatives and patrons of literature I would exert myself for having this undertaken. Here I can only send out ' a voice from the mountains ' for it ; and this on every opportunity I will not fail to do."

The effort made at this time may have led to the publication of the *Glossary* in 1832, as mentioned by MR. WARD. I will only add that if I may judge of the whole by a part I quite endorse Mr. Southey's opinion. D. M. STEVENS.
Guildford.

CRICKET : THE LYTTELTON CRICKET MATCH (5ᵗʰ S. ix. 165, 253.)—MR. C. F. S. WARREN is quite wrong in stating that " the Lyttelton cricket match was ' Lytteltons *v.* Hagley.' " I myself played in the match, and I well remember all the incidents connected with it. The match was " Lytteltons *v.* King Edward's School, Bromsgrove " ; it was played in Hagley Park, on Mon-

scored 150 and 51, the Lytteltons 191 and 12 (without the loss of a wicket) ; so that the family won by 10 wickets. I have the full score before me at this moment, and no less than four long accounts of the match, one of them particularly amusing and interesting as having been written by one of the Lytteltons for the *Hagley Parish Magazine* of Sept., 1867. But perhaps the most interesting of the many productions which appeared at the time anent this " great match " are the lines by the late lord himself, which I copied from the original MS., and which, as having been written by a constant and valued contributor to "N. & Q.," I now forward for preservation in your columns. The references I have added, as they may not be evident to all.

Lines by the late Lord Lyttelton on the " Great Match " at Hagley, played on Monday, August 26, 1867.

" Sing the song of Hagley cricket,
  When the peer and all his clan
Grasped the bat to guard the wicket
  As no other household can.

Fair the dawn and bright the morning
  When the great eleven rose,
Toil and heat and danger scorning
  Till the day's triumphant close.

But the peer and *Marshal* * *courtly*
  Yielded not one single notch ;
Nor, alas ! did *parson*† *portly*
  Fail alike his game to botch.

Yet the peer, to mend his glory,‡
  One and eke another caught ;
While the parson—mournful story—
  Miss'd the two his hands that sought.

Charles and *Albert*,§ broad and lankey,
  Well maintained the old renown ;
Yelled the field to bowler, ' Thank ye,'
  When at length the stumps came down.

Nevy,‖ pride of England's army,
  Kept the wicket, hit out free ;
Spencer shouts, ' 'Tis I shall harm ye,'
  Reached the top of goodly tree.

Arthur and the sober *Bobbin*
  Gird them to the task sublime ;
Vain the attempts to drop the lob in,
  Vain the fielding—for a time.

But the *small undaunted heroes*,¶
  Trained in Walker's school to fame,
Scorned papa's and uncle's zeros,
  Swelled the score and graced the name.

---

* The late peer's younger brother, Spencer, late H.M.'s Marshal of Ceremonies.
† The Rev. the Hon. W. H. Lyttelton, Rector of Hagley.
‡ In making one of these catches he turned a complete somersault.
§ The present peer, better known among cricketers as " C. G.," and the Rev. the Hon. Albert Victor Lyttelton.
‖ Capt. the Hon. Neville Lyttelton, Rifle Brigade.
¶ The Hon. Edward and the Hon. Alfred, at present the great heroes in the Cambridge eleven.

Good to bat, to bowl, to fag,
Vanquished in the strife uneven,
Strike the ancient Bromsgrove flag.

Ne'er again in mingled labours
  Shall we willow weapon wield ;
Ne'er again such thronging neighbours
  Shall surround the famous field.

Sing the song of Hagley cricket.
  ' Come whate'er eleven may,'
Quoth the peer, ' my boys shall lick it,
  My eight boys shall win the day.'

Sept. 10, 1867."

J. B. WILSON, M

St. Helen's Rectory, Worcester.

MR. ARBER'S REPRINTS (5ᵗʰ S. ix. 243, 2 The tone, though hardly the matter, of DR. Nₑ son's reply seems to require some notice froı 1. The writer says that I shall find in Mr. A prospectus the reason why the spelling of the G is modernized, or, as he puts it, why the repɩ not " in fac-simile." Before I wrote the notic course read Mr. Arber's prospectus, as well ɩ book itself. I have now read the prospectus and I do not find in it a single reason, stat implied, to account for the modernized spₑ 2. The writer insinuates, with much ingₑ and possibly with truth, that I am not s very advanced student after all. This is ɩ sonal matter into which I must decline to ɩ him. 3. The writer is pleased to conjectur(I am a teetotaller. This argument may pₑ be dismissed as somewhat irrelevant. 4 writer charges me with having called a c paper " a wine merchant's bill " which is n wine merchant's bill." The paper which] described is headed thus : " Report to Lord leigh of the cost of delivering a tun of Gasₑ wine in England in November, 1583." It cₒ a number of items of cost, added up at foot total of 12*l*. 14*s*. 10*d*. And on the page fac is printed a poem entitled " The Bride's Morrow." 5. The writer's argument in favₑ accents in English is that "nowadays we ma past -*ed* for distinction's sake -*èd*." *Stat pro* ɩ *voluntas*. But the question who *we* are, anɗ right *we* have to accentuate thus, remains considered. 6. The writer says that A. ɩ " either does not know, or is unable to unders a certain very simple matter. There are things, and simple matters too, which A. does not understand. For instance, he do understand why a published literary notice, ʋ in good faith and within the just limits of cism, should subject the author of it to a (if reply it can be called) such as that whi called forth these remarks.   A. J.

** The Rev. Dr. Collis, late Head Master of grove School.

UNENCLOSED COMMONS (5ᵗʰ S. ix. 268, 297.)—
Permit me to say, in answer to A. J. K., that
there is no list extant of the commons and open
spaces of England. Up to a very recent time the
extent of such lands was unascertained, and much
misconception existed as to the quantity. The
Inclosure Commissioners for England and Wales
(a body presumed to be specially conversant with
this subject) stated, in their Report of 1872 :—
"The estimate of 1844 of 'common' and 'commonable' land together, at somewhat over 9,000,000 acres,
may, we think, be accepted as fairly accurate. In the
twenty-five years since the passing of the General Inclosure Act, 670,000 acres of these lands have been, and
are in course of being, inclosed, an extent equal to an
average English county. This leaves fully 8,000,000
acres still to be dealt with, which is more than one-fifth
of the entire acreage of England and Wales. Of this
vast extent of country there is reason to believe that
upwards of 3,000,000 acres will be found in the lowland
counties of England, and the remainder in the mountainous and moorland counties, and in Wales. A large
proportion of the 'commonable lands,' which are situated
chiefly in the lowland counties, is undoubtedly suscep-
tible of more profitable use and cultivation after inclosure. In addition to the 'commonable land' (which
at present is more or less under cultivation), we think it
may be assumed as a very moderate estimate that, out of
the 'commons,' one million acres might still be added to
the productive area of agricultural land in England. To
accomplish this at the rate of progress hitherto made
with inclosures many years must necessarily elapse.
Even when that is completed, there would remain about
one-sixth of the area of the entire country still open and
subject to rights of 'common,' an extent so great as must
show how erroneous have been the apprehensions expressed of the speedy inclosure of every common in England."

This estimate the Commissioners themselves found
to be erroneous, as in 1874, after a careful examination of the Tithe Commutation Awards, they
then estimated the area of commons and common
field lands at 2,632,000 acres for England and
Wales, 1,500,000 acres of which they regarded as
apparently unsuitable for cultivation. But, from
a still more recent return of landowners, prepared
by the Local Government Board from parish rate-
books, it appears that the common lands consist of
no more than 1,524,648 acres, of which 326,972
are said to be situate in Wales, and by far the
greater proportion of the remainder in the mountain districts of England, thus leaving a comparatively small extent for the rest of the country.

EDWARD W. FITHIAN.
Commons Preservation Society,
1, Gt. College Street, S.W.

PRINCESS SCHWARZENBERG (5ᵗʰ S. ix. 287.)—
This lady, the Princess Pauline Charlotte of Arem-
berg, born in 1775, and married to Prince Joseph
Jean of Schwarzenberg, was burnt to death at
Paris on July 1, 1810. She was the mother of
nine children. She had safely escaped from the
burning ballroom, when, being under the impression that one of her daughters was still in it, she

returned to seek for her. Madame d'Abrantes
says (Laurent, Hist. Napoleon):—
"A lustre fell from the ceiling on the head of the
princess and fractured her skull. She fell through an
aperture, and her body, with the exception of her bosom
and one part of her arm, was burnt to a cinder. She
was recognized only by a gold chain which she wore
round her neck, and to which was suspended a locket
set round with jewels. She was one of the most charming women of her time, beautiful, amiable, graceful, and
accomplished."

Sir A. Alison (History of Europe) says that her
remains could only be identified by a gold ornament which she had worn on her arm, and adds
that her death "is one of the noblest instances of
maternal heroism recorded in the annals of the
world." It is said that the prince her husband
went out of his mind ; but he survived her till
1833 (Almanach de Gotha). F. R. C. P. does not
state in what works the statement he mentions is
to be found. It is, to say the least, highly improbable ; but in the case of the Princess Pauline
Schwarzenberg it is, I think, impossible.

EDWARD SOLLY.
Sutton, Surrey.

ENGLISH TRANSLATIONS OF DANTE (5ᵗʰ S. viii.
365, 417.)—Was the Joseph Hume who published
a translation of the Inferno in blank verse, in
1812, the well-known M.P. of that name ? The
Dictionary of Living Authors ascribes it to him ;
but a correspondent who kindly pointed out to me
the omission of this version from my list of Dante
translations says, Query.

Mr. Charles Tomlinson's version of the Inferno,
in terza rima, has already been noticed by the
editor in the last volume of " N. & Q.," p. 520.

Did Lieut. Griffith, R.N., whose translation of
the Gerusalemme Liberata was published post-
humously in 1863, also translate Dante ? The
preface mentions him as a translator of Dante, but
I am inclined to think this is a misprint for Tasso,
more especially as this is not the only error (if
error it be) that the writer of the preface has fallen
into. He says that in Lieut. Griffith's version
Tasso's metre is exactly reproduced, whereas this
is not the case. As far as the fourth line Lieut.
Griffith's stanzas resemble Tasso's ; then instead
of, as in ottava rima, making the fifth line rhyme
with the first and third, and the sixth with the
second and fourth, the translator has for some
unaccountable reason made the fifth and sixth
lines rhyme together. His seventh and eighth
lines rightly rhyme together, as in Tasso's stanza.

Again, the writer of the preface speaks of Tasso
as the most esteemed poet of his country, a piece
of criticism that would considerably astonish an
Italian. What would an Englishman think if an
Italian writer, oblivious of Shakspeare and Milton,
were to call Spenser the most esteemed poet of
England ? Yet the distance between Milton and

Spenser is hardly so great as that between Dante and Tasso. The writer does not seem to be aware that Tasso was a great poet, but Dante a gigantic one. It is true that Byron calls Tasso "victor, unsurpassed in modern song"; but Byron's literary judgments are well known to have been singularly capricious and uncertain. In fact, he seems to have been nearly as poor as a critic as he was great as a poet. JONATHAN BOUCHIER.
Bexley Heath, Kent.

There is a MS. translation of the *Inferno* by Thomas Wade, author of *Mundi et Cordis Carmina*. It is in what is usually called *terza rima*, and a specimen of it may be seen in the *London Quarterly Review* for April, 1877. In the *Monthly Packet* some years ago there was a serial translation attempted in *terza rima* with dissyllabic rhymes, but not done at all strictly. There is also, privately printed, an experimental version of four cantos in absolute *terza rima* (all rhymes strictly dissyllabic) by Alfred Forman, translator of Wagner's *Der Ring des Nibelungen*. If it be worth while to add to the catalogue the two versions of the *Vita Nuova* named by JABEZ, it must surely be far better worth while to add that of Dante Gabriel Rossetti, which is one of the most exquisite exotics we can boast, and which, with other poems from Dante, is in *The Early Italian Poets*, 1861, renamed *Dante and his Circle* when republished in 1874. H. BUXTON FORMAN.

JUNIUS (5th S. ix. 147.)—May it not be that MR. C. ELLIOT BROWNE has erred in writing thus of the authorship of the *Contest*, a political satire against H. Fox (Lord Holland), 1756-7 : "I am aware it is usually attributed to Dr. Francis." Horace Walpole, in his *Memoires of the last Ten Years of the Reign of George II.*, 1822, vol. ii. p. 109, under Dec., 1756, says :—"Two weekly papers called the *Test* and *Contest*, besides occasional pamphlets, were the vehicles of satire. Murphy, a player, wrote the former on behalf of Fox, and Francis, a poetic clergyman, signalized himself on the same side." Murphy was, of course, Arthur Murphy, the well-known dramatist, author of *A Life of Garrick*, &c.; while Francis I take to be quite another than he who was supposed to have had to do with the *Letters of Junius*. O.

DEATH OF EDWARD, DUKE OF YORK, 1767 (5th S. vii. 228, 274, 294; viii. 192, 215, 238, 397; ix. 95, 131.)—I have just discovered another bit of scandal about this royal duke, which has not, I think, been referred to by MR. SOLLY or any of your correspondents. In the *Town and Country Magazine* for 1771, p. 672, it is said :—

"Notwithstanding the various reports about a Duchess of York, his late Royal Highness the Duke of that title never was married. Being once in company with some ladies who were rallying him on a declaration which he

made of determined celibacy, one of them laugh resolved to marry him that instant; and accordi getting a Prayer Book, read some part of the cerem between Miss Flood and him. This is the sole found on which the report of marriage is founded, and i James's the matter is treated wholly as a jocula cumstance."

Could this supposed marriage have suppli motive for the duke's pretended death abandonment of rank, country, and fortune, posing G. D. P.'s strange story to be well foun Has MR. THOMS ever heard of it ? Ha alluded to that gentleman, may I ask if the l which scattered to the winds the Hannah Li foot scandal and exposed the fraudulent pre sions of the Princess Olive has lost its cunnin why has one who has criticized so unsparingly scandals of the last century left this new unnoticed ? Can he not throw any light upon duke's supposed marriage, death, or disappearai Y. N. l

COLLECT FOR ASH WEDNESDAY (5th S. ix. 2 —If MR. CROMIE refers to the *Annotated l of Common Prayer*, part i. p. 92, he will find this collect is "partly a translation of one use the benediction of the ashes, and partly a c position of 1549 on the basis of other coll of the day." At p. 91 he will find the orig of the portion described as a translation, "o potens sempiterne Deus qui misereris omniun nihil odisti eorum quæ fecisti, dissimulans pec hominum propter pœnitentiam." The English sion is, as usual, free, not literal ; but the ph commented on by MR. CROMIE is in the L As for its origin, is it not scriptural ? Per from Wisdom xi. 24, "Thou lovest all the th that are, and abhorrest nothing which thou l made ; for never wouldest thou have made i thing if thou hadst hated it." A. (

MR. CROMIE will find the origin of the ph to which he refers in the introit for Ash Wed day in the Salisbury use, "Misereris omn Domine et nihil odisti eorum quæ fecisti," &c. same phrase occurs in the Benedictio Cinei "Omnipotens sempiterne Deus qui misereris nium et nihil odisti corum quæ fecisti," &c. " great storehouse, from which four-fifths of our vice book were taken," is to be found in the anc English service books, mainly in those of the S bury use, not in the Roman Breviary.
JOHNSON BAIL
Pallion Vicarage.

I hardly think that the quotation given by CROMIE shows the origin of the prayer for the day in Lent. St. Augustine, who quotes libe from the Vulgate in his writings, no doubt obta the idea from the Apocrypha ; in fact, he taken the very words of *Liber Sapientiæ*, xi. 2 "Diligis enim omnia quæ sunt, et nihil o

eorum quæ fecisti; nec enim odiens aliquid con-
stituisti, aut fecisti."   HUGH A. KENNEDY.
·Waterloo Lodge, Reading.

A "COTTACEL" (5ᵗʰ S. ix. 288.)—Is T. F. R.
quite sure of his word, and, if so, quite sure that
his authority speaks of "a cottacel of land"? I
suspect that the deed in question speaks of *cot-
setlas*, and, if so, we have to deal with cultivators
of the land, not with the land itself. But what is
the date of this "deed of grant"?
                                A. JESSOPP.

"MARQUIS" v. "MARQUESS" (5ᵗʰ S. ix. 167.)—
Sir Robert Naunton, 1630, speaks of "Paulet,
Marquesse of Winchester," while Stow, in his
edition of 1598, refers to the same title, if not the
same individual, as "Marquis of Winchester."
Pepys uses the two words as though to distinguish
male from female possessors, namely, "My Lord
Marquis Dorchester" and "Marquis Ormond," and
then "My Lady Marquess Winchester." In the
Life and Reign of Queen Ann, 1738, we read of
the "Marquis of Kent," "Marquis of Lothian,"
&c., and the *Peerage* of 1792 calls the dignity
"Marquis"; and yet, with these proofs that the
title should be "Marquis," on my own commission
as an officer in the Reserve Forces, under the hand of
the late Lord Lieutenant of Middlesex, he describes
himself as "James Brownlow William Gascoyne,
Marquess of Salisbury."   W. PHILLIPS.

MANOR OF MERE, STAFFORDSHIRE (5ᵗʰ S. ix.
248.)—Maer, near Whitmore, is a reputed manor
which is in the same hands with the advowson.
It formerly belonged to the Chetwynds. As there
is a considerable natural mere there, from which
the place doubtless takes its name, it is pretty
certain that the original spelling would be *Mere.*
                                H. W.

THE ROYAL CROWN OVER A CIVILIAN CREST
(5ᵗʰ S. ix. 167.)—A county militia regiment is
stated by C. T. J. M. to have lately adopted for
its badge the crest of its colonel. A regimental
badge is an honorary distinction granted by the
sovereign as a mark of special approbation, and,
as such, a regiment cannot adopt for itself a badge,
any more than a private individual is at liberty to
assume for himself a title or an "augmentation"
to his arms. Several years ago, when a button of
universal pattern was adopted for the regiments of
infantry in the British army, such regiments were
authorized to wear what, in default of a better
term, was styled a "collar-badge," which was intended to display such device as had formerly
appeared upon the buttons. The introduction of
these collar-badges gave rise to the adoption of
various new devices, which were duly sanctioned
by proper authority. It is presumably some such
device to which C. T. J. M. refers, but it cannot

with propriety be styled the badge of the regiment,
which, as already indicated, must be specially
granted. Such device certainly would not be
allowed to appear upon the regimental colour, but
whether it could be used upon the plate or paper
of the regiment is a somewhat different question.
It would certainly seem to be more appropriate
than the so-called "county arms" which are borne
by so many regiments of militia. With regard to
the main question, viz. whether the crest of the
colonel should be placed immediately beneath the
royal crown, or whether it should be divided in
some way from the crest or badge, there can be no
doubt but that the latter arrangement only would
be correct. The crest and motto of the late Duke
of Wellington form the badge of the 33rd Regiment,
whilst the boar's head—the Campbell crest—is
borne by the 91st Highlanders. I would suggest
that C. T. J. M. should ascertain in what manner
these crests are borne by the regiments in question.
Unfortunately for the case in point, the 33rd
and the 91st are not "royal" regiments, and the
crest of its colonel hardly appears to be an appropriate badge for a regiment bearing a royal title.
                                A. E. L. L.

THE PREVIOUS QUESTION (3ʳᵈ S. i. 345.)—The
"previous question" is a mode of disposing of a
subject at a public meeting by an amendment
which has considerably increased in use of late
years. There are two distinct forms of it, and
confusion is now not unfrequently caused by those
who adopt it not bearing this in mind. The old
Parliamentary form was practically to move, as an
amendment, "Shall we divide upon this question
or not?" The more modern form is different; it
amounts to putting as an amendment some admitted fact which no one disputes. Both forms of
"previous question" of course lead to the same
end, namely, to dismiss a question without taking
a direct vote upon it; but in the old form, if the
previous question passes in the affirmative, then
the original motion has to be put to the vote,
whereas, in the modern form, if the previous question (the admitted platitude) is carried, then the
original motion is lost, or rather cannot be put.
It would be well if all chairmen would adhere to
the old form, which is clearly the better.
                                EDWARD SOLLY.

DEATH OF CHARLES II. : P. M. A. C. F. (2ⁿᵈ
S. i. 110, 247; ix. 470.)—Accidentally opening
vol. i. of *The Phœnix; or, a Revival of Scarce and
Valuable Pieces*, London, 1707, I came upon "A
True Relation of the late King's Death," which
seems to be identical with the broadside under the
same title in Somers, viii. 429. In addition to
this account of the death of Charles II. there are
two papers found in the king's strong box, and
containing arguments in favour of the Roman
Catholic Church. The *True Relation* contains the

much trouble (*History*, i. 440), and referring to the person who first instigated the Duke of York to bring a priest to his brother's bedside. From "N. & Q." (2ⁿᵈ S. ix. 470) and Ranke's *History of England* (iv. 201), it appears that it was the duke's confessor who gave the first exhortation. Now this confessor was a Capucin, Père Mansuète. In the *True Relation* the initials of proper names are all printed in italic capitals, the initials of titles and dignities in roman capitals. Now Macaulay's P. M. A. C. F. is printed *P. M. a C. F.* The "a" is printed in ordinary small roman type. Thus P. M. would be a name, C. F. a title, and the whole, being translated, would mean "Père Mansuète, a Capucin Friar." I think, thanks to the *Phœnix*, this little mystery may be considered solved ; and as the explanation agrees with the account given in "N. & Q.," it raises the value of the evidence as to the circumstances of Charles's death to be derived either from the *True Relation* or the Benedictine account given, as said in "N. & Q.," by F. C. H.

W. K. GRIFFIN.

THOMAS CURNICK (NOT CHURNICK) (5ᵗʰ S. ix· 188) was the author of *Vortigern and Rowena*, a poem in three cantos, 12mo., 1814, also *Jehoshaphat and other Poems*, 12mo., 1815, Bristol, M. Bryan, Corn Street. Beyond the fact that this gentleman was an accountant, and that I believe his descendants to be living in Bristol, I can say nothing. Probably John Curnick, Esq., Agincourt Villa, Hampton Park, Redland, or John Curnick, Esq., Greenway Road, Redland Park, could give MR. INGLIS more information.

J. F. NICHOLLS, F.S.A.
Free Library, Bristol.

"DANDY PRATTE" (5ᵗʰ S. ix. 187.)—I am not prepared to answer this query, but I venture to record an anecdote from No. 5 of the Camden Society publications, which at any rate establishes the minuteness of the coin, and connects it with one of my own ancestors.

" Sir Richard Bingham," we are there told, " was a man eminent both for his spiritt and martiall knowledge, but of very small stature ; and, understanding that a proper bigg-bon'd gentleman had traduced his little person, or corpusculum, with the ignominious tearme of *Dande pratt*: ' Tell' him from me,' says he, ' that when it comes to the tutch, he shall find there is as good silver in a Dandepratt (which is a very small kind of coine) as in a brodd-fac't groate.'"

Camden (*Remaines*, p. 188) tells us that "K. Henry VII. stamped a small coine called *Dandy prats*."
C. W. BINGHAM.

SIR HUMPHRY DAVY (4ᵗʰ S. xi. 304.)—The liquefaction of the blood of St. Januarius was the subject of a long controversy in the *Catholic Magazine*, 1831-2, and an anonymous writer states

it was quite certain that a liquefai but not so certain that it was believe he was inclined to think The writer gives no reason for thi: rests merely on the words which] it can hardly be said to have any ɪ A few years later, however, this jecture was transformed into a ɪ by a Sicilian priest, Antonio de ˙ a book entitled *Sopra una cele dibattuta in Inghilterra negli aɪ intorno alla Liquefazione del Sang Vescovo e Martire* (4to., Napoli, 1ɛ says, " Il celebre chimico Davy testante, inchinava a tener per ˅ liquefazione " (p. 74).

I have reason to believe that t. Luca (now a cardinal) was the aɪ book (or pamphlet) on art, or thɪ lished at Rome about the year 1ɛ much obliged to any of your corɪ will enable me to find the exact ti
FRɪ
7, King Street, Covent Garden.

" HEADS OF THE PEOPLE ' (5ᵗʰ have not seen the book for thirɪ not be quite right in my details,] passing through the press I had ɪ " reader " at Vizetellys', who wa the accuracy of the printers' worɪ MS. of Jerrold's paper, " The Yo brought into his room by a compos sentence of which not a man in room could make out. It so ha best hand at deciphering MS. establishment was the boy who rɪ my brother when he read the p admitted into the consultation, aɪ of laughter, pronounced the word pigs are born to teats and some ɪ boy was right.
Croeswylan, Oswestry.

DANA (5ᵗʰ S. ix. 106.)—In the ɪ this name there are two (perhaps The Christian name should be E parish Wroxeter. In our local *Shɪ* March 15, 1876, there is the follɪ
" THE PROPOSED AMERICAN MINɪ with great satisfaction that the propɪ of the United States (in place of Ge this country is Mr. Richard Henry] an American born, comes of a good o He is a great-nephew of the late Re sometime Vicar of Wroxeter in this cɪ 1823, after whom the Dana Walk aɪ formerly in front of the county prison

My parents were married in V by the Rev. Edmund Dana in 18]

the same name lived in the Gay in the Abbey Foregate when I was a pupil at the Schools, 1842-1849.
BOILEAU.

Shrewsbury.

LICENCE TO EAT FLESH IN LENT (5th S. ix. 226, 274.)—The following is recorded in Phillips's *History of Shrewsbury* :—

"Whereas John Tomkies, M.A. and public preacher of the word in the town of Salop, is notoriously visited with sickness, insomuch that he is desirous to eat flesh, for the recovery of his former health, during the time of his sickness.

"By the minister of the parish next adjoining, according to the statutes in that behalf provided.

"I, therefore, Andrew Duker, minister of the parish of St. Alkmond's, do licence the aforesaid John Tomkies to eat flesh during his sickness, and no longer, according to the true meaning and intent of the afore-mentioned statute. In witness whereof I have subscribed my name, this 15th day of February, 1591.   AND. DUKER."

John Tomkies was minister of St. Mary's from May, 1582, to June, 1592.   W. HUGHES.

Shrewsbury.

"WHIG" AND "TORY" (5th S. ix. 25, 211.)—Webster gives, among other derivations, Whig "from the initial letters 'We Hope In God' as a motto of the club from which the Whig party took its rise." And Tory, "said to be an Irish word, denoting a robber or a savage, or from *toree*, 'Give me your money.'"   JOHN COLLINS FRANCIS.

DRAYTON (5th S. ix. 87, 137.)—Are there any other instances of British *tre* changed into English *dray* ? The difference in sound between the *Dray* of *Drayton* and the *try* of *Coventry*, *Oswestry*, *Daventry*, would make even a Celtophile (will MR. JACKSON allow me to call myself one ?) wish for some circumstantial evidence in the matter of the former. Again, even in the face of isolated cases like that of Torpenhow, is it likely that the Saxons remained, all the time it took them to conquer and rename these Draytons, so utterly ignorant of the language of the Briton as not to know the word he used for a town, and that, after committing one such blunder on their landing in the East, they went on repeating their tautological " town-town " at every *tre* they met with throughout their slow progress westward, up to and including Drayton in Shropshire? Lastly, what is to be done with the *Draycots* ? To one inclined to credit the Saxons with the naming of some, at least, of these towns, there is one fact which cannot but seem remarkable. I have gathered notes on most Draytons and Draycots in England, and invariably find one or other of the following characteristics in their geographical description : "hilly country," " very hilly," "dry soil," "light soil," " gravelly soil." Might this suggest the derivation of *Dray* from A.-S. *dreg* (dry), even as we have *hay* from *heg* ? Lambton, co. Durham, with its clayey soil and pasture lands would then supply us with the

counterpart of *Drayton* (cf. *Lambeth*, *Lambourne*, &c.), whilst we should find a pendant to *Draycot* in *Lambcote*, a hamlet near Ettington (Stratford-on-Avon), the soil of which does not belie its name.   ALPHONSE ESTOCLET.

THE TRUE ORIGIN OF THE WORD "PUMPER-NICKEL" (4th S. xi. 136, 226 ; 5th S. ix. 257.)—The following extract from a letter by Earl Marischal to ——, quoted in Lord Mahon's *History of England*, v., appendix, illustrates the phrase, " Bon pour Nicole," and carries it back to 1743 at least :—

" Le 'Starve donc' vient de ce qu'on dit que le pain manquait deux jours parmi les Anglais pendant que les Hanoveriens en avaient abondamment. ' Bon pour Nicole ' est une histoire qu'on fait d'un François à Hanovre qui ne pouvait pas trouver dans ce pays du pain mangeable, et en ayant fait apporter du meilleur il dit, ' Bon pour Nicole,' son cheval, à qui il le donna."

That the phrase was perfectly understood in 1743 is proved by an inscription on a satire of that date, styled *The H—v—n* (Hanoverian) *Confectioner General* (British Museum, Satirical Print, No. 2584), in which the British Lion is represented as lamenting that he is "Starv'd on Bon pour Nicole." Another print, No. 2605 of the same collection, comprises a pot of filth inscribed " Bon pore Nicole." This satire is called *A List of Foreign Soldiers in daily Pay for England*, and it assails the Hessian and Hanoverian mercenaries employed under General Ilton and others by the Granville ministry at the period in question—troops who were said to have behaved disgracefully at Dettingen. Ilton was called the " Confectioner General " because he boasted that he had "preserved" the troops by not sending them into action.   F. G. S.

"THE LASS OF RICHMOND HILL" (5th S. ix. 169, 239.)—I have a note that this song was written by Leonard McNally (born Sept. 27, 1752), a man of some repute in his day as a barrister as well as an author, in honour of Miss I'Anson, the daughter of William I'Anson of Richmond Hill, Leyburn, Yorkshire, a lady to whom he was married at St. George's, Hanover Square, Jan. 16, 1787. I had before heard the authorship of it attributed to James Hook. But see " N. & Q.," 2nd S. ii. 6 ; xi. 207, from which it would appear to have been written by William Upton and to have been sung by Incledon at Vauxhall, with such success as to cause his withdrawal from that place of amusement to the stage. Perhaps MR. CHAPPELL can settle the question.
GEORGE WHITE.

St. Briavel's, Epsom.

See " N. & Q.," 1st S. ii. 103, 350.
H. G. C.

[It is distinctly stated, *ante*, p. 239, that " the Richmond is in Surrey."]

Though I have been on the Severn in years long past, I do not propose to say a word about the wave occurring in that river, though I may remark that I have never heard of a wave forty feet high happening in that or any other river. My object is to point out that certain tidal estuaries, usually, I believe, mouths of rivers, are liable to this phenomenon, especially those where there is great rise and fall of tide at the springs.

I am aware that in some places there is an excessive rise and fall—for instance, in the Bay of Fundy, N. America, New Brunswick, and Nova Scotia ; but there are no great rivers with wide jaws there, and I have not heard of any bores there. The Hoogly of Bengal is subject to a bore, but if boats and ships are prepared for it no harm occurs. I was at turn of tide exposed to one, the boatmen all asleep, the boat lying across the course of the incoming wave, the roar of which I heard. I had the boat's head quickly turned to meet it and took no damage.

Later I was in Burmah, when a sad catastrophe occurred. A regiment had to go from Maulmain up the Sittang river in boats. They were over-taken by the bore, and great loss of life ensued. I have since seen the bore on that shallow river, a wave perhaps six feet high and two miles across. I then learned what the natives thought to be the cause of the disaster and their means of avoiding it. It was told me the officers would insist on the boats going off, at hours fixed by themselves, by sound of bugle irrespective of any other consideration, and also stopping in like manner when they pleased. Time and tide wait for no man. I learned that the Burmese practice was, when bores were expected, to ground their boats at half ebb, so that when the tidal wave made the boats were beyond its reach. I make this a present to you for the benefit of those beyond the seas.　　　　J. C. H.

This is not seen in the Humber, which is too wide for it, but begins to make its appearance some few miles up, as the banks become closer, in the Trent and Ouse, where it is called the "Ager." I have seen it rolling grandly up at Owston Ferry, and as it is coming one hears shouts of "Ware ager !" to warn persons in charge of boats, &c. See Peacock's *Lincolnshire Glossary*, E.D.S., *s.v.*, and Stonehouse's *Hist. of the Isle of Axholme*.　　　　J. T. F.

There is no bore in the Humber. It commences as the tide rushes up Ouse and Trent, and is called the "agar." Finn Magnusen derives the Scandinavian god Ægir from *œgia, aga*, to flow (Mallet's *Northern Antiquities*, Bohn, p. 546). The agar is only important at spring tides. The sailors give warning (as the Norsemen would do ages ago) by the cry, " War' agar !"　　　　W. G.

Quincey gives a quaint and graphic descriptio this phenomenon as he saw it in the Dee.
W. J. BERNHARD SMIT Temple.

For a graphic description of the bore or ægi the river Trent, see Stonehouse's *Isle of Axhc* p. 50.　　　　J. ;

"SHACK" (5ᵗʰ S. viii. 127, 413.)—I had t more care than one of the respondents supp and it was after a conversation with another c spondent of "N. & Q.," and in consequence o that I sent the query. I am obliged to A. B his remarks. Those who are familiar with appearance of the open fields will call to n that they very frequently were partitioned ou strips, which were formed by the lands of different proprietors, and the balks of rough g by which they were separated. The homily c mends the proprietors who make their balks w for the better shack of their neighbours' cattl harvest, and the Clarendon editor inclines Richardson's interpretation. The fact that : for use in harvest time seems to point to ano period than that of the common occupation of feeding ground after harvest ; and the fact th is the balk which is in question, and which sists of grass, also appears to preclude the sup tion that it is to be referred to shaken out c as some think, which would be anywhere rather than on it. And again, the circumst that the balk was very narrow, as being a r boundary, and that to make it wide enough f cart would have caused a waste of corn-produ land, appears to throw a doubt upon Richard interpretation that it was for a road.

In the supposition which I hazarded, the broader balk would be a great advantage for feeding of the animals employed in carting harvest home, I sought for an explanation w would agree with all the circumstances of the (In this I am confirmed by A. B.
ED. MARSHAL

This word explains the derivation of the cal pigs common in Lincolnshire. When pigs called home out of the fields, the caller ("Sheck, sheck !"　　　E. LEATON BLENKINSOF

"CRY MATCHES !" (5ᵗʰ S. viii. 491 ; ix. 5! F. R. F. I believe must give to England the c of the above exclamation of surprise rather to America. It was in schoolboy use fifty } ago to my personal knowledge, at which tim deemed it to be no more nor less than "Gra'mercy" of old, modified by time, whil word "Crimes," which was as much used similar sense, we took to be its abbreviatior though since I have been partly persuaded th might be that slang expression of the sixte century, "Cry aim," so frequently mentioned by the old dramatists, and which was used as an hortatory exclamation by the bystanders at archery meetings.   W. PHILLIPS.

SUTTON MUTTON (5th S. ix. 88, 175.)—The version of this saying with which I have been familiar makes Walsall to have been famous for "bow legs" instead of "bandy legs." I imagine that legs of the latter character have their crooked-ness of a knock-kneed description, turning inwards and not outwards, as in bow legs. I always under-stood that the bow legs at Walsall were attributable to the continued tramping up and down the stone steps that led to so many of the houses.
                                        CUTHBERT BEDE.

The rhymes under this heading have called to my mind a verse upon four villages in the neigh-bourhood of Banbury ; whence I got them I know not :—

" Aynho on the hill,
    Clifton in the clay,
    Drunken Deddington,
    And Yam Highway."

Yam, it must be explained, is the local pronun-ciation of *Hempton*, a hamlet in the parish of Deddington.   EDWARD H. MARSHALL.
The Temple.

I am sorry to say that in the rhyme communi-cated from oral tradition by MR. HOPPUS, but which is also printed in Dr. Giles's *History of Witney*, for "Duckington dogs" should be sub-stituted "Ducklington dogs," the inhabitants of the village from which I write being those who are thus uncomplimentarily designated. But it is not for one of those inhabitants to say whether the epithet is in the present day deserved or not. Also for "Fawder" read "Fawler."
                                        W. D. MACRAY.
Ducklington Rectory.

A TIRLING-PIN (5th S. ix. 88, 229.)—I have seen and tirled at an original tirling-pin on the chief entrance door of the vicarage house at Oving-ham-on-Tyne, Northumberland, which has been in use from time immemorial. It is similar to the one described in *Peveril of the Peak*.   J. T. F.
Winterton, Brigg.

"HOPING AGAINST HOPE" (5th S. ix. 68, 94, 258, 275.)—I suppose that the change in the Rheims version was made by Bishop Challoner. It is found in his edition, issued in 1749, while in the edition printed by Cousturier, in 1633, the original reading of 1582, "contrarie to hope," is preserved. I do not find this text cited among the many which are referred to by Dr. H. Cotton in his volume entitled *Rhemes and Doway*.
                                        W. D. MACRAY.

Miscellaneous.

NOTES ON BOOKS, &c.

The Holy Bible according to the Authorized Version (A.D. 1611). With an Explanatory and Critical Com-mentary and a Revision of the Translation by Bishops and other Clergy of the Anglican Church. Edited by F. C. Cook, M.A., Canon of Exeter, &c. New Testa-ment. Vol. I., S. Matthew, S. Mark, S. Luke. (Murray.)

Two years have elapsed since the publication of the sixth and last volume of the Old Testament division of that edition of the Holy Scriptures which the enlightened Churchmanship of the late Lord Ossington had sug-gested as necessary to supply a far-spread and yet growing want. During these two years the success which has attended this attempt "to put the general reader in possession of whatever information may be requisite to enable him to understand the Holy Scrip-tures, to give him as far as possible the same advantages as the scholar, and to supply him with satisfactory answers to objections resting upon misrepresentation of the text," has steadily increased ; and the appearance of this, the first volume of the New Testament with the Speaker's Commentary, will be welcomed by a large body of readers. It contains the Gospels of St. Matthew, St. Mark, and St. Luke, with a long and interesting introduction by the Archbishop of York, who, it will be remembered, undertook to organize the plan for carrying out the Speaker's suggestion by the co-operation of scholars selected for their Biblical learning, a task which he has thoroughly accomplished. The commentary and critical notes on the first twenty-six chapters of St. Matthew are by the late Dean Mansel, while for those to the two concluding chapters (which, owing to the Dean's death in July, 1871, were left incomplete) the editor, the Rev. Canon Cook, is responsible, as he is also for the commentary and critical notes on the Gospel of St. Mark. The Bishop of St. Davids prepared his com-mentary on St. Luke some years ago, but having been unable to get it ready for the press, owing to the pressure of episcopal duties, that task has devolved upon the editor, who has added many valuable additional notes. Three more volumes will complete this important work, creditable to all who have had any share in its prepara-tion, and eminently calculated to awaken and spread among us a reverent and intelligent study of the Holy Scriptures.

The Great Dionysiak Myth. By Robert Brown, Jun., F.S.A. Vol. II. (Longmans & Co.)
WE shall have to wait yet awhile ere the veil be entirely lifted from the myth of Dionysus, in so far at least as that unveiling depends upon the unwearied exertions of Mr. Robert Brown. But even now his βακχικόν δώρημα is an imposing one, crowded with many a strange name and still more strange orthography. We fear we are still in so unregenerate a condition as to prefer the old-fashioned Bacchus to the modern "Bakchos," concerning whom we always feel a latent doubt whether he may not be identified with that other potent Oriental divinity, "Baksheesh." Mr. Brown's minuteness of research on his favourite topic is worthy of a sounder cause than we are at present persuaded that he has embraced. Re-serving the possibility of conviction by means of the arguments to be adduced in his concluding volume, we do not yet feel able to give in our adhesion to the view which appears to be the cardinal point of Mr. Brown's theory, viz. that the Dionysiak Myth "covers the entire field of research" necessary to demonstrate the con-clusion that "man has not gradually raised himself by his own unaided efforts from the lowest depths of belief

or conjecture, but that his career reveals a falling away from a simple trust in the supreme to complicated systems of perverted truth." We should willingly grant that the careful and patient investigation of any myth, Solar, Dionysiak, Arthurian, or by whatsoever name called, may throw much light on the primitive religion of man. And within such limits Mr. Brown has done a great deal of good hard work. But we cannot admit that any one myth covers the entire field of research, and herein therefore lies, in our judgment, the radical weakness of Mr. Brown's theory. In all such attempts to make a part do the work of the whole there is a necessary one-sidedness, an inevitable straining of meanings, however unconsciously to the writer. Having got hold of a "horned divinity," Mr. Brown cannot let the unfortunate island Kerastis take its name from the simple fact of its shape, but must press that name into the service of his divinity. His presentment of a Japanese Dionysus is truly formidable, not to say repulsive. We should not be surprised if those who may worship here it were to do so, as we lately heard a Hindoo gentleman state to be his own habit, with closed eyes. Mr. Brown must surely have been nodding, like the good Homer, when he introduced, at p. 137, a reference to "Porphery, De Antro Nymph," a writer and a title alike unknown to us.

Memories of our Great Towns, with Anecdotic Gleanings concerning their Worthies and Oddities (1860-1877). By Dr. John Doran, F.S.A. (Chatto & Windus.)

Memories of our Great Towns, a posthumous work of Dr. Doran, which as the latest outcome of his genial, versatile, and scholarly mind has a special interest for readers of "N. & Q.," consists of a series of notices, which first appeared in the *Athenæum*, of places selected for annual meetings of the British Association for the Advancement of Science. The period between 1860 and 1877 is comprised in the series, the latest paper describing Plymouth, the scene of last summer's gathering. One of Dr. Doran's latest tasks was to complete the revision of the sheets, and restore them with his own hand to the printer. The volume constitutes thus his latest accomplishment. It has every grace of his singularly happy and attractive style. It is a mere commonplace of criticism to say that no living writer could furnish information so curious, so varied, and so full of interest. Whether gossiping about the muster of Yorkshire squires at Doncaster; chronicling the appearance of those "famous wits" to whom Cambridge, albeit not always an *alma mater*, proved herself "native or hospitable"; depicting the strife for precedency between Dundee and Perth; dwelling upon the presence at Norwich of "beauty so abounding, so dazzling, so intoxicating," that the place has ever since remained famous; describing the growth of Brighton beneath princely patronage; or crystallizing into a few delightful sentences the comic history of the Plymouth stage, Dr. Doran is always unapproachable.

In the account of the coach journey to Bath before the days of railways, and in the picture of the gentlemen between Marlborough and Sandy Lane looking in anticipation of highwaymen "to their silver-hilted rips," hiding "their watches in their boots," and stowing "away their guineas in places where robbers always looked for them," we have a perfect reproduction of old life, and at the same time a capital specimen of Dr. Doran's gentle humour. How pleasantly expressed, too, is the contrast between Bath in 1720 and the same place in 1864 ! "To-day the philosophers may communicate through the telegraph wires with friends at a distance, at a low tariff, and in a few minutes. A hundred and fifty years ago the Bath express letter office would carry your message to London, at any time, in a day and night, and charge 2l. 1s. for the service." Apropos of Liverpool Dr. Doran chronicles the answer of G. F. Cooke of Thomas Walsingham, who, when too drunk to play Richard III. as announced and confronted with a demand for an apology, exclaimed "with a haughty scorn and a halting logic, 'Apology from me to you? Why there isn't a brick in your town that is not cemented with the blood of a slave !'" Glasgow clubs furnish a chapter of capital gossip, second describes with incomparable fidelity the eccen tricities of Bradford dialect, and a third presents a full and picturesque account of the nobility of Devon. It i needless to say that there is not in the volume a dull pag or a page that the seeker after amusement or informa tion can afford to omit.

———

Mr. H. T. Riley, M.A., Barrister-at-Law, so well known as the editor of the *Liber Albus*, the *Chronicle of Thomas Walsingham*, and other historical work of the Middle Ages, died at Croydon last Sunday, afte an illness which had been brought on by hard menta work.

Mr. Murray announces, amongst other works in the press:—*The Student's Edition of the Speaker's Com mentary on the Bible,—Memoir of Bishop Stanley*, revise and enlarged by the Dean of Westminster,—*A New Lif of Albert Dürer,—The Psalter of David, according to th Great Bible of* 1539, with introduction and notes b Prof. Earle of Oxford,—and *Murray's Alphabetica Handbook for England and Wales*.

Notices to Correspondents.

We must call special attention to the following notice:—

On all communications should be written the name an address of the sender, not necessarily for publication, bu as a guarantee of good faith.

W. H. F.—The inscription merely signifies that the instrument was made at Cremona, formerly celebrate for its violins and musical strings.

Rob Roy is referred to our notice of Dr. Rogers' *Genealogical Memoirs of the Scottish House of Christie ante*, p. 220.

Kingston.—We shall be glad to forward the cutting t A. J. M.

J. C. F.—The passage quoted from Macaulay's *Histor* is well known.

Gwavas will greatly oblige by writing his communica tions on separate pieces of paper.

A. S. (Princeton, New Jersey.)—Have you consulte Murray's *Handbook to Italy?*

A. Burrell.—We hardly think that, under the cir cumstances, the subject is suited to our columns.

W. G. D. F.—Most probably an ordinary visitor' handbook to the cathedral would answer your purpose.

T. C. Adams (Malta.)—Your query is simply in explicable.

W. Gallatly.—Apply to a second-hand bookseller.

George White.—It will appear.

St. Swithin.—Letter forwarded.

NOTICE.

Editorial Communications should be addressed to " Th Editor of 'Notes and Queries'"—Advertisements an Business Letters to "The Publisher"—at the Office, 20 Wellington Street, Strand, London, W.C.

We beg leave to state that we decline to return com munications which, for any reason, we do not print ; an to this rule we can make no exception.

NOTES AND QUERIES.

LONDON, SATURDAY, APRIL 27, 1878.

CONTENTS.— N° 226.

Notes.

MATHIAS ON CHATTERTON AND ROWLEY.

I have in my possession a manuscript bearing the following title and memorandum in the handwriting of Mr. Thomas James Mathias :—

"Two original Poems by Chatterton—On our Lady's Chirch and The Tournament—Two others by Rowley ; two of the Poems which Chatterton transmitted to Mr. H. Walpole, & which the latter returned to him—A present to me from Dr. Glynn, Fell. of King's Coll. Cam.— T. J. M."

Whether the manuscript is really in the handwriting of Chatterton, or whether Mathias was mistaken in this, as I shall give reasons for thinking he was in another part of his memorandum, is immaterial to my main purpose in writing this. Suffice it that the handwriting of Mathias is unquestionable, and that he believed the manuscript to be what he described it. It may possibly have been three separate documents ; but they are all on paper (quarto post) bearing the same water-mark, and have every appearance of having been written at the same time. They consist of—1. a sheet of two unnumbered leaves :—

"On oure Ladys Chirch (not to be copied).
In auntient days, when Kenewalchyn Kynge
.   .   .   .   [32 lines ending]
And as aforesed mickle much of Land."

2. Four sheets, forming leaves numbered from 1 to 7 and one blank :—

"The Tournament (not to be copied).
The matten Belle han sounded longe
.   .   .   .   [108 lines ending]
And then one Howre was gone & past.
Ende of the fyrste Canto."

3. Two sheets, forming leaves numbered 1 to 3 and one blank :—

"John Seconde Abbat of Sayncte Augustyn was a Manne well learned in the Languages of yore, he wrote ynn the Greke Tonge a Poem on Roberte Fitz Hardynge, whyche as nie as Englyshe wyll serve I have thus transplaced—
Wythe daitive steppe Relygyon dyghte yn Greie
.   .   .   .   [19 lines ending]
And spende mie daies upponn Fitz Hardynges Breste.
Nor was hee lackynge ynn descriptions of Battles and drear accounts, as ye maie see under bie himself onn Kynge Rycharde.
Harte of Lyon ! shake thie Sworde
.   .   .   .   [12 lines ending]
Yn thy banner Terrour standes.
Thus moche for Abbat Johannes Pamics he was inducted 20 yeeres and dyd act as Abbat 9 yeeres before hys induetyon for Phylyp then Abbat, hee dyed yn MCCXV heeing buryed yn hys Abbe yn the Mynster."

The first two pieces, "On oure Ladys Chirch" and "The Tournament," bear titles which were assigned to two of the alleged Rowley poems, as published by Tyrwhitt, but have nothing in common with those pieces except the names. Those in the present manuscript were published in the *Supplement to the Miscellanies of Thomas Chatterton*, 8vo., London, 1784, with the euphonious description of Imitations of our old poets, and with the date assigned to them of 1769 ; but they contain important variations in spelling and otherwise, showing clearly that they have not been printed from this manuscript. The two pieces which Mr. Mathias supposed to have been those sent to and returned by Horace Walpole are printed (with at least as much variation from the present manuscript) in Barrett's *History of Bristol*, but with no apparent connexion between them, the poem on Fitz Hardynge being printed at p. 246 with somewhat similar particulars as to the induction and death of Abbat John, while that on King Richard appears at p. 641 as incorporated in Chatterton's note to "The Ryse of Peyncteynge in Englande." These latter documents and some others are stated by Barrett to be "printed from the very originals, in Chatterton's handwriting, sent in two letters to Horace Walpole, Esq." Nothing is more probable than that the papers returned by Walpole should have come into the hands of Barrett ; but unless he has taken great liberties in rearranging his materials, on which I will observe presently, it follows that the manuscript now in question (in which the two last named pieces form part of one document, connected together by the biographical notice of Abbat Johannes Pamies and criticism on his merits) is not that sent to Walpole ; and it may be inferred that he was not the only person on whom Chatterton tried the experiment of seeking a patron by communicating specimens of antique lore.

Mathias's note does not mention the date of Dr. Glynn's present ; but from the first two pieces being described in the note as by Chatterton, while it says the others are by Rowley, I suppose it to have been written subsequent to the publication of the *Supplement to the Miscellanies* in 1784. But Dr. Glynn was engaged, as early as 1778, in inquiries as to Chatterton at Bristol, where he may have obtained the manuscript ; and, if so, Mathias, who has left a record of his intimacy with Dr. Glynn in the notes to the *Pursuits of Literature*, and, independent of such intimacy, knew of his researches from Bryant's *Observations on Rowley* (see p. 527, &c.), cannot have failed to communicate with his friend and see this manuscript before publishing, in 1783, his own essay on the evidence relating to the poems attributed to Rowley.

In the following year a letter printed in "N. & Q.," 2nd S. xii. 221, seems to imply that Dr. Glynn's faith in Rowley had been shaken ; for his phrase, when he wished to impute a literary forgery to Sir William Jones, was that his translation of the *Moallákat* "was damnably like the manner of Chatterton's writing." Now Horace Walpole, writing from memory nine years after Chatterton's manuscripts had been in his possession, was in doubt whether the poem on Richard I. had been represented as of contemporary date or of the age of Edward IV., but believed the former to have been the case. In relation to this very controversy there has been some dispute whether Homer was known in England in the reign of Edward IV. ; but Walpole, if this had been the manuscript submitted to him, could scarcely have failed to notice or remember the astounding fact of a poem on an English subject being alleged to have been written *in Greek* by an English monk who died in 1215, and translated by another in the fifteenth century. But here we have Thomas James Mathias, a professed critic and a scholar of pretensions infinitely superior to Walpole's, accepting the fact without question, and in his own handwriting, on the very document containing this egregious statement, attributing the two later poems to Rowley.

If this was the manuscript known to Barrett, he must have dealt with it in the manner above pointed out, and suppressed the statement as to translation from the Greek as too damaging to the Rowleian cause. I am not confident that this was not the case, for Barrett's Chatterton papers passed, on his death in 1789, to Dr. Glynn, who bequeathed them to the British Museum (see "N. & Q.," 2nd S. x. 282), and this may have been one of the documents which he so acquired. But if this were the history of the manuscript, the donor should have been called Dr. Glynn-Clobery, which name

he had assumed before the publication (... *History of Bristol*, the dedication of whi... April 15, 1789 ; for the name of Clobery the list of subscribers, though incorrect as if it had been part of Dr. Glynn' Even if, on the above or other grounds, gested, in defence of Mathias's candou manuscript may only have come to his after the publication of the essay in maintained the authenticity of Rowley the fact that in editions of the *Pursuits* ture published after the death of Dr. anonymous author retained a note on (... dated 1794, in which he adopts "the ge of this controversy in Mr. Mathias's c comprehensive essay on the evidence, ex internal, on the subject of Rowley's poer

If I thought there yet survived any b Rowley, I would ask what they think of author ; but, as a question more imme teresting to myself as the owner of the n I should be glad to know whether (as being in Chatterton's handwriting, as there exist materials of easy access f a comparison) any further light can be its history before it reached the hands of I also, whether the "Ryse of Peyncteyn lande" is one of the MSS. now in the Museum, and, if so, whether it has the Abbat John and his poem on King I printed by Barrett. JOHN FITCHETT
Hardwick House, Chepstow.

A SALISBURY MISSAL.

In order to complete the descripti(... volume, a partial sketch of which was (p. 221, I add a list of the saints com(... in the Sanctorale and of the votive mass are as follows :—

1. St. Andrew.
2. St. Nicholas. [The addition of "In t' p'... the Officium, Offertorium, and Communio this service was intended to do duty also for the saint's translation, May 9.]
3. In conceptiõe sancte marie ad missã omT in natiuit' eiusdš verbis tñ natiuit' mutat' s' sine " Glia in excels " & Ite missa c̃.
4. St. Thomas.
5. Purification of B.V.M.
6. St. Matthias.
7. Annunciation of B.V.M.
8. St. Mark.
9. SS. Philip and James.
10. Invention of the Cross. [To the "... martyribus alexandro sociisque ejus," the M m' de oīb' scĩs."]
11. Nativity of St. John the Baptist. [Thi the introduction of two rubrics in the Seq " Iste v dr' in natiuitate," " Iste v dr' in dec(made also to serve for the two festivals of th beheading of the Baptist.]
12. SS. Peter and Paul. [A rubric pr(Offertorium, " R* in cathedra scĩ pet'," is str

service for the festival Cathedra Petri is given in the MS.]
15. Translation of St. Thomas of Canterbury.
14. St. James.
15. Assumption of B.V.M. [Only one sequence is given, not seven, i.e. one for each day during the octave.]
16. St. Bartholomew.
17. St. Giles.
18. Nativity of B.V.M.
19. Exaltation of Holy Cross.
20. St. Matthew.
21. St. Michael.
22. SS. Simon and Jude.
23. All Saints.
24. In Natali' uni' apli. Under this head are given:—
Offm. Mihi autem nimis. Ps. Dnē probasti me. Ep. ad Ephesios, ii. 19-22. Gr. Nimis honorati. V. Dinumerabo. Gr. In omnē terram. V. Celi enarrant. V. In omnē terrā. V. Nimis honorati. Seq. Clare sanctor' senatus. Alia seq. Alla nunc decantet. Offr. Michi aūt nimis... Constitues eos principes...Confitebunt' celi...Justus ut palma...Euang. S. John, xv. 1-7 and 17-25. Cō. Vos qui secuti estis.
25. In Natali' uni' eu'ngeliste. Under this head are given:—Offm. Protexisti me deus. Ps. Exaudi deus orōm. Offm. Os iusti meditabitur. Ps. Noli emulari. Lc. ezechielis prophete, i. 10-14 V. Primus ad syon. Seq. Laus deuota mente. Offr. Posuisti dnē in capite eius. Cō. Magna est gl'ia eius.
26. Missa de scā maria cotidie per aduentū.
27. Missa de scā maria ī die Nat' dnī & cotidie ab hinc usq ad purific'.
28. Missa de scā maria cotidie a purific' usq ad'aduentū dni.

Missæ Votivæ.
1. De Trinitate.
2. De sancta Cruce.
3. De sancto Spiritu.
4. Pro fratribus et sororibus. [Sometimes called missa "Salus Populi," from the first words of the Introit.]
5. Pro pace. [Those that follow should strictly be classed as Memoriæ Communes, as under each head only the Oratio, Secreta, and Post Communio are given.]
6. Pro serenitate aëris.
7. Ad pluviam postulandam.
8. In tempore belli.
9. Pro quacumque tribulatione.
10. De Angelis.
11. De omnibus Sanctis.
12. Pro papa.
13. Pro universali ecclesia.
14. Pro pontifice.
15. Pro prelatis et subditis.
16. Pro rege.
17. Pro rege et regina.
18. Pro semetipso.
19. Pro salute amici.
20. Pro spirituali amico.
21. Contra temptationem carnis.
22. Contra malas cogitationes.
23. Ad invocandam gratiam Sci Spiritus.
24. Pro penitentia lachrymarum.
25. Pro peccatoribus.
26. Pro mortalitate hominum.
27. Pro iter agentibus.
28. Pro pœnitentia.
29. Contra aereas potestates.
30. Pro inspiratione divinæ Sapientiæ.
31. Ad poscendum donum sce caritatis. [The heading given in a Missal printed at Paris, 1514, is Ad poscēdum donum spūs sancti.]
32. Pro eo qui in vinculis detinetur.

33. Contra invasores.
34. Pro navigantibus.
35. Pro tribulatione cordis.
36. Pro infirmo.
37. Pro benefactoribus vel pro salute vivorum.
38. Contra adversantes.
39. Pro peste animalium.
40. Missa pro defunctis. [This is followed by Memoriæ Communes, viz.:—]
41. In die sepulturæ.
42. In anniversariis.
43. Pro episcopo.
44. Pro abbate.
45. Pro sacerdote.
46. Pro quolibet defuncto.
47. Pro patre et matre.
48. Pro parentibus et benefactoribus.
49. Pro benefactoribus.
50. Pro fratribus et sororibus.
51. Pro trigintalibus.
52. Pro trigintalibus evolvendis.
53. Pro morte prevento.
54. Pro familiaribus.
55. Pro amico.
56. Pro amico defuncto.
57. Pro familiaribus feminis.
58. Pro quiescentibus in cimiterio.
59, 60, 61, 62, 63. Missa generalis. [The first of these Missæ generales corresponds to the Pro oib' fidelib' defūctis the printed Missal. Nos. 60, 61, and 62 are headed in it "Oratio generalis," whilst No. 63 follows the rubric defining the Trigintale sancti Gregorii.]

A few Communia follow, marked in the margin for convenience of reference with a capital letter. They are:—
A. Gr. Constitues eos p'ncipes.
B. Tract. Beatus vir qui timet.
C. Offr. In omēm terram.
D. Coio. Ego sum vitis vera.
E. Eung. Scdum Matheum. Venit ihs in p'tes cesaree philippi.
F. V. Non vos me elegistis.
G. Offr. Michi autē nimis.
H. V. Vitam petiit.
I. V. Inquirentes a' dn'm.

Three prayers, the Oratio, Secreta, and Communio of the second of the Missæ Generales, are copied in handwriting of the sixteenth century on a blank page at the end of the MS. There are two important alterations in the first of these prayers; for "dominum papam regem et episcopum nostrum et onnem plebem illis commissam," the copy reads "reges, episcopos et abbates nostros," &c., omitting all mention of the pope, whilst at the close the words, "et iter famulorum tuorum in salutis tuæ prosperitate dispone," are left out. The copy of the Secreta, "Deus qui singulari corporis tui hostia totius mundi solvisti delicta," &c., is almost erased. In the copy of the Communio the only important change is the addition before the name of the Blessed Virgin of the words, "semperque virginis."

A strange rubric occurs in the Canon of the Mass: "Hic eregat sacerdos manus et conjungat et postea tergat digitos et elevet hostiam dicens. 'Qui pridie q' pateretur': ita quod non videatur a populo et sic debet tenere quousque dixerit verba consecrationis quia si ante consecrationem elevetur et populo ostendatur sicut faciunt fatui sacerdotes faciunt populum ydolatriare adorando panem purum tanquam corpus Christi et in hoc peccant."

A canon of the Synod of Exeter, A.D. 1287, quoted by Maskell (*Ancient Liturgy of the Church of England*, second edit., p. 92, n.), may be cited in connexion with the above :—

"Quia vero per hæc verba, *Hoc est enim Corpus meum*, et non per alia, panis transubstantiatur in corpus Christi, prius hostiam non levet sacerdos, donec ista plena protulerit verba, ne pro creatore creatura a populo veneretur."

The description has, I fear, run to a somewhat inordinate length, but I have made it as brief as I could consistently with accuracy.

JOHNSON BAILY.

Pallion Vicarage.

THE BIBLIOGRAPHY OF ARCHERY.

In the following list works relating to archery societies are grouped and given first, then follow a group of MSS., then the general list. The works are ranged in the order of their age, excepting that the several editions of one work are grouped with the first edition. Excepting those works to the titles of which the words "not seen" are appended, and the few imperfectly given titles authorities for which are cited, copies of all the works noted were in my hand at the time I described them. A few entries are taken from *A Transcript of the Registers of the Company of Stationers of London*, 1554-1640, A.D., edited by Edward Arber, privately printed, London, 1875, &c., 4to. : they are distinguished by the letters "T. S. R.," followed by the numbers of the volume and page from which the entry is taken. The letters B., G., M. following a title denote that a copy of the work so distinguished should be found in the Bodleian, Oxford; Guildhall, London; and the British Museum libraries respectively.

Works relating to Robin Hood and to the William Tell group of mytho-historical tales are not included in this, but are reserved for separate lists.

The most valuable works noted in the list on the theory and practice of archery are the second edition of H. A. Ford's work, 1859 ; the lecture by Sir J. F. W. Herschel, 1866 ; the papers by James Spedding and F. Townsend in *The Archer's Register* for 1866-67 ; and the articles by Maurice Thompson in Harper's and Scribner's magazines, 1877. The article by the Hon. Daines Barrington in the *Archæologia*, 1783, is perhaps the most complete on the history of archery in England. To the gentlemen who have helped me to perfect this list I tender my thanks.

To the Secretary of the Royal Company of Archers, Edinburgh (who forwarded a parcel of rare books to London for me to examine), and to the Honorary Secretary of the Roya Society, London, I am especially inc courteous ways in which they comp requests for information.

SOCIETIES.

Royal Guard of Scottish Archers, L'Escosse Françoise. Discours des mencees depuis l'an sept cents septante sep jusques à present, entre les couronnes d'Escosse....A Paris, chez P. Mettayer,...1(Dedication signed A. Houston [de Losse].

Papers relative to the Royal Guard of S(in France. From original documents. Constable] at Edinburgh, 1835. 4to. pp x 84, Reprint of a work by A. Houston, entit Françoise. A Paris, chez P. Mettayer, 16 the Maitland Club, Glasgow. M.

The Scot abroad. By John Hill Burt(wood & Sons, Edinburgh, 1864. 2 vols pp. 47-59, R. G. of S. A. M.

Fraternity of St. George, afterwards the Artillery Company, 1537.

29° Nouembris, 1615. John Trundle— Copie vnder the handes of Master Taverr Lownes Warden a poeme called *The Ar* by Thomas Dekker....vj^d. (T. S. R., i poem was published in 1616. I cannot h sent existence of a copy.

Londons Artillery, briefly containing th(of that wo[r]thie Societie : with the mode1 martiall exercises, natures of armes, vertue antiquitie, glorie and chronography of tl cittie....By R. N. Oxon. London, print Creede and Bernard Allsopp for William to be sold at his shop in Paules Church Y(of the Swan, 1616. 4to. pp. viii-104. Ded Richard Nic[c]olls. Pp. 86-88, 93 94, Ar(12th April, 1639. Ra[l]ph Mabb—F copie under the bandes of Master Wyk(Rothwell Warden The summons or bills f(Garden. Vj^d. (T. S. R., iv. 464.)

The bowman's glory ; or, archery reviv(account of the many signal favours vouchs and archery by those renowned monarch VIII., James, and Charles I. As by their s commissions here recited may appear. relation of the manner of the archers several days of solemnity. Published by marshal to the regiment of Archers. L(by S. R., and are to be sold by Edward (Cross, 1682. 12mo. pp. xvi-80. The firs Pp. 33-80, A remembrance of the worthy s ing by the Duke of Shoreditch, and his worshipful citizens of London, upon Tues(September, 1583. Set forth according thereof to the everlasting honour of the ga in the long bow. By W. M. M., G.

Royal patents, and letters, for inco1 encouraging the H. A. C., viz.:—

1. The patent of Henry VIII. 1537.
2. The patent of James I. 1605.
3. The patent of Charles I. 1633.
4. The letter of William III. 1690.
5. The letter of Queen Anne. 1702.
6. The letter of George I. 1715.
7. The letter of George III. 1766.

London, printed by Stephen Clark,...1777 Folding plan of Finsbury Fields.

The history of the H. A. C., of the city o(its earliest annals to the peace of 1802.

Highmore....London, printed for the author by R. Wilks, ...and sold by J. White...and Messrs. Richardson,...1804. 8vo. pp. xvi-600. Frontispiece and two folding plates (one of the marks in the Finsbury Fields, 1737). G., M.
Captain Raikes is said to be compiling a history of the II. A. C.

Company of Finsbury Archers.
19th Novr., 1590. John Pyrryn—Entred for his copie under Master Cawoodes hand The Tectonicon of Ffinsbury feildes. Vjᵈ. (T. S. R., ii. 568.)—Perhaps by Leonard Digges the elder.
Ayme for Finsburie Archers, or, an alphabeticall table of the names of every marke within the same fields, with their true (or due) distances, both by the map and by dimensuration of (or with) the line, published for the ease of the skilfull and behoofe of the younge beginners in the famed exercise of Archerie. By I. I. (or T. T.) and E. B. (or B. E.). Printed at London by R. F., and are to be sold at the sign of the Swan in Grub Street by T. Sergeant, 1594. 16mo.
Another edition—" to be Sold at the sign of the Frier, in Grub Street," 1601.
Another edition—1604. (Not seen.)
MS. Archers' Marks in Finsbury Fields. — Per me Henricus Dickmanus nomine : scribebam hunc librum et scriptus erat in anno Domini 1601, quarto die Mayij.— London, 1601. 24mo. ff. 93, paper.—The Marks are in a b c order. This MS., which is in the library of the Society of Antiquaries of London, I was courteously shown by the secretary.
Aim for Finsbury Archers, or an alphabetical table of ye names of every mark within ye fields, with ye true distance according to ye true dimension of ye line and pulley, gathered and amended, ye 2nd impression by James Partridge and by him dedicated to ye Archery of Finsbury with ye rules for ye use of ye same by I. N. Printed for J. Partridge at ye sign of ye Sun in Sᵗ. Pauls Church Yard, 1626. 4to., 138 pages. (B. M. MS. Sloan 5900, f. 35, note by John Bagford.)
Ayme for Finsbury archers. Or an alphaticall table of the names of every marke within the same fields, with their true distances according to the dimensuration of the line. Newly gathered and amended by James Partridge. London, printed by G. M. for John Partridge, and are to be sold at the signe of the Sunne in Paul's Church Yard, 1628. 24mo. pp. x-148. Preface signed I. N. M.
Aim for Archers, 1638. 12mo. (" N. & Q.," 4ᵗʰ S. iv. 330.)—Possibly the date is an error for 1628 or 1738.
Collection of the names of marks in Finsbury fields. London, 1728. 24mo. (Watt, B. B.)—Possibly the date is an error for 1628 or 1738.
Aim for Finsbury Archers : or, a table of all the names of the marks now standing in the fields of Finsbury; with their true distance from each other. Also a plan of the said fields and marks by which one may know their true bearing. Likewise a list of all the names of such as have been Captains or Lieutenants of the Easteror Whitson· Target, from the year 1717 to this present year 1738.—London, 1738. 24mo., pp. 16. An engraved frontispiece and a folding plate, inscribed :—A plan of all the marks belonging to the Company of Finsbury Archers, in the said fields of Finsbury, with the true distance from each other as they now stand. May the 20th, 1737. (M. copy mislaid.) G.
Articles agreed on by the Society of Archers for the well ordering and regulateing of their game yearely to be shott at in Finsbury Fields or other place nere adjoyning and more especially for the present yeare 1687. (Around the margin of which is :—)
An account of the number of the Archers that have shott at the Generall Targett from the year of our Lord

1658 unto this present yeare 1687 [and continued to 1757] in company with the severall Captains and Leiuetenants whose severall and respective names are here under written in the severall collums.—On a sheet of parchment in B. M. MS. Add. 28801.
Rules and records of the Society of Finsbury Archers, from 1652 to 1761, &c. In the handwriting of William Latham. In B. M. MS. Add. 29792. 4to. ff. 100.
Londinium redivivum, or, an ancient history and modern description of London....By James Peller Malcolm....London, printed by John Nichols & Son...and sold by Longman,...1802-1807. 4 vols. 4to. Vol. iv. p. 26, and plan of Finsbury Fields, by William Hole, copied from original (undated, but late sixteenth cent.) in the Bodleian Library, Oxford. M.

FRED. W. FOSTER.

45, Beaufort Street, S.W.

(To be continued.)

"THE BELLMAN'S DROWSY CHARM." — Nares quotes from Herrick a poetical version of the charm, and I find a notice of the bellman, some years later than Milton's allusion, in Pepys's *Diary* (1659-60, Jan. 16) : "I staid up till the bellman came by with his bell just under my window, as I was writing of this very line ; 'past one of the clock, and a cold, frosty, windy morning.'" What could our forefathers have been made of to endure their sleep being broken by this wholly unnecessary disturbance? I well remember the London watchman's "Past three o'clock and a cloudy morning." His drone could awaken none but the lightest sleepers. What if the watch had had a bell to ring ! It seems from a line of Pope's that the bell-ringing continued down to his time :

" To drink and droll be Rowe allow'd
Till the third watchman's toll."
Farewell to London, 1715.

JAYDEE.

FIELD NAMES.—I desire to make an appeal to your country contributors and readers for their help in a very important historical matter. Even with the priceless treasures of the British Museum, London students must often appeal to students resident in the country for information on matters that have not yet found their way into our printed literature. I therefore simply state the plea of necessity in asking the aid of "N. & Q." on the question of field names in England. In many localities, especially agricultural districts, a local custom exists of calling certain fields within the neighbourhood by particular names : see Maine's *Village Communities*, p. 126, quoted by me in "N. & Q.," 5ᵗʰ S. vii. 344, and MR. WOOLLEY gives a peculiar instance at 5ᵗʰ S. viii. 192. Many of these field names are trade names, and are as well identified with the particular fields as personal names with their owners. I have collected some few from olden-time records, but what I am anxious to obtain now is a record of any existing customs of the kind. They are fast dying out ;

they are eminently of historical value, being so indicative of local legend ; they cannot be collected without aid, and I do not therefore think my appeal will be in vain. Instances forwarded to me direct I will, if permitted, insert in " N. & Q." when I have a sufficiently long list.

G. LAURENCE GOMME.
Castelnau, Barnes, S.W.

A MALAY SUPERSTITION. — Surgeon - Major Davie, of the Buffs, in his " Medical History of the Laroot Field Force," given in the appendix to the Army Medical Department Report for 1876, mentions a curious custom which exists among the Malays in cases of dangerous illness, which are attributed to the influence of evil spirits. The Malays imagine that if they can remove the evil spirits they are all right ; so, with this object, they construct a miniature prahu, or war boat, of wood, complete in every way, with mast, rigging, black flag, paddles, and a rudder. The boat is filled with various articles, a bag of rice at the stern, and a lamp made out of a cockle-shell at the prow ; the body of the boat is stuffed with cups made of leaves, containing liquors of various sorts, entrails of fowls, sweetmeats of all kinds, tobacco, flowers, and copper coins. The boat is supported oy a slender square bamboo platform, surrounded with pendent grass, to the ends of which are tied all sorts of eatables, and at the corners the legs and wings of a chicken. About eighteen inches below the boat are figures of turtles, crocodiles, and lizards, made of rice, resting on a plantain leaf ; the whole being supported by four straight branches about seven feet high (the top leaves forming a canopy) stuck into a raft made of plantain trees. Slips of bamboo are stuck round the raft with partially burned red rags tied to them. The raft is set afloat, and it is supposed that the evil spirits, enticed away by the food in the boat, leave the patient and attach themselves to the boat. Should any Malay, by accident or otherwise, touch this raft after it has been set afloat, he or she becomes afflicted with the disease from which the person for whose benefit the raft was set adrift suffered.

EVERARD HOME COLEMAN.
71, Brecknock Road, N.

THE POET MICKIEWICZ.—About a week ago the *Daily News* contained a genial article on this poet, so celebrated among Slavonic peoples, on the occasion of the honours lately done to his memory at Rome. The writer quotes triumphantly the high opinion passed upon the poet by Mr. George Borrow. Without wishing at all to depreciate the merits of the author of *The Bible in Spain* and *Lavengro*, whose works I remember to have read with so much pleasure when a boy, I must add that the praises of Mickiewicz have been heard in higher quarters. The Polish poet called upon Goethe just before the death of the great Cory-

phæus of German literature, and when 1 him farewell, the veteran is recorded to hav " You are now the greatest poet of Euro Goethe is fast going to his grave."

W. R. MOR

RUSSIAN HISTORY.—The following no possibly have interest for Russian studen Bolingbroke's *Correspondence* (edited by Parke), 1798, vol. i. p. 128, there is this foo " Charles Whitworth had been Envoy extraord the Czar's court, and was now appointed Aml extraordinary. From this gentleman the Secre State received an account of. Muscovy, writte judgment and accuracy, which is in the possessio editor."

This was probably in MS. ; was it ever pub The papers of Bolingbroke were kept at Sto in Norfolk, by his secretary, Thomas Hare descendant handed them over to Parke f lication. Parke, in his preface, says the remained till the death of Thomas Hare, i " little known or noticed." In *Fugitive P Various Subjects*, vol. ii., 1762, one of the is an account of Russia in 1710, by Baron worth. If this is from the same MS. as th to Bolingbroke it must, I suppose, hav taken from among his manuscripts, printe put back again, to come by-and-by into the of Parke. Observe, Parke says the pape little noticed till 1760 ; this may impl they then received some attention, and *F Pieces* was published in 1762. The accou probably the same. At all events, here account of Russia in 1710 which all can but of which perhaps all do not know.

THOS. FAIRMAN OR

" THE PASTON LETTERS."—I write to p a slight error in Mr. Gairdner's edition *Paston Letters.* In the preliminary r No. 939 (iii. 389) Isabel, wife of John L Addington, co. Surrey, is stated to have b daughter of Agnes Paston (*née* Morley) second husband, John Isley, of Sundric Kent. But Isabel's monument in Ad Church, wherein she is called " sole syste George Harvye," proves her to have be daughter of Agnes by her first husband Harvye, of Thurleigh, co. Beds. Isabel (o beth, as she is called in her brother Sir Harvey's will, 1520) married secondly \ Atclyff, and died 1545.

The letter No. 939 is undated, and Mr. G assigns no date to it beyond saying that have been written after 1495. Its date fixed almost to a year. The writer, Si Paston, speaks of his wife, the above-me Agnes, as being about to ride into Kent ' wydow, hir doughtir Leghe." John Leghe, ing to the monument in Addington Churc

April 24, 1502, and Sir John Paston himself was dead in September, 1503.   S. H. A. H.

Queries.

[We must request correspondents desiring information on family matters of only private interest, to affix their names and addresses to their queries, in order that the answers may be addressed to them direct.]

DID MORLAND EVER PAINT "FISH PICTURES"? —I have possessed for nearly thirty years a beautiful fish picture, about 26 by 20, not signed, and respecting which I have endeavoured in vain to obtain some definite information. All I ever did learn was some twenty-five years since from a gentleman advanced in years, who had a similar picture, and that was that his father had, many years ago, bought it off the easel of the artist, who was a very celebrated painter, and who had, in some freak perhaps, painted twelve fish pictures and no more, all differing merely in the grouping of the fish, pike, carp, perch, &c., and every one having the same background—fish-basket, sedges, and bit of blue sky, through clouds. The price my friend's father paid the artist was 100l., but he could not recollect the name. On showing the picture to a distinguished animal painter the other day he pronounced the whole treatment to be Morland's. To show its excellence, I may be permitted to mention that the picture was so admired by my friend Sir Daniel Macnee, P.R.S.A., that he begged the loan of it and kept it a long time in his studio.   J. D. DOUGALL.
Kensington.

THE VENERS came over at the Conquest; they then called themselves Venoure. They then were connected with the Earls of Chester, and are alluded to under the name of Venator. It is my impression that a band of them settled in London. I know that William Venour was a merchant in London in 1350; that another William Venour was (Alderman) Sheriff 1388, and Lord Mayor in 1389 (he was of the Grocers' Guild); he, with his wife Elizabeth, was buried at Great St. Helen's, A.D. 1400, whose son William was Sheriff 1402, and was at the battle of Agincourt, 1415. I find that another Venour, who spelled his name Henry Vainor, of the Vintners' Guild, was buried at St. Martin's in the Vintry, A.D. 1391. These, or some of them, certainly were alive when these guilds were founded, and I doubt not a succession of them existed in some or other guild until a late period, for I find that Sir Thomas Viner (the name then was changed into Viner and Vyner) was Lord Mayor in 1654, and Sir Robert Sheriff 1667 and Lord Mayor in 1675. I see that Sir Henry Vynar (it was then Vynar) was of the Merchant Taylors' Guild in 1571, and Nicholas Vynar half a century later; again, 1459,

William Vener was Warden of the Fleet, and his son Walter after him. I am collecting historical facts concerning this family, and shall esteem it a favour if any of your correspondents will give me information on the subject.

HENRY W. VINER.

P.S.—The name has also been spelled Vynour. It would not surprise me if William Joyner, Sheriff 1223, William Joynour, Lord Mayor 1239, was really a Venour. Certainly I think Rauffe Fenour, Sheriff 1278, was a Venour. Three centuries later evidence at the British Museum and elsewhere shows that Vyner and Fyner were indiscriminately used, therefore I do not see why Venour and Fenour should not be one and the same.

AN ANTIQUE SILVER BELL.—I was shown the other day a very small silver bell, a copy of an antique one in gold about an inch long, found as I understood at Rome, and belonging to H.M. the Queen of Italy. The bell has the following inscription on the four sides, for the solution of which I shall be much obliged to any of your contributors:

TOI   COM   MAC   IN
VIIO   TGT   AΓM   AI
W. M. B.

PORTUMA.—Will any of your readers kindly tell me what place in England this is? Bishop Sherborne says of himself, "bis Richmundie, ac semel turris Portume, cum propugnaculo ei herente, edificiis prepositus fuit." Porchester (Porcestria) has been suggested to me, and Portsmouth (Portesmuthia, Portus Magnus), but I think without a show of likelihood.

MACKENZIE E. C. WALCOTT.

CALLING CARDS: CRAPE AS MOURNING.— When did these come into fashion and use in Great Britain?   GREYSTEIL.

NUMISMATIC.—I shall be obliged for information regarding any of the following:—
1. What does the following bronze medal commemorate?—Obv., Pope Gregory XIII. seated, and in the act of blessing a number of ecclesiastics; on a tablet on the wall is inscribed ITE OPERAMINI IN VINEAM DOMINI, and round obv. is legend SEMINANS IN BENEDICTIONIBUS DE BENEDICTIONIBUS ET METET; on reverse is the following, GREGORIVS | XIII PONT MAX | COLLEGIVM | SOCIETATIS IESV | OMNIVM NATIONVM | SEMINARIVM | PRO SVA IN CHRISTIANAM | RELIGIONEM ET ORDINEM | ILLVM PIETATE | A FVNDAMENTIS | EXTRVXIT | ET DOTAVIT. AN SAL | CIƆIƆLXXXII | PONT SVI X, and below, ROMAE. As the Society of Jesus was founded some years earlier, this has a little puzzled me.
2. A sixpence of Charles I., mint mark an anchor. Obv., crowned head to the left and VI; legend, CAROLVS D. G. MAG BRIT. FR. ET HIB REX;

on rev., shield with arms—1 and 4, quarterly, Engl. and France; 2, Scotland; 3, Ireland; legend (with the following misprint) CHISTO (*sic*) AVSPICE REGNO. It is in good preservation, which was the cause of my buying it at a silversmith's, and I did not at first detect the mistake on the reverse. Are other examples known?

3. What is the explanation of a franc of the first Napoleon bearing on the obverse the legend NAPOLEON EMPEREUR, and on reverse REPUBLIQUE FRANÇAISE, and date AN 13? T. M. FALLOW.
Chapel Allerton, Leeds.

OVID'S "METAMORPHOSIS."—The other day I came across an old and curious verse translation of Ovid's *Metamorphosis*, and I shall feel obliged if any of your readers can give me some idea as to the value or rarity of the book by the following description. It is 12mo. or 16mo., engraved frontispiece, with tablet in centre bearing the following title :—

" Ovid's | Metamor- | phosis. | Englished by | G. S. | London, | printed by | Robert Young ; | are to be sold | by F. Grismond. | 1628."

The volume is dedicated to "The most high and mightie prince Charles, King of Great Britaine, France, and Ireland." WILSON BATTY.

HERALDIC.—What were the arms of Clarke of Lavington Gernon, whose heiress married Nicholas Englefield about A.D. 1390? W. F. C.

" EVERY MAN HAS HIS PRICE."—This cynical saying is attributed to Sir Robert Walpole. On whose authority? Mr. Ewald, in his recent *Life* of the statesman, suggests that he may have said, pointing to his supporters in the House of Commons, "All *these* men have their price." Mr. Lecky (*Hist. of England*, vol. i. ch. iii.) makes the same suggestion. This gives quite a different turn to the cynicism. Walpole might well apply it to men whose votes he had already bought, or was ready to buy. The late Sir Benjamin Brodie, in that most charming book, *Psychological Enquiries*, thus alludes to the saying :—

" The anecdote may or may not be true, but if it be so the answer to such an ungracious doctrine is sufficiently obvious. He drew his conclusions from a too limited experience, and did not bear in mind that those who had not their price were just the persons with whom it was least likely that he should come in contact."

JAYDEE.

HENRY ANDREWS.—I have an engraved portrait, dated 1798, of Henry Andrews, with a globe at his side. Underneath is printed the following :— " Henry Andrews, the celebrated author of *Moore's Almanac*." Any information respecting the life of the above, where born, &c., will greatly oblige.
E. C. H.

A " YOTING STONE."—Quite recently in a West-country paper appeared a letter from the Vicar of

Bishop's Hull, Somerset, contai[n] I have not seen answered, and t an extract in the hope that son butors will enlighten me :—
" I should be very much obliged i me what a ' yoting-stone ' is. I fin[d] [Here follow several quotations fro[m] 1578 to 1651, in which it is variou[s] stone,' ' yowting-stones,' and ' yeoti[n] " We know that ' yote,' or ' yoat,' men are said to ' yote in ' metal t[o] railings. The word ' yote ' also s pour water on.
" Instances of its use :—Grose grains must be well *yoted* for the pi ' My fowls found feeding at thei[r] wheat.' "
May I suggest, without prete derivation of the word, that it i[s] to a grindstone or the stone of a

THE RIGHTS OF WOMEN.—] *Brésil Littéraire*, par F. Wolf, so long ago as 1820 the Viscon[d] the Brazilian deputy to the Cor in favour of the political eman I fancied this a movement of a was it mooted in any other pub period ?

THE ABBEY OF ST. VICTO annals of the once powerful and of St. Victor, Paris, the abbey of Canterbury made a brief sta[y] there is a long list of the sacred once preserved there. Two of curious that I transcribe their [c]
" De oleo quod fluit ex imagin similitudinem Beatæ Mariæ Virgin facta est."
" De oleo Imaginis B. Mariæ q quæ crescit et decrescit sicut Luna caro."
I should be very glad if any ents would kindly inform me ever met with any notice of th[e] in the course of their reading. and Husenbeth could most pr[o] something on the subject ; p[e] Gould or Dr. Lee will do so.
W.]
Gravesend.

ELEANORA NUGENT.—Can [a] were her parents? She was w[i] Kerr of Newfield, son of Lord grandson of the first Marqui[s] died at Ayr, N.B., Sept. 9, 17[8]
HA[l]

SAINTE-BEUVE ON BOSSUE in his *Sainte-Beuve* (Paris, L[e] says :—" Il (Sainte-Beuve) dé parle d'un ton dégagé des absurdités de Bourda-loue." In what work does Sainte-Beuve make these attacks? I cannot find any blackening of Bossuet or jeering at Bourdaloue in the *Nouveaux Lundis*.   L. H. T.

MARY QUEEN OF SCOTS.—Are there any means of finding out what needlework was done by Mary Queen of Scots and where it now is?   C. P.

LETTERS OF WASHINGTON. —Ex-President Grant, when passing through Leicester last sum-mer, was presented with copies of four unpublished letters of Washington's, the originals being in the Leicester Museum. Is there any reason why they should not be published, seeing they are public property? At least, I believe the museum is a public institution.   KINGSTON.

COL. MICHAEL JONES, GOVERNOR OF DUBLIN IN 1649.—What were his arms? Are there any descendants of his now living?   T. S.

JOHN HUNTER.—Who was "John Hunter, Esq.," who published *A Tribute to the Manes of Unfortunate Poets*, 1798, second edit. 1803—also a volume of *Poems*, third edit. 1805, with portrait and plates, this latter including the "Tribute"? Hunter seems to be only known to the biblio-graphers by his name or the titles of the above.   J. O.

MRS. PIOZZI'S TEA-POT.—In a note to Marryat's *Pottery and Porcelain*, p. 307, mention is made of a tea-pot formerly in the possession of a Mrs. Marryatt, of Wimbledon, who is stated to have purchased it at the sale of Mrs. Piozzi's effects at Streatham. The tea-pot was supposed to hold more than three quarts. In whose possession is this tea-pot at the present time?   G. ROSS.

CERACCI THE SCULPTOR.—Can any of your readers give me information respecting him? He modelled the figures on the top of Somerset House; also the heads of Napoleon Bonaparte, Marquis of Buckingham, Admiral Keppel, and General Paoli.   A. F.

AUTHORS OF BOOKS WANTED.—

An Essay on Religion and Morality; or, the Scorn and Evidence of True Religion. 8vo. pp. 77 in verse. Glas., for David Baxter, 1767. With copious notes in dialogue between A., C., G., M., and W., in which the real or imaginary parties these initials indicate freely criticize the poet.

A Few Verses, English and Latin. Motto from Petrarch. 8vo. Cawthorn, 1812. Probably by an Englishman at Glasgow College.

Momentary Musings: Poems. By K. D., Esq. Hurst, 1840.

The Summer Day: a Poem in Four Cantos. London, 1769.

The Sportsman's Progress: a Poem. Sherwood, 1820.

Metrical Miscellanies. By A. C. S. Printed for Private Circulation. 1854.   J. O.

AUTHORS OF QUOTATIONS WANTED.—

Can any one tell me where to find the passage in Tennyson in which the poet speaks of "the walls of Ilion," I think, being built up by invisible hands, "and therefore built for ever"? The other allusions to the same fact in *Œnone* and *Tithonus* are neither of them the quotation I want.   B.

Replies.

WILLIAM (*NOT* CHARLES) CLARKE, AUTHOR OF "THE CIGAR," &c.
(5th S. ix. 286.)

I fear I have been the cause of error in ascribing this work in the *Handbook of Fictitious Names* (pp. 139, 145, and 197) to "Charles" instead of William Clarke. I am sorry that I am now able to give MR. BLANCHARD JERROLD so little infor-mation. During the last ten years I have col-lected the following notes relative to W. Clarke, and am pleased to be able to publish them in order that your numerous readers may have an oppor-tunity of supplementing and correcting what must be so imperfect. I think, however, it will readily be admitted that the information has not been collected without difficulty, which must be my excuse for asking you to print portions which may probably not be generally interesting. By search-ing through the *Gentleman's Magazine* I found the exact date of his death, which I did not know when the *Handbook of Fictitious Names* was pub-lished. The *Gentleman's Magazine* for 1838 says (p. 335) he died suddenly at his house near Hamp-stead of an apoplectic attack, on June 17 in that year, at the early age of thirty-seven, leaving a young family and their mother unprovided for. It does not say where he was born. The *Gentle-man's Magazine* for January, 1836, p. 98, records the death of William Clarke, who died at Lambeth on November 22, 1835, aged forty, who was "for several years connected with the public press." The name is spelled with the final *e*, but I imagine should have been without. I find no notice of either in the *Annual Register*.

The first book I have in my list is autonymous, and it will be observed that the name is spelled without the final *e*. These two facts incline me to think that the work may possibly be by the W. Clark who died in 1835, and not the author of the *Cigar*, who would not be likely to spell his name wrong in his first book, though such things have happened.

The literary scrap book, or a variety of beauties from the most esteemed ancient and modern authors; in which are interspersed a number of interesting anec-dotes: selected by William Clark [motto]. London, printed (by T. White) for James Paul 42 Holland Street Southwark 1824. Small 8° pp. 193.

This was published periodically in twopenny num-bers.

The following works I believe to be by, or to

emanate from, William Clarke, author of the *Cigar*, &c., and they are without exception anonymous or pseudonymous :—

The Cigar [vignette]. London, T. Richardson 98 High Holborn 1825. In two volumes, 16° of 382 pages each.

The booksellers call it a "magazine of wit, humour, and instruction." "The only permanent mark left by this ephemeris was changing the spelling *Segar*, then universal, to *Cigar*" (" N. & Q.," 4ᵗʰ S. ix. 528). I have not been able to find it in the British Museum Catalogue, but presume it must be there nevertheless.

The terrific register or record of crimes, judgments, providences and calamities. London, published by Sherwood, Jones & Co. and Hunter, Edin. 1825, printed by T. Richardson 98 High Holborn. 8°.

The illustrations round the title are signed "Seymour de" and " M. Byfield Sᶜ," the cuts throughout only " M. Byfield Sᶜ." " Terrific" indeed it is. I inadvertently perused the first horrible description of a frightful execution. It was published in numbers. I should be surprised if this production, which is more horrible than the *Newgate Calendar*, were Clarke's, and yet it is advertised with other books which he published.

Every man's book or useful companion for 1826. London, T. Richardson 98 High Holborn [1826]. 8°.

After 1828 this was published by Vizetelly, and it ceased in 1830. At the end of the issue for 1828 are advertised *Old English Tales, Legends of Terror*, the *Terrific Register*, the *Cigar*, and *Gymnastics*.

Every night book, or life after dark; by the author of the Cigar [illustration "Mason sc" and motto]. London, published by T. Richardson 98 High Holborn 1827. 12° pp. 192.

A gossiping book, treating of the theatres, Almack's, the Cole Hole, fairs, taverns, and the different sights in London.

The book of health, a compendium of domestic medicine...London, Vizetelly, Branston & C° 135 Fleet Street 1828. 8° pp. 119.

At the end are advertised *Every man's book* for 1829 and *The Boy's own book*. Another edition (of the title-page) is dated 1829.

The boy's own book, a complete encyclopædia of all the diversions, athletic, scientific and recreative, of boyhood and youth [motto]. London, Vizetelly, Branston and Co. Fleet street 1828. Square 16°.

Mr. Henry Vizetelly, to whom I am indebted for several facts about W. Clarke, told me Clarke was editor and principal author of this book. The second edition is advertised in the *Book of Health*, 1828.

Boy's own book &c. London, D. Bogue 86 Fleet Street [1849]. Sm. sq. 8° pp. 611.

This edition has an index. The preface says that twenty editions, comprising eighty thousand copies, had been sold. The above edition, printed by Vizetelly & Co., was the first that received much alteration. It was edited and revised by Mr. Henry Vizetelly, who also engraved some of

the additional illustrations from d Harvey. The preface describes it a improved, every article having und ful and competent revision, and s subjects been entirely rewritten, &c.

The boy's own book &c. London, W. I Street (late D. Bogue) 1859. Sm. sq. 8° p]

This edition, printed by Thomas reprint. The preface says twenty comprising ninety thousand copies, This book brought the printers a between 500*l.* and 600*l.* a year, an two thousand copies a year were pri at about 8*s.* 6*d.*, the original cost b a fourth of that sum.

Every family's book for 1829 contain that is most useful and necessary to be kr in the different situations of maid, wit continued annually...London, T. Richar pp. 64.

Advertised at the end : *Every n Cigar, Old English Tales, Legends Terrific Register*, and *Gymnastics*.

The young lady's book, a manual of tions, exercises and pursuits. London, Vi and C° 1829. 12° pp. 504 and 1, with illu

Three courses and a dessert; the de Cruikshank [motto]. London, Vize pp. 432.

" By Mr. Clarke who wrote the Cruikshank in the *New Monthl* (Reid's *Descrip. Cat. of Cruikshank's* vol. i. p. 322).

Three courses and a dessert comprisi tales, West Country, Irish and Legal ; with fifty-one illustrations by G. Cruiks tion [motto]. London, Vizetelly 1836. 8°.

Third edition of the title-page only in Bohn's Illustrated Library.

The Georgian Era, memoirs of the m sons who have flourished in Great Br accession of George the first to the demi fourth, in four volumes...London, Vizetel C° Fleet Street 1832. 8° pp. 582; vol. i vol. iii. 1834 pp. 588; vol. iv. the same : in double columns with portraits.

This work, of which Clarke was edit good character, and contains muc not to be found elsewhere. The a chronological, classified according t first volume containing the royal far preface says " all the lives have l compiled and entirely rewritten . . . exertion has been made, both on tl editor and his assistants, to eluci points," and he "fearlessly asserts a able claim to strict impartiality."

Twelve maxims on swimming, by th Cigar. London, Charles Tilt 1833. 16° p] the title-page. It is signed C. " Very g written " ; see A list of works on Swim Hamst [1868], p. 6.

Wm. Clarke also wrote a work entitled *Old English Tales*, but I have not been able to see this, nor do I find it mentioned in any catalogue. He wrote a story called *The love and child*, and another *Mrs. (somebody's?) boarding-house*, or some such titles, and scores of others in the *Monthly Magazine*, of which he was editor, and wrote nearly half each number just before Charles Dickens began editing it.

The *Gentleman's Magazine* refers to a *Natural History* he was preparing at his death, "upon which an enormous expenditure must have been incurred." Query whether this was ever published.

His most successful work was the *Boy's own book*. The *Athenæum* (Nov. 22, 1874, p. 721) said, "and it is an oversight that, when writing of old toys, our contemporary [the *Graphic*] did not lay a wreath on the tomb of the illustrious author, whoever he was, of the *Boy's own Book*." For thirty years it held its place, and was without a competitor until the publication of *Every Boy's Book*, edited by the Rev. J. G. Wood.

Though Clarke's books have sold by thousands, he is still unknown. He has nevertheless left his mark behind him in his works, which one meets as constantly in booksellers' catalogues as almost any others.

For half a century the publishers have had a rich harvest from the *Boy's own Book*, and two generations of boys have had delightful and rich gleanings. What was the author's reward?

OLPHAR HAMST.

KING ALARIC'S BURIAL (5ᵗʰ S. ix. 248.)—The only poem of any note on the burial of Alaric in the bed of the river Busento is by Count von Platen. It is to be found not only in the five volumes of his collected works, but also in all the books composed of specimens of the best German poets. Indeed, this ballad, a few other ballads, and his fine lines descriptive of the rise of German poetry, have done more than Platen's many other elaborate works to perpetuate his name. I am not aware that any of his poems have been translated into English. I fancy that he is but little known in this country even to readers of German. Hence I append his exquisite ballad in the original for the enjoyment of those persons who can appreciate it in that form, and I add a not unfaithful 'rendering in English for the partial information of those persons whom the German words do not enlighten:

"*Das Grab am Busento.*

Nächtlich am Busento lispeln, bei Cosenza dumpfe Lieder,
Aus den Wassern schallt es Antwort, und in Wirbeln klingt es wieder ! ,
Und den Fluss hinauf, hinunter, ziehn die Schatten tapfrer Gothen,
Die den Alarich beweinen, ihres Volkes besten Todten.

Allzufrüh und fern der Heimat mussten hier sie ihn begraben,
Während noch die Jugendlocken seine Schulter blond umgaben.
Und am Ufer des Busento reihten sie sich um die Wette,
Um die Strömung abzuleiten, gruben sie ein frisches Bette.
In der wogenleeren Höhlung wühlten sie empor die Erde.
Senkten tief hinein den Leichnam, mit der Rüstung, auf dem Pferde.
Deckten dan mit Erde wieder ihn und seine stolze Habe,
Das die hohen Stromgewächse wüchsen aus dem Heldengrabe.
Abgelenckt zum zweitenmale, ward der Fluss herbei gezogen:
Mächtig in ihr altes Bette schäumten die Busentowogen.
Und es sang ein Chor von Männern: 'Schlaf' in deinen Heldenehren !
Keines Römers schnöde Habsucht soll dir je das Grab versehren !'
Sangen's, und die Lobgesänge tönten fort im Gothenheere ;
Wälze sie, Busentowelle, wälze sie von Meer zu Meere ! ''

"*The Grave in the Busento.*

On Busento at Cosenza muffled lays are whispered nightly ;
From the water sounds an answer, by the ripples echoed lightly.
And beside the stream the spectral forms of valiant Goths are roaming,
Him, the chief among their people, slain, their Alaric bemoaning.
Here untimely and remote from home must they lay him underground,
While the flaxen locks of morning-tide still his shoulders circle round.
And they range them on Busento's banks, in emulation bending
To bar the path of the rushing wave, aside the water sending.
In the flood-deserted cavity, the earth first upward heaving,
They lower deep down the mail-clad corse, still to his charger cleaving.
Then upon him and his panoply the earth again are flinging,
That from out the hero's sepulchre may river plants be springing.
For a second time diverted is the torrent backwards veering,
Till Busento's waves again are in their olden bed careering.
Then a choir of men are chanting : 'Sleep in thy heroic glory,
Never Roman insult to thy tomb shall desecrate thy story.'
Sang, and the host of Goths prolongs the strain with a mighty motion ;
Roll, Busento's billows, roll it on from ocean unto ocean."

W. FRASER RAE.

Reform Club.

DAINES BARRINGTON : WHITE'S "SELBORNE" (5ᵗʰ S. ix. 304.)—To call Barrington a "pompous

Pompous he may have been, for anything I know
to the contrary, and an antiquary he was ; but
the union of the two words (and these alone)
very ill describes the man, while his papers on
scientific, and especially zoological, subjects, however mistaken he may at times have been, justify
a protest in his defence. But will MR. P. W.
TREFOLPEN give the date of the disallowed charge
for sparrow poisoning? We shall then know
whether it was before or after (and if after, how
long) he made White's acquaintance, which appears to have been in 1769 or thereabouts. Granting, however, as seems possible, that the charge
was made after they were known to each other, I
do not know that we can complain very much of
Barrington on this account. Are there not still
estimable people in London who find their water-
spouts occasionally blocked up by sparrows' nests
and take measures accordingly? And is it not
possible that White himself might not have objected to such measures? Look at what he says
in Letter xvi. to Pennant about willow-wrens
eating pease—a passage over which I would willingly pass, because it contains one of the very few
grave errors of observation that White ever made
—and one can hardly doubt that he would not
scruple much as to the means he might take to
rid himself of the "horrid pests" when scaring
them failed.

The mistake of "Gray" for "Gay," as the author
of The Beggars' Opera, is not due to Prof. Bell's
printer. It stands in the note as originally printed
in the Transactions of the Norfolk and Norwich
Naturalists' Society, and it failed to attract any
attention until it was pointed out to me by a kind
correspondent.

I may perhaps be allowed here to add to my
last note on " The Published Writings of Gilbert
White" (ante, p. 150) that since writing it I have,
by favour of MRS. MORTIMER COLLINS, become
aware of another edition of his famous book—one
that I am all the more glad to know since I formerly doubted its existence. Its description is
thus :—

*1825. The | Natural History | of | Selborne, | by the
late | Rev. Gilbert White, A.M. | Fellow of Oriel College,
Oxford. | To which are added, | The Naturalist's Ca-
lendar, | Miscellaneous Observations, | and Poems. | A
new edition, with engravings. | In two volumes. | Lon-
don : | Printed for C. and J. Rivington; J. and A. Arch,
Long- | man, Hurst, Rees, Orme, Brown and Green;
Harding, | Triphook and Lepard ; Baldwin, Cradock and
Joy; | J. Hatchard and Son; S. Bagster; G. B. Whit-
taker ; | James Duncan; W. Mason; Saunders and Hodg.
son ; and | Hurst, Robinson and Co. | 1825. | 8vo. Vol. i.
flyleaf, title-page, and advertisement, pp. viii; text,
pp. 351. Vol. ii. pp. 364.

The plates are the same as in the 8vo. edition of
1813, of which indeed the present is very nearly a
page for page reprint.   ALFRED NEWTON.
Magdalene College, Cambridge.

—This refers to the authority of Parliament which
had to be obtained to enable the wardens of Wadham College, and (unless I mistake) the principals
of Jesus College also, to marry. Dorothy Wadham,
who carried out the intentions of her deceased
husband, Nicholas Wadham, was the foundress of
the college bearing their name in or about the year
1610. Though this date was post-Reformation,
celibacy was enjoined on the wardens. Dr. Tournay, who was warden from 1806 to 1831, was instrumental in obtaining the removal of this
restriction. But he did not avail himself of the
privilege obtained, considering, it is said, that he
was not released thereby from the pledges voluntarily given by him when elected warden.
Dr. Tournay resigned in 1831, and Dr. Benjamin
Parsons Symons became warden, and not long
afterwards married Miss Masterman. Dr. Symons
has just died at the great age of ninety-three or
more. Like his predecessor he resigned the government of the college. He is the only warden of
Wadham who as yet has committed matrimony.
About ten years previously Dr. Ffoulkes, the
Principal of Jesus College, married, I believe,
under sanction of the same authority, and no
disability now exists in any headship to prevent
marriage, though it happens, at the present time,
that about one-third are unmarried.

Now with regard to the obtaining authority of
Parliament, it happened that, wishing to avoid
expense and notoriety in passing a special Act for
the purpose, the matter was arranged by simply
adding a clause to a Turnpike Bill which was
passing through the House. A notice of these
facts will be found in Recollections of Oxford by
G. V. Cox, M.A., pp. 183-4. GIBBES RIGAUD.
18, Long Wall, Oxford.

[Dr. Symons died on the 11th inst.]

MAYNELLS OR MANELL (5th S. ix. 287.)—These
words are of French origin, and were originally
applied to the bells rather than the tower in which
they hung. In mediæval Latin we find mee-
nellum, maanellus, monellus. Thus, in a con-
cessionary charter A.D. 1235, we read, "Concessit
etiam eis quod ad pulsationem campanorum quæ
chori appellantur et aliarum quæ mediocres sive
maanelli appellantur, quamdiu vixerint, minime
teneantur." Again, in another charter of the same
year, "Et quando meenella vel grossiora signa
sonabunt." In another document, bearing date
A.D. 1497, respecting the ringing of bells (Statuta
Capit. Tullensis), "In Dominicis et profestis
ultimæ cum duabus mediocribus campanis simul ;
et in duplicibus cum monellis." In French the
equivalents were moisneau, moineau, or moinel.
So in a MS. of Eccl. S. Wulfran, "Campanis
Guillelmo majore et les deux moisneaux." In all
these cases the word has the same meaning, that

of a moderate sized bell, Lat. *medianellum*. In the *Glossaire François* attached to Ducange, *moisneau* is interpreted "moyenne cloche." Ménage, *sub voce*, says, "Dans l'église de N. D. de Paris, on appelle *moineaux* les clroches qui sont entre les dessus et les basses.'

The transition in England, where the word was foreign, from the bell to the tower in which it was hung, is not unnatural.   J. A. PICTON.
. Sandyknowe, Wavertree.

This has an analogous derivation with *campanile*. *Maanellus* or *mannellus*—there are both forms—is a bell. The word occurs in Ducange.
ED. MARSHALL.

EDMUND WALLER (5th S. ix. 286.)—Some confusion is introduced by the expression "authorized." Waller's poems were at first handed about in MS. as copies of verses, and as small printed pamphlets. There was no collected edition of them till after his imprisonment, and, therefore, whilst he was living in France. It is said that an English lady of his acquaintance desired him to make a collection of his poems, and send them to her from France. Waller did so, and accompanied them with a letter, which is prefixed to the first collected edition of his poems, printed in 1645. The name of the lady is not given, and Waller's biographers have failed to identify her. From a note by MR. W. C. HAZLITT in "N. & Q.," 3rd S. vii. 435, it would appear that she was the Lady Sophia Bertie, daughter of the first Earl of Lindsey, who married Sir Richard Chaworth, Kt., and died in 1689, aged seventy-two. It has generally been stated that Waller's Lady Amoret was the Lady Sophia Murray, and this appears to rest solely on Fenton's recollection of what he had heard the late Duke of Buckingham say many years previously (Fenton's *Waller*, ed. 1729, p. lxii). Whether this was correct might perhaps, as Dr. Johnson observes, be ascertained from family traditions. The note just referred to may fairly raise the question whether Waller was devoted to two Ladies Sophia, Bertie and Murray. It is possible that the duke was speaking of his own Lady "Amoretta," and not of Waller's Lady "Amoret."

Whether Waller did or did not design that the lady should print the volume of his poems is doubtful; but it is certain that, on his subsequent return to England, he was displeased with the little book, and that in 1664 he published his poems, which bear upon the title-page the words "never till now corrected and published with the approbation of the author," and with a preface or notice from the printer stating that, "when the author returned from abroad some few years since, he was troubled to find his name in print, but somewhat satisfied to see his lines so ill rendered, that he might justly disown them." The printer further adds that, for the last twelve years, he had

importuned Mr. Waller to enable him to print a complete and correct edition.

The first collected edition was, therefore, that printed in 1645, but the first authorized one was that published in 1664. The notice of Waller's works in Watt's *Bibliotheca Britannica* is very imperfect. He calls him "a poet of popularity in his day," and does not even mention the first edition of his poems. Lowndes and Allibone give good lists of the chief editions, but they both err in calling that of 1645 the first genuine edition.
EDWARD SOLLY.

SIR RICHARD GRENVILLE (5th S. ix. 222.)—May I be allowed to draw the notice of your correspondents to a difficulty in the Grenville pedigree on which I should be glad to have some light—the place in it rightly belonging to Honor, Viscountess Lisle ? All the pedigrees—known to me —which notice her at all enter her as a daughter of Sir Thomas Grenville (d. 1515) and Isabel Gilbert. Now, while I do not presume to assert that it is not so, I find but one statement in the *Lisle Papers* that harmonizes with it, and several that seem difficult to accommodate to it. I append the extracts in question, and I shall be obliged to any one who will favour me with an opinion upon them.

"My cousin John Granfile and his wife . . . have given me good cheer at their house" (James Basset to his mother, Lady Lisle, dat. London, 1539, *Lisle Papers*, i. 72).

"Your Ladyship hath two nyeces with the Queen, which are daughters unto Mr. Arundell" (John Husee to Lady Lisle, dat. London, May 25 [1536] ; *ib.*, xii. 35).

"Mr. Diggory Graynfield and his wife, my Lady's mother" (Tho. Pectree to Lady Lisle, no date [1532-40]; *ib.*, xiii. 46).

"Your brother, Mr. John Graynfield" (Rev. Tho. Raynolde to Lady Lisle, dat. Paris, April 19 [1534-40] ; *ib.*, xiii. 63).

" [Signed] by yr loving and lowly Sister, Mary Seyntaubyn" (to Lady Lisle, dat. Clowens [Clowance], Midsummer Day [1533-9] ; *ib.*, xiii. 101).

"Yr nieces my daughters. . . . My daughter Phelypp is departyd on Crstmas Day, Almyghtie pardon her soule, and my wyffe hath take greatte discomfort therbye" (Tho. St. Aubyn to Lady Lisle, dat. Jan. 31 [1534-40] ; *ib.*, xiii. 102).

By examination of such pedigrees as I know, I find that Sir Thomas Grenville had two daughters married to gentlemen named Arundel—Jane, wife of John A. of Trerice (mother of Sir Humphrey A. and Mary, Countess of Sussex), and Katherine, who married Sir John A. of Lanherne. This looks as if Lady Lisle were Sir Thomas's daughter, since I find no Arundel marriage among the daughters of his son Sir Roger. But I find a John among

Sir Thomas. I see a Mary (not a Mary St. Aubyn, whom I cannot discover anywhere) among the daughters of Sir Roger, and none among those of Sir Thomas. And I am told that Diggory was the son of Sir Roger, while no such name appears among the family of Sir Thomas. How, moreover, would Lady Lisle's niece be her nurse—even if it mean her children's nurse? Was Lady Lisle, then, the daughter of Sir Thomas and Isabel Gilbert, or was she the daughter of Sir Roger and Margaret Whitleigh? HERMENTRUDE.

"LIBERTY AND PROPERTY" (5th S. ix. 129.)—The latest use known to me of this long-popular cry was during the furious agitation against the "Excise" scheme, or so-called "Cyder Act," of Lord Bute's most injudicious ministry, the term of office held by Sir Francis Dashwood, otherwise Lord Le Despenser, of Medmenham Abbey infamy, as Chancellor of the Exchequer. As such it was said that "a sum of five figures was to him an impenetrable mystery." At this period, i.e. 1761 to 1763, no cry was so frequently in men's mouths as "Liberty, Property, and no Excise." The last part of the denunciation was expressive of so strenuous a degree of wrath that the apple farmers of the West publicly announced their resolution to cut down their apple trees, and let their stocks of cider run to waste, rather than submit to the hated inquisitorial excise law of the chancellor ignoramus, whose attempt thus to tax the people was the more stupid, insomuch that not more than a quarter of a century before the catastrophe of Sir R. Walpole culminated in his proposal to impose an excise. *Pasquin* was published in 1756. There are numerous satirical prints in the British Museum collection which illustrate the use of the cry in question in Lord Bute's day. F. G. S.

SAMUEL BAILEY, OF SHEFFIELD (5th S. ix. 182, 216.)—Since my communication to "N. & Q." at the former reference I have seen a French work entitled "*La Psychologie Anglaise Contemporaine*, par Th. Ribot, ancien élève de l'Ecole Normale, agrégé de Philosophie, Paris, 1870," in which there is a chapter devoted to Bailey. I give the following extract from the chapter referred to :—

"Par le nombre de ses publications philosophiques, dont quelques-unes remontent à une époque déjà fort ancienne, M. Samuel Bailey mériterait une étude à part, si nous nous étions proposé ici autre chose qu'une courte esquisse de la psychologie Anglaise contemporaine. Il n'est guère possible de le classer. Partisan déclaré de l'expérience, il forme comme une transition entre l'école Ecossaise et les psychologistes dont nous venons de parler. Par sa manière nette, exacte, précise, non sans quelque sécheresse, il diffère totalement de la psychologie descriptive dont M. Bain nous a offert le type le plus complet ; il rappelle plutôt le xviii° siècle et la clarté un peu maigre de Condillac et de Destutt de Tracy. Il est, comme eux, plus logicien que psychologue, et son analyse verbale ne pénètre pas assez dans une science ' aussi

enfoncée dans les faits que la psychologie. Dép... pénétrant qu'étendu, avide de clarté, il pours ennemi acharné les métaphores, la phraséologie les arguments de rhétorique qui usurpent la plac science, les explications qui font semblant de ré les difficultés : il demande pour la psychologie une aussi précise que possible. Il n'est point cepen épris d'algèbre qu'il ne céde aux entraîneme l'éloquence, quand c'est le lieu : et il a revendi droits de la science dans un langage si ferme et s' qu'il faut traduire " (here follows a long quotatio *Letters on the Philosophy of the Mind*, by S. Bail Series, Letter 21).

ALEX. IRELA

THE OXFORD AND CAMBRIDGE BOAT-RACE (5th S. ix. 246, 271, 280, 292.)—We hav record of the dimensions of the eight-oared used in the above race, but we should be to show SCULLER a small photograph of a p of an eight-oar which we built for Univ College, Oxford, and which was second o river in 1827. SEARLE & SO Lambeth, S.E.

[Have our correspondents seen the note at the l ference from the pen of the stroke in the race of 1 The Cambridge boat was built by Sear Lambeth. J.

WHOEVER "HEARS THE WHISTLERS" WII (5th S. ix. 309.)—The novel in which the superstition is alluded to is *Edina*, by Mrs. 1 Wood. C. W.

AN "AQUÆBAJALUS" (5th S. ix. 268.)—"We do decree " (Boniface) " that the offices fc water be conferred upon poor clerks."—Lindwood, "For the understanding of which constitutior to be observed that parish clerks were heretofoi clerks, of whom every minister had at least one, tr under him in the celebration of divine offices; and better maintenance the profits of the office of a, *jalus* (who was an assistant to the minister in ca the holy water) were annexed unto the office parish clerk by this constitution ; so as in after *aquæbajalus* was only another name for the cle ciating under the chief minister."—From Burn's *Law*.

H. T.

Dr. Oliver, in his *Monasticon Diæcesis Exon* p. 260, says—

"Aquebajuli were persons who carried the ve the holy water in processions and benedictions. Se In the minor orders were always to be preferred f office (*vide* Synod. Exonien., A.D. 1287, cap. 2C small parishes the aquebajulus occasionally ac sacristan, and rang the bell. See Abp. Bor decree, lib. iii. Lynwode's *Provinciale*."

The word also signifies "parish clerk." in 1613, William Cotton, Bishop of E licensed John Randall to exercise "Officium bajuli sive clerici parochialis apud Gwenn: docendi artem scribendi et legend;" ($H_{2}^{1}st$. *wall*, vol. ii. p. 135). E. H. W.

"Aquæbajulus " was originally the bearer holy vase of water in the church. After th formation the office merged into the office of parish clerk. Bishop Hall, in 1627-8, licensed a John Lyle to the parish church of St. Paul in Exeter : "Emanavit licentia exequenda officium aquæba-juli sive clerici parochialis ecclesiâ S. Pauli Exon Johanni Lyle."   T. E. D.

URCHENFIELD (5th S. ix. 168.)—The *Liber Landavensis* will probably explain the origin of the peculiar legal customs prevalent in Urchen-field. This part of Herefordshire belonged originally to the diocese of Llandaff, which was formed (we are told) by Germanus and Lupus in the fifth century :—

"They consecrated the eminent doctor St. Dubricius, who was elected by the king and the whole district to be archbishop. Having received this dignity, they granted to him, with the consent of King Meurig and of the princes, clergy, and people, the episcopal see, which was founded in the district of Llandaff in honour of St. Peter the apostle ;......the diocese to have five hundred wards, the bay of Severn, *Ergyng* and Anergyng, from Mochros {now written Moccas] on the banks of the Wye as far as the island Terthi [probably Barry Island, in the Bristol Channel]."—*L. L.*, pp. 310, 311.

The editor adds in a note that "Ergyng or Archen-field comprehended the portion of Herefordshire S.W. of the river Wye, of which the present ecclesiastical deanery of Archenfield, or Irchen-field, constitutes a part."

In the twelfth century this territory was claimed by the Bishop of Hereford, and Urban, Bishop of Llandaff, appealed to Pope Honorius II. against the claim. Honorius summoned the Bishop of Hereford, and also the Bishop of St. Davids, to appear before him in order that the dispute might be determined. He complains in a bull issued in the year 1129 that "they neither came nor sent persons to answer for them." Honorius con-tinues :—

"Thou, however, our brother Urban, in the appointed term, didst present thyself in our sight ready with wit-nesses, and we, having for some time waited for those who were invited, took the oaths of six witnesses, two of whom, that is, a certain intelligent priest and a layman, swore that thy portion, respecting which the lawsuit had been instituted, that is Gower, Kidwelly, Cantrebychan, Ystradyw, and *Ergyng*, was contained within the bounds of the diocese of Llandaff, that is, between the rivers Towy and Wye.... ..We, therefore, with the common deliberation of our bishops and cardinals, have determined that the aforesaid districts should be held and possessed by thee, and thy successors for ever, without any in-terruption from the churches of Hereford and St. Davids, or either of them."—*L. L.*, pp. 580, 581.

The peculiar customs of the district belong to the Keltic races (see *Laws of Howel, Myv. Arch.*). This fact and the long continuance of this part of Herefordshire as a portion of the diocese of Llandaff lead to the inference that the district was occupied, even to the middle ages, by a predominant Keltic people, who adhered to the customs of their fore-fathers.

It is worth a passing notice that the name Archenfield, or Erchenfield, is Keltic in the first part. This hybrid form is found in many other names of places, as Ewyas Harold ; Maesbury (W. *maes*=field) ; Nantwich (W. *nant*=valley) ; Pendle, prim. Pen-hull (W. *pen*, head or hill ; A.-S. *hull*, hill) ; Glenfield (Ir. and O.W. *Glenn*, a valley or dell) ; and many other instances. With these may be compared the name Cel-bridge, in Kildare, the first part of which has been taken from the O. Irish name *Cill-droichid*, and Man-chester, which was called, according to Dr. Whi-taker, *Man-cenion* by its Keltic inhabitants, and Latinized by its Roman conquerors into *Man-cunium*.   J. D.

Belsize Square.

SIR NATHANIEL RICHE (3rd S. xi. 256, 392.)—A writer from Boston, U.S., inquires who this individual was, and does not appear to have re-ceived any satisfactory reply. Having had occa-sion to investigate the subject, and found it by no means easy to attain a tolerable certainty, the sub-joined results may perhaps interest some readers. Sir N. Riche is referred to, about 1630, in a MS. history of Bermuda in the British Museum (Sloane MS. 750), as "a near kinsman of the Earl of War-wick, and a very temperate and honest gentleman." He had a sister Jane Riche, married to Thomas Grimsditch, who is reputed by her descendants to have been a niece of Sir Henry Riche, first Earl of Holland, and a brother of the second Earl of Warwick. A close connexion of some sort, there-fore, stands on good evidence. Notwithstanding this, there is a total silence as to both Nathaniel and Jane Riche in all accounts of the Warwick family. See, for example, Morant's *Essex*, Banks's *Dormant and Extinct Peerages*, and Collins's *Peerage;* but one of these works, which I have neglected to note which, does say that Robert Riche, first Earl of Warwick, left one illegitimate son and three illegitimate daughters, and here appears the key to the whole mystery. Sir Nathaniel Riche was, I apprehend, an illegitimate son of Robert, first Earl of Warwick, who died in 1619. He sat in Parliament for Retford, 1614 and 1620 ; for Harwich, 1623 to 1629 ; and died in 1636, be-queathing four shares of land in Bermuda for school purposes, and six shares to the Earl of Man-chester in trust for one of the children of his sister Jane. He was knighted between 1614 and 1620.
                                                J. H. L. Y.

CHEDDLE (5th S. ix. 248.)—This name in both mentioned counties was formerly *Chedle*. The last part of the word is *dale*. Three of the Cheadles are situated on or near rivulets, from which, how-ever, they could not have derived their names. The first syllable of Cheadle is no doubt the ancient appellation of such rivulets, say the *Ched*, *Chet*, *Chat*, *Cad*, *Cat*, *Ket*, or *Kit*. Conf. *Chet*win in

Speed's map of Staffordshire; *Chatburn*, co. Lancaster; *Quatford*, co. Salop; the Göta river in Sweden; the Gade in Herts.

R. S. CHARNOCK.

Junior Garrick.

PRIMITIVE COFFINS (5th S. ix. 285.)—It has been a common practice in all ages whereof we have records to inter relics of mortality in the simple manner described by MR. R. P. HAMPTON ROBERTS. The most interesting example of this practice, as it obtained in this country, is in the Scarborough Museum, being the bones and coffin of a Bernician (?) chief. At any rate, there is a gigantic male human and absolutely perfect skeleton, comprising even the smallest sesamoid and the hyoid bones, and its inclosure the cleft trunk of an enormous oak, which, together with several weapons and ornaments, were found in a tumulus on Gristhorpe Cliff, between Scarborough and Filey. Qwing to the presence of a large proportion of ferruginous earth in the tumulus, and the occurrence of a considerable quantity of water in the oak cist, the gallates of the timber had produced a fluid of the nature of black ink, so that, having been saturated for centuries in this fluid, every bone, implement, and other relic of this peculiarly important interment is now "as black as ink." These relics have been more than once engraved, but never in a manner which is sufficient to give a fair idea of their extraordinary interest.

O.

There is a fine example of a coffin formed out of the trunk of a tree in the museum at Scarborough. It was dug up in that part of England, and has a rudely cut representation of the head of the dead man on the outside, giving it something of the appearance of a mummy case. The skeleton is singularly perfect, of great size, and the front teeth are worn down in a remarkable way, reminding one of the times when it is said that man lived upon acorns. Some ornaments of jet were, I believe, found in the coffin.   J. C. J.

"GALY HALFFENNY" (5th S. ix. 187.)—The following quotation from Camden's *Remains*, under "Money," will illustrate this term :—

"Gally halfpence, brought hither by the gallies of Genoa, who had great trade in England, was prohibited by Parliament in the time of King Henry IV."

GWAVAS.

"Galihalpens were a kind of coin with which Suskins and Dotkins were forbidden by the stat. 3 Hen. V. 1. They were a Genoa coin, brought in by the Genoese merchants, who, landing hither in gallies, lived commonly in a lane near Tower Street, and were called Galley Men, landing their goods at a certain Thames Street called Galley Key, and trading with their own small silver coin called Galley halfpence. See Stow's *Survey of London*, 137. Sir Francis Bacon writes them Gauls halfpence; and 'tis like, more truly."—Cowel, *Interpreter.*

R. S. CHARNOCK.

TOUCHING FOR THE KING'S EVIL : FORMS OF PRAYER (5th S. ix. 49, 236, 251, 273.)—Thanking your correspondents very much for their replies may I remark that no one of them has answered my first and main question, "When [*i.e.* at what date] did James I. of England first perform this ceremony ? " I am strongly convinced that, if only for politic reasons, he commenced it very early after his accession ; but I wish much for the actual date, and thereby for the proof of my belief.

With all thanks also to MR. J. C. Cox, will he permit me without offence to say that, as was meant to be shown by the very form of my query —" James I. of England "—I never supposed (nor I believe, any other) that James VI. of Scotland and heir of England, ever touched for the evil Tradition and its historical following never gave the power to the heir while heir, but only to the legal and actual monarch. Moreover, Elizabeth would have had more than a word to say to such an infringement and usurpation of her rights.

B. NICHOLSON.

I am in possession of a copy of the Book of Common Prayer, printed in 1728, the first year of George II., without printer's name, which contains the form "At the Healing" in the usual place after the three state forms. As the service for the king's accession is for August 1 (*i.e.* Geo. I.) the book must have been printed before the date given on the title-page. It is an exact copy of Baskett's quarto edition of 1715, of the same size but with a smaller though beautifully clear type so as to bring the whole within 124 pages, Baskett's extending to 160 pages. It is not mentioned in Lowndes. Like Baskett's, it does not give the Epistles and Gospels in full, but only the reference and the first three words. When did this practice commence ? In what other editions is it found ? Does it not imply that the reader must turn to the Bible in order to find and read thence these Epistles and Gospels ? And, if so, does it not imply that the practice then must have been to read the Communion Service, not from the altar, but from the reading-desk where the Bible was ?

G. B. BLOMFIELD.

Chester.

The queen of 1717 was a very different person from her predecessor. Before we can consider MR. FERREY's book as exceptional, it would be well to know whether Queen Sophia was ever prayed for in England.   GWAVAS.

The form of prayer is found in a quarto Prayer Book printed by Baskett at Oxford, in 1732, as have mentioned in my short notice of the office printed in Blunt's *Annotated Prayer Book*, p. 580 Of this edition a copy was purchased by the Bodleian Library in 1866.   W. D. MACRAY.

HENRY INGLES (5th S. vi. 490; vii. 14, 99; ix. 256.)—If H. W. and J. P. E. were to apply to Henry Ingles-Chamberlayne, Esq., of Maugresbury Manor, Stow-in-the-Wold, Gloucestershire, they would probably obtain information relative to their queries.   J. R. S.

"THE BRISTOL MEMORIALIST" (5th S. ix. 188, 236.)—From the style of "Sayings of my Uncle" I should ascribe those articles to the Rev. John Evans, of Park Row Academy, Bristol, author of *The Ponderer*, 12mo., 1812. He was a friend of Tyson.   J. F. NICHOLLS, F.S.A.

JOHN FLEETWOOD (5th S. viii. 335; ix. 232.)— Lowndes, in *Bibl. Man.*, mentions this John Fleetwood as the author of a *Christian Dictionary; or, a True Guide to Divine Knowledge*, Lond., 1773, 4to.   ED. MARSHALL.

CHRONOGRAMS (1st S. ix. 60; 5th S. ix. 69, 112.) —The following may interest DR. SPARROW SIMPSON:—

"De spIrItaLI IMItatIone ChrIstI,
aDMonItIones saCræ et VtILes,
pIIs In LVceM Datæ.

A. R. P. Antonio Vanden Stock Societatis Jesu. Ruræ-mondæ, apud Gasparem du Pree." Sm. 8vo. pp. 92, engraved frontispiece.

This is the *Imitation of Christ*, by Thomas à Kempis, travestied into chronograms, each line giving the date 1658. The author in a short preface ("aVthorIs aD LeCtores præMonItIo") explains why he was induced to compose this curious work:—

"Tum tut optimus ille ac saluberrimus animæ cibus, alio quam unquam fortasse fuit modo coctus, magis lec. torum palato arrideat."

"ChrIsto aDhærens non aMbVLat In tenebrIs.
ChrIstI Mores attenDe, et seqVI Labora.
et Interne sentIes LVMen CorDIs.
freqVenter MeDItare ChrIstI Labores."

This book is of considerable rarity. I have never seen a copy. (Cf. De Backer, *Écrivains de la Compagnie de Jésus*, second ed., *sub nomine*.)
                                EDMUND WATERTON.

I send three from Devonshire:—1. William, Earl of Bath, 1623, at Tawstock:—

"EXIIt en bon teMps nVnCq' VIenDra patet."

2. Thomas Ford, 1658, at Ilsington:—

"DorMIo et vt spero CIneres sIne Labe resVrgent."

3. Mary Elford, aged 25, 1642, at Widdecombe-in-the-Moor:—

"A° ætat } { VIXIt obIIt sVperIs.

MarIa GaLe IohannIs ELforD VXor tertIa heV obIIt pVerperIo."
                                        T. F. R.

LEEDS POTTERY (5th S. viii. 409, 455; ix. 78.) —I saw a plate, very much like one of those re. ferred to by Chaffers as having been made on

the occasion of Prince William V.'s marriage, in a shop window at Whitby in 1876. The embellish-ment consisted of two busts, a lighted candle, and some orange branches. There was also a legend in Dutch, of which I have a copy made by the shop-man, and accompanied by what is said to be a "literal translation," due to himself or to one of his friends:—

"ik brand Light Voor de
Prins Zÿn Nigt
En ook de Oranje Sprúit
Die het Niet Wil
Zien die blaast het U'it."

"Literal Translation.—I burn a light for the Prince's Niece and also for the Orange ᵇᵘᵈ / sprout who will see it. He blows it out."
                                        ST. SWITHIN.

I give the modern Dutch and a translation of the inscriptions on B. J.'s bottle:—

"Ziet wat
recht
van achteren
Staat."

—"See what there is behind."

"Bidt voor uwen
Vorst wenscht
voor geen
Kwaad."

—"Pray for your king and wish no harm."

The date indicated by the initials of William V., Prince of Orange, are certainly before Leeds pro-duced earthenware. Is the bottle Delft?
                                        HUGH OWEN.

G. AND H. CABOT, OF BOSTON (5th S. ix. 9, 112.) —The Cabots of Boston, Mass., have claimed to descend from Sebastian Cabot. The family of the late Mr. C. C. Foster, of Cambridge, Mass., a relation, I suppose, of the Boston Cabots, possess an heirloom, a mourning ring, over two hundred years old, with the name "Sebastian Cabot" en-graved on it. Mr. Payne says, in regard to the Cabots, "The eldest branch of this family, which formerly held much landed property in the parish of St. Trinity [Jersey], emigrated to America in the person of George Cabot [son of François]," &c. (*Armorial of Jersey*, p. 50). This was about 1700. Besides proving the descent of the Cabot family from that of Jersey, my authority (of whom presently) states the claim, as a lineal ancestor to Sebastian Cabot, to be doubtful, though he appears to have been of the same stock. M. de la Roque (*Armorial de Languedoc*) has said he died without issue, but gives no proof of his assertion. The name Cabot is found in England, France, Belgium, and Italy. "The coat of arms of the Jersey family is perfectly defined and well known. The device is three fishes, or, in the Jersey phrase, 'three chabots.'" The motto of the Boston family is "Semper cor caput Cabot." There are other details in the work from which the above is de-

rived, which is, by the way, a valuable contribution to American political history—*Life and Letters of George Cabot*, by Henry Cabot Lodge, Boston, 1877. This George Cabot, born Dec. 16, 1751, died April 18, 1823, was the grandson of John, a younger brother of the first George who came to America. WILLIAM JOHN POTTS.
Camden, New Jersey.

PROVINCIAL FAIRS (5th S. vi. 108, 214, 278, 353; vii. 99, 437; viii. 156, 269.)—No mention has been made in any of the notes on this subject of the continental fairs, and I agree with K. P. D. E. that some information about them would be valuable. I was in Rotterdam last year in the middle of the fair there (Aug. 21), and the variety of costumes alone was remarkable, interesting, and amusing. On Aug. 29 I arrived at Arnhem at the annual fair time, which should have lasted from Aug. 27 to Sept. 2. The burgomaster and town authorities, however, had given notice a few days before that the fair would not be permitted to be held, as it was contrary to their religion (Lutheran). This was of course injudicious, and the consequence was that the people determined to have the fair, while the Roman Catholics and Jansenists from Utrecht took it up as an insult to their religion and determined to revenge themselves. Accordingly on Monday the 27th, the first day of the usual fair, a great number of people came from neighbouring towns, filled the streets, and began breaking the shop windows. The military were called out, and, firing on the mob, killed two or three and wounded several. This checked them for that night. Every succeeding evening the streets were crowded with people, principally women. All the shops which possessed no shutters were boarded up, and soldiers in bodies of about twelve infantry and six cavalry paraded the streets throughout the night. On Aug. 30, which was the maid-servants' fairing night, a riot was expected. But, alas! I was obliged to return to England that day, and have not heard what happened. I was told that at Zaandam in 1876 the fair was stopped in the same way by the authorities; but the mob seized the burgomaster, and, carrying him off to the Stadhuis, made him sign a paper giving them permission to continue holding the fair for five more years.
A great movement is being made throughout Holland for the suppression of the annual fairs, principally on account of the immorality which it is alleged they produce. Knowing hardly any Dutch, I was unable to ascertain all the particulars I should have liked; but I hope some attempt will be made, if it has not yet been made, to gather together the customs of the fairs before these interesting festivals become a thing of the past.   H. C. DENT.

Gunning, in his *Reminiscences of the University*

and *Town of Cambridge*, gives an amusing account of Stourbridge fair as it existed in his early days at Cambridge. Also in the *Musæ Anglicanæ* may be found a poem upon it entitled "Nundinæ Sturbrigienses."   JOHN PICKFORD, M.A.
Bushey Rectory, near Watford.

"CATALOGUE OF FIVE HUNDRED CELEBRATED AUTHORS" (5th S. viii. 428; ix. 72.)—I see in Bohn's *Lowndes*, as precisely and usefully indicated by MR. POCOCK, a record of the book, and it states that Marshall bought up the copies and destroyed them, but it does not say it was edited by Rivers of Highgate, as reported by Lowndes. I conclude from this that MR. POCOCK has Bohn's *Lowndes* and also Lowndes's own work, which, oddly enough, Bohn does not chronicle at all under the head of Lowndes. I have never had an opportunity to compare these books together. Can MR. POCOCK say whether Bohn is in the habit of omitting such important facts as that Rivers edited this *Catalogue of Five Hundred Authors* when it is mentioned by Lowndes? If so, both the works are necessary; for Bohn's becomes merely a work based on Lowndes, and not a reprint with valuable additions, as it ought to have been, and as I supposed that it was. It is ridiculous to see the diversity of the estimates given of the value of the book. One calls it libellous, another a contemptible catchpenny, a lady devotes her time to covering it with MS. notes, and Lowndes, who was the best possible judge of such a thing, calls it "a useful work to the time when it was published." No doubt but Mr. Marshall, ensconced in his snuggery at Epsom, wrote just what he thought of a great number of the said five hundred who passed as *littérateurs*, and taken anywhere would always be more or less a contemptible and laughter-moving lot. Having published, he would suddenly find his Epsom bower converted into a hornets' nest, would lament past peace and the pleasant honey stowage of his industry, and hurriedly set about buying up copies to make a bonfire on the lawn, and from the funeral pyre hope to revivify that domestic Phœnix, peace.   C. A. WARD.
Mayfair.

RUSSIA IN THE BIBLE (5th S. vii. 306; viii. 56.) —The etymology of the word *Russia* is thus explained by Dr. V. Thomsen, Professor of Comparative Philology in the University of Copenhagen :—
There is an old Swedish word *rother* (O.N. *róðr*), meaning "rowing, navigation," from which is derived *Roslagen*, the coast of Upland, formerly *Rother, Rothin*, the people of this district being called *Rods*-Karlar, now *Rospiggar*, "rowers, seafarers." From *Rods*-Karlar or *Róðs*-Karlar the Finns have *Ruotsi*=Sweden, *Ruotsa-lamen*=a Swede. From the Finns, who came first in contact with the Northmen, the Slavs borrowed the word *Rus'* as a designation of the Scandinavians. The evolution of the word in Russian history is as follows:—

(1) it was the name of a foreign dominant clan, whose homestead was the coast of Sweden, opposite the Gulf of Finland; (2) the land under the sway of the *Rus'*, ruling at Kiev; (3) the inhabitants, Slavs as well as North-men.—See Thomsen, *Origin of the Ancient Russ*, Lect. iii.

A. L. MAYHEW.

CHEVALIER D'EON (5th S. ix. 307.)—Most of the documents are said by M. Gaillardet himself to have been deposited in the public library at Tonnerre.   K. H. B.

THE FIRST INSTITUTION OF SUNDAY SCHOOLS (5th S. viii. 367 ; ix. 110, 156, 271) is ascribed by Catholics to Cardinal Borromeo, Archbishop of Milan (born 1538, died 1584). Their chief object was the oral instruction and repetition of the Catechism. Another "pious practice" may per-haps be traced to the saintly reformer of Church discipline. It was the custom of the archbishop to leave devotional books on the tables of his waiting-rooms, in order that visitors to his house might occupy themselves profitably whilst waiting for an audience.* Is not this same idea reproduced in the Bibles, &c., placed in most, if not all, of our railway station waiting-rooms ?   F. C. V.

AUTHORS OF BOOKS WANTED (5th S. ix. 268.)—
Poems for Youth, by a Family Circle, was the united work of the Roscoe family (one of the ladies acting as editor), and contains poems by the head of the house, William Roscoe, William Stanley Roscoe, William Cald-well Roscoe, Margaret Roscoe, Robert Roscoe, Mary Anne Roscoe, Henry Roscoe, and Jane E. Roscoe. It consists of two parts, and is dated not 1820, as given by T. W. C., but 1821 in my copy. As I possess only part i., I should feel greatly obliged if T. W. C. would kindly inform me whether part i. contains William Roscoe's famous sonnet *On Parting from his Books*, beginning—
" As one who, destined from his friends to part";
and, if so, quote page, title, and, if not too much trouble, exact text as there given.   WM. BUCHANAN.
87, Union Street, Glasgow.

Miscellaneous.

NOTES ON BOOKS, &c.

Notes on some Passages in the Liturgical History of the Reformed English Church. By Lord Selborne. (Murray.)
Did Queen Elizabeth take "other order" in the "Adver-tisements" of 1566? A Letter to Lord Selborne. By James Parker, Hon. M.A. Oxon. (Oxford and London, Parker & Co.)
THE "Queen of Festivals" can hardly be said to have brought the gift of a cessation from controversy to the parties who are at issue within the comprehensive limits of the Church of England as by law established. In the eyes of some, perhaps, such a gift would be a doubtful blessing, a sign of lethargy rather than of life. What-ever be the true view of the benefits of controversy it is certain that there is "a very pretty quarrel" between Lord Selborne and Mr. James Parker. It is needless to say that the disputants are both learned in

* See *Life of S. Charles*, edited by Edward Healy Thompson, M.A.

the special lore of their subject, and that they are as courteous towards each other as the gentlemen of the English Guards who requested the gentlemen of the French Guards to fire first. How the difference between the two is to be bridged over, it is not for us to suggest. If Lord Selborne's view be accepted, Queen Elizabeth did take in the Advertisements of 1566 precisely the "other order" reserved to her in sec. xxv. of I Eliz. cap. 2. But a difficulty still seems to remain, involved in the very fact of the *cadit quæstio* which we presume to be the intended result of the learned Lord's argument. The difficulty is, if we may be allowed the comparison without suspicion of an intention to derogate from his lordship's authority, somewhat similar in kind to that which was felt by M. Jourdain when he found that he had been always talking prose without knowing it. The "bright Occidental Star" took "other order," which settled for ever in 1566 questions still rife in 1878, only we did not know it. We much fear that notwithstanding the deference which naturally attaches to so illustrious a name as that of Lord Selborne, the last word has not yet been spoken on these controverted matters, and that the liturgical history of the Reformed Church of England is not so easily to be settled on the basis of 1566. We need scarcely say that the author of the *Introduction to the History of the Successive Revisions of the Book of Common Prayer*, to which Lord Selborne in his own opening words pays a graceful tribute of praise, makes a very good and stubborn fight in his Letter on the Advertise-ments. How Queen Elizabeth took "other order" in 1561, and what was the nature of that "order," and how far oppugnant to the supposed effect on the ornaments of the minister of any "order" in 1566, we must leave the readers of Mr. Parker's valuable and interesting pam-phlet to find out for themselves. The disputants are both before the world, and their respective works should be in the hands of the same reading public for the forma-tion of an impartial judgment.

The Works of Robert Burns. Poetry. 3 vols. (Edin-burgh, W. Paterson.)
IT is seldom that a more satisfactory book than Mr. W. Scott Douglas's edition of Burns's poetry presents itself for review. Its object is to supply, in handsome library form, a strictly chronological edition, as faithful to the poet's own MSS. and copies as may be, with variations noted, particulars as to MSS. and bibliography carefully recorded, biographical and other illustrative notes added, and in fact everything done to present the poet before us in a connected story told by himself in verse and by his editor in prose. And yet the result is not such a work as that of Robert Chambers, half life and half works, but, in the strictest sense, a library edition of the works; for the notes are unobtrusive in extent, and full of closely packed information. The text is copiously supplied with glossarial foot-notes, and these are supplemented by a combined glossary from Burns's editions, enlarged, and appended to the third volume. Many of the songs are furnished with the music to which they were composed. Each volume has an alphabetical list of first lines prefixed as well as the usual numerical table of contents; and then there is a general list of first lines for the three volumes at the end of vol. iii. This and the glossarial arrangement of course involve a certain lavish consumption of space; but this is not to be regretted when the advantages are so manifest. No pains seem to have been spared in carrying out an unusually exacting programme; the material arrange-ments, typographical and other, are most excellent; the text bears close examination, and is as readable as it is scholarly. The illustrations are well chosen and ex-cellently engraved, though in the mechanical style of the

poet's MSS., only need to be printed on the paper of the latter part of last century to be first-rate. The first volume contains, besides other illustrations, a pretty and useful map of the principal portions of Ayrshire at the close of last century, and the title-pages bear a beautifully engraved vignette of the Scottish Muse, in appropriate if not in the highest taste. There has been no such full edition of Burns yet; and it may be fairly questioned whether a fuller is desirable. We should be very sorry to assume the editorial responsibility of adding to the transgressions currently admitted into the body of Burns's writings; and yet we cannot deny that the tabooed book, *The Merry Muse*, contains verses no whit more inadmissible than much which has been too long included to be thrust forth from any standard edition. The editor's views on this and many other subjects may be expected to be set forth at large in a general preface which is to accompany the prose works; and we can hardly doubt that a book executed in a manner so lavish of trouble and expense will contain what we miss very much at the point already reached—a subject index. As long as the three volumes of poetry and valuable notes be duly indexed, it is no matter whether now or at the end of the series. This series can hardly fail to be, when completed, *the* edition of Burns: the three volumes before us are certainly *the* edition of his poetry ; for though, for students and others who can give room to more than one edition, this does not supersede the beautiful set of books known as the Kilmarnock edition, based upon a fac-simile of the *editio princeps* of *Poems chiefly in the Scottish Dialect*, it yet covers more ground than that or any other edition.

THE current *Quarterly Review* (Murray) contains much of general interest, but the paper that will attract of course chief attention at the present time is that on "The Aggression of Russia and the Duty of Great Britain." Of Lord Salisbury's now celebrated despatch of the 1st inst. the writer says, " Manly and dignified in tone, it does not mince matters, or shrink from saying the plainest truths in the calmest words."

THE May number of the *Law Magazine and Review* will contain an exhaustive article on Parish Registers, by the editor, Mr. Taswell-Langmead, B.C.L., who drew attention to this important subject in "N. & Q." some years ago.

A DANTE CURIOSITY.—According to the *Times* a Padua publisher is to send to the Paris Exhibition an edition of Dante scarcely longer than the thumb-nail, and intended for a watch-chain appendage. The letters are so small as to resemble grains of sand, and few, of course, can decipher them without a magnifying-glass. It being impossible to distribute the type after the edition had been worked off, it was returned to the foundry. This *Iliad* in a nutshell will be bound in red velvet, with silver clasps.

MR. EDWARD R. VYVYAN is now engaged on a biographical sketch of the bishops of Gloucester from the creation of the distinct diocese in 1541 to the present day. MR. VYVYAN would be glad to receive any information about the more obscure occupants of the See.

Notices to Correspondents.

We must call special attention to the following notice:—
ON all communications should be written the name and address of the sender, not necessarily for publication, but as a guarantee of good faith.

EARLSCOURT. — Legitimation *per subsequens matrimonium* is common to the laws of France and other

it was one of the three modes of legitimation known to the later Roman Civil Law, the other two modes bein *per oblationem curiæ* (now extinct) and *per Rescriptu Principis* (still obtaining on the Continent). It appear to have originated in the Civil Law through a constitu tion of Constantine, renewed by Zeno. It passed from the Civil into the Canon Law, in which it is said to hav been established by two constitutions of Pope Alex ander III., preserved in the Decretals. It has neve been received into the English Common Law. Where i has been followed this has arisen, as Lord Mackenzi points out, "not by authority of the Decretals, but i itself." Reference may be made to *Code Civil*, Art. 331-3 Lord Mackenzie, *Studies in Roman Law ;* Mackeldey *Systema Juris Romani*, &c.

M.—The Calendars of State Papers published unde the authority of the Master of the Rolls are ver; numerous. There are eight volumes of the reign o Henry VIII., edited by Rev. J. S. Brewer; twelve volume of the "Domestic Series," including the reigns o Edward VI., Mary, Elizabeth, and James I., edited b; Mr. Lemon and Mrs. Green; and of the subsequen reigns of Charles I. and Charles II., edited by Mr Bruce, Mrs. Green, and Mr. Hamilton, no less tha twenty-five volumes have been issued. Our correspon dent should consult the catalogue of *Record Publication* on sale. It could, we presume, be procured from Messrs Longman, and may also be found in the *Annals of England* (Parker).

SIGMA (Brooklyn, U.S.) thanks MR. WOODWARD for hi reply, *ante*, p. 114. SIGMA is anxious to place himself ir communication by mail with HIRONDELLE in reference to the book, *Casa de Sousa*, mentioned by HIRONDELLI in our last volume, p. 179.

F. L. D. asks for information concerning the airs to which the songs in Shakspeare's plays are sung. [We shall be happy to forward prepaid communications.]

J. W. writes that he has extracts from two newspapers of the day giving a description of the Oxford and Cam bridge boat-race (1829) which are at the service of SCULLER.

ACADEMICUS should consult *The Coins of England*, by H. Noel Humphreys (London, Wm. Smith, 113, Flee Street).

W.—You should go to the British Museum. Knight' *Cyclopædia* (biographical division) might answer you purpose.

W. GARNETT.—The "D. G." was accidentally omittec —hence the epithet. The florin was withdrawn as fai as possible from circulation.

J. J. H.—A general article on the subject of the assumption of baronetcies might prove acceptable.

GEO. A. M. will now find that he has been anticipated *ante*, p. 174.

E. R. VYVYAN.—We have not seen the work referred to in the latter part of your letter.

A. S. ELLIS.—" Chauncy Family " next week.

C. ROGERS.—It was from you.

NOTICE.
Editorial Communications should be addressed to "The Editor of 'Notes and Queries'"—Advertisements and Business Letters to "The Publisher"—at the Office, 20, Wellington Street, Strand, London, W.C.
We beg leave to state that we decline to return com· munications which, for any reason, we do not print ; and to this rule we can make no exception.

LONDON, SATURDAY, MAY 4, 1878.

CONTENTS.—N° 227.

Notes.

BURNS'S EDINBURGH PRIVATE JOURNAL.

The world has been long familiar with the introductory part, and sundry extracts from this document, dated "Edinburgh, April 9, 1787," which were included by Dr. Currie in the poet's biography.

In D'Israeli's *Curiosities of Literature*, vol. i. p. 136, occurs the following passage concerning this journal :—

"Once we were nearly receiving from the hand of genius the most curious sketches of the temper, the irascible humours, the delicacy of soul, even to its shadowiness, from the warm *sbozzos* of Burns, when he began a diary of his heart—a narrative of characters and events, and a chronology of his emotions. It was natural for such a creature of sensation and passion to project such a regular task, but quite impossible to get through it."

Lockhart, in 1828, thus referred to the same manuscript, after quoting the portions printed by Currie :—

"This curious document, it is to be observed, has not yet been printed entire. Another generation will, no doubt, see the whole of the confession; meanwhile, it may be surmised, indicates sufficiently the complexion of Burns's prevailing moods during his moments of retirement at this interesting period of his history."

Dr. Currie evidently was put in possession of the original journal. His words are these :—

"Of the state of the poet's mind at this time an authentic though imperfect document remains in a book which he procured in the spring of 1787, for the purpose of recording in it whatever seemed worthy of observation, ...The intentions of the poet in procuring this book (so fully described by himself) were very imperfectly executed. He has inserted in it few or no incidents, but several observations and reflections, of which the greater part that are proper for the public eye will be found interwoven in the volume of letters. The most curious particulars in the book are the delineations of characters he met with. These are not numerous; but they are chiefly of persons of distinction in the republic of letters, and nothing but the delicacy and respect due to living characters prevents us from committing them to the press."

The only delineations of character included by Currie in his printed extracts from that journal are those of the Earl of Glencairn and of Dr. Blair. Can any person inform the present inquirer what became of the book after Currie's death, which event happened in 1805 ? Is it known to be still in existence ? and if so, where is it ?

From another jotting-book used by Burns (of date 1788) Cromek printed in his *Reliques of Burns* a few pages, headed "Fragments, Miscellaneous Remarks, &c.," but these consist almost entirely of scraps, every one of which can be traced to some particular letter in the "Clarinda Correspondence." These form no portion of the journal now inquired after. Allan Cunningham, who in his edition has tagged together those scraps from Cromek with the extracts given by Currie from the missing journal, quotes from Cromek's manuscript notes a most absurd story, to the effect that the journal in question was stolen from the poet's lodging (at Mrs. Carfrae's, Baxter's Close, Lawnmarket) by a carpenter working in Leith who often called to see Burns, and which carpenter shortly thereafter sailed for Gibraltar. That story is easily accounted for. Cromek had evidently seen a letter, hitherto unpublished, addressed by Burns on April 19, 1787, to an intimate friend, Mr. George Reid of Barquharrie, in which he narrates the fact that, during his absence, "a fellow now gone to Gibraltar" had entered his room and stolen some of his manuscripts.

It remains further to be stated that the poet has described the missing book as a clasped volume, with "lock and key—a security at least equal to the bosom of any friend whatever." W. S. D.

SHAKSPEARIANA.

"CORIOLANUS," ACT I. SC. 1, LL. 82-5 (CAM. ED.).—

"*Menen.* I shall tell you
A pretty tale,—it may be you have heard it,—
But since it serves my purpose I will venture
To scale't a little more."

So run the folios. But Dyce, the Cambridge editors, and, I believe, all moderns, following Theobald, substitute "stale't" for "scale't." The

substitutes a phrase more in use with and more understood by modern readers than one that is somewhat antiquated. The rule, however, is beginning to be better understood (except by some emending critics) that a change which the emender believes to be an improvement is not to be adopted if the old reading give a sufficient sense. Here I believe it gives not only a sufficient but a better sense.

To " scale a fish " is to disfurnish or clear or clean it from its scales that it may be used by man. To " scale a piece of old and rusty metal" is to clear off its rusty scaling, and so furbish it up anew for use or ornament. To " scale a bone " as practised by the old surgeons was to scrape off the diseased surface, and so clear or clean it.

The ordinary supposition (founded on the reading " stale 't ") is that Menenius only intends to say that " he will tell the tale again." But he does not merely do this, nor intend to do it. What he intends to do and afterwards does do is intimated in the words " but since it serves my purpose." In accordance therewith he not only tells the tale, but also takes off its covering and lays bare its meaning or moral to their use, or, to use other synonyms, clears it or shells it open to their apprehensions, that they may see and taste it in all its goodness. Nor are we without contemporary examples of a similar use of the word. A very pertinent one is to be found in James I.'s *Dæmonologie*, a work probably read by Shakspere, though the royal author may not be complimented on his collocation of terms :—" The brightness of the Gospell . . . scaled [= cleared off] the cloudes of all these grosse errors [*i.e.* all these gross clouds of error]" (bk. ii. ch. vii. p. 53, first ed.).

This example is sufficient for the reinstatement of " scale" as Shakspere's word. Richardson, in his *Dictionary*, following Skinner, also reads " scale" in this passage, though he quotes it as showing that it always implies " dividing " or " division " ; as that here " the tale was scaled by being divided more into particulars and degrees," more circumstantially and at length. The phrase in *Measure for Measure* (iii. 1, 241, Cam. ed.), " the corrupt deputy scaled," he however explains " by slipping off his covering of hypocrisy," and here I fully agree with him, and claim this as a second or third example.

B. NICHOLSON, M.D.

" THE MOBLED QUEEN," " HAMLET," ACT II. SC. 2 (3ʳᵈ S. vi. 66, 111.)—" *Mab-led* or *mob-led* in Warwickshire signifies being led astray by a will-o'-the-wispe " : thus Longstaffe, in his *History of Darlington*, p. 14, where he gives a long list of the *aliases* borne by the *ignis fatuus*. Brand makes the same statement (*Antiquities*, vol. iii. p. 397, Bohn). The Warwickshire poet may have applied

the word . . . . because she ran windy about *mab-led* or *mob-led*, as it were, by the drea(fascination of the flames. ST. SWITHIN

[See *ante*, p. 255.]

" HAMLET," ACT I. SC. 4 (5ᵗʰ S. ix. 103.)—
" The dram of eale
Doth all the noble substance of a doubt
To his own scandal."

Adopting Knight's reading *ill* for *eale*, that Steevens, *dout* (*i.e.* do out) for *doubt*, and *oft* of *a*, and *its* for *his*, which, as Malone observe so common in Shakspear that every play furnis us with examples, the lines would read as follo
" The dram of ill
Doth all the noble substance oft do out
To its own scandal."
F

" THE TAMING OF THE SHREW."—In the lection of Lord de Tabley (*Hist. MSS. Commiss* vol. i. p. 49) is a 12mo. volume of poems by P. Leycester, containing an " Epilogue to *Tam of the Shrew*, acted at Nether Tabley, by the S vants and Neighbours there, at Christmas, 1(
P. L." ALICE B. GOMMI

" MERCHANT OF VENICE."—In the *Annales Crime et de l'Innocence* (Paris, 1813) I read :—
" Un Turc ayant prêté à un Chrétien 300 livres, condition que le Chrétien ne rendait pas cette som au jour fixé, le Turc lui couperait deux onces de c sur le corps. Le Chrétien n'ayant pas pu rendre l'arg Amurath premier en fut averti. Il fit venir devan ces deux hommes, et dit au Turc que si il coupait ou moins que les deux onces, il lui serait fait autant.'

Where could the writer have met this i version of the old legend ? Amurath I. reignec the fourteenth century. Amurath III. died 1595-6. Shakspear says (*Henry IV.*, part Act v. sc. 2) :—
" Not Amurath an Amurath succeeds,
But Harry Harry."
PHILIP ABRAHAM
Gower Street.

CHAUCER AND LYDGATE FRAGMENTS.
I. ON MISRULE AND GOOD RULE IN CONDUCT ANI MANNERS.*
[Mr. Hy. Huth's paper MS. of Chaucer and Lydgate f ments, &c., about 1460-70 A.D.; last leaf, 144]
1.
Hit/ is ful harde to knowe ony estate
Double visage loketh oute of/ euery hood
Sewerte is loste / Truste is past/ the date
Thrifte hathe take his leue ouer/ the flood
Lawe can do no thyng/ with/ -outen good
Thefte bathe leue / to goo oute at/ large
Of/ the communes/ mysreule / hathe take the charge.
2.
And thou desire thy self/ to auaunce
Poure or riche / whether that/ thou be
Be lowly and gentyl in thy gouernaunce

* Possibly part of two or more poems.

Good reule douteles/ may best/ preserve the
Yf/ thou be gentyl/ hurte not/ thy degre
And thou be poure / do alle that/ thou canne
To vse good maners/ for maner/ maket/ man. /

3.

Atte thy mele be glad in countenaunce
In mete and drynke/ be thou mesurable
Beware of/ surfete and mysgouernaunce
They cause men ofte to be vnresonable
Suffre no thyng/ be sayde at/ thy table
That/ ony man may hurte or displese
For good mete and drynke axeth Ioye and ese

4.

Yf/ thy goodes to the not/ suffyse
Conforme the euer to that/ thou hast/
Gouerne so thy self/ in suche a wyse
In thyn expences/ make no waste
Grete excesse causeth vnthrift/ in haste
Beware be tyme bere this in thyn herte
Misrewle maketh/ ofte many men to smerte. /

5.

Beware of/ nouellis that/ be new brought/
Thoughe they be plesant// lokke fast/ thy lyppe
An hasty worde may be to sore bought/
Close thy mouthe / leste thy tounge trippe
To thy self/ loke thou make not/ a whyppe
Hurte not/ thy self/ lest/ thou sore rewe
For/ thyn owne ese / keepe thy tonge in mewe. /

II. BALADE MADE BY HALSHAM.*

1.

The worlde so wyde / the ayre so remeuable
The sely man so lytel of/ stature
The graue and grounde / of clothyng/ so mutable
The fyre so boote / and subtylle of/ nature
The water/ neuer in oon/ what/ creature
That/ made is of these foure thus flyttyng/
Maye endure stable and perseuere in abydyng/

2.

The further I goo / the more behynde
The more behynde / the ner my weyes ende
The more I seche / the werse can I fynde
The lyghter leue / the lother for to wende
The truer I serue / the ferther oute of/ mynde
Though I goo loose I am teyde with a lyne
Is hit/ fortune or Infortune thus I fynde. /

EXPLICIT.

III. WOE TO SEVEN EVILS.†

Wo worthe debate. þat/ neuer may haue pease. /
Wo worthe penaunce. þat/ asketh no pyte. /
Wo worthe Vengeaunce. whiche mercy may not sease./
Wo worthe þat Iugement. þat/ hathe none equite. /
Wo worthe þat trouthe. þat/ berethe no charite. /
Wo worthe þat Iuge. þat/ may no gilt[y] / saue. /
Wo worthe þat right/. þat/ may no fauor haue. /

Can any one tell me of other copies of the first
and third poems?

* According to Shirley, in his MS. Addit. 16165, Brit.
Mus., leaf 244. Often printed as Chaucer's, as part of his
Proverbs; see Aldine ed., 1866, vi. 303.
† In a different but contemporary hand.

RECIPE FOR EDWARD IV.'S PLAGUE MEDICINE.

[From Mr. Huth's paper MS. of Chaucer and Lydgate
pieces, &c., about 1460–70 A.D. ; leaf 150 bk.]

Ihesus.

Thys ys þe medesyn þat þe kyngis grace vsythe
every day for The raynyng seknys þat now raynthe
þe wyche bathe ben prowyd & be þe grace of god yt
hathe olpyn þys ȝere lxxi personys   he most take a
hanfvll of rewe, a hanfvll of marygoldis, halfe a hanfvll
of fetherfev, a hanfvll of bvrnett, a hanfvll of sorell, a
qvantyte of dragonys—þe crop or þe rovte :—then take
a potell of rvngyng water, Fyrst wasche them clene &
let them sethe esely tyl yt be a-moste cvm from a
potell to a qvarte of leker : then take a clene clothe,
& strayne ytt & drynke yt ; & yt be byttyr, pvt
ther-to a lytyll svger of candy, & thys may be
dronkyn oftyme ; & yf yt be drokyn be-fore eny
pvrpyl a-pere, By þe grase of god ther schall be no
perell of no dethe.

F. J. F.

THE LAST OF THE WYCLIFFES.

As our great Reformer, John Wycliffe, has recently been brought before the notice of the English
public, perhaps an account of one who was the last
of the family who bore that name may be thought
worthy of a place in your columns.

Some years ago I copied the following inscription from a tombstone in the churchyard of Whit-
kirk, Yorkshire:—

"Sacred to the Memory of
Mrs. Catherine Wade,
of Halton,
the last descendant
of the family which in the 14th century
produced the Reformer,
Wickliffe.
She died in great peace, Jany 29th, 1838.
Aged 75 years.
Precious in the sight of the Lord is the
death of his saints. Ps. cxvi. 15."

Being anxious to gain some particulars of Mrs.
Wade, I made inquiries in the neighbourhood, and
learned that Walter Sellon Gibson, Esq., her son
by her first husband, resided at York. I called
upon him, and was most courteously received, and
took down from his lips the following, among
other, recollections of his mother, whose memory
he venerated in no ordinary degree. They showed
that Mrs. Wade inherited in no small degree the
uncompromising fearlessness and decision of character for which her great ancestor was famed.
Mrs. Wade (née Catherine Wickliffe) was remarkable not only for uncommon powers of mind, but
for great beauty of person. Mr. Gibson showed me
two portraits of her, both taken after she was
seventy years of age—one by Noel Carter, an artist
of York, the other by some artist unknown. Both
are on ivory, and show that she must have been
not only very handsome, but that the expression
of her features was remarkably intellectual.
A specimen of her handwriting at sixty-one,

beauty and character. She had a great taste
for music, and could bring harmony out of almost
any instrument. At forty she began to learn
Latin, and attained some proficiency ; having also
made some progress in the Hebrew language.
She invariably read her Bible in Wickliffe's translation, and never used the Authorized Version.
She had some talent for painting, and indeed
appeared to have a genius for everything she
engaged in. Among her other accomplishments
was a remarkable skill in carpentering !

She was engaged to Richard Hey, the eldest son
of the celebrated surgeon, but he died within three
days of their intended marriage. Mr. Hey's house
was the head-quarters of John Wesley when at
Leeds, and by that means she became intimately
acquainted with him, as also with several of the
early Wesleyans. Samuel Bradburn thought very
highly of her. She was a member of the Metho-
dist Society from an early age, and continued in it
to her death. A short account of her appeared in
the *Wesleyan Magazine* in 1838.

Her first husband was Walter Sellon Gibson,
Esq., of Leeds, the father of my informant. He took
a black fever when visiting some poor in Leeds,
and died a few months after the birth of his son.
Mr. Gibson was the nephew of the Rev. Walter
Sellon, Vicar of Ledsham, near Castleford—a man
remarkable not only for his piety, but for his learning, being one of the first Greek scholars of his
time. He was the almoner of Lady Betty Hastings, and is frequently mentioned in the life of
the Countess of Huntingdon. As a proof of the
high esteem in which Mr. Sellon held Mrs. Wade,
he left his property to her personally, and not to
his nephew. Mr. Sellon died before the birth of
Mr. Gibson's son, who was to have been baptized
by the names of John de Wycliffe, but in consequence of Mr. Sellon's death he was called after
him.

After fourteen years of widowhood Mrs. Gibson
married Edward Wade, Esq., of Stourton Grange.
He died after they had been married about fourteen
years. The latter part of her life she lived at
Halton.

Mrs. Wade had several brothers, but they all
died young, except Thomas, who was brought up
to the law. At his death he left Mrs. Wade
about 2,000*l.* per annum. He was the last male
heir, the only surviving children of his father
being three daughters, of whom Catherine, Mrs.
Wade, being the last to marry, was the one who
longest bore the venerated name of Wickliffe.

Mrs. Wade was greatly beloved in the village in
which she lived, not only for her extensive benevolence, but for her consistent piety. Her death
was sudden, though not unexpected by herself.
She breathed her last in her arm-chair.

Mr. Gibson furnished me with many interesting

many interesting documents—arms, seal:
singular relic I must mention, and then
long account, fearing I have sadly tre:
your valuable columns. This was a
ring, cut out of the metal, and given t₀
Thomas Wickliffe by the Duke of N₀
land, as being found in Palestine, a
another ring belonging to the Percy fa₁
ring is stamped, and not engraved, with
liffe arms and crest.

Two years ago I was in York, and ha₀
to have called on Mr. Gibson and to h
to my information about the Wickliffe f₁
to my great regret, I learned that he
dead some time. I find in "N. & Q.,'
484, there is an account of one Francis
That person was not named in my co
with Mr. Gibson, but had the latter liv
seen me again he might have thrown ₛ
upon the matter.   H. E. WIL
Anerley, S.E.

JUDGES IX. 53.—A controversy is g₀
the correspondence columns of the *Gua₁*
regard to the expression in Judges ix.
a certain woman cast a piece of a mill₅
Abimelech's head, and all to brake]
Upon this Mr. R. Druitt pointed out, wi
illustrations from Chaucer, what one w
thought was obvious enough, that the wo:
be printed "all to-brake." In the glos:
little edition of *Piers the Plowman*, pu
the Clarendon Press Series, Mr. Skeat s₁
  "*To- prefix ;* (1) apart ; answering to G₀
Old Frisian *to-, te,* Old High German *za,*
Gothic *dis-,* Latin *dis-,* with the force of
asunder ; examples, *to-broke, to-lugged,* to
exceedingly, a modification of the former ; ₀
bolle."

In Chaucer there also occur *to-burst,* ₁
beten, to-go, to-hewen, to-race, to-rent, t
and *to-sterte.* The Bishop of Bath a₁
however, says that the letter has n₀
conviction to his mind, and that "till ℕ
can produce passages in English of th₀
teenth or early seventeenth century in ⱳ
prefixed to verbs as it was in the Angl
he "must think his point very defecti·
bishop goes on in happy unconsciousness
very thing, for he cites the following :—
  "She fell in hand with him (he told me)
rated him."—*Sir T. More.*
  " With briers and bushes all to rent and scr

  "She to be quit with them will all to fini:
both the fox and the cubs."—Holland's *Plinie*
      "She plumes her fethers and lets grow h₀
      That in the various bustle of resort
      Were all to ruffled."

Who does not see that the words he:

rated, to-rent, to-ruffled? In the well-known nursery rime—

" This is the man all tattered (*i.e.* to-teared) and torn
That kissed the maiden all forlorn "

—nobody would think of reading " all-to teared " and " all-for lorn."   C.

CURIOSITIES OF HISTORY.—The following is copied from *The Perils of War : a Discourse delivered March* 31, 1878 :—

" In the last century Vandreuil brought from America to France a famous Indian chief who had been fighting for the French. He was presented to the king, and when he came into the royal presence the Sagamore lifted up his hand and said, 'This hand has slain 150 of your majesty's enemies in the territory of New England.' This so pleased the king that he knighted the chief on the spot, and ordered a pension of eight livres a day to be paid to him during life. On the Sagamore's return to New England he was so impressed by the popularity of his deeds of slaughter that he set about murdering everybody he met. After he had gone on adorning a state of peace with the arts of war which had gained him knighthood and fortune, his neighbours combined against him, and he was forced to flee the country."—P. 17.

The story is new to me, but I may have read it in another form. I could not have forgotten the strange variations, such as " knighting on the spot " by a king of France, and the New Englanders being obliged to combine against a man who " murdered everybody he met," instead of trying him for the first murder and hanging him in the ordinary way. Any reference which may enable me to get at realities will oblige.

           FITZHOPKINS.

Garrick Club.

SURNAMES NOW OBSOLETE.—The records of the ancient borough of Wallingford contain a large number of surnames of persons which have now wholly disappeared from our nomenclature. The following, which are given in the *Sixth Report of the Historical Manuscripts Commission,* are selected as being some of the most remarkable :—Threehalfpence, Scaldwater, Mainwrench, Brokenfoot, Timeofdaye, Peekepeni, Waps, Hurlebat, Petipas, Pesewips, Brusebaston, Putti, Pelekoc, Moppe, Tredewater, Cake, Goldeye, Skylli, Kykaw, Hentekake, Wrawe, Scikerwit, Wholeheart.

It will be observed that the name " Pelekoc " was known to Shakspeare, as evidenced by the passage in *King Lear,* iii. 4 :—

" Pillicock sat on pillicock's hill."

The female names occurring in these records are of a no less singular character, and all in total disuse at the present time. Many of them, it will be seen, are of Roman and some of Greek origin :—Estrilda, Scolastica, Eliwiz, Claria, Asselina, Claricia, Hawis, Bona, Yngeleis, Gunnild, Dionisia, Sabelina, Alota, Edelota, Evelota, Orenge, Sueta, Basille, Limota, Elmita, Agasa, Juiveta, Pimma, Ydelota, Deonira, Wymarca, Piancia, Ysoda,

Helietta, Adula, Marcilia, Gunelina, Cinelote, Magota, Tomason, Ybbe.

           HUGH A. KENNEDY.

PRICE OF FOOD IN 1801.—The following is copied from writing on the fly-leaf of an old family Bible :—

" 1801· February, butter sold at Shaftesbury and Wincanton, 1s. 4½d. per lb. March, meat sold—viz., beef and mutton at 9d. per lb., veal at 8d., fat pigs 15 and some at 16 shillings per score. Wheat at Shaftesbury 5 guineas per sack, other places the same ; flour at Pin Mill and Long Lane Mill 7 guineas per bag ; barley flour 3lb. for a shilling ; fine garkins 5lb. for a shilling for people to eat. Potatoes 12 and 14 shillings per sack ; Castle Cary, 1l. 1s., and at many other places. Cheese 14d. per lb. Malt 54 shillings per sack. Beer 9d. [per gall.]."

           JOSIAH MILLER, M.A.

PROVERBS WHICH HAVE CHANGED THEIR MEANING.—Archbishop Trench gives examples of words which have, through lapse of time and usage, lost their primitive meaning, and adopted a secondary one, very different from the first. There are some proverbs which have gone through a similar process with a like effect.

" The schoolmaster is abroad." Forty years ago this proverb meant that ignorance prevailed, because the schoolmaster had shut up shop and gone abroad. To-day it is generally used to signify that knowledge is universal, because the schoolmaster is to be found everywhere.

" To put a spoke in his wheel." This now means putting a block between the spoke and the carriage so that the wheel cannot turn, thus impeding motion. It had not always this meaning. It once meant that the more spokes a wheel had the stronger it was ; thus :—

" If, when th' oud Mester wur alive himsel,
The Justices, for fear he shid rebell,
Had used him as yo done other foke,
Yoar wheels had wanted monny a pratty spoke."

A dialogue about compelling a person to take the oaths to the government (Byrom's *Poems*).

The mistake in the common use of the proverb, " Exception proves the rule," has already been pointed out in " N. & Q."

           E. LEATON BLENKINSOPP.

BEDFORDSHIRE PROVERBS.—Amongst the personal or nominal proverbs of this county there are two which relate to Crawley :—1. As crooked as Crawley ; 2. 'Crawley ! God help us. The first is most probably derived from the brook of that name, which runs a distance of eighty miles in a space of eighteen ; and the second may refer to the same, or it may possibly be derived from Judge Crawley, 1632-1645. May I venture to express a hope that the Folk-Lore Society, from which so much may be expected, will not disdain to collect, collate, and explain these local sayings ?

           EDWARD SOLLY.

1814 the *History of the University of Oxford* was issued in quarto form by the enterprising publisher Rudolph Ackermann,* of the Strand. It is a book that will always prove interesting to old Oxonians, and forms one of a series of works of a similar kind hitherto unparalleled, as *The Microcosm*, *Westminster Abbey*, *History of the University of Cambridge*, *History of the Public Schools*. There are contained in the two volumes eighty-four engravings of different public buildings in Oxford, thirty-two of the founders, and seventeen of the costumes of the members of the university.

Having frequently heard that the portraits of the wearers of the academicals were those of resident members at the time, it would be useful to ascertain if their names have been preserved, and, as many old Oxonians collect "Oxoniana," it occurs to me that the information may be supplied from these sources. A former rector of mine, a contemporary of Thomas Arnold and John Keble, and who is still flourishing in a green old age (*diu vivat*), once told me that the portrait of the Scholar was intended for him when an undergraduate of C. C. C., and gave me the names of some others, but unfortunately they have been forgotten. The portraits are cleverly executed, and the academical dress is much the same as that worn at the present time, though the fashionable attire of stiff cravats, knee-breeches, silk stockings, shoes, watch-ribbons with seals appended, &c., belonging to the period of the Regency, has long since departed. How very few survivors are there of the Oxford of that day, sixty-four years ago ! The senior member of the university at the present moment seems to be, from the Calendar, the Rev. Arthur Gibson, M.A. of Queen's College, who graduated as B.A. in 1804, ten years prior to the publication of the book referred to, and who is still Rector of Chedworth in Gloucestershire. The date assigned by the same authority to the graduation of the present respected Warden of Merton College, Dr. Bullock Marsham, is 1807.

JOHN PICKFORD, M.A.
Newbourne Rectory, Woodbridge.

TOBACCO SMOKING IN FRANCE.—The late Dr. Munaret makes the following remark as to the date of the introduction of tobacco smoking into France :

" L'introduction du tabac en France, date-t-elle seulement du règne de François Ier? J'ai la preuve d'une ancienneté bien plus reculée ; c'est une pipe en fer, rongée par la rouille, dont je vous transmets le croquis, qui a été déterrée par la soc d'une charrue, sur le champ de la célèbre bataille dite des *Tard-Venus*, arrivée à Brignais, en 1362, d'après les *Chroniques* de Froissart."— *Bulletin de la Société contre l'Abus du Tabac*, 1877, p. 25.

This ancient pipe would in all probability, like

* See an interesting account of Rudolph Ackermann and of his many and varied publications in " N. & Q.," 4th S. iv. 109, 129.

Further details respecting the find would be accep able.   WILLIAM E. A. AXON.
Bank Cottage, Barton-on-Irwell.

ANTWERPIAN SPANISH INQUISITION TORTU DUNGEONS.—A young friend has told me th he had lately seen at Allmannshooven,† sixte English miles from Antwerp and five from L (station on direct Antwerp-Louvain Railway), the ruined palace of those times (probably Duke Alva's period), with the rack, pictures (to be h for asking), secret panels, &c., as I saw at Ratisbo on the Bavarian Danube. Since humanity is mc concerned with these realities than with minu criticisms on picture galleries, I recommend tl to public notice and insertion in the guide-book further antiquarian information being doubtl very desirable to the English tourist's personal i spection of the barbarous tortures of those tim which quite sickened me when seeing them Ratisbon, Nuremberg, Venice, Münster, &c.
S. M. DRACH.

FRENCH HERALDRY.—It is proposed by t present directors of the French Protestant Hospit to decorate the Court-room with the armori bearings of the past governors, deputy governo: and some of the more distinguished early directo: Will any of your correspondents versed in Fren heraldry supply information as to the arms bor by any of the following persons ?—Philip Hervart, Baron d'Huningue, elected govern 1720 ; Jean Robethon, Conseiller Privé, do. 172 Guy de Viçouse, Baron de la Court, do. 172: Moise Pujolas, do. 1728 ; Paul Buissiere, d 1729 ; Pierre Cabibel, deputy governor 172 governor 1739 ; Jaques Gaultier, elected govern 1745 ; Jean Buissiere, do. 1776 ; Jean de Blagn do. 1781 ; Jaques Baudoin, elected deputy gove nor 1718 ; Henri Guinand, do. 1739 ; Pier Gaussen, do. 1756 ; Claude Desmarets, do. 175! André Girardot-Buissieres, do. 1763 ; Jac Albert, do. 1779 ; Francois Duroure, do. 178! René Briand, do. 1797. Philippe Hervart, Bar d'Huningue, gave 4,000*l.* towards the foundati of the hospital. Pierre Cabibel was probably r lated to the wife of Jean Calas. All the perso mentioned must after the dates given have liv in or near London, as their attendance at tl hospital, or "La Providence," then situated Bath Street, St. Luke's, was very frequent. B

† Jardin de tous les hommes.

sides their armorial bearings, I shall be glad of any other authentic information relating to any of them.   ARTHUR GIRAUD BROWNING,
Hon. Sec. French Protestant Hospital.
3, Victoria Street, Westminster Abbey, S.W.

ACRE.—Had the word *acre* (or rather *half-acre*) ever the sense of a plot of ground without any hint of dimensions? Piers the Plowman (Pass. vi.) says :—

"I haue an half acre to erye by þe heighe way;
Had I eried þis halfacre and sowen it after,
I wolde wende with ȝow and þe way teche."

Then he sets the whole company, which is described (Pass. v. 517) as "a thousand of men," to work at ploughing this *half-acre*, which is represented as taking many days—in fact till harvest. Further on he says :—

"And þanne seten somme and songen atte nale
And hulpen erie his halfacre with 'How! trolli-lolli!'"

Hence I infer that *half-acre* could only mean a field without regard to size. But why *half* acre?
                                           A. R. C.

PORTRAITS AFTER VANDYCK, &c.—I lately picked up a thin undated quarto consisting of plates only, without any letter-press, entitled "*Sketches after Antᵒ Van-Dyck*." Dedicated by permission to Henry Raeburn, Esq., R.A., by his obliged servant, Edward Mitchell, Engraver, Edinburgh." It contains twenty portraits, with their names attached, but nineteen only are by Vandyck, as the last portrait is a bust of Canova "se stesso scolpi in Roma l' anno 1812."
I have been able, after some little research, to identify them all, with the exception of the following, and shall be glad if some one of your learned correspondents can inform me who these were, with date of birth, where born, and time of death :—1. Hubertus Vanden Eynden ; 2. Adam De Coster; 3. Theodorus Vanlonius. As regards the last mentioned, there was a Belgian painter so called, said to have been born in 1629 ; but it cannot be his portrait, Vandyck having died in 1641, unless his birth be wrongly dated ; or was there an earlier painter of the same name?
I shall also be glad of any information respecting the two following engraved portraits :—1. A full-length figure, apparently, from the costume, of the latter part of the seventeenth century, under which is inscribed :—

"This is no Muckle John, nor Summers Will,
But here is Mirth drawn by yᵉ Muses quill;
Doubt not (kinde Reader) be but pleasᵈ to view
These witty Jests ; they are not ould but new."

It probably formed the frontispiece to a book of jests.
2. In a small oval the bust of a man in profile, with falling band, a pen behind his ear, and his right hand raised across his breast, with one out-stretched finger pointing beyond his shoulder. Over his head in two lines across the field :—

"Toe but a Windy-bancke, and
Thou art out of thier reach."

I am disposed to think this has reference to the persecution of the Scotch Covenanters.
                                           JOHN J. A. BOASE.
7, Albion Terrace, Exmouth.

PRIVATE PROPERTY IN LAND UNKNOWN IN ENGLAND.—I venture to appeal again to. MR. PICTON, or any other reader of "N. & Q." who may be conversant with the subject, for information on the following points :—1. Is there any historic authority for MR. PICTON'S belief, expressed in "N. & Q.," 5ᵗʰ S. viii. 109, that among the "Anglo-Saxons," or other Teutonic or Scandinavian settlers in Britain, the customs of their original country, as described by Tacitus and Cæsar, prevailed after their immigration, and that private property in land was unknown? Mr. Wingrove Cooke, whose opinion on the subject is certainly entitled to consideration, writes as follows in his *Treatise on the Law of the Rights of Common* :—"In our own country we have neither record nor tradition anterior to the existence of a property in land. Without entering upon the question of the origin of feuds and of manors, we may sufficiently understand that, since the time when the history of this island begins, a title has never been wanting in some person to every rood of land in Britain."
2. Can MR. PICTON'S allegation in the same paper, that the "folc-land" was, in England, divided every year into convenient portions, according to the wants of the families, be supported by evidence? If so, I am further curious to learn MR. PICTON'S authority for his description of the mode of division adopted, namely, the "running of furrows to a certain distance," and for his statement that forty times the width of the ridge was the length of the furrow.
                                           T. SMITH WOOLLEY.
South Collingham, Newark.

EDITH, WIFE OF THOMAS FOWLER, ESQ., AND "GENTILLWOMAN" TO MARGARET, MOTHER OF HENRY VII.—Of what family was she? The arms on her brass in Christ's College Chapel are, quarterly, 1 and 4, four fusils conjoined in fess ; 2 and 3, three arches (?), two and one.   W. F. C.

BARTLETT=GREEN.—Who were the ancestors of Benjamin Bartlett, of Bradford, Yorkshire, who married a Miss Green? Their son Benjamin married Martha Heathcote, a niece of Sir John Rodes. Their only son Newton died s.p. about the end of the last century. One of these B. Bartletts was a surgeon, to whom the celebrated Dr. Fothergill was a pupil.   R. H. J. GURNEY.
Northrepps Hall, Norwich.

works which treat of the French, German, and other popular names of plants as Dr. R. C. A. Prior has treated those of England? I know of H. C. L. von Jenssen-Tusch, *Plantenavne i forskellige Europæiske Sprog.*   W. G. PIPER.

ALEXANDER TAIT.—I want to find the name of the wife of Alexander Tait, of Edinburgh, who lived at the end of the seventeenth century. Her daughter Catherine married William Blair of Blair. Alexander Tait was probably a merchant.   HASTINGS C. DENT.

HOTEL.—When did this word come into use in England as signifying an inn? Latham has it in his *Dictionary*, but no example. In *St. Ronan's Well*, ch. i., note, Scott writes:—"This Gallic word (hôtel) was first introduced in Scotland during the author's childhood, and was so pronounced [*i.e.* hottle] by the lower class."
     T. LEWIS O. DAVIES.
Pear Tree Vicarage, Southampton.

"BRISTOL AND WEST OF ENGLAND ARCHÆOLOGICAL MAGAZINE."—How many numbers of this quarterly periodical were issued? It was "in connexion with the Bristol and West of England Architectural and Heraldic Society," and No. i. is dated May 1, 1843. I have Nos. i.-iii.
     ABHBA.

"IT IS AN ILL WIND," &c.—Thomas Fuller is said to be the father of this well-known saying (see Chambers's *Book of Days*, vol. i. p. 367). Can any of your readers supply an earlier author?
     W. H. C.

JAMES, FOURTEENTH EARL OF GLENCAIRN, the patron of Burns, died at Falmouth on the 30th of January, 1791, and was buried in the chancel of the church there. Is there any memorial to his memory in the church? and if so, will some of your readers kindly copy the inscription? The earl was returning from Lisbon, where he had been for the benefit of his health, and only landed a few days previous to his death.
     JAMES GIBSON.
Liverpool.

THE POET BERONICIUS.—Who was he, what was his nationality, where was he born, what did he write, and what information can be found about him? are all questions I should like your (almost) all-wise readers to answer me if possible.
     DACCARP AIKONE.

THE ARMS OF NOTTINGHAM AND COLCHESTER. —Can any of your readers explain to me the reason why the arms of Nottingham are the same as those of Colchester save only in respect of tinctures? Had the two towns ever any connexion? And how are the arms of Southwark blazoned?   TIRO.

Cout of Keeldar, the following verse occurs:
   "The iron clash, the grinding sound,
     Announce the dire sword-mill;
   The piteous howlings of the hound
     The dreadful dungeon fill."
The author says in a note that "he is una produce any authority that the execrable ma the sword-mill, so well known on the Cont was ever employed in Scotland; but he be the vestiges of something very similar have discovered in the ruins of old castles."
What was this machine, and where can I description of it? I do not remember any al to it in Sir Walter Scott's writings. As, a ing to Leyden, it appears to have been an i ment of torture or execution employed by t and oppressors on the Continent, one naturally expect to find some mention of *Quentin Durward* or *Anne of Geierstein.*
     JONATHAN BOUCH

ROBERT SMALL, MUS. DOC.—I possess a portrait by "Geo. Dance, May 6, 1801," mother's uncle, Dr. Robert Small. Who wa Dance? Is anything known of Dr. Small tradition he was organist in some London c and teacher in the royal family. It is sai he lent the Prince Regent 3,000*l.*, the savi a lifetime, and that the non-payment o money broke his heart. In the portrait he a to be about fifty years of age.
     WM. J. BAI
35, Molesworth Street, Dublin.

TWO IRISH FAMILIES.—I should be oblig any information concerning the families of I and Dolphin. The former were seated—ar name is there yet—about Kilkee (Clare). Dolphins had lands along the south-eastern of Loughrea (Galway); and tradition make: to have been the owners of the old castle town of that name. The Four Masters reco slaying of John Dolifin in the year 1270. families are, as would seem, of English origi
     D
Hammersmith.

WASHINGTON IRVING.—In the *Echo* of N last was "A Little Sermon," attribut Washington Irving, and commencing, "The for the dead is the only sorrow from whi refuse to be divorced." Not being able to . in those of his works which are accessible to should esteem it a very great favour if you help me.   CHISLEHU

CLERICAL TITLES.—When did the ti "Venerable" for an archdeacon and "Very rend" for a dean come into use? In a list c scribers to Borlase's *Natural History of Cor* 1758, I find the following names :—"*R*

D'Oiley, Archdeacon of Chichester"; "*Rev.* Mr. Hole, Archdeacon of Barum"; "*Rev.* Charles Lyttelton, LL.D., Dean of Exeter"; "*Rev.* Mr. Sleech, M.A., Archdeacon of Cornwall." In the *Gentleman's Magazine* I find the following work noticed :—"*A Charge delivered in August,* 1823, &c. By the *Ven.* and *Rev.* Francis Wrangham, M.A."

H. BOWER.

BIBLICAL ERRORS.—Prof. Robertson Smith, in his *Answer to the Form of Libel now before the Free Church Presbytery of Aberdeen*, says, at p. 43 (third edit.):—

"All the leading reformers are at one in admitting the existence of verbal errors in the Biblical text, and supposing that the authors did not always write with scrupulous exactness, or observe in their narratives the order of events. Some of these opinions are quite as startling as anything I have said, and the list might easily be added to."

Can any of your readers tell me where I can find a list of such errors and inaccuracies ?   B.

THE BROSELEY REGISTERS.—In searching the Broseley church registers the name of Huxley occurs—it also occurs in the burgess roll, 1662 ; that of Ffosbrooke, 1637, and that of Jevons, 1733. No families of that name have lived here for many years. Roger Ffosbrook de Madeley occurs in 1620. Can any of your readers inform me whether these are likely to have been ancestors of the men of the same name so well known in our time in literature and science ?

JOHN RANDALL.
Madeley, Salop.

THE LATE BISHOP OF LICHFIELD.—So far as I have observed no obituary notice of this lately deceased prelate has noted his ancestry. Was he a direct or collateral descendant of his namesake, the wit of the last century ?   W. C. J.

T. W. JONES, CHEMIST, 1767.—I am interested in knowing whether one Thomas William Jones, a chemist and druggist, resided in or near Petticoat Lane, Whitechapel, about the year 1767 ; and, if so, at what time the business was relinquished by him, and who succeeded him.   H.˙ C.

FEMALE FREEMASONS.—Marie Antoinette writes to her sister Marie Christine, Feb. 26, 1781 :—

"Ces jours derniers la princesse de Lamballe a été nommée *grande maîtresse* dans une *loge*, elle m'a raconté toutes les jolies choses qu'on lui a dites......il n'y a pas de mal à tout cela......tout le monde en est, on sait tout ce qui s'y passe, où donc est le danger ? "

She is saying that Freemasonry is thought little of in France, as it is so public. Have other women been made *grandes maîtresses* of any lodge ?
K. H. B.

DARTMOOR : SCOTLAND.—I have heard from various sources of some half-savage families that lived a short time ago, or live now, on Dartmoor, and I believe also in parts of Scotland. I should be much obliged if you could give me any information on the subject through the medium of "N. & Q."   Z. Y. X.

JEAN MONNET went to London in 1749 with a company of French actors, and gave some representations of French plays at the Haymarket Theatre. His enterprise gave rise to much discussion, to articles in the journals, pamphlets, &c., *pro* and *contra*. I should be thankful for any information concerning Jean Monnet and his undertaking which would aid me in a work I am at present writing upon the subject.

ARTHUR HEULHARD,
Rédacteur du "Moniteur du Bibliophile."
34, Rue Taitbout, Paris.

ROMANO-CHRISTIAN REMAINS IN BRITAIN.—I am anxious to ascertain whether any Christian inscriptions or symbols have been found on the Roman remains discovered in this island, and should feel greatly obliged for any trustworthy information on the point.   T. S. H.
Vicar's Close, Wells.

"THE MIGHT AND MIRTH OF LITERATURE."— I want some information about the author and the literary merits of this work. Is it a trustworthy authority on figures of speech ?   W. S. R.

AUTHORS OF BOOKS WANTED.—
The Unfortunate Author : an Elegy. By Motte Facetum, Esq. Oxford, Talboys, 1840.
Essays, Religious, Moral, Dramatic, and Poetical, addressed to Youth, and Published for a Benevolent Purpose. By a Lady. Charleston, S.C., 1818.—The only copy I have seen or heard of. Internal evidence seems to point at the name of Pinckney as the authoress. Not in Allibone or any other authority.
Poems, principally founded upon the Poems of Meleager. Cadell, 1817.
The Exhibition : a Poem. By a Painter. Lond., 1819.
Poetical Compliments to Painters of Eminence in Scotland. Edin., 1797.
Mischief of the Muses. Bogue, 1847.
Ex Oriente : Sonnets on the Indian Rebellion. 12mo. Chapman, 1858.   J. O.

AUTHORS OF QUOTATIONS WANTED.—
" O consistency, thou art a jewel."
EDWARD P. TENNEY.

Replies.

ST. GEORGE.

(5th S. viii. 447 ; ix. 189, 209.)

The festival of St. George was ordered to be observed by Archbishop Chichele, by general desire of the clergy, as a Major Double, like Christmas Day, in the reign of Henry V., 1415, on the ground that he was "martyr gloriosissimus B. Georgius, tanquam patronus et protector nationis specialis : cujus (ut indubitanter credimus) gentis Angligenæ armata militia contra incursus hostiles bellorum tempore regitur" (Lynd., App., 68, 69). I find no notice of St. George in the Council of 1222. The church of St. George, Botolph Lane, London, was in existence before 1321 ; St. George's, Colegate, Norwich, before 1349; St. George's, Seaton, about the same date. The priory church of Dunster is dedicated to St. George, and, like St. George's, Thetford, Oxford, and Southwark, dates from the reign of William I. Gresley Priory was founded in the time of Henry I. The dedication is most frequent in the diocese of Norfolk ; but there were few altars of St. George in English cathedrals : these occurred at Hereford, Chichester, Lichfield, St. Paul's, and York. There was a St. George's guild at Wolverhampton.

There are figures of St. George on brasses at Elsing, Norfolk, 1347, and Cobham, Kent, 1407. On the famous chest of the latter part of the reign of Henry V. in York Minster St. George appears with a cross upon his shield.

Edward I. had banners with the arms of St. George, St. Edmund, and Edward the Confessor. At the siege of Calais Edward III. raised the war cry, "Ha, St. Edward ! Ha, St. George!" and, in Spenser's words, he became his " owne nation's frend and patrone; St. George of mery England, the sign of victoree."

It must be borne in mind, however, that the old English war cry, in recollection of the Rood of Waltham, was " Holy Cross," and the " Red Cross Knight " was a familiar term.

MACKENZIE E. C. WALCOTT.

H. W. is mistaken in supposing that "the red cross was first displayed on the English flag when the first Union Jack was formed, and a national ensign invented, under James I., in 1606." England was certainly not without a national ensign up to the year 1606. The very name "Union Jack" tells us how the new flag of 1606 was formed, i.e. by the union of the two previous national ensigns of England and Scotland. The cross of St. George and that of St. Andrew were then placed together on the same flag. Before 1606, the " jack flag " of the English navy was a plain white flag bearing a red St. George's cross. Representations of it may be seen in many old engravings of ships, the fight with the Spanish Armada, &c.

From 1606 to the union with Ireland in 1801 this same Union Jack remained the national ensign, with the exception of the period of the Commonwealth, when, in 1649, the authorities replaced the Union Jack by the old St. George's Ensign or Jack, which was itself supplanted by a new Union Jack (of a different design) ordered by the Protector Oliver in 1658. See an article of mine on " The National Flags of the Commonwealth, 1649

—1660," printed in vol. xxxi. (1875) of the *Journal of the British Archæological Association.* I have to apologize for taking up your space with ; subject perhaps not very closely connected with the original query about St. George, but I hop you will allow me thus to enter my protest against H. W.'s ignoring the St. George's Jack—the fla; under which Howard, Drake, Hawkins, Frobisher Grenville, Blake, Penn, Monk, and other admiral; gained their glorious naval victories, and rendered the English the acknowledged masters of the sea.

HENRY W. HENFREY.

"THE PASTON LETTERS" (5ᵗʰ S. ix. 205, 326.)— I am under obligations to two of your recent corre spondents for pointing out errors in my edition o the *Paston Letters.* All corrections are to me mos! valuable, and particularly any correction simila: to that furnished by S. H. A. H., where informa tion derived from a monument in a church, or some other local source, leads to the true identification of a person and the correct dating of a letter. In a work attended with so great difficulty and labour. it is impossible but that there must be many such slips, unknown to me, as those above referred to, and I shall be very glad if future contributors to your columns will help to point them out. 1 should be much disposed, if a sufficient number were discovered, to publish, at some future date. a sheet of corrections to be inserted in the work.

Let me add that I should be the more willing to follow this course if the gentleman who owns the originals of the letters printed in Fenn's third and fourth volumes could be induced in some manner to make these and the other Paston documents in his possession more available for the purposes of historical research. These documents, invaluable in themselves, are simply of no value whatever so long as they remain shut up in a country house in Norfolk, and if Mr. Frere is not disposed to sell them to the British Museum, it is greatly to be wished that he would place them in such custody as would really enable literary men to study them at leisure. If they were thus accessible it might be worth while to collate minutely every one of the newly recovered originals reprinted from Fenn, and to print all the omitted passages, together with the letters as yet unedited, as a supplement to the last edition. JAMES GAIRDNER.

THE ORDER OF THE LION AND SUN (5ᵗʰ S. ix. 188, 255.)—Since the publication of the works of Burke, Carlisle, and Schulze, the Persian order of the Lion and Sun has undergone a complete reorganization at the instance of Ferukh Khan, ambassador at Paris. It was remodelled on the lines of the Légion d'Honneur, and, like it, consists of five classes. The form of the decoration resembles that of the Turkish Medjidié. The ribbon is of green silk. By the first class the decoration (consisting of six groups of silver or brilliant rays, separated by as many rays of green enamel, and having in enamel, on the circular centre, a lion couchant on a mound proper in front of the rising sun) is worn *en écharpe* from the right shoulder to the left side. The decoration is attached to the ribbon by a sun surrounded by rays. A star similar to the badge, but of course without the link group, is worn on the left breast. The second class (Grand Officers) wear the badge at the neck, and a smaller star on the right breast. The third class (Commanders) also wear the badge *en sautoir*, but have no star. The fourth class (Officers) wear the badge, of a smaller size, on the breast ; while the fifth (or Chevaliers) have the same without the sun in splendour, or group of solar rays, which surmounts the badge of the preceding class. Besides these there are certain minute differences in the badges which, without drawings, could only be rendered intelligible by a long description. Probably the above will suffice for ordinary inquirers. Mr. Cleghorn will see that there is not " much uncertainty about it."

JOHN WOODWARD.
Montrose, N.B.

This order was conferred upon Sir Robert Ker Porter, the celebrated artist and traveller, by the Shah on the occasion of his painting his Majesty's portrait.   E. H. A.

CODEX DIPLOMATICUS, No. DXXXIV., EADGAR, A.D. 967 (5th S. ix. 300.)—I do not think it would be impossible to identify the two localities quoted from this charter. But they are not, as Mr. Coote appears to have thought them, in Cornwall, but in the southern limb of Glamorgan. It is true that a name Lismanoch or Lesmanaek does occur in Cornwall, among the endowments of Mount St. Michael (Oliver, *Mon. Exon.*, Nos. iii. and vii.), but this is not the one conveyed by King Edgar's charter. In this the landmark names of Lesmanaoc most likely include the district of Nash Point, St. Donat's, and Marcross. Of the boundary names, the only ones that I will presume to have realized are " Lembroin " and " Alan " river. There can be no doubt that Lembroin is the place of which the church town is now known as Llanvrynach, with the still surviving dedication of St. Brynach, called the Irishman, though the place is perhaps better known as Penlline, the name of the castle and principal village in the parish. That the Lembroin of the charter is identical with this Llanvrynach we are helped to believe by the intermediate evidence of Leland, who, minutely describing this coast, calls it " Llesbroinuith." This Anglo-Saxon corruption of St. Brynach may be compared with those at another of his dedications, " Braun " and " Barum," at Braunton, on the opposite coast of Devon. Leland also says that " this Alein " river riseth at " Llesbroinuith, about a 4 miles above

the Place wher it cumnith by itself into Severn," and that its mouth is three miles beyond St. Donat's, which would be near Dunraven Castle.

Perhaps the property conveyed by the charter may be the same as in what appears to be a Welsh charter, " De Lann mocha," printed in *Monasticon Angl.* (Llandaff, No. vii.). One of the landmarks in this is " Castel merych," and one of those in King Edgar's is " Cestell-merit." The Welsh *Llan-* and Cornish *Lan-* appear to be liable to English corruptions such as *Lem-* and *Les-*.

As to " Pennarth," the smaller property granted by King Edgar, it is evidently the small eastern promontory of the same southern cape of Glamorgan, now well known by the same name. The simplicity of the landmark—" from the sea along the dike to the rill, then along the rill to the sea " —could only apply to such a small peninsula.

That this is the true placement of the charter will appear more likely when it is found that King Edgar was at this very time actively and personally concerned in the affairs of this very district of Glamorgan, as may be seen by the entries under A.D. 952 and A.D. 967 in the Gwentian Chronicle. Besides, the witnesses to the charter are nearly the same as those to Archbishop Dunstan's consecration of the Bishop of Llandaff (*Liber Lland.*, p. 509), and it is most probably one of the acts of the same council, and thus it would also fix the date of that consecration, which otherwise seems to be hitherto uncertain. In these South Wales expeditions, perhaps to and from Bath, King Edgar used the port of Bristol (Caer Odornant) for the left side of the channel, and Caerleon upon Usk for the right side.

Mr. Coote appears to be justified in citing the charter for the word " hide "; for although the text of it grants Lesmanaoc as " iii. mansas," in the vernacular landmarks it is described as " iii-hida."   THOMAS KERSLAKE.
Bristol.

SIR SAMUEL FERGUSON (5th S. i. 288, 335.)— Under the latter of the above references, I was able to inform a correspondent that the author of the vigorous poem, *The Forging of the Anchor*, was Mr. Samuel Ferguson, Q.C., M.R.I.A. I did not, however, answer that other portion of your correspondent's inquiry, " Did he ever write anything else ? " As Sir Samuel Ferguson has just had the honour of knighthood conferred upon him, for literary as well as official reasons (he is the Deputy Keeper of the Records, Dublin), it may be here as well to state, on the authority of the *Athenæum*, March 23, that

" Sir Samuel Ferguson's spirited *Forging of the Anchor* is well known. He is the author also of *Congal, Lays of the Western Gael*, and various stories and essays, including the very humorous ' Father Tom and the Pope,' which originally came out in *Blackwood* many years ago. In the same periodical appeared, a few months ago, a poem signed by him called ' The Widow's Cloak,' a symbolical expression denoting the Queen's sovereignty over India. Sir S. Ferguson is also a distinguished worker in the field of Irish archæology."

To this I may add that " Father Tom and the Pope; or, a Night at the Vatican," originally appeared in *Blackwood*, May, 1838, and was reprinted in *Tales from Blackwood*, No. 7. It was supposed to be written by "Mr. Michael Heffernan, Master of the National School at Tallmactaggart, in the County of Leitrim." The author of the *Handbook of Fictitious Names* might make a note of this. CUTHBERT BEDE.

THE PREVIOUS QUESTION (3ʳᵈ S. i. 345 ; 5ᵗʰ S. ix. 315.)—MR. SOLLY's explanation of the previous question is itself erroneous, as all may see who will refer to Sir T. Erskine May's *Law and Practice of Parliament*, or to Mr. Palgrave's *Chairman's Handbook*. T. P. Q.

INVITATIONS WRITTEN ON PLAYING CARDS (5ᵗʰ S. ix. 168, 214, 239, 276.)—My great-great-uncle, a great traveller and *savant* during the concluding twenty years of last century, preserved a quantity of cards of callers on him. They form probably the most extensive and curious collection in existence, and are now lying before me. Among them are an invitation to a ball from the Ambassador and Ambassadress of Spain, written on the back of the nine of diamonds ; a printed invitation to a ball at Geneva, in 1784, on the king of diamonds; and the following calling cards :—The Chamberlain of the Elector of Bavaria, on half the three of diamonds, written over the pips ; Le Baron de Lille, on the queen of diamonds ; Mr. Stapleton (the future Lord Despencer), on half the six of clubs ; "Mrs. Morris of Philadelphia," the loyalist who was attainted of high treason, the quondam flame of Washington, printed within a border on half the four of clubs.

Calling cards in those days were either printed or written on card or paper indifferently. Those of Cardinal Rerius, Earl Cowper, Mr. Piozzi, Sir John Hawkins, &c., in the above collection, are on paper.

It was greatly the fashion to write the name on cards engraved with views of classic ruins, which were evidently bought in packs, as two cards of Lord Clive have entirely different pictures. Mr. Townley had a card engraved by Skelton, with his favourite busts of Isis, Pericles, and Homer, which he only left at particular houses, however. Sir Richard Worsley (the author of the *Museum Worsleyanum*) had a card engraved by the same artist, with a view of the Acropolis at Athens. Sir ˢ ⁿᵃ Reynolds's card was engraved by Barto-
Ibzzλ.

In the fourth plate of " Marriage à la Mode," engraved in 1745, may be seen some cards on the floor, viz. the five and six of diamonds, and four

other cards, evidently written on the bac playing cards, which read as follows :—

" Count Basset begs
to no how lade
Squander sleapt
last nite."

" Lady Squander's
Com. is desir'd at
Lady Heathans
Drum Major on
Next Sunday."

" Lady Squander's
Company is desir'd at
Miss Hairbrane's Rout."

" Ly. Squander's Com.
is desir'd at Lady
Townly's Drum
Munday next."
JOHN W. Fᴏ

A good illustration of the undoubtedly fre practice of writing notes on playing cards ι in the well-known legend to the effect th; Duke of Cumberland wrote cruel orders to ι his troops, after the fight at Culloden, on the of a nine of diamonds, which is said (?) to thenceforth been called " The Curse of Scotl;

[See 4ᵗʰ S. vi. 194, 289 (" The Nine of Diamoɴ Curse of Scotland "). At the latter reference GORT states that he has a letter on a matter of bɩ written by a right reverend prelate in 1767 on th of an ace of hearts.]

GREAT SEAL OF CORSICA (5ᵗʰ S. ix. 308.) arms described by MR. SOLLY as engraved the great seal of Theodore, King of Corsic the personal arms of that unfortunate ɩ impaling those of his realm. Theodore ᵥ member of the German family of Neuhc Neuenhof, which bore the arms, Sa., a chain posed of two links and a half in pale arg. (*v.* macher, *Wappenbuch*, ii. plate 117). As were the personal arms of Theodore, MR. Sc ingenious suggestion that they may have assumed to commemorate the breaking o Moorish dominion over Corsica, or the casti of the equally heavy yoke of Genoa, is obv untenable. The arms of Corsica are simp coat which Theodore impaled with his own— a Moor's head in profile, couped at the nec wreathed round the temples of the first. I ι know when these were first assumed. S says : " Quâ tesserâ hæc utatur insula no vidisse memini " (*Opus Heraldicum*, p. lib. i. xxxviii. 169). But the Moors' heads a also in the arms of the adjacent island of Sar which were, Arg., a cross gu. betw. four ɪ heads in profile ppr., wreathed of the first. are the arms of Genoa, differenced by the ɪ heads, which indicate the Saracenic occupat the island. Spener says that this coaʀ assumed by the kings of Arragon in mem a victory gained over the Saracens by Pedro of Arragon at Sarragossa in 1096, by the miraculous aid of St. George, whose cross, together with the heads of four Moorish princes who fell in the battle, appears in the shield. I have, however, never seen the smallest evidence that this coat was used in Arragon, and we must, for more reasons than this, incline to the belief that we have here another of those old legends with regard to the origin of national arms which are utterly without foundation in fact. My own explanation given above appears in every way a more probable one. I have only to add that the arms of Corsica are borne as a " chief of augmentation " in the arms of the Earls of Minto, who descend from Sir Gilbert Elliot, fourth baronet, viceroy of the island during its tenure by Great Britain. He was created Baron Minto on his return from the island in 1797.

JOHN WOODWARD.

Montrose.

"MARQUIS" v. "MARQUESS" (5th S. ix. 167, 315.) —A mere reference to peerages will not give much evidence on this point, for out of nineteen which I am now using in compiling the "Index of British Titles" for the Index Society, nine give Marquess, nine Marquis, and one gives both. The same nearly may be said of dictionaries, which vary according as the word is assumed to be derived from the Latin, German, French, or Italian. I trust I shall not be accused of making a bull when I say that the first English title of this order was an Irish one, but the oldest English patent is that by which Robert de Vere was created Marquess of Dublin in 1385. In this he is styled Robertus de Vere Marchionis Dublinæ. Selden, in Titles of Honour (third edit., 1672, p. 628), observes that the designation of Marchiones, as applied to the Lords Marchers, had been long previously used, but was not employed as a distinct title before 1385. At this time Court documents were drawn up in Latin or French indifferently ; and John de Beaufort, the son of John of Gaunt, who was created Marquess of Dorset in 1397, but from whom the title was taken in 1400, petitioned the king in 1402 not to restore the marquessate to him—he "molt humblement pria au Roy, que come le noun de Marquis feust estrange noun en cest roialme, q'il ne luy vorroit ascunnement doner cet noun de Marquis" (Selden, p. 629). It does not seem certain, however, that the title was spelt Marquis in this petition, for in Courthope's edition of Sir H. Nicolas's Historic Peerage of England, 1857, lx, this same passage is quoted as from the Rolls of Parliament, and it is there given as Marquys. The Rev. Mr. Webb, in Archæologia, xx. p. 193, says that contemporary writers called Beaufort "the Marquess"; but he gives no authority for this mode of spelling.

There is of course no evidence how the title was

at that time pronounced ; but in all the earliest documents which I have examined, when the title is written in English, it is spelt Marques. It is thus in Willoughby's letter to the Lord Cromwell, 1539 (Ellis, Orig. Let., first series, ii. 105), and in that of the Lords of Council to Lord Shrewsbury, 1549 (Lodge, Illustrations, 1791, i. 133). In nearly all the best old writers of authority, such as Hollinshed, 1586 ; Speed, 1605 ; Vincent, 1622 ; Walkley, 1642 ; Ashmole, 1672 ; Selden, 1672 ; and Dugdale, 1682, it is spelt Marquess. On comparing the three versions of Camden's History of Elizabeth, in the Latin it is Marchionem, in the French Marquis, and in the English (ed. 1675) it is Marquess. I am therefore led to conclude that precedents are in favour of Marquess.

EDWARD SOLLY.

PUBLIC-HOUSE SIGNS (5th S. ix. 127, 174, 257, 293.)—Some doubts have occurred to my mind while reading CLARRY's interesting and valuable communication. I would invite his consideration of such signs as " The Bull and Mouth," " The Bull and Bush," " The Bull and Gate," and " The Bull and Last." These incongruous combinations, not to be accounted for by any principle of heraldry with which I am acquainted, I have always referred to Henry VIII.'s expedition to France. Doesn't Butler in Hudibras make his knight wear

" Breeches of woollen
That had been at the siege of Boullen " (Boulogne) ?

I take it that Boulogne was considered by the English the gate or mouth (Fr. bouche) of France. Thus the first three signs mean the same thing, " The Boulogne Mouth," " La Boulogne Bouche," and " The Boulogne Gate." The derivation of the fourth seems less apparent, but we have only to remember that there is a village near Paris which gives name to the celebrated wood in that vicinity, and which is legally known as Boulogne l'Est, in contradistinction to Boulogne-sur-Mer, which, of course, is l'Ouest, to detect the derivation at once. Some innkeeper with a superficial knowledge of European topography I conceive to have started the title, in contradistinction to the numerous Bulls or Boulognes of his competitors ; or, even discarding our hypothesis, which may perhaps be considered somewhat fanciful, Boulogne l'Ouest itself might serve as the basis of the corruption. Anyhow, I should like CLARRY to explain whether he holds that this sign (actually that of a public-house at Kentish Town) has anything to do with that article to which we are proverbially told it is the cordwainer's duty to adhere.   S. P.

HOMER'S " NEPENTHES " (5th S. viii. 264, 316; ix. 57.)—Any one who will compare the description of the effects of the use of the Egyptian drug, as detailed in the fourth book of the Odyssey—taking the plain meaning of the words, without the

...medium of a poetical translation—with those produced by the use of the Indian hemp, or *bhang*, so well known to all acquainted with daily life in India, Persia, and Scinde, must, I think, be struck with the great similarity between them. The use of the drug is universal in the countries named. It is either smoked or used as a beverage; in the latter case the leaves of the hemp are prepared by washing in three waters, then they are pounded and mixed in any drink, oftenest in a bowl of milk. This mixture is said to be sweet, rather sickly, and to taste as of pepper, but not unpleasantly. I question if a quantity of opium sufficient to produce the results described by Homer would form, when mixed with wine, a very palatable drink. As to the effects of *bhang*, it is said to intensify to a wonderful degree the feelings of the drinker, according to what may be his peculiar temperament or momentary excitement, besides being, like Helen's drug, "grief-assuaging and relieving from sorrow." For these reasons, amongst others, its use is very common among Indian soldiers of the swashbuckler class in the Native states.* Few of our Indian campaigns have been without instances of most determined, sometimes almost irresistible charges made on our troops by native horsemen. These were executed by men maddened and infuriated with *bhang*, who are for the moment literally "forgetful of all perils" possible from British bayonets. To men in this state it must be a small matter though their "fathers and mothers should die," or anything conceivable happen "before their eyes" from "the brazen sword" to their "brothers or sons," or, what is more to the purpose, to themselves.

At the risk of some little injury to Indian romance, it may be said that it is believed that in many cases the wonderful self-devotion of the *sattee* was in great measure attributable to this "well-adapted drug" causing "forgetfulness" (or unconsciousness) "of peril," till the wretched child, as it might be, was choked by the smoke of the funeral pyre. Perhaps it may bear a little against the argument of *bhang* being *nepenthes* that the effects of the former on a beginner are said to be anything but pleasant.† *Hashish* is the Arabic name of *bhang* in the prepared state.

ALEX. FERGUSSON, Lieut.-Col.
Edinburgh.

DE QUINCEY : ALDORISIUS (5th S. viii. 369.)— On the principle that "half a loaf is better than no bread," I beg to offer to my friend MR. NORVAL CLYNE's still unanswered question the following

---

* "...the Nuwab Subzee Khan....It is a pity he is so addicted to *subzee* or *bhang*, from which, however, he has gained a name which it is well known has struck terror into his enemies on the battle-field."—*Confess. of a Thug*, by Col. Meadows Taylor, ii. 136.

† On this point see *Scinde ; or, the Unhappy Valley*, by Capt. R. F. Burton, i. 259-262.

---

crumbs of a reply. Aldorisius was a philosopher of Geneva who flourished in the sixteenth century. This is all I know about him ; but I would ask any of your readers who have access to Leu's *Dictionnaire de la Suisse* (a great authority with Gibbon) to kindly jot down any particulars therein contained, if our mysterious friend is there noticed at all.   J. MYERS DANSON.

ST. MARK'S DAY A FAST (5th S. ix. 266.)—The fast is attached to April 25, and it is accidental that it comes on the same day as the feast of St. Mark. On this day, as well as on the Rogation Days, which are the three days which precede the feast of the Ascension, the Litanies are sung in procession in Catholic countries, and they are considered days of penance and special prayer to avert the evils of pestilence, famine, and war. These processions and supplications on April 25 are at least as early as the time of St. Gregory the Great.
C. J. E.

THE WORD "READ" (5th S. ix. 28, 134.)—The word is by no means so irregular as it seems at first sight, but it is necessary to go back a thousand years to see this. The Anglo-Saxon forms were inf. *rédan*, imperf. *rédde*, p. part. *réded*. The like are the verbs *laédan*, *laédde*, *laéded*; *fédan*, *fédde*, *féded*; *maénan*, *maénde*, *maéned*. In the fourteenth century the forms are already shortened ; we have *rede*, *redde* and *radde*, *rad*; *lede*, *ledde* and *ladde*, *ladde*; *fede*, *fedde*, *fed*; *menen*, *mente*, *ment*(?). At that time the inf. *e* was long, the imperf. and part. *e* were short. Very soon, I suppose, the final *e* of the inf. as well as of the imperf. was dropped, and then all forms were written alike, as one *d* of the imperf. was dropped too, for a double *d* cannot stand at the end of a word. Thus we must have had the forms *réd*, *rĕd*, *rĕd*. In the sixteenth century a new change took place, though only for the eye, the pronunciation being the same as to-day. The long *e* in the infinitive was changed to *ea*, and the short *e* of the imperfect and p. part. too, without giving up the short sound. For what reason the two latter forms got *ea*, instead of retaining the spelling *e*, is not easily to be seen ; but this word is not the only one with a short *ea*—to *mean*, to *spread*, and others have it likewise. In to *spread* the short vowel has even gone into the infinitive, which of old had a long vowel. This MR. SPURRELL would call "a change for the worse." Whether that expression is correct I will not dispute. The fact is that the vowel of some tense has frequently been of influence upon the vowel of another tense, not in English alone, but in all Teutonic languages, and the spelling has certainly done very little to this. It is true if at present we wrote "to read, red, red," it would be quite correct, and we should accommodate the spelling to the pronunciation, and thus meet the aims and

endeavours of the spelling reformers ; but then we ought to be consistent and write also *ment* for *meant*, *dremt* for *dreamt*, and even *lernt* for *learnt*. Besides this, we ought to spell the infinitives in the same way, either with *ea* or *ee*, as to *feed*, to *heed*, to *speed*, to *deem*, to *read*, and even to *lead*, to *leave*, and to *mean* might receive the same vowels, though in Anglo-Saxon they have *aé*, whilst the others have *é*. If Byron wrote *redde* he used an archaic form, and therefore, I suppose, he only did so when he was compelled by the metre. If the verb to *eat* has undergone such a change in pronunciation as MR. SPURRELL assumes, it only proves what I said before, viz. that one tense frequently changes another one. As to the verb to *beat*, this is as regular as a word only can be. The A.-S. was *beátan*, *beót*, *beáten*. Now the A.-S. *eá* as well as *eó* generally gives a long *e* in English, which can be written *ea* or *ee*. So the A.-S. *nedd* is English *need; A.-S. beám*, Eng. *beam; A.-S. beán*, Eng. *bean; A.-S. fleá*, Eng. *flee; A.-S. hleápan*, Eng. to *leap;* likewise A.-S. *fredsan*, Eng. to *freeze; A.-S. cleófan*, Eng. to *cleave; A.-S. cneó*, Eng. *knee; A.-S. hreód*, Eng. *reed; A.-S. deóp*, Eng. *deep*. The verb to *beat* had in the fourteenth century the forms inf. *bete*, imperf. *bete* and *beet*, p. part. *beten*, all three with a long vowel. The next change was the dropping of the *e* in the inf. and imperf., giving the forms *bet*, *bet*, *beten*, and the modern forms to *beat*, *beat*, *beaten*, must necessarily arise from those old forms. Thus the spelling and pronunciation are quite regular, and we are wrong if we say the spelling had corrupted the pronunciation. We might, of course, write both tenses with *ee* instead of *ea*, which would not make any difference, since we have seen that A.-S. *eá* and *eó* turn into English *ea* or *ee*, which two different signs denote one and the same sound, viz. a long *e*.   F. ROSENTHAL.
Hannover, 17, Burgstrasse.

FANS (5ᵗʰ S. ix. 88, 137.)—Please permit me to offer my sincere thanks to the gentleman, unknown to me, who has kindly sent me the catalogue of the loan collection of fans exhibited at the Liverpool Art Club.   J. BRANDER MATTHEWS.
Lotos Club, N.Y.

JUNIUS : DR. FRANCIS (5ᵗʰ S. ix. 147, 314.)—Bibliographers give little or no information about the *Test* and *Contest*. The *Test* is sometimes called a pamphlet and sometimes a newspaper. The truth is there were two publications of the name. In June, 1756, the *Test* was printed under the auspices of Charles Townshend ; it was intended to have been a weekly publication, but no second number was issued. In November, 1756, a second paper of the same name was brought out by the other side in politics, to assist Fox, by Murphy. This was met by the immediate publication of the *Contest*, and the two continued as twopenny weekly papers for about six months ; the *Test* terminating on the 9th of July, 1757, and the *Contest* on the 6th of August, 1757. There is a review of these two papers, said to be by Dr. Johnson, in the *Literary Magazine* for 1756, pp. 453-61, which commences thus :—

" The change of Ministry has produced a paper called the *Test*, written in favour of Mr. H. F., to defame Mr. P., who is insulted with every invidious recollection of the past and anticipation of the future ; the charge which has been urged with most Humour and Spirit is, that since his Engagement in the Administration he has not freed himself from the Gout. To this *Test* a zealous Writer has opposed a *Con-test*."

The reviewer ends by saying :—

" Of the motives of the author of the *Test*, whoever he be, I believe every man who speaks honestly speaks with abhorrence.......Wit is frequently attempted, but always by mean and despicable imitations, without the least glimmer of intrinsic light, without a single effort of original thought."

It is generally stated that the *Test* was written by Arthur Murphy and the *Contest* by Owen Ruffhead (*Biographia Dramatica*, 1812, i. 536 ; Chalmers's *Bio. Dictionary*, xxvi. 457 ; Gorton's *Bio. Dictionary*, 1833, iii.). I am not aware that the name of Francis has been put forward as writing the *Contest;* it used to be associated with Murphy as that of a writer on the same side as the *Test* (Walpole, *Memoires of George II.*). The Francis here spoken of as the " poetic clergyman " was the Rev. Philip Francis, best known as the translator of Horace, but who, employing his pen in defence of Government, acquired the patronage of Henry Fox, Lord Holland, who rewarded him with the rectory of Barrow, in Suffolk, and the chaplaincy of Chelsea Hospital. His political writings, together with his Church preferment, drew upon him the wrath of Churchill, in *The Author*, in lines of terrible satire. Dr. Francis died in 1773. He was the father of Sir Philip Francis, who held so distinguished a part in Parliament at the end of the last century.
EDWARD SOLLY.

MILTON QUERIES (5ᵗʰ S. ix. 107, 176, 256.)—I doubt if any of the suggestions hitherto made in explanation of the line in *Il Penseroso* are quite satisfactory. They all seem to me to put more upon the words than they will fairly bear. I would suggest (but with great diffidence) that *hist* may not be a verb at all, but a participle—in fact, identical with *whist* = hushed. Then the passage would read thus : " First, with thee bring . . . the cherub Contemplation, and [next *bring*] the *mute hushed Silence* along." This position of a noun between two epithets is distinctly Miltonic, *e.g.* " mortal sin original," " temperate vapours bland," &c.   C. S. JERRAM.

The word *haste* is so spelled in the 1645 edition of Milton's *Poems*, in the passage referred to in

MR. DIXON'S reply. As a further answer to his inquiry I extract from that volume the following particulars, the references to the numbers of the lines being from Cleveland's *Concordance* to Milton's works :—

"*Haste* (verb), L'Allegro, l. 25; Arcades, 58; Comus, 920, 956; Ode on the Nativity, 23.
"*Haste* (noun), L'Allegro, 87.
"*Hast* (verb), Ode on the Nativity, 212.
"*Hast* (noun), Comus, 568."

MR. DIXON is quite correct in stating that *haste* is always printed *hast* in the first editions of *Paradise Regained* and *Samson Agonistes* (1671). It occurs twice as a verb and four times as a noun in those poems.   J. F. MARSH.
Hardwick House, Chepstow.

"And the mute Silence *hist* along."

The meaning suggested by DR. ROSENTHAL (p. 176) will scarcely commend itself to students of Milton, for the idea of *mute* Silence going about "saying to every one *hist!* so as to bring all to silence," is not only almost ludicrous in itself, but entirely out of harmony with the rest of the poet's address to Melancholy. MR. DIXON'S substitution of *haste* for *hist* at once makes the interpretation clear. In *Paradise Regained* and *Samson Agonistes* he finds *haste* always printed *hast*, and it may support his supposition that *hist* is a misprint for *hast* to know that in the first edition of *Paradise Lost* (Pickering's reprint, 1873) *hast* is found three times—i. 357, ix. 17 (now x. 17), and x. 115 (now xi. 104). I hope, however, that MR. DIXON would not propose to alter *hist* into *haste*. Even although no other example of *hist* as a verb could be adduced, I should be loth to see it pass from the familiar place. It is possible the word was a coinage of Milton's own—an onomatopœia—more suitable in the line than *haste*. Anyhow, the ejaculatory meaning is quite impossible.
WILLIAM GEORGE BLACK.
1, Alfred Terrace, Hillhead, Glasgow.

THE DE STUTEVILLE FAMILY (5th S. viii. 447; ix. 17, 110.)—I am afraid SYWL will find that what he states of the early part of the Skipwith pedigree rests on no better foundation than a "Family Genealogy" of the seventeenth century,* which Sir Bernard Burke perpetuates apparently from the old baronetages. A younger son of the Norman family of De Estoteville *might have been* settled by the head of the family at Skipwith, but nothing more can be said. Whether Erneburga was daughter and heiress (or co-heiress) of Hugh fitz Baldric or not there is no certain evidence, though Robert de Estoteville seems to

have claimed, as her son perhaps, which he some of the lands of Hugh fitz Baldric, who, ever, was not a "great Saxon thane," but a man, of whom there is a notice before he Normandy. Wido, a *son-in-law* of Hugh, is tioned in Domesday Book, 1086 (fo. 356), ¿ had at this date at least one married daugh John, or William, son of Osbert de Schip gave a toft, essart, and lands in Skipwith to ¿ Abbey, apparently in the reign of John Henry III. (Burton's *Monasticon Ebor.*, 400) neither figures in the pedigree.   A. S. ELL
Westminster.

Pedigrees of this family are given in Ba Dormant and Extinct Baronage, vol. i. p. Baker's *Hist. of Northamptonshire*, vol. i. p. See also Watton's *Engl. Baronetage*, vol. iv. p. *The Patrician*, vol. ii. p. 268; and other ¿ referred to under the name in Bridger's *Ind Pedigrees of English Families*. For the fa arms, see Berry's *Heraldic Encyclopædia*. first of the name in England was Robert d'Es ville, so called from Estouteville, formerly Es villa, now Etouteville in the present arrondisser of Yvetot, in France. He came in the trai William, Duke of Normandy, at the Conque 1066. His name appears on the Roll of Kni as the "Sire D'Estoteville." In the parcellir lands by the Conqueror he was granted ¿ estates in various parts of the realm, principal Yorkshire. In the time of Edward I. Walte Stuteville, who had as his patrimony land Latton in North Wilts, assumed the nam Latton, and from him descended the La of Upton in Berks, of Esher in Surrey, anc family which settled at Morristown Latti Kildare.   J. J. LATTIN
64, Madison Avenue, New York, U.S.A.

HERALDIC (5th S. viii. 147, 254; ix. 27 There are two old maxims which seem to app MR. HYDE's note at the last reference : "The no rule without an exception," and "The ex tion proves the rule." If Margery Cater had entitled by descent to bear the arms and cre her family, she would not have needed any "g ratification, or confirmation" to authorize her her issue to do so. Indeed, this grant would ¿ to imply a doubt whether John Cater himself previously entitled to the arms in question, ¿ will be observed that Hervye's (misprinted Her grant was made not only to Margery and her i but "unto all the posteritie of the saide ¿ Cater." What I have urged, and do urge, is a *crest*, unlike arms, is not *inherited* throu¿

---

* Elaborated perhaps by the same ingenious hand from which came the genealogies of the old Yorkshire families of Brodrick, Cave, Eastoft, Hotham, which last begins with Sir John de Trehouse, *Lord of Kilkenny in Ireland*, who served under the Conqueror !

† An account of Hugh fitz Baldric, who was Sher Yorkshire, will be found in "Biographical Notes o Yorkshire Tenants named in Domesday Book" ii *Yorkshire Archæological and Topographical Jou* vol. iv. p. 237.

woman, and neither this grant nor twenty such grants would prove the contrary. Undoubtedly under this "special grant" it must be admitted that Margery and her issue have a right to use the arms and crest so granted.　　　JOHN MACLEAN.
Bicknor Court, Coleford, Glouc.

"THE LITTLE DUSTPAN" (5th S. ix. 199.)—This was the sign of a general ironmongery shop in High Holborn, close to Museum Street. It was opened in opposition to a then famed house hard by known as "The Big Dustpan." The date was prior to the opening of New Oxford Street, about 1830-1. The clue I have to this date is memory of a famous waxwork show within a few doors of "The Little Dustpan." Here I remember at ten years of age seeing a representation of the murder of Maria Martin, and Corder digging her grave in the barn. This was then the only permanent waxwork exhibition in London. Madame Tussaud used then to "meander" the country.
SEPTIMUS PIESSE.

THE GREAT BELL AT BRAILES, CO. WARWICK (5th S. ix. 166, 255.)—The lines—

"Gaude quod post ipsum scandis,
Et est honor tibi grandis
In cœli palatio"

—occur in the hymn of the "Seven Earthly Joys of the Blessed Virgin Mary," commonly attributed to St. Thomas, Archbishop of Canterbury, and refer to her Assumption. Some readings give *Christum* for *ipsum*. The concluding lines are (a comma occurring usually after *palatio*) :—

"Ubi fructus ventris tui
Per te nobis detur frui
In perenni gaudio. Amen."

These stanzas are given in many modern Latin prayer books, and they are to be found in all the Sarum Horæ and Prymers. Mone gives several versions from different early MSS.
EDMUND WATERTON.

SWALE FAMILY (5th S. i. 188, 253, 297, 476; ii. 78.)—This baronetcy has at length been formally claimed by the Rev. John Swale, O.S.B., as the eldest male descendant of William Swale, son of Dr. Robert Swale, and grandson of the first baronet. There seems to be good documentary evidence in support of his claim. Can any readers of "N. & Q." give me any information as to the representatives of the last baronet, Sir Sebastian Fabian Enrique Swale? He is said to have married Elizabeth, daughter of a Mr. Smith, of Poole, in Dorsetshire, and to have died in Spain, leaving three daughters —1. Elizabeth Easter (?), 2. Frances Theodora, 3. Dorothy Fabiana.
JOHN H. CHAPMAN, M.A., F.S.A.
Woodgreen, Witney.

WEST INDIES : BARBADOES (5th S. ix. 249, 297.) —Bristol and London were the ports from which

ships usually sailed to the West Indies. The first ship which touched at Barbadoes was the Olive, in 1605. The only lists of ships and their passengers that I have heard of are to be found in the Record Office (Colonial dep.), London. While answering this question it will probably prove interesting to many of your readers to know that in the Col. Sec. Office, Barbadoes, there is an immense mass of genealogical information to be obtained, as wills and deeds are to be found there in large numbers which date from about 1645. Some of the parish registers, such as St. Philip, Christ Church, and St. James's, are perfect from about this date. I fancy that many a missing link in old English and Scotch families is to be found in the Sec. Office, Barbadoes, judging from what I have seen during my researches there.　　　N. FORTE, Jun.
7, The Paragon, Clifton.

THE EAR-LOBE (5th S. ix. 146.)—Where does the "orthodox faith" mentioned by DR. HYDE CLARKE prevail? In a paper read by Mr. H. G. Kennedy before the Indian section of the Society of Arts, on May 1, 1874 (DR. HYDE CLARKE himself presiding), "On the Antiquities of Siam and Camboja," Mr. Kennedy referred to the practice of piercing the ears prevalent among the Cambojans ; and, in the discussion that followed, Mr. Parke Harrison remarked :—

"One very singular case was the enlargement of the lobe of the ear, which had been referred to by Mr. Kennedy : he [the speaker] had paid some attention to it, and would briefly trace its extent. In the southern part of India and Ceylon, and again in the north, this custom prevailed, which had been alluded to by ancient authors as that of making windows in the ears, the ears of children being pierced when very young, and the aperture gradually enlarging by inserting leaves and other materials, until at last it would receive a metal disc of two or three inches in diameter. When the disc was removed, the ears hung down on the shoulders or chest, as was seen in the images of Buddha. Col. Hamilton and others, who visited Burmah 150 years ago, described the kings, priests, and nobles as having their ears enlarged in this singular manner, and the same was found in the Solomon Islands, the Fiji Islands, and even Easter Island, probably the most isolated island in the world, being about two thousand miles from any other island, or from the coast of Peru. When the Spaniards conquered the latter country they found a similar custom prevailing principally among the nobles, though imitated to a certain extent by the common people. It was curious to find such a singular custom prevailing in such widely separated countries, and as he had mentioned at Bradford last year, other customs were also found associated with it."

And Mr. Thompson remarked that this peculiarity had been noted by him in almost all the sculptures and antiquities of Camboja, and would therefore seem to have been practised by the ancient Cambojans.

After noting the wide field over which Mr. Harrison's remarks travelled, the "orthodox faith" referred to by DR. CLARKE cannot prevail in a large part of the world, or the whole population of each place mentioned would be hanged, and the last survivor in each case reduced to the extremity of suicide—a martyr to his superstition. Dr. Clarke's note would seem to imply that the superstition is well-nigh universal, his only exception apparently being England.

Might I conclude by asking whether any of your readers know what the " other customs," mentioned by Mr. Harrison at Bradford in 1873, are ?
R. P. Hampton Roberts.

Gipsies in England (5th S. ix. 149, 295.)—For information as to the first arrival of Gipsies in Great Britain, K. P. D. E. should refer to Simson's *History of the Gipsies*, Lond., 1865, chap. iii. pp. 99, 100, or to *Blackwood's Magazine*, vol. i. (April, 1817), p. 167.
H. T. C.

At present I do not remember any mention of Gipsies in England earlier than 1530. The works mentioned by Dr. Charnock contain much information relative to the early history of the Gipsies. In Scotland their first appearance, according to Simson, was about 1506. At that date they were called new-comers. Although the name Tinkler can be traced in the Scotch records as far back as 1165, it does not prove that the term was then applied to Gipsies. The term seems to have been applied to any one pursuing the trade of a tinsmith. When the Gipsies came into Scotland about 1506, many of them being tinsmiths and workers in horn, it is not singular that they should be called Tinklers and Horners. Mr. H. T. Crofton, the joint author with Dr. Bath C. Smart of an admirable *Vocabulary of the English Gipsy Dialect*, has some very valuable observations upon this subject in " N. & Q.," 5th S. v. 129.

With regard to the period of time the Gipsies have been in Europe, much information may be obtained from a recent publication by the well-known and reliable author M. Paul Bataillard, entitled *État de la Question de l'Ancienneté des Tsiganes en Europe*. It is a work full of interest, and the result of much careful investigation and research.
Hubert Smith.

British and Continental Titles of Honour (5th S. ii. 23, 95, 195, 351; iii. 252.)—I trust I may be permitted finally to fortify my position by quoting an authority which puts the whole matter in the clearest possible light. I came upon the passage while reperusing my *Coke upon Littleton* the other day. It will be found in Butler's long note to *Co. Litt.*, 191 a, and runs thus :—

"V. 4. The difference between the English nobility and English Parliament and the nobility and Parliaments of the nations on the Continent is very remarkable. The three states and three orders of the state on the Continent have been mentioned. In almost every country on the Continent, the third state, or third order of the state, was originally distinguished from the nobility, and con-

sisted of the commonalty only. In England all the barons or lords of those manors which were held immediately of the king were entitled to a seat in the national council. In the course of time they became numerous, and the estates of many of them became very small. This introduced a difference in their personal importance. In consequence of it, the great barons were personally summoned to Parliament by the king ; the small barons were summoned to it in the aggregate by the sheriff. They assembled in distinct chambers. The king met the great barons in person, but, except when he summoned their personal attendance, left the latter " [qy. lesser ?] " to their own deliberations. These, and some concurrent circumstances, elevated the great to a distinct order from the smaller barons, and confounded the latter with the general body of the freeholders.
" In the mean time a considerable revolution took place in the right to the English peerage. From being territorial it became personal......when they were granted in this way, if the party had not a baronial dignity the king conferred it on him, and thus entitled him to a seat in the higher house. Where the dignity was hereditary, if he had more than one male descendant, his eldest son only took his seat in the house, and the brothers and sisters of that son were commoners. Thus a separate rank of nobility, unknown to foreigners, was introduced in England ; and thus, in opposition to a fundamental principle of the French law, that every gentleman in France is a nobleman, it became a principle of the English law that no English gentleman is a nobleman unless he is a peer of the upper house of Parliament."
Middle Templar.

Perrott and Sharpe Families (5th S. viii. 369, 458, 516.)—According to the *Gentleman's Magazine* for Feb., 1770, p. 59, the *elder* brother of " Dick Parrott " was an apothecary, but then practised as a physician at Tewkesbury " by virtue of a diploma from Leyden." The subject of my query is stated to have practised as a surgeon for " near forty years " in Earl's Shilton. I hardly think, therefore, that he was, as suggested, the " James, M.D.," of Kimber and Johnson's mendacious pedigree, though as his " lady wife " is asserted to have been the widow of a personage whose name (like Sir John Maclean) I was unable to find in any baronetage, I own that I had my suspicions. But in propounding my query I had no intention of reviving this unpleasant subject. I am interested in a Worcestershire family of Perrott (whose descent I may mention en passant, is very inaccurately given in Mr. Barnwell's book), and thinking it possible that the Earl's Shilton surgeon might be a member of that family, I asked about him in " N. & Q."

The replies which my query has elicited from Sywl and others almost compel me to add that I have read Mr. Barnwell's *Perrot Notes*, and also the article by the late Mr. Gough Nichols in the *Herald and Genealogist*, and that in the course of my researches I have turned up documents which have revealed to me the true pedigree of the personage known as " Sir Richard Perrott, Bart.," who, I need scarcely say, was not in any way allied to " the great and eminent house of Perrott of Haroldstone."
H. S. G.

CHAUNCY FAMILY (5th S. viii. 427.)—EBOR is referred to Clutterbuck's *History of Hertfordshire* for a pedigree amplified from that given by Sir Henry Chauncy in his history of the same county (pp. 55-61). But the commencement is not quite correct in either, and it should begin not with a William, but with that Anfrid or Alfreit de Canceio or Canci mentioned in that valuable fragment—all that remains—of a survey of Lincolnshire made for Henry I. soon after he came to the throne (1100-8), which is preserved in the Cottonian Library (Claudius C. v.).*

This is the first time the name occurs, and it is found herein five times. Anfrid was tenant in capite of lands in Wilgeton (fo. 4), Duneham (fo. 6), Walesby (fo. 11), Swincopa (fo. 12), Blesebi (fo. 23). In the second and last instances his name is spelt Alfreit and Alfræit. This difference is curious, but I do not think there were two persons with similar Christian names, for Anfrid, son of Walter, is once called Alfrid in the Whitby cartulary.

This valuable document furnishes us with proof that as early as 1100-8 Anfrid was already in possession of some at least of the lands belonging to Odo Balistarius at the time of the Domesday Survey, 1086. It follows, then, that in all probability Odo's estate in Yorkshire (Skirpenbeck, Bugthorp, &c.) was also then in his hands. The family pedigree says William de Canci bought it; but this is less likely than that it was a royal reward to Anfrid for his support of Henry I., being an escheat of one of the king's vanquished enemies.

Anfrid was no doubt the father of Walter de Canceio, the son's name suggesting for his wife a daughter of one or other of his influential neighbours in Yorkshire and Lincolnshire, Walter de Perci or Walter de Gaunt, or of the family of Scotney. The father was dead 1131 (Pipe Roll, 31 Hen. I.), when Walter fined 15*l.* with the king to marry whom he wished, also 20*s.* of the pleas of Blythe, and he had paid that year—being pardoned the 20*s.* by the king's brief—7*l.* 3*s.* 4*d.*, but the rest he owes. I think it will be found the lady of his choice was a sister of Simon de Kyme, which would account for the introduction of the names of Simon and Philip into the family. This is the Walter who, with the assent of his son and heir Anfrid, gave the advowson of Skirpenbeck to the monks of Whitby. Simon de Canci, who

seems to have been another son, witnessed the charter of Philip de Kyme, dated 1162, to the monks of Kirkstead (*Mon. Angl.*, i. 809). Walter was dead 1168, when Amfrid de Canci, his son, returns himself as a tenant in chief of five knights' fees, all of the old feoffment, *i.e.* held "the year and day when King Henry [I.] was alive and dead." One knight's fee only he kept in his own hands (*Liber Niger*, i. 318, where for "Guggetorp" read Buggetorp).†

Westminster.   A. S. ELLIS.

MR. ARBER'S REPRINTS (5th S. ix. 243, 295,. 312.)—I answered A. J. M. because, though I have not the pleasure of Mr. Arber's personal acquaintance, I think that that gentleman has done, and is doing, excellent service in our old English literature. I must express my regret that A. J. M. and myself cannot read Mr. Arber's circular with the same eyes, and that A. J. M. does not understand the words in what seems to me their plain and obvious sense.   B. NICHOLSON.

AUTHORS OF BOOKS WANTED (5th S. ix. 309.)—
Hermit in London is by Capt. Macdonough. Let your correspondent consult the Index to the Fourth Series; he will be able to get further information.   O. H.

(5th S. ix. 329.)
Momentary Musings.—I venture to suggest that the author is Kenelm Digby, Trin. Coll., Camb., B.A., 1819.
K. H. S.

AUTHORS OF QUOTATIONS WANTED (5th S. ix. 309.)—
"Vast plains and lowly cottages forlorn," &c.
The "old poet" is Dr. Henry More, and the lines occur (only "with" for "and") in the twenty-fifth stanza. of *The Argument of Psychathanasia, or the Immortality of the Soul.* I am just about completing my edition of More's complete poems in the Chertsey Worthies' Library, and in preparing the full Glossarial-Index, *s.v.* "glowing," I penitently confess that the original word "gloring" (which I took to be a misprint) has a more More-ish sound, and ought at any rate to have been left. J. D. will do well to read and re-read the whole very. vivid stanza and its context. See as above, p. 168.
A. B. GROSART.
(5th S. ix. 329.)
"For, an ye heard a music, like enow
They are building still, seeing the city is built
To music, therefore never built at all,
And therefore built for ever."
These lines, which refer not to Ilion, but to Camelot, occur in *Gareth and Lynette*, at p. 19 of the edition of 1872.   R. R. LLOYD.

* It is not improbable that this unique fragment of the original is all that exists of a return of all the tenants and their lands throughout the realm ordered by Henry I., but this refers only to the three ridings of the parts of Lindsey. The leaves were formerly pasted together. It was printed by Hearne in the second volume of *Liber Niger*. Mr. Stapleton has pointed out that it cannot be later than 1108, because Odo, Count of Champagne, is named, who must have died that year.

† Charlton, in his *History of Whitby*, gives this ridiculous story of the origin of the family (p. 118): "When William the Conqueror came into England he gave considerable possessions near Battle Bridge, now called Stamford Bridge, to an adventurer that came along with him, called Cancy or Chancy." Where he got it from I do not know. The charters of the Cancis. to Whitby Abbey will be found in this volume, but translated unskilfully.

Miscellaneous.

NOTES ON BOOKS, &c.

The Annals of England. Library Edition. (Oxford and London, Parker & Co.)

THIS old-established favourite will be found a very useful companion to the works by which Prof. Stubbs and Mr. J. R. Green and others are shedding new light on English history. The plan of the *Annals* being, as the compiler fairly claims for it, substantially identical with the mode of studying history recommended by Mr. J. A. Froude, and found most useful in practice by both Mr. Goldwin Smith and Mr. Stubbs, has unimpeachable authority in its favour. It provides, in fact, the dry bones of our history, which any lecturer who knows his subject can with ease make instinct with life for his hearers. Year by year the facts recorded by our annalists, and embodied in our statute-book, are unrolled before the student, while a profusion of drawings illustrating the art, the science, and the manners and customs of the past, cannot but add alike to the interest and the value of the book in its altered and greatly improved shape. The herald and the sigillographer will both find their favourite studies called into constant requisition. The Appendix on the "Materials of English History" contains lists not only of the chroniclers, and the best printed editions of their works, but also of the publications of the various Government Commissions, and of the principal publishing societies of the United Kingdom. By means of this list the student can unearth Mr. Freeman's life of Earl Godwine from the depths of the volumes of *Archæologia* in which it is buried, as well as the numerous papers in the same *Transactions* in which Dr. Guest's learning has illustrated Romano-British and early English history. But we must note with a view to strict accuracy that Mr. Richard Sims, the author of the well-known *Manual for the Genealogist* which is noticed at p. 591, writes his name with a different orthography from that given in the *Annals*. And we cannot but regret that the author did not consult vol. viii. of the 3ʳᵈ S. of "N. & Q." (pp. 533-4) before repeating an old error, handed down from Douglas, in the statement that the last pre-Revolution Archbishop of St. Andrews was Arthur Ross. This prelate was a *Rose*, whose descent is clearly deduced from Hugh, eighth Baron of Kilravock, the chief of that name in Scotland. He was successively Parson of Glasgow, 1660; Bp. of Argyle, 1676; Bp. of Galloway, 1678; Abp. of Glasgow, 1679, on Burnet's removal, whom he succeeded as Abp. of St. Andrews in 1684, and so continued till the Revolution.

Shelley: a Critical Biography. By George Barnett Smith, Author of *Poets and Novelists*, &c. (Edinburgh, David Douglas.)

THIS little book is free from party spirit and very prettily printed; but it is not in any strict sense a biography, or critical. An omission of some importance and significance strikes us at the outset: Mr. Smith does not say on what authority any new statement or contradiction to be met with in his book is founded. Consequently we must receive with great caution such statements as are unfamiliar. At p. 21 it is alleged that Shelley's coadjutor in the *Original Poetry by Victor and Cazire* was his sister Elizabeth, and not his cousin Harriet Grove, as sometimes supposed, and that Shelley ordered the whole edition to be destroyed. We know no reason against believing this; but we want more encouragement in belief than Mr. Smith gives us. Shelley's order to destroy the edition need not set aside the hope of finding a copy, because Stockdale's statement that about

siderable number of small deviations from received indicate, not special information, but want of car copying or in reading. One of the most remarkabl these is at p. 142, where the story of the figure : beckoned Shelley into "the saloon" is reproduced f the *Memorials* with the strange gloss that the incid happened on board the Don Juan. "The saloon" of course in Casa Magni; but Mr. Smith seems to pose the deckless and cabinless boat had a saloon! have noted many deviations of this kind, but f scarcely demand a detailed setting forth. As a critic Smith does not seem to grasp thoroughly any one p of Shelley's; we look in vain for a happy charac ization, but find plenty of mistakes almost as enorm as that of supposing that when Shelley wrote *The A of Anarchy* he was aiming at "the witty or the morous" (p. 229).

THE REV. J. MACRAY writes that a paper on b plates, by the Rev. D. Parsons, is contained in Third Annual Report of the Oxford University Arch logical and Heraldic Society, Oxford, 1837.

Notices to Correspondents.

We must call special attention to the following notice

ON all communications should be written the name address of the sender, not necessarily for publication, as a guarantee of good faith.

GEORGE ELLIS.—For Dr. Dee and his magic mir see "N. & Q.," 5ᵗʰ S. ii. 86, 136, 218, 376. J. B. describes the mirror, from personal knowledge, "a flat mirror of polished coal."

A. J. K. (Clifton.)—"Portuma." Please send n and address according to our rule.

F. G. HILTON PRICE.—We have forwarded your c munication.

JOSEPH SIMPSON.—For Palm Sunday called Fig ᘠ day, see "N. & Q.," 4ᵗʰ S. iii. 553; iv. 286.

PROF. NEWTON (Cambridge.)—We shall be very gla have the proposed comments.

RIVUS.—It is impossible to set up, with ordinary t the inscription forwarded.

NOLENS VOLENS. — Pronounced, and often writ *Brake.*

H. C. F. (Herts.)—For Adam and Lilith, see 5ᵗ i. 387, 495; ii. 132, 217.

JONATHAN BOUCHIER.—Try the *Sunday at Home* (Tract Soc.).

R. R. LLOYD.—Please send the will.

C. L. D.'s wish shall be complied with.

J. O.—We quite concur. Pray act as you suggest.

H. I. C. and HIRONDELLE.—Letters forwarded.

M. (ante, p. 340.)—We have a letter for you.

H. J. L.—Apply to a general publisher.

K. H. SMITH.—Query next week.

ST. SWITHIN is thanked.

LONDON, SATURDAY, MAY 11, 1878.

CONTENTS. — N° 228.

Notes.

MIGUEL SOLIS, AGED 180.

In the two years which followed the publication of my little book, *The Longevity of Man*, I was overwhelmed with such a mass of correspondence asking my opinion and challenging my investigation of what the writers all believed to be undoubted cases of ultra-centenarianism, that in 1875 I was obliged, in self-defence, to explain in the *Times* that I had been compelled to give up the investigation of cases of supposed exceptional longevity, and to print a circular to the same effect. From that time, with one or two rare exceptions, such as the undoubted case of Canon Beadon and the hoax of Mr. Edward Morgan, said to be 106, I have not troubled myself nor any of the public journals on the subject of longevity. But the astounding account reported in the *Pall Mall Gazette* of the 20th ult. as given by "Dr. Luiz Hernandez to a meeting of physicians at Bogota, of a visit which he had paid to a half-breed farmer named Miguel Solis, living in the Foot Hills of the Sierra Mesilla, who *confesses* to being 180 years old, but is believed by his neighbours to be *really much older*," has made me such a target for the paper bullets of the brain of all my friends that I venture to ask you to find room for a few words of comment upon it.

That a member of the medical profession in any part of the civilized world should be found, in the year 1878, to consider seriously the case of a man who modestly " confesses " to being 180 years old, but is believed by his neighbours to be really much more than 180, did not, until I read this article, " stand within the prospect of my belief."

Dr. Hernandez's credence in this story of Miguel Solis (for if he had not believed it he certainly would not have brought it forward) appears to have been based upon the evidence of three witnesses. First, on that of Miguel Solis himself, " who confesses to being 180 years old " ; secondly, on that of the oldest inhabitants of the district, who remembered him as a reputed centenarian when they were boys ; thirdly, on that of the abbot of a Franciscan monastery near San Sebastian, who is satisfied that the present Miguel Solis is the identical Miguel Solis who was, in 1712, a contributor to the building fund of the monastery. San Sebastian is obviously a locality favourable to longevity, since the abbot (I wonder how much he is under 200) can identify the living party to a transaction which took place 166 years ago.

It is clear that age cannot wither Miguel Solis. He is robust and active, and when the doctor visited him was working in his orchard ; his " teeth are as sound as they were 180 years ago"; his snow-white hair is twisted turban fashion round his head, and his eyes are " so bright that the doctor felt quite uncomfortable when they were turned upon him." I suspect the learned gentleman's " uncomfortable feeling " has misled him as to the expression of old Miguel's eyes, and that they were really twinkling with malicious glee at the doctor's gullibility.

The Indians say Miguel has sold himself to the Devil. Miguel says the same thing of the Indians. There is no ground for supposing Dr. Hernandez to have acted in that way. Gentlemen who do so sell themselves generally claim from the purchaser the two gifts of long life and supernatural power. If the doctor has been seduced into any such compact, it is to be hoped he will at least obtain the promised length of days, for it is obvious from his present " interesting account " that he is no conjurer. Had he been, he would have eliminated from the story of Miguel Solis the small error on which it is founded—have struck out the first of the three figures of his reputed age, and have left " the half-breed farmer living at the Foot Hills of the Sierra Mesilla " the eighty years, or thereabouts, which he has probably attained.

In conclusion, will you kindly give me the following canon on centenarianism the advantage of publicity in your columns ?—

" The age of an individual is a fact, and like all other facts is to be proved, not inferred ; to be established by evidence, not accepted on the mere assertion of the individual or the belief of his friends ; not deduced from his physical condition if living, or from his autopsy if dead ; but proved by the register of his birth or baptism, or some other authentic record; and in proportion as the age claimed is exceptionally extreme ought the proof of it to be exceptionally strong, clear, and irrefragable." It has received the approval of many eminent authorities, and will, I believe, point out to those who only desire to know the truth with respect to cases of exceptional longevity some suggestions as to how that truth may be arrived at.

WILLIAM J. THOMS.
40, St. George's Square, S.W.

THE SEE OF CAITHNESS.

In using Father Theiner's *Vetera Monumenta* (Hib. et Scot.) lately, I came upon three letters respecting the see of Caithness which puzzled me for a time. They are Nos. DCXLI., DCXLVI., and DCLX.

In the first, dated May 11, 1360, Pope Innocent VI. writes to Thomas, Bishop of Caithness, directing him upon his consecration to proceed to his diocese. In the second, dated July 8 following, we find Innocent addressing a letter to George, Archbishop of Cashel, in consequence of certain accusations and objections made by the Bishops of Killaloe, Limerick, Ardfert, and Cloyne against the appointment of Bishop Thomas to the see of Caithness, and directing the archbishop to report concerning the condition of that see—" præsertim si dicta ecclesia Cathayensis cathedralis existat, et a quanto tempore cathedralis fuit, et si habuit et habet civitatem et diocesim distinctas, ac si alios episcopos habuit, et qui fuerunt," &c. The Archbishop of Cashel was, however, drowned in 1362, and seems to have passed away without making the report directed by the letter of the Pope. Innocent also died about the same time, and on June 24, 1363, we find his successor, Pope Urban V., writing to Thomas, Bishop of Lismore, directing him to make the required report as to the status of the see of Caithness.

In these letters there were two things which seemed to me to require explanation: first, how the Pope and his officials could have the smallest doubt with regard to the existence of the see of Caithness, seeing that, as we find in Theiner, the Papal archives contained the fullest records of many former appointments to the bishopric. And again, it seemed almost inexplicable that, with a regular hierarchy existing in Scotland, the Pope should direct first an Irish archbishop and then an Irish bishop to report concerning the status of a Scottish see. But I believe I may say that I have discovered the explanation. On turning over Graesse's *Orbis Latinus* (" Oder Verzeichniss der Lateinischen Bennenungen der Städte," &c.), Dresden, 1861, I find that there was another *Cathanasia* besides the Scottish county and see of Caithness, viz. the town of Dunmore in Ireland. It is therefore clear, I think, that the Irish bishops who

objected to the appointment of Bishop Th the see of Caithness were, or affected to b that the Pope had been persuaded to n him, and cause him to be consecrated, as t an Irish see which had not then, and (appear ever to have had, any existence interference and the reference of the matt Irish archbishop and bishop are thus expla is still not easy to understand how it there was no one at hand to explain tha Thomas had been nominated to a Scottish to a non-existent Irish one.

The residence of the Papal Court at *A* from whence the above letters are dated, : for the inability of the officials to con archives in the Vatican. Still, among tho must have been preserved at Avignon, the at least two Papal nominations to the see c ness, viz. that of Alan, by Benedict XII., and of Thomas de Fingast (Fingask), by VI., in 1341 (Theiner, Nos. DXLVIII. ai which, had they been consulted, would h quite sufficient to clear up the matter, prove that the see of Caithness had a (existence in the kingdom of Scotland.

JOHN WOOD
Montrose.

P.S.—I have just remembered to look a son's excellent edition of the *Orkneyin*(The succession to the see of Caithness is forth, and I observe that the editor is awa difficulty, but is unable to offer any ex except that it may have been (as I have was) a "series of mistakes." Mr. Ande leaves out the name of the Bishop of the ("Thomas Laoniensis") as one of the c With reference to his note I may also : from the difference of dates, it seems c the objection could not have been to de Fingask (*Orkneyinga Saga,* Intr pp. lxxxvi, lxxxvii).

PANCIROLLUS AND SALMUTH.

I ask leave to correct, in "N. & Q.," a which has now extended so far as to see to obtain the undying character which i belong to falsifications. My note is mad hope of stopping its progress.

When the late Mr. John Ward of Bur publishing his work upon the *Borough upon-Trent*, I translated and sent to him : from the chapter of Pancirollus, edited by " De Porcellanis." I have his letter b now, in which he enclosed to me a proof c had sent, asking me to correct the p return it to him. I did so. I will now title-page of Pancirollus at length, from copy which I then used. The title-pag two volumes differ slightly, as will be see!

"Guidonis | Pancirolli | JC, Clariss | *Rerum Memora-bilium.* | Libri Duo. | *Quorum prior* | Deperditarum. | *Posterior* Noviter inventa- | *rum est* | ex Italico Latiné redditi & No- | tis illustrati | ab | Henrico Salmuth. | *Editio Tertia.* | Cum Privelegio Sacræ Cæsareæ Majestatis. | Ambergæ | Typis Michaelis Forsteri | M.DC.XII."

The title-page of the second volume is :—

"Nova | Reperta | sive | *Rerum Memorabilium* | recens | Inventarum | & | veteribus Inco- | gnitarum Guidonis Pancirolli | JCti Clarissimi. | Liber Secundus," with the rest as in vol. i.

On the appearance of Mr. Ward's work I was shocked to see (p. 591) that some one had been guilty of the folly (to speak mildly) of altering the name of Salmuth into *Salmutti*. The following passages (p. 591) would be incredible, previously to that bitter experience which conceited ignorance inflicts upon mankind :—" So far the venerable author" (Pancirollus) ; " what follows is the commentary of Signior" (so spelt) " Salmutti." It has been seen that Salmuth printed his book " Ambergæ." On the same page (591) is this :—"(Printed at Antwerp, 1612, the third edition)."

In 1857, Mr. Marryatt, in his *History of Pottery and Porcelain*, p. 189, second edition, gave the passage translated by me, but without mentioning the place from which he obtained it. He describes the book quoted by me as being edited "ab Henrico Salmutti," following what he saw in the *History of Stoke-upon-Trent.*

In 1865, Mr. Binns of Worcester, in his *Century of Potting*, quotes Mr. Ward's book, and very naturally adopts " Salmutti," but adds to the delusion by saying " Signor "—he knew better than " Signor"—"*Henrico* Salmutti." In a visit which Mr. Binns in 1871 obliged me by making to this house I put my Pancirollus into his hands. He was amazed. I hope that what I have produced will give back to Salmuth his real name, and abolish the ludicrous fiction of "Salmutti," and restore Amberg to the Palatinate, whenever the quotation which has been travestied so long is again made use of by any writer on porcelain.

D. P.

Stuart's Lodge, Malvern Wells.

EPIGRAMS FROM THE GREEK.

Will you oblige by adding to the epigrams already given in " N. & Q." (5th S. i. 226 ; ii. 445 ; viii. 264) the following imitations from the Greek?

DRINKING CUPID.

(*From the Greek of Julian.*)

Wreathing once a garland gay,
'Mid the roses Cupid lay ;
Seizing on the boy divine,
Straight I dropped him in the wine :
Well, what next ? I raised the cup,
And with laughter drank him up.
Now, alas ! he sports and sings
Round my heart with feathery wings.

BEAUTY AND FLOWERS.

(*From the Greek of Strato.*)

Boast not of your beauty rare,
Like a rose-bud fresh and fair,
Since the rose, its freshness past,
On the mouldering heap is cast.
Flowers and beauty quickly fade,
Flung by envious time to endless shade.

WELCOME DEATH.

(*From the Greek : author unknown.*)

More sweet than life
Art thou, O Death, to me,
Who from unceasing strife
And gout dost set me free.

A GRAVE.

(*From the Greek of Heracleitus and Isidorus.*)

This mound's a grave : stay, labourer, stay,
And turn thy ox and plough some other way,
For thou disturb'st the dead, and here
Thou shouldst not sow thy wheat, but shed a tear.

ON A MAIDEN.

(*From the Greek of Plato.*)

In life, like Phospher on the morning's brow,
Thy beauty shone ;
Alas ! like Hesper art thou shining now,—
Too quickly gone !

ENVY.

(*From the Greek : author unknown.*)

Envy's a thing that all, no doubt, should shun ;
Yet even envy has one worthy part :
It dims the eyesight of the envious one,
And wears away his heart.

THE WRECK.

(*From the Greek of Theodoridas.*)

A shipwrecked traveller calmly sleeps below ;
Yet fear not thou to cross the waves, for know
That when his vessel sank within the sea,
A score of others sailed triumphantly.

EPITAPH ON A GIRL.

(*From the Greek of Paul the Silentiary.*)

A grave, and not a bridal chamber bright,
O maid beloved, thy parents' hands prepare ;
For thou hast passed beyond our earthly night,
Whilst we life's chilling clouds of grief must bear.
In thee the flower-like beauty of a child,
Mixed with the fruits of age, serenely smiled.

THE ISLANDS OF THE BLEST.

(*From the Greek : author unknown.*)

Thou art not dead, O friend beloved : thou hast but gained thy rest,
And rovest o'er th' Elysian plains with ever-fresh delight :
Thou sharest in the banquets of the Islands of the Blest,
Where far from every mortal ill soft blossoms cheer thy sight.
Thou fearest not the winter storm nor summer's scorching glow,
Nor dost thou now regret the life of man that once was thine ;
No dread disease can trouble thee, nor sorrow lay thee low,
But the pure splendours of the gods upon thy dwelling shine.

(*Imitated from the Greek of Palladas.*)
If you, my foolish friend, by chance 'mid learned wights are flung,
To seem a sage you only need—do what? why hold your tongue.

CUPID'S SPORT.
(*Imitated from the Greek.*)

Young Love is gone out with his bows and his arrows
To shoot—do you think 'tis to shoot at the sparrows?
Ah no; by his merry bright eyes and his curls,
I tell you, my boy, 'tis to shoot at the girls.

H. BOWER.

THE THAMES: KENT AND ESSEX.—Generally speaking, the river Thames is considered the dividing line between the counties of Kent and Essex, except at Woolwich; but that this has always been so is by no means certain. First with regard to Woolwich: a small portion of this parish at the present hour lies on the opposite side of the river, entirely surrounded by the county of Essex, and yet it is accounted as a portion of Kent. Then in the description of Chalk, near Gravesend, given in Domesday, it is stated that "In Exesse there is one hide which justly pertains to this manor," and again in the Domesday description of Higham is this, "And in Exesse pasture for 200 sheep." Now, although these outlying parts of Chalk and Higham are said to be in "Exesse," yet the idea intended to be conveyed was plainly that they formed parts of Kent—there was no other way of expressing the fact without a long periphrasis; and if Woolwich had been described in Domesday we should doubtless have found the same expression. These peculiarities of Chalk and Higham seem to have been overlooked by Hasted and the other historians of Kent; and I think it is certain that at the present day neither Chalk nor Higham has any jurisdiction on the northern side of the Thames. Considering that three Kentish waterside parishes stretched across the stream, and that stream of no mean width, a question thus proposes itself to the curious inquirer, whether all the waterside parishes from Deptford downwards had not each a portion on the other side of the stream. The river Thames is a convenient but not necessarily a natural division of the two counties. It may be that the Isle of Dogs, close to the metropolis, is justly a portion of the county of Kent, though not now claimed as such. Its peculiar position within the fantastic bend of the river at that point, and its contiguity to such an important locality as Greenwich, seem to strengthen the idea. But without definite evidence one way or the other all this must be left to conjecture. The abstract point, however, *i.e.* whether the river Thames has always been the boundary between Kent and Essex, is worthy of careful consideration and investigation; and I beg leave to submit the same to your readers. W. H. HART, F.S.A.

lowing letter, from the Marquis of Argyll to his dependent, Dugald Campbell of Inverawe, contains instructions for destroying the house of Lord Ogilvie, eldest son of the first Earl of Airlie, on which deed of feudal vengeance the fine old Scottish ballad called The Bonnie House of Airlie is founded:—

"DOWGALL,—I mynd, God willing, to lift from thir the morrow, and therefor ye shall meitt me the morrow at nicht at Stronarnot, in Strathardill: and caus bring alonges with you the haill nolt and shiepe that ye have fundine perteineing to my lord Ogilbie. As for the horse and mearis that ye have gottine perteining to him, ye shall not faill to direct thame home to the Stranemoor. I desyre not that they be in our way at all, and to send thame the neirest way home. And albeit ye shoulde be the langer in followeing me, yeit ye shall not faill to stay and demolishe my lord Ogilbies hous of Forthar. Sic how ye can cast off the irone yeattis and windowis, and tak doun the rooff: and if ye find it will be langsome, ye shall fyre it weill, that so it may be destroyed. Bot you neid not to latt know that ye have directions from me to fyir it: only ye may say that ye have warrand to demoleishe it, and that, to mak the work short, ye will fyr it. Iff ye mak any stay for doeing of this, send forward the goodis. So referring this to your cair, I rest, your freynd, ARGYLL."

The postscript is holograph of the marquis:—

"You shall heawe for your pains of that beis send hame. You shall delyver bak to Rob Griver such of his goods as are not sufficient for present use, and thir presentis shall be your warrand. ARGYLL.
"For Dowgall Campbell, fiar of Inverawe."

The original of the above letter is preserved at Inverawe, and dated July, 1640, the season which corresponds with the opening lines of the ballad:—

"It fell on a day, a bonnie simmer day,
When the leaves were green and yellow."

And one of the verses commemorates how "Dowgall" carried out but too completely the furtive and confidential orders he had received from his lord:—

"Clouds o' smoke and flames sae hie
    Soon left the wa's but barely;
And she laid her doon on that hill to die
    When she saw the burnin' o' Airlie."

HUGH A. KENNEDY.

COLLEGIATE OR SCHOLASTIC BIOGRAPHIES.—I should be glad if any reader could add to the following list:—

Cooper (C. H. and T.). Athenæ Cantabrigienses. Vols. i. ii., 1500-1609. Camb., 1858-61, 8vo.
Graduati Cantabrigienses, MDCLIX.—MDCCCXXIII. Cantab., 1823, 8vo.
Romilly (J.). Graduati Cantabrigienses, MDCCLX.—MDCCCLVI. Cantab., 1856, 8vo.
Todd (J. H.). Catalogue of Graduates who have proceeded to Degrees in the University of Dublin, from the earliest recorded Commencements to July, 1866. With Supplement to December 16, 1868. Dubl., 1869, 8vo.
Taylor (W. B. S.). History of the University of Dublin. With Biographical Notices of many Eminent Men educated therein. Lond., 1845, 8vo.

Ward (J.). The Lives of the Professors of Gresham College. Lond., 1740, folio.

Smith (Rev. J. Finch). The Admission Register of the Manchester School. With some Notices of the more distinguished Scholars. A D. 1730—1837. Printed for the Chetham Society, 1866-74, 4 vols., 4to.

Wood (Anthony à). Athenæ Oxonienses. To which are added the Fasti. New Edition, with Additions and a Continuation by Philip Bliss. Lond., 1813, 4to., 4 vols.

Munk (Wm.). The Roll of the Royal College of Physicians of London, 1518—1800. Lond., 1861, 8vo., 2 vols.

Knight (Samuel). The Life of Dr. John Colet, Dean of St. Paul's, and Founder of St. Paul's School. With an Appendix containing some Account of the Masters and more eminent Scholars of that Foundation. New Edition. Oxford, 1823, 8vo.

List of the Queen's Scholars of St. Peter's College, Westminster, admitted to that Foundation since 1663. Lond., 1852, 8vo.

C. W. SUTTON.

7, Moss Grove Terrace, Brooks' Bar, Manchester.

A BALL AT DUBLIN CASTLE IN THE REIGN OF GEORGE II.—The following is an extract from a letter of Benjamin Victor to Colley Cibber, dated Dublin, Nov. 17, 1748, published in the *History of the Theatres of London and Dublin*, by the former writer, London, 1761 :—

"Nothing within the memory of the oldest Courtier living ever equalled the Taste and Splendor of the Supper-Room at the Castle on the Birth Night. The Ball was in the new Room design'd by Lord Chesterfield,* which is allowed to be very magnificent. After the Dancing was over, the Company retired to an Apartment form'd like a long Gallery, where as you pass'd slowly through, you stopp'd by the Way at Shops elegantly form'd, where was cold Eating, and all Sorts of Wines and Sweetmeats ; and the whole most beautifully disposed by transparent Paintings, through which a Shade was cast like Moon-light. Flutes and other soft Instruments were playing all the while, but, like the Candles, unseen. At each End of the long Building were placed Fountains of Lavender Water constantly playing, that diffused a most grateful Odour through this amazing Fairy Scene, which certainly surpass'd every Thing of the Kind in Spencer ; as it proved not only a fine Feast for the Imagination, but, after the Dream, for our Senses also, by the excellent Substantials at the Sideboards."

H. W. S.

GRAY, THE POET, ON THIRLMERE.—In Gray's *Diary*, under date October 8, 1769, he writes :—

"Came to the foot of Helvellyn, along which runs an excellent road, looking down from a little height on Lee's-water (called also Thirl-meer, or Wiborn-water), and soon descending on its margin. The lake from its depth looks black (though really as clear as glass), and from the gloom of the vast crags that scowl over it. It is narrow and about three miles long, resembling a river in its course. Little twinkling torrents hurry down the rocks to join it, with not a bush to overshadow them or cover their march. All is rock and rugged grass, where the very brow, which lies so near your way that not half the height of Helvellyn can be seen."

In a *Descriptive Tour and Guide to the Lakes, Caves, Mountains, &c., in Cumberland, Westmore-*

* Lord Lieutenant 1745-46.

land, Lancashire, &c., by John Housman, Esq., published at Carlisle in 1814, the author writes of Leathes-water, or Thirlmere Lake, while in the map accompanying the engraver calls it Thurlmere.
W. N. STRANGEWAYS.

[See 5th S. viii. 469 ; ix. 34, 79.]

A COINCIDENCE.—
"To M. Isidore Geoffrey St. Hilaire belongs the credit of having first induced his countrymen to try horseflesh, concerning which innovation Alphonse Karr remarked, that since the horse had so long carried man it was but fair that now man should carry the horse."—*Standard*, April 23, 1878.

Wit generally suffers by translation, and Alphonse Karr is so neat in his good things that I am curious to see his words, if any correspondent will cite or refer to them. The thought is not new.

"Bene me admonuit domina mea. In prospectu habuimus ursinæ frustum, de quo cum imprudens Scintilla gustasset, pœne intestina sua vomuit. Ego contra plus libram comedi, nam ipsum aprum sapiebat. Et si, inquam, ursus homuncionem comest, quanto magis homuncio debet ursum comesse."—Pet. Arbitri, *Satyricon*, c. lxvi., p. 156, ed. Anton, Lipsiæ, 1781.

H. B. C.

U.U. Club.

HOT CROSS BUNS.—Mr. Cuming's paper at the Brit. Arch. Assoc.† attributes these sacred cross-notched cakes to Greek sculpture. The decree of Canopus in honour of the deceased young princess Berenice orders sacred cakes to be given to the virgins at the annual processions in her honour. Jewish sacred Sabbath loaves (chollo) חלב are of oval form, with intertwined serpent - forms of dough at top and caraway seeds sprinkled thereon. A gigantic one is used abroad at circumcision breakfasts. The double three harder Passover biscuits at the home night services are notched or perforated with one, two, and three holes, to mark their position on the bitter-herb central plate. Was the *cross* originally the Egyptian life-mark Tau, transferred by the Christians to their new faith ? I know a still living pious Jew, who got up a (Scandinav.) Christmas tree, which he named a Maccabee lights tree, so as to give his children the fashionable winter diversion without violating his scruples of conscience.
S. M. DRACH.

HUNTINGDON IN 1807.—"At this period it was remarkable at Huntingdon that there were four churchyards, three steeples, two churches, and but one clergyman" (*Gent. Mag.*, 1807, p. 312).
MACKENZIE E. C. WALCOTT.

RUE.—The process of the degradation of speech is curiously illustrated in the sale of rue by the small grocers and herbalists. This herb of grace is constantly advertised as "Herby grass."
GWAVAS.

† *Times*, April 18, 1878.

CHAUCER AND LYDGATE FRAGMENTS (*ante*, p. 342.)—The heading to this paper should have been "Early English Scraps from Mr. Huth's MS. of Chaucer and Lydgate Fragments, &c."

Queries.

[We must request correspondents desiring information on family matters of only private interest, to affix their names and addresses to their queries, in order that the answers may be addressed to them direct.]

A RESIDENCE FOR ROYALTY IN IRELAND.—On the property of Earl Fitzwilliam in co. Kildare, Ireland, are the ruins of an unfinished mansion, built of Dutch bricks, which the Earl of Strafford, when Viceroy of Ireland, commenced for the purpose of its becoming the permanent residence of some member of the royal family, and I am told that he impressed the policy of this arrangement on Charles I. Can any one refer me to any letter or document left by the great and unfortunate Strafford in which, with such remarkable prescience, he advised a royal residence in Ireland?

ALFRED GATTY, D.D.

"FORTITER ET SUAVITER."—I have long been in search of this proverbial expression, and think that I have at last discovered it in the Book of Wisdom (viii. 1). The Vulgate translates the verse thus : "Attingit ergo a fine usque ad finem *fortiter, et disponit omnia suaviter.*" Can any of your correspondents suggest a more likely origin?

C. T. RAMAGE.

SCLAVONIC OR SLAVONIC.—Which of these two appellations is the more correct? Sclavonic seems to sever its connexion in English with that disgraceful original meaning of a slave, whilst Slavonic (if retraced to the Russian word *slava* = glory, or *slovo* = speech) points to a glorious nation, or well spoken of race. In German the distinction is made between *sclavisch* = slavish and *slawisch* = Slavonic, whilst in French no such distinction of the root-word is found, and a difference appears only in the termination, viz. *esclave* = slave, *Esclavon* = Slavonic. Lastly, is it not contrary to the formation of English nouns to introduce the new appellation "Slav" instead of "Slavonian"?

H. KREBS.
Oxford.

COL. ALURED, THE REGICIDE.—Do his descendants yet exist? If not, with whom did they fail? His daughter (heiress?) Jane married William Pincke, "Citizen and Drugster of London," second son of Henry Pincke, or Pinke, of Kempshott, Hants, and grand-nephew of Dr. Robert Pinke, Warden of New College, and Vice-Chancellor at Oxford *temp.* Charles I. The surviving issue of this marriage—as per a monumental tablet—was two sons and four daughters. A descendant,

probably grandson, Thomas Alured Pincke, of Kent, quartered the arms of Alured of Heydon with those of Pincke of Kempshott. I should be obliged for information respecting the descendants of William Pincke and Jane Alured.

W. D. PINK.
Leigh, Lancashire.

THE WELSH AP SHENKIN AND THE IRISH FAMILY OF SHINKWIN.—I should be very much obliged if any one would enable me to trace the connexion between these two families. The latter is now resident in Florence, and their arms are—Azure, between three escallop shells or, on a fess argent, a lion's head gules. Crest : Out of a ducal coronet a lion's head.

W. M. M.

THE NAMES OF THE MISTLETOE.—J. St. Hilaire, in his *Plantes de France*, gives *gillon* and *verquet* as names of the mistletoe. What is their etymological explanation?

W. G. PIPER.

RICHARD WILSON'S "BATHERS."—Can any one tell me whether a picture by Richard Wilson—a landscape with three great trees on the right-hand side, and one on the left, has been engraved? There is a pool with dark shadow on the right, and three men standing in the centre, one undressing, another holding a fishing-rod. There is a weeping willow overhanging the water, between the second and third trees.

J. C. J.

THE STATES PRISON AT THE HAGUE.—In a small room of the States Prison at the Hague, on the walls of which are many devices and inscriptions similar to those in the Beauchamp Tower of the Tower of London, is a well-executed and accurate carving of the bear and ragged staff, the cognizance of the Dudleys, and almost identical with that carved by Lord Guildford Dudley in the Tower. Was any member of this great house ever imprisoned by the Dutch, to account for the appearance of so celebrated an English device in the prison at the Hague?

J. F. B.

THE YOKI.—In a leading article of the *Daily News* the following words appeared :—
"Persons in the enjoyment of leisure sit on board and contemplate the floats at the end of their lines as devoutly as the Yoki stares at the fixed point which is the centre of his reverie."

What is the Yoki? Is the word a mistake for Goghi?

W. S. R.

THE FAMILY OF GOLDING OF COLSTON BASSET. —Can any reader supply information with regard to this family? A pedigree of the family appeared in the *Gentleman's Magazine* for the year 1795, p. 284. Edward Golding and John his son were Capuchin friars at Rouen during the Commonwealth. Is it possible to find further particulars about them?

C. E. D.

THE AMERICAN ROBIN.—To what bird is the name robin given in the United States? Our red-breast is, I believe, unknown there. Longfellow, in his recently published poem *Kéramos*, has the following lines :—

" The wind blows east, the wind blows west ;
The *blue* eggs in the robin's nest
Will soon have wings and beak and breast,
And flutter and fly away."

The European robin has white eggs with brown spots.   J. DIXON.

BIOGRAPHICAL PARTICULARS WANTED.—Can any of the readers of " N. & Q." kindly *write me direct* any particulars respecting :—

Roger Clopton, M.A., Rector of Downham, I. of Ely, 1661. Wanted his pedigree.

Messenger Mouncey (Dr.).

Dr. Hutton, Dean of York, 1567. Pedigree.

Nicholas Felton, Bishop of Ely, 1619. Whom did he marry? Pedigree. Had he a son Nicholas?

Robert Westfield, D.D., Bishop of Bristol, 1644. Any particulars.

Penie, Dr., Master of Peterhouse, 1554? Pedigree.

Wren—Matthew, Bishop of Ely, 1638 ; Francis? Pedigrees.

John Nowell, Rector of Downham, I. of Ely, 1640. Was he a son of the Dean Nowell?

The smallest information respecting any of the above will be thankfully received by

K. H. SMITH (Clk.).

The Cambridge Road, Ely.

"BOLSHUNS."—A few days ago a friend of mine was sitting in her room when her maid came in and said : " Oh, please, ma'am, I have found a blackbird's nest in the garden, and there are three *bolshuns* in it." My friend, not knowing what *bolshuns* were, was informed that they were eggs just on the point of being hatched. Can anybody tell me the etymology of this word, and the correct spelling of it? The maid is a Northamptonshire woman. Is it a Northamptonshire word?

J. B. WILSON.

St. Helen's Rectory, Worcester.

EASTER SUNDAY ON ST. MARK'S DAY.—I have seen a French prophecy which says the end of the world will come when Easter Sunday falls on St. Mark's Day. This will be the case in 1886. When did it last happen? I subjoin the prophecy :—

" Quand Georges Dieu crucifiera,
Et Marc le suscitera,
Et Jean le portera,
La fin du monde arrivera."

The third allusion is to Corpus Christi Day. Is the date of the prophecy known?   HADJI.

CLIPPING THE CHURCHES.—Brand gives an account of this curious custom (Bohn, 1849, vol. i.

p. 181). Can any of your readers tell me how the custom originated, and when the ceremony was last performed at Birmingham?   W. S. RANDALL.

[See Dyer's *British Popular Customs*, Bell & Son.]

GEN. SIR JOHN GUNNING.—Information wanted as to the date of his birth. He was son of John and Hon. Bridget Gunning, and brother of the celebrated beauties.

RICHARD SHELLEY, son of Sir John Shelley third baronet, married a lady named Fleetwood. Who was she?   HASTINGS C. DENT.

THE REV. GEORGE WICKHAM, CIRCA 1720.—On a gravestone in the chancel of Badgworth Church, Somerset, is an inscription to the Rev. George Wickham, " Rector of this parish near Fifty years, who died July 9th, 1720, aged 73." Can you supply me with any information as to his parentage? From a search in the diocesan registry at Wells I find that he was ordained March 3, 1671, and instituted to the living of Badgworth May 9, 1672, on the presentation of John Prowse, Esq., but the register supplies no further particulars. His will was proved in the Wells Probate Court July 30, 1720, and is sealed with Arg., a chev. sa. between three roses. Calculating his age at the date of his death he would have been born in 1647. Also I should be glad to be supplied with the like information as to Thomas Wickham, his successor, who was instituted to the same living Nov. 22, 1720, on the presentation of Abigail Prowse, guardian of Thomas Prowse, and who died in 1754.   EDWARD FRY WADE.

Axbridge, Somerset.

FLORAL CHIEF RENTS.—I shall be glad of notices of any. I can mention two.

1. A damask rose is payable, by deed dated in 1636, to the mayor of Leicester for the time being, on the feast day of St. John the Baptist, by the owner of land upon which now stands the " Crown and Thistle " Inn, Loseby Lane, Leicester.

2. A chief rent in the form of a garland of flowers (which must contain three roses) is sent every year by the owner of Rushy-field, in the parish of Woodhouse, Leicestershire, to the lord of the manor residing at Beaumanor Park. This garland is hung in the hall at Beaumanor, and there remains until replaced by the fresh garland of the succeeding year.

THOMAS NORTH, F.S.A.

FOLEY'S " ENGLISH-IRISH DICTIONARY."—*An English-Irish Dictionary.* By Daniel Foley, B.D., Prebendary of Kilbragh, Cashel, and Professor of Irish in the University of Dublin. Dublin, 1855. From what part of Ireland was Foley, and consequently what dialect of the language is chiefly represented in the above-named useful vocabulary?

D. F.

Hammersmith.

Is it known in which house he lived ? J. T. SMITH
and Peter Cunningham give no information.

The Athenæum, Liverpool. E. S. N.

"THE NEW GROUND, MOORFIELDS."—I am desirous of finding out if any record is extant of burials in "The New Ground, Moorfields." I have before me a copy of the will of Christopher Thomlinson, made 1678, proved 1681 ; in it he desires to be buried in the ground above mentioned. JAMES ROBERTS BROWN.

"IT IS THE INTRODUCTION OF THE THIN END OF THE WEDGE."—What is the source or earliest use of this expression? ED. MARSHALL.

MERCHANTS THROUGH EIGHT GENERATIONS.— We have here a family (the Stirlings) who have been merchants since the end of the seventeenth century, through eight generations from father to son. Is this a unique commercial pedigree ? If it can be matched, I believe it must be among the Spanish or German Jews. M.
Glasgow.

EASTER DAY, EAST AND WEST.—Our first Sunday after Easter is Easter Day in the Eastern Church. How is this? Full moon was on the morning of April 17, three days before Easter Day in the West. Why is the Sunday after, ten days after the full moon, the Easter Day of the East ?
E. LEATON BLENKINSOPP.

"CYNTHIA; with the Tragical Account of the Unfortunate Loves of Almerin and Desdemona : being a Novel. Done by an English Hand. The Sixth Edition corrected. London : Printed for Eben. Tracy, at the Three Bibles on London Bridge." (Date erased.)
Who was the "English Hand," and what was the date of publication ? G. POTTER.

AUTHORS OF BOOKS WANTED.—
Is anything known regarding the authorship of the pieces named below ?—
The Poetical Duenna : a Comic Opera. Philadelphia, 1778. 8vo.
Occurrences of the Times; or, the Transactions of Four Days : a Dramatic Piece. [Boston, 1789.] 12mo.
The Politicians; or, a State of Things : a Drama. Philadelphia, 1798. 8vo.
Savonarola : a Drama. By J. C. M. Harrisburg, 1831.
The Maid of Midian : a Drama. Philadelphia, 1833.
12mo. A third edition of this drama was published in 1836.
David and Uriah : a Drama. Philadelphia, 1835. 12mo.
The Bride of Fort Edwards : a Drama. New York, 1839. 12mo.
Ormusd's Triumph : a Drama. New York, 1842. 12mo.
Rhodomanthus, &c. [Providence, Rhode Island] 1858. 12mo.
America : a Dramatic Poem. New York, 1863.
R. INGLIS.

(5th S. ix. 309.)

Your correspondent C. R. L. speaks of a miniature of King Charles I., measuring two inches by one and three-quarters, and says that the sentence of death had been passed upon king. It seems strange that, during the short interval between the sentence on the king and execution, Sir Peter Lely should have taken the likenesses of him. But however this may be, soon after the Restoration four somewhat similar miniatures of the king to those described by C. R. and two of Queen Henrietta, were painted. One of these is in the possession of Miss Whitmore Jones, of Chastleton House. It is beautiful, painted on copper. It is oval, and measures two inches by one and three-quarters. It represents the king with the order of St. George. It was found some years ago in a secret drawer of an old bureau in Chastleton House, in a small wooden box, which also contained eighteen separate paintings on talc of the same size and shape as the miniature, but with an aperture in each large enough to admit the king's head, and these, as they were placed one after the other on the miniature, were intended to represent the king in the different conditions of his life, from his coronation to his execution. The one which represents Bishop Juxon reading to him in prison makes the bishop look like a florid young man, and the others are not particularly well painted, and of course no proportion to the portrait of the king. Chastleton House is a grand old mansion, built in the early part of the reign of Charles I., and the parish of Chastleton adjoins that of Little Compton, which was the property and residence of Archbishop Juxon. An intimacy naturally existed between his family and his neighbours the Joneses, proprietors of the adjoining lands ; and as I. Juxon, the wife of Sir Charles Juxon, the nephew and heir of the archbishop, gave to Mr. J. Jones, the then proprietor of Chastleton, the Bible that Charles had on the scaffold, it is very probable that she also gave the miniature to him or on the family, and, being placed in a secret drawer became forgotten. The Bible is bound in brown leather, with the royal arms and small fleurs-de-lis and thistles and roses, and "C. R." stamped in gold on it. The date is 1629. The house of Bishop Juxon still exists, but the relics of King Charles which were said to exist there have now disappeared, and among the rest the scaffold and his favourite chair. J. W. LODOWICK

My brother, the Rev. John Rigaud, of Magdalen Coll., has here a miniature on copper of Charles and C. R. L. would confer a great favour by say where he found the fact stated that Sir Peter Lely took three such likenesses after the king was sentenced to death, and whether there are ·any particulars by which one of these copies might be identified. Dr. Routh, the late venerable President of Magdalen College, who died in his one hundredth year, was well known for his interest in the Stuarts. After his death his widow presented my brother with one of these box miniatures, which the old president always carried in his pocket. The miniature is on copper. The box is of silver; the size is exactly two and a half inches by two inches : the shape oval. There is a small bow on the top for a ribbon to wear it by round the neck. The king has on a black dress, with the ribbon of the Garter over it. The lace collar is carefully painted, and the first sight of the painting gives any one the impression that he is looking at a genuine and contemporaneous portrait of Charles. Unfortunately, Mrs. Routh could give no information as to the history of the miniature. My brother has shown it to more than one expert, and the conclusion come to was that it was not by Vandyck, as at first surmised, but by some pupil—perhaps by Dobson, "the English Vandyck," who died in 1646. Mr. Scharf, the Keeper of the National Portrait Gallery, "thought it probably a copy (perhaps a copy of a copy) of the Duke of Northumberland's picture at Sion House." He added that an original may have been taken out of the case, which was perhaps richly enamelled, and the present copy put in. Mr. Hogarth in the Haymarket also told my brother that he had seen two or three such box portraits. They were painted, he said, for the adherents of the king after his martyrdom. Mr. Hogarth said he knew of one copy in the possession of a Roman Catholic family at Manchester. He could not recall the name at the instant, but it was the same as the name of the college there (qy. Owens).

I should be very glad if anything I have said should help C. R. L., and still more so if anything he may learn should throw light on the box portrait which belonged to President Routh.

GIBBES RIGAUD.

18, Long Wall, Oxford.

SCOTT FAMILY: THE PARENTAGE OF ARCHBISHOP ROTHERHAM.

(5th S. vii. 89, 139, 158, 292, 330, 375, 416, 470, 490, 509 ; viii. 29, 79, 370, 389, 410 ; ix. 37.)

I have carefully examined the list of Archbishops of York (Cottonian MSS., Titus, A. xix., fo. 150) referred to by MR. EDWARD SCOTT. It appears to me to be in a hand coeval with Archbishop Rotherham, but is continued in another, quite distinct, in different ink, and of a very much later date. The original list merely speaks of the archbishop as "Thomas." The continuator adds,

"Roderam or Scote"; but this addition affords no evidence one way or the other, beyond showing doubt in the later writer's mind.

I was certainly under the impression that I had rigidly abstained from putting myself forward in any way as an authority ; and that, in every instance, I had simply printed extracts from original records, giving invariably exact references. At least the readers of "N. & Q." have before them ample materials, of the most incontrovertible character, from which they may draw deductions for themselves with regard to the inaccuracies called in question.

I am surprised that MR. SCOTT should imagine I had any intention of charging him with inserting the archbishop in the pedigree of Scott of Scotts' Hall without authority, because he himself in the first instance recited a long list of those persons upon whom he relied. And G., F.S.A., another correspondent, evidently looked upon it in the same light, for he speaks of them as a "cloud of witnesses called up by MR. SCOTT, who, like a multitude of counsellors, only seem to darken knowledge" (5th S. vii. 511).

MR. S. O. ADDY has apparently taken umbrage because I am inclined to ignore his very unimpartial notes. One side of a question is often considered good until the other is heard. MR. ADDY furnishes examples, to suit his own particular ideas, from a certain register, while an antiquary of great talent and experience sends me the following six entries from another :—

"Names taken from a list of those who received the first tonsure at the hands of Rigaud de Asserio, Bishop of Winchester, in 1321:—
    Radulfus de Overton, de Alresford.
    Rogerus de Clatford, de Andover.
    Robertus de Clatford, de eadem.
    Ricardus de Hyrtyng, de Havonte.
    Walterus de Molland, de Cheryton.
    Bartholomeus de Molend, de Chelmeston.'

He pertinently remarks in connexion with them :—"Ask if these theorists will explain which are their birthplaces, or can they venture to claim both? Overton is many miles distant from Alresford ; Clatford two miles from Andover ; Harting, I should think, was at least twelve or fourteen from Havant."

JAMES GREENSTREET.

The claims of the Kentish family of Scott to be connected with Rotherham, Archbishop of York, appear to be based by MR. JAMES R. SCOTT on rather indefinite grounds. To part of that gentleman's second suggestion, 5th S. vii. 330, I would reply :—
1. That the archbishop's first preferment was the rectory of Ripple, co. Worcester, not co. Kent, vide Nash's Worcestershire, ii. 299 : "Mag. Thomas Rotheram, S. Th. Bac., 12 July, 1461, Regist. Carp. f. 162 b ; successor appointed 11 Feb., 1465, ib. f. 192 a."
2. That the lands at Ash, Preston, Staple, and

Wingham were held by the archbishop in his official capacity as Provost of Wingham, from which circumstance no personal relationship with the Kentish Scotts can be inferred.

With regard to the third suggestion, I would remark that the archbishop bought Barnes Hall of Robt. Shatton on Feb. 7, 1477, and bequeathed it to the Scotts. If, then, Richard-a-Barne, who signs a Scotshall deed in 1473, be identical with Richard of Barnes Hall, we must make the assumption, for which there exists no evidence or even countenance, that the Scotts lived at Barnes Hall before the date of its purchase by the archbishop.

Again, the presence in Kent of John Rotheram, brother of the archbishop, may be due to the fact of his appointment as joint collector of customs at the port of Sandwich; see Fine Roll, 9 Edw. IV., No. 278, memb. 9, 10, 12. Probably in this way he was brought into contact with his future wife, who had in the eastern part of the county considerable properties; and these were bequeathed by John to his second son, George Rotherham. The latter is described in the numerous legal proceedings connected with these properties, at one time as a gentleman of Canterbury, and at another as resident at Someries. He was married twice : first to Johanna, dau. of Richard Lowell, by whom he had one child, Margaret, wife of John Crisp (*Originalia*, Ld. Treas. Rem.'s side of Excheq., 30 Hen. VIII., Rot. 10); secondly to Jane, widow of Thomas Astry, by whom George left no issue (see her will, proved at Bedford 1546). The Kentish properties appear to have gone to the Crisps. And the pedigrees unanimously concur in assigning to this George Rotherham a bastard son, who was also called George Rotherham; and, from the latter's obtaining by purchase extensive grants of possessions belonging to the suppressed religious houses (*Originalia*, 5 Par. Rot. 94, 1 Marie), we may infer that his father must have made large provision for him, either by will, which has not yet been discovered, or otherwise. This illegitimate George had numerous descendants, the elder line of whom was seated at Farley, near Luton, for several generations; and I may mention that none of the wills, patent or claus rolls, inquisitions p.m., &c., of which there are a great many, contain the least suggestion of any connexion with the Scotts either of Barnes Hall or Kent, and uniformly employ the surname Rotherham. This assertion is true with regard to the documents connected with the line also of the archbishop's elder nephew, Sir Thomas Rotherham ; and similarly no document (apart from St. George's impudently fraudulent pedigree) belonging to the Scotts of Barnes Hall conveys even the feeblest intimation of any connexion with the Bedfordshire Rotherhams or Kentish Scotts.

W. ROTHERHAM.

(*To be continued.*)

"THE PASTON LETTERS" (5th S. ix. 205, 326, 350.)—I venture to point out that both MR. GAIRDNER and S. H. A. H. are somewhat in error in their account of Isabel Leghe. She was the only daughter of John Harvye, of Thurley, co. Beds, Esq., by Agnes, daughter of Nicholas Morley, of Glynde, co. Sussex. The Inquisition p.m. of John Legh her husband (Chancery Inquis. p.m. 19 Hen. VII. No. 7) recites a charter of Aug. 20, 8 Hen. VII. (probably his marriage settlement), by which divers lands in Surrey were by him conveyed to Isabella Harvy, daughter of John Harvy, Esq., deceased, and Agnes, wife of John Isted, formerly wife of John Harvy. In 1493, therefore, this Agnes was the wife of John Isted. The marriage of Annis, daughter of Nicolas Morley of Glynde, with John Isley of Sundridge and remarriage with Sir John Paston are given in a pedigree of Isley (*Top. and Gen.*, vol. iii. p. 196). John Isley, as appears by his monument in Sundridge Church, died Jan. 8, 1484 (*id.*, p. 197), so that, if she were the same person, he must have been her second husband, John Isted her third, and Sir John Paston her fourth.

The inscription on the monument of Isabel Leghe in Addington Church proves her, as S. H. A. H. says, to have been the daughter of Agnes by John Harvy, besides which she quarters the arms of Nernuit and Buckland, both quarterings of the Harvy family, which were afterwards assumed by the Leighs of Addington. She is not mentioned in her brother Sir George Harvy's will, which is dated April 8, 1520, and was proved on May 8, 1522 (P.C.C., 3, Ayloffe), nor is she the Elizabeth referred to therein. He mentions "Margaret Smarte" (she was his illegitimate daughter), "wife of William Smart ; her son Gerard" (he afterwards took the name of Harvy, and was M.P. for Bedford, 1 Ed. VI.) ; "one John Harvey, eldest son of said William ; Elizabeth Atclyff, wife of William Atclyffe, suster to said 'George.'" This George clearly does not refer to himself, and as no George has been mentioned before, it is doubtless an error in the copyist. Had Isabel Leghe married again, some notice of it would surely have appeared on the monument at Addington. Her eldest daughter, Ann Legh, married Thomas Atcliff, some relation probably of William Atcliff mentioned above. Collins (*Peerage*, iv. 321), confounding her with her daughter, says that she first married Thomas Atcliff, secondly John Leigh, Esq.

The date of John Legh's death, as given on the monument at Addington, is MCCCCCIX., but that this is an error is clear from the inquisition upon his death, which was taken at Southwark on Feb. 12, 19 Hen. VII. (1504), and which states that he died on April 24, 18 Hen. VII. (1503), leaving Isabella his wife surviving. The two statements made by Blomefield, *Hist. of Norfolk* (vol. v. p. 489, and vol. viii. p. 99), viz., that "Sir Thomas Paston, fifth son of Sir William Paston, *temp.* Hen. VIII., married Anne, daughter and co-heir of Sir John Leigh, of Addington in Surrey," and again, "Sir Edward Paston, son and heir of Sir Thomas Paston by Agnes, daughter and heir of Sir John Leigh, of Addington in Surrey," are I am satisfied, from a careful investigation into the pedigree of Leigh of Addington, void of foundation, and arise probably out of some confusion as to this connexion between Agnes Paston and Isabel Legh.   G. L. G.

"EVERY MAN HAS HIS PRICE" (5th S. ix. 328.) —JAYDEE, after remarking that "this cynical assertion is attributed to Sir Robert Walpole," observes that Mr. Ewald, in his recent life of Walpole, throws out the suggestion that that statesman may have said, pointing to his supporters in the House of Commons, "All *these* men have their price," and adds that Mr. Lecky makes the same suggestion. The opinions of those authors might have been reproduced by JAYDEE with greater correctness. Mr. Ewald, instead of suggesting that Walpole may have said, "All *these* men have their price," makes the positive assertion that he did say so. Instead of limiting Walpole's remark to his own supporters, Mr. Ewald makes it include the hireling members of the Opposition. Mr. Lecky is equally emphatic in asserting that Walpole's observation on "a group of members" has been turned into the general assertion quoted by JAYDEE. These gentlemen are right; the popular expression is a popular error, often corrected, but never completely rooted out. In West Cornwall the tradition runs that Walpole, after saying, "All *these* men have their price," added the solitary exception, "except the little Cornish baronet." The Cornishman thus honoured was Sir John St. Aubyn, the third baronet, who represented the county in Parliament from 1722 to 1744. He was an active member of the band of "patriots." Many of his speeches in the House in opposition to Walpole's policy are printed in the early volumes of the *Gentleman's Magazine*, and on Walpole's fall the little Cornish baronet was a member of the committee appointed to inquire into the minister's conduct.

W. P. COURTNEY.

15, Queen Anne's Gate.

It would appear not only that there is no evidence that Sir Robert Walpole thought or said this, but that there is reasonable evidence that he did not. Coxe, in his *Memoirs of Sir Robert Walpole* (1798, 4to., i. 757), says, on the authority of Lord Orford and Lord John Cavendish, that speaking of pretended patriots who had interested views for themselves or for their relatives, that he despised their flowery oratory, and said of them, "All those men have their price." Those who

quoted his saying chose to leave out the defining word "those." But Walpole well knew that all men were not to be bought—not even all members of Parliament, for he said of one of his most consistent opponents, "I will not say who is corrupt, but I will say who is not, and that is Shippen"; and this was after he had ceased to be minister.

EDWARD SOLLY.

A common compliment, though not a very neat one, is to use this phrase with the addition, "except So-and-so." Early in this century a prime minister expressed the exception in favour of Colonel Gore-Langton.   TREGEAGLE.

A TURNPIKE ACT MARRIAGE (5th S. ix. 267, 332.)—I must ask to supplement my own remarks, and to correct my own errors. This expression doubtless referred to the marriage of the Warden of Wadham, and Mr. Cox, in his *Recollections of Oxford*, has given his authority to the story of the clause added to a Turnpike Bill. I may add that this story is almost universally believed; but yet I must add further that there is *not a word of truth in it.* If reference be made to an octavo volume called—

"Enactments in Parliament. | Specially concerning | the Universities of Oxford and Cambridge. | Collected and Arranged by the Rev. John Griffiths, M A , Keeper of the Archives of the University of Oxford. Clarendon Press, 1869"

—it will there be found at p. 121 that "46 Geo. III. cap. cxlvii." is "an Act for enabling a married person to hold and enjoy the office of Warden of Wadham College in the University of Oxford." So my mistakes will be—1st. That there was not a special Act, but a clause tacked on to a Turnpike Bill. 2nd. That Dr. Tournay was instrumental in obtaining it. It was passed in 1806, just after Tournay had been made warden; but Dr. John Wills, who died warden in 1806, was the acting warden in the matter. 3rd. That Jesus College was included in the same Parliamentary authority as Wadham College.

In the time of Dr. James Gerard, who was warden before Wills, an effort was made to get a special Act for the two colleges; but the Bill was set aside because the two were in one Bill. After an interval of some years the special Act of 46 Geo. III. was obtained for Wadham alone; and I find, in the vol. of enactments, no mention of any Act releasing the principals of Jesus College from their disability.   GIBBES RIGAUD.

18, Long Wall, Oxford.

JONATHAN BOUCHER'S "GLOSSARY OF ARCHAIC WORDS" (5th S. ix. 68, 311.)—MR. STEVENS's communication has interested me very much. I was a subscriber to the work to which I suppose he alludes, but I never received more, I believe, than two numbers, ending "Blade." To my great dis-

duction printed subsequently, I imagine, have neither title-page nor date, nor anything to determine the year in which they were published. I have often wondered whether the materials collected by Mr. Boucher had been published in any other form, or incorporated in any other work, and had an extreme desire to learn what had become of them. I have a very lively impression that when the publication was interrupted by the author's death, I saw a notice by the publishers that the work was completed for the press, and would be continued under the superintendence of a competent editor. The Rev. Joseph Hunter, the well-known historian of Hallamshire, was, I think, the intended editor ; than which nothing more satisfactory could have been arranged. But I never heard anything more about the original publication or the intended continuation. If MR. STEVENS, or any other correspondent, could give the readers of " N. & Q." some further information as to the existence and state of the materials or their ultimate fate, he would confer on me, and probably on many of your readers, a great gratification, and a considerable advantage possibly on the cause of English archaic literature.   S. R.

ROBERT PALTOCK (5th S. ix. 186.)—MR. CROSSLEY, in his note to " N. & Q." (1st S. x. 712), gave satisfactory proof of Paltock's authorship of *Peter Wilkins*, and promised to identify another work by the same hand in a future communication, which he failed to do. At the period I had a similar intention of attributing to him another fiction entitled *Memoirs of the Life of Parnese*, but standing aside for your esteemed correspondent, I put my note into the volume from whence I have just disinterred it, seeing that the subject has again turned up. The full title to this second book of mine has not yet been given in " N. & Q." It is, *Memoirs of the Life of Parnese, a Spanish Lady*, translated from the Spanish by R. P., Gent. (Lond., Owen, 1751), which from a general similarity in style, initials, and plate seems to be a second publication of this mysterious author. As in *Peter Wilkins*, this last is dedicated to a lady, Mrs. F. Mitchell, in a like complimentary style, showing in both the gallantry of the writer in resting the success of his novels upon the assurance that, if the smiles of the sex are accorded him, " nothing so common as a frown can possibly be exacted." But I have still another string to my bow, and submit that the following also comes from " Clement's Inn " :—

"Virtue Triumphant and Pride Abased in the Humorous History of Dicky Gotham and Doll Clod. Digested from Ancient Tractates and the Records of those Admirable Families now Extant at Addle Hall in Nottinghamshire. By R. P., Biographer." 2 vols., 1753.

if you like.   J

KING ALARIC'S BURIAL (5th S. ix. 248, 3 The poem of Count von Platen is not quite s known in England as MR. FRASER RAE su] but he has done excellent service to English i by directing attention to it. From my bec acquainted with it in *Der Poetischer Hausse* Wolff (Leipzig, 1847), I have enjoyed it, most graphic picture of the event. Some ago, when great things had been found at and there was an allusion to the possibility covering the treasure buried with Alari translation appended was made. It is inc with trifling variations, in a volume of *Ecl Old Cumberland*, Carlisle, 1876 :—

" *The Grave in the Busento.*

From the German of August von Platen.

On Busento nightly whisper by Cosenza hollow d
And in eddies, there re-echoing, come answers fr
  surges,
As up the stream and down the stream shades o
  Goths are sweeping,
Who for their people's bravest—best—for Ala
  weeping.
All too early, far from their own land, here they
  must bind him
O'er whose fair shoulders but so late youth's brig
  flowed behind him.
On Busento's shore they rank themselves, in en
  burning,
Into a channel newly dug the waters swiftly turn
And far below the emptied depths the earth they
  deeper,
And on his steed, in armour full, they sink the
  sleeper.
Then o'er his corpse, his state, his wealth, th
  restored upheaping,
For water-growths to root, and hold the hero's g
  keeping ;
Turned back again, the stream o'erflowed the
  earth-entombing,—
Rushed mightily to their own bed Busento's
  foaming.
Then sang the men a chorus deep—' Sleep, in t
  glory !
No greed of Rome shall spoil thy grave, or e
  fane its story ! '
With the song of warrior praise from the Got
  rebounding,
Roll, ever roll ! Busento waves, from sea to sea
  ing."
                                                            M
Cumberland.

"As " (5th S. ix. 188, 256, 275.)—It is strange that this expression should be brar G. L. G. as a vulgarism of middle-class 1 and at the same time be a common idiom classical languages. That this is the case i every tyro knows : take the construction, (in Thucydides, Σικελίας περίπλους ἐσ ὀκτὼ ἡμερῶν = The voyage round Sicily i about eight days, where ὡς (= as it were) means *about* or *thereabout*, for ὡς with numerals (see Liddell and Scott, *sub voce*, p. 1621) marks that they are to be taken only as a *round* number, *about* nearly, like Latin *quasi*, or *admodum*; ἀπέθανον ὡς πεντακόσιοι, Xen.; also ὡς πέντε μάλιστα, Herodotus, vii. 30 = as it were, five at most, about five at most, five or thereabout. And so we would render HERMENTRUDE'S sentences by "thereabout." The meaning, for instance, of the last would be "Yesterday or thereabout." So that on the whole I would that (*pace* G. L. G.), where the genius of the Greek language and the idiom of our mother tongue coincide, such expressions, however Miltonian and middle-class, were more often heard in the retirement of a Gloucestershire parsonage.   F. S.

I have certainly never heard "which his" for "whose" in the impossible connexion suggested by HERMENTRUDE, viz. as an interrogatory, but very often in such a sentence as the following, "He lived with a gent ' which his ' name were So-and-so." I am afraid that exception is taken to my use of the words "middle-class English"; it is too wide a term, but I employed it for want of a better. I have often heard among the upper classes the outrage upon grammar mentioned by HERMENTRUDE, or a question like the following put to a shopman, "What ' are ' the price of these?" The English of the upper classes is often ungrammatical, that of the lower classes provincial, but the middle class have a language of their own. The type that I had in my mind is to be seen to perfection at Margate or at so-called " watering " places in the month of August. With them the doctor is the " medical man "; they " ride " in carriages, and don't walk but " promenade "; they pronounce the second word in " piano-forte " as a monosyllable; the words " elegant" and " genteel" are for ever on their lips; they use long words of the meaning of which they are ignorant, *e.g.* I heard the following from a retired tradesman at a board of guardians: " The water in the well," he said, " was full of 'organized' matter," meaning, of course, " organic."

In face of the instances of the use of the word "as" given by HERMENTRUDE (*ante*, p. 256), and of the fact that in a letter from the Hon. Mrs. Boscawen, dated July 8, 1788, I find " He was to be at Badminton ' as ' yesterday," I ought perhaps somewhat to modify my former remarks. This use of the word has, however, I am satisfied, disappeared from good English ; it is redundant and inexpressive, and, if not positively wrong, is as disagreeable to listen to as the omission of the *h* in the word " humble " which one sometimes hears even from educated lips.   G. L. G.

RHODES FAMILY (5th S. ix. 208.)—The Rodes family of Horbury claim descent from the eldest son of Judge Rodes. He was disinherited. Great Houghton in Yorkshire and Barlborough in Derbyshire are the two parishes in which BARBATUS will find the good old Puritan family of Rhodes seated in the centuries he mentions. In the times of careless spelling the *h* was often used and as often omitted, but in the last century the name had settled into Rhodes. The present name De Rodes has been assumed by a gentleman who by female descent inherited the blood and part of the estates of Rhodes, and who has ventured to record in connexion with the name some allusion to the Greek island, which never yet was named without the aspirate.   GWAVAS.

Entries relating to this family occur in our parish registers (which commence in 1574) from 1586 to the present time.   S. M.
Calverley, near Leeds.

A family of this name was settled at Hipperholme, near Halifax, three centuries ago, as shown by the church registers ; and six centuries ago as shown by the manor rolls.
    J. HORSFALL TURNER.
Idel, Leeds.

SAINTE-BEUVE ON BOSSUET (5th S. ix. 328.)—L. H. T. should consult the *Causeries du Lundi*, not the *Nouveaux Lundis*. At the end of the eleventh volume he will find a copious index. One of the articles on Bossuet will be found in the twelfth volume. Of Bossuet Sainte-Beuve says, " il n'avait pas d'esprit "; of Bourdaloue, " c'est Despréaux en prose."   L. A. R.
Athenæum.

THE HEIR OF JOHN, LORD WENLOCK (5th S. viii. 462.)—In the matter of Lord Wenlock's lands more was done to strengthen the title of Archbishop Rotherham. In 1488 John Cornwall, Esquire, natural son of Sir John Cornwall, K.G., Lord Fanhope,* by writings under seal released to Thomas, Archbishop of York, and William Skelton, clerk, all his right, title, and demand, which he had or might have in the manor of Grethampstede Someris, in the parish of Luton, &c., in the counties of Bedford and Hertford (the precise lands released and quit-claimed by the two Lawleys), which were of John, late Lord Wenlock, or of any other to his use : with warranty against the Abbot of Westminster and his successors. Two writings were brought on May 17, 3 Hen. VII.

* Dugdale, who is followed by Beltz in *Memorials of the Order of the Garter*, says that he died on the *first day* of December (*Baronage*), although his will had before been mentioned as made Dec. 10, 1443. The date of decease should be Dec. 11, 1443, as found by the inquisition taken at Ampthill, though that taken for the county of Cornwall gives Dec. 10, 1443 (22 Hen. VI. No. 21). Sir John Cornwall's will was proved at his manor of Ampthill, January 6, 1443-4 (Reg. Stafford and Kempe, fo. 119).

(1488), by John Cornwall to the Court of Common Pleas for inrolment and acknowledged to be his deed (factum suum). Both these are of this date and are exactly alike, except that, in the first, the greeting clause has, " Johannes Cor[n]wall, Armiger, bastardus filius Johannis Cornwall, Militis, nuper domini Fawnhope"; and, in the second, "Johannes Cornwall Armiger" without other addition (De Banco Roll, Easter, 3 Hen. VII. *Deeds inrolled*).   JOHN A. C. VINCENT.

AN OLD BOOK OF TREATISES ON AGRICULTURE (5ᵗʰ S. ix. 208.)—The prices of several editions of two of the works in question are stated by Lowndes, *Bibl. Man.*, "Fitzherbert." But it does not appear that the editions, as contained in the volume which forms the subject of the query, are priced. The following notice of Fitzherbert's *Boke of Husbandrie*, in J. Donaldson's *Agricultural Biography from 1480 to the Present Time*, shows the position of this work in the literature of agriculture :—

" Our lengthy notice and quotations from Fitzherbert's book are intended to show the reader a specimen of the writing contained in the first English work on practical agriculture, and also the heads of the divided matter which forms the volume. The author was the first native of Britain that studied the nature of soils and the laws of vegetation with philosophical attention. As these he formed a theory confirmed by experience, and rendered the study pleasing as well as profitable by realizing the principles of the ancients to the honour and advantage of his country. These books, being written at a time when philosophy and science were but just emerging from that gloom in which they had so long been buried, were doubtless replete with many errors, but they contained the rudiments of true knowledge, and revived the study and love of agriculture."—P. 7, Lond., 1854.

Xenophon's *Treatise of Householde* was translated by Gentian Hewet (Lowndes, "Xenophon").   ED. MARSHALL.

FRANCIS FOSTER BARHAM, THE "ALIST" (5ᵗʰ S. ix. 268.)—From the *Memorial of Francis Barham*, Bath, 1873, your Barton-on-Irwell correspondent may glean the titles of the numerous works this earnest Biblical scholar wrote or translated. The *Memorial* is edited by Mr. Isaac Pitman, of Bath, the eminent phonographer. Included in its 493 pages are several articles selected from the 116lbs. of *manuscript* that Mr. Barham left at his death. Mr. Barham corresponded with me on business affairs for nearly twenty years, and a very kindly and friendly man I found him. My copy of his *Memorial* is a gift "from the editor." In it I have preserved his last note to me, written a few weeks before his death :—

"Bath, Decr. 12, '70.
" My dear old friend George,—Thanks for your nice and very creditable catalogue. As an old man, half blind and half stupid, and possessing 5,000 volumes, I do not now want many books. Like Southey, I look at the backsides of them instead of the insides. Many of them came through your hands. To cut a long story short pray send me *Grotius on War*, folio, 5s. Pitman has just printed Solomon's Proverbs for me. Yours,
" FRANCIS BARHAM."

He died at Bath suddenly on Feb. 9, 1871, aged sixty-two. His books were bequeathed to various Bath libraries. On founding the Alistic Association about 1843, he dropped his second Christian name (Foster), and did not resume it again.   W. GEORGE.
Bristol.

MR. AXON will find as complete a list of the Alist's publications as could be made in the *Bibliotheca Cornubiensis*, where three columns are devoted to him (vol. i. pp. 11-12). Messrs. Boase and Courtney, however, were unable to see the following works, which they state were written by Barham. Perhaps the mention of the titles may be the means of eliciting bibliographical descriptions :—*A Life of Edward Colston of Bristol*; *The Fables of Lokman*, translated from the Arabic ; *The Copernican Astronomy of the Bible*.   OLPHAR HAMST.

MILTON'S FIRST WIFE, MARY POWELL (5ᵘ S. ix. 308.)—Your correspondent MR. JOHN E. BAILEY will find an answer to his question in the *Fifth Report of the Royal Commission on His torical Manuscripts*, p. 111 :—

"1643, Oct. 26. Application for a pass for Mrs. Mary Powell, wife of the schoolmaster of Paul's School, into Berkshire and back, with a manservant, maidservant, a coach and four horses, and a saddle horse.—L. J.; vi. 273."

I take down the first life of Milton which comes to hand, Gilfillan's memoir prefixed to his edition of Milton's *Poetical Works*, and at vol. i. p. xv, it is stated that Milton married in 1643 " about Whitsuntide." If this date is correct, the above extract from the journals of the House of Lords shows that the Mary Powell there spoken of could not have been Milton's first wife, inasmuch as in October, 1643, she was " wife of the schoolmaster of Paul's School." Knight, in his *Life of Colet* tells us that John Langley was " elected chief master of St. Paul's School in Jan., 1640," and that " he died in his house, joining to St. Paul's School, Sept. 13, 1657." His immediate predecessors were Alexander Gill, senior, 1608-1635 and Alexander Gill, junior, 1635-1640 ; so that Mr. Powell was not Head Master of St. Paul's School. The wretched index to Knight's *Colet* does not include Mr. Powell's name.   W. SPARROW SIMPSON.

THE PROVOSTS OF ST. EDMUND'S, SALISBURY BISHOPS COURTENAY AND THIRLBY (5ᵗʰ S. ix 267.)—Your correspondent G. H. B. is right in identifying Peter Courtenay and Thomas Thirlby who were Provosts of St. Edmund's, Sarum, in 1464 and 1534, as the Bishops of Winchester

(1487) and Westminster (1540) respectively. He will find much concerning the former in Oliver's *Lives of the Bishops of Exeter* (p. 111), and something about the latter in Brady's *Episcopal Succession in England, &c.* (i. p. 17). They both of them held prebends in the cathedral of Salisbury, and the former was also, from 1464-1478, Archdeacon of Wilts. The institutions to the office of Provost of St. Edmund's, Sarum, are contained in the Episcopal Registers, it being in the patronage of the bishop. They are entered under their respective years in Sir Thomas Phillipps's *Wiltshire Institutions.*   W. H. JONES, Canon of Sarum.
Bradford-on-Avon Vicarage.

SCHOOL BOOKS (5ᵗʰ S. ix. 265.)—"Budens" may be for Budæus (Budé); "Mintius" for Minsheu, *Duct. ad Ling.*, fo., Lond., 1617; "Martineus" for Martinius (M. M.), *Lex. Phil.*, fo., Utrecht, 2 vols.; "Votius" for Vossius (G.), *Etym. Ling. Lat.*, fo., Amst., 1662, or for Voetius (G.), *i.e.* Voet; "Skynlau" for Skinner (S.), *Etym. Anglic.*, Lond., 1671; "Goldman" for Gouldman, *Lat. Dict.* "Calopin" refers no doubt to Calepin (Ambr.), the celebrated grammarian and lexicographer of the fifteenth century; whence *calepin,* formerly a common name for a lexicon, and still used in French for a memorandum book, scrap-book, commonplace book.
R. S. CHARNOCK.
Junior Garrick Club.

CERACCI THE SCULPTOR (5ᵗʰ S. ix. 329.)—Ceracci, or Ceracchi, was concerned with Arena, Diana, Topino, Lebrun, and other of the old Republican party in a plot to assassinate the First Consul in 1800, for which, upon the explosion of the infernal machine, they were executed. The conspirators of the latter plot were Royalists. A very fine and interesting bust of Napoleon as First Consul by Ceracci, in bronze, may occasionally be found in London. A copy of it, however, by Barbedienne is very inferior. The tradition is that Ceracchi intended to assassinate the First Consul while he was sitting to the sculptor; but his courage failed him, and he adjourned his foul intention to behind the scenes of the French opera, when the police, already informed of the plot, captured him. He was a Corsican by birth.
H. HALL.
Lavender Hill.

TABLING (5ᵗʰ S. ix. 265.)—A similar custom of pricking obtained at Oriel College, Oxford, in my time, and I have no doubt is continued now. The Bible clerks (of whom there were two, doing duty a week alternately) pricked the attendances of those who kept chapel on a printed list for the special purpose, each such list lasting a week. A certain number of attendances at chapel were of obligation in the course of the week.   H. A. W.

LETTERS OF WASHINGTON (5ᵗʰ S. ix. 329.)—As the honorary curator of the department of antiquities in the museum of this town, I have pleasure in answering the inquiries of KINGSTON, who is right in supposing that institution to be a public one. The nucleus of the present extensive collection, which had been formed some nine years previously, was in the year 1849 conveyed by deed of gift by the Leicester Literary and Philosophical Society to the Town Council, and it has since been in charge of the Corporation under the powers of the Museums Act. There is, of course, no reason why these four letters of Washington's should not be published, and, if it be thought desirable, I shall be happy to send copies of them for insertion in "N. & Q."
The letters are addressed to the historian, Mrs. Catherine Macaulay-Graham (who was connected with this town and county), and are dated respectively "Mount Vernon, Jan. 10, 1786"; "Mount Vernon, Nov. 16, 1787"; "New York, Jan. 9, 1790" (a long letter of five pages on his election as president, the state of affairs in the country, &c.); and, lastly, "Philadelphia, Feb. 10, 1791."
The lady, who had visited America in 1785, entertained, as is known, strong republican principles, and, from the tone of these letters, had evidently expressed her hearty congratulations on the successes which the general and his compatriots had achieved against the mother country.
WILLIAM KELLY, F.R.H.S.
Leicester.
[We shall be glad to print the letters in "N. & Q." if they have not hitherto been published.]

"A FORLORN HOPE' (5ᵗʰ S. ix. 266.)—The Dutch word *hoop,* translated band, only expresses a band or external edge, not a troop of men. A forlorn hope, or band of men, volunteers or otherwise, to attack a breach in a fortress, is nearly identical with the French *enfans perdus,* namely *verlorene kinderen* (lost children). I do not think it ever was understood in Holland in any other sense.   H. HALL.

WILLIAM JACKSON OF EXETER (5ᵗʰ S. ix. 268.)—In Watt's *Bibliotheca Britannica* I find the following reference to W. Jackson (formerly Organist of Exeter Cathedral) :—
"Jackson, William, a musical composer of Exeter, where he was born about 1730, died 1803 :—*Observations on the Present State of Music in London,* London, 1791, 8vo.—*Thirty Letters on Various Subjects,* London, 1782, 2 vols., 12mo.; second edit., corrected and improved, London, 1784, 2 vols., 12mo.; third edit., with considerable additions, London, 1795, 8vo.; principally consisting of essays on the *belles lettres.*—*The Four Ages,* together with *Essays on Various Subjects,* London, 1798, 8vo.—*Eighteen Musical Works,* consisting of hymns, songs, canzonets, elegies, and an Ode to Fancy."
E. C. HARINGTON.
The Close, Exeter.

of the above. GWAVAS.

There is a notice of him and his works by Dr. Burney in Rees's *Cyclopædia*, *sub nom*. See also Brydges's *Censura Literaria*, iv. 303-5. "Jackson, the musician, was a man of rare genius in his own art, and eminently gifted in many ways" (Southey's *Wesley*, 1820, vol. ii. p. 63).
Bristol. W. GEORGE.

In a notice of this variously accomplished gentleman written by the late Rev. Dr. Oliver, about twenty years ago, mention is made of the *Elegies* as the most admired of his works. His *Four Ages* and *Thirty Letters* will be found in the library of the Devon and Exeter Institution, as well as an oil portrait by Keenan.
R. DYMOND.
Exeter.

"GERMAN" SILVER (5th S. ix. 129.)—PROF. ATTWELL, in speaking of "German" as a title for spurious silver, seems unaware that in Germany the composition known to us as "German silver" is called "English silver." I remember occasioning much amusement to some Germans by applying our name to it, when I was informed that they always understood "English" silver to be false. W. S. H.

AN ANTIQUE SILVER BELL (5th S. ix. 327.) —Obviously the inscription is τοῖς ὄμμασιν ὑποτέταγμαι, "I am subjected to the eyes." I can only suggest that the bell was intended for show on the table rather than for common use.
Oxford. FAMA.

WASHINGTON IRVING (5th S. ix. 348.)—CHISLE-HURST will find the quotation he seeks in the *Sketch-Book*, article "Rural Funerals."
D. M. STEVENS.
Guildford.

CLERICAL TITLES (5th S. ix. 348.)—I may refer your correspondent to "N. & Q.," 1st S. iii. 437; vi. 246; 2nd S. ix. 483; and 3rd S. vii. 121; xii. 26. The prefix of "Venerable" for archdeacons and "Very Reverend" for deans did not come into common use till about the close of the first quarter of the present century (obituaries of *Gentleman's Magazine*; *Sacred Archæology*, 504, 505). In the *Clerical Guide*, 1822, all the deans are "Very Reverend" and archdeacons "Venerable." MACKENZIE E. C. WALCOTT.

I have searched many documents, ancient and bordering on modern, and can find no title of "Very Reverend" or "Venerable" applied to either dean or archdeacon. They are simply styled land styles itself "Venerable," and I can or presume that the term has been obtained fr(thence. I can find no authority anywhere 'for t title of "Very Reverend" assumed by deans, a it is only of comparatively recent time that it h been so assumed. If there were any authoritati grant in either case it would be duly recorded.
S. L.

[At the first reference will be found a paper on t subject by the late JOHN WILSON CROKER.]

ST. MARK'S DAY A FAST (5th S. ix. 266, 35 —The fast belongs not to St. Mark, but to t greater litanies and procession which were ce. brated on that day. Thus the fast was moved the day according to that on which the Litany w said. The fast has nothing to do with the feast St. Mark, for no feasts during Paschal-tide ha fasted eves or vigils. On the general question litanies I would refer to Durandus, *De Lætani* cap. 122, in his "Explicatio Divini Officii." T writer of the query having given the rule for t transference of the Litany according to Sarum u it may be worth while to give the rule accordi to Roman use at the present day. On St. Mar] Day the Mass *de Rogationibus*, i.e. *Exaudivit*, said at the procession, which means to say that different Mass from that which is celebrated on ! Mark's Day is said, being the Mass, in fact, whi is said on the Rogation Days, when the Lita] again is said. The procession is not transferr except when the feast occurs on Easter Day, a then it is transferred to Tuesday in Easter wee For instance, this year the Litany would have be said on April 25, and the procession made (wi violet vestments), and the Mass *Exaudivit* sai but the feast of St. Mark itself is translated to t first vacant day after the octave of Easter, whicl observe the *Ordo Recitandi* says is May 13. Apj rently the day on which the Litany is said is n observed as a fast, herein again differing from t Sarum custom. H. A. W.

HERALDIC (5th S. viii. 147, 254; ix. 277, 35(—MR. HYDE's instance of a lady's right to a cre is very curious and interesting. May I ask if t reason of the concession is known? and may I a other correspondents if they can contribute simil cases? We know the Queen uses the crest England, and in the seventeenth century we som times find the lady's family crest placed over h half of the shield on monuments; but this w either a caprice of fashion or a mistaken comp ment, except in such a case as Margery Cater's.
P. P.

THE ANCIENT BARONY OF COURTENAY OF OK HAMPTON (5th S. ix. 268, 296) was (*i.e.* the lan &c.) by co-heirs dispersed into divers families.

was held by the Mohuns until 1712. Charles, Lord Mohun, quarrelled with the Duke of Hamilton about an estate, &c., and challenged him to a duel in which he was himself killed, Nov. 15, 1712. He left no issue, and so the honour became extinct. A. Saville, Esq., was lord of the manor in 1810.   H. W. ESTRIDGE.

SIR RICHARD GRENVILLE (5th S. ix. 222, 333.) —HERMENTRUDE inquires if Honor, Viscountess Lisle, is correctly entered in the pedigrees as a daughter of Sir Thomas Grenville (d. 1515) and Isabel Gilbert, as it appears from the Lisle papers in the Record Office (1) that the Lady Lisle had two nieces with the queen, "daughters unto Mr. Arundell"; (2) that she had a brother called John Grenville, and a sister called Mary St. Aubyn; (3) that the wife of Digory Grenville is spoken of as "my lady's nurse"; and (4) that James Basset, the son of Lady Lisle by her first husband, John Basset, was cousin to John Grenville. The Visitation of Cornwall (1620), printed by the Harleian Society in 1874, enables me to confirm the correctness of the pedigrees, and to settle the doubts of your correspondent. (1) Jane, daughter of Sir Thomas Grenville by his first wife, Isabella Gilbert, was married to John Arundell of Trerice, and another married (in C. S. Gilbert's Cornwall, i. 507, called Catherine) was the wife of Sir John Arundell of Lanherne. (2) John Grenville, "a priest," was the son of Sir Thomas by his second wife. Mary, daughter of Sir Thomas by his first wife, was married to Richard Blewet, and after his death to Thomas St. Aubyn. (4) John Grenville was the second son of Lady Lisle's brother, Roger Grenville, and consequently cousin to her own son John Basset. As regards (3) I may state that Digory Grenville was the nephew of Lady Lisle, and suggest that his wife may possibly have nursed Lady Lisle in some sickness in London or elsewhere.   W. P. COURTNEY.
15, Queen Anne's Gate.

HERMENTRUDE, on consulting Polwhele's Cornwall, will find there an engraving of a brass to "Thomas St. Aubyn of Clowance, Esq., and his wife Mary, daughter of Sir Thomas Granville of Stow, Knt." See also Harl. MS. 14315; Harleian Society's pub. Cornwall.
    W. J. ST. AUBYN.
Rochester.

SURNAMES NOW OBSOLETE: PELEROC, PILLICOCK, PETIPAS (5th S. ix. 345.)—There is a living French caricaturist (a frequent contributor to the Petit Journal pour Rire) by the name of Jules Pellecocq. Most of us remember the renowned French ballet dancer, M. Petipas.
    G. A. SALA.

GRIMALDI (5th S. ix. 208, 296.)—Is not MR. WYLIE rather bold in stating that "The Memoirs

of Joseph Grimaldi (edited by 'Boz') furnish all the information your correspondent is likely to get," &c.? Dickens's Memoirs were taken, I believe, from Grimaldi's own MS. journal, which is of the greatest interest, and I should say would form, if printed, several volumes of the size of the Memoirs. Mr. Henry Stevens gave me the pleasure of inspecting this most interesting MS. volume some years ago.   O. H.

GIUDECCA (5th S. ix. 273, 297.)—MR. BOUCHIER's inquiry as to whether the pronunciation Zuecca for Giudecca is Venetian only, or of general acceptance, may be meant to draw from me a confession that the case of this word is not a case in point. Nor do I venture to say decisively that it is; for every one knows that Venice is not as the rest of Italy. There must be many local abbreviations, as there are many patois, in different parts of Italy, which may or may not be taken into account when you speak or think of Italian generally. At Genoa, I believe, the word signora is abbreviated into scia. A lady known to me was always called "Scia Lydia" by the servants there.   A. J. M.

CHIOGGIA (5th S. ix. 49, 138, 234, 272, 297) is called Chioza solely in the Venetian dialect. In Italian, dialects apart, most names are pronounced as written. The soft Venetian patois eliminates all hard sounds, and makes Chioggia Chioza, Doge Dose, Giovanni Zuane, bella bea, and is the prettiest and most engaging dialect of Italy.
    K. H. B.

LICENCE TO EAT FLESH IN LENT (5th S. ix. 226, 274, 317.)—Several correspondents have given particular instances of licences granted by the Protestant clergy from the time of Queen Elizabeth to that of Charles I. as if they were something very extraordinary. But was not the custom of this abstinence almost universal in England at the periods spoken of? I imagine it was, and that the majority of the people—certainly all good Protestants—would have thought they were committing a great sin, both against religion and law, in not observing it, unless a dispensation were granted by a clergyman.

    "The cut-throat butchers, wanting throats to cut,
    At Lent's approach their bloody shambles shut;
    For forty days their tyranny doth cease,
    And men and beasts take truce, and live in peace."
    Jack a Lent.

At Hull in 1636, where the plague was then prevailing, the mayor and aldermen of that place sent a petition to the Archbishop of York for a general dispensation during the ensuing Lent. The reasons assigned were the plague, and that the town was not served with fish as formerly. His grace returned answer, that he did not know what power he had to grant such indefinite licence

" but that in all cases of sickness, and other extraordinary circumstances, the ministers upon certificate from their physicians might grant permission to particular persons to eat flesh during that holy season."

These quotations very clearly point to its universality even at so late a period as this, when the Puritans were becoming very strong.

Lent was the fishmonger's harvest and the butcher's holiday. No doubt a good deal of smuggling was going on. Those who had no religion at all would have their " pound of flesh," and if we may credit our Water Poet (writing some six years earlier) the Puritans, who doubtless regarded this fasting as a Romish practice, openly defied the law.

" Sir Francis Drake's ship at Deptford, my Lord Mayor's barge, and divers secret and unsuspected places, and there they make private shambles with kill-calf cruelty, and sheep-slaughtering murder, to the abuse of Lent, and the great grief of every zealous fishmonger."—
Jack a Lent.

" I have often noted, that if any superfluous feasting or gormandizing, paunch-cramming assembly do meet, it is so ordered that it must be either in Lent, upon a Friday, or a fasting day : for the meat doth not relish well, except it be sauced with disobedience and contempt of authority. And though they eat sprats on a Sunday, they care not, so that they may be full gorged with flesh on the Friday night.

" Then all the zealous puritans will feast
In detestation of the Romish beast."
Idem.
MEDWEIG.

THE FIELDFARE, &c. (5th S. viii. 286, 354, 376, 478 ; ix. 136.)—There is a reddish worm which leaves a considerable amount of slime along its path. This slime, too, is slightly phosphorescent, and on a dark night I have traced its track for nearly two feet. C. L. PRINCE.

" GIVE PEACE IN OUR TIME " (5th S. ix. 148, 289.)—On one point L. A. R. is correct. The apparent incongruity between the versicle and the response has been pointed out before now. Mr. Charles Reade has pleasantly and lightly touched upon the subject in his *Hard Cash*, in which the hero, in one of the conversations wherein he attempts to demonstrate his sanity to the " mad doctors," remarks upon the illogical character of this petition.

I think it is rather beside the question to discuss the pacific or non-pacific nature of our Prayer Book. But, as the topic has been entered upon, I may be allowed to maintain that the Prayer Book is distinctly peaceful in its character. In praying for the Parliament, we ask that " peace may be established among us for all generations " ; in the Litany is, " give to all nations unity, peace, and concord " ; and in the service for the Queen's accession are the petitions, " let peace flourish in her days," " that our posterity may see peace upon Israel." In all these instances it is clearly political and not religious peace that is made the object of our prayers. EDWARD H. MARSHALL.

" HOPING AGAINST HOPE " (5th S. ix. 68, 94, 258, 275, 319.)—C. C. M. is referred to the following instance of the expression in the sixteenth century, not later than 1586 :—
" Yit houp hings by ane hair,
Houping aganes all houp."
" Luve-sang on Houp," Pinkerton's *Ancient Scotish Poems*, vol. ii. p. 264.
G. F. S. E.

LOWLAND ABERDEEN (5th S. ix. 5, 111.)—The following rhyme may possibly belong to those mentioned by I. M. P. When young I frequently heard it called after Highlandmen by street boys in Belfast :—
" There 's naething in the Hielans
But lang kail an' leeks,
An' lang-leggit Hielanmen
Wantin' the breeks."
I imagine the " leeks " is merely a necessity to rhyme with " breeks." P. DREWETT-KING.
Dublin.

AN OIL PAINTING (5th S. ix. 189, 256.)—I am much obliged to GWAVAS for his information. The oil painting is a large one with large tree, and there is a ruddy tone over the whole of the painting. Would GWAVAS still further oblige with any particulars of Gerard Edema—when and where he lived, and if his works are of any value ?
T. McM.

William Oram is thus noticed in H. Walpole's *Anecdotes of Painting* (reprint Lond., 1872) p. 351 :—
" Wm. Oram was bred an architect, but taking to landscape painting arrived at great merit in that branch and was made master carpenter to the Board of Work by the interest of Sir E. Walpole, who has several of his prints and drawings."
ED. MARSHALL.

PARSONS WHO WERE ALSO PUBLICANS (5th S. ix 164, 253.)—In a book entitled *Eat, Drink, and be Merry*, by Harry Blyth, and published by J. A. Brook & Co., occurs the following : " This reminds us of a clergyman whose living was so poor that he humbly petitioned that the parsonage might be licensed as an ale-house—and it was." Can this be verified ? R. MILLS.

THE FOURTH ESTATE OF THE REALM (5th S. ix 167, 213, 277.)—Was not Carlyle the author of this expression ? He says in his *Hero-Worship* Lect. v., as follows : " Burke said there were three estates in Parliament, but in the Reporters Gallery yonder there sat a fourth estate more important far than they all."
JOHN CHURCHILL SIKES.
Godolphin Road, Shepherd's Bush, W.

"CRAZYS" (5th S. v. 364, 454.)—
"Crazy or craisey, in Wilts and the adjoining counties, the buttercup; apparently a corruption of 'Christ's eye,' L. *oculus Christi*, the mediæval name of the marigold, which through the confusion among old writers between Caltha and Calendula has been transferred to the marsh marigold, and thence to other Ranunculaceæ."—Dr. Prior's *Popular Names of British Plants*.
                                      T. F. R.

AUTHORS OF BOOKS WANTED (5th S. ix. 268, 339.)—
Poems for Youth, by a Family Circle (part i.), 1820, pp. iv-106; part ii. 1821, pp. 78.—In reply to MR. BUCHANAN's query, Roscoe's sonnet *On Parting with his Books* does not appear in the above book. Your correspondent can hardly be right in including among the authors of the poems the name of William Caldwell Roscoe, as he was not born until September 21, 1823. It may be worth while to note that in 1821 another little volume was published, with the following title, *Poems, by one of the Authors of " Poems for Youth, by a Family Circle,"* second edition, London, 1821, pp. 66. This was written by Jane Elizabeth Roscoe, daughter of the historian of Lorenzo de' Medici, and afterwards wife of Mr. Francis Hornblower.   C. W. SUTTON.
Manchester Free Library.

AUTHORS OF QUOTATIONS WANTED (5th S. ix. 268.)—
" Ratio ultima regum."—This motto is the subject of a query, 3rd S. xii. 436, where there is a note by the editor: " This motto was engraved on the French cannon by order of Louis XIV." The subject is taken up in the first volume of the next series. At p. 19 it is stated that the motto was perhaps taken from Calderon, in whose *Heraclius*, Jorn. ii. t. i. p. 594, edit. Keil, there is this line:—

          " Ultima razon de Reyes";

but was possibly an earlier proverb. At p. 90 there is an examination of the question whether Calderon borrowed it from Corneille, or Corneille from Calderon. The same occurs, in more particulars, pp. 174-176; and at p. 184 it is maintained, with reference to a statement by Voltaire, that Calderon did not borrow it from Corneille.   ED. MARSHALL.

Drifting is a poem by the late J. Buchanan Read, of Philadelphia, Penn., artist and author. It will be found in his collected poems, and also in the volume on Italy of Mr. Longfellow's new series of " Poems of Places."
                              J. BRANDER MATTHEWS.

Miscellaneous.

NOTES ON BOOKS, &c.

Outlines of General or Developmental Philology: Inflection. By R. G. Latham, M.A., M.D. (Longmans & Co.)

IN this volume Dr. Latham professes to treat of the "method" of philological investigation rather than of its "results," and of "the principles governing the processes by which languages are changed rather than of the changes themselves." Part I. is taken up with a classification of languages under the heads of Analytic and Synthetic, Agglutinative, and Monosyllabic; a sketch is given of the relations between the various members of each group, and familiar examples illustrate the meaning of the nomenclature employed. In all this there is

nothing very novel, and Dr. Latham had only to follow a beaten path. But in Part II., where he analyzes the ideas conveyed by the inflections, by the changes which are used to denote case, person, mood, &c., he is on more dangerous ground. And here, as it seems to us, lies the weakness of his treatment, which is altogether too speculative. He relies too much, we think, on *à priori* reasoning from one or two instances, and does not bring sufficient evidence from a wide comparison. Hence many of his ideas, though ingenious, are not convincing. Thus it is suggested, without being proved, that inflections the last lost were the first developed. The Greek aorist (i) is considered to have had for its original ending -κα, as in ἔδωκα and ἔθηκα, and this κ is said to have been changed to σ by sibilation, under the influence " of the small vowel (ἔγραψε)." In favour of this theory is quoted Bopp's view that the h (κ) which is the sign of the past tense in Slavonic represents the σ of Greek. But surely this is not enough to account for the supposed sibilation in the latter. It is true that κ becomes σ in many cases, but always before a y sound. Still less evidence is brought to support the supposed transference of this aorist κ to the perfect, though the confusion of the two tenses might have been illustrated from the Latin. As to the person-endings of the verb, Dr. Latham holds, with Garnett, that *scrib-o*= "writing-my," not "writing-I"; and he claims that nouns as well as verbs are provided with inflections denoting person and voice. The section on Gender is interesting; but it is somewhat paradoxical to say that the only inflection in English which has any precise and constant meaning is the *t* of *it, what*, and *that*, for very few Englishmen recognize it as a sign of the neuter.

MESSRS. GEORGE BELL & SONS have sent us the second edition, revised, of Mr. H. M. Westropp's *Handbook of Archæology, Egyptian-Greek-Etruscan-Roman*, valuable as a work of reference, but rendered doubly so by its capital index.—*Pius IX.*, by J. F. Maguire, M.P. (Longmans), is a new edition of the late Mr. Maguire's work, and has been revised and brought down to the accession of Pope Leo XIII. by Monsignor Patterson. To it all may refer for a full description of the latter days of the last pope, and of the formularies attending the election of his successor.—For the benefit of English readers the Rev. E. Marshall has translated *The Explanation of the Apocalypse*, by Venerable Beda (James Parker & Co.).—From Messrs. Parker we have also received Mrs. Stapley's *History of the English Church*, which was so highly commended by the late Dean Hook, and has now reached a fourth edition; and *Memorials of T. G. Godfrey-Faussett*. These *Memorials* possess a public and a private interest, and therefore should be prized not only by the personal friends of the late Auditor of the Canterbury Chapter on account of some personal recollections with which the small volume is prefaced, from the pen of one who signs himself with the well-known initials " W. J. L," but also by those who are collectors of Latin renderings of well-known Church hymns.—*Studies in Spectrum Analysis* (Kegan Paul & Co.), by J. Norman Lockyer, F.R.S., one of the useful International Scientific Series, has reached a second edition.—*A Lexicon of New Testament Greek on a New Plan* and *A Companion to the Lexicon* (Elliot Stock) are devised on a plan "by which the Greek New Testament may be translated into English with demonstrable accuracy by the simplest method." Of the "plan" and "method" we can only say that they seem to us decidedly intricate.

AN article on "Political Clubs and Party Organization," by Mr. W. Fraser Rae, in the *Nineteenth Century*, contains some interesting particulars concerning the

Mrs. Oliphant, in *Within the Precincts* (*Cornhill*), describes a minor canon as "a singing man in the highest grade," his duty as "not (to) be called work at all." But to such humble "duty" was poor Mr. Ashford compelled to settle down, all through having been discovered to have perpetrated in early life a wrong accent upon a Greek word! Readers of "N. & Q." will do well not to forget the effects of so heinous a crime, for "it weighed him down for the rest of his days."

WE have received part viii. of Mr. Helsby's edition of Ormerod's *Cheshire*. On the completion of vol. ii. we hope to speak at some length on the merits of this valuable work.

CAMDEN SOCIETY.—At the annual meeting of the society on the 2nd instant, the Earl of Verulam in the chair, the Very Rev. the Dean of Westminster, F. W. Cosens, Esq., F.S.A., and Sir Albert Woods (Garter) were elected on the Council in the place of the three retiring members, and the Report of the Council expressed a hope that the General Index to the First Series of the Publications of the Camden Society would be put to press and published during the ensuing year.

Notices to Correspondents.

We must call special attention to the following notice:—
ON all communications should be written the name and address of the sender, not necessarily for publication, but as a guarantee of good faith.

W. T. M.—*The Christian Year.* Reference, it may be inferred, was made by Prof. M. Burrows to the hymn for Gunpowder Treason. One verse of that hymn runs now:

"O come to our Communion feast:
There present, in the heart
As in the hands, th' eternal Priest
Will his true self impart."

"*Not* in the hands" was originally written, but Keble altered the phrase as it stands above in the edition of *The Christian Year* that was printed off before, but not issued till just after, his death.

W. H. should submit his engraving to the inspection of some authority in such matters. The description given is wholly insufficient.

ED. J. M.—The writer has expressed a wish to remain anonymous, a wish that in all similar cases ought to be respected.

E. L. BLENKINSOPP.—Is not the word of East Indies origin?

BELWELBY.—The title is always accorded, if only by courtesy, to any one placed in command.

A. C. S.—The ballad, *The Happy Old Couple*, tells the story of Darby and Joan.

JON. BOUCHIER.—"G. M." not remembered. Other papers as soon as possible.

J. S. ATTWOOD.—Letter forwarded.

NOTICE.

Editorial Communications should be addressed to "The Editor of 'Notes and Queries'"—Advertisements and Business Letters to "The Publisher"—at the Office, 20, Wellington Street, Strand, London, W.C.
We beg leave to state that we decline to return communications which, for any reason, we do not print; and to this rule we can make no exception.

LONDON, SATURDAY MAY 18, 1878.

CONTENTS.—N° 229.

Notes.

SHELLEY'S "ŒDIPUS TYRANNUS, OR SWELL-FOOT THE TYRANT."

Some crumbs of information for Shelley students are to be found in a book which came under the hammer of Messrs. Puttick & Simpson on Wednesday last, and which is something of a curiosity, independently of what is written in it, in virtue of its extreme scarcity. It is a copy of Shelley's *Œdipus Tyrannus*, published anonymously in 1820, and immediately suppressed—" stifled," says Mrs. Shelley, " by the Society for the Suppression of Vice, who threatened to prosècute it if not immediately withdrawn." At the top of the title-page has been written, "Bought 16 Dec., 1820, M. G." The " 20 " has been cut off in binding, but 1820 must have been the year, to judge from the well-known facts of the case, and " M. G." would seem to have been, not Maria Gisborne, but some virtuous inhabitant of the Ward of Cheap, who bought this copy for purposes of warfare, for in the same handwriting is written all over the title-page the following note :—

"This work was published by Johnson in Cheapside at the commencement of the Caroline Phobia ; was bought by me, and presuming it to be highly libellous, some Inhabitants of the Ward determined to have it prosecuted in accordance to the resolutions of the Ward-mote ; it was, however, suppressed by the interference of Alderman Rothwell without coming before a Jury, the publisher giving up the whole impression, except 7 what [*sic*] he said was the whole number sold. He gave up as the Author (or at least his Employer) Smith, the

Author of *Rejected Addresses*, *Horace in London*, &c. Smith, however, said it was sent to him from Pisa in Italy, at that time the residence of Lord Byron, Shelly [*sic*], and others."

If this is genuine (and its general air is that of the most convincing genuineness), we learn from it that, whatever part the Society for the Suppression of Vice may have taken in the matter, the attack did not originate with that society ; that the sale, according to Johnston (not Johnson), only extended to seven copies, the rest falling into hands not likely to preserve them very carefully ; that Shelley's friendly agent was Horace Smith ; and that that estimable gentleman staunchly refused to give up the name of his principal at Pisa, for " M. G." would certainly have said which of the " Satanic school " was the author, had he known. This copy of " M. G.'"s was, of course, one of the seven, and if Johnston and his intimidators were all good men and true, there are now only three copies to come to the surface, for this is the fourth known to Shelley specialists. There are none in any of the public libraries, except the copy in the Dyce collection at South Kensington ; Mr. Trelawny has the second copy ; I have the third ; and this fourth, a closely cropped one, was knocked down to Messrs. Ellis & White, of Bond Street, for 25*l.* I believe no copy has ever come to the hammer before, and it will not be surprising if no further copy makes its appearance, for pamphlets of twenty leaves are perishable things ; and even if some of the high-minded "inhabitants of the Ward" followed the example of "M. G." in preserving copies for their own reading (for "M. G.'"s copy is marked in the margin throughout), still four copies would be a good percentage of survivors.   H. BUXTON FORMAN.

MR. J. PAYNE COLLIER'S REPRINTS.

I have beside me such a list of Mr. Collier's reprints as M. C. R. asks for (5th S. ix. 226), and as the editor of " N. & Q." has kindly accepted it, I hope the following may be useful to collectors of these admirable exemplars of our early literature.

Red Series (in two volumes or twenty-four parts).

Vol. I.—1. A Piththy Note to Papists, by T. Knell, 1570.
2. Murder of John Brewen, by Thos. Kydde, 1592.
3. History of Jacob and his xii. Sonnes, n.d.
4. The Wyll of the Deuyll, and Last Testament, n.d.
5. The Metamorphosis of Tabacco, 1602.
6. Murder of Lord Bourgh, and Arnold Cosby's Verses, 1591.
7. Enterlude of Godly Queene Hester, 1561.
8. Complaynte of them that ben to late Maryed, n.d.
9. Censure of a Loyal Subject, by G. Whetstone, 1587.
10. Lyrics for Old Lutenists. *Temp.* Eliz. and James I.
11. Calverley, and the Yorkshire Tragedy, 1605.
12. A Complaint of the Churche, 1562.
Vol. II.—1. Report of the Royal Commissioners, and Decree of the Star-Chamber, regarding Printers and Stationers, 1584.
2. Parry's Travels of Sir A. Sherley, 1601.

3. Becke Against the Anabaptists, 1550.
4. The Comedy of Tyde taryeth no Man, 1576.
5. Voyage of Richard Ferris to Bristol, 1590.
6. Broadsides and Speeches to Monck, 1660.
7. R. Johnson's Look on me London, 1613.
8. W. Bas's Sword and Buckler, 1602.
9. A Good Speed to Virginia, 1609.
10. Copies of Early Love-Letters, &c., n.d.
11. R. Johnson's Walks of Moorfields, 1607.
12. Verses by Walton, Arnold, and Clinton, n.d.

These two volumes are titled *Illustrations of Early English Popular Literature.*

Green Series (in three volumes or twenty-four parts).
Vol. I.—1. Lamentation against London, 1548.
2. Pasquil's Palinodia, 1619.
3. Respublica, An Interlude, 1553.
4. Lady Pecunia, by Richard Barnfield, 1605.
5. Mirror of Modestie, by T. Salter, n.d.
6. Passion of a Discontented Mind, 1602.
7. Encomion of Lady Pecunia, 1598.
8. News from the Levant Seas, 1594.

Vol. II.—1. Pancharis, by Hugh Holland, 1603.
2. Horestes, An Interlude, 1567.
3. Preservation of Henry VII., 1599.
4. Reformation of Rebellion, 1598, and Shore's Wife, 1593, by Thomas Churchyard.
5. Seven Deadly Sins of London, by T. Dekker, 1606.
6. Love's Court of Conscience, by H. Crowch, 1637.
7. William Longbeard, by Thomas Lodge, 1593.
8. Triumph of Truth, by T. Proctor, n.d.

Vol. III.—1. Mirror of Modesty, by Robert Greene, 1584.
2. Life and Death of Gamaliel Ratsey, 1605.
3. Ceyx and Alcione, by W. Hubbard, 1569.
4. Apology for England's Joy, by R. Vennar, 1614.
5. History of Plasidas, by J. Partridge, 1566.
6. Anatomy of Absurdity, by Thomas Nash, 1589.
7. Royal Arbor of Loyal Poesie, by Thomas Jordan, 1664.
8. Instructions for the Lord Mayor of London, &c., by Thomas Norton, 1573.

These three volumes are titled *Illustrations of Old English Literature.*

Blue Series (containing twenty-five parts).
1. Tottel's Miscellany, 1557, three parts.
2. Turberville's Songs and Sonets, 1567, two parts.
3. Whetstone's Rock of Regard, 1576, three parts.
4. Churchyard's Chippes, 1575, two parts.
5. Churchyard's Miscellaneous Poems, 1579, one part.
6. Churchyard's Charge, 1580, one part.
7. A Gorgious Gallery of Gallant Inuentions, 1578, one part.
8. The Paradyse of Daynty Deuises, 1578, one part.
9. The Phoenix Nest, 1593, one part.
10. England's Helicon, 1600, two parts.
11. England's Parnassus, 1600, five parts.
12. Davison's Poetical Rapsody, 1602, two parts.
13. An Antidote Against Melancholy, 1661, one part.

The fifth part of *England's Parnassus* contains a general introduction to *Seven Poetical Miscellanies.*

Yellow Series (containing seventeen parts).
1. Perimedes the Blacke-Smith, by Robert Greene, 1588.
2. Strange Newes, by Thomas Nash, 1592.
3. A Qvip for An Vp-Start Courtier, by Robert Greene, 1592.
4. Skialethia, by Edward Guilpin, 1598.
5. Foure Letters, and Certaine Sonnets, by Gabriel Harvey, 1592.

6. Pierce Penilesse his Svpplication to tne Thomas Nash, 1592.
7. A New Letter of Notable Contents, Harvey, 1593.
8. Pierces Supererogation : or a new prayse Asse, by Gabriel Harvey (in three part
9. Have with you to Saffron-Walden, k Nash, 1596.
10. Hvmors Looking Glasse, by Samuel 1608.
11. The Anatomie of Abuses, by Phillip Stub 1583.
12. The Trimming of Thomas Nashe, Gen Gabriel Harvey, 1597.
13. The Pastorals and other Workes of Wil 1653.
14. Good Newes and Bad Newes, by San lands, 1622.
15. A True Coppie of a Discourse written b man, employed in the late Voyage of Portingale, 1589.

I may mention that No. 13 (Basse's *Past* printed from manuscript for the first tir series. The whole of the tracts in th literary "flyting" between Thomas N Gabriel Harvey are also included ; and ir thorough way Mr. Collier has added *Trimming of Thomas Nashe* an introdu taining the order in which they should b

Magenta Series (four parts).
1. Delia. Contayning certayne Sonnets : complaint of Rosamond, by Samuel Dai
2. Idea. The Shepheards Garland, by Mic ton, 1593.
3. The Complaint of Rosamond, by Samu 1592.
4. Endimion and Phœbe. Ideas Latmvs, b Drayton, n.d.

Brown Series (one part).
Nine Historical Letters of the Reign of Hei

Ballads (one part).
Broadside Black-Letter Ballads, printed in teenth and Seventeenth Centuries.

Shakespeare.
In eight volumes, including the Poems an as well as the doubtful plays of "Edward I Two Noble Kinsmen," "Mucedorus," and "A Tragedy."

In addition to the foregoing—and p may not be out of place to mention tl seeing that some of them have appeare catalogues since their issue—Mr. Collie most generous and liberal manner, pre his friends the following :—

1. An Old Man's Diary Forty Years Ago, fo
2. Trilogy. Conversations between Three the Emendations of Shakespeare's Text, three
3. Odds and Ends for Cheerful Friends, one
4. Twenty-five Old Ballads and Songs : Fr scripts in the possession of J. Payne Collier, o part.
5. King Edward the Third. A Historic William Shakespeare, one part.

It may not be unnecessary to add th foregoing were printed for private circu

small 4to., and—excepting the *Shakespeare* (of which fifty-eight copies were printed) and the *Twenty-five Old Ballads* (of which only twenty-five copies were printed)—limited to an impression of fifty copies each.   S.

THE BIBLIOGRAPHY OF ARCHERY.

(*Continued from p.* 325.)

Body-Guard of Archers of Mary, Queen of Scots.
Miscellany of the Maitland Club, consisting of original papers and other documents illustrative of the history and literature of Scotland. Vol. I....Printed at Edinburgh, 1840. 4to. Pp. 25-36, The archearis of our soverane ladyis gaird, 1562-1567 (Roll of the Body-Guard of Archers of Mary, Queen of Scots).   M.

Scorton Arrow Meetings, 1673.
An old parchment roll on which the articles agreed to by the society of archers at Scorton on the 14th May, 1673, for the regulating of the annual exercise of shooting at the targets for a silver arrow, are engrossed. Excepting for the years 1682, 1698, 1699, 1701, 1747-1786, 1789, 1799-1809, this roll also contains the names of the annual captains and lieutenants from 1673 to the present time.
Account of the annual shooting for the ancient silver arrow, commonly called the Scorton arrow, from 1673 to 1866.—MS. fol. pp. 200. Contains the "articles," localities and dates of meetings, names of annual captains and lieutenants, and signatures of the archers present at the different meetings. At the end of the "articles" is the following entry:—"N.B. The original articles of this society being almost defaced and obliterated, the gentlemen archers present on the eighteenth of June 1766 bought this book for the same to be fairly transcribed herein (and also to enter any new rules or orders)." Fifteen signatures attest the accuracy of the transcript. The annual accounts are not consecutive; the long omission in the parchment roll described above, 1747 to 1786, with the exception of the years 1773, 1774, 1777, 1779, and 1780, is supplied in this book.
Account of the annual shooting for the ancient silver arrow, commonly called the Scorton arrow, from 1867.—MS. fol. 27 pages of this book are at present written in. [The Scorton silver arrow and MS. records are held by the captain during his year of office ; his duties are to perpetuate the records and manage the affairs of the next annual meeting. I am indebted to Wm. Butt, captain of the Scorton arrow, 1877, for these particulars.]

Royal Company of Archers, 1676.
Archerie reviv'd: a poëtical essay, penn'd upon occasion of the intended muster of the [R.] C. of A. in Scotland, June 11, 1677....Edinburgh, printed by the heir of Andrew Anderson,...1677. 4to. pp. viii-10. Dedication signed W. C. [William Clark, or Clerk, or Clerke].
Poems in English and Latin on the Archers, and R. C. of A. By several hands. Edinburgh, printed in the year 1726. 12mo. pp. 108. M.
La parade des Archers Ecossois, poeme dramatique, adressé au très-haut et puissant Prince Jacques Duc d'Hamilton et Brandon, &c., Capitaine General, et a tous les Officiers de la Compagnie Royale des Archers Ecossois. Imprimée à Edimbourg, l'an 1734. 4to. pp. 12. By James Freebairn. (M. copy lost.)
A short history to the commendation of the R. [C. of] A., with a description of six of the dukes in Scotland, especially Argile. Written by the Tinklarian Doctor in the year 1734, in the 65th year of his age. With a de-

scription of the great dukes in Scotland. [Edinburgh] Printed in the year 1734. 8vo. pp. 8. By W. Mitchel. M.
The Scots Magazine, Edinburgh. Vol. xxxviii. p. 385 (July, 1776), On Mr. St. Clare of Roslin and his band of Royal Scots Archers. (Four eight-line verses, dated July 8, 1776, and signed) Wal[ter] Johnston. Also a Latin version in twenty lines. M.
Chronological list of the R. C. of Scottish A....Edinburgh, printed by P. Neill, 1819. 8vo. pp. 64-16.—The second part contains the names of members who have gained prizes.
List of the R. C. of A., the King's Body-Guard for Scotland. 1st January, 1834. Edinburgh, printed...by W. Burness, 1834. 4to. pp. ii-24.
List of the R. C. of A., Queen's Body-Guard for Scotland. Edinburgh, printed by W. Burness,...1859. 4to. pp. 86. Pages 39-86 is a "List of archers who have gained prizes."
Domestic annals of Scotland from the Revolution to the Rebellion of 1745. By Robert Chambers [Publisher]...W. & R. Chambers, Edinburgh,...1861. 8vo. Pp. 495-497, Historical note on R. C. of A. M.
The history of the R. C. of A., the Queen's Body-Guard for Scotland, by James Balfour Paul, Advocate of the Scottish bar, one of the members of the Royal Company of the Council. William Blackwood & Sons, Edinburgh and London, 1875. 4to. pp. x-394. 12 plates, 42s. M. (Reviewed in the *Spectator*, London, May 13, 1876.)

Toxophilite Society, afterwards Royal Toxophilite Society, 1781.
Rules and orders of the T. S., instituted at Leicester House anno Domini 1781. Together with the by-laws of the society.—London, 1784(?). 12mo. pp. 20. M.
The laws of the T. S., instituted in the year 1781, revised and altered in the year 1791.—London, 1791 24mo. pp. 24. M.
Names of the members of the T. S. for the year 1792. —London, 1792. 24mo. pp. 24. M.
The laws of the T. S., instituted in the year 1781, revised and altered 1791. Printed 1793.—London. 24mo. pp. 24. M.
The laws of the T. S., instituted in the year 1781, revised and altered in the year 1821. London, printed for Rowe & Waller, 49, Fleet Street. 24mo. pp. 20.
The rules and regulations of the T. S., instituted in the year 1781, revised and altered 1834. London, Roake & Varty, printers, 31, Strand, 1834. 12mo. pp. ii-18.
The T. S. 1834 [List of members]. Roake & Varty, printers, 31, Strand. 12mo. pp. 4.
The rules and regulations of the R. T. S., instituted in the year 1781, revised and altered 1837. London, printed by T. Brettell,...1837. 24mo. pp. 26.
The T. S., 1841 [List of members]. Printed by T. Brettell, Rupert Street, Haymarket. 24mo. pp. 4.
The rules and regulations of the R. T. S., instituted in the year 1781, revised and altered 1837 and 1847. London, printed by W. Creswick, 5, John Street, Oxford Street, 1847. 24mo. pp. 24.
The rules and regulations of the R. T. S., instituted in the year 1781, revised and altered 1851. London, George Odell, printer,...1851. 24mo. pp. 22 (Rule 33 lithographed on an errata leaf).
The rules and regulations of the R. T. S., instituted in the year 1781, revised and altered 1858. London, printed by A. D. Mills,...1808[=1858]. 24mo. pp. 30.
The R. T. S., 1865 [List of members]. 24mo. pp. 6.
The rules and regulations of the R. T. S., instituted in the year 1781, revised and altered 1866. London, printed by Witherby & Co.,...1866. 24mo. pp. 30.
A history of the R. T. S., from its institution to the present time. Edited by a Toxophilite. 1867. Printed

[by H. Abraham, Taunton] for private circulation only. 8vo. pp. ii-126, and errata leaf. By Thomas Dawson.

A history of the R. T. S., from its institution to the present time. Edited by a Toxophilite. Second edition, 1870. Printed [by H. Abraham, Taunton] for private circulation only. 8vo. pp. iv-308. By Thomas Dawson. Pp. 294-303, List of works on archery.

The R. T. S., 1867-8 [List of members]. London, 1868. 24mo. pp. 8.

The rules and regulations of the R. T. S., instituted in the year 1781, revised and altered 1870. London, printed by Witherby & Co. 24mo. pp. 32.

Account of the Toxophilite season of 1870, with an introductory notice of part of the year 1869.—1871. 12mo. pp. 10. By William Butt, Hon. Sec. R. T. S. M.

Account of the Royal Toxophilite season of 1871, with an introductory notice of part of the year 1870.—London, 1872. 12mo. pp. 10. By William Butt, Hon. Sec. R. T. S. M.

The rules and regulations of the R. T. S., instituted in the year 1781, revised and altered 1874.—London, printed by Witherby & Co. 24mo. pp. 36.

Account of the Toxophilite season for [of] 1875.—London, 1876. 12mo. pp. 14. By William Butt, Hon. Sec. R. T. S. M.

The rules and regulations of the R. T. S., instituted in the year 1781, revised and altered 1876.—London, printed by Witherby & Co. 24mo. pp. 36.

Account of the Toxophilite season for [of] 1876.—London, 1877. 12mo. pp. 30. By William Butt, Hon. Sec. R. T. S. M.

Account of the Toxophilite season for [of] 1877.—London, printed by Witherby & Co., 1878. 12mo. pp. 28. By William Butt, Hon. Sec. R. T. S. M.

My former article (ante, p. 324) needs amending, thus :—Third paragraph, second line, after the word "are" insert "Roger Ascham's Toxophilus, 1545 "; sixth line, a full stop instead of the semi-colon, erase the word " and," begin a new sentence with the word " The "; eighth line, after " 1877 " insert " are interesting from the fact of their being the only writings I know of on hunting with the long-bow." P. 325, eleventh line, erase all and read " Thomas Digges." F. W. F.

(To be continued.)

ST. PAUL AND ROMAN LAW.

Readers of Sir Henry Maine's *Ancient Law* will remember how that learned writer remarks on the influence which the ideas and principles of Roman jurisprudence have exercised upon the thought, and especially the theological thought, of the Western world. The subject is well worthy of exhaustive treatment ; particularly, I think, that part of it which regards the influence of Roman law on the writings of St. Paul. That the great teacher Gamaliel instilled a knowledge of the civil law into his yet greater pupil is of itself not unlikely, and the internal evidence derivable from St. Paul's Epistles strengthens the hypothesis.

I have jotted down a few passages in which the mind of the apostle appears most clearly to have been influenced by his study of Roman law, and should be very glad if any of your readers, who may have more capacity for the task than I have

myself, would point out others. Gaius, our e authority, flourished in the second century Christian era, and no doubt drew much material from older sources. Most of my pa I have taken from his *Institutes*, and have them in juxtaposition with St. Paul's wor represented in the Vulgate translation [whi have collated with the edition of Paris, 1870 the *imprimatur* of Abp. Darboy—Ed.]. Pa from the *Institutes* of Justinian are marked and from the *Digest* by the usual abbreviati [These have been collated with the *Corpus* of the brothers Kriegel.]

Justice.

Reddite ergo omnibus debita.—Rom. xiii. 7.	Justitia est const perpetua voluntas jus
Dilectio proximi malum non operatur. Plenitudo ergo legis est dilectio.— Rom. xiii. 10.	cuique tribuens.—*In:* quoted from Ulpian died A.D. 228.
Omnis enim lex in uno sermone impletur: Diliges proximum tuum sicut teipsum.—Galat. v. 14.	Juris præcepta sun honeste vivere, alteru lædere, suum cuiqu huere.— *Inst.*, i. 1, quoted from Ulpian.

Freemen and Slaves—Modes by which Roman Citiz was attained.

Et respondit tribunus : Ego multa summa civilitatem hanc consecutus sum. Et Paulus ait : Ego et natus sum.—Acts xxii. 28.	Latini multis mo civitatem Romanam veniunt.—Gaius, i. 28 Rursus liberorum num alii ingenui sun libertini.
	Ingenui sunt, qui nati sunt; libertini, justa causa manumiss Rursus libertorum tri genera ; nam aut civ mani, aut Latini, aut ticiorum numero s Gaius, i. 10-12.

The Authorized Version confuses this passa; inserting the word " free" in St. Paul's an The point is, the apostle was a Roman citize birth—inhabitants of Cilicia having this privi whereas the chief captain obtained citizensh purchase, either upon receiving his freedo subsequently, having been formerly a *libertu*

Patria Potestas.

I'co autem : Quanto tempore heres parvulus est, nihil differt a servo, cum sit dominus omnium ; sed sub tutoribus et actoribus est usque ad præfinitum tempus a patre.—Galat. iv. 1, 2.	Nec me preterit G rum gentem crede potestate parentum l esse.—Gaius, i. 55. Præterea, qui ad c tempus testamento tutores, finito eo dep tutelam.—*Inst.*, i. 22.

This passage from Gaius is a remarkable illu tion of St. Paul's desire to be all things to all To the Galatians, among whom a *patria po* resembling that of Rome prevailed, he writ the position of the heir under tutors and cui (*actores*), and takes an illustration from their known custom. Dr. Lightfoot (Galatians, *in* refuses to see any special significance in words, but assigns no particular reason for so doing. *Actores* are mentioned by Justinian, *Inst.*, i. 23, 6, and *D.*, xxvi. 7, 24.

Marriage, Monogamy, &c.

Nam quæ sub viro est mulier, vivente viro, alligata est legi: si autem mortuus fuerit vir ejus, soluta est a lege viri. Igitur, vivente viro, vocabitur adultera si fuerit cum alio viro: si autem mortuus fuerit vir ejus, libera est a lege viri: ut non sit adultera si fuerit cum alio viro.—Rom. vii. 2, 3.

Omnino auditur inter vos fornicatio, et talis fornicatio, qualis nec inter Gentes, ita ut uxorem patris sui aliquis habeat.—1 Cor. v. 1.

Item eam quæ nobis quondam socrus aut nurus aut privigna aut noverca fuit (nefas est ducere uxorem) ideo autem diximus quondam, quia si adhuc constant eæ nuptiæ per quas talis adfinitas quæsita est, alia ratione inter nos nuptiæ non possunt, quia neque eadem duobus nupta esse potest, neque idem duas uxores habere.—Gaius, i. 63.

Socrum quoque et noveram prohibitum est uxorem ducere, quia matris loco sunt.—*Inst.*, i. 10, 7.

The seventh chapter of the Epistle to the Romans is especially worthy of notice, as St. Paul in the opening of it expressly says that he is writing *scientibus legem.*

Heirs and Inheritance.

Si autem filii, et heredes: heredes quidem Dei, coheredes autem Christi.—Rom. viii. 17.

Sui autem et necessarii hæredes sunt veluti filius filiave, &c.—Gaius, ii. 156.

Wills.

Ubi enim testamentum est, mors necesse est intercedat testatoris, testamentum enim in mortuis confirmatum est: alioquin nondum valet, dum vivit qui testatus est.—Heb. ix. 16, 17.

Mentis nostræ justa contestatio, in id solemniter facta, ut post mortem nostram valeat.—Ulpian, *Reg.*, xx. 1.

Testamentum est voluntatis nostræ justa sententia de eo, quod quis post mortem suam fieri velit.—*D.*, xxviii. 1, 1.

Whatever may have been the case with St. Paul, it is evident that St. Jerome had no knowledge of Roman law, for the most rudimentary acquaintance with the subject would have made him write *jus* for νόμος in its abstract sense of *law*, and not *lex*, which is merely a *statute*.

EDWARD H. MARSHALL.

The Temple.

THE TEN ORDERS OF ANGELS.—Mr. Skeat, in his most valuable body of notes upon *Piers the Plowman* (E. E. T. S., 1877), draws attention, at p. 33, to the ten orders of angels mentioned in Text C., Passus ii. 105, and he illustrates the passage by a quotation from *O. E. Homilies*, ed. Morris (E. E. T. S., 1868), p. 219. An interesting parallel will be found in J. de Amundesham, *Annales Monasterii S. Albani* (Rolls Series), vol. i., Appendix (C.), which contains an account, written c. 1428, of the altar of the Holy Cross (and St. Laurence), in the north transept of St. Alban's Abbey Church:—

"Assunt etiam ibidem duo angeli, a curiâ cœlesti destinati, unigenitum Dei Patris Filium in agonia suæ Passionis consolaturi, et ejusdem gloriosam victoriam hominum salvationem, et decimi ordinis angelici deperditi restaurationem, eidem cœlesti curiæ relaturi."—P. 420.

R. R. LLOYD.

St. Albans.

BLACKBURN COTTON MILLS.—The following account of the origin of the names of various Blackburn mills seems to me worth a corner in "N. & Q." It is from the *Standard* of April 18:—

"The constant patter of feet over the flags and pavement announced the cessation of labour in the cotton mills. Last night some wag announced that a meeting would be held at the Exchange Hall to be addressed by the strike delegates, and many thousands assembled for the purpose of taking part in the proceedings, but no meeting was held, as the hall had not been hired for any such occasion. The anxious crowds discussed the probabilities of the struggle, stating that the 'Rat Hole' was going on, that was a portion of the Throstle Nest Mill, once the property of Mr. Turner, M.P. The mill of Messrs. J. and F. Johnston was running, because the members of the firm had not joined the masters' union. Tom Abbott had pulled down his notice and withdrawn from the Masters' Association—he was going on. Another master had seceded from the Masters' Association, who had a place at Coppy Nook, on the ground that he could not afford to stop. The speakers in the crowd seemed perfectly conversant with all that was going on in the mills. 'The Physic,' a colossal concern, so called from its founder having been a physician, was adjusting its machinery for a stoppage. Hollin-bank Mill, built about twenty years ago, was stopping, but its proprietor, it was alleged, had promised his hands 5s. per head per week if they would remain away four weeks. The 'Cat Hole' was just preparing to stop. This appellation was applied to the mill of Mr. Eli Heyworth, one of the active colleagues of Colonel Jackson. The 'Butter Tub,' known as the Messrs. Lewis, originally wholesale grocers, and 'The Smut' had stopped; and so had 'The Twelve Apostles,' 'The Glory,' and 'The Hallelujah,' small weaving shed. 'The Twelve Apostles' refers to a weaving shed of which the original promoters, eighteen years ago, were total abstainers, who failed; their building and machinery were sold for very little to an enterprising manufacturer, and the original proprietors were returned 10l. each in place of the 100l. they had invested. 'The Glory' and 'The Hallelujah' refer to mills whose proprietors were revivalists. Another mill, 'The Mushroom,' denotes a fabric that was created by a man who was not supposed to possess a single penny. Another very large concern, both for spinning and weaving, but principally spinning, is known as 'The Lather Box,' its possessor having once been a barber, who shaved at one halfpenny each, but now owns seven large mills, chiefly spinning mills, and is the fortunate possessor of the extensive estates that formerly belonged to Lord De Tabley in the valley of the Ribble. 'The Sand Hole' is the next mill to the Lather Box, and its origin was the excavation of as much red sand as realized the money to build the mill."

JAMES BRITTEN.

British Museum.

WHIMSICAL PARLIAMENTARY EPITOME.—We usually expect, on the assembling of each new Parliament, to see in *Punch* some of the names of representatives placed in odd conjunction. It would appear that this is no new idea. As far back as 1802 I find the following "Whimsical Epitome of the New House of Commons" in the papers :—

"A Gardner, with a Garland, and two Roses, without a Thorn.—Twelve Smiths, with many Stewards, Butlers, and Cooks.—An Orchard, with Lemons.—A Cartwright, with a Pole.—A Martin, and two Rooks.—A Park, with a Huntingfield, a Warren, a Fox, and a Hare.—Two Bastards, with two Wards.—A Hill, with two Towns-ends. —Two Brooks, and a Trench.—A Taylor, with a Spencer. —A Wood, with a Forrester.—Three Camels, a Bullock, and two Lambs.—A Moor, with Birch, Broom, Hawthorne, and Beech.—A Bishop with Parsons, a Chaplain, and an Abbot.—A Temple, and five Fanes.—Two Pitts, with Coals.—A Baker, with Whitebread.—And a Mann and a Hussey, with only one Patten."

I copy this from the *Salopian Journal* of Oct. 13, 1802, but it is doubtless taken from a metropolitan paper. A. R.
Croeswylan, Oswestry.

A BISHOP IN MASQUERADE.—On the occasion of a masqued ball at Prior Park in the time of Ralph Allen, Bishop Warburton was asked by his wife to join the party, without a mask, but in disguise. The lady ordered a post-chaise to be in readiness in the courtyard, and equipped the bishop in the wig and uniform of a general officer who was one of the guests. A report was spread that a gentleman from India was expected, the carriage drew up at the door, and she entered the ball-room "with a veteran-like officer whom she presented gravely to the company, saying, 'Gentlemen and ladies, give me leave to introduce to you Brigadier-General Mores'" (*Gent. Mag.*, 1802, p. 423). Bishop Hoadley wrote a prologue to *All for Love*, which was recited by Lady Bateman in 1718 at Blenheim. As a preaching bishop no prelate exceeded Matthews. As Dean of Durham during eleven years and a half he preached 721, as Bishop of Durham in twelve years 556, and as Archbishop of York 722 sermons.
MACKENZIE E. C. WALCOTT.

GENOESE PROVERBS.—
" Homo sine pecuniâ est viva imago mortis."
" Viginti Oves faciunt Gregem :
Decem Boves faciunt Armentum :
Tres Canonici faciunt Capitulum :
Quo majores sunt bestiæ, eo minor requiritur numerus."
This last is from Rome.
W. J. BERNHARD SMITH.

ROBERT FLOWER, THE LOGARITHMIST. — Mr. Alexander J. Ellis has found the date of his burial, Feb. 23, 1774, at the age of sixty-three. This would give his birth as 1710 or 1711, for which the register should be looked after. I have a notion he may be Scotch. HYDE CLARKE.

ST. MARGARET'S, WESTMINSTER.—The beautiful east window of St. Margaret's, Westminster, being regarded as a " monument of superstition and idolatry," was very nearly removed o Puritan spirit displayed by certain volume in its defence, called *The O1 Churches*, was published by Dr. Wils cumbent. It was the composition Hole, B.D., Fellow of Exeter College, of Exeter, Rector of Menheniot, and of Barnstaple. Dr. Wilson's share in was limited to the introduction, pp. 15- seventh section, pp. 136-143 (Chalm xxxii. 182 ; *Gent. Mag.*, 1817, p. 2 always a just matter to detect plagiaris vice of all times. MACKENZIE E. C. V

POPULONIA AND SARDINIA.—
" From sea-girt Populonia,
Whose sentinels descry
Sardinia's snowy mountain-tops
Fringing the southern sky."
Macaulay's *Horatius*

Sardinia here is clearly an error ; Mace to say Corsica. Populonia is (or rath believe it does not exist now) on the coas in a line with Cape Corso at the norther of Corsica, and just opposite the island A sentinel stationed at Populonia wo ingly hardly see the mountains of Sard might on a clear day see those of Corsic considerably higher than the mountains island. The highest mountain in Sard Genargentu, is over five thousand feet but Monte Rotondo, in Corsica, is thousand, and Monte d' Oro not much epithet " snowy " is accordingly much cable to the Corsican than to the Sardi tains. It would never do to lay profar the text of Macaulay's stirring lay, bi editions the error might be corrected in
JONATHAN B

" GIVING THE STRAIGHT TIP."—I s primarily, this was a turf phrase ; but I hear it applied in other ways in run Thus, a farmer, in speaking of his inte his landlord's steward, said, " I gav straight tip ! I told him that if I co the barn floor made good, and the bul built, I should give up the farm." speaking of a rustic engagement that existing several years between his dau young man, said, " Then she gave him tip ! ' If you don't want me,' she saj another man as does ; so you 'd better and make up your mind at once !'" T the dilatory lover to book, and the bar riage were put up within a fortnight.
" Giving the straight tip," as thus used means speaking plainly and decisively- an *ultimatum*. CUTHBEE

CHESTER MYSTERY PLAYS.—In a 4 seventeenth century, a short notice is gi

Chester mystery plays (*Historical Manuscripts Commission*, vol. i. p. 49) :—"The ancient Whitson playes in Chester were set forth at the cost and charges of these occupations, and played yearly on Monday, Tuesday, and Wednesday in Whitsun week, being first made and . . . put into English tongue by one Randall Higden, a monk of Chester Abbey, A.D. 1269." The companies as they have joined and the parts that they played at their own costs here follow. The *Drama of the World* was presented in twenty-five portions, the first being the fall of Lucifer and the last being Doomsday. Nine of these were given on the first day, nine on the second day, and seven on the third day. On the first day the Barbers and Tanners bring forth the falling of Lucifer ; the Drapers and Hosiers bring forth the creation of the Worlde. On the second day the Cooks, Tapsters, Hostelers, and Innkeepers presented the Harrowing of Hell. The last on the third day was Doomsday.
　　　　　　　　　　　　ALICE B. GOMME.

Queries.

[We must request correspondents desiring information on family matters of only private interest, to affix their names and addresses to their queries, in order that the answers may be addressed to them direct.]

THE CHANGE IN THE ENGLISH PRONUNCIATION OF LATIN.—I wish to know the particulars and the date of the change in the pronunciation of the Latin language in England. I assume at the outset, as I believe that I am entitled to do, that the proper method of pronouncing that language is that which, broadly speaking, is used by all Roman Catholic priests, whether in or out of church; and that the same pronunciation prevailed in pre-Reformation times—in fact, in a few words, that the "Church" or "Roman Catholic" pronunciation is and has ever been the correct method. This being so, it is obvious that the English method, or that which I and hundreds of others in years past have been taught, must have been introduced into this kingdom at some particular date, and by some particular person or influence. I wish to know when and by whom. I have a recollection of reading some document or other in which it is stated that the change was made and adopted by certain English persons in the reign of Queen Elizabeth, so that they should not be mistaken for Roman Catholics by their speech ; and that this change took root, and eventually established what we may call the "Protestant" or English pronunciation. I should be exceedingly glad of any information on the point.　　　　　　W. H. HART.
Gravesend.

[In the present day theological partisanship cannot fairly be charged upon any pronunciation of Latin. The Public Schools scheme has introduced into England some of the principal characteristics of the continental method, and Presbyterian Scotchmen have never altered their pronunciation, which is identical in principle with what our correspondent calls the "Church" or "Roman Catholic" method. There are ethnic differences between the French, German, and Italian pronunciations which may be observed in the chanting in those several countries. See 2ⁿᵈ S. iii. 108 ; vi. 313, for some observations on this curious point by MR. ASHPITEL.]

POPE ALEXANDER VI.—I find the following on the fly-leaf of an old book in my possession :—
"N.B.—Alexander VI. Papa.
　Vendit Alexander Claves, altaria, Christum
　　Vendere jure potest, emerat ille prius.
　Sextus Tarquinius, Sextus Nero, Sextus et ipse ;
　　Semper et à Sextis, perdita Roma fuit.
　De vitio in vitium, de flammâ cessit in ignem,
　　Roma sub Hispano deperitura jugo.
N.B.—Borgia (Cesar) Cardinal, 2ᵈ fils a Alexandre VI.,
avoit p. devise : aut Cæsar, aut nihil. Ce qui donne occasion à quelque poëte de son tems de lui faire ce distique.
　Borgia Cæsar erat, factis et nomine Cæsar
　　Aut nihil, aut Cæsar dixit, utrumque fuit.
Sennaar fit les 2 épigrammes qui suivent :—
　Aut nihil, aut Cæsar vult dici Borgia : quidni?
　　Cum simùl et Cæsar possit et ess......
　Omnia vincebas, sperabas omnia, Cæsar,
　　Omnia deficiunt, Incipis esse Nihil."
Who is intended by Sennaar ? The letters following " ess " are destroyed; would the end of the line read " esse nihil " ? Are these lines known to any of your readers ?　　　　　　　　　　H. A. W.

THE "PASS-BOOK" OF A BANK.—I am asked why a bank " pass-book " is so called ; a question to which I confess myself unable to give an absolutely convincing and satisfactory reply, though a probable and plausible one is ready to hand. Can any reader kindly answer the inquiry? I should feel obliged by even conjectures on this point, but very much more so by *facts*, that is, by authentic instances of the use of the term, exhibiting its origin and history, and accompanied with dates.
　　　　　　　　　　　　　　BANKER.

HOLMAN, PAINTER.—Can you give me some information about a marine painter named Holman, who lived during the latter half of the last century? I know a very good and interesting painting of his representing part of the Channel Fleet off St. Mary's, Scilly. The date on the picture is 1778. I should be glad to know if there are many paintings by this artist extant, and in what repute as a painter he was held.　　　　　　UNIT.

J. S. JONES, M.D., OF BOSTON, AMERICA, is author of *The Surgeon of Paris*, a drama, Boston, 1856, 12mo., and also of many other pieces, produced within the last forty years. Is Dr. Jones still living ?

" THE ANNIVERSARY SPEAKER."—A book thus named, by Rev. Newton Heston, was published at Philadelphia in 1862. Of what church was Mr. Heston a minister, and is he resident in Philadelphia? R. INGLIS.

ALL SAINTS' CHURCH, LOUGHBOROUGH.—The deep cavetto of the western window of this church is filled with carved crests and armorial shields. Though now much weathered, many are still distinguishable. Among others are the rose, portcullis, and Agnus Dei. The last, I believe, was the crest of the Henson family. Will some reader of "N. & Q." kindly say where I can find a complete list of these crests and shields? JAMES SCOTT.

BUCKLES IN SHOES.—Is the following the earliest notice of buckles in shoes? St. John Baptist in a sermon of 1547 is said to have counted himself "unworthy to unbuckle our Saviour's shoes" (Homily, Misery of Man, p. 11, attributed to Harpsfield). Kemp mentions his host at Rockland with black shoes shining and made strait with copper buckles of the best, in his Nine Days' Wonder. This was in the reign of Elizabeth. MACKENZIE E. C. WALCOTT.

EARLY DOUBLE NAME.—In Mr. Millett's new volume, The Parish Register of Madron, there is mention of Nicholas Arthur de Tyntagel, who was instituted vicar in 1309. Mr. Millett's habitual accuracy forbids suspicion of error, but is not this a very rare instance of the use of a double Christian name? TREGEAGLE.

SIR CHARLES WHITWORTH.—Whom did this brother of Earl Whitworth marry? Wanted also pedigree of Francis Whitworth of Blowerpipe, M.P. for Stafford about the time of the Revolution.

JOHN SOLE, LL.D.—Whom did he (b. circ. 1660), registrar of the diocese of Dublin, and M.P. for Carysfort, marry?

THOMAS SCOT (OR SCOTT).—Wanted the pedigree and descendants of this regicide. HASTINGS C. DENT.

NORFOLK POLLS, &c.—Where can I see the original polls, or copies of same, for Norfolk prior to 1714? And beside wills and parish registers, how can I trace a Norfolk yeoman previous to 1674? JAMES H. HARRISON.
Burgh Castle, Suffolk.

HERALDRY.—The following arms and crest are said to be borne by a family of the name of Jenkins in Wales, but of what part of Wales I am not informed. As there are many Jenkinses in the principality, any information tending to identify this branch is particularly requested. Arms: Party per pale, argent and sanguine, three fleurs-de-lis. Crest: Battle-axe on a wreath. LLALLAWG.

INSCRIPTION ON A BELL.—Can any of your readers throw light on the following inscription, which appears on the tenor bell in the parish church of Yarnscombe, in North Devon? The bell bears the date of 1500, is marked with the arms of the Cockworthys (three cocks gules), and is said to be the finest in the northern part of the county after that at Sheepwash. The inscription of which a solution is desired is simply the following letters : s . R . Q . P . O . N . M . L. D. C. BOULGER.

PETTY TREASON.—Miss Cobbe, in an article in last month's Contemporary, on "Wife Torture in England," states in a note, p. 63 : "A woman was burned to death under this atrocious law at Chester in 1760 for poisoning her husband." Where can I find an account of this? E. LEATON BLENKINSOPP.

"PAW WA'."—Defoe, in his Modern History of the Devil, Bohn, 1854, p. 488, uses this expression : "The Pope has a cloven foot, with which he paw wa's upon the world, wishes them all well, and at the same time cheats them." Of course the dictionaries do not give the word. Defoe uses it again at p. 492 : "As often as it is needful for her to paw wa for half-a-crown." In the first instance it is written paw wa's, in the second paw wa. Does it mean pawing away, palming? C. A. WARD.
Mayfair.

"A DESCRIPTION OF THREE ANCIENT ORNAMENTAL BRICKS, FOUND AT DIFFERENT PERIODS IN LONDON AND GRAVESEND. LONDON, 1825."—The above octavo of thirty-two pages is before me. It contains a description of an ornamented brick on which is represented the story of St. Hubert. This brick was found in the year 1808 in a well on the premises of Thomas Johnson, Esq., adjoining the Catherine Wheel in High Street, Gravesend (now pulled down), opposite the Town Hall. The author's name is not appended. Can any of your readers enlighten me on this point? Also, as to where the brick in question now exists. W. H. HART.
Gravesend.

JOSEPHUS.—In the works of Josephus given by Whiston there is a treatise on Hades. Can any reader inform me whether it is in any other list of the works of Josephus? W. J. BIRCH.

AUTHORS OF BOOKS WANTED.—
Royal Recollections on a Tour to Cheltenham, Gloucester, Worcester, and Places adjacent, in the Year 1788. Ninth edition. London, 1788. 8vo.
Historical Collections relative to the Town of Belfast. Belfast, 1817. 8vo. ABHBA.
Musomania ; or, the Poet's Purgatory. Baldwin, 1817.
A Walk from the Town of Lanark to the Falls of the Clyde : in Verse. 8vo. Glas., Chapman, 1816.

A *Trip to Portsmouth and the Isle of Wight: in
Rambling Verse.* By a Friend of Britain. 8vo. Edin.,
for A., 1797.

*The Mad-Cap : a Comedy for the Digestion by A. V.
Kotzebue.* By R***** H***** (query Hunter). 8vo.
Edin., 1800.—Not mentioned anywhere.

*Pizarro : a Tragedy differing widely from all other
Pizarros.* By a North Briton. 8vo. Lond., n.d. (1800 ?).

The Psalms of David: Specimens of a New Version.
Privately printed. Lond., 1829.—The author says he
has the whole ready if called for. Not mentioned by
any who have treated of the Psalms, and not continued,
I think.   J. O.

AUTHORS OF QUOTATIONS WANTED.—

"Hark, from the tomb a doleful sound !
Mine ears, attend the cry !
Ye living men, come view the ground
Where ye must shortly lie."   J. R. M.

" Unfading in glory, unfailing in years,
The mother of Churchmen and Tories appears."
These lines refer to Oxford University.
NORVAL CLYNE.

Replies.

PRIVATE PROPERTY IN LAND IN ENGLAND.
(5ᵗʰ S. ix. 347.)

In response to the appeal of MR. SMITH
WOOLLEY, I beg to offer the following remarks on
the state of the land tenure amongst our Teutonic
ancestors. The principal authorities on the subject
are Cæsar and Tacitus for the pre-historic period,
the Anglo-Saxon charters as contemporary records,
and the works of Sharon Turner, Kemble, Lappenburg, Sir Henry Maine, Palgrave, and Freeman for
historical information. Cæsar (*Bell. Gall.*, vi. 22)
says of the Germans as to their occupation of land :

" Neque quisquam agri modum certum aut fines habet
proprios ; sed magistratus ac principes in anuos singulos
gentibus cognationibusque hominum, qui una coierint,
quantum, et quo loco visum est, agri adtribuunt atque
anno post alio transire cogunt."

Tacitus (*Germania*, xxvi.) states :—

" Agri, pro numero cultorum, ab universis per vices
occupantur, quos mox inter se secundùm dignationem
partiuntur ; facilitatem partiendi camporum spatia
præstant. Arva per annos mutant ; et superest ager."

It is clear, then, that in their original continental
seat the land was the property of the community,
partitioned out from time to time for the usufruct
of individuals or families.

When the Saxons invaded Britain, they necessarily brought with them their old laws and institutions. From a very early period after their
invasion private interest to a certain extent in land
was recognized, but the very name *alod* given to
these estates shows that they were *allot-ments*
awarded by the community for services or distinction of some kind. Mr. Kemble says :—

" It is certain that not all the land was so distributed ;
a quantity sufficient to supply a proper block of arable
to each settler was set apart for division ; while the
surplus fitted for cultivation......and a great amount of

fine grass or meadow land remained in undivided
possession as commons."

Mr. Kemble has here allowed speculation to out-
run known fact. We have no record of such early
appropriation of land. Sir Henry Maine (*Village·
Communities*, 10) says :—

" The mark or township was an organized and self-
acting group of Teutonic families exercising a common
proprietorship over a definite tract of land, its *Mark*,
cultivating its domain on a common system, and sustain-
ing itself by the produce. It is described by Tacitus as
the *Vicus*. It is well known to have been the proprietary
and even the political unit of the earliest English society."

Mr. Freeman (*Hist. Norman Conquest*) takes much
the same view. See also Palgrave, vol. i. p. 72.
Lappenburg (vol. ii. p. 323) says :—

" The land conquered by the Germanic tribes belonged
to them in common, hence among the Anglo-Saxons its
denomination of Folc-land, or land of the people (*ager
publicus*). This was the property of the community,
though it might be occupied in common or possessed in
severalty ; in the latter case it was probably parcelled
out to individuals in the Folc-gemôt, or court of the
district, the grant being sanctioned by the freemen
present."

Baron von Haxthausen, who has investigated
closely the rural institutions of Germany, states
that there is a considerable district in the Hoch-
wald of Thor in which all the lands still belong to
the respective communities, among whose members
they are divided anew after the lapse of some years.

The system of run-rig tenure, which has subsisted
to our own times, particularly in Orkney, Shetland,
and the Hebrides, where the Norsemen settled, is
a relic of the ancient common proprietorship. In
this case the land is laid out in long ridges, the
several farmers having different ridges allotted to
them from year to year, according to the nature of
their crops.

It is not difficult to see how private ownership
grew out of this state of things. The *alods*, or
lots granted to individuals, first by the community
and subsequently by the chiefs or kings as representing the community, would naturally become,
in process of time, heritable property, until at
length the possession of land was essential to every
freeman. But amidst all this, surviving even the
feudal system, which vested all lands in the Crown,
the common lands, which remain to this day, and
which require legislative authority for their appropriation, bear irresistible testimony to the original
common ownership of the lands in each mark or
township.

Probably the above succinct statement may
suffice, at least to point out to MR. WOOLLEY
from what sources he can complete the information
he seeks.

And now for a short notice on the mode of
division adopted, or, in other words, the origin of
the land measures in England.

Our lineal and square measures are drawn from
different sources and from several groups. The

inch, foot, cubit, yard, fathom, are personal measures derived originally from the human frame, and do not square integrally with our land measures, which start from a different point of departure. We cannot, of course, quote the chapter and verse of history showing the when and the where these measures were invented, but the terms themselves and the relations in which they stand may help us to tolerably safe conclusions. It must be self-evident that the terms perch, rood, furlong, acre, had a meaning when they were first applied, and if it can be shown that this meaning would naturally arise out of certain circumstances, the knowledge of which we derive from other sources, the inference seems fair that we have hit on the right explanation.

When the Saxons took possession of Britain a large portion of the country was dense forest. The first thing to be done before cultivating the land was to clear away the superfluous timber. This would be done by degrees. Every patch thus cleared was called a *rood*, or clearing; A.-S. *wrotan, rodan*, to root up; Lat. *terra rodata*. These cleared patches would be very precious to the new settlers, and means would necessarily be taken to measure and set them out. The foot and yard measures were too short for practical use. It was therefore natural to take a pole or perch of convenient length as the unit from which to start. The length of the pole differed in different parts of the country, being five and a half yards, seven yards, and in Lancashire and Cheshire eight yards long. Forty of these square poles constituted a rood. They might of course be arranged in any form, but for the purpose of ploughing—these clearings being arable—setting them out lengthways was the most convenient. A furrow would be the natural boundary between the clearings and the furrow-length; *furleng* or *furlong* would thus be the length of the forty poles constituting the rood. This is confirmed by the fact that the furlong is not a definite measure, but varies according to the length of the perch, being 220 yards in England and 280 yards in Ireland. In England the perch of five and a half yards became the standard or statute measure, though the provincial measures of seven, seven and a half, and eight yards continued in use down to our own day. Spelman, under "Furlongus," explains it thus: "Quasi a *furrowlonge*, hoc est quòd longitudine sulci determinatur, . . . et continet plerumque 40 perticas."

The Anglo-Saxon mile was doubtless derived from the Roman *mille-passuum*, but had to be accommodated to the perch, the unit of Anglo-Saxon land measures. The Roman mile was 1,518 English yards, equal to a thousand paces of a fraction over a yard and a half each. Eight times the length of the furlong or rood, based on the normal perch of five and a half yards, equal to 1,760 yards,

was sufficiently near for all practical purposes, whilst a definite principle was laid down connecting the measures of length and area. Of course, where the perch was seven or eight yards, instead of five and a half, the mile had to be extended in similar proportion, making the Irish mile 2,240 yards compared with the English 1,760.

The term *acre* in its various forms is perhaps, next to the words expressive of domestic relations, one of the most widely diffused in existence, there being no Aryan tongue, from Sanskrit to Cymric, in which it is not found. Its application as a definite measure of area is of comparatively late introduction, the A.-S. *æcer*, like Gr. αγρος, Lat. *ager*, Goth. *akrs*, meaning simply a cultivated field. Spelman says, "*Æcer* apud Saxones non tantùm definitam terræ quantitatem, sed latum quantumvis agrum significabat, quod adhuc in Germania remanet, et appellatione et usu." Ducange adopts the same view, referring to this passage in confirmation.

When the rood, or small clearing, assumed a definite area, it was natural that the *ager*, or larger holding, should also be brought into a defined quantity. The most obvious way of doing this was to place several roods together side by side; so Spelman quotes, "Continet autem *acra* secundùm stadii longitudinem 40 *rodas*, seu perticas; in latitudine tantum quatuor. Perinde etiam *roda* terræ 40 perticas in longitudine; unam vero, solummodo in latitudine."

Though the acre was thus brought into correspondence with the units of land measure it has never thoroughly coalesced with them. A square perch, a square rood or furlong, a square mile have their sides exactly expressed by integers. Not so with the acre. Its square root, whether in perches or yards, cannot be expressed without several places of decimal fractions. It is evident, therefore, that the acre as a definite area has been an adaptation subsequent to the adoption of the unit of land measure.

When we extend our inquiries beyond the acre, and endeavour to estimate the area of the virgate, the hide, the bovate, &c., we find the subject surrounded with insuperable difficulties. The documents vary so widely as to render it impossible to establish any common measure. There can be no doubt that the Norman Conquest introduced great confusion into the nomenclature as well as the tenure of the holdings. Virgates and bovates were not Saxon terms. In many cases in the Domesday survey arable land alone was estimated, in others pasture, forest, and even waste were included. Many documents, however, agree in laying down as a normal rule, subject to very wide deviations, the following scale:—

A square furlong or fardel contained 10 acres.
4 fardels = 40 acres = 1 virgate.
4 virgates = 160 acres = 1 hide.

4 hides = 640 acres, or 1 square mile, constituted a knight's fee.
5 knights' fees = 3,200 acres = 1 barony.

J. A. PICTON.

Sandyknowe, Wavertree.

SCOTT FAMILY: THE PARENTAGE OF ARCHBISHOP ROTHERHAM.

(5th S. vii. 89, 139, 158, 292, 330, 375, 416, 470, 490, 509; viii. 29, 79, 370, 389, 410; ix. 37, 369.)

Materials have not yet been found to dispose of the question whether Scott or Rotherham was the correct name of the archbishop. To me it seems little less than certain that Leland's two statements are the *fons et origo* of the practice of succeeding authors in writing the *alias*. Doubtless a closer study of the transfer of Wenlock's Luton estates may result in unearthing the requisite data. The quotation from Pote's *Catalogus Alumnorum* of "Thomas Scot *alias* Rotheram, 1444," can have little weight in the face of the declaration in the preface that the catalogue was "prepared *with the assistance* of a MS. in the possession of the Rev. Dr. Evans, &c.," for we have but to consult any current calendar to see what emendatory liberties can proceed from an editorial hand. And, strange to say, in Pote's work there is, anno 1449, a John Rotheram proceeding to King's College. It is extremely probable that he was the brother of the archbishop; but none of the annotators or compilers of the lists were drawn to attach the same *alias* to his name, doubtless from his comparative obscurity, and their ignorance of the fraternal relationship.

Observing that Wolsey was Cardinal of St. Cecilia, I offer the natural conjecture that some confusion affording the opportunity of applying the title to Rotherham—of course in mistake, as it cannot be supposed that the latter in his last will would describe himself as "Archiepiscopus Eboracensis," and omit the higher dignity.

In a note to the new edition of the archbishop's will, published in the Surtees Society's last volume of York wills, Can$_{on}$ Raine, who apparently had access to the originals for his statements, says that "on Jan. 14, 1493-4, William Grayberne, Provost, and the fellows of the College of Jesus of Rotherham, quit claim to John Scott and his heirs their interest in Houseley and le Chapell, in accordance with a charter thereof made to the said John by the archbishop himself. On Nov. 4, 1507, John Scott makes Houseley Hall over to trustees as part of the jointure of Agnes his wife."

I presume this is the John Scott, consanguineus, of the archbishop's will; if so, we have a fair starting point for further investigation.

I notice that MR. GATTY does not give the contents of the will of Thomas Scott, father of Sir Richard. Eastwood (*Hist. of Ecclesfield*) refers to it as dated Nov. 1, and proved Dec. 21, 1585.

If these few hints (and they pretend to be no

more) succeed in putting your combative correspondents on a fresh scent, I shall be glad to intervene in future discussion.

W. ROTHERHAM.

PUBLIC-HOUSE SIGNS (5th S. ix. 127, 174, 257, 293, 353.)—I hasten to reply to the appeal of S. P. I ought to have added to my former letter that the rebus, another means of communicating with the illiterate, was a source of inn signs. The "Bolt in Tun," which formerly existed in Fleet Street, from the rebus of Bolton, with which every antiquary is acquainted, is an illustration.

I do not hesitate to express my firm belief that the "Bull and Last" was a sign to claim the adherence of cordwainers. It must be borne in mind that the benefit clubs attached to trades have always been held at public-houses, and nothing could be more simple than a sign to attract the wayfarers of a particular class.

I cannot for a moment believe that any innkeeper could ever be inspired by "a superficial knowledge of topography" to erect a sign, especially in those times when they were adopted for the obvious purpose of attracting those who could not read.

The bush was the primitive sign of a public-house, hence the old adage which S. P. must remember.

"An anonymous head by Hollar of a monopolizer of sweet wines; near him are three barrels, over which is the word 'Medium'; he holds another small one under his arm. *Sign of the Bell and Bush;* over the sign is inscribed 'Good wine needs no bush nor a Bell.' The sign of the Bell and a capital A near it is evidently a rebus upon this man's name, which was Abel."—See Granger's *Biographical History, temp.* Charles I., vol. ii. p. 406.

I have seen in country towns a real bush put on a sign-post; the last one I noticed was at Pershore. The addition of the bull to distinguish one inn from another was a very easy process. The "Bull and Gate" admits of a like explanation.

If S. P. had ever noticed the illustration of the "Bull and Mouth," in Aldersgate Street, he would have been puzzled to refer it back to the *bouche* of France. Had the siege of Boulogne produced a strong national or political feeling or sentiment, there would have been a more general illustration of it, as in the numerous "Royal Oaks" that are to be found all over the country. One "Bull and Mouth," or one "Bull and Bush," is a very poor proof of "the basis of the corruption."

If S. P. will look at the *London Directory* he will see forty-four signs of the "Ship"; then follow eight signs with something added for a distinction. The same will be found with regard to tinction. The same will be found with regard to "King's Heads," "Bull's Heads," "Mitres," "Green Man," "Horns," &c.

In conclusion, let me ask S. P., or any other correspondent who "has doubts," to exercise his ingenuity in conjecturing, or, what would be better, give the slightest evidence, how the following signs, all of which exist in London, could be identified with Boulogne, either through the medium of "breeches that had been worn at the siege," or any other association that would give a clue to their origin : the "Bull and Anchor," the "Bull and Bell," the "Bull and Butcher," the "Bull in the Pound," the "Bull and Pump," and the "Bull and Ram." CLARRY.

TOUCHING FOR THE KING'S EVIL : FORMS OF PRAYER (5ᵗʰ S. ix. 49, 236, 251, 273, 336.)—I have a Prayer Book of Queen Anne's reign, which after the thanksgiving for her accession contains the service "For the Healing." It is large octavo, very well printed, with black-letter heads to the pages, as "For the King's Restauration"; but the title-page is lost, and printer's name and date. The metrical version of the Psalms, which occupies 232 numbered pages, seems of the same type, but has no black letter; but has "London. Printed by E. Powell, for the Company of Stationers, 1713"; and also bound with it is, "A Supplement to the New Version of the Psalms, by Dr. Brady and Mr. Tate. Containing the Psalms in *Particular Measures :* the *Usual Hymns, Creed, Lord's Prayer, Ten Commandments,* for the *Holy Sacrament,* &c., with *Gloria Patri's,* and *Tunes (Treble* and *Bass)* proper to each of them, and all of the rest of the *Psalms.* The Sixth Edition, Corrected and much Enlarged." There is a long description of "near 30 new Tunes, composed by several of the Best Masters, &c. The Whole being a Compleat Psalmody" (sixty pages). (The Order in Council for the allowance of the use of this Supplement in churches and chapels and congregations is dated from the Court at Hampton Court, July 30, 1703, the second year of her Majesty's reign.) It bears the imprint, "In the Savoy. Printed by *John Nutt ;* and sold by *James Holland,* at the Bible and Ball, at the West End of St. Paul's, 1708." The directions for "All *Psalms* of *Prayer, Mourning, Distress,* &c., to be sung to *grave, flat Tunes,*" &c., and "All *Psalms* of *Thanksgiving, Praise,* &c., to *airy, sharp Tunes,* as," &c., are very quaint and curious.

The name of my great-grandmother, which is my own, is elaborately printed (with pen and ink) Roman capitals, lengthwise at the end of the book, and with an apostrophic *s ;* date 1755. The print is so good that I often find it a saving of eyesight to use this old book in dark weather, and wish I could recover the date, if any correspondent of "N. & Q." has, and would kindly communicate, it. M. P. Cumberland.

A NONAGENARIAN (5ᵗʰ S. iv. 205.)—Some of your readers who are interested in the question of longevity may perhaps call to mind that at the above reference I demonstrated, or (to speak with

more becoming modesty) made it in a very high degree probable, that Esther Sharpe, a pauper, wh was given as one hundred years of age in th *Statistical Account of the Glanford Brigg Union* was at that time only ninety-four or, at the mos ninety-five. This rectification of mine was accepte by the poor law authorities, and her age is reduce in subsequent issues of the *Statistical Accoun* Esther Sharpe is still alive, aged, as I believe ninety-seven or ninety-eight years. A correspon dent of the *Gainsburgh News* for March 30 ha revived the old story in the following paragraph :-

"LONGEVITY.—Our correspondent writes : 'There : now living at Messingham Esther Sharp, aged 103 year She has never been known to take laudanum or any othe stimulant. She has been married twice.'"

It is important that this error should be onc more pointed out, or it will be by-and-by assume as proved that Esther Sharpe is really a cer tenarian. EDWARD PEACOCK.
Bottesford Manor, Brigg.

COLERIDGE OR WALPOLE (5ᵗʰ S. ix. 128.)- "Summer has set in with its usual severity" is phrase commonly attributed to Sydney Smitl The style of the thought and the turn of the ex pression are both more like Smith than either c the other two. There is a conversational littlenes about it that it would be impossible for Coleridg to have stumbled into, and its flavour has to much of the nineteenth century to come from th fine gentleman of Twickenham. C. A. WARD.
Mayfair.

GERMAN MEASLES (5ᵗʰ S. ix. 129.)— "*German Measles, Rötheln, Rubeola.*—The ter Rubeola was brought into use by German physiciar about the middle of the last century, to characterize disease which it was considered could belong to no or of the acute contagious or non-contagious eruption though closely resembling measles and scarlet feve Opinions with regard to it have greatly varied ; b latterly it has been shown that it is an independer disease by distinct epidemics of it, and by the fact th while it insures against a second attack of itself, affords no protection from measles or scarlet fever."

The above definition is from Prof. Charteri *Practice of Medicine,* and has the advantage being perfectly intelligible to a non-profession reader. MEDICUS.

I would beg to quote some remarks from the p of the late Dr. Hillier (see *Diseases of Childre* p. 303) :—

"There is a disease which is said to be more freque on the Continent than in Great Britain, but which l been seen here, and described by numerous observe It partakes of the characters both of measles and scar tina. It has been called Rötheln and Rubeola in G many; in England, *Rubeola notha,* epidemic Roseo Rosalia (Richardson), bastard measles and bastard sc latina. The eruption appears on the second or thi day, and at first resembles that of measles, becoming su sequently more like that of searlatina."

It is considered a spurious form of measles in England, and from its greater frequency in Germany than here is thus denominated German measles. It has been termed a hybrid of measles and scarlet fever.   JOHN COLEBROOK.

This disease takes its technical name, *Rötheln*, from the Germans, who were amongst the earliest to observe and discuss this hybrid malady between scarlet fever and measles. Hence its popular name, "German measles."   M. D.

COAT OF ARMS (5ᵗʰ S. ix. 148.)—The shield about which JAYDEE inquires bears the arms of Wheatley or Whetley of Fakenham, Norfolk—Argent, a bend sable between two bears salient of the second, chained and muzzled or, impaling those of Pepys of Southcreke in the same county—Sable, on a bend or, between two nags' heads erased argent, three fleurs-de-lis of the first. It points to the marriage of William Whetley, Esq., Chief Prothonotary of the Court of Common Pleas, with Clemence Pepys of Southcreke, who died in 1565. It is noteworthy that in 1813 the Rev. John Whateley, Vicar of Cookham, Berks, married Isabella Sophia, daughter of Sir William Pepys of London.   B. J.

The sinister coat is the same as that borne by the Hughes, a Scotch family.   SYWL.

The arms mentioned by JAYDEE are probably—dexter : Argent, a bend between two bears salient sable, chained and muzzled or (Wheatley of Fakenham, co. Norfolk), impaling Sable, on a bend or, between two nags' heads erased argent, three fleurs-de-lis of the field (Pepys).

GEO. J. ARMYTAGE.
Clifton Woodhead, near Brighouse.

THE LORD OF BURLEIGH (5ᵗʰ S. ix. 168.)—
"Lord Burghley, under the name of Jones, married in 1791, when he was thirty-seven years of age, a country maiden, Sarah Hoggins, became Marquis of Exeter 1793, and takes his wife, to her surprise, to Burghley House, near Stamford Town, where she died in 1797. He died in 1804. He made ample provision for her parents. Her quiet manners were greatly admired by Queen Charlotte. Grandparents of the present Marquis and Earl of Exeter."—From the appendix to Hubert Smith's *Tent Life in Norway*.
H. C. B.

A prose version of the story of *The Lord of Burleigh*, upon which the Laureate has recently founded a poem, is to be found in a number of Hazlitt's *Table Talk*, published in the *New Monthly Magazine* for May, 1822. A fuller account appeared in a work published last year in London, entitled *Tales of the Higher Classes*.
UNEDA.
Philadelphia.

The prose version of Tennyson's ballad, respecting which your correspondent MR. TAYLOR

inquires, and also of Moore's "You remember Ellen, our hamlet's pride," is to be found in Seward's *Spirit of Anecdote and Wit*, vol. iv. p. 285 (1823).   WILLIAM KELLY, F.R.H.S.
Leicester.

A "FEMALE HERCULES" (5ᵗʰ S. ix. 288.)—A. J. M. will find a short account of this woman in Timbs's *Romance of London*, vol. iii. p. 92. She was a Frenchwoman. One of her feats was to lift up an anvil by the hair of her head, and then have the same anvil placed on her bare bosom, while three smiths forged a horseshoe with their hammers, she talking and singing all the while. John Carter, the antiquary, is Timbs's authority.
E. LEATON BLENKINSOPP.

MELLON (5ᵗʰ S. ix. 208.)—I have heard that the village of St. Mellons, in Monmouthshire, was so called after St. Melan, an early bishop of Rouen, to whom the church is dedicated.   D. K. T.

THE TWO ROBBERS, ST. LUKE XXIII. (5ᵗʰ S. ix. 225.)—I would refer MR. MARSHALL to the sermon on the *Cluster of Grapes*, sub-division iii., by Faber Matthias (A.D. 1620). In 1859 Francis Ferrante published at Naples a reprint of Faber's sermons, 1,163 in number, in five 4to. vols. See Ashley's *Promptuary, in loc.*   F. S.
Churchdown.

SIR CHRISTOPHER ROBINSON, JUDGE OF THE ADMIRALTY COURT FROM 1828 TO 1833 (5ᵗʰ S. ix. 288.)—He died April 21, 1833, not 1853 as your correspondent states. An interesting notice of him will be found in the *Law Magazine*, vol. x. p. 485 (London, Saunders & Benning, 43, Fleet Street, 1833). Besides being the author of the first series of *Admiralty Reports*, 1798 to 1808, he was the author of the following treatises :—*Collectanea Maritima; being a Collection of Public Instruments tending to Illustrate the History and Practice of Prize Law* (London, printed by W. Wilson, St. Peter's Hill, Doctors' Commons, for J. White and J. Butterworth, Fleet Street, 1801) ; *A Translation of the Chapters CCLXXIII. and CCLXXXVII. of the Consolato Del Mare relating to Prize Law* (same publishers, 1800) ; and *A Report of the Judgment of the High Court of Admiralty on the Swedish Convoy, pronounced by Sir W. Scott Jan.* 11, 1790, which last I have not seen. His son, William Robinson, D.C.L. and Advocate of Doctors' Commons, reported in the Admiralty Court from 1838 to 1850.

If J. R. B. has not means of access to the *Law Magazine* I shall be happy to send him the substance of the notice I have referred to.
HUGH F. BOYD.
12, Doughty Street, W.C.

WORDS ONCE OBSCURE (5ᵗʰ S. ix. 226.) — A very useful list of "Words obsolete or rare in form, meaning, or construction," as occurring in the *Two Books of Homilies*, may be seen in the edition of the Clarendon Press, 1859, "General Index," pp. 624-9. ED. MARSHALL.

MIGUEL SOLIS, AGED 180 (5th S. ix. 361.)—MR. THOMS speaks of Dr. Hernandez's credence of this story as based apparently "upon the evidence of three witnesses." The second "witness" is stated by MR. THOMS to be "the oldest inhabitants of the district." Suppose half-a-dozen persons aged seventy or upwards, and uncontradicted by the "oldest inhabitant," were to agree in stating that "they remembered him (Miguel Solis) as a reputed centenarian when they were boys," would MR. THOMS consider this evidence to be lightly treated? "Reputed centenarianism" may often no doubt admit a deduction of fifteen or twenty years, but even then there would be tolerable evidence of an antiquity of 130 or 140 years. However, unless the witnesses were separately cross-examined as to the reality, and especially the independence, of their alleged recollection, the value of their evidence is at least uncertain, though it surely does not deserve to be placed on the same level as the "confession" of Miguel himself, or the "satisfaction" of the abbot. C. C. M.
Temple.

EDITH, WIFE OF THOMAS FOWLER, ESQ., AND "GENTILLWOMAN" TO MARGARET, MOTHER OF HENRY VII. (5th S. ix. 347.)—The arms on the brass in the chapel of Christ's College—as described —are Dinham quartering Arches. Sir John Dynham, Kt., married Joan, daughter and heiress of Richard de Arches. We may therefore conclude that Edith was one of their daughters, and sister of John, Lord Dynham, K.G.
B. W. GREENFIELD.
Southampton.

JOHN GILPIN (5th S. ix. 266.)—Among the critics of cavalry many a man has earned the nick-name of Johnny Gilpin who was no captain of London train-bands. GWAVAS.

CURIOUS NAMES (5th S. ix. 265.)—Some twenty-five or thirty years ago a child was baptized in our parish church by the name of Sigismunda, a name queer enough. In due course of time she was married and became Sigismunda Jones ; but when she brought her baby to be christened all persons seem to have forgotten how to spell her Christian name, which then became "Sydgister-mondayer," a much queerer name than Sigis-munda. BOILEAU.
Shrewsbury.

L,NCOLN'S INN (5th S. ix. 267.)—The northern side of Old Square, or at least a part of it, was pulled down five or six years ago to make room for the new block of buildings facing the garden and south of Stone Buildings. Henry VIII.'s Gate-way, dated 1513, stands and will (I believe) re-main ; but the quaint masses of chambers north and south of it, honeycombed with old stairs and passages, are doomed. A. J. M.
[How much of Henry VIII.'s Gateway is left?]

I may refer R. M. to Thomas Lane's *Student's Guide through Lincoln's Inn*, second edit., 1806. It is said to have a "neat ground plan."
MACKENZIE E. C. WALCOTT.

WINGREAVES (5th S. ix. 228.)—Why BARBATUS should inform the readers of "N. & Q." that this "name has disappeared" I am at a loss to conceive. Under no more than the usual variety of spellings I have met with the name, as applied to an estate in the parish of Pentrich, Derbyshire, in every century, from the twelfth to the nine-teenth. The Ordnance Survey and the last edition of the *Post Office Directory* now give it as "Wain-groves," but the first syllable has been frequently spelt without the *a*. J. CHARLES COX.

There is an old farmhouse, called now Wain-groves Hall, situated about a mile and a half from the town of Ripley. Not far away is a hamlet known as Waingroves, which has recently sprung up, owing to the proximity of a coal mine opened a few years ago by the Butterley Company. It may be further (if at all) interesting to BARBATUS to know that Waingroves is still in the parish of Pentrich, though three or four miles from that place, and although the large parish of Ripley intervenes. JOHN B. SLACK, B.A.
Green Hill House, Ripley, Derby.

OLD PROTESTANT BIBLES IN IRELAND (5th S. ix. 228.)—I regret to say that there is not an old Bible in any of the Cork churches. In the Cathe-dral of St. Fin Barré there are two folio Prayer Books containing the Epistles and Gospels, the Communion Office, and subsequent forms of prayer, ending with the service "At the Healing." They were printed about 1704. The binding is of recent date, and they are lettered on the back, "Altar." In the cathedral lately taken down they always were placed on the communion table, leaning against the wainscot at the back. These are the oldest books now in any of the Cork churches.
R. C.
Cork.

WEATHERLEY FAMILY (5th S. viii. 9) of Garden House, in the county of Durham. I have an en-graving of the armorial bearings of Edward Oswald Weatherley, Esq., of Garden House, in the county of Durham, as follows, viz. :—Quarterly, 1 and 4, Sa., a chev. erm. between three rams trippant ar. for Weatherley ; 2 and 3, Sa., a fosse erm. betw. three bells ar. for Bell. Crest : A ram's head ar. Motto : SIT SINE LABE. According to some notes on the back of the engraving this gentleman married Mary Anne, daughter of John Bell, Esq., M.D., formerly surgeon in the Royal Navy, who died Sept. 24, 1847, in his seventieth year, at Houghton-le-Spring, in the county of Durham.

MARK NOBLE S. WADE.

25, Brewer Street, Regent Street, W.

A RESIDENCE FOR ROYALTY IN IRELAND (5th S. ix. 366.)—The passage which DR. GATTY asks for is in a letter from Wentworth to Laud, Sept. 27, 1637 (Strafford Letters, ii. 105).

SAMUEL R. GARDINER.

EASTER DAY AND ST. MARK'S DAY (5th S. ix. 367.)—Easter Day coincided with the festival of St. Mark (April 25) in the years 1666 and 1734. It will do so again in 1886 and (si la fin du monde n'arriverait pas antérieurement) in 1943.

J. WOODWARD.
Montrose.

In the Guardian for June 7, 1871, these lines are described as "an old prediction repeated by Nostradamus in his Centuries." He published that work in 1555.   R. R. LLOYD.

St. Albans.

"BOLSHUNS" (5th S. ix. 367.)—Fifty years ago at Rugby a balch or balchin signified an unfledged young bird, and that was doubtless the meaning of the bolshuns in MR. WILSON's blackbird's nest. The name is in all probability from an imitation of the sound made by the fall of a soft lump to the ground. Mrs. Baker, in her Northamptonshire Glossary, has, " Balch, to fall suddenly and heavily. He came down full balch." In the same way, from a representation of the sound of the fall of the young bird by the syllable squab, the name of squab is given to an unfledged bird, a young rook. "The eagle took the tortoise up into the air and dropped him down squab upon a rock, that dashed him to pieces " (L'Estrange).

" No, truly, sir, I should be loth to see you
Come fluttering down like a young rook, cry squab !
And take ye up with your brains beaten into your
    buttocks."   Beaumont and Fletcher.

H. WEDGWOOD.

In my younger days, which were principally passed in the county of Northampton, I was in the habit of hearing this word constantly. It is in common use amongst the peasantry, and I have always understood them to mean by it a bird just hatched and entirely featherless. By them it is pronounced as if it were spelt bolchin.

EDMUND TEW, M.A.
Patching Rectory.

AN ENGRAVING (5th S. ix. 168.)—I have an engraving which answers exactly to L.'s description. It was painted by William Barraud and engraved by W. T. Davey. It is entitled " The Fathers of

the Flock : Hounds of the Pytchley Hunt," and was published June 3, 1850, by W. and H. Barraud, 79, Park Street, Grosvenor Square. The names of the hounds are Fairplay, Helicon, and Watchman.   W. SMITH.

Oxford.

NUMISMATIC (5th S. ix. 228.)—The leaping bock (Capra ibex) on a white field was the ensign armorial of the ancient counts of Rhetia, a pagus which embraced what is called now the canton of Grisons, Switzerland. In course of time that scutcheon became the arms of the bishopric, then of the capital, Chur, Coire, Curia (Latin), and finally of the whole canton.   G. A. M.

Washington, D.C.

The coin is of Coire in the Grisons, whose ancient name is Curia. There was twenty years ago a very miscellaneous small copper coinage in that part of Switzerland. Several counts possessed the right of coining till, say, 1750, and the money passed within the present generation in that neighbourhood. The leaping goat on the grated doorway is probably the town arms. The last word should be RETHICÆ (Rhætian).   J. B.

The coin described is surely one of Chür, or Coire, in the Grisons.   J. WOODWARD.

IRISH NAMES (5th S. ix. 229.)—Agh in Irish means generally field : Cavanagh equal to hollow field ; Curragh, race field, &c. Armagh, literally high field, is, however, supposed to be named from Queen Macha, a Firlbog princess, as its Latin equivalent in the Book of Armagh, A.D. 807, is Altitudo Machæ—Machas, height. See Joyce's Irish Names of Places, pp. 71 and 213.

H. HALL.
Lavender Hill.

Agh has a variety of meanings according as it is or is not joined to a preceding consonant. But its general meaning is allowed to be meadow or field. May it not be allied to ager, acre, and such words ? Ardag would thus signify high field. Its meaning ish not changed by a preceding m. Thus Armagh would also mean high field. Castlereagh would, however, mean the castle of the king, ric, reagh, roi, being allied to rex, and meaning king. Moy, ma, magh, at beginning or middle of words would also mean field. Thus Macroom, the sloping or slanting field. Might I suggest that in the word aftermath, which means the second crop of grass mown in the same summer, math and magh are identical ?   J. HENRY.

"CHARLOTTE " (5th S. ix. 168, 236.)—Is this word, applied to a dish, not older than supposed by G. L. G. ? " Charlotte " is a generic culinary name : Charlotte russe, Charlotte aux pommes, &c. As to the word itself, don't we have it in Charlet ? See the Antiquitates Culinariæ, by the Rev. Chas.

... santon mentioned in the recipe was there to colour the dish. Another darker substancé may have been mixed with it, hence perhaps the epithet of *rousse* given to the *Charlet.* G. A. M.
Washington, D.C.

WALKING ON THE WATER (5th S. iii. 304, 366, 446, 495 ; iv. 17, 276 ; v. 38.)—I, a few weeks ago, saw an oil painting of this scene in Mr. Attenborough's window in the Strand, in which the water-walker was distinctly prominent. I immediately recollected the scene at which, when a boy, like your correspondent MR. BULLEN, I was present. On inquiry, however, Mr. Attenborough's people called it the embarkation of Lord Nelson previous to the battle of Trafalgar, the Hill of Howth in the distance being supposed to be the Isle of Wight. I do not know who the artist was, but this I know, that a very excellent Dublin one, George Peacock, was engaged on the subject for some time. The water-walker's foot machinery, however, came to nothing, and has been since often imitated. H. HALL.
Lavender Hill.

CRICKET: THE LYTTELTON CRICKET MATCH (5th S. ix. 165, 253, 311.)—In the lines by the late Lord Lyttelton what is the allusion in this ?—

" Trained in Walker's school to fame."

Is the reference actually to some school noted for its cricket, or to the family of Walker at Southgate, so well known for their cricketing powers ? There were seven brothers of this family all noted. H. A. W.

"SKAL" (5th S. viii. 509 ; ix. 117, 199, 231.)— An excellent engraving of "The Mug of a Celt"— a drinking-bowl made of a skull—will be found, p. 52, in *Cups and their Customs* (J. Van Voorst, 1863), an anonymous work, written by Dr. Porter, F.G.S., and George E. Roberts, F.G.S., Clerk to the Geological Society of London, both of whom have been dead several years. They also give Byron's poem, " Lines inscribed upon a Cup formed from a Skull." At pp. 2, 3, they enter fully into the origin of the word *cup* and the words *skull, skoll, skal, skyllde, schale, skala, kalt-skaal, skiel, scutella, scodella, écuelle,* and our own *skillet,* with historical notices, to which I refer those who are interested in this subject. CUTHBERT BEDE.

PARCHMENT LACE (5th S. ix. 7, 75, 231.)—In the price list of a gold and silver laceman just published, I find the word " Vellum " used to describe a certain *pattern* of lace. Query, are the words used in a similar sense? B. B.

THE MARQUIS ESTERNULIE (5th S. ix. 147, 237.)—In the first volume of the late Mr. Simpson's *School of Shakspere,* DR. LEARED will find a biography of Sir Thomas Stucley, on p. 128 of which

quess of Leinster," &c. ; on p. 127 a letter, in which " Parsons at Rome to Campion at Prague" says, " You shall understand that Sir Thomas Stewkly, who was made here marquis before his departure, is now dead in Africa with the King of Portugal ; the particulars of his death I have not received " (Nov. 28, 1578) ; in a bracket, " Simpson's *Life of Campion,* p. 9." L. P.

RACINE'S "ATHALIAH " (5th S. ix. 208, 236.)— In reference to translations of this tragedy, I may mention one not generally known, made by a Spanish Jew, David Franco Mendes, into the Hebrew language, for the benefit of his co-religionists. I picked up a copy of this work many years ago at Amsterdam, where it was printed and published. The translation is not a literal one, but the plot, characters, and scenes are all taken from Racine, whose name, however, is not given ; and the Hebrew title of the book is *The Recompense of Athaliah.* The text is in the Hebrew character, and the introduction, notes, and stage directions in the Rabbinic character. The only piece of European writing the volume contains is a Dutch poem in its praise, superscribed as follows :

" Op het Vorstelyk Treurspel
Athaliah
Door den Heer
David Franco Mendes, A.z.
In't Hebreeuwsch beschreeven."
M. G. KENNEDY.
Waterloo Lodge, Reading.

FRISIAN SONGS AND LEGENDS (5th S. ix. 168, 252.)—*De Vrije Fries,* Twaalfde Deel, Nieuwe Reeks, Zesde deel, Tweede stuk, 1870, te Leeuwarden bij G. T. N. Suringar, contains "De Bruidshoogten, eene oude Vertellung in Rijm," in North and West Frisian and Dutch. H. T. C.

"DON'T SIKE " (5th S. ix. 154, 238.)—*Sike,* the substantive and the verb, is used in Salop as well as in Staffordshire. The other day I saw a letter from a Shropshire woman, who, describing the death of a mother in childbed, said, " Her give a great sike, and then died." A. J. M.

MAFFLED : MUFF (5th S. viii. 446 ; ix. 255.)— T. J. M. speaks of the word *muff* as a "vulgarism of late years." It is, however, to be found in print at least as far back as the early part of the seventeenth century. In Thomas Shelton's translation of *Don Quixote* (part ii. chap. x.), when Sancho presents to his master a " blub-faced wench " astride on an ass as the veritable Dulcinea, and the knight has knelt to her accordingly, she replies as follows : " Marry, muff (quoth the Countrey-Wench), I care much for your courtings !" Here the word is evidently used in the same sense which it has at the present day.

There is in the East Riding a word *mafting,*

cognate, as I suppose, with *maffling.* It occurs in a local ballad, thus :—

" An' sky was thick wi' maftin' fog,
An' neet begun te fall."

A. J. M.

BIOGRAPHIES OF MR. GLADSTONE AND THE EARL OF BEACONSFIELD (5th S. viii. 108, 215.)—The following work may be added to those mentioned by other correspondents as giving an account of the latter statesman : *Benjamin Disraeli, Earl of Beaconsfield, being Forty Years and upwards of Political Life, from Bradenham, Bucks, to Bulgaria,* 1876. This was published in eight parts by Goubaud & Son shortly after the elevation of Mr. Disraeli to the peerage, and attracted a very considerable amount of attention at the time.

D. C. BOULGER.

I add the following notices. Mr. Gladstone :—

1. "The Right Honourable William Gladstone, M.P." Part i. p. 240, part ii. p. 261, *Blackwood's Magazine,* Feb. and March, 1865, vol. xcvii.
2. A Chapter of Autobiography. By the Right Hon. W. E. Gladstone, M.P. London, Murray, 1868.
3. The Goblin of Crotchets in the Gladstone Mind : being a Reply to Mr. Gladstone's Autobiographical Apology for a Propensity to Wild Innovation, which renders his Holding of the Helm of State a Dangerous Pilotage for the Vessel of England's Weal. By a South Hants Liberal Conservative. Salisbury, Bennett, Printer, *Journal* Office, v.d.

Earl Beaconsfield :—

1. "The Right Honourable Benjamin Disraeli." No. 1, p. 129, No. 2, p. 369, No. 3, p. 491, *Blackwood's Magazine,* Sept., and October, 1868, vol. civ.
2. The Best of all Good Company. By Blanchard Jerrold. "A Day with the Right Hon. B. Disraeli, M.P." London, Houlston & Sons, 1872.

ROBT. GUY.

Shawlands, Glasgow.

LEEDS POTTERY (5th S. ix. 287.)—This plate reminds me of one in the South Kensington Museum (Spanish), about the fifteenth·century, bearing the following legend, " Cum sis yn mensa et vino de paupere pensa." R. H. WOOD.

Rugby.

Free Translation.

" Freedom oft bends a bow of might*
Its freedom to obtain ;
But Freedom from its seat on high†
Earth's freedom doth restrain."‡

The lines refer doubtless to the·struggle of the Seven United Provinces (seven arrows, &c., being arms) on behalf of a religious and civil freedom in subjection to the higher laws of God (eye in cloud). The open book is also doubtless, in both cases, the Bible, but the letters ENG DIENS and " Voor V. Fied " must be miscopied ; the latter ought pro-

* Literally "A great bow."
† "Which lives on high."
‡ "Silences," *i.e.* Heaven's freedom superimposes itself on man's.

bably to be "Voor Vryheid"=for freedom, and the former comes nearest to " In Gedienst " or " In Gods Dienst "=in God's service. A. Y.

JOHN PHILIPS: " THE SPLENDID SHILLING " (5th S. ix. 148, 216, 258.)—In the year 1878 a correspondent of " N. & Q." pronounces oracularly that the *Splendid Shilling* is " of no literary value whatever." A hundred and fifty years earlier, in 1728, Mr. George Sewell, in his *Life* prefixed to Philips's works, pronounces as follows concerning the same poem. The first of Philips's published pieces was, says he,

" the *Splendid Shilling ;* a Title as new and uncommon for a Poem as his Way of adorning it was, and which, in the Opinion of one of the best and most unprejudiced Judges of this Age, is *the finest Burlesque Poem in the British Language* [here he refers to No. 250 of the *Tatler*]; nor was it only the finest of that kind in our Tongue, but handled in a manner quite different from what had been made use of by any Author of our own or other Nations; the Sentiments and Style being in this both New; whereas in those. the Jest lies more in Allusions to the Thoughts and Fables of the Ancients, than in the Pomp of the Expression."

The biographer then goes on to expound the merits of the poem at length, and to speak of the " universal applause " which it gained for its author.

At the present day, and after a long course of English burlesque poems—including *Hudibras,* which the *Tatler* and Mr. Sewell seem to have forgotten—one may perhaps be allowed to think that the *Splendid Shilling : an Imitation of Milton,* is a very good imitation of Milton, and a very clever piece of solemn fooling ; smooth and harmonious in numbers, and only deficient in incident and purpose. A. J. M.

OLD SPELLING OF "VELVET" (5th S. ix. 306.)—I have called attention to the substitution of *w* for *v* in *Ripon Chapter Acts,* Surtees Soc., vol. lxiv., preface, p. viii. I ought to have referred to pp. 58 (Glower for Glover), 73, 97 (Wersa for Versa), 14 (Willæ for Villæ). I have met with *wox* for *vox* at Wivelsfield, in Sussex, in the common bell inscription, " Vox Augustine sonet in aure Dei," and have just received from my friend Mr. Peacock, of Bottesford, the following out of " hundreds of examples" which he informs me he has met with but not noted. He has also found *v* for *w.*

" It. pewd' *wessell* w't all other stuff in the howse the pc. xlvj· viijᵈ."—*Invent.* of Ric. Allele of Scalthorp in par. of Scotter, 1551.

" Hev halifax my sonne to haue the hooll draughte enew as it gois and Alis my daughture to haue so moche in *walewe* as it is worthe."—Will of Katherine Halifax of Epworth, 1551.

" Forasmuch as hyt ys *conwenient* and necessary for every man to declare the trewth."—Declaration of Ric. Beddyr in *Mon. Anglic.,* iii. 292.

" Item duæ peciæ albæ *velvet.*"—*Inv.* of goods in York Minster, *circa* 1530, in *Mon. Anglic.,* viii. 1207.

... ior expens of the archedekyns *wisitacon* at lanceston, xvj^t.^b"—Stratton (co. Cornwall) Ch. Acc., 1526, 14 a (an unpublished MS.).
" Although my *waise* [voice] is small I will be heard a maingst yov all."—Bell ins. at Churchill, Ellacombe's *Bells of Somersetshire*, 39.
" In provisione cujusdam navis *wocate* le Kowcow."— Acc. of Chamberlain of Fife, 1496-1497, in Dickson's *Acc. of Lord High Treasurer of Scotland*, i. clii. n.
"For......qware *wellome* to prykesong booke."—Louth Ch. Acc., 1505-1506 (unpublished MS.).
"Mendyng coppys & *westment*."—*Ibid.*, 1507.
"1 *wessell* for the holy water for the Sondais."—*Ibid.*, 1486.

Winterton, Brigg.

JOHN BANCKS, OF SUNNING (5th S. viii. 335 ; ix. 232.)—The statement, whatever its original source, that this author " published all his works anonymously " is erroneous, for his *Weaver's Miscellany*, 1730, *Miscellaneous Works*, 2 vols., 1738, and *Hist. of the House of Austria*, n.d., bear his name on their title-pages, and moreover the spelling in all three is Bancks, which, besides having his own authority, will be useful to distinguish him from his namesake (save the c), the dramatic author of a former generation.

W. H. ALLNUTT.
Oxford.

VARANGIANS (5th S. i. 113, 358 ; ix. 218.)— Whatever may be the opinion of Prof. Thomsen as to the Scandinavian etymology of this word, and his claim to rank the people with his own race, yet if Englishmen were more attentive to the history of their race they would know there is another title. This is founded on the connexion with the Varini of Tacitus, a tribe or league constantly associated with the Angli. This has now been accepted by some leading authorities on English history. For the evidence see my treatise on the *Varini of Tacitus* (1868), published also in the *Journal* of the Ethnological Society.

HYDE CLARKE.

"PLATFORM" (5th S. ix. 146, 195, 214.)—King James I. is represented as speaking of Laud in these terms :—". . . For all this he feared not mine anger, but assaulted me again with another ill-fangled *platform* to make that stuborn Kirk stoop more to the English pattern " (*Mem. of the Great Deservings of John Williams, D.D.*, by John Hacket, late Bish. of Litch. and Cov., p. 64). If this speech were ever uttered by the king, and the fact has been doubted, it must have been about the year 1624. ALEX. FERGUSSON, Lieut.-Col.
Edinburgh.

TOKENS OF THE SACRAMENT (5th S. ix. 248.)— As no dates are given, and I have not seen the books mentioned, I hardly like to hazard a conjecture ; but it seems not unlikely that the tokens in question were the certificates of having received

the Sacrament as a qualification for holding an office under Government.
EDWARD H. MARSHALL.
The Temple.

THE SCALLOP SHELL (5th S. ix. 248) was the badge of the pilgrim to St. James at Compostella. The pilgrims to the Holy Land were designated by a palm, and those to St. Thomas at Canterbury by a little leaden phial. See *Life of St. Thomas*, by Canon Morris, p. 354. F. C. V.

SLANG PHRASES (5th S. ix. 263.)—A mistake occurs here under the heading " A Caffre's Tightner," quoted from Lady Duff Gordon's *Letters from the Cape*. The word " troak," or prison, should be " tronk " (trunk), a slang phrase in Cape Dutch for a gaol, just as in our slang a prison is called a " stone jug." H. HALL.
Lavender Hill.

CHARLES HOWARD (5th S. ix. 266.)—Brydges's *Collins* gi_es 1719 as the date of Mr. Charles Howard's birth. I find it difficult to ascertain who two single ladies of the Suffolk and Berkshire family could have been. They resided at Bury St. Edmunds, and they signed my great-great-grandfather's marriage settlement in 1739 with the names Henrietta and Martha Maria Howard. The sisters of Earl Henry Bowes are named in the peerages Ann, Mary, and Dorothy. One of the daughters of Philip, the seventh son of Thomas, the fourteenth earl, was named Henrietta, and she was buried at Bury in 1744, but then her only sister's name is usually given as Mary Lucy. That they belonged to the Suffolk branch is certain ; I have a letter from the Countess Catherine and other correspondence showing this.
GWAVAS.

THE NANFAN FAMILY (2nd S. viii. 228, 294, 357 ; 5th S. viii. 472 ; ix. 129.)—In reply to MR. BOWER's request, I may mention that I remember calling in 1869 on a person of this name (a substantial farmer, I think) in Buckinghamshire, and no great distance from High Wycombe.
E. A. WHITE, F.S.A.
Old Elvet, Durham.

MANORBEER (5th S. ix. 248.)—Giraldus (*Iter.*, p. 851) says : " The castle called Maenor Pyrr, *i.e.* Mansio Pyrri, is about three miles distant from the castle of Pembroke." See note on Giraldus Cambrensis (edit. by J. S. Brewer, M.A., Lond., 1861) in *Rer. Brit. Med. Ævi Script.*, vol. i., preface, p. 1, note. Lewis (*Topograph. Dict.*) writes " Manorbeer (Maenor-býr)," and says :—
" Giraldus, in his *Itin.*, calls it Maenor Pyrr, which he interprets ' the mansion of Pyrrus ' (Pyrrhus ?), who, he says, also possessed the island of Caldey. According to Sir Richard Colt Hoare, the name literally signifies ' the manor of the lords,' and appears to be derived from its occupation by the lords of Dyved, who were also pro-

prietors of the neighbouring island of Caldey. The castle probably owed its name to M. de Barri, one of the Norman lords that accompanied Arnulph de Montgomery into Britain."

Carlisle says:—

"Maenor Bŷrr, *i.e.* the manor of the lords. The castle was the property of the Barri family. The Comot probably takes its name from Caldey Island, or the Isle of the Lords, which lies at a distance from it."

The last part of the local name Manorbeer might even be from Barri. Giraldus's real name was Giraldus de Barri.   R. S. CHARNOCK.

Junior Garrick.

Gerald de Barri, in describing his birthplace, Maenor Pyrr, says : "That is the mansion of Pyrrus, who possessed also the island of Chaldey, which the Welsh call Inys Pyrr, or the island of Pyrr." Pyrrus is evidently a Latinized form of Pyrr, a Welsh mythical hero, generally known as Pyrr of the East. I rather doubt if Prof. Rhys would admit *Maenor* as a pre-Norman Welsh word. If in its place we substitute either Maen y or Menhir, then the meaning of Manorbeer would be either Pyrr's stone, or Pyrr's Menhir, or long stone. Within half a mile of the castle there is a cromlech, and the farm it stands on is called Skrinkle. This name may well be derived from the Norse (we have a vast number of Norse names in this district) ; Kringla in that tongue means a circle. If this supposition is correct, then in the time of the Viking raids there must have been pre-historic remains at Manorbeer which have now disappeared. These same Norsemen altered the name of Inys Pyrr to Caldy, or the Bleak Island.

EDWARD LAWS.

Tenby Museum.

ROWE FAMILY (5th S. vi. 289, 375, 494 ; vii. 74, 372 ; ix. 257.)—I have in my library an odd volume of the *Odes of Horace*, translated by Philip Francis, D.D., London, 1765, containing the bookplate of Jane and Frances Rowe (both members of the Durham family), with the following arms on a lozenge-shaped shield : Gu., three holy lambs, staff, cross, and banners arg. If ANON. would like the book I shall be most happy to give it to him, if he will let me have his address.

EDWARD J. TAYLOR, F.S.A. Newc.

Bishopwearmouth.

PORTRAIT OF BEATRICE CENCI (5th S. viii. 407 ; ix. 17, 199.)—That such a head-dress was worn as painted in the supposed Guido portrait is evident, for in a letter of Madame de Sévigné, July 17, 1676, especial mention is made of a "suit of plain head-cloths" worn by "la Brinvilliers" on her way to execution. Her head was shaved after she had mounted the scaffold.   EMILY COLE.

Teignmouth.

NOTES ON BOOKS, &c.

Old English Plate: Ecclesiastical, Decorative, and Domestic; its Makers and Marks. With Improved Tables of the Date Letters used in England, Scotland, and Ireland. By Wilfred J. Cripps, M.A. (Murray.)

IF you are an owner of plate, a collector of plate *in esse* or *in posse*, or merely an admirer, some such book as Mr. Cripps has written is indispensable. Mr. Morgan's book is out of print. He went to the fountain head, and wrote one of the earliest, if not the earliest, book on hall marks. This volume Mr. Cripps has taken in hand, greatly amplified, revised, and made complete to the date of its issue, and it is frank of him that he gives the fullest weight to his predecessor's labours. The scope of Mr. Cripps's book is, within the title he has given, a treatise on British plate from early time, and the test by which its genuineness may be recognized ; the result is a complete and careful work, the best, if not the only, guide in the province with which it deals. The hall marks of the London Goldsmiths' Company, the marks of the Scotch, Irish, and provincial Halls, are here recorded, and by Mr. Cripps's aid any one may test the age and fineness of any British plate under consideration. To many this knowledge will be interesting, archæologically ; and, as ascertaining the marketable value of the metal (*i.e.* whether standard of the realm or not), Mr. Cripps's will recommend itself to a larger, because less æsthetic, section of the public. Incidentally the perusal may lead to another result—a desirable one, in our mind. We have but little doubt that the reader will recognize the value of maintaining in full efficiency the Government test on gold and silver, and will see that to throw open the market and permit the sale, as silver and gold, of any metal that it may please a vendor so to denominate, is to hand over the public helplessly to the seller, and to apply the maxim of *caveat emptor* to transactions where the technical knowledge of the article vended is confined to the vendor.

History of the English People. By J. R. Green, M.A. Vols. I. and II. (Macmillan & Co.)

WITH greater space for the display of his special power, Mr. Green is at once a more interesting and a more tantalizing writer for the students of the Library edition of his *History*—more interesting, because he has wider scope for illustrating his subject from contemporary history, and contemporary life, in the other countries of the West ; more tantalizing, because he persists in his refusal to give us any other than a general idea of the sources of his many apt quotations and vivid illustrations. In this respect he resembles Sir Francis Palgrave rather than those later masters of the modern school of English historians to whom his present book is dedicated. We think this circumstance even more to be regretted in the fuller expression of Mr. Green's views than in the *Short History* which gained its author such speedy and deserved popularity. But we must take Mr. Green as he is, or not at all. And having uttered our protest, we are bound to say that readers of the Library edition, still in process of completion, will find the story of England's history told with all that was to be expected of sympathy for the tiller of the soil, and contempt for the mere pomp and circumstance of war ; of fellow-feeling for Earl Simon and John Wyclif, and all, whether in Church or State, who by quickening men's thought helped in any way to make men realize that they were citizens of a country which demanded their best energies, and was worthy of their deepest devotion. And it is quite in accordance with such a conception of his functions as we already knew Mr. Green to entertain, that in his new work he should devote to the "Peasant

of the Roses," and that he should give not less than forty pages to the "Revival of Learning." Equally charącteristic is it that the present instalment of Mr. Green's book should close with the England of Shakspeare. It is not, of course, to be supposed that we can set out here all those points on which we do not agree with Mr. Green. We may remark, however, that we do not understand on what genealogical principle the Earl of Morton is called "head of the house of Douglas," and we were under the impression that the inspirer of the first lectures on Greek at Oxford was the Byzantine exile Chalcondylas, not "Chancondylas." Again, we would ask, is there a necessity for coining the word "Renascence"? But inasmuch as perfect agreement on all points is not to be looked for, and even perhaps the truth shines out more clearly through the clash of differing treatments, we may commend Mr. Green's volumes to the student with the exhortation to read them carefully, with constant reference to original and other authorities, while for ourselves we may say, in conclusion, that we look forward to much pleasant reading as still in store for us in the volumes yet to come.

Poetical Works of Geoffrey Chaucer, with Poems formerly Printed with His, or Attributed to Him. Edited, with a Memoir, by Robert Bell. Revised Edition, in Four Volumes. With a Preliminary Essay by Rev. W. W. Skeat, M.A. (Bell & Sons.)
IF the establishment of the Chaucer Society a few years since furnished evidence of increased attention to the writings of Chaucer on the part of scholars and students, the appearance of an edition of his poems in that cheap and popular series known as "Bohn's Standard Library" is a strong proof of a growing interest in the works of the father of English poetry by the large body of general readers, and a good sign it is. The edition thus prepared for their use is moreover not a mere reprint of one hastily got up for popular use, but it is a reproduction of that prepared some years since by Mr. Jephson under the supervision of the late Mr. Robert Bell, and it has had the advantage of being revised by no less competent an authority than the Rev. W. W. Skeat, the new Professor of Anglo-Saxon at Cambridge, who has written a preliminary essay, in which he explains the improvements which have been made in it for the purpose of increasing the convenience and value of the work, and furnishes much valuable information as to the character of many of the poems formerly attributed to Chaucer, but now known to be spurious, but which are wisely retained as being in themselves of considerable interest and value, while they throw great light upon the genuine writings of the author.

SOCIETY OF ANTIQUARIES.—The complimentary dinner to Mr. Ouvry, on his retirement from the presidency, by the Fellows on the 31st instant, under the chairmanship of Lord Carnarvon, promises to be a great success. Of the 120 tickets which alone can be issued, owing to the size of the room, one half were immediately secured.

COWPER, BLAKE, AND HAYLEY AUTOGRAPHS.—The sale of autographs on Monday next at Messrs. Sotheby's will contain not only a number of remarkable letters which Mr. Bruce was examining at the time of his death with a view to a new life of Cowper, but between thirty and forty letters of that remarkable artist and poet, Blake, as well as of Flaxman, Lady Hamilton, Sir Walter Scott, &c.

MISS MARGARET STOKES, to whom was entrusted by the late Earl of Dunraven the duty of editing his valuable *Notes on Irish Architecture*, has in the press another work likely to be acceptable to all interested in Irish archæology. It is entitled *Early Christian Architecture*

many fine wood engravings. Messrs. G. Bell & Sons are the publishers.

WE are glad to be able to refer our readers to an exhaustive account of the Round Tower of Kinneigh, co. Cork, in the *Cork Constitution* of the 9th inst., a tower whose history is as peculiar as its architecture is unique.

THE Rev. W. W. Skeat was on Wednesday last elected Professor of Anglo-Saxon at Cambridge.

LONDON, SATURDAY, MAY 25, 1878.

CONTENTS.—N° 230.

Notes.

THE KILDAVIE FOLK, CANTIRE.

The parish of Southend occupies the extremity of the peninsula of Cantire, Argyleshire, and among the many spots in this parish prefixed with the word Kil—the most notable of which is Kilcolmkill, "the Church of St. Columba, the founder of churches"—are several, such as Kildavie, Kilblaan, Kilravan, Killeolan, and Killoran, where all traces of the churches and cemeteries have been lost. Kildavie glen lies between Coniglen on its west and the sea on its east, the Pennyland being on the eastern side of the glen. This district of Kildavie was peopled by the followers of Ralston of Ralston, who had fled from the persecutions in Renfrewshire to seek the protection of the Marquis of Argyll, when the Act Recissory had been passed in the year 1662. Other families from Renfrewshire and Ayrshire had also, at this troublous period, sought refuge in Cantire, and had been protected by its people, with the sanction of Argyll. Labourers from the same two counties had previously been sent by Argyll to Cantire, to make good the loss sustained by the population in the great plague that swept over the peninsula in the year 1648. The Laird of Ralston died in Cantire, but the greater portion of the Covenanters —Hamilton of Wishaw, Dunlop of Garnkirk, and the Maxwells of Williamwood, Milnwood, and South Barr—went back to Ayrshire and Renfrewshire when it was safe for them to do so, leaving their followers in the various farms at Kildavie and elsewhere, where the Ralstons, Dunlops, Colvilles, Reids, and Huies have lived from generation to generation, keeping "themselves to themselves," and mixing but little with the native West Highlanders.

A lady in Cantire has written to me as follows concerning these descendants of the old Covenanters :—

"The Kildavie folk—as they were called—never intermingled or intermarried with the natives of Cantire, but retained their own peculiar language and customs ; and many amusing anecdotes are told of their manners and modes of expressing themselves. They spoke in a very broad and drawling tone. A story is told of their manner of making love. 'Dae ye tak me, Jeannie?' said the sweetheart; and she replied, in a slow and bashful tone, 'Aye, some.' 'Will ye gie me a kiss, Jeannie?' was the next inquiry. 'Nae, but ye may tak it,' was her cautious answer. Their phrase for calling the reapers home to dinner was, 'Come hame fast, the meat is wul!' When the day was wet they described it as 'A bluisterin' day; nae day ava, man!' and it was accordingly struck out of the calendar. But the point of these stories of the Kildavie folk is lost when transferred to paper, as the peculiar twang that accompanied them was what made them so extremely comical. The Kildavie folk established a separate form of worship, called the Relief Church, which was almost similar to the Independent sect. The greater part of them are now emigrated ; and I fancy that not more than two families, descendants of the first settlers, are now to be reckoned as genuine Kildavie folk."

I may add to what my correspondent has here mentioned, that the church in question was built in the year 1798, together with a house for the minister, on ground given by the Duke of Argyll, the erection of the church being a necessity, as many of these Lowlanders were unable to join in a Gaelic service from ignorance of the language. The minister, too, was not always resident. They also preferred to have a burial-ground of their own, separated from that set apart for the Highlanders. The pendicle of ground that was added to the cemetery of Southend originated in the difficulty which the Lowlanders encountered in obtaining accommodation for the disposal of their dead when they first settled in the parish. It is natural to suppose that the West Highland descendants of the Macdonald clansmen would not look with a favourable eye upon the Lowland settlers whom their new master Argyll had brought into the country ; and as the influence of feudalism in Cantire prevailed till the middle of the past century, it would give birth to a strong feeling against the followers of Argyll, and more especially against his Lowland immigrants. Thus the prejudice which, unhappily, divided the two races may have had a much stronger hold on the Celtic than the Saxon mind ; and the poor Kildavie folk would thus be driven to their own devices through the churlish jealousy of their neighbours. CUTHBERT BEDE.

Before this note can be published that well-known firm, Messrs. Sotheby, Wilkinson & Hodge, will have dispersed the "Illustrated and general library," &c., "of the late distinguished artist." A perusal of the catalogue and a search through the interesting collection of books reveal several curious facts, if facts they be.

The first is as to a book called *Sunday in London*, illustrated in fourteen cuts by G. Cruikshank . . . London, Wilson, 1833, as to which the following note occurs on the first leaf (Lot 244): "This work is my own original idea ; my dear friend Wight (the author of *Mornings at Bow St.*) wrote the text from my suggestion.—George Cruikshank, 1874."

As to Ainsworth's *Tower of London* (Lot 371), the edition published by G. Routledge, the following note is made :—"The etchings all spoilt by being re-bit—by a stranger—instead of being done, as they ought to have been, by Geo. Cruikshank." And certainly a comparison with the earlier edition fully justifies the remark.

"Lot 552, *Miser's Daughter*, the story suggested to Harrison Ainsworth by George Cruikshank."

The library is full of anonymous books ; the authors of some I should like to know, *e.g.* Lot 26, *Isn't it odd ?* by Marmaduke Merrywhistle ; in three vols. [motto] London, Whittaker, 1822. Inside is the author's note of presentation, but not signed. *Mirth and Morality*, a collection of original tales by Carlton Bruce, London, Tegg, 1835, is Lot 231, and Cruikshank has made a note that the illustrations are by him. In faded ink is written "Auldjo." Is Carlton Bruce a pseudonym ? I do not find it in Allibone. *Truth without fiction and religion without disguise, or the two Oxford students in College, London, and the country* . . . [and so on] by a country rector, London, Emans, 1837, large 8vo. pp. xvi–ii–519. This work forms Lot 339. I do not find it in the *London Catalogue*, nor in the continuation of it, the *English Catalogue* ; and yet, as will be gathered from the above, it is a work of some pretensions. It is illustrated by several full-page plates—by G. Cruikshank, I presume. Who was the author?   OLPHAR HAMST.

"SHE, THE CAT'S MOTHER."—I cannot find any mention of this saying in the General Indexes of "N. & Q." or in books of proverbial expressions, but it is one with which I have been acquainted from my youth, and which I still hear from time to time. For example, a little girl runs in to her mother, and says excitedly, "O mamma, we met her just as we were coming home from our walk, and she was so glad to see us !" Upon which the mamma says, "Who is 'she'? the cat's mother?" Then the child laughs merrily, and replies, "No ; it was Lucy Jones." "But how could I know that, when you did not mention her name?" Thus,

cuity of speech and precision in reference.
                                    CUTHBERT BED.

THE HUNDRED.

Now that so many of the old local institution England are being swept away by the active tralizing spirit of modern legislation, it is wel put on record any information bearing upon relationship between the old and the new stat things. To this end, therefore, with the permis of the editor of "N. & Q.," I propose sending f time to time, say monthly, a series of tables w] I have carefully drawn up relating to the hund These tables are arranged in counties, and I w suggest that they be inserted alphabetically, ginning, however, with Berkshire, because the formation respecting that county is more im diately illustrative of the usefulness of the ta than Bedfordshire. The headings of the colu explain themselves ; but I would observe, reference to column 1, that (*a*) Roman cap numerals are used where the old hundreds represented in the modern system, (*b*) Ro "lower-case" numerals where the old hund are not so represented, and (*c*) ordinary figures the modern hundreds.

It has always appeared to me that the hun has not received that attention at the hand historians which its position in the Teutonic pc should give it. One of the means by which may get to know more of its early history is studying the names applied to it in the diffe parts of England.

Mr. Coote, in a paper read at the Societ Antiquaries, and published in *Archæologia*, enti "The Milites Stationarii considered in Relatio the Hundred and Tithing of England," says : " hundred being named in Anglo-Saxon times (a still is in our own) from a vill or large villag follows that the head-quarters of the hundred-i and his assistants were in that vill " ; and he re to the Anglo-Saxon text published by Sir H.] in his *General Introduction to Doomsday* (i. 18; Now, this document gives the Anglo-Saxon na of the hundreds of Northampton, eight of modern names of which are *not* identical v town names ; and it is noticed in the Ce; *Report*, 1851 (p. lxiv), that "in all England out of 799 names of hundreds, wapentakes liberties are the same as names of parishes, to ships, or places separately returned within t limits." This small proportion is very signific and an analysis of the tables I have prep shows the proportion to be still smaller.

But of this hereafter. I do not pretend that tables are perfect ; I present them as being us especially if added to or corrected by the rea of "N. & Q."   G. LAURENCE GOMM
Castelnau, Barnes, S.W.

NOTES AND QUERIES.

County of Berkshire.

Columns 2, 4, 5 from Lysons's *Magna Britannica*; 3, 6, from Census Tables; 7, from Reports of Common Law Commissioners and Municipal Corporation Commissioners.

No.	Names of Hundreds.			Towns having Names identical with the Hundred.		Particulars as to Hundred Court.
	Early Names.	Modern Names.	Early Hundreds not represented in Modern System.	Early.	Modern.	
(1) I.	Beners or Benes	Beynhurst	—	(Bras ?)	—	[Hundred Court of Burnham? disused in 1851.]
ii.	Blitberie	—	Now included in the hundreds of Moreton and Reading	Blitberie	Blewbury	(None.)
iii.	Borchedeberie or Borcheldeberie	—	Now included in Faircross and Reading	Borcheldeberie	Bucklebury	(None.)
(2) IV.	Bray	Bray	—	Brai	Bray	Manor Crt. of Bray disused in 1851.
(3) V.	Cerledone	Charlton	—	—	Charlton	Hundred Court disused in 1851.
4.	—	Compton	—	Contone	Compton	(None.)
5.	—	Cookham	—	Cocheham	Cookham	(None.)
vi.	Eletesford, Helitesford, or Hesliteford	—	Now included in Moreton, Reading, and Cookham	—	—	(None.)
6.	—	Faircross	—	—	—	(None.)
7.	—	Faringdon	—	Ferenedone	Faringdon	Hundred Court disused in 1851.
(8) VII.	Gamesfel	Gaufield	—	—	—	Hundred Court disused in 1851.
viii.	Hilleslau	—	Now included in Shrivenham	Hildeslei, Hilslei, or Hislelew	Ilsley	(None.)
(9) IX.	Hornimere	Hormer	—	—	—	Hundred Court disused in 1851.
(10) X. XI.	Cheneteberie } Eglei }	Kintbury-Eagle.	—	Cheneteberie	Kintbury	(None.)
(11) XII.	Lamborne	Lambourn	—	Lamborne	Lambourn	(None.)
xiii.	Merceham	—	Now included in Ock and Hormer	Merceham	Marcham	(None.)
12.	—	Moreton	—	Mortune	Moreton	Hundred Court disused in 1851.
xiv.	Nachededorne	—	Now incl. in Compton and Faircross	—	—	(None.)
13.	—	Ock	—	—	—	Hundred Court disused in 1851.
(14) XV.	Radinges or Redinges	Reading	—	Radinges	Reading	Court Leet held by the Corporation.
(15) XVI.	Riplesmere	Ripplesmere	—	—	—	(None.)
xvii.	Roeberg	—	Now included in Faircross	—	—	(None.)
(16) XVIII.	Shrivenham	Shrivenham	—	Seriveham	Shrivenham	Hundred Court disused in 1851.
17.	—	Sonning	—	Soninges	Sonning	Hundred Court disused in 1851.
xix.	Sudtone	—	Now included in Ock, Wanting, and Gaufield	—	Sutton-Courtney	(None.)
18.	—	Theale	—	—	—	(None.)
xx.	Taceham	—	Now included in Faircross and Reading	Taceham	Thatcham	(None.)
(19) XXI.	Wanating	Wantage	—	Wanetinz	Wantage	Hundred Court disused in 1851.
20.	—	Wargrave	—	Weregrave	Wargrave	Hundred Court disused in 1851.
xxii.	Wifol	—	Now incl. in Faringdon and Shrivenham	—	—	(None.)
	Wallingford	Wallingford	—	(Borough)	(Borough)	Court Leet held by the Corporation.
	Windsor	Windsor	—	(Borough)	(Borough)	Court Leet held by the Corporation.

"MACBETH," ACT II. SC. 1, LL. 56-8.—

"*Macbeth.* ... ... Thou fowre and firme-set earth
Heare not my fteps, which they may walk, for feare
Thy very ftones prate of my whereabout.*"*

Sowre is the first folio reading, and the three other folios follow it, as they do in the other blunders of this scene, spelling the word respectively *sowre*, *sowr*, and *sour*. It need not be said that these are unquestionably press errors. Pope, apparently on the suggestion of the fourth folio spelling, altered the word to *sure*, and this has been generally adopted. But though press errors are sometimes not to be explained, their causes may usually be suggested and understood. Now no known spelling of *sure* will explain the error *sowre*. A more convincing argument is that while " sure and firm-set " is, as a general epithet of the earth, unexceptionable, it is here no poet's epithet, but a mere poetaster's, for it has no relevancy. It is like the epithet of a schoolboy who has racked dictionary and memory for a phrase which, irrespective of its being germane to the matter, and therefore poetic, will fill up the scansion of a halting hexameter. Looking to the context, and to the circumstances under which Macbeth is speaking, I should as soon expect Shakspere to make him use such an epithet as to hear Richard talk of " Blushing Aurore, morn of our discontent." What is the " earth" of which Macbeth speaks ? The pebbled courtyard, or the stone-paved corridors looking on it, in one or other of which places all editors are agreed that the scene takes place. What are the circumstances ? Macbeth and his servant have trod there, and heard the clank and echo of their own footsteps, and also those of Banquo and Fleance. Any who have ever been in such a courtyard or corridor will at once understand the effect these noises must have had on one whose mind is full of a secret deed of darkness, and thinks of the would-be stealthy pace of a murderer or other wolfish miscreant. His thoughts and fears are naturally attracted to these noises, and hence both in these lines and in those preceding he dwells on them, " Hear not my steps which way they. walk." I propose, therefore, by adding one letter to *sowre*, to read, " Thou s[*t*]*owre* [*i.e.* stour] and firm-set earth." (Here and in all succeeding quotations I substitute *s* for the long f.) Halliwell (Phillipps), in his *Dictionary*, gives *stour* as still an eastern counties provincialism for "stiff or inflexible," and quotes from Palsgrave, " *Stoure*, rude as coarse cloth is, *gros*," and " *stowre* of conversation, *estourdy*," some of the meanings of *estourdi* being, as Cotgrave gives them, " sottish, blockish, lumpish." So also Ray's *Glossary· of South and East Country Words* (Eng. D. Soc.) : " *Stowre*, adj., inflexible, sturdy, and stiff, spoken also of cloth [Palsgrave's *gros*] in opposition to limber." Again, in Col. Leigh's *Cheshire Glossary*,

" *Stor* ·or *storr*, v.—When a horse, from bad roads, deep snow, too great a load, or vice, stops in harness, he is said to be *storred.*" " *Staw* also has the same meaning as applied to a cart." Again, in writings just prior to or contemporaneous with Shakspere's, we have (*Prompt. Parv.*) : " *Stoor (store*, MS. K. Coll., Cam.), hard or boystous. *Austerus, rigidus* " (*boystous* here not being our *boisterous*, but as explained s.v. *rudis, rigidus*).

" Thys pange was greater......then when the *stower* nayles were knocked and driven throughe hys bandes and fete.*"*—Latimer, Serm. 7, Arber's repr., p. 185.

" Looke on the fedders of all maner of birdes, you shall se some so lowe, weke, and shorte, some so course, *stoore*, and harde."—Ascham, *Toxoph.*, Arber's repr., p. 129.

"A fenny goose euen as her flesh is blacker, *stoorer*, vnholsomer, so is the feder for the same cause courser, *stoorer*, and rougher."—*Ib.*, p. 151.

I am informed also by Mr. John Payne that another example is to be found in the earlier part of Gervase Markham's *English Husbandman*, 1620. By this change Macbeth is made to refer to the hard, unyielding, and therefore resounding stones of the court, and we thus get epithets in exact accord with both his natural and his expressed thoughts. It now remains to explain how the error arose. This scene so bristles with errors that one is forced to the conclusion that the compositor was either a new or a very careless hand, or (as is extremely likely) that he was dazed and dulled by over much malt liquor. Hence in reading he confounded the *t* with the long line and loops of the preceding *s*. Nor is this mere supposition, for he did the same in the very line above, printing " Tarquin's ravishing sides," where, *pace* Mr. Knight, " the word must be either *strides* or *slides.*" I may add that exactly the same mistake, as I think, occurs in Herbert's *Church Porch*, st. xx. l. 3 :—

" When thou dost purpose ought within thy power,
  Be sure to doe it, though it be but small ;
Constancie knits the bones, and   ʃ *sowre* (Wm.'s MS.)
              makes us ᒾ *stowre* (pr. edds.)
When wanton pleasures beeken, us to thrall."

My friend Dr. Grosart, relying on the MSS., not however in Herbert's handwriting, reads *sowre*. But, with all deference to him and the MSS. (Wm.'s and Bodl.), I cannot accept it for, as seems to me, two good reasons. The first is that a compositor is very unlikely to have changed by error the familiar *sowre* into the all but obsolete and unknown *stowre*. The second, that while *sowre* gives, were there no alternative, a passably sufficient sense, *stowre* is almost infinitely preferable, giving a better sense because fuller and in more exact accord with the context.

Thus ends my plea for *stour* both in *Macbeth* and Herbert. But I would add a little digression on the word as it occurs in the first extract by Halliwell from Palsgrave. Some might refer this *stoure* to the Yorkshire *store* (*Gloss.*, C. C. Robinson, Eng. Dia. Soc.), which, say Mr. Atkinson and Mr. Skeat, is to be connected not with the familiar English *store*, but with the Icelandic *stórr*, *great.* With all deference, however, to these authorities, I fail to see either the proof or the necessity of this. And in explanation of Palsgrave's *gros*, I would refer to the latter part of the quotation from Ray's definition of *stoure* given above, and to Cotgrave, s.v. *gros*. It is also noteworthy that both our *stours*, *stour*, a conflict, or cloud of dust, and *stour*, hard, *rudis*, *rigidus*, as well as our *sturdy*, have their analogues in the old French *estour*, *estourbillon*, and *estourdi*.

B. NICHOLSON.

"THE TEMPEST," ACT IV. SC. 1, L. 64 (5th S. viii. 385.)—

" Banks with pioned and twilled brims."

Your correspondent E. E. F. directs my attention to the above passage and to the common names of the marsh marigold (*Caltha palustris*). I have never heard the " peony " applied to the marsh marigold, or found any one who had. The marsh marigold is the " winking marybuds " of Shakespeare, and is known as May-blobs, water-blobs, and Moll-blobs—the last, however, is more a Worcestershire than a Warwickshire term. I have asked many of the country people during the past three weeks the name by which they know the marsh marigold, and they have replied, almost without exception, "water buttercup," though the *Ranunculus aquatilis* has white petals and not yellow. With respect to the line quoted, and which some commentators have amended(?) into " peonied and lilied brims," I can only read it as you print it. To me it is the pioned, the pied, parti-coloured, or variegated edges of the twilled or ribbed banks—the wave-marked shore, which " spongy April " betrims at the "hest" of Ceres with the flowers "to make cold nymphs chaste crowns." *Pied* and *piedness* are common terms in the Midlands, and are frequently used by Shakespeare. Though the peony is a native of Lundy Island in the Severn, it is not a riverside plant, and is called the "sheepshearing rose" by many from the rough juice of filling the folds of its petals with pungent snuff or pepper at sheep-shearing feasts, in order to enjoy the torments of those who innocently smell it at that period. Sidney Beisley in *Shakespeare's Garden* suggests that the water-lily might be intended by Shakespeare, but only the yellow variety, *Nuphar lutea*, is found wild in Warwickshire. The only habitat of the white water-lily is near Sutton Coldfield and in the streams that are in the Trent watershed, not in those flowing into the Avon.

J. TOM BURGESS, F.S.A.

Worcester.

WILL OF JOHN ARCHOR, OF BISHOP'S HATFIELD, CO. HERTS.—The original has never before been printed :—

" In dei noi'e ame' the xix day off noue'ber the yere off owr lorde god A Mⁱ vᵒ & xixᵒ I Jhon archor off boshp* at ffeld in the dioc off lincoll beyng seke in my body fferyng the pe(r)ell off dethe but wᵗ good Reme'brans & holle mynd I make & ordynd thys my last wyll & testment ffyrst I be quethe my sowll to yᵉ merci off all myghty god & to owre lady sent mari & to all yᵉ holy co'peny off evyn my body to be beryd in yᵉ cherche yerd off send audry† afforsed I be quethe to yᵉ moder cherche off lyncoll ij^d also I be quethe to yᵉ hy aw't' ffor my tythys & offryng nellyge't‡ fforgottyn iiij^d also I be quethe to Rychard archor my ffader my Best gone§ & my Best dublett also I Bequethe to my wyffeys ffader hew swenson on grynkott|| also I be quethe to yᵉ byldyng off yᵉ cherche howsse my best stoflekott¶ also my howse sett & lyyng att sent albons I gyuff & be quethe to Elezabethe my wyffe terme off hyr naturallyffe & aft' yᵉ dessesse off my sed wyffe I be quethe yᵉ sed howsse to Jhon my son ffor eu'more ffaylyng yᵉ sed Jhon my wyll ys the sayd howsse be solde & yᵉ mony there off Reservyd ffor to hyer a pryst to syñg ffor my solle & al cristin sowlls yᵉ Resydu off all my goodys movabull & on movabull nott be quethe I geue & be quethe to Elezebethe my wyffe wome I make myne ex sextryx & Rychard archor my ffader over seyer wytthes hete off sr Robertt ffrouik pryche** pryst Rychar archar Jamys ffost."

Proved Sept. 25, 1520.

R. R. LLOYD.

St. Albans.

ARMS OF POPE LEO XIII.—The following paragraph is extracted from the *Times* of Tuesday, April 30, 1878 :—

" The Pecci arms consist of a field gules, bearing a cypress or pine—' pitch tree ' (from *pece*)—crossed by a bar argent, and the shield so quartered bears on the upper left quarter a comet or, and on the two lower quarters two French lilies, *fleurs-de-luce*, also or. Over the shield is a comital crown, though the Pecci were no counts but merely untitled patricians."

The writer of the above does not seem to have a clear apprehension of the rules of blazon, but for all that we may make out from his description what is intended. The coat is, of course, not " quartered," and we may perhaps be safe in assuming that the tincture of the pitch pine is " proper."

Perhaps a better blazon would be, Gu., a pitch pine (eradicated ?) pr., between in sinister chief a comet, and in base two fleurs-de-lis or, over all a fess arg.

The adoption of the count's coronet by the Pecci of Carpineto is in accordance with a very general Italian use, or abuse. I have before noted in " N. & Q." the same custom as existent in France ; and some who are not aware of this fact have

* Bishop's Hatfield.
† St. Etheldreda, to whom the church is dedicated.
‡ Negligently.
§ Gown.
|| Green coat.
¶ Stofle (duffle) coat.
** Parish priest.

been led to assume for themselves and their ancestors an hereditary rank and title to which they had not the shadow of a claim. It is a curious fact that the arms of the present Pope contain a comet, while the motto under which he was predicted in the famous prophecy of St. Malachi is, "Lumen in cœlo."

Perhaps I may fitly place on record here the Ultramontane pasquinade which was circulated in Rome on the occasion of the late Papal election and the assumption by the Holy Father of the title of Leo XIII.:—

"Non è Pio, non è Clemente,
Ma è Leone,—senza dente."

Montrose.   J. WOODWARD.

BELLS WITH ROYAL HEADS.—My friend Mr. North, who is about to publish an account of the bells of Northants, informs me that he has found the following, the intervening stops being the heads of Edward I. and Queen Eleanor.

At Manton St. Lawrence, two bells :—
2nd. + PRO . THOME . LAUDE . RESONABO . MODO . SINE . FRAUDE.
3rd. + EDWARDI . NOTA . SONET . NEC . DULCISIMA . TOTA.

At Potterspury :—
4th. + AVE . MARIA . GRACIA . PLENA.

At Grafton Regis :—
3rd. + AVE . MARIA . GRACIA . PLENA.

For the heads and crosses see North's *Leicester Bells*, pp. 25, 28, and 29.

At Stow-Nine-Churches, with Edward III. and Queen Philippa :—
+ AVE . MARIA GRACIA . PLENA.

At Slapton :—
+ VLTIMA . SU- . TRINA . CAMPANA . VOCOR . KTERINA.

At Duddington and Great Oakley the head of Edward I. is repeated several times without inscription.   H. T. ELLACOMBE.

PIC-NIC.—In 1802 *pic-nic* meant a dance and supper given to friends and neighbours, who at a joint expense contributed bread, cold meat, cakes, wines, and spirits, the gentlemen also paying the owner of the house for the expense of the music (*Gent. Mag.*, 1802, p. 225). The term is not in Bailey. The *Dictionnaire de l'Académie* gives "*Pique-nique*, a meal where every one pays his shot"; but what is the origin? Another word has been corrupted. We say of a rough, gamblesome boy, "He is a pickle"; Littleton gives "A pickled rogue as full of mischief as he can be."
                      MACKENZIE E. C. WALCOTT.

TEMPLE BAR.—The removal of Temple Bar being a fact so recently accomplished, perhaps the following remarks respecting it, extracted from Samuel Ireland's *Picturesque Views; with an Historical Account of the Inns of Court in London and Westminster*, published in the year 1800, may

be worthy of preservation in the pages of "N. & Q.":—

"In the view prefixed Temple Bar is introduced, as a good finish to the scene (Middle Temple Gate), but it has a still higher claim to our respect, having infinite merit in its design.

"As we are led to believe," &c. [Here follows a suggestion that the Bar should "be placed either as a foot entrance to the Inner Temple opposite Chancery Lane, or near Mitre Court, in such a spot as to command a view of that grand area, the King's Bench Walk." See "N. & Q.," 5th S. vii. 466.] "But perhaps our anxious desire to lay open this delightful scenery to the view of the public may have dictated the suggestion of a plan which even the liberality of these gentlemen has not the power of carrying into execution.

"We are well aware that many obstacles stand in the way of so great an improvement, and we sincerely lament that the spirit of national munificence, generally prevalent in civilized countries, but in so eminent a degree the characteristic of England, should in the instance before us feel its energies so crippled by circumstances as to prevent it from rescuing from unmerited seclusion some of the most striking specimens of architecture that are to be found in the first city of the world."

The worthy man little thought that seventy-eight years would elapse before the "short time" would be accomplished, and the demolition of Temple Bar be effected.
                      WILLIAM ENGLAND HOWLETT.
Kirton in Lindsey.

HAYDN'S "UNIVERSAL INDEX OF BIOGRAPHY," 1870.—It is singularly unfortunate that this work, as regards the biography of ecclesiastics, both ancient and modern, swarms with blunders. I give a few. St. George is confounded with George the Arian. St. Chrysostom is said to have been "deposed at the Council of Chalcedon for his faithfulness." Of course, every one would think that this happened at the Œcumenical Council of Chalcedon instead of the "Synod of the Oak." Of Gregory the Great it is said he "established the Gregorian rite for uniformity"; this, of course, means his reforming the Kalendar. St. Clement of Rome is said to be the "*reputed* author of two Epistles to the Corinthians." Jeremy Taylor is said to have "published *Antiquitates Christianæ* in 1675," and to have died 1667! Jeremy Collier is credited with the authorship of "*Histryo-Mastix.*" A new edition was, I believe, issued last year, which I have not seen; it is as well, however, to note the above errata in that of 1870.
                      E. LEATON BLENKINSOPP.

ROGATION SUNDAY.—An old gardener near Exeter was bewailing the destruction of apple blossom by the frost, and explained that it was never safe until after Rogation Sunday. "And do you know why? Old Rogation was a maltster, and couldn't abide cider."
                      PAUL Q. KARKEEK.
Torquay.

CHARLES COLLINS.—In the possession of Dr. J. Gardner Dudley is a painting of three jungle pheasants, with other birds, well executed, but with inferior background, and signed "Chas. Collins, 1740." It is said to have been painted for some one who attempted to acclimatize the birds.

HYDE CLARKE.

Queries.

[We must request correspondents desiring information on family matters of only private interest, to affix their names and addresses to their queries, in order that the answers may be addressed to them direct.]

AN OLD BALLAD.—The following fragment of a ballad I have from the recital of a Norfolk gentleman. He can remember no more than what is here given, nor can either he or I ascertain that it occurs anywhere in print. I shall be obliged to any reader of "N. & Q." who can furnish me with a complete copy. I am also anxious to know who Captain Ward was, and to what feat of his these verses refer:—

"Captain Ward sent to our king,
    'Twas on the third of January,
To know whether he might come in
    And all his company—

To know whether he might come in,
    And not to be controlled,
And if he might his ransom was
    Full . . . tons of gold.

'Oh, nay, oh, nay,' replied our king,
    'Oh, nay, that ne'er can be;
He is so much then of a knave,
    He and I should never agree.'

With that the king prepared
    A ship of noble fame,
'Twas called the Royal Rainbow,
    When by its proper name.

Oh, then it was prepared,
    And sent unto the sea;
Full fifteen hundred men on board
    To bear her company.

.   .   .   .   .
But if you are the king's own ship
    I'd have you to pass by.

At four o'clock the next morning
    They did begin to fight,
And so they did continue
    Till late it was at night.

'Fight on, fight on,' cried Captain Ward,
    'I value you not one pin,
For if you are good brass without
    We are good steel within.

Fight on, fight on,' cried Captain Ward,
    'This sport doth pleasure me,
For if ye fight until . . . ,
    I will your master be.'

With that the Royal Rainbow
    Returned from whence she came;
Saying Captain Ward was on the seas,
    And there he would remain.

'Alack, alas!' replied our king,
    'Have I lost jewels three;
Had the worst of them but been alive
    He'd brought proud Ward to me.'"

M. G. W. PEACOCK.

Bottesford Manor, Brigg.

"CORNELIANUM DOLIUM." BY T. R.—Is there any valid reason for ascribing this comedy to Thomas Randolph the poet? A copy is before me dated 1638, of which the following is the title:—

"CORNELIANVM DOLIUM. Comœdia lepidissima, optimorum judiciis approbata, & Theatrali Coryphœo, nec immeritò, donata, palma chorali apprimè digna. Auctore, T. R. ingeniosissimo hujus ævi HELICONIO.

Ludunt dum juvenes, lasciviunt Senes,
Senescunt juvenes, juvenescunt Senes.

Londini, Apud Tho. Harperum. Et væneunt per Tho. Slaterum, & Laurentium Chapman. 1638." 8vo.

Some former owner, who seems to have been "Jo: Gibson, Trin: Coll: Cantab: 1649, Pension:," has thus annotated the initials:— "Thomas Randolph, Trin: Coll: socio." According to Mr. Hazlitt (Poetical and Dramatic Works of Thomas Randolph, 1875, p. viii), the poet was admitted a minor Fellow of Trinity September 22, 1629, and major Fellow March 23, 1631-2, when he proceeded M.A. The comedy itself is dedicated "Alexandro Radcliffe, Baiensi Militi."

JOHN E. BAILEY.

Stretford, Manchester.

THE "PITCH" OF CHEESE.—At the Gainsburgh Mart a newspaper account informs us that "the pitch of cheese was not equal to last year." Is this use of the word "pitch" peculiar to cheese, or is it a local term?

E. LEATON BLENKINSOPP.

HERALDRY.—Wanted the correct armorial bearings of the Reed family of Chipchase Castle and Troughend, Northumberland; also of the Northumbrian families of Weldon.

E. J. DE RUELYAT.

ORIENTAL NAMES.—Rumphius describes the Aleurites Moluccana, W., under the name of Camirium. He gives the Malayan names as Camirin and Camiri, and the Dutch equivalent as Camiriboom. Loureiro gives Juglans camirium as a synonym, and Gaertner describes it as Camirium cordifolium. Hasskarl gives Kamirie as the Malayan and Javanese name, and Ed. Balfour gives Kamiri as the Malay. The Malayan is also spelt Kemiri. Kamiri and Camiri are partly naturalised French names for fruit best known as candle-nuts. J. Crawfurd, in his Malay-English Dictionary, gives Kámiri as the Malay and Javanese name of the tree, and says that its hard nuts are used in playing a game of chance. He also gives Kámiling as the equivalent in the Malay of Bencoolen. Can any of the readers of "N. & Q." help me to the etymology of this name,

or direct me to works in which I shall find this and other Eastern words explained etymologically?
W. G. PIPER.

"THE RURAL LOVERS," BY GAINSBOROUGH.—Can you tell me where this picture now is—"The Rural Lovers, by Thos. Gainsborough, in the possession of Mr. Panton Belew" (3 ft. 11¼ in. wide, 2 ft. 5¼ in. high), as given in a good engraving I have of the picture, published by F. Vicars, Aug. 4, 1760?   J. NIGHTINGALE.

RICHARD SAPP : RICHARD SOPP.—According to Boyne (*Seventeenth Century Tokens*, Nos. 134, Southwark, and 91, Dorsetshire, respectively) both these persons issued tokens. Information respecting their trades, family, &c., will be welcome, and should any collector possess duplicates of their tokens I shall be happy to purchase them. While on the subject of tokens, I may say that I am anxious to obtain specimens of those issued by Barffoot and Trimmer, both of this town. Has a supplement to Boyne's work (1858) yet appeared, as contemplated by the author? Vide Introd., p. xxiii.   H. G. C.
Basingstoke.

GILES SEXTON.—When Gov. Winthrop arrived at Boston in 1630, he had with him a Nonconformist minister named Giles Sexton, who after a few years returned to England and became Vicar of Leeds. I shall be glad of any information respecting this Giles Sexton, his family, or descendants.   GEO. SEXTON.

KENSAL GREEN CEMETERY. — Is there any printed book which gives the inscriptions on the tombstones in Kensal Green Cemetery?
J. R. B.

BESIEGERS OF WORCESTER, 1646. — In the appendix to Nash's *History of Worcestershire*, vol. ii. p. c, there is an account of the siege of Worcester, including, amongst other correspondence, a summons to surrender. The list of names attached to the latter is concluded with those of Thomas Younge and Edward Younge, and it is respecting these that I would ask for information. Can any one inform me whether they were natives of the county, to what family they belonged, and where they were buried? Were they related to the William Younge of Evesham who, a few pages further on, is mentioned as being one of those who entered the city after the surrender?
S. G.

NIGHTINGALES AND COWSLIPS.—I have heard country folk say that nightingales are not seen or heard in places where cowslips are not to be found in profusion. Does this rustic belief rest on fact, or is it a mere poetic pastoral?
CUTHBERT BEDE.

IRISH HERALDIC BIBLIOGRAPHY.—I shall be glad of references to any bibliographical descriptions of, or any information respecting, heraldic works printed or published in Ireland or written by Irishmen. I am of course acquainted with Moule's *Bibliotheca Heraldica*.   HIRONDELLE.

FLORIO'S ITALIAN BIOGRAPHY OF LADY JANE GREY.—Where was the rare and remarkable work printed which bears the title *Historia de la Vita e de la Morte de l' Illustriss. Signora Giovanna Graia, gia Regina eletta e publicata d' Inghilterra,*&c., by Michelangelo Florio, in 12mo. size, "stampato appresso Richardo Tittore, 1607," without naming the place of its publication? There are only three copies of it known to me—one at the British Museum, another at the Bodleian, and a third recently acquired for the Taylorian Library at Oxford. Could any of your readers oblige me with a reference to another copy of the same work, or to another book printed by "Richardo Tittore"?   H. KREBS.
Oxford.

GRATTAN FAMILY.—There is a tradition that a sister of the Right Hon. Henry Grattan, M.P., was drowned in a pond near Belcamp, in this parish of Santry. Her father, James Grattan, Recorder of Dublin, died 1766, and mentions in his will his daughters Anne, Catharine, Elizabeth, and Mary. Which of these was drowned, or was it another daughter? Is this occurrence mentioned in any newspaper or published work? Near this pond is a small mound under which a general of William III., wounded at the Boyne, is said to be buried. What was his name?   B. W. ADAMS, D.D.
Santry Rectory, co. Dublin.

THE LARK AND THE LINNET.—On these two rivers Bury St. Edmunds is built. Popular opinion regards them as named from the birds. But this derivation will not stand. I ask whether Lark is a corruption of Lech or Leach, from *leced*, dead. No name could better describe the sluggish stream. Lech seems to survive in Lackford; which in Doomsday is generally Lacforda, once Lac. Forda (p. ccxxii), and once Leacforde (p. clvi). Is the Linnet *hlynna*, brook? I shall feel greatly obliged to your etymological correspondents if they will consider and answer my queries.
WILLIAM COOKE, F.S.A.
The Hill House, Wimbledon, Surrey.

WILLIAM OF ORANGE AND BENTINCK.—In Macaulay's *History of England*, chap. vii., he refers to private letters, on the subject of hunting and horses, that passed between Prince William and Bentinck. Are these letters printed in English or French, and can they be seen? I wish to refer to them for the second edition of my *Book of the Horse*, which I am now preparing.
S. SIDNEY.

WINCHESTER COLLEGE.—It is stated that " the Winchester scholars, headed by Dr. Warton, dressed in their *gowns and caps*, attended the royal review at Winchester in the summer of 1778." When were the caps left off?
MACKENZIE E. C. WALCOTT.

AUTHORS OF BOOKS WANTED.—
The Isle of Arran : a Poem. Cantos 1 and 2. (Not Hetherington's.) 8vo., Edin., 1848.
Faith's Telescope ; and other Poems. Edin., 1830.
Edinburgh Delivered ; or, the World in Danger : a Dramatic Poem. 8vo., Edin., 1782.—The only copy I have seen or heard of.
The Fortune-Hunters ; or, the Gamester Reclaimed. 8vo., printed for author (1736).—Scene at Bath. Not known to the bibliographers.
The Pettyfogger Dramatized. Lond., for A. (1797).
Attack upon Lord Kenzon. Ditto.
Bruce, Wallace, and the Bard. Verse. 1844.
J. O.

AUTHORS OF QUOTATIONS WANTED.—
" Flower of eve, the sun is sinking
Far beneath the western main ;
Thirsty shrubs the night-dews drinking,
Moonbeams stealing o'er the plain."
G. E. B.

Replies.

NEVILLE QUERIES.
(5th S. ix. 266.)

Reference to the will of Anne, Duchess of Exeter (who was eldest daughter of John de Montacute, third Earl of Salisbury, and widow of John Holand, Duke of Exeter), in register Stockton, fol. 87, shows that what is given in Nicolas's *Testamenta Vetusta*, 293, as an abstract of the will of Margaret (Neville of Hornby), wife of Thomas Beaufort, Duke of Exeter, is an entire error. It is, in fact, an imperfect summary of the last clause (omitted in Dugdale's extract, *Bar.*, ii. 81) of the will of Anne, Duchess of Exeter, above mentioned, wherein she disposes of the residue of her effects (after providing for her burial in the church of St. Katherine beside the Tower of London, and the religious ceremonies in connexion therewith). My abstract—taken from the register itself—of that part of the will omitted by Dugdale is as follows :
"Residue to Sir Thomas Tirill, Kt., Thomas Lowmell, John Aps the elder, and Robert Boyton, whom I make executors of this my will, and I appoint overseers thereof my 'nevew' the Earl of Warwick and Mr. John Pynchebeke, Doctor of Divinity. Dated 20 April, 1457, and proved 15 May, 1458." Thus the expression *nephew* becomes perfectly intelligible ; for the Earl of Warwick of 1457 (the renowned Earl of Warwick and Salisbury of after days) was that Richard Neville who was declared and confirmed, by patent in 1449, Earl of Warwick, in consequence of his marriage with Anne Beauchamp, the great heiress.

He was eldest son and heir of Richard Neville, Earl of Salisbury, by his wife Alice, sole child and heir of Thomas de Montacute, fourth and last Earl of Salisbury of that stock, who was killed at the siege of Orleans in November, 1428. Anne, Duchess of Exeter, was eldest sister of this Thomas, Earl of Salisbury ; consequently she was aunt to Alice, wife of Richard Neville, Earl of Salisbury, and great-aunt to their son the Earl of Warwick.

Dugdale, in his account of John Holand, Duke of Exeter (*Bar.*, ii. 82), has wrongly made this Anne, who was his third wife, mother of his daughter Anne ; whereas the latter was daughter of Anne (Stafford), his first wife ; and, whilst stating the two previous marriages of Anne de Montacute (*Bar.*, i. 651), Dugdale makes no mention of her issue by those marriages. The following particulars will throw light on these several points.

Anne Holand, only daughter of John, Duke of Exeter, married, before February, 1442, John Neville, only son of Ralph, second Earl of Westmorland ; consequently she could not have been the issue of the duke's third wife, Anne de Montacute, who was not married to him before 1443.

Regarding the marriages and issue of this Anne de Montacute : she married firstly Sir Richard Hankford, Kt., of Annery, Devon, grandson and heir of Sir William Hankford, K.B., Chief Justice of England, and was his second wife. By him she had an only child, Anne Hankford, who was twelve weeks old at the time when her father Sir Richard Hankford died in February, 1430-1 (Inq. p.m. 9 H. VI. No. 54). This daughter became the wife of Thomas Butler, seventh Earl of Ormond and Baron of Rocheford, Essex, who died in August, 1515, and by him was great-grandmother of Queen Anne Boleyn. As widow of Sir Richard Hankford, Anne married secondly—before 1434—Sir John Fitz-Lewis, Kt., of West-Horndon, Essex, and was his second wife. By him—who died Oct. 27, 1442 (Inq. p.m. 21 H. VI. No. 16)—she had two daughters, Elizabeth and Margaret. On his death she married thirdly Sir John Holand, Earl of Huntingdon and Duke of Exeter, K.G. (being his third wife), by whom she had no issue. He died August 5, 1447 (Inq. p.m. 25 H. VI. No. 25), and by his will, dated July 16 in that year, ordered that his body should be buried in the church of St. Katherine beside the Tower of London, in a tomb which he had prepared for himself, Anne his first wife, Constance his sister, and for Anne, his wife then living. The Duchess of Exeter—surviving him for more than ten years—by her will (as shown above) gave order for her burial in the church of St. Katherine, where the corpse of the duke, her last husband, lay interred. Pursuant to writs dated February 6, 36 H. VI. (1457-8), inquisitions were taken on

when she died and who were her nearest heirs :—

" Prædicta Anna, Ducissa Exoniæ obiit 28° die Novembris ultimo præterito (1457). Et quod Anna uxor Thomæ Ormond est una filiarum et hæredum prædictæ Annæ nuper Ducissæ Exoniæ et est ætatis 25 annorum et amplius. Et quod Elizabetha uxor Johannis Wynkfeld est altera filiarum et hæredum prædictæ Annæ nuper Ducissæ Exoniæ et est ætatis 22 annorum et amplius. Et quod Margareta uxor Willielmi Lucy militis est tertia filiarum et hæredum prædictæ Annæ nuper Ducissæ Exoniæ et est ætatis 18 annorum et amplius."

I may here remark that Margaret Neville of Hornby, wife of Thomas Beaufort, Duke of Exeter, died before her husband, and was buried in the abbey church of St. Edmundsbury, Suffolk. He died December 29, 1426, and his remains were, according to the directions in his will, laid beside hers in the same abbey.

Sir William Lucy, the husband of Margaret Fitz-Lewis, does not appear to have been connected with the Lucys of Charlcote. He sprang from a Geoffery de Lucy, who held lands in the counties of Cambridge, Northampton, Bucks, Herts, and Surrey, and was summoned to Parliament as Baron Lucy in 49 H. III., 1264. By the death of his mother Eleanor, daughter and co-heir of Sir Warine Archdekne, in 1447, Sir William acquired the lordship of Ricards Castle, in Herefordshire, and other manors in Worcestershire and Cornwall (Inq. p.m. 26 H. VI. No. 13). He was over forty years of age at the time of his father Sir Walter Lucy's death, in 1444 (Inq. p.m. 23 H. VI. No. 9). According to HERMENTRUDE, Magaret Neville of Raby must have been his first wife. His second wife was Elizabeth, widow of Thomas Borough, mother of Thomas, first Lord Borough, and daughter and co-heir of Sir Henry Percy of Athol. By her—who died in 1455 (Inq. p.m. 34 H. VI. No. 16)—he had no issue. In the following year, 1456, when he was more than fifty-two years old, he married thirdly Margaret Fitz-Lewis, the Duchess of Exeter's youngest daughter, who was only eighteen years of age. He did not long survive this marriage ; for, an intrigue occurring between his wife and John Stafford, Esq., Sir William was slain, on July 10, 1460, by Stafford's servants : whereupon John Stafford married the young widow (Stevenson's Letters and Papers, &c., ii. 773, and Inq. p.m. 1 E. IV. No. 16). Dying without issue and intestate, administration of Sir William's effects was granted in the Prerog. Court of Canterbury July 29 following (Register Bourchier, 46ᵇ, at Lambeth Palace). This John Stafford was a younger son of Sir Humphry Stafford, Kt., of Grafton, co. Worcester, Lieutenant of Calais, and commander of the royal forces in the encounter with the Kentish rebels at Sevenoaks, in which action Sir Humphry was killed, June 18, 1450. John Stafford's lawless and precipitate acts were soon followed by his death,

1464 Margaret had married a third husband named Wake ; and she died August 4, 1466, leaving issue a son, John Wake, who was found to be her nearest heir, and then aged two years (Inq. p.m. 6 E. IV. No. 29).

The following remarks will furnish a solution to HERMENTRUDE's third query, viz. as to the parentage of Margaret Neville, wife of Sir William Gascoyne. Jane, only child and heir of John Neville of Wymersley, only son and heir of Sir Ralph Neville, Kt., Lord of Oversley, married Sir William Gascoigne of Gawthorpe, great-grandson of the Chief Justice. Their grandson, Sir William Gascoigne of Gawthorpe, married Margaret, eldest daughter of Richard Neville, Lord Latimer (who died in 1529), by his wife Anne (married in 1494), daughter of Humphry Stafford, Esq., of Grafton.   B. W. GREENFIELD.

Southampton.

Ralph Neville, third Earl of Westmorland, according to Courthope's Historic Peerage, died 1523, and was succeeded by his grandson, another Ralph. Is it a fact that his son Ralph, who died during his lifetime, had two wives ? I thought his only wife was Edith, daughter of William, Lord Sands, of Hampshire.

Anne, wife of William, Lord Conyers, is always, I believe, said to have been daughter of Ralph, the third Earl of Westmorland, and aunt to Ralph, the fourth earl of that name.   SYWL.

THE LATE BISHOP OF LICHFIELD (5ᵗʰ S. ix. 349.)—George Selwyn, the famous wit, represented the city of Gloucester in Parliament for many years, and lived at the family seat, Matson House, near that city, where Charles I. and the royal princes took up their abode during the siege of Gloucester. The Gloucestershire Chronicle of April 20, in an able notice of the late Bishop of Lichfield, says :—

" Although the bishop was born and reared elsewhere, and his visits to this neighbourhood were few and hurried, yet there were times when his thoughts would turn to an old manor-house nestling peacefully amidst the firs on the eastern slopes of Robin's Wood Hill. The bishop always spoke of Matson as the loved home of his race ; and some years ago, when he came here to plead the cause of foreign missions in our noble cathedral, he walked out and spent a quiet hour there...As he stood in the quaint little church, and thought of his ancestors who for many generations had worshipped there, he could scarcely have failed to feel a pride in the name he bore ; and yet none of them had done so much to honour that name as he had done...The bishop was a schoolboy again as he roamed through the old house of his forefathers at Matson, and searched for the traditional marks which the two princes had left on the window-sill of an upper room. By chance some workmen were employed on the inside of the roof, and the bishop climbed up the ladder and wrote the well-known autograph, ' George Augustus Selwyn,' on one of the beams. May be in the distant future those words will be more honoured than the sword clefts, or any relic of the well-known eighteenth century wit.

"Pedigrees are very dull things to outsiders; but some of your readers may like to know exactly what was the bishop's connexion with Matson, and where his family branched off from the parent stock. General William Selwyn, the fourth Selwyn who owned Matson, died in Jamaica, in 1702, leaving three sons and several daughters. John, the eldest son, succeeded to the estates, and was the father of George Selwyn, so distinguished for his *bons mots* a hundred years ago. Charles, the second son, died in 1749, and left no heirs. Henry, the youngest, married in early life Ruth, daughter of Anthony Compton, of Gainslaw, and was the ancestor of Bishop Selwyn. The Matson property was entailed on the male heir; but Colonel John Selwyn and his eldest son, John, shortly before they both died in 1751, broke the entail and re-settled the property on the heirs of Albinia Townshend. But for this Henry Selwyn's children would have come into it on the decease of George Augustus. Henry Selwyn died in 1734 in the prime of life, and was buried at Matson. His mother Albinia Selwyn, who rebuilt the little church, begged on her death-bed that her body might rest by his, beneath the north-east window of the nave. He had two sons— Charles Jasper and William. Charles Jasper, the eldest son, married Elizabeth Coxeter, of Bampton, and was the father of Henry Charles Selwyn, whose son, the Rev. Townshend Selwyn, was Canon of Gloucester not many years ago. Many of your readers have seen the inscription which he wrote for a fountain in his garden near the cathedral. He loved the old Matson home, which he felt ought to have been his own, and when he tasted the sparkling water which came to him from the springs on Matson Hill, it seemed to him in his old age as though he were a boy once more. The canon's son, Admiral Frederick Leopold Selwyn, but for the re-settlement on the Townshends, would be the present proprietor of Matson.

"To return to the younger branch of the family. Henry Selwyn's second son, William, was a barrister-at-law, and several of his descendants have highly distinguished themselves in that profession. He married Elizabeth Dodd, of Woodford, and had a son, William, who was an eminent Nisi Prius lawyer, and was selected to instruct the late Prince Consort in the constitutional history of this country. He married Letitia Kynaston, of Witham, and was the father of Bishop Selwyn and his two no less distinguished brothers—William, who became Canon of Ely and Lady Margaret's Professor of Divinity; and Charles Jasper, who was so successful at the bar that he became Lord Justice Selwyn before his death."

　　　　　　　　　　　　　　　　J. H. B.
Gloucester.

A RESIDENCE FOR ROYALTY IN IRELAND (5th S. ix. 366, 395.)—In 1637 Lord Strafford was building a mansion house at Naas, and his enemies took occasion to make this a ground of misrepresentation to the king. Lord Strafford mentions this in a letter to the Archbishop of Canterbury (Laud), dated Sept. 27, 1637. He says :—

"Next they say I build up to the sky. I acknowledge that were myself only considered in what I build, it were not only to excess, but even to folly......but his Majesty will justify me that, at my last being in England, I acquainted him with a purpose I had to build him a house at the Naas, it being uncomely his Majesty should

not have one here of his own, capable to lodge him with moderate conveniency, which in truth as yet he hath not ; in case he might be pleased sometimes hereafter to look upon this kingdom......that when it was built if liked by his Majesty it should be his, paying me as it cost; if disliked, *a suo damno*, I was content to keep it and smart for my folly. His Majesty seemed to be pleased with all, whereupon I proceeded, and have in a manner finished it, and so contrived it for the rooms of state and other accommodations which I have observed ever to have cast it for a private family. Another Frame of wood I have given order to set up in a park I have in the county of Wicklow. And gnash the Tooth of these Gallants never so hard, I will by God's leave go on with it.......Yet lest these magnificent structures might be thought those of *Nebuchadnezzar*, the plain truth is, that at the *Naas* with the most may stand in six thousand pounds.......to profess a truth to your Grace, but that I did consider his Majesty might judge it hereafter for his service to visit this kingdom, in that case foresaw no part able to give him the pleasure of his summer hunting like that park and the country adjacent......I protest there had not been one timber of it fastened to another."

Lord Strafford goes on to complain that a foul-mouthed Scotchman, one Mr. Barre, tells lies of him to the king, which he calls " Bodadoes stuffed with untruths and follies."

On the 24th of October, 1637, the archbishop writes to him in reply :—

" His Majesty was well pleased with what you writ, and the manner of your buildings, and your end proposed in it, and the offer made to himself to take or refuse them."—*The Earl of Strafford's Letters and Despatches,* vol. ii. pp. 105, 126, folio, Dublin, 1740.

　　　　　　　　　　　　　　　　EDWARD SOLLY.

EMBLEMS OF THE PASSION (5th S. ix. 261.)—CUTHBERT BEDE's article may be illustrated by a description of a curious little engraving, a tracing of which lies before me, which stands at the commencement of the " Missa de Quinque Vulneribus," in a copy of the Salisbury Missal, Paris, 1514, preserved in Bp. Cosin's Library, Durham. A canopy of three arches surmounts the whole ; the cross stands to the right of the engraving, its upright dividing it into two unequal portions, that to the left being double the width of that to the right of the cross. Our Lord, whose body is entirely nude save for a waistcloth, stands with his left arm round the stem of the cross, whilst his right supports the spear with which his side was pierced. The wounds on the hands and feet and in the side are indicated, and on the brow are large drops of sweat. On the left arm of the cross stands a chalice, probably referring to our Lord's words, " The cup which my Father hath given me, shall I not drink it ?" The larger space on the left is occupied by a pillar, round which a rope is coiled, a whip with a double thong having its handle thrust through the upper coil of the rope ; on the pillar stands a cock. In the lower part of this compartment is an open tomb, close to which lies a hammer ; the rest of the space is occupied by a face with tongue protruded, the crown of thorns,

. — ———- (.... .... xix. .), three large nails, and a bundle of rods, looking very like an ordinary birch. In the narrower or right hand space are depicted, on the ground, the seamless garment and three dice with a large lantern ; a long rod supports a sponge ; there are pincers for drawing out the nails, a reed, probably that placed in our Lord's hand in mockery, the head of Judas, with the bag slung round his neck, and a strange-looking object, that may possibly be intended to represent the thirty pieces of silver. The terms "right" and "left" are intended to apply to a person looking at the engraving. JOHNSON BAILY.
Pallion Vicarage.

About the year 1850 I was on a visit to the Rector of Kilmeen, near Clonakilty, in the county of Cork. My friend brought me to visit the ruins of an old castle. Over the open fireplace in the great hall there was a stone, about two or three feet square, carved in the rudest fashion, and evidently representing our Lord's sufferings. There were the cross, the nails, the hammer, and the scourge ; but there was one piece of sculpture which I could not understand. It was a sort of rude semicircle, the curve below and the diameter above, and at the junction a figure intended to represent a bird. My friend asked me what it meant. I confessed my ignorance. " That," said he, " is the cock ; the servants were boiling him for supper, but when the moment came to convict the apostle he started up, perched on the side of the pot, and astonished the assembly by his salutation of the morning." This is a fact I had never heard of. Perhaps some of your correspondents can give me the authority, or some trace of the legend. H.

PAPAL MEDALS (5ᵗʰ S. ix. 207.)—We have three medals of Clement XII. :—1. CLEMENS XII. PONT. MAX. AN. III. Of extraordinary size, by young Otto Hamerani. The Pope, with the tiara on head, is giving the benediction. Rev., the façade of St. John Lateran as it was in 1733 ; ADORATE DOMINUM IN ATRIO SANCTO EIUS. Above, in the centre, is seen the statue of St. John holding the Cross, and on his right and left ten other statues. In the exergue are the words, LATERAN BASIL. PORTICUS. This medal is so finely executed that every detail can be seen clearly without a glass.
2. RECTIS . CORDE . LÆTITIA. A female figure, standing, holds the scales in her right hand and a palm in the left. OTTO in the exergue. The attitude of the figure is extremely graceful. Canova drew inspiration from this composition to improve one of his nymphs.
3. FONTE . AQVÆ . VIRGINIS . ORNATO. The celebrated fountain of Trevi. In the exergue, O and H, and a she-wolf, the symbol of Rome. Venuti found in the private collections of princely libraries other medallic riches of this reign

(sixteen). One of these is that mentioned i View of the Loretto of Ancona, with vessels ai the city in the distance. In the exergue, DORIC VRBIS LOEMOCOMIVM ; the she-wolf and initial Otto Hamerani. Clement fortified . Ancona ai gave it a lazaretto.
Short as was the reign of Francis Todeschi Piccolomini (Pius III.), there was time in tl twenty-six days to strike three medals. The fir₤ without being an exact restoration of that Pius II., has the same legend on the revers GLORIA SENENSI. D. C. PICCOLOMINI. In tl middle of the shield, surmounted by the tiara an keys, are the arms of the family. Second repr₤ sents the Pope in his tiara, throned, blessir a warrior, who has his right arm extended and h₤ left on his breast ; two mitred cardinals right an left of the throne. Du Molinet very plausibl₤ supposes this warrior to be Cæsar Borgia. Legen₤ SVB VMBRA ALARVM TVARVM. M.D.III. Borgi₤ menaced by the Orsini, had sought the Pope's pr₤ tection. Before Cæsar is a cardinal's hat. Th₤ prince is armed as a warrior, with gauntlets an greave. Third, reverse : Three staffs interlaced i a crown. Legend, TENTANDA VIA. All the ex planations of this are mysterious. Typotius, i his Symbola Divina Pontificum (1603), speaks ₤ it at length. The three staffs are, according t him, the aids offered by the Holy Trinity to trea₤ the paths of life and win the eternal crown. I these three medals the obverse is the same. Th head entirely bare, with the legend, FIVS III. PON꞊ MAX MDIII. (see Montor's Lives of the Popes).
With regard to the fifteen medals of Clement XI₤ alluded to above, if NEPHRITE wishes for a descrip tion of them, and will forward me his address, shall be happy to supply it. It would take up to much space in " N. & Q." JOHN THOMPSON.
The Grove, Pocklington.

" SOLILOQUIES OF ST. AUGUSTINE " (5ᵗʰ S. i₤ 246.)—It should be stated that these have n claim to be considered St. Augustine's—they ai relegated to the appendix in the Benedictine ed tion of his works ; also that " Et nihil odis eorum quæ fecisti " is the Vulgate version ₤ Wisdom xi. 24 ; in A. V., " And abhorrest nothin which Thou hast made." It occurs in the Sali₤ bury Missal in the Collect for Ash Wednesda꞊ and in the Roman Missal in the Introit, on tl same day. ED. MARSHALL.

" BETWEEN YOU AND I " (5ᵗʰ S. ix. 275.)- Every one who possesses an ear for grammar mu agree with HERMENTRUDE about the atrocity " between you and I." The only advantage I c₤ think of as springing from this and similar gra₤ matical blunders is that they teach one a lesson ₤ self-control, as it is extremely difficult when o₤ hears people make such mistakes to avoid imitati₤

John Kemble, who would correct any one, no matter how exalted in station. With regard to this particular mistake of "I," Herrick, in his charming lyric, *Go, Happy Rose*, makes the verb govern the nominative case of the personal pronoun:—

> "Lest a handsome anger fly
> Like a lightning from her eye
> And burn thee up as well as I."

I do not say that this justifies the error, unless poets are to be considered the masters of language.

JONATHAN BOUCHIER.

HAMPDEN PEDIGREES (5ᵗʰ S. ix. 287.)—I think I have some papers which may be of use to O. C. They are the manuscript collection of Browne Willis on the family of Hampden, consisting of (1) extracts of all that concerns the Hampden family from the "Alesbury Register"; (2) extracts of wills "out of the Prerogative Office"; (3) baptisms from Hartwell register; (4) copy by Lord Trevor of some papers " wrote by my mother of the several times when her children were born," April, 1724 ; (5) "the pedigree of Hampden of Hampden, co. Buckingham : Lords of Great Hampden, Kimbell, Dunton, Hartwell, &c., all co. Buckingham, and divers other demeasnes in Oxfordshire, Berkshire, &c." (this is in the handwriting of Browne Willis, and extends down to 1743); (6) letters from Browne Willis on various miscellaneous matters in connexion with the family, and addressed " to John Hampden, Esqʳᵉ, member of Parliamᵗ, att His House in Conduit Street, near Hannover Square, London " (for whom these researches were made). I was assured by your learned correspondent A. S. A., a short time ago, that these papers had not been printed. They came into my possession from the library of James Gomme, F.S.A., of High Wycombe, who was a personal friend of Browne Willis. At my leisure moments I am transcribing them for the pages of " 'N. & Q.,' " if acceptable to the editor ; but I shall be happy to show them to O. C. in the mean time. G. LAURENCE GOMME.
Castelnau, Barnes, S.W.

RUSSIAN HISTORY (5ᵗʰ S. ix. 326.)—Lord Whitworth's *Account of Russia*, as it was in the year 1710, was printed by Horace Walpole at Strawberry Hill in 1758. In the advertisement it is stated :—

> "Lord Whitworth's MS. was communicated to me by Richard Owen Cambridge, Esq., having been purchased by him in a very curious set of books collected by Monsieur Zolman, secretary to the late Stephen Poyntz, Esq. This little library relates solely to Russian history and affairs, and contains in many languages everything that perhaps has been written on that country."

The Right Hon. Stephen Poyntz was Governor to the Duke of Cumberland 1731, and afterwards steward of his household. He died in December, 1750. The curious Russian library referred to by Horace Walpole must therefore have been sold to Cambridge between the years 1750 and 1758. Mr. Cambridge died in 1802, and it may be of interest to inquire what became of this Russian library. EDWARD SOLLY.

"IT IS AN ILL WIND," &c. (5ᵗʰ S. ix. 348.)—Camden, in his *Remains*, gives the saying as a proverb. He was born fifty-seven years before Fuller. Nathan Bailey, *s.v.* " Wind," explains the proverb, and gives its Latin, French, Greek, and Hebrew equivalent. And Shakespeare, in 2 *Henry IV.*, which play, according to Malone, was written in 1598, makes Pistol say (v. 3, 90), " Not the ill wind which blows no man to good." From the above references it cannot be Fuller's offspring. FREDK. RULE.

> " Ill blows the wind that profits nobody."
> 3 *Hen. VI.*, Act ii. sc. 5.
> G. PERRATT.

> " Except wind stands as never it stood,
> It is an ill wind turns none to good."
> Thomas Tusser, *Moral Reflections on the Wind*.
> H. F. W.

JUDGES IX. 53 (5ᵗʰ S. ix. 344.)—Permit me to say in behalf of the Bishop of Bath and Wells that C. has hardly made out his case. The fact, as I believe now known, is that by 1611 the use of *to*=*zer* was nearly obsolete, and that *all*=quite having previously often preceded this prefix *to*, became corrupted into *all to*, with, or mostly without, the hyphen. *All to* thus came to mean *altogether* when *to* alone was dying out, and it seems more likely, as *all* is present in every one of the passages quoted, that this usage had become fixed by 1611. *Tattered* is surely not *to-teared*. In *Peres the Ploughmans Crede*, 753, we have, "His teeth with toylinge of lether tatered as a sawe," *i.e.* jagged, and Skeat compares Icelandic *tæta*, to card wool. H. F. W.

ARMS ON THE STALLS IN THE CHOIR OF THE CATHEDRAL AT HAARLEM : THE GOSPEL AND EPISTLE SIDES OF THE ALTAR (5ᵗʰ S. ix. 61, 101.) —Your learned and very accurate correspondent in his notice of the above arms speaks pointedly of the north side of the cathedral as the Epistle side, and the south as the Gospel side. Is this the usual arrangement in Roman Catholic churches ? In the English Church the opposite use prevails. The Gospel is read from the north side and the Epistle from the south side of the altar in those churches where most pains are taken to have all according to Catholic usage and liturgiology scrupulously observed. Is there any authority for the English usage ? CROWDOWN.

FIELD NAMES (5ᵗʰ S. ix. 325.)—I have often felt the want expressed by MR. GOMME, and, in addition to the tithe map, have found the convenience of having access to a quantity of old

depends on an antiquity which may sometimes exceed that of the *political* divisions of the country. These latter are almost universally English, while it is among the names of non-political objects and areas that one may find the remnants of a previous system of nomenclature. TREGEAGLE.

MRS. CRANMER'S MARRIAGE (5th S. ix. 308.)— Cranmer was twice married. About 1516, shortly after his admission as a Fellow of Jesus College, Cambridge, he married the niece of the landlady of the "Dolphin," a tavern of good repute in Cambridge. This of course forfeited his fellowship; but his young wife died within the first year, and the Fellows of his college re-elected him at once, "for his towardlinesse in learning." He became a divinity lecturer, and took orders in 1520. In 1530 Cranmer was sent to Rome by Henry VIII. as one of our embassy, and in 1531 was appointed to be king's orator at the emperor's court, at which time he resided for about six months at Nuremberg. He there saw much of Osiander, the celebrated Lutheran pastor, and married his niece Margaret about the year 1532. In the August of that year Archbishop Wareham died, and Henry summoned Cranmer from Germany to be his successor. He was consecrated in March, 1533. Early in 1534 his wife joined him in England, but she lived apart from him, and very privately; for Cranmer, though he felt quite justified in marrying as one of the secular clergy, was well aware that it was not right for an archbishop. Gilpin (*Life of Cranmer*) says :—" The affair of his marriage was made easy to him, and the king's message brought him immediately to England." In 1539 Cranmer fell rather under the king's displeasure, because Henry desired to sequestrate the revenues of the abbeys to his own use, and Cranmer deemed this wrong, and had the courage to say so openly. His enemies then were enabled to pass the celebrated Act known as the "Six Articles," which was energetically put forward by Gardiner, Bp. of Winchester. Under this it was death for a priest to have a wife, and Cranmer at once sent his wife back to Germany.

When Edward VI. became king an Act was passed, not only permitting the clergy to marry, but "repealing all laws and canons that had been made against it " (Burnet's *Hist. of Reformation*, 1681, ii. 89). On this Cranmer's wife returned to England, and was openly received and acknowledged. On the death of King Edward, Cranmer at first took the part of Lady Jane Grey. Under Queen Mary he was found guilty of high treason and attainted, was partly pardoned by the queen for the time, yet was eventually burned on March 21, 1556. After the accession of Elizabeth a special Act was passed to restore his children in blood ; the date of this was March 9, 1563

because Henry VIII. had, without Cranme given to his wife the revenues of Welbeck Abb in Nottinghamshire (Strype's *Life of Cranm* 1694, p. 418). Mrs. Cranmer survived the ar bishop many years; she afterwards married Wh church the printer, who died in 1561, and in 15 she married, for the third time, Bartholomew Se (Cooper's *Athenæ Cantabrigienses*, 1858, i. 457).
EDWARD SOLLY.

There is no reason to doubt the truth of Cra mer's first marriage at Cambridge before I ordination, the death of Joan his first wife childbed, and his subsequent marriage at Nür berg about 1532 with a niece of Osiander.
TREGEAGLE.

RELAYED OR RELAID? (5th S. ix. 308.)—*Del* and *allay* are not compounds of *lay*. *Delay* is tl Latin *differo*, sup. *dilatum; defer* is another for of the same word. *Allay* is the French *allég[e* and it is a general rule to end all verbs in -*e* except those from our native strong conjugation *Lay* is the Ang.-Sax. *lecg[an*], past *legede*, pa part. *leged*, and the form *laid* is corrupt, as *paid* i being from the French *payer*. *Said* has mo right to its peculiar spelling, being the Ang.-Sa *sæd*, from *sæcg[an*], to say. The best thing woul be to abolish the absurd form *laid* and resto *layed;* but if this restoration is looked on wit disfavour, then all the compounds of *lay* shoul follow one pattern, as *re-*, *mis-*, *way-*, *in-*, *ove [lay*], but by no means should such words as *dela* and *allay* be allowed to falsify their parentage b being made to appear of the same family.
E. COBHAM BREWER.
Lavant, Chichester.

JOHN NOWELL (5th S. ix. 367.)—*A* John Nowel bapt. Mar. 26, 1589, was *great-grandson* of th dean's half-brother, John Nowell, who had died i 1526, though the dean survived "almost fort years after he had begun to reckon himself an ol man," till 1601-2.
H. W.
New Univ. Club.

THE AMERICAN ROBIN (5th S. ix. 367.)—I woul refer MR. DIXON to the *Life of Canon Kingsle* vol. ii. p. 427. Writing from Boston (U.S.) o March 23, the canon says : "Oh, dear, I wi spring would come, the winter here is awful. . . But the bluebird and the robin (as they call great parti-coloured thrush) are just beginning come, to my intense delight."
E. C. PERRY.
King's Coll., Camb.

"THE PASTON LETTERS" (5th S. ix. 205, 32 350, 370.)—That Agnes, daughter of Nichol Morley and wife of John Harvey, is the san person as Agnes, wife of John Isley and Joh

Paston, is proved beyond a doubt by her will, an abstract of which is given in the *Paston Letters* (new edit., iii. 471). Is not John Isted, mentioned by G. L. G., a misreading for John Isley? That her daughter Isabel Legh is the same person as Isabel (or Elizabeth) Atclyff cannot be proved quite so satisfactorily. It certainly does seem strange that there should be no mention of a second marriage on Isabel Legh's monument in Addington Church. On the other hand, Agnes Paston, whom we know to be mother of Isabel Legh, in her will mentions her son-in-law, William Hatteclyff, and her daughter, Isabel Hatteclyff, as well as her daughter Isabel Isley. There is also the passage in Sir George Harvey's will, quoted by G. L. G. : "Elizabeth Atclyff, wife of William Atclyff, suster to the said George." As no George has been mentioned before, the supposition of Lord Arthur Hervey (*Family of Hervey*, p. 72) that by "the said George" is carelessly meant the testator himself seems most natural. Margaret Smarte was not Sir George Harvey's illegitimate daughter, as G. L. G. says, but the mother of his illegitimate son Gerard. Also the date of John Legh's death, as given on the monument at Addington, is 1502, not 1509. If he died in 1503, as G. L. G. then the date of the letter, No. 939, in the *Paston Letters* can be fixed yet more nearly than was done ante, p. 326.   S. H. A. H.

"A FORLORN HOPE" (5ᵗʰ S. ix. 266, 375.)—George Gascoigne, a scholar and a soldier, who both fought for the Dutch and understood their language, furnishes a good example of the use of this term. I regret that I have only Hazlitt's reprint, which evidently is not a literal one :—

> " But I by Miser meane the very man,
> Which is enforst by chip of any chaunce
> To steppe aside and wander now and than,
> Till lowring lucke may pipe some other daunce,
> And in meane while yet hopeth to aduaunce
> His staylesse state by sworde, by speare, by shielde ;
> Such bulwarkes (loe) my Misers braine doth builde."

> *The forlorne hope* which haue set vp their rest
> By rash expence, and knowe not howe to liue,
> The busie braine that medleth with the best,
> And gets dysgrace his rashnesse to repreue,
> The man that slewe the wight that thought to theeue,
> Such and such moe which flee the Catchpols fist,
> I compt them Misers, though the Queene it wist."

Hazlitt's *Gascoigne*, vol. i. p. 165.
R. R.
Boston, Lincolnshire.

AN OIL PAINTING : GERARD EDEMA (5ᵗʰ S. ix. 189, 256, 378.)—T. McM. may find two or three Edemas in a small room at Hampton Court. I sold one at Christie's for a trifle in 1861 or 1862. They are usually large upright oblongs. They are about a hundred and twenty years old, and will, I think, some day be valued because they were either painted in Canada or from sketches

there made by the artist in early life. But I suppose the picture in question to be by Mr. Oram.   GWAVAS.

BALLAD : "NUTTING" (4ᵗʰ S. vii. 162.)—This ballad may be found in the *Portfolio*, a Philadelphia weekly, for August 16, 1806, p. 93. The authorship and first appearance are said to be unknown.   M. N. G.

POPULATION OF ROME UNDER AUGUSTUS (5ᵗʰ S. ix. 248.)—MR. KREBS will find the first part of his query fully discussed in Dr. Smith's edition of Gibbon's *Decline and Fall*, vol. iv. p..89, note.
EDWARD H. MARSHALL.
The Temple.

TONY LUMPKIN (5ᵗʰ S. ix. 286.)—Surnames which go out in *kin* are usually formed on some Christian name, as Wil*kin* or Wat*kin*; but what can *Lump* represent, unless it is Lionel?
GWAVAS.

THE NAME SKELHORN (5ᵗʰ S. ix. 289.)—This word is of Norse or Danish origin. If the locality is on the sea coast it would mean "the shell prominence or promontory." If in the interior it is probably a corruption of Old Norse *skilja*, to divide or separate, and would mean the boundary eminence. Compare *Skelbrook*, the boundary brook, *Skelmeresdale*, the dell of the boundary pool, &c.   J. A. PICTON.
Sandyknowe, Wavertree.

SHELLEY'S PLACE IN ENGLISH LITERATURE (5ᵗʰ S. vi. 341, 361, 392, 478, 517 ; vii. 189.)—Rather more than a year ago you were kind enough to insert an article of mine under this heading, in which I endeavoured to combat the views of two of your correspondents who, as I considered, held a very extravagant estimate of Shelley's genius, and more especially of one of them, who said that he considered Shelley Milton's equal. Some time after this article appeared I received a letter from the latter gentleman, remonstrating with me strongly, but I must say most courteously, for having, as he expressed it, "done scant justice to Shelley's marvellous poetic gifts." The result of his letter was that I promised him I would read Shelley more fully and closely than I had done before, and then let him know what conclusion I had come to. I wish now to state that after reading Shelley with much attention I frankly and willingly acknowledge that, although I do not now, and am quite sure that I never shall, consider him equal to Milton (probably not even to Spenser), I did him an injustice in saying that his place in the poetic hierarchy was *far* below John Milton's. I now retract the word *far*. My correspondent justly observed that "I could scarcely say anything more depreciatory of such small bards as Tom Moore, Beattie, or Montgomery." After a

the criticism that has been written on Shelley, I do not know of any more just and intelligent than that of Lord Macaulay in his essay on the *Pilgrim's Progress :*—

"Some of the metaphysical and ethical theories of Shelley were certainly most absurd and pernicious. But we doubt whether any modern poet has possessed in an equal degree some of the highest qualities of the great ancient masters. The words bard and inspiration, which seem so cold and affected when applied to other modern writers, have a perfect propriety when applied to him. He was not an author but a bard. His poetry seems not to have been an art but an inspiration. Had he lived to the full age of man, he might not improbably have given to the world some great work of the very highest rank in design and execution."

The last sentence appears to me to hit the mark in the very centre. It shows that although Macaulay thought the *Prometheus* and the *Cenci* sufficiently great to warrant our judging it highly probable that their author would, if he had lived, have taken his place by the side of the great patricians of Parnassus, he differed from those who think that he is side by side with them as it is. It seems presumptuous in me to say that I agree with such a critic as Macaulay (this will, I fear, suggest the comparison of the very small M.P. who said " ditto to Mr. Burke"); still, if I may say so, I think Macaulay's estimate of Shelley perfectly just. Those ardent lovers of Shelley who, in their certainly pardonable enthusiasm for such a genius, speak of him as Milton's equal, should " inwardly digest" the following words of Mr. J. R. Green in his *Short History of the English People :*—

" The romance, the gorgeous fancy, the daring imagination, which Milton shared with the Elizabethan poets, the large but ordered beauty of form which he had drunk in from the literature of Greece and Rome, the sublimity of conception, the loftiness of phrase, which he owed to the Bible, blended in this story of 'man's first disobedience.' It is only when we review the strangely mingled elements which make up the poem that we realize the genius which fused them into such a perfect whole."

Would not Mr. W. M. Rossetti, Mr. Buxton Forman, or any other of Shelley's most devoted lovers, hesitate before applying such a criticism as this either to the *Prometheus Unbound*, the *Cenci*, or *Adonais ?*

I trust your readers will not imagine that I have written this note because I suppose that my opinion is of any importance either to Shelley or to the public. But it is of some importance to myself; and as I feel that I did Shelley an injustice in my former article in underrating his genius, it will be a satisfaction to me if you will allow me to take this opportunity of making his *manes* the *amende honorable*, and of doing more justice to our own or most highly gifted geniuses either in our own or any other literature.   JONATHAN BOUCHIER.
Bexley Heath, Kent.

ROBERT PALTOCK (5th S. ix. 186, 372.)—J. O. (*ante*, p. 372) has made a mistake which will

amuse him when pointed out. It seems to me have arisen in this way. In 1867 I wrote the n J. O. refers to, attributing the *Memoirs of the 1* of *Parnese* to Paltock. J. O. seems to me to h copied out that note at the time, but without a. ing the reference, and, having now " disinterr(his copy, regardless of my actually having laid cl: to it in my last communication (*ante*, p. 186), to g it as his own. The title which I gave (3rd S. 445) will show how incorrectly J. O. has gi what he states to be the full title. I should l to add that I do not take any credit to myself my suggestion as to the authorship, for experie has shown me that, without some corroborat evidence, an attribution on the ground similarities is next to worthless. The second w J. O. refers to I am unable to find in the Brit Museum Catalogue.   OLPHAR HAMST

EASTER SUNDAY AND ST. MARK'S DAY (5tt ix. 367, 395.)—St. Mark's Day, April 25, is last day on which Easter Sunday can possibly f It is therefore often marked in calendars " Ultimum pascha"; similarly March 22, earliest day on which the festival can fall, marked " Primum pascha." March 27 is often calendars described as " Resurrectio Domini," fr a belief that the resurrection of our Lord actus took place on that day. Hampson (*Medii A Kalendarium*) has been led into a curious er by an entry of the kind described above ir calendar brought under his notice. Noting it a fourteenth century calendar, he asserts that must have been written in one of the three yer 1323, 1334, 1345, in which Easter Day fell March 27 in that century. During the last i years Easter Day has coincided with St. Mai Day on only seven occasions, viz. in the ye 1014, 1109, 1204, 1451, 1546, 1641, 1736. Dur the same period it has fallen eight times March 22, viz. in the years 1041, 1136, 1383, 14 1573, 1668, 1761, 1818. It will not again fall this day during the present century.
    JOHNSON BAILY
Pallion Vicarage.

In stating that Easter Day coincided with festival of St. Mark in 1666 and 1734, I thinl would be right to add that this was according *New Style*; for, according to the old calendars, i coincidence took place in 1641 and 1736. If prophecy is to be looked for in accordance w Old Style, I think the years now predicted for end of the world, 1886 and 1943, may be decla quite safe, as in them Easter Day and St. Mai Day will not be identical.   EDWARD SOLLY

" HOT COCQUAILLE " OR " COCQUALE " (5th ix. 87, 151.)—In Canada and the Northern St: a cake is eaten hot which I thought very n Strips of sweetened dough are twisted and foli so that the ends come together ; they are then dropped into boiling lard or other fat, and when brown are taken out and served at once. They are called "cookies."   BOILEAU.

FIRE-SHIPS (5th S. ix. 149, 217.)—From my early school training in Holland, I recollect they were used by the Dutch at the siege and reduction of Damietta, I believe in 1218, and since then they have formed an important part of the equipment of every Dutch fleet or squadron. The fire-ships, or "branders," did important service in the war of independence against Spain, the conquest of the Portuguese settlements in the East, and the wars with France and England, not forgetting the destruction of the British fleet at Chatham in 1666.   T. A. ROCHUSSEN.

"KEX" (5th S. viii. 169, 454 ; ix. 113.)—Kex or kexes are, at least in Derbyshire, the dry stalks of all hollow-growing plants. A kex is, in fact, the common name for a dry stalk. As a boy I remember that we called the dry, upright stalks of hemlock, bracken, nettle, dock, &c., but especially nettle, kexes. A favourite amusement with us was "kex.shooting." We made bows, and then betook ourselves to a nettle bed where the kexes stood strong and dry, a good yard high, and, cutting them close by the ground, trimmed them and shot them away from the bow against the wind at an angle which carried them so high that often they went out of sight.

Sixty or seventy years ago my grandfather, who was the first schoolmaster in Belper, used to make his lead pencils out of dry kex and molten lead. The kexes were cut just below the "joints," stuck deep into a pot of sand, and the lead poured carefully in. In this respect at least my grandfather was not the schoolmaster "abroad."

THOMAS RATCLIFFE.

Worksop.

The word kex is universally applied by the common people in the West Riding of Yorkshire to the Chærophyllum tenulentem, one of the most troublesome of the Umbelliferæ, and the word is pronounced invariably kex, and not kence. The real hemlock, Conium maculatum, is by no means common. Any of the umbelliferous tribe which is not a kex is summarily called a humlock (so pronounced).   H. E. WILKINSON.

Anerley.

I perfectly remember an old lady, who died in 1843, in her eighty-fourth year, telling me that in her youth children in Guernsey used to make toy candles by filling the hollow stalk of the kex with grease. Does not this explain what is meant by kex candles? Mr. George Metivier, in his Dictionnaire Franco-Normand, ou Recueil des Mots particuliers au Dialecte de Guernesey (Williams & Norgate, 1870), says :—

"Caisses ou quesses, s.f.pl. Branc-ursine, ou acanthe d'Allemagne. Lat. Heracleum spondylium. Son nom guernesiais vient de la même source que l'angl. kash, kex, plante à tige tubuleuse, canon de sureau, la ciguë. Ainsi le gaél. cas, au génitif cais, pied, jambe, tige, représente le lat. tibia, flûte, jambe. On séchait autrefois les tiges creuses de notre branc-ursine pour faire des alumettes de ses éclats."

Lucifers have banished all other matches. Paraffine lamps have driven out the old crasset or cresset, and bid fair to render tallow dips as much things of the past as kex candles.

EDGAR MACCULLOCH.

Guernsey.

"CAT-IN-THE-PAN" (1st S. xii. 268, 374, 415 ; 3rd S. iii. 144, 191 ; iv. 17 ; 5th S. viii. 148, 454.) —One form of the proverb was Cat in the band. But cate is not a cake, pace Addison. There is no such word. Manchet and chetebred occur in 1577. Cates is the recognized form ; it means provisions (Bullinger, i. 424), and is the corruption of "household achates" (Parker, xii.). Shakspeare thus uses the word—Taming of Shrew, ii. 1 ; 1 Hen. IV., iii. 1 ; 1 Hen. VI., ii. 3 ; Comedy of Errors, iii. 1 ; Pericles, ii. 3. Bullinger says in the passage already quoted : "Neither glut thyself with present delicates nor long after deintrels. Let thy diet be of cates good cheap." Niceties was a later meaning, when what was bought seemed preferable to home fare. There can be no mistake. Littleton gives "To turn cat in pan, transfugere, prævaricari," to be a turncoat.

MACKENZIE E. C. WALCOTT.

ST. GEORGE (5th S. viii. 447 ; ix. 189, 209, 349.) —The following is from the Army and Navy Gazette of April 27 last :—

"5TH FUSILIERS.—The 2nd Bat. was en fête at Chatham on Tuesday, St. George's Day. Early in the morning every man, woman, and child was supplied with a rosette of white and red roses, specially procured from France. Athletic sports were provided for the men, valuable money prizes being offered. A tug of war, open to the whole of the corps in garrison, created interest. In all previous contests the Marines have proved the victors, but this time they lost their laurels, which were won by the Fusiliers."

QUO FATA VOCANT.

In the Percy Reliques may be found the ballads of The Birth of St. George and St. George and the Dragon, pieces which did not come from the old folio which so long slumbered in the archives of Ecton Hall. Prefixed to the former of them is a learned preface. In the same work is to be found, in addition, the ballad of St. George for England, the first and also the second part. The badge of St. George, "Argent, a cross gules," was the banner of England, and worn on the breast of her soldiers, certainly as late as the fourteenth century ; but the date of its original adoption would be a far more difficult point to ascertain. How finely has Sir Walter Scott described it in

is supposed to be 1513! When the sun was setting on Norham's castled steep, and Tweed's fair river broad and deep, and Cheviot's mountains lone, he goes on to say :—

"St. George's banner, broad and gay,
Now faded, as the fading ray
Less bright and less was flung;
The evening gale had scarce the power
To wave it on the donjon tower,
So heavily it hung."
Canto i. stanza 2.

Another illustrative poetical passage is from *The Faerie Queen* by Edmund Spenser :—

"And on his brest a bloodie Cross he bore,
The deare remembrance of his dying Lord,
Upon his shield the like was also scored."
L. i. 2.

JOHN PICKFORD, M.A.
Newbourne Rectory, Woodbridge.

JOHN GILPIN (5th S. ix. 266, 394.)—I would put it on record, before the feet of the passers by have obliterated the inscription, that in the church-yard of St. Margaret's, Westminster, between that church and the Abbey, lies a large slab, on which is engraven MR. JOHN GILPIN. Of course Cowper's hero ought to lie in the city of London, but here his name is to be seen.

W. J. BERNHARD SMITH.
Temple.

THE LORD OF BURGHLEY* (5th S. ix. 168, 393.) —At vol. ii. p. 93 of Mr. Walter White's *Eastern England, from the Thames to the Humber*, is an extract from the parish register of Great Bolas, setting forth the marriage of John Jones and Sarah Hoggins.

H. Y. N.

THOMAS, SECOND BARON LEIGH (4th S. v. 316.) —I should feel extremely obliged if the gentleman who wrote on the above subject, and signed him-self R. L., would communicate with me.

J. HENRY WHITEHEAD.
24, Clarendon Street, Cambridge.

BELL INSCRIPTION AT YARNSCOMBE (5th S. ix. 388.)—Thanks to MR. BOULGER for calling atten-tion to the mysteriously inscribed (4th and tenor) bell at Yarnscombe, Devon.

When I was *campaning* in 1864 and 1865 for all the bells in the county, I went twice to Yarns-combe, wishing to make out the inscription alluded to. I have referred to my notes and rubbings and casts now before me. I find that your correspondent has omitted to notice what are of the greatest in-terest to bell-hunters—the founder's stamps. First there is a crown (Fig. 36 in my *Devon Bells*), then a ship (Fig. 31 in the same book), then the letter "S" with a crown over it, then the crown as before is repeated, and then in unusually small mediæval

* As the title should be spelt.

correspondent—what they mean I cannot unravel—next the crown as at the beginning, then another crowned letter, then a puzzling stamp. I have no note of any coat of arms, certainly nothing "in gules," and no date. I don't think I could have omitted a date, visiting the same bell twice. Judging from the stamps, the bell is certainly older than 1500.

There is a similar bell at Sheepwash, in the same locality, with the *ship* stamp and two different crowns, and also a mysterious initial inscription in large mediæval letters. These two bells are the most unintelligible I found in the county ; they are from the same foundry, and are very uncouth, high-shouldered, clumsy castings. That at Sheep-wash is cracked, and therefore cannot be "the finest" in North Devon.

They are the only two bells in the county with the *ship* stamp, such as is often met with in Somerset and Glouc.

H. T. ELLACOMBE.

VENOUR FAMILY (5th S. ix. 327.)—The pedigree of Venour contained in Mr. Berry's compilation of Berkshire pedigrees is headed Venour *alias* Hunter. The instance of a family using two names, or rather the same name in two languages, is curious because modern, and I mention it here to warn MR. HENRY W. VINER in his inquiries.

TREGEAGLE.

MR. VINER may like to make a note of Robert le Venour, sheriff of the county of Lincoln, 1294-7, if he has not already done so. This personage (Pipe Rolls, 1299) agreed to convey 1,400l. of the new customs of the king from Boston to West-minster for 10l., a further sum of 1,750l. for 8l., and to convey and conduct 3,888l. of the same customs to London, by three modes or ways, for twelve marks, all under the king's writ. His name and arms are thus recorded in the Roll of Edward II., edited by Nicolas : "Sire Robert le Venour, de argent, crusule de goules, a un lion rampand de goules, la couwe forchie."

W. E. B.

ILLUSTRATED VISITING CARDS (5th S. ix. 306.) —Canova's card represented a block of marble, rough hewn from the quarry, drawn in perspective, and inscribed in large Roman capitals, A. CANOVA. Miss Berry and her sister used one whereon were portrayed two nymphs, in classical drapery, pointing to a weed-grown slab, on which is engraved MISS BERRYS. It looks like a tombstone. One of the nymphs leads a lamb by a ribbon, to typify Miss Agnes Berry. I possess a specimen of each of these cards.

W. J. BERNHARD SMITH.
Temple.

ST. VALENTINE (5th S. ix. 289.)—In the Nor-man-French dictionaries of Duménil and Dubois, *Valentin, Valantin*, are given as the forms used for *Galantin*="futur époux." *Valantin* is generally explained as signifying "petit galant," *v* for *g*. From a confusion of names Bishop Valentine has been long considered both in England and France the patron saint of lovers.

A. L. MAYHEW.

Oxford.

BYRON'S "PRISONER OF CHILLON" (5th S. ix. 268.)—Byron does not imply that the whole of Bonnivard's dungeon was under or below the level of the lake (see stanzas ii. and vi.):—

"Through the crevice and the cleft."

" I have felt the winter's spray
Wash through the bars when winds were high."

Other passages are to the same effect. The fact is, the floor of the dungeon is about four feet below the surface of the lake at an average, but the water rises and falls according as the season affects the snow range. I visited Chillon a few years past, and was struck with Byron's correct description of it; but I have failed to find any account of the "murder or drowning well." There is a passage out of the dungeon, through which the guide conducted me, by descending two steps, to the brink of a well, which he said was in fact joined to the lake, adding an account of its terrible use. Thus said he: "When they wanted to make away with any prisoner, the governor would pretend to make friends with him, offering for a bribe the means of escape. In due time he was conducted to the well-passage, and was confidentially told that by following it he would find an open door in the Villeneuve road. Of course the victim was drowned." Has this legend been fixed in print anywhere?

SEPTIMUS PIESSE.

Chiswick.

The dungeon at Chillon is below the surface of the lake, if I may trust my own sensations not otherwise verified. Standing in it, and looking out on

" The little isle
Which in his very face did smile,"

you seem to be about as far below the water level as if you were standing in the hold of a laden barge of light draught. So recollection reports to me; but on my last visit I did not go into the dungeon.

A. J. M.

ANNIS-WATER ROBBIN (5th S. ix. 287.)—This personage is, I take it, identical with Annel-seed Robin, whose epitaph is to be found amongst Charles Cotton's poems. He appears to have possessed the peculiarities attributed to the Chevalier d'Eon.   W. J. BERNHARD SMITH.

"THE CHRISTIAN YEAR": THE ALTERED LINE (5th S. ix. 380, 400.)—

" (Not) As in the hands, th' eternal Priest."

In your "Notices to Correspondents" (ante, p. 380) you say :—" Keble altered the phrase . . .

in the edition of the *Christian Year* that was printed off before, but not issued till just after, his death." This is inaccurate. The last edition of the *Christian Year* printed in Mr. Keble's lifetime exhibited the line "Not in the hands," &c., as it had stood from the beginning.   OXONIENSIS.

[The difference between ourselves and OXONIENSIS seems to us chiefly verbal. Literally the edition of the *Christian Year* to which he refers was the "last printed in Mr. Keble's lifetime" which the author lived to see published. But the edition to which we referred was correctly described by us in the words to which OXONIENSIS takes exception. We have since consulted the edition of 1876, bearing the imprimatur of Messrs. Parker, and in a note on the disputed verse, signed by the authoritative initials "T. K.," under the date of St. Mark's Day, 1866, we find the following account of the nature and reason of the alteration, which we submit, amply bears out our statement :—" It was the anxious wish of the Author, repeatedly expressed, that these words should be understood with the modification implied, as in other passages of Holy Scripture, so, very emphatically, in Jer. vii. 22: 'I spake *not* unto your fathers,' &c.......The Author understood the words himself, and wished them to be understood to mean, that to have Christ 'in the hands, not in the heart' is, not to be a 'partaker of Christ.'......Fearing, however, that he was misleading others, a few weeks before his departure he determined that the verse should stand as it now appears." We think it well to add the following passages from letters on the subject by the Dean of Chichester and Canon Liddon.

In the *Times* of the 14th inst. Dean Burgon wrote:—" It was Dr. Liddon, not Mr. Keble, who wrote the line in the *Christian Year* which has reasonably created so much offence, and led to the excision from the volume of one of its most faithful poems. I cannot think that this grave offence belongs to the department of 'forgotten controversy.'" And in the *Times* of the following day, May 15, Canon Liddon replied:—" You will allow me to say that the dean is, unintentionally, I am sure, but seriously inaccurate in his account of my supposed share in the alteration of a well-known line in the *Christian Year*."]

AUTHORS OF QUOTATIONS WANTED (5th S. ix. 389.)—

" Hark, from the tomb a doleful sound," &c.
See Dr. Watts's *Hymns*, book ii. hymn 63.   W. K.

Miscellaneous.

NOTES ON BOOKS, &c.

History of the Life and Reign of Richard the Third. To which is added the Story of Perkin Warbeck. By James Gairdner. (Longmans & Co.)

THE value of this book lies chiefly in the fact that it is the work of a ripe scholar. Mr. Gairdner does not follow the lead of Walpole in his manner of discussing the deeds which are inseparably connected with the career of the last of the Plantagenets. He prefers to tell his tale in his own way; and in the course of the narrative he shows his opinions to be that Richard took his share along with his own party in the murders of Edward, Prince of Wales, and Henry VI.; that he was not guilty of Clarence's death; that the executions of Rivers and Hastings were unjustifiable, and that Richard was guilty of the princi-

But with all this Richard III. is not represented to us as the hated tyrant of dramatic tradition: he was certainly a wise statesman and not a bad king. We think that Mr. Gairdner's views are urged very powerfully, for he adds original research to forcible argument. In the case of the execution of the Rivers party, however, he relies principally upon Sir Thomas More's history, which, on this point, is certainly ably opposed by Walpole. Surely the account of Richard presenting his withered arm before the Council is inconsistent with Mr. Gairdner's own views as to the king's personal appearance. Occasionally, too, it appears to us that while the evidence seems to point in favour of Richard, the text of the author speaks against him. Thus the reign of terror mentioned on p. 99 comes upon us very suddenly; and, though the evidence quoted on p. 147 certainly bears out the conclusion that Richard was highly popular "with the common people generally," two pages further on the author, without apparent evidence, asserts that Buckingham was instigated to rebellion by "the general hatred of the king." We notice that Mr. Gairdner quotes the *Historical Manuscripts Commission Reports* once; we would point out that Lord Bagot's "grant of part of the earldom of Hereford to Buckingham" (iv. 328), the account of the king's coronation by an eye-witness belonging to the Duke of Northumberland (iii. 114), the Shrewsbury correspondence of Sir Gilbert Talbot (i. 50), and other documents, might have been consulted with advantage.

The Complete Poetical Works of Percy Bysshe Shelley. The Text carefully Revised, with Notes and a Memoir, by William Michael Rossetti. 3 vols. (E. Moxon, Son & Co.)

MR. ROSSETTI is indefatigable in his labours on the poetry and life of Shelley. In 1870 he published the first critical edition of Shelley's poetry, and the first systematic attempt to examine the whole accessible evidence concerning the poet's life from the cradle to the grave. That edition has been very hotly criticized on account of the liberties taken with the text; and, in the time that has passed since its issue, Mr. Rossetti has seen reason to modify some of his views. Very many changes made in the edition of 1870 are recanted in that now before us, wherein, however, the right is still claimed to rectify "absolutely wrong grammar,... rhyming,...and metre," as well as to "systematize" the punctuation. There will always be a class of readers allowing, and a class disallowing, this editorial claim. For our own part, we cannot think it an editor's duty to bind a poet's text down by laws that did not bind the poet himself; and grammar of all things could never wring from Shelley an unmusical line when the creative impulse sent his spirit flaming across the ethereal heights of imagination and thought. Thus to cite at once what is perhaps the most remarkable instance of honest adherence to a principle, we cannot imagine that Mr. Rossetti's fine critical ear felt no shock when he contemplated the ruined loveliness of the lines in *Epipsychidion*,

"Thou too, O Comet beautiful and fierce,
Who drew the heart of this frail Universe..."
altered under the inexorable laws of grammar to
"Thou too, O Comet, beautiful and fierce,
Who drew'st the heart of this frail universe..."
The less can we imagine the editor as free from the pain inflicted on some of his readers when we turn to an identical case in the poem *To a Skylark*, and find that Mr. Rossetti deems "the sound of the lovely line,"

"Thou lovest; but ne'er knew love's sad satiety..."
"would be so spoiled by changing the word into

sible." The case cited from *Epipsychidion* is an instance of form marred for the sake of rigorou rence to rule; but, in a minor degree, sound frequently sacrificed for strictness, in cases wh poet had sacrificed strictness for sound; and whole, careful as Mr. Rossetti's textual work abounding with fine points of perception and pretation, moderate as are the changes compare those of 1870, we should prefer a text based on t babilities of what Shelley did, to a text based probabilities of what he might have done had he person of rigidly exact habits of mind. But whe fixing the text, in annotating it, or in examining t Mr. Rossetti has been most laudably watchful f data. Those who compare the Life and Notes edition with those in that of 1870 will find evide untiring and enthusiastic prosecution of what is a labour of love—the labour of throwing light on t and his works; and the present edition, as a col of data, is still more valuable to all Shelley st than its predecessor of 1870.

MR. EDWARD PEACOCK (Bottesford Manor, writes:—"I shall be very much obliged to any on will lend me for a short time 'A Perfect List of a Persons as by Commission under the Great Seal o land are now Confirmed to be Custos Rotuloru Justices of Peace in the several Counties......withi land and Wales. London, printed by Thomas ......1660,' 12mo."

LONDON, SATURDAY, JUNE 1, 1878.

CONTENTS.—N° 231.

Notes.

LETTERS OF GENERAL WASHINGTON.

Agreeably to the editorial note (ante, p. 375) at the foot of my previous communication on this subject, I now send transcripts of the four letters of General Washington, copies of which were lately presented to General Grant, the originals being now preserved in the museum at Leicester.

No. I.

Mount Vernon, Jany 10th, 1786.

Madam,—I wish my expression would do justice to my feelings, that I might convey to you adequate ideas of my gratitude for those favourable sentiments with which the letter you did me the honour to write to me from New York is replete. The plaudits of a lady, so celebrated as Mrs Macauly Graham, could not fail of making a deep impression on my sensibility; and my pride was more than a little flattered by your approbation of my conduct through an arduous and painful contest.

During the time in which we supposed you to have been on your journey to New York, we participated the distresses which we were sure you must have experienced on acc^t of the intemperate of the air, which exceeded the heats common in this Country at the most inclemnet season; and though your letter was expressive of the great fatigue you had undergone, still we rejoiced that the journey was attended with no worse consequences.

I hope, and most sincerely wish, that this letter may find you happily restored to your friends in England, whose anxiety for your return must, I am persuaded, have been great, and that you will have experienced no inconvenience from your voyage to America.

Mrs Washington, who has a grateful sense of your favourable mention of her, and Fanny Bassett and

Major Washington, who since we had the honor of your company have joined their hands and fortunes, unite with me in respectful compliments to you, and in every good wish that can render you and Mr Graham happy. The little folks enjoy perfect health. The boy, whom you would readily have perceived was the pet of the family, affords promising hopes from maturer age. With sentiments of great respect and esteem, I have the honor to be, Madam,

Y^r most Obed. & very H^ble S.
G°. WASHINGTON.

Mrs Macauly Graham.

No. II.

Mount Vernon, Novr 16th, 1787.

Madam,—Your favor of the 10th of Oct^r, 1786, came duly to hand, and should have had a much earlier acknowledgment, had not the business of the public (in which I have been, in a manner, compelled to engage again) engrossed the whole of my time for several months past; and my own private concerns required my unremitted attention since my return home.

I do not know to what cause I shall impute your not receiving my letter of the 10th of Jan^y, 1786, till the last of June; it went by the common rout, subject to the common incidents.

Mr Pine's Historical painting does not appear to go on very rapidly. He informed me, when I was in Philadelphia, that he had been collecting materials to enable him to proceed with it, but that it must be a work of time to accomplish it. You will undoubtedly, before you receive this, have an opportunity of seeing the plan of Government proposed by the Federal Convention for the United States. You will very readily conceive, Madam, the difficulties which the Convention had to struggle against. The various and opposite interests which were to be conciliated. The local prejudices which were to be subdued. The diversity of opinions and sentiments which were to be reconciled—and in fine, the sacrifices (sic) wch were necessary to be made on all sides, for the general welfare, combined to make it a work of so intricate and difficult a nature, that I think it is much to be wondered at, that any thing could have been produced with such unanimity as the Constitution proposed.

It is now submitted to the consideration of the people and waits their decision. The legislatures of the several states have been convened since the Constitution was offered have readily agreed to the calling a Convention in their respective States—some by an unanimous vote, and others by a large majority; but whether it will be adopted by the People or not remains yet to be determined. Mrs Washington and the rest of the family join me in compliments and best wishes for you and Mr Graham. I have the honor to be, Madam,

Y^r most Obed. & very H^ble Servant,
G°. WASHINGTON.

Mrs Macauly Graham.

No. III.

New York, Jany 9th, 1790.

Madam,—Your obliging letter, dated in October last, has been received; and, as I do not know when I shall have more leisure than at present to throw together a few observations in return for yours, I take up my Pen to do it by this early occasion.

In the first place I thank you for your congratulatory sentiments on the event which has placed me at the head of the American Government; as well as for the indulgent partiality, which it is to be feared, however, may have warped your judgment too much in my favor. But you do me no more than justice in supposing that, if I had been permitted to indulge my first and fondest wish, I should have remained in a private Station. Although neither the present age or Posterity may possibly give me full credit for the feelings which I have experienced on the subject; yet I have a consciousness, that nothing short of an absolute conviction of duty could ever have brought me upon the scenes of public life again. The establishment of our new Government seemed to be the last great experiment for promoting human happiness by reasonable compact in civil Society. It was to be, in the first instance, in a considerable degree a government of accommodation as well as a government of Laws. Much was to be done by *prudence*, much by *conciliation*, much by *firmness*. Few who are not philosophical spectators can realize the difficult and delicate part which a man in my situation had to act. All see, and most admire, the glare which hovers round the external trappings of elevated office. To me there is nothing in it, beyond the lustre which may be reflected from its connection with a power of promoting human felicity. In our progress towards political happiness my station is new ; and, if I may use the expression, I walk on untrodden ground. There is scarcely any action whose motives may not be subject to a double interpretation. There is scarcely any part of my conduct wch may not hereafter be drawn into precedent. Under such a view of the duties inherent to my arduous office, I could not but feel a diffidence in myself on the one hand ; and an anxiety for the Community that every new arrangement should be made in the best possible manner on the other. If after all my humble but faithful endeavours to advance the felicity of my Country and mankind, I may indulge a hope that my labours have not been altogether without success, it will be the only real compensation I can receive in the closing scenes of life.

On the actual situation of this Country under its new Government I will, in the next place, make a few remarks. That the Government, though not absolutely perfect, is one of the best in the world, I have little doubt. I always believed that an unequivocally free and equal Representation of the People in the Legislature, together with an efficient and responsable (*sic*) Executive, were the great Pillars on which the preservation of American Freedom must depend. It was indeed next to a Miracle that there should have been so much unanimity, in points of such importance, among such a number of Citizens, so widely scattered, and so different in their habits in many respects as the Americans were. Nor are the growing unanimity and encreasing goodwill of the Citizens to the Government less remarkable than favorable circumstances. So far as we have gone with the new Government (and it is completely organized and in operation) we have had greater reason than the most sanguine could expect to be satisfied with its success.

Perhaps a number of accidental circumstances have concurred with the real effects of the Government to make the People uncommonly well pleased with their situation and prospects. The harvests of wheat have been remarkably good—the demand for that article from abroad is great—the encrease of Commerce is visible in every Port—and the number of new manufactures introduced in one year is astonishing. I have lately made a tour through the Eastern States. I found the country, in a great degree, recovered from the ravages of War, the Towns flourishing, and the People delighted with a good. The same facts I have also reason to believe, from good authority, exist in the Southern States. By what I have just observed, I think you will be persuaded that the ill-boding Politicians who prognosticated that America would never enjoy any fruits from her Inde-

pendence, and that she would be obliged to a foreign Power for protection, have mistaken.

I shall sincerely rejoice to see that Revolution has been productive of happ on both sides of the Atlantic. The rer French Constitution is indeed one of the . events in the history of mankind ; and th Marquis de la Fayette in a high degree h character. My greatest fear has been, would not be sufficiently cool and mode arrangements for the security of that li it seems to be fully possessed.

Mr Narville, the French Gentleman yo been in America and at Mount Vernon ; b sometime since to France.

Mrs Washington is well and desires h may be presented to you. We wish th your fireside, as we also long to enjoy tha and I think that our plans of living will : reasonable by the considerate part of our wishes coincide with my own as to sim[and everything which can tend to suppo character without partaking of the follie ostentation. I am, with great regard, M[Your most Obedient and most Humble :

G^o. \

Mrs Cath^e Macaulay* Graham.

No. IV.

Philadelphia, Fel

Madam,—At the same time that I ac receipt of your letter of June last, with been honored, I must beg you to accept r for your treatise on Education which acco

The anxiety which you express for the country demands a proper acknowledgn political sentiments which are contained merit a more particular reply than the m important business in which I am cons (especially while Congress are in Session) to make. I must therefore, Madam, r goodness to receive this short letter a ledgment of your polite attention, and I assured that my not entering at this time : the subject of your favor does not procee of that consideration with which I have tl Madam,

Your most Obed. H^{ble} S

G^o. V

Mrs C. Macauly Graham.

The foregoing letters were presentec museum many years ago, whilst it perty of the Leicester Literary and] Society. It is believed that they h viously been printed.

WILLIAM KELLY,

Leicester.

_____

ISTAMBOUL AND ISLAMBOUL : . FORMATION OR MODIFICATION

A short time ago Mr. Catafago, th(teacher of Arabic and author of an A1 and English-Arabic dictionary, sent : a little book entitled (in English) 7

_____

* The lady's family name was in this rectly written.

NOTES AND QUERIES.

graphy of the Constantinopolitan Story-Teller, and edited by himself (Quaritch, 1877). On looking at the Arabic title I noticed that the equivalent of Constantinopolitan was اسلا مبولي (Islāmboolee) instead of استانبولي (Istānboolee),* the usual form. It immediately occurred to me that the form *Islāmbool*, in which only two letters are changed, had been adopted for the sake of making the word mean "the city of Islam." I did not, however, like to write a note upon the subject without first obtaining the opinion of an Arabic scholar, and I therefore wrote to Mr. Catafago about it; and it was so. He very obligingly wrote me a long letter in reply, of which I will give a very condensed summary. It appears that my conjecture was perfectly correct, and that the change was made for the reason I assigned. But it must not be supposed that the modified form was invented by the author of the book I have named, or that it has been or is in frequent use. It is to be found on all the gold and silver Turkish coins struck at Constantinople during the reign of Selim III. and some of his predecessors; and it seems, as far as I understand Mr. Catafago, that it is also sometimes used in Turkish official documents, whilst any good Mahometan who wishes to show his zeal for Islamism is at liberty to use it.

Nor is this the only word which, according to Mr. Catafago, has been, or is, so modified. Scriptural names, such as Moses, Aaron, and Joseph, are frequently modified in a similar manner when they belong to Israelites or Christians. Thus they write حرون instead of هرون, *Haroon*=Aaron; موسي instead of موسي, *Moosa*=Moses; يوصف instead of يوسف, *Yoosoof*=Joseph,† changing, as

---

* The Turks and Arabs call Constantinople *Istanboul*, with an *n*, and not *Istamboul*, with an *m*, as is commonly written in English. I know that the usual derivation is εἰς τήν (or εἰς τάν) πόλιν ("into the city"), but I should like to know upon what authority this derivation rests. These words *in Greek* cannot surely have been the war cry of the *Turks*. It seems to me much more natural to suppose that *Istanbool* is a contraction of (*Con)stan(tino)ple*, the three syllables included in parentheses having disappeared, one from the beginning and two from the middle. Comp. *Brighton*, contracted from *Bright(helms)ton(e)*. The *I* would naturally be added on in Arabic, as no Arabic word commences with a double consonant; and so, if it is wished to Arabize a foreign name which does so begin, it is necessary to add an *alif* with a vowel (cf. the old French *escrire*, from *scrivere*), so as to divide the double consonant between two syllables. See my note 4ᵗʰ S. xii. 456.

† For the sake of making this intelligible to those who cannot read the Arabic letters, I will observe that in Arabic there are two *h*'s and two *s*'s, which differ much more in form than in pronunciation, so that by substituting one of them for the other the three names given above can be changed in appearance without any great change in pronunciation. Mr. Catafago says, "If you ask them why they write in such a way, they

will be observed by those who can read the Arabic alphabet, one letter in each word.‡ I have already written several little notes in "N. & Q." on the arbitrary formation or modification of words, and I suspect that a few similar cases would be found in nearly every language. My notes will be found in 4ᵗʰ S. vii. 533; xi. 461; 5ᵗʰ S. ii. 216; iii. 177. F. Chance.
Sydenham Hill.

THE PURY FAMILY.
(*Concluded from p. 305.*)

Thomas Pury the younger, son of Alderman Pury before mentioned, was born July 16, 1619. In *The Mystery of the Good Old Cause* it is said that in the first year of the Parliament (1640-1) "he was servant to Mr. Townshend, an attorney of Staples Inn"; but if this implies that he served in a menial or inferior capacity, it is an invidious statement. He may have been intended for his father's profession, and have spent some time in the office of his father's agent, or some other London solicitor, as is still customary; and I have met with a statement (which I have failed to verify) that in 1642 he was keeping terms for the Bar. When the siege commenced, and Gloucester was garrisoned for the Parliament, there were two regiments there—one of them under the command of the Earl of Stamford, with Massey as Lieut.-Colonel and Governor of the City; the other under Colonel Henry Stephens, which apparently consisted of volunteers, for the captains were all citizens, the Purys father and son, being amongst them. Young Pury, as well as his father, signed the reply of the garrison and city to the king's summons, and proved himself, during the siege, a very active officer. He was engaged in the first act of hostility against the king's army before Gloucester. Dorney says :—

"On Sunday, August 6, before the king's arrival in person, upon General Garret's facing the city with a brigade of horse on Tredworth field, a small party of horse and foote commanded by Captain Blunt, and assisted by Lieutenant-Colonel Matthews, Captain White, Captain Pury the younger, and Captain Lieutenant Harcus, issued forth of the Northgate, and at Wooton took about ten prisoners."—*Exact Relation.*

"The next day young Pury with Captain Evans and Lieut. Pierce skirmished with the enemy at Brockthroppe, killed one, hurt or killed others, and took one prisoner and seven horses."—*Id.*

And again :—

"Aug. 25. This night (it being suspected that false rumours of our being taken might be spread abroad to

---

answer, 'We cannot grant the names of prophets to the unfaithful.'"

‡ I have given only one modified form of each name for the sake of simplicity, but many other modifications are used. Thus يوسف is also written يوصيف, يوزيف, يوزيف, موسف, &c., in the last of which an *h* is actually substituted for the *y*.

be set up on the Colledge-Tower (College is the local name of the cathedral) to give notice abroad 'of our holding out: the performance whereof was committed to the care of Captain Pury, Junior, who performed it accordingly. The enemy vexed thereat levelled some shot at the Tower, one whereof came close by the said Captain Pury,. as he was looking towards Lanthony, whence their fiery bullets came, who for all that continued the burning of his linkes till the moone was fully risen."

Mr. Brett, who had been returned with Alderman Pury to the Long Parliament, having attended the Parliament summoned by the king at Oxford in 1644, was expelled the House, and it is said that the younger Pury was elected in his place ; but this is doubtful, though he was certainly returned for the city with General Desborough in 1656. His father had become possessed of the manors of Minsterworth and Taynton, between Gloucester and the Forest of Dean, and the parish church of Taynton having been destroyed during the troubles, an order of Parliament was obtained for rebuilding it, and it was rebuilt, chiefly by his exertions, on a new site, and in accordance with his peculiar views in such matters, the new church being made to stand north and south, instead of in the usual manner, the communion table being placed in the centre of the building. He appears to have been a man of literary tastes, and being one of the commissioners to whom the care of the cathedral was entrusted, he exerted himself with his fellow commissioners in founding the cathedral library, which was done at considerable expense in 1648, he and Sir Matthew Hale being amongst the principal contributors. Evelyn, who saw it in 1654, calls it "a noble tho' a private designe" (*Memoirs*, i. 282). In 1656 it was settled on the mayor and burgesses, who, Puritans as they were, took more care of it than their successors, the clergy, appear to have done after the Restoration, for there are now very few books there, and all of importance have disappeared. Neither of the Purys was molested after the Restoration, though Charles did not forget the part which the citizens of Gloucester had taken in the civil war ; for although they seem to have veered with the times, and professed great joy at the Restoration, and proclaimed him with great pomp, and subsequently set up his statue in the Southgate Street, he ordered the walls which had excluded his father to be razed, gave their outer gates to the "faithful city" of Worcester, and took away their charter that he might grant a new one by which he constituted better affected persons members of the corporation. After his father's death Pury retired to Taynton, and lived in comparative retirement for many years, "loved and respected for his piety, learning, great abilities and extensive charity." Mr. John Washbourn, editor of the *Bibliotheca Gloucestrensis*, Lond. (1825), states that he had in his

possession an interleaved almanac, longed to the younger Pury, and some memoranda in his handwritir some of the above information. P. married Barbara, daughter of Jan of Walford Court, in Herefordshire "The Man of Ross," and died A aged seventy-four.

He was buried at Taynton, an friend penned for his tombstone a scription, in which, after describing a disposition vigorous by nature highest ends, and so cultivated b studies and godly piety that he h equal in his own rank of life, he any human frailty attached to him the time rather than his own) it w to be blamed as it was to be wo one who had joined the rebels shou in piety and religion, arts and present representative of the famil the estate is Captain Stanhope Gro Gloucestershire.

Like Massey and many others Pury favoured the Restoration, missions as captain and colonel un (see Pury papers, " N. & Q.," 3rd S.

Temple.

"SUBMIT."—The Russians are u with the possession of much talen languages, but, if newspaper reports pended upon, they have just com blunder in their interpretation of th

It has been stated that the lat Russia of the proposal made by Gre the former should *submit* the whole San Stefano to the intended Congress Russia taking offence at the harmle in question. Now there certainly i attached to that word which would offensive, and that meaning is w phrase would be called "knocking no person of common sense (query, a always blessed with that commodity such a meaning to it when used ir style of diplomatic correspondence.

Without any intention of acting to Russian philologists, I may refe following different meanings of *subn* may find in any good English, Fren German dictionaries, and none of w have any insult concealed in them :-

English.—To *submit* sometimes (Johnson and Webster).

French.—*Soumettre à l'analyse*, " analysis."

Italian.—*Sottomettere*, to refer another.

German.—*Ueberlassen*, to commit to the care of. If, also, we regard the derivation from the original Latin *submitto*, the literal meaning is to "place under"; and it is difficult to conceive how Russia could find ground of offence in being asked to "bring the whole treaty under the notice of the Conference."

I may add that in the craft to which I belong (the law) the term "*submitting* a case to counsel for his opinion" is quite a common phrase, signifying little more than presenting, without expressing any intention of being bound by the opinion.
M. H. R.

GARLANDS IN CHURCHES.—At Grinton, Yorkshire, a garland used to be hung up, for which the young men of the place used to run a race yearly up a steep hill. It was given in the last century by a young woman of Askrigg. The competitors were regaled at a garland feast.

"SING OLD ROSE AND BURN THE BELLOWS." —This seems to have been a jovial version of our famous Wykehamical song, *Dulce Domum*,

"Musa libros mitte fessa,"

as though "et burn libellos." Walton makes one of his characters say, "Let's sing 'Old Rose.'" The *British Apollo* has a silly explanation of the latter, attributing it to a drunken dance at Nottingham round an alewife in the reign of King Stephen. It appears thus (1708-9) in the *Flowers of Harmony*:—

"Now we are met like jolly fellows,
 Let us do as wise men tell us,
 Sing Old Rose, and burn the bellows,
 Let us do as wise men tell us.

When the jowl with claret glows,
 And wisdom shines upon the nose,
 O then 's the time to sing Old Rose,
 And burn, burn the bellows."
MACKENZIE E. C. WALCOTT.

THE ASLOAN MANUSCRIPT, 1512-1520.—This extraordinary and valuable historical manuscript, commonly known under the name of the "Auchinleck Chronicle," was considered to be one of the gems in the library of the Boswells of Auchinleck. It appears to have been missing since the year 1845. But from a communication "Respecting some of the Early Historical Writers of Scotland" made to the Society of Scotish Antiquaries by David Laing, Esq. (since printed in the *Proceedings* of the society, vol. xii. part i.), and also from the "Minutes of the Evidence" submitted to the House of Lords in the Annandale Peerage Case, July, 1876 (since printed), it is shown that the said manuscript has at length—after a lapse of thirty years—been discovered, and said to have been sold in the year 1867 to an Edinburgh bookseller by a person who is understood to have been in no manner of way related to the Boswell family.

From the very remarkable, instructive, and important evidence which has now been printed, it must be apparent that the manuscript was originally the undoubted property of the Boswell family. Moreover, no mention is made that such had ever been presented away or sold to any one by the family. In such circumstances I humbly conceive that there is here a duty to be performed by the trustees and also the heirs of the late Sir James Boswell, so that immediate measures may be adopted by them for its recovery and restoration to the shelves of the fine and curious library at Auchinleck.
T. G. S.
Edinburgh.

PETRARCH AND LAURA.—The following passage may interest those who are never weary of speculating about Laura's influence on Petrarch:—

"Consortium feminæ, sine quo interdum æstimaveram non posse vivere, morte nunc gravius pertimesco: et quamquam sæpe tentationibus turbarer acerrimis, tamen, dum in animum redit quid est femina, omnis tentatio confestim avolat, et ego ad libertatem et ad pacem meam redeo."—*De Rebus Familiaribus*, Liber Decimus, Epistola v., Gerardo Fratri Suo; vol. ii. p. 100 of Fracassetti's edition.

If this passage is to be found in any biographies of Petrarch, it is at least not in the two or three I have read—not in Sade's, not in Foscolo's, not in Reeve's little book, which is founded on the Latin letters.
E. S. R.
Edinburgh.

BURNS.—Mr. F. T. Palgrave, in the preface to his selection from Herrick's poems, recently published in the Golden Treasury series, quotes eight lines "by some old unknown Northern singer":—

"When I think on the happy days
 I spent wi' you, my dearie,
 And now what lands between us lie,
 How can I be but eerie!

How slow ye move, ye heavy hours,
 As ye were wae and weary!
 It was na sae ye glinted by
 When I was wi' my dearie."

Mr. Palgrave truly says that "there is an intensity here, a note of passion beyond the deepest of Herrick's"; but it would be very remarkable if it were otherwise, seeing that the "unknown Northern singer" is no less a person than Robert Burns. I have consulted three different editions of Burns (one the Golden Treasury edition, edited by Alexander Smith), and in none of these is there a hint that the verses are not really by Burns himself. I daresay Mr. Palgrave had the lines in his mind, and forgot at the moment that they were by Burns.
JONATHAN BOUCHIER.
Bexley Heath.

"THE ACTS OF TO-DAY BECOME THE PRECEDENTS OF TO-MORROW."—These words, used by Mr. Herschell, Q.C. (in his speech in support of Lord Hartington's resolution), May 23, 1878, are

THE "TIDE OF FATE."—Some time ago I took occasion to refer to this subject (I forget the precise title I prefixed to the note), and spoke of the "epidemical" character which seemed frequently to be attached to casualties, accidents, and misfortunes, as, for example, the occurrence of three or four fires in rapid succession ; suicides, under similar circumstances, to the number of perhaps three or four ; railway and mining catastrophes, shipping disasters, and so on. Crime of all descriptions seems at times to be actuated by the same law, especially after some new device or agent has been introduced, and any special notoriety has been gained in consequence of its adoption. May I now quote an illustration from the *Pall Mall Gazette* ?—

"There are few more interesting objects for study than the peculiar virulence displayed occasionally by the ' tide of fate' towards certain persons or classes. At present it runs strongly against detectives, and it is almost impossible to glance at a newspaper without the eye falling on an account of some detective in trouble."

Four or five instances of detectives being "in trouble" within the space of two days are then recorded, and the *Pall Mall Gazette* proceeds :—

"It is worthy of note that it is not merely detectives in the metropolitan police, but detectives public, private, and provincial everywhere, who seem to be getting into scrapes or out of them."

The subject is a curious one.   KINGSTON.

FOX-DAY.—In Col. Townley's *Journal in the Isle of Man*, 1791, he notes :—

"January 25th. In my long ramble met with a farmer, whom I had ten minutes' chat with ; and observing upon the uncommon fineness and pleasantness of the day *for the month of January*, he replied, Yes ; but he feared it would be only another Fox-day ; for there was a great hoar upon the ground early in the morning, though very little frost. A *Fox-day* is a very common expression in the island ; and by it I believe they mean a single fair day, that is sure to be closely pursued by a rainy one."
    W. N. STRANGEWAYS.
Stockport.

"GOD SAVE THE MARK." — This expression, equivalent to the "Salvum sit quod tango" of Petronius, is connected with an Irish superstition. If a person in telling the story of some injury of limb or wound to another person should touch the corresponding part of his own or a bystander's body, he averts the omen of similar mischief by saying, " God bless (or save) the mark," as a sort of charm.   MACKENZIE E. C. WALCOTT.

BELLIES OF FINGERS.—The inside muscles of the phalanges of the hands are called " bellies," and in some districts it is considered a merit that they should belly when bent.   HYDE CLARKE.

THE OAK AND THE ASH.—It is [...]ing that in the middle of this extre[...] the oak was in leaf about ten day[...] before the ash ; indeed, in this part the ash can hardly be said to ha from its buds.   E. LEATON B[...]
Gainsborough.

PRICE OF PROVISIONS IN IRELAN[...] following extract from the *Dubli[...]* May 8, 1742, may prove interesting "We hear from Derry that provisio[...] there as they were ever known ; ther pounds of meal for ninepence, twenty [...] for twopence halfpenny, eighteen egg and potatoes for threepence per bushel."

PRINSEP'S "LINEN GATHERERS."-[...] of the *Standard*, May, 1878, in his Royal Academy exhibition, writes tl "Art, as long as it seeks to be popular content not to rise above the agreeable late years has been more successfully realization of agreeable sentiment, and than Mr. G. D. Leslie, the painter of Home,' No. 64 in the present exhibition. since, in the great picture of the washir down the hillside, Mr. Leslie strove man his more popular charms the element o: and if the picture failed at all, it was r design was wanting, after all, in nobil. because the design was more obviously n tural than the subject could bear. As pu treatment (for wall-painting) of a theme r but suggested by, English country life, been well ; but as the realization of a sc painted under the conditions of frankl; stead of decorative art, it was more, studiedly noble than it ought to have beer of the Academic, though its flow of line and measured, but gracious and free. In Home,' Mr. Leslie has re-entered the habitual work," &c.

The picture of "the washing girls" "every one" knows) by G. D. Leslie, Prinsep. In the catalogue for 18: "Gallery No. V., No. 411, The Lin Val. C. Prinsep." It is engraved Mr. Henry Blackburn's *Academy N* year.   CUTHB

BOOKSELLERS' CATALOGUES : (LIBRARIES.—Olive Payne, of Round (is said to have originated the practic catalogues ; the first issued by him 29, 1740.* Daniel Brown, of the "] without Temple Bar, and Mears and N followed out the same idea. Circula[...] were projected by S. Fancourt, of (Fleet Street, and there were subscr[...] new venture in 1741.
    MACKENZIE E. C.
[* See date given by MR. VERNON,

Queries.

[We must request correspondents desiring information on family matters of only private interest, to affix their names and addresses to their queries, in order that the answers may be addressed to them direct.]

KIT'S COTY HOUSE.—Can any of the readers of "N. & Q." explain whence this very ancient cromlech, near Aylesford, in Kent, has received its name? There is no record of any person of the name of Christopher or Kit in the neighbourhood who may in bygone times have owned the place; and if there were, the question would still remain, What is the meaning of "Coty"? It is recorded by the earliest Saxon historians, and the story is reproduced in Stowe's *Annales*, that the Britons delivered battle here against the Saxon invaders Hengist and Horsa, and were defeated after a severe conflict, in which Horsa was slain. The name of Vortigern, the British king whose kingdom was invaded, signifies in Gaelic the "True Lord," from *fior*, true, and *tighearn*, a lord, a chief, a ruler. The name of his brother Catigern, slain in this battle, signifies in like manner the "Lord of Battle," from *cath*, a battle, and *tighearn*; and if the name of Kit's Coty House be also traceable to the same language, it would seem to be an Anglo-Saxon corruption of *ceud* (pronounced *kid* or *kit*), first, and *coda*, a victory. The victory at Aylesford was claimed both by the Saxons and by the Britons; and if Catigern was buried at the spot where he fell, and the cromlech erected over his remains in memory of the event by the Britons, as tradition records, the fact would fully account for the Keltic name, which I have ventured to suggest as the true meaning of Kit's Coty.

CHARLES MACKAY.

HOGARTH.—Can any of your "art" readers inform me whether the satirical print which Hogarth presented to Dr. Kirby, and which was afterwards used by the latter as the frontispiece to his edition of Dr. Taylor's work on perspective, was ever reproduced by Hogarth as a painting? I have come across an old engraving of it, underneath which is written at the left-hand corner, "Hogarth pinx.," whereas in Nichols's *Works of Hogarth* the words are, "Hogarth inv. et delin." If a painting were made, where can it be seen?

G. WOLFERSTAN.

Arts Club.

ALCHEMY AND MODERN SCIENCE.—Professor Alexander Campbell Fraser, in his edition of Berkeley's *Works* (1871), says in a note to *Siris* (vol. ii. p. 417), speaking of alchemy: "The most advanced science of our day has not abandoned the idea of this scientific transubstantiation." Comparatively few persons are aware of the amount and force of historical evidence which alchemy can adduce, or of the extent to which occult researches

generally are privately prosecuted at the present day. But can any acknowledged scientific authority be cited for Prof. Fraser's rather surprising statement? It is well known to students of these subjects that the transmutation of metals was always associated (except by the mercenary charlatans who first brought it into discredit) with a philosophy that has far more sublime though analogous applications; and whenever the principles of this philosophy revive in the human mind, its physical-experimental side is sure to obtain renewed attention.

C. C. M.

A RUSSIAN MARRIAGE. — "A traditionary story widely celebrated in Europe," says Mrs. Ellet, in her interesting *Popular Legends* (Dublin, 1850, pp. 235, 236), is that of a mysterious marriage, "said to be connected with events occurring in Russia after the death of Peter the First and Catharine." A priest of Rörwig hamlet, in Iceland, was called on late at night by two strangers, who promised him a large fee if he came with them to perform the marriage ceremony: his refusal would cost him his life. He was led blindfold to the church, which was brilliantly lit up; "the stern bridegroom and pale bride present themselves, and are united; he is then led out of the church, but lingers near enough to hear a sound of disputing, the report of a pistol, and the groans of one expiring. Next morning the strange company set sail again, and the inhabitants of the village, conducted by the priest to the church, find in the vault the body of the newly murdered bride. . . . An agent of the Russian Government, coming to inquire into the matter," binds all who know of it to secrecy. "It is suspected that the deed was committed by the sanction, if not the express direction, of persons near the throne." This story is related with much ability by Henry Steffens, and translated in *Foreign Tales and Traditions* (Glasgow, 1828, vol. i. pp. 241-248). What is the foundation for it, if any, in fact? And is there any older version than that given above?

DAVID FITZGERALD.

Hammersmith.

THOMAS BALDWIN : MODELS OF BATH.—In the *Bath Journal* of April 6, 1789, was an advertisement of " Proposals for publishing by subscription various designs in Architecture" executed in Bath and elsewhere by Thomas Baldwin, architect. It was stated that the work was in "great forwardness," and the first number would be published the second week in July.. I cannot, however, find any notice, by advertisement or otherwise, of these designs in the *Journal* for July 13, 20, or 27, in the same year. I should like to know whether the work ever was published, and, if so, where a copy of it can now be seen.

In the *Bath Journal* of the same year there are advertisements of two models of the city—one by

Sheldon, on a scale of 24 feet to an inch, and the other by C. Harcourt Masters, on a scale of 30 feet to the inch. Is either of these models, or any portion of either of them, still in existence, and, if so, where?
C. P. EDWARDS.

STUDLEY ROYAL.—Wanted, coat of arms of Sir J. Le Gras, owner of Studley Royal prior to 1400. Also the name of Isabel de Aleman's husband. She was heiress of Studley about 1251.
C. R.

GUARINI, "PASTOR FIDO," &c.—By whom is the translation of this poem, published by R. Montagu, 1736, and stated in the letter of "The Publisher to the Reader" to be "by an Ingenious Gentleman, who would not prefix his name, but had made great improvements on the translation of Sir Richard Fanshaw"? If by Elkanah Settle, it has not the dedication to Lady Elizabeth Delaval mentioned in "N. & Q.," 5th S. vii. 458. In the same volume with the above is bound *Comus, now adapted to the Stage, as altered from Milton's Mask*, Dublin, 1738. By whom was it altered, and was it ever performed?
W. M. M.

SIMONBURN, NORTHUMBERLAND.—I want the name of the saint to whom the parish church of Simonburn, in Tynedale, Northumberland, was dedicated. County histories and the Ordnance map say St. Simon; tradition says St. Mungo. There is a well known as St. Mungo's Well in the neighbourhood.
W. B.

THE "ROUND HOUSE," LIVERPOOL.—There is an old house in this neighbourhood which has been known for the last hundred and fifty years at least as the "Round House," and it is still so called by the old people living in and about West Derby, where the house is situated, but none of them can give any reason for the name. It was about fifty years ago used as a farmhouse, and the land about it was called the Round House farm. The house (which is of some considerable size) is rectangular in plan, and has a high pitched roof, flat on the top, and dormer windows to the attics, which are in the roof. There is nothing in the appearance of the house to suggest the appellation "Round House," and I should feel much obliged to any of your readers who would supply me with the probable reasons for the name. Perhaps other houses in the country may be so called without being circular or oval in plan, and the reason for the name "Round" being given to them may, if known, furnish the information I am in want of.
NEMO.

BANDDELROWES.—In a list of the "Townes Armore," in the Constables' Accounts of Repton for the year 1616, mention is made of "one payre of Banddelrowes." Can this be intended for bandoleers, *i.e.* separate charges of powder, contained in small cylindrical boxes, attached to

belts? Is there any more likely sugge confirming my surmise, I may mentic list also includes "one flaske or tucb "2 Culivers."
J. CHAR

THE "WATCH."—What is supposec origin of the above expression, whic monly used by insane persons, who are under an impression that they are wa is interesting to trace some of the i tained by persons mentally afflicted, have "reason in their madness," and th sions, though exaggerated and distc perhaps have been originally caused by genial conditions of their surroundings.
PSYCH

SACRAMENT MONEY.—Where can I s or buy a copy of the following work a tract only), the title of which I c Lintott's *Monthly Catalogue*, June, 171 "The Rules which have obtained for t of Sacrament Money since the Restorati Charles II. compared with those which we before."
T. BOWATER

"BEATI POSSIDENTES."—Whence co Bismarck's version of "a bird in hand,"
C

[The full form of the phrase, "Beati in ju possidentes," sufficiently shows its origin in t commentators on the Civil Law, and may l with the English proverbial expression, "I nine points of the law."]

"HISTOIRE DES SEIGNEURS DE GAVR DU XVe SIÈCLE, publié par Van Dale, —Can any reader of "N. & Q." suppl when this work was published? It i volume, containing an exact fac-simile o MS. as it appears, with ornamental in miniatures. Van Dale seems to have editor as well as the publisher. The after the title adds to the name "Le Gavres": "Se vend chez Vandale à Br
H.

Oxford.

"MALLIA CADREENE."—Can you gi better explanation of the legend "Mallia which occurs upon the Oxford seventeer token of Thomas Applebee, than the "Mal y a Car. de regne," or, as I per freely translate it, "Evil be to th Charles"? The date is about 1650 moneyers of the period being very illi have condensed it into its first form as t tioned.
J

HERALDIC.—A friend of mine he number of old silver and other seals them bearing coats of arms. Will any

dent kindly let me forward him the impressions in order to inform me to what families they belong ?
P. BERNEY BROWN.
St. Albans.

Co. CAVAN.—In which historical work can I find the greatest amount of information concerning the county of Cavan in Ireland and the lords of Cavan during the sixteenth and seventeenth centuries ? It appears O'Reilly was created Baron of Cavan about 1561. Where can I find a genealogy of this family ?   LA ROCHE.

THE KNIGHTS OF ST. JOHN.—Are there any monuments or tombs of the Knights of St. John (Hospitallers) existing, like those of the Templars in the Temple Church ? Where could I get a description or a sketch of one ?   F. R. DAVIES.
Hawthorn, Black Rock, Dublin.

FUNERAL ARMOUR.— On revisiting some village churches with which I was well acquainted many years ago, I remark, both in the restored(?) and the unrestored, that the funeral armour is going very fast, and, there being no source of supply or reparation, will soon be gone. What is this armour ? There are instances (such as that of Clive) of its use in the middle of the last century when armour was no longer worn, and where the helmets and swords are plainly no more than undertaker's trappings of a very perishable quality. I hope, though not without doubt, that the older armour is the genuine wear of the deceased, and therefore worthy of careful preservation.
TREGEAGLE.

AN OLD BOOK.—I lately came across an old book containing a vast amount of very curious matter. I should like to inquire if it is well known :—

"The Secretes of Maister Alexis of Piemont by hym Collected out of Divers Excellent Aucthours and newly Translated out of French into English, with a General Table of all the Matters contained in the sayde Booke. By Willyam Ward. Printed at London by Rouland Hall for Nicholas Englande, 1563."

The book is a small quarto in three parts. The colophon to part one is, "Printed at London by Roulande Hall for Nycholas Englande, 1562." The colophon to part three is, "Printed at London by Rouland Hall dwelling in Gutter lane, at the Signe of the half Egle and the Keye, 1562." Willyam Ward the translator dedicates the book to "Lord Russell, Earle of Bedford."
W. H. PATTERSON.
Belfast.

STREET NOMENCLATURE.—In Dudley is a thoroughfare bearing the singular name of "Inhedge," and in Wednesbury there is a street known as "High Bullen." Are these names to be met with in any other towns, and what is their derivation ?   FREDERIC WAGSTAFF.

EDBURTON, SUSSEX. — Can any reader of "N. & Q." supply the last words of the following inscription on a tablet in the church of Edburton, Sussex ? It is suggested that the lines may be a quotation ; in any case, some copy of them may be in existence.

"Here lieth the body of William Hippisley, Esq., who married to wife Katherine, yᵉ Daughter of John Pellett, of Bolney, Esq., by whom he had issue John, Katharine, & Mary, all yet survivinge. He dyed November the 4ᵗʰ,* ...... Aged 51.
And seeing stones can speak......
Both who he was and what lie......
He that Court, City, Country life......
And finding none that pleased fell......
He dyed if dead he can be said......
That knew no life besides E.,......"
H. H.

"ALLAH."—Which of the Popes asserted that the Christian "God" and the Mohammedan "Allah" were different beings, and what is the authority ?   D. D.

AUTHORS OF BOOKS WANTED.—
The Student of Padua : a Play. Privately printed. 1836.
Fits of Fancy. By Anybody. Cambridge.
New Year's Tribute to the New Reign. Sonnets. Edin., 1838.
Anglo-Indian Domestic Sketch. 8vo. Calcutta, 1849.
Calcutta : a Poem. Lond., 1811.
Rival Uncles ; or, Plots in Calcutta : a Play. Cal., 1819.   J. O.

Revelations of Russia ; or, the Emperor Nicholas and his Empire in 1844. By One who has Seen and Describes. Henry Colburn, Great Marlborough Street.—Who now possesses the copyright ? There is no copy in the British Museum.   E. TARLETON.

Hymn to the Daylight.—Was this poem, published in *Tait's Magazine*, No. 17, July, 1833, and commencing "Come from the crystal chambers of thy rest," and signed "V.," written by David Vedder, author of *The Covenanters' Communion,* &c. ?   WM. PEACE.

Replies.

ROMANO-CHRISTIAN REMAINS IN BRITAIN.
(5ᵗʰ S. ix. 349.)

This very interesting subject is treated in the *Councils and Ecclesiastical Documents relating to Great Britain and Ireland,* by Haddan and Stubbs. Vol. i. p. 37, appendix C, is devoted to the "monumental remains of the British Church during the Roman period," and shows how excessively rare they are. The very learned and laborious authors are only able to mention a single Roman-Christian inscription, which is let into the wall of the church of St. Mary-le-Wigford at Lincoln. An engraving of this is given in the *Archæological Journal* for 1860, vol. xvii. p. 15, with a description by the Rev. E. Trollope, M.A., and Arthur

* By the register, 1657.

Trollope, who state that it is very indistinct, and that no satisfactory explanation of it has been given. But in Prof. Emil Huebner's valuable work, the *Corpus Inscriptionum Latinarum Britanniæ*, Berlin, 1873, p. 53, No. 191, he gives this inscription, and says plainly that it is a work of the sixteenth century; and in his introduction, after noticing that his plan was to admit all the Latin inscriptions which were probably anterior to the sixth century, he says : " Exclusi autem titulos Christianos fere quotquot in variis Britanniæ partibus reperti sunt. *Ii enim omnes* videntur seculo sexto recentiores esse." There are, however, a very few instances of the ancient Christian monogram, the " Chi-rho," found on Roman pavements in England, sometimes combined with the symbolic Alpha and Omega. These are engraved in the *Journal* of the British Archæological Association for 1867, vol. xxiii. pp. 221–230, accompanied by a very interesting article by Mr. J. W. Grover on " Pre-Augustine Christianity in Great Britain, as indicated by the Discovery of Christian Symbols." In Prof. E. Huebner's work he also gives engravings of six gold rings of the Roman period found in England with Christian symbols, two of them having the words " vivas in Deo " (p. 234, Nos. 1305, 1307).

As some of the Roman-British Christians, therefore, had tesselated pavements, and wore gold rings, it seems we can hardly ascribe the total absence of Roman-Christian monumental inscriptions in Britain to the poverty of the Christians, especially as Constantine embraced the faith about a hundred years before the legions departed. I cannot help thinking that some of these interesting relics may yet be turned up in the excavations which are everywhere going on for railway and other purposes, and that the numerous clerical correspondents of " N. & Q." might contribute some further information of the existence of such relics.

I am informed that Prof. E. Huebner has since published a work entitled *Inscriptiones Britanniæ Christianæ*, but I have not been able to find it in the library of the British Museum. His other work above mentioned appears to be a monument of faithful and exhaustive labour and learning, and will soon be in every great library.

JOSEPH BROWN.
Temple.

The Roman villa at Chedworth in the Cotswold Hills contains several slabs of stone on which the Christian monogram, representing X P, is inscribed. This villa is by far the most interesting, so far as I know, in Britain. Its situation is charming ; its discovery recent and romantic. A keeper of the Earl of Eldon's was shooting rabbits, about fifteen years ago, in a lonely combe of the Cotswolds, Forcombe by name, the lower end of which is crossed by a Roman road, that runs into Ermine Street. The upper end of the combe is enclosed by a nobl cirque of woods, and just under these the keeper' dog scratched up out of a rabbit-hole certai: curious little pieces of stone, some white, som blue, some red. They were, of course, *tesseræ;* and the judicious keeper sent them off to one of th earl's relatives, who at once sent men to dig They dug, they found, they laid bare, under thi gentleman's guidance ; and now the whole head o great Roman country house : built, too, to suit th climate, in what one may call an English fashion and looking wondrous like an Elizabethan home stead with its pleasaunce and its range of office: and stabling. The house stands on a terrace, over looking the vale, and sheltered by the encircling woods. Its stone walls, about five or six feel high, are nearly perfect, and have been roofed in so that the tesselated pavements (one of which contains a figure of the British Roman as he appeared in winter, hunting) and the *caldarium*; &c., of the baths are now weatherproof. The timbered upper part of the house, which is supposed to have rested on these walls, has of course perished. A flight of well-worn steps leads down from the hall door to the terrace, which extends round three sides of a large square, the fourth and lowest side being open to the valley. The space within the square, which I have called the pleasaunce, is now a lawn, traversed by new-made gravel paths, which look, however, as if they had a right to be there. The two sides of the terrace are flanked by out-buildings and offices ; those on the left have in front an arcade of stone pillars, and they exhibit the remains of the granary, the bakehouse, the forge (with pigs of iron lying about), and such like appendages of a large rural homestead. In the angle between the upper end of this range of buildings and the house is a bare green slope, which I may call the ladies' garden ; for just at its highest point, where the retaining walls that enclose it on two sides are about to meet, the corner is cut off by an open circular summer-house or bower, walled in, except in front, with stone, and backed by the solid green hill, and overhung by the woods. In the centre of this bower, surrounded by a broad margin of flags, is a cylindrical fish-pond of hewn stone, some four feet deep. And when the earth which filled this up had been removed, a spade chanced to tap the very spring which had supplied it. At once the clear water bubbled up again ; and now, after more than fifteen hundred years, the pool is as full and as bright as when the Roman road-master's wife and daughters watched their tame fish there, looking out over their garden upon the fair green valley and the wooded hills, just as we do now.

In a neat cottage, built for the purpose on vacant ground, Lord Eldon has established a *custos* of the ruins, and a most interesting museum of things found on the spot, among which the slabs that I have mentioned appear.   A. J. M.

In the years 1794-96 some very fine tesselated pavements were found in a meadow between Frampton and Maiden Newton in Dorsetshire. On one of these was represented Constantine's Christian monogram. For details see Lysons's *Figures of Mosaic Pavements discovered near Frampton, Dorsetshire*, Lond., 1808, imp. fol.; Hutchins's *History of Dorset*, vol. ii. p. 250, second edit.; and Warne's *Ancient Dorset*, p. 192.

T. W. W. S.

T. S. H. will find some trustworthy information on the subject in E. Hübner's recent work, *Inscriptiones Britanniæ Christianæ* (London, Williams & Norgate, 1876).   H. Krebs.
Oxford.

MAC MAHON FAMILIES (5th S. ix. 7, 59, 97, 133.)—The following notes on the three Mac Mahons successively archbishops of Armagh, in Ireland, are derived from authentic sources, as stated afterwards, and give the information wanted by MR. BONE, correcting also some of the dates assigned to their respective episcopates by MESSRS. SHIRLEY, FISHER, and WARREN.

1. Hugh Mac Mahon, born 1660, in co. of Monaghan, said to have been a lineal descendant of the ancient princes there; educated in Irish College, at Rome, from 1682; a secular priest and professor there, as also doctor in theology; canon of the Collegiate Church of St. Peter, at Cassel, in French Flanders (of which chapter his uncle Arthur was then provost; and elected vicar-general of Clogher, his native diocese, in 1703; nominated bishop of Clogher, by brief of Pope Clement XI., March 15, 1707 (after a vacancy of nearly twenty years in that see from death of its last occupant, Fr. Patrick Tyrrell, O.S.F. Min. Observ.), and after consecration abroad (probably at Rome) arrived in Dublin shortly before October, 1708, " after many difficulties and dangers"; translated to archbishopric of Armagh by decree of Propaganda Aug. 6, 1713, as approved by the same pope on 26th of that month. On July 9, 1715, the new primate had another papal brief, enabling him to exercise all archiepiscopal acts without receiving the pallium, which it would have been dangerous to grant him in open Consistory, during that period of the persecuting penal laws against the clergy in Ireland. In 1728 he published, in 4to., a learned work on the long contested question of the primatial precedency of the see of Armagh, entitled *Jus Primatiale Armacanum, in omnes Archiepiscopos, Episcopos, et Universum totius Regni Hiberniæ—assertum per H.A.M.T.H.P.* Abp. Mac Mahon died at Dublin, Aug. 2, 1737, an. ætat. 77, epis. 30, and was interred in St. Peter's Church at Drogheda.

2. Bernard Mac Mahon (or " Brian "), educated in Irish College at Rome, and said, but erroneously, to have been brother of the above, though he may have been a nephew; a secular priest, appointed vicar-apostolic of Clogher by brief of Pope Clement XI. August —, 1718; and bishop of that see April 7, 1727, by brief of Pope Benedict XIII.; thence translated to Armagh Nov. 8, 1737, by brief of Pope Clement XII. He had a second brief from the same pope, dated Sept. —, 1738, setting forth the primatial dignity of his new see; and in Dec. following another, enabling him to exercise all the archiepiscopal acts without the pallium. He resided for many years in a humble cottage at a place called Ballymascanlan, in his diocese, co. Louth, where his assumed name was " Mr. Ennis," so insecure was the condition of Catholic prelates little more than a century ago; and he died May 27, 1747, ætat. 69, epis. 20 circa. Interred in the old churchyard of the chapel at Errigall, in barony of Trough, near village of Rockcorry, co. Monaghan, and diocese of Clogher.

3. Roche Mac Mahon (or " Ross "), secular priest, also educated at Irish College, Rome, and younger brother of above; nominated bishop of Clogher May 17, 1738, by brief of Pope Clement XII., and consecrated on Sunday, August 27 following, O.S., by Fr. Stephen Mac Egan, O.S.D , Bishop of Meath and Clonmacnois, before whom he took the usual oath, and made the profession of faith required at consecration. He was translated to Armagh Aug. 3, 1747, as successor to his brother in both sees, by brief of Pope Benedict XIV., and received a grant of faculties, as archbishop, January 8, 1748; but his primatial rule was short, as he died October 29 following, ætat. 49, epis. 11; his remains being interred beside those of his brother and predecessor in churchyard of Errigall, where is a monument to the memory of the two archbishops, with a Latin inscription:—

" Hic jacent Bernardus et Rochus Mac Mahon, fratres germani; uterque successive Archiepiscopus Armacanus, totius Hiberniæ primates, quorum nobilissimi generis memor pietas, atque æmula doctrina, vitaque titulis non impar mœrentem patriam decoravere. Bernardus obiit die 27 Maii 1747, ætat. 69. Rochus die 29 Oct. 1748, ætat. 49. Ambo pares virtute, pares et honoribus ambo. This monument was erected by Mr. Roger McMahon, brother to the deceased primates, A.D. 1750."

From the above it will be seen that three prelates of the name of Mac Mahon—the last two being brothers-german—were successively translated from Clogher to Armagh between 1713 and 1747; and, in conclusion, it may be noticed that Fr. Dominic Mac Guire (or "Maguire"), O.S.D., was elected abp. of Armagh, by decree of Propaganda, Dec. 14, 1683, as confirmed by Pope Innocent XI. Jan. 12, 1684; had a pension of 300l. a year from King James II. Mar. 12, 1686; received his pallium in 1687; and was obliged to

ny from Ireland, after surrender of Limerick, in October, 1691 (and shameful breach of treaty by the English), when he obtained refuge in France ; dying there, in exile, at Paris, Sept. 21, 1707, æt. 63 circa, epis. 24 ; and was buried in church of Irish College of the Lombards, under a tomb with an inscription. He was a native of Fermanagh, and friar in Dominican convent at Gaula, in diocese of Clogher, becoming afterwards for many years hon. chaplain to the Spanish Ambassador in London, until raised to the primacy of his native land and church.

Authorities.—De Burgo, *Hibernia Dominicana*, Colon. Agripp., 4to., 1762, pp. 331-3, 499 ; Harris, *Writers of Ireland*, fol., Dublin, 1764, p. 195 ; Ware's *Bishops*, Dublin, fol., 1739, p. 80, by Harris ; Beaufort, *Memoir of Map of Ireland*, 4to., Dublin, 1792, *passim* ; King, *Primer of Church History of Ireland*, small 4to., 1851, pp. 1244-46 ; Brenan, *Ecclesiastical History of Ireland*, 8vo., Dublin, 1864, pp. 573-75 ; M'Carthy and Renehan, *Collections on Irish Church History*, 8vo., Dublin, 1861, vol. i. pp. ix, x, and 79-100 ; Lynch, *Life of St. Patrick*, &c., 12mo., Dublin, 1828, p. 294 ; Stuart, *Historical Memoir of Armagh*, 8vo., Newry, 1819, pp. 399-406 ; Brady, *Episcopal Succession in England, Scotland, and Ireland*, 8vo., Rome, 1876, vol. i. pp. 229-30, 257-58 ; *Registrum Sacrum Hibernicum*, MS. *penes me.*   A. S. A.
Richmond.

JOHN THEODORE AND JACOB HEINS (5ᵗʰ S. ix. 308.)—The seventeen portraits bearing this name at Norwich were all painted by John Theodore Heins. His son Jacob is also said to have painted portraits, but the only one I can find at all likely to have been by him is that of Sir James Burrough (erroneously called Burroughes in Chambers's *Norfolk Tour*, p. 1131) at Caius College, Cambridge. Burrough was master of the college from 1759 to 1765, and there is reason to believe that John Theodore Heins died at the end of 1756 or in January, 1757. Chambers gives a very confused account of these two artists, for after saying that "J. Heins" made the drawings for Bentham's *History of Ely Cathedral*, and that he painted the portraits of Sir Benjamin Wrench and Mr. Emerson in the Guildhall at Norwich, he adds, "An artist of this name, and probably the same person, painted fifteen of the portraits of mayors hanging in St. Andrew's Hall," whereas every one of the seventeen portraits (only *eleven* of them were mayors) was, as I have said, painted by the father, and the drawings for Bentham's book were made by his son Jacob, who could not have been more than about sixteen years old when the last of the Heins portraits at Norwich were painted.

FR. NORGATE.
7, King Street, Covent Garden.

Heins painted portraits of Thomas Esq., and Sir Benjamin Wrench, now in tl chamber at the Guildhall, Norwich : alsc of Robert, Earl of Orford ; John, Lord the Hon. Horatio Walpole, M.P. ; and Si Vere, M.P. ; and of eleven mayors of (Benjamin Nuthall, Robert Marsh, Franc Timothy Balderstone, Thomas Harwood Clarke, William Wiggett, Simeon Walle: Harvey, Thomas Hurnard, and Nockol(son) in St. Andrew's Hall, Norwich. I note at p. 1131 of the *Norfolk Tour* (1£ said to have painted a portrait of Sir Ja roughes at Caius College, Cambridge, an died probably in 1757.   G. W.
Norwich.

Heins was a German artist who liv years at Norwich, where he painted portr was also an engraver. His son, who wa Norwich about 1740, became a better a his father, both in oil and miniatures. engraved in a good style, but died young a in 1770.   EMILY
Teignmouth.

WITCHCRAFT TRIALS (5ᵗʰ S. viii. 169, 255, 297.)—I have a very curious coll cases relating to judicial combat (wager c ordeal, and witchcraft. Amongst these the accompanying curious case of which I a translation :—

"The heresy of the Waldenses or poor of L; this time arose against Christ our Lord, which heresies disturbed us much, whose inventor, de diabolical inspiration, was a certain Vaudois, a Lyons. He when rich, abandoning everythin life of evangelical poverty, having great zeal fo not according to knowledge. He caused som(the Bible to be translated into the vulgar tongu with some lives of saints......For these wretch seeing themselves resisted and contradicted b lates and pastors, by preachers and religious they were no longer able to be malicious pu openly, had recourse to other means of perditi "Many of them, becoming invokers of demo tering into an agreement with them, became having wicked conversations with the ener human race : they formed an alliance with th("I remember in my youth, before I entered hearing many things concerning sorcerers of who are generally called *scobaces*.* For then wards many were taken in our province and bu being closely questioned, confessed horrible tl cerning one of whom, if however you see no o it, I think I ought not to be silent. "......Wherefore, as I have already said, be ing this order, there was a certain person nam Edeline, formerly professor of sacred theolo; was patent afterwards to everybody, a persecu: being first a Carmelite, then entered the Cartl not long after leaving them, being dispensec expelled the order, he betook himself to the Be

* Scobaces : Scoba=Scopæ=a broom. T were called *scobaces* from the notion of thei broomsticks—scrub, scroob.

he afterwards, consumed with ambition, became so diabolically dishonest, and, in order to obtain the much coveted dignities which he had set his heart on, made a compact with the cruel enemy, and adored him first in human form, that he may more easily deceive by kissing his wicked hand on bended knees......
"I am silent concerning the denial of the Holy Trinity, of Jesus Christ our Lord and his most holy Mother, of the noble standard of the Cross, of the holy Sacraments, and of other matters which the faithful are bound to believe and observe, for they are terrible to our ears. For he after he had lived a long time in such error, dead in life, was seized and captured and given into the hands of the Bishop of Evreux, who also conferred on me all my holy orders in the very city of Evreux.
"I have given this narration thus diffusely for a two-fold cause, namely, as a caution for many who may be seduced by these Waldenses or scobaces, of whom many, I doubt not, although unknown, still survive." *

JAMES MORRIN.

Dangan House, Thomastown.

I think the following interesting account from the Standard of October 18, 1877, is worthy of permanent preservation in the pages of "N. & Q." :

"THE WHITE WITCH OF DEVON.—The case of the North Devon White Witch came before Earl Devon and other magistrates at quarter sessions at Exeter yesterday. The name of the so-called witch is John Harper. He is eighty-three years of age, appears in his younger days to have been a good deal connected with mines in the neighbourhood of Combmartin, in the north of Devon, and he now described himself as a mining proprietor. He, however, did a considerable business as a herbalist, or quack doctor, and was commonly known as the 'White Witch' of North Devon. In visiting patients he usually took with him a number of sticks or rods of wood or metal, with small pieces of parchment attached, on which were inscribed the names of different planets, and these rods were supposed to have some mysterious instrumentality in the cures he professed to effect. The proceedings leading to his being brought before the magistrates arose in consequence of the death of the wife of a cattle doctor. A medical man attended her for some time, but on his pronouncing her case as hopeless, her husband went a journey of twenty miles to see the White Witch. He came to the woman, and inquired as to the day, the hour, and the planet under which she was born. From a box he produced some rods with the names of the planets written on the parchment attached, and, placing these one at a time in the woman's hands, directed her to strike a piece of metal which he produced, and as she complied with his directions he spoke some words in a low tone. He also prescribed some bitters, and gave a powder which was to be mixed in boiling water, and which, he added, he always used in every fever but typhus. He stated that though the woman was very weak there was no reason why she should not recover. She, however, died a day or two afterwards. When asked what his charges were, the so-called witch said twenty-five shillings, and that sum was paid him. For the defence it was stated that the rods were struck by the patient on a piece of manganese, and this produced an electric shock. It was further contended that the different planets actually did exercise a powerful influence over the human frame and the electric currents permeating the system. Some persons spoke as to cures effected by Harper in some cases after medical men had given up all hopes.

* Anonymous tract on history of Carthusians, chap. xxv.

When he first came to the house he said he was a humble instrument in the hands of God, and he was not sure he could do anything. It was denied that he said there must be three persons of one faith in the room before he could do any good. The magistrates in petty sessions sentenced Harper to one month's imprisonment, but owing to his age they did not impose hard labour. The defendant now appeared against the conviction, on the ground that the use of certain means and devices to deceive or to impose on her Majesty's subjects had not been proved, and objection was also taken to the form of conviction, the words 'hard labour' having been inserted in the copy now before the court, whereas no hard labour was imposed. It was explained that these words were inserted as after the committal of the defendant it was found that he could not be imprisoned without hard labour. The objection was held to be fatal, and the conviction was quashed."

R. P. HAMPTON ROBERTS.

"IT IS EASIER FOR A CAMEL," &c. (5th S. ix. 106, 268.)—The result arrived at by the writer of the article referred to by K. P. D. E. coincides entirely with the judgment of one or two literary friends whom I have since consulted, and I think the question may now be considered as being settled beyond dispute in the following manner—1. That there is no valid ground for changing the Scriptural "camel" into a "cable"; and 2. that the term "needle's eye," as applied to a small door or wicket in an Eastern town, has been familiar to writers and travellers in those countries for hundreds of years; hence the propriety of the image contained in the text referred to is established beyond all doubt.   CH. A. MURRAY.

Villa Victoria, Cannes.

[An "Aquæbajalus," see ante, p. 334.]

BUCKLES ON SHOES (5th S. ix. 388.)—There are numerous examples of buckles on belts or girdles. Thus we have "the bocle of the gerdle" (Ayenbite of Inwit, ed. Morris, p. 236). As to buckles on shoes, they were certainly used in the fourteenth century. There is a well-known line in Chaucer, alluding to St. Mark i. 7, "Ne were worthy vnbokele his galoche" (Squieres Tale, C. T. Group F, 555). Wyclif uses the word thwong, i.e. thong, not buckle.   WALTER W. SKEAT.

I hardly think that the writer of the Homily, when he used the word "unbuckle," desired to suggest shoe buckles, but rather that he meant "to unfasten." According to Hone (Every-day Book, ii. 677), shoe buckles were fashionable in England many years before the time of Queen Mary (see Fosbroke). They were, however, then articles of luxury, and Holinshed (Description of England, 1586, p. 139) speaks with disgust of the priests before the Reformation, who had their "shoes buckled with silver."

In the Paraphrase on the Gospells, by Erasmus, printed by Whitchurch, 1548, the word "unbuckle" is used several times. Thus, under John i. 27, the translator, who I believe was the Princess Mary, renders it, "unworthie to leuse the buckles of his shoes." And again at Luke 1ii. 16, Nicholas Udal, who translated that part, renders it, "unworthy to unbuccle the latchet of his shooes." The word "buckle," as then used, did not, I think, necessarily mean that there was a "fibula," but signified, in general, union or bringing together. Thus Udal, in the same page just quoted from, speaks of "two armies buckling together." EDWARD SOLLY.

MILTON : "PARADISE LOST" ILLUSTRATED BY GEORGE CRUIKSHANK (5th S. ix. 289.)—The following letter from Cruikshank to myself, dated March 14, 1877, supplies the information asked for by MR. W. G. BLACK :—

"Previous to the year of 1825 I was engaged to illustrate Milton's *Paradise Lost*. A friend of mine, Mr. Lewis, was to be the editor, and a bookseller in the Strand, near Holywell Street, named Birch was, I believe, to be the publisher.

"For this work I made two drawings on wood, one was 'Satan, Sin, and Death at the Gates of Hell,' and the other 'Satan calling up the Fallen Angels' :—

'Awake ! arise ! or be for ever fallen.
They heard, and were abashed, and up they sprung
Upon the wing.'

"This illustration was very crowded with figures, and the best drawing that I ever did in my life; but when the wood engraver saw it he said he was afraid he could not engrave it. However, it was done and published. But the block is missing. However, there is an impression of it (No. 116) now exhibiting in the selection of my works at the Royal Aquarium, Westminster, London.

"I expect there had been some kind of arrangement made as to a partnership between the editor and the publisher. But some disagreement followed, which stopped the work, and this is the reason why the subject you mention of the large figure in perspective,

'Lay floating under a rood,'

was not published; and since then I have had so many matters to attend to that I don't think I shall ever publish it, nor be able to do an oil painting of the subject, as I always wished to do, being now too much overwhelmed with various engagements."

I have contributed a copy of this letter, with other matter, to Mr. Blanchard Jerrold for his forthcoming work on Cruikshank as an artist and as a temperance reformer.

J. POTTER BRISCOE, F.R.H.S.
Free Public Library, Nottingham.

BLECHYNDEN AND BACHE (5th S. ix. 289.)—I should have been glad to have given MR. DUANE more information, but the place of birth is never recorded on entrance to college. I thought, however, that some clue might be obtained by the way in which the father is described, and I have therefore got from the President of St. John's the fact that Richard Blechynden the elder is called in the college books "Londinensis plebeii filius." The younger Richard Blechynden is styled "of Surrey, generosi fil." As they were both "Merchant Taylor" boys, it is probable they were both

Londoners, only the younger one's parents the Surrey side of the river. The elder college living of Crick or Creek, in amptonshire. The family, I was told, still Kent. At Christ Church the Buttery Bo 1679 to 1696 is wanting. But in an old lation book there is the entry of the matri of "Gul. Bach, April 22, 1686, as a Servit therefore was not in prosperous conditio start in life. GIBBES RIC
18, Long Wall, Oxford.

At the east end of the south aisle of th church of Swanscombe in Kent is a tomb memory of Thomas Blechyndon, Lord of the of Swanscombe, who died in 1740, aged thir also to Lydia his widow, who died in 174 thirty-one, leaving two sons, co-heirs. in his *History of Kent*, gives the follow scription of the arms engraved upon the mental slab : "Quarterly, 1 and 4, a fess between three lions' heads erased, impalin ermine between three cinquefoils."

J. A. SPARVEL-BAYLY, F

PETTY TREASON (5th S. ix. 388.)—I can in my list of executions one for petit-tre 1760, but on April 13, 1753, Ann Willia burned at Gloucester for this offence. account of her execution will be found in and Baldwin's *Newgate Calendar* (Lond., 8vo., 1824-6), vol. ii. p. 177. Petit-treas sisted in the breach of civil or eccles connexion coupled with murder, as w servant killed his master, a wife her hust an ecclesiastical person (either secular or his superior, to whom he owed faith and obe The punishment in a man was to be dra hanged, and in a woman to be drawn and This punishment of burning may be trace laws of the ancient Druids (vide *Cæs. de Bel* l. vi. c. 19). It was, however, the usual ment (until lately) for *all* treasons commi those of the female sex. The crime of petit was abolished by stat. 9 Geo. IV. c. 31, s. ;
GEORGE W
St. Briavel's, Epsom.

It is stated in the *Annual Register* f that a woman, for poisoning her husbar sentenced at the Chester Spring Assizes burned the third day after conviction, but tence was respited by the judge till t [April], on which day she was executed at Another case of a woman burned for poiso husband will be found on p. 211 of Phillip *tory of Shrewsbury*, which occurred a earlier than the Cheshire one, viz. 1647.
Croeswylan, Oswestry.

NUMISMATIC (5th S. ix. 327.)—1. This refer to the founding of the *Society* of Jesu the *college* of that order, which was founded by Gregory XIII. at Rome in the year 1582, which was the tenth of his pontificate. This pope was a great patron of the Jesuits, granted them many privileges, and, as we are told, founded and endowed no fewer than twenty-seven seminaries in different parts of the world—four even in Japan—for the instruction of youth in the Roman Catholic faith. The medal, no doubt, was struck to commemorate the founding of the college at Rome.

EDMUND TEW, M.A.

3. The official style of the French Republic, with its computation of time from the abolition of monarchy in 1792, its decades, decade-days, and "days without breeches," was not done away till some months after the establishment of the empire under Napoleon.　　　TREGEAGLE.

EARLY DOUBLE NAME (5th S. ix. 388.)—TREG-EAGLE is under a misapprehension. The case he cites is not an instance of a double name. The surname of Arthur is not at all an uncommon one, at least in Cornwall, and the "de Tyntagel" was simply to distinguish the said Nicholas Arthur from others of the same name, or to show to what particular family he belonged. The family of Arthur was settled at a very early date in the parish of Tyntagel. John Arthur was one of the jurors upon an inquisition *ad quod damnum* concerning certain lands in that parish, taken on July 11, 1306 (Esch. 34 Edw. I. No. 217). Possibly he was the father of Nicholas. I do not find the name in the Subsidy Roll for Tyntagel of 1 Edw. III., but many of the names in the record are illegible. John Artur was one of the venditors of the Ninths in the adjoining parish of Trevalga in 1341. Thomas Arthur was a freeman of the manor of Tyntagel in 1493. John Arthur was assessed to the subsidy in 1543, and the name is one of the earliest which occurs in the parish register, which commences in 1569. There are gravestones in the churchyard as late as 1798.

JOHN MACLEAN.
Bicknor Court, Coleford, Glouc.

THE BLESSING OF CRAMP RINGS (5th S. ix. 308.) —The service for the blessing of cramp rings may be seen in Maskell's *Monumenta Ritualia Ecclesiæ Anglicanæ*, iii. 335. Cf. Brand's *Popular Antiquities*, ed. 1813, i. 128; Nares's *Glossary*, sub voc. ; *Pro. Soc. Ant.*, first series, ii. 292 ; *Journal of British Archæolog. Ass.*, xxvii. 287.

EDWARD PEACOCK.
[See Dyer's *British Popular Customs* (Bell & Sons), under "Good Friday," p. 149.]

FOLEY'S "ENGLISH-IRISH DICTIONARY" (5th S. ix. 367.)—The late Rev. Prof. Foley, D.D., was a native of Kerry. He had been originally educated for a Catholic clergyman. At the time of his death

he was incumbent of Templetuchy in the diocese of Cashel.　　　JOSEPH FISHER.

ROMAN CITIES IN BRITAIN (5th S. ix. 288.)— These two works might interest your correspondent:
Somner's Treatise on the Roman Ports and Forts in Kent; with Life. Edited by Brome. 12mo. Portrait by Burghers. Oxf., 1693.
The Durobrivæ of Antoninus identified and illustrated in a Series of Plates, exhibiting the Excavated Remains of that Roman Station, in the Vicinity of Castor, Northamptonshire, including the Mosaic Pavements, Inscriptions, Paintings in Fresco, Baths, Iron and Glass Furnaces, Potters' Kilns, Implements for Coining, and the Manufacture of Earthen Vessels, War and other Instruments in Brass, Iron, Ivory, &c. Discovered by E. T. Artis, F.S.A., F.G.S., &c. London: Printed for the Author, 1828. Folio.

HIRONDELLE.

"A PROVERB IS THE WISDOM OF MANY AND THE WIT OF ONE" (5th S. ix. 187.)—This definition of a proverb (which has been aptly termed "the child of experience") is attributed to Lord John Russell in the *Memoirs of Mackintosh*, vol. ii. p. 473. It bears a strong resemblance to a passage in Pope's *Essay on Criticism:*—

"True wit is nature to advantage dress'd,
What oft was thought, but ne'er so well express'd."
WM. UNDERHILL.
[See 1st S. viii. 243, 304, 523; 4th S. ix. 320; 5th S. ii. 452.]

AN OLD BALLAD (CAPTAIN WARD) (5th S. ix. 407.)—This is one of the old ballads in the Roxburghe collection, which will be reprinted for the members of the Ballad Society. Its old title is "*The Famous Sea-fight between Captain Ward and the Rainbow.* To the tune of *Captain Ward.*" Ward was a famous sea-rover, or pirate, who flourished near the end of Elizabeth's reign and in the earlier years of that of James I. He succeeded in beating off his Majesty's ship the Rainbow, which was sent to take him. This is the subject of the ballad. The recital of the Norfolk gentleman from whom MISS PEACOCK received a traditional version begins at the third stanza. The old printed copies commence thus :—

"Strike up, you lusty gallants,
　　With music and sound of drum,
For we have descry'd a rover
　　Upon the sea is come.

His name is Captain Ward,
　　Right well it doth appear
There has not been such a rover
　　Found out this thousand year."

There are twelve stanzas in the first and twelve in the second part. Copies in Rox. coll., vol. iii., at folios 56, 652, 654, and 861 ; other editions are in the Bagford and in the Pepys collections. It was reprinted about the commencement of the present century in Aldermary Churchyard, so that the tradition is not necessarily one of early date.

WM. CHAPPELL.

OVID'S "METAMORPHOSIS" (5th S. ix. 328.)—
This is the well-known translation of the *Meta-morphoses* by George Sandys, a traveller and a poet, who lived from 1577 till 1643 (see Watt's *Bibliotheca Britannica*, vol. ii. p. 832). How popular and commonly sought for it must have been may be gathered from the fact that it has seen nine different editions, at least, during the seventeenth century. Lowndes (vol. iii. p. 1745) quotes eight successive editions of this translation, but omits that of 1628. Having another copy of the very same edition before me, I find, as far as I compared the translation with the Latin poem, it deserves the praise of an elegant version, which, at the same time, conveys a fair understanding of the original sense by consulting its valuable notes. Two competent judges, moreover, have given their opinion as to its poetical merits, viz. Dryden and Pope. "Sandys is pronounced by Dryden to be the best versifier of the last age; and Pope affirmed that English poetry owed much of its present beauty to Sandys's translations" (Lowndes, *l.c.*). H. KREBS.
Oxford.

The work inquired for is evidently the translation made by George Sandys, the traveller and poet. I do not know it as a 12mo. or 16mo., but the folio copies range in mercantile value from 15s. or 16s. up to a guinea, according to condition.
A. J. M.

MARY, QUEEN OF SCOTS (5th S. ix. 329.)—
C. P. will find needlework done by the unfortunate queen in Hardwicke Hall, near Chester-field, in the bedroom bearing her name, and also in the minstrel's gallery. G. H. A.
Pendleton.

In North Derbyshire and the neighbourhood of Sheffield it has become usual to attribute most of the old framed silk needlework to Queen Mary and her ladies. TREGEAGLE.

To "FAVOUR" (5th S. ix. 225.)—The expression is not uncommon in this neighbourhood; and I have frequently heard it elsewhere. The very words quoted by COL. FERGUSSON were used to me only the other day by a clergyman, who said that my daughter decidedly "favoured her mother." W. D. SWEETING.
Peterborough.

Should COL. FERGUSSON have occasion to visit North-east Lancashire, I will engage, if he keep his ears open, that it will not be long before he will hear of some small child that "it favvers it fayther" or some other relative. (The compositor is respectfully requested not to print *its;* we have no *s* in our possessive case.) HERMENTRUDE.

Peacock's *Glossary of Words used in the Wapen-takes of Manley and Corringham* gives it thus:

"Favour, *v.* to resemble in feat bairn *favours* Bill strangely."'"

In Westmorland the word *favou* used in the sense alluded to by Co Kendal.

This expression, which I suppose use of the substantive *favour*, is Lancashire. One day, in the min county, I was coming along by a v of which sat two blackfaced little ɡ pitfolk; and one of them, looking the other, "Eh, doesn't he favve Which may have been true enou just come from a neighbouring pitl

WILLIAM FISHER, 1576 (5th S the Campo Santo of Bologna ther tion to Robertus Fisheir, dated 4 N just above it is a slab inscribed:—
"Hoc situs in tumulo est Gulielmus Anglorum quem Mors traxit ad Ely Nam modo festivos dum spectat lue Bombardæ fractus viribus occubuit Proh dolor ergo homini quæ nam fi Si jugulant etiam quos putat ille jo
In the long arcade is a tablet ɩ "Fr. Julius Borius," orator of Jɛ Pope, and "Eques Hierosolym Angliæ Prior," dated 1702. The second line is evidently a ɩ Domitius Marsus's epitaph on Tibu
"Mors juvenem campos misit ad

"DANDY PRATTES," &C. (5th S. I had hoped some one better ver: currency would have answered this this, I will give the best informatiɩ the subject. It appears that previ giving permission for the issue of tokens, no other coins than in gold ever been issued in this country, aɪ for some currency of less value at the price of provisions and labot small is sufficiently obvious. Freq were made to Parliament in conse matter, with however, so far as the iɪ in a metal other than gold or silver no result. The people remedied th by using for minor payments variou as mailes, brabants, crokards, sus pollards, galley penys, nurnbergs, Jews have the credit of introducinɡ with ever an eye to the main chan much of their money, which was silver, and closely resembled the Edwards, into the country; and i complaint to the king in 1406 the Scots brought as much as 100l. with them, to the defrauding of the poor people who could not distinguish the difference in the coins. Various statutes, with fearful penalties, were passed to prevent the circulation of this base money, but seemingly without effect. The particular coins of which E. M. T. speaks :—

1. *Dandy prattes.* This name was probably applied to the silver farthings of the Edwards and Henries IV., V., VI. Possibly a jocose name in reference to their smallness.

2. *Romans grottes.* These were certainly the gros, groats, or great penny of the continental states, which being of silver, of worse fineness than our standard, the design or type being very similar, were imported in large numbers by the merchants, and passed off amongst the people.   .

3. *Galy halfpeny*, or *galley pence.* These were pennies of base money brought to England by the merchants trading from Venice and who came in galley ships. They are specially mentioned in a writ to the Mayor of London in 1414, commanding him to search the galleys coming to London, and to warn the possessors of the coins therein not to attempt to pass the same, but if they wished they might take them to the Mint and have their value in sterlings (English pennies), or might have the base money melted and recoined.

E. M. T. might with advantage consult the numismatic works of Snelling, Ruding, Hawkins, Burns (Jacob Hy.), and Boyne upon the subject of the base money circulating in England from the twelfth to the seventeenth century.   J. HENRY.
Devonshire Street, W.C.

"THE CHRISTIAN YEAR" : THE ALTERED LINE (5ᵗʰ S. ix. 380, 400, 419.)—Canon Liddon's reply that the Dean of Chichester is " seriously inaccurate in his account " of the altered line appears to me scarcely to bear the construction you put upon it in " Notices to Correspondents " (*ante*, p. 400), that it is an entire denial. A person may be " seriously inaccurate " without being " wholly so," and, as it appears to me, something lies concealed under this distinction which it would be fair to the Dean of Chichester to have made clear. If Canon Liddon is able to substitute " wholly " for " seriously " the matter is at an end. In the contrary case something seems reserved, and the truth rather fenced with than dealt with.   G. B.
Upton, Slough.

ROBERT PALTOCK (5ᵗʰ S. ix. 186, 372, 416.)—Inasmuch as I overlooked OLPHAR HAMST's communication of Nov. 30, 1867, I am amenable to his strictures ; but in the matter of Paltock I simply deny that I am indebted to him or to anybody else. The subject was started by MR. CROSSLEY in 1854, long before OLPHAR HAMST came to our assistance in " N. & Q.," and having both *Peter Wilkins* and *Parnese*, the ." R. P." in

both obviously suggested to me one author, and it was then, I reassert, that I wrote my suppressed note to " N. & Q." to await MR. CROSSLEY's further revelations, which never came. When OLPHAR HAMST honoured me with a visit I showed him my *Parnese* with my jotting in it, and still remaining. I do not, of course, say that what he wrote in 1867 could be derived from anything I told him in 1874, but I do say that there is no novelty in independent workers in the same line arriving at the same conclusions, and that this may be an example of it.

Meeting lately with a cutting which brought to light a third " R. P.," with a title which seemed to me to favour MR. CROSSLEY's idea that the author of *Peter Wilkins* was a lawyer, I ventured to bring them altogether under the eye of your readers.
                                            J. O.

MILTON'S FIRST WIFE, MARY POWELL (5ᵗʰ S. ix. 308, 374.)—I am obliged for DR. SIMPSON's reply to my query, from which it appears that the entry of the Lords' order in the *Report of the Historical MSS. Commission* is calendared with greater care than is manifested by the editors of the *Journals*. As to the Mr. Powell, who is not enumerated amongst the masters of St. Paul's School in Knight's *Life of Colet*, there was one of his name who in 1661 was schoolmaster of Stafford (Plume's *Life of Hacket*, ed. 1675, p. xxx).
                                            JOHN E. BAILEY.

THE ISLE OF MAN (5ᵗʰ S. viii. 127, 251, 298, 470 ; ix. 177, 214.)—MR. W. G. WARD, in his notes on the Isle of Man, gives me credit for more knowledge than I profess to have. I did not express any pain or astonishment at his statement that " the sovereignty of this island was never purchased by Government," well knowing that many statements are made respecting the island by those who have not given sufficient attention to its early history. I quoted several authorities, which I thought would be sufficient for the purpose. One of the earliest records in the Rolls Office, Castletown, speaks of the " king." This was not an empty title only, for upon summons to his barons to come in and do their fealty, upon refusal or neglect to do so in proper time, their lands were forfeit to the king or lord's use. The power of life and death was in his sole hands, without any appeal to any other sovereign, of which instances are to be met with among the records in the Rolls Office; also treasure trove, a sovereign right which the Crown is very jealous of to the present time, of which I could give a good instance ; mines royal; the right of minting money, which probably MR. WARD may not know was exercised here before the revestment of the island in the Crown of England— the particulars respecting this last have been copied from the records, and may perhaps be published before long : these, with other matters, might be adduced as instances of sovereign rights of the Isle of Man, without any appeal to any other power.

The legislative power in the Isle of Man has been independently exercised, it may be truly said, from time immemorial by the local kings, or lords if they were pleased to be so styled, in conjunction with the other estates, without any reference to the Crown of England previously to 1765 ; and since that date the first estate in the legislature has been the sovereign of England; hence the submitting the Acts of Tynwald to the Sovereign in Council for approbation, previously to being promulgated on Tynwald Hill before they became the law of the land, the only existing ceremony of the kind in Europe.

The Attorney and Solicitor General of England very recently were of opinion that the insular legislature had not the power, even with the consent of the Crown, to pass a measure for the redistribution and rearrangement of the revenues of the see of Man after the next avoidance ; but on reconsidering the matter, after arguments advanced by the Attorney-general for the Isle of Man, they state, " We are led to the conclusion that the insular legislature *have power* to pass a measure for the rearranging the revenues of the see of Sodor and Man."

" N. & Q." is not the place in which to enter into a lengthened history of matters connected with the Isle of Man, but if your readers will consult the authentic records of the island, they will find much that will dispel many erroneous opinions respecting it. When the boxes and boxes of documents resting in the archive-rooms at Knowsley, Dunkeld, Lord Dunmore's, and other places, come to be examined, much no doubt will be found to throw light upon matters connected with the early history of this little kingdom of Man.

I shall not trouble you again as to its "sovereign rights." WILLIAM HARRISON.
Rock Mount, Isle of Man.

"SUMMER HAS SET IN," &c. (5th S. ix. 128, 392.) —The sarcastic description of an English summer is not quite accurately given by MR. C. A. WARD (*ante*, p. 392), and I think he is wrong also in ascribing the authorship to the witty canon of St. Paul's. My impression is that the sarcasm runs thus, " The English summer has set in with all its usual severity," and that this passage may be found in a volume of travels by Prince Puckler Muskau, a German nobleman who visited this country more than once in the reign of George IV., and who latterly committed his observations to the press.
J. SCOTT.
Bath

GERMAN MEASLES (5th S. ix. 129, 392.)— Having under very favourable circumstances seen an epidemic of this disease at Corfu, I had intended

answering this query, but forgot it. tion from Prof. Charteris's *Practice of .* exceedingly good so far as it goes. But a hybrid between measles and scarlet stated by some writers, is wholly wron; known theory as to the origin of fever be no *hybridity* between two such distin and to make or adopt such a statement an error similar to that of old times wl and scarlatina were accounted but c *Rubeola* or German measles is a s distinct eruptive fever, the result ol poison, and one as distinct as are those scarlet fever, and small-pox. It wou long and out of place to go into more every marked case has one or more possibly four, different eruptions. No can, by an accurate eye, be confounde eruption in measles, and the red flush sembles that of scarlatina is nearly a partial, and always more transient. seeing it on a man's chest I carefully c up, and yet when within an hour I unc to show it to another it was gone. A in the severer or more marked cases, th peels in films as in scarlet fever, but the secretion which is so formidable in t wholly wanting. From the peeling, and from the supposition that no British s have, or was entitled to have, a disea down in the Medical Regulations, the hig authorities in the island called it scarl from investigations made for the pur fully convinced of the correctness of the in the quotation given from Prof. Char (p. 392). A very good account of the be found in Copland, *s.v.* " Rubeola,' learnt the name of the disease that l first time come under my observation.
BRINSLEY NICHOLSON, N
At that time Surgeo

CHARLES HOWARD (5th S. ix. 2 Martha Maria Howard, daughter Howard, of Bury St. Edmunds, was Ickworth Church, on Dec. 31, 1740, t and Rev. Charles Hervey, fifth son of Earl of Bristol. He died s.p. in 178 nothing more about her. S. :

THE CHANGE IN THE ENGLISH PRO OF LATIN (5th S. ix. 387.)—May I be] support the query of MR. HART? T has much vexed me, and been a sou difficulty and inconvenience. I have ver made similar inquiries of personal frie far I have never received a clear and reply. Certain it is that the pron Latin in this country is almost a sure " theological partisanship " of the sp(am extremely anxious, with your corre know when and why the alteration took place. I feel convinced that an exhaustive article on the subject would be exceedingly interesting to a large number of your readers.   H. N.

PUBLIC-HOUSE SIGNS (5th S. ix. 127, 174, 257, 293, 353, 391.)—Will our good friend CLARRY tell us the origin of the sign of the "Apple Tree and Mitre"?   H. Y. N.

DID MORLAND EVER PAINT "FISH PICTURES"? (5th S. ix. 327.)—Most probably he did not. I have two pictures, one of which answers MR. DOUGALL's description; the second is a fellow to it by the same hand, but saltwater fish, lobster, oysters, &c., with sea birds, and a ruined fort in the background, and this one is signed "W. Sartorius ft." At the back of the freshwater fish is in pencil, "painted by 'Sartorius.'" I shall be glad to communicate directly with MR. DOUGALL, if he requires further evidence and will send his address through you to me.   BOILEAU.
Shrewsbury.

I am not aware that Morland ever painted a picture of fish alone, but it is likely enough that he did, as he was fond of coast scenes, with fishermen pursuing their various avocations, and he introduced fish more than once into his pictures. I have myself a copy of one of his works representing a cottage door, near which is a piece of water with a boat drawn up to the bank. A woman and a man are at the door conversing, and on the ground is a large fish, the species of which, though "a brother of the angle" to some small extent, I am unable to give, the copyist having apparently caught little of the spirit of his original. Hassell, in his Life of Morland, though he gives a copious list of works, describes none of fish only. He has one called "Selling Fish": scene, a coast; man on grey horse bargaining with fisherman's wife for fish. Another is fishermen landing fish, and this he describes as a "little elegant cabinet piece on panel." Is not your correspondent's picture more likely to be by Coleman?   A. H. BATES.
Edgbaston.

PORTUMA (5th S. ix. 327.)—It is probable that this word signifies the Island of Portland opposite Weymouth, which according to Cowell bore the name of Portunia.   A. J. K.

GOD's CHURCH AND DEVIL's CHAPEL (5th S. ix. 267.)—There is a similar old saying in German, viz., "Keine Kirche so klein, der Teufel baut seine Kapelle daneben." The analogous French and Italian proverbs are, "A côté de l'église le diable a sa chapelle"; "Laddove Iddio ha una chiesa, il diavolo ha la sua capella." I have found also the corresponding proverb in Polish, viz., "Gdzié Pan Bóg Kosciol buduje, tám Diabel Káplice stáwia."   H. KREBS.

Miscellaneous.

NOTES ON BOOKS, &c.

The Student's Ecclesiastical History. By Philip Smith, B.A. (Murray.)
The Student's English Church History. By Rev. G. G. Perry, M.A. (Same publisher.)

IN these two new volumes of the Student's series Mr. Murray provides for two different but equally widely felt requirements—a compendious history of the period known among Anglicans as the Undivided Church, and a clear but succinct account of the post-Reformation Church of England. Mr. Smith's Ecclesiastical History is profusely illustrated by woodcuts representing diptychs, frescoes, early Christian symbolic pictures, churches in far East and far West, from Syria to the Cornish Land's End, and is enriched by notes and references to original authorities. But we should have been glad to have known the source of some of the illustrations, notably of the "Ancient Syrian Church of the Sixth Century at Kalb Louzeh," figured at p. 192, and the exterior view of what is vaguely described as an "Ancient Syrian Church of the Sixth Century," at p. 348, and which is probably a restoration. It is not to be supposed that every reader will agree with Mr. Smith's views, though the part which he desires to play is rather that of an exponent of facts than a propounder of theories. But he leans too much on Dr. Schaff, we think, in the sub-apostolic and early conciliar periods to be quite fair to the Ignatian and Cyprianic views of Episcopacy. And his suggestion of interested motives for the supposed heresy of the Gregorian Armenians is, to say the least of it, gratuitous, and almost certainly not warranted by the true history of the Armenian separation, which appears in its origin to have been rather accidental than intentional.

Mr. Perry treats an important period in the history of the National Church temperately, and with considerable tact as well as scholarship. On the whole, he meets his difficulties fairly, neither avoiding them nor going out of his way to seek them. "Advertisements" and Injunctions, Seminary priests and Puritans, all pass in review. But Mr. Perry uses Lingard and Tierney no less than Evelyn and Burnet, and so his readers are not kept in ignorance of the different sides of the numerous questions, whether of doctrine, ritual, or discipline, which have from time to time arisen since the Reformation settlement. Mr. Perry is not blind to the shortcomings either of individual Churchmen or of the Church itself, but he closes his survey of religious affairs during the latter part of the eighteenth century with words of hope for the future, which are justified to his mind by the many "striking outward manifestations of increased zeal" and "growth in religious energy," undeniably characteristic of the Church of England in the present day.

Transactions and Proceedings of the Conference of Librarians held in London, Oct., 1877. (Whittingham.)

MR. E. B. NICHOLSON and Mr. H. R. Tedder, the editors of this report, may well be congratulated on the accuracy and general appearance of the volume before us. The papers read are of great interest, and some of considerable value, but the good done by the Conference of Librarians must not be estimated by the original matter or new ideas which are to be found in the report. Nevertheless a large amount of information is brought together, and if in a somewhat desultory manner, that is compensated for by a good table of contents, and, what is still better, and indeed a very noticeable feature in the report, a most exhaustive index which Mr. Tedder has rendered a very model of its kind. It is well that such a good example should thus be set, and if librarians would take every available opportunity of following it, and insisting on the prime importance of good indexes, much would assuredly be accomplished in the way of relieving the labours of authors.

DEATH OF DR. CARRUTHERS.—A worthy man, a valuable and frequent contributor to "N. & Q." in years gone by, and to whom the admirers of Pope are indebted for an excellent edition of their favourite's works, has just gone to his rest. Dr. Robert Carruthers, who had only lately retired from a fifty years' editorship of the *Inverness Courier*, died at Inverness on Sunday last, in the seventy-ninth year of his age.

AT the recent sale of the Hayley collection of autograph letters Mr. W. H. Collingridge (owner of Cowper's house at Olney) became the purchaser of the *Yardley Oak*, 10 pp., 4to., in the handwriting of Cowper. It fetched 11*l.*

Notices to Correspondents.

We must call special attention to the following notices:

ON all communications should be written the name and address of the sender, not necessarily for publication, but as a guarantee of good faith.

CORRESPONDENTS are requested to bear in mind that it is against rule to *seal* or otherwise *fasten* communications transmitted by the halfpenny post. Not unfrequently double postage has to be paid on their receipt, because they have been "closed against inspection."

POSTULATA is informed that, in accordance with the Code Napoléon, marriage must be celebrated in France before a civil officer of the domicile of one of the contracting parties in presence of four witnesses, after due public notice has been given. This, which alone is the obligatory marriage, may be *followed* by the religious ceremony; but any minister of public worship who should perform the religious rite *before* the civil marriage would be liable to heavy punishment under Arts. 199, 200, of the Penal Code. The rules of French law respecting marriage are given in Book I. Arts. 63-76 and 144-228 of the Civil Code, while the legal effects of marriage upon the property of the spouses will be found, under the title "Contract of Marriage," in another part of the Civil Code, Book III., Arts. 1387-1581. The ecclesiastical powers of the bishops in France regarding dispensations of various kinds must, it is presumed, be governed by the extent of the powers conferred in the quinquennial faculties granted to them by the Pope. But it may be observed that the decrees of the Council of Trent have never been received in France, and that Pothier calls the decree of 1563, which first required the presence of the parish priest and two witnesses for the ecclesiastical regularity of marriage, "a clerical usurpation which never had any authority in France." Care should therefore be taken to ascertain that any licence which may be granted by a bishop within his ecclesiastical competence be not in conflict with the powers allowed to him and recognized in him as the minister of a "culte" acknowledged by the State. The civil officer would, in the case put by our correspondent, no doubt require the production of the bridegroom's register of birth (*not* baptism), in order to establish his being of full age. In France a man under eighteen and a woman under fifteen cannot intermarry without a dispensation from the State. A son under twenty-five, or a daughter under twenty-one, must prove the consent of their parents, or of the survivor of the parents, or, in case of difference between them, that of the father. Failing all these, the consent of a "conseil de famille" must be obtained. Even above the ages specified respectful

application for consent must 'be made to t] according to forms prescribed by authority (Arts. 144-160),

A. W. C. BAKER.—The principal translati works of Ariosto are by Sir John Harington edition, 1634), W. S. Rose (8 vols., sm. 8vo., 18 J. Hoole (6 vols., 12mo., 1807). Probably the ful critical edition of the original text (but translation) is that by Panizzi (1834), which : by memoirs of Ariosto's life and bibliographi of the editions of his works. As to the relati the various translations opinions will natur Leigh Hunt, in the preface to his *Stories from Poets*, expresses himself strongly in regard 1 them. "With all due respect," he says, "to I lators as Harington, Rose, and Wiffen, their not Ariosto and Tasso, even in manner. I the gay 'godson' of Queen Elizabeth, is not like Ariosto; but when not in good spirits 1 as dull as if her Majesty had frowned upon h was a man of wit, and a scholar, yet he has un turned the ease and animation of his original sion and insipidity.......As to Hoole, he is below It will, of course, be understood that we si Leigh Hunt's views *quantum valeant*, in orde correspondent may be placed in a position to himself which translation he is likely to prefei

A. C. S.—The ballad of *Darby and Joan* is the *Gentleman's Magazine* for March, 1735, vo and in Plumptre's *Collection of Songs, Moral* Cambridge, 1805, p. 152, with the music. ' have been attributed to Prior. It is entitle *Never Forgot*, and the first line begins, "Dear C thus beyond measure." It is in eight-line st the third stanza begins, "Old Darby with Jo side," &c.

GEO. ADAMSON.—Your note in reference to *ante*, p. 288, cannot be called a reply; moi history of the family is too well known to ne tulation in these columns. The other paper s to partake rather of the nature of an essay, and not to fall within the scope of "N. & Q."

MEDWEIG.—You seem to have missed the p query, which was simply as to the authority foi statement with regard to Sir H. Davy. A di; the reality of the "miracle" itself would be q place in our columns.

ABHBA.—*The Athenæum*, a *monthly* maga edited by Dr. John Aikin. It lasted only two a half, viz., January, 1807, to June, 1809. a copy in the London Library, St. James's : which a former possessor has written the nai various anonymous contributors.

IGNORAMUS.—Consult Lord Derby's *Hom* Smith's *Classical Dictionary*.

S. F. CRESWELL, D.D. (The High School, Du did not receive your communication till th WOODWARD had appeared. See *ante*, p. 405. be glad to hear from you further.

STEPHEN RICHARDSON.—A matter of taste.

NOTICE.

Editorial Communications should be addresse Editor of 'Notes and Queries'"—Advertiser Business Letters to "The Publisher"—at the Wellington Street, Strand, London, W.C.

We beg leave to state that we decline to re munications which, for any reason, we do not 1 to this rule we can make no exception.

LONDON, SATURDAY, JUNE 8, 1878.

CONTENTS.—N° 232.

Notes.

WHITSUNTIDE.

The origin of the word Whitsun, which has been warmly discussed in these columns,* is still an undecided question, and seems likely to remain so. It is certainly a misfortune that an expression which serves to denote one of the greatest events in the history of Christianity should remain unsatisfactorily explained. It has been suggested that we should look for its derivation in the word Pentecost, which has become in German Pfingst; but this is mere conjecture, as etymologists have been unable to show how the transition from Pentecost to Whit or to Whitsun was effected. Dr. Neale, however, in his essay on Church Festivals and their Household Words, favours this view, and says, " It is neither White Sunday (for, in truth, the colour is red), nor Huit Sunday, as the eighth after Easter, but simply by the various corruptions of the German Pfingsten, the Dansk Pintse, the various patois Pingsten, Whingsten, &c., derived from Pentecost." Some have sought for its origin in Wytsonday, i.e. Wit or Wisdom Sunday, because of the light and knowledge which were shed upon the Apostles on this day, a derivation we find suggested by a writer of the fourteenth century :—

* 2nd S. ii. 154; 3rd S. vii. 479; 4th S. xi. 437; 5th S. i. 401-403; viii. 2 (Mr. Picton's article should be consulted), 55, 134, 212, 278.

" This day Witsonday is cald,
For Wisdom and Wit seuene fold
Was gouen to the Apostles as this day."

In Yorkshire it is called Whissun-day, i.e. Wisdom-day, an appellation much used by the common people.

Others, again, have derived the term from White Sunday, in supposed allusion to the white garments of the neophytes, as Whitsunday was one of the two chief seasons for baptism. Against this view it has been argued that the newly baptized were for the most part infants, except in national or apostolical conversions. Wheatley quotes a letter from Gerard Langbain, in which he cites a passage from some MS. in the Bodleian Library, where it is said that the day is called Witsonenday or Vitsonenday, because our ancestors were in the habit of giving to the poor on that day all the milk of their ewes and kine, which was called, in some places, " the whites of kine," in others, " whitemeat." Once more, it has been asked whether we can find any festival of the White Sun to assist us in ascertaining the history of the word. " It appears," says a correspondent of " N. & Q.," " possible that a heathen but religious custom prevailed in spring of asking for a white, clear summer sun, and that Whitsun-day took its name from this observance." This, however, seems highly fanciful and improbable. As far as the arguments in favour of the other derivations are concerned, the evidence for each is very equally balanced. It is, indeed, to be hoped that etymologists and others interested in the subject will not relax their efforts to bring it to a satisfactory solution.

In Spain the day is usually called Fiesta del Espirito Santo ; in Portugal, Pascoa do Espirito Santo. In Italy it goes by the name of Pasqua Rosata, because at this season the roses are in full bloom. In Russ it is Trinity Day, probably as filling up the commemoration of the Blessed Trinity.†

Much interesting and gorgeous ritual was anciently associated with this festival. It was usual, in the Catholic times of England, to dramatize the descent of the Holy Ghost, a practice alluded to in Barnaby Googe's translation of Naogeorgus. A remnant of the old customs of Whitsuntide is retained at St. Mary Redcliffe, Bristol, which is annually strewn with rushes. The same practice was also kept up at Heybridge Church, near Maldon, Essex. Formerly at Monk Sherborne, Hampshire, the parish church was decorated with birch ; a similar custom also was followed at King's Pion, near Hereford. Whitsuntide was also the season, in bygone times, for much festivity and merriment. Our ancestors had their Whitsun Ales—meetings usually held in some barn near the church, in which feasting formed the prominent

† See Kalendar of the English Church, 1865, p. 72

feature. The ale, which had been brewed specially for the occasion, was sold by the churchwardens, and any profit that resulted from its sale was expended on the repairs of the church. Miss Baker, in her *Glossary of Northamptonshire Words* (1854, ii. 433), describes the celebration of a Whitsun Ale early in the present century, in a barn at King's Sutton, fitted up for the entertainment, in which the lord, as the principal, carried a mace made of silk, finely plaited with ribbons, and filled with spices and perfumes for such of the company to smell as desired it. Six morris dancers were among the performers.* At last, however, these gatherings occasioned so many abuses that they were put down.

The Whitsun mysteries, which were acted at Chester during Whitsun week, were costly pageants, each mystery having been set down at fifteen or twenty pounds present money. The dresses were obtained from the churches until, this practice being denounced as scandalous, the guilds had to provide the costume and other necessaries. For full information on this subject the reader should consult the *Edinburgh Essays*, 1856.

Various customs were formerly observed at this season, but the majority of these have long ago fallen into disuse.† At St. Briavels, Gloucestershire, after divine service on Whitsunday bread and cheese were distributed to the congregation; to defray the expenses every householder paid a penny. At Hinckley, in Leicestershire, a fair took place on Whitsun Monday, when the millers from various parts of the county walked in procession, with the "King of the Millers" at their head.‡ The Court of Array, or view of men and arms, was held on Whitsun Monday in the vicinity of Lichfield, Staffordshire, when every householder failing to answer his name was fined a penny. On Whitsun Tuesday, the Eton Montem, a time-honoured ceremony peculiar to Eton, was observed biennially, but latterly triennially, down to the year 1844, when it was abolished. It originally took place on the festival of St. Nicholas, the 6th of December, but was afterwards held on Whitsun Tuesday. It was a procession of the scholars to a small mound on the south side of the Bath Road, where they exacted money for salt, as the phrase was, from all persons present and from travellers passing.§

Among the customs still kept up may be mentioned the Flower Sermon which is preached on

* See *Journal of the Archæological Society*, 1852, vii· 206; also Brand's *Pop. Antiq.*, 1849, i. 276-283; and Chambers's *Book of Days*, i. 637.
† See Thiselton Dyer's *British Popular Customs*, 1876 (Bell & Sons), pp. 278-292.
‡ Nichols's *Hist. of Hinckley*, 1813, p. 678.
§ For a full account of this custom consult Lysons's *Magna Britannia*, 1813, vol. i. pt. ii. 558 : *Gent. Mag.*, 1820, xc. 55; "N. & Q.," 1st S. i. 110, 322; 2nd S. ii. 146.

Whitsun Tuesday at St. James's Church, N Court, Aldgate, from a text having special rence to flowers. On the same day, at St. Leon: Church, Shoreditch, a Botanical Sermon is livered, for which purpose funds were left Thomas Fairchild, who died in 1729. Throug' the country a good many fairs are held, and s the institution of the Bank Holiday, Whi Monday has become a general holiday. Whit tide, too, is not without its superstitions, but s will not permit us to mention more than the fol lowing one, which formerly prevailed in country : "Whatsoever one asks of God t Whitsunday morning, at the instant when sun rises and plays, God will grant it him."

THE BIBLIOGRAPHY OF ARCHERY.

(Continued from p. 384.)

Royal Kentish Bowmen, 1785.
Rules of the Society of R. K. B. [Dartford?] Augus 1789.—24mo. pp. 64. Contains a list of members to 29th Aug., 1789. M.

Robin Hood's Bowmen, 1787.
Rules and orders of the society of archers na R. H. B., instituted anno Domini 1787. Lon printed in the year 1790. 24mo. pp. 16. M.

Royal British Bowmen, 1787.
Regulations of the Society of R. B. B., establi Feb. 27th, 1787. Wrexham. 48mo. ("N. & Q.," 4 iv. 330.) (Not seen.)

John of Gaunt's Bowmen, 1788.
Rules and orders of the Society of J. of G. B., rev at Lancaster anno Domini 1788. Revised and pri 1791.—Lancaster? 16mo. pp. iv-18. M.

Loyal Archers : Lady Well Lodge, 1789.
B. M. MS. Add. 6299. 12mo. ff. 31. Ff. 7-18, Ger rules and orders of the L. A. : L. W. L., May 29, (List of members).

United Woodmen of Arden.
Present state of the Society of the U. W. of Broughton Archers, and the Lancashire Bowme Boden, printer, Stafford.—1791. 8vo. pp. 10. M.

Mercian Archers.
B. M. MS. 6299. 12mo. ff. 31. Ff. 19-31, The rul the Society of M. A., July 9, 1804 (List of members)

Grand National Archery Meetings, 1844.
Accounts of the Annual Meetings, by the Hon Secretaries for the time being, were printed annu from 1844 to 1868, and for 1870 and 1871, by Me Hargrove at York, under the direction of the (mittees. The account of the first meeting (1844) is single sheet folio, the rest are 8vo. pamphlets of fro to 24 pages each. 1 to 3—1844-1846—J. Higginson H. Peckitt, Hon. Secs. 4 to 18—1847-1861—O. L and J. C. Pigott, Hon. Secs. In 1861 the G. N Soc'ety was instituted. 19 to 28—1862-1871—O. Lu Hon. Sec.
No account of the twenty-sixth meeting, held in 1 was issued. Accounts of meetings 29-33—1872-18 are given in "The Archer's Register for 1877."

Manuscripts at the British Museum.
Harl. 135, sixteenth cent. fol., ff. 110. An answer favour of archery] to contrarie opynions militarie.

and in the handwriting of, Sir John Smythe. A reply
to A breefe discourse, &c., by Humfrey Barwick, 1590.
Lans. 160, paper, fol. Fol. 338, Minute of statutes re-
lating to archery fit to be repealed, A.D. 1610.
Arundel 359, paper, sixteenth cent. 8vo. ff. 29. Ff. 26-
29, " The order of shoting with the crosbow." A poem
in sixteen seven-line stanzas. At end, " Quod M. Beele."
Sloan 1950, paper, seventeenth cent. 4to. ff. 112.
Ff. 47-48, Notes on archery. By Nehemiah Grew.
Ends : " Take your bow in ye night & shoote at two
lights, & it will compell you to looke at your marke."
Add. 6299, 12mo. ff. 31. Rules and lists of members of
archery societies.
Add. 6314, 8vo. ff. 52. Extracts and cuttings from
newspapers relative to archery, 1727-1818.
Add. 6315, 8vo. ff. 83. Archery collections chiefly in
the handwriting of Lady S. S. Banks : arranged chrono-
logically.
Add. 6316, fol., ff. 47. Archery collections. By Lady
S. S. Banks.
Add. 6317, 4to. ff. 108. Extracts, notes, cuttings from
magazines, &c., relating to archery. By Lady S. S.
Banks.
Add. 6318, fol., ff. 88. Notes, extracts, cuttings from
books, &c., relating to archery. By Lady S. S. Banks.
Ff. 2-3, Bibliography of Archery (notes several re-
ferences to archery not given in this list).
Add. 6319, fol., ff. 21. Collections relating to archery.
By Lady S. S. Banks. Ff. 11-14, Bibliography of Archery.
Add. 6320, 24mo. size, ff. 63. Patterns of archery
ribbons (three copies bound together, ff. 1-22, 23-46, 47-
63). Issued by Thomas Waring of Bloomsbury to his
customers. The ribbons are numbered for facility in
ordering. The names of some of the wearers of the
ribbons are given.
Add. 23489, ff. 139. Arabic. Taibugha Al-Ashrafi
Ghunyat Al-Tullab Fil-Ramy Bil-Nushshab. Treatise
on archery.
Add. 28801, fol., ff. 160. Extracts, anecdotes, observations, &c., relating to archery. By Sir Samuel Rush
Meyrick.
Add. 29788, 4to. ff. 261. Collections for a history of
archery. In the handwriting of William Latham,
1787-89.
Add. 29789, 4to. ff. 158. Collections for a history of
archery. In the handwriting of William Latham,
F.A.S., 1787.
Add. 29790, fol., ff. 136. ΤΟΞΟΓΡΑΦΙΑ, or anecdotes
of archery. Mostly in the handwriting of William
Latham. Ff. 109-110, An autograph letter from W. M.
Moseley, author of An essay on Archery, Worcester,
1792, 8vo.
Add. 29791, 4to. ff. 72. Extracts from books, &c., and
anecdotes relating to archery. In the handwriting of
William Latham. Collected at the request of the Society
of Kentish Bowmen. Dated May 3, 1788.
Add. 29792, 4to. ff. 100. Extracts from books, &c.,
relative to archery. In the handwriting of William
Latham.

General List.

Toxophilus, the schole of shootinge conteyned in
two bookes. Londini. In ædibus Edouardi Whyt-
church,...1545.—24 sheets, 4to. ff. viii-50-38. The folioing
is erratic ; between sheets S and T the numbers 23-26 are
omitted, the leaves of sheets T, U, X, Y, are thus ante-
numbered by four, the last leaf shows as f. 42. The
dedication is signed Roger Ascham. (See the Retrospec-
tive Review, London, 1821, vol. iv. pp. 76-87.) M. has
two imperfect copies.
Toxophilus, the schole, or partition of shooting contayned in ij. bookes, written by Roger Ascham, 1544.
And now newlye perused...Anno 1571. Imprinted at

London in Fleet Streate neare to Saint Dunstones Church
by Thomas Marshe. 4to. ff. iv-63. Black-letter. M.
Toxophilus : the schoole, or partitions of shooting
contayned in two bookes, written by Roger Ascham, and
now newly perused....At London, printed by Abell Jeffes
[dwelling in Phillip Lane, at the signe of the Bell] by
the consent of H. Marsh. Anno 1589. 4to. ff. iv-63. M.
23rd(?) June, 1591. Thomas Orwyn. Granted unto
him by the consent of Edward Marshe, theis copies
insuinge, which did belonge to Thomas Marshe, deceased,
viz.,...in English...in folio....Schoole of Shootinge....
(T. S. R., ii. bookes.
The English works of Roger Ascham....With notes
and observations and the author's life. By James
Bennet....London, printed for R. and J. Dodsley,...1761.
4to. pp. x-xvi-396. Pp. 51-186, Toxophilus. M.
Reissued without date.
Toxophilus, the schole, or partitions of shooting.
Contayned in II. bookes. Written by Roger Ascham,
1544....To which is added a dedication and preface by...
John Walters....Wrexham, reprinted by R. Marsh, 1788.
12mo. pp. xxiv-230. M.
The English works of Roger Ascham....London, printed
[by S. Hamilton, Weybridge, Surrey] for White, Coch-
rane & Co.,...1815. 8vo. pp. ii-xxviii-392. Pp. 47-174,
Toxophilus. M.
Reissued with extra leaf (half title) and different
paging.
Reissued without date.
Toxophilus, the schole, or partitions, of shooting....By
Roger Ascham....Dedication and preface by...John
Walters....Wrexham, reprinted by J. Painter, 1821.
8vo. pp. xxii-232. M.
The whole works of Roger Ascham. Edited by J. A.
Giles. London, J. R. Smith, 1864-5. 4 vols. 8vo. M.
—Toxophilus is a part of vol. ii. It is separately paged,
vi-168. Vols. of a " Library of old authors."
Toxophilus also issued alone.
English reprints. Roger Ascham. Toxophilus, 1545.
Carefully edited by Edward Arber....London, Alex.
Murray & Son,...1 July, 1868. One shilling. 8vo.
pp. 168. M.
23rd August, 1577. Richard Jones. Receaued of him
for his licence to imprinte A merye reioisinge historie of
the notable feastes of Archerye of the highe and mightie
prince William Duke of Shordiche....iiijd and a copie.
(T. S. R., ii. 318.)
19th August, 1579. Edward White. Receyued of him
for printinge ij ballates, ye one of Ye skratchinge of ye
wytche, ye other of Ye Renovacon of Archery, by prince
Arthure and his companions, viijd. (T. S. R., ii. 358.)
Positions wherin those primitive circumstances be
examined, which are necessarie for the training up of
children, either for skill in their booke, or health in their
bodie. Written by Richard Mulcaster....Imprinted at
London by Thomas Vautrollier,...1581. 4to. Pp. 100-
102, chapter 26, Of Shooting. M.
25th Sept., 1581. Richard Jones. Lycenced unto him
under th[e] [h]andes of the wardens, A joyfull songe of
the worthie shootinge in London the XIXth of September, 1581....iiijd. (T. S. R., ii. 401.)
The auncient order, societie, and unitie laudable, of
Prince Arthure, and his knightly armory of the round
table. With a threefold assertion frendly in favour and
furtherance of English archery at this day. Translated
and collected by R[ichard] R[obinson]....London, imprinted by [R. I. for] John Wolfe dwelling in Distaffe
Lane neere the signe of the Castle, 1583. 4to. 53 leaves.
Black-letter.—The dedication is signed. On leaves 4, 5,
is "A praise of the bowe and commendation of this
booke, written by Thomas Churchyard, gent.," in
verse. The threefold assertion occupies the last 14

leaves. I 3 b—K 3 b, The first assertion and is sacred historicall. K 3 b—L 3 b, The second assertion and ys prophane hystoricall. L 3 b—M 4 b, The thirde assertion Englishe hystoricall. M.

A remembrance of the worthy show and shooting by the Duke of Shoreditch and his associates the worshipful citizens of London upon Tuesday the 17th of September, 1583. Set forth according to the truth thereof to the everlasting honour of the game of shooting in the long bow. By W. M.—I have not seen this. It was reprinted in the Bowman's Glory, by W. Wood, Lond., 1682, pp. 33-80; in the Monthly Register, London, 1792-93; and in the English Bowman, by T. Roberts, Lond., 1801, pp. 253-284.

The discoverie of witchcraft...by Reginald Scot.... 1584.—Imprinted at London by William Brome. 4to. Book 3, chap. xv. p. 65, "A skilful archer punished by an unskilfull justice." At Malling in Kent an archer was "severelie punished" by "one of Q. Maries justices," ..." to the great encouragement of archers and to the wise example of justice; but speciallie to the overthrowe of witchcraft,"...." bicause he shot so neere the white [i.e. centre] at buts." M.

A new Yorkshyre song, intituled:—
  Yorke, Yorke, for my monie.
[22 eight-line stanzas, with a four-line chorus.] From Yorke by W. E[lderton]. Imprinted at London by Richard Jones: dwelling neere Holburne Bridge, 1584. Broadside, folio. (M., Rox. I. i.; T. S. R., ii. 416; also cf. iv. 80, 493, 514; reprinted in Thomas Evans's Old Ballads and in Joseph Ritson's Yorkshire Garland.)

F. W. F.

(*To be continued.*).

SHAKSPEARIANA.

Touchstone's "Feature" ("As You Like It," Act iii. sc. 3, l. 3).—When the late famous Dr. Stokes, of Dublin, saw a vulgar brute of a countryman of his bring over a beautiful rich English bride, he was wont to explain the anomaly, says Prof. Mahaffy, by declaring that "the Saxon beast has no power of analysis." It seems that the same poor animal has no power either of seeing a joke of Shakspere's until an Irishman explains it to him. In As You Like It, Act iii. sc. 3, l. 3, Touchstone says to Audrey, "Doth my simple feature content you?" On which the latest and most careful editor, Mr. W. Aldis Wright, comments: "There is possibly some joke intended here, the key to which is lost" (p. 140, Clar. Press ed.). And, as far as I know, none of us English fellow-dullards of Mr. Wright, living or dead, ever did see what the joke was, till Mr. W. Wilkins, an undergraduate of Trinity College, Dublin, told us at the New Shakspere Society some months ago. He said that feature here meant "composition," the early English "making," even the "verses," of which Touchstone complains in l. 9 that "when a man's verses cannot be understood ... it strikes a man more than a great reckoning in a little room." This meaning at once accounts for Touchstone's "most capricious poet," &c., and is as plainly right as anything can be. (Shakspere's occasional going back to the original meaning of words is as well known as his love of wo As I find that Mr. Wilkins's happy exp of this joke has not reached even all the of young folk who are preparing *As You* for the nearing examination, one may as w it more public, together with the neares *feature*, by Ben Jonson, that I have been find—in the Prologue to his play of the F(

"In all his poems still hath been this measure,
  To mix profit with your pleasure;
And not as some, whose throats their envy fa
Cry hoarsely, 'All he writes is railing':
  And when his plays come forth, think they
  them,
With saying, he was a year about them.
To this there needs no lie, but this his creatu
Which was two months since no *feature:*
And though he dares give them five lives to n
'Tis known, five weeks fully penn'd it,
From his own hand, without a co-adjutor,
Novice, journey-man, or tutor."

Now, though the contrast may be betw *creature* or creation, the fully-shaped pl *feature* in its known sense of the vague s form, the magical appearance, or phanton by art, which did not exist even in Jonson yet the use of the word in connexion ' dra-ma, po-em, mak-ing, shape shaped shaper's hands (A.-S. *scóp*, maker, poet), d Touchstone's under meaning of his *feature*.

F. J. Furni

"Macbeth," Act i. sc. 2, l. 3.—
  "*Mal*[*colm*]. This is the Serjean
  Who like a geed and hardie Souldier foug
  'Gainst my Captiuitie."

Yet this "Serjeant" is called, in the folic personages who enter on the scene, "A 1 Captaine," and, according to the same aut his three speeches are spoken by a "Cap The Cambridge editors, Dyce, and others, n apparent inconsistency, alter all the "capt: "sergeants." I venture, however, to maint: the folios are right, that there is no incons and that the modern change destroys the tional and visible proof that Shakespeare p Macbeth's then loyalty to his cousin Dunc enhancing his after fall through the devili gestions of the witches.

It is quite clear from Malcolm's words had previously told his royal father the s his danger and his rescue. And he now known to his father that the wounded m: meeting them is the sergeant who rescue But Malcolm is a generous youth, as is suff shown by what he at once exclaims, and subsequent "Hail, brave friend." Nor wa beth other at this time than a loyal kinsn subject, and the king's general. For the therefore, of the heir to the throne the serg speak after the language of our day, wa moted for distinguished valour in the fiel

promoted by a death vacancy and made a captain. Hence the spectators seeing the quondam sergeant now wearing the insignia of his new rank—and the readers—grasp at the outset these facts: that Macbeth is a loyal soldier ; Malcolm, who at the close is crowned king, a generous young prince and hopeful heir ; and lastly are prepared for diction too poetic and ambitious to come from an ordinary "ranker," but which is not out of place in one so valiant in fight.   B. NICHOLSON.

"KING LEAR," ACT III. SC. 4, L. 77.—
    "'Twas this flesh begot
    Those pelican daughters."

Dr. Johnson has thought it necessary to annotate this passage by telling us that " the young pelican is fabled to suck the mother's blood." Where is such a fable to be found? The attitude of the pelican, pressing her red-tipped bill against her breast, for the purpose of squeezing out the contents of her pouch, has given rise to the fable of her drawing blood from her own breast to feed her young; but the mother's "piety," as the heralds call it, reflects no discredit on her offspring. The strongest imputation I have met with upon pelican daughters, to lay them open to Lear's invidious comparison with his own, is in Bartholomew Glanville, De Proprietatibus Rerum. In bk. xii. ch. xxix. he states, on the authority of Jacobus de Vitriaco (De Mirabilibus Orientalium Regionum), that

"in Egypt is a byrde that hyght Pellicanus, a byrde with greate wynges and moost leane.......Whan the mother passeth oute of the neste to gette meate, the serpente clymeth on the tree and styngeth & infecteth the byrdes. And whan the mother commethe agayne, she maketh sorowe three dayes for her byrdes, as it is sayde. Than, he saythe, she smyteth her selfe in the breste, and springeth bloudde vpon them, and rereth theym fro deathe to lyfe, and then for great bledynge the mother wexeth feble, and the byrdes bene compelled to passe out of the neste to gette them selfe meate. And some of them for kynde loue fede the mother that is feble: and some ben vnkynde and care not for the mother, and the mother taketh good hede therto, and whan she cometh to her strengthe, she nourysheth and loueth those byrdes that fedde her in her nede, and putteth away her other birdes, as vnworthy and vnkynde, and suffreth them not to dwelle nor lyue with hir."

After all, then, there are Cordelias, as well as Gonerils and Regans, among the pelican daughters, and their reputation has suffered from Lear's too hasty generalization. It is remarkable that Shakespeare has again in Richard II. (Act ii. sc. 1, l. 126) charged the bird with murderous propensities, though in Hamlet (Act iv. sc. 5, l. 142) he calls it " the kind life-rendering pelican."
                    JOHN FITCHETT MARSH.

MEXICO: MOSARABIC SERVICE.—The following, from the Echo, May 29, 1878, seems worthy of note and preservation :—

" According to Dr. Riley, a bishop of the Protestant Episcopal Church in America, the Pope is being wounded even more severely in Mexico than in Germany and Switzerland. Dr. Riley, who has lately been visiting Mexico in the interests of Christian unity, gives a wonderful report of the exceeding rapid and decisive development of an Old Catholic revolt in the bosom of the Mexican Church. Seventy-one congregations have recently declared, by an unanimous vote, their definitive separation from Rome, and their return to a purer, more primitive, and more national form of Catholicism. They have secured for themselves the legal possession of some of the handsomest churches in Mexico, and have already placed themselves in communication with the Old Catholics of Europe. The movement appears to have originated in national as much as in religious causes. They declare that they wish to recover the spirit of nationality and patriotism which was once so strong in the Church. They have already abolished the Roman Mass and make use of the ancient Spanish Mass, so well known to liturgical scholars as the Mozarabic, which dates from the earlier Christian centuries."

What would St. Leander, St. Isidore, or St. Hildefonso—what would C. Archbishop Lorenzana—what would that other cardinal, the great Ximenes himself—think of such a movement, for such a purpose, accompanied with such an old-world spirit, and to be accomplished by such means?

What would St. Ambrose think, to say nothing of the Cardinals Borromeo, if North Italy were to revolt from under the Vatican, and, adopting the same line of action, were to assume the use of Milan for its rite, so far as it could possibly extend? What if the Two Sicilies, on the same principle, were to assert their independence of Rome by reinaugurating, if I may use the expression, and generalizing the rites of the king's chapel in Naples and those of Palermo and Sicily proper—leaving to Rome herself, if she chose to adopt it, the venerable old service of the Lateran—their ancient monastic and collegiate use?
                    W. J. BLEW.

GEORGE CRUIKSHANK.—In April, 1863, I remember seeing an exhibition at Exeter Hall of a very large collection of the etchings and engravings of this celebrated artist, to the best of my recollection more than three thousand in number, and certainly the most complete that had ever been got together, or in all probability ever will be.

It has often occurred to me that it would be worth the attention of some book collectors or librarians to endeavour to form as complete a collection as could be amassed of the books illustrated with the productions of this clever and industrious artist, and which have the effect of making their readers more fully appreciate the text. Perhaps an entire one could not be formed, and even a moderate one would embrace some hundreds of volumes. The Waverley Novels, Roscoe's Modern Novelists, most of W. Harrison Ainsworth's novels, The Ingoldsby Legends, The Comic Almanacs, Cruikshank's Omnibus, Max-

Well's *History of the Irish Rebellion in 1798*, may, for example, be instanced, and many other 'books in addition will suggest themselves. How much more sensible than merely collecting the illustrations alone! And, it may be added, how often, in order to obtain them, has a copy of the book which they enriched been rendered imperfect by having had engravings abstracted! To use the language of John Hill Burton, in *The Book-Hunter*,

"The Illustrator is the very Ishmaelite of collectors; his hand is against every man, and every man's hand is against him. He destroys unknown quantities of books to supply portraits or other illustrations to a single volume of his own; and as it is not always known concerning any book that he has been at work on it, many a common book-buyer has cursed him on inspecting his own last bargain and finding that it is deficient in an interesting portrait or two. Tales there are fitted to make the blood run cold in the veins of the most sanguine book-hunter about the devastations committed by those who are given over to this special pursuit."—Pp. 80-81.

JOHN PICKFORD, M.A.
Newbourne Rectory, Woodbridge.

MILES CORBET.—In the north aisle of the church of St. Mary and St. Margaret, Sprowston, co. Norfolk, is a monument, with kneeling figure and effaced inscription, to the memory of Miles Corbet (second son of Sir Thomas Corbet, who was knighted by Charles I. at Royston), one of the judges who sat at the trial and signed the death warrant of the king. This Miles Corbet, at the time of the Long Parliament in 1642, was one of the registrars in Chancery, and chairman of the Committee for Scandalous Ministers. He is said also to have been Chief Baron of the Exchequer. At the time of the Restoration he fled to Holland, and having been seized by Downing, the king's envoy, and brought to England in 1661, he was afterwards executed as a traitor.

WALTER P. HIGH.
Norwich.

TEA was taxed at 8d. the lb. in 1660. On Sept. 25, 1661, Pepys drank his first "cup of tea, a Chinese drink." It was sold first in "drink, and in leaf from 16s. to 60s. the lb.," in the reign of Charles II. by one Thomas Garraway at Garraway's, in Exchange Alley, being first sweetened with sugar candy. He says that till 1651 it had been sold from 6l. to 10l. the lb. weight, and therefore only used as a regalia in high entertainments or given as a present to princes and grandees. Catherine of Braganza and Boutelloc, a Dutch physician, 1678, rendered it fashionable. Came either from Portugal or Holland. In 1794 there were at least 30,000 tea-dealers in Great Britain. In 1786 16,000 lbs. of tea were annually consumed in England. A writer in 1797 says that his father told him that tea was introduced into England by Christopher Bur-roughes. The *Kingdom's Intelligencer*, 1662, announces the sale of " tea or chaa according to

its goodness" at the coffee-house in E; Alley. In 1665 a gallant is described as for tea. It was often pronounced *tay*. Th Kenelm Digby's " receites," 1669, inform Mr. Waller adopted the Chinese fashion of tea with eggs. A century ago a Cumberla: served up a dish of tea with butter and In the time of William of Orange it was sol the lb. Lord Clarendon, in his diary fo: says that he and le Père Couplet had t€ supper. The tea was boiled with the wat kettle. Tea at length replaced bevers as a MACKENZIE E. C. WAL

HOGARTH.—In the ordinary books Hogarth I observe no mention made of which forms the frontispiece to a pamphlet *An Address of Thanks to the Broad Bottom* which," as the title-page goes on to say, " fixed a curious emblematic Frontispiece, from an original painting of the ingeniou H****th." The date is 1745. The plate scribed above " Broad Bottoms," and bel« the words:—

" Believing, we lifted ye up among the Mighty,
Yet our Drivers have ye join'd, increasing our

PENZA

[The print is not by Hogarth; see *Catal«Satirical Prints in the British Museum*, No. 2621.

" BANDANA " POCKET-HANDKERCHIEFS.
George Birdwood, in p. 80 of his elaborate . *book to the British Indian Section of the Exhibition*, observes that " We must w: Colonel Yule to give us the etymology of *Ba* pocket-handkerchiefs." The sledge-hammer learned and gallant colonel is scarcely wai crack so small a nut; for the word app« come from *bandh, bundh, bandhan*, in most dialects derived from the Sanscrit, and sig1 binding, confining, tying, a use to whic article is commonly put. See Wilson's *G of Indian Terms*. T

[We must request correspondents desiring infoi on family matters of only private interest, to affi names and addresses to their queries, in order tl answers may be addressed to them direct.]

ELECTORAL FACTS.—Can any one tell me I can find accurate information regarding tl didates, successful as well as unsuccessful, a polls taken at parliamentary elections held the union with Ireland and the meeting first Imperial Parliament in 1801? I am tol since the Reform Act of 1832 these statistic been published from time to time in parliam returns, but I have not been able to tra« such returns among the series of parliame papers and blue-books sent out to this country. I know that a republication of Dod's annual volume in 1853, under the title of *Electoral Facts*, contained much information on this subject ; but this volume is, I find, in places not very accurate as to names and dates.

I am also anxious to ascertain whether the journals of the House of Commons were published before 1832 in such a form as would enable an inquirer to ascertain readily what writs were issued for new elections, on the occurrence of vacancies in the representation between general elections, and the names of members so returned. The later volumes of Hansard state these facts very precisely, and though the earlier volumes do not contain any abstract of these facts, they can be easily extracted from the body of the work ; but for the period before the existence of Hansard the journals of the House supply, I suppose, the only source of information.

FREDERIC LARPENT.
Lahore.

[Has our correspondent consulted Oldfield's *Representative History*, 6 vols., which will give him the information he desires down to 1816 ? The general indexes to the journals of the House of Commons will give him a reference to all writs issued for new elections on vacancies.]

EXELBY FAMILY.—This old Yorkshire family is apparently descended from Whyomar, a Breton, who accompanied his feudal lord, Count Alan of Brittany, afterwards first Earl of Richmond, to England at the Conquest. This Whyomar was dapifer or steward to the earl, and one of his chief under lords. He had large estates granted to him in Richmondshire, including the lordship of Aske ; and the position of dapifer to the earls remained in his family for several generations. His son Warner had two sons : Conan de Aske, from whom descended the family of Aske of Aske, whose pedigree is given in Whitaker's *Richmondshire*; and Wimar, or Wymar, de Eskelby, from whom, through his granddaughter* and

* Whyomar, Lord of Aske, &c., dapifer to Alan, Earl of Richmond, A.D. 1070.

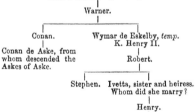

```
                        Warner.
          ┌───────────────────┴───────────────────┐
        Conan.                          Wymar de Eskelby, temp.
          │                                  K. Henry II.
  Conan de Aske, from                            │
  whom descended the                         Robert.
  Askes of Aske.                                 │
                              ┌──────────────────┴──────────────────┐
                           Stephen.        Ivetta, sister and heiress.
                                           Whom did she marry ?
                                                 │
                                              Henry.
                                                 │
                                      Alan de Eskelby, A.D. 1277,
                                      from whom descended the
                                      family of Exelby.
```

heiress Ivetta, descended the family of Exelby, which, for a long period, held considerable property in Yorkshire. I have been unable to discover the name of the husband of this Ivetta, although it seems probable that it is somewhere recorded, in consequence of the feudal custom under which, in the cases of heiresses, the Crown had the disposal of their hands or received a fine in lieu. Some interesting particulars of this family are given by the late Mr. J. R. Walbran in *Memorials of Fountains Abbey* (Surtees Society). Can any of your readers refer me to further information of any kind, or say if there is any pedigree of this family extant ? Their arms were Argent, a chevron gules within a bordure sable bezantee, but I have been unable to find the crest. Can any of your readers give it ?   BEDALE.

THE RIGHT TO SEARCH THE PUBLIC RECORDS.— Some time since legal proceedings were taken to try the right of individuals to search the public records at the Rolls House. The attempt to establish such right failed, I believe ; but, strange to say, I cannot trace a report of the case in any of the legal journals. The subject is one of great interest, especially to students of "N. & Q.," and I should be obliged by a reference to any full report of the case.   P. R. R.

"PLOTINUS," ed. princeps Ficini, Florence, 1492, red morocco, a fine copy.—The above has on cover, inside, the royal arms, and bearing the label of apparently the Duke of Sussex, and underneath is the motto, "Si Deus pro nobis quis contra nos?" I shall be much obliged if any reader can say to whom it probably formerly belonged.   H. H.

"COMPARISONS ARE ODIOUS."—Who will give me an earlier use than this ?—" *Comparationes* vero, *Princeps*, ut te aliquando dixisse recolo, *odiosœ reputantur*" (Fortescue, *De Laudibus Legum Angliœ*, fol. 42, ed. 1616). The prince was the son of Henry VI. Fortescue was about to compare the Common and Civil Laws. Cf. *Much Ado*, Act iii. sc. 5, l. 18.   WALTER D. STONE.

PETRARCH AND BYRON.—In the highly interesting sketch of Petrarch by Mr. Henry Reeve, one of the volumes of "Foreign Classics for English Readers," at p. 76 is the translation of an extract from Petrarch's *Africa*, the subject being "The Death of Mago," the Carthaginian. The translation is ascribed to Lord Byron. Tolerably familiar with his works, the "Death of Mago" is a piece I never before heard of. It is certainly not Byron at his best, though it might have appeared in *Hours of Idleness*, or even amongst *Occasional Pieces*; but I fail to find it in either. The indexes to Mr. Murray's editions are excellent, but I find no reference to any such verses under either of the letters P (Petrarch), or M (Mago), or C (Cartha-

gmuau), ... ⅅ \ᴅeath of). Will any reader of "N. & Q." inform me in what collection of Byron's works the piece referred to can be found, or on what authority it is ascribed to Byron?
GEO. JULIAN HARNEY.
Boston, U.S.

THE LAW OF GRAVITATION.—In *Supernatural Religion*, second ed., ii. 54, the following passage is quoted (*inter alia*) from Trench's *Notes on Miracles*, p. 292:—

"In regard to this very law of gravitation, a feeble, and for the most part unconsciously possessed, remnant of his power survives to man in *the well-attested fact that his body is lighter when he is awake than sleeping;* a fact which every nurse who has carried a child can attest. From this we conclude that the human consciousness, as an inner centre, works as an opposing force to the attraction of the earth and the centripetal force of gravity, however unable now to overbear it."

Has the fact expressed in the words italicized been "well attested" by some authority more likely to be exact than a nurse? And if so, what is the scientific explanation of the difference?
FREDERIC WAGSTAFF.

THE REBELLIONS OF 1715 AND 1745.—In the Scotch troubles of 1715 or 1745 a young lady, named Debby Carnegie, waylaid and killed a trooper who was carrying an order for the execution of her lover or father. Where can I obtain the particulars?   H. B. HYDE.
34, Oxford Gardens, W.

"PEACE AT ANY PRICE."—Is the following the origin of this familiar phrase, or is there an earlier instance of its use?—

"Paris, May 14, 1848.......The bourgeoisie are eager for war.......Lamartine having proclaimed, 'Paix à tout prix,' is therefore thought an obstacle."—A. H. Clough's *Letters and Remains*, p. p., Lond., 1865, p. 105.
ED. MARSHALL.
Sandford St. Martin.

BACKWELL CHURCH, SOMERSETSHIRE.—In this church there is an ancient chapel, and on the north side of the chancel is an ancient tomb, on which lies the effigy in stone of one of the Rodney family, whose burial-place was in the chapel. On this tomb on a scroll is the following inscription:—

"Within this Chapel lieth Elizabeth the first founderys of this Chapel, and of the floke of shepe to the quarter tymes lat......Knight, and before that wyff to Sir Walter Rodney, Knight, and syster to Sʳ Wylliam Comptor, Knight, which Elizabeth departed the......in the yere of grace MCCCCCXXXVI."

The two hiatus in the inscription I can supply from other sources, as Elizabeth Comptor was first the wife of Sir John Chaworth, and died on June 3, 1536; but I should be glad to have an explanation of the "fioke of shepe to the quarter tymes." My own idea is that "floke" is not a flock, a collection of sheep, but means wool, as when we say a flock bed, a bed stuffed with wool, and that the inscrip-

tion probably refers to a payt ... the ember weeks, or four s(fasting. Probably the will of was proved in London short June 3, 1536, and an inspec petent person would throw inscription.
Clifton.

ENGLISH VERSIONS OF THE any one kindly say where ... Iræ" may be found? The ˑ hymn-book is Isaac Willia Slater's may be found, and wl mentioned in 3ʳᵈ S. xii. 482.
C. F. S
Farnborough, Banbury.

THE OPERA.—In a letter Newport to her brother Sir Dec. 14, 1658, and calendare MSS. Commission, vol. v. p. passage occurs: "It is thou speedily go down; the Godlʸ discontented with it." What mentioned—not, I imagine, w stand by the word?

MISS E. BERRIE is author a farce in one act, adapted fr(*Nearer and Dearer.* It was p Cross Theatre, April 1870, vol. lxxxix. of Lacy's *Play* "Ernie Berrie" is a *nom de p* real name of the authoress? ⸀ entitled *Little Fibs*, was pⅰ Cross Theatre in Sept., 1869, ⸴ the same lady, having the titlⅇ performed at the Amphitheat 1874.

CHARLES FLEMING.—Abου a French translation of Shaksⲣ Charles Fleming was publis⅃ Charles Fleming (a native of ⅼ years Professor of the Englis Polytechnic School, Paris. Ⅰ the French metropolis?

"VIEWY."—This is a word paper—and no one else, so far fond of. I can find it in no ⸀ invention of the *Spectator*, an it mean? It appears to have about it, like plausible or suⲣ but I cannot quite translate it

THE PASSING OF THE Rⴸ correct in believing that Ea Howick, is the only survivor o of both Houses of Parliam appear in Samuel Reynolds's

Walker, of the Reform Bill receiving the royal assent in 1832? Earl Russell, if I am right, was the last survivor but one. The engraving is in a shop window in St. James's Street.

WM. THORNELY.

"IF THE COACH GOES AT SIX, PRAY WHAT TIME GOES THE BASKET?" is a line from a song popular some fifty years ago. Some one, I think Hood, published a humorous engraving, of which this is the motto. Where shall I find the song at length?

K. P. D. E.

GERARD FAMILY.—"Sir Thomas Gerard, the first baronet, was living at Higlecar(?). He succeeded his father, Sir Thomas Gerard, Knt., in Sept., 1601." I shall be glad if any one can inform me where Highlecar (?) is ; also, who was the widow "Annie" (Gerard ?) who resided there in 1590.

W. L. J.

[Highclere, Hants?]

FRANCIS SMITH, THE BOOKSELLER, OF CORNHILL, who had figured in other prosecutions, was proceeded against in the year 1681 or thereabouts, by information, for publishing on October 1, 1681, an alleged seditious libel on the king intituled *A Raree Show*, accompanied by an engraving. The passage complained of commenced thus, " That monstrous foul Beast, with a Hey, with a Hey, has houses twain in 's chest with a Ho." Where can I find a copy of this publication—a broadside, I presume?

W. H. HART, F.S.A.

Gravesend.

AUTHORS OF BOOKS WANTED.—

Oxford and Cambridge Nuts to Crack. Second edition, corrected and enlarged. London, A. H. Baily & Co., 83, Cornhill, MDCCCXXXV. 12mo. pp. 270.

Reminiscences of Thought and Feeling. By the Author of *Visiting my Relations*. London, William Pickering, 1852. 12mo. pp. 290.—Appended to the preface are the initials M. A. K.

Papers on Preaching and Public Speaking. By a Wykehamist. London, Bell & Daldy, 186, Fleet Street, 1861. 12mo. pp. 268.

JOHN PICKFORD, M.A.

A Statement regarding the New Lanark Establishment. Edinburgh, 1812. 8vo.

The Gaol of the City of Bristol compared with what a Gaol ought to be. Bristol and London, 1815. 8vo.

Rationale of Justification by Faith. By a Layman. Second edition. London, 1859. 8vo.

ABHBA.

Replies.

BOWING TO THE ALTAR.

(5th S. ix. 189.)

Though I have occasionally seen an educated person bow to the altar on entering and leaving a (Protestant) church—such person being a member of the Church of England—yet I have repeatedly seen, and still do see, nearly every Sunday, among a rustic congregation, an act of reverence or re-

spect that might very easily be taken for " bowing to the altar." For many years I looked upon it in that light, and considered it to be the lingering relic of an old custom. But after awhile, by closely watching this custom for myself, and getting others to attend to it for me, I came to the conclusion that it was bowing to the clergyman, and not to the altar. This opinion I still hold after twenty-seven years' experience of the matter in small country churches in Huntingdonshire and Rutland, where, among other old customs, the women and men sit apart in places specially reserved for them by their own traditional habits. It is plain that the bowing is to the parson, and not to the altar, because it is only done by some late comer. It is chiefly the old men who do this, though I have occasionally seen boys do it. I cannot remember seeing a woman do it. If the man comes into church after the service has commenced, he makes a slight pause at the end of the nave—on his way to the men's seats in the north transept—and respectfully turns towards the east and pulls his forelock. This might easily be taken, at first acquaintance, for bowing to the altar, but it is really a mark of respect for the clergyman in the reading desk, or a token of humble apology for coming in late. I saw this done only on Sunday, March 10 last, and it is an act of very common occurrence. Twelve years ago, I remember an old-fashioned farmer in a small Huntingdonshire church, who, by virtue of possessing the glebe farm, had a seat in the chancel. When the old man came late into church, and hobbled up the nave with difficulty, he used to reserve his bow until he came close to the reading desk, when he pulled his forelock and made a deep obeisance. But this was to the rector, and not to the communion table, a few feet in front of him, although some of the rector's town visitors, who were not accustomed to these rural habits, were disposed to put down this old farmer as a very advanced Ritualist, who made a practice of bowing to the altar. I never saw this done on leaving church, which is a further proof that the bowing was to the person, as a token of respect and apology for coming late. I do not say, however, that it may not be a modern rustic relic of the more ancient custom of bowing to the altar.

CUTHBERT BEDE.

The traditional reverence towards the east or altar, that is, in honour of God (Bishop Morton [Collier, pt. ii. bk. ix. p. 94] ; Hall's *Satires*, bk. v. sat. iii. 20 ; Herbert's *Priest to the Temple*, ch. viii.), at entering the choir in various cathedrals in the seventeenth and eighteenth centuries, will be found illustrated in my *Traditions and Customs of Cathedrals*, sect. iv. pp. 135-7, second edition, published by Longmans. Hammond mentions bowing to the east on entering a

the Puritans objected to the "bowing towards the
altar or towards the east many times with three
congees, but usually in every motion access and
recess in the church" (Cardw., *Conf*, 272). Bishop
Williams, 1641, speaks of clergy who "make three
courtesies towards the communion table, and en-
join the people at their coming into the church to
bow towards the east or towards the communion
table" (*Comm. on Ritual*, app., 552). At Windsor
and Oxford I believe a trace of the custom still
remains. It is a relic of the ancient "ante et
retro facere sive inclinare," as at St. Paul's in
1518. "Residentes ingressi chorum ad orientem
in ipso chori medio primum Deo reverenter in-
clinent" (*Registrum S. Pauli*, p. 237, ed. W.
Sparrow Simpson). At the installation of Knights
of the Garter, in the present century, this "reverence and obeisance" to God was paid in solemn
form. It was ordered by the canons of 1640
(Wilkins, *Conc.*, iv. 550). The statutes of Canterbury, c. 34, require all "in ingressu chori Divinam
majestatem devota mente adorantes humiliter se
.nclinare versus altare," according to the ancient
statutes of certain churches.

MACKENZIE E. C. WALCOTT.

"N. & Q.," 1st S. vi. 182 : St. vi. and ix. of
Statutes of St. Patrick's Cathedral, Dubl., 1692,
an extract from Mason's *Hist. of St. Patr. Cath.*,
p. 92. *Constitutions and Canons Eccl. of Canterb.*
and York, 1640, Can. viii., and "Declaration concerning some Rites and Ceremonies," in Sparrow's
Collection, p. 361, ed. Lond., 1684. Abp. Bram-
hall, *Discourse of the Sabbath and Lord's Day*
(first publ. in 1676), vol. v. p. 77, ed. A. C. L., Oxf.,
1845, where there is reference in the notes to
Mede's "Disc. of the Altar," in *Works*, pp. 486-99,
and "On Ps. cxxxii. 7," and to the Dublin statutes,
as above, and to Bingham. Compare, for the
general subject, Jer. Taylor, "Of the Reverence due
to the Altar," in vol. v. of Eden's edition of *Works*.

ED. MARSHALL.

Sandford St. Martin.

See a sermon preached at the opening of the
new chapel at Cornhill-upon-Tweed, 1752, by
Thos. Sharp, D.D., Archdeacon of Northumberland and Prebendary of Durham :—

"If it be asked if there be any piety or religion in
bowing towards the altar, or at the Name of Jesus, or in
turning sometimes to the east at the repetition of the
creeds, &c., which are customs received from the undated usage of the Christian Church, I answer, they are
only points of order and decency; but still they do *so*
accompany religion, and they do *so* suit it that we know
not how they can be well separated from it."—P. 17.

See also *Decency and Order recommended in Three
Discourses preached in Hereford Cathedral*, by
Thos. Bisse, D.D., 1723, pp. 72-80. See also
Hierurgia Anglicana, 1848, Contents.

E. H. A.

The origin of this, as of most
ecclesiastical customs, must, I im
for in pre-Reformation usage.
may observe, has no sacred archæ
than it has a sacred art or—excep
—a theology. The Catholic bows
and the Anglican follows his pr
this difference—that the Catholic
altar, but the presence of God whi
be thereon ; whereas the Anglica
times an altar on which the Sacra
only for a few minutes each day, '
quarter.

As F. W. L. dates from Oxfor
to end these remarks with a qu
Church there is a custom for
leaving the cathedral to turn rou
wards the altar. The chaplains a
perform the same ceremony, and I
ask, Is this bow on the part of the
ence to the altar, or is it merely a
tion to the chaplain before he tu
choir vestry, in the same way as
cellor bows to the University pre
latter ascends the pulpit ?

EDWARD H

The Temple.

Bingham in his *Christian Antiq*
chap. x.) says that in all probal
primitive practice, and there certai
reason to doubt it. It was eviden
given up in England at the Refo
1640 it was recommended in on
formed by Archbishop Laud. C
Durham, was charged by the Purit
ing in a custom of "cringeing anc
altar." There is an article on t
Brand's *Popular Antiquities*, in
tions a book called *Altar Worship*,
*Communion Table, considered by 2
buter, but proved Enemy to the I*
Bishop Jeremy Taylor also recomn
The custom has not yet died out.
about twenty years ago, numerous
given of the custom in remote co
In Christ Church Cathedral the d
on entering or leaving the choir,
round and bow to the altar. This
done at Westminster, and, I hav
many other cathedrals and chu
exists in a corrupted form; fi
Durham the clergy bow to one anc
the choir, or they did some yea
also done at St. John's College,
Fellows and Scholars. In 1843,
communion table was sanctioned
Anglican bishops, and the High C
reintroducing this primitive ci
churches.

Oxford.

The custom of bowing on entering church (curt-sying by women) was common among old people when I was curate at Ormskirk, some thirty years ago. Two old women regularly curtsied before entering their seats in this church (Springthorpe) when I came here fifteen years ago.

E. LEATON BLENKINSOPP.

A good deal of information and discussion with respect to this custom, as existing now and in times past, has recently appeared in correspondence in the *Church Times* for Jan. 18, 25, and Feb. 8, and in the *Durham Advertiser* for Feb. 8, 15, 22, and March 1, 1878.   J. T. F.

Bp. Hatfield's Hall, Durham.

THE CHOIR STALLS AT HAARLEM: THE GOSPEL AND EPISTLE SIDES OF THE ALTAR (5th S. ix. 61, 101, 413.)—The present Roman and the modern Anglican uses are identical. In both the Gospel is read on the north side, the Epistle on the south. (I so read them myself a hundred times in every year.) But the older and more correct way is the reverse.

Mr. Mackenzie Walcott in his *Sacred Archœ-ology* (p. 22, *s.v.* "Altar") gives the explanation :—

" It (the altar) was divided into three parts in front, *medium altare*, before the altar, and the right-hand, or Epistle side, and the left-hand, or Gospel side, according to the English use ; but in Roman churches, since 1458, the position is reversed, being assumed from the crucifix on the altar, and not, as before, from the celebrant's arms facing the reredos."

It might, perhaps, have been better if, in my paper on the stalls, I had avoided any ambiguity by calling the sides of the choir simply after their geographical position. There can be no contro-versy about north and south, though there may be about Epistle and Gospel sides. I almost wonder that no critic with a little knowledge has availed himself of the chance to point out my supposed deficiency in that accuracy on which CROWDOWN is pleased to compliment me.

There are two corrections which should be made, nevertheless, in my paper. No. 2, south side (p. 61), should read thus :—2. Quarterly, 1 and 4, Bavaria ; 2 and 3, Flanders quartering Holland. In No. 6, north side (p. 102), it is obvious that Arkel is in the third, not in the fourth, quarter.

J. WOODWARD.

Montrose.

[MR. WALCOTT'S article next week.]

THE FIRST LOCAL NEWSPAPER (3rd S. i. 287, 351, 398, 435, 479 ; ii. 38, 92 ; 5th S. viii. 72, 140, 153, 179, 232, 330 ; ix. 12, 98, 155, 214.)— This subject, so far as Nottingham is concerned, has received in my leisure moments a fair share of attention, but, as one of your correspondents has truly said, it is somewhat "surrounded with diffi-culties." The historians of Nottingham, from Deering downward, give a poor, meagre, and dis-connected account of the first newspapers printed in Nottingham, the best, it may be, that could be given at the time, with the information then at hand ; but, through the medium of " N. & Q.," more light has been thrown upon the subject, and, if I may, I would briefly recapitulate the evidences already adduced, offer some new facts, and fathom the right of the *Nottingham Journal* of to-day in appropriating the date of 1710 as the year of its commencement.

MR. WHITE says (*ante*, p. 12) : " I have now before me a copy of the *Nottingham Post*, No. 42, July 11 to July 18, 1711." On calculation it will be found that, assuming it was published weekly, the first number was issued on Wednesday, Sep-tember 20, 1710. MR. S. F. CRESSWELL says (3rd S. i. 479) : "The *Nottingham Weekly Courant* appeared first on Monday, November 27, 1710. The second number gives the Queen's speech." We have it then unquestionably proved that both the *Nottingham Post* and the *Nottingham Courant* appeared in 1710, and that to the former must be awarded the honour of being the first in the field. MR. DUNN himself "has no doubt of it." This paper changed its name into that of the *Notting-ham Mercury*, of which I am in possession of a copy, dated October 10, 1721, but, there being no number upon it, I am unable to fix the date of its appearance under a new title. Under this head-ing it went on till, I believe, 1724, when it re-assumed its former title of the *Nottingham Post*. The latest number I have seen is dated April 5, 1739. Open to correction, I incline to the opinion that it came to a close about this time.

From evidence at command I am able to say that the *Nottingham Courant* continued its career until Saturday, March 27, 1762, when it came to an end. This last number is marked vol. 51, thus claiming a beginning in the year 1710. On the week following the *Nottingham Journal* of April 3 contains this notice :—

" Mr. George Ayscough, printer of the *Nottingham Courant,* being determined to leave off the printing busi-ness, takes this method of returning his sincere thanks to all his customers for supporting the newspaper which has been carried on by his father, mother, and self for more than half a century in so genteel and credit, and which will be continued by Samuel Cresswell, printer, under the new change, who is determined to spare neither expence nor labour in his endeavours to make this journal a truly useful and entertaining newspaper, and he assures the public that as soon as proper correspon-dence can be settled the *Nottingham Journal* will be constantly circulated in the following towns " (here follows a list of eighteen towns, and a winding up of the advertisement).

Here then we have proof of the incorporation of the *Nottingham Courant* with the *Nottingham Journal*, and on this basis, no doubt, the latter paper grounds its claim to having commenced in 1710. A word now as to the *bonâ fide* age of the *Nottingham Journal*. The copy just referred to,

April 3, 1762, is numbered 62, vol. ii., which places the *Nottingham Journal's* first publication on Saturday, January 31, 1761. Besides ' the amalgamation just mentioned, it coalesced ·with *Burbage's Nottingham Chronicle* in July, 1775, a paper which had a run of three and a half years only, and so has continued under different proprietorships to the present time. Finally this claim of the *Nottingham Journal* is of recent origin. The files for 1849 say established 1741, those for 1850 say 1716, and those in 1852 say 1710 ; thus by a simple imprimatur, and within four years, the *Nottingham Journal* added the respectable sum of thirty-one years to its score.

It will be noticed that I have passed over the *Leicester and Nottingham Journal*, as I consider it in no wise connected with the *Nottingham Journal* proper. It was printed at Leicester, began, I believe, in 1753, and the latest number I have seen is dated December 31, 1768. I ask pardon for the length of this paper. F. D.

Nottingham.

I willingly comply with MR. DUNN's request, and give the name of the printer of my copy of the *Nottingham Post.* The exact title is—

"The Nottingham Post : being a Faithful Account of all the Publick News, &c. Impartially Collected from the Best Accounts. Numb. 42. From Wednesday, July 11, to Wednesday, July 18, 1711. Nottingham : Printed and Sold by John Collyer, Bookseller in Long-Row."

The size of the sheet is seven and a half inches by twelve inches, printed on both sides. I have examined my copy carefully, but find no evidence to support MR. DUNN's opinion that it was printed "at uncertain intervals." The legitimate inference appears to be that it was printed weekly.

ROBERT WHITE.
Worksop.

MOORE AND REBOUL (5th S. ix. 104, 233.)— An elaborate paper on this subject appeared in the March number of the *Irish Monthly,* which, as it contains a few facts not mentioned by either of your correspondents, may be interesting to readers of " N. & Q." The writer in the *Irish Monthly* gives from a letter of Moore himself the exact date at which his sacred song, "This world is all a fleeting show," was written. In Messrs. Puttick & Simpson's catalogue of Moore's unpublished letters, London, 1853, pp. 9 and 10, copious extracts are given from three letters written from Kegworth, in Leicestershire, and dated respectively 1st, 10th, and 23rd November, 1813. In the second of these, addressed to his musical publisher, Mr. Power, Moore says : "I like your idea of keeping ' Oh fair, oh purest !' for a set of sacred songs exceedingly, and the possibility of making such a work very interesting between Stevenson and me struck me so much that I set to and wrote the following words for it, which I am sure you

will like." Here follow three verse mentary corrections of "This world is ι show." "I like these as well as anyt written," continues Moore, "but do nc to Stevenson yet, as I mean first t myself."

Few will consider that Moore e: estimate of the beautiful song he had j particularly as his self-criticism was a severe and apologetic kind. The ever, would have been in singular ba the lines been a translation from any ' ever distinguished. They were finall to Stevenson, who completed the mus to Moore's satisfaction before Octobe Finally, the song appeared for the fi print in the volume of his sacred s Moore dedicated to his friend Dalton of 1816.

In 1813, when Moore wrote "This a fleeting show," Jean Reboul, the bι Nismes, was only in his seventeenth yι not until 1820 that his poetical instin have been awakened. About this tin anonymous author of a sketch of his ̀ to his poems in the *Bibliothèque Chɩ* 1840),—

"Reboul était membre d'un cercle de jo: Ils se réunissaient dans un café. Ce fut là d'abord la verve poétique de Reboul. Entr bière un cigare il y composa des cha satires qui ne sortaient pas de ce cercle ami

"It is quite plain from this naïve d says the writer in the *Irish Monthly,*

"that even if M. Reboul's poetical yeast fer years earlier, and had been coincident with experience as a baker, no strain so pure, so sacred as that of the stolen melody of Moor received much favour or could have lived the most retentive memory of this select ci: admiring ears, amid the raptures of a cigɛ of beer, the earliest ' inspiration of his soι confided."

MR. BATES, in his interesting reply ject, gives Madame Beloc's French pros(of Moore's song, which evidently w which Reboul worked. Perhaps he wɩ ment his paper by publishing in "Ɲ original foundation of Reboul's most fa "L'Ange et l'Enfant," which, as in Moore's song, he gave to the world composition. The latter appeared in *dienne* in 1828, but it is stated in t *Biographie Générale* to have been tal(German of Franz Grillparzer, the dramatist.

"The Angel and the Child" is readers of English poetry from Longfe ful translation of it (Boston ed., 1876, not unworthy companion to this vers by the editor of the *Irish Monthly* in article which first drew attention to these "rogueries" of Jean Reboul.

D. F. Mac Carthy.
Notting Hill Terrace, W.

Moses with Horns (5th S. ix. 145.)—See Coleridge's *Biographia Literaria*, chap. xxi. :—
" When I was at Rome, among many other visits to the tomb of Julius II., I went thither once with a Prussian artist, a man of genius and great vivacity of feeling. As we were gazing on Michael Angelo's Moses our conversation turned on the horns and beard of that stupendous statue; of the necessity of each to support the other; of the superhuman effect of the former, and the necessity of the existence of both to give a harmony and *integrity* both to the image and the feeling excited by it. Conceive them removed, and the statue would become *un*-natural without being *super*-natural. We called to mind the horns of the rising sun, and I repeated the noble passage from Taylor's *Holy Dying*. That horns were the emblem of power and sovereignty among the Eastern nations, and are still retained as such in Abyssinia; the Achelous of the ancient Greeks; and the probable ideas and feelings that originally suggested the mixture of the human and the brute form in the figure by which they realized the idea of their mysterious Pan, as representing intelligence blended with a darker power, deeper, mightier, and more universal than the conscious intellect of man, than intelligence ;—all these thoughts and recollections passed in procession before our minds."

See also Sir Thomas Brown's *Vulgar Errors*, bk. v. chap. ix.   C. F. S. Warren, M.A.
Bexhill.

Of course Michael Angelo followed the regular traditional mode of representation derived from the Vulgate. Who ever saw a mediæval representation of Moses *without* horns? As to the Hebrew, Gesenius has the following in his *Thesaurus* :—

" *Qaran*—1. pr. ut videtur, *feriit*.........2, denom. a *qeren* significatu radii (No. 4) : *radiavit, radios sparsit*, de facie Mosis, postquam splendorem Dei communis viderat, Ex. xxxiv. 29, 30, 35. LXX., δεδόξασται τὸ πρόσωπον αὐτοῦ. Targ. Pesch. Saad. et Abalw. splenduit facies ejus. Ridicule Aqu. κερατώδης ἦν. Vulg. *cornuta erat* (facies) quo factum est, ut pictores Mosen cornutum depingerent, v. *Deylingii Observatt.*, s. iii., 81 *sqq*."

The Hebrew word is קָרַן (not לָקַן). It occurs in Hab. iii. 4, where see A. V. and marg. ; also LXX. and Vulg., both which render " horns," though " lightning flashes " would seem nearer the true sense.   J. T. F.
Bishop Hatfield's Hall, Durham.

I have many photographs of the interior of Roslin Chapel, giving numerous details of its marvellously intricate architectural beauties. Two of these, by Mr. J. Thomson of Roslin (or " Rosslyn," as he prefers to spell the word), four by three inches in size, represent two brackets or corbels. On the lower portion of one is a beautifully carved figure of a woman (half-length) holding and guiding a child, the end of whose clothing

is held by a grim-looking demon with horns and long ears. The other bracket is supported by a fine figure of Moses (nearly half-length), with bearded face, long curling hair, and two horns, which are not straight, but slightly curved inwards. The figure of Moses is amply draped. In his right hand he bears the Table of the Law ; in his left hand a knotted staff. The date of the erection of Roslin Chapel was (about) 1446, and, as Michael Angelo was not born till 1569, it follows that the Roslin sculptor anticipated that great artist in representing Moses with horns. Col. Fergusson's opinion is thus supported by an accomplished fact.
Cuthbert Bede.

The passage quoted by Col. Fergusson from " *Talks about Art*. By W. M. Hunt. With a Letter from J. E. Millais, R.A.," is not to be allowed to obscure the probable explanation of Michael Angelo's employment of horns—veritable horns of a bull-calf—in his much admired statue called Moses. Old Dunton's remark—it was doubtless his—in the *Athenian Mercury*, to the effect that a blundering reading of the Vulgate originated the practice in question, is much more likely to be correct. Long before Buonarotti's day a custom obtained to represent Moses, not with bull-calf's horns, but with sheafs of rays issuing from his temples, exactly as Parmigiano in a later day depicted the prophet in that glorious design where, in sublime wrath, he dashes to the earth the first received Tables of the Law.   O.

May not the horns have reference to the sun's having entered into Aries at the Vernal Equinox in or about Moses's time?   M. M. H.

Ember Days (5th S. ix. 308.)—There is no such Gotic word as *ryne*; but in Anglo-Saxon we have *ymbyrnan*, *i.e. yrnan* (*irnan* for *rinnan*, Lat. *currere*)=to run, and *ymb* (Old Saxon *umbi*, Frisian *umbe*, Old German *umpi*, Mod. Germ. *um*)=round. (Thus in Beowulf, l. 67, "him on môd bearn"=it occurred to his mind.) *Ymbyrnan* is, however, not the word which gave rise to the name " ember days," for any other day might claim the same title, and there is no historical evidence of such an origin. If we consider that the ember days are institutions of the Roman Catholic Church, and have no special name in Anglo-Saxon, it is clear that we must look to the language of the Romish ritual for an explanation. Now in Italian the ember days are called *quattrò-tempora*, in French *quatre-temps*, and German adopted the original mediæval Latin name *Qua-tember*, formed after the analogy of September, November, December, from *quatuor*, because ember days are (Church) quarterly fasting days. The language which curtails *omnibus* into '*bus* made of *Quatember* *ember*. This is the whole secret of the etymology. Embers, hot cinders,

could, of course, not be used in crossing people's foreheads ; yet it is possible, even probable, that the existence of this word *embers* may have caused the shortening of *Quatember*. *Ember* is in Anglo-Saxon *aemyrje*; Old Norse *eimyrja* (fire-shower), from *eymr* (glowing fire) ; Old German *eimer*; Modern German *Ammer* (in Luther). I may add, in conclusion, that the Scandinavian languages have no special term to denote ember days, but simply call them fast days (*fastedagar* in Swedish).
G. A. SCHRUMPF.
Tettenhall College.

Another derivation, at least as likely as that from Sax. *ymb* and Sax. (not Goth.) *ryne*, a course, is from *quatuor tempora*, the liturgical term, through the German *Quatember*, of which *ember* may well be a contraction. I am not aware that in the Church of England embers or hot ashes have ever been connected with days of abstinence, or ashes with any day except the Dies Cinerum, or Ash Wednesday, but speak under correction, not having the pre-Reformation service-books at hand.   J. T. F.
Winterton, Brigg.

This word is evidently a contraction of the German word *Quatember*, *i.e.* *quatuor tempora* (*quat' tempor'*), "four times" (a year), viz., Quadragesima Sunday, Whitsunday, Holyrood Day in September, and St. Lucia's Day in December.
E. COBHAM BREWER.
Lavant, Chichester.

"LORD ELLIS," 1708 (5ᵗʰ S. ix. 268.)—Dom. Philip Ellis, monk of the Holy Order of St. Benedict, and of the English congregation, consecrated in the chapel at St. James's Palace, in Westminster, May 6, 1688, with the title of " Episcopus Aurelio-polis" (Dod's *Church History*), one of the chaplains and preachers to King James II., retired at the time of the revolution with the royal family to St. Germains, and subsequently was made Bishop of Segni, in the Ecclesiastical State in Italy. An engraving from a picture of the bishop in the possession of Viscount Clifden is given in the first vol. of the *Ellis Correspondence*, edited by the Hon. George Agar Ellis (Colburn, 1829). Mr. E. M. Thompson, the editor of the *Prideaux Correspondence*, published by the Camden Society, 1875, in a foot-note to his preface, p. vii, writes that the account of the Ellis family in the *Ellis Correspondence* " is incorrect in some details." I do not know if Mr. Thompson impugns the pedigree or not, but curiously enough, in a foot-note by Dr. Bliss (*Athenæ Oxonienses*) to the notice of John Ellis, father of the bishop, introduced into the *Life of Henry Hickman* (vol. iv. col. 368), the maternity of the bishop is assigned to one of the three daughters of Henry Wilkinson mentioned (vol. iii. col. 231). On the other hand, Mr. George Agar Ellis quotes this notice from the *Athenæ in extenso*, without alluding to Dr. Bliss's note, and in

the pedigree Susannah, d. of W. Welbore, appears as the mother of the bishop. A notic Philip Ellis appears in Granger's *Biograph History of England.* Several of his letters, d Rome, 1695, are in the possession of the Bisho Southwark, addressed to Father Sherburne ; *Royal MSS. Commission Third Report*, Appen p. 233. The series of six sermons preached be their Majesties, 1685–6, are of frequent occurre
E. W.

H. A. S. is referred, for the best account of D Philip Ellis, Bishop of Segni, in print I know to "N. & Q.," 1ˢᵗ S. vi. 125, 298 ; vii. 242 ; for an engraved portrait of him to Lord Do *Ellis Correspondence*, with a slight notice of in the preface. It is there stated that his fa Rev. John Ellis, Rector of Waddesden, " w younger son of the family of Ellis of Kiddal, elder branch of which is now extinct ";* whic by no means correct, for his parentage is as unknown, although he probably came from neighbourhood of Doncaster, being of St. Ca rine's Hall, Cambridge. While there he was st " junior," to distinguish him from a contempo namesake, a Welshman, " Cambro-Britannic Dr. Welbore Ellis, Bishop of Kildare, fathe Lord Mendip, was Dom. Philip's younger brot
A. S.

No doubt this was Philip Ellis, Ord. S. F one of King James II.'s court preachers, and a bishop *in partibus*. Dod says that he, " at going to *Rome*, obtained a bishoprick in *It* Dr Oliver says that it was " the vacant se Segni" to which he was preferred in 1708, that he died Nov. 16, 1726. He adds that "] Leo XII. kindly gave Bishop Ellis's library ring to Bishop Baines for the use of his succes in the Western district." When the library of college founded by Bishop Baines at Prior] was sold some twenty years since, many b

* In Burke's *Commoners* (iii. 554), and the f volume edition of *Landed Gentry*, " Burroughes of] Stratton," it is asserted Welbore Ellis, Bishop of dare, " sprang" from Henry Ellis. As the former born about 1660, and the latter in 1672, it is impos Mrs. Burroughes was the heiress *of her father only*. co-heiresses of this ancient family were the siste Capt. William Ellis, R.N., of H.M.S. Gosport, who at New York in 1743, viz. (1) Mary, wife of Tim Smith, of Brotherton, co. York, yeoman ; (2) Annal wife of Matthew Snowdon, of London, sadler ; (3) C rine ; (4) Elizabeth ; and (5) Mildred, wife of Jone Wainwright, of London, salter ; to raise portion whom their father had vested the manor of Kid trustees for ninety-nine years. But the male line i now extinct, and the present representative is the s the late Sir William Charles Ellis, M.D., whose f was the compiler of *Ellis's Exercises*, formerly a known school book. *Notices of the Ellises*, by ' Ellis, Esq., of the Middle Temple, a privately pr work, and very rare now in its complete form, ma] be consulted, but some of these particulars are new.

appeared in which Bishop Ellis had written his name, and some also in the Stowe Library.

THOMAS KERSLAKE.
Bristol.

See Maziere Brady's *Succession of English Bishops* (Burns & Oates).   C. PARFITT.

JUDGES IX. 53 (5th S. ix. 344, 413.)—The argument of H. F. W. and of the Bishop of Bath and Wells is somewhat affected by the fact that the phrase is not a new one, inserted by the translators of the Authorized Version of 1611, but is of older date. How much older I cannot say, but it is in the Bishops' Bible, "and al to brake his brayne panne," and probably comes from an earlier version. It is therefore not the idiom or usage of 1611 which has to be considered in settling the point so much as that of an earlier date. "To-break" is very common in the older translations, *e.g.* in the passage in the Gospels of the new wine bursting the old bottles. Thus Matthew ix. 17 (*Anglo-Saxon Gospels*), " the bytta beoth *to brocene*," which Wiclif keeps in " the botels ben *to brokun*"; Mark ii. 22, "to brycth"; while Luke v. 37 has the simple form " brycth" or " breceth," as Tyndale " breaketh." Though the prefix was dying out in the sixteenth and seventeenth centuries, it would be easily understood when brought on from an older translation. And though the later examples of the phrase do show that *all*=utterly was generally prefixed, yet other instances may be found, as

" Then let them all encircle him about
And fairy-like *to pinch* the unclean knight."
Merry Wives of Windsor, iv. 4, 55.

The verb "pinch," without the prefix, follows five lines later. A late use of the phrase is found (1678) in Bunyan's *Pilgrim's Progress*, " missed but little of *all to breaking* Mr. Greatheart's skull."   O. W. TANCOCK.

AN "AQUÆBAJULUS" (5th S. ix. 268, 334.)—I had already communicated the meaning of this word to MR. HART, but had not the historical evidence contributed by your other correspondents. Perhaps, however, a few words on the origin of *bajulus* will not be out of place. It is a Latin word, and means " a porter," probably from Baiæ, the Campanian watering-place. Thus *bajulus* originally denoted "a (Baian) porter." The Latin verb derived from *bajulus* is *bajulare*, "to carry a burden." Isidorus, however, derives the name *Baiæ* from the verb *bajulare:* "hunc portum veteres a bajulandis mercibus vocabant Baias." Frisch connects *Baiæ* with the Old Romance *ba(d)are*, "to open the mouth" (probably an onomatopœia). Others* suggest that it is a Basque word, as *baia*, " harbour "+*ona*, " good "=Bay-

* Boudard, *Numismatique Ibérienne*, Paris, 1852, and, after him, Heiss and Philipps.

onne, the name of a French town. Grimm traces it to the German *biegen*, "to bend." Lastly, it is believed that it is the same as the Gaelic *bâdh*, *bâgh*, "a bay, harbour, creek, estuary." This etymology is the more probable as it accounts for the phonetic transformations of the word, viz. French *baie*, Span. *bahía*, Ital. *baia*. Either *Baia* was at first a local name, and then extended to other places, or it was a general name, and in the case of the Campanian town signified the Baia *par excellence*. At any rate, *baia* seems to be the primitive, and *bajulare*, *bajulus*, the derived words. The French still use the term *bajule* to denote a cross and candle bearer in religious processions.

G. A. SCHRUMPF.
Tettenhall College.

The constitution of Archbishop Boniface, or Winchelsey, lays down that the *aquæbajulus* should be a poor clerk, holding his office as an ecclesiastical benefice conferred by the curate of the church and maintained by the alms of the parishioners, in all parishes within ten miles of a city or castle throughout his province. He served the priest at the altar, sang the responses, read the epistle, and carried the holy water vat (*aquâ benedictâ*) ; he was required to read also the lections and sing the gradual ; to assist at the canonical hours and the ministration of the sacraments and sacramentals : in fact, he was the prototype of the parish clerk (Lyndw., lib. iii., tit. 7, pp. 142-3, app. 21). The *aquæbajulus* was a poor scholar and his office was an exhibition, "ut ibidem proficeret ut aptior et magis idoneus fieret ad majora." The bishops of Lichfield, Salisbury, Worcester, and Exeter, in the thirteenth century, also interfered on behalf of poor scholars in a similar way. In 1393, Archbishop Courtenay required the parishioners to pay the clerk for bringing the holy water to them, as a laudable English custom (Wilkins, iii. 220). He seems to have kept school on week-days, and after mass visited the houses in the parish and sprinkled the whole family—a custom which prevailed in parts of France even in the time of Ducange. Erasmus mentions that in Holland people guarded their houses with holy water, holy bread, and a wax taper.   MACKENZIE E. C. WALCOTT.

SCLAVONIC OR SLAVONIC (5th S. ix. 366.)—According to Mahummadan historians generally, derived apparently from the Talmud or other Hebrew authority, Suklub or Saklab, the progenitor of the Sclavonic races, was the third of the nine sons of Japhet, the son of Noah, viz.,* Toork, Hirz, Suklub, Roos, Munsukh, Cheen, Komari, Kymul, and Mazukh.

Unless, therefore, this Oriental account, which is confirmed by the extant nomenclature of coun-

* *Shajrát ul Atrák*, or *Genealogical Tree of the Turks*, translated by Col. Miles, 1838, p. 22.

tries in Europe as well as Asia and Africa, is to be rejected as altogether fabulous, it appears to me there can be no doubt that Sclavonic would be the more correct mode of writing the word.

R. R. W. ELLIS.
Dawlish.

INDEXES (5ᵗʰ S. viii. 87.)—In his pleasant anecdote about John Baynes, MR. THOMS makes mention of "Lord Campbell's well-known denunciation of all such offenders," to wit, authors who omit to supply their books with alphabetical indexes. Will he, or any correspondent who may be able to do so, be good enough to give the exact reference to this denunciation?   APIS.

"IMP" OR "IMPE" (5ᵗʰ S. ix. 46.)—Trench, in English, Past and Present, p. 199, says :—

"Imp was once a name of dignity and honour, and not of slight or of undue familiarity. Thus Spenser addresses the Muses in this language,

' Ye sacred imps that on Parnasso dwell ';

and imp was especially used of the scions of royal or illustrious houses. More than one epitaph still existing of our ancient nobility might be quoted beginning in such language as this, ' Here lies that noble imp.' "

In Tooke's Diversions of Purley a great many notices of the same kind are given. For example, "Imp was antiently a term of dignity. Lord Cromwel, in his last letter to Henry VIII., prays for the imp his son."

Many instances are found in Shakspeare and still older writers, together with at least a score of passages from Spenser's Faerie Queene and other works, all of which may be found under this heading in the book first mentioned. Somewhere I have read, but cannot now find the reference, that an old divine calls our Lord "that blessed Imp."   GEORGE RAVEN.

[See 4ᵗʰ S. iii. 81, 202, 418 ; vi. 323, 420, 579 ; 5ᵗʰ S. vi. 66 ; vii. 146, 276.]

COLLEGIATE AND SCHOLASTIC BIOGRAPHIES (5ᵗʰ S. ix. 364.)—Permit me to add the following works to MR. SUTTON's list of books on the above subject :—

Bloxam (Rev. J. R.). Register of the Presidents, Fellows, Demies, Instructors in Grammar and in Music, Chaplains, Clerks, Choristers, and other Members of St. Mary Magdalen College......Oxford. Oxford, 1853, &c., 8vo. [Still in progress.]

Burrows (Prof. Montagu). Worthies of All Souls': Four Centuries of English History. Lond., 1874, 8vo.—The information in this list may be supplemented by " Catalogue of the Archives in the Muniment Rooms of All Souls' College. Prepared by Charles Trice Martin, F.S.A. Printed by Spottiswoode & Co......London, 1877." 8vo. pp. xiv-467.

Boase (Rev. C. W.). History of Exeter College, Oxford.—Now being printed. The part containing biographical particulars of the Rectors and Fellows has nearly passed through the press.

Harwood (T.). Alumni Etonenses. Birmingham, 1797, 4to.

Hawes (Robert) and Loder (R.). History of Fᵣ ham......including Notices of the Masters and Fe Pembroke Hall in Cambridge......Begun by R. With Additions and Notes by R. Loder. Woo 1798, 4to.

Marlborough College Register from 1843 to ' clusive. With Alphabetical Index. Lond.,1870

Mayor (Rev. J. E. B.). History of the Colleg John the Evangelist, Cambridge. By Thomas B.D., ejected Fellow. Edited for the Syndics University Press by John E. B. Mayor......Camb¡ the University Press, 1869, 2 vols., 8vo.—Mr refers in his advertisement to " Mr. Searle's e history of Queens'."

Sidebotham (Rev. J. S.). Memorials of the School, Canterbury : comprising Brief Notices therein Educated. Canterbury, 1865, 8vo.

Stapylton (H. E. C.). The Eton School Li 1791 to 1850. London [Eton printed], 1863, 4to.; ed., 1864, 4to.

Steven (William). History of the High S Edinburgh. Edinburgh, 1849, 8vo.

Wilson (Rev. H. B.). History of Merchant School from its Foundation. Lond., 1812-14, 4to. —A new history of this school by Mr. C. J. Rot in preparation.

W. P. COURT
15, Queen Anne's Gate.

A correspondent wishes additions to tl already has. The medical graduates of th versity of Edinburgh from the year 1705 t are given in a volume of 280 pages, pri Edinburgh in 1846 by Neill & Co.—1 Eorum qui Gradum Medicinæ Doctoris i demia Jacobi Sexti Scotorum Regis, quæ burgi est, adepti sunt. The names are in t by the year and then alphabetically. It custom each year to print on four octavo pa medical graduates of that year, so it is keep up the record. Between the years 1' 1845 the degree of doctor of medicine was cc on the alarming number of five thousa ninety-six persons.

THOMAS STRATTON, M.D.]

MR. SUTTON may add to his list :—
The History of the College of Corpus Christi B. Virgin Mary (commonly called Bennet), in ' versity of Cambridge, from its Foundation to the Time. In Two Parts. I. Of its Founders, Ben and Masters ; II. Of its other Principal Memb Robert Masters, B.D., Fellow of the College. Ca: 1753, 4to.

William of Wykeham and his Colleges. By M E. C. Walcott, M.A. Winchester, 1852, 8vo.

The Rugby School Register from the Year 16: Present Time. Second edition, Rugby, 1838, 8 another edition to 1860.

J.]

HOGARTH (5ᵗʰ S. ix. 427.)—There are three prints describing the frontispiece to Perspective :—1. inscribed " Hogarth pinx Ireland sculp'," produced for Graphic 1 tions of Hogarth, by S. Ireland, the text o¡ edit. 1794, i. 158, accounts for the inscrip ferred to by MR. WOLFERSTAN. S. Ireland wrote thus :—

"The original drawing is in my possession, and like-wise the sketch in oil, from which the annexed etching is made. Each of these designs has its respective merit; but I suspect the sketch in oil to have been the first thought. The design is very different from that which has been published," &c.

An aquatint engraving, entitled "Satire on false Perspective, from the orig¹ Drawing," with the publication line, "Hogarth del¹, Le Cœur sc¹, pub. for S. Ireland, May 1, 1799," indicates an original drawing for the "frontispiece," and is referred to in the edition of *Graphic Illustrations* published in 1799, ii. 134, as "an engraved fac-simile of the original drawing in Indian ink, given to the editor of this work by the daughter of the late Mr. Kirby." 2. An illustration to *The Genuine Works of William Hogarth*, by J. Nichols and G. Steevens, 1810, ii. 201, with the signatures, "Hogarth pinx¹, T. Cook & Son sc." This print was republished in *The Works of William Hogarth*, by the Rev. John Trusler, 1821, i. 3. Another copy, signed "W. Hogarth, Pinx., J. Moore, Sculp.," published in *The Complete Works of William Hogarth*, by the Rev. J. Trusler and E. F. Roberts, n.d. The print pub-lished as a frontispiece to Kirby's *Perspective*, 1753, is signed "W. Hogarth inv. et delin., L. Sullivan Sculp." *The Genuine Works*, see above, 1808, i. 244, gives a letter from Kirby to Hogarth, thanking him for the drawing which supplied the original of this print. This drawing is, I believe, now in the possession of Dr. Percy. It is very likely that "pinx¹" refers to the draw-ing in Indian ink. I do not know what has become of the oil painting which S. Ireland possessed. Old sale catalogues are unfortunately not often enriched with the names of purchasers.

F. G. S.

"ACRE" (5ᵗʰ S. ix. 347.)—The word *acre* was formerly used with its original signification, viz. any open ground or field, without reference to dimensions. In this sense it seems to be pre-served in the names of places, as Castle Acre, West Acre, &c. In the churchwardens' accounts of Bishop's Stortford, *temp.* James I., the following items occur :—

"Of Thomas Leaper for the Land called Spittleacre in Apton feild next Sandpitts."
"Of Thomas Barnard for his peece of land in Shepho al's wyndhillfeild next Vicar's Acre."
"Of land belonging to the Chauntry, viz. for a peece in moche *halfe acres* called Shortland."

The land referred to in the last item is known by the name of Half Acres at the present time. The *acre* was, I believe, first limited to a definite quantity by an Act of Parliament in the time of Edward I. G.

[See 5ᵗʰ S. viii. 109.]

NEVILLE QUERIES (5ᵗʰ S. ix. 266, 409.)—In a note to the will of Margaret, Duchess of Exeter, in the *Testamenta Vetusta*, it is stated that Richard Neville, Earl of Warwick, certainly was *not* her nephew. Raphe Brooke, York Herald, in his *Catalogue of the Earls of Westmoreland*, 1619, says that Anne, wife of Sir William Cogniers, Knight, was the daughter of Ralph, the third earl.

J. H. COOKE.

AN OLD PRINT (5ᵗʰ S. ix. 289.)—The old print mentioned by B. B. represents an ancient road-side cabaret at Whittington in the county of Derby, near Chesterfield, which was called Revolu-tion House. In the early part of 1688 the Earl of Devonshire, Lord Danby, and other leading men, are said to have met together in the little parlour of this humble hostelry, and then to have concocted a plan which ultimately was the means of bringing about the Revolution of 1688. At its centenary in 1788 Dr. Samuel Pegge, the learned antiquary, preached a sermon on the subject in the parish church of Whittington, of which he was then in-cumbent. See for further information on this subject Chambers's *Book of Days*, vol. ii. pp. 745-6, and Lewis's *Topographical Dictionary of England*, under "Whittington, co. Derby."

JOHN PICKFORD, M.A.
Newbourne Rectory, Woodbridge.

THE NANFAN FAMILY (2ⁿᵈ S. viii. 228, 294, 357; 5ᵗʰ S. viii. 472; ix. 129, 398.)—MR. BOWER has given an extract from *Berrow's Worcester Journal* of January, 1870, recording the death of Mr. William Nanfan, who claimed to be the male representative of the Nanfans of Corn-wall and Birtsmorton Court, Worcestershire. I was well acquainted with William Nanfan, though I never saw the pedigree that he relied upon. But I think it probable that he was descended from John Nanfan, who was esquire of the body to Henry VI., and which said John Nanfan, according to Dr. Nash, in his *History of Worcestershire*, was Lord of Birtsmorton in 9 Henry VI., and in the twenty-fourth of that king's reign was member of Parliament for Worcestershire, with John Throg-morton. An altar tomb, though despoiled of its brasses, yet exists in Birtsmorton Church, which Dr. Nash has ascribed to Sir John Nanfan, Knt., father of the John Nanfan just mentioned. Bridges Nanfan, who died in June, 1704, was the last male heir who possessed the mansion and estate at Birtsmorton, and he left an only child, Catharine, who was married to Richard Coote, Earl of Bella-mont. The surviving son of this marriage died in 1776, and had an only child, Lady Judith Coote, who died unmarried in 1771, leaving, Dr. Nash says, the manors of Birtsmorton and Berrow to her cousin Charles Coote, who, in 1767, was created Earl of Bellamont, and retained possession of the Birts-morton property. The Nanfans, however, had not died out, for William Nanfan, the grandfather of Bridges, left two younger sons, Thomas and William, and Bridges himself had two younger brothers, one of whom, if the estates had been entailed, should have been entitled to them on his death. But no claim appears to have been made at that time by any descendant of the Nanfan family, though branches existed both at Tewkesbury and the Berrow, and from one of these William Nanfan was descended.

It does not clearly appear how the Nanfans became possessed of Birtsmorton, which must originally have been a part of the Forest or Chace of Malvern ; but William Nanfan believed that it was a royal grant, and contended that as such the estate could only descend to male heirs, and that Lady Judith Coote had no legal right to alienate it from the Nanfan family.

The father of the late William Nanfan was a provision dealer in Worcester, and had a shop at the Cross ; but he gave himself no trouble about the Birtsmorton estate, which no doubt even then would have been useless, though it was the visionary idea of his son, which he maintained to the close of his chequered life, always asserting his descent from and his sole representation of the Nanfan family. It was, in fact, his habit to be ever talking on the subject, and affecting to be collecting papers and information. He obtained a living by timber measuring, at which he was deemed very expert ; but towards the close of his life a long and severe illness placed him in circumstances requiring assistance, and a worthy and benevolent friend procured his entrance as a patient into the Worcester Infirmary. Here he died, and was buried in the new cemetery. I have ascertained that he left a son and two daughters, who came down from London to his funeral, and I suppose paid all expenses. I have inquired as to this son Thomas, the last of the Nanfans, and it appears that a few years since he was acting as a waiter at an hotel in Oxford Street, London, and may possibly be there now, but he has not lately been heard of. He makes another instance of the vicissitudes in families once occupying a position of wealth and distinction.

EDWIN LEES, F.L.S.

PRINSEP's "LINEN GATHERERS" (5th S. ix. 426.) —The art critic of the *Standard* corrected his error on this subject in the succeeding notice of the R. A. Exhibition.   J. T. M.

ROMANO-CHRISTIAN REMAINS IN BRITAIN (5th S. ix. 349, 429.)—MR. BROWN states, in speaking of "*Inscriptiones Britanniæ Latinæ consilio et avctoritate Academia Litterarvm regiæ Barvssicæ.* Edidit Æmilivs Hübner. Berolini apvd Georgivm Reimervm, 1873, fol.," that he had not been able to find it in the library of the British Museum. It may perhaps be of service to him to state that I

saw the book there last week. It under Huebner, Emil, and is press r It forms the seventh volume of the of the Academia Regia Scientiar which was originally known unde Societas Regia Scientiarum.   GEO.

INSCRIPTION ON THE TENOR BEl COMBE (5th S. ix. 388, 418.)—Th present Vicar of Yarnscombe, the Dixon, M.A., sends me the followi wishes to submit to the learne " N. & Q." as a possible solution of t inscription on this bell : " Sonorus Pro Operariis Narrat Matutina Læti   D. C

A TIRLING-PIN (5th S. ix. 88, I mentioned the tirling-pin at Ovingl have noted that it is combined ' rapidly disappearing "sneck," the which raises the "sneck" passing just below the upright "pin," whic the handle of the ordinary "snecks" short lever at the top. The ring h thumb-piece of the little lever withi and the "pin" on which it rattles twisted iron. I said it was "origi meant was that it is not a mo Extensive alterations were made in 1694, and the front door seems to be so probably is its tirling-pin, though : one of earlier date. I imagine that the "snecked" door is a "survival" pin.
Ovingham-on-Tyne.

CHEDDLE (5th S. ix. 248, 335.)—Tl of the Cheshire Cheadle, near Stockp capable of another explanation than *Taxatio* of Pope Nicholas, 1291, it form Sheddeleye.   JOHN
Southport.

Is it not more reasonable to refer names to St. Ceadda, the apostle of :
                                                        ']

SIR RICHARD GRENVILLE (5th S. 377.)—I beg to refer HERMENTRUD series of Lady Llanover's *Autobiogi* *Delany* (Mary Granville), where she particulars she requires stated and 1 removed.   (

THE TIDAL "BORE" (5th S. ix. 8] This tidal wave is called in some pai as, for instance, in Lincolnshire and *eygre* or *ager*. Will your reader those who have written upon this me to draw their attention to a char Jean Ingelow called *The High Tid of Lincolnshire in* 1571? The scene of it is laid near Boston, and no one could have described more pathetically or exquisitely than she has done the devastation committed by the tidal wave rolling up the river and overflowing the surrounding country. She narrates how the bells in the grand old tower of St. Botolph's Church at Boston rang out the alarm called *The Brides of Enderby :—*

" Play uppe, play uppe, O Boston bells !
  Ply all your changes, all your swells,
  Play uppe *The Brides of Enderby.*
    *   *   *   *   *
  They sayde, And why should this thing be?
  What danger lowers by land or sea,
  They ring the tune of Enderby?"
                    JOHN PICKFORD, M.A.
Newbourne Rectory, Woodbridge.

WEEPING CROSS (5ᵗʰ S. ix. 246.)—It is interesting to know of such in any locality, but the occurrences of them cannot be rare. There is notice of one such in a book often referred to by one at least of the correspondents of " N. & Q.," Beesley's *Hist. of Banbury.* At p. 2 there is a discussion as to the use; at p. 115 there is a description of the one formerly existing between Banbury and Adderbury, and of its final removal in 1803 ; at p. 612 it is stated that there is a paper on " Weeping Crosses" in the *Gentleman's Magazine* for Aug., 1841, in which their origin is discussed.
                    ED. MARSHALL.

An instance of this phrase occurs in Wallington's *Historic Notices:—*

" At Stone is said that the Cavaliers have taken their cattle, and drave them to their quarters, but do sell cheap pennyworths of other men's goods. A butcher went to make a purchase amongst them, took a sum of money, and bought cattle at an easy rate, making account of a very great gain ; but as he returned, another troop met him, and took his bargain out of his hand, and sent him home by *weeping cross.*"—Vol. ii. p. 112.

The date is October, 1642. It is quoted from *Speciale Passages,* No. 7.   EDWARD PEACOCK.
Bottesford Manor, Brigg.

There was a weeping cross near Stafford (*Archæol.,* xiii. 216). At Shrewsbury it was a station on Corpus Christi day, when the various guilds, religious and corporate bodies, visited it, and, having offered prayers for an abundant harvest, returned to hear mass in St. Chad's Church. The broken shaft and steps of one remain at Banbury ; and the base of another at Ripley has niches which would cause positive pain to penitents in a kneeling position. It was probably of a penitential character, as though the last tears of penitents were shed upon it.   MACKENZIE E. C. WALCOTT.

In an editorial note at p. 154, 1ˢᵗ S. i., three places are mentioned where there are, or were, weeping crosses, viz., one between Oxford and Banbury, another near Stafford, and a third near Shrewsbury.   H. G. C.

AUTHORS OF BOOKS WANTED (5ᵗʰ S. ix. 429.)—The Catalogue of the Advocates' Library, Edinburgh, ascribes *Revelations of Russia,* 1844; *The White Slave and the Russian Prince,* &c., to Charles Frederick Henningsen.   W. H. ALLNUTT.

𝕸𝖎𝖘𝖈𝖊𝖑𝖑𝖆𝖓𝖊𝖔𝖚𝖘.

NOTES ON BOOKS, &c.

The Constitutional History of England. By William Stubbs, M.A. Vol. III. Clarendon Press Series. (Macmillan & Co.)

THE Regius Professor of Modern History in the University of Oxford has now concluded the task which he had set before him of examining our constitutional history "in its origin and development." It has been a work of considerable time, even to one so familiar with his subject as Prof. Stubbs. But the time which has elapsed since we were carried from the struggle for the Charter down to the deposition of Richard II., in Mr. Stubbs's second volume, has been spent, as might have been expected, not only in preparing the last portions of the historical narrative, but also in thinking over the many problems necessarily presented to us for solution in the course of the history of a nation's constitution. Of some of these Mr. Stubbs says frankly that "the careful study of history suggests many problems for which it supplies no solution." The questions, for instance, which are at issue more or less throughout Western Europe at the present moment, regarding the relations between Church and State, between the Church and education, and between the State and education, have to be grappled with in the history of the Middle Ages, and they meet us no less in the history which we are making for the future by our action in the present. The "exact harmonizing" of the respective courses of the Church and the State in these, as in various other departments of life and action, must no doubt be left for a " distant future and altered conditions of existence." But it is well to seek out the roots of these questions, deep down in the history of the Middle Ages. It is well to study periods of transition, such as that which forms the subject of Mr. Stubbs's concluding volume, when the knell of the Middle Ages had rung, although the men of Bosworth Field and of Fornovo heard it not. It is well also to be reminded that "the greatest treasure of kings is their possession of the heart of their people," as Sir Arnold Savage reminded Henry IV. in 1401. It is well to mark, in the acts of the kings of England of the House of Lancaster, the recognition of the duty of the king "to rule lawfully, of the people to obey honestly"; to note the "share of the three estates in all deliberations"; to observe the " limitations and responsibilities, as well as the prerogatives of royal power." Looking back upon the work of Mr. Stubbs as a whole, we may say of it, as has been said of the *Divina Commedia,* that it is a " hard book," but that we doubt whether the author would have had it be other than a hard book. He has written for the student, certainly not for the *dilettante.* And the student will find that it requires all his faculties to be on the stretch that he may not lose the thread with which the Regius Professor of History offers to guide him through the many dark and winding passages of the history of the English Constitution. If the student follows Mr. Stubbs to the end, he will. we believe, "turn his back on the Middle Ages with a brighter hope for the future, but not without regrets for what he is leaving." With similar regrets we take our own leave of Prof. Stubbs.

Die Alliterierende Englische Langzeile im XIV. Jahrhundert. Von F. Rosenthal. (Halle-a-S., E. Karras.) In this inaugural dissertation for the Doctorate of Philosophy of the University of Leipzig, our learned correspondent Herr Rosenthal carries us back to the days when the forgotten glories of Alexander of Macedon were revived on the Levantine shores of the Mediterranean, and when Langland showed himself to be the last of the old school of English poets in form, the first of the new school in genius and spirit. Of the eight poems on which the present essay is founded one only, the *Vision of William concerning Piers the Plowman*, is of certain attribution, the authorship of the others being either unknown or disputed. Dr. Rosenthal makes proof of a close and critical study of Mediæval English versification, as well as of the most modern commentators upon it, whether English or Continental, such as Skeat, Ten Brink, Trautmann, and others. His notes on the various forms of alliteration, and his comparative tables, illustrating the three texts of *Piers Plowman*, render the essay an unusually rich storehouse of references and examples for the student of English poetry in the Middle Ages.

MR. T. KERSLAKE, in a reprint from the *Journal of the Royal Archæological Institute*, vol. xxxiv., asks the question, *What is a Town?* and devotes much curious lore, and somewhat intricate special pleading, to the elaboration of a theory that "in its natural state a town was essentially uninclosed"; that it has "three principal approaches, meeting at a central triangular space"; and that the word "town" may be closely allied to "two," and signify *bivium*.—In the April number of the *Journal of the National Indian Association* (C. Kegan Paul & Co.) will be found an interesting account, by an eye-witness, of an agricultural show in rural Bengal, and a paper, by a native writer, on the history of the caste system in India, showing clearly that sea voyages and other acts, which would now expose a Hindu to the loss of caste, were not unusual in the Vedic period.—*The Future of the Australian Race*, by Marcus Clarke (Melbourne, A. H. Massina & Co.), deals with a subject of considerable ethnological and social interest in language more forcible than philosophical. Mr. Clarke considers that vegetarians are Conservatives, and "Red Radicals" for the most part meat-eaters, while "fish-eaters are invariably moderate Whigs." He thinks that "the Australasians will be content with nothing short of a turbulent democracy," and that in five hundred years the Australasian race will have "changed the face of nature, and swallowed up all our contemporary civilization," but it is fortunately "impossible that we should live to see this stupendous climax." Après nous, le déluge !

ATTEMPTS ON THE LIVES OF ROYAL PERSONAGES.—The following list, taken from the *Times* of June 5, 1878, seems worthy of preservation in "N. & Q.":—
"One of the papers gives the following catalogue of twenty-eight attempts on the lives of royal personages and rulers during the last thirty years:—The Duke of Modena attacked in 1848 ; the Prince of Prussia (now the Emperor William) at Minden in June, 1848 ; the late King of Prussia in 1852 ; Queen Victoria (by an ex-lieutenant) in 1852; an infernal machine discovered at Marseilles on Napoleon III.'s visit in 1852 ; the Austrian Emperor slightly wounded by the Hungarian, Libenyez, in 1853 ; attack on King Victor Emmanuel in 1853 ; also on Napoleon III. opposite the Opéra Comique ; the Duke of Parma mortally stabbed in 1854; Napoleon III. fired at by Pianori in the Champs Elysées in 1855; a policeman seized Fuentes when about to fire at Queen

Isabella in 1856 ; Milano, a soldier, dinand of Naples in 1856 ; three Ita convicted of conspiracy against Nap the Orsini plot against Napoleon III Prussia twice fired at, but not hit, by at Baden in 1861; Queen of Greece sh Brusios in 1862; three Italians from conspiring against Napoleon III. i Lincoln assassinated in 1865; the C Petersburg in 1866 and at Paris in 18 of Servia assassinated in 1868 ; King attacked in 1871 ; President of Peru a President of Bolivia in 1873 ; Presi 1875 ; President of Paraguay in 1877 on the life of the German Emperor ii
A.

ENGLISH COMIC FOLK-LORE.—I bel floating about the country many sati illustrate the simpleness of the inhab districts, such as the Gothamites, th and the Wiltshire moon-rakers. I sl the communication direct to myself however fragmentary. Wi
40, St. George's Square, S.W.

Notices to Correspor
We must call special attention to the
On all communications should be wi
address of the sender, not necessarily
as a guarantee of good faith.

CORRESPONDENTS are requested to t
is against rule to *seal* or otherwise *fas*
transmitted by the halfpenny post.
double postage has to be paid on th
they have been " closed against inspe

MR. TAYLOR (Northampton) wri
FIDELIS will perhaps be glad to add to
counties magazines as under :—' *North*
or *Monthly Amusements*, &c. Vol.
(pages 129-168). Northampton: Pri
and W. Dicey ; and Sold by Henry W
Boston ; John Weale in Bedford ; (
borough ; P. Gibson in Wisbech ; an
St. Bennet's Church in Cambridge. (
Octavo."

BIBLIOTHECAIRE DE LA VILLE DE G
not find the passage to which you ref
for 1874, but we are able to say tl
readers at the British Museum ext
We shall be glad to see your Report w

FAMA (*ante*, p. 458) will see a pr
there is given on the bell "part of tl
backwards."

W. M. M. will find the arms of the :
in Debrett's *House of Commons and*
for 1878.

J. SHELLY is thanked. He will fi
mation has been given, *ante*, p. 357.

J. H. WHITEHEAD.—Letter forward
H. T. E.—Received.

NOTICE.

Editorial Communications should be
Editor of ' Notes and Queries ' "—A
Business Letters to "The Publisher".
Wellington Street, Strand, London, W
We beg leave to state that we decl
munications which, for any reason, we
to this rule we can make no exceptior

LONDON, SATURDAY, JUNE 15, 1878.

Notes on Books, &c.

‎𝕹otes.

LORD JAMES AND LADY ELIZABETH RUSSELL.

It will be noticed, in all the printed accounts of the Russell family, that the surname of the wife of Lord James Russell, fifth son of William, first Duke of Bedford, is never given. No knowledge of her family, if ever sought for, appears to have been obtained, and this hiatus continues to exist in the latest pedigrees of both the Russells and the De Hoghtons. Having accidentally come upon the details of her history while pursuing another matter, it seems well that they should be placed upon record. I will make the statement as brief as possible.

Richard Lloyd, citizen and mercer, and evidently a considerable merchant of London, married early in 1668, being then a widower, Jane, one of the daughters of Henry Ireton, and granddaughter of Oliver Cromwell, who did not long survive, and by whom he had an only daughter. At his death in 1686 he left a widow (evidently his third wife), Tryphena, and two daughters by her, Elizabeth and Alicia. Six years later, viz. early in 1692, the widow Tryphena remarried Robert Grove, Esq., of Ferne, co. Wilts (ancestor of the present Sir Thomas Grove, Bart.), who died in 1695, she surviving him some thirty years. Her elder and apparently only surviving daughter by her first husband, viz. Elizabeth Lloyd, became the wife of Lord James Russell. The marriage licence, issued

from the Faculty Office, is dated August 11, 1698, he being described as a bachelor, aged above twenty-one (he was really fifty-two or fifty-three), and she as a spinster, aged about seventeen. They had issue an only daughter, Tryphena, who subsequently married Thomas Scawen, Esq., of Carshalton, Surrey, and was buried there January 28, 1757. Lord James Russell died June 22, 1712, in his sixty-seventh year, and was buried at Chenies, in Bucks. In his will he directed that, in case of his daughter's minority, his mother-in-law, Mrs. Tryphena Grove, should become one of her guardians, the Marquis of Granby being the other. One of these contingencies arose, as on April 14, 1721, Lady Elizabeth Russell became the second wife of Sir Henry Hoghton, fifth baronet, of Hoghton Tower. On February 7, 1725-6, letters to administer the estate of Tryphena Grove, late of Ferne, co. Wilts, but who died at Hampstead, co. Middlesex, were granted, by the Prerogative Court of Canterbury, to her daughter Elizabeth, Lady Russell, *alias* Hoghton, wife of Sir Henry Hoghton, Bart. Mrs. Tryphena Grove was buried at Donhead St. Andrew, Wilts, then the burial-place of the Grove family. Lady Elizabeth Russell died Sept. 1, 1736, at Reading, while on her journey homeward from Bath. In her will, made with her husband's consent, dated November 14, 1735, she left all her possessions to her daughter, Mrs. Scawen. She directed to be privately buried near her mother, that only two coaches should attend her funeral, and that no monument should be placed over her grave. She was buried at Donhead St. Andrew on September 13, 1736.

This mysterious lady being thus identified, it is to be hoped that the publication of the facts may elicit some further information respecting her father and mother, Richard and Tryphena Lloyd. The former had a brother Edmund, citizen and grocer of London, who died in 1692, leaving issue.

JOSEPH LEMUEL CHESTER.

THE UNIVERSITY OF BREDA: LETTER FROM EDWARD NORGATE, WINDSOR HERALD, TO SIR ABRAHAM WILLIAMS.

The following letter is from a MS. (Lansdowne, 1238) in the British Museum, which, although itself only a copy, bears evident marks of being a careful transcript of the original autograph. Edward Norgate was one of Fuller's "Worthies"; some account of him may also be seen in Noble's *College of Arms* and in Walpole's *Anecdotes of Painting*. His name also occurs frequently in Mr. Sainsbury's *Life of Rubens*, but on one point Mr. Sainsbury has been misled, viz. as to the time of his death, for relying on the Bodleian MS. of Norgate's work, *On the Art of Limning*, which he says is dated July 8, 1654, he adds (p. 212),

"Fuller is therefore in error when he says Norgate died December 23, 1650." If this MS. is really dated 1654, I can only say that the date was not written by Norgate, for although Fuller appears to have made a slight mistake as to the day, he is quite right as to both the month and the year. The parish register of St. Benet, Paul's Wharf, records that he was *buried* December 23, 1650. Moreover, his will was proved in the following January.

"Worthie Sir Abraham Williams,—Upon recoverie of my late grievous sicknesse, I left Utrecht, with intention for England, but finding at Rotterdam the Winds contrarie, the Cheshire Shipp not come, and leasure more then enough, I was easily invited by the vertuous and noble young Ld. Stanhope to accompany him to Breda, to the inauguration of the new Academie, founded by the Prince of Orange, to his Eternall honour: the Celebritie whereof is now become the Argument of this letter: I hope I shall not neede to begg yᵉ pardon, for it is not my meaning to doe anything that needes it, my ignorance and impertinence rather deserve yᵉ pitty. Bee pleased therefore to imagine the great Church pulpitt and pewes richlie sett out and adorned with arras, the Towne in their holyday cloths, the horse-troops and foot companies making a goodlie Guard from the Castle to the Church, between whom the seven Professours were orderly ledd and attended severally one between two the principall Magistrates of the Citty. The Professours names, nation and offices will as I conceive best come in here: They are Monsʳ Renesse of Utrecht for Divinitie, Rector and Regent of this new Universitie, Monsʳ Dauberus an Almaine for yᵉ Civill Law, Kiperus of Prussia for Phisick, Brosterhusius a Hollander for Plantes, hearbes and Greeke, Mʳ Pell an Englishman and of Cambridge for the Mathematiques, Philemon a Bohemian for Historie, and Bornius of Utrecht for Logick and Ethickes. The Secretarie and Bibliothecarius is one Housman of the Palatinate, the Curatores or Stewards are Sʳ Constantine Hugins, that noble Virtuoso, the Heere Van Henflett, and Dʳ Rivett: thus much for the men, now for the matter: In this Order and Equipage they were on Munday the 16th of this moneth brought to the great Church, ushered with blew officers in Liveries, and blew musick, besides a formall Bedell, upon whose Ebon staffe was perch't a silver Statue of Minerva, a graven image it was, but sure no Papisticall Pallas, but very conformable, for shee went to Church and ushered her new Mʳˢ into the Chancell, where they were entertained with varietie of excellent Musick, with voices and other Instruments to the Organ:—In this interim came the Princesse of Orange, a great Patronesse of Arts and friend to this soe great and good a worke, a goodlie Lady and of a noble aspect and presence, richly besett wᵗʰ Orientall Pearle and flaming Diamonds; shee was ledd by Count Willᵐ of Freesland and surrounded and attended wᵗʰ a Corona of beautifull Ladies, among whom were the Princesses her daughters, the Princesse of Portugall, Madame Dona and Madame Brederode, &ᶜ, being seated under a seate neere and opposite to yᵉ Pulpitt: an anthem was sung to yᵉ Organ with verses and Chorus, during which time the Professours were brought to their places neare the Pulpitt, which was ascended by Dʳ Rivett, who made a grave and learned Oration in Latine, containing a gratefull acknowledgment of Gods mercies towards the Prince for soe many great & remarkeable victories, specially for regaining this town of Breda, now designed a Seate for Arts, yᵉ Graces and yᵉ Muses, that was formerly a Stage for Warre, death and desolation. This

speech ended they had another bout at Musick, and then went upp Housman their secretarie, who reade yᵉ booke of Statutes for regulating the Universitie, wᵗʰ the Priviledges and immunities of the Professours and Students, too long for a Letter. This done the Princesse departed, and all the Professours, Curatores, with many a Countrie Parson and Predicant, returned to the Castle, guarded and attended as before. In the great Hall they were entertained with a Royall feast. The rest of that day was spent in Collations, Musick, fireworkes and Drinke. The great Gunnes were heard as farr as the high Steeple was seen flaming wᵗʰ artificiall fires till midnight. The next morning the Curatores and Professours went to take possession of the new Colledge, made of an old Nunnerie, and now called Collegium Auriacum; a handsome Chappell there is for the Auditorie, and soe called, being newly furbasht, and fitted wᵗʰ seates and Deskes for yᵉ purpose. In an upper Chappell preparation was made for yᵉ Princesse and her attendants, who being sett, an Oration was made in Latine by Renesse the magnificus Rector (for soe he called himselfe). It was as Long, Leane and drie as the Speaker, among other passages he saide, there needed noe greater miracle to shew Gods good liking of this good worke then the fair weather, which instantly changed before his speech was done, for it presently began to rain, and so continued till night. To sweeten this was heard a service of very good Voices to a portative organ, which done, an affected frenchified high German mounts, being for the Civill Law, himselfe of a small Volume, as was his discretion, his discourse in folio, interlarded with a great deale of Hebrew, wherein he told yᵉ Princesses and Ladies, to their great Edification, what were the Lawes among the Jewes concerning Circumcision, (a strange impertinence, their persons and sex considered). Yet the Princesse with admirable patience satt him out, and to shew shee was not in her way as Victorious and invincible as her husband in his, shee returned in yᵉ afternoone and letts the Prussian Kiperus doe his worst, whose businesse being Physick, the stony-hearted fellow had yᵉ Conscience to hold these poore Ladies three long houres wᵗʰ comparing yᵉ Princesse to yᵉ moone, and the Ladies attending to lesser Constellations, but not a word of his own occupation. This dayes worke ended, the next beginnes wᵗʰ Brosterhusius, who, the Princesses sett, and yᵉ usuall preface of Musick done, beginns to expresse the many and various uses of Plants, herbes, trees &ᶜ for Nutriment, Medicament, Navigation &ᶜ and how in America shipping, tackling, and Anchors too, were all made of the Coco tree, and other trees; this was the honestest man appeared as yet, and of Laudable Brevitie, and was succeeded by our Countrieman Mʳ Pell, for the Mathematiques, who with admirable elocution, and most gracefull Deliverie deserved and gott soe great Commendations of all his auditory as it was a measuring cast, whether his skill in his Art or Oratory exceeded. Hee was little above halfe an hour, and yett found time to tell us soe much concerning the use and dignity of that Studdy, the Antiquity it had and Patronage it found from great Kings and Princes, wᵗʰ ample answeres to the usuall objections of those that deterr men from the study of the Mathematiques, as sufficiently shewed him a full Mʳ in his profession, an honour to his Countrie, and worthy the favour of soe great a Prince; his conclusion was very respective, and excellently worded, wᵗʰ particular thankes to yᵉ Princesse, mentioning the late* Royall marriage and his double obligation thereupon: A Complement to his Colleagues and Students ended yᵉ Oration, and this forenoones work. In the afternoone

* Mary, daughter of Charles I., married to the Prince William (second) of Orange.

yᵉ, Princesse returnes, and yᵉ Musick ended, a sage Bohemian beginnes his Historicall Oration, in praise of his owne profession, as yee know, Chacun Loüe sa Marchandise ; he was an honest man, and made it short and good. Bornius for Logick (an excellent Scholler) ne're appeared to speake, being reserv'd against the Prince of Orange his coming, to whom the Princesse went to Berghem the next morning. Thus as you see I have presumed upon yʳ patience (since I can live no where out of your service) to make an occasion, when I find none, that though it signifie nothing but il poco ch'io posso, yet it may serve for the testimonio del molto che vorrei. soe Sʳ I wish you as much happinesse as I want, and will be found in all fortunes and occasions

Yoʳ most affectionate Servant
EDW: NORGATE.

Bredæ, 22° Sept: 1646."

FR. NORGATE.

7, King Street, Covent Garden.

"CELTS."

The origin of this word as applied to the stone and bronze implements of the pre-historic ages has always been a "crux antiquariorum." The question has been recently brought under public notice by a paper read at a meeting of the Society of Antiquaries by Mr. C. Knight Watson, M.A., the secretary, and reported in the *Times* of May 15. Several letters have since appeared in the *Times* referring to Mr. Watson's paper. The question is interesting in itself, but much more so as leading to the examination of a Biblical text in which there is an important difference between the Hebrew, the Septuagint, and the Vulgate versions. The pages of " N. & Q." seem to be a more suitable vehicle for the permanent record of a discussion of this nature than the columns of a daily newspaper. I propose to call attention to the leading points involved.

The substance of Mr. Knight Watson's paper is briefly as follows. Mr. J. Evans, F.S.A., in his work on ancient stone implements, derives the word *celt* from Latin *celtis* or *celtes*, a chisel, adding that the word is only found in the Vulgate translation of Job, and is considered as a derivative from *cælo*, to engrave, and the equivalent of *cælum*, a graver or chisel. After the Vulgate the word is next met with in Beger's *Thesaurus*, 1696. From this source it was borrowed by Borlase in his *Antiquities of Cornwall*. From thence it has crept into glossaries and works on archæology until it has been generally accepted as a generic term for a definite class of archaic implements.

Mr. Watson, in the examination of a certain Latin MS. of the Bible, found in Job xix. 23-4 the word written *certe*, and on further investigation discovered that other copies, especially the Codex Amiatinus, the oldest existing MS. of the Vulgate, gave the same reading, implying, as stated, that the patriarch wished his words to be engraven on the rock for surety, not repeating any expression for the burin or graving tool. It was further

stated that in one MS. of the twelfth century (Harl. 4773) *certe* is found changed into *celte*, and in another, bearing date A.D. 1148, part of the *r* is erased to make *celte*.

A remark was made by Mr. Thomson, of the British Museum, which does not appear to have attracted the notice it deserved, that "in the earlier centuries, say from the eighth to the twelfth, the *rt* was written exactly as the *lt* came to be written afterwards, so that copyists might very easily make the mistake." Thus far the discussion at the Society of Antiquaries.

On May 17 a letter appeared in the *Times* pointing out that the alleged discovery was nothing new, and quoting Ducange (*sub voc.* "Celtis") with precisely the same information. Another correspondent suggests that there are signs of the Vulgate having been translated, not from the Hebrew, but from the Septuagint, in which, as he alleges, there is no word answering to *certe*, and that the mistake may have been in the Codex Amiatinus, but he goes into no particulars.

The subject presents a tempting opportunity for a little verbal criticism, to which the philological fraternity are rather prone, and in many points of view it possesses remarkable interest.

The question turns upon a single word in the Vulgate version of Job xix. 24, whether it should be *certe* or *celte*. It cannot be dismissed in the summary manner it was disposed of at the Society of Antiquaries, as the solution there given raises more difficulties than it allays.

We have three principal sources from which to derive our knowledge of the Old Testament :— 1. The Masoretic text of the Hebrew, from which our authorized version is translated ; 2. The Greek Septuagint, the Hebrew original of which is unknown ; 3. The Latin Vulgate, adopted by the Roman Catholic Church as its standard. These three authorities in regard to the text under consideration differ rather materially. It is necessary to take the twenty-third and twenty-fourth verses together, as the words "for ever," or their equivalents, which in the Hebrew occur in the twenty-fourth verse, are in the Septuagint transferred to the twenty-third, or if the division of the verses be overlooked, they may be read with either. In the Vulgate they do not occur. The twenty-third verse, as it stands in the Hebrew, may be thus literally translated : "Who will cause now that my words be written ? Who will cause them to be inscribed in a book ?" The twenty-fourth verse then proceeds thus :—

בְעֵט־בְּרוֹל וְעֹפֶרֶת לָעַד בַּצּוּר יֵחָצֵבוּן

yechatsbhun batsur lä(y)ad ve(y)ophåreth barzel be(y)ét —"with an iron style and lead for ever on the rock they shall be cut." The Septuagint is as follows : twenty-third, τίς γὰρ ἂν δοίη γραφῆναι τὰ ῥήματά μου, τεθῆναι δὲ αὐτὰ ἐν βιβλίῳ εἰς τὸν αἰῶνα ; twenty-fourth, Ἐν γραφείῳ σιδήρῳ καὶ μολίβῳ, ἢ ἐν πέτραις ἐγγλυφῆναι. This would be literally, "Who will give my words to be inscribed, to be placed in a book for ever with an iron style and lead, or on the rocks to be graven?" Without much violence to the text the "for ever" may apply either to the first or last clause of the passage.

We now come to the Vulgate, which presents much more difficulty. It reads :—V. 23. "Quis mihi tribuat ut scribantur sermones mei? quis mihi det ut exarentur in libro." V. 24. "Stylo ferreo, et plumbi lamina, vel celte sculpantur in silice?"

It will be observed that the Hebrew láad, the Greek εἰς τὸν αἰῶνα, "for ever," is altogether omitted, and the words vel celte introduced.

A comparison of the texts shows that the Latin Vulgate must have been translated from the Greek rather than from the Hebrew, and it is in this transition that the difficulty arises. The disjunctive conjunction ἢ would be rightly rendered in Latin by vel; if the ἢ were by the translator mistaken for the adverb of confirmation ἦ, certe would be the correct rendering ; but here we have both. The literal translation would then be, "with an iron style and lead, or verily on the rock to be graven." There is no authority in the Greek for the insertion of both vel and certe, nor is there any for the introduction of celte. If it be supposed that certe is intended to represent the εἰς τὸν αἰῶνα of the Greek, it is the only instance of such rendering. The phrase is common in the New Test., but is usually expressed by in æternum, or in one or two instances by in sæcula. If we inquire how the passage has been understood by the English translators of the Vulgate, we find in Wickliffe's version (A.D. 1380) the following :— "Who giveth to me that my woordes be writen ? Who giveth to me that thei be graven in a boc with an iren pointel, or with a pece of led ; or with a chisell that thei be graven in flint ?" The first edition of the Douay version, printed in 1609, has the passage as follows :—"Who wil grant me that my wordes may be writen ? Who wil geve me that they may be drawen in a booke, with yron penne, and in plate of leade, or els with stile might be graven in flintstone ?" Coverdale translates it : "O that my wordes were written ; O that they were put in a boke ; wolde God they were graven with an iron pen in lead or in stone." This is taken direct from the Greek, omitting the expression "for ever." It is clear that the MSS. from which Wickliffe, about A.D. 1370, and the Douay authors, A.D. 1609, formed their version gave the passage vel celte.

At the meeting of the Society of Antiquaries Mr. Thomson remarked on the close resemblance of the contractions for rt and lt in the old MSS. On this subject Chassant, in his Paléographie des Chartes, remarks on a certain abbreviation :—

Il tient lieu fréquemment de la syllabe er. Quand le signe est fixé à un b ou à une l, il montre dans certaine cas que ces lettres sont mises pour ub, el, comme en vel, libellis."

He adds :—

" Ainsi, à l'égard du style informe de la basse latinité, il se présentera bon nombre des mots qui feront hésiter dans le déchiffrement, par l'impossibilité de s'en rendre compte."

The question is not one to dogmatize about, but on the whole the balance rather inclines in favour of the authenticity of celte. The strongest argument in its favour is the fact that St. Jerome, who was undoubtedly the translator or the recensionist of the Vulgate text, in his Epist. ad Pammachium, quotes the passage in question, and gives the word as celte. So far as I am aware, neither the authenticity of the epistle nor the genuineness of the text has ever been called in question.

Ducange, sub voc. "Celtis," gives no opinion of his own, but quotes Brito's vocabulary, where it is stated, "in originali ut antiquæ Bibliæ habent certe et nullus sanctorum expositorum poni celte." An inscription, "Sed malleolo et celte literatus silex," was said to have been discovered at Pola in Istria. It is given in Gruter's Corpus Inscriptionum, p. 329, with a foot-note, "Ex Fabricio Manutio aliisque hanc inscriptionem fabulosam et ridiculam esse ait." This may probably be so, but the evidence is scarcely less strong than if it were genuine. The introduction by a forger of an unknown word would be so likely to throw discredit on the authenticity of the forgery that it is the very thing he would take care to avoid. If no such word was in existence, how did the forger come by it ?

Beger (Thesaurus Numismatum, &c., 1696), vol. iii. p. 418, introduces a plate of a celt with a description. The text is in Latin in the form of a dialogue between two friends, Archæophilus and Dulodorus. The former says : "Both the name and instrument are strange to me." The other replies : "It is a tool used by the statuaries in cutting and polishing their figures. By the Greeks it is called ἐγκοπεὺς, which word is used by Lucian in his Somnium, ἐγκοπέα γὰρ τινα μοι δοὺς, which Johannes Benedictus turns into ' Celte data.'" "Celte ?" exclaims Archæophilus ; "unless I am mistaken this word is unknown in Latin." "It is found," replies his friend, " in the Vulgate version of the Book of Job, ch. xix., although some read certe instead of celte, which seems less suitable. An old glossary gives, ' Celtem, instrumentum ferreum.' If, however, this does not commend itself to you, a softer vocable may be employed, and you can call it cœlum."

Mr. Ben. Street in the Athenæum of June 11, 1870, has a note on the word. After referring to St. Jerome's quotation above mentioned, he says : "The word seems genuine, and the root of culter and cultrus. Marianus Victorius defends the reading *celte,* and appeals to the Septuagint for confirmation."

I think I have given above pretty nearly all the information extant on the subject. It is not at all improbable that Cymric *cellt,* a flint stone ; Lat. *celtis,* a chisel ; *culter,* a knife ; *cultrus,* Low Lat. a sword ; A.-S. *culter,* a ploughshare, were all from the same root *cael,* to cut.   J. A. PICTON.

Sandyknowe, Wavertree.

TARVIN PARISH CHURCH.

A few miles from Chester, on the highway to London, is the old village of Tarvin. It has still many curious timbered houses, but most of the interest of the place centres in the church. A few years ago it presented the usual appearance of one which had escaped the hand of the restorer: the pulpit (a typical "three decker," comprising pulpit, reading desk, and clerk's desk in one) was placed about the middle of the building, and all around it straggled the big "loose-box" pews. A year or two ago all this was changed ; funds were raised, architects employed, and the church given over to their tender mercies. This "restoration" has, however, revealed some interesting facts, and on the whole been conducted with commendable care. Before proceeding further, however, I would wish to quote the description which I find in the last published part of the new edition of Ormerod's *Cheshire.*

It, he says, "has been a fine specimen of the enriched Gothic of the fifteenth century, and such of the battlements, friezes, and corbels as have remained unaltered exhibit a profusion of carved ornaments. One entrance is by a south porch, *the doorway of which appears to be of earlier date than the rest of the fabric.* The other is by an arch with an ogee canopy under the tower between two highly decorated niches. The tower is of four stories embattled. The body of the church is separated from the side aisles by six arches, one of which, attached to the east end of the south aisle, is considerably narrower than the others. The pillars have foliaged capitals. At the end of the nave is a chancel; a small chancel or oratory (built by the Bruens of Bruen Stapleford, and confirmed * to the Bruens by Thomas Kingsley, LL.B., and Richard Strete, commissioners of the Dean and Chapter of Lichfield at a visitation 1 Henry VIII.) is situated at the east end of the south aisle and separated from the aisle by a carved screen."—Ormerod's *History of Cheshire,* ed. by Thomas Helsby, part viii. p. 312.

The writer of the above, it will be seen, gives the church a date about the fifteenth century, though he acknowledges a doorway on the south seems of earlier date. I cannot but think that if more consideration had been given to the building different conclusions might have been arrived at. Obviously all the windows in the north aisle have been Perpendicular, but all have been long ago changed into "churchwarden gothic," save a fine window at the east end. But the south aisle is

* Harl. MS. 2022, 52 Bruen deeds.

altogether different, and the only two windows that remain unaltered belong very clearly to the Decorated period, and the doorway, to which Ormerod vaguely alludes, is Decorated, much as described in Parker's *Introduction to Gothic Architecture,* p. 177. But it is on entering that the difference of age between the south aisle and the rest of the church becomes most striking. The screen before referred to is a good specimen of the Decorated rood-screen which divided the choir from the nave. During the recent restoration a small piscina was discovered in the south side of the east end of the chapel, close to where the altar formerly stood. It is probable that much of the elaborate ornamentation which distinguished the piscinæ of the Decorated period has been destroyed, and we have now only left rude remains, sufficiently preserved, however, to show clearly what once it must have been. In the wall between the east end of the chapel and the chancel is a "squint," to enable persons in the former to see the elevation of the Host at the high altar. This appears to be another proof that the Bruen chapel belongs to an earlier date, as there is no such opening on the north side of the chancel, but only a large arch, the requirements of the congregation of the northern aisle being evidently considered at the erection of the later or Perpendicular portions. The remaining features of the building are Perpendicular. What I now desire information upon is this : Am I right in supposing that the south aisle was the original church, and that when the new centre aisle and north aisle were built, the space behind the screen in the south aisle was assigned to the Bruens as a private chapel ? If so, is there any documentary proof ? Or is all the building of one age, and am I altogether wrong ? If so, how is the striking difference in architecture to be explained ? The register of the church might attract the attention of some students ; it contains among other records a notice of one of the Bruens of Stapleford (an estimable man, it seems, but rather fanatical, who made his influence felt in Tarvin by destroying all the fine old coloured glass), who was thus (1623) commemorated by an admiring and poetical parish clerk :—

> "An Israelite in whom no guile
> Or fraud was ever found;
> A Phœnix rare
> Whose virtues fair
> Through all our coasts do sound."

Into Ormerod's other statements relating to church I shall not now enter, but may mention that only the pillars on the south side have foliaged capitals.   WILLIAM GEORGE BLACK.

1, Alfred Terrace, Glasgow.

DIXWELL THE REGICIDE.—By the courtesy of Mr. Maggs, the well-known bookseller of Church

Street, Paddington Green, I have had an opportunity of examining a rare ultra-Liberal periodical, the *Democratic Review* for 1849-50, in which I expected to find some information respecting an historical question which I am investigating. The book is a very curious one, and contains many articles by Kossuth, Mazzini, Louis Blanc, &c. It commenced in June, 1849, and came to an end in September, 1850, when it was succeeded by the *Red Republican*, conducted by the same editor, G. Julian Harney. In looking through this volume (which is, I believe, as scarce as it is curious, and therefore deserving to be noticed in "N. & Q.") I came across an account of John Dixwell, one of the Regicides, from which I venture to extract the following passage. Noble mentions his death at New Haven, but says nothing of his having lived there under a feigned name.

"GRAVE OF A TYRANNICIDE.—The New Haven (U.S.) newspapers contain accounts of an incidental opening of an ancient grave in the process of erecting a monument. One hundred and sixty years ago—that is, on or about the first day of April, 1689—there were deposited in that grave the remains of an old man who, for twenty years before his death, had lived in New Haven, but had been known intimately only to a very few. He had been a member of the Church (now known as the First Church in New Haven), and had been much respected for his intelligence and piety, no less than for the dignity of his manners as if he had been familiar with great things. The rumour had spread abroad in the little village that this mysterious old man was one of those who, for the part they had acted as champions of 'the good old cause,' in the then recent times of revolutionary conflict, had been compelled to flee with a price on their heads. The grave was that of John Dixwell, whose name had been subscribed with his own hand to the death warrant of ' the man Charles Stuart,' King of England. In his seclusion he had borne the name of James Davids.

"Soon after his death, 'the Revolution,' which had already taken place in England, became known on the American side of the Atlantic. The faithless dynasty of the Stuarts had been again expelled, and the secrets of that mysterious grave, with the equivocal epitaph, 'J. D., Esqre, deceased March ye 18th, in ye 82nd year of his age, 1688-9,' were no longer so perilous. The widow and children of James Davids resumed the name of Dixwell; and papers were placed upon record in the Probate Office, which demonstrated the identity of the deceased with the Colonel John Dixwell of the Parliamentary army. In one of those papers subscribed by the deceased, he had used the following words, which showed that he was still of the same mind as when he subscribed the death warrant of an anointed king :—' I am confident that the Lord will appear for his people, and the good old cause for which I suffer, and that there will be those in power again who will relieve the injured and oppressed.' This confidence he carried with him to his grave."

D. T. R.

THE FAVOURITE CHAIR OF CHARLES I. : THE ALBERT CHAIN.—At an art exhibition held in Birmingham about 1846, among other rare sights were the chair once belonging to Charles I. and several other curious things, that belonged to the same monarch. They were exhibited by Dr. Sands Cox, who was in some way descended from

Archbishop Juxon. Dr. Cox is dead, but I ha no doubt that the chair is now in the possession some one of his family.

Prince Albert visited the exhibition, and it believed in these parts that what he then saw ga· him the idea of the great Exhibition of 1851.] show what great things often grow from ver small ones, I may mention that when the Prin· visited Birmingham the jewellers of the town pr· sented him with a gold watch-chain of beautif· workmanship. That chain begat the fashic which has brought hundreds of thousands pounds into the town, finding employment f· hundreds of people, and *now* who among us b· wears an Albert chain?   FATHER FRANK. Birmingham.

To "DEMUR."—The above is one of sever· popular misapplications of terms of art. Ev· good writers are accustomed to speak of "demu ring" to a statement or proposition in the sense denying it. The derivation of "demur" is · course the (old) French *demorrer*, to delay ; hen· it was used in pleading to denote "that the ol jecting party *will not proceed* with the pleading because no sufficient statement has been made o· the other side, but will wait the judgment of th Court whether he is bound to answer" (Stephen o Pleading). In law a demurrer admits the a· legations of the pleading demurred to, only puttin· in issue the legal question of their sufficienc). The analogous use of the term in popular languag· would be to aver the irrelevancy of a fact to a· argument, and to this purpose it would be mor correct to confine it.   C. C. M. Temple.

SIXTEENTH CENTURY BOOK INSCRIPTION.—Th· following lines are written by a sixteenth centur· hand in a copy of Horace printed at Antwer· 1540. In lines 5 and 6 are allusions which ar· obscure, and after the capital letter *G* in line 6 syllable is wanting—a small *m* with a curve over i· appears there, the meaning of which I canno· find :—

"My money to me this booke did geve,
    I hope to keepe it as long as it last ;
whose booke it is if you will knowe
    by letters twaine I will you shewe,
the one is H : that shines so bright,
    thother is G....all men fight.
if that you chance this name to misse
    Look downe belowe and there it is.
                                Hennrey Gouldinge."

In the second line we should naturally expect t· find " I live" instead of "it last," as better rhym· and quite as good sense.   BOILEAU.

DIMPLES AND SHORT TONGUES.—It is th· opinion of nurses that babies which have dimple· have short tongues, and will lisp.   H. C.

Queries.

[We must request correspondents desiring information on family matters of only private interest, to affix their names and addresses to their queries, in order that the answers may be addressed to them direct.]

VOLTAIRE.—How many of the works of Voltaire have ever been published in English? It would seem that his writings are very little known to the majority of English people, for on this his centenary I find him very commonly spoken of as an atheist; and the *Rock* revives the old but often refuted calumny describing the philosopher of Ferney as " the man whose war-cry was *Ecrasons l'infâme* (meaning our Saviour)." Was not Dugdale's edition of the *Philosophical Dictionary* translated by a brother of Leigh Hunt?
W. M. G. W.

[A probable explanation of the phrase cited by W. M. G. W. is given in our Paris contemporary, *L'Intermédiaire*, for March 25 last, where the writer compares it with a recent *mot* of almost equal celebrity, "Le cléricalisme c'est l'ennemi," and considers "Ecrasons l'infâme" to have been aimed against the Jesuits, not against the Christian religion or its founder.]

PRINCESS DASCHKOFF.—Horace Walpole tells us that this celebrated Russian lady, when in England in 1770, translated into French the eulogium on Peter the Great which the Archbishop of Moscow had pronounced upon the occasion of the Russian victory over the Turkish fleet, and that Dr. Hinchcliffe, Bishop of Peterborough, was to translate it into English. Did such a translation ever appear? If so, the title, date, &c., will oblige.
AN OLD READER.

" ARTHURUS SEVERUS O'TOOLE NONESUCH, ÆTATIS 80."—I have fallen in with a small oval print of an aged gentleman in armour, of, I should say, about the time of Queen Elizabeth, and bearing a peculiarly ornamented rod or sceptre in his right hand. Round the print is the superscription, "Arthurus Severus O'Toole Nonesuch, ætatis 80 "; and beneath are the following verses :—

" Great Mogul's landlord, of both Indies king,
Whose self admiring fame doth loudly sing,
Writes four score years, more kingdoms he hath right to,
The stars say so, and for them he will fight too :
And though this worthless age will not believe him,
But clatter, spatter, slander, sc ff, and grieve him,
Yet he and all the world in thisagree,
That such another Toole will never be."

Can you or any of your readers tell me who this King O'Toole was, or whose the verses are?
I. M. P.
Curzon Street, W.

SWEDISH PROVERB.—
" Es ist nicht gut trinken aus des Korporal's Kanne."
In Cramer's *Denkwürdigkeiten der Gräfin Königsmark*, vol. i. p. 239, this is given as a Swedish proverb by Count Löwenhaupt to his wife. She

had previously warned him against over-conviviality; and he writes :—
" Um Dich hinsichtlich meiner zu beruhigen, will ich Dir ein Sprichwort sagen, woraus Du das Uebrige errathen kannst."
And then follows the proverb. What is the meaning of it? and has it reference to his imbibing or not?
R. C. S. W.
Reading-Room, British Museum.

PHILOLOGICAL.—I send the following quotation with the hope that the query may receive attention from "N. & Q." :—

" We commend as an agreeable puzzle to comparative philologists the task of determining the relation in which the following words stand to each other: *Ding, thing, saka, sache, chose, causa;* and to antiquarian legists that of ascertaining how the notion of *thing* or *chose* became permanently attached to the notion of a law court. At the risk of putting our foot into a wasp's nest, we will throw out the following suggestion. The further we penetrate into the border land between historic and prehistoric times, the more the political business and the judicial business of the earliest Aryan assemblies melt into one common mass as *public* business, into *one* Court as *the* Court in which all business is transacted. Could not then the *Dinghof*, or *Thing-court*, or some analogous term, have originally designated *the* Court *par excellence* in which the public business, the *public thing, res publica*, was transacted? The public business would very naturally get to be looked upon as 'the business,' the public things as 'the thing,' and the public Court as 'the Thing-Court.' The analogy of *res publica* is, at all events, a curious one, and that *public* business generally, and not *judicial* business specifically, was the early idea connected with *Ding* and *Thing* seems clear from the fact that the Scandinavian Parliamentary bodies have to this day retained the name (*e.g.* in Denmark the Upper and Lower Houses are respectively the *Landsting* and the *Folksthing*)."—*Local Government and Taxation of Germany*, by R. B. D. Morier, Cobden Club Essays, p. 371, note *.
G. LAURENCE GOMME.

" FAMILIARITY BREEDS CONTEMPT."—On the subject of proverbs I would ask, Which is the original and legitimate meaning of "Familiarity breeds contempt"? Is it (1) too familiar intercourse breeds contempt in your associates; or (2) long familiarity with benefits, &c., leads us to under-value them? I have seen the proverb quoted in both senses.
H. C. D.
Woodbridge.

KITTESFORD BARTON, NEAR WELLINGTON, SOMERSETSHIRE.—Can any of your readers give me information about this old building?
E. A. S.

ORIENTAL TITLE.—Can any of your readers tell me the literal meaning and precise value of the title of Punt Sucheo, held by the ruler of Bhore, in Western India? He is described as the last relic of Brahmin sovereignty in India. TREGEAGLE.

" PATTERROONE " OR " PUTTERROONE."—In a MS. deposition of the year 1655 I find that George

Haybeard was accused of saying that Mr. Wm. Collings, Vicar of Modbury, " had a necke as bigg as a bull, and that he was a *patterroone* to his kinsman Thomas Shepheard." Is this word known ? I am not sure that it is not *putterroone*. In another place I find it spelt with one *t*.

A. H. A. HAMILTON.

HERALDIC.—In the *Book of Family Crests*, ninth edition, p. 212, pub. by Bell & Daldy, Fleet Street, appears the following :—

" Greenhill, Lond. and Midd., a demi griffin, gu. (powdered with thirty-nine mullets,* or), Pl. 27, No. 35.
'Honos alit artes.'

" * The number of mullets with which this crest is charged is stated to have originated in the fact that the first bearer was the thirty-ninth child of the same parents."

Can any of the readers of " N. & Q." oblige me by answering the following questions :—Who were the persons referred to in the above foot-note ? Have there been, in modern times, any or many instances recorded in Haydn's *Index of Biog.* same parents " ? And is it usual to grant to a man heraldic honours on account of being one of an unusually numerous family ?   H. G. H.

BRADSHAW THE REGICIDE.—Did any other of the name of Bradshaw hold a seat in the House of Commons, either before or after the Protectorate ?
D. H. B.

GARDINER'S " PSALMODY."—Can any of your readers inform me whether this was the work of Wm. Gardiner, author of the *Music of Nature?* and, if so, where can one get any tidings of him ? He is not mentioned in Haydn's *Index of Biog.* nor in Phillips's *Biog. Dict.* It would appear that the characteristic of his work was that he had contrived to adapt passages of Haydn, Mozart, and Beethoven to the Psalms of David. It was sanctioned by the Prince Regent and the Archbishop of Canterbury. What has become of the work ? Was it ever largely adopted? and, if so, why has it fallen so utterly into disuse ?   C. A. WARD.
Mayfair.

POPULAR LEGAL FALLACIES.—Some time ago (I believe in some work on jurisprudence) I came across a list of popular fallacies on legal subjects, such as " that one must cut off one's heir with a shilling," " a corpse cannot be seized for debt," &c. Could you, through the medium of your valuable journal, give me any insight as to what work it probably was I saw the list in, or where else I can find such a list ?   INQUIRER.

THE " TE DEUM."—Why is not " white-robed " used instead of " noble," as applied to the army of martyrs ? The translator in the first English Prymer (see Maskell's *Monumenta Ritualia Ecclesiæ Anglicanæ*, vol. ii. p. 13) is much happier

in catching the spirit of the original w " Thee, preisith the white oost (Throughout the ordinary translations o ficent hymn there are, to my mind, 1 fections, and a great failure in the just of the original.   W. H. HAI
Gravesend.

[MR. HART will find the first clause of discussed at length in " N. & Q .," 5ᵗʰ S. i 112, 312 ; v. 330, 397, 514; vi. 76, 136, 450 172.]

ADMIRAL VERNON.—In what rel noble house of Vernon of Sudbury a did this hero of Porto Bello stand ? that branch which settled in Ireland sixteenth century, and possessed Clo co. Dublin ?   A. I

THE ARRANGEMENT OF AUTOGR some correspondent kindly advise n best mode of arranging a large and 1 lection of autograph letters, so as to el easily shown to one's friends ? To pe applied to the corners or only to one averse, as it renders the autograph without destruction ; neither are slits so as to admit the four corners satisf cially when the letter consists of mor one. To bury them in drawers or am also disinclined, as this prevents generally and readily accessible. C be suggested for making a collection (letters as accessible as (say) an ordin photographs better than slipping t between the blank leaves of large vol of course, for the purpose ?

Perhaps any one who will be goo reply to this query will also advis details it is desirable to mention whe catalogue.
Oxford and Cambridge Club.

ZOFFANY. — The painter Zoffany worked for some years in Lucknow. your readers give me any information detailed information concerning the 1 of this painter can be found ? Did he any account of his life and experienc Are his letters, or possibly a journal, i or private collection ? He painted " 1 of Hyderbeck," " Tiger Hunt," and fight," all engraved by Earlom, in Luc information concerning the present these paintings and the Indian caree will be thankfully received.   I ha *History of the Royal Academy* and 1 *of Painters.*
Lucknow.

PROHIBITING THE BANNS.—I thin ing cutting from the *Elgin Courant, 1* is worthy of a corner in the pages of " N. & Q.," especially as I nowhere find a record of a similar "ancient usage" in its well-stored volumes. My query is, Why and for what did the "strapping young damsel" throw down a shilling as she made her protestation ?—

"On Sunday last, in the Gaelic church of Inverness, the church officer was, before the beginning of the service, making the usual proclamation of banns of marriage. When the names of a certain couple were mentioned, however, a strapping young damsel got to foot and protested, and, according to the ancient usage, threw down a shilling. The incident is somewhat curious, and certainly unusual, and created no ordinary sensation in the church."

C. H. STEPHENSON.

Barnes, Surrey.

AUTHORS OF BOOKS WANTED.—

A Faithful Abridgment of the Works of that Learned and Judicious Divine, Mr. Richard Hooker. With an Account of his Life. By a Divine of the Church of England. Lond., 1705. 8vo. pp. lvii-350.

ED. MARSHALL.

The Old House at Home.—Who wrote this song, and who set it to music ? I have not heard it or seen it since the days of my boyhood.   JOHN PICKFORD, M.A.

AUTHORS OF QUOTATIONS WANTED.—

"Arise, and hail the happy day,
    Cast all low cares of life away," &c.

"The Saviour ! O what endless charms
    Dwell in the blissful sound !" &c.
DEXTER.

"As bees on flowers alighting cease their hum,
So settling in their places Whigs are dumb."
JONATHAN BOUCHIER.

"Si vis pacem, para bellum."
H. A. B.

Replies.

DANTE: NIMROD, "INFERNO," XXXI. 67.

(5ᵗʰ S. ix. 288.)

" Rafèl mai amèch zabi almi."

J. T. F. asks if "these words are mere non-sense, or can be explained as an attempt at some Shemitic words." There is hardly a commentator on Dante, either English or Italian, who has not something to say about this strange passage. In Bianchi's excellent Florentine edition of the Divina Commedia, 1857, I find the following note :—

" Il sig. ab. Lanci in un suo dotto discorso stampato in Roma l'anno 1819 intese di mostrare che queste parole di Nembrotto sono dell' idioma arabo, e che significano : 'esalta lo splendor mio nell' abisso, siccome rifolgorò per lo mondo.' L' ab. Giuseppe Venturi veronese opinò che le parole di Nembrotto siano del linguaggio siriaco, e ne dava questa spiegazione : ' Rafel, per Dio ! o poter di Dio ! maì, perchè io, amèch, in questo profondo, o pozzo? zabì, torna indietro ; almi, nasconditi.' A me però pare più probabile l' opinione di chi crede che questo verso sia un miscuglio di parole senza alcun senso tolte da diversi dialetti orientali, e stia a rappresentare la confusione

delle lingue avvenuta presso la torre elevata da quel superbo."

Fraticelli, in his notes to the Divina Commedia (edit. of 1877), says :—

" Tra le varie opinioni intorno al significato di queste strane parole, parmi la più probabile questa : che le cinque voci siano ciascuna d' un diverso linguaggio ; la prima dell' ebraico, le altre de' quattro principali dialetti, che si vogliono da quello derivati nella confusione di Babel. Che il verso compongasi di voci di dialetti babelici, par che lo accenni il Poeta medesimo, dicendo poco appresso : ' Egli stesso s' accusa : Questi è Nembrotto, ec.' In questa ipotesi il significato ne sarebbe : ' Poter di Dio ! perchè son io in questo profondo ? Torna indietro ; t' ascondi ': come, traducendosi nello spagnuolo-latino-tedesco-francese-italiano, si direbbe : ' Pardiez ! —cur ego—hier?—va-t-en ;—t' ascondi.'"

Leigh Hunt says (Stories from the Italian Poets, 1846, vol. i. p. 137) :—

"The gaping monotony of this jargon, full of the vowel a, is admirably suited to the mouth of the vast half-stupid speaker. It is like a babble of the gigantic infancy of the world."

Another of the poet's commentators, Raffaele Andreoli, speaks with some scorn of those who attempt to explain the passage. He says :—

" Dante says that to Nimrod no language is known, and that his language is known to no one. After this formal declaration could he ever have believed that the learned would have wasted so much time in searching for the meaning of Nimrod's strange accents ? "

J. T. F. speaks of "Nimrod's howl of fury," in inverted commas, as though he were quoting these words from some one. I do not know from whom, as there is no such phrase in Dante, or in Cary's version, which he mentions. He also gives the last word of the line as alams; it should be almi, in order to rhyme with palmi and salmi.

J. T. F. may be interested in comparing the above passage with a somewhat similar one in the earlier part of the poem, which is also a great crux to the poet's commentators. I allude to the words with which Plutus greets the two poets on their entrance into the fourth circle, in which the misers and the spendthrifts are punished—"Pape Satan, pape Satan aleppe" (Inferno, vii. 1); of which Longfellow says, "This outcry of alarm is differently interpreted by different commentators, and by none very satisfactorily."   JONATHAN BOUCHIER.

Bexley Heath, Kent.

No wonder that J. T. F., or any linguist, should be puzzled to extract any meaning from this passage. Venturi, in his admirable commentary (Divina Commedia, Verona edition, 1750), clearly shows that the words have no meaning at all—that they are, in fact, and were intended by the poet to be, pure gibberish. The matter is thus explained, and the whole of it is strikingly characteristic of Dante's style. One of the monstrous giants approached by Dante and his guide bellows out the passage quoted, and is immediately rebuked by Virgil, who tells him to resort again to his horn (which the giant had blown previously) rather than attempt uncouth and unintelligible speech. The confusion of tongues following the dispersion on the plain of Babel is alluded to ; and the noisy giant is supposed to be Nimrod, and that after the dispersion he would not be able to make himself understood by speech. In the context the poet refers to the Titans trying to scale heaven by piling mountain on mountain, and Jupiter conquering them with his thunder. This mixing up of Bible history and heathen fables is frequent in the *Divina Commedia*, and is to my mind a fatal blemish in a wonderful work. At the risk of raising a nest of hornets, I must say that I consider the whole plan of Dante's *Inferno* revolting to the mind of a Christian. M. H. R.

Your correspondent J. T. F. has lighted on one of the greatest difficulties of the *Divine Comedy*. It might almost be said that volumes have been written on this one line. Commentators differ very greatly as to its meaning. Some suppose the words to be mere gibberish (*guazzabuglio* is the expression of one editor) ; others say it is a string of sounds meant to represent the confusion of Babel. It is not easy, however, to imagine Dante inventing mere nonsense. Accordingly the Abbate Lanci endeavours to show that these words are Arabic, and that the meaning is, "Exalt my splendour in hell as it shone on earth." Venturi supposes the sentence to be Syriac, and would translate, "In God's name, why am I in this pit? Turn back, hide thyself." Fraticelli, again, maintains that each word is taken from a different language. With deference to these authorities, I cannot think their theories at all tenable. I would venture to inquire whether the sentence may not be very corrupt Hebrew. Dante, in the treatise *De Vulgari Eloquio* (i. § 6), asserts that Hebrew was the primitive language of the world ; and Nimrod is represented as living before the confusion of tongues. Surely, then, there can be little doubt that Dante believed him to speak Hebrew. In a somewhat parallel manner Arnault Daniel, the troubadour, is introduced speaking Provençal, and his words, in all editions of the *Divine Comedy* (*Purgatorio*, xxvi. 140, *sqq.*), are, according to M. Raynouard, as corrupt as I imagine this Hebrew sentence to be. Every reader of Dante knows that there is another line in the *Inferno* (vii. 1) which is as great a *crux* as this, and which perhaps is also meant for Hebrew. It may be added that there are many variants of the line under discussion. A comparison of the four early editions reprinted by Lord Vernon seems to show that the line originally stood :

"Raphel mai amech zabi almi."
GWAVAS.

If J. T. F. had consulted Cary's foot-note, he would have seen that "These unmeaning sounds,

it is supposed, are meant to express of languages at the building of Babel." R. M. Sr
Manse of Arbuthnott, N.B.

PROVERBS WHICH HAVE CHANGED ING (5th S. ix. 345.)—This is a sugg siderable interest, but in discussing taken to ascertain the true foundatio sayings. "The schoolmaster is abrc common expression just half a cer was a saying of Lord Brougham (J "The schoolmaster is abroad, and I armed with his primer, against the military array." This was short Brougham had been instrumental in of the Society for the Diffusion of ledge. The saying was at once adopt everywhere, but there were many wl it, and ridicule was cast upon it, a many other things that Brougham There was a caricature of a counti up, bearing a notice that the sch gone abroad, and an inference was had gone at the public cost to "Be This was a pictorial sneer at the At this time—and these were the "Stinkomalee"—if a teacher, lectu master made any mistake, it was t say, "The schoolmaster is *abroad*— a distinct saying, this expression h fifty years always meant "means of i open to all." But attempts have oft to pervert its meaning, just as the of a text of Scripture. This sayin scribed as a temporary proverbia meaning of which will pass away a learning increase.

The expression, "To put a spoke is one of which the original meanin clear. There are old illustrations meaning to help and to prevent. Th notes on this question in "N. & Q 269, 351, 522, 576, 624 ; ix. 45, 601 the last reference a quotation is give 1689 as meaning to check or stop progress.

Old sayings of this sort have in s got quite a new meaning, because purport is forgotten. Amongst sea was common to say, "Do not lose sparing a ha'perth of tar." But in i this saying takes the form of "D sheep for sparing a ha'perth of tar." question which of these two forms of saying is the older. Here the in same, though the illustration is so the case of the wheel there are clearl the real one and the ironical one, bu older ? EDW

Mr. Blenkinsopp is mistaken in supposing that "forty years ago this proverb meant that ignorance prevailed because the schoolmaster had shut up shop and gone abroad." It had the opposite meaning then, as it has now. The phrase was first used by Brougham when the Duke of Wellington was first minister in 1828. In one of his speeches in the House of Commons, Brougham, referring to the fact of the soldier being abroad, comforted himself with reflecting that the schoolmaster also was abroad. It was merely a bit of party glorification, and its application was evident. Brougham, however, lived to form a juster estimate of the great soldier-statesman, and gave utterance to it on a remarkable occasion in a noble oration. "Spoke in the wheel." May not this be a corruption of *spike?* A spike put into a wheel, though it would not prevent its use, as in the case of a cannon, would certainly impede its action.

C. Ross.

The history of this *supposed* proverb and its change of meaning is this : Lord Brougham threatened all opposers of the Reform Bill, enemies of "progress," &c., with speedy extinction, because "The schoolmaster is abroad." Seymour the caricaturist published in return a series of nine lithographic sketches (1834), in which he illustrated the comic results of the schoolmasters being "abroad" in another sense.   W. G.

In the seventeenth century "To put a spoke in his wheel" had exactly the same meaning as it has now, and is so used by Beaumont and Fletcher in *The Loyal Lover*, Act iv. sc. 6.

H. Fishwick, F.S.A.

The Choir Stalls at Haarlem : the Gospel and Epistle Sides of the Altar (5th S. ix. 61, 101, 413, 451.)—The Ambrosian rite is this, "Diaconus se transfert ad cornu exterius altaris in parte epistolæ, subdiaconus vero ad cornu evangelii, sibi versâ ad invicem facie stant." The Gospel was read on the south side of the church up to the middle of the ninth century towards the men (*Gemma Animæ*, lib. i. c. 22), the women seated on the north side being supposed to learn from their husbands at home (1 Cor. xiv. 35). The church had its proper orientation, so that north side was to the left and south side on the right hand of a person entering by the west door (Amalar, c. 820, *De Eccl. Off.*, l. iii. c. 2). Remigius of Auxerre, c. 882, says that for mystical reasons —symbolically of opposing the approach of the Evil One (Is. xiv. 13 ; comp. *Vita S. Hugonis, Epis. Lincoln.*, v. 940 ; Rupert, *De Div. Off.*, lib. iii. c. 22), as distinguished from the divine quarter (Hab. iii. 3)—the deacon read the Gospel towards the north. The lectern used by the deacon at Aix-la-Chapelle was the gift of St. Henry, 1011, and is placed on the right side of the choir entry. Some time later Micrologus complains of the read-

ing of the Gospel on the north side as an innovation (*De Eccles. Observ.*, c. ix.). Possibly the position was originally determined according to the axis of the church ; but tradition, by way of compromise, kept its place till recently at Notre Dame, Paris, where the deacon sang the Gospel in the southern ambon (upon the site of the rood-loft) facing northward. Where there was a rood-loft the subdeacon, ascending by the north stairs, read southward, and the deacon, who used the south staircase, faced northward. Durandus says the Epistle was read in *dextra parte* facing the altar (*Rationale*, lib. iv. fo. xc), "lecturus evangelium transit ad partem sinistram et opponit faciem suam aquilonare juxta illud Esa. xliii. 6" (fo. xcviii b). In England the rood-loft was used only on great festivals. The socket for the Gospel lectern remains in the altar step on the north side at St. David's ; at Canterbury it was on the north side adjoining the choir transept. At Durham "at the north end of the high altar there was a goodly fine letteron of brasse where they sunge the Epistle and Gospell" (*Rites*, vii. p. 11), clearly because the Gospel was read from it. At Hereford, "Evangelium a diacono (legebatur) super superiorem gradum converso ad partem borealem," which harmonized with the use at Seville. In the Bourges Missal little tonsured heads mark the positions of deacon and subdeacon. At Salisbury the rule was "semper legatur evangelium versus aquilonem." An English will, however, dated 1438, mentions "the south side of the altar where the Gospels are usually read " ; but it was not till 1485 that the Roman rule required the north and south sides to be taken from the arms of the crucifix upon the altar (Maskell, 20), with a remarkable though unexpressed relevancy to the ancient position of the celebrant facing westwards in the Basilica, as the Pope still stands. Possibly the change in England from south to north arose in conventual, cathedral, and collegiate churches, where the celebrant in front of a choir of men only did not turn, but read from the book lying on the north or left hand of the altar, the gospeller and epistoler only attending at high or chapter masses. The Gospel and Epistle sides of the altar coincided with the cantoris and decani of the choir stalls. The MS. statutes of St. David's, 1368, require, in consequence of some abuses, "diaconum et subdiaconum ministrantes in missâ ad continuam stationem in suis locis, nisi quando officii missæ necessitas exposceret, simul concelebrantes, districtius arctari." I may remark that two sets of double stairs (of access and egress) for the epistoler and gospeller remain at St. John's, Brecon, marking the site of the rood-loft ; and that the traces of a peculiar Benedictine arrangement—the choir entry, or interspace between the rood and choir screens—may be observed in that church, although obliterated at St. Alban's, Peterborough, Durham, Rochester, and Dunster.

I do not notice any special use in the Missal of Utrecht, which would account for the change of terms at Haarlem; neither do I in an article on that church stating that "the stalls are late and poor, and the subsellæ" (misericords) "have been destroyed" (*Ecclesiologist*, 1852, vol. x. p. 400). A very interesting trace of the old English use occurs in 1636, when Bishop Wren enjoined that "in very long Churches the Minister may come nearer to read the Epistle and Gospell," that is, remove from "the Communion Table" to do so (*Rit. Comm. Rep.*, 564). It stood "close vnder theast wall of the chancell where the altar in former times stood, the ends thereof being placed north and sowth" (p. 557).

MACKENZIE E. C. WALCOTT.

FLORIO'S ITALIAN BIOGRAPHY OF LADY JANE GREY (5th S. ix. 408.)—I have a copy of this volume, and there is another in the library of Mr. Henry Huth. It appears to have been printed at London. I cannot at present recollect any other volume printed by Richardo Pittore (not Tittore).

R. S. TURNER.
A 5, Albany.

WILL OF JOHN ARCHOR, OF BISHOP'S HAT-FIELD (5th S. ix. 405.)—One of the witnesses to this will was "Robert ffrouik parish priest." Can MR. LLOYD tell if "Robert ffrouik" was then rector of Bishop's Hatfield, or was he only a chantry priest? H. FISHWICK, F.S.A.
Carr Hill, Rochdale.

PROVINCIAL FAIRS (5th S. vi. 108, 214, 278, 353; vii. 99, 437; viii. 156, 269; ix. 338.)—I was present at the kermesse at Amsterdam in September, 1873, and though to a stranger it was an interesting sight from the variety of the costumes of the Frisian and other peasants who attended it, I am not at all surprised that the government have determined to put an end to it. (I believe that this determination caused a regular riot last autumn, which required the employment of military force for its suppression.) Having already had some experience of English "Statute Fairs," Gloucestershire "Mops," and Scotch term-day hirings, I can say that though all these might surely be suppressed with advantage to the morals of the rural population, I never in them witnessed anything even approaching the scenes of frenzied debauchery and oblivion, or disregard, of common decency which were common at the Amsterdam kermesse. In other years I have happened to be present at kermesses in Belgium, at Antwerp, Brussels, &c., but these were, by comparison, tameness and innocence itself. Some of the very "peculiar arrangements" of the Dutch kermesses are alluded to in Baedeker's guide-book, *La Belgique et la Hollande*, 1864, among "les particularités hollandaises," in a passage which has

been judiciously excluded from my last Er edition (1876). J. WOODWA

ROMANO-CHRISTIAN REMAINS IN BRITAII S. ix. 349, 429, 458.)—MR. BOASE has by sight supposed that I had said, *ante*, p. 430, E. Huebner's *Inscriptiones Britanniæ Lo* &c., was not to be found in the library o British Museum, whereas the work I spoke o the professor's later work, *Inscriptiones Brite Christianæ*, published in 1876, as may be by the last paragraph of my article, and whic not in the Brit. Mus. Catalogue a fortnigh when I looked for it, though I found the fo work to which MR. BOASE refers.

I fear there is delay in putting new work; the B. M. Catalogue, and it is quite possible Huebner's late work may be in the library, bi yet indexed. JOSEPH BRO'
Temple.

"BANDANA" POCKET-HANDKERCHIEFS (5 ix. 446.)—T. S. notwithstanding, the origin word *bandana* may still be left, as suggest Dr. Birdwood, to Colonel Yule. There is no in any language of India a word resembling *dana*, taking it either as "three long," or a and two short," or as a dissyllable, which i kerchief, handkerchief, turband, towel, or girdle, and the term could not have passed the native languages and have remained in mercial English.

As *calico* from Calicut on the western coas *madapolliams* from the town of Madapollie the eastern coast, it is most probable that the is from the name of some place whence spotted silk or cotton pieces were first expor
R. B.

PUBLIC-HOUSE SIGNS (5th S. ix. 127, 174 293, 353, 391, 439.)—I can only refer H. Y. Hotten's *History of Signboards*, p. 239, f that can be said of the apple tree as a The addition of the mitre was doubtless t tinguish the house from others that had the emblem. The "Apple Tree and Mitre" Cursitor Street; there is an "Apple Tree" Gray's Inn Road; and the "Mitre" will be as a sign for several places in the vicinity.
CLAI

The well-known explanation of the sign "Goat and Compasses," as a corruption of encompasses us," I look upon as an instance practice of following the most misleading guides—similarity of sound. Allow me to e another possible origin. The arms of the wainers' Company are Azure, a chevron tween three goats' heads erased argent. could be more natural than that, in ignor; the meaning of the chevron, the sign of the wainers' Arms should be described as the '

and Compasses," from which the transition to a single goat is easy?   J. F. MARSH.
Hardwick House, Chepstow.

"CORRODY" (5ᵗʰ S. viii. 448.)—

"*Corodie* is an allowance of meat, bread, drink, money, cloathing, lodging, and such like necessaries for sustenance. *Corodies* are of common right, as every founder of abbeys and other houses of religion had authority to assign such in the same houses for father, brother, cousin, or other that he would appoint.......And this *corody* was due as well to a common person Founder as where the King himself was Founder. But where the House was holden in Frankalmoigne there the tenure itself was a discharge of *corodie* against all men, except it were afterward charged voluntarily; as when the King would send his writ to the abbot for a *corodie* for such a one, whom they admit, there the House should be thereby charged for ever, whether the King were founder or not. See the writ *de Corodio habendo* in Fitzh. *Nat. Brev.*, fol. 230."—*Les Termes de la Ley*, edit. 1685.

Primarily the *corrody* was a supply of food and other necessaries given by the vassals of a lord whenever he chose to quarter himself and his dependents upon them, or, as it is explained in Migne's edition of Ducange, "convivia quæ dominis præstabantur a vassallis quoties per illorum terras pergebant." The custom was of Celtic origin, and was called *coshering* in Ireland. It is named by Sir John Davies, in his *Discovery of the True Cause why Ireland was never brought under Obedience of the Crown of England*, as one of the exactions by which the Irish people were oppressed by their native chiefs :—

"This extortion of coin and livery (levies of food and money) was taken for the maintenance of their men of war; but their Irish exactions, extorted by their chieftains and taniata, by colour of their barbarous seigniory, were almost as grievous a burden as the other, namely *coshering*, which were visitations and progresses made by the lord and his followers among his tenants, wherein he did eat them (as the English proverb is) out of house and home."—P. 134, edit. 1787.

The term *corrody* was at length applied to any grant of permanent subsistence by any one who had a right to make it. It was primarily written *conrody* (hence the Fr. forms *conroit, conroi,* Roquefort), and is probably from Celt. *cyn* (con. Lat. *cum*), and *rhodd* (rod), a gift, a contribution, meaning a gift in unison or by many contributors, which the *corrody* originally was. In Welsh the word *corodyn* was formerly used in the general sense of "a giver of alms or bounty."   J. D.
Belsize Square.

From *conredium* or *corredium:*—

"Quidquid ad alimentum, ad cibum, ad mensam datur, cibus, mensæ apparatus, alimonium, convivium."—Du Fresne, *sub voc.*

"*Corody*......signifies in common law a sum of money or'allowance of meat, drink, and clothing, due to the king from an abbey, or other house of religion, whereof he is the founder, towards the reasonable sustenance of such a one of his servants, being put to his pension, as he thinketh good to bestow it on. And the difference beween a *corody* and a pension seemeth to be that a

corody is allowed towards the maintenance of any of the king's servants that liveth in the abbey, a pension is given to one of the king's chaplains for his better maintenance in the king's service until he may be better provided of a benefice."—Cowel, *Law Dict., sub voc.*
                                        K. P. D. E.

A *corrody, corody,* or *corodie* was practically a kind of rent charge on an abbey or other religious endowment. Blount in his *Law Dictionary* defines it as a sum of money or allowance of meat, drink, and clothing due to a founder "towards the reasonable sustenance of such a one of his servants or vadelets as he thinks good to bestow it on." A *corody* was for life, for a term of years, in tail, or in fee, and might be certain or uncertain (see Fitzherbert's *Natura Brevium*). In the *Termes de la Ley* it is said that a *corody* on a monastery cannot be held by a woman, neither can one on a nunnery be held by a man. The question of *corodies* became of very general interest at the time of the dissolution of religious houses, and the 34-35 Hen. VIII. cap. 19, provides for " pensions, portions, *corrodies,* indemnities, sinodies, and proxies " (see Bishop Gibson's *Codex Juris Eccl. Ang.*). The usual dictionary derivation, such as that given by Minshew, 1627, " a lat. *corrodo,*" is by no means satisfactory. It was a monkish word, like *cordone* (*i.e.* reward), and surely could not be derived from " fretting or gnawing bones."
                                        EDWARD SOLLY.

A *corodie, corrodium* alias *corredium,* Lat.; *corredo,* Ital. Provision ; a right of sustenance or to receive certain allotments of victual and provision for one's maintenance. The founder of an abbey or other religious house had the right to claim a provision out of the common fund for his servant or vadelet. The king, whether founder or not, had this privilege. It was the subject of grant for life or less term, and even in fee simple or fee tail. If the charge were upon a house of monks, the grantor could not send a woman to take it, or if it were due from a nunnery, it was not lawful to appoint a man to receive it. Where the religious house was holden in Frankalmoigne it was discharged of all *corodies* (stat. 1 Edw. III. cap. 10), except the *corodie* were voluntarily charged, as when the king sent his writ and the beneficiary was admitted, in which case the house would be thereby charged for ever. A *corodie* differed from a pension, which was given to one of the king's chaplains for his better maintenance until he should be provided with a benefice. It was an ancient law, for in the statute of West. 2, cap. 25, it was ordained that an assize should lie for a *corodie.* It is also apparent by the stat. 34 and 35 Hen. VIII. cap. 26, that *corodies* belonged sometimes to bishops and noblemen from monasteries. Sir Matthew Hale says that a *corodie* was due of common right, and that no prescription would discharge it (2 *Inst.,* 647). If the house did not submit a writ would lie (see *Reg. of Writs*, fo. 264). Fitzherbert, in his *Nat. Brev.*, fo. 30, sets down all the *corodies* and pensions certain that any abbey when they stood was bound to perform to the king. See Blac., *Com.*; *Termes de la Ley*; Spelman, *Gloss.*

GEORGE WHITE.

St. Briavel's, Epsom.

See Spelman's *Glossary*, Jacob's *Law Dictionary*, or Halliwell's *Glossary*. C. J. E.

"IT IS AN ILL WIND," &c. (5ᵗʰ S. ix. 348, 413.)— The following extract from the *Times* of some months since gives an early instance of the occurrence of this proverb in what is now the less common form :—

"AN ILL-USED PROVERB.—The *Theatre*, commenting on the proverb generally quoted as 'It's an ill wind that blows nobody any good,' says: 'In Heywood's *Proverbs*, 1562, is this, "It is an ill wind that blows no man to good." Shakspere uses it in *Hen. VI.*, pt. iii. Act ii. sc. 5, "Ill blows the wind that profits nobody," a change of form made for the sake of the metre. In *Hen. IV.*, pt. ii. Act v. sc. 3, Pistol says, "Not the ill wind which blows none to good," which is very nearly the popular form as given by Heywood.'"

ED. MARSHALL.

DEMOGRAPHY (5ᵗʰ S. ix. 247, 295.)—I should think there is scarcely a Greek scholar worthy of the name who would endorse M. Lagneau's doctrine that "the terms Ethnology, Ethnography, and Demography are almost synonymous in their etymological signification." For if etymology is to be the test (and there can be no better), then M. Lagneau has pitched upon the very one which, far beyond all others, tells directly against his view. Passing by the first, let us break up the others into their component parts. We have thus ἔθνος-γράφω and δῆμος-γράφω, the radical or root meaning of the former being a nation comprising people of every class ; of the latter, people of the lower class only, the exact equivalent of the Latin *plebs* ; so that the two words, or "terms," are no more synonymous than are *genus* and *species*, which, in their mutual relation, they really are.* Hence, as ἔθνος comprehends within its signification *nobles* as well as *commoners*, it would be quite as legitimate to say that *nobles* and *commoners* are nearly one and the same, as that ἔθνος and δῆμος are "almost synonymous." But authority is dead against all this ; for, not to mention others, both Homer and Herodotus put the words in opposition. In the *Iliad* (ii. 188) we find ὅντινα μὲν ἔξοχον ἄνδρα, and in l. 198 of the same book, ὃν δ᾽ αὖ δῆμου τ᾽ ἄνδρα, where the speaker is represented as addressing the former, ἀγανοῖς ἐπέεσσιν, with *bland words*, and as striking the other σκήπτρῳ, with his sceptre. In Herodotus (i. 196) we have between εὐδαίμονες and δῆμος a contrast set up

* What I mean is that, as correlatives, ἔθνος and δῆμος are respectively to each other *genus* and *species*.

exactly similar. According to the "etymological signification," therefore, Ethnography must mean the science, or whatever we may call it, which is conversant about nations *collectively*, Demography that which is conversant about a certain part of them *distinctively*. EDMUND TEW, M.A.

Patching Rectory, Arundel.

There is an able periodical issued in Paris entitled *Annales de Démographie Internationale*. Amongst other matter the last number announces that Dr. Bertillon, a former president of the Société d'Anthropologie, is giving a "cours public de démographie et de géographie médicale." WILLIAM E. A. AXON.

Barton-on-Irwell.

THE "TIDE OF FATE" (5ᵗʰ S. ix. 426.)—The consideration raised by KINGSTON is a very curious one. I have for many years observed the effects, or the *apparent effects*—for I know not which is the more correct term—of the phenomena referred to, and have asked myself this question, Do events and casualties, which appear beyond the control or influence of the human will, occur in cycles ? Take railway accidents. No sooner does one serious casualty of this class occur than the newspapers teem with others of the same class, but of less magnitude ; then comes a lull. I feel certain that to a very large extent there is nothing more than coincidence here, arising in this form. The public mind becomes excited upon the subject, everything bearing upon it is consequently recorded in the newspapers, and so there seems to be a cycle of such occurrences, when in truth nothing more than ordinary events are happening. This view as to railway accidents may be proved to be correct by reference to the Board of Trade returns of persons killed by such casualties. These show a steady increase in regard to the number of miles of railway opened and the increase of persons travelling, and rarely anything more.

This view therefore arises : Events of all kinds are happening constantly around us, but we do not take conscious note of them, unless the mind is directed towards them by some overwhelming incident ; then for a time we see all the events of the same class, whether small or large.

But there are some classes of events which may really occur in proximity from one common influence, as that of the weather, *i.e.* the condition of the temperature—there are explosions of fire-damp in coal mines, perhaps also gunpowder-mill explosions and steam-boiler explosions. It is clear that the number of shipwrecks occurring in any given space of time may depend much upon the condition of the elements in relation to storms, fogs, &c. It is possible that here we may trace a relation to the sun spot theory.

I have long been a director of a leading accident insurance company. It is quite certain that in this business we do have cycles of casualties, as, for instance, a certain district of the country will sustain an unusual proportion of accidents, or that accidents of a certain distinct type, as distinguished from other types, will prevail for a given period. I have endeavoured to deduce a law in all this, but without success hitherto, yet I do not despair. Certain states of the atmosphere superinduce to fatal terminations of simple injuries, as erysipelas and other species of blood-poisoning.

In fire insurance losses are observed to run upon certain classes of risk, as at one period woollen mills, at another cotton mills, and (about quarter days!) on the shops of struggling tradesmen; but in all this cause and effect are always to be traced, as depression of certain branches of trade, &c. In some countries fires will be very numerous in one province, and hardly any in another and perhaps a neighbouring one, the solution being political discontent, unusual fiscal burdens, &c.

It is clear, then, that in many of the observed facts the operations of the human will are apparent and direct. May it not be that in other cases the cause is the same, but its operation concealed? This operation may be indirect as well as direct. In the case of railway accidents their prevention depends greatly upon the nerves of numerous pointsmen, breakmen, and other officials. Fear, affecting the nervous energies, may produce the very results which are sought to be avoided.

I note down these thoughts as they occur to me, without exact logical sequence, and simply in the spirit of inquiry. What we want, in view of the solution of all such questions, is accurately recorded facts, complete over a series of years. Chance jottings are always incomplete, and therefore necessarily misleading. I have sometimes (mentally) resolved to start an " Event and Occurrence " Society, whose business it should be to prepare and publish records. Would it go?

CORNELIUS WALFORD, F.I.A., F.S.S.
Belsize Park Gardens, N.W.

If KINGSTON will refer to Buckle's *History of Civilization in England*, vol. i. cap. i. pp. 22-26, edition 1871, he will find this subject, and " the proof we now possess of the regularity with which mental phenomena succeed each other," very ably discussed.   CLARRY.

"COPPER": "KOPPER": "COP" (5ᵗʰ S. ix. 187, 297.)—MR. SCHOU connects the word *cop* = head with Gr. κεφαλή, Lat. *caput*. This, of course, is an impossible etymological equation. The Teutonic cognates of *caput* are Goth. *haubith*, A.-S. *heáfod*, O.N. *höfuð*, Eng. *head*, &c. The O.H.G. *choph*, Germ. *kopf* (= head), Icel. *koppr* (= cup), Eng. *cop*, a round hill, head, is a different word, cognate probably with the Celtic *cop*, top, summit.   A. L. MAYHEW.
Oxford.

THE OPERA (5ᵗʰ S. ix. 448.)—As Rachell New-port's letter is dated in Dec., 1658, it may be assumed that she refers to the performance of operas at the Cockpit Theatre in Drury Lane, rather than to those at Rutland House in Charter House Yard, which preceded the others. The first inhibition of " stage plays " was in 1642, and the second on Feb. 13, 1647-48. In Dec., 1648, Captain Betham was appointed provost martial, " with power to seize upon all ballad-singers, and to suppress stage plays." But in 1656 the government had fallen into less fanatical hands. Cromwell was in the ascendant, and he was known to be a great lover of music. Then Sir William Davenant, with the countenance and support of Lord Whitelocke, Sir John Maynard, and others, fitted up Rutland House as a theatre, and produced *An Entertainment after the Manner of the Ancients*, in which the dialogue was declaimed throughout to music, as by the ancient Greek Rhapsodists in their recitations of the Homeric and other poems. This was the first English opera, the vocal and instrumental music having been composed by Dr. Charles Coleman, Captain Henry Cook, Henry Lawes, and George Hudson. The evasion of the Act of Parliament having been tolerated, Davenant produced in the same year *The Siege of Rhodes*. Finding his venture successful, he next took the Cockpit Theatre in Drury Lane, and produced there *The Cruelty of the Spaniards in Peru*, which Cromwell is said to have read and approved before its representation, and *The History of Sir Francis Drake*. The former was published in 1658 and the latter in 1659. Spoken dialogue was reverted to after the Restoration, as in Matthew Locke's opera of *Psyche* and others.
WM. CHAPPELL.

THE AMERICAN "ROBIN" (5ᵗʰ S. ix. 367, 414) is the *Turdus migratorius* of Linnæus and other naturalists, and has its common name from its red breast, which reminded the settlers in New England of the " household bird " of their old country. Mr. Longfellow is, of course, perfectly right in calling its eggs *blue*. They are spotless, and coloured almost exactly like those of our hedge-sparrow, but greatly superior in size.
ALFRED NEWTON.
Magdalene College, Cambridge.

DRAYTON (5ᵗʰ S. ix. 87, 137, 317.)—It is quite true that Market Drayton is a *dry* town, built, as it is, on an eminence. But are Drayton Fen and Fenny Drayton so named from their particularly dry sites? There is an instance of A.-S. *dreg* in the Domesday " Dregetone," modernized, not Drayton, but Drineton. In the same place Market Drayton is written " Draitune." This orthography marks a striking difference, then and now, in the pronunciation of the first syllable of each word. May I quote in support of my suggestion of the

Salop, ii. 107?—" This town is certainly a place of great antiquity, and is supposed to be the Roman station of Mediolanum " (a similar claim has, I believe, been advanced on behalf of Middle, co. Salop). " Ninnius enumerates this as one of the principal cities of the Britons." He speaks of Market Drayton. In the first number of the *Old Cross*, a magazine for Warwickshire, just published, I notice that the derivation of Coventry is asked for. I am sorry that I cannot anticipate the answer. But the *try* in Oswestry is not the British *tre* ; the place was originally called Maserfield, and was called subsequently Oswaldstree, in commemoration of a great victory gained there by Oswald, King of Northumberland, fighting under the ensign of the cross. Daventry is pronounced Daintry : this sounds like Danes-town. Perhaps Dr. Lee, in his history of Market Drayton, says something about the origin of the name. May I ask, in conclusion, whether the Anglo-Saxon words *Bur* and *Cot*, interpreted as they are some forty times by the addition of *ton*, are not also tautological curiosities ?   W. F. MARSH JACKSON.

ROBIN HOOD SOCIETY (5th S. viii. 351, 378 ; ix. 257.)—In *Rodondo*, a satire on W. Pitt the first and his party, written by Mr. Hugh Dalrymple, 1763, canto i. p. 21, the following refers to C. Churchill :—

> " Towards the City then he rode ;
> But halted at the *Robin Hood ;*
> Cry'd, ' D—n my Eyes and Limbs, but here
> I 'll have a double Pot of Beer.
> Here mighty *Henley*, Type of me,
> Gave Lectures of true Orat'ry.
> Here first he publish'd to the Nation
> His own, and my Divine Legation.
> Here left to me his Parts and Flock ;
> But he had none ! That Gown, behold,
> So torn, so rusty, and so old !
> That Cassock see, of Nut-brown Hue ;
> That Gown was his, that Cassock too !
> But, here 's the Cure of all my Woes.
> Sorrow is dry,—Come, *W(il)ks*,—here goes.'
> So drain'd the Pitcher to the Dregs."

" Henley " was, of course, " Orator Henley."
O.

TWIN TOES (5th S. ix. 286.)—A male child was born on February 16, 1878, at a cottage on a part of my estate called the Spring Valley, in the parish of Worfield, in Shropshire, having the first and second toes next the big toe of each foot webbed together. The parents are now residing in another part of the same parish, and the child is living and tolerably healthy.   HUBERT SMITH.

PORTRAITS AFTER VANDYCK (5th S. ix. 347.)— Can the engraved portrait No. 1, of which MR. BOASE speaks, be that of Richard Tarlton or Tarleton, who lived in the end of the sixteenth and beginning of the seventeenth century ? He was

the earliest English comedian a very rare old pamphlet entit *Dream*, by Henry Chettle, 4to., lished in December, 1592, he is " The next by his suite of russet his taber—his standing on the to knew to be either the body or rese who living for his pleasant conceits and dying for mirth left not his lik In 1611 a book was publishe *Jeasts*. The portrait in questio the frontispiece to this book.

" THE ACTS OF TO-DAY BECOM OF TO-MORROW " (5th S. ix. 42t to that of Mr. F. Herschell Junius's dedication of his lett nation : " What yesterday w doctrine."
Newcastle-on-Tyne.

" BEATI POSSIDENTES " (5th *New Dictionary of Quotations* me, the form is given as "beat the following passage is cited, without a reference to its autho! " Henry VIII. silenced the profes at the universities, forbade the g it, and nominated a commission *beati possessores !* is a maxim of th the science of defence have always l own behalf."

Reading.

THE POET BERENICIUS (5th following extract from *A New graphical Dictionary*, 15 vol probably the answer to yo! query :— " Berenicius, a man utterly unk in Holland in the year 1670. H a Jesuit, or a renegade from a fraternity. He got his bread by sv grinding knives. He died in a bog drunkenness. His talents, if the hi him are to be credited, were extrao! with so much ease that he would r in tolerably good poetry, whatever prose. He has been seen to tr gazettes from that language into (standing on one foot. The dead languages, Greek, Latin, French, familiar to him as his mother tong by heart Horace, Virgil, Homer several pieces of Cicero, of the one and, after reciting long passages f the book and the chapter from whe It is supposed that the *Georgarchon*

In my turn I should like to : remarkably named work may b
G.

Is not Berenicius intended. gives an account in his *Univer* poet lived in Zeeland in the m teenth century, and was wonderfully skilled in languages and in impromptu verse. He used at times to fall into ecstasies, and speak so quickly that it was impossible to write down his words. He was entirely negligent of the comforts of life, travelled from country to country, and was at last found dead in a ditch near Rotterdam. His poems were published in that city in 1691.

JOSIAH MILLER, M.A.

A PSEUDO-CHRIST (5ᵗʰ S. viii. 488; ix. 17, 298.)—Were not these personations of Christ due then, as they are now, to mental derangement? The case is better understood in the present day.

P. P.

JOHN LOCKE (5ᵗʰ S. viii. 307, 356.)—The *Correspondence between the Earl of Sunderland and the Bishop of Oxford respecting Mr. Locke* is quoted in appendix ii. to Charles James Fox's *History of James II.* The first letter is so curious that it may be permissible to quote it :—

"To the Lord Bishop of Oxford.

"Whitehall, Nov. 6, 1684.

"My Lord,—The King being given to understand that one Mr. Locke, who belonged to the late Earl of Shaftesbury, and has, upon several occasions, behaved himself very factiously and undutifully to the Government, is a student of Christchurch, his Majesty commands me to signify to your Lordship that he would have him removed from being a student, and that in order thereunto your Lordship would let me know the method of doing it. I am, my Lord, &c., SUNDERLAND."

The bishop acknowledges, on Nov. 8, the honour of his lordship's letter, and writes :—

"I have for divers years had an eye upon him, but so close has his guard been on himself that after several strict inquiries I may confidently affirm there is not any one in the college, however familiar with him, who had heard him speak a word either against, or so much as concerning, the Government."

The bishop goes on to explain how vain efforts had been made to entrap him, without eliciting any expression of concern "in word or look," so that, he adds, "I believe there is not in the world such a master of taciturnity and passion." He then explains how Mr. Locke "is now abroad upon want of health," but has been summoned to return, and that if he fails to do so he may be expelled "for contumacy." He thinks it possible that Mr. Locke may be caught tripping in London, "where a general liberty of speaking was used, and where the execrable designs against his Majesty and his Government were managed and pursued." Dr. Fell concludes by saying that if the method suggested "seem not effectual or speedy enough, and his Majesty," their founder and visitor, shall please to command his immediate remove, it shall accordingly be executed by his lordship's "most humble and obedient servant, J. Oxon." His Majesty accordingly, on Nov. 11, signified his will and pleasure that Locke should be removed from his student's place. On Nov. 16 Dr. Fell wrote to

say the command was "fully executed"; and an undated acknowledgment from Lord Sunderland intimates that his Majesty "is well satisfied with the College's ready obedience to his commands for the expulsion of Mr. Locke."

D. BARRON BRIGHTWELL.

"THE BRISTOL MEMORIALIST" (5ᵗʰ S. ix. 188, 236, 337.)—In reference to my reply (*ante*, p. 236) as to who was the author of "Sayings of my Uncle" in the above-named work, MR. J. F. NICHOLLS says that "from the style" he should "ascribe" them to the "Rev. John Evans," author of *The Ponderer*. My information was obtained from a copy of the *Memorialist*, in which the name of the contributor is prefixed to each article by Mr. W. Tyson, the editor. Under the heading of the papers in question he has written, in his plain handwriting, "by John Evans, *printer*." This evidence of their authorship is of more value than any assumptive "ascriptions." The minister and the printer, though bearing the same names, were in no way related—only "a cosmopolitish affinity," writes the latter.

W. GEORGE.

ANNIBAL CARACCI (5ᵗʰ S. ix. 27, 75, 298.)—The information given by MR. RUTLEY agrees with what I find in dictionaries. I have been told by one of the most eminent English artists now living that he knew of only two (perhaps three) engraved copies of the Marys—one in London and one in St. Petersburg. Are there any others known? I should be glad to have this question answered.

GEO. A. M.

Washington, D.C.

There is one fine engraving of the celebrated picture of the three Marys, unfinished, by Sharp, without letters, which is sometimes met with. Rouillet's is very scarce. Sharp's engraving is mentioned by Bryan. H. HALL.

Lavender Hill.

BREAD AND SALT (5ᵗʰ S. ix. 48, 138, 299.)—A. J. M. asks if the custom of presenting bread and salt to a baby continues in Yorkshire. It does in the East Riding, for I have frequently seen babies given not only bread, salt, and money; but, in addition, an egg and matches. I do not know the meaning of the various gifts, but imagine that the last, at least, must be a comparatively recent addition.

There is another custom prevailing in the same part of the country which I should be glad to see explained, *i.e.* that of "letting in" Christmas and New Year. I cannot recollect the different minutiæ comprised in it accurately, as it is many years since I was in Yorkshire, but, as far as I can remember, Christmas was always represented by a fair man, and was the first person admitted into the house after midnight on the eve. Certain questions were put and answered before the guest was allowed to enter, and on coming in he was presented with bread, salt, and a groat. The same, or almost the same, occurred at the New Year, except that, I believe, the representative must on that occasion be dark. The contrary was supposed to bring ill luck. I shall be glad of correction in the details. Is this only a local custom ?

W. S. H.

A " FEMALE HERCULES " (5ᵗʰ S. ix. 288, 393.)— I have a vivid recollection of being taken when a very little child to see a female Hercules. I can vouch for her taking up a heavy anvil with her hair, which was arranged in two thick plaits, fastened to each end of the anvil, which was afterwards put upon her breast, and some hard blows were struck upon it with a very large hammer. I do not remember if a horse-shoe were forged, or if she talked and sang during the performance ; but what I did see is as distinctly fixed in my mind as if it happened but yesterday.

H. E. WILKINSON.

Anerley, S.E.

DROWNED BODIES RECOVERED (5ᵗʰ S. ix. 8, 111, 218.)—The idea of throwing a loaf of bread containing quicksilver into the water to find the body of a drowned man still prevails in North Lancashire, though in a slightly different form from that described as existing at Swinton. Here the belief is that the loaf containing the quicksilver will float until it arrives immediately over the drowned man, when it will sink, and thus denote the position of the body.

In January, 1849, when the pier at Morecambe was being constructed, the stone for which was procured near Halton, the boat conveying the workmen from the quarry across the river Lune to the village was upset, and eight of the men were drowned. The villagers were confident that quicksilver placed inside a loaf would enable them to find the bodies, but the last corpse was not discovered until nearly three months after the accident.

A few years ago, when two young men were drowned in the Lune, I believe the same expedient was tried. Guns also were fired over the water, and gunpowder was so contrived as to explode in the bottles containing it beneath the surface, but one of the bodies has never been found.

ROSPEAR.

Lancaster.

In looking through the chronicle of the *Annual Register* for 1767, I came across the following entry, which clearly shows that the superstition referred to by MR. COLEMAN was at that time current in Berks :—

" The following odd relation is attested as a fact. An inquisition was taken at Newbury, Berks, on the body of a child near two years old who fell into the river Kennet and was drowned. The jury brought in their

verdict *Accidental death.* The body ᵥ a very singular experiment, which was diligent search had been made in the ᵣ to no purpose, a twopenny loaf with a ₁ silver put into it was set floating from the child, it was supposed, had fallen its course down the river upwards of ₁ a great number of spectators, when thᵥ to lay on the contrary side of the ri denly tacked a ut and swam acros gradually sunk bear the child, when b loaf were immediately brought up witl for that purpose."

MR. COLEMAN can perhaps tell ᵤ result of the trial at Swinton. Cᵣ

GEORGE CRUIKSHANK (5ᵗʰ S. answer to OLPHAR HAMST'S queᵣ Bruce a pseudonym ?" I answer yᵢ *Morality* was written by the lᵢ Mogridge, who wrote also undeₑ *plume* of " Old Humphrey." T book arose thus : Cruikshank and met and dined at my late father' Cheapside ; one day while at dinnᵢ full of mirth, and Mogridge staᵢ Mr. Tegg laughingly remarked t gentlemen seem so opposite in feelᵢ that I think an interesting book cocted between you." " Good," sa " what think you ? I will take the —you know I *can draw ;* let fᵣ take ' Morality.' " Mr. Tegg repl to work to-morrow, and let the ᵥ ' Mirth and Morality.' "

No doubt the remark, " In fadeᵢ ' Auldjo,' " alludes to the work e *Ascent of Mont Blanc*—a note think, to procure or refer to the wo often made " notes " on slips of pap I hold many such with his pen when he had no paper I have knoᵥ notes and even sketches on his thᵤ he did in the case of the portrait ᵢ ing, which was afterwards copied a Thomas Hood's poem of *Eppin* dinner where this sketch was madᵢ and given by Rounding ; among tᵢ sent were Thomas Hood, Cruikshan &c. Wᵢ

Pancras Lane.

AN OLD BALLAD (CAPTAIN W 407, 435.)—MR. CHAPPELL has aᵢ his answer to this, and probably kᵣ Ward than I do. Hence, having the matter, I would ask him what notice of Ward's beating off of thᵢ will, I am sure, allow me to reᵢ degree the favour by the correc lapse. Ward did not " flourish [the end of Elizabeth's reign." Hᵢ

one till the second (or perhaps third) year of James I. Born at Feversham, he was a fisherman at Plymouth, and afterwards a seaman in his Majesty's cruiser the Lion's Whelp. Thence, with some of the crew, he deserted to rob a ship, and partly failing turned pirate (Barker, 1609).

Two plays were written on him. The first, not now extant, dealt, as we learn from the prologue to the second, with his base birth and with his piracies. The second, *A Christian turned Turk* (4to., 1612), a miserable play, deals chiefly with his becoming a renegado and with his death. Mr. (Halliwell) Phillipps, in his *Dict. of Old Plays*, says that "the story [of this play] is taken from an account of the overthrow of these two pirates [Ward and Danseker] by Andrew Barker, 4to., 1609." This would have been correct had he not omitted the word "not" before "taken." For example, their overthrow is not narrated by Barker, for it had not then taken place.

B. NICHOLSON.

FIELD NAMES (5th S. ix. 325, 413.)—MR. GOMME in his appeal for names of fields has suggested an interesting and a very wide subject for inquiry. He did not give instances of the speciality named by him—field names which are trade names—and such a combination surely must be rare. But ancient field names are curious and often exceedingly valuable for elucidation of local history, and it is much to be regretted that under the system of enclosing and laying in severalty tracts of commons and open fields, which used to exist throughout England (as they still do in continental countries), great numbers of curious names have been obliterated, along with the subdivisions of furlongs, and together also with curious local customs and habits. Romantic names bespeaking old legendary tales, such as Devil's Eyes, Devil's Back-Bones, Hoar Stones, and Holy Wells, which carry back the thoughts through the centuries of Christianity to times of our wild "untamed ancestors," have given place to prosaic titles, as North Field and South Field, or Twenty Acre or Forty Acre Field. With the papers (if still existing) of old chieftains amongst the land agents and surveyors of a past generation, such as Fuljames of Gloucester, Dixon of Oxford, Davis of Banbury, and many others, who acted as commissioners in the "palmy" days of field enclosures, might be found mention of names and customs materially helpful to searchers into parochial history. Many old names undoubtedly remain, and many which at first sight are unpromising deserve to be mused over, and to have their meanings tested by comparison; for in primitive times there was a reality and simplicity in names of persons and places, names which bespoke their occupation, trade, or attendant or surrounding circumstance; but variations in language, lack of scholarship, carelessness, and other causes have

introduced strange corruptions and alterations in them, which baffle etymological knowledge and give occasion to much conjecture and fancy.

I will conclude with the mention of a few names out of many in this immediate neighbourhood which seem to bear upon the subject, and may serve to call forth further questions and remarks.

1. Round Hill Field in Broughton parish. At first sight it is difficult to discover the hill in this flat piece of arable land, but closer examination shows that, notwithstanding continual levellings with the plough, there is a circular patch of rising ground, sufficient to indicate it as the remnant of that which in former generations gave occasion to the name, and as one of the many tumuli about the country, probably the burial-place of some old pagan inhabitant.

2. Chaddels, also in Broughton parish. This name is applied to some arable fields, the property of Lord Saye and Sele. And upon seeking for the meaning of the queer-sounding name, it appeared that the fields once formed one grass field, in which was a shady dell with a clear spring or well rising out of the ironstone rock just above, and the water was held in repute even so late as amongst the elders of the present generation, who resorted thither for the cure of weak eyes. But the picturesque village Holy Well has disappeared before axe and ploughshare. The spring still gushes forth, but the water is diverted by drain-pipes into a ditch cut by the side of the footpath dividing the fields; and the corrupt name of "Chaddels" remains to testify not indistinctly to "Chad's Well," recalling a bit of early history when this part of the country was the border land of the Saxon kingdom of Mercia, with its one bishopric, and pointing to some now forgotten connexion with St. Chad, the first bishop, the founder and patron saint of Lichfield Cathedral—perhaps to a visit of the holy man to this distant part of his diocese, when the pure spring was first brought into notice, and afterwards, in accordance with the feelings of the times, became an object of veneration.

3. The Berry Moor with the Bear Garden in Banbury parish. This is a grass field just beyond the site of the old walls on the south-west side of the town. "Berry Moor" implies that it was the Anglo-Saxon *Bury, Berg, Burg*, or town moor or common, and the "Bear Garden" is an earthwork of a still more ancient age, and supposed to have been the amphitheatre when Banbury was a Roman station. It is semicircular in form, cut in the concave face of the hill, and has three grass terraces, from which spectators had a view of the sports in the arena immediately below.

FREDERICK J. MORRELL.

Wilberforce make the remarks, in answer to a question from him, which are alluded to as "the advice of one of the bishops" (p. 58).   ED. MARSHALL.

Reminiscences of Thought and Feeling is by Mary Ann Kelty. She gives her name in *Solace of a Solitaire*, Lond., 1869, as author of *Visiting my Relations*, &c.   J. T. CLARK.

See *The Handbook of Fictitious Names*, p. 86.   O. H.

(5th S. ix. 429, 459.)
That Charles Frederick Henningsen is the author of *Revelations of Russia*, 1844, as stated in the Catalogue of the Advocates' Library, Edinburgh, may be verified by consulting that author's *Past and Future of Hungary*, Lond., 1852, where a list of his works is given.   J. T. CLARK.

AUTHORS OF QUOTATIONS WANTED (5th S. viii. 49.)—
"The anchor's weighed," &c.
There is a song by Geo. Bennett, commencing, "Oh! the anchor's heaved, and the sails unreeved," &c., set to music by T. Crampton, which may be that inquired for.   H. G. C.

(5th S. ix. 349.)
"O consistency, thou art a jewel."
"Consistency's a jewel" appeared originally, I believe, in Murtagh's *Collection of Ancient English and Scotch Ballads*, 1754. In the ballad of "Jolly Robyn Roughhead" are the following lines:—
"Tush, tush, my lasse! such thoughts resign,
Comparisons are cruell;
Fine pictures suit in frames as fine,
Consistencie's a jewel.
For thee and me coarse clothes are best,
Rude folks in homelye raiment drest,
Wife Joan and goodman Robyn."   H. A. GOULD.

(5th S. ix. 389, 419.)
"Hark, from the tomb a doleful sound," &c.
No doubt this is found in Dr. Watts's *Hymns*, book ii. hymn 63, but six lines of the first two stanzas are marked as a quotation. I understand your querist to require the original author. He would find it (I think) in Miller's *Singers and Songs of the Church*.   S. SHAW.

Miscellaneous.

NOTES ON BOOKS, &c.

Lives of Famous Poets. By William Michael Rossetti. (E. Moxon, Son & Co.)
UNDER the title *Lives of Famous Poets* Mr. W. M. Rossetti has collected into one volume the biographical and critical notices prefixed to the several volumes of "Moxon's Popular Poets," completing the survey of English poetry by adding notices of Chaucer, Spenser, Shakspeare, Butler, Dryden, Gray, and Goldsmith, and interpolating tabular lists of the otherwise unnoticed poets born between the dates of birth of each two in the series. The lives that have appeared before have been revised, so as to bring them to the level of advancing knowledge in each case—for our knowledge of poets' lives is continually advancing—and the book really forms what Mr. Rossetti diffidently suggests, a supplement to Johnson's *Lives*. Facts are carefully collected and clearly stated, critical opinions advanced temperately, and yet with sufficient strength and enthusiasm, and the book is altogether as instructive and useful as it is readable. Severn's portrait of Keats, engraved by Robinson, appears as frontispiece; the plate being badly worn, the picture might be re-engraved with advantage.

SENHOR DAVID CORAZZI has just issued a prospectu a new *édition de luxe* of the works of Camoens which l about to publish. The issue will be confined to f copies, costing about 12*l.* each. The work will be troduced by a critical notice of the great poet by Lai Coelho of the Academy, and the issue will be in numb to be completed in June, 1880, the third centenar the death of Luiz de Camoens.

Notices to Correspondents.

We must call special attention to the following notice
ON all communications should be written the name a address of the sender, not necessarily for publication, as a guarantee of good faith.

CORRESPONDENTS are requested to bear in mind tha is against rule to *seal* or otherwise *fasten* communicati transmitted by the halfpenny post. Not unfrequer double postage has to be paid on their receipt, beca they have been "closed against inspection."

FOLK-LORE.—We would strongly urge on those co spondents who are good enough to send us commun tions on Folk-Lore that, before doing so, they sho consult Brand's *Popular Antiquities*, Chambers's *B of Days*, Hone's *Every-Day Book*, but especially Thi ton Dyer's *British Popular Customs*, this last being most recent work on customs connected with Calendar.

HELEN.—For notices of "borrowed days," "N. & Q.," 1st S. v. 278, 342; 3rd S. iii. 288; viii. l The following is one version of the lines about the and the ash:—
"If the oak's before the ash,
Then you'll only get a splash;
If the ash precedes the oak,
Then you may expect a soak."
For "Beltane" Day, the old name of May Day, must refer our correspondent to "N. & Q.," 3rd S. 263, 354, 478, 516. At these references some very teresting articles on the subject will be found.

H. FORDE (Tenby) writes:—"Who was St. Julian] find nothing about our Welsh saint in Baring-Gou *Lives of the Saints*." [There was a St. Julian, Ai bishop of Toledo, who died 690.]

A CORRESPONDENT writes to us that the Flower Serr (*ante*, p. 442) was preached at St. Katherine Cree, church of St. James, Aldgate, having been taken do and the benefice united to that of the former church.

H. M. R. asks whether Vincent Priessnitz, the coverer of hydropathy, who for many years practise Graefenberg in Austria, is still alive, and, if so, whet he still carries on the establishment.

W. P. BARKER (Ipswich) should send prepaid lett with paginal references to "N. & Q." on the envelo to be forwarded.

DISCIPULUS asks to be informed as to the best bool use in studying Norwegian.

G. E. A.—"The streak of silver sea." See 5th S. 459.

W. RENDLE.—We shall be very glad to hear from y H. A. B.—"Talis cum sis," &c. See *ante*, p. 118.

NOTICE.

LONDON, SATURDAY, JUNE 22, 1878.

CONTENTS.—N° 234.

Notes.

CLERICAL WIGS.

Bits of quaint and amusing reading may often be met with in unexpected quarters. The treatise of Pope Benedict XIV., *De Synodo Diœcesana*, does not, as to its title, promise much of general interest, yet some of its chapters are sufficiently amusing, not the least so being the ninth chapter of the eleventh book, which is devoted to the discussion of the use of false hair, popularly called a "perruque" (*vulgo* "parrucca"), by the clergy.

It seems from the opening of the chapter that many of the clergy had complained of what they deemed the needless severity of certain diocesan synods in condemning the use of false hair by the clergy, and of the enforcing of their condemnation by the most stringent ecclesiastical censures. The pope's object is to clear the synods from this charge of harshness. Amongst those which had taken action in this matter Benedict mentions that of Malta, 1703; of Pisa, 1708; of Monte Fiascone, 1710; and of Partalegri, 1714. Sarnellus, Bishop of Bisaglia, had on his own responsibility pronounced on the question in 1697, declaring all clerics who should wear false hair as *ipso facto* excommunicate. An appeal was not unnaturally (one would think) made to the Apostolic See against this sweeping decree; but the appellants gained little by their action, for at a special congregation, held on May 20, 1699, the decree was

confirmed in its entirety as far as it concerned those who belonged to the higher orders or were beneficed clergy, and relaxed only as far as the penalty was concerned in regard to those who had received the lesser orders or were unbeneficed. The Bishop of Melfi in 1721 issued an injunction to his clergy in exact harmony with the above-mentioned decree, as modified by the Congregation of Rites; but opposition was again aroused, and a renewed appeal made to the Apostolic See, only to result, Aug. 8, 1722, in a confirmation of the bishop's order. Benedict, who was then secretary to the congregation, drew up an elaborate statement of the authorities on which the judgment rested, with a condensed *résumé* of which he concludes his chapter.

He traces the use of false hair to the vanity of women who were anxious to disguise the ravages of advancing years, citing two epigrams from Martial in illustration :—

> "Jurat capillos esse, quos emit, suos
> Fabulla. Numquid illa, Paulle, pejerat ?"

And again :—

> "Dentibus, atque comis, nec te pudet, uteris emptis:
> Quid facies oculo, Lælia? non emitur."

A similar allusion he finds in Ovid (*De Art. Amandi*, lib. iii.) :—

> "Fœmina procedit densissima crinibus emptis.
> Proque suis, alios efficit ære suos."

Leaving profane sources, the good pope turns to patristic literature. St. Jerome, in a letter to Marcella (*Epist.*, 38), complains that there are old women (he uses the diminutive *vetulæ*: compare the γυναικάρια, *mulierculæ*, of 2 Tim. iii: 6 as a mark of contempt) who deck their heads with alien hair; and in a letter to another female friend, Demetrias, he reminds her how, in the days of her vanity, she had been wont to build up a tower-like headdress for herself of false hair. Tertullian, too (*De Cult. Fœminar.*, lib. ii. cap. 7), inveighs against a Christian woman fitting on herself the spoils of some strange head, a filthy one perchance—nay, worse, of a head perhaps doomed to hell. Clemens Alexandrinus (*Pædag.*, lib. iii. cap. 11) seeks to deter his female hearers from the use of such adventitious aids by asking, To whom is the blessing conveyed when the priest lays his hand on a head so adorned? Does not the blessing light on the assumed locks, and through them pass to their original possessor?

Since the Fathers never direct their invectives against men, it has been supposed that women alone were guilty in this matter, and I have gone so far as to assert that male wigs were a late invention of English origin, and first used in this country in the reign of William II. or Henry I., and that after they had long lurked in our island they gradually passed into other lands. That, however, they who so assert are in error is plain from the fact that Rufus Festus Avienus, a

describes in a short poem the misadventure of a certain bald knight whose wig was carried away by a sudden gust of wind. Still, argues the pope, although some men might be found to rival women in luxury, it is utterly incredible that priests can have ever so far forgotten themselves in old time; for were they not consecrated to their holy office by the cutting off of the hair, and were they not expressly forbidden, when once they had received the tonsure, to cultivate luxuriant locks?

Councils had not deemed it beneath their dignity to legislate on this matter; witness an Irish synod held under the presidency of St. Patrick A.D. 450, and the fourth Council of Toledo, can. 41, A.D. 633; whilst the Council of Agde, A.D. 506, provided a practical remedy for abuse by ordering that a priest who let his hair grow unduly was to be clipped, even against his will and active opposition ("etiam invitus et reluctans"), by the archdeacon in whose jurisdiction he might be. In modern synods, provincial and diocesan alike—*e.g.* of Milan; of Bourges, 1584; of Ravenna, 1607; of Lucca, 1625; and of Amalphi, 1639—clergy are warned to take care that the tonsure shall not be obscured by the growth of hair, that their hair dressing shall be of the simplest, that they abstain from brushing up the hair over their foreheads, from curling it or frizzing it with curling-irons; but not one word is said of wigs. The evidence is overwhelming that the use of them by clergy is a modern enormity. The decree forbidding this abuse cannot therefore be accused of severity. Yet, in spite of the general prohibition, there may be cases in which health requires some such protection for a bald head.

The diocesan synods of Bononia, 1698, and of Ascoli, 1718, have both permitted the bishop on just and reasonable cause to grant a dispensation. He is, however, to proceed warily in the matter, and must satisfy himself not only that there is just cause for granting the indulgence, but must personally inspect the wig, so as to be quite convinced that it can in no way minister to the vanity of the wearer, and must see that it is curled with such moderation and modesty that it may be evident to all that it is worn from sheer necessity—not as an article of luxury, state, or as an ornament for the head, but simply as a covering. Care must also be taken that no such licence shall be construed as permitting the wearing of the wig when the priest celebrates the Holy Eucharist, although certain canonists, Theophilus Raymundus and Pasqualigus, have held that it may be so worn, provided only that it be so fitted to the head as to be indistinguishable from true and natural hair; and although there is a licence in existence from Cardinal Jerome Grimaldi, Archbishop of Aqua, granting to a priest the privilege of so wearing it.

That the canonists are wrong, and that the arch-bishop exceeded his authority in granting such a licence, is evident from the fact that it is declared by canon 57 of a Roman Council held under Pope Zachary in A.D. 743, to be unlawful for even a bishop to minister at the altar with his head covered, and from the consequent consideration that a bishop cannot relax a law passed by his superior, or grant a licence to another to enjoy a privilege that he cannot claim for himself.

To set matters at rest, at meetings of the Congregation of Rites, held January 31, 1626, and April 24 of the same year, it was decreed that henceforth no one should dare to wear a skull-cap (*pileolum*) during the celebration of masses without express licence of the Apostolic See, any contrary custom notwithstanding; and since some evaded the decree by asserting that a wig was not a skull-cap, at a special congregation, held under Alexander VIII., 1690, it was, after solemn discussion, decided that the terms of the decree were to be so construed as to include every possible covering for the head, and that it was unlawful for a priest to celebrate in a wig, however comely and moderate in dimensions, without an express papal dispensation.

May I close this long article by asking whether the Church of Rome is still so explicit on this matter of clerical wigs? Did we not find it so solemnly discussed, we might in our irreverent haste have been inclined to settle the whole question by an appeal to the maxim, "De minimis non curat lex."   JOHNSON BAILY, F.R.H.S.
Pallion Vicarage.

THE DUKEDOM OF CUMBERLAND.

It will be curious to note how the precedence of the new Duke of Cumberland is fixed in the next roll of peers. If the law of England is followed his place will be between the Dukes of Northumberland and Wellington. The special precedence given to members of the royal family extends only to the king's children, which has been held to include his nephews and grandsons. I think the present sovereign extended this special precedence to her first cousins by an Order in Council. The new Duke of Cumberland is great-grandson to one sovereign, great-nephew to two others, and first cousin once removed to Her Majesty. No pretence whatever can be found for extending any special precedence to him by law, though of course the sovereign, by her prerogative as the fountain of honour, may do so; but we can hardly anticipate that such a slight will be passed on the twenty great peers (including the two archbishops, the Lord High Chancellor, and the Duke of Cambridge) who will thereby be displaced.

We now see, for the first time in four hundred years, a descendant of a king of England in the strict male line who takes by law no precedence or privilege from his royal descent, but ranks according to the date of his peerage.

WILLIAM WICKHAM.
Athenæum Club.

WATERLOO DAY.

The present week has brought round to us the sixty-third anniversary of Waterloo. Three years ago I counted, so far as I could ascertain, eighty-two surviving officers who had taken part in the battle. Of these, I reckon the following thirty to have in the intervening period passed away from amongst us :—

General Sir George Bowles, K.C.B. (1st W.I. Regiment).
Lieut.-General B. Cuppage (Royal Artillery).
Major-General R. G. B. Wilson (Royal Artillery).
Colonel Horton (7th Dragoon Guards).
   ,,   Linton (Coldstream Guards and Enniskillen Dragoons).
   ,,   Wildman (1st Dragoon Guards).
   ,,   Thomas Smith (95th Rifles), late Barrack Master at Aldershot.
   ,,   Charles Wood (10th Hussars).
Lieut.-Colonel Sedley (3rd W.I. Regiment).
   ,,   Browne (11th Dragoons).
   ,,   Drought (15th Regiment).
   ,,   Johnston (Grenadier Guards).
   ,,   Luard (30th Regiment).
   ,,   Sir J. C. Stepney, Bart. (Guards).
   ,,   G. Schreiber (38th Regiment).
   ,,   Dickson, K.H. (Grenadier Guards).
   ,,   Parchall (Depôt Battalion).
Major Bacon (17th Dragoons).
   ,,   Sir F. Head, Bart., K.C.H. (Royal Engineers).
   ,,   Methold (3rd Dragoon Guards and 23rd R.W.F.).
   ,,   Austin (56th Regiment).
   ,,   Webb (3rd W.I. Regiment).
Captain Bowlby (4th King's Own).
Lieutenant James (Military Knight of Windsor).
   ,,   Cox (71st Regiment).
   ,,   Lord Grantley (Guards).
   ,,   Sir F. Frankland (quondam Barrack Master at Gibraltar).
Surgeon-Major Thomas Smith.
Surgeon Gildea (Coldstream Guards).
Paymaster F. Feneran, Lieut.-Col. (95th Regiment).

The remaining fifty-two veterans are, to the best of my belief, those whose names I now append ; and here let me add, the fewer errors I have made the more shall I be satisfied :—

Field-Marshal Sir Wm. Rowan, G.C.B. (52nd Regiment).
   ,,   Sir Charles Yorke, G.C.B. (Rifle Brigade).
General Sir Thomas Reed, K.C.B. (44th Regiment).
   ,,   Lord Rokeby (77th Regiment).
   ,,   G. Whichcote (52nd Regiment).
   ,,   J. A. Butler (Guards).
   ,,   G. Macdonald (16th Regiment).
Lieut.-General Sir J. Bloomfield, K.C.B. (R.A.).
   ,,   Sir F. Warde, K.C.B. (R.A.).
   ,,   Sir W. Ingilby, K.C.B. (R.A.).
   ,,   Earl of Albemarle (Guards).
   ,,   T. Charlton Smith (27th Enniskillen).
Major-General Lloyd.
   ,,   Trevor (R.A.).
   ,,   Sir John Woodford, K.C.B., K.C.H. (Guards).
Colonel J. M. Harty.

Colonel Le Blanc (46th Regiment).
   ,,   Riddlesden (27th Regiment).
   ,,   Vandeleur (4th Dragoons).
Lieut.-Colonel Webster (18th Regiment).
   ,,   Burney, K.H. (44th Regiment).
   ,,   Jackson (Staff Corps).
   ,,   Cadell, K.H. (94th Regiment).
   ,,   Colthurst (18th Regiment).
   ,,   Molloy (9th Regiment).
   ,,   Hewett (53rd Regiment).
   ,,   Home (Guards).
Major Nugent (7th Dragoon Guards).
   ,,   Brady (36th Regiment).
   ,,   Drewe (88th Regiment).
   ,,   Fraser (34th Regiment).
   ,,   Hare (51st Regiment).
Captain White (Military Knight of Windsor).
   ,,   R. C. Elliott (30th Regiment).
   ,,   W. Harris (16th Light Dragoons).
   ,,   W. C. Shaw (Royal Horse Guards Blue).
Lieutenant Spurling (Royal Engineers).
   ,,   Bramwell (92nd Regiment).
   ,,   Butler (Guards).
   ,,   Gardner (27th Regiment).
   ,,   Parry (28th Regiment).
   ,,   Robinson (50th Regiment).
   ,,   J. R. Smith (38th Regiment).
   ,,   Tighe (Guards).
   ,,   Watson (24th Regiment).
   ,,   Wright (Rifle Brigade).
   ,,   Henry Leeke, the Rev. (52nd Regiment).
Surgeon Young (28th Regiment).
   ,,   George Jenks (10th Hussars).
Assistant-Surgeon Evans (14th Regiment).
Paymaster Hilliard (68th Regiment).
Quarter-Master Hardy (New Brunswick Fencibles).

The above lists are necessarily imperfect, but I think they are as nearly correct as a private individual can make them. They are offered for revision and correction, and will at any rate, and even in their present form, interest the public. I cannot guarantee that the regiment opposite each officer's name was that in which he served during the battle—indeed, in most cases I see it could not have so been—but I have in almost every case attached a regiment to which at some time or other such officer did belong, and through which he may, therefore, be traced. It would be interesting to get this list as perfect as possible, and, as I am trying towards this end, I ask a place for these names in the columns of "N. & Q.," for the present collection of correct information, and also for future and enduring record.

Let me add that, were it possible, I should like to see added the names of the rank and file still among us, of whom, though the individual life is not likely to be so long, a goodly force, from their numerical advantage, is likely to survive ; but it might be a difficult task to arrive at this more detailed information.   W. T. M.
Reading.

LOCAL PROVERBS, &c., OF BERWICKSHIRE.—Having lately had occasion to consult the *History of the Berwickshire Naturalists' Club* (Edinburgh, 1834), I came across some papers on the local pro-

these may not be known to the readers of "N. & Q.," and the place of their record is not very likely to be searched by persons interested in such matters, it may be as well that I should indicate it. At pp. 119-123 are sixteen of these proverbs, with comments "by Mr. [George] Henderson, Surgeon, Chirnside"; and at pp. 145-152 the subject is continued by the same gentleman as regards the "Popular Rhythmes" of the county, of which seventeen are given, while a few more are added by him at pp. 217-219. Perhaps as a zoologist I may be permitted to subjoin from the same volume (p. 216) the Roxburghshire version of the skylark's song, with which I think I never met before :—

"Up in the lift we go.
Tehee, tehee, tehee, tehee !
All the sutors in Selkirk can't make a shoe to me.
Why so ? Why so ?
Because my heel is as long as my toe."

ALFRED NEWTON.
Magdalene College, Cambridge.

LIST OF RELICS IN THE COLLEGE CHURCH OF ST. MARY, WARWICK.—The following list of relics, taken only seven years after Chaucer's death, and which I owe to the kindness of a friend in the Public Record Office, shows that our poet did not exaggerate in putting the Virgin's veil and a bit of the sail of St. Peter's boat among the relics of the Pardoner in the Prologue to the *Canterbury Tales.*

[Exch. Q. R. Miscellaneous Books, No. 30, fo. 204ᵈ.]

Hic specificantur reliquie que sunt in ecclesia Collegiata beate Marie de Warrewico nono die Julii anno Domini Millesimo ccccl. quinto. Secundum antiquum co[n]tentum de eisdem.

Quedam pars de cruce in qua crucifixus est Jbesus.
§ De capillis beate Marie et de vestimentis eius.
§ Quedam zona eiusdem beate Marie virginis et de tumba ejusdem beate Virginis.
§ Ossa beati Egidii abbatis et stola eiusdem cum aliis diversis reliquiis.
§ Quedam pars de lacte beate Marie Virginis.
§ De oleo sancte Katerine Virginis.
§ Reliquie sanctorum Edwardi Regis Swithuni et Alkemundi Wolfadi et Rufini, videlicet, ossa eorum.
§ Quedam reliquie sancti Jacobi Apostoli.
§ Quoddam Cilicium * sancti Thome Cantuariensis Archiepiscopi.
§ De Tumba Domini nostri Jhesu Christi et de spina que posita fuit super capud Jhesu.
§ De dente et ossibus Sancti Laurencii Martiris.
§ Quedam pars de Cathedra Patriarche Abrahe.
§ Oleum in quo venit ignis in vigilia Pasche de celo.
§ Quoddam os beate Andree Apostoli.
§ Pecten beati Edmundi Cantuariensis Archiepiscopi.
§ Quedam pars de manutergio Nichodemi quando sustinuit corpus Domini deponi supra humeros.
§ Quedam pars de arboribus Montis Caluarie.
§ De Rubo quem viderat Moyses incombustum.
§ Cornu eburneum Sancti Georgii Martiris.
§ Oleum Sancti Nicholai episcopi cum aliis reliquiis.

* A garment made of goat's hair.

§ De ossibus Sanctorum Innocencium.
§ Reliquie de Sancta Margareta Sancta dalena.
§ Reliquie Sancti Blasii Sancti Taddei apost
§ Reliquie Sancti Hugonis Lincolniensis E tiris.
§ De Sepulcro Domini et de petra Montis C
§ De præsepe Domini et columpna ad quam quando fuit flagellatus de petra supe vnctus post mortem.
§ De Sepulcro Sancte Katerine Virginis.
§ De genu Sancti Georgii et de petra supe guinauit in Martirio suo. De oss Brendani.
§ De facie Sancti Stephani.
§ De veste et capillis beate Marie Magdalen
§ De rupe in qua Sancta Anna iacet.
§ De capillis beati Francisci.
§ De vestimento Sancte Agnetis.
§ De velo et tunica beate Clare.
§ De reliquiis Sancte Cecilie.
END.

There is a curious inventory of goods syluer berneys, vestments, surplices relikes ") in English on folios 201ᵈ, 20⅔ dated the feast of the Purification of Mary (Feb. 2), 1407. F. J. Fui

CONVENTUAL CHURCHES STILL IN Us it may be interesting to have a record i of " N. & Q." of all the conventual ch in use. I have no sympathy with the vulgar sentimentality about ruins, or w enthusiasts who have no higher thoug schools of archæology. I heartily wish berately repeat my desire, that as se religious and useful learning, or as rest of God, we may one day see roof and c Bolton, Lanercost, Lilleshull, Cymmer, Rievaulx, Kirkstall, and Buildwas, w ancient feature of interest is spared, an or specious demolition is permitted in abused name of restoration. Brinkburr once more given back to the worship o a service was sung recently in the roofl Valle Crucis. The choir of the Gi Chichester, and the nave of Stamford, c no longer secularized.

Cathedral Churches of the New F Benedictine.—Canterbury, Worcester, and with chapter houses destroyed, chester, Rochester ; with Lady chapel Norwich ; and left incomplete at the R Bath (Priory not Abbey).

Cathedral Churches since the Reforma dictine.—Chester, Westminster, Glouc with chapter house and Lady chapel Peterborough ; and with chapter house St. Alban's.

Monastic Churches, Benedictine.—Sell Abergavenny, Usk, St. Bee's, Kidwell Peverell, Dunster ; and with Lady (

stroyed, Great Malvern, Tewkesbury ; and with Lady chapel desecrated and western church destroyed, Sherborne ; and with naves only, Leominster, Lynn, Shrewsbury, Binham, Tutbury, Wymondham, Chepstow, Bromfield, Deerhurst, Malmesbury ; Croyland, north aisle only ; Thorney, deprived of its aisles ; and with choirs only, Pershore, Boxgrave, Little Malvern, Milton Abbas ; and mutilated, Ewenny. The transept remains at Boxgrave and Milton, and one wing has been preserved at Pershore.

Nunnery Churches, Benedictine.—Romsey (Lady chapel destroyed), St. Helen's (Bishopsgate), Easebourne, Folkestone, Shepey le Minster.

Monastic Churches, Cistercian.—Conway ; Margam, Scarborough, Holm Coltram (nave-aisles and) choir destroyed ; Dore, with nave destroyed. Scarborough has one wing of the transept left.

Monastic Churches, Carthusian.—Charterhouse, London.

Cathedral Churches, Regular Canons of St. Austin.—Of the New Foundation, Carlisle ; since the Reformation, Bristol, Oxford, with naves which have suffered curtailment.

Conventual Churches, Austin Canons.—Christchurch (Twyneham), Cartmel, Brinkburne, Bruton, Bethgelert, Dorchester ; with naves destroyed, St. Mary's Overye, St. Bartholomew's (Smithfield), Hexham ; with choirs destroyed, Bridlington, Worksop, St. German's, Dunstable, Waltham ; or in ruins, Bolton, Lanercost ; and one aisle only, Dunmow.

Conventual Churches, Gilbertine Canons.—Old Malton, nave only, aisles and all eastward destroyed.

Friary Churches.—Dominicans, Brecon, choir only ; Austins (Dutch meeting), London, nave only, Atherstone ; Franciscans, Reading, part of choir only.   Mackenzie E. C. Walcott.

Randolph and "Aristippus."—Mr. Halliwell-Phillipps, in his *Dict. of Old Plays*, gives, " Aristippus ; or, the Jovial Philosopher. By T. Randolph. Demonstrativelie proveing," &c. Giving all thanks and justice to Mr. Halliwell-Phillipps for his labour, might I ask why "By T. Randolph" is inserted between the transcript titles of the work ? And again, on whose authority is Randolph fixed on as the author ? It seems to me not improbable that this and *The Conceited Pedlar*, always printed with it, were by Th. Randolph, but neither in the first edition of 1630 (not 1631) nor in that of 1668, both of which I possess, is there any name on the title-page, nor in any part of the after text.

Mr. Halliwell-Phillipps also says that "there is a ridicule of the prologue of *Troilus and Cressida*." Now, if both prologues were armed, that does not prove ridicule ; and there is no allusion, not even the most remote, in one prologue to the other, nor any other similarity than that they were " armed." Again, if there were no other armed prologues, it could hardly be that a prologue in 1630 should ridicule one produced years before. Thirdly, the prologue in *Aristippus* is not, in my opinion, armed in armour. He is an enchanter, and, "shews having been long intermitted and forbidden by Authority for their abuses, could not be raysed but by conjuring," and, " standing in a circle," these are his words :—

" I come an armed Prologue[,] arm'd with arts,
Who by my sacred charmes and mystique skill,
By virtue of this all-commanding wand," &c.

Afterwards, too, he tells the shew (represented by a person) to "take these purer robes." Fancy an armoured prologue laden with robes, who afterwards tells the audience, if they find no jest worth laughing at in what is to come, they can laugh at him.   B. Nicholson.

Election Expenses.—The following bill, sent to Sir Marcus Somerville, who represented county Meath, after an election, was amongst a few papers left by the late John Timbs, the popular antiquary :—

" *Copy of an Account sent to Sir Marcus Somerville by a Publican after an Election.*

To eating 16 freeholders for Sir Marke above stairs at 3s. a head	2	12	6
To eating eleven more below stairs and 2 clergymen after supper	1	15	0
To 6 beds in one room & four in tother at 2 Guineas for every bed	22	15	0
23 horses in the yard all night at 13d. every one of them, & for a man watching them all night	5	5	0
Breakfast & Tea next day for every one of them & as many as they brought with them as near as I can guess... ...	4	12	0
For Beer & Porter & Punch for the first day & first night. I am not sure but I think for 3 days & ½ of the Election as little as I can call it, & to be very exact is in all or thereabouts as near as I can guess	79	15	5½
Shaving & Dressing & cropping the heads off 24 freeholders for Sir Marke at 13d. every one of them, & cheap enough, God noes	2	5	6

In the name of Tinny Car,   Brian Garraty."

There is a humour in the remarks which accompany the charges made by Brian Garraty on behalf of one Tinny Car which makes the bill worth preserving in "N. & Q."   G. B.
Upton, Slough.

" Guy Mannering."—The last time I read this romance I noticed what appears to be a slip of the author, and which I do not think ever struck me before. In chap. xii. Col. Mannering, in writing to his friend Mervyn, says that his uncle the bishop "at his death bequeathed him his blessing, his manuscript sermons, and a curious portfolio containing the heads of eminent divines of the Church of England." Further on (chap. xx.) we read of " Dominie Sampson being occupied, body

library, which had been sent from Liverpool by sea, and conveyed by thirty or forty carts from the seaport at which it was landed." Scott evidently forgot the meagreness of the bishop's legacy to his nephew, as described in chap. xii.—a legacy which was not much more valuable than the famous one left by the licentiate Sedillo to Gil Blas, which struck such bitter disappointment to the soul of that worthy. One cannot regret the author's forgetfulness, because, had Scott not endowed Col. Mannering with the bishop's large library, we should have lost one of the most characteristic scenes in the romance, namely the one in which the Dominie is represented as engaged with all his faculties in cataloguing the books, oblivious of every other mundane concern whatsoever, including even what Byron calls " the tocsin of the soul, the dinner-bell." JONATHAN BOUCHIER.
Bexley Heath.

" COALS TO NEWCASTLE."—This homely proverb has many equivalents, ancient and modern, but it is in the kaleidoscope of Shakspere's fancy that the general notion of superfluousness which it localizes has assumed its most brilliant forms. " Therefore," says Salisbury, seeking to show the superfluity of the double coronation of King John,—

> " Therefore, to be possessed with double pomp,
> To guard a title that was rich before,
> To gild refinéd gold, to paint the lily,
> To throw a perfume on the violet,
> To smooth the ice, or add another hue
> Unto the rainbow, or with taper-light
> To seek the beauteous eye of heaven to garnish,
> Is wasteful and ridiculous excess."
> *King John,* iv. 2.

The " wit and wisdom " of the proverb have received in the above passage perhaps their highest literary expression ; at the same time it is worth noting that, long before Shakspere wrote, they had already been set forth in still wider range of exemplification. A Latin poet of the eleventh century, Joannes Garlandius, thus begins his *Opus Synonymorum* (Leyser's *Historia,* p. 312) :—

> " Ad mare ne videar latices deferre, camino
> Igniculum, densis et frondes addere sylvis,
> Hospitibusque pyra Calabris. dare vina Leæo,
> Aut Cereri fruges, apibus mel, vel thyma pratis,
> Poma vel Alcinoo, vel mollia thura Sabæo.
> Ad veterum curas curo superaddere nostras."
> A. C. MOUNSEY.
Jedburgh.

IRISH CHARACTERISTICS.—I do not remember to have met in " N. & Q." the following, given to me recently by an Irish lady :—

> " Leinster for breeding,
> And Ulster for reeving,
> Munster for reading,
> And Connaught for thieving."
> G. B.
Upton, Slough.

DIRTY HALF HUNDRED."—I cannot bu that the following scrap touching the nickr this regiment, taken from the *Scotsman* of 1878, is worthy of a firmer abiding-place t somewhat fleeting pages of a daily newspa]

" It was on its return from the Egyptian e: under Sir Ralph Abercrombie that the gallant the name of ' The blink half hundred,' on ac the number which it had lost during the camp on the prevalence of ophthalmia among the mt the remnant. This popular designation was, soon lost in that of ' The dirty half hundred,' wh acquired in the Peninsula. At that time the f the regiment were black, and it was no uncomm for the men during their marches, in the hot summer, to wipe their faces with the cuffs tunics, and the black of the facings not beii ' fast,' much of the colour was left on their face

Glasgow.

" ALL ROUND ROBIN HOOD'S BARN."—1 find this proverbial saying in the General : of " N. & Q." It is used thus. " Whe you been to-day ?" " All round Robin barn ! I have been all about the countr here and then there." Or thus : " Did y the house ?" " Yes, I did at last ; but I work to discover it. I should think that have gone all round Robin Hood's barn l lighted upon the place." CUTHBERT B

" NAILED TO THE STREET LIKE AN A DAMSE GAAPER."—In Drummond's *Travels* in describing Augspurg, he says :—

" Here I must observe that all the houses i countries being painted according to the taste proprietor or tenant, the eye of a stranger is irr attracted by something, I know not what ; and times such diverting oddities occur that he manner nailed to the street like an Amstt Gaaper."

W. N. STRANGEW
Stockport.

Queries.

[We must request correspondents desiring info on family matters of only private interest, to afl names and addresses to their queries, in order t answers may be addressed to them direct.]

LUCY, DAUGHTER OF EARL MORCAR (' COUNTESS OF CHESTER.—The doubt that over the connexion of the Saxon fan Mercian Earls and the Palatine Earls of Ch not yet dispelled (see a note to Mr. Helsby *tory of Chester,* vol. i. p. 50, and writer: cited). The fact of the connexion itself hat excited a doubt : that the victorious N should seek to confirm the title of the sw that of the inheritance was in the nature of and in accordance with the practice and pc all times. The example, indeed, was follow the throne itself, in the popularly approved instance of Henry I. But who the ladies were whose marriage thus quieted possession and rendered foreign intrigue hopeless appears from the note above mentioned not to be so well ascertained. The assumption that there were two Lucies of that family might perhaps be accorded ; that they were also mother and daughter is an additional assumption credible enough did no other Lucy appear. But Stebbing Shaw (*Topographer*, vol. ii. p. 256) tells us that the Earl Ralph " died 1120 [it should be 1129] (29 Hen. I.), leaving issue by Lucia, *daughter of Morcar*, Earl of Northumberland, &c. Now this Morcar was brother of Earl Edwin ; both were sons of Algar and grandsons of Leofric and Godiva." If this be so, there were two Lucies, and the latter, Morcar's daughter, giving us an additional generation, may be substituted as the wife of at least one of the three husbands assigned (under the circumstances incredibly) to Lucy, daughter of Earl Algar. My query is, Does any authority exist for Shaw's Lucy ? He made the statement without citing any at a time—which is important—when no doubt had as yet been thrown upon the exactitude of the MS. pedigree cited in *Monast.*, vol. ii. p. 204, from the copy of Florence of Worcester, in the hands of the Archbishop of Armagh—the pedigree which has been so much commented upon.   T. J. M.

Stafford.

A BUST OF NAPOLEON BY CERACCI.—Previous to Napoleon embarking for Egypt in the year 1798, Ceracci the sculptor, who was afterwards guillotined by Napoleon for an attempt upon his life, obtained permission to make, and made, a model of his head. This model was at one time in the Louvre. Can you or any of the readers of " N. & Q." give me any information as to this piece of sculpture, or say where I am likely to obtain any information ? I ask this as I own what I firmly believe to be the work in question. It was bought by my father of a Frenchman in London in 1816. It is a remarkably handsome head, circled with a wreath of laurels, and carved in the finest marble. In height it is about eighteen inches.   H. W. MACKIETH.

[See *ante*, pp. 329, 375.]

PORTRAITS OF CROMWELL AND DANTE.—Can any one give me any information about the two following portraits in my possession ? An engraved portrait of Oliver Cromwell, about 14½ inches high by 8½ broad, a side face. In the lower compartment of the picture is a quaint representation of a group of persons, one of whom on bended knee is presenting a crown to the Protector, whilst the latter is motioning it away from him. In the right-hand lower corner is a plumed helmet, in the left a cornucopia, between these a sword and axe. Neither the painter's nor the engraver's name is stated. Oliver's own portrait is clearly from Cooper's miniature of him, but by whom is the remainder of the picture ?

An engraved portrait of Dante, about 4½ by 3½ inches. The poet's brows are wreathed with laurel, and he has a frightened look in his eyes, or, as Macaulay expresses it, " the dilated eye of horror . . . . with which he tells his fearful tale." It is the poet of the *Inferno* rather than of the *Purgatorio* or *Paradiso*. Under the picture are the words " Coll^on de la Sorbonne. Dante Alighieri, 1321 " (that is, the date of the poet's death). Above is the number 1727. Does this mean the number of the picture in the Sorbonne collection ? Who was the painter of this portrait ?
    JONATHAN BOUCHIER.

Bexley Heath, Kent.

DIVINATION "PER TABULAS ET CAPRAS."—The late Prof. De Morgan, who is well known to have been the author of the shrewd and caustic preface to a book (attributed to his wife) entitled *From Matter to Spirit* (Longmans, 1863), makes in it the following suggestion :—

" One of the Fathers, but I have mislaid the reference, speaks of divination *per tabulas et capras*, by tables and *goats*—an odd association. The word *crepa* would be the legitimate companion substantive of *crepo*, and would mean a crack or rap. But the word is only found in Festus (*teste* Forcellini), who says that *crepæ* are goats, *quod cruribus crepent*. There is enough in this to raise a suspicion that *crepa* did actually exist in what would have been its primitive sense, and that the Father who is cited was speaking of divination by *tables and raps*. There is also *crepus*, for which see any account of the Lupercalia."

Whatever may be said of the modern practice, the learning of divination is certainly obsolete ; but perhaps some student of patristic divinity may be able to supply the reference mislaid ·by Prof. De Morgan, and then the context might possibly throw light on the interpretation.   C. C. M.

OLD CHINA.—I have inherited some china, of which the following is the device :—Ermine, on a bend cotised sable, three griffins' heads erased or ; crest, a boar's head erased azure, crested or (the red head of Ulster is in chief). Motto round the coat, " Tria juncta in uno " ; motto beneath the coat, " Laudat qui invidet." Supporters, a boar azure, crested, &c., or ; a griffin argent, winged, &c., or. For whom was it painted, and when ?   S. SMITH.

Rickmansworth.

THOMAS POWELL OR POEL, DRAMATIC WRITER. —Whilst wandering about in London amongst the old book-stalls some few years ago I met with a MS. play entitled *Camillus and Columna; or, the Sleeping Beauty*. On the back of the title-page is written, " Story invented, executed, &c., by Ts. Poel, 1764." I have not found the name of this writer in any dramatic or biographical dictionary ;

volume by him called the *Works of Thomas Powell, Esq.*, 1805, and in its catalogue he is spoken of as "of Monmouth." His works consist of poems, prologues, &c., and at p. 160 is this note :—" These prologues and epilogues belong to plays which have never yet been shown to any one." The titles of the plays are the following :— *The First Part of Henry II.*; *Courcy, Earl of Ulster*; *Camillus and Columna*; *The Children in the Wood*, written 1780; *The Gipsies*, and a play without a name. The epilogue to *Camillus and Columna*, as there given, is not in the MS.

The Museum Catalogue has also the following works entered under his name :—*Edgar and Elfrida : a Drama*, by Taliesin de Monmouth ; *Blind Wife ; Student of Bonn*, 2nd ed., 1845 ; *The Shepherd's Well : a Play*, 1844 ; *The Wife's Revenge*, 1843. At the end of *The Shepherd's Well* is a poem entitled " Mary ; or, the First Love : a Recollection of an Octogenarian." But if he wrote *Camillus and Columna* in 1764, he must in 1844 have been a hundred at least. Perhaps the author of *The Shepherd's Well* may have been a son of the author of *Camillus*. Any information respecting either writer will be gratefully accepted. I may add that my MS. play is very neatly written ; it has been so freely corrected by the author as to lead one to suppose that it may have been a first copy, and consists of 110 pages of fcap. 8vo. I bought it for twopence.   H. Bower.
Brighton.

"Ear-aches"=the Field Poppy.—The popular name for field poppies, as well as cultivated ones, in this district is " ear-aches." Why this name is given I am unable to discover. It is said that if the ear are gathered and put to the ear a violent attack of ear-ache will be the result. Is this the popular idea of poppies elsewhere ? In some parts of Derbyshire poppies are called " ear-aches."   Thos. Ratcliffe.
Worksop.

The Wife of a Baron of the Cinque Ports entitled " Dame."—I have seen " Dame" put upon the tombstone of a lady. I am told it is the title of a baronet's or knight's wife. The inscription in question said " wife of a Baron of the Cinque Ports." Probably in virtue of it the lady thought she had a right to the title. Can any of your readers give information as to it ?
W. J. Birch.

Character of James I.—In vol. iv. of the *Harleian Miscellany* there is reprinted a pamphlet on the legitimacy of the Duke of Monmouth ; it contains the following curious description of King James I. :—

" Let me upon this occasion remind your Lordship of a story, of a Scots nobleman to my Lord Burleigh, upon

James, long before he ascended the English thr your Lordship, saith the blunt Scotsman, know napes, you cannot but understand, that if I have my hands, I can make him bite you, whereas if him into your hands, you may make him bite me

Is the author of this contemporary word-' known ?   J. H. Chapman, M.A., F
Woodgreen, Witney, Oxon.

Clocks upon Bells, 1552.—Where can planation be found of the mechanism of affixed upon bells, and were they in c use ? At Winwick, Lancashire, in the yea named, there were four bells in the church " where of a clokke sticketh upon one Horsley, West Hallam, and at Ashbou Derbyshire, there were similar instances same kind (*Reliquary*, xi. pp. 6, 7, 12).
John E. Bai
Stretford, Manchester.

Bartholomew Howlett.—My grand Bartholomew Howlett, was born somewl Norfolk in the year 1739. I should lik much to ascertain where it was. Perhap Norfolk reader of " N. & Q." can help me. lieve he came to Lincolnshire as a young m settled at Louth. He married for his seco Catharine Rogerson, of Sotby, Linc., on I 1789. He had a son by a former marriag named Bartholomew Howlett, somewha brated as an engraver, who died about tl 1825. Perhaps it may not be deemed un of remark that 139 years is rather a long stretch back to the birth of the grandfath man aged fifty-six, which is the age of
W. E. How:
Kirton in Lindsey.

Rev. Lewes Hewes or Hughes.—Whe croft was Bishop of London, a minister Lewes Hewes dwelt in Great St. Helen's, I gate Ward, which was then his living.
Among the first ministers sent to Bermu a Lewes Hewes. In 1633 a Lewes Hewes, c of White Lion Jail, Southwark, was dismi five years of nonconformity. I desire t whether Lewes Hewes of St. Helen's, Be and White Lion Prison was the same perso
Del
Minneapolis, Minnesota, U.S.

Authors of Quotations Wanted.—
" With heart and lips unfeign'd
We praise Thee for Thy word," &c.
" How happy is the Christian's state !
His sins are all forgiven," &c.
" Sing to the Lord a new-made song,
Let earth, in one assembled throng,
Her common patron's praise resound
" Praise the Lord, whose mighty wonder
Earth, and air, and seas display," &c
D:

"Hush, oh, hush, for the Father knows what thou
        knowest not—
The need, and the thorn, and the shadow linked with
        the fairest lot;
Knows the wisest exemption from many an unseen
        snare,
Knows what will keep thee nearest, knows what thou
        canst not bear."   JOHN TAYLOR.

Replies.

"ALL TO BRAKE," JUDGES IX. 53.

(5th S. ix. 344, 413, 455.)

There can be no question of the original identity
of the intensitive prefix to with the zer in many
German verbs, and its identity in the present
passage is illustrated, as I showed in a letter to the
Guardian, by a comparison with the High and
Low German versions. In Luther's translation the
corresponding words are, " Und *zerbrach* ihm den
schedel"; and in a Low German version, printed
about 1479, "Unde *tho brak* eme syn harnschedel."
Then the phrase descended regularly through the
successive English versions, excepting Wiclif—who
indeed uses the prefix very frequently, but in this
passage reads, "And brak his brayn" (" nol " in
marg.)—and Coverdale (1535), who follows Wiclif
in 2 Chron. xxv. 12, " They all *to barst* in sunder "
(*all* being there *omnes*, not *omnino*), but here has,
" And brake his brane panne," and the Geneva
version, 1560, " And brake his braine pan."
    Thus Matthew's version, 1537, Cromwell's, 1539,
Taverner's, 1539, Cranmer's, 1540, Daye's (or
Beke's), 1551, Cranmer's second, 1553, and the
Bishops', 1568, all have " *All to brake* hys brayne
panne."
    So that the makers of the Authorized Version of
1611, in reading " All to brake his skull," adopted
no new phrase, but, as MR. TANCOCK suggests,
took the phrase inherited from the earlier versions
of about one hundred years before. The question
is, then, not so much what *they* understood by the
phrase as what the maker of Matthew's version
understood by it.
    Now 1. Was *to* obsolete in 1611 as an intensi-
tive prefix? 2. Could *al-to*, as the Bishop of Bath
and Wells and others have thought, have been
then used as an adverb? 3. Was *all*, as the bishop
thinks, then obsolete as an adverb?
    1. *To* is admitted to have been in common use
as an intensitive prefix in Wiclif and Chaucer;
and it is easy to give a catena of writers who used
it from the latter's time to the date of Matthew's
version.
    Thus, 1430, *Sir Generydes*:—

"A hundred houndes on a throm
    He saw that were thider com
    And al the bodie had *to rent*."   L. 2951.
"Ismaels shelde in the midward
    He *to rofe* and al *to brast*."   L. 4453.
"His shelde *to sheuered* euen in twoo."   L. 5156.

1440, *Morte Arthur*:—
"Alle *to stonayede* with þe strokes of þa steryne
    knyghtes."   L. 1436.

1460, *Holy Grail*:—
"The schip on fowre partyes *to rof*."   C. 35, l. 394.
"He dide brenne and *to brast* Every where."
                                                C. 16, l. 498.
"They *to brosed* him both body and bak."
                                                C. 14, l. 410.
"Helmes and hauberkis *to kraked* he then."
                                                C. 14, l. 196.

C. 1470, *The Flower and the Leaf*:—
"Forshronke with heat, the ladies eke *to brent*."
                                                L. 358.

1490, *Lancelot of the Laik*:—
"His suerd atwo the helmys al *to kerwyth*"   L. 868.
"His face was al *to hurt* and al *to schent*" L. 1221.
His newis [fists] swellyng war, and al *to rent*."

1500, *Partenay*:—
"All hys Armure he *to breke* and tere."   L. 5893.
"Paynims thay will make *to stoniste* incline." L. 2198.
"Tham all *to chapped* and kerue."   L. 2272.
"And this said leuer *to rent* thorughly."   L. 4290.
"All the skyn tho was torn and *to rent*,"   L. 5648.
"Hauberke broken and *to tore*."   L. 5872.

1535, Coverdale, Matt. vii. 6 :—
"Turne agayne and all *to rente* you."

So *all* is not once used with the *to* prefix in the
Holy Grail ; and in *Partenay* only once could it
belong to the verb, and need not in any of the
passages. In line 4290 " *to*-rent thoroughly " is
precisely equivalent to *all to-rent*.
    The author, then, of *Partenay* knew little if
anything of *all-to*, but used *to-tore* and its kindred
verbs freely. Is it not, then, probable that Coverdale, only thirty-five, and Matthew, only thirty-
seven, years later, knew very well what they were
writing, and, in using the perfects *to-rente* and *to-
brake*, only used words current in their youth, and
used *all*=utterly only to intensify the phrase still
further ?
    No doubt in later days the *to* prefix *alone* was
fast becoming obsolete, and instances of its use are
rare ; but it was not only by the translators of the
passage in Judges that it was handed down, for
we find it in Foxe and Shakspere, and, in its longer
form, in writers from 1562 to 1726.
    The following list from the index to Foxe's
works in Stevenson's *Church Historians* shows a
very frequent use of the longer phrase in 1562, and
two instances of the *to* prefix alone. The complete series is difficult to come by, but it must, I
suppose, have been printed, or a correct index
could not have been made :—*To*, without *all*, vol. v.
395 [853] ; with *all*, [v. 424, 425, 470; vi. 669,
682; vii. 512, 561, 719; viii. 635, 774, 790];
all-to-be, i. 131; ii. 100, 382 [871]; iii. 110, 382;
[v. 424, 425; vi. 340]. The references in brackets
are in volumes which I cannot find.

I should add that the first instance of *to* alone (v. 395) is a doubtful one. It is on p. 1358, col. 2, of ed. 1570 :—" Sodeinly at the voice of the Lord Cromwell's commyng, the campe brake vppe, and the Ruffins *togoe* " (*sic*). Comp. Summer's last will and testament, 1600 :—" The lustye courser, if he . . . spye better grasse, . . . breakes ouer hedge and ditch, and *to goe*, ere he will be pent in " ; where the construction seems the same, but *goe* is plainly the infinitive, and *to* = *zu*.

1562, A. Brooke, *Romeus and Juliet*:—
"Mercutious ysy hand had *all to frozen* myne
And of thy goodness thou agayne hast warmed it with thyne."

1571, Lord Buckhurst, *Ferrex and Porrex*:—
" Done her villanie, and after *all-to-be-scratched* her face."

1590, Sir P. Sidney, *Arcadia*, p. 156 :—
"Now forsooth as they went together, often *all to* kissing one another."

1591, Harrington, *Ariosto*, xxxiv. 48 :—
"That did with dirt and dust him *all to dash*."

1596, Spenser, *Fairy Queen*, iv. 7, 8 :—
" With briers and bushes *al to rent* and *scratcht*."

1596, Shakspere, *Merry Wives*, v. 4 :—
" Then let them all encircle him about,
And Fairy-like *to pinch* the vncleane Knight."

1598, Shakspere, *King John*, v. 2 :—
" Where these two Christian Armies might combine
The bloud of malice in a vaine of league,
And not *to spend* it so vnneighbourly."

1609, Shakspere, *Pericles*, iv. 6 :—
" Now the Gods *to-blesse* your honour " (4to.) : " bless," third and fourth folios.

1601, Phil. Holland, *Pliny*, x. 74 :—
" She againe to be quit with them will *all to pinch* and nip both the Fox and her cubs."

C. 1620, Beaumont and Fletcher, *Philaster*, v. 3 :—
" I 'll have you chronicled, and chronicled, and cut and chronicled, and *all to be praised* and sung in sonnets."

1629, Bernard's *Terence*, p. 16 :—
" I will *all to becurry* thee, or bethwacke thy coate."

1632, Ben Jonson, *Magnetic Lady*, v. 2 :—
" See who is here ! She has been with my lady, who kist her, *all to be kist* her, twice or thrice."
Chorus, Act I. " And at last come home lame, and *all to be laden* with miracles."

1634, Milton, *Comus*, i. 376 :—
" Plumes her feathers and lets grow her wings,
That in the various bustle of resort
Were *all to ruffled*."

1644, Cleveland, *Character of a London Diurnall*:
" I wonder my Lord of Canterbury is not come more *all-to-be-traytored* for dealing with the lyons to settle the commission of array in the Tower."

1684 (not 1678, as MR. TANCOCK has it), Bunyan, *Pilgrim's Progress*, pt. ii. p. 110 :—
" And the Giant mist but little of *all to breaking* Mr. Greatheart's Scull with his Club."

1726, Swift to Pope, Dec. 5 :—
" A letter from my Lord Peterborow for whi treat you will present him with my humble resp thanks, though he *all-to-be-Gullivers* me by vei insinuations."

In all these cases it is certain, I thin whether some of the writers knew it or not is the very *to* prefix of Wiclif and Chaucer, of the Low Dutch version of the Bible, and of the High Dutch ; and not at all what the of Bath and Wells was inclined to think the *to* (*zu*) of hitherto and thereto.

But Shakspere, at least, must have what he meant when he wrote to-blesse, and to-pinch ; and Holland had no difficult the last word, though he strengthened *all*. Nor were the translators of the Bible in doubt when they " *al* to-brake Abin skull."

To without *all* was the commonest form prefix in early writers ; *to* with *all* in later and in later still *be* was more frequently i lated to add to the strength and quaintness almost obsolete form of speech.

But none of the writers, early or late, have said, if asked to parse the sentence, adverb ; pinch or bepinch, the verb to whic adjoined.

2. But can *all-to* be called an adverb ? T the second question proposed. Is it an equ of *omnino*, of *altogether*, as the bishop sugge It would be indeed a strange sort of which is never used with adjectives, and ne far as I can learn, with any verbs except which could take the *to* prefix. Let us sub it in a few passages in which *altogether* occu
" They are *all to* lighter than vanity itself."
" Make thyself *all to* a prince over us."
" Why are ye thus *all to* vain ? "
" Or saith he it *all to* for our sakes ? "
" Thou, O God, knowest it *all to*."
" Behold thou hast blessed them *all to*."
I think we shall never find *all to* used in way. The last instance might be turned to blessed them," because bless takes the *to* pref the one before it could not be so turned, k know does not take it.

I conclude, then, that the answer to the question would have been, on the part o who did not think about it, " Oh, it is a phr use when we mean to speak strongly." clearer answer would be " *To* is a prefix ; prefix ; all, though an adverb, has the char a prefix, as in *allutterly*, almighty, almos they are all intensive, and are in common compounded together, so as to add more f the verb to which they belong. They h adverbial character, as prefixes always ha they are inseparable from the verb, and f intensitive variety of it."

Everybody knew that the verb *to-brenne*

"to burn up"; *to-brent*, "utterly burnt"; *be-brent*, if it existed, would have a like meaning ; *all-be-brent*, the same intensified ; *all-to-brent* (Wiclif), the same ; and if one wished to be very energetic indeed, like Bernard, one had no scruple in saying all one could, *all-to-be-brent*.

The whole thing was in all cases a compound verb, a verb with a prefix, and that a prefix which neither in its compound state, nor in its several parts, *to*, or *be*, or *al-to*, could ever be used apart from the verb.

3. As to the third question, the bishop seemed to consider *all* obsolete as an adverb, but it appears that it was only as to its use with an indicative that he had doubts, and that this led him to think *all tobrake* an unlikely use at the time of our version. But *all* is and was used as an adverb in every other possible way : With a substantive preceded by a preposition, "*All* in gore blood up to the elbows" (Foxe) ; "*All* in the Downs" (eighteenth century) ; with another adverb, "And then he spake to me *all* angerlie" (Foxe) ; "*all* abroad" (nineteenth century) ; with an adjective, "If a man had not *al* steady belief" (Foxe) ; "All forlorn" (nineteenth century) ; with a participle, "But Hildebrand *all* set on wickedness " (Foxe) ; "*all* tattered and torn" (nineteenth century). Wiclif moreover uses it with an infinitive, as in Eccles. ii. 10, "ne I forfendide myn herte, but that of all voluptuouste he shuld take frut, and *al* delicen hym self in these thingus," and with an indicative, as in Ps. liv. 6 (lv. 6 of our version), "Drede and trembling camen vp on me, and *all* couereden me dercnesses" ; in both of which cases *all* is rather a prefix.

All to-brake then would have been quite a possible construction with earlier writers, and probably with later ones also ; but I think it clear that at least down to 1611 they would have read the whole thing, whether *al-to* or *al-to-be*, as a compound prefix inseparable from the verb ; and that Priscian would have complained, and loudly, at the notion of *all-to* being ranked as an adverb.

HENRY H. GIBBS.

St. Dunstan's, Regents Park.

THE RUSSELL FAMILY (5ᵗʰ S. ix. 461.)—Why does COL. CHESTER throw difficulties in the path of inquirers by speaking of Lady Elizabeth Russell ? That title implies that she was the daughter of an earl, a marquis, or a duke. Correctness in names is a great help in many cases, and many students have been led wrong by the foolish practice of speaking of the William, Lord Russell, executed under Charles II. as "Lord William Russell." William, Lord Russell, marks an eldest son, Lord William Russell a younger son.   A. H. C.

Allow me to notice a mistake into which your valued correspondent COL. CHESTER has fallen.

Elizabeth Lloyd by her first marriage became Lady James Russell ; and to style her "Lady Elizabeth Russell" is certainly incorrect.   G. A. W.

THE RIGHT TO SEARCH THE PUBLIC RECORDS (5ᵗʰ S. ix. 447.)—The decision was given in the Court of Appeal at Lincoln's Inn, Aug. 2, 1876, in the matter of the Keeper of the Public Records *ex parte* Carr, before Lords Justices James, Mellish, and Baggallay, and is reported in the *Times* of the next day. The result of the application, as there stated, is :—

"The Court dismissed the appeal, on the ground that there is no general right in all the queen's subjects to inspect the documents in the Record Office. Some particular right must be shown. The appellant was in the position of a mere stranger, and the public time could not be wasted in hearing such an application."

There is also a full report of the previous decision of the Divisional Court at Westminster in the previous number of the *Times*. It was held that the right to consult the records was subject to the limitations of the Public Records Act, 1 & 2 Vic. c. 94, one of which was that the Keeper of the Records had power to make rules.

ED. MARSHALL.

The question of the right of the public to search the public records was argued before Lord Coleridge, the Lord Chief Baron, and Mr. Justice Archibald on July 31, 1876 (see *Times* and *Daily News* of Aug. 2 in that year). The decision was against any such right. An appeal against the decision was heard before Lords Justices James, Mellish, and Baggallay on Aug. 2, 1876 (see *Times* of Aug. 3), and was dismissed.   C.

NIGHTINGALES AND COWSLIPS (5ᵗʰ S. ix. 408.) —I have lived during the past half century in Devonshire, and have never, to my knowledge, seen a cowslip growing wild in the county, though they abound within a few miles of its borders. During the same period I have never known a well-authenticated case of the notes of the nightingale having been heard within the county of Devon, though exceptional cases are sometimes reported. A clerical friend of mine in this county, who had studied this subject for thirty years, had travelled many a mile in search of a nightingale, and sat up till a very late hour during many a night in the hope of hearing its note (attracted to Ringmore Vale and elsewhere by delusive promises), has often told me that in no case had his hopes been fulfilled.   E. C. HARINGTON.

The Close, Exeter.

On this subject allow me to cite the following from Yarrell's *British Birds* (4th ed., vol. i. p. 316, note) :—

"Walcott, in his *Synopsis of British Birds* (vol. ii. p. 228), says that the nightingale 'has been observed to be met with only where the *cowslip* grows kindly,' and

…the association receives a partial approval from Montagu; but whether the statement be true or false, its converse certainly cannot be maintained, for Mr. Watson, in his *Cybele Britannica*, gives the cowslip (*Primula veris*) as found in all the 'provinces' into which he divides Great Britain as far north as Caithness and Shetland, where we know that the nightingale does not occur."

ALFRED NEWTON.

Magdalene College, Cambridge.

It may interest your correspondent to know that the nightingales have been in full song here since April 12, the day on which they first appeared, but that in the immediate neighbourhood cowslips are not at all plentiful. At Albury, a mile and a half distant, they are abundant, but in the adjacent field I have rarely met with them. It was Cobbett, I think, in his *Rural Rides*, who said that in the Vale of Chilworth the nightingales sing earlier than in any part of England.

G. UNWIN.

Chilworth, Surrey.

In East Sussex, on the border of Kent, the cowslip is quite unknown, but nightingales are as common as blackberries there.   T. W. W. S.

DARTMOOR: SCOTLAND (5th S. ix. 349.)—In an article in the *Pall Mall Gazette* of Sept. 20, 1869, reference is made to the evidence of Mr. J. Mackie before a Select Committee on the Poor Law, Scotland, as to Caithness Tinkers, who, he said, were a race different, and had little or nothing in common with, the other inhabitants of that part of Scotland. Mr. Mackie is also said to have stated that about twenty years previously they were only about twelve or fifteen in number, living in the open air, and wandering about; but since that time they had rapidly increased to several hordes, two colonies of whom had located themselves in natural caves on the side of Wick Bay, and the others occasionally wandered about the five northern counties. They were also stated to be a savage, drunken, lawless people, and that all efforts to reclaim them had hitherto failed. In a more recent issue of the *Pall Mall Gazette*, Oct. 29, 1870, an account is given of a singular family living on their own land at Nymet Rowland, North Devon ; and reference is made in the same article to a savage community called "Broom Squires" who had infested the west of Somerset. A very graphic account of the family at Nymet Rowland will be found in the interesting work of Mr. Greenwood (the "Amateur Casual"), entitled *Strange Company*, published by Messrs. Henry S. King & Co. in 1874. In the chapter headed "The North Devon Savages" an account is given of his visit to the Cheriton family, who seem to have been as irreclaimable as their Northern prototype, the Tinkers of Caithness.   HUBERT SMITH.

Z. Y. X. will find a long account of "The North Devon Savages, by our Special Commissioner,"

and a leading article thereon, in the *graph* for Oct. 23, 1871.   W.

FEMALE FREEMASONS (5th S. ix. never was any order of female Freen was, however, an order of *Mopses*, con of men and women. In a book writ and published at Amsterdam in either author's or publisher's na *L'Ordre des Franc-Maçons trahi, e Mopses révélé*, an account of the found. The following is what we ar When Pope Clement XII. excom Freemasons, certain persons formed a Germany under the patronage of m Government and others of high rar and passwords, and all the parapher masonry ; they set up a dog as th sign of fidelity, and called themselve dogs. To avoid the appearance o masons, they admitted women into over each of their lodges they set a Grand Mistress, each ruling f six months, who were addressed as C On the admission of a candidate, i sword, &c., in use among Freema collar and chain were attached to which he or she was led blindfolded immediately the Mopses began to b like dogs. The final ceremony is to described here.   E. LEATON BL

On the French lodges of female F Clavel, *Histoire Pittoresque de la nerie* (Paris, 1844), partie 1re, chap. female lodge appears to have been 1730, and many others were institut beyond the period of the great Fren The Princesse de Lamballe was pi Loge du Contrat Social. Some o admitted members of both sexes. too good reason to fear that some of such as L'Ordre des Chevaliers et de la Rose, were designed, or, to were employed, to cover the grossest J.

PERSONAL PROVERBS (5th S. ix. 4 Would HORATIO kindly give the ref Donne, mentioned in his note *ante*,

ALCHEMY AND MODERN SCIEN 427.) — It has often occurred to apparent success (if we may believ evidence of which C. C. M. speaks) mediæval alchemists was due to the knew how to *extract* gold from th and this would often appear like In antimony ore, for instance, gold and may be extracted in a solid lun

"Allah" (5th S. ix. 429.)—Is D. D. serious in the question he puts? Had he prefaced his query with an express statement that he believed or understood a Pope to have really given utterance to the proposition quoted by him, we might have received the fact as something to go upon ; but as he only leaves this to be inferred, we are at liberty to reflect on the warning example of Charles II. and the Royal Society in the matter of the difference of weight between the fish alive and the fish dead. Does D. D. mean to say positively that any Pope is responsible for seriously asserting, as though it were a new discovery, that the Christian God differs from the Allah of Mohammedanism?

W. T. M.

Reading.

"Pizarro" (5th S. ix. 389.)—The *Biographia Dramatica* makes the edition of this play written by a North Briton, and differing from all other editions, to have been written, on supposition, in 1799, but never acted. It adds, "a despicable production abounding with grammatical blunders."

J. Keith Angus.

The Thames: Kent and Essex (5th S. ix. 364.)—In *The History of South Britain*, by Henshall, 1798, pp. 78-81, the question of these outlying portions of certain Kentish manors is considered. He concludes that Alestan, the Bailiff of London, held them as representative of the Bishop and Church of London, who then had custody of the course of the Thames, and were proprietors of all lands recovered from the encroachments of the tide, and that as an ecclesiastic he was permitted to continue the holding, which was confirmed to his nephew Helto. In the time of the Saxons the Thames estuary was probably wider than it is at present, and many of the marsh lands must have been subject to frequent inundations ; but I have met with no evidence tending to support the suggestion that what is now called the Isle of Dogs ever formed part of the lands of the Çant-wara-rice. It is probable that the main current of the Thames flowed south of this district from the earliest times, and that it was included in the lands north of the Thames, as defined by Alfred and Godrun in 878.

Edward Solly.

A "Yoting Stone" (5th S. ix. 328.)—In this word *yote* the English dialects have preserved one of the oldest European roots, viz., GHU, *ghud*, "to pour"; Greek χέω (κέ-χυ-μαι); Latin *fundo* (fudi, f = gh); Gotic *giutan* (giutan vein in balgins = to pour wine into bottles), past *gaut*, plur. *gut*: this *gut* is the Teutonic root; Old Saxon *giotan* (blôd geotan = to shed blood ; geotan is Frankish), past *gôt*, plur. *gut*, the root again ; Anglo-Saxon *gɛ́otan*, past *we guton*, also showing the root *gut* (*Beowulf*, 1691, gifen geótende = the sea pouring, *i.e.* the flood); Old High German

giozan, kiozan ; Middle High German *giezen* (er hôrte wazzer giezen = he heard water roar, *Nibelungen*, v. 1533). So far the word means "to pour," but it gradually obtains the additional meaning of "to cast," *i.e.* metals. Thus *Kudrun*, v. 1129, "ir anker wâren von glocken spîse gozzen," her anchors were cast of bell metal. In Old English we find :—

"hys mase* he toke in his honde tho
that was made of *yoten* bras."
Richard Coer de Lion, 370.

"the lazar† tok forth his coupe of gold
bothe‡ were *yoten* in o § mold."
Amis and Amiloun, 2024.

Modern German *giessen, goss*, means both "pour" and "cast" (as Glockengieszerei, "bell-foundry ").

Now with regard to the phonetic changes at the beginning of the root, they appear in Frisian (g)*iata*, and in the Swedish *gjutan*, "to cast, pour " (as gjutstâl = cast steel), from Old Norse *giota*. Thus the English *yote* will be accounted for.

Yote means in the present dialects "to pour water on, to soak in or mix with water." A yoting stone may therefore be a trough where the corn is soaked before being given to the fowls. In German the word *gosse* (or *gossenstein* = yoting stone) means a sink, as in a kitchen. *Gosse* further denotes a trough-like excavation in a rock where waters sink; also a trough destined to receive the portion of a mill where the corn is "poured in " to be ground.

G. A. Schrumpf.

Tettenhall College.

T. W. Jones, Chemist, 1767 (5th S. ix. 349.)—I have a copy of Baldwin's *Directory of London* for 1770, which gives the name of Thomas Jones, chymist, 43, Newgate Street, and also the name of William Jones, druggist, Russell Street, Covent Garden. These are the only two in the list in that trade. Perhaps one of these will be the party inquired for by H. C.

Edward J. Taylor, F.S.A.Newc.

Bishopwearmouth.

A Sword-Mill (5th S. ix. 348) was revolving barrels set with sword-blades which received the victim from the maiden or virgin (of Nuremberg, &c.), and chopped the body past recognition. The working of the execrable machine is described at length in Reynolds's *The Bronze Statue; or, the Virgin's Kiss*, illustrations by Anelay.

Henry Llewellyn Williams.

"Paw wa'" (5th S. ix. 388.)—What Defoe meant by this word, and whence he derived it, will readily be ascertained by a reference to the eleventh chapter of his *Modern History of the Devil*, which

* Mace.
† Leper.
‡ *I.e.* the cup brought to him and his own.
§ One.

treats of "Divination, Sorcery, the Black Arts, and Pawawing," &c. He says there is amongst the Indians of North America a kind of magic which they call pawawing; their divines, or witches, they call pawaws.

Neal, in his *History of New England* (1720, i. 33), says the Indians recognize a secondary deity which they call Hobbamocko, that is in English the devil, who appears only to the powaws or priests. Blome, in the *Present State of America* (1687, p. 207), describes how, when an Indian is very ill, at last they send for a pawnaw or priest, who sits down and asks no questions, but expects a fee or gift, according to which he proportions his work; and Capt. Smith, as quoted in Beverley's *History of Virginia* (1705, pt. iii. p. 36), describes how, when Col. Byrd's plantations were perishing from drought, the Indians brought a powaw who for two bottles of rum undertook to procure a shower of rain, and did so. *Paw wa* therefore means conjuring by evil spirits; Defoe only adopted the Indian word. EDWARD SOLLY.

"SHE, THE CAT'S MOTHER" (5th S. ix. 402.)—This is familiar to me as a Yorkshire expression, but certainly not as an illustration of perspicuity of language and precision of reference. On the contrary, I have always heard it employed for confusion of reference and ambiguity of language. Nor is it ever, that I know of, used by the classes which supply "mammas" and little girls to literature. It was considered, in my time, a most vulgar form of speech, fit only for the mouths of servant-maids, who, in discussing their mistress, had this adage ready to baffle inconvenient inquiries as to what "unexpressive she" they were talking of. In the nursery, therefore, it was rigidly tabooed, and the rather because in the presence of children a vulgar nursery-maid would be strongly tempted to use it. A. J. M.

SIR CHARLES WHITWORTH (5th S. ix. 388.)—There must be some mistake in this question. Sir Charles Whitworth, created a peer in 1800, was an only son. He married the Dowager Duchess of Dorset, and died s.p. His father, Sir Charles Whitworth, married Miss Shelley (see *Peerage*, 1811). A. S.

PIC-NIC (5th S. ix. 406.)—This word was adopted for the title of

"The Pic Nic Papers: by Various Hands. Edited by Charles Dickens, Esq., Author of *The Pickwick Papers*, *Nicholas Nickleby*, &c. With Illustrations by George Cruikshank, Phiz, &c. In Three Volumes" (H. Colburn, 1841).

The title was a happy thought, as it suggested the *Pickwick Papers*, and also that the volumes were made up of the free gifts of several contributors. The work was published for the benefit of the widow and children of Mr. John Macrone,

the original publisher of the *Sketches* i realized the sum of 300*l*. Dickens's c was "The Lamplighter's Story," whic thirty-two pages of vol. i. (see Forster's viii.). CUTHBER

HERALDRY (5th S. ix. 407.)—Reed of and Troughend: "Or, on a chevron bet garbs gules, as many ears of wheat si leaved arg. Crest, a griffin rampant worth and Burke). Weldon of Northum a cinquefoil gu.; on a chief of the secor lion rampant of the field" (Burke).
T. F. RAVI
Pewsey Rectory, Wilts.

KENSAL GREEN CEMETERY (5th S. i have a volume entitled *A Handbook f to Kensal Green Cemetery*, by Benjar published by Joseph Masters (Lonc 1843); also *Highgate Cemetery* (1845), lisher, by "Thomas Dolby," with au Thomas William King, Rouge Dragon. be happy to let your correspondent see t
JAMES ROBERTS
84, Caversham Road, N.W.

Your correspondent will find a very trated account of this cemetery, with co chief inscriptions on the tombstones, in *day at Home* for May, 1878, pp. 299, article is written by the author of *Epis Obscure Life*. CUTHBER:

IN-HEDGE LANE, DUDLEY (5th S. i This is a corruption of Innage. MR. W will find "the Innage" and the "Innage the neighbouring borough of Bridgnor and to the north of the old town wall. an old English term signifying a field or and is derived from the Anglo-Saxon *in*, For further illustrations of derivatives root consult Eusebius Salverte's *History of Men, Nations, and Places*, translatec dacque, vol. ii. p. 185.
WM. P. PHILLIMOR
Nottingham.

THE "ROUND HOUSE," LIVERPOOL 428.)—Johnson gives:—
"Roundhouse, n. s. (*round* and *house*) stable's prison, in which disorderly persons, ! street, are confined.
"They march'd to some fam'd *roundhouse*
and, more recently, "Constables came me to the *Roundhouse*" (*Anti-jacobin*).

THE BARONY OF COURTENAY OF OR (5th S. ix. 268, 296, 376.)—This baro by writ 1299, became finally forfeit attainder of Thomas, sixth Earl of Dev brothers, 1 Edward IV. This Thoma sisters, his co-heirs—Elizabeth (who di issue), wife of Sir Hugh Conway, and Jane, wife first of Sir Roger Clifford, and secondly of Sir Wm. Knyvett (his will is given in Nicolas's *Testamenta Vetusta*). Jane Clifford had two sons, and a daughter married to William Coe, but at this moment I cannot give my authority for this statement, nor have I been able to trace any later descendants of this lady, in whom, if they exist, and if the attainder were reversed, the barony of Courtenay would be vested.

In the first year of Henry VII., Edward Courtenay, "late of Bournoe, Esquire," the heir male of the family, was created Earl of Devon, his own attainder having been previously reversed ; but no barony was restored at that time, nor by any later patent, so that I much doubt if any barony existed which could fall into abeyance between the descendants of the four great-great-aunts and (in their issue) co-heirs to Edward, Earl of Devon, who died 1553, one of whom is Sir R. Vyvyan, Bart.

Mr. Vyvyan makes a most erroneous statement as to the marriage of John Vyvyan, whose wife was Elizabeth, dau. and co-h. of Thomas Trethurfe, son and heir of John Trethurfe and Elizabeth Courtenay, and not Elizabeth Courtenay herself.

By the Inq. p.m. taken April 11, 1556, after the death of Edward, Earl of Devon, the following persons were found to be his co-heirs : Reginald Mohun ; Alexander Arundell ; John Vyvyan, junior, and Margaret Buller, widow ; and John Trelawney ; the representatives of the earl's four great-great-aunts—(1) Isabella, wife of William Mohun ; (2) Matilda, wife of John Arundell ; (3) Elizabeth, wife of John Trethurfe ; and (4) Florence, wife of John Trelawney, who must themselves have been long dead.

I regret that I cannot name the present representatives of Isabella Mohun and Matilda Arundell, though I believe the Hunter-Arundell family represent the latter ; but the present co-heirs of Elizabeth Trethurfe are—Sir R. Vyvyan, Bart. ; Isabella, Dowager Marchioness of Exeter ; John, fifth Earl Spencer ; and Richard, ninth Earl of Cork and Orrery ; and those of Florence Trelawney are—Sir J. S. Trelawney, Bart., W. Buller, of Downes, Esq., and the representatives, if any, of Elizabeth Trelawney and the Ven. George Allanson, Archdeacon of Cornwall.

EDMUND M. BOYLE.
14, Hill Street, W.

"THE LASS OF RICHMOND HILL" (5ᵗʰ S. ix. 169, 239, 317.)—Leonard McNally was the author of the *words* of this song ; James Hook the composer was the author of the *melody*. It was written in praise of Miss I'Anson, who resided at Hill House, Richmond, Yorkshire, whom he afterwards married. Hill House is an old mansion built on the highest point of the hill on which the town reclines, and is truly enough described in the song. (Richmond Hill, Leyburn, Yorkshire, quoted by MR. GEORGE WHITE, *ante*, p. 317, is a manifest error. Leyburn is a small town eight miles from Richmond, and has no hill so named.) Hill House, Richmond, was at a later period, I believe, occupied by Sir Ralph Milbanke. See Lord Byron's *Life*, where many of his letters to Miss Milbanke have this address given.

McNally was a well-known member of the Irish Bar, and was associated with Curran in several of the political causes of the period. Two in particular to which I have been able to refer are the cases of Henry Sheares, tried for high treason, July, 1798, and of Robert Emmet and others, September, 1803.

Miss I'Anson's father was, I believe, a solicitor, and I find a record of the marriage as having taken place in London in 1787 (see *European Magazine* of that date, where the name I'Anson is spelt Janson). Her brother, whom I well remember, was brought up to the Bar, but lived many years in Richmond as a private gentleman, and died there at an advanced age in 1846 or thereabouts, leaving an only daughter, the wife of Captain Hampton Lewis, of Beaumaris.

The history of the song was well known to the late Henry Blegborough, M.D., a native of Richmond, Yorkshire, whose *sister married the brother of Miss I'Anson*, and he communicated the facts to me at the time that a contradiction of the story popularly believed appeared in the *Biographical Reminiscences of Lord William Lennox* (1863, vol. i. p. 79).

Corroborative testimony might probably be furnished by the family of the late Mr. Hook. His widow died April 5, 1863. In the following year Mr. Augustus A. Hook, a son of the composer, was residing at 1, Elizabeth Terrace, St. Ann's Road, Wandsworth.   JOHN BELL.
Lime Grove, Shepherd's Bush.

INDEXES (5ᵗʰ S. viii. 87 ; ix. 456.)—APIS wishes the exact reference to the whereabouts of Lord Campbell's denunciation of authors who omit the necessary index. He will find it in the last paragraph of the preface to the third volume of the *Lives of the Chief Justices*, as follows :—

"So essential did I consider an index to be to every book that I proposed to bring a Bill into Parliament to deprive an author who publishes a book without an index of the privilege of copyright ; and moreover to index him, for his offence, to a pecuniary penalty."

W. T. M.
Reading.

ST. GEORGE (5ᵗʰ S. viii. 447 ; ix. 189, 209, 349, 417.)—MR. PICKFORD, at the last of the above references, says that the badge of St. George was worn on the breast of English soldiers certainly as late as the fourteenth century. According to Sir

.at any rate on their helmets, so late as the middle
·of the sixteenth century. A Lancashire archer is
thus described in the third canto of the *Lay of the
Last Minstrel* :—

" His coal-black hair, shorn round and close,
  Set off his sun-burned face ;
  Old England's sign, St. George's cross,
  His barret-cap did grace."

The period of the *Lay* is the reign of Edward VI.
JONATHAN BOUCHIER.

WEEPING CROSSES (5th S. ix. 246, 459.)—There
is a clump of elm trees at four cross-roads just outside Salisbury, on the London road, known as
" the weeping cross trees "; but I am so far unable
to trace the existence of a cross. The popular
notion is that friends here took leave of friends at
the outset of a long coaching journey in the olden
time.   C. H.

JOHN THEODORE AND JACOB HEINS (5th S. ix.
308, 432.)—In addition to the pictures mentioned
at the latter reference are Rev. William Ford and
Mrs. Ford, 1731 ; Thos. Gainsborough and Elizabeth his wife, 1731 ; Samuel and Thomas Gainsborough, sons of the above, 1731 (these were the
uncle and aunt and the cousins of the great Gainsborough) ; Mary Ford ; Rev. John Ford and Mrs.
Ford. The last three are not known to be still in
existence, and any information about them will be
acceptable. Heins also painted the picture on
which Cowper wrote the beautiful lines beginning,
" Oh ! that those lips had language."
This last is still in possession of the family of
Donne. All these are by Heins the elder.
                                    T. FORD FENN.
Trent College.

THE FIRST INSTITUTION OF SUNDAY SCHOOLS
(5th S. viii. 367 ; ix. 110, 156, 271, 339.)—Are not
these a simple development of Sunday catechizing
in the churches?   HYDE CLARKE.

HERALDIC (5th S. viii. 147, 254 ; ix. 277, 356,
376.)—In reply to SIR JOHN MACLEAN and P. P.,
I may say that the crest confirmed and granted to
Margerye Cater, wife of William Hyde, was not a
new one. The grant (which is published in the
·*Genealogist* for May), after the usual opening,
says :—
" And being requyred of Margerye Cater......to make
Search in the Registers and Records of myne Office for
the Armes and Creast belonging to the said John Cater
her father and his Auncestors and I fownde the same
accordinglie. And so considering the antiquitie thereof
could not alter or change the same nor no parte nor
parcele thereof but to the great prejudice of the said
Margerye," &c.
I regret I am not aware of the reason for the
grant.   H. B. HYDE.
   34, Oxford Gardens, W.

—Has MR. KENNEDY or any other
of "N. & Q." interested in obso
ever come across the almost unf
name of Hilcock, and where ?
                              HILCOCI

The name of T. Hurlbatt occurs
Anerley.   H. E.
Anerley, S.E.

COCKER'S "ARITHMETIC" (5th S
35, 232.)—The following is an extra
Romance of London, vol. ii. pp. 2
think gives a better explanation
" According to Cocker." After th
Murphy recorded by GEN. RIGAUD
  " Without doubting its authenticity
that Cocker's *Arithmetic* was the first
excluded all demonstrations and reasoni
itself to commercial questions only, w
the secret of its extreme circulation.
attained in the saying to denote accurac
Cocker.' A copy of the edition of 1678
8*l*. 10*s*. Cocker was buried, accordin
evidence, in the church of St. Georg
Southwark, near which lived his publisl
  I read the account some time sinc
a copy for about the same pric
remember where. It was some t
between May and November. T
London.

" GERMAN " SILVER (5th S. ix. 1
introduction of nickel into the whit
are used as cheap substitutes fo
German invention. The result wa
creased hardness, and the new mate
with the stamp, or, as it were, th
" Neu silber." It was consequentl
distinguished by our traders as (
while our own invention, known t
Britannia metal and on the Co
English, is a cheaper and softer ma
many purposes for which hardne
solutely necessary.

CHRONOGRAMS (1st S. ix. 60 ;
ix. 69, 112, 140, 215, 337.)—
  " Wither (George), Sigh for the Pit
out in a personal Contribution to the N
tion, the last of May, 1666, in the Citi
Westminster upon the near approach
then expected between the English an
Imprinted in the sad year expressed i
chronogram, LorD haVe MerCIe Vpon
                                       (

WILL OF JOHN ARCHOR, OF BISH
(5th S. ix. 405, 472.)—I am sorry t
furnish COL. FISHWICK with the
seeks. The name of "Robertt ffr
appear either in the list of the rect
the chantors of Bishop's Hatfield g

buck's *History of Hertfordshire*, nor is the name to be found in Chauncy's *History of Hertfordshire*. He was probably a member of the family of Frowick, one of whom was Lord of Weld and of North Mimms, a parish adjoining that of Hatfield, *temp.* Henry VII.　　　R. R. LLOYD.

St. Albans.

THE CHOIR STALLS AT HAARLEM : THE GOSPEL AND EPISTLE SIDES OF THE ALTAR (5th S. ix. 101, 413, 451, 471.)—The headings of my papers, "Gospel, or South Side," "Epistle, or North Side," are those which occur in the pencil notes of my visit in 1873.

MR. MACKENZIE WALCOTT, in his interesting reply at the last reference, says that he has not noticed any special reason for a change of terms at Haarlem.

Now, since reading this, I seem to remember, and I cannot shake off the impression, that the high altar at Haarlem is at the west, not at the east, end of the church. Perhaps some more recent visitor than myself can tell us whether this is so or not.　　　JOHN WOODWARD.

Montrose, N.B.

AN OLD BALLAD (CAPTAIN WARD) (5th S. ix. 407, 435, 478.)—The ballad in question is the only authority known to me for this pirate's having beaten off a king's ship which fell in with him. The original ballad was probably a contemporary production, because Ward's later adventures and death are not recounted in it, and because one of the extant copies is of the reign of Charles I., when there were many living who could remember the time. I accept with thanks DR. NICHOLSON's limitation of the dates during which Ward "flourished." Not having felt any particular interest in Ward, I had not read Barker's pamphlet.　　　　　　　　　　　WM. CHAPPELL.

THE TOMB OF EDMUND OF LANGLEY, DUKE OF YORK (5th S. viii. 443 ; ix. 251, 276.)—I am greatly obliged to H. Y. N. for his kind answer to my query. If the skeleton of the young woman were indeed that of Anne Mortimer, Mr. Evans was right in saying that her age could not have exceeded twenty-five. Twenty-three was her probable age at the latest. Dugdale says that she was born Dec. 27, 12 R. II. ; but since her father's marriage was granted to Thomas, Earl of Kent, only on October 7 previous (Rot. Pat., 12 R. II., part i.), this is plainly an error. There is every reason to believe that she was the eldest of the family, and she was probably born in 1389. Since her husband (beheaded Aug. 6, 1415) was twice married, she can scarcely have died later than 1413 ; and the real probability is that she died at the birth of her son Richard, which took place Sept. 20-21 (Inq. Post Mort., 7 membranes), 1410 (*ib.*, 26 membranes), 1411 (*ib.*, 9 membranes), or

1412 (Rot. Pat., 13 H. IV., part ii., seems to show that it was not before Feb. 18, 1412). The other child of Anne, Isabel, Countess of Essex, was affianced Feb. 18, 1412 (Rot. Pat), and must therefore have been the senior of her brother.
　　　　　　　　　　　HERMENTRUDE.

"FAMILIARITY BREEDS CONTEMPT" (5th S. ix. 467.)—To the "too familiar intercourse," or the "long familiarity with benefits," offered for selection as the original and legitimate meaning of the proverb, I add another version, which I have often heard Whately enunciate, namely, "Familiarity with *danger* breeds contempt for it." He did not urge that this was the original and legitimate meaning of the proverb, but I am not aware that he ever patronized any other application of it.
　　　　　　　　　　　JOHN PIKE, F.S.A..

The equivalent phrase among the negroes of Sierra Leone is, "Too much freedery breeds despisery."　　　　　　　　X. P. D.

FLORAL CHIEF RENTS (5th S. ix. 367.)—Walter de Camhon granted land, &c., in Leighton to Newminster Abbey for a rent of one rose on the feast of St. James (Newminster Cartulary, Surtees Soc., vol. lxvi. p. 93).　　　J. T. F.

Bishop Hatfield's Hall, Durham.

1357, August 1. Lionel, Earl of Ulster, grants the bailiffry of Cork to Geoffrey Stukeley by tenure of a rose, to be paid on St. John Baptist's Day (Rot. Pat., 32 E. III., part ii.).

1340, Feb. 10. Edward the Black Prince remits to John de Molynes three weeks' service, and 33 sols 10 deniers, which he was bound to pay by the year, in consideration of a rose, to be paid every year on the feast of St. John Baptist, at the request of the king his father (Rot. Pat., 14 E. III., part i.).　　　　　　　　　HERMENTRUDE.

The Darels of Buckinghamshire held the manor of Fulmer by the "reddendo" of a red rose annually.　　　　　　　　J. WOODWARD.

Montrose.

THE "PASS-BOOK" OF A BANK (5th S. ix. 387.)—In reply to BANKER's query I think the following may help him. In the early days of banking, *i.e.* in the seventeenth and early part of the eighteenth centuries, a customer was wont to go down to his goldsmith's or banker's periodically to pass his accounts, and would write at the foot of the credit or debit side, "I allow this account," and sign his name, the banker signing the other. About the same time bankers were in the habit of furnishing a statement of account copied from the ledger for the benefit of the customer who wished to check or pass his account. The Earl of Litchfield, writing to Mr. Child on May 30, 1713, says :—

... suppose my account is ready in your Bookes for my Mich' rents and a duplicate of it for me, and I will come and passe it y' first opportunity I have leisure. This writing need not be set to y' account till I come because some small matter perhaps may be drawne upon you between this and then."

From statements upon paper it was found to be more convenient to write the account in small books. The first mention of a pass-book I have met with was in 1715, when Lady Carteret, writing to Mr. Child about her affairs, stated :—

"Y' person I thought of sending to examine y' accounts is sick. I should be glad of a Book, as I used to have at Mr. Mead's, with an account of all that you have received upon this article."

Mr. Mead was a goldsmith keeping running cashes in Fleet Street, I believe at the "Black Lion." I know a pass-book which has been in existence since 1717 or earlier, and still in use.

F. G. HILTON PRICE.
Temple Bar.

I find in Bailey's *Dictionary*, "To pass (*passer*, F.; *passare*, Ital.), to be current as money." Pass-book is, therefore, the book in which the current account is entered. S. L.

"THE NEW GROUND, MOORFIELDS" (5th S. ix. 368.)—Among the burials in the register of All Hallows on the Wall, the first three books of which are being privately printed, there are several entries in which mention is made of the "new buryall place." The first is :—

"Mr Will'm Martine, Minister and preache', was Buryed the xvj. day of March, 1573, in the new buryall place in Bethealem founded by Sir Thom's Rooe, late knyght and alderman of london."

Stow states (vol. i. p. 426, ed. 1754) that Sir Thomas Roe caused this ground to be enclosed in 1569, and that it was part of Bethlehem Hospital. That portion of the present Broad Street Railway Station at the corner of Liverpool Street and Eldon Street stands on this "new buryall place." The portion of these registers being printed ends with 1674. T. N.

THE YOKI (5th S. ix. 336.)—The extract which your correspondent takes from the *Daily News* respecting the Yoki is in the main correct, and a passing notice from Vaughan's *Hours with the Mystics* may throw some light on the subject. In vol. i. p. 45, I read as follows :—

"The Yoki constantly exerciseth the spirit in private. He is recluse, of a subdued mind and spirit, free from hope and free from perception. He planteth his own seat firmly on a spot that is undefiled, neither too high nor too low, and sitteth upon the sacred grass which is called *koos*, covered with a skin and a cloth. There he whose business is the restraining of his passions should sit, with his mind fixed on one object alone—in the exercise of his devotion for the purification of his soul keeping his head, his neck, and body steady, without motion; his eyes fixed on the point of his nose, looking on no other place around."

Such silent contemplation and self-absorption may tend to excite a smile in the minds of those who feel the cravings of a more elaborate mode of worship. But the history of the religious sentiment proves its universality, and the peculiarity of its exercise which the Yoki enjoys is an instance in point in support of the statement.

A. CUTLER.

This seems to be the Sanskrit *yoki*, in var. dial. *jogi*, which Wilson renders "a follower of the *yoga* philosophy, a practiser of ascetic devotion, in common use, a religious mendicant, and reputed conjurer or magician." See Wilson's *Glossary of Indian Terms*, under "Yoga," "Yogí," "Yoginí."

R. S. CHARNOCK.
Junior Garrick.

MILES CORBET (5th S. ix. 446.)—Is your correspondent quite sure that the monument at Sprowston is a memorial to the Miles Corbet who was put to death after the Restoration for acting as one of the late king's judges ? I am not in a position to deny the fact, but I think it unlikely, as the bodies of persons who suffered the high treason punishment were not commonly given to their friends for burial. K. P. D. E.

"GIVING THE STRAIGHT TIP" (5th S. ix. 386.)— I think this very common phrase did not take its rise from the turf, for I can remember it nearly fifty years, which, I think, is before such things as "tips" were spoken of in connexion with the turf. In this part of the country it means something direct and to the point, either in words or actions. A good knock-down blow delivered right from the shoulder into an opponent's eye is "a straight tip." To knock over is to "tip over." *Tip* is often used nearly in the same sense as *tap*=a smart blow.

R. R.
Boston, Lincolnshire.

This phrase is largely used in rural townships and villages of Essex, where it "evidently means speaking plainly and decisively—delivering an *ultimatum*," as CUTHBERT BEDE tersely defines it, and also something more ; and the "straight tip," as given at Dunmow and within a considerable radius, not only means a direct reply without either evasion or reservation, but also a spirit of in-difference and defiance—very often an insult is intended. *Straight* is also much in vogue in Essex, and whether applied to speaking or dealing it is equivalent to "square," "fair and above board"= *e.g.* honest and mutually satisfactory.

J. W. SAVILL.
Dunmow, Essex.

See Hotten's *Slang Dictionary*, s. v. "Tip," "Tipster." The phrase relates to private information of any kind. FREDK. RULE.
Ashford.

Miscellaneous.

NOTES ON BOOKS, &c.

Foreign Classics for English Readers.—Goethe. By A. Hayward. (Blackwood & Sons.)

PERHAPS there is no more trying subject for the respectable or "Philistine" mind than the life of Goethe. Gretchen, Aennchen, Frederica, Charlotte, Christine, and the rest—*ed in Italia, mille e tre*—all this monstrous regiment of women defiles before us through the great man's life, and we know not what to make of them. It is therefore not the least among the merits of an able and very interesting monograph that Mr. Hayward, for one, does know what to make of them; and when sketching, with pure and delicate hand, the many courtships of his hero, is not afraid to speak freely of that "aloofness" and introspective self-control which made Goethe fall in love after the manner of Firmilian, the student of Badajoz, as if he merely gave himself up to love for the sake of studying the passion in a series of differing manifestations. There is another and a still more important subject, too, on which Mr. Hayward is equally judicious—Goethe's religion, or his want of it. Beyond an allusion to "the angry God of the Old Testament," and a recital of the fact that Goethe came back from Italy "a confirmed unbeliever," hardly anything is said about a matter which, and the consequences of which, could not be adequately dealt with in so small a book. Yet within this little compass of 222 pages Mr. Hayward, with the ease and skill of a veteran *littérateur*, has managed to draw out a vivid and sufficient sketch of Goethe's career as poet, dramatist, philosopher, man of science; a sketch which, to a reader who does not yet know the longer biographies, will be of this great use, that it will show him how largely *Werther*, and *Wilhelm Meister*, and *Faust*, not to mention lesser works, are informed by the history and experience of their author. The book, too, is rich in apt allusion and illustrative anecdote; and, if we had space, we might say something of the humour and point which its criticisms display, and of the clearness of its analysis of the poet's chief labours.

Mr. Hayward ends by declaring Goethe to be "the most splendid specimen of cultivated intellect ever manifested to the world"; a verdict that seems to us as just in what it suppresses as in what it affirms; for how much of human excellence is left untouched by such a meed of praise! He quotes too, most appropriately, concerning Goethe some noble lines (*O si sic omnia!*) of Moore's on Rousseau; lines of which it is sad indeed to think that they are applicable to one of the greatest of mankind.

Halleck's International Law. A New Edition, Revised, with Notes and Cases, by Sir Sherston Baker, Bart., of Lincoln's Inn, Barrister-at-Law. (C. Kegan Paul & Co.)

BY turns soldier, practising lawyer, and publicist, General Halleck forms a striking example of that wonderful many-sidedness of character in which our Transatlantic cousins seem to rival the Italians of the Renaissance. It was during a period of national peace, but of personal hard work as a San Francisco lawyer, that the ex-Secretary of State for California composed the valuable work on International Law which Sir Sherston Baker now brings afresh before the English reader, at a very opportune moment. There are few subjects rendered prominent by recent events in Europe which are not touched upon or illustrated, either in General Halleck's original text or in Sir Sherston Baker's notes. Many of our readers are probably asking themselves what is likely to be the issue of the Berlin Congress. If they turn to the pages of General Halleck, they will find the obvious remark that, "in order to afford a prospect of success in these deliberations, the plenipotentiaries should be actuated by a sincere desire to effect a just and amicable settlement of the questions to be discussed," tempered by the caustic word of criticism, "this, however, has not often been the case." Let us hope that our present plenipotentiaries may be among the brilliant exceptions which shall deserve to be enshrined in a future edition of Halleck. Among the notes with which Sir Sherston Baker has enriched the original text we observe an interesting *précis* of the principal divergences between the representatives of the various Powers at the Brussels Conference of 1874 (vol. i. p. 418), and a valuable list of extradition treaties between the chief States of the civilised world (vol. i. p. 210). The second volume is rendered specially useful in regard to Military Law by the insertion at full length of Dr. Francis Lieber's remarkable "Instructions for the Government of Armies of the United States in the Field," drawn up for the War Department at Washington in 1863. The history of the second volume carries us down the stream of Time to the foundation of the Italian kingdom and the German empire. Since it was being prepared for press some famous names have disappeared from the roll of the living. Victor Emmanuel and Pius IX., the first elective embodiment of United Italy, and the last hereditary embodiment of the temporal power of the mediæval Papacy, have both migrated *ad plures*. The warrior king, who was saluted "Kaiser in Deutschland" amid the relics of Bourbon and Bonaparte glories at Versailles, has all but followed in their wake. At a time when peace and war seem still to be trembling in the balance, those who wish to understand the principles of the Law of Nations will do well to consult Sir Sherston Baker's timely and interesting gift from the "Golden Gate of the Pacific."

Rivista Europea: Rivista Internazionale. (Florence, Pancrazi.)

THE May number of this review, which was long associated with the name of the distinguished Italian Orientalist, Prof. de Gubernatis, contains much of an international interest, including an essay on Edgar Poe's correspondence, a translation from Poushkine, and an article on English universities. But we would suggest to the Editor that, in order to maintain the high character of the *Rivista Europea*, it would have been well to have given one so competent to inform the Italian public on English academical questions as Signor de Tivoli an opportunity of correcting the proof of his article. We are quite sure that the Taylorian teacher of Italian knows and loves Oxford far too well to be answerable for the strange dichotomy of the late Regius Professor of Modern History into the "Professori Goldwin, Smith," and the no less remarkable change of the present Master of Balliol into Prof. "Jurett." The same observation applies also to the case of the correspondent who reviews English literature. We should always coincide with his criticisms, but we can feel for his anguish on seeing in print such impossible forms as "nolveists" for "novelists," "Sir Kenelms" for "Sir Kenelm Digby," and "Hing-Kens" for "Hong-Kong." A review which, although young, has already made so considerable a name, should ensure the permanence of its renown by adding accuracy to the brilliancy which gained it so early a reputation.

SIR THOMAS DUFFUS HARDY.—It is with deep regret that we have to record the death of Sir Thomas Duffus Hardy, Deputy-Keeper of the Public Records, who expired, after a brief illness, on Saturday night, the 15th inst., at his house, 126, Portsdown Road, Kilburn. The event leaves a vacancy in the public service which it will not be easy to supply, and, in his own special department of literature, not likely to be supplied at all. Born in Jamaica in 1804, he was the eldest son of Major Hardy of the Royal Artillery. Devoted at an early age to the public service, he was appointed in 1819 a junior clerk in the Record Office in the Tower of London. Under the tuition of Mr. Petrie he became an expert in the reading and interpretation of ancient MSS., a faculty which, combined with a close and accurate study of early English history, soon led to important results. Ere long he distinguished himself by some papers in the *Archæologia* and in the *Excerpta Historica*, chiefly in illustration of the reign of King John. He afterwards edited several important works for the Record Commission, among which were two large folio volumes of the early Close Rolls, one of the Patent Rolls, and others of the Charter Rolls, Norman Rolls, and other series of records at that time preserved in the Tower. His Introductions to the Close and Patent Rolls were so valuable that they were published separately. His publication of the celebrated *Modus tenendi Parliamentum* was an important contribution to constitutional history. Some time after Mr. Petrie's death he completed for publication and wrote an introduction to the first volume of that gentleman's unfinished work, the *Monumenta Historica Britannica*. But the scheme of that publication being afterwards superseded by the now voluminous series of chronicles issued under the direction of the Master of the Rolls, he undertook the compilation of his elaborate *Descriptive Catalogue of MSS.*, a work of which it is impossible to over-estimate the utility to the historical student.

On the death of Sir Francis Palgrave in 1861, Mr. Hardy was appointed Deputy-Keeper of the Public Records, and in 1870 he received from the Queen the honour of knighthood in recognition of his services. He was beyond question the foremost palæographer and the most experienced record scholar of his day, and with him there dies an amount of curious learning which was always placed most courteously at the disposal of every inquirer. Of his personal character it is enough to say that the warmth and kindliness of his disposition made him beloved by almost every one with whom he ever came in contact.

MORWENSTOWE CHURCH, CORNWALL.—A fund is being formed (bankers, East Cornwall Bank, Launceston) for the purpose of restoring this ancient church, which derives much of its interest from the poems of the Rev. R. S. Hawker, its late vicar, who was an occasional contributor to "N. & Q." The restoration is under the countenance of the Bishop of Truro, who has made the gratifying announcement that " nothing should be done away with that showed there had been a human brain to plan and contrive, a human heart to love, a human hand to work." One marked feature of the edifice is to be found in the massive pew carvings, and a tracery of the vine plant,

" A leafy line,
With here and there a cluster,"

running round the church, was alluded to by the priest-poet in one of his sonnets. It would be unfortunate if these and other features of Hawker's " Saxon shrine," which are commemorated in the poems, were obliterated.

THE ALDERMEN OF ALDERSGATE, 1451-1616.—Mr. F. C. Price, the fac-similist, is proposing to reproduce subscription copies of John Withie's list of the names and arms of the above civic dignities. The document, which belongs to a period when the traders of the metropolis were of the best *generose* families of England,

and when Leigh (in his *Accidence of Armory*, p. 41) compared the heralds to angels and to Aaron, will prove be an important adjunct to the *Visitation of London* now under the care of the Harleian Society.

MR. P. LE NEVE FOSTER's many friends will rejoice hear that some members of the Society of Arts, with Lo Hatherley at their head, have associated themselv together to present him, on the occasion of his completing twenty-five years' service as secretary of the Society of Arts, with a substantial testimonial in mone as an expression of their respect.

THE Flower Sermon at St. Katharine Cree, Leadenha Street, is not an ancient custom, but was introduced Dr. Whittemore, the present rector of the united parishe about twenty-five years since. W. R. TATE.

Notices to Correspondents.

We must call special attention to the following notices:

ON all communications should be written the name an address of the sender, not necessarily for publication, bu as a guarantee of good faith.

CORRESPONDENTS are requested to bear in mind that is against rule to seal or otherwise *fasten* communication transmitted by the halfpenny post. Not unfrequentl double postage has to be paid on their receipt, becaus they have been " closed against inspection."

FOLK-LORE.—We would strongly urge on those corr spondents who are good enough to send us communic tions on Folk-Lore that, before doing so, they shou consult Brand's *Popular Antiquities*, Chambers's *Boc of Days*, Hone's *Every-Day Book*; but especially Thise ton Dyer's *British Popular Customs*, this last being th most recent work on customs connected with the Calendar.

E. CORNER.—The Muggletonians are the followers Lodowicke Muggleton, who in 1651 declared that he an his companion John Reeve were the " two witnesses mentioned in Revolation xi. 3 7. Muggleton was trie at the Old Bailey for blasphemy, and convicted Jan. 1 1676. He died March 14, 1697.

G. F. S. E. (*ante*, p. 118.)—H. A. B. will be glad if yc will say in what Latin version of Plutarch's *Agesilai* " Talis cum sis utinam noster esses " is to be found.

C. A. WARD.—" Aula Cervina," Oxford, now Hert Hart Hall, which became Hertford College in 1740. was subsequently named Magdalen Hall, and agai recently, Hertford College. See " N. & Q.," 5th S. i. 5 74, 133, 178.

DISCIPULUS.—A good grammar of the Norwegian la guage (southern division) is Sargeant's *Outlines of No wegian Grammar* (London, Rivingtons).

A. F.—Before inserting your second communicatio please read the notes, *ante*, pp. 435, 478, 497.

R. S. B.—The writer wishes to remain anonymous.

A. Z. (Cork Club), L. C. M. (Cobham, Surrey), ai " SHAKESPERE."—Name and address required.

G. H. A.—Letter forwarded.

J. FISHER.—Yes, if not too long.

VINCENT S. LEAN.—It will appear possibly next wee

R. F. C. and H. KERR.—Next week.

NOTICE.

Editorial Communications should be addressed to " Tl Editor of ' Notes and Queries ' "—Advertisements an Business Letters to " The Publisher "—at the Office, 2 Wellington Street, Strand, London, W.C.

We beg leave to state that we decline to return con munications which, for any reason, we do not print; ar to this rule we can make no exception.

LONDON, SATURDAY, JUNE 29, 1878.

Notes.

LITERATURE AT THE INTERNATIONAL CONGRESS IN PARIS.

I remember long ago being gravely asked by a
very young lady, "What is Literature?" Unfortunately my fair friend is not in Paris just now, or
she might learn something, and perhaps something
that would enlighten her. "What is Literature?"
was a question both asked and answered by Victor
Hugo, who defined it in one place as the impulse
given to the mind of man, "la mise en marche de
l'esprit humain," and in another place as the
government of the human race by the mind of
man, "le gouvernement du genre humain par
l'esprit humain." And he claimed an essential
identity as subsisting between literature and
civilisation. "On peut dire," he exclaimed, "que
littérature et civilisation sont identiques." For
the greatness of a people, he continued, is measured
by their literature. "Xerxes had a vast army,
but no poet. His army melted away; the Iliad
remains. Small in the actual extent of her territory, Greece is rendered great by Æschylus.
Summon up Spain ; Cervantes comes before us.
Call upon Italy; Dante appears. Name England ;
Shakespeare presents himself. Rome is but a
town, yet through Virgil, Tacitus, Lucretius,
Juvenal, her renown has filled the whole world."
In this last sentence, so striking in its antithesis,
we seem to catch a sort of unconscious echo of

that most touching poem known as The Emperor
Otto III.'s Lament :—

> "O Welt, du bist so nichtig !
> Du bist so klein, O Rom !"

It would be a long tale were I to tell of all the
countries represented at this literary "Festival of
Peace," where Russians, Belgians, Germans, Bra-
zilians, Italians, Swedes, Norwegians, Dutchmen,
and Danes have joined with Americans and Britons
in discussing with their French hosts the common
interests of that literature which is the lamp of
knowledge in all countries. "Light, always and
everywhere! we need more light!" said Victor
Hugo. It is much to be noticed that the
point of the great writer's earnest appeals to his
audience lay repeatedly in these two factors of
prosperity, knowledge and peace, both to be diffused
throughout the world by literature, which is only
to make war against hatred and bloodshed—a
great idea, worthily brought before a great people
by one of the masters of their literature of whom
they are deservedly most proud. I only regret
that it is really impossible for me to go through
some of the other extremely able addresses which
we heard both at the Châtelet and in the hall of
the Grand Orient. The display of oratorical power
has been all that the names of the chief speakers
would have led one to expect. I do not think
that the business qualities shown by members in
the practical working of details have been by any
means equal to their facility of speech. The
debates were often marred by what I can only
express as "un décousu déplorable." The actual
president of our general sittings has been that most
charming Nestor of Russian literature, Tourgenieff,
at once venerable in aspect and gentle in manner.
At the public assembly in the Châtelet Theatre,
Victor Hugo was ably supported by the admirable
gesture-language and eloquent words of M. Jules
Simon. Italy was represented at this sitting by
the Deputy Mauro Macchi, and Germany by Dr.
Löwenthal, while Brazil brought the proceedings to
a most happy conclusion by demanding the raising
of the cry, "Vive la France !" So far as I have
been able to judge of the feeling of members on
the questions connected with Copyright, there
appears to be a sharp division between the views
prevailing, with slight differences of detail, on the
Continent, and those which would be likely to find
favour in Great Britain. I do not see how
this gulf is to be bridged over. I do not suppose
it will be bridged over by the present Congress.
But it is something to know what one's neighbours
want ; and from that point of view, at any rate,
as well as on account of the eloquence which it
drew forth, the Paris Literary Congress of 1878
may fitly take its place among meetings which
have deserved well of the Republic of Letters.

Nomad.

Paris.

THE BIBLIOGRAPHY OF ARCHERY.
(Continued from p. 444.)

14th August, 1589. William Jones. Entred for his copie, a ballad intytuled, Discrybinge the vallure of our Englishe Archers and shott that accompanied the Blacke Prince of Portugall their governor into the feildes on Twesdaie the 12 of August with the welcome into Lyme Streete by Master Hugh Offley under th[e] [b]andes of Master R. Judson and bothe the wardens iiij^d. (T. S. R., ii. 528.)

A briefe discourse of warre. Written by Sir Roger Williams, Knight; with his opinion concerning some parts of the martiall discipline....Imprinted at London by Thomas Orwin, dwelling in Paternoster Row, over against the signe of the Checker, 1590. 4to. pp. iv-62, and errata leaf. Pp. 46-48, To proove bowmen the worst shot used in these daies. M.

Certain discourses, written by Sir John Smythe, Knight: concerning the formes and effects of divers sorts of weapons, and other very important matters militarie, greatlie mistaken by divers of our men of warre in these daies; and chiefly of the Mosquet, the Caliver, and the Long-bow: as also of the great sufficiencie, excellencie, and wonderful effects of archers....At London, printed by Richard Johnes, at the signe of the Rose and Crowne neere Holburne Bridge, I. Maij, 1590. 4to. M. The practice, proceedings and lawes of armes described. ...By Matthew Sutcliffe....Imprinted at London by the deputies of Christopher Barker,...1593. 4to. pp. xxiv-342. Pp. 181, 189-190 (cap. xii. pt. ii.), Wherein the use of...archers...is declared. M.

A breefe discourse, concerning the force and effect of all manuall weapons of warre and the disability of the long bowe or archery, in respect of others of greater force now in use....Written by Humfrey Barwick....At London, printed for Richard Oliffe, and are to be solde in Paul's Church Yard at the signe of the Crane.—1594? 4to. ff. vii-35, and folding plate. Black-letter. (In answer to two works, both published in 1590, by Sir John Smythe and Sir Roger Williams.) M.

Instructions, observations and orders mylitarie....Composed by Sir John Smithe, Knight, 1591....Imprinted at London by Richard Johnes, at the signe of the Rose and Crowne next above S. Andrewes Church in Holborne, 1595. 4to. pp. xxxii-220. Pp. 150-154, The advantage that archers have of mosquetiers. M.

A briefe treatise, to proove the necessitie and excellence of the use of archerie. Abstracted out of ancient and moderne writers. By R. S. Perused, and allowed by Aucthoritte....At London, printed by Richard Johnes, at the Rose and Crowne; next above S. Andrewes Church in Holburne, 1596. 4to. 12 leaves. Black-letter. By R. Sharpe, to whom William Hole dedicated his map of Finsbury, a copy of which is in the Bodleian Library, Oxford. M.

The Survey of Cornwall. Written by Richard Carew of Antonie, Esquire. London, printed by S. S. for John Jaggard,...1602. 8vo. Ff. 72-73, Archery. M.

The lives of the III. Normans, Kings of England. William the first, William the second, Henrie the first. Written by [Sir] J[ohn] H[ayward]. [Motto and device] Imprinted at London by B., anno 1613. 4to. pp. viii-316. The dedication is signed. Pp. 77-79, Reasons for preferring the English bow to fire arms. Quoted in Archæologia, xxii. 72. M.

The tactiks of Ælian,...Englished...with notes...by [Captain] J[ohn] B[ingham]....At London for Lawrence Lisle,...1616. Fol. pp. vi-166, plates. Pp. 24-27, Note on Archery. M.

Taylor's goose.—London, printed by E. A. for Henry Gosson, 1621. (Not seen.)

All the workes of John Taylor, the water-poet. Beeing sixty and three in number. Collected into one volume by the author:..with sundry new additions, corrected, revised, and newly imprinted, 1630. At London, printed by J. B. for James Boler; at the signe of the Marigold in Pauls churchyard, 1630. Folio, pp. xii-148-344-146, inaccurate. Pp. 104-111, Taylors goose: describing... the honourable victories of the grey-goose-wing... ; pp. 106-108, The prayse of the grey goose wing. 208 lines. B. (Not seen.)

Works of John Taylor the water-poet comprised in the folio edition of 1630. Printed for the Spencer Society, [Manchester] 1869. Folio, pp. vi-630. Pp. 114-121, Taylor's goose: describing...the honourable victories of the grey-goose-wing...; pp. 116-118, The prayse of the grey goose wing. M.

The double-armed man, by the new invention, briefly shewing some famous exploits atchieved by our British Bowmen, with severall portraitures proper for the pike and bow. By W[illiam] N[eade], Archer. Printed for J[ohn] Grismand, at the signe of the Gun in Pauls Alley, 1625. 4to. pp. 36, seven full-page woodcuts of positions. The dedication is signed. M. (T. S. R., iv. 136.)

A new invention of shooting fire-shafts in long-bowes: wherein, besides the maner of making them, there is contained a briefe discourse of the usefulnesse of them in our moderne warres, by sea and land. Published by a true patriot for the common good of his native countrey of England. [Device.] London, printed by H. L. for John Bartlet at the Gilt Cup in Cheape-side, anno Dom. 1628. 4to. M.

The art of archerie. Shewing how it is most necessary in these times for this kingdome, both in peace and war, and how it may be done without charge to the country, trouble to the people, or any hinderance to necessary occasions. Also of the discipline, the postures and whatsoever else is necessarie for the attayning to the art. London, printed by B. A. and T. F. for Ben. Fisher...at the signe of the Talbot without Aldersgate, 1634. 8vo. pp. xxii-172, 1 plate. Dedication signed Gervase Markham. M.

F. Marini Mersenni minimi cogitata physico mathematica. In quibus tam naturæ quàm artis effectus admirandi certissimis demonstrationibus explicantur. [Device.] Parisiis, sumptibus Antonii Bertier, viâ Jacobæâ. 1644. Cum privilegio regis. 4to. The pagination is in seven series, of which one series is twice broken by other series. Pp. (30)-40-(22)-41 to 224-(8)-225 to 370-(32)-140-(6). Collation: general title, dedication, licences, " præfatio præfacionem," list of contents, and " præfatio generalis," (24) ; " Tractatus de mensuris ponderibus, atque nummis tam Hebraicis, quàm Græcis & Romanis ad Parisiensia expensa." Dedication and preface, (6), the text, 40 ; " Hydraulica pneumatica ; arsque navigandi. Harmonia theoretica, practica. Et mechanica phænomena. Autore M. Mersenno M. [Device.] Parisiis, sumptibus Antonii Bertier, viâ Jacobæâ. 1644. Cum privilegio regis." Sub-title, dedication, and preface, (22) ; " De hydraulicis et pneumaticis phænomenis," 41 to 224 ; " Ars navigandi super, et sub aquis, cum tractatu de magnete, et harmoniæ theoreticæ, practicæ, & instrumentalis. Libri quatuor. [Device.] Parisiis, sumptibus Antonii Bertier, viâ Jacobæâ, sub signo Fortunæ. 1644. Cum privilegio regis " Title and dedication, (8) ; " Ars navigandi," 225 to 244 ; " Tractatus de magnetis proprietatibus," 245 to 260 ; " Harmoniæ," 261 to 370 ; Index to the whole volume, (20) ; " F. Marini Mersenni minimi ballistica et acontismologia. In qua sagittarum, jaculorum, & aliorum missilium jactus & robur arcuum explicantur. [Device.] Parisiis, sumptibus Antonii Bertier, viâ Jacobæâ, 1644. Cum privilegio regis." Title, dedication, and preface, (12) ; the text, 140 errata to the whole volume, (6).

· Aime for the archers of St. Georges fields. Containing the names of all the marks in the same fields, with their true distances according to the dimensuration of the line. Formerly gathered by Richard Hannis. And now corrected by Thomas Bick and others. London, printed by N. Howell for Robert Minchard and Benjamin Brownsmith, and are to be sold at the sign of the Man in the Moon in Blackman Street, 1664. 16mo. pp. vi-110. M.

Archerie reviv'd; or, the bow-man's excellence. An heroick poem : being a description of the use and noble vertues of the long-bow, in our last age, so famous for the many great and admired victories won by the English, and other warlike nations, over most part of the world. Exhorting all brave spirits to the banishment of vice, by the use of so noble and healthful an exercise. Written by Robert Shotterel and Thomas Durfey, Gent. London, printed by Thomas Roycroft, ann. Dom. 1676. 8vo. pp. xxii-80. M.

Selecta poemata Archibaldi Pitcarnii Med. Doctoris, Gulielmi Scot a Thirlestane, equitis, Thomæ Kincadii, civis Edinburgensis, et aliorum....Edinburgi, excusa anno 1727. 12mo. pp. xii-156. Edited by Robert Freebairn. Issued with a new title-page :—Editio secunda. Londini : apud A. Millar,...1729. M.

Ordonnances pour le noble exercice de l'arc. 1773, 8vo. (Bodleian Douce Cat., p. 12; not seen.)

Memoirs of the life of the late Charles Lee, Esq.... Dublin,...P. Byrne,...1792. 8vo. M. Pp. 239-242, letter from B. Franklin to C. L.:—"Philadelphia, Feb. 11th, 1776....I still wish, with you, that pikes could be introduced, and I would add bows and arrows : these were good weapons, not wisely laid aside: 1st. Because a man may shoot as truly with a bow as with a common musket. 2d. He can discharge four arrows in the time of charging and discharging one bullet. 3d. His object is not taken from his view by the smoke of his own side. 4th. A flight of arrows seen coming upon them terrifies and disturbs the enemies' attention to his business. 5th. An arrow striking in any part of a man puts him hors du combat till it is extracted. 6th. Bows and arrows are more easily provided every where than muskets and ammunition...." (This excerpt is reprinted in the Critical Review, London, March, 1792, p. 319.)

Archæologia : or miscellaneous tracts relating to antiquity. Published by the Society of Antiquaries of London. 4to. Vol. vii. pp. 46-68, Observations on the practice of archery in England. By the Hon. Daines Barrington. Read Feb. 27, 1783.—Copies of this article, with the signatures omitted and new paging (pp. 1-24), were issued.

Republished in the Annual Register...for 1784 and 1785, London, vol. xxvii. pp. 64-75, and in the European Magazine, London, vol. viii. pp. 177-181, 257-261 (Sept.—Oct., 1785). M.—D. B. notes a MS. treatise on archery by a Manchester saddler. Where is this now?

An historical essay on the dress of the...Irish.... A memoir on the armour and weapons of the Irish....By Joseph C[ooper] Walker....Dublin,...Grierson, 1788. 4to. pp. xii-182. Pp. 128-132, 165-166, Archery. M.

The Scottish journal of topography, antiquities, traditions, &c. Edinburgh. Vol. i. p. 96 (No. 6, Oct. 9, 1847), Duel with bows and arrows on the 10th of Feby., 1791, in the Meadows, Edinburgh. M.

Anecdotes of archery, ancient and modern. By H[enry] G[eorge] Oldfield. Printed for the author; and sold by T. and J. Egerton,...1791. 12mo. pp. xii-78, and errata leaf, 2 plates. M.

An essay on archery: describing the practice of that art, in all ages and nations.—By Walter Michael Moseley, Esq.—Worcester, printed by T. and I. Holl, and sold by

I. Robson. London, 1792. 8vo. pp. ii-x-348, errata leaf 5 plates and engraved title. M. (See " N. & Q.," 4th S iv. 463.)

Anecdotes of archery ; from the earliest ages to the year 1791. Including an account of the most famous archers of ancient and modern times ; with some curious particulars in the life of Robert Fitz-Ooth, Earl of Huntington, vulgarly called Robin Hood. The present state of archery, with the different societies in Great Britain, particularly those of Yorkshire, Lancashire, and Durham. By E[ly] Hargrove. York, printed for E. Hargrove, Bookseller, Knaresboro',...1792. 12mo. pp. 104, 3 plates. M.

The Sporting Magazine. London, 1792, &c. 8vo. Contains articles, songs, &c., on archery. M.

Anthologia Hibernica. Dublin, 1793, 1794. 4 vols. 8vo. Vol. ii. pp. 275-277, Review of J. C. Walker's " Memoir," 1788. Vol. iii. pp. 6-9, Theory of Archery. By an Old Finsbury Archer. M.

The Biographical Mirror. London, S. and E. Harding, 1795-98-1803. 3 vols. 4to. (portraits and text ; the latter by F. G. Waldron). Vol. i. pp. 66-69, portrait, William Wood. M.

" Pro aris et focis." Considerations of the reasons that exist for reviving the use of the long bow with the pike in aid of the measures brought forward by his Majesty's ministers for the defence of the country. By Richd. Oswald Mason, Esqr. London, printed for T. Egerton, Military Library, Whitehall, 1798. 8vo. pp. 60, 2 folding plates, 3s. 6d. M.

(To be continued.)

F. W. F.

INVENTORY OF "SPUILZIE" ON THE SCOTTISH BORDER, 1572.

The following curious inventory of goods plundered in 1572 by the burghers of Jedburgh (famous for its justice), assisted by certain of their neighbours, from the house of Woodhead of Ancrum, Roxburghshire, then the seat of Robert Kerr of Ancrum, ancestor of the present Marquis of Lothian, seems interesting enough to deserve a place in " N. & Q." It is copied from the (unpublished) Privy Council Register in the General Register House, Edinburgh, and indicates a degree of comfort and even refinement such as is not usually associated in our minds with a squire's home on the Scottish Borders in the middle of the sixteenth century.

"That is to say, furth of the said place of Ancrum, xl bollis heippit meill, price of the boll iij lib.; xxx bollis cleine qubeit, price of the boll iiij lib.; fyftie bollis malt, price of the boll lvjs.; xxx martis of salt heif, price of the mart iiij lib. ; the aill of xij bollis brewing of malt, estimat to ten gallownis the boll, price of the galloun iiijs.; ane twn of wyne, to wit, three puncheonis of clarett and ane punscheoun of qubyte wyne, price of the twn lxvj lib. xiijs. iiijd.; fiftie stane of cheis, price of the stane xvjs.; xxiiij stane of butter, price of the stane xxvjs. viijd.; xvj stane wycht of candill, price of the stane xiiijs.; ane barrikin of vinagre, contenand vj quartis, price of the quart overheid xld.; ane quart of oy doleif, price thairof xxiiijs.; iiij siluer tassis weyand xij vnce, price of the vnce owerheid xxxs.; ane siluer maser, dowbill owergilt, weyand xviij vnce, price of the vnce xxxs.; twa dosane of siluer spvins, weyand ane vnce and ane half the pece, price of the vnce xxxs.; twa siluer saltfattis, ane quhairof partiall gilt with gold, with the cover, weyand xij vnce, price of the vnce xxxiijs.; the vther weyand vij vnce, price of the vnce xxxs.; ane siluer fute to ane coupe, weyand v vnce, price of the vnce xxxs.; thre dosane of flander pulder plaittis, wey- and fyve stane wecht, price of the pund vs.; v dosane of flander poyder truncheoneis, weyand the dosane viij pund, price of the pund vs.; twa basingis, twa lawers of flanders poyder, price of the basing and lawer owerheid ls.; v tyn flaconis of flanders work, tua thairof full of aqua vite, extending to v pyntis, price of the pynt xs.; price of the pece of the saidis flaconis owerheid xxxs.; tuelf pottis les and mair, price of the pote xls.; aucht pannis of flanders work les and mair, price of the pece owerheid xvjs.; foure irne rakkis, the pece weyand xxiiij pundis weycht, price of the stane xvjs.; viij irne speittis weyand fyve stane, price of the stane xvjs.; tua frying pannis, price of the pece xxs.; tua rosting irnis, price of the pece xs.; xl furneist fedder heddis, with scheittis, coveringis, coddis, bousteris, blankattis, price of the furneist bed owerheid xx merkis; thre stand napery of fyne flanderis dernick work, price of the stand x lib.; thre stand of small lyning clayth, price of the stand ten merkis; thre gentill womanis gounis, to wit, ane gown of blak champlott silk, begareit with veluet, price thairof xl lib.; ane vther of frenche blak, begareit with veluet, price thairof xxx lib.; and the thrid of scottis russat, begareit with veluot, price thairof xx lib.; thre mennis dowblattis, ane thairof blak satine, price thairof x lib.; ane vther of violat armosie taffatie, price vj lib.; and the thrid dowblatt of blak bumbassy, price iij lib.; thre hattis to gentill wemen, ane of blak veluet, price iij lib.; ane vther of blak armosy taffatie, price ls.; and the thrid of blak felt, with ane string to it, price xls.; ane mekill brasen watter fatt, price x lib.; tuentie scoir of crouuis of the sone, price of the pece xxxvjs.; jc auld angell nobillis, price of the pece lvjs.; xl rois nobillis, price of the pece iiij lib. xvjs.; fyve portingall ducattis, price of the pece xx lib., and fyve hundreth merkis in quhite money, sic as Scottis xxxs. pecis, Scottis vs. testanis, plakkis, and babeis; And furth of the barnis of Ancrum of Wodheid sex scoir bollis threschin aittis, price of the boll xxxs.; fiftie bollis of threschin beir, price of the boll xls.; xxiiij bollis threschin quheit, price of the boll iiij lib.; ane chalder threschin peis, price of the boll ls.; And furth of the barnzard of the same, vj stakkis of aittis, ilk stak contenand foure scoir thravis, estimat to fiftie bollis aittis, price of the boll with the fodder xxxvs.; fyve stakkis of beir, ilk stak contenand owerheid foure scoir thravis, estimat to xl bollis beir, price of the boll with the fodder xliiijs.; twa stakkis of quheit, contenand owerheid thre scoir thravis quheit, estimat to xxx bollis quheit, price of the boll with the fodder iiij lib. money of oure realme, as is allegeit, And thairfoir the saidis personnis," &c.

Jedburgh.
A. C. MOUNSEY.

THE GLOBE EDITION OF SHAKSPEARE. — In reading *Hamlet* with the first Quarto for my series of Shakspere Quarto Fac-similes—for which I hope a good number of the readers of "N. & Q." will subscribe, at 6s. a quarto—I find two accidental printer's slips in printing a prose line as verse, and *vice versâ*, which your readers may be glad to correct in their copies. P. 836, col. 1, Act iv. sc. 5, l. 57, " *Oph*. Indeed, la, without an oath, I 'll make an end on 't." Plain prose, of course. Other editors leave out the " la," and thus make an extra-syllable verse line of the passage ; but if

you print the " la," you must treat the line as prose, and not read " 'Deed la " as one syllable. P. 836, col. 2, Act iv. sc. 5, l. 74-5, " *King*. Follow | her close ; | give her | good watch, | I pray | you," clearly an extra-syllable verse line, and not two lines of prose.

For the blank in p. 833, col. 1, Act iii. sc. iv. l. 169, " And either . . . . the devil or throw him out," I suggest " tame." You want a *t* word for euphony, I think. " Throne " is out of the ques- tion—as are all words of its class—for the context plainly requires *subjection* of the devil, to go along with the *ejection* of " throw him out." Hamlet is not discussing with his mother the general question of the opposite forces of habit, but telling her that the custom of abstaining from Claudius's bed will enable her either to subdue in herself, or drive out from herself, the devil of lust. Malone's " curb," for my " tame," contrasts well with " change " in l. 168. The " easiness " of l. 166, the " easy " of l. 167, and the alliteration with " either," might tempt one to suggest that Shakspere wrote in l. 169 the Early English verb *eathe*, soothe, lessen the force of—see *eathien* in Stratmann, and "*ethede* his sorye " (sorrow) there quoted—and that the printer left the word out because he could not understand it. But I believe in the accidental omission of a word like " tame " or " curb," and am glad that the Cambridge editors have rejected the weak, metre-spoiling, two-syllable " master " of Quarto 5, &c.
F. J. FURNIVALL.

P.S.—Our editor of *Henry V.*, Mr. W. G. Stone, calls my attention to a slip in the Globe numbering of that play. In Act v. sc. 2, l. 201 is made 301, and consequently all the subsequent numbers in the scene are wrong by 100.

" DUCDAME."—" Ducdamè " is a word that occurs in *As You Like It*, where Jaques (Act ii. sc. 5) adds a verse to the old ditty, " Under the Green- wood Tree," and sings it to Amiens :—

> " If it do come to pass
> That any man turn ass,
> Leaving his wealth and ease,
> A stubborn will to please,
> Ducdamè, ducdamè, ducdamè ! "

Amiens asks what the word means, and Jaques replies, " 'Tis a Greek word to call fools into a circle." None of the editors of Shakspere can make anything of " ducdamè." Sir Thomas Han- mer turned it into Latin, and thought it a misprint for " Duc, ad me "; Charles Knight was of opinion that " Ducdamè " was " some country call of a woman to her ducks "; while Mr. J. Payne Collier thought it an abbreviation of " Dear me " or " Dearie me." Mr. Howard Staunton, rejecting all these interpretations, inclined to the belief that it was " mere unmeaning babble coined for the occasion." Mr. Halliwell, in his archæological dictionary, calls it the burden of an old song which he found under the form of "Dusadamè! me ! me !" in a MS. in the Bodleian Library. This form appears to be an error of the transcriber. Jaques in using the phrase had some vague idea that it related to a "circle," and called it "Greek," just as at the present time a person will say of anything unintelligible that it is "all Greek to me." The word, however, resolves itself into the Keltic or Gaelic *duthaich* (the *t* silent before the aspirate, pronounced *duhaic*), signifying a country, an estate, a territory, a piece of land ; *do* signifying to, and *mi*, me, *i.e.* "this territory or ground is to me," or "belonging to me"; "it is my land or estate." This old British phrase appears to have been used in England long after the British language had given way to Saxon English, and was repeated by children in the game now called "Tom Tiddler's ground," in which a circle is drawn to signify the hill or piece of ground, of which one of the players holds possession, and from which all the other players attempt to oust him, while he dares them to do so by exclaiming *Duthaich do mi*, corrupted into "duedamè," or "this is my country," dispossess me if you can. "Tom Tiddler's ground," notwithstanding its very Saxon sound, is in like manner a corruption of the Keltic. It is described by the Rev. E. Cobham Brewer, in his *Dictionary of Phrase and Fable*, as "The ground or tenement of a sluggard." "Tidler," he adds, is a contraction of "the idler," or "t' idler." "Tom Tidler stands on a heap or mound of stones, gravel, &c.; other boys rush on the heap, crying, 'Here I am on Tom Tidler's ground, picking up gold and silver,' and Tom bestirs himself to keep the invaders off."

The Keltic meaning clears up all these obscurities and mistakes. The true derivation is the Gaelic *tom*, a hill, a mound, a mount, a hillock, a heap, and *tiodlach*, a gift, an offering, a boon, a gratuity. Thus *Tom-tiodlach*, or "Tom Tidler's ground," where gold and silver were to be had for the seeking, signified the hill of gifts or abundance. It is much to be wished that philological antiquaries would look into the ancient British more than they have done. They would find much to reward them for their trouble.

CHARLES MACKAY.
Fern Dell, Mickleham, Surrey.

CAMBRIDGE ACADEMIC COSTUME ABOUT 1820.— The following extract from the report of the address of the Rev. R. E. Hooppell, LL.D., the retiring president of the Tyneside naturalists' field club, is taken from the *Auckland Times* of the 17th of May last. It will prove of interest to many of your Cambridge readers.

"The late Rev. G. C. Abbes was an undergraduate of St. John's College, Cambridge, when the Princess Charlotte died. That terrible blow to the nation's hopes diffused universal grief; the national sorrow found vent in national mourning. Up to that time the young men of Cambridge had never been allowed to lay aside the eighteenth century knee breeches. The Blue-coat boys of London are still doomed to wear a similarly antiquated attire. By the resolution of our lamented friend, however, the undergraduates of Cambridge were delivered from the bondage full sixty years since. It came about thus :—The mourning, as I have said, was general. An edict went forth at Cambridge that undergraduates should appear in trousers one term as mourning ; the next term to resume their ordinary attire. The mourning trousers were duly worn ; the ordinary breeches were resumed by all but George Abbes. Having experienced the pleasure and relief of the change of dress, he was averse to return to the ancient style. The Dons remonstrated with him; he manifested obstinacy ; they deprived him of his term. He nevertheless stood out. The next term came, and he still appeared in trousers. Again he was deprived of his academical reckoning ; but as the term drew near to its end other undergraduates, admiring his boldness, and stimulated by his example, began to tread in his steps. The third term many did so, and the authorities began to doubt their power to resist the general rebellion which seemed threatening to set in. They yielded to Mr. Abbes's persistency ; they good grace, cancelled the long-standing æsthetic regulation, restored him to his collegiate status, and saw before long the substitution of modern trousers for the more ancient garb universally adopted. Mr. Abbes's undergraduate career terminated in 1821, when he took his degree of Bachelor of Arts."

W. P. COURTNEY.
15, Queen Anne's Gate.

PROVINCIALISMS.—There are a few curious provincialisms in common use in my own county, Lancashire, which it may be well to embalm for the future philologist, before we are all reduced to one uninteresting dead level of correct English. These are not peculiarities of the dialect, but are to be constantly heard from the lips of more or less educated persons. The sentences I give will show their use better than any description.

A. "He is a rich man, is Mr. Smith." "She sings well, does Mary." "He didn't say so, didn't William."

B. "I should have done it, only I forgot." "John called at your office, only you were gone."

C. "All these books belong the library." "That man belongs the mill." "Does this hat belong you ?"

D. "Nay" for *no*. ("Ah," or "yea," for *yes*, doubtless from *aye*, is confined to the uneducated class.)

E. "Did you insense him well with the whole affair ?" "Just insense him about that business." John Husee, writing to Lady Lisle in 1538, says, "I wonder who first incensyd my Lord Privy Seal with Painswick" (*Lisle Papers*, xii. 8). This is evidently not the modern incense=to anger, but our Lancashire insense=to put into one's head, to make him understand thoroughly.

HERMENTRUDE.

NEWS FOR THE MARINES.—The following extract is from a pamphlet on *The Study of Anglo-Saxon*, by F. A. March, LL.D., Professor of the

English Language and Comparative Philology in Lafayette College at Easton, Pa. The italics stand as in the original.

"This is great progress for any linguistic study to make in these times when the natural sciences are crowding everywhere. The time is all full in the old colleges, and the supply of good teachers for the new study is very scant. The professors of rhetoric who are oftenest turned to are not often linguists; it is better to try the Latin or Greek professor, as is done at Haverford. But special attainments are needed. To the coming generation of scholars, Anglo-Saxon has prizes to offer as tempting as any. There are professorships, and then the eminence which waits on successful original work in a prominent field. There is nowhere in the world so much of this study as in America. Professor Child says, in his answer to the circular of the bureau, that 'Anglo-Saxon is *utterly* neglected in England—at present there is but one man in England that is known to know anything of it—and not *extensively* pursued anywhere in America.' The Germans, he adds, 'cannot do their best for want of properly edited texts. Two or three American scholars, devoted to Anglo-Saxon, would have a great field to distinguish themselves in, undisputed by Englishmen.'"

ST. SWITHIN.

THE ARCHBISHOP'S MITRE.—The first mitre of a primate distinguished from that of a bishop is Gilbert Sheldon's in Sandford's *Genealogical History*, p. 442. It has a circlet with pearls, like a viscount's coronet. Sancroft and Tillotson are given that of a marquess by R. White in his engravings ; whilst Wake and Blackburn, in the *British Compendium*, 1731, pt. ii. pp. 58, 82, have the mitre rising from a ducal coronet. This is done wholly without authority.

MACKENZIE E. C. WALCOTT.

THE SCHOOLMASTER ABROAD.—The following is a copy of a letter received recently by a member of my family, and it strikes me as almost too good to lose, as a specimen of the march of intellect in the nineteenth century. The writer is a photographer, who has been employed to take views of a house and to copy some family portraits.

"Sir,—I Forwarded By Passenger train on Saterday Last 5 Photographs from Oilpainting Witch I trust Will Sute I also Inclose 5 Cart De V. from *Sam*, the Weather Being So unsetled As Prevented Me From Photographin the Redesants * So I Han Posponed it for a Feue dayes untill Grass Has Been Cut And then I Will Forward a Coppy Of Sam, In the Meen time Plese say if you Would Like to Han Gardener on the *Frunt* or any Figger I am Sir you Obently."

I am happy to add that this gentleman's photographs are of a quality much superior to his spelling. HERMENTRUDE.

OLD SURNAMES AND SIGNS.—In examining the particulars of Exchequer depositions and commissions of the reigns of Elizabeth and James I., I met with several curious names which struck me as worthy of a special note. Some of them,

* I venture to suggest " residence."

I have reason to think, have survived to t present day :—Dunce, Milksop *alias* Mellsop Littlepage, Pepperknight, Tiplady, Catchma Crakbone, Walklate, Standanaught, Quicklo Sweetaple, Thickpenny, Shortgrave, Bestpitc Cockcomb, Rumbelowe, Hob *alias* Nob, Panckc Phipers, and Zinzan.

From the same source it appears that a certa messuage was called "The Robin Hodd" (si and that other tenements known by the name of "The weeping eye" and "The angel in t house." WM. UNDERHILL.

ABIGAIL.—The first use of this name as a wo meaning a waiting woman is commonly attribut to Pope and Swift, who, as is supposed, took tl idea from the fact of Mrs. Masham's name beir Abigail. It is, however, found in a pamphlet r printed in the *Harleian Miscellany*, iv. 416, " New Bill, drawn up by a Committee of Grievanc in reply to the Ladies' and Batchelors' Petition an Remonstrances" [1694]. The following is tl passage :—

"But, whereas they [the Chaplains] petition to l freed from any Obligation to marry the Chambermai we can by no means assent to it, the *Abigail*, by inm morial Custom, being a *Deodand*, and belonging to Ho Church."

TREGEAGLE.

[We must request correspondents desiring informatio on family matters of only private interest, to affix the names and addresses to their queries, in order that th answers may be addressed to them direct.]

THE BURIAL OF A KNIGHT : CONSUETUDINA OF THE MONASTIC ORDERS.—While the fulle and most exhaustive particulars have descende to us regarding the ceremonial observed at th funeral of a mediæval prince or baron, the manne of conducting the obsequies of a simple knigh (banneret or bachelor) seems wrapt in comparativ obscurity. Can any of your correspondents ac quaint me whether it was customary to parad the steed at the funeral of the latter at any or eac period from the institution of chivalry to the tim of Henry VIII.? From Froissart, whose Chronic is a repertory of the more stately pageantry, I ca: recall no passage shedding any light upon th subject (such an important one to the antiquar, and romancist) ; while Strutt, generally so explici an authority, is absolutely silent in the matter o the observance obtaining previous to Henry VIII.' time, when, apparently by sumptuary law, th horse of any one beneath the rank of an earl wa forbidden to be led in procession at his intermen (see Horda, vol. iii. p. 162). Certainly, during thi reign at least, the knight's courser was not pre sented in the church, whether pursuant to ordin ance or not. Brand is silent till we arrive at th

Elizabethan era. Chaucer, no doubt, who invests his Arcite with all the characteristics of a contemporary warrior, and describes him as a mere knight, represents no less than three mounted steeds as accompanying the bier (the number usually assigned to a sovereign prince), but the poet's words seem to imply that this was intended as a special compliment on the part of Theseus the monarch.

I likewise desire to learn the best consuetudinal of the monastic orders in England, especially the Cistercian and Benedictine. Fosbroke is superficial; and Walcott, though sound, is not sufficiently full. Flete's narrative, if published, were excellent for the Benedictines. A reference or citation will confer no small boon.

WILLIAM WHITTY, Clk.

"EYESERVICE."—Can any reader of " N. & Q." help me to the proper meaning of this word ? "Eyeservice" is the rendering, literal enough, of the Greek ὀφθαλμοδουλεία, and in the A.V. represents the latter word in the two places in the New Testament where it occurs—Ephesians vi. 6, Colossians iii. 2. Now, the meaning commonly assigned to this word is "service rendered only while under inspection," and the two texts are generally used as pegs whereon to suspend exhortations to srevants to do their work as well in their masters' absence as in their presence. But I venture to say that this view of the texts can hardly be correct; for St. Paul in both passages is exhorting servants—whether slaves or freemen is not to the point—who are Christian converts. Their duties, he argues, are not to be performed with eyeservice as menpleasers, but "in singleness of heart," "fearing God," "as servants of Christ." It is evident that an "eyeservice" which was done only when the masters were present and neglected when they were away would soon be found out, and would make the doers of it anything but "menpleasers."

The word, I think, must bear a different interpretation. May I, while inviting criticism, suggest the following ? "Eyeservice" is not the deceitful performance of services while under inspection, but the thorough, unhesitating compliance with every command and wish of the master, the watching upon the master's eye to anticipate all his wants, the "waiting upon the eyes" of the 123rd Psalm. Such a devotion to a master, laudable though it might be under some circumstances, would easily degenerate into serving a master when his commands were opposed to the Divine law, and it is against such an obedience as this that the apostle warns his converts. The two passages I will paraphrase thus :—You servants must remember you have a duty to God as well as to man. Your obedience to your masters must be regulated by your Christian principles. Devotion, eyeservice, to your masters' interests is not all

that is expected of you ; you must not try to be menpleasers only—you have a master in heaven also, whose commands must be your first consideration.

The question I wish to ask is, Will ὀφθαλμοδουλεία bear without violence such a construction as I have here put upon it? and, if so, is my view of the two passages a reasonable one ?

EDWARD H. MARSHALL.
The Temple.

POPE'S "ESSAY ON CRITICISM."—Has it ever been noticed that in this essay no less than *twelve* lines end with the same word, "wit"? Five times, too, it rhymes with "fit," and three times with "writ." Once it is linked to the very unrhyming word "light," and once to "delight." So much for criticism ! "Quis custodiet custodes ?"
ZOILUS.

OLD COIN.—I seek to identify a coin dated 1607. It is of copper, the size of a modern penny. On one side is a half-clothed figure, meant, I suppose, to typify Hope, as there is an anchor in the background. The legend is the familiar REDEANT SATURNIA REGNA. On the reverse is a coat of arms, with many quarterings, between four heraldic shields. The legend, CAMERÆ RATONUM (or RATIONUM) GELRIA, altogether beats me.
D. J.

"THE HISTORY AND ANTIQUITIES OF WINTERTON."—I give the following extract from Gough's *Anecdotes of British Topography*, found under the head of "Lincolnshire":—"The MS. History and Antiquities of Winterton, collected by Abraham De La Pryme, corrected and enlarged by Warburton, was purchased at the sale of the latter's books, 1759, by Mr. Goodman." Can any reader of "N. & Q." give further information as to the existence and ownership of this MS. or a copy of it ?
J. T. F.
Winterton, Brigg.

"UPON CONTENT."—Is this phrase, as equivalent to "upon trust," used by any other author than Pope ? If the expression was a familiar one in his day instances of it must surely be found.

"Their praise is still,—the style is excellent;
The sense they humbly take upon content."
Essay on Criticism, part ii.

"Consent" would seem to have more meaning than "content," but the latter is the word in all the editions I have looked at, and Johnson quotes the lines as illustrating the use of "content" in the sense of acquiescence.
JAYDEE.

HOGARTH AND BIRDS.—Has the absence of birds from Hogarth's pictures ever been noticed and accounted for ? Geese and ducks, or hens and chickens, would have added a suitable element in the confusion of the "March to Finchley," or the

election plates; nor would they have disturbed the rustic quiet of "Evening." Fighting cocks do appear in "The Cockpit," in one of the "Stages of Cruelty," and a monstrous owl in "Debates on Palmistry." None of these are happy instances. Two pictures in "The Rake's Progress" of cocks are more like a scrawl of a schoolboy on a slate than the work of a great painter. Is it that Hogarth was really unable to draw a bird correctly, and that he was aware of his deficiency?
E. LEATON BLENKINSOPP.

THE DUTCH MASTER METSU.—Has any reader, acquainted with the works of this celebrated master, seen amongst his pictures, or engravings from them, the exterior of a Dutch tavern and butcher's, where a pig recently killed is being cut up, with figures drinking or looking on? The writer is so impressed with the valuable replies given in "N. & Q." that he would fain have recourse to the same channel for information. In the painting he possesses the pig is so truthfully drawn, and the lights and shades are so skilfully arranged, that the animal seems to come out of the canvas; the object to fastidious and unartistic eyes becomes offensively prominent, and sight is lost of the admirable grouping of the figures as well as of the perfection of the drawing and harmonious colouring of the picture. G. G.

THE "HUE AND CRY."—Constant charges (generally of twopence) occur for this in constables' accounts of the eighteenth century. Was it a kind of gazette? MARTYN.

TENNYSONIANA.—In an American edition of Tennyson's works published in Boston in 1866 are *Three Sonnets to a Coquette*. I cannot find these in any English edition of the poet's works. Where did they first appear? This edition also contains another little poem which seems to have dropped out of later editions, namely, *The Ringlet*, which I find in the volume containing *Enoch Arden* and *Aylmer's Field*, published in 1864. Several years ago I cut out of a newspaper a poem of thirty lines, entitled *Trodden Flowers*, signed Alfred Tennyson. Is this really Tennyson's? and if so where did it first appear? The mystery of *The Old Seat*, included in a Rotterdam edition of Tennyson, about which inquiries have been made in "N. & Q." both by myself and another correspondent, has not yet been cleared up. Is this also a *bonâ fide* Tennyson?
I am sure all admirers of Tennyson must share my disappointment at finding that the delightful one-volume edition of the poet's works just published, and stated by the publishers in their advertisement to be complete, does not contain the fine ballad of *The Fight in the Revenge*.
JONATHAN BOUCHIER.
Bexley Heath, Kent.

JEWISH SURNAMES AND SH· be glad to know when the Jew adopted surnames; also, if I am that the otherwise catholic-minde be excused for drawing his Jew villain, because there were no Je sit as models to the great master.

Lavender Hill.

WOOLLEN CAPS.—MR. NIC "Tucking Mill" (5th S. ix. 156) me a query as to the meaning entry, taken from a book of re manorial courts held in Dorset, 1: stables of Pimperne Hundred he report "omnia bene ad hunc diem of various parishes follow suit. de Blandforde" (?) makes the f ment:—"Et q'æ statut' pr' wei capps n'o est execut' per tot' hi omnia bene." Is the statute rel Edw. IV., I wonder? THO: Weymouth.

LEGEND OF HOLME CHURCE Riding of Yorkshire, six or se Market Weighton, is a village cal church is on the top of a hill, a used to be believed by the village

"Some persons commenced to build bottom of the hill, and they were wa to build it at the top, but they took the church was nearly finished it was They recommenced to build, but the in ruins again; and they started a t was again spoiled by the fairies. Th the top, where it now remains."

Are any other similar legends of·

INSCRIPTION ON A PORTRAIT.— quarter-length portrait (in oil c five feet by four feet) of a youn; on a pilaster the following inscri capitals : BAᴰIOIOMAVᶜ ARE favour me with an interpretation

MONASTERY : CONVENT.—Can respondents give me the distincti words? I believe a difference use; but no book that I have Italian, English, or Church dict plain wherein the true distinctior

Worle Vicarage.

MOUNT JEROME CEMETERY, D inform me whether there is in p (at least the principal) monumen this well-known cemetery, which mains of a large number of I

highly distinguished in their respective stations?
If there is not, there ought to be.   ABHBA.

THE "BUCK OF BEVERLAND."—Goldsmith, in
the *Vicar of Wakefield*, chap. vi., says :—
"He" (Mr. Burchell) " sang us old songs, and gave
the children the story of the *Buck of Beverland*, with
the history of Patient Grissel, the adventures of Catskin,
and then *Fair Rosamond's Bower*."

Where is Beverland, and where is the story of
the *Buck of Beverland* to be found? An early
reply will oblige   W. J. T.

JACK MITFORD.—Where can I find any account
of him, or ascertain the date of his death? I have
searched your four indexes in vain. There are
several references to the quondam editor of the
Gentleman's Magazine, Reverend John, but not
one to the *irreverend* Jack.   K. D.

PASCAL.—What meaning do these letters bear
which are appended to the third *Provinciale*:
E. A. B. P. A. F. D. E. P.? All the other *Pro-
vinciales* are unsigned.   GWAVAS.
Penzance.

AUTHORS OF BOOKS WANTED.—
The *Foster Brothers: being a History of the School and
College Career of Two Young Men*. London, Arthur
Hall. Virtue & Co., 25, Paternoster Row, 1859. Fcap.
8vo. pp. 423.   JOHN PICKFORD, M.A.
The *Chronicles of Camber Castle : a Tale of the Refor-
mation*. London, Hatchard, 1855.—Is this a real or
imaginary history? Camber Castle was built by
Henry VIII. in the low ground between Rye and Win-
chelsea for defence in the event of an enemy landing.
                    ED. MARSHALL.

AUTHORS OF QUOTATIONS WANTED.—
"So burly Luther breasted Babylon."
Blanchard Jerrold quotes it in his *Life of Napoleon III.*,
vol. iii., in reference to M. Rouher.   L. E. WILLIS.

"And knew not but the Ganges rolled
Near as the neighbouring Thames."
                    WM. P. MENDHAM.

"Scilicet a superis etiam fortuna luenda est,
Nec veniam, læso numine, casus habet."
                    J. F. M.

Replies.

THE SEE OF CAITHNESS.

(5th S. ix. 362.)

I think that a more probable explanation of
"ecclesia Cathayensis," as referred to in Theiner's
Vet. Mon. Hib. et Scot. (Nos. 641, 646, 660, pp. 316,
317, 324), is as follows ; and, with all deference to
MR. WOODWARD'S "discovery" of *Cathanasia*, or
"the town of Dunmore in Ireland," as being the
place mentioned, I venture to submit my solution
of the difficulty as a more correct and probable
one.

The see of Caithness—"ecclesia Cathanensis"
—in Scotland was occupied by Thomas (Murray)
of Fyngask from Nov. 29, 1342, until his death,
which is stated to have occurred at Elgin in the
year 1360, apparently in March (Gordon's *Gen.
History of Earldom of Sutherland*, p. 52 ; *Orkney.
Saga*, lxxxvi), and the next bishop of Caithness
certainly known, from authentic records, was
Malcolm of Alnes, who was "elect. Cathanensis"
before March 5, 1367-8 ("Compota Custumar'
et Balliv' de Abirden.," cf. Chamberlain Rolls of
Scotland, vol. i. No. 48, p. 487), and confirmed, or
rather "provided," to the see by Pope Urban V.,
Feb. 21, 1369, at Rome, in the room of "bone
memorie *Thoma* episcopo Cathanensi" (Theiner,
No. 681, pp. 333-4). The chief difficulty here lies
in identifying this Thomas, and whether he is the
bishop of that name, formerly mentioned as dying
in 1360, or an intermediate one of the same name,
during the interval 1360-67. This vacancy—if
such intervened, and as I am inclined to think—it
is impossible to fill up satisfactorily from any
known historian of the succession here. It, *primâ
facie*, affords grounds for the belief that the second
Thomas, provided to the church of Cathay by
Pope Innocent VI. on May 11, 1360, and consecrated
at Avignon by Pierre de Prez, Cardinal-Bishop of
Palestrina (most probably on the Sunday previous,
May 10), had really succeeded to the Scottish
bishopric, but, unfortunately, there is no mention in
the bull of provision as to his previous ecclesiastical
station which might give a clue to his nationality ;
still the accompanying facts, hereafter stated, are
too strong in favour of Cathay having been an
Irish see. The ancient though small see of Inis-
Cathay, vulgo "Inis-Scattery"—"ecclesia *Cathayensis*"—is said to have been founded in the fifth
century by St. Patrick, and it existed as a distinct
bishopric until the end of the twelfth or beginning
of the thirteenth century, when it was united to that
of Limerick ; while portions of this island diocese
were, at the same time, annexed to the surrounding sees of Killaloe and Ardfert, all of which were
in the province of Cashel, and under its metropolitan archbishop.

Inis-Cathay—"insula Cathayensis"—so designated from the island near the mouth of the river
Shannon, which formed the limits of the diocese,
has now, I hope, been satisfactorily identified with
Cathay, or "ecclesia Cathayensis," as distinct from
"ecclesia Cathanensis," and it is only necessary to
allude to the confirmatory evidence of the see being
an *Irish* one. The first papal commission, of
July 8, 1362, to George (De Rupe, or Roche),
Archbishop of Cashel, was for the purpose of his
inquiring into the complaint and petition of
"Thome Epi' Cathayensis," against the accusations and obstructions of "Thomas Laoniensis"
(Thomas O'Cormacain, Bishop of Killaloe,
1355-82/7), "Stephanus Limiricensis" (Stephen

de Valle, or Wale, Bishop of Limerick, 1360-69), "Joannes Ardfertensis" (John de Valle, Bishop of Ardfert, 1348-72), and ". . . Clonensis" (see *vacant*, John Whittock, Whitcock, or "Whytekot," Bishop of Cloyne—*not* "Clonmacnoise"—from 1351, having died Feb. 7, 1361-2, and no successor being nominated till 1363). These prelates were naturally opposed to the appointment of a bishop to the long extinct see of Cathay, which had been divided and annexed to the neighbouring dioceses, over which they ruled, upwards of a century and a half before, and which was then only a parochial church, as correctly asserted by them, and no longer a cathedral, according to Bishop Thomas's statements to the Holy See. Archbishop George of Cashel had only been nominated to that metropolitan see on June 17 previous (his bull of provision is misplaced in Theiner, being No. 670, p. 329, but correctly in *Argumenta*, p. xxiv), and was drowned, it is believed, on his way home from the Roman Curia at Avignon (not "Rome," as in Ware, Cotton, &c.), so no report was made by him on the state of the church of Cathay, whether parochial or cathedral. Pope Innocent VI. also died about the same time, Sept. 12, 1362, but the succeeding pontiff, Urban V., in the first year of his reign, issued a fresh commission of inquiry on June 24, 1363, addressed to "Thome Episcopo Lismorensi (et Waterfordiensi)," directing him to make the necessary report (the metropolitan see of Cashel being then vacant, and so continuing till Feb. 27, 1365); but the result of this attempt to revive the bishopric of Cathay is not recorded, or what became of its titular occupant Thomas, and the matter rests in that obscurity, and is never likely to be ascertained, I fear (cf. Harris's *Ware*, i. 34, 502, 590, *et passim;* Cotton's *Fasti Eccles. Hib.*, i. 372, 431-2 ; Lenihan's *Limerick*, pp. 4, 46, 564). The last writer relates, on the authority of the White MSS., that "about the year 1742 the chapel of Inis Catha, or Scattery island, at the mouth of the river Shannon, was recovered from the diocese of Killaloe, and a second time joined to that of Limerick, by Bishop Robert Lacy," who held the see from 1737 to 1759. It also seems that the previous recovery of the island was during the episcopate of Bishop Cornelius O'Dea, who records (in the *Black Book of Limerick*) that Inis-cathy was "formerly of the lands belonging to Limerick, which were not before me for many years in the possession of the church." The date given is "A.D. 1542, Sept. 30," which must be wrong, and seems to refer to Cornelius O'Dea, Bishop of Limerick, 1400-26, and certainly not to Cornelius O'Dea, Bishop of Killaloe, 1546-55 ; but confusion, "or a series of mistakes," appears to be inseparably connected with Inis-Cathay. Sir James Ware states :—

"Neque hic prætermittendum, sub exitum seculi xii. vel initium insequentis, Episcopatus Limericensem et

Cathayensem sive de Insula Gatha coaluisse."—*Ant qutates Hibernicæ*, ed. secunda, London, 1658, p. 323. The island was evidently a subject of disput between the sees of Limerick and Killaloe.

If any other explanation of the "puzzling documents in Theiner can be given by some c your numerous learned correspondents, wit sufficient proofs in support of a different theory and a more probable one than MR. WOODWARD' "discovery," I am quite ready to submit, an acknowledge my error. I may mention that in conversation and correspondence with Mr. Ander son, the able editor of the *Orkneyinga Saga*, on the question of this see of Cathay, he coincided in my views of its being an *Irish* bishopric, and having no reference whatever to Caithness in Scot land ; although he admitted having been, at on time, doubtful about the preferment of this Bishop Thomas, and whether it was to the Scottish o Irish see.

In conclusion I would merely remark that the usual accounts of the succession of bishops o Caithness are about the most unsatisfactory and imperfect of any see in Scotland, and whoever can supply this desideratum will be rendering a service to ecclesiastical literature, which future historian will be thankful for.   A. S. A.
Richmond.

THE RUSSELL FAMILY (5th S. ix. 461, 491.)— I submit myself with all due humility to my anonymous critics, and hope that their verdict may not be followed by an order for my instant decapi tation. If one is to be held so strictly to account for using a convenient and familiar formula, which could by no possibility mislead any one, and for which there is ample precedent, it will be well to be more exact, and I therefore hasten to relieve myself from the imputation of ignorance by de scribing the lady in question in the only manner in which, during the period of her first marriage and widowhood, she had any right to be described viz. as *Madam*, or *Mistress*, Elizabeth Russell From the instant of her second marriage she, o course, lost all right to the name of Russell, with or without any prefix, and became *Dame* Eliza beth Hoghton. I should be glad if the second o my critics would refer me to any authority, civil o ecclesiastical, by virtue of which a lady on her marriage changes her Christian name as well as her surname. I am not to be put off with a mere reference to any social custom. If I am to be hel to the strict letter of the law, so must he be, an I therefore challenge him to prove his assertion that "*Elizabeth* Lloyd by her first marriage becam Lady *James* Russell."

But "le jeu n'en vaut pas la chandelle," and should not have returned to the subject if it had not afforded me the opportunity of expressing th opinion that contributors to "N. & Q." migh employ themselves better than in rushing into print with such trivial criticisms.

JOSEPH LEMUEL CHESTER.
Linden Villas, Blue Anchor Road, S.E.

I do not think that COL. CHESTER has committed an error. The object of persons who write about matters of genealogy is, or should be, so to express themselves as to leave no room for doubt. If the Christian name of a married woman be suppressed, and her husband's given her in its stead, confusion will be introduced in many cases, and where a man has been married several times positive blunders will be sure to be made. The pathways of genealogy have a sufficient number of pitfalls beside and across them already, without our permitting modern fashion to add another. I say modern fashion, for I do not believe that this custom of giving the wife her husband's Christian name has much antiquity to boast of. I have carefully gone over many name-lists of the seventeenth century, but do not remember ever to have seen a single instance of this practice of an earlier date than the Restoration.

How are married ladies described in modern legal documents? EDWARD PEACOCK.
Bottesford Manor, Brigg.

[In the Chronological Diary issued with the *Historical Register*, among the deaths in September, 1736, is that of "*Lady Russel*," mother of the wife of Thomas Scawen, Esq." In the record of administration to the estate of her mother, the same person is called "*Elizabeth, Lady Russell*, alias Hoghton," &c. In the probate act attached to the will of her first husband, who, by the way, called himself "James Russell, Esquire, commonly called Lord James Russell," she was described as the "*Honourable Elizabeth Russell*." She commenced her own will thus: "I, *Dame Elizabeth*, the wife of Sir Henry Hoghton, Baronet, but usually styled the *Lady Russell*," &c. And in the administration act Sir Henry Hoghton is described as "husband of the Right Honourable the *Lady Elizabeth Russell*." We know of but one instance where she was called *Lady James Russell*, and this is in the will of her step-sister, Mary Grove; but, strange to say, this was considered so remarkable by the official who transcribed the will into the register, that he took occasion to justify himself by writing in the margin the words "So in the original." As a matter of fact, she was never "Lady Russell," "Elizabeth, Lady Russell," "Lady Elizabeth Russell," nor, according to ancient practice, "Lady *James* Russell." So long as she was the wife or widow of her first husband, she was simply "Mrs. Elizabeth Russell," even the prefix of "Honourable" being hers only by courtesy. The instant she married Sir Henry Hoghton she ceased to have any right to the name of Russell at all, either with or without prefixes, and her only proper title thenceforth was "Dame Elizabeth Hoghton."]

GIPSIES IN ENGLAND (5th S. ix. 149, 295, 358.) —The earliest mention of Gipsies in these islands seems to be that of 1506, found by Mr. Simson, and alluded to by MR. HUBERT SMITH. It is, however, possible that they may have visited England as early as 1427, when a number came from the South or East to Paris, and on leaving went towards Pontoise, as if going north. M. Bataillard (*De l'Apparition, &c., des Bohémiens en Europe*, Paris, 1844, p. 53) surmises that their first appearance on this side of the Channel was probably not before 1440 or 1450, and Mr. Borrow (*Lavolil*, 212) asserts that they first came to England in 1480. S(amuel) R(id), in *The Art of Juggling*, published in 1612, says: "This kind of people about 100 years ago, about the 20th year of King Henry the Eighth, began to gather an head, at the first heere, about the southern parts," which puts the advent about 1528, two years before the passing of the Act of 1530 (22 Hen. VIII., c. 10), which, from internal evidence, was not passed immediately on their arrival, but during the immigration. We know, moreover, that the Gipsies were ordered to be expelled from Spain in 1492, causing an exodus into France; from the German empire in 1500, causing a further exodus into the more attractive France; and from France in 1504, when we may anticipate that there was a general overflow of the race into England; and in 1506 we know that a band had wandered into the Land of Cakes. In addition to this Mr. Simson (*Hist. of the Gipsies*, 99) alludes to a Scotch tradition, which may relate to a still earlier visit from Gipsies, under the name of Saracens.

Hall, in his *Chronicles*, under the dates 1510 and 1520, mentions Egyptians in a manner which leads one to imagine that he meant Gipsies; and Mr. Bright (*Travels in Lower Hungary*, Lond., 1818, p. 538) notes that in *A Dyalogue of Syr Thomas More* (1514) an "Egipcyan" is mentioned who had returned to France. About 1517 Skelton, in his *Elynoure Rumminge*, alludes to the costume of the Gipsies. In 1521 we find a gentleman giving what was then the large sum of forty shillings to a probably large band of Egyptians. In 1527, at Aberdeen, Ekin Jako (Jacques?), "maister of the Egiptians," was accused of stealing "twa silver spounis" ("N. & Q.," 5th S. v. 52); and a translation, made possibly in 1527, of Josafa Barbaro's *Travels to Tana* (Hakl. Soc., 1873, p. 18) mentions Gipsies in plain terms. So far this seems all that is known of Gipsies in Great Britain prior to 1530. From that time to 1600 about forty additional notices could be specified, and those of your readers who ferret through those bugbears, unindexed county histories, would render a service to myself and others if they would kindly chronicle in your columns any early references to Gipsies across which they may come. In conclusion it may be stated that *Gipsy* is no modern corruption of *Egyptian*, for Skelton, in his *Garlande of Laurell*, 1455, alludes to S. Maria Ægyptiaca and her marvellous Romany-like powers of deception in the line, "By Mary Gipcy, quod scripsi, scripsi."

H. T. CROFTON.
Manchester.

THE CREST OF THE GREENHILL FAMILY (5th S. ix. 468.)—H. G. H. will find some remarks on this subject in "N. & Q.," 1st S. vi. 303. In answer to his first query, I may state that the person to whom the augmentation in his crest was granted in 1698 was Thomas Greenhill, a surgeon of some repute, who contributed two papers to the *Philosophical Transactions* (July, 1700, and June, 1705), and was the author of the *Art of Embalming*, published in 1705. His father was William Greenhill, of Greenhill at Harrow, Middlesex, a counsellor-at-law and secretary to General Monk. He married Elizabeth White, daughter and co-heir of William White, of London, by whom he had thirty-nine children, all (it is said) born alive and baptized, and all single births except one. There is a portrait of this lady, with an inscription at the back, in the possession of Sir Thomas Woollaston White, Bart., of Walling Wells, near Worksop; and another similar portrait and inscription at Lowesby Hall, Leicestershire, the seat of Sir Frederick Fowke, Bart. William Greenhill lived and died at Abbot's Langley, Herts, where he was buried in 1681, and where it is believed his children were born. About ten years ago I had (through the courtesy of the Rev. Dr. Gee, the vicar) an opportunity of examining the parish registers, in the hope of finding some confirmation of the family tradition. I found numerous entries relating to the family, from the early part of the seventeenth century to the beginning of the eighteenth; but between 1652 and 1690 (that is, the exact time when these thirty-nine children were born) two or more leaves had been cut out of the register, probably by some one who was in some way interested in the entries contained in them. I have an additional motive for mentioning the mutilation of the register, in the hope that this notice may possibly reach the eye of some one who may be able to give some information respecting the missing leaves. The mutilation is not of recent date, as it is noticed in the "Parish Register Abstract" connected with the Census Report of 1831.　　　　　　　　　　　　　W. A. G.
Hastings.

Thomas Greenhill was a London surgeon, who, in 1705, published a quarto volume entitled NEKPOKΔEIA ; *or, the Art of Embalming,* to which is prefixed the author's portrait by Nutting, after T. Murray. There was a small portrait of his mother Mrs. Greenhill at Wallingwells, near Worksop, the seat of Sir Thomas Wollaston White, Bart., an account of which is to be found in the *Gentleman's Magazine* for 1805, pt. i. p. 405. There was on this picture an inscription, attested by a clergyman named Rich. Ashby, setting forth that

"She had thirty-nine children by one husband. They were all born alive and baptized, and all single births save one. The last child, who was born after his father's

death, was a chirurgeon in King Street, Bloom She was heard to say by a credible witness, wit was well acquainted, that she believed if he had lived she might have had two or th children.

"There was an addition made to the arms of to commemorate this extraordinary case, whic is thirty-nine stars on the crest of a griffin's h

I have tried in vain to trace any rel between this Mrs. Greenhill and either Greenhill, *circa* 1590-1677, the exposito kiel ; John Greenhill of Salisbury, the Lely, who died in 1676, and left a wi several children ; or Thomas Greenhill of who died in 1633, and whose curious br Beddington Church, Surrey.　　EDWARD Sutton, Surrey.

"THE PASTON LETTERS" (5th S. ix. 350, 370, 414.)—I have referred to th p.m. of John Legh, and find that S. H. right in his conjecture, and that "Isted" reading for "Islee." But a difficulty still inasmuch as the charter therein recited noticed before is dated Aug. 30, 9 Hen. 1493-4—and mentions "Agnes, the wife Islee, formerly wife of John Harvy," wo seem to show that John Isley was aliv time. The inscription, however, upon his Sundridge Church (now no longer existi by Philpott in his MS. collections, an by a writer in the *Topographer and G* (vol. iii. p. 197), states that he died in 14 same writer, in a pedigree of the Isle makes Sir John Paston to have been a band to John Isley, stating that the for in 1478, and citing in support of it an e 20 Ed. IV., No. 15. This, however, as a the letter No. 939, the date of which mus or 1503, must be an error.

The inquisition taken upon the death Paston (Chancery Inquis. p.m., 1-2 He Kent, No. 4) throws a little further light history. It is headed "Inquis. p.m. Ag fuit uxor Johannis Isley, armigeri," a that on Nov. 3, 15 Ed. IV., 1475 or 147 the wife of John Isley, inasmuch as it conveyance of that date whereby divers l conveyed to the use of Agnes, then th John Isley, for the term of her life. It at Farningham on Sept. 20, 2 Hen. V and gives the date of her death as June 7

The original of Sir George Harvy's wi the P.C.C., and therefore it is impossible tain the correctness of the passage, " Atclyff, suster to the said George." The i upon his death states that Elizabeth W wife of Edward Wanton, was his dau heir, and twenty-four years old, so that the words "said George" refer to himsel is an error for "daughter." The followi are, I think, almost conclusive against his sister Isabel, formerly the wife of John Harvy, being meant:—1. She is called Elizabeth, not Isabel, and although these names are sometimes used the one for the other in old documents, they are not commonly so used. 2. As I said before, the absence of any mention of her second marriage upon her tomb, and, in addition to the coat of Legh impaling Harvy, there is a coat of her own arms quarterly in a lozenge. With regard to the date of John Harvy's death upon this tomb, I can say positively that it is MCCCCCIX. I have rubbed the brass myself, and the date 1509 is given by Aubrey, Lysons, Manning, and Brayley in their histories of Surrey. It is an error of the graver's, of course, because we know from the inquisition that he died on April 24, 1503.

It was, as S. H. A. H. says, Margaret Smarte who was the mother of Sir George Harvy's illegitimate son Gerard. In a *Visitation of Beds* (H. 9, p. 16, College of Arms) there is a pedigree of Harvy which gives the descent thus: Sir George Harvy, Kt., eldest son and heir to John Harvy, had issue Gerrard Harvy, his son natural; Gerrard Harvy, of Thurley, Esq., son and heir by adoption unto Sir George Harvy, Kt., married Jane, widow to Cheyney of Callice, and daughter to Sir John Williams, of Binfield, co. Berks, Kt., and sister to the Lord Williams of Thame.	G. L. G.

EMBLEMS OF THE PASSION (5th S. ix. 261, 411.)— These are singularly introduced in a representation of what is styled "Redemptoris mundi arma," as stamped upon the binding of books which are supposed to have belonged to the library of Henry VIII. The crest is the cock in the act of crowing. He stands upon the pillar, round which is the rope or thong ; on each side a scourge, and below them the bundles of rods. Over the shield is a full-faced helmet with mantling. Arranged within the shield appear the head of Judas with the bag suspended from his neck, the pieces of silver, the lantern, the seamless garment and the dice, the branch or reed which was held in the right hand, the palm of the open hand which smote, the nails, the hammer, the sponge upon the reed, the spear, the pincers, and the open sepulchre. The central object on the shield is the cross, surmounted by the crown of thorns and the inscription. The supporters are unicorns, and the motto is—"Redemptoris mundi arma." Over the shield are two small ones, each containing a monogram.

The book itself from which this description has been taken is a copy of the *Paraphrasis in Evangelium Lucæ* by Erasmus, printed by Froben in 1523, and dedicated to that "Rex invictissimus," Henry VIII. himself, in a long epistle. On the other side it bears the royal arms, and also a large scroll held up by two angels and encircling a rose, with the motto :—

"Hæc rosa virtutis de cœlo missa sereno
Eternum florens regia sceptra feret."

The binder is said to have been John Reynes, who bound for Henry VIII., and kept his shop in St. Paul's Churchyard.	NIGRAVIENSIS.

In the *British Architect and Northern Engineer*, May 17 and 24, is an illustrated report of "Pen and Pencil Sketches in Brittany," a lecture given before the Society for Encouragement of the Fine Arts, Conduit Street, Regent Street, by J. S. Phené, LL.D., F.S.A., &c., May 16, 1878 ; and in the *Building News*, May 17, is a briefer report of the same lecture, with a sheet of sketches by Dr. Phené. One of these represents an enormous menhir, commanding a view of the Island of Aval, or Avalon, the burial-place of King Arthur, for the full and very interesting particulars concerning which, and Dr. Phené's discoveries there, readers are referred to the published reports of the lecture. The face of this menhir, ten feet wide and twenty-five feet high, is entirely covered with sculptured emblems of the Passion, surmounted by the sun and moon, and a figure (possibly) of the Deity. Dr. Phené says :—

"The quaintest of all is the great menhir which commands the way to the Grand Island, now literally covered with sculptured masonic emblems, in juxtaposition with such florid Christian exhibitions as the reed and sponge, hammer and nails, dice and lot-cast garment, and in the centre a life-size representation of the great death on Calvary, all in supposed proper colours."

In addition to the emblems above mentioned I can make out (on the sketch) the lantern, ladder, cock on a pillar, spear, pincers, and ewer (for vinegar?). There are also other implements, an open hand, a face, and two cross-bones. Dr. Phené says that

"in Brittany each place has its special emblems, illustrating its special traditions. Penmarc'h means 'horse's head,' and the parish church is decorated with horses' heads. 'La Torche,' at Penmarc'h, 'La Clarté,' near Tregastel, &c., are evidently places of Phoenician lighthouses, and perpetuated by modern lighthouses and modern names. Arthur was the great light—the great Christian warrior ; and here we have La Clarté. Avalon is the place of his tomb, and here we have the grand menhir sculptured with the emblems of the great Christian death, and with the sun, or sun-myth, adapted to the true light which Arthur (as a warrior) represented. This is the great tombstone of Arthur, though not on the island, but commanding it and all the Avalonian district."

The estate on which stands Arthur's tomb was purchased by Dr. Phené, who, after several years' exploration, has succeeded in tracing the ancient Avalon. A large stone, used in former times for pressing the apples that were once grown on the island, has been brought to England by Dr. Phené, and is now in his grounds at Chelsea.
	CUTHBERT BEDE.

J. S. JONES, M.D. (5th S. ix. 387), dramatic writer, died within the year in Boston, America.

He wrote *Six Degrees of Crime*, &c., and was thought a good actor in his day. L. G. W.

CRAMP RINGS (5ᵗʰ S. ix. 308, 435.)—I beg to present your querist with the following extracts as a contribution to the history of cramp rings :—

"Four bunches of cramp rings, some silver and some gold.—Jewlls in the exchequer."—Inventory of the Lord Lysley's [Lisle's] Goods, July 7, 1540 ; Domestic State Papers, Calais, uncalendared.

James Basset writes to his mother, Lady Lisle, for six cramp rings, three gold and three silver. Paris, Aug. 20 [1537?].—*Lisle Papers*, i. 73.

Sir George Douglas sends Lady Lisle a dozen of cramp rings, from London, "this Wednesday, the 8 January" [1533 or 1539].—*Ib.*, x. 93.

"I have sent your lordship cramp rings, both of gold and silver." John Grenville to his sister's husband, Lord Lisle.—*Ib.*, iii.

"I send you by Mr. Degory Gramefilld [Grenville] 59 cramp rings of silver, that Christofer Morys giveth you, and one of gold." London, April 17 [1535], John Husee to his mistress, Lady Lisle.—*Ib.*, xi. 111.

"Madam, I think verily that if all the books and cronycles were totally revolved and to the uttermost proscruted and tried, which against wymen hath been pennyd, contryvyd, and wryten, syns Adam and Eve, these same were I think verily nothing in comparison of that which hath been done and committed by Anne the Queen......I think not the contrary but she and all they shall suffre. John Williams hath promised me some cramp rings for your ladyship." Husee to Lady Lisle, London, May 13 [1536].—*Ib.*, xii. 58. Be it remembered that the virtues of the cramp rings were solely due to the touch of Anne the Queen aforesaid !

"Your ladyship shall receive of this berer 9 cramp rings of silver. John Williams says he never had so few of gold as this year. The king had the most part himself ; but next year he will make you amends." Ditto to ditto, May 10 [1536].—*Ib.*, xii. 60. Queen Anne had been beheaded that morning. Probably Mr. John Williams had good reason for supposing that there would be another by next year.

"Lord Herts showed me that he sent you one dozen cramp rings." Ditto to ditto, London, April 7 [1537].—*Ib.*, xii. 32.

"I will tell Lord Herts you received the cramp rings." Ditto to ditto, St. Katherine, July 17 [1537].—*Ib.*, xii. 106.

"Cramp rings I can get none out of the jewel-house. Mr. Wyll"'s says the king had the most part of gold, but has promised me twelve silver." Ditto to ditto, London, May 2 [1538].—*Ib.*, xii. 43.

"To-morow Mr. Williams shall give me 12 silver cramp rings." Ditto to ditto, London, May 5 [1538].—*Ib.*, xii. 44.

"I send 2 dozen silver cramp rings. Gold is very skant." Ditto to ditto, London, May 8 [1538].—*Ib.*, xii. 37.

"I send you 24 cramp rings, 8 of gold, and 16 of silver." Ditto to ditto, London, April 23 [1539].—*Ib.*, xi. 67.

"Hussy told me you were very desirous to have some cramp rings against the time that you should be brought a bedd :......I send by the present messenger 18 cramp rings, which you should have had long ago." Edward Seymour, Earl of Hertford [afterwards Duke of Somerset], to Lady Lisle, 1537.—*Ib.*, xi. 13.

HERMENTRUDE.

EAR-ACHES = THE FIELD POPPY (5ᵗʰ S. ix. 488·)—Field poppies seem to have an evil reputa-

tion. In South Lincolnshire we used to ca[l] "head-aches," and if ever I smelt one it w[a] fear and trembling lest I should have to su my rashness. ST. SWI[T]

THOMAS POWELL (5ᵗʰ S. ix. 487.)—Se[e] bone's *Dictionary of English and An* *Authors.* F.

CONVENTUAL CHURCHES STILL IN USE ix. 484.)—To the list given by MR. W[,] should be added the parish church of Elsto[n] fordshire, formerly belonging to the con[v] Benedictine nuns founded in the reign of V the Conqueror by Judith, Countess of Hunti W. [F] Worle Vicarage.

HAGWAYS (5ᵗʰ S. ix. 68.)—In the glos[s] my edition of Burns (Bewick) "hag" is (as "a scar, or gulf, in mosses and moors." acquainted with Scottish moors well kn[o] dangerous gulfs called "moss hags." Scott, *Lay of the Last Minstrel*, uses the word i sense when he refers to the moss-trooper's

"Small and shaggy nag,
That through a bog, from hag to hag,
Could bound like any Bilhope stag."

But the word "hag," in the south of Scotla[n] nacular, has another meaning, which I do n[o] in the glossary ; and this gives a clue to the[m]ing of "hagways," a word, according to CUT BEDE, applied by a Rutland gamekeeper to paths cut "through the thick undergrowth i woods to enable the keepers and beaters t[o] the game." "Hag," *Scotticè*, means to cut, (with an axe, hence hagging (cutting) with a "Hagways" in Rutland, in all probability, fore means cutways, having been cut, or l with an axe. I cannot at present lay my h an Anglo-Saxon dictionary, but I imagi word "hag," to cut, comes direct from the or Norse. H. K

Stacksteads, Lancashire.

Five and twenty years ago or more I [r] note of a similar expression, used by a man when I was consulting him as to th means of getting away timber which had be down in a plantation thick with underwood. mun cut a hag *roo-ad* thro' t' underbrush, m was his reply ; and upon my asking for an e[x] tion of the word "hagroad," he described ride or drive through the wood. Halliwell "hag" to hew, chop, or hack ; and in anoth[e] a certain division of wood intended to be (The wood on the east side of the river Der[w] Matlock Bath, in which the lovers' wal situate, is called the Hagwood. JOHN PA[F] Idridgehay, Derby.

To "hag" is a North-country verb in c[o] use, to cut, hew down ; and "hagways" n

roads cleared in a forest by cutting down lines of trees. A portion cleared at one time is termed a "hag" in a wood, and a cutting in a peat-moss is called a "peat-hag." When Waverley first inquired for the Baron of Bradwardine, and his servant said that "his honour was wi' the folk that were getting down the dark hag," the visitor's puzzle only ceased when Miss Bradwardine explained that "the dark hag had no connexion with a black cat or a broomstick, but was simply a portion of oak copse which was to be felled that day." May not this word have something to do with "ha-ha" fences?   M. P.
Cumberland.

Burns describes the old sportsman Tam Samson shooting grouse for the last time:—

"Ower mony a weary hag he jumpit,
And aye the tither shot he thumpit."

Hack, hag, haggle, have all one meaning—to cut.
                                        J. C. M.

While residing in Northamptonshire I frequently visited Weekley Hall Wood, where a keeper pointed out to me a recently cleared path, which he described as the "hacked way," saying that it saved him a walk of half a mile, besides enabling him to more easily overtake trespassers.
                                  JOHN PLUMMER.
Canonbury.

See Taylor's *Words and Places*, p. 81.
                                  SEDBERGHIAN.
Ind. Coll., Taunton.

"BERNARDUS NON SCIT OMNIA" (5th S. ix. 284.) —Inquiry has been made as to this phrase. Whether there be anything to account for the "Bernardus" or not, the sentiment at least has been a common one at all times. In Homer, *Il.*, N. 729, *sqq.*, Polydamas, when he incites Hector, says :—

ἀλλ' οὔπως ἅμα πάντα δυνήσεαι αὐτὸς ἑλέσθαι·
ἄλλῳ μὲν γὰρ ἔδωκε θεὸς πολεμήϊα ἔργα·
.   .   .   .
ἄλλῳ δ' ἐν στήθεσσι τίθεῖ νόον εὐρύοπα Ζεὺς
ἐσθλὸν.

In a similar manner Maharbal remonstrates with Hannibal to make him use his opportunity: "Non omnia nimirum eidem dii dedere. Vincere scis Hannibal: Victoria uti nescis" (Liv. xxii. 51). In one of the dialogues of Plato it is asked, εἰ πάντα ἐπίστασθαι τινὰ ἀνθρώπων ἐστὶ δυνατόν; (*Sophist.*, *Opp.*, p. 155, B. Lugd., 1590).
In Gaisford's *Paroem. Grœc.*, p. 292, Oxon., 1836, on the proverb εἷς ἀνὴρ οὐδεὶς ἀνήρ, there is mention in a note of "Euripideum illud" [sc. Phœniss., v. 752], εἷς ἀνὴρ οὐ πάνθ' ὁρᾷ. And there is a similar Latin proverb, "Nullus omnia scire potest" (*Adagia*, Typ. Wech., 1629, p. 34).
                                  ED. MARSHALL.
Sandford St. Martin.

WHY IS "AXE" SPELT "AX" IN THE OXFORD PRAYER BOOKS? (5th S. ix. 227.)—Both spellings are equally correct, but the former is at present the usual. In a New Testament printed by the University Press, Oxford, 1856, I find the reading *ax* at Matt. iii. 10 and *axe* at Luke iii. 9, whilst in a Bible printed by John Bill and Christopher Barker, London, 1666, both passages have *ax*. Wycliffe wrote *axe*, Layamon, i. 196, *ax*; this latter spelling is also to be found in *Havelock*, l. 1894, *Seven Sages*, l. 613, *Gawayn*, ll. 208 and 289, and in Rob. of Gloucester, p. 490. In *Ancren Riwle* we have *eax* on pp. 128 and 384 ; in Layamon, i. 98, *eaxe*, whilst *eax*, *ib.*, i. 276. The different forms in Middle English are *ax*, *eax*, *aex*, *ex*, *axe*, *exe*, and in Anglo-Saxon *acas*, *äx*, *eax*.
Such variety of spellings in old texts will, I think, justify *axe* and *ax* in modern texts.
                                  F. ROSENTHAL.
Hannover.

The reason why it is so printed at the Clarendon Press is, that this is the spelling of the Sealed Book. See A. J. Stephens's reprint, Lond., 1854. The spelling does not appear to have been uniformly one way or the other at any time. In Tyndale's N. T., ed. 1626, as reprinted by Offor, Lond., 1836, it is *ax* at St. Matt. iii., *axe* at St. Luke iii. In a bl.-l. copy which I have of A. V., of which the title is lost, it is *ax*; in another, bl.-l., Lond., 1625, it is *axe*. In the Pr. Bk., Lond., 1614 and 1621, it is *axe*. In the Scotch C. P., Edin., 1637, it is *ax*. But Keeling, *Lit. Brit.*, Lond., 1851, has no notice of this, and spells *axe*. Coverdale, reprint Lond., 1836, and all the versions in Bagster's *Hexapla*, and also Tyndale's ed., Zurich, 1550—at least, at St. Luke iii., for the copy is imperfect at St. Matt. iii.— have *axe*, and this is also in the Bishops' Bible, ed. Lond., 1595.   ED. MARSHALL.

I return to CUTHBERT BEDE's query about *axe* or *ax* the very same answer which I gave two years ago to his *penny* or *peny* one. The Oxford Prayer Books of course spell *ax* simply and purely because such is the spelling of the Sealed Books. Dr. Stephens's or any other reprint will show this at once. Why the Cambridge and Queen's printers' books are less faithful to their standard is quite another matter.   C. F. S. WARREN, M.A.

SENSITIVE PLANT TOY (5th S. ix. 288.)—Although I am the fortunate possessor of one of these curious toys, I fear I shall not be able to give much help as to the means of getting one. Mine consists of a lady and gentleman, two large fish, and two small. These are enclosed in a printed paper, in English and French, giving a description of the way in which these leaves are to be used. I will merely quote a few lines, as the whole would, I fear, take up too much space in "N. & Q.":—

" This is an account of the remarkably sympathetic power of the Chinese sensitive leaf, invented by one of the most celebrated operators, by name Jan Pertista Chaseretto, from China. The largest leaves are for the gentlemen and the smallest for the ladies," &c. There is no date, but the water-mark of the paper is " Edmonds, 1808." EMILY COLE.
Teignmouth.

This old Dutch toy was formed of a thin shaving of horn cut into various shapes and painted on one side in water colour. When it was laid on the palm of the open hand, with the painted surface upwards, the heat expanded the lower surface and caused the whole to curl up. I lately found two of these antique toys in an old volume, where it is probable I myself put them sixty years ago.
HUGH OWEN, F.S.A.

I remember these things ; they curled up by the heat of the hand, as goldbeater's skin does, but they were whiter, stouter, and more sensitive. I think they professed to tell one's fortune or one's temper by the way they twisted. "Plant" was no doubt a blind, for they could have no connexion with the mimosa. Some sort of skin was more likely the material. P. P.

I have one of these sensitive leaves. It is at least thirty years old, and is wrapped in its original cover, which sets forth that they are sold by J. Howlett, 17, South Street, Park, Sheffield.
H. FISHWICK, F.S.A.

The toy referred to by MR. BONE is of French origin, and can be procured at any of the French toy warehouses in the City, and sometimes at the West-end drapery establishments. Above twelve months since I purchased a box, at a very small cost, in Bond Street. A. CUTLER.

ANGUS PARLANCE (5th S. ix. 248.)—The name märt, marte, or mairt, applied to a cow or ox fattened, killed, and salted for winter provision, is an old and familiar Scottish word, still extensively used and understood in many parts of Scotland besides Forfarshire. It is so called from Martinmas, October 31 (Old Style), "the term" at which beeves are usually killed for winter use in North Britain. For further explanation MR. CARRIE is referred to Dr. Jamieson's Dictionary of the Scottish Language (sub voce), where the origin of the word is attributed to "Acts of King James IV." (1488-1513). A. S. A.

" Mart, a beef, a cow " (O'Reilly's Irish Dictionary).
" Sir Morogh O'Flaherty of Bunowan was buried Anno D. 1666.
" In his lifetime better known by the name of Morogh na Mart, or Morogh of the Beeves."—Roderic O'Flaherty's Chorographical Description of West or H-Jar Connaught, p. 83, Hardiman's note.
CPL.

PLAGUE MEDICINE (5th English Mans Treasure, p there is the following :—
" A maruellous secret to p plague, and hath bene prooue Physitians, in that great and yeare 1348 which crept thro there was neuer man which va preserued from the plague.
" Take Aloe epaticum or Si Mirrhe, of each of them thre Lignum Aloe, Masticke, Bole them halfe a dragme : let a stamped in a cleane morter, th and after keepe them in some e euery morning two penny we white Wine, with a little wa morning at the dawning of the the grace of God) goe hardly ayre and plague."

There follow many other tilence, which the author " prooued," one of them in tl the yeare 1523, in Aleppe, whom the author saw.
" The | English Mans | Trea tomie | of mans bodie : Compil | rurgion, M. Thomas Vic Chirurgion to | King Henry 1 the 6, To Queene | Marie, An Ladie Queene | Elizabeth, And to Saint Bartholmewes Hospita
The book is of 224 pages printed in black-letter, and thing known of it ?

DROWNED BODIES RECO\ 218, 478.)—In the south of England it is still a p body of a drowned person loaf containing quicksilver stream. The loaf so charge stationary over the place wl I have never seen this fooli it is a wide belief in the B years ago, when I was a sch accidentally drowned in a recollect that several men f of the river, in the belief body would rise to the sur is to be presumed. By foundation for the popula body of a man always floe the body of a woman face u this insisted upon repeate sions I have seen at least tl floating in rivers and in tl the faces were downwards.
Bacup, Lancashire.

It was on arriving in the Morecambe Bay that Lor aspect of the sea, asked if there, and received for an

had never known an instance in which they had not been recovered within a week.
TREGEAGLE.

PROHIBITING THE BANNS (5th S. ix. 468.)—This was probably an unusual proceeding, but "tabling" a shilling is the recognized mode in Scotland of claiming that a decision be confirmed or an appeal entered, and the usual term which one sees used in the squabbles in the church courts is, "Mr. A. protested and *took* instruments." Dr. Jamieson explains that this is a corrupted phrase; it should be "asked or required" instruments. The shilling is the clerk's fee for recording the requirement, or a pledge that the party is in earnest, and will pay the expense of the documents. The phrase occurs often in the proceedings on Bothwell's trial for the murder of Darnley. See Dr. Jamieson, "Instrument."
W. G.

SHELDON HALL, WARWICKSHIRE: SHELDON FAMILY (5th S. viii. 285; ix. 132, 229.)—Dugdale mentions but little about the Sheldon or the Bromwich families, particularly the latter, although these two places are little more than two miles apart.
I send a few extracts out of a great number of family charters, and extracts from a pedigree of Chattock, compiled at great expense from the records and charters of England; and although the Hayes and Chattocks have held large quantities of land in Warwickshire, &c., from very early times to the present day, their names are not mentioned in Dugdale, and his account of Castle Bromwich, &c., is very meagre.
The *Heraldry of Worcestershire*, by H. Sydney Grazebrook, gives a good account of the Sheldon family, a branch of the Warwickshire Sheldons; also see the *County of Dorset*, by John Hutchins, M.A., third edition, by Ship and Hodson, vol. iv. p. 74, pedigree of Percye and Chattock, &c., of Shaftesbury and Manston, under "Manstone."
Extracts from a few of Chattock charters, &c.:—
Let persons now and hereafter know that I, Henry son of Richard de Brockhurst, have given to my brother John, &c., land, &c., lying between the lands of Mar. garete de Scheldon, to have and to hold, &c. Wit. nesses, Anselm de Bromwiz, Thomas de Castello, Roger de Somerloue, and others. (No date; temp. Hen. III.)
Let persons now and hereafter know that I, Richard son of Hugh of the Hay, have given, granted, and this my charter confirmed to Roger, son of Richard, son of Henry de Bromwich, &c. Witnesses, Roger of the Somerloue, Henry son of Richard, Henry son of Ranulf, and others. (No date; temp. Hen. III.)
Let people now and hereafter know that I, Alice, formerly wife of William, son of Alan de Bromwich, in my pure and lawful widowhood, have given, granted, &c., to Hugh of the Hay, &c. Witnesses, Henry de Castro, Geoffrey of the Clyf, Adam son of Henry, Ranulf de Altredemor, Sir William, Chaplain, and others. (No date; temp. Hen. III.)
To all the faithful in Christ who shall see or hear the present writing, &c., John de la Hay, greeting in the Lord: know that I have remitted, &c., to Geoffrey, son of Hugh de la Hay, &c., and have put my seal. Dat. at Bromwyche, Tuesday in the feast of S. John ante Port. Lat. 2 Ed. II. Witnesses, William de Bromwyche, Clerk, Henry atte Somerloue, Thomas de la Hay, Richard, Clerk, and others.

Hugh de la Haye,=Alice	Chattok, and sister		
2, 12, and 16 Ed.	and co-heir to her brothers,		
II.	3 Ed. II.		
Geoffrey de la=Emma,dau,	Ralph =Isabbella,ward		
Haye, 2 and	and heir to	Chattok,	of William de
18 Ed. II.	Richard de	son of	Bromwyche.
Land in Wodi	Brom-	Ralph,16	250 acres of
Bromwyche,	wyche.	Ed. II.	land in Brom-
Erdynton,			wyche and
Egebaston,&c.			Erdyngton.*

The following extract from rolls will show the name of Chattok as known in Warwickshire as early as Hen. III.:—
[4 Ed. I., A.D. 1276.] Names of the rebels and enemis of King Henry and Edward his son in the counties of Warwick and Lancaster. [Among the said names are] John de la Haye, John son of Adam de Somery, and John...Chattok.
Let the present and future know that William de Berwood has given, granted, &c., to Alice all the lands, &c., which I had, &c., from Henry de Castello in Wodybromwiz, &c., and all the land which I had from Anselm de Bromwiz, &c. In testimony whereof to the present writing I have put my seal. Witnesses, Henry de Castello, Ralph de Sheldone, Clerk, Adam Lovecoe, Thomas Annsel, Henry Monford, and others. Dated at Wodibromwiz, Wednesday next after the feast of the Circumcision of the Lord, 29 Edw. I.
[16 Ed. II.] Charter between Ralph, son of Ralph de la Chattok, Isabella his wife, and William de Bromwyche, sometime guardian of the said Isabella, and Henry son of Anselm, respecting lands, &c. 100 shillings rent, &c., with the appurtenances, &c., in Ennedeworth, Sutton, and Mokeshull.
RICHARD F. CHATTOCK.
Holms Hill, Barnet, Herts.

DRAYTON (5th S. ix. 87, 137, 317, 475.)—The Rev. J. R. Lee (not Dr. Lee), in his *History of Market Drayton*, says:—
"The name is common to no fewer than twenty-six towns or villages in England, and probably is to be referred to the early British period. Dr. Wilkes derives it from *drai*, a river. Mr. Baxter prefers to deduce it from *draith rut-dun*, a village on a road. But these conjectures are by no means satisfactory, and the original meaning of the word has never been clearly and decisively explained. Perhaps it may be connected with *deru*, an oak, and with *Druid*; but it is impossible to speak positively on such an uncertain point. The most ancient book which contains the name is a history of the Britons, written in Latin by Nennius, a monk of Banchor, about a thousand years ago. He gives a list of ancient British cities, and among them we find a place which he calls

* May I put an inquiry here? What became of the family of Erdington? The last mentioned by Dugdale is Thomas, "but what became of him after 7 Ed. IV. we can't discover." Did the name become extinct with this Thomas?

'Cair Draithon.' Where Cair Draithon was situated no one seems to know, and Bishop Kennett maintains that it is quite useless to inquire; but the historians who copied their account of British cities from Nennius seem to have been acquainted with the spot, for Hollinshead speaks of 'Cair Draiton, now a slender village,' as if he knew the locality, and Henry of Huntingdon mentions 'Cair Draiton, or the town of Draiton.' Now we find that in the Saxon times Drayton in Hales was a place of some importance, as appears clearly from Domesday Book. There is, therefore, some reason to suppose that it is the place alluded to by Nennius; but, of course, this is mere conjecture."

Mr. Lee makes no further allusion to the origin or derivation of the name of *Drayton.* He no doubt felt a difficulty in dealing with the fact that so many other places, under varied conditions of site and position, bear the same name.

WM. HUGHES.

A SIXTEENTH CENTURY BOOK INSCRIPTION (5ᵗʰ S. ix. 466.)—The lines copied by BOILEAU are a variation of a well-known formula, of which examples will be found in "N. & Q.," 1ˢᵗ S. vii. 554; viii. 591; and xii. 243. On referring to these it will be found that the allusions in lines five and six are not so very obscure. The capital letters in these lines are simply the initials of the name of the owner of the book, Hennrey Gouldinge, who seems to have been so uneducated as not to know how to spell correctly his own Christian name, which we may presume to have been Henry. It is not to be wondered at if he made other blunders in transcribing the lines, such as " it last " for " I live," and " all men fight " for " all men's sight."

EDGAR MACCULLOCH.
Guernsey.

POPULAR LEGAL FALLACIES (5ᵗʰ S. ix. 468.)— Mr. Henry Broome, Lecturer to one of the Inns of Court—I think it was the Middle Temple—published under the head of *Legal Maxims* a work such as that sought by INQUIRER.

JOSEPH FISHER.
Waterford.

LENGTH OF GENERATIONS (5ᵗʰ S. ix. 488.)— MR. HOWLETT and myself are coeval, but whereas he counts 139 years from the birth of his grandfather, and calls it a long stretch back, I can reckon 161 from the birth of mine in 1717.

W. T. M.

JOHN BANCKS, OF SUNNING (5ᵗʰ S. viii. 335; ix. 232, 398.)—To the literary works of this writer may be added the *Life and Reign of William III.*, 12mo., 1744, and the editing of Prior's *Miscellaneous Works*, Lond., 2 vols., 8vo., 1740. Prior died 1721, leaving his MSS. to Adrian Drift, who copied them, and entrusted the copy to Charles Forman. Drift died in 1738, and then Forman intended to complete the work and publish it; before he could do this, however, in 1739 he too died, and the incomplete work was entrusted to

John Bancks, to connect the MSS. a whole a form such as Prior himself wou have desired. Bancks's name does no the title-page, but he signed the dedic: Earl of Oxford, and added his init preface, in which the above facts are st

The correction of the name from Bancks is very noteworthy, and may p the present confusion. Most biogri Cibber, who wrote 1753, two years aft spell it Banks; and it was so prir *Gentleman's Magazine*, 1751, p. 187, a deaths, where he is called "author treatises, and editor of books appro publick." It has resulted from this graphers have made two men of hir Lowndes and Allibone give—Bancks, *cellaneous Works*, 1738-9; Banks, Jc *Cromwell*, often reprinted.

It is plain that he wrote "Bancks" to 1740, and it is most probable that 1 true name; but it is possible that close of his life he may have left out t name. As he died in easy circumstal at his house at Islington, and was prot there, perhaps there may be some mon scription or record still existing; if so would be of interest. Anyhow, it is (Bancks, as the name which he did use books to which his name appeared, n applied to all those works which h anonymously.

EDWAR

I am glad MR. ALLNUTT has put me to the reputed absence of Bancks's nai of his titles, and also settled the ort both authors bearing that name. The find as often calls himself Bankes as our subject in Cibber's index is givei although rightly Bancks at the referen

Having only one of the works I ad by Bancks, I jumped to the conclusion altogether an anonymous writer. My *cellaneous Works, Serious and Hu Verse and Prose. Design'd for the A the Fair Sex*, 8vo., Reading, 1740.

This does not well assort with the L he is said to have written, althoug another instance of a serious and c rolled into one. But his biographer, 1 a margin for his versatility when 1 "he (Bancks) had the talent of rel humorously in verse," which is here ex

I don't see the Reading book any tioned, and the proof that it is a curio in my copy having the witty book-pla Clark, "A Pleader to the Needer whe which I never find but in rare books.

THE AMERICAN ROBIN (5ᵗʰ S. i 475.)—Was not Mr. Kingsley wron that the American robin was not the blue-bird, but "a great parti-coloured thrush"? And is not the American robin the blue-bird, *Saxicola sialis?* In Alexander Wilson's poem, *The Blue-bird* (six verses of eight lines each), are the following lines :

" The slow lingering schoolboys forget they'll be chid,
While gazing intent as he warbles before them
In mantle of sky-blue, and bosom so red,
That each little loiterer seems to adore him."

It is stated that in his shape and size, as well as in his habits and song, the blue-bird is very similar to the English robin, the only difference being the sky-blue "mantle" instead of the brown-olive coat.　　　　　　　　　　　　CUTHBERT BEDE.

One more query on this subject. I am just now away from all books, and cannot remember whereabouts the scene is laid where the American robin is mentioned. Will any reader of " N. & Q." who has *Kéramos* at hand kindly inform me as to this ?
　　　　　　　　　　　　　　　　J. DIXON.

" MARQUIS " v. " MARQUESS " (5th S. ix. 167, 315, 353.)—Marquess, certainly. A MS. notebook of a herald, *temp.* Henry VIII., formerly in Sir Charles G. Young's collection, now before me, which contains copies of several early orders of precedence, affords good evidence of that. I extract from " The order of all Estates of nobilitye & getry of Englãd set forthe the 8 of Octob. in the yeare of or Lo. God 1399," " It'm. my Lo. Marquesse. A newe honr " ; and from " The order of all Estates of wor and gentrie of England as they were ordered by the Lo. Protectors grace & by the Earle Marshall of England against the kings coronatiõ & set forthe by the Herolde and by me Registred at Petrborough. Anno. Dni MCCCCXXXI," " It'm. Marquesses, brought in of Late." There are many similar instances, in more than one handwriting of about the same period, in this volume. The title appears so written by all the old heraldic authorities.　　　　　　　　　　　　W. E. B.

" AN UNLAWFUL COTTAGE " (5th S. ix. 207, 275.)—Cowel says :—

" A *cottage* is a house without land belonging to it, anno 4 El. I. stat. 1. By a later statute, 31 Eliz. c. 7, no man may build a *house* unless he lay four acres of land to it ; so that a *cottage* is properly any little house that hath not four acres of land belonging to it."
　　　　　　　　　　　　　　　R. S. CHARNOCK.
Junior Garrick.

LEEDS POTTERY (5th S. viii. 409, 455 ; ix. 78, 337.)—The translation of a Dutch inscription quoted by ST. SWITHIN needs correction. It should be :—" I burn a light for the Prince's Niece and also for the Orange branch. He who will not see it blows it out."　　　　HUGH OWEN, F.S.A.

RHODES FAMILY (5th S. ix. 208, 373.)—In *Recollections of Oxford,* by G. V. Cox, M.A., New

College, late Esquire Bedell and Coroner in the University of Oxford (8vo., London, 1868), it is stated, under the date of 1792 :—

" In April died Mr. Evton, M.A. of Jesus College, and for forty-seven years Esquire Bedell in Medicine and Arts. He was succeeded by his nephew, Mr. (*sic*) Rhodes, M.A. and Fellow of Worcester, who had acted as Mr. Eyton's deputy during a long illness and absence from Oxford."

Some amusing particulars further on in chap. xii. are added respecting Mr. Rhodes, who died in 1815.
　　　　　　　　　　　　　　J. MACRAY.

AUTHORS OF QUOTATIONS WANTED (5th S. ix. 469.)—

" The Saviour ! O what endless charms
Dwell in the blissful sound ! " &c.

This is the second stanza of a piece of thirty-nine stanzas, entitled *Redeeming Love,* written by Anne Steele in 1760, and given in Daniel Sedgwick's reprint (1863) of her *Hymns on Various Subjects.*　　　　JOSIAH MILLER.

" Si vis pacem," &c.

Cicero has a thought very near akin to this when he says (*De Officiis,* i. 23) : " Bellum autem ita suscipiatur, ut nihil aliud nisi pax quæsita videatur."
　　　　　　　　　　　　EDWARD H. MARSHALL.

The phrase, " Qui desiderat pacem præparet bellum," occurs in Vegetius, *Rei Milit. Inst.,* l. iii., prol. Compare, " Nam paritur pax bello ; itaque qui ea diutina volunt frui, bello exercitati esse debent," in Cornelius Nepos, *Epam.,* p. 163, ed. Foulis, Glas., 1777.
　　　　　　　　　　　　ED. MARSHALL.

" As bees on flowers alighting," &c.

These lines of Thomas Moore, slightly misquoted by MR. BOUCHIER, are to be found in his poem of *Corruption,* which, with a kindred satire entitled *Intolerance,* he published anonymously in 1808.　　　D. F. MACCARTHY.

Miscellaneous.

NOTES ON BOOKS, &c.

A History of Blackburn, Town and Parish. By W. Alexander Abram. (Blackburn, Toulmin.)

MR. ABRAM deserves praise for the careful and painstaking way in which he has produced his excellent and exhaustive volume. Blackburn now possesses a written history of which it may well be proud. Indeed, few towns can boast of a more conscientious and diligent historian than Mr. Abram, for while many writers rely on the work of others for their information, he has searched out facts for himself from their original sources, and consequently his book possesses that invaluable charm, accuracy. The first part comprises a general history extending from the Roman and Saxon periods up to the present day ; whereas the latter portion is devoted to township history and topography. In narrating the part Blackburn has played in history Mr. Abram has introduced many well-known facts which, though interesting, might yet, we think, have been somewhat curtailed, as unnecessarily increasing the bulk of the volume. The chapter devoted to the modern history of Blackburn is highly interesting, and is well worth the perusal of the reader ; for Mr. Abram has given a capital account of the introduction of cotton spinning into this part of Lancashire, and briefly traversed some of the changes and processes by which the manufacture has reached its present perfection.

Indeed, the cotton trade, as Mr. Abram truly remarks, has a history as interesting as any of the developments of human energy the world has witnessed. The history of the township is valuable from a biographical point of view, because the author, as he tells us in the preface, "has bestowed much space and expended an unusual amount of work upon the account of old native families" of our yeomen and lesser gentry, gathered from parish registers and public records, in conjunction with family papers and title deeds. We cannot over-estimate the value of this part of Mr. Abram's labours, for the number of families and distinct branches of families genealogically noticed is nearly three hundred. The illustrations, too, which embellish the volume are excellent, and we congratulate the people of Blackburn on this new history of their town written by such competent hands.

The Position and Prospects of Catholic Liberal Education. By the Hon. and Rev. William Petre. (Burns & Oates.)
"Is there a cause?" Such is a question which has been frequently asked of late years with regard to various movements of the day. We have carefully considered Mr. Petre's earnest plea for the liberal education of his co-religionists in England, and we are clearly of opinion that "there is a cause" for his pamphlet as the visible exponent of his plea. So far as outsiders to the Roman communion in this country can judge from the language of a writer belonging to that communion, Mr. Petre's orthodoxy is of the severest purity. All who are not of his Israel are in his eyes wandering "without the gates." He and his "walk in light," while they who are not of his theological company walk "in darkness." And from Mr. Petre's point of view the freedom of "Protestant public schools" is likely, all too readily, to "lapse into licence." But setting aside such expressions as parts of the theological rather than the literary or scholastic armour of Mr. Petre, we cannot but sympathize strongly with his keen sense of past shortcomings, and his sincere desire to help forward the establishment of schools in which English Roman Catholic boys can be made "English gentlemen, strangers to no culture which is bestowed upon their Protestant fellow-countrymen," and able to compete "in society with the best educated scholars in the kingdom." Mr. Petre urges many very serious arguments to enforce his thesis, of which we would say, as well as of his pamphlet as a whole, "Judicent qui judicare queant." But, in order to be in a position to judge, those who are interested in education must read Mr. Petre's work for themselves, and not take it at second hand.

An Attempt to Determine the Chronological Order of Shakespeare's Plays, by the Rev. H. P. Stokes, B.A. (Macmillan), the Harness (triennial) Essay for 1877, must not be classed in the usual category of university prize essays, as it contains much really instructive matter for Shaksperian scholars.—"Ballad" to "Boieldieu" is the portion comprised in part ii. of Macmillan's *Dictionary of Music and Musicians.* To the notice of Beethoven is appended the well-known "G.," a guarantee that the subject is worthily treated.—Mr. Stevens's admirable bibliographical description of *The Bibles in the Caxton Exhibition,* 1877 (Henry Stevens, Trafalgar Square), should be in the possession of all collectors of the various editions of the Bible; its interest is for all times.—We have received from Messrs. Rivingtons *Homer's Iliad,* books i., ii, by A. Sidgwick, M.A., in which all is done that seems possible to mitigate the troubles of beginners in reading Homer; and Mr. G. L. Bennett's *First Latin Writer, with Accidence, Syntax Rules, and Vocabularies.*

WE learn that an International Bibliographical Congress, organised under the auspices of the Société Bibliographique, will be held in Paris, at the rooms of the Société d'Horticulture, 84, Rue de Grenelle, from the 1st to the 4th July.

A NEW and considerably enlarged edition of a general *History and Literature of the Art of Quick Writing* has just been published at Dresden by Prof. Zeibig, of the Royal Stenographic Institute of that city. The work enters with commendable minuteness into the bibliography of English shorthand literature, and Prof. Zeibig expresses his obligations to Mr. J. E. Bailey, of Manchester.

Notices to Correspondents.

We must call special attention to the following notices:

ON all communications should be written the name and address of the sender, not necessarily for publication, but as a guarantee of good faith.

CORRESPONDENTS are requested to bear in mind that it is against rule to *seal* or otherwise *fasten* communications transmitted by the halfpenny post. Not unfrequently double postage has to be paid on their receipt, because they have been "closed against inspection."

FOLK-LORE.—We would strongly urge on those correspondents who are good enough to send us communications on Folk-Lore that, before doing so, they should consult Brand's *Popular Antiquities,* Chambers's *Book of Days,* Hone's *Every-Day Book,* but especially Thiselton Dyer's *British Popular Customs,* this last being the most recent work on customs connected with the Calendar.

C. L. PRINCE (Crowborough.)—Hakewell's verses will be found in the second volume of our present series, p 483. The reference must be to ink. For other papers on the electric telegraph foreshadowed, see " N. & Q.," 2nd S. iv. 266, 318, 392, 461 ; vi. 265, 359, 422 ; viii. 503 ; xii. 166, 277.

L. N. T.—
"Lord of himself, though not of lands;
And having nothing, yet hath all"
(Wotton, *Description of a Happy Life*), is the correct rendering.

L. L. N.—The Court of Arches was formerly held in the church of St. Mary-le-Bow (ecclesia Sanctæ Mariæ de Arcubus).

Q. Q.—*The Abbey Walk* is a ballad by Robert Henrysoun (d. 1508), and is included in Lord Hailes's collection of *Ancient Scottish Songs.*

RURAL BOTANIST asks to be informed of any books that treat of the derivations, meanings, and origin of the technical botanical names of plants.

"THE LASS OF RICHMOND HILL."—See " N. & Q.," 3rd S. xi. 343, 362, 386, 445, 489.

J. C. ("Lord Barnard") has sent no name and address.

G. M.—*Hamlet,* Act v. sc. 1.

F. C. BROOKE.—Forwarded.

ERRATUM.—P. 495, col. i., line 12 from top, for "of Bournoe," read *of Boconnoc.*

NOTICE.

Editorial Communications should be addressed to "The Editor of 'Notes and Queries'"—Advertisements and Business Letters to "The Publisher"—at the Office, 20, Wellington Street, Strand, London, W.C.

We beg leave to state that we decline to return communications which, for any reason, we do not print; and to this rule we can make no exception.

INDEX.

FIFTH SERIES.—VOL. IX.

[For classified articles, see ANONYMOUS WORKS, BOOKS RECENTLY PUBLISHED, EPIGRAMS, EPITAPHS, FOLK-LORE,
PROVERBS AND PHRASES, QUOTATIONS, SHAKSPEARIANA, and SONGS AND BALLADS.]